T
CRICK
WHO'S WHO
2005

Introduction by
NICK KNIGHT

Edited by
CHRIS MARSHALL

Statistics by
RICHARD LOCKWOOD

Photographs by
GETTY IMAGES
and
BILL SMITH

Queen Anne Press

QUEEN ANNE PRESS
a division of Lennard Associates Limited
Mackerye End, Harpenden, Herts AL5 5DR

Published in association with
The Cricketers' Who's Who Limited

First published in Great Britain 2005

British Library Cataloguing in Publication is available

ISBN 1 85291 661 3

Typeset in Times and Univers Condensed
Editor (for Queen Anne Press): Kirsty Ennever
Quiz compiled by Peter Brierley
Cover design by Paul Cooper

Printed and bound by Butler & Tanner

ACKNOWLEDGEMENTS

Cover photographs by Getty Images

The publishers would also like to thank the county clubs, the players
and their families for their assistance in helping to assemble
the information and photographs in this book.

Extra information has also been gathered from the pages of *The Wisden Cricketer*,
The Times, *The Sunday Times*, CricInfo.com and CricketArchive.com

County photocall photographers for Getty Images:
Derbyshire/Gary M Prior; Durham/Laurence Griffiths; Essex/Christopher Lee;
Glamorgan/Bryn Lennon; Gloucestershire/Bryn Lennon; Hampshire/Mike Hewitt;
Kent/John Gichigi; Lancashire/Ross Kinnaird; Leicestershire/Matthew Lewis;
Middlesex/Clive Rose; Northamptonshire/Clive Mason;
Nottinghamshire/Gary M Prior; Somerset/Stu Forster; Surrey/Ian Walton;
Sussex/John Gichigi; Warwickshire/Stu Forster; Worcestershire/Stu Forster

Thanks also to the following for providing additional photographs:
Bucks Free Press, Carlisle News and Star, Neville Chadwick Photography,
Cricket Images, Cricket World, Derby Evening Telegraph, Empics,
Exeter Herald Express, Ken Grime, Vic Isaacs, Kent Messenger Group,
Kent Regional Newspapers, Lancashire Evening Post, Leicester Mercury,
Pete Norton Photography, Rutland Times, SWPix

CONTENTS

INTRODUCTION
7

THE PLAYERS
9

THE UMPIRES
787

ROLL OF HONOUR 2004
818

FIRST-CLASS AVERAGES 2004
820

INDEX OF PLAYERS BY COUNTY
827

ANSWERS TO QUIZ
832

INTRODUCTION

As I sit down to write this, I've just returned from New Zealand, having been with the FICA Masters for three ODIs against New Zealand. FICA (the Federation of International Cricketers' Associations) came of age in 2004, and it was a privilege to be one of those asked to step into the breach when Sri Lanka were forced to postpone their tour after the devastation caused to their country by the Boxing Day tsunami.

What a year 2004 was for cricket! On the international front, England went from strength to strength as if the whole year were a deliberate and thrilling preamble to 2005 and the arrival of the Aussies. Excitement has been mounting for months, and the magnificent results have not just been encouraging the faithful but also calling to a new audience as attendances swell. The domestic game weighed in with another epic year (I would say that, wouldn't I?), with Warwickshire winning the Frizzell County Championship, Leicestershire the Twenty20 Cup, Gloucestershire the C&G Trophy and Glamorgan the totesport League. All good news, of course, but the reason you buy this book is because you recognise that what makes the game of cricket really exciting, really worth your time and attention, is the people who play it. 2004 was not just a good year for the game of cricket but also a good year for its principal stakeholders. You buy this book because you want to know more about us, and we contribute to it because we want to be more than just statistics to you. We're proud of who we are and of what we do and, collectively, we've made massive strides during 2004 and will continue to do so in 2005.

Last year saw the introduction of the new standard contract negotiated between our PCA and the ECB. Along with new Qualification and Registration Regulations, we at last saw the end of Lists One and Two, which, for decades, kept us severely restricted in our choices and kept cricket locked in an anachronistic master-and-servant relationship between players and counties. A new TV deal was announced at the end of the year that creates financial stability for the game through to 2009, and an historic '3G' deal was brokered that, for the first time ever, saw all the game's stakeholders uniting to centralise their rights so all could benefit.

A few years ago the PCA asked its members – us, the players – to endorse their strategy of working with, rather than against, the other stakeholders in cricket. There were more than a few of us who doubted that it would work – distrust ran deep – but we only had to look at the culture of 'us and them' that has developed in football to question whether that way can work in the long run. 2004 saw the PCA's strategy take massive strides and they have become, on all the players' behalf, increasingly central to the game and increasingly influential. This is only right as, after all, we are the product.

We still have issues to deal with, but we do it against a background of vibrant stability and a sense of collective and individual excitement. Pre-season is the time of dreams, plans, strategies and hard yards trying to ensure we start the season in the best possible shape. This pre-season we can also start proud that cricket, in an unprecedented show of community and effort of will, raised over 15 million Australian dollars in an international one-day game just two weeks after the tsunami. I am not aware of any other sport doing as much, and it is largely down to FICA and its energetic leadership, who galvanised the cricket community to contribute. The same spirit ensured that the ODIs I've just played in in New Zealand not only took place but continued to raise money for tsunami relief. 2004 was a great year in cricket overshadowed by an overwhelming tragedy in the real world. Here's to 2005 being a greater year in cricket and a safe year for everyone.

I will close by congratulating the staff and players at Warwickshire County Cricket Club on winning the Frizzell County

Championship. Disciplined thought and hard work combined creates a powerful unit; the challenge ahead is for us to build on the standards set in 2004.

Nick Knight
February 2005

2005 Benefits and Testimonials

Essex	Paul Grayson	Notts	Jason Gallian
Glamorgan	Matthew Maynard	Somerset	Michael Burns
Glos	Tim Hancock	Surrey	Mark Butcher
Hants	Alan Mullally	Sussex	Mark Robinson
Kent	Martin Saggers	Warwicks	Dougie Brown
Lancs	Gary Yates		

PCA County Representatives

Derbys	Kevin Dean	Middx	Paul Hutchison
Durham	Neil Killeen	Northants	Ben Phillips
Essex	Paul Grayson	Notts	Darren Bicknell
Glamorgan	Ian Thomas	Somerset	Simon Francis
Glos	James Averis	Surrey	Ian Salisbury
Hants	Dimitri Mascarenhas	Sussex	Richard Montgomerie
Kent	Martin Saggers	Warwicks	Dougie Brown
Lancs	Mark Chilton	Worcs	Stephen Peters
Leics	Paul Nixon	Yorks	Richard Dawson

THE PLAYERS

KOLPAK

If a cricketer is a national of a country that has an Association Agreement with the EU (such as South Africa or Zimbabwe) and also has a valid UK work permit, he enjoys the same right to work within the EU as an EU citizen and may be eligible to play county cricket as a domestic (that is, non-overseas) player. Cricketers playing in England under this system are commonly referred to as Kolpak players, after the Kolpak ruling, a judgement in the European Court of Justice that found in favour of Maros Kolpak, a Slovakian handball goalkeeper who challenged his status as a non-EU player in Germany.

THE WIDER WORLD OF INTERNATIONAL CRICKET

Throughout the book there are 100 quiz questions relating to the most recent additions to Test cricket (Sri Lanka, Zimbabwe and Bangladesh) and other aspiring ICC countries.

Editor's Notes

The cricketers listed in this volume include all those who played 1st XI cricket for a first-class county at least once last season, in any form of cricket, and all those registered (at the time of going to press at the beginning of March) to play for the 18 first-class counties in 2005, even those who have yet to make a first-team appearance. We also include the Scottish Saltires, pen portraits of the 2005 squad appearing at the end of the players' section. All players' statistics are complete to the end of the last English season (the Stop press sections for individual players cover subsequent highlights); Test and One-Day International tallies for umpires are up to and including 2 March 2005. Figures about 1000 runs, 50 wickets and 50 dismissals in a season refer to matches in England only. All first-class figures include figures for Test matches, which are also extracted and listed separately. One-Day 100s and One-Day five wickets in an innings are for the English domestic competitions (including the Twenty20 Cup and the now discontinued Benson and Hedges Cup) and all One-Day Internationals, home and abroad. Career records include 'rebel' tours to South Africa. In the interests of space 2004 statistics are not given for those whose appearances in first-class cricket or one-day competitions were only for teams other than the county for which they are now registered – i.e. universities, minor counties etc (excluding international cricketers on tours to England). These appearances are, however, reflected in their career statistics and reference is made in the Extras section to the team for which they played.

The figures for batting and bowling averages refer to the full first-class English list for 2004, followed in brackets by the 2003 figures. Inclusion in the batting averages depends on a minimum of six completed innings; a bowler has to have taken at least ten wickets and bowled in a minimum of six innings. Strike rate refers to a bowler's record of balls bowled per wicket taken.

The following abbreviations apply: ODI means One-Day International; * means not out. In statistics tables All First means all first-class matches; 1-day Int – One-Day Internationals; C&G – C&G Trophy (including NatWest); totesport – totesport League (including previous one-day and Sunday leagues); Twenty20 – Twenty20 Cup.

Please note that Worcestershire ceased awarding caps in 2001 and now present 'colours' to each player who appears for the county in the Championship; in addition, beginning in 2004 Gloucestershire have awarded caps to players on making their first first-class appearance for the county.

A book of this complexity and detail has to be prepared several months in advance of the cricket season, and occasionally there are recent changes in a player's circumstances or the structure of the game which cannot be included in time. Many examples of facts, statistics and even opinions which can quickly become outdated in the period between the compilation of the book and its publication, months later, will spring to the reader's mind, and I ask him or her to make the necessary commonsense allowance and adjustments.

Chris Marshall, March 2005

ACKERMAN, H. D. Leicestershire

Name: Hylton Deon Ackerman
Role: Right-hand bat, right-arm medium bowler, county captain
Born: 14 February 1973, Cape Town, South Africa
County debut: No first-team appearance
Test debut: 1997-98
Tests: 4
1st-Class 50s: 38
1st-Class 100s: 17
1st-Class 200s: 1
1st-Class catches: 89
Family links with cricket: Father (H. M. Ackerman) played first-class cricket in South Africa (1963-64 – 1981-82) and also for Northamptonshire
Overseas tours: South Africa U24 to Sri Lanka 1995; Western Province to Australia

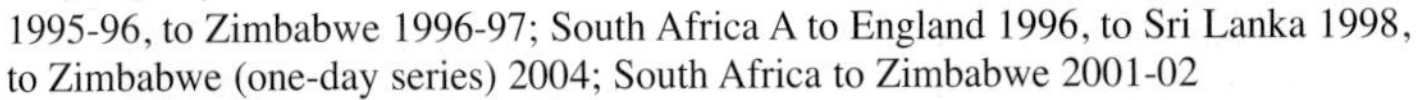

1995-96, to Zimbabwe 1996-97; South Africa A to England 1996, to Sri Lanka 1998, to Zimbabwe (one-day series) 2004; South Africa to Zimbabwe 2001-02
Overseas teams played for: Western Province 1993-94 – 2002-03; Gauteng 2003-04; Lions 2004-05
Extras: Scored maiden first-class double century (202*) v Northerns at Centurion in the SuperSport Series 1997-98, in the process breaking Barry Richards's record for the most first-class runs by a South African in a domestic season (ended 1997-98 with 1373 at 50.85). Scored century (145) for South Africa A v Sri Lanka A at Matara 1998, winning Man of the Match award. Man of the SuperSport Series 2000-01. His other domestic awards include Man of the Match v Griqualand West at Kimberley (81) and v KwaZulu-Natal at Durban (86*), both in the Standard Bank Cup 2003-04. Joined Leicestershire for 2005 and appointed captain. Is not considered an overseas player
Best batting: 202* Western Province v Northerns, Centurion 1997-98

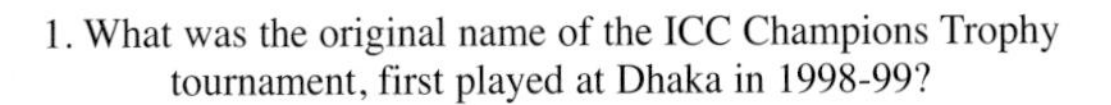

1. What was the original name of the ICC Champions Trophy tournament, first played at Dhaka in 1998-99?

2004 Season (did not make any first-class or one-day appearances)

Career Performances

	M	Inns	NO	Runs	HS	Avge	100s	50s	Ct	St	Balls	Runs	Wkts	Avge	Best	5wI	10wM
Test	4	8	0	161	57	20.12	-	1	1	-							
All First	110	179	19	6776	202 *	42.35	18	38	89	-	90	54	0	-	-	-	-
1-day Int																	
C & G																	
totesport																	
Twenty20																	

ADAMS, A. R. — Essex

Name: André Ryan Adams
Role: Right-hand bat, right-arm fast-medium bowler
Born: 17 July 1975, Auckland, New Zealand
Height: 5ft 11in **Weight:** 14st 7lbs
Nickname: Dre, Doctor
County debut: 2004
County cap: 2004
Test debut: 2001-02
Tests: 1
One-Day Internationals: 31
1st-Class 50s: 6
1st-Class 100s: 1
1st-Class 5 w. in innings: 5
1st-Class catches: 16
One-Day 5 w. in innings: 1
Place in batting averages: 184th av. 24.50
Place in bowling averages: 17th av. 24.39
Strike rate: 41.13 (career 46.36)
Parents: Felise du Chateau and Keith Adams
Wife and date of marriage: Ardene, 5 April 2003
Children: Danté, 24 February 2004
Family links with cricket: 'Parents West Indian!'
Education: West Lake Boys, Auckland
Off-season: Playing for Auckland
Overseas tours: New Zealand to Sharjah (ARY Gold Cup) 2000-01, to Australia 2001-02 (VB Series), to Sharjah (Sharjah Cup) 2001-02, to Pakistan 2002, to Africa (World Cup) 2002-03, to Sri Lanka 2003 (Bank Alfalah Cup), to England (NatWest Series) 2004, to Bangladesh 2004-05 (one-day series)

Overseas teams played for: Takapuna, Auckland; Auckland 1997-98 –
Career highlights to date: 'Test victory against England in final game (Auckland) in 2002, my Test debut'
Cricket moments to forget: 'Losing to India in 2003 World Cup'
Cricket superstitions: 'None'
Cricketers particularly admired: Viv Richards, Michael Holding
Young players to look out for: Alastair Cook, Will Jefferson, Ravi Bopara, Rob Nicol (Auckland)
Other sports followed: Rugby (Auckland Blues, All Blacks)
Favourite band: Ryan Edwards
Relaxations: Xbox
Extras: Member of New Zealand team to 1998 Indoor Cricket World Cup. Leading wicket-taker in 1999-2000 Shell Cup one-day competition (28; av. 13.50). Played for Herefordshire in the C&G 2001, winning Man of the Match award v Gloucestershire Board XI at Brockhampton (2-29/46). His ODI match awards include Man of the Match v India at Queenstown 2002-03 (5-22) and v West Indies at Port Elizabeth in the 2002-03 World Cup (35*/4-44). Called up from club cricket in Lancashire to New Zealand squad for NatWest Series 2004. Was an overseas player with Essex July to September 2004, first deputising for Danish Kaneria, absent on international duty, then for the injured Scott Brant; has returned for 2005. Scored maiden first-class century (91-ball 124) v Leicestershire at Leicester 2004 in his first Championship innings and batting at No. 9. Awarded Essex cap 2004
Best batting: 124 Essex v Leicestershire, Leicester 2004
Best bowling: 5-40 Auckland v Northern Districts, Hamilton 2003-04

2004 Season

	M	Inns	NO	Runs	HS	Avge	100s	50s	Ct	St	O	M	Runs	Wkts	Avge	Best	5wI	10wM
Test																		
All First	7	8	0	196	124	24.50	1	-	4	-	157.4	23	561	23	24.39	5-93	1	-
1-day Int	1	0	0	0	0	-	-	-	-	-								
C & G																		
totesport	6	2	0	28	17	14.00	-	-	2	-	24	1	146	2	73.00	1-32	-	
Twenty20	1	1	0	7	7	7.00	-	-	-	-	3	0	33	2	16.50	2-33	-	

Career Performances

	M	Inns	NO	Runs	HS	Avge	100s	50s	Ct	St	Balls	Runs	Wkts	Avge	Best	5wI	10wM
Test	1	2	0	18	11	9.00	-	-	1	-	190	105	6	17.50	3-44	-	-
All First	36	53	1	1073	124	20.63	1	6	16	-	6306	3170	136	23.30	5-40	5	-
1-day Int	31	24	7	338	45	19.88	-	-	3	-	1438	1238	44	28.13	5-22	1	
C & G	2	2	0	55	46	27.50	-	-	2	-	120	98	4	24.50	2-29	-	
totesport	6	2	0	28	17	14.00	-	-	2	-	144	146	2	73.00	1-32	-	
Twenty20	1	1	0	7	7	7.00	-	-	-	-	18	33	2	16.50	2-33	-	

ADAMS, C. J. Sussex

Name: Christopher (Chris) John Adams
Role: Right-hand bat, right-arm medium bowler, slip fielder, county captain
Born: 6 May 1970, Whitwell, Derbyshire
Height: 6ft **Weight:** 13st 7lbs
Nickname: Grizzly, Grizwold
County debut: 1988 (Derbyshire), 1998 (Sussex)
County cap: 1992 (Derbyshire), 1998 (Sussex)
Benefit: 2003 (Sussex)
Test debut: 1999-2000
Tests: 5
One-Day Internationals: 5
1000 runs in a season: 6
1st-Class 50s: 72
1st-Class 100s: 37
1st-Class 200s: 4
1st-Class catches: 313
One-Day 100s: 18
One-Day 5 w. in innings: 1
Place in batting averages: 47th av. 47.76 (2003 102nd av. 35.77)
Strike rate: (career 78.31)
Parents: John and Eluned (Lyn)
Wife and date of marriage: Samantha Claire, 26 September 1992
Children: Georgia Louise, 4 October 1993; Sophie Victoria, 13 October 1998
Family links with cricket: Brother David played 2nd XI cricket for Derbyshire and Gloucestershire. Father played for Yorkshire Schools and uncle played for Essex 2nd XI
Education: Chesterfield Boys Grammar School; Repton School
Qualifications: 6 O-levels, NCA coaching awards, Executive Development Certificate in Coaching and Management Skills
Off-season: 'Drinking, eating, travelling and training'
Overseas tours: Repton School to Barbados 1987; England NCA North to Northern Ireland 1987; England XI to New Zealand (Cricket Max) 1997; England to South Africa and Zimbabwe 1999-2000; Sussex to Grenada 2001, 2002; Blade to Barbados 2001
Overseas teams played for: Takapuna, New Zealand 1987-88; Te Puke, New Zealand 1989-90; Primrose, Cape Town, South Africa 1991-92; Canberra Comets, Australia 1998-99; University of NSW, Australia 2000-01
Career highlights to date: 'Lifting the County Championship trophy [in 2003] for the first time in Sussex's history'
Cricket moments to forget: 'The death of Umer Rashid in Grenada'

Cricketers particularly admired: Ian Botham
Young players to look out for: Matt Prior, Tim Ambrose, 'Georgia Adams!'
Other sports played: Golf, football, 'dabbled a bit with ice hockey'
Other sports followed: Football ('Arsenal!')
Favourite band: Spandau Ballet, Duran Duran
Relaxations: 'Family time'
Extras: Represented English Schools U15 and U19, MCC Schools U19 and, in 1989, England YC. Took two catches as 12th man for England v India at Old Trafford in 1990. Set Derbyshire record for the highest score in the Sunday League (141*) v Kent at Chesterfield 1992 and record for the fastest century by a Derbyshire batsman (57 minutes, finishing on 140*) v Worcestershire at Worcester 1992. Set record for the highest score by a Derbyshire No. 3, 239 v Hampshire at Southampton 1996. Released by Derbyshire at the end of the 1997 season and joined Sussex for 1998 as captain. Scored 135 and 105 v Essex at Chelmsford 1998, becoming the third player to score centuries in each innings of a match for two counties; he had also done so for Derbyshire. Sussex Player of the Year 1998 and 1999. Set individual one-day record score for Sussex of 163 (off 107 balls) v Middlesex in the National League at Arundel 1999; the innings included nine sixes, a Sussex Sunday/National League record. Sussex 1st XI Fielder of the Season 2000. BBC South Cricketer of the Year 2001. Scored century (115*) v Middlesex at Hove in the NCL 2003, sharing with Murray Goodwin (118*) in a new record third-wicket partnership for the one-day league and a competition record for any wicket for Sussex (228*). One of *Wisden*'s Five Cricketers of the Year 2004. Scored 200 v Northamptonshire at Hove 2004, in the process becoming the third batsman (after Mark Ramprakash and Carl Hooper) to score a century against all 18 counties
Opinions on cricket: 'It's still the greatest game on earth and it's up to the current players and administrators to ensure it remains so. We've got to evolve to survive, but we must never forget the truth of the game.'
Best batting: 239 Derbyshire v Hampshire, Southampton 1996
Best bowling: 4-28 Sussex v Durham, Riverside 2001

2004 Season

	M	Inns	NO	Runs	HS	Avge	100s	50s	Ct	St	O	M	Runs	Wkts	Avge	Best	5wI	10wM
Test																		
All First	16	25	4	1003	200	47.76	4	2	14	-	10	2	35	0	-	-	-	-
1-day Int																		
C & G	2	2	0	119	68	59.50	-	2	-	-								
totesport	18	18	2	557	93	34.81	-	4	7	-	0.3	0	3	0	-	-	-	
Twenty20	4	4	2	106	38 *	53.00	-	-	1	-								

Career Performances

	M	Inns	NO	Runs	HS	Avge	100s	50s	Ct	St	Balls	Runs	Wkts	Avge	Best	5wI	10wM
Test	5	8	0	104	31	13.00	-	-	6	-	120	59	1	59.00	1-42	-	-
All First	273	447	33	15753	239	38.05	41	72	313	-	3211	1890	41	46.09	4-28	-	-
1-day Int	5	4	0	71	42	17.75	-	-	3	-							
C & G	30	29	7	1382	129 *	62.81	4	10	11	-	114	91	1	91.00	1-15	-	
totesport	215	206	34	6757	163	39.28	11	43	112	-	887	817	27	30.25	5-16	1	
Twenty20	9	9	2	219	38 *	31.28	-	-	4	-							

ADAMS, J. H. K. Hampshire

Name: James Henry Kenneth Adams
Role: Left-hand bat, left-arm medium bowler
Born: 23 September 1980, Winchester
Height: 6ft 1in **Weight:** 14st
Nickname: Jimmy, Bison, Nugget
County debut: 2002
1st-Class 50s: 5
1st-Class 100s: 1
1st-Class catches: 11
Place in batting averages: 143rd av. 30.05 (2003 169th av. 26.44)
Strike rate: 69.00 (career 57.00)
Parents: Jenny and Mike
Marital status: Single
Family links with cricket: 'Dad played a bit for Kent Schoolboys. Brothers Ben and Tom played/play for Hampshire age groups'
Education: Sherborne School; Loughborough University
Qualifications: 9 GCSEs, 3 A-levels, Level 1 coaching
Overseas tours: England U19 to Sri Lanka (U19 World Cup) 1999-2000; West of England to West Indies 1995; Sherborne School to Pakistan
Overseas teams played for: Woodville, Adelaide 1999-2000; Melville, Perth 2000-01
Career highlights to date: 'County debut. First first-class 100 v Somerset for Loughborough'
Cricket moments to forget: 'Kidderminster, June 2000'
Cricketers particularly admired: 'M. Parker, R. Smith, B. Lara …'
Young players to look out for: 'J. Francis, J. Tomlinson, K. Latouf, C. Benham …'
Other sports played: Hockey (Dorset age group when 14); 'fair interest in most sports'
Other sports followed: Football (Aston Villa); 'follow most ball sports'

Favourite band: Led Zeppelin, The Who, Blind Melon
Relaxations: Music, PlayStation, 'kick about with mates'
Extras: Played in U15 World Cup 1996. Hampshire Young Player of the Year 1998. Represented England U19 2000. Part of Hampshire's 2nd XI Championship winning side 2001. Played for Loughborough University CCE 2002 to 2004, scoring a century in each innings (103/113) v Kent at Canterbury 2002; captain of LUCCE 2003, scoring maiden first-class century (107) v Somerset at Taunton. Represented British Universities 2002, 2003 (captain 2003) and v New Zealanders and Sri Lanka A 2004
Best batting: 107 LUCCE v Somerset, Taunton 2003
Best bowling: 2-16 Hampshire v Durham, Riverside 2004

2004 Season

	M	Inns	NO	Runs	HS	Avge	100s	50s	Ct	St	O	M	Runs	Wkts	Avge	Best	5wI	10wM
Test																		
All First	12	20	3	511	75	30.05	-	2	2	-	23	6	77	2	38.50	2-16	-	-
1-day Int																		
C & G																		
totesport	3	3	0	74	40	24.66	-	-	2	-								
Twenty20																		

Career Performances

	M	Inns	NO	Runs	HS	Avge	100s	50s	Ct	St	Balls	Runs	Wkts	Avge	Best	5wI	10wM
Test																	
All First	28	51	5	1260	107	27.39	1	5	11	-	342	223	6	37.16	2-16	-	-
1-day Int																	
C & G																	
totesport	6	6	0	102	40	17.00	-	-	4	-	1	6	0	-	-	-	
Twenty20																	

2. Who was the enthusiastic Essex seamer who coached Zimbabwe in the 1991-92 World Cup?

ADSHEAD, S. J. Gloucestershire

Name: Stephen John Adshead
Role: Right-hand bat, wicket-keeper
Born: 29 January 1980, Worcester
Height: 5ft 8in **Weight:** 13st
Nickname: Adders, Top Shelf
County debut: 2000 (Leicestershire), 2003 (Worcestershire), 2004 (Gloucestershire)
County cap: 2003 (Worcestershire colours), 2004 (Gloucestershire)
1st-Class 50s: 5
1st-Class catches: 46
1st-Class stumpings: 4
Place in batting averages: 87th av. 38.06
Parents: David and Julie
Marital status: Engaged to Becky
Family links with cricket: Father and brother play club cricket in Worcester; mother keen spectator
Education: Brideley Moor HS, Redditch
Qualifications: 9 GCSEs, 3 A-levels, ECB Level 2 coaching
Career outside cricket: Coaching
Off-season: Playing club cricket in Queensland
Overseas tours: Leicestershire to Potchefstroom, South Africa 2001
Overseas teams played for: Fish Hoek, Cape Town 1998-99; Witwatersrand Technical, Johannesburg 1999-2000; Central Hawke's Bay, New Zealand 2000-01
Career highlights to date: 'Winning C&G final at Lord's 2004'
Cricket moments to forget: 'The whole 2002 season was a fairly miserable one'
Cricket superstitions: 'None'
Cricketers particularly admired: Alec Stewart, Steve Waugh
Young players to look out for: Steve Davies (Worcs)
Favourite band: U2
Relaxations: 'Spending as much time as possible with my fiancée Becky; gym, eating'
Extras: Released by Leicestershire at the end of the 2002 season. Played for Worcestershire in 2003 as an uncontracted player; also played for ECB XI in 2003. Joined Gloucestershire for the 2004 season. Scored 187-minute 57* to help save match v Lancashire at Cheltenham 2004
Opinions on cricket: 'Too many players forget to enjoy the game, which is why we all got good at it in the first place.'
Best batting: 63 Worcestershire v Glamorgan, Cardiff 2003

2004 Season

	M	Inns	NO	Runs	HS	Avge	100s	50s	Ct	St	O	M	Runs	Wkts	Avge	Best	5wI	10wM
Test																		
All First	15	23	7	609	61	38.06	-	4	39	2								
1-day Int																		
C & G	5	3	1	25	17 *	12.50	-	-	8	4								
totesport	15	13	2	133	32 *	12.09	-	-	18	6								
Twenty20	5	4	1	101	81	33.66	-	1	2	3								

Career Performances

	M	Inns	NO	Runs	HS	Avge	100s	50s	Ct	St	Balls	Runs	Wkts	Avge	Best	5wI	10wM
Test																	
All First	18	28	8	711	63	35.55	-	5	46	4							
1-day Int																	
C & G	9	7	2	172	77 *	34.40	-	1	13	6							
totesport	15	13	2	133	32 *	12.09	-	-	18	6							
Twenty20	7	6	2	103	81	25.75	-	1	3	3							

AFZAAL, U. Northamptonshire

Name: Usman Afzaal
Role: Left-hand bat, slow left-arm bowler
Born: 9 June 1977, Rawalpindi, Pakistan
Height: 6ft **Weight:** 12st 7lbs
Nickname: Saeed, Gulfraz, Usy Bhai, Trevor
County debut: 1995 (Nottinghamshire), 2004 (Northamptonshire)
County cap: 2000 (Nottinghamshire)
Test debut: 2001
Tests: 3
1000 runs in a season: 4
1st-Class 50s: 44
1st-Class 100s: 17
1st-Class catches: 72
One-Day 100s: 1
Place in batting averages: 14th av. 59.34 (2003 107th av. 34.07)
Strike rate: 77.25 (career 94.42)
Parents: Firdous and Shafi Mahmood
Marital status: Single
Family links with cricket: Older brother Kamran played for NAYC and for Nottinghamshire U15-U19 ('top player'); younger brother Aqib played for Notts and England U15; 'Uncle Mac and Uncle Raja great players'

Education: Manvers Pierrepont School; South Notts College
Qualifications: Coaching certificates
Career outside cricket: Printing company
Overseas tours: Nottinghamshire to South Africa; England U19 to West Indies 1994-95, to Zimbabwe 1995-96; 'the great ZRK tour to Lahore, Pakistan' 2000; England A to West Indies 2000-01; England to India and New Zealand 2001-02
Overseas teams played for: Victoria Park, Perth
Career highlights to date: 'Playing for England in the Ashes'
Cricket moments to forget: 'Every time I get out'
Cricketers particularly admired: David Gower, Saeed Anwar, Ian Botham, Clive Rice, Uncle Raja and Uncle Mac
Young players to look out for: Bilal Shafayat, Aqib Afzaal, Nadeem Malik
Other sports played: Indoor football
Other sports followed: Football ('a bit of Man U')
Relaxations: 'Praying; spending time with friends and family; listening to Indian music'
Extras: Played for England U15 and U17. Broke the U16 bowling record in the Texaco Trophy. Won Denis Compton Award 1996. Took wicket (Adam Gilchrist) with third ball in Test cricket v Australia at The Oval 2001. C&G Man of the Match award for his 3-8 (from four overs) and 64* v Ireland at Clontarf 2002. Left Nottinghamshire at the end of the 2003 season and joined Northamptonshire for 2004
Best batting: 167* Northamptonshire v Sussex, Northampton 2004
Best bowling: 4-101 Nottinghamshire v Gloucestershire, Trent Bridge 1998

2004 Season

	M	Inns	NO	Runs	HS	Avge	100s	50s	Ct	St	O	M	Runs	Wkts	Avge	Best	5wI	10wM
Test																		
All First	16	28	5	1365	167 *	59.34	4	7	9	-	51.3	7	196	4	49.00	3-65	-	-
1-day Int																		
C & G	3	3	0	45	27	15.00	-	-	-	-	3	2	4	3	1.33	3-4	-	
totesport	15	15	2	444	86 *	34.15	-	4	4	-	6.1	0	58	3	19.33	2-9	-	
Twenty20	5	4	1	12	9	4.00	-	-	1	-	3	0	27	0	-	-	-	

Career Performances

	M	Inns	NO	Runs	HS	Avge	100s	50s	Ct	St	Balls	Runs	Wkts	Avge	Best	5wI	10wM
Test	3	6	1	83	54	16.60	-	1	-	-	54	49	1	49.00	1-49	-	-
All First	146	254	25	8057	167 *	35.18	17	44	72	-	6610	3543	70	50.61	4-101	-	-
1-day Int																	
C & G	13	11	2	355	71	39.44	-	2	2	-	162	102	8	12.75	3-4	-	
totesport	80	73	10	2123	105	33.69	1	17	24	-	633	627	24	26.12	3-48	-	
Twenty20	9	8	1	56	17	8.00	-	-	1	-	18	27	0	-	-	-	

AGARKAR, A. B. — Middlesex

Name: Ajit Bhalchandra Agarkar
Role: Right-hand bat, right-arm fast-medium bowler
Born: 4 December 1977, Mumbai, India
County debut: 2004
Test debut: 1998-99
Tests: 21
One-Day Internationals: 131
1st-Class 50s: 6
1st-Class 100s: 2
1st-Class 5 w. in innings: 8
1st-Class catches: 22
One-Day 5 w. in innings: 1
Place in bowling averages: 64th av. 32.30
Strike rate: 56.10 (career 54.50)
Overseas tours: India U19 to Sri Lanka 1996-97; India A to Pakistan 1997-98; India to Zimbabwe 1998-99, to Bangladesh (Wills International Cup) 1998-99, to UK, Ireland and Holland (World Cup) 1999, to Australia 1999-2000, to Kenya (ICC Knockout Trophy) 2000-01, to Bangladesh 2000-01, to Zimbabwe 2001, to South Africa 2001-02, to West Indies 2001-02 (one-day series), to England 2002, to Sri Lanka (ICC Champions Trophy) 2002-03, to New Zealand 2002-03, to Australia 2003-04, to Pakistan 2003-04, to England (ICC Champions Trophy) 2004, to Bangladesh 2004-05 (one-day series), plus other one-day tournaments in Sharjah, Sri Lanka, Toronto, Bangladesh, Holland and England
Overseas teams played for: Mumbai 1996-97 –
Extras: Took fewest matches (23) to reach 50 ODI wickets. One of *Indian Cricket*'s five Cricketers of the Year 1998. Has won several ODI match awards, including Man of the Match for his 67* (50 in 21 balls) and 3-26 v Zimbabwe at Rajkot 2000-01. Scored maiden Test century (109*) in the first Test v England at Lord's 2002. Was an overseas player with Middlesex July to early August 2004, deputising for Nantie Hayward, absent on international duty
Best batting: 109* India v England, Lord's 2002
Best bowling: 6-41 India v Australia, Adelaide 2003-04

2004 Season

	M	Inns	NO	Runs	HS	Avge	100s	50s	Ct	St	O	M	Runs	Wkts	Avge	Best	5wI	10wM
Test																		
All First	3	4	2	27	22	13.50	-	-	2	-	93.3	20	323	10	32.30	5-81	1	-
1-day Int	3	2	0	69	47	34.50	-	-	-	-	26	2	135	3	45.00	1-33	-	
C & G																		
totesport	2	2	1	2	2	2.00	-	-	-	-	12	1	67	3	22.33	3-22	-	
Twenty20																		

Career Performances

	M	Inns	NO	Runs	HS	Avge	100s	50s	Ct	St	Balls	Runs	Wkts	Avge	Best	5wI	10wM
Test	21	33	3	420	109 *	14.00	1	-	4	-	4095	2306	52	44.34	6-41	1	-
All First	56	75	12	1440	109 *	22.85	2	6	22	-	9483	4893	174	28.12	6-41	8	-
1-day Int	131	83	26	1024	95	17.96	-	3	41	-	6499	5539	197	28.11	6-42	1	
C & G																	
totesport	2	2	1	2	2	2.00	-	-	-	-	72	67	3	22.33	3-22	-	
Twenty20																	

ALI, K. — Worcestershire

Name: Kabir Ali
Role: Right-hand bat, right-arm medium-fast bowler
Born: 24 November 1980, Birmingham
Height: 6ft **Weight:** 12st 7lbs
Nickname: Kabby, Taxi
County debut: 1999
County colours: 2002
Test debut: 2003
Tests: 1
One-Day Internationals: 1
50 wickets in a season: 2
1st-Class 50s: 5
1st-Class 5 w. in innings: 10
1st-Class 10 w. in match: 2
1st-Class catches: 12
One-Day 5 w. in innings: 1
Place in batting averages: 262nd av. 11.62 (2003 196th av. 23.81)
Place in bowling averages: 63rd av. 32.10 (2003 16th av. 23.16)
Strike rate: 53.14 (career 46.12)
Parents: Shabir Ali and M. Begum

Marital status: Single
Family links with cricket: Father played club cricket. Cousin Kadeer plays for Gloucestershire. Cousin Moeen plays at Warwickshire
Education: Moseley School; Wolverhampton University
Qualifications: GNVQ Leisure and Tourism, coaching
Overseas tours: Warwickshire U19 to Cape Town 1998; ECB National Academy to Australia and Sri Lanka 2002-03; England to Australia 2002-03 (VB Series), to South Africa 2004-05 (one-day series); England VI to Hong Kong 2003, 2004
Overseas teams played for: Midland-Guildford, Perth
Career highlights to date: 'Playing for England'
Cricketers particularly admired: Wasim Akram, Glenn McGrath
Young players to look out for: Moeen Ali, Omer Ali, Aatif Ali
Other sports played: Football, snooker
Other sports followed: Football, snooker
Relaxations: 'Playing snooker and spending time with family and friends'
Extras: Warwickshire Youth Young Player of the Year award. Won Gold Award on B&H debut for his 4-29 v Glamorgan at Worcester 2000. Represented England U19 2000. NBC Denis Compton Award for the most promising young Worcestershire player 2000. Junior Royals Player of the Year 2001. Worcestershire Player of the Year 2002. PCA Young Player of the Year 2002, 2003. His 8-53 v Yorkshire 2003 was the best return at Scarborough since Bill Bowes's 9-112 v Essex in 1932. Made Test debut in the fourth Test v South Africa at Headingley 2003, taking a wicket (Neil McKenzie) with his fifth ball. Worcestershire Young Player of the Year 2003. Don Kenyon Award 2003 for the best Championship match-winning performance by a Worcestershire player (8-58 v Derbyshire, following 68 in Worcestershire's only innings)
Best batting: 84* Worcestershire v Durham, Stockton 2003
Best bowling: 8-53 Worcestershire v Yorkshire, Scarborough 2003
Stop press: Took 1-12 and struck an 11-ball 34 to win Player of the Final award as England retained the Hong Kong Sixes title in 2004

2004 Season

	M	Inns	NO	Runs	HS	Avge	100s	50s	Ct	St	O	M	Runs	Wkts	Avge	Best	5wI	10wM
Test																		
All First	8	9	1	93	31	11.62	-	-	2	-	248	45	899	28	32.10	5-60	1	-
1-day Int																		
C & G	3	1	0	11	11	11.00	-	-	-	-	24	3	117	2	58.50	1-29	-	
totesport	7	6	1	86	33	17.20	-	-	-	-	40.3	6	190	11	17.27	3-28	-	
Twenty20	4	3	1	52	49	26.00	-	-	2	-	15	0	108	3	36.00	2-25	-	

Career Performances

	M	Inns	NO	Runs	HS	Avge	100s	50s	Ct	St	Balls	Runs	Wkts	Avge	Best	5wI	10wM
Test	1	2	0	10	9	5.00	-	-	-	-	216	136	5	27.20	3-80	-	-
All First	56	75	15	1178	84 *	19.63	-	5	12	-	9455	5542	205	27.03	8-53	10	2
1-day Int	1	0	0	0	0	-	-	-	-	-							
C & G	17	10	4	85	23 *	14.16	-	-	3	-	752	572	19	30.10	4-2	-	
totesport	53	31	8	335	92	14.56	-	1	9	-	2064	1747	80	21.83	5-36	1	
Twenty20	4	3	1	52	49	26.00	-	-	2	-	90	108	3	36.00	2-25	-	

ALI, K. — Gloucestershire

Name: Kadeer Ali
Role: Right-hand bat, right-arm medium-fast bowler
Born: 7 March 1983, Birmingham
Height: 6ft 2in **Weight:** 13st
Nickname: Kaddy
County debut: 2000 (Worcestershire)
County colours: 2002 (Worcestershire)
1st-Class 50s: 5
1st-Class catches: 10
Place in batting averages: 206th av. 21.60 (2003 139th av. 30.42)
Strike rate: 126.00 (career 228.00)
Parents: Munir Ali and Maqsood Begum
Marital status: Single
Family links with cricket: 'Brother Moeen plays for Warwickshire CCC and England U19; cousin Kabir Ali plays for Worcestershire; younger brother Omar Ali plays for Warwickshire U17'
Education: Handsworth Grammar; Moseley Sixth Form College
Qualifications: 5 GCSEs, Level 1 coach
Off-season: 'Spending it playing cricket somewhere abroad'
Overseas tours: England U19 to India 2000-01, to Australia and (U19 World Cup) New Zealand 2001-02; England A to Malaysia and India 2003-04
Overseas teams played for: WA University, Perth 2002-03
Career highlights to date: 'Being in the national academy. Really enjoyed it'
Cricket moments to forget: 'First-class debut – got a pair against Glamorgan'
Cricket superstitions: 'None'
Cricketers particularly admired: Rahul Dravid, Graeme Hick
Young players to look out for: Moeen Ali ('brother')
Other sports played: Snooker

Other sports followed: Football (Birmingham City FC)
Injuries: Out for six weeks with a fractured elbow
Relaxations: 'Just chilling, spending time with mates, music, movies'
Extras: Young Player awards at Warwickshire CCC. Represented England U19 v Sri Lanka U19 2000, v West Indies U19 2001 and v India U19 2002; scored 97 and 111 in the third 'Test' at Northampton 2002, in the process sharing with Bilal Shafayat in partnerships of 212 and 256. NBC Denis Compton Award for the most promising young Worcestershire player 2001, 2002. Represented ECB National Academy v England XI at Perth 2002-03, scoring a century (100). Contributed century (182, as captain) to Worcestershire 2nd XI record total (686), v Warwickshire 2nd XI at Barnt Green 2003. ECB National Academy 2003-04. Scored 221 v Somerset 2nd XI at Kidderminster 2004. Became first player to hit a ball over the Basil D'Oliveira Stand (opened 4 May 2004) when he struck a six off Daniel Vettori v New Zealanders at Worcester on 7 May 2004. Left Worcestershire at the end of the 2004 season and has joined Gloucestershire for 2005
Opinions on cricket: 'Twenty20 is the way forward.'
Best batting: 99 Worcestershire v Yorkshire, Worcester 2003
Best bowling: 1-15 Worcestershire v Middlesex, Worcester 2004

2004 Season

	M	Inns	NO	Runs	HS	Avge	100s	50s	Ct	St	O	M	Runs	Wkts	Avge	Best	5wI	10wM
Test																		
All First	6	10	0	216	66	21.60	-	1	4	-	21	1	106	1	106.00	1-15	-	-
1-day Int																		
C & G																		
totesport	2	2	0	67	51	33.50	-	1	-	-								
Twenty20																		

Career Performances

	M	Inns	NO	Runs	HS	Avge	100s	50s	Ct	St	Balls	Runs	Wkts	Avge	Best	5wI	10wM
Test																	
All First	25	43	1	810	99	19.28	-	5	10	-	228	163	1	163.00	1-15	-	-
1-day Int																	
C & G	4	4	0	140	66	35.00	-	1	-	-	27	25	1	25.00	1-4	-	
totesport	10	10	1	249	57	27.66	-	3	-	-							
Twenty20	5	5	0	122	53	24.40	-	1	2	-							

3. At which home venue do Scotland normally play their international matches and Saltires fixtures?

ALI, M. M. Warwickshire

Name: Moeen Munir Ali
Role: Left-hand bat, right-arm off-spin bowler; 'batter who bowls'
Born: 18 June 1987, Birmingham
Height: 6ft **Weight:** 10st 7lbs
Nickname: Moe, Eddy, Bart, Elvis
County debut: No first-team appearance
Parents: Munir Ali and Maqsood Begum
Marital status: Single
Family links with cricket: Father is a cricket coach; cousin Kabir Ali plays for Worcestershire and England; brother Kadeer Ali plays for Gloucestershire; younger brother Omar plays youth cricket
Education: Moseley School
Qualifications: GCSEs and Leisure and Tourism
Career outside cricket: Student
Overseas tours: 'Streets to Arena' to Pakistan 2002; England U19 to India 2004-05
Career highlights to date: 'Becoming one of the youngest professional cricketers at 15 years old. Hitting 195* in 20 overs'
Cricket moments to forget: 'None'
Cricket superstitions: 'None'
Cricketers particularly admired: Nick Knight, Sanath Jayasuriya, Saeed Anwar, Wasim Akram, Kabir Ali, Kadeer Ali, Mohammed Sheikh
Young players to look out for: Omar Munir Ali, Atif Ali, Behram Ali
Other sports played: Football
Other sports followed: Football (Birmingham City)
Favourite band: B21
Relaxations: 'Playing snooker at Premier in Balsall Heath and listening to music (chilling out)'
Extras: Represented England U15 2002. Has won five Warwickshire youth awards since age of 11. Represented England U19 v Bangladesh U19 2004
Opinions on cricket: 'Youngsters should be given more chances at international standard and first-class.'

ALLEYNE, D. Nottinghamshire

Name: David Alleyne
Role: Right-hand bat, wicket-keeper
Born: 17 April 1976, York
Height: 5ft 11in **Weight:** 13st 7lbs
Nickname: Bones, Gears
County debut: 1999 (one-day, Middlesex), 2001 (first-class, Middlesex), 2004 (Nottinghamshire)
1st-Class catches: 23
Parents: Darcy and Jo
Marital status: Engaged to Dawn
Family links with cricket: Father played for local club Northampton Exiles
Education: Enfield Grammar; Hertford Regional College, Ware; City and Islington College
Qualifications: 6 GCSEs, City and Guilds, BTEC Diploma in Leisure Studies, Level 3 coaching award
Career outside cricket: Coaching; teaching
Overseas tours: Middlesex to Johannesburg 2000-01
Overseas teams played for: Stratford, New Zealand; Inglewood, New Zealand 1997-98; Sturt, Adelaide 1999-2000; Midland-Guildford, Perth 2000-01; Karori CC, Wellington, New Zealand 2001-02
Cricketers particularly admired: Viv Richards, Desmond Haynes, Carl Hooper, Jack Russell, Alec Stewart, Keith Piper
Other sports played: Judo, football (Middlesex U15, U16; Enfield Borough U16)
Other sports followed: Football (Liverpool FC)
Relaxations: 'Relaxing with Dawn and family'
Extras: Represented Middlesex U11 to U17. London Cricket College (three years). Represented Middlesex Cricket Board. Middlesex 2nd XI Player of the Year 1999, 2000, 2002. Left Middlesex at the end of the 2003 season and joined Nottinghamshire for 2004
Best batting: 49* Middlesex v Derbyshire, Derby 2002

2004 Season

	M	Inns	NO	Runs	HS	Avge	100s	50s	Ct	St	O	M	Runs	Wkts	Avge	Best	5wI	10wM
Test																		
All First	4	4	2	112	43 *	56.00	-	-	11	-								
1-day Int																		
C & G																		
totesport																		
Twenty20																		

Career Performances

	M	Inns	NO	Runs	HS	Avge	100s	50s	Ct	St	Balls	Runs	Wkts	Avge	Best	5wI	10wM
Test																	
All First	9	11	3	260	49 *	32.50	-	-	23	-							
1-day Int																	
C & G	5	5	0	30	19	6.00	-	-	3	-							
totesport	25	20	2	226	58	12.55	-	1	19	6							
Twenty20	5	2	1	11	6 *	11.00	-	-	3	-							

ALLEYNE, M. W. — Gloucestershire

Name: Mark Wayne Alleyne
Role: Right-hand bat, right-arm medium bowler, occasional wicket-keeper, county club and one-day captain
Born: 23 May 1968, Tottenham, London
Height: 5ft 10in **Weight:** 14st
Nickname: Boo-Boo
County debut: 1986
County cap: 1990
Benefit: 1999
One-Day Internationals: 10
1000 runs in a season: 6
50 wickets in a season: 1
1st-Class 50s: 71
1st-Class 100s: 21
1st-Class 200s: 1
1st-Class 5 w. in innings: 9
1st-Class catches: 273
1st-Class stumpings: 3
One-Day 100s: 4
One-Day 5 w. in innings: 3
Place in batting averages: (2003 228th av. 19.30)

Place in bowling averages: 5th av. 20.63
Strike rate: 36.27 (career 64.24)
Parents: Euclid (deceased) and Hyacinth
Wife and date of marriage: Louise Maria, 9 October 1998
Children: Jasper, 6 April 2004
Family links with cricket: Brother played for Gloucestershire 2nd XI and Middlesex YC. Father played club cricket in Barbados and England
Education: Harrison College, Barbados; Cardinal Pole School, East London
Qualifications: 6 O-levels, NCA Senior Coaching Award, volleyball coaching certificate
Overseas tours: England YC to Sri Lanka 1986-87, to Australia 1987-88; England XI to New Zealand (Cricket Max) 1997; England A to Bangladesh and New Zealand 1999-2000 (captain), to West Indies 2000-01 (captain); England to Australia 1998-99 (CUB Series), to South Africa and Zimbabwe 1999-2000 (one-day series), to Kenya (ICC Knockout Trophy) 2000-01, to Pakistan and Sri Lanka 2000-01 (one-day series)
Career highlights to date: '1) England debut in Brisbane 2) England Man of the Match in East London, South Africa 3) Each one of our five consecutive trophies'
Cricket moments to forget: 'Missing promotion in the Championship and being relegated in the Norwich Union League in the same week [2001]'
Cricketers particularly admired: Gordon Greenidge, Viv Richards, Jack Russell, Steve Waugh
Other sports played: Basketball, football
Other sports followed: 'Still follow Tottenham religiously but support our local football and rugby teams'
Relaxations: 'Sport crazy but also an avid gardener. Keen historian'
Extras: Graduate of Haringey Cricket College. In 1986 became (at 18 years 54 days) the youngest player to score a century for Gloucestershire, with his 116* v Sussex at Bristol. In 1990 became the then youngest to score a Championship double hundred for the county, with his 256 v Northamptonshire at Northampton. In 1992 struck then highest Sunday League score for Gloucestershire (134*) v Leicestershire at Bristol. Cricket Select Sunday League Player of the Year 1992. Scored 112 in the B&H Super Cup final v Yorkshire at Lord's 1999, winning the Man of the Match award. Leading all-rounder in the single-division four-day era of the County Championship with 6409 runs (av. 32.53) and 216 wickets (av. 31.18) 1993-99. Captain of Gloucestershire's one-day double-winning side (NatWest and B&H Super Cup) 1999 and of treble-winning side (NatWest, B&H and Norwich Union National League) 2000. Man of the Match in ODI v South Africa at East London February 2000 (53, 3-55 and a catch to dismiss Jonty Rhodes). Played 393 consecutive competitive games, a Gloucestershire record, between 28 July 1990 and 24 June 2000. One of *Wisden*'s Five Cricketers of the Year 2001. Honorary fellowship from University of Gloucestershire, October 2001. Gloucestershire captain 1997-2003; Gloucestershire player/coach, club and one-day captain since 2004. Awarded MBE in the New Year honours list 2004. His 5-71 v Surrey at Bristol 2004 included his 400th first-class wicket for Gloucestershire (Nadeem Shahid)

Best batting: 256 Gloucestershire v Northamptonshire, Northampton 1990
Best bowling: 6-49 Gloucestershire v Middlesex, Lord's 2000

2004 Season

	M	Inns	NO	Runs	HS	Avge	100s	50s	Ct	St	O	M	Runs	Wkts	Avge	Best	5wI	10wM
Test																		
All First	5	6	1	171	77 *	34.20	-	2	5	-	66.3	19	227	11	20.63	5-71	1	-
1-day Int																		
C & G	5	4	1	8	4 *	2.66	-	-	-	-	44.1	2	188	11	17.09	4-33	-	
totesport	12	12	4	176	42	22.00	-	-	3	-	95	3	501	17	29.47	4-39	-	
Twenty20	5	3	1	34	18 *	17.00	-	-	1	-	13	0	115	1	115.00	1-27	-	

Career Performances

	M	Inns	NO	Runs	HS	Avge	100s	50s	Ct	St	Balls	Runs	Wkts	Avge	Best	5wI	10wM
Test																	
All First	327	535	52	14876	256	30.79	22	71	273	3	26599	13575	414	32.78	6-49	9	-
1-day Int	10	8	1	151	53	21.57	-	1	3	-	366	280	10	28.00	3-27	-	
C & G	52	40	7	671	73	20.33	-	1	16	-	2260	1437	61	23.55	5-30	1	
totesport	271	248	54	5530	134 *	28.50	3	23	110	-	9445	7623	249	30.61	5-28	1	
Twenty20	10	6	4	74	21 *	37.00	-	-	6	-	186	252	6	42.00	2-33	-	

AMBROSE, T. R. — Sussex

Name: Timothy (Tim) Raymond Ambrose
Role: Right-hand bat, wicket-keeper
Born: 1 December 1982, Newcastle, New South Wales, Australia
Height: 5ft 7in
Nickname: Shambrose, Freak, Mole
County debut: 2001
County cap: 2003
1st-Class 50s: 14
1st-Class 100s: 2
1st-Class catches: 62
1st-Class stumpings: 8
Place in batting averages: 238th av. 17.13 (2003 72nd av. 40.47)
Parents: Raymond and Sally
Marital status: Single
Family links with cricket: 'Cousin played Sydney first grade; father is captain of local grade D4 team'

Education: Merewether Selective High, NSW
Career outside cricket: Greenkeeping
Off-season: 'Training in South Africa'
Overseas tours: Sussex to Grenada 2001, 2002
Overseas teams played for: Wallsend, NSW 2000; Nelson Bay, NSW 2001; Newcastle, NSW 2002
Career highlights to date: 'Winning the Championship 2003. Maiden first-class century, 149 v Yorkshire. Playing with Tony Cottey'
Cricket moments to forget: '2004'
Cricketers particularly admired: Alec Stewart, Ian Healy, Steve Waugh, Mushtaq Ahmed
Young players to look out for: Andrew Hodd, Matt Prior, Luke Wright
Other sports played: Football, squash, golf, rugby league, rugby union, AFL, 'I'll have a go at anything'
Other sports followed: Rugby league (Newcastle Knights), Australian Rules (Sydney Swans), football (Tottenham Hotspur)
Favourite band: Jeff Buckley, Ben Harper, Jack Johnson
Relaxations: Guitar, music
Extras: Captained Newcastle (NSW) U16 1999 Bradman Cup winning side. 'Scored 138 in first ever game.' Played for New South Wales U17. Won NSW Junior Cricketer of the Year three years running. Scored 52 on first-class debut v Warwickshire at Edgbaston 2001. C&G Man of the Match award for his 95 v Buckinghamshire at Beaconsfield 2002. Holds a British passport and is not considered an overseas player
Opinions on cricket: 'Great game. Love it.'
Best batting: 149 Sussex v Yorkshire, Headingley 2002

2004 Season

	M	Inns	NO	Runs	HS	Avge	100s	50s	Ct	St	O	M	Runs	Wkts	Avge	Best	5wI	10wM
Test																		
All First	10	15	0	257	60	17.13	-	2	21	1								
1-day Int																		
C & G	1	1	0	14	14	14.00	-	-	2	-								
totesport	5	4	0	57	21	14.25	-	-	9	2								
Twenty20																		

Career Performances

	M	Inns	NO	Runs	HS	Avge	100s	50s	Ct	St	Balls	Runs	Wkts	Avge	Best	5wI	10wM
Test																	
All First	40	66	4	2078	149	33.51	2	14	62	8	6	1	0	-	-	-	-
1-day Int																	
C & G	6	6	0	173	95	28.83	-	1	4	-							
totesport	32	29	1	569	87	20.32	-	1	35	5							
Twenty20	5	5	2	108	54 *	36.00	-	1	5	3							

ANDERSON, J. M. Lancashire

Name: James Michael Anderson
Role: Left-hand bat, right-arm fast-medium bowler
Born: 30 July 1982, Burnley
Height: 6ft 2in **Weight:** 13st
Nickname: Jimmy
County debut: 2001 (one-day), 2002 (first-class)
County cap: 2003
Test debut: 2003
Tests: 11
One-Day Internationals: 36
50 wickets in a season: 1
1st-Class 5 w. in innings: 7
1st-Class 10 w. in match: 1
1st-Class catches: 10
Place in bowling averages: 11th av. 22.80 (2003 60th av. 30.04)
Strike rate: 41.81 (career 43.95)
Parents: Michael and Catherine
Marital status: Single
Family links with cricket: Father and uncle played for Burnley
Education: St Theodore's RC High School; St Theodore's RC Sixth Form Centre – both Burnley
Qualifications: 10 GCSEs, 1 A-level, 1 GNVQ, Level 2 coaching award
Off-season: Touring with England
Overseas tours: Lancashire to Cape Town 2002; ECB National Academy to Australia 2002-03; England to Australia 2002-03 (VB Series), to Africa (World Cup) 2002-03, to Bangladesh and Sri Lanka 2003-04, to West Indies 2003-04, to Zimbabwe (one-day series) 2004-05, to South Africa 2004-05
Career highlights to date: 'Receiving Lancs cap. Playing for England'
Cricket moments to forget: 'England v Australia – 2003 World Cup'
Cricketers particularly admired: Darren Gough, Nasser Hussain, Peter Martin
Young players to look out for: Jonathan Clare, David Brown
Other sports played: Golf (12 handicap), football
Other sports followed: Football (Arsenal FC), rugby league, darts
Favourite band: Oasis, U2
Relaxations: 'Watching TV, playing PlayStation, music'
Extras: Represented England U19 2001. Took 50 first-class wickets in his first full season 2002. NBC Denis Compton Award for the most promising young Lancashire player 2002. England's leading wicket-taker in the 2002-03 World Cup (10 wickets;

av. 22.50), winning two Man of the Match awards. Became youngest bowler to take a hat-trick for Lancashire (aged 20 years 9½ months), v Essex (Robinson, Hussain, Jefferson) at Old Trafford 2003. Became youngest bowler to record a five-wicket innings return on England Test debut (5-73) in the first Test v Zimbabwe at Lord's 2003. Became the first England bowler to take an ODI hat-trick (Abdul Razzaq, Shoaib Akhtar, Mohammad Sami) v Pakistan at The Oval in the NatWest Challenge 2003, having also dismissed Imran Nazir with the first ball of the match. Cricket Writers' Club Young Player of the Year 2003. Recorded maiden first-class ten-wicket match return (6-49/4-32) v Worcestershire at Old Trafford 2004. ECB contract 2004-05

Best batting: 21* England v South Africa, Lord's 2003
Best bowling: 6-23 Lancashire v Hampshire, West End 2002

2004 Season

	M	Inns	NO	Runs	HS	Avge	100s	50s	Ct	St	O	M	Runs	Wkts	Avge	Best	5wI	10wM
Test	3	4	2	23	12	11.50	-	-	2	-	55.1	8	219	7	31.28	4-52	-	-
All First	7	8	3	29	12	5.80	-	-	3	-	181.1	35	593	26	22.80	6-49	1	1
1-day Int	5	2	1	13	11	13.00	-	-	1	-	38.5	2	202	7	28.85	3-37	-	
C & G	2	0	0	0	0	-	-	-	-	-	20	0	95	2	47.50	2-56	-	
totesport	5	2	1	10	5 *	10.00	-	-	-	-	39.1	6	172	12	14.33	3-26	-	
Twenty20	3	1	1	0	0 *	-	-	-	-	-	10	0	73	2	36.50	2-28	-	

Career Performances

	M	Inns	NO	Runs	HS	Avge	100s	50s	Ct	St	Balls	Runs	Wkts	Avge	Best	5wI	10wM
Test	11	16	12	68	21 *	17.00	-	-	4	-	1830	1125	33	34.09	5-73	2	-
All First	33	40	25	145	21 *	9.66	-	-	10	-	5363	3110	122	25.49	6-23	7	1
1-day Int	36	13	5	41	11	5.12	-	-	5	-	1741	1391	57	24.40	4-25	-	
C & G	7	3	3	12	7 *	-	-	-	2	-	384	288	11	26.18	3-14	-	
totesport	9	3	2	11	5 *	11.00	-	-	1	-	403	318	18	17.66	3-26	-	
Twenty20	3	1	1	0	0 *	-	-	-	-	-	60	73	2	36.50	2-28	-	

4. Which West Indian opener, who scored 104 v England at Antigua in 1997-98, top-scored for USA v New Zealand in the 2004 ICC Champions Trophy?

ANDERSON, R. S. G. — Northamptonshire

Name: Ricaldo (Ricky) Sherman Glenroy Anderson
Role: Right-hand bat, right-arm medium-fast bowler
Born: 22 September 1976, Hammersmith, London
Height: 5ft 10in **Weight:** 11st 11lbs
County debut: 1999 (Essex), 2002 (Northamptonshire)
50 wickets in a season: 1
1st-Class 50s: 2
1st-Class 5 w. in innings: 8
1st-Class 10 w. in match: 1
1st-Class catches: 7
Strike rate: 63.00 (career 51.05)
Parents: Heather and Junior
Marital status: Single
Education: Alperton High School; Barnet College; NWL College; London Cricket College
Qualifications: 6 GCSEs, BTEC National in Engineering
Overseas tours: Middlesex U16 to Jersey; BWIA to Trinidad and Tobago 1998, 1999, 2000
Overseas teams played for: Coronation CC, South Africa 1996-97
Cricketers particularly admired: Malcolm Marshall, Stuart Law, Carl Hooper
Other sports followed: Football (Liverpool)
Relaxations: Music
Extras: Took 50 first-class wickets in his first season 1999. Left Essex in the 2001-02 off-season and joined Northamptonshire for 2002; released by Northamptonshire at the end of the 2004 season
Best batting: 67* Essex v Sussex, Chelmsford 2000
Best bowling: 6-34 Essex v Northamptonshire, Ilford 2000

2004 Season

	M	Inns	NO	Runs	HS	Avge	100s	50s	Ct	St	O	M	Runs	Wkts	Avge	Best	5wI	10wM
Test																		
All First	1	1	1	33	33 *	-	-	-	-	-	21	3	54	2	27.00	1-11	-	-
1-day Int																		
C & G																		
totesport																		
Twenty20																		

Career Performances

	M	Inns	NO	Runs	HS	Avge	100s	50s	Ct	St	Balls	Runs	Wkts	Avge	Best	5wI	10wM
Test																	
All First	40	52	6	683	67 *	14.84	-	2	7	-	6229	3452	122	28.29	6-34	8	1
1-day Int																	
C & G	1	1	0	4	4	4.00	-	-	-	-	42	53	1	53.00	1-53	-	
totesport	19	15	2	102	22	7.84	-	-	-	-	780	678	15	45.20	3-30	-	
Twenty20	1	1	1	0	0 *	-	-	-	1	-	24	29	4	7.25	4-29	-	

ANDREW, G. M. Somerset

Name: Gareth Mark Andrew
Role: Left-hand bat, right-arm fast-medium bowler; all-rounder
Born: 27 December 1983, Yeovil
Height: 6ft **Weight:** 13st 8lbs
Nickname: Gaz, Brad, Sobers
County debut: 2003
1st-Class catches: 4
Place in bowling averages: (2003 64th av. 31.00)
Strike rate: 34.28 (career 41.64)
Parents: Peter and Susan
Marital status: Single
Family links with cricket: 'Dad and younger brother are club cricketers'
Education: Ansford Community School; Richard Huish College, Taunton
Qualifications: 10 GCSEs, 3 A-levels, Level 1 coach
Career outside cricket: 'Open University studying business'
Off-season: 'Training hard'
Overseas tours: West of England U15 to West Indies 1999; England U17 to Australia 2001; Somerset Academy to Western Australia 2002; Aus Academy to Perth 2003
Overseas teams played for: Swanbourne CC, Perth 2002-03
Career highlights to date: '4-48 against Scotland in totesport League [2004]'
Cricket moments to forget: 'Whenever bowling in the Twenty20'
Cricket superstitions: 'Keep eyes open!'
Cricketers particularly admired: Ian Botham, Andrew Flintoff, Chris Cairns
Young players to look out for: Mike Munday, Ivan Short, Bert Cox
Other sports played: Football (Bruton Town FC, Yeovil District U11-U16, Castle Cary AFC)

Other sports followed: Football (Yeovil Town, Man Utd)
Injuries: Out for three months after an operation in January 2004 for a SLAP (Superior Labrum Anterior-Posterior) lesion of the shoulder
Favourite band: 'Too many to mention'
Relaxations: 'Going home; chilling in Esporta; people-watching from Starbucks with the boys'
Extras: Played for Somerset Board XI in the NatWest 2000 and the C&G 2002. Represented England U19 v South Africa U19 2003
Opinions on cricket: 'Too much cricket. Longer game should be shortened by a day to get more competitive, resultful cricket.'
Best batting: 44 Somerset v Sri Lanka A, Taunton 2004
Best bowling: 4-63 Somerset v Sri Lanka A, Taunton 2004

2004 Season

	M	Inns	NO	Runs	HS	Avge	100s	50s	Ct	St	O	M	Runs	Wkts	Avge	Best	5wI	10wM
Test																		
All First	2	3	0	59	44	19.66	-	-	2	-	40	5	179	7	25.57	4-63	-	-
1-day Int																		
C & G																		
totesport	9	6	1	40	18	8.00	-	-	2	-	49.1	2	314	10	31.40	4-48	-	
Twenty20	5	3	1	9	5	4.50	-	-	-	-	13.3	0	128	2	64.00	1-31	-	

Career Performances

	M	Inns	NO	Runs	HS	Avge	100s	50s	Ct	St	Balls	Runs	Wkts	Avge	Best	5wI	10wM
Test																	
All First	6	8	0	95	44	11.87	-	-	4	-	708	489	17	28.76	4-63	-	-
1-day Int																	
C & G	2	1	0	1	1	1.00	-	-	1	-	53	35	0	-	-	-	
totesport	18	12	2	91	23	9.10	-	-	6	-	525	536	21	25.52	4-48	-	
Twenty20	8	5	1	11	5	2.75	-	-	-	-	117	181	4	45.25	2-36	-	

ANYON, J. E. Warwickshire

Name: James Edward Anyon
Role: Left-hand bat, right-arm fast-medium bowler
Born: 5 May 1983, Lancaster
Height: 6ft 2in **Weight:** 13st 7lbs
Nickname: Jimmy
County debut: No first-team appearance
1st-Class catches: 2
Strike rate: 45.00 (career 90.00)
Parents: Peter and Christine

Marital status: Single
Family links with cricket: 'Dad used to play village cricket'
Education: Garstang High School; Preston College; Loughborough University
Qualifications: GCSEs, 3 A-levels, BSc Sports Science with Management, Level 1 coaching
Career outside cricket: Building/labouring
Off-season: 'In Australia for one month playing club cricket for Claremont-Nedlands'
Overseas teams played for: Claremont-Nedlands, Perth 2004-05
Career highlights to date: 'Bowling at Brian Lara'
Cricket moments to forget: 'Losing UCCE final 2004'
Cricketers particularly admired: Glenn McGrath, Michael Atherton
Young players to look out for: Moeen Ali
Other sports played: Football, golf
Other sports followed: Football (Man Utd, Preston North End)
Favourite band: Nuse
Relaxations: 'Playing football; socialising with mates; spending time with girlfriend'
Extras: Young Player of the Year awards at Preston CC. Bowler of the Year award at Farsley CC (Bradford League) 2004. Played for Loughborough University CCE 2003, 2004. Played for Cumberland in the first round of the C&G 2004, which was played in August 2003
Opinions on cricket: 'Too many non-England-qualified players. Too many teams go up and down – no stability in the Championship and one-day league.'
Best batting: 21 LUCCE v Leicestershire, Leicester 2003
Best bowling: 3-57 LUCCE v Gloucestershire, Bristol 2004

2004 Season (did not make any first-class or one-day appearances for his county)

Career Performances

	M	Inns	NO	Runs	HS	Avge	100s	50s	Ct	St	Balls	Runs	Wkts	Avge	Best	5wI	10wM
Test																	
All First	5	4	1	23	21	7.66	-	-	2	-	630	494	7	70.57	3-57	-	-
1-day Int																	
C & G	1	1	0	0	0	0.00	-	-	1	-	42	46	1	46.00	1-46	-	
totesport																	
Twenty20																	

AVERIS, J. M. M. Gloucestershire

Name: James Maxwell Michael Averis
Role: Right-hand bat, right-arm fast-medium bowler
Born: 28 May 1974, Bristol
Height: 5ft 11in **Weight:** 13st 7lbs
Nickname: Avo, Fish, Goat
County debut: 1994 (one-day), 1997 (first-class)
County cap: 2001
1st-Class 5 w. in innings: 5
1st-Class catches: 12
One-Day 5 w. in innings: 4
Place in batting averages: 208th av. 21.42
Place in bowling averages: 116th av. 39.25
Strike rate: 61.14 (career 71.78)
Parents: Mike and Carol
Wife and date of marriage: Anna, 26 October 2002
Family links with cricket: 'Father and grandfather played and have lots of advice'
Education: Bristol Cathedral School; Portsmouth University; St Cross College, Oxford University
Qualifications: 10 GCSEs, 3 A-levels, BSc (Hons) Geographical Science, Diploma in Social Studies (Oxon), FPC I and II
Overseas tours: Bristol Schools to Australia 1990-91; Gloucestershire to Zimbabwe 1997, to South Africa 1999, to Cape Town 2000, to Kimberley 2001, to Stellenbosch 2002; Bristol RFC to South Africa 1996; Oxford University RFC to Japan and Australia 1997
Overseas teams played for: Union CC, Port Elizabeth, South Africa; Kraifontaine, Boland, South Africa 2001
Career highlights to date: 'Winning treble in 2000'
Cricket moments to forget: 'Dropping the biggest dolly in 2000 NatWest final'
Cricket superstitions: 'Must eat on way to ground. Always use same toilet'
Cricketers particularly admired: Viv Richards, Malcolm Marshall, Ian Botham
Other sports played: Football (Bristol North West), rugby (played for Bristol RFC, captain of South West U21 1995, Oxford Blue 1996)
Other sports followed: Rugby (Bristol RFC), football (Liverpool FC)
Relaxations: 'Reading, surfing, eating out'
Extras: Double Oxford Blue in 1996-97. Played in every one-day game in Gloucestershire's treble-winning season 2000. Gloucestershire Player of the Year 2001. Had figures of 4-23 in the C&G final v Worcestershire at Lord's 2004, including hat-trick (Leatherdale, G. Batty, Hall) with the last ball of his ninth over and the first two balls of his tenth

Best batting: 48* Gloucestershire v Surrey, The Oval 2004
Best bowling: 6-32 Gloucestershire v Northamptonshire, Bristol 2004

2004 Season

	M	Inns	NO	Runs	HS	Avge	100s	50s	Ct	St	O	M	Runs	Wkts	Avge	Best	5wI	10wM
Test																		
All First	13	11	4	150	48 *	21.42	-	-	2	-	285.2	51	1099	28	39.25	6-32	2	-
1-day Int																		
C & G	2	0	0	0	0	-	-	-	-	-	19	4	55	5	11.00	4-23	-	
totesport	11	4	2	22	10 *	11.00	-	-	3	-	84.4	10	425	17	25.00	3-28	-	
Twenty20	5	1	0	4	4	4.00	-	-	2	-	14	0	111	10	11.10	3-7	-	

Career Performances

	M	Inns	NO	Runs	HS	Avge	100s	50s	Ct	St	Balls	Runs	Wkts	Avge	Best	5wI	10wM
Test																	
All First	56	70	16	662	48 *	12.25	-	-	12	-	9045	5408	126	42.92	6-32	5	-
1-day Int																	
C & G	17	6	5	33	12 *	33.00	-	-	2	-	829	592	33	17.93	6-23	1	
totesport	80	43	20	202	23 *	8.78	-	-	11	-	3603	2900	119	24.36	5-20	3	
Twenty20	7	1	0	4	4	4.00	-	-	3	-	126	170	12	14.16	3-7	-	

AZHAR MAHMOOD — Surrey

Name: Azhar Mahmood Sagar
Role: Right-hand bat, right-arm fast-medium bowler; all-rounder
Born: 28 February 1975, Rawalpindi, Pakistan
Height: 6ft **Weight:** 13st 5lbs
Nickname: Aju
County debut: 2002
County cap: 2004
Test debut: 1997-98
Tests: 21
One-Day Internationals: 134
1st-Class 50s: 25
1st-Class 100s: 4
1st-Class 5 w. in innings: 14
1st-Class 10 w. in match: 3
1st-Class catches: 84
One-Day 5 w. in innings: 5
Place in batting averages: 142nd av. 30.36 (2003 96th av. 37.08)

Place in bowling averages: 47th av. 29.94 (2003 65th av. 31.34)
Strike rate: 53.13 (career 49.06)
Parents: Mohammed Aslam Sagar and Nusrat Perveen
Wife and date of marriage: Ebba Azhar, 13 April 2003
Education: FG No. 1 High School, Islamabad
Qualifications: 'A-level equivalent'
Career outside cricket: 'Property'
Overseas tours: Pakistan Youth to New Zealand 1994-95; Pakistan A to Bangladesh 1996, to England 1997; Pakistan to India (Pepsi Independence Cup) 1997, to South Africa and Zimbabwe 1997-98, to Bangladesh (Wills International Cup) 1998-99, to India 1998-99, to UK, Ireland and Holland (World Cup) 1999, to Australia 1999-2000, to Sri Lanka 2000, to Kenya (ICC Knockout Trophy) 2000-01, to New Zealand 2000-01, to England 2001, to Bangladesh 2001-02, to Australia (Super Challenge II) 2002, to Morocco (Morocco Cup) 2002, to Zimbabwe 2002-03, to Africa (World Cup) 2002-03, to England (NatWest Challenge) 2003, to New Zealand 2003-04, to England (ICC Champions Trophy) 2004, to Australia 2004-05 (VB Series), plus other one-day tournaments in Toronto, Kenya, Sharjah, Bangladesh and Singapore
Overseas teams played for: Islamabad; United Bank; Rawalpindi; Pakistan International Airlines
Career highlights to date: 'First Test match (debut) against South Africa in 1997 in Pakistan (Rawalpindi). I scored 128* in the first innings and 50* in the second, plus two wickets – Man of the Match'
Cricket moments to forget: 'World Cup 1999 – final against Australia (which we lost)'
Cricket superstitions: 'None'
Cricketers particularly admired: Imran Khan, Wasim Akram, Steve Waugh
Young players to look out for: Bilal Asad, Rikki Clarke
Other sports played: Snooker, basketball, kite flying
Other sports followed: Football (Man U)
Relaxations: 'Listening to music, training, spending time with my family'
Extras: Made first-class debut for Islamabad 1993-94. Scored 128* and 50* on Test debut in the first Test v South Africa at Rawalpindi 1997-98; during first innings shared with Mushtaq Ahmed (59) in a tenth-wicket stand of 151, equalling the world tenth-wicket record in Tests. Scored century (136) in the first Test v South Africa at Johannesburg 1997-98, becoming the first Pakistan player to score a Test century in South Africa and achieving feat of scoring a century on Test debuts home and away. Took 6-18 v West Indies in the Coca-Cola Champions Trophy in Sharjah 1999-2000 and 5-28 v Sri Lanka in the final of the same competition, winning the Man of the Match award on both occasions. Was Surrey's overseas player at the start of the 2002 season, pending the arrival of Saqlain Mushtaq, absent on international duty; returned as an overseas player 2003. Topped English first-class bowling averages 2002 with 20 wickets at 17.25. Awarded Surrey cap 2004
Opinions on cricket: 'State of sport now – there's a lot more cricket now than when I started. Hardly any off time. Cricketing standards have improved through fielding,

third umpiring, and cricket is a lot faster, hence viewed by a wider audience. Because of the fast pace, we are able to get results in Test matches; before, most Test matches were drawn. Having overseas players in county [cricket] is very good because it's become more competitive and helps groom younger players.'
Best batting: 136 Pakistan v South Africa, Johannesburg 1997-98
Best bowling: 8-61 Surrey v Lancashire, The Oval 2002

2004 Season

	M	Inns	NO	Runs	HS	Avge	100s	50s	Ct	St	O	M	Runs	Wkts	Avge	Best	5wI	10wM
Test																		
All First	12	20	1	577	84	30.36	-	4	8	-	336.3	77	1138	38	29.94	5-54	1	-
1-day Int																		
C & G	1	1	0	13	13	13.00	-	-	-	-	9.2	0	60	2	30.00	2-60	-	
totesport	10	9	2	187	67	26.71	-	2	4	-	72	6	299	15	19.93	5-24	1	
Twenty20	3	3	0	35	13	11.66	-	-	2	-	10.1	0	73	2	36.50	2-22	-	

Career Performances

	M	Inns	NO	Runs	HS	Avge	100s	50s	Ct	St	Balls	Runs	Wkts	Avge	Best	5wI	10wM
Test	21	34	4	900	136	30.00	3	1	14	-	3015	1402	39	35.94	4-50	-	-
All First	108	169	20	4323	136	29.01	4	25	84	-	18399	9421	375	25.12	8-61	14	3
1-day Int	134	103	23	1435	67	17.93	-	3	37	-	5976	4572	120	38.10	6-18	3	
C & G	4	4	0	49	20	12.25	-	-	2	-	212	172	8	21.50	4-49	-	
totesport	23	20	4	464	98	29.00	-	4	6	-	976	775	34	22.79	6-37	2	
Twenty20	8	7	1	149	57 *	24.83	-	1	3	-	174	196	14	14.00	4-20	-	

5. Which former Australia Test cricketer was born in Colombo and coached Bangladesh in the 2004 ICC Champions Trophy tournament?

BAILEY, T. M. B. Northamptonshire

Name: Tobin Michael Barnaby Bailey
Role: Right-hand bat, wicket-keeper
Born: 28 August 1976, Kettering
Height: 5ft 11in **Weight:** 13st 8lbs
Nickname: Bill, Mad Dog, Scruff
County debut: 1996
County cap: 2003
1st-Class 50s: 6
1st-Class 100s: 1
1st-Class catches: 97
1st-Class stumpings: 18
Place in batting averages: (2003 192nd av. 24.00)
Parents: Terry and Penny
Marital status: Single
Family links with cricket: 'Step-dad watches a lot'
Education: Bedford School; Loughborough University
Qualifications: 3 A-levels, BA (Hons) Politics, Level II coaching award
Career outside cricket: Coaching
Overseas tours: Bedford to South Africa 1994, to Bermuda; Northamptonshire to Grenada 2000, 2001
Cricketers particularly admired: Jack Russell, Mike Atherton, Alan Knott
Other sports played: Hockey and tennis (both for Beds at youth level), golf ('badly')
Other sports followed: Rugby (Bedford RFC), football (Leicester City FC)
Relaxations: Watching videos, playing golf and eating out
Extras: Bedfordshire Young Player of the Year and Northants County League Young Player of the Year in 1995. Holmwoods Schools Cricketer of the Year. Played for England Schools U19 and was a reserve for the England U19 tour to Zimbabwe 1995-96. Won the BUSA Championship with Loughborough University in 1996 and captained the university to BUSA Championship shared win with Durham University in 1998 (final washed out by rain). Represented British Universities 1997 and 1998. Northamptonshire Young Player of the Year 2000. NBC Denis Compton Award for the most promising young Northamptonshire player 2000. Left Northamptonshire at the end of the 2004 season
Best batting: 101* Northamptonshire v Somerset, Taunton 2003

2004 Season

	M	Inns	NO	Runs	HS	Avge	100s	50s	Ct	St	O	M	Runs	Wkts	Avge	Best	5wI	10wM
Test																		
All First	3	5	2	89	52 *	29.66	-	1	3	4								
1-day Int																		
C & G	1	1	0	19	19	19.00	-	-	1	-								
totesport	7	5	2	54	26	18.00	-	-	9	2								
Twenty20	2	0	0	0	0	-	-	-	-	2								

Career Performances

	M	Inns	NO	Runs	HS	Avge	100s	50s	Ct	St	Balls	Runs	Wkts	Avge	Best	5wI	10wM
Test																	
All First	52	71	12	1324	101 *	22.44	1	6	97	18	6	3	0	-	-	-	-
1-day Int																	
C & G	5	5	0	56	19	11.20	-	-	3	4							
totesport	47	30	15	486	44 *	32.40	-	-	52	15							
Twenty20	5	2	2	1	1 *	-	-	-	-	5							

BALL, M. C. J. — Gloucestershire

Name: Martyn Charles John Ball
Role: Right-hand bat, off-spin bowler, slip fielder
Born: 26 April 1970, Bristol
Height: 5ft 9in **Weight:** 12st 10lbs
Nickname: Benny, Barfo
County debut: 1988
County cap: 1996
Benefit: 2002
1st-Class 50s: 15
1st-Class 5 w. in innings: 12
1st-Class 10 w. in match: 1
1st-Class catches: 210
One-Day 5 w. in innings: 2
Place in batting averages: 170th av. 25.83 (2003 181st av. 25.33)
Place in bowling averages: 151st av. 55.36 (2003 96th av. 36.00)
Strike rate: 99.81 (career 79.50)
Parents: Kenneth Charles and Pamela Wendy
Wife and date of marriage: Mona, 28 September 1991
Children: Kristina, 9 May 1990; Alexandra, 2 August 1993; Harrison, 5 June 1997

Education: King Edmund Secondary School, Yate; Bath College of Further Education
Qualifications: 6 O-levels, 2 A-levels, advanced cricket coach
Overseas tours: Gloucestershire to Namibia 1991, to Kenya 1992, to Sri Lanka 1993, to Zimbabwe 1996, 1997, to South Africa 1999; MCC to New Zealand 1998-99; England to India 2001-02
Overseas teams played for: North Melbourne, Australia 1988-89; Old Hararians, Zimbabwe 1990-91
Cricketers particularly admired: Ian Botham, Vic Marks, John Emburey, Jack Russell
Other sports played: Rugby, football (both to county schoolboys level), 'enjoy golf and skiing'
Other sports followed: 'All sport – massive Man City fan'
Relaxations: 'Spending some quality time at home with family'
Extras: Represented county schools. Played for Young England against Young New Zealand in 1989. Produced best match bowling figures for the Britannic County Championship 1993 season – 14-169 against Somerset at Taunton. Called up for England Test tour of India 2001-02 after withdrawal of Robert Croft
Best batting: 75 Gloucestershire v Somerset, Taunton 2003
Best bowling: 8-46 Gloucestershire v Somerset, Taunton 1993

2004 Season

	M	Inns	NO	Runs	HS	Avge	100s	50s	Ct	St	O	M	Runs	Wkts	Avge	Best	5wI	10wM
Test																		
All First	8	10	4	155	38	25.83	-	-	5	-	183	25	609	11	55.36	3-96	-	-
1-day Int																		
C & G	4	2	2	52	33 *	-	-	-	2	-	35.2	2	174	6	29.00	2-29	-	
totesport	12	8	3	71	17 *	14.20	-	-	6	-	85	2	405	12	33.75	3-59	-	
Twenty20	4	2	1	8	6 *	8.00	-	-	6	-	13	0	110	2	55.00	2-22	-	

Career Performances

	M	Inns	NO	Runs	HS	Avge	100s	50s	Ct	St	Balls	Runs	Wkts	Avge	Best	5wI	10wM
Test																	
All First	180	274	53	4408	75	19.94	-	15	210	-	28302	13349	356	37.49	8-46	12	1
1-day Int																	
C & G	36	21	8	221	33 *	17.00	-	-	29	-	1741	1187	42	28.26	3-39	-	
totesport	172	121	44	1019	45	13.23	-	-	67	-	6402	5203	164	31.72	5-33	2	
Twenty20	10	4	2	21	11 *	10.50	-	-	7	-	222	246	10	24.60	2-21	-	

BARRICK, D. J. Durham

Name: David James Barrick
Role: Right-hand bat, leg-spin bowler; all-rounder
Born: 4 January 1984, Pontefract
Height: 5ft 8in **Weight:** 12st 7lbs
Nickname: Bac, Butterbean, John Smith
County debut: No first-team appearance
Parents: Janet and Dave
Marital status: Single
Education: Malet Lambert School; Wilberforce College
Qualifications: 10 GCSEs, 3 A-levels, Levels 1 and 2 cricket coaching
Career outside cricket: 'Housewife'
Off-season: 'Training at home; working!'
Overseas tours: England U17 to Australia 2001
Overseas teams played for: Adelaide Buffalos CC 2002; Bulleen Bulls CC, Melbourne 2003-04
Career highlights to date: 'Playing for England U17'
Cricket moments to forget: 'Involved in run-out, missed ball, broke finger, whilst doing 12th man – right laugh!'
Cricket superstitions: 'None'
Cricketers particularly admired: Ricky Ponting, Shane Warne, Herschelle Gibbs
Young players to look out for: Chris Grey
Other sports played: Golf, football
Other sports followed: Football (Sheffield Wednesday)
Injuries: Out for two months with a damaged tendon in the spinning finger; for three months with a damaged ligament in the left thumb (operation needed)
Favourite band: Linkin Park
Relaxations: 'Music, watching sport and films, eating out, and the gym?!'
Extras: Has played for Durham 2nd XI since 2002. Is a Durham Development Player
Opinions on cricket: 'More technical – looked at in greater detail these days. The game's faster. More professional. Not enough publicity compared to football.'

BASSANO, C. W. G. Derbyshire

Name: Christopher Warwick Godfrey Bassano
Role: Right-hand bat, leg-spin bowler
Born: 11 September 1975, East London, South Africa
Height: 6ft 2in **Weight:** 13st 7lbs
Nickname: Bass, Bassy
County debut: 2001
County cap: 2002
1000 runs in a season: 1
1st-Class 50s: 18
1st-Class 100s: 5
1st-Class catches: 30
One-Day 100s: 5
Place in batting averages: 69th av. 42.84 (2003 254th av. 14.57)
Parents: Brian and Allison
Marital status: Single
Family links with cricket: 'Father played throughout his life, was a radio commentator, provincial manager, and held development positions in South Africa; also wrote books on cricket etc.'
Education: Grey School, Port Elizabeth; Launceston Church Grammar School, Tasmania; University of Tasmania, Hobart
Qualifications: Bachelor of Applied Science (Horticulture)
Career outside cricket: Trout fishing guide
Overseas teams played for: Launceston CC, Tasmania 1990-2002; Kingborough CC, Hobart 2003; Tasmania 2002-03
Career highlights to date: 'Being selected to play representative cricket or to play at a higher level is always a highlight'
Cricket moments to forget: 'Losing'
Cricketers particularly admired: Graeme Pollock, Steve Waugh
Other sports played: Hockey
Other sports followed: Rugby union
Injuries: Out for two games with diabetic complications
Favourite band: Roxette
Relaxations: Fly fishing and fly tying
Extras: Captained Eastern Province U13 1987-88. Played for Tasmania U16, U17, U19 (captain), U23 (captain) and 2nd XI. Became the first player to score a century in each innings of his Championship debut, 186* and 106 v Gloucestershire at Derby 2001; his first innings lasted 8¾ hours and also produced the highest score by a Derbyshire batsman on Championship debut. Scored 100-ball 121 v Glamorgan at

Cardiff in the C&G 2003, winning Man of the Match award and sharing with Andrew Gait (87*) in a new competition record third-wicket partnership for Derbyshire (191). Made Pura Cup debut for Tasmania v South Australia at Bellerive Oval, Hobart 2002-03. Is diabetic. His ancestry includes a set of brothers from Venice who were musicians at the court of Henry VIII. Is not considered an overseas player
Opnions on cricket: 'The general standard of the pitches needs to improve to more closely mimic those of Test cricket. One-day pitches are particularly poor in general. There is too much cricket played. With the amount of talent we have in England, there is no reason why England can't be number one in the world for years.'
Best batting: 186* Derbyshire v Gloucestershire, Derby 2001

2004 Season

	M	Inns	NO	Runs	HS	Avge	100s	50s	Ct	St	O	M	Runs	Wkts	Avge	Best	5wI	10wM
Test																		
All First	14	22	3	814	123 *	42.84	2	6	4	-								
1-day Int																		
C & G	1	1	0	18	18	18.00	-	-	-	-								
totesport	15	15	1	328	100 *	23.42	1	1	4	-								
Twenty20	4	4	0	43	30	10.75	-	-	-	-								

Career Performances

	M	Inns	NO	Runs	HS	Avge	100s	50s	Ct	St	Balls	Runs	Wkts	Avge	Best	5wI	10wM
Test																	
All First	50	87	9	2703	186 *	34.65	5	18	30	-	12	11	0	-	-	-	-
1-day Int																	
C & G	5	5	0	283	121	56.60	2	-	-	-							
totesport	50	49	5	1300	126 *	29.54	3	6	11	-							
Twenty20	9	7	0	119	43	17.00	-	-	3	-							

6. Which former Sussex batsman became, at the time,
the second youngest player to score a fifty in a World Cup match
when he made 54 for Holland v England in the 1995-96 competition?

BATTY, G. J. Worcestershire

Name: Gareth Jon Batty
Role: Right-hand bat, off-spin bowler, county vice-captain
Born: 13 October 1977, Bradford, Yorkshire
Height: 5ft 11in **Weight:** 12st 4lbs
Nickname: Batts, Boris, Ronan
County debut: 1997 (Yorkshire), 1998 (one-day, Surrey), 1999 (first-class, Surrey), 2002 (Worcestershire)
County colours: 2002 (Worcestershire)
Test debut: 2003-04
Tests: 5
One-Day Internationals: 5
50 wickets in a season: 2
1st-Class 50s: 8
1st-Class 100s: 1
1st-Class 5 w. in innings: 7
1st-Class 10 w. in match: 1
1st-Class catches: 43
Place in batting averages: 134th av. 31.33 (2003 211th av. 22.04)
Place in bowling averages: 53rd av. 30.68 (2003 35th av. 26.25)
Strike rate: 65.62 (career 64.09)
Parents: David and Rosemary
Marital status: Single
Family links with cricket: 'Dad is Yorkshire Academy coach; brother played for Yorkshire and Somerset'
Education: Bingley Grammar
Qualifications: 9 GCSEs, BTEC Art and Design, coaching certificate
Career outside cricket: 'Property'
Off-season: England tour to South Africa
Overseas tours: England U15 to South Africa 1993; England U19 to Zimbabwe 1995-96, to Pakistan 1996-97; ECB National Academy to Australia and Sri Lanka 2002-03; England to Bangladesh and Sri Lanka 2003-04, to West Indies 2003-04, to Zimbabwe (one-day series) 2004-05, to South Africa 2004-05
Overseas teams played for: Marist Newman, Australia 1999
Career highlights to date: 'Playing for England'
Cricket moments to forget: 'Whenever we don't win'
Cricket superstitions: 'None'
Cricketers particularly admired: Adam Hollioake
Young players to look out for: Daryl Mitchell
Other sports played: Golf, rugby

Other sports followed: Rugby league (Leeds Rhinos)
Favourite band: Maroon 5, Frank Sinatra
Relaxations: Going to the gym
Extras: National U15 bowling award. *Daily Telegraph* Young Player of the Year 1993. Surrey Supporters' Club Most Improved Player Award and Young Player of the Year Award 2001. Surrey CCC Young Player of the Year Award 2001. ECB 2nd XI Player of the Year 2001. Released by Surrey at the end of the 2001 season and joined Worcestershire for 2002, taking 56 first-class wickets. Leading all-rounder in the inaugural Twenty20 Cup 2003. Made Test debut in the first Test v Bangladesh at Dhaka 2003-04, taking a wicket (Alok Kapali) with his third ball. Scored maiden first-class century (133) v Surrey at The Oval 2004. Recorded maiden first-class ten-wicket match return (7-52/3-61) v Northamptonshire at Northampton 2004. Appointed vice-captain of Worcestershire for 2005
Opinions on cricket: 'I think Twenty20 is great and keeps kids interested.'
Best batting: 133 Worcestershire v Surrey, The Oval 2004
Best bowling: 7-52 Worcestershire v Northamptonshire, Northampton 2004

2004 Season

	M	Inns	NO	Runs	HS	Avge	100s	50s	Ct	St	O	M	Runs	Wkts	Avge	Best	5wI	10wM
Test																		
All First	12	18	3	470	133	31.33	1	2	7	-	492.1	129	1381	45	30.68	7-52	2	1
1-day Int																		
C & G	4	3	1	47	32 *	23.50	-	-	2	-	29	1	115	3	38.33	2-38	-	
totesport	14	13	3	123	22	12.30	-	-	6	-	100.4	3	429	13	33.00	3-22	-	
Twenty20	6	5	0	41	23	8.20	-	-	1	-	10	0	88	3	29.33	2-14	-	

Career Performances

	M	Inns	NO	Runs	HS	Avge	100s	50s	Ct	St	Balls	Runs	Wkts	Avge	Best	5wI	10wM
Test	5	8	1	144	38	20.57	-	-	2	-	1304	689	10	68.90	3-55	-	-
All First	61	96	14	1834	133	22.36	1	8	43	-	12562	5921	196	30.20	7-52	7	1
1-day Int	5	3	0	4	3	1.33	-	-	3	-	252	217	4	54.25	2-40	-	
C & G	13	10	2	101	32 *	12.62	-	-	8	-	533	362	11	32.90	2-25	-	
totesport	65	58	14	898	83 *	20.40	-	4	20	-	2311	1770	53	33.39	4-36	-	
Twenty20	11	10	0	191	87	19.10	-	1	2	-	180	260	12	21.66	3-45	-	

7. Which Dublin-born Middlesex batsman averages over
70 for Ireland in the ICC Trophy and qualifies for England this year?

BATTY, J. N. Surrey

Name: Jonathan (Jon) Neil Batty
Role: Right-hand bat, wicket-keeper
Born: 18 April 1974, Chesterfield
Height: 5ft 10in **Weight:** 11st 6lbs
Nickname: JB
County debut: 1997
County cap: 2001
50 dismissals in a season: 2
1st-Class 50s: 16
1st-Class 100s: 9
1st-Class catches: 284
1st-Class stumpings: 38
Place in batting averages: 116th av. 34.55 (2003 18th av. 56.94)
Strike rate: (career 78.00)
Parents: Roger and Jill
Marital status: Single
Family links with cricket: Father played to a high standard of club cricket
Education: Wheatley Park; Repton; Durham University (St Chad's); Keble College, Oxford
Qualifications: 10 GCSEs, 4 A-levels, BSc (Hons) in Natural Sciences, Diploma in Social Studies (Oxon)
Overseas tours: Repton School to Holland 1991; MCC to Bangladesh 1996; Surrey to South Africa 1997, 2001
Overseas teams played for: Mount Lawley CC, Perth 1997-2002
Career highlights to date: 'Winning three County Championships'
Cricket moments to forget: 'None!'
Cricketers particularly admired: David Gower, Alec Stewart, Jack Russell
Other sports played: Golf, squash
Other sports followed: Football (Nottingham Forest)
Relaxations: Reading, listening to music, movies
Extras: Represented Combined Universities 1994, 1995. Oxford Blue 1996. Has also played for Oxfordshire and represented Minor Counties. Surrey Supporters' Club Most Improved Player 2002, 2003. Carried his bat for 154* v Lancashire 2003, becoming the first Surrey batsman to achieve the feat at Old Trafford since Harry Jupp in 1870. BBC Radio London Listeners' Cricketer of the Year 2003. Became second wicket-keeper (after Kent's Steve Marsh in 1991) to take eight catches in an innings (a new Surrey record) and score a century (129) in the same match, v Kent at The Oval 2004. Made 56 dismissals and scored 933 runs in first-class cricket 2004. Captain of Surrey 2004

Best batting: 168* Surrey v Essex, Chelmsford 2003
Best bowling: 1-21 Surrey v Lancashire, Old Trafford 2000

2004 Season

	M	Inns	NO	Runs	HS	Avge	100s	50s	Ct	St	O	M	Runs	Wkts	Avge	Best	5wI	10wM
Test																		
All First	17	29	2	933	145	34.55	3	3	50	6								
1-day Int																		
C & G	1	1	0	8	8	8.00	-	-	-	-								
totesport	14	13	1	351	66	29.25	-	4	17	-								
Twenty20	7	6	3	39	18	13.00	-	-	4	-								

Career Performances

	M	Inns	NO	Runs	HS	Avge	100s	50s	Ct	St	Balls	Runs	Wkts	Avge	Best	5wI	10wM
Test																	
All First	111	164	24	4284	168 *	30.60	9	16	284	38	78	61	1	61.00	1-21	-	-
1-day Int																	
C & G	8	6	2	117	55 *	29.25	-	1	5	-							
totesport	92	68	14	935	66	17.31	-	4	101	15							
Twenty20	14	12	6	103	19 *	17.16	-	-	12	-							

BELL, I. R. — Warwickshire

Name: Ian Ronald Bell
Role: Right-hand bat, right-arm medium bowler
Born: 11 April 1982, Coventry
Height: 5ft 10in **Weight:** 11st
Nickname: Belly
County debut: 1999
County cap: 2001
Test debut: 2004
Tests: 1
1000 runs in a season: 1
1st-Class 50s: 22
1st-Class 100s: 9
1st-Class 200s: 1
1st-Class catches: 37
One-Day 100s: 1
One-Day 5 w. in innings: 1
Place in batting averages: 5th av. 68.56 (2003 138th av. 30.50)

Place in bowling averages: 32nd av. 27.37
Strike rate: 56.12 (career 64.17)
Parents: Terry and Barbara
Marital status: Single
Family links with cricket: Brother Keith has played for England U18
Education: Princethorpe College, Rugby
Overseas tours: Warwickshire U19 to Cape Town 1998-99; England U19 to New Zealand 1998-99, to Malaysia and (U19 World Cup) Sri Lanka 1999-2000, to India 2000-01 (captain); England A to West Indies 2000-01, to Sri Lanka 2004-05 (captain); ECB National Academy to Australia 2001-02, to Sri Lanka 2002-03; England to Zimbabwe (one-day series) 2004-05, to South Africa 2004-05
Overseas teams played for: University of Western Australia, Perth 2003-04
Career highlights to date: 'Test debut at The Oval against West Indies 2004'
Cricket moments to forget: 'Being bowled for a duck when making county debut'
Cricketers particularly admired: Michael Atherton, Steve Waugh, Alec Stewart, Nick Knight
Young players to look out for: Keith Bell
Other sports played: Football (was at Coventry City School of Excellence), rugby, golf
Other sports followed: Football (Aston Villa), rugby union (Northampton Saints)
Relaxations: Golf, listening to music
Extras: Played for England U14, U15, U16, U17; captained England U19. NBC Denis Compton Award for the most promising young Warwickshire player 1999, 2000, 2001. Gray-Nicolls Trophy for Best Young Schools Cricketer 2000. Scored maiden first-class century (130) v Oxford University CCE at The Parks 2001, becoming (at 19 years 56 days) the youngest player to score a first-class century for Warwickshire. Scored maiden Championship century (103) v Nottinghamshire at Edgbaston 2001, becoming (at 19 years 115 days) the youngest Warwickshire batsman to score a Championship 100. Cricket Society's Most Promising Young Cricketer of the Year Award 2001. B&H Gold Award for his 65* in the last B&H final, v Essex at Lord's 2002. Recorded maiden one-day century (125) and maiden one-day five-wicket return (5-41) v Essex at Chelmsford in the NCL 2003. Scored maiden first-class double century (262*; a ground record) v Sussex at Horsham 2004, in the process becoming (at 22 years 39 days) the youngest player to score a double hundred for Warwickshire and equalling with Tony Frost (135*) the county's record partnership for the seventh wicket (289). Scored 155 and 96* v Surrey at Guildford 2004, in the second innings passing 1000 first-class runs in a season for the first time (ending season with 1714). Scored century in each innings (112/181) v Lancashire at Old Trafford 2004, during the first innings sharing with Dougie Brown (162) in a new ground record partnership for the fifth wicket (254). Made Test debut in the fourth Test v West Indies at The Oval 2004, scoring 70 in his only innings. Cricket Writers' Club Young Cricketer of the Year 2004. PCA Young Player of the Year award 2004. ECB National Academy 2004-05
Best batting: 262* Warwickshire v Sussex, Horsham 2004
Best bowling: 4-4 Warwickshire v Middlesex, Lord's 2004

Stop press: Made ODI debut in the first ODI v Zimbabwe at Harare 2004-05, scoring 75 and winning Man of the Match award. Called up to England Test squad in South Africa 2004-05 after wrist injury forced Mark Butcher to leave tour early

2004 Season

	M	Inns	NO	Runs	HS	Avge	100s	50s	Ct	St	O	M	Runs	Wkts	Avge	Best	5wI	10wM
Test	1	1	0	70	70	70.00	-	1	2	-								
All First	18	29	4	1714	262 *	68.56	6	7	12	-	149.4	34	438	16	27.37	4-4	-	-
1-day Int																		
C & G	4	3	1	126	68	63.00	-	2	2	-	19	2	70	1	70.00	1-33	-	
totesport	15	15	0	424	89	28.26	-	4	7	-	73	3	346	10	34.60	2-17	-	
Twenty20	6	5	2	32	18	10.66	-	-	3	-	13	0	106	1	106.00	1-30	-	

Career Performances

	M	Inns	NO	Runs	HS	Avge	100s	50s	Ct	St	Balls	Runs	Wkts	Avge	Best	5wI	10wM
Test	1	1	0	70	70	70.00	-	1	2	-							
All First	68	114	10	4342	262 *	41.75	10	22	37	-	1861	999	29	34.44	4-4	-	-
1-day Int																	
C & G	10	9	1	261	68	32.62	-	3	5	-	147	103	1	103.00	1-33	-	
totesport	46	45	4	1401	125	34.17	1	11	9	-	683	593	19	31.21	5-41	1	
Twenty20	11	10	2	83	20	10.37	-	-	3	-	108	150	2	75.00	1-29	-	

BENHAM, C. C. — Hampshire

Name: Christopher (Chris) Charles Benham
Role: Right-hand bat, right-arm off-spin bowler
Born: 24 March 1983, Frimley, Surrey
Height: 6ft 2in **Weight:** 13st
Nickname: Benny, Beano, Benoit
County debut: 2004
1st-Class 50s: 1
Parents: Frank and Sandie
Marital status: Single
Family links with cricket: 'Both older brothers, Nick and Andy, played local club cricket'
Education: Yateley Comprehensive School; Yateley Sixth Form College; Loughborough University
Qualifications: 10 GCSEs, 3 A-levels
Overseas tours: West of England U15 to West Indies 1998

Cricketers particularly admired: Ricky Ponting, V.V.S. Laxman, Sachin Tendulkar, Michael Vaughan
Young players to look out for: Andrew Hodd, David Wigley, Nick Ferraby
Other sports played: Football (school, district and county sides; trials with Swindon and Crystal Palace), tennis, golf
Other sports followed: Football (Reading FC)
Favourite band: Kings of Leon
Relaxations: 'Listening to music; watching DVDs; spending time with my girlfriend; going to the gym'
Extras: Played for ESCA U15 v Scotland. Represented England U16 v Denmark. Played for Hampshire Board XI in the C&G 2001. Played for Loughborough University CCE 2002, 2004. Represented British Universities v Sri Lanka A at Grace Road 2004. Scored 74 on Championship debut v Derbyshire at Derby 2004
Best batting: 74 Hampshire v Derbyshire, Derby 2004

2004 Season

	M	Inns	NO	Runs	HS	Avge	100s	50s	Ct	St	O	M	Runs	Wkts	Avge	Best	5wI	10wM
Test																		
All First	4	6	1	202	74	40.40	-	1	-	-								
1-day Int																		
C & G																		
totesport																		
Twenty20																		

Career Performances

	M	Inns	NO	Runs	HS	Avge	100s	50s	Ct	St	Balls	Runs	Wkts	Avge	Best	5wI	10wM
Test																	
All First	4	6	1	202	74	40.40	-	1	-	-							
1-day Int																	
C & G	1	1	0	0	0	0.00	-	-	-	-							
totesport																	
Twenty20																	

8. Which bowler took a hat-trick with the first three balls
of the match against Bangladesh in the 2002-03 World Cup?

BENKENSTEIN, D. M. Durham

Name: Dale Martin Benkenstein
Role: Right-hand bat, right-arm off-break or medium bowler
Born: 9 June 1974, Harare, Zimbabwe
County debut: No first-team appearance
One-Day Internationals: 23
1st-Class 50s: 33
1st-Class 100s: 11
1st-Class 200s: 2
1st-Class catches: 74
Strike rate: (career 87.67)
Family links with cricket: Father, Martin, and two brothers, Brett and Boyd, played first-class cricket
Education: Michaelhouse, KwaZulu-Natal
Overseas tours: KwaZulu-Natal to Australia (Champions Cup) 2000-01; South Africa U24 to Sri Lanka 1995; South Africa A to Sri 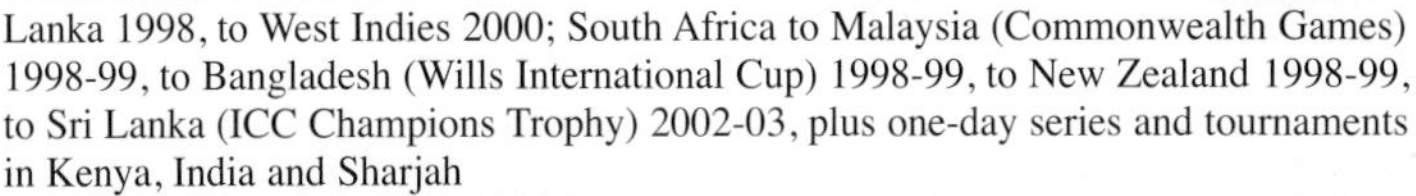Lanka 1998, to West Indies 2000; South Africa to Malaysia (Commonwealth Games) 1998-99, to Bangladesh (Wills International Cup) 1998-99, to New Zealand 1998-99, to Sri Lanka (ICC Champions Trophy) 2002-03, plus one-day series and tournaments in Kenya, India and Sharjah
Overseas teams played for: Natal/KwaZulu-Natal 1992-93 – 2003-04; Dolphins 2004-05 –
Extras: Captained Natal Schools and South Africa Schools. Represented South Africa A against various touring sides. One of *South African Cricket Annual*'s five Cricketers of the Year 1997. Was captain of KwaZulu-Natal, leading the side to the double (SuperSport Series and Standard Bank Cup) in 1996-97 and 2001-02. Has won numerous domestic awards, including Man of the Match in the final of the Standard Bank Cup 2001-02 at Durban (77*). Is not considered an overseas player
Best batting: 259 KwaZulu-Natal v Northerns, Durban 2001-02
Best bowling: 2-4 KwaZulu-Natal v Northerns, Durban 2001-02

2004 Season (did not make any first-class or one-day appearances)

Career Performances

	M	Inns	NO	Runs	HS	Avge	100s	50s	Ct	St	Balls	Runs	Wkts	Avge	Best	5wI	10wM
Test																	
All First	104	152	15	5742	259	41.91	13	33	74	-	2718	1245	31	40.16	2-4	-	-
1-day Int	23	20	3	306	69	18.00	-	1	3	-	65	44	4	11.00	3-5	-	
C & G																	
totesport																	
Twenty20																	

BENNING, J. G. E. — Surrey

Name: James Graham Edward Benning
Role: Right-hand bat, right-arm medium bowler; batting all-rounder
Born: 4 May 1983, Mill Hill, London
Height: 5ft 11in **Weight:** 13st
Nickname: Benno
County debut: 2002 (one-day), 2003 (first-class)
1st-Class 100s: 1
1st-Class catches: 3
Place in batting averages: 167th av. 26.50
Strike rate: 147.00 (career 112.50)
Parents: Sandy and David
Marital status: Single
Family links with cricket: 'Dad played for Middlesex'
Education: Caterham School
Qualifications: 12 GCSEs, 3 AS-levels
Overseas tours: Surrey YC to Barbados 1999-2000, to Sri Lanka 2002
Overseas teams played for: North Dandenong, Australia 2001-02
Career highlights to date: 'Making County Championship debut'
Cricket moments to forget: 'Dropping two catches in front of a lively crowd at Canterbury, live on Sky'
Cricket superstitions: 'Order in which I put my kit on'
Cricketers particularly admired: Alec Stewart, Adam Hollioake
Young players to look out for: Neil Saker, Scott Newman, Ben Scott
Other sports played: Rugby, football
Other sports followed: Football (Watford)
Favourite band: 'Listen to almost all music apart from thrash metal'

Relaxations: 'Going to the gym, music, spending time around friends'
Extras: Played for Buckinghamshire in the C&G 2002. Played for England U15-U19. First recipient of Ben Hollioake Scholarship. NBC Denis Compton Award for the most promising young Surrey player 2003. Scored maiden first-class century (128) v Oxford University CCE at The Parks 2004
Best batting: 128 Surrey v OUCCE, The Parks 2004
Best bowling: 1-28 Surrey v OUCCE, The Parks 2004

2004 Season

	M	Inns	NO	Runs	HS	Avge	100s	50s	Ct	St	O	M	Runs	Wkts	Avge	Best	5wI	10wM
Test																		
All First	6	11	1	265	128	26.50	1	-	3	-	24.3	5	92	1	92.00	1-28	-	-
1-day Int																		
C & G	1	1	0	27	27	27.00	-	-	-	-								
totesport	9	8	0	164	71	20.50	-	2	2	-	25.1	0	188	6	31.33	2-54	-	
Twenty20	5	5	0	91	30	18.20	-	-	1	-	2	0	24	1	24.00	1-24	-	

Career Performances

	M	Inns	NO	Runs	HS	Avge	100s	50s	Ct	St	Balls	Runs	Wkts	Avge	Best	5wI	10wM
Test																	
All First	8	14	1	352	128	27.07	1	-	3	-	225	173	2	86.50	1-28	-	-
1-day Int																	
C & G	3	3	0	70	27	23.33	-	-	1	-	18	26	1	26.00	1-26	-	
totesport	12	11	0	205	71	18.63	-	2	4	-	247	289	12	24.08	4-43	-	
Twenty20	10	10	0	164	30	16.40	-	-	1	-	24	36	1	36.00	1-24	-	

9. Which former Warwickshire opener was Kenya's coach in the 2004 ICC Champions Trophy tournament?

BETTS, M. M. — Middlesex

Name: Melvyn Morris Betts
Role: Right-hand bat, right-arm fast-medium bowler
Born: 26 March 1975, Durham
Height: 5ft 11in **Weight:** 12st
Nickname: Betsy
County debut: 1993 (Durham), 2001 (Warwickshire), 2004 (Middlesex)
County cap: 1998 (Durham), 2001 (Warwickshire)
1st-Class 50s: 5
1st-Class 5 w. in innings: 14
1st-Class 10 w. in match: 2
1st-Class catches: 37
Place in batting averages: 251st av. 14.50 (2003 155th av. 29.00)
Place in bowling averages: 132nd av. 44.38 (2003 104th av. 37.30)
Strike rate: 68.15 (career 51.87)
Parents: Melvyn and Shirley
Wife and date of marriage: Angela, 3 October 1998
Children: Chloe, 16 July 1999; Meghan, 14 May 2002
Family links with cricket: 'Dad and uncle play for local team Sacriston'
Education: Fyndoune Community College
Qualifications: 9 GCSEs, plus qualifications in engineering and sports and recreational studies
Overseas tours: England U19 to Sri Lanka 1993-94; England A to Zimbabwe and South Africa 1998-99; Durham CCC to South Africa 1996; MCC to Namibia and Uganda 2004-05
Career highlights to date: '9-64 v Northamptonshire'
Cricketers particularly admired: David Boon
Other sports played: Football, golf
Other sports followed: Football (Newcastle United FC), darts
Favourite band: U2
Relaxations: 'Local pub with friends outside cricket'
Extras: Played for England U19 v India U19 1994. Left Durham at the end of the 2000 season and joined Warwickshire for 2001. Took 5-22 on his Championship debut for Warwickshire against his old county, Durham, at Edgbaston 2001. Left Warwickshire at the end of the 2003 season and joined Middlesex for 2004
Best batting: 73 Warwickshire v Lancashire, Edgbaston 2003
Best bowling: 9-64 Durham v Northamptonshire, Northampton 1997

2004 Season

	M	Inns	NO	Runs	HS	Avge	100s	50s	Ct	St	O	M	Runs	Wkts	Avge	Best	5wI	10wM
Test																		
All First	7	8	2	87	31 *	14.50	-	-	3	-	147.4	30	577	13	44.38	5-89	1	-
1-day Int																		
C & G	1	0	0	0	0	-	-	-	-	-	7	2	15	4	3.75	4-15	-	
totesport	8	5	0	40	18	8.00	-	-	2	-	43	5	211	11	19.18	3-23	-	
Twenty20	4	1	1	13	13 *	-	-	-	2	-	9	0	79	1	79.00	1-13	-	

Career Performances

	M	Inns	NO	Runs	HS	Avge	100s	50s	Ct	St	Balls	Runs	Wkts	Avge	Best	5wI	10wM
Test																	
All First	106	154	35	1743	73	14.64	-	5	37	-	16653	9797	321	30.52	9-64	14	2
1-day Int																	
C & G	10	7	1	40	14	6.66	-	-	2	-	594	442	19	23.26	4-15	-	
totesport	58	40	17	236	21	10.26	-	-	11	-	2371	1958	64	30.59	4-39	-	
Twenty20	4	1	1	13	13 *	-	-	-	2	-	54	79	1	79.00	1-13	-	

BEVAN, M. G. — Kent

Name: Michael Gwyl Bevan
Role: Left-hand bat, slow left-arm wrist-spin bowler
Born: 8 May 1970, Canberra, Australia
County debut: 1995 (Yorkshire), 1998 (Sussex), 2002 (Leicestershire), 2004 (Kent)
County cap: 1995 (Yorkshire), 1998 (Sussex)
Test debut: 1994-95
Tests: 18
One-Day Internationals: 232
1000 runs in a season: 3
1st-Class 50s: 75
1st-Class 100s: 54
1st-Class 200s: 5
1st-Class 5 w. in innings: 1
1st-Class 10 w. in match: 1
1st-Class catches: 117
One-Day 100s: 10
One-Day 5 w. in innings: 1
Place in batting averages: 257th av. 12.85

Strike rate: (career 74.36)
Wife: Tracy
Education: Australian Cricket Academy (1989)
Overseas tours: Australia YC to West Indies 1990; Australia to Sharjah 1994, to Pakistan 1994-95, to India and Pakistan (World Cup) 1995-96, to Sri Lanka 1996-97, to India 1996-97, to South Africa 1996-97, to England 1997, to New Zealand 1997-98, to India and Sharjah 1997-98, to Pakistan and Bangladesh 1998-99 (one-day series), to West Indies 1998-99 (one-day series), to UK, Ireland and Holland (World Cup) 1999, to Sri Lanka 1999-2000 (one-day series), to Zimbabwe 1999-2000 (one-day series), to New Zealand 1999-2000 (one-day series), to South Africa 1999-2000 (one-day series), to Kenya (ICC Knockout Trophy) 2000-01, to India 2000-01 (one-day series), to England 2001 (one-day series), to South Africa 2001-02 (one-day series), to Kenya (Nairobi Triangular) 2002, to Sri Lanka (ICC Champions Trophy) 2002-03, to Africa (World Cup) 2002-03, to West Indies 2002-03 (one-day series), to India (TVS Cup) 2003-04, to Sri Lanka 2003-04 (one-day series)
Overseas teams played for: South Australia 1989-90; New South Wales 1990-91 – 2003-04; Tasmania 2004-05 –
Extras: Struck century (114) for South Australia v Western Australia at Perth on first-class debut 1989-90. In 1990-91 he became the first player to score a century in five successive Sheffield Shield matches. Played for Yorkshire 1995-96 (vice-captain 1996). Scored 78* to shepherd Australia to victory v West Indies in World Series ODI at Sydney 1995-96; at one point Australia were 38-6 in pursuit of 173. Sussex overseas player and vice-captain 1998 and 2000. Scored 150-plus (166/174) in each innings v Nottinghamshire at Hove 2000. Scored 106 in the inaugural indoor ODI v South Africa at Melbourne 2000. Topped English first-class batting averages in 2000 with 1124 runs at 74.93; also top run-scorer in the 2000 National League with 706 runs at 117.66. Sussex Player of the Year 2000. Scored 135* v Western Australia in the 2000-01 Mercantile Mutual Cup final at Perth, winning the Man of the Match award. New South Wales Player of the Year 2000-01. Scored 203* v Western Australia 2001-02, in the process becoming the highest first-class run-scorer in New South Wales cricket history. Played for Leicestershire as overseas player 2002. His international awards include Man of the Match for a World XI v an Asia XI in Dhaka 2000 (132-ball 185*), Man of the Match v New Zealand in the VB Series at Melbourne 2001-02 (93-ball 102*; Australia were at one point 82-6 chasing 246), and Man of the Match v New Zealand at Guwahati in the TVS Cup 2003-04 (84*). Was an overseas player with Kent late July to August 2004, deputising for Andrew Symonds
Best batting: 216 New South Wales v Tasmania, Sydney 2003-04
Best bowling: 6-82 Australia v West Indies, Adelaide 1996-97

2004 Season

	M	Inns	NO	Runs	HS	Avge	100s	50s	Ct	St	O	M	Runs	Wkts	Avge	Best	5wI	10wM
Test																		
All First	4	7	0	90	66	12.85	-	1	2	-	6	0	25	0	-	-	-	-
1-day Int																		
C & G																		
totesport	4	4	1	128	52	42.66	-	1	-	-	3	0	19	0	-	-	-	
Twenty20																		

Career Performances

	M	Inns	NO	Runs	HS	Avge	100s	50s	Ct	St	Balls	Runs	Wkts	Avge	Best	5wI	10wM
Test	18	30	3	785	91	29.07	-	6	8	-	1285	703	29	24.24	6-82	1	1
All First	218	364	63	16938	216	56.27	59	75	117	-	8552	5207	115	45.27	6-82	1	1
1-day Int	232	196	67	6915	108 *	53.60	6	46	69	-	1966	1655	36	45.97	3-36	-	
C & G	11	10	2	456	91 *	57.00	-	5	2	-	223	174	4	43.50	2-47	-	
totesport	61	59	18	2451	103 *	59.78	2	21	23	-	734	665	38	17.50	5-29	1	
Twenty20																	

BICHEL, A. J. Worcestershire

Name: Andrew (Andy) John Bichel
Role: Right-hand bat, right-arm fast-medium bowler
Born: 27 August 1970, Laidley, Queensland, Australia
Height: 5ft 11in **Weight:** 13st 13lbs
Nickname: Bic, Andre
County debut: 2001
County cap: 2001; colours 2002
Test debut: 1996-97
Tests: 19
One-Day Internationals: 67
50 wickets in a season: 1
1st-Class 50s: 13
1st-Class 100s: 5
1st-Class 5 w. in innings: 25
1st-Class 10 w. in match: 5
1st-Class catches: 74
One-Day 100s: 1
One-Day 5 w. in innings: 3
Place in batting averages: 72nd av. 42.17
Place in bowling averages: 141st av. 46.93

Strike rate: 72.51 (career 49.91)
Parents: Trevor and Shirley
Wife and date of marriage: Dionn, 18 April 1997
Children: Keegan, 26 October 1999; Darcy, 24 October 2002
Family links with cricket: 'Dad played local Queensland country cricket. Uncle Don played for Queensland. Best game was against England'
Education: Laidley High; Ipswich TAFE
Qualifications: Carpentry; cricket coaching
Career outside cricket: Project management
Off-season: Playing for Queensland Bulls
Overseas tours: Queensland Academy to South Africa 1994; Australian Academy to South Africa 1996; Australia A to Scotland and Ireland 1998; Australia to South Africa 1996-97, to England 1997, to New Zealand (one-day series) 1997-98, to Malaysia (Commonwealth Games) 1998, to West Indies 1998-99, to South Africa 2001-02, to Kenya (PSO Tri-Nation Tournament) 2002, to Sri Lanka (ICC Champions Trophy) 2002-03, to Sri Lanka and Sharjah (v Pakistan) 2002-03, to Africa (World Cup) 2002-03, to West Indies 2002-03, to India (TVS Cup) 2003-04; FICA World XI to New Zealand 2004-05
Overseas teams played for: Queensland 1992-93 –
Career highlights to date: 'World Cup 2003'
Cricket moments to forget: 'Being sick on the field against India in India'
Cricket superstitions: 'Like my gear in its place before the game'
Cricketers particularly admired: Allan Border, Sachin Tendulkar, Glenn McGrath, Dennis Lillee
Young players to look out for: Shaftab Khalid, Kadeer Ali, Aaron Nye (Queensland)
Other sports played: Rugby league (first grade TRL); tennis (first grade LTA)
Other sports followed: Rugby league (Brisbane Broncos), AFL (Brisbane Lions)
Injuries: Groin strain
Favourite band: U2, Cold Chisel
Relaxations: 'Beach, fishing, golf, hanging out on the islands just off Queensland coast'
Extras: Sheffield Shield Player of the Year 1996-97. Queensland Player of the Year 1998-99. Took 60 first-class wickets at 20.11 in the 1999-2000 Australian season, including 6-47 in Victoria's first innings in the Pura Milk Cup final. Was Worcestershire's overseas player 2001-02, returning in 2004. Won the Dick Lygon Award 2001 as Worcestershire's Player of the Year; was also the Worcestershire Supporters' Association Player of the Year 2001 and the winner of the inaugural Don Kenyon Award for the season's best first-class match-winning performance (113 runs and seven wickets v Glamorgan). Man of the Match v South Africa at Sydney in the VB Series 2001-02 (5-19). His 9-93 v Gloucestershire at Worcester 2002 was the best innings return by a Worcestershire bowler since Neal Radford took 9-70 v Somerset at Worcester in 1986 and the best innings return in April in Championship history. Man of the Match v England at Port Elizabeth in the World Cup 2002-03 (34* following 7-20, the third best bowling return in ODI history). C&G Man of the Match award for

his 4-17 and 38* v Somerset at Worcester 2004. Had first innings figures of 5-87, then scored century (142) v Northamptonshire at Worcester 2004. Has same birthday as the late Sir Donald Bradman. Left Worcestershire at the end of the 2004 season
Opinions on cricket: 'The game is looking a lot better because Australia were ahead by a lot and the field has got better. Now England are getting things together the future is brighter – they need to be strong. But we need the West Indies to become stronger for world cricket. Great to see India and Pakistan becoming more consistent in recent times.'
Best batting: 142 Worcestershire v Northamptonshire, Worcester 2004
Best bowling: 9-93 Worcestershire v Gloucestershire, Worcester 2002

2004 Season

	M	Inns	NO	Runs	HS	Avge	100s	50s	Ct	St	O	M	Runs	Wkts	Avge	Best	5wI	10wM
Test																		
All First	14	18	1	717	142	42.17	3	2	3	-	398.5	75	1549	33	46.93	5-87	2	-
1-day Int																		
C & G	5	5	2	68	38 *	22.66	-	-	1	-	40.1	2	160	10	16.00	4-17	-	
totesport	12	12	1	161	42	14.63	-	-	2	-	83.3	6	369	15	24.60	4-60	-	
Twenty20	6	6	3	180	58 *	60.00	-	1	5	-	21	1	162	8	20.25	3-36	-	

Career Performances

	M	Inns	NO	Runs	HS	Avge	100s	50s	Ct	St	Balls	Runs	Wkts	Avge	Best	5wI	10wM
Test	19	22	1	355	71	16.90	-	1	16	-	3337	1870	58	32.24	5-60	1	-
All First	132	170	14	3699	142	23.71	5	13	74	-	26158	13747	524	26.23	9-93	25	5
1-day Int	67	36	13	473	64	20.56	-	1	19	-	3257	2464	78	31.58	7-20	2	
C & G	10	9	2	110	38 *	15.71	-	-	1	-	475	305	20	15.25	4-17	-	
totesport	32	27	2	322	42	12.88	-	-	11	-	1421	949	49	19.36	5-21	1	
Twenty20	6	6	3	180	58 *	60.00	-	1	5	-	126	162	8	20.25	3-36	-	

10. Where was the final of the second ICC Champions Trophy tournament, then known as the ICC Knockout Trophy, played?

BICKNELL, D. J. Nottinghamshire

Name: Darren John Bicknell
Role: Left-hand opening bat, occasional slow left-arm bowler
Born: 24 June 1967, Guildford
Height: 6ft 4½in **Weight:** 14st 9lbs
Nickname: Denz, Bickers
County debut: 1987 (Surrey), 2000 (Notts)
County cap: 1990 (Surrey), 2000 (Notts)
Benefit: 1999 (Surrey)
1000 runs in a season: 8
1st-Class 50s: 77
1st-Class 100s: 42
1st-Class 200s: 2
1st-Class catches: 102
One-Day 100s: 10
Place in batting averages: 65th av. 43.20 (2003 117th av. 33.42)
Strike rate: 39.66 (career 51.00)
Parents: Vic and Valerie
Wife and date of marriage: Rebecca, 21 September 1992
Children: Lauren Elizabeth, 21 September 1993; Sam, 9 November 1995; Emily, 16 December 1997
Family links with cricket: Brother Martin plays for Surrey
Education: Robert Haining County Secondary; Guildford County College of Technology
Qualifications: 8 O-levels, 2 A-levels, senior coaching award, Diploma in Golf Club Management, 'Sage Accountancy 10-day passport to competency'
Career outside cricket: Scottish Courage brewery account manager
Off-season: 'Working and training'
Overseas tours: Surrey to Sharjah 1988, 1989, to Dubai 1990, to Perth 1995; Nottinghamshire to Johannesburg 2000, 2001, 2002; England A to Zimbabwe and Kenya 1989-90, to Pakistan 1990-91, to Bermuda and West Indies 1991-92
Overseas teams played for: Coburg, Melbourne 1986-87
Career highlights to date: 'England A call-up. Debut for Surrey. Being capped by Notts and Surrey. Every time I reach a hundred. Second division championship with Notts 2004'
Cricket moments to forget: 'My first-ball dismissal in my debut A "Test" match v Zimbabwe, and brother Martin getting me out twice'
Cricket superstitions: 'Try and wear same clothes if successful previously'
Cricketers particularly admired: Mark Taylor, David Gower, Angus Fraser, Martin Bicknell

Young players to look out for: Kevin Pietersen, Samit Patel, Josh Meerkhaus (Notts Academy)
Other sports played: Golf (11 handicap), five-a-side football
Other sports followed: Football (West Ham United, Nottingham Forest)
Favourite band: Anastacia
Relaxations: Family, golf and TV
Extras: Shared Surrey record third-wicket stand of 413 with David Ward v Kent at Canterbury in 1990. Surrey Batsman of the Year four times. Left Surrey and joined Nottinghamshire for 2000. Became first English cricketer to take part in more than one Championship partnership of 400-plus when he scored 180* in a first-wicket stand of 406* with Guy Welton (200*) v Warwickshire at Edgbaston 2000; the stand broke several records, including that for the highest Nottinghamshire partnership for any wicket and that for the highest unbeaten first-wicket partnership in Championship history. Was acting captain of Nottinghamshire in 2001 during the absence through injury of Jason Gallian. Scored 108 v Middlesex at Trent Bridge 2002, in the process sharing with Kevin Pietersen (254*) in a record partnership for any wicket in matches between Nottinghamshire and Middlesex (316)
Opinions on cricket: 'Am enjoying watching England improve – central contracts being a big part of it. English net facilities appalling – general. Teams should socialise more! I would like to see teams in division one being more positive in trying to win games!'
Best batting: 235* Surrey v Nottinghamshire, Trent Bridge 1994
Best bowling: 3-7 Surrey v Sussex, Guildford 1996

2004 Season

	M	Inns	NO	Runs	HS	Avge	100s	50s	Ct	St	O	M	Runs	Wkts	Avge	Best	5wI	10wM
Test																		
All First	17	26	1	1080	175	43.20	5	1	4	-	39.4	2	135	6	22.50	3-33	-	-
1-day Int																		
C & G																		
totesport	1	1	0	8	8	8.00	-	-	-	-								
Twenty20																		

Career Performances

	M	Inns	NO	Runs	HS	Avge	100s	50s	Ct	St	Balls	Runs	Wkts	Avge	Best	5wI	10wM
Test																	
All First	289	504	40	17858	235 *	38.48	44	77	102	-	1479	928	29	32.00	3-7	-	-
1-day Int																	
C & G	25	25	5	939	135 *	46.95	1	5	1	-							
totesport	148	142	16	4441	125	35.24	6	31	35	-	42	45	2	22.50	1-11	-	
Twenty20																	

BICKNELL, M. P. Surrey

Name: Martin Paul Bicknell
Role: Right-hand bat, right-arm fast-medium bowler
Born: 14 January 1969, Guildford
Height: 6ft 4in **Weight:** 15st
Nickname: Bickers
County debut: 1986
County cap: 1989
Benefit: 1997
Test debut: 1993
Tests: 4
One-Day Internationals: 7
50 wickets in a season: 11
1st-Class 50s: 22
1st-Class 100s: 3
1st-Class 5 w. in innings: 41
1st-Class 10 w. in match: 4
1st-Class catches: 97
One-Day 5 w. in innings: 3
Place in batting averages: 160th av. 27.93 (2003 74th av. 40.00)
Place in bowling averages: 41st av. 29.44 (2003 47th av. 27.82)
Strike rate: 54.00 (career 52.03)
Parents: Vic and Val
Wife and date of marriage: Loraine, 29 September 1995
Children: Eleanor, 31 March 1995; Charlotte, 22 July 1996
Family links with cricket: 'Brother plays, but with no luck'
Education: Robert Haining County Secondary
Qualifications: 2 O-levels, NCA coach
Career outside cricket: 'Running "Martin Bicknell Golf"'
Overseas tours: England YC to Sri Lanka 1986-87, to Australia 1987-88; England A to Zimbabwe and Kenya 1989-90, to Bermuda and West Indies 1991-92, to South Africa 1993-94; England to Australia 1990-91
Career highlights to date: 'A *Wisden* Cricketer of the Year 2001'
Cricket moments to forget: 'It's all been an experience!!'
Cricketers particularly admired: 'All honest county trundlers'
Young players to look out for: Tim Murtagh
Other sports played: Golf
Other sports followed: Football (Leeds United), golf
Relaxations: 'Playing golf, reading; spending time with my children'
Extras: Took 7-30 in National League v Glamorgan at The Oval 1999, the best Sunday/National League return by a Surrey bowler. His 16-119 (including 9-47 in the

second innings) v Leicestershire at Guildford in 2000 is the second best match return in Surrey history behind Tony Lock's 16-83 v Kent at Blackheath in 1956. One of *Wisden*'s Five Cricketers of the Year 2001. Scored maiden first-class century (110*) v Kent at Canterbury 2001 out of a total of 193-8. Wetherell Award for the Cricket Society's leading all-rounder in English first-class cricket 2000 and 2001. Surrey Supporters' Player of the Year 1993, 1997, 1999, 2000, 2001. Surrey Players' Player of the Year 1997, 1998, 1999, 2000, 2001. Surrey CCC Bowler of the Season Award 2001. Took 6-42 v Kent at The Oval 2002, in the process achieving the feat of having recorded a five-wicket innings return against all 17 counties besides his own. Recalled to the England side for the fourth Test v South Africa at Headingley 2003, 10 years (and a world record 114 Test matches having passed) after his last appearance, taking a wicket (Herschelle Gibbs) with his second ball. Took Test best 4-84 (6-155 the match) in the fifth Test v South Africa at his home ground of The Oval 2003. His 5-128 v Kent at The Oval 2004 included his 1000th first-class wicket (Matthew Dennington)
Best batting: 141 Surrey v Essex, Chelmsford 2003
Best bowling: 9-45 Surrey v Cambridge University, The Oval 1988

2004 Season

	M	Inns	NO	Runs	HS	Avge	100s	50s	Ct	St	O	M	Runs	Wkts	Avge	Best	5wI	10wM
Test																		
All First	13	19	3	447	47 *	27.93	-	-	4	-	387	95	1266	43	29.44	5-128	1	-
1-day Int																		
C & G	1	1	0	16	16	16.00	-	-	-	-	10	0	55	1	55.00	1-55	-	
totesport	6	5	1	51	22	12.75	-	-	-	-	48	2	220	6	36.66	3-21	-	
Twenty20																		

Career Performances

	M	Inns	NO	Runs	HS	Avge	100s	50s	Ct	St	Balls	Runs	Wkts	Avge	Best	5wI	10wM
Test	4	7	0	45	15	6.42	-	-	2	-	1080	543	14	38.78	4-84	-	-
All First	280	341	83	6237	141	24.17	3	22	97	-	53333	25405	1025	24.78	9-45	41	4
1-day Int	7	6	2	96	31 *	24.00	-	-	2	-	413	347	13	26.69	3-55	-	
C & G	44	21	9	232	66 *	19.33	-	1	17	-	2691	1559	60	25.98	4-35	-	
totesport	204	106	47	837	57 *	14.18	-	1	43	-	8888	6241	247	25.26	7-30	3	
Twenty20	3	2	2	11	10 *	-	-	-	1	-	66	61	4	15.25	2-11	-	

BISHOP, J. E. Essex

Name: Justin Edward Bishop
Role: Left-hand lower middle order bat, left-arm fast-medium opening bowler
Born: 4 January 1982, Bury St Edmunds
Height: 6ft **Weight:** 13st 8lbs
Nickname: Bish, Bash, Basher, Tractor Boy
County debut: 1999
1st-Class 50s: 4
1st-Class 5 w. in innings: 1
1st-Class catches: 5
Place in batting averages: (2003 220th av. 20.83)
Place in bowling averages: (2003 82nd av. 33.54)
Strike rate: 81.00 (career 60.56)
Parents: Keith and Anne
Marital status: Single
Family links with cricket: 'Dad played for Bury St Edmunds and Suffolk; Mum does teas!'
Education: County Upper School, Bury St Edmunds; Durham University
Qualifications: GCSEs, 1 A-level (PE), GNVQ (Advanced) Science, BA (Hons), Level 1 coaching awards in cricket and athletics
Off-season: Playing for Claremont CC in Cape Town
Overseas tours: England U19 to Malaysia and (U19 World Cup) Sri Lanka 1999-2000, to India 2000-01; British Universities to South Africa 2002, 2004
Overseas teams played for: Claremont CC, Cape Town 2004-05
Career highlights to date: 'Taking seven wickets in an U19 "One-Day International" for England v West Indies'
Cricketers particularly admired: Mark Ilott ('ability to swing ball back into right-handers')
Young players to look out for: Craig Estlea, Sken Reece, Bernie Rutterford
Other sports played: Football (Suffolk U15; John Snow College, Durham – 'uni champions 2003-04')
Other sports followed: Football (Ipswich Town FC)
Injuries: Out for six weeks with a hamstring injury
Favourite band: The Thrills
Relaxations: 'Watching with delight as Norwich get relegated from the Premiership'
Extras: Represented England U15 and U17. Took 7-42 for England U19 v Sri Lanka U19 in third 'Test' at Worcester 2000. Took 7-41 for England U19 v West Indies U19 at Chelmsford 2001, the best England U19 figures in an 'ODI'. Played for Durham University CCE 2002, 2003, 2004. Scored 50 for DUCCE v Nottinghamshire at Trent

Bridge 2003 and also took 4-111 in the county's only innings. Represented British Universities 2003 and v Sri Lanka A 2004
Best batting: 66 DUCCE v Northamptonshire, Northampton 2004
Best bowling: 5-148 Essex v Leicestershire, Chelmsford 2001

2004 Season (did not make any first-class or one-day appearances for his county)

Career Performances

	M	Inns	NO	Runs	HS	Avge	100s	50s	Ct	St	Balls	Runs	Wkts	Avge	Best	5wI	10wM
Test																	
All First	24	33	5	433	66	15.46	-	4	5	-	3331	2197	55	39.94	5-148	1	-
1-day Int																	
C & G	3	3	0	3	3	1.00	-	-	-	-	127	78	3	26.00	2-34	-	
totesport	20	13	6	55	16 *	7.85	-	-	4	-	701	666	23	28.95	3-33	-	
Twenty20																	

BLACKWELL, I. D. — Somerset

Name: Ian David Blackwell
Role: Left-hand 'aggressive middle order' bat, slow left-arm bowler; all-rounder
Born: 10 June 1978, Chesterfield
Height: 6ft 2in **Weight:** 16st
Nickname: Blackie, Blackdog, Donkey, Ledge (Window)
County debut: 1997 (Derbyshire), 2000 (Somerset)
County cap: 2001 (Somerset)
One-Day Internationals: 23
1000 runs in a season: 1
1st-Class 50s: 20
1st-Class 100s: 12
1st-Class 200s: 1
1st-Class 5 w. in innings: 7
1st-Class catches: 39
One-Day 100s: 1
Place in batting averages: 11th av. 61.71 (2003 28th av. 50.43)
Place in bowling averages: 87th av. 36.00 (2003 102nd av. 37.11)
Strike rate: 76.70 (career 87.93)
Parents: John and Marilyn
Marital status: 'Spoken for – Beth'
Family links with cricket: Father played for Derbyshire Over 50s and is also involved at Chesterfield CC

Education: Manor Community School (GCSEs); Brookfield Community School (A-levels)
Qualifications: 9 GCSEs, 1 A-level, NCA senior coaching award
Off-season: 'Training and travel (Oz and New Zealand)'
Overseas tours: Somerset to Cape Town 2000, 2001; England VI to Hong Kong 2001; England to Sri Lanka (ICC Champions Trophy) 2002-03, to Australia 2002-03 (VB Series), to Africa (World Cup) 2002-03, to Bangladesh and Sri Lanka 2003-04 (one-day series), to West Indies 2003-04 (one-day series); ECB National Academy to Australia 2002-03
Overseas teams played for: Delacombe Park CC, Melbourne 1997, 1999
Career highlights to date: 'Winning C&G final 2001. 247* off 156 balls with 11 sixes against old county Derbyshire'
Cricket moments to forget: 'My numerous noughts for England!'
Cricket superstitions: 'None of note'
Cricketers particularly admired: Phillip DeFreitas, Jamie Cox, James Hildreth, Ricky Ponting
Young players to look out for: James Hildreth
Other sports followed: Golf, football (Chesterfield FC)
Injuries: Out for two weeks with a hamstring injury; for one week with a back spasm
Favourite band: Eminem
Relaxations: 'Golf, Internet, PlayStation; spending time with my better half Beth'
Extras: Played for Derbyshire from the age of eight through to the 1st XI. Set record for number of balls lost (seven) in a score of 213* off 156 balls at Bolsover, which included 21 fours and 15 sixes and equalled the Bassetlaw League 1A record. Left Derbyshire at end of 1999 season and joined Somerset for 2000. Became first batsman in Championship history to score two centuries (103/122) in a match batting at No. 7, v Northants at Northampton 2001. C&G Man of the Match award for his 53-ball 86 in the semi-final v Kent at Taunton 2002. Scored a 68-ball 82 in his second ODI, v India at Colombo in the ICC Champions Trophy 2002-03. Scored 134-ball double century (the fastest by an Englishman in terms of balls received) v Derbyshire at Taunton 2003, finishing with 247*; in the process shared with Nixon McLean (39) in a new record tenth-wicket partnership for Somerset (163). Returned career best innings figures of 7-90 v Glamorgan at Taunton and again v Nottinghamshire at Trent Bridge 2004
Best batting: 247* Somerset v Derbyshire, Taunton 2003
Best bowling: 7-90 Somerset v Glamorgan, Taunton 2004
7-90 Somerset v Nottinghamshire, Trent Bridge 2004

2004 Season

	M	Inns	NO	Runs	HS	Avge	100s	50s	Ct	St	O	M	Runs	Wkts	Avge	Best	5wI	10wM
Test																		
All First	11	16	2	864	131	61.71	2	6	5	-	345.1	85	972	27	36.00	7-90	2	-
1-day Int	2	2	0	9	5	4.50	-	-	-	-								
C & G	1	1	0	27	27	27.00	-	-	-	-								
totesport	12	12	1	236	69	21.45	-	1	1	-	80	1	427	10	42.70	2-23	-	
Twenty20	3	3	1	21	13 *	10.50	-	-	1	-	8	0	69	0	-	-	-	

Career Performances

	M	Inns	NO	Runs	HS	Avge	100s	50s	Ct	St	Balls	Runs	Wkts	Avge	Best	5wI	10wM
Test																	
All First	94	144	9	4976	247 *	36.85	13	20	39	-	13718	6390	156	40.96	7-90	7	-
1-day Int	23	19	1	291	82	16.16	-	1	5	-	648	485	15	32.33	3-26	-	
C & G	18	16	2	369	86	26.35	-	2	5	-	576	436	9	48.44	2-34	-	
totesport	94	89	7	2271	111	27.69	1	15	22	-	3098	2590	81	31.97	4-24	-	
Twenty20	8	8	1	95	29	13.57	-	-	3	-	140	185	0	-	-	-	

BLAIN, J. A. R. Yorkshire

Name: John Angus Rae Blain
Role: Right-hand bat, right-arm fast-medium bowler
Born: 4 January 1979, Edinburgh
Height: 6ft 2in **Weight:** 13st 7lbs
Nickname: Blainy, Haggis, William, JB
County debut: 1997 (Northamptonshire), 2004 (Yorkshire)
One-Day Internationals: 5
1st-Class 5 w. in innings: 2
1st-Class catches: 6
One-Day 5 w. in innings: 2
Place in batting averages: 254th av. 13.42
Place in bowling averages: 30th av. 26.80 (2003 85th av. 34.53)
Strike rate: 37.60 (career 52.77)
Parents: John and Elma
Marital status: Single
Education: Penicuik HS; Jewel and Esk Valley College
Qualifications: 8 GCSEs, 1 A-level, HNC Leisure and Recreation, Level 1 coaching award
Off-season: Tour to UAE in November with Scotland; 'working in Edinburgh'

Overseas tours: Northants CCC to Zimbabwe 1997, to Grenada 2001, 2002; Scotland U19 to Holland (International Youth Tournament) 1994-95, to Bermuda (International Youth Tournament) 1997, to South Africa (U19 World Cup) 1997-98 (captain); Scotland to Denmark (European Championships) 1996, to Malaysia (ICC Trophy) 1996-97, to Malaysia (Commonwealth Games) 1998, to Sharjah ('World Cup warm-up') 1999, to Canada (ICC Trophy) 2001, to UAE (ICC Six Nations Challenge) 2003-04, to UAE (ICC Inter-Continental Cup) 2004-05
Overseas teams played for: New Plymouth Old Boys, New Zealand 1998-99; Taranaki Cricket Association, New Zealand 1998-99
Career highlights to date: 'World Cup 1999, England. Signing for Yorkshire CCC'
Cricket moments to forget: 'Not qualifying for the 2003 World Cup, failing to qualify by losing the last match by six runs in Canada 2001; not qualifying for the Champions Trophy in England 2004, losing last game to the USA in Dubai 2004' (*USA qualified for the Champions Trophy ahead of Scotland by virtue of a net run rate that was superior by just 0.028 runs*)
Cricket superstitions: 'Keeping a tidy kitbag'
Cricketers particularly admired: Devon Malcolm, Darren Lehmann
Young players to look out for: David Wainwright
Other sports played: Football (schoolboy forms with Hibernian FC and Falkirk FC, making youth and reserve team appearances)
Other sports followed: Rugby
Relaxations: 'Listening to music, going out for a beer; spending time with my girlfriend and going home to Scotland to see family; watching football, going to the gym, and sleeping!'
Extras: In 1996 became then youngest ever cricketer to play for Scotland national side, at 17 years and 114 days. Played for Scotland in the B&H and NatWest competitions; has also played for Scottish Saltires in NCL. Made his first-class debut for Scotland against Ireland in 1996. Took 5-24 on Sunday League debut for Northamptonshire v Derbyshire at Derby 1997. Represented Scotland in the 1999 World Cup, taking 10 wickets and finishing top of the strike rate chart for the tournament. Released by Northamptonshire at the end of the 2003 season and joined Yorkshire for 2004
Opinions on cricket: 'Too many so-called British- or English-qualified imports coming into the game. County players are underestimated in world cricket. The instant success of "newcomers" to the England team shows just that.'
Best batting: 34 Northamptonshire v Surrey, Northampton 2001
Best bowling: 6-42 Northamptonshire v Kent, Canterbury 2001
Stop press: Played in Scotland side that won the ICC Inter-Continental Cup in the UAE, November 2004, returning match figures of 7-55 (3-27/4-28) in the final v Canada in Sharjah and winning Man of the Match award

2004 Season

	M	Inns	NO	Runs	HS	Avge	100s	50s	Ct	St	O	M	Runs	Wkts	Avge	Best	5wI	10wM
Test																		
All First	9	13	6	94	28 *	13.42	-	-	1	-	188	26	804	30	26.80	4-38	-	-
1-day Int																		
C & G	1	0	0	0	0	-	-	-	-	-	7	3	8	2	4.00	2-8	-	
totesport	5	2	2	1	1 *	-	-	-	3	-	22.5	0	142	4	35.50	3-34	-	
Twenty20																		

Career Performances

	M	Inns	NO	Runs	HS	Avge	100s	50s	Ct	St	Balls	Runs	Wkts	Avge	Best	5wI	10wM
Test																	
All First	29	35	14	244	34	11.61	-	-	6	-	4169	3117	79	39.45	6-42	2	-
1-day Int	5	5	1	15	9	3.75	-	-	1	-	223	210	10	21.00	4-37	-	
C & G	3	1	0	6	6	6.00	-	-	1	-	168	111	6	18.50	2-8	-	
totesport	14	6	6	10	5 *	-	-	-	6	-	525	486	16	30.37	5-24	1	
Twenty20																	

BLAKEY, R. J. — Yorkshire

Name: Richard John Blakey
Role: Right-hand bat, wicket-keeper
Born: 15 January 1967, Huddersfield
Height: 5ft 10in **Weight:** 11st 4lbs
Nickname: Dick
County debut: 1985
County cap: 1987
Benefit: 1998
Test debut: 1992-93
Tests: 2
One-Day Internationals: 3
1000 runs in a season: 5
50 dismissals in a season: 6
1st-Class 50s: 86
1st-Class 100s: 10
1st-Class 200s: 3
1st-Class catches: 778
1st-Class stumpings: 57
One-Day 100s: 3
Place in batting averages: (2003 160th av. 27.52)
Strike rate: (career 63.00)
Parents: Brian and Pauline

Wife and date of marriage: Michelle, 28 September 1991
Children: Harrison Brad, 22 September 1993
Family links with cricket: Father played local cricket
Education: Rastrick Grammar School
Qualifications: 4 O-levels, Senior NCA Coach
Overseas tours: England YC to West Indies 1984-85; Yorkshire to Barbados 1986-87, to Cape Town 1990-91; England A to Zimbabwe and Kenya 1989-90, to Pakistan 1990-91; England to India and Sri Lanka 1992-93
Overseas teams played for: Waverley, Sydney 1985-87; Mt Waverley, Sydney 1987-88; Bionics, Zimbabwe 1989-90
Cricketers particularly admired: Martyn Moxon, Dermot Reeve, Ian Botham, Alan Knott
Other sports followed: All
Relaxations: All sports, particularly golf and squash, eating out, drawing, photography
Extras: Made record individual score for Yorkshire 2nd XI (273*) v Northamptonshire 2nd XI 1986. Scored 204* v Gloucestershire at Headingley 1987, becoming the youngest player (20 years 225 days) to score a Championship double century for Yorkshire. Yorkshire's Young Player of the Year 1989. Was awarded a citation by the International Committee for Fair Play in 1995, the only cricketer among the 25 winners worldwide. Vice-captain of Yorkshire 2002. Yorkshire Players' Player of the Year and Club Player of the Year 2002. Scored 206-ball 223* v Northamptonshire at Headingley 2003
Best batting: 223* Yorkshire v Northamptonshire, Headingley 2003
Best bowling: 1-68 Yorkshire v Nottinghamshire, Sheffield 1986

2004 Season

	M	Inns	NO	Runs	HS	Avge	100s	50s	Ct	St	O	M	Runs	Wkts	Avge	Best	5wI	10wM
Test																		
All First																		
1-day Int																		
C & G	3	3	2	21	10 *	21.00	-	-	3	-								
totesport	4	2	1	49	27	49.00	-	-	5	2								
Twenty20	2	1	0	18	18	18.00	-	-	-	1								

Career Performances

	M	Inns	NO	Runs	HS	Avge	100s	50s	Ct	St	Balls	Runs	Wkts	Avge	Best	5wI	10wM
Test	2	4	0	7	6	1.75	-	-	2	-							
All First	348	554	87	14674	223 *	31.42	13	86	778	57	63	68	1	68.00	1-68	-	-
1-day Int	3	2	0	25	25	12.50	-	-	2	1							
C & G	48	35	13	516	75	23.45	-	2	54	5							
totesport	249	218	52	5531	130 *	33.31	3	27	244	48							
Twenty20	7	5	1	119	32	29.75	-	-	5	1							

BLEWETT, G. S. — Surrey

Name: Gregory (Greg) Scott Blewett
Role: Right-hand bat, right-arm medium bowler
Born: 28 October 1971, Adelaide, Australia
Height: 6ft **Weight:** 11st
Nickname: Blewy
County debut: 1999 (Yorkshire), 2001 (Nottinghamshire), 2003 (Kent), 2004 (one-day, Surrey)
County cap: 1999 (Yorkshire), 2001 (Nottinghamshire)
Test debut: 1994-95
Tests: 46
One-Day Internationals: 32
1000 runs in a season: 1
1st-Class 50s: 81
1st-Class 100s: 39
1st-Class 200s: 4
1st-Class 5 w. in innings: 1
1st-Class catches: 169
Place in batting averages: (2003 129th av. 31.41)
Strike rate: (career 81.42)
Parents: Bob and Shirley
Wife and date of marriage: Jodie, 26 June 1998
Family links with cricket: Father played for South Australia
Education: Prince Alfred College, Adelaide
Overseas tours: Australian Institute of Sport to Sri Lanka 1990-91; Australia YC to England 1991; Australia A to South Africa (one-day series) 2002-03; Australia to New Zealand (Bank of New Zealand Centenary Series) 1994-95, to West Indies 1994-95, to South Africa 1996-97, to England 1997, to India 1997-98, to West Indies 1998-99, to Sri Lanka 1999-2000, to Zimbabwe 1999-2000, to New Zealand 1999-2000; FICA World XI to New Zealand 2004-05
Overseas teams played for: South Australia 1991-92 –
Cricketers particularly admired: Greg Chappell, Gordon Greenidge, Viv Richards
Other sports played: Golf
Other sports followed: Australian Football League (Adelaide Crows)
Relaxations: Golf, films, socialising
Extras: Scored centuries (102* and 115) in his first two Test matches, v England at Adelaide and Perth in 1994-95. Scored 214 in the first Test at Johannesburg 1996-97, sharing in record fifth-wicket partnership for Australia in Tests v South Africa, 385 with Steve Waugh. Was the only Australian to make 1000 Test runs in 1997 calendar

year. Holds the unenviable record of being the first Australian to be out for 99 twice in Test cricket. In 1998-99, made 1175 first-class runs (av. 146.86 and including five 100s and a 200) before Christmas in the Australian season, breaking David Hookes' record of 1163 set in 1982-83. Was Yorkshire's overseas player in 1999. Leading run-scorer in the Pura Cup 2000-01 with 1162 runs (av. 68.35), including a match-saving 260* v Queensland at Brisbane. Was Nottinghamshire's overseas player in 2001. Scored 133 v Durham at Trent Bridge 2001, becoming only the second player to score a century on Championship debut for Notts. Has a share in record South Australian Sheffield Shield/Pura Cup partnerships for the second wicket (386 with Darren Lehmann v Tasmania at Hobart 2001-02) and the third wicket (286 with Darren Lehmann v Tasmania at Adelaide 1993-94). Leading run-scorer in the Pura Cup (843; av. 49.58) and the ING Cup (486; av. 54.00) 2002-03. Was an overseas player with Kent April to June 2003, deputising first for Andrew Symonds and then for Mohammad Sami. Was an overseas player with Surrey in July 2004, deputising for the injured Azhar Mahmood

Best batting: 268 South Australia v Victoria, Melbourne 1993-94

Best bowling: 5-29 Australian XI v West Indies, Hobart 1996-97

2004 Season

	M	Inns	NO	Runs	HS	Avge	100s	50s	Ct	St	O	M	Runs	Wkts	Avge	Best	5wI	10wM
Test																		
All First																		
1-day Int																		
C & G																		
totesport	1	1	0	36	36	36.00	-	-	-	-	3.1	1	19	1	19.00	1-19	-	
Twenty20	3	3	0	37	32	12.33	-	-	2	-	6	0	61	1	61.00	1-23	-	

Career Performances

	M	Inns	NO	Runs	HS	Avge	100s	50s	Ct	St	Balls	Runs	Wkts	Avge	Best	5wI	10wM
Test	46	79	4	2552	214	34.02	4	15	45	-	1436	720	14	51.42	2-9	-	-
All First	215	386	26	16464	268	45.73	43	81	169	-	10992	5685	135	42.11	5-29	1	-
1-day Int	32	30	3	551	57 *	20.40	-	2	7	-	749	646	14	46.14	2-6	-	
C & G	7	7	1	178	77	29.66	-	2	3	-	196	110	7	15.71	4-18	-	
totesport	35	35	0	883	89	25.22	-	3	12	-	524	527	8	65.87	1-14	-	
Twenty20	6	6	1	57	32	11.40	-	-	3	-	42	71	1	71.00	1-23	-	

11. For how many were the West Indian tourists bowled out in their one-day defeat at the hands of the Irish at Sion Mills in July 1969?

BLIGNAUT, A. M. — Durham

Name: Arnoldus Mauritius (Andy) Blignaut
Role: Left-hand bat, right-arm medium-fast bowler
Born: 1 August 1978, Harare, Zimbabwe
Height: 6ft **Weight:** 12st 12lbs
County debut: 2004
Test debut: 2000-01
Tests: 15
One-Day Internationals: 47
1st-Class 50s: 7
1st-Class 100s: 2
1st-Class 5 w. in innings: 3
1st-Class catches: 26
Strike rate: 63.00 (career 57.12)
Overseas tours: Zimbabwe A to Sri Lanka 1999-2000; Zimbabwe to West Indies 1999-2000, to England 2003, to Australia 2003-04, to South Africa 2004-05, plus one-day tournaments in Singapore, Kenya and Sharjah
Overseas teams played for: Mashonaland 1997-98 – 2003-04; Tasmania 2004-05 –
Extras: Returned best Test debut analysis by a Zimbabwe bowler (5-73) in the first Test v Bangladesh at Bulawayo 2000-01. Took hat-trick (Hannan Sarkar, Mohammad Ashraful, Mushfiqur Rahman) in the first Test v Bangladesh at Harare 2003-04. Has a share in the record Test partnerships for Zimbabwe for the seventh and eighth wickets (154 and 168 respectively, both with Heath Streak). Represented Zimbabwe in the World Cup 2002-03, scoring a 28-ball 54 v Australia at Bulawayo and winning the Man of the Match award. Played for Durham July to early August 2004 after Shoaib Akhtar departed on international duty; is not considered an overseas player. Has worked as a male model
Best batting: 194 Mashonaland v Manicaland, Mutare 2003-04
Best bowling: 5-73 Zimbabwe v Bangladesh, Bulawayo 2000-01

2004 Season

	M	Inns	NO	Runs	HS	Avge	100s	50s	Ct	St	O	M	Runs	Wkts	Avge	Best	5wI	10wM
Test																		
All First	2	4	0	90	56	22.50	-	1	-	-	42	3	200	4	50.00	2-109	-	-
1-day Int																		
C & G																		
totesport	3	2	0	24	19	12.00	-	-	-	-	13	0	70	0	-		-	-
Twenty20																		

Career Performances

	M	Inns	NO	Runs	HS	Avge	100s	50s	Ct	St	Balls	Runs	Wkts	Avge	Best	5wI	10wM
Test	15	28	2	638	92	24.53	-	3	11	-	2808	1664	51	32.62	5-73	3	-
All First	42	64	4	1712	194	28.53	2	7	26	-	6512	3901	114	34.21	5-73	3	-
1-day Int	47	36	8	533	63 *	19.03	-	4	10	-	2059	1779	41	43.39	4-43	-	
C & G																	
totesport	3	2	0	24	19	12.00	-	-	-	-	78	70	0	-	-	-	
Twenty20																	

BLOOMFIELD, T. F. — Middlesex

Name: Timothy (Tim) Francis Bloomfield
Role: Right-hand bat, right-arm fast-medium bowler
Born: 31 May 1973, Ashford, Middlesex
Height: 6ft 2in **Weight:** 14st
Nickname: Bloomers, Boof, Frank
County debut: 1997
County cap: 2001
50 wickets in a season: 1
1st-Class 5 w. in innings: 6
1st-Class catches: 8
Strike rate: 120.00 (career 55.15)
Parents: Richard and Pauline
Marital status: Engaged to Emma
Education: Halliford Independent School
Qualifications: 8 GCSEs, NCA coaching award
Overseas tours: Berkshire U25 to Barbados 1996; Middlesex to South Africa 2000; MCC to Sri Lanka 2001, to Kenya 2002
Career highlights to date: 'Getting capped by Middlesex at Lord's'
Cricket moments to forget: 'All of the 2002 season, having not played due to injury'
Cricketers particularly admired: Ian Botham, Viv Richards, Angus Fraser
Young players to look out for: Nick Compton
Other sports played: Football, golf, tennis, snooker
Other sports followed: Football (Liverpool)
Relaxations: Sport, music
Extras: Has also played for Berkshire. Took 4-17 v Somerset at Southgate in the NatWest 2000, winning the Man of the Match award. Released by Middlesex at the end of the 2004 season
Best batting: 31* Middlesex v Northamptonshire, Northampton 2002
Best bowling: 5-36 Middlesex v Glamorgan, Cardiff 1999

2004 Season

	M	Inns	NO	Runs	HS	Avge	100s	50s	Ct	St	O	M	Runs	Wkts	Avge	Best	5wI	10wM
Test																		
All First	1	1	0	8	8	8.00	-	-	-	-	20	3	55	1	55.00	1-55	-	-
1-day Int																		
C & G																		
totesport	1	1	1	0	0 *	-	-	-	-	-	3	0	23	0	-	-	-	
Twenty20	1	0	0	0	0	-	-	-	-	-	4	0	46	2	23.00	2-46	-	

Career Performances

	M	Inns	NO	Runs	HS	Avge	100s	50s	Ct	St	Balls	Runs	Wkts	Avge	Best	5wI	10wM
Test																	
All First	58	62	25	306	31 *	8.27	-	-	8	-	8660	5291	157	33.70	5-36	6	-
1-day Int																	
C & G	6	2	1	7	7 *	7.00	-	-	-	-	259	191	6	31.83	4-17	-	
totesport	47	17	7	71	15	7.10	-	-	10	-	2004	1528	47	32.51	4-25	-	
Twenty20	5	1	0	0	0	0.00	-	-	1	-	108	168	6	28.00	2-44	-	

BOPARA, R. S. — Essex

Name: Ravinder (Ravi) Singh Bopara
Role: Right-hand top-order bat, right-arm medium bowler
Born: 4 May 1985, Newham, London
Height: 5ft 10in **Weight:** 12st
Nickname: Puppy
County debut: 2002
1st-Class catches: 14
Place in batting averages: 200th av. 22.28
Strike rate: (career 140.00)
Parents: Baldish and Charanjit
Marital status: Single
Education: Brampton Manor School; Barking Abbey Sports College
Qualifications: 7 GCSEs, ECB Level 1 coaching
Overseas tours: England U19 to Australia 2002-03, to Bangladesh (U19 World Cup) 2003-04
Career highlights to date: 'Playing against India and Pakistan overseas teams. Meeting Sachin Tendulkar; facing Shoaib Akhtar and Mohammad Sami'
Cricket moments to forget: 'I went out to bat once and didn't realise I didn't have a box on until I got hit there'

Cricketers particularly admired: Sachin Tendulkar, Viv Richards, Carl Hooper
Young players to look out for: Bilal Shafayat, 'and any players who are hungry for success'
Other sports followed: Football (Arsenal)
Favourite band: Tupac and the Outlawz
Extras: Played for Development of Excellence XI (South) v West Indies U19 at Arundel 2001. Played for Essex Board XI in the C&G 2002. Represented England U19 2003 and v Bangladesh U19 2004
Opinions on cricket: 'Too much time and money is spent on looking for young players in private schools. We should be looking at youngsters in the inner cities and state schools. Players to be as natural as they can.'
Best batting: 48 Essex v Durham, Colchester 2002
48 Essex v Middlesex, Lord's 2003
Best bowling: 1-23 Essex v Surrey, The Oval 2003

2004 Season

	M	Inns	NO	Runs	HS	Avge	100s	50s	Ct	St	O	M	Runs	Wkts	Avge	Best	5wI	10wM
Test																		
All First	5	8	1	156	40 *	22.28	-	-	5	-	24	1	108	0	-	-	-	-
1-day Int																		
C & G	1	1	0	11	11	11.00	-	-	1	-	4	0	18	2	9.00	2-18	-	
totesport	8	7	2	149	55	29.80	-	1	2	-	21	0	110	6	18.33	2-10	-	
Twenty20	5	3	0	48	26	16.00	-	-	1	-	10	0	80	4	20.00	3-18	-	

Career Performances

	M	Inns	NO	Runs	HS	Avge	100s	50s	Ct	St	Balls	Runs	Wkts	Avge	Best	5wI	10wM
Test																	
All First	13	22	5	484	48	28.47	-	-	14	-	420	304	3	101.33	1-23	-	-
1-day Int																	
C & G	2	2	0	12	11	6.00	-	-	1	-	24	18	2	9.00	2-18	-	
totesport	17	16	4	231	55	19.25	-	1	3	-	211	207	7	29.57	2-10	-	
Twenty20	10	6	1	78	26	15.60	-	-	2	-	60	80	4	20.00	3-18	-	

BOTHA, A. G. — Derbyshire

Name: Anthony (<u>Ant</u>) Greyvensteyn Botha
Role: Left-hand bat, slow left-arm bowler
Born: 17 November 1976, Pretoria, South Africa
Nickname: Boats, Both, Botox
County debut: 2004
County cap: 2004
1st-Class 50s: 6
1st-Class 100s: 1

1st-Class 5 w. in innings: 3
1st-Class 10 w. in match: 1
1st-Class catches: 41
Place in batting averages: 174th av. 25.31
Place in bowling averages: 88th av. 36.07
Strike rate: 67.15 (career 68.24)
Parents: Elise and Ian
Marital status: Single
Education: Maritzburg College; Maritzburg Technikon
Career outside cricket: 'Was sales manager for glass company in South Africa'
Off-season: 'Rehab on groin injury'
Overseas tours: South Africa U19 to India 1995-96
Overseas teams played for: Natal/KwaZulu-Natal 1995-96 – 1998-99; Easterns 1999-2000 – 2002-03

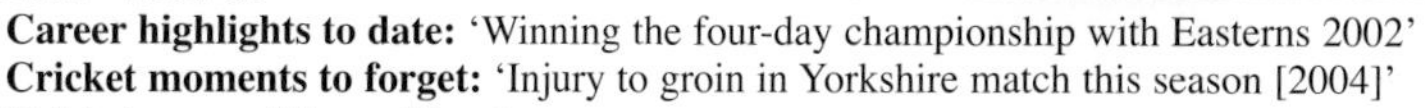

Career highlights to date: 'Winning the four-day championship with Easterns 2002'
Cricket moments to forget: 'Injury to groin in Yorkshire match this season [2004]'
Cricket superstitions: 'None'
Cricketers particularly admired: Jonty Rhodes
Other sports played: Hockey, tennis, watersports
Other sports followed: Rugby, football
Favourite band: Barry Manilow
Relaxations: Fishing, watersports
Extras: Represented South African Schools 1995. Played for South African Academy v New Zealand Academy in home series 1997. Man of the Match v Boland at Paarl in the SuperSport Series 2000-01. Man of the Match v Eastern Province at Benoni in the Standard Bank Cup 2001-02. Played for Derbyshire Premier League and Premier Cup double winners Clifton 2003, scoring 200* v Denby. Scored maiden first-class century (103) v Durham University CCE at Derby 2004, then took 5-55 in the DUCCE second innings to become the first Derbyshire player since 1937 to score a century and record a five-wicket innings return in the same first-class match. Awarded Derbyshire cap 2004. Has English father and is not considered an overseas player
Opinions on cricket: 'I think the game is in a healthy state. Two sides down and up rather than three. My view on English-qualified players is simple – if you are good enough you will play!'
Best batting: 103 Derbyshire v DUCCE, Derby 2004
Best bowling: 8-53 KwaZulu-Natal B v Northerns B, Centurion 1997-98

2004 Season

	M	Inns	NO	Runs	HS	Avge	100s	50s	Ct	St	O	M	Runs	Wkts	Avge	Best	5wI	10wM
Test																		
All First	11	18	2	405	103	25.31	1	1	5	-	291	62	938	26	36.07	5-55	1	-
1-day Int																		
C & G	1	1	0	4	4	4.00	-	-	-	-	5	0	28	0	-	-	-	
totesport	10	8	2	95	24	15.83	-	-	2	-	67	3	285	12	23.75	3-24	-	
Twenty20	4	3	2	21	13 *	21.00	-	-	2	-	11	1	77	3	25.66	2-28	-	

Career Performances

	M	Inns	NO	Runs	HS	Avge	100s	50s	Ct	St	Balls	Runs	Wkts	Avge	Best	5wI	10wM
Test																	
All First	55	88	12	1610	103	21.18	1	6	41	-	9759	4454	143	31.14	8-53	3	1
1-day Int																	
C & G	1	1	0	4	4	4.00	-	-	-	-	30	28	0	-	-	-	
totesport	10	8	2	95	24	15.83	-	-	2	-	402	285	12	23.75	3-24	-	
Twenty20	4	3	2	21	13 *	21.00	-	-	2	-	66	77	3	25.66	2-28	-	

BOWLER, P. D. — Somerset

Name: Peter Duncan Bowler
Role: Right-hand opening bat, occasional off-spin bowler, occasional wicket-keeper
Born: 30 July 1963, Plymouth
Height: 6ft 2in **Weight:** 13st 10lbs
Nickname: Tom
County debut: 1986 (Leicestershire), 1988 (Derbyshire), 1995 (Somerset)
County cap: 1989 (Derbyshire), 1995 (Somerset)
Benefit: 2000 (Somerset)
1000 runs in a season: 10
1st-Class 50s: 101
1st-Class 100s: 42
1st-Class 200s: 3
1st-Class catches: 232
1st-Class stumpings: 1
One-Day 100s: 7
Place in batting averages: 42nd av. 49.23 (2003 106th av. 34.07)
Strike rate: (career 97.11)
Parents: Peter and Etta
Wife and date of marriage: Joanne, 10 October 1992

Children: Peter Robert, 21 September 1993; Rebekah, 25 August 1995
Education: Scots College, Sydney, Australia; Daramalan College, Canberra, Australia; Nottingham Trent University
Qualifications: Australian Year 12 certificate, LLB
Career outside cricket: Solicitor
Cricketers particularly admired: Gus Valence, Rob Jeffery, Bill Carracher, Phil Russell
Other sports followed: Rugby union
Relaxations: Family and reading
Extras: First Leicestershire player to score a first-class century on debut (100* v Hampshire at Leicester 1986). Moved to Derbyshire at the end of the 1987 season and scored a hundred (155*) on debut v Cambridge University at Fenner's 1988, becoming the first player to score hundreds on debut for two counties. His 241* v Hampshire at Portsmouth 1992 is the highest score by a Derbyshire No. 1. First batsman to 2000 runs in 1992, finishing equal leading run-scorer (2044) with Mike Roseberry of Middlesex. Derbyshire Player of the Year 1992. Joined Somerset for 1995. Took over the Somerset captaincy mid-season 1997; relinquished captaincy after 1998 season. Top-scoring English batsman in first-class cricket in his benefit season (2000) with 1305 runs (av. 62.14). Retired at the end of the 2004 summer, having scored 1034 first-class runs (av. 49.23) in his final season
Best batting: 241* Derbyshire v Hampshire, Portsmouth 1992
Best bowling: 3-25 Somerset v Northamptonshire, Taunton 1998

2004 Season

	M	Inns	NO	Runs	HS	Avge	100s	50s	Ct	St	O	M	Runs	Wkts	Avge	Best	5wI	10wM
Test																		
All First	16	27	6	1034	187 *	49.23	3	3	11	-	2	1	2	0	-	-	-	-
1-day Int																		
C & G																		
totesport	1	1	0	12	12	12.00	-	-	-	-								
Twenty20																		

Career Performances

	M	Inns	NO	Runs	HS	Avge	100s	50s	Ct	St	Balls	Runs	Wkts	Avge	Best	5wI	10wM
Test																	
All First	318	542	59	19567	241 *	40.51	45	101	232	1	3302	2051	34	60.32	3-25	-	-
1-day Int																	
C & G	36	36	0	1108	111	30.77	2	5	13	-	36	26	0	-	-	-	
totesport	221	214	19	6348	138 *	32.55	3	51	80	1	308	323	8	40.37	3-31	-	
Twenty20																	

BOYCE, M. A. G. Leicestershire

Name: Matthew (Matt) Andrew Golding Boyce
Role: Left-hand opening bat, 'very occasional' right-arm off-spin bowler
Born: 13 August 1985, Cheltenham
Height: 5ft 10in **Weight:** 10st 12lbs
Nickname: Boycey
County debut: No first-team appearance
Parents: Anne and Andrew
Marital status: Single
Family links with cricket: 'Father played recreational cricket for over 20 years and coached youth cricket for ten years. Aunt played for Cambridge University. Brother played for Oakham School for three years in 1st XI'
Education: Oakham School; Nottingham University ('studying Management Studies and Economics; in first year')
Qualifications: 9 GCSEs, 3 A-levels
Off-season: 'Studying at university'
Overseas tours: Leicestershire U13 to South Africa 1998; Oakham School to South Africa 2000
Overseas teams played for: Hoppers Crossing, Melbourne 2003-04
Career highlights to date: 'Scoring first century (105) v Northants for Leics 2nd XI. Scoring 2570 runs in 2004 season for Egerton Park and Market Overton and Leics, including record score of 225 (150 balls; 30 x 4, 5 x 6) in the Rutland Championship side v Peterborough. Playing for England Development Squad v Bangladesh 2004'
Cricket moments to forget: 'Walking out to bat against Northamptonshire without a box on and facing the first over before admitting to that fact!'
Cricket superstitions: 'None'
Cricketers particularly admired: David Gower, Andrew Strauss, Brian Lara
Other sports played: Hockey (Leicestershire and Midlands Schoolboys, England trialist), rugby (Oakham School; played scrum half in two *Daily Mail* Cup final winning sides at Twickenham), football (for university), squash (for hall at university)
Other sports followed: Football (Manchester United), rugby (Leicester Tigers)
Favourite band: Midtown, Queen
Relaxations: Sport – squash, gym, swimming, football, rugby; socialising, PlayStation, music
Extras: County Council Special Award for Youth Cricket. *Rutland Times* Young Cricketer of the Year. Sporting Moment of the Year (225; *see above*). Rutland League Teenage Cricketer of the Year. Leading batsman in Leicestershire League

Opinions on cricket: 'I am just starting out in the professional game, having been awarded a two-year contract with Leicestershire. I have played for the county since I was nine. I have always enjoyed success at all levels, but I am sure that the moment will come when success comes hard. However, like many counties, Leicestershire concentrate on the whole person and not just cricket in terms of training the mind as well as the body. Today's game has many support features which would have been anathema to bygone cricketers. Physios, sports psychologists, nutritionists, biomechanics are all the rage, and whilst they play an invaluable role they can't play for you. Therefore it is still a game to be played by fostering your own talent, organising yourself and perhaps not taking yourself too seriously!'

BRACKEN, N. W. — Gloucestershire

Name: Nathan Wade Bracken
Role: Right-hand bat, left-arm fast-medium bowler
Born: 12 September 1977, Penrith, New South Wales, Australia
Height: 6ft 5in **Weight:** 14st 13lbs
County debut: 2004
Test debut: 2003-04
Tests: 3
One-Day Internationals: 17
1st-Class 5 w. in innings: 4
1st-Class catches: 11
Strike rate: 46.80 (career 68.17)
Marital status: Single
Education: Springwood High School, NSW
Overseas tours: New South Wales to New Zealand 2000-01; Australia to India 2000-01 (one-day series), to England 2001, to Africa (World Cup) 2002-03, to India (TVS Cup) 2003-04; Australia A to South Africa (one-day series) 2002-03
Overseas teams played for: New South Wales 1998-99 –
Career highlights to date: 'Test debut and winning the World Cup'
Extras: Represented Australia U19 v New Zealand U19 1995-96. Attended Commonwealth Bank [Australian] Cricket Academy 1997. Had figures of 5-38 (including hat-trick – White, Berry, Harwood) v Victoria at Melbourne in the ING Cup 2001-02, winning Man of the Match award. Man of the Match v England at Adelaide in the VB Series 2002-03 (3-21). Was an overseas player with Gloucestershire towards the end of the 2004 season
Best batting: 38* New South Wales v Victoria, Melbourne 2002-03

Best bowling: 5-22 New South Wales v Western Australia, North Sydney 2000-01
Stop press: Returned innings figures of 7-4 (7-5-4-7) as New South Wales dismissed South Australia for 29 at Sydney in the Pura Cup 2004-05

2004 Season

	M	Inns	NO	Runs	HS	Avge	100s	50s	Ct	St	O	M	Runs	Wkts	Avge	Best	5wI	10wM
Test																		
All First	2	2	1	21	13 *	21.00	-	-	-	-	39	12	106	5	21.20	2-12	-	-
1-day Int																		
C & G																		
totesport	2	0	0	0	0	-	-	-	-	-	18	2	83	4	20.75	3-37	-	
Twenty20																		

Career Performances

	M	Inns	NO	Runs	HS	Avge	100s	50s	Ct	St	Balls	Runs	Wkts	Avge	Best	5wI	10wM
Test	3	3	1	9	6 *	4.50	-	-	1	-	768	351	6	58.50	2-12	-	-
All First	38	51	21	449	38 *	14.96	-	-	11	-	7636	3350	112	29.91	5-22	4	-
1-day Int	17	1	1	7	7 *	-	-	-	2	-	852	552	28	19.71	4-29	-	
C & G																	
totesport	2	0	0	0	0	-	-	-	-	-	108	83	4	20.75	3-37	-	
Twenty20																	

12. Who scored 127* at his home ground, Sydney,
to secure a draw against West Indies in 1981-82 and later coached
Sri Lanka in the 2004 ICC Champions Trophy?

BRANDY, D. G. — Leicestershire

Name: Damian Gareth Brandy
Role: Right-hand bat, right-arm fast-medium bowler; all-rounder
Born: 14 September 1981, Highgate, London
Height: 6ft 1in **Weight:** 14st 2lbs
Nickname: Damo, Brandytime
County debut: 2002
1st-Class 50s: 1
1st-Class catches: 3
Place in batting averages: (2003 217th av. 21.14)
Strike rate: (career 38.25)
Parents: Judy-May and Winston
Marital status: Single
Family links with cricket: 'Dad was very good club cricketer, playing for Essex and London league clubs'
Education: St John's C of E Secondary, Epping; Harlow College
Qualifications: 11 GCSEs, 3 A-levels, Level 1 coaching
Overseas teams played for: Bankstown, Sydney 2000-01; Potchefstroom Boys High, South Africa 2002-03
Career highlights to date: 'First-team debut v Somerset under lights in September 2002'
Cricket moments to forget: 'Being left out of Twenty20 squad for finals 2003'
Cricketers particularly admired: Viv Richards, Sachin Tendulkar, Rahul Dravid, Devon Malcolm
Young players to look out for: Tom New, Luke Wright
Other sports played: Golf, football (West Ham Youth)
Other sports followed: Football (Arsenal, Leicester City)
Favourite band: Maxwell, Eric Benet
Relaxations: 'Reading autobiographies; holidays; eating nice food; spending time with girlfriend and family'
Extras: Played for Essex from U11 to 2nd XI. Scored century in first 2nd XI game for Leicestershire, v Durham 2001. Released by Leicestershire at the end of the 2004 season
Opinions on cricket: 'Not sure county cricket should panic or be forced to change its entire structure. We have a unique game in our country, with conditions and amount played different to the rest of the world. We also have a lot of very talented players and need all 18 counties to give maximum opportunity. No EU players! Young players to be given more guidance.'

Best batting: 52 Leicestershire v Kent, Canterbury 2003
Best bowling: 2-11 Leicestershire v LUCCE, Leicester 2003

2004 Season

	M	Inns	NO	Runs	HS	Avge	100s	50s	Ct	St	O	M	Runs	Wkts	Avge	Best	5wI	10wM
Test																		
All First	1	2	0	11	7	5.50	-	-	-	-								
1-day Int																		
C & G																		
totesport	3	3	0	40	23	13.33	-	-	-	-	2	0	26	0	-		-	-
Twenty20	1	0	0	0	0	-	-	-	-	-								

Career Performances

	M	Inns	NO	Runs	HS	Avge	100s	50s	Ct	St	Balls	Runs	Wkts	Avge	Best	5wI	10wM
Test																	
All First	9	14	2	187	52	15.58	-	1	3	-	153	172	4	43.00	2-11	-	-
1-day Int																	
C & G																	
totesport	6	6	1	90	35	18.00	-	-	-	-	12	26	0	-		-	-
Twenty20	4	3	2	27	13	27.00	-	-	2	-							

BRANT, S. A. — Essex

Name: Scott Andrew Brant
Role: Right-hand bat, left-arm fast-medium bowler
Born: 26 January 1983, Harare, Zimbabwe
Nickname: Woody
County debut: 2003
County cap: 2003
1st-Class 5 w. in innings: 1
1st-Class catches: 7
Place in batting averages: 284th av. 5.57 (2003 294th av. 4.62)
Place in bowling averages: 152nd av. 55.50 (2003 61st av. 30.18)
Strike rate: 94.16 (career 62.41)
Education: Nudgee College, Brisbane; Bond University, Queensland
Overseas teams played for: Norths (Northern Suburbs), Brisbane; Queensland 2001-02 –

Other sports played: Hockey, swimming, triathlon, athletics (all at Zimbabwe Youth level; pole vault gold medallist at South African junior championships)
Extras: Born in Zimbabwe and moved to Australia with his family in 1999. Played for Queensland U19 2000-01. Had match figures of 6-54 (3-23 and 3-31) v Victoria at Brisbane 2001-02 in his second first-class game, winning the Man of the Match award. Joined Essex as an overseas player in 2003. Scored 19 v Nottinghamshire at Southend 2004, in the process sharing with Ronnie Irani (122*) in the first century partnership for the tenth wicket in first-class cricket at the Southchurch Park ground (105). Left Essex at the end of the 2004 season
Best batting: 23 Essex v Lancashire, Old Trafford 2003
Best bowling: 6-45 Essex v Nottinghamshire, Trent Bridge 2003

2004 Season

	M	Inns	NO	Runs	HS	Avge	100s	50s	Ct	St	O	M	Runs	Wkts	Avge	Best	5wI	10wM
Test																		
All First	7	8	1	39	19	5.57	-	-	-	-	188.2	42	666	12	55.50	2-34	-	-
1-day Int																		
C & G	3	1	1	3	3 *	-	-	-	-	-	24	3	117	7	16.71	4-54	-	
totesport	9	4	4	20	10 *	-	-	-	-	-	60.5	1	330	12	27.50	4-49	-	
Twenty20	4	1	1	5	5 *	-	-	-	1	-	11.2	0	59	5	11.80	4-20	-	

Career Performances

	M	Inns	NO	Runs	HS	Avge	100s	50s	Ct	St	Balls	Runs	Wkts	Avge	Best	5wI	10wM
Test																	
All First	23	26	9	111	23	6.52	-	-	7	-	3745	2008	60	33.46	6-45	1	-
1-day Int																	
C & G	5	1	1	3	3 *	-	-	-	-	-	258	216	12	18.00	4-54	-	
totesport	16	7	6	40	14 *	40.00	-	-	4	-	687	624	25	24.96	4-25	-	
Twenty20	9	3	2	6	5 *	6.00	-	-	3	-	188	241	11	21.90	4-20	-	

13. Which Scotland cricketer played rugby in the same school 1st XV as a future British Lions prop and later became a Test cricket captain?

BREESE, G. R. — Durham

Name: Gareth Rohan Breese
Role: Right-hand bat, right-arm off-spin bowler
Born: 9 January 1976, Montego Bay, Jamaica
County debut: 2004
Test debut: 2002-03
Tests: 1
1st-Class 50s: 16
1st-Class 100s: 2
1st-Class 5 w. in innings: 9
1st-Class 10 w. in match: 3
1st-Class catches: 47
Place in batting averages: 156th av. 28.54
Place in bowling averages: 120th av. 41.53
Strike rate: 65.92 (career 61.48)
Overseas tours: West Indies U19 to Pakistan 1995-96; Jamaica to Malaysia (Commonwealth Games) 1998-99; West Indies A to England 2002; West Indies to India 2002-03

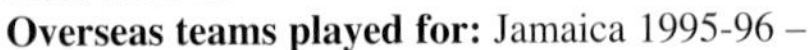

Overseas teams played for: Jamaica 1995-96 –
Extras: Represented West Indies U19 in home series v England U19 1994-95. Second-highest wicket-taker in the Busta Cup 2000-01 with 36 av. 15.11 and in 2001-02 with 44 av. 20.18. Captain of Jamaica since 2004. Scored 165* as Durham made 453-9 to beat Somerset at Taunton 2004 in the fourth-highest successful run chase in the history of the County Championship. Is a British passport-holder and is not considered an overseas player
Best batting: 165* Durham v Somerset, Taunton 2004
Best bowling: 7-60 Jamaica v Barbados, Bridgetown 2000-01

2004 Season

	M	Inns	NO	Runs	HS	Avge	100s	50s	Ct	St	O	M	Runs	Wkts	Avge	Best	5wI	10wM
Test																		
All First	14	25	1	685	165 *	28.54	1	3	12	-	307.4	44	1163	28	41.53	5-41	2	1
1-day Int																		
C & G	1	1	0	25	25	25.00	-	-	-	-	8	0	49	1	49.00	1-49	-	
totesport	18	13	2	240	52 *	21.81	-	1	4	-	117.3	1	538	12	44.83	3-37	-	
Twenty20	5	5	1	38	24 *	9.50	-	-	3	-	20	0	120	7	17.14	4-14	-	

Career Performances

	M	Inns	NO	Runs	HS	Avge	100s	50s	Ct	St	Balls	Runs	Wkts	Avge	Best	5wI	10wM
Test	1	2	0	5	5	2.50	-	-	1	-	188	135	2	67.50	2-108	-	-
All First	63	101	15	2438	165 *	28.34	2	16	47	-	11314	4747	184	25.79	7-60	9	3
1-day Int																	
C & G	1	1	0	25	25	25.00	-	-	-	-	48	49	1	49.00	1-49	-	
totesport	18	13	2	240	52 *	21.81	-	1	4	-	705	538	12	44.83	3-37	-	
Twenty20	5	5	1	38	24 *	9.50	-	-	3	-	120	120	7	17.14	4-14	-	

BRESNAN, T. T. — Yorkshire

Name: Timothy (Tim) Thomas Bresnan
Role: Right-hand bat, right-arm fast-medium bowler
Born: 28 February 1985, Pontefract
Height: 6ft **Weight:** 13st
Nickname: Brezy Lad, Brez
County debut: 2001 (one-day), 2003 (first-class)
1st-Class 50s: 1
1st-Class catches: 4
Place in batting averages: 261st av. 11.91
Place in bowling averages: 68th av. 32.76
Strike rate: 56.64 (career 59.91)
Parents: Julie and Ray
Marital status: Single
Family links with cricket: 'Dad played local league cricket'
Education: Castleford High School; Pontefract New College
Qualifications: 8 GCSEs
Overseas tours: Yorkshire U16 to Cape Town 2001; England U17 to Australia 2000-01; England U19 to Australia and (U19 World Cup) New Zealand 2001-02, to Australia 2002-03, to Bangladesh (U19 World Cup) 2003-04
Career highlights to date: 'Winning [U19] "Test" series against India [2002]'
Cricket moments to forget: 'Eight ducks in a row in 2000 season, for various teams'
Cricket superstitions: 'None'
Cricketers particularly admired: Ian Botham
Young players to look out for: Joseph Sayers, Chris Gilbert, David Stiff
Other sports played: Golf, football
Other sports followed: Football (Leeds United)
Favourite band: Girls Aloud

Relaxations: Golf, PlayStation
Extras: Bunbury Festival Best All-rounder and Most Outstanding Player. Made one-day debut v Kent at Headingley 2001 aged 16 years 102 days, making him the youngest player to represent Yorkshire since Paul Jarvis in 1981. NBC Denis Compton Award for the most promising young Yorkshire player 2002, 2003. Represented England U19 2002 and v South Africa U19 2003, taking 5-81 in first 'Test' at Headingley 2003. Scored maiden first-class fifty (52) v India A at Headingley 2003
Best batting: 52 Yorkshire v India A, Headingley 2003
Best bowling: 3-32 Yorkshire v Durham, Scarborough 2004

2004 Season

	M	Inns	NO	Runs	HS	Avge	100s	50s	Ct	St	O	M	Runs	Wkts	Avge	Best	5wI	10wM
Test																		
All First	10	15	3	143	35	11.91	-	-	3	-	160.3	31	557	17	32.76	3-32	-	-
1-day Int																		
C & G	4	3	1	12	7	6.00	-	-	1	-	32	3	151	2	75.50	1-44	-	
totesport	18	12	3	215	49	23.88	-	-	2	-	118	11	602	17	35.41	3-31	-	
Twenty20	5	4	0	89	42	22.25	-	-	3	-	18.2	0	143	3	47.66	1-21	-	

Career Performances

	M	Inns	NO	Runs	HS	Avge	100s	50s	Ct	St	Balls	Runs	Wkts	Avge	Best	5wI	10wM
Test																	
All First	14	19	3	224	52	14.00	-	1	4	-	1438	816	24	34.00	3-32	-	-
1-day Int																	
C & G	7	4	1	26	14	8.66	-	-	2	-	318	242	6	40.33	2-53	-	
totesport	46	30	9	484	61	23.04	-	1	12	-	1798	1451	46	31.54	3-29	-	
Twenty20	10	6	1	107	42	21.40	-	-	5	-	218	259	10	25.90	3-31	-	

BRESSINGTON, A. N. — Gloucestershire

Name: Alastair Nigel Bressington
Role: Left-hand bat, right-arm fast-medium bowler; all-rounder
Born: 28 November 1979, Bristol
Height: 6ft 1in **Weight:** 14st
Nickname: Magic, Bressy
County debut: 2000
County cap: 2004
1st-Class 50s: 1
1st-Class catches: 4
Strike rate: 126.00 (career 57.05)
Parents: Adrian and Marjorie
Marital status: Single

Family links with cricket: Brother Nathan played for Gloucestershire 2nd XI
Education: Marling Grammar School, Stroud; UWIC
Qualifications: 12 GCSEs, 4 A-levels
Cricketers particularly admired: Jack Russell, Ian Botham
Other sports played: Rugby (Gloucestershire Colts; Gloucester RFC U21; Newbury)
Other sports followed: Rugby (Bristol RFC), football (Liverpool FC)
Relaxations: Music, reading
Extras: Took wicket with third ball in first-class cricket v Glamorgan at Bristol 2000 and took five wickets in debut match, including that of Matthew Maynard. Captain of Cardiff University CCE 2001 and 2002. Released by Gloucestershire at the end of the 2004 season
Best batting: 58* Gloucestershire v Kent, Bristol 2004
Best bowling: 4-36 Gloucestershire v Glamorgan, Bristol 2000

2004 Season

	M	Inns	NO	Runs	HS	Avge	100s	50s	Ct	St	O	M	Runs	Wkts	Avge	Best	5wI	10wM
Test																		
All First	3	3	3	83	58 *	-	-	1	1	-	21	2	138	1	138.00	1-38	-	-
1-day Int																		
C & G																		
totesport																		
Twenty20																		

Career Performances

	M	Inns	NO	Runs	HS	Avge	100s	50s	Ct	St	Balls	Runs	Wkts	Avge	Best	5wI	10wM
Test																	
All First	9	9	6	125	58 *	41.66	-	1	4	-	970	584	17	34.35	4-36	-	-
1-day Int																	
C & G	3	2	0	98	54	49.00	-	1	2	-	150	86	5	17.20	3-21	-	
totesport	4	3	0	42	22	14.00	-	-	2	-	150	118	1	118.00	1-31	-	
Twenty20																	

BRIDGE, G. D. Durham

Name: Graeme David Bridge
Role: Right-hand bat, slow left-arm bowler
Born: 4 September 1980, Sunderland
Height: 5ft 8in **Weight:** 12st 12lbs
Nickname: Bridgey, Teet
County debut: 1999
1st-Class 50s: 3
1st-Class 5 w. in innings: 1
1st-Class catches: 18
Place in batting averages: 210th av. 21.40 (2003 193rd av. 24.00)
Place in bowling averages: 86th av. 35.78 (2003 116th av. 39.84)
Strike rate: 74.21 (career 70.55)
Parents: Anne and John
Wife and date of marriage: Leanne, 2 October 2004
Children: Olivia Molly, 13 September 2003
Family links with cricket: 'Dad and brother played club cricket'
Education: Southmoor School, Sunderland
Qualifications: 5 GCSEs, Level 1 coaching
Career outside cricket: 'Admin, office work'
Off-season: 'Netting in new indoor school; tour to India; training'
Overseas tours: England U19 to New Zealand 1998-99, to Malaysia and (U19 World Cup) Sri Lanka 1999-2000; Durham to South Africa 2002; Durham Academy to India
Career highlights to date: 'Making first-team debut'
Cricket moments to forget: 'Pulling up with twisted ankle on TV'
Cricket superstitions: 'Don't be late'
Cricketers particularly admired: Martin Love, David Boon
Young players to look out for: Phil Mustard, Dave Harrison, Mark Wallace
Other sports played: Football
Other sports followed: Football (Sunderland AFC 'home or away')
Injuries: Out for four weeks with a broken finger
Favourite band: 'Anything'; Stone Roses
Relaxations: 'Horse racing (jumps)'
Extras: Played in U15 World Cup 1996. Represented England U19 v Australia U19 1999. C&G Man of the Match award on county one-day debut for his 3-44 v Gloucestershire at Bristol 2001
Opinions on cricket: 'Enjoy.'
Best batting: 52 Durham v Leicestershire, Riverside 2004
Best bowling: 6-84 Durham v Hampshire, Riverside 2001

2004 Season

	M	Inns	NO	Runs	HS	Avge	100s	50s	Ct	St	O	M	Runs	Wkts	Avge	Best	5wI	10wM
Test																		
All First	11	18	3	321	52	21.40	-	2	1	-	235	60	680	19	35.78	4-64	-	-
1-day Int																		
C & G																		
totesport	9	5	2	33	15 *	11.00	-	-	2	-	49.4	4	230	9	25.55	3-14	-	
Twenty20	5	3	0	19	11	6.33	-	-	1	-	18.5	0	101	7	14.42	2-16	-	

Career Performances

	M	Inns	NO	Runs	HS	Avge	100s	50s	Ct	St	Balls	Runs	Wkts	Avge	Best	5wI	10wM
Test																	
All First	37	61	10	881	52	17.27	-	3	18	-	5927	2952	84	35.14	6-84	1	-
1-day Int																	
C & G	8	6	2	63	19	15.75	-	-	1	-	368	276	7	39.42	3-44	-	
totesport	32	23	8	156	24	10.40	-	-	5	-	1350	939	38	24.71	4-20	-	
Twenty20	5	3	0	19	11	6.33	-	-	1	-	113	101	7	14.42	2-16	-	

BRIGNULL, D. S. — Leicestershire

Name: David (Dave) Stephen Brignull
Role: Right-hand bat, right-arm fast-medium bowler
Born: 27 November 1981, Forest Gate, London
Height: 6ft 4in **Weight:** 15st 10lbs
Nickname: Briggers, Brig-Dog
County debut: 2002 (one-day), 2003 (first-class)
Strike rate: 87.00 (career 65.11)
Parents: Sharon Penfold and Stephen Brignull
Marital status: Single
Family links with cricket: 'Uncles on both sides of family played for Essex Schools'
Education: Lancaster Boys School; Wyggeston and Queen Elizabeth I College
Qualifications: 11 GCSEs, 3 A-levels, Level 1 coaching
Overseas tours: Leicestershire U19 to South Africa 2000-01
Overseas teams played for: Lafarge CC, Lichtenburg, South Africa 2000-01
Career highlights to date: '3-48 on Sky against Glamorgan in the National League – a game we won off the last ball'

Cricket moments to forget: 'Being hit for 26 in one over in club cricket'
Cricketers particularly admired: Robin Smith, Darren Gough
Young players to look out for: Tom New, Luke Wright
Other sports played: Rugby (Wigston RFC), volleyball (for college team that came fourth in nationals)
Other sports followed: Rugby (Leicester Tigers), football (West Ham), American football (Oakland Raiders)
Favourite band: Eminem
Relaxations: 'Music, socialising'
Extras: Represented England U17 at the ECC Colts Festival in Northern Ireland 1999. Leicestershire Youth Bowler of the Year and U19 Player of the Season 2001. Hat-trick against Derbyshire U19
Best batting: 46 Leicestershire v Middlesex, Leicester 2003
Best bowling: 2-30 Leicestershire v Kent, Canterbury 2003

2004 Season

	M	Inns	NO	Runs	HS	Avge	100s	50s	Ct	St	O	M	Runs	Wkts	Avge	Best	5wI	10wM
Test																		
All First	1	2	2	0	0*	-	-	-	-	-	29	3	121	2	60.50	2-78	-	-
1-day Int																		
C & G																		
totesport	1	0	0	0	0	-	-	-	1	-	4	0	32	0	-	-	-	
Twenty20																		

Career Performances

	M	Inns	NO	Runs	HS	Avge	100s	50s	Ct	St	Balls	Runs	Wkts	Avge	Best	5wI	10wM
Test																	
All First	4	6	2	58	46	14.50	-	-	-	-	586	356	9	39.55	2-30	-	-
1-day Int																	
C & G	3	3	1	20	9*	10.00	-	-	3	-	154	129	4	32.25	2-35	-	
totesport	9	5	3	11	4*	5.50	-	-	3	-	278	264	10	26.40	3-40	-	
Twenty20																	

BROAD, S. Leicestershire

Name: Stuart Broad
Role: Left-hand bat, right-arm medium-fast bowler; all-rounder
Born: 24 June 1986, Nottingham
Height: 6ft 5in **Weight:** 11st
Nickname: Broady
County debut: No first-team appearance
Parents: Carole and Chris

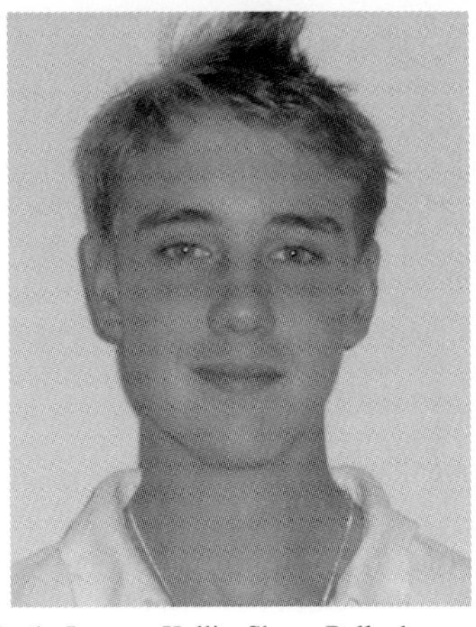

Marital status: Single
Family links with cricket: 'Father played for Gloucs CCC, Notts CCC and England; sister plays for Exeter Uni Ladies 1st XI'
Education: Oakham School
Qualifications: 10 GCSEs, 3 A-levels
Off-season: 'Playing with Hoppers Crossing CC in Melbourne'
Overseas tours: Oakham School to South Africa 2001
Overseas teams played for: Hoppers Crossing CC, Melbourne 2004-05
Career highlights to date: 'ECB Schools v Bangladesh U19; Development of Excellence XI v Bangladesh U19; 190 v Derbys U17'
Cricket superstitions: 'Right pad on first; scrape my mark three times before a new delivery'
Cricketers particularly admired: Glenn McGrath, Jacques Kallis, Shaun Pollock
Young players to look out for: Matthew Boyce, Paul Cook, Mark Collier
Other sports played: Hockey (Midlands age-group), golf
Other sports followed: Football (Nottingham Forest), rugby (Leicester Tigers)
Favourite band: 'Whatever's playing on the radio'
Relaxations: 'All sports, especially a round of golf; travelling'
Extras: Leicestershire Young Cricketers Batsman Award 2003
Opinions on cricket: 'Cricketers should be on 12-month contracts, and the Twenty20 should be kept a novelty and not overplayed. There should be at least eight players eligible to play for England in each county side.'

14. Who was Man of the Match in Sri Lanka's 1995-96 World Cup final victory over Australia?

BROPHY, G. L. Northamptonshire

Name: Gerard Louis Brophy
Role: Right-hand bat, wicket-keeper
Born: 26 November 1975, Welkom, South Africa
Height: 5ft 11in **Weight:** 12st
Nickname: Scuba, Broph
County debut: 2002
1st-Class 50s: 11
1st-Class 100s: 5
1st-Class catches: 119
1st-Class stumpings: 7
Place in batting averages: 130th av. 32.34 (2003 9th av. 62.28)
Parents: Gerard and Trish
Wife and date of marriage: Alison, 3 January 2004
Education: Christian Brothers College, Boksburg; Wits Technikon (both South Africa)
Qualifications: Marketing Diploma, Level 2 coach
Off-season: 'Working in my tooth-whitening clinic. Studying'
Overseas tours: South Africa U17 to England 1993; South African Academy to Zimbabwe 1998-99
Overseas teams played for: Gauteng 1996-97 – 1998-99; Free State 1999-2000 – 2000-01
Career highlights to date: 'Captaincy of Free State 2000-01. First dismissal [in collaboration] with Allan Donald'
Cricket moments to forget: 'Messing up a live TV interview'
Cricket superstitions: 'Right pad on first and right glove on first'
Cricketers particularly admired: Ray Jennings, Ian Healy, Allan Donald, Hansie Cronje
Young players to look out for: Jacques Rudolph
Other sports played: Golf, rugby
Other sports followed: Golf, rugby
Favourite band: Coldplay
Relaxations: 'Fishing, travelling, braais, scuba diving'
Extras: Captained South Africa U17. Played for Ireland in the NatWest 2000. Parents live in Brisbane, Australia. Holds a British passport and is not considered an overseas player
Best batting: 185 South African Academy v President's XI, Harare 1999-2000

2004 Season

	M	Inns	NO	Runs	HS	Avge	100s	50s	Ct	St	O	M	Runs	Wkts	Avge	Best	5wI	10wM
Test																		
All First	16	25	2	744	181	32.34	1	4	27	2	1	0	1	0	-	-	-	-
1-day Int																		
C & G	2	1	0	24	24	24.00	-	-	1	1								
totesport	13	10	3	238	50 *	34.00	-	1	13	3								
Twenty20	4	3	1	39	18	19.50	-	-	2	-								

Career Performances

	M	Inns	NO	Runs	HS	Avge	100s	50s	Ct	St	Balls	Runs	Wkts	Avge	Best	5wI	10wM
Test																	
All First	50	83	13	2456	185	35.08	5	11	119	7	6	1	0	-	-	-	-
1-day Int																	
C & G	4	3	0	52	24	17.33	-	-	1	1							
totesport	26	22	4	433	54	24.05	-	2	24	6							
Twenty20	6	5	2	59	18	19.66	-	-	3	1							

BROWN, A. D. — Surrey

Name: Alistair Duncan Brown
Role: Right-hand bat, right-arm off-spin bowler, occasional wicket-keeper
Born: 11 February 1970, Beckenham
Height: 5ft 10in **Weight:** 12st 7lbs
Nickname: The Lord
County debut: 1992
County cap: 1994
Benefit: 2002
One-Day Internationals: 16
1000 runs in a season: 7
1st-Class 50s: 51
1st-Class 100s: 34
1st-Class 200s: 2
1st-Class catches: 207
1st-Class stumpings: 1
One-Day 100s: 14
One-Day 200s: 2
Place in batting averages: 31st av. 52.50 (2003 180th av. 25.47)
Strike rate: (career 483.50)
Parents: Robert and Ann
Wife and date of marriage: Sarah, 10 October 1998

Children: Max Charles, 9 March 2001; Joe Robert, 11 March 2003
Family links with cricket: Father played for Surrey Young Amateurs in the 1950s
Education: Caterham School
Qualifications: 5 O-levels, Level II coach
Career outside cricket: 'Poker player, cricket coach, amateur gambler and horse owner'
Off-season: 'Jury service; coaching'
Overseas tours: England VI to Singapore 1993, 1994, 1995, to Hong Kong 1997; England to Sharjah (Champions Trophy) 1997-98, to Bangladesh (Wills International Cup) 1998-99
Overseas teams played for: North Perth, Western Australia 1989-90
Career highlights to date: '118 v India at Old Trafford 1996; 203 v Hants at Guildford 1997; 268 v Glamorgan at The Oval 2002'
Cricket moments to forget: 'A great couple of days in Ireland!'
Cricket superstitions: 'Always get to the ground before 11 a.m.'
Cricketers particularly admired: Ian Botham, Viv Richards
Young players to look out for: Timothy Murtagh ('should bat at three for England next year and give up bowling altogether')
Other sports played: Football, golf
Other sports followed: Football (West Ham United), rugby union (London Wasps)
Injuries: Out for one week with a torn hamstring; 'for six months sulking'
Favourite band: Roachford, Snow Patrol
Relaxations: 'Golf and sleep (when the children allow) – would be interested in the Warwickshire relaxation programme!'
Extras: Scored three of the eight fastest centuries of the 1992 season (71, 78 & 79 balls). Awarded Man of the Match for his 118 against India in the third One-Day International at Old Trafford 1996. Recorded the highest-ever score in the Sunday League with 203 off 119 balls against Hampshire at Guildford in 1997 and received an individual award at the PCA dinner for that achievement. Scored 72-ball century v Northamptonshire at The Oval to become joint winner (with Carl Hooper) of the EDS Walter Lawrence Trophy for the fastest first-class 100 of the 1998 season. Scored 31-ball 50 v South Africa in the Texaco Trophy at Headingley 1998, the fastest 50 in the history of the Texaco Trophy. Surrey CCC Batsman of the Season Award 2001. C&G Man of the Match award for his 160-ball 268 out of 438-5 v Glamorgan at The Oval 2002; it set a new record for the highest individual score in professional one-day cricket worldwide and Brown also became the first batsman to have scored two double centuries in one-day cricket. Scored 154 v Lancashire at Old Trafford 2004 to complete full set of first-class hundreds against all 17 other counties
Opinions on cricket: 'Twenty20 is here to stay and should not be tampered with too much. Looking forward to the ECB bringing out next year's first-class veterans' fixtures for the over 35s!'
Best batting: 295* Surrey v Leicestershire, Oakham School 2000
Best bowling: 1-11 Surrey v Warwickshire, The Oval 2003

2004 Season

	M	Inns	NO	Runs	HS	Avge	100s	50s	Ct	St	O	M	Runs	Wkts	Avge	Best	5wI	10wM
Test																		
All First	15	24	2	1155	170	52.50	4	6	15	-	13.3	3	43	0	-	-	-	-
1-day Int																		
C & G	1	1	0	67	67	67.00	-	1	1	-								
totesport	12	11	0	251	54	22.81	-	1	4	-	5	0	42	1	42.00	1-18	-	
Twenty20	7	7	0	180	64	25.71	-	1	8	-	0.2	0	2	0	-	-	-	

Career Performances

	M	Inns	NO	Runs	HS	Avge	100s	50s	Ct	St	Balls	Runs	Wkts	Avge	Best	5wI	10wM
Test																	
All First	199	312	30	12206	295 *	43.28	36	51	207	1	967	504	2	252.00	1-11	-	-
1-day Int	16	16	0	354	118	22.12	1	1	6	-	6	5	0	-	-	-	
C & G	35	31	2	937	268	32.31	1	4	12	-	18	26	0	-	-	-	
totesport	206	200	5	6060	203	31.07	12	26	71	-	315	320	10	32.00	3-39	-	
Twenty20	14	14	1	331	64	25.46	-	2	14	-	2	2	0	-	-	-	

BROWN, D. R. — Warwickshire

Name: Douglas (Dougie) Robert Brown
Role: Right-hand bat, right-arm fast-medium bowler; all-rounder
Born: 29 October 1969, Stirling, Scotland
Height: 6ft 2in **Weight:** 14st 7lbs
Nickname: Hoots
County debut: 1992
County cap: 1995
One-Day Internationals: 9
1000 runs in a season: 1
50 wickets in a season: 3
1st-Class 50s: 40
1st-Class 100s: 8
1st-Class 200s: 1
1st-Class 5 w. in innings: 19
1st-Class 10 w. in match: 4
1st-Class catches: 110
One-Day 100s: 1
One-Day 5 w. in innings: 2
Place in batting averages: 39th av. 50.36 (2003 40th av. 46.72)
Place in bowling averages: 65th av. 32.32 (2003 89th av. 35.38)
Strike rate: 63.85 (career 53.90)

Parents: Alastair and Janette
Children: Lauren, 14 September 1998
Family links with cricket: 'Both grandads played a bit'
Education: Alloa Academy; West London Institute of Higher Education (Borough Road College)
Qualifications: 9 O-Grades, 5 Higher Grades, BEd (Hons) Physical Education, ECB Level III coach
Career outside cricket: PE teacher
Off-season: 'Benefit!'
Overseas tours: Scotland XI to Pakistan 1988-89; England VI to Hong Kong 1997, 2001, 2003; England A to Kenya and Sri Lanka 1997-98; England to Sharjah (Champions Trophy) 1997-98, to West Indies 1997-98 (one-day series), to Bangladesh (Wills International Cup) 1998-99; Scotland to UAE (ICC Six Nations Challenge) 2003-04
Overseas teams played for: Primrose, Cape Town 1992-93; Vredenburg Saldhana, Cape Town 1993-94; Eastern Suburbs, Wellington 1995-96; Wellington, New Zealand 1995-96
Career highlights to date: 'Playing first Lord's final v Northants 1995. England debut in Sharjah'
Cricket moments to forget: 'Phone call from David Graveney (chairman of selectors) saying you are dropped!'
Cricket superstitions: 'None'
Cricketers particularly admired: Ian Botham, Wasim Akram, Dermot Reeve 'and everyone who gives 100 per cent'
Young players to look out for: Ian Bell, Jonathan Trott, Kadeer Ali
Other sports played: Golf
Other sports followed: Football (Alloa Athletic, 'and all the Midlands football teams')
Favourite band: Oasis, U2
Relaxations: 'Music, time with Lauren'
Extras: Played football at Hampden Park for Scotland U18. Has played first-class and B&H cricket for Scotland. Scored 1118 runs and took 109 wickets in all first-team county cricket 1997. Set record for the earliest Championship 100 in an English season with his maiden first-class century (142) v Northamptonshire at Edgbaston on 15 April 1999. Scored maiden first-class double century v Sussex at Hove 2000 (203; the highest score recorded by a Warwickshire No. 7), during which he shared in a record Warwickshire partnership for the seventh wicket (289 with Ashley Giles; equalled by Ian Bell and Tony Frost 2004). Vice-captain of Warwickshire 2002-03. Warwickshire All-rounder of the Year 2002. Scored 108 v Essex at Edgbaston in the C&G 2003, winning Man of the Match award and sharing with Ashley Giles (71*) in a competition record seventh-wicket partnership (170). Scored century (140*) v Lancashire 2003, sharing with Jonathan Trott (126) in a new record sixth-wicket partnership for Warwickshire at Edgbaston (216). Scored century (162) v Lancashire at Old Trafford 2004, in the process sharing with Ian Bell (112) in a new ground record

partnership for the fifth wicket (254). Scored century (108*) then returned first innings figures of 5-53 v Northamptonshire at Northampton 2004. Granted a benefit for 2005
Opinions on cricket: 'Still a great game!'
Best batting: 203 Warwickshire v Sussex, Hove 2000
Best bowling: 8-89 First-Class Counties XI v Pakistan A, Chelmsford 1997

2004 Season

	M	Inns	NO	Runs	HS	Avge	100s	50s	Ct	St	O	M	Runs	Wkts	Avge	Best	5wI	10wM
Test																		
All First	17	22	3	957	162	50.36	3	2	7	-	425.4	97	1293	40	32.32	5-53	2	-
1-day Int																		
C & G	4	1	0	47	47	47.00	-	-	2	-	37.3	7	154	13	11.84	5-43	1	
totesport	16	10	2	202	41	25.25	-	-	2	-	111	5	639	19	33.63	3-48	-	
Twenty20	6	5	0	76	37	15.20	-	-	1	-	19	1	104	8	13.00	2-5	-	

Career Performances

	M	Inns	NO	Runs	HS	Avge	100s	50s	Ct	St	Balls	Runs	Wkts	Avge	Best	5wI	10wM
Test																	
All First	179	270	36	7467	203	31.91	9	40	110	-	25714	13619	477	28.55	8-89	19	4
1-day Int	9	8	4	99	21	24.75	-	-	1	-	324	305	7	43.57	2-28	-	
C & G	31	27	3	632	108	26.33	1	4	9	-	1487	1030	40	25.75	5-43	1	
totesport	162	129	20	2444	82 *	22.42	-	11	39	-	5991	4769	186	25.63	4-37	-	
Twenty20	11	9	0	81	37	9.00	-	-	3	-	192	235	10	23.50	2-5	-	

15. Which Worcestershire left-arm spinner has an uncle who won the Open [Golf] Championship at Turnberry in 1994?

BROWN, J. F. Northamptonshire

Name: Jason Fred Brown
Role: Right-hand bat, off-spin bowler
Born: 10 October 1974, Newcastle-under-Lyme
Height: 6ft **Weight:** 13st
Nickname: Cheese, Fish, Brownie
County debut: 1996
County cap: 2000
50 wickets in a season: 2
1st-Class 5 w. in innings: 14
1st-Class 10 w. in match: 3
1st-Class catches: 17
One-Day 5 w. in innings: 2
Place in batting averages: 269th av. 9.11 (2003 250th av. 15.16)
Place in bowling averages: 123rd av. 42.30 (2003 22nd av. 23.71)
Strike rate: 97.41 (career 68.25)
Parents: Peter and Cynthia
Wife and date of marriage: Sam, 26 September 1998
Children: Millie
Education: St Margaret Ward RC School, Stoke-on-Trent
Qualifications: 9 GCSEs, Level 1 coaching qualification
Overseas tours: Kidsgrove League U18 to Australia 1990; Northants CCC to Zimbabwe 1998, to Grenada 2000; England A to West Indies 2000-01; England to Sri Lanka 2000-01
Overseas teams played for: North East Valley, Dunedin, New Zealand 1996-97
Cricketers particularly admired: John Emburey, Carl Hooper
Other sports played: Golf
Other sports followed: Football (Port Vale)
Relaxations: 'Reading, listening to music'
Extras: Represented Staffordshire at all junior levels, in Minor Counties, and in the NatWest 1995. Once took 10-16 in a Kidsgrove League game against Haslington U18 playing for Sandyford U18. Took 100th first-class wicket in 23rd match, v Sussex at Northampton 2000, going on to take his 50th wicket of the season in the same game, only his seventh of the summer. Took 5-27 v Somerset at Northampton in the Twenty20 2003. C&G Man of the Match award for his 5-19 v Cambridgeshire at Northampton 2004
Best batting: 38 Northamptonshire v Hampshire, Northampton 2003
Best bowling: 7-69 Northamptonshire v Durham, Riverside 2003

2004 Season

	M	Inns	NO	Runs	HS	Avge	100s	50s	Ct	St	O	M	Runs	Wkts	Avge	Best	5wI	10wM
Test																		
All First	13	15	6	82	34	9.11	-	-	4	-	584.3	133	1523	36	42.30	5-113	1	-
1-day Int																		
C & G	3	2	0	1	1	0.50	-	-	1	-	30	1	113	6	18.83	5-19	1	
totesport	15	6	4	19	9*	9.50	-	-	5	-	133.5	3	562	17	33.05	4-33	-	
Twenty20	5	0	0	0	0	-	-	-	-	-	16	0	127	2	63.50	2-17	-	

Career Performances

	M	Inns	NO	Runs	HS	Avge	100s	50s	Ct	St	Balls	Runs	Wkts	Avge	Best	5wI	10wM
Test																	
All First	75	88	39	376	38	7.67	-	-	17	-	19385	8659	284	30.48	7-69	14	3
1-day Int																	
C & G	12	8	5	9	3	3.00	-	-	1	-	720	515	15	34.33	5-19	1	
totesport	74	26	15	65	16	5.90	-	-	22	-	3430	2376	75	31.68	4-26	-	
Twenty20	10	0	0	0	0	-	-	-	2	-	203	249	13	19.15	5-27	1	

BROWN, M. J. — Hampshire

Name: Michael James Brown
Role: Right-hand bat, occasional wicket-keeper
Born: 9 February 1980, Burnley
Height: 6ft **Weight:** 12st
Nickname: Brownstone, Dawson, Browndog
County debut: 1999 (Middlesex), 2004 (Hampshire)
1st-Class 50s: 10
1st-Class 100s: 2
1st-Class catches: 24
Place in batting averages: 132nd av. 32.23
Parents: Peter and Valerie
Marital status: Single
Family links with cricket: 'Father played league cricket for 30 years. Mum makes great tuna sandwiches. Brother David plays for DUCCE'
Education: Queen Elizabeth's Grammar School, Blackburn; Durham University
Qualifications: 10 GCSEs, 4 A-levels, 2.1 Economics/Politics
Off-season: 'Shoulder operation followed by playing grade cricket for Fremantle'
Overseas teams played for: Western Province CC, Cape Town 1998-99; Fremantle CC, Western Australia 2002-05

Career highlights to date: 'Maiden hundred v Leicestershire and winning game in two days; 90 and 109* v Glamorgan in same game; winning promotion to first division; playing in side captained by Shane Warne'
Cricket moments to forget: 'Getting out to James Hildreth'
Cricket superstitions: 'Always tap non-striker's end four times at end of over when at that end'
Cricketers particularly admired: Dale Benkenstein, Gary Kirsten, Wasim Akram, Mike Atherton, James Foster
Young players to look out for: David Brown, Ravi Bopara, Jacques Rudolph
Other sports played: Football ('town team')
Other sports followed: Football (Burnley FC)
Favourite band: Counting Crows 'and all "cheese"'
Relaxations: 'Sleeping; prowling round Perth'
Extras: Represented ECB U19 A v Pakistan U19 1998. Played for Durham University CCE 2001 and 2002, scoring two fifties (55 and 60*) for DUCCE v Worcestershire at Worcester 2001. Represented British Universities 2001 and 2002. 'Was at non-striker's end as five wickets fell in one over, Middlesex 2nd XI v Glamorgan 2nd XI, July 2001.' 'Kept wicket for Middlesex v Zimbabwe [at Shenley 2003] after both wicket-keepers were injured before and on morning of game', also scoring 98 in Middlesex's first innings. Left Middlesex at the end of the 2003 season and joined Hampshire for 2004. Scored maiden first-class century (102*) v Leicestershire at West End 2004
Opinions on cricket: 'Standard of first-class wickets, especially in second division, is poor. Too many games, not enough practice time. (Does anyone taken any notice??) Two up/two down in promotion/relegation. Great to see England looking and performing like a top side.'
Best batting: 109* Hampshire v Glamorgan, West End 2004

2004 Season

	M	Inns	NO	Runs	HS	Avge	100s	50s	Ct	St	O	M	Runs	Wkts	Avge	Best	5wI	10wM
Test																		
All First	16	28	2	838	109 *	32.23	2	6	12	-								
1-day Int																		
C & G																		
totesport	4	4	0	60	35	15.00	-	-	2	-								
Twenty20	3	3	0	19	14	6.33	-	-	-	-								

Career Performances

	M	Inns	NO	Runs	HS	Avge	100s	50s	Ct	St	Balls	Runs	Wkts	Avge	Best	5wI	10wM
Test																	
All First	28	47	5	1326	109 *	31.57	2	10	24	-							
1-day Int																	
C & G																	
totesport	5	5	0	78	35	15.60	-	-	2	-							
Twenty20	3	3	0	19	14	6.33	-	-	-	-							

BRUCE, J. T. A. Hampshire

Name: James Thomas Anthony Bruce
Role: Right-hand bat, right-arm medium-fast bowler
Born: 17 December 1979, Hammersmith, London
Height: 6ft 1in **Weight:** 13st 10lbs
Nickname: Brucey, Bula, Bear, Eugene
County debut: 2003
1st-Class catches: 5
Place in batting averages: (2003 282nd av. 8.50)
Place in bowling averages: (2003 131st av. 43.63)
Strike rate: 58.66 (career 69.09)
Parents: Andrew and Claire
Marital status: Single
Family links with cricket: 'All three of my brothers have played youth cricket for Hampshire'
Education: Eton College, Durham University
Qualifications: BA (Hons) Geography, Level 1 coaching
Off-season: 'Playing for South Perth CC, December 2004-March 2005'
Overseas tours: West of England U15 to West Indies 1995; Eton College to South Africa 1998-99; Yellowhammers to South Africa 2001-02; Durham University to South Africa 2001
Overseas teams played for: Balmain Tigers, Sydney 2002-03; South Perth CC, Perth 2003-05
Career highlights to date: 'Making my Championship debut against Somerset. Making my NCL debut in a day/night game on Sky v Notts at Trent Bridge [2003]. Playing in Twenty20 competition 2004'
Cricket moments to forget: 'Having my box split in two by Mike Kasprowicz'
Cricket superstitions: 'Too many to mention'
Cricketers particularly admired: Robin Smith, Shaun Udal, Wasim Akram, Brett Lee
Young players to look out for: Kevin Latouf, Mitchell Stokes, Edward Bruce
Other sports played: Rugby, golf
Injuries: Out for 20 weeks after thigh surgery in January 2004
Favourite band: Powderfinger
Relaxations: 'I like spending time on the beach, watching TV and sleeping'
Extras: Played for DUCCE in 2001 and 2002. Played for Cumberland in the C&G 2002

Opinions on cricket: 'I think the introduction of Twenty20 has helped improve the popularity of county cricket to the general public and helped players to develop new aspects to their game. I also strongly believe that too many EU passport qualified players can only hinder the development of local young players and their transition from youth to first-class cricket.'
Best batting: 21* Hampshire v Glamorgan, West End 2003
Best bowling: 3-42 Hampshire v Glamorgan, West End 2003

2004 Season

	M	Inns	NO	Runs	HS	Avge	100s	50s	Ct	St	O	M	Runs	Wkts	Avge	Best	5wI	10wM
Test																		
All First	4	5	1	10	9	2.50	-	-	1	-	88	11	375	9	41.66	3-74	-	-
1-day Int																		
C & G																		
totesport																		
Twenty20	6	3	0	18	12	6.00	-	-	3	-	18	0	141	8	17.62	3-21	-	

Career Performances

	M	Inns	NO	Runs	HS	Avge	100s	50s	Ct	St	Balls	Runs	Wkts	Avge	Best	5wI	10wM
Test																	
All First	18	22	7	105	21 *	7.00	-	-	5	-	2280	1593	33	48.27	3-42	-	-
1-day Int																	
C & G	1	1	0	0	0	0.00	-	-	-	-							
totesport	3	1	1	6	6 *	-	-	-	-	-	120	100	4	25.00	3-45	-	
Twenty20	6	3	0	18	12	6.00	-	-	3	-	108	141	8	17.62	3-21	-	

BRYANT, J. D. C. — Derbyshire

Name: James Douglas Campbell Bryant
Role: Right-hand bat, right-arm medium bowler
Born: 4 February 1976, Durban, South Africa
Height: 6ft **Weight:** 11st 10lbs
Nickname: JB
County debut: 2003 (Somerset), 2004 (Derbyshire)
1st-Class 50s: 19
1st-Class 100s: 7
1st-Class 200s: 1
1st-Class catches: 53
Place in batting averages: 263rd av. 11.26 (2003 144th av. 29.90)
Strike rate: (career 38.00)
Parents: Nick and Helen
Marital status: Single
Education: Maritzburg College; University of Port Elizabeth

Qualifications: BComm (Hons) Business Management, Level 2 coach
Career outside cricket: Entrepreneur
Overseas tours: South African Academy to Ireland and Scotland 1999; South Africa A to West Indies 2000-01
Overseas teams played for: Eastern Province 1996-97 – 2002-03
Career highlights to date: '234* v North West and achieving South African highest first-class batting partnership – 441; and playing for South Africa A'
Cricket moments to forget: 'The whole 2004 season'
Other sports played: Golf, tennis, squash
Other sports followed: Rugby (Natal Sharks)
Injuries: Out for six weeks with a broken hand
Relaxations: 'Reading, watersports, golf'
Extras: SuperSport Recruit of the Year 2000. Scored career-best 234* v North West at Potchefstroom in the SuperSport Series 2002-03, in the process sharing with Carl Bradfield (196) in a new record partnership for any wicket in South African domestic first-class cricket (441). Is a British passport holder and is not considered an overseas player. Left Somerset in the 2003-04 off-season and joined Derbyshire for 2004
Opinions on cricket: 'Still too many county fixtures.'
Best batting: 234* Eastern Province v North West, Potchefstroom 2002-03
Best bowling: 1-22 Eastern Province B v North West, Fochville 1998-99

2004 Season

	M	Inns	NO	Runs	HS	Avge	100s	50s	Ct	St	O	M	Runs	Wkts	Avge	Best	5wI	10wM
Test																		
All First	9	16	1	169	30	11.26	-	-	3	-								
1-day Int																		
C & G																		
totesport	14	12	0	118	42	9.83	-	-	-	-								
Twenty20	4	4	1	97	41	32.33	-	-	2	-								

Career Performances

	M	Inns	NO	Runs	HS	Avge	100s	50s	Ct	St	Balls	Runs	Wkts	Avge	Best	5wI	10wM
Test																	
All First	79	142	16	4156	234 *	32.98	8	19	53	-	38	37	1	37.00	1-22	-	-
1-day Int																	
C & G	2	1	0	9	9	9.00	-	-	-	-							
totesport	20	18	1	202	56 *	11.88	-	1	-	-							
Twenty20	5	5	1	97	41	24.25	-	-	2	-							

BURNS, M. — Somerset

Name: Michael Burns
Role: Right-hand bat, right-arm medium bowler, occasional wicket-keeper
Born: 6 February 1969, Barrow-in-Furness
Height: 6ft **Weight:** 13st 7lbs
Nickname: Burner, Bunsen, George
County debut: 1991 (Warwickshire), 1997 (Somerset)
County cap: 1999 (Somerset)
1000 runs in a season: 2
1st-Class 50s: 49
1st-Class 100s: 7
1st-Class 200s: 1
1st-Class 5 w. in innings: 1
1st-Class catches: 138
1st-Class stumpings: 7
One-Day 100s: 2
Place in batting averages: 94th av. 36.65 (2003 82nd av. 39.06)
Place in bowling averages: (2003 113th av. 39.53)
Strike rate: 89.33 (career 69.35)
Parents: Robert and Linda, stepfather Stan
Wife and date of marriage: Carolyn, 9 October 1994
Children: Elizabeth, 12 January 1997; Adam, 3 August 2000
Family links with cricket: 'Grandfather was a great back-garden bowler'
Education: Walney Comprehensive; Barrow College of Further Education
Qualifications: 'Few CSEs, couple of GCEs', qualified fitter at VSEL in Barrow, coaching award
Overseas teams played for: Gill College, South Africa 1991-92; Motueka, Nelson, New Zealand 1992-93; Alex Sports Club, Harare 1993-94; Lindisfarne, Tasmania 1999-2000

Career highlights to date: '2001 C&G final'
Cricket moments to forget: 'Losing the 1999 NatWest final to Gloucestershire'
Cricket superstitions: 'None'
Cricketers particularly admired: Marcus Trescothick
Young players to look out for: Adam Burns ('if he's no good at golf'), Arul Suppiah
Other sports played: Rugby league ('had trials for Barrow RLFC and Carlisle RLFC'), golf
Other sports followed: Football (Liverpool FC), rugby league (Walney Central ARLFC)
Injuries: Out for two weeks with a hamstring strain
Favourite band: Eminem, Scissor Sisters, Snow Patrol
Relaxations: TV, family, cinema, Indian food
Extras: Player of the Tournament at Benson and Hedges Thailand International Cricket Sixes in 1989. Left Warwickshire and joined Somerset for the 1997 season. Scored club record of 217 for Lindisfarne (Tasmania) in 1999-2000 season. Scored 160 v Oxford Universities at Taunton on 7 April 2000, setting new record for the earliest ever 100 in a first-class cricket season in this country. His 221 v Yorkshire at Bath in 2001 set a new record for the highest score by a Somerset player at the ground and for the highest score by a Somerset player against Yorkshire. C&G Man of the Match award for his 83-ball 71 in the quarter-final v Kent at Canterbury 2001. Captain of Somerset 2003-04. Granted a benefit for 2005
Opinions on cricket: 'It is always going to be difficult finding a balance between cricketers needing more time to prepare and recover and county clubs needing to play games to generate revenue. I think we need to play our first few games of this season in March, but like the European golf tour (where they play in Australia and South Africa), we should maybe start in a country where the sun shines – maybe Spain or Portugal! Just a thought.'
Best batting: 221 Somerset v Yorkshire, Bath 2001
Best bowling: 6-54 Somerset v Leicestershire, Taunton 2001

2004 Season

	M	Inns	NO	Runs	HS	Avge	100s	50s	Ct	St	O	M	Runs	Wkts	Avge	Best	5wI	10wM
Test																		
All First	16	22	2	733	124 *	36.65	1	4	17	-	44.4	7	155	3	51.66	3-46	-	-
1-day Int																		
C & G	2	2	0	59	59	29.50	-	1	-	-								
totesport	15	15	0	398	97	26.53	-	3	14	1	8	0	54	1	54.00	1-54	-	
Twenty20	5	4	0	61	36	15.25	-	-	2	-								

Career Performances

	M	Inns	NO	Runs	HS	Avge	100s	50s	Ct	St	Balls	Runs	Wkts	Avge	Best	5wI	10wM
Test																	
All First	145	231	13	7164	221	32.86	8	49	138	7	4508	2743	65	42.20	6-54	1	-
1-day Int																	
C & G	27	26	3	698	84 *	30.34	-	5	8	-	378	337	10	33.70	2-13	-	
totesport	152	143	15	3051	115 *	23.83	2	18	80	12	1236	1216	38	32.00	4-39	-	
Twenty20	9	7	0	108	36	15.42	-	-	3	-	36	55	2	27.50	1-15	-	

BURROWS, T. G. — Hampshire

Name: Thomas (Tom) George Burrows
Role: Right-hand middle-order bat, wicket-keeper
Born: 5 May 1985, Reading
Height: 5ft 8in **Weight:** 10st 10lbs
Nickname: T
County debut: No first-team appearance (*see* ***Extras***)
Parents: Anthony and Victoria
Marital status: Single
Family links with cricket: 'My father was briefly on Gloucestershire ground staff and played club cricket'
Education: Reading School
Qualifications: 12 GCSEs, 4 AS-levels, 3 A-levels, Level 1 cricket coach
Overseas tours: MCC to Namibia and Uganda 2004-05
Overseas teams played for: Melville CC, Perth 2003-04
Career highlights to date: 'Keeping wicket in second innings v Yorkshire 2002'
Cricket moments to forget: 'The entire game against Somerset 2nd XI 2003'
Cricket superstitions: 'Never wear a jumper to bat'
Cricketers particularly admired: Steve Waugh, Jack Russell
Young players to look out for: David Wheeler, Kevin Latouf
Other sports played: Rugby, football
Other sports followed: Rugby (London Irish RFC), football (Chelsea FC)
Favourite band: R Kelly
Relaxations: 'Listening to music; watching rugby'
Extras: Appeared as substitute wicket-keeper for Hampshire v Yorkshire at West End 2002 but has yet to make full debut. Played for Berkshire in the C&G 2003
Opinions on cricket: 'Too many overs are played per day. I believe that 90 overs in a

day would allow players to concentrate on how to get batsmen out and set plans rather than rushing to get the overs through.'

2004 Season (did not make any first-class or one-day appearances)

Career Performances

	M	Inns	NO	Runs	HS	Avge	100s	50s	Ct	St	Balls	Runs	Wkts	Avge	Best	5wI	10wM
Test																	
All First																	
1-day Int																	
C & G	1	1	0	1	1	1.00	-	-	1	-							
totesport																	
Twenty20																	

BUTCHER, M. A. Surrey

Name: Mark Alan Butcher
Role: Left-hand bat, right-arm medium bowler, county captain
Born: 23 August 1972, Croydon
Height: 5ft 11in **Weight:** 13st
Nickname: Butch, Baz
County debut: 1991
County cap: 1996
Test debut: 1997
Tests: 69
1000 runs in a season: 7
1st-Class 50s: 79
1st-Class 100s: 27
1st-Class 200s: 2
1st-Class 5 w. in innings: 1
1st-Class catches: 216
One-Day 100s: 1
Place in batting averages: 139th av. 31.00 (2003 10th av. 61.15)
Strike rate: (career 61.41)
Parents: Alan and Elaine
Children: Alita, 1999
Family links with cricket: Father Alan played for Glamorgan, Surrey and England and is now coach with Surrey; brother Gary played for Glamorgan and Surrey; uncle Ian played for Gloucestershire and Leicestershire; uncle Martin played for Surrey
Education: Trinity School; Archbishop Tenison's, Croydon
Qualifications: 5 O-levels, senior coaching award

Career outside cricket: Singer, guitar player
Off-season: Touring with England
Overseas tours: England YC to New Zealand 1990-91; Surrey to Dubai 1990, 1993, to Perth 1995; England A to Australia 1996-97; England to West Indies 1997-98, to Australia 1998-99, to South Africa 1999-2000, to India and New Zealand 2001-02, to Australia 2002-03, to Bangladesh and Sri Lanka 2003-04, to West Indies 2003-04, to South Africa 2004-05
Overseas teams played for: South Melbourne, Australia 1993-94; North Perth 1994-95
Cricketers particularly admired: Ian Botham, David Gower, Viv Richards, Larry Gomes, Graham Thorpe, Alec Stewart, Michael Holding
Other sports followed: Football (Crystal Palace)
Relaxations: Music, playing the guitar, novels, wine
Extras: Played his first game for Surrey in 1991 against his father's Glamorgan in the Refuge Assurance League at The Oval, the first-ever match of any sort between first-class counties in which a father and son have been in opposition. His 259 v Leicestershire 1999 is the highest score by a left-hander at Grace Road and the fifth highest individual score recorded there overall. Captained England in third Test v New Zealand at Old Trafford 1999, deputising for the injured Nasser Hussain. His 4-42 in the first Test v Australia at Edgbaston 2001 included four wickets in 14 balls. Scored 145* v Glamorgan 2001, becoming the first Surrey batsman to carry his bat at The Oval since Grahame Clinton did so in 1984. Man of the Match in the fourth Test v Australia at Headingley 2001 for his match-winning 173*, having also scored 47 in the first innings; England's Man of the Series v Australia 2001 with 456 runs (more than any other batsman on either side) at an average of 50.66. His other Test awards include England's Man of the Series v Sri Lanka 2002 and v Zimbabwe 2003. Slazenger Sheer Instinct Award 2001 for the cricketer who has impressed the most in the recent season. Captained Surrey in Adam Hollioake's absence during the first part of the 2002 season. Recorded song 'You're Never Gone' in memory of the late Ben Hollioake. Appointed captain of Surrey for 2005. Granted a benefit for 2005. ECB contract 2004-05
Best batting: 259 Surrey v Leicestershire, Leicester 1999
Best bowling: 5-86 Surrey v Lancashire, Old Trafford 2000
Stop press: Forced to return home early from England Test tour of South Africa 2004-05 with wrist injury

2004 Season

	M	Inns	NO	Runs	HS	Avge	100s	50s	Ct	St	O	M	Runs	Wkts	Avge	Best	5wI	10wM
Test	3	6	1	105	59	21.00	-	1	2	-								
All First	7	14	1	403	184	31.00	1	1	3	-								
1-day Int																		
C & G																		
totesport	3	3	0	1	1	0.33	-	-	-	-								
Twenty20	3	3	0	148	60	49.33	-	2	-	-								

Career Performances

	M	Inns	NO	Runs	HS	Avge	100s	50s	Ct	St	Balls	Runs	Wkts	Avge	Best	5wI	10wM
Test	69	127	7	4191	173 *	34.92	8	22	62	-	901	541	15	36.06	4-42	-	-
All First	230	396	30	14498	259	39.61	29	79	216	-	7616	4190	124	33.79	5-86	1	-
1-day Int																	
C & G	20	20	5	673	91	44.86	-	6	10	-	318	231	5	46.20	2-57	-	
totesport	97	84	14	1523	104	21.75	1	5	27	-	1717	1571	37	42.45	3-23	-	
Twenty20	3	3	0	148	60	49.33	-	2	-	-							

BUTLER, I. G. Kent

Name: Ian Gareth Butler
Role: Right-hand bat, right-arm fast bowler
Born: 24 November 1981, Middlemore, Auckland
County debut: 2003 (Gloucestershire), 2004 (Kent)
Test debut: 2001-02
Tests: 7
One-Day Internationals: 14
1st-Class 50s: 2
1st-Class 5 w. in innings: 2
1st-Class catches: 8
Place in batting averages: 140th av. 30.83
Place in bowling averages: 119th av. 40.54 (2003 52nd av. 28.11)
Strike rate: 55.36 (career 50.66)
Overseas tours: New Zealand U19 to Sri Lanka (U19 World Cup) 1999-2000;
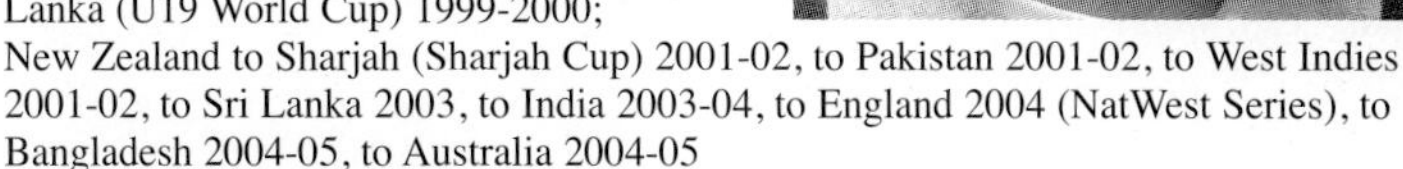
New Zealand to Sharjah (Sharjah Cup) 2001-02, to Pakistan 2001-02, to West Indies 2001-02, to Sri Lanka 2003, to India 2003-04, to England 2004 (NatWest Series), to Bangladesh 2004-05, to Australia 2004-05
Overseas teams played for: Northern Districts 2001-02 –
Extras: Represented New Zealand U19 v South Africa U19 2000-01. Took 4-60 v England at Wellington 2001-02 in his second Test match. Was an overseas player with Gloucestershire in May and early June 2003, deputising for Ian Harvey, absent on international duty. Recorded maiden Test five-wicket return (6-46) in the second Test v Pakistan at Wellington 2003-04. Was an overseas player with Kent July to August 2004, deputising for Mohammad Sami, absent on international duty. Scored career best 68 v Surrey at Canterbury 2004, in the process sharing with Rob Ferley (29) in a new record ninth-wicket stand for Kent in matches v Surrey (103)
Best batting: 68 Kent v Surrey, Canterbury 2004
Best bowling: 6-46 New Zealand v Pakistan, Wellington 2003-04

2004 Season

	M	Inns	NO	Runs	HS	Avge	100s	50s	Ct	St	O	M	Runs	Wkts	Avge	Best	5wI	10wM
Test																		
All First	5	8	2	185	68	30.83	-	1	2	-	101.3	11	446	11	40.54	4-114	-	-
1-day Int	4	1	1	0	0 *	-	-	-	1	-	24.2	0	123	6	20.50	3-41	-	
C & G																		
totesport	6	6	2	27	18 *	6.75	-	-	-	-	37.4	1	224	5	44.80	2-11	-	
Twenty20	2	2	1	14	8	14.00	-	-	3	-	7.5	0	52	3	17.33	3-19	-	

Career Performances

	M	Inns	NO	Runs	HS	Avge	100s	50s	Ct	St	Balls	Runs	Wkts	Avge	Best	5wI	10wM
Test	7	9	1	61	26	7.62	-	-	4	-	1272	842	24	35.08	6-46	1	-
All First	34	41	13	460	68	16.42	-	2	8	-	5523	3261	109	29.91	6-46	2	-
1-day Int	14	6	4	6	3	3.00	-	-	5	-	545	500	13	38.46	3-41	-	
C & G	1	0	0	0	0	-	-	-	-	-	54	40	0	-	-	-	
totesport	8	7	2	27	18 *	5.40	-	-	-	-	306	312	6	52.00	2-11	-	
Twenty20	2	2	1	14	8	14.00	-	-	3	-	47	52	3	17.33	3-19	-	

CADDICK, A. R. — Somerset

Name: Andrew Richard Caddick
Role: Right-hand bat, right-arm fast-medium bowler
Born: 21 November 1968, Christchurch, New Zealand
Height: 6ft 5in **Weight:** 14st 13lbs
Nickname: Des, Shack
County debut: 1991
County cap: 1992
Benefit: 1999
Test debut: 1993
Tests: 62
One-Day Internationals: 54
50 wickets in a season: 8
100 wickets in a season: 1
1st-Class 50s: 6
1st-Class 5 w. in innings: 65
1st-Class 10 w. in match: 15
1st-Class catches: 75
One-Day 5 w. in innings: 3
Place in batting averages: 216th av. 20.40
Place in bowling averages: 89th av. 36.17

Strike rate: 62.01 (career 49.98)
Parents: Christopher and Audrey
Wife and date of marriage: Sarah, 27 January 1995
Children: Ashton Faye, 24 August 1998; Fraser Michael, 12 October 2001
Education: Papanui High School, Christchurch, New Zealand
Qualifications: Qualified plasterer and tiler
Career outside cricket: Plasterer and tiler
Overseas tours: New Zealand YC to Australia (U19 World Cup) 1987-88, to England 1988; England A to Australia 1992-93; England to West Indies 1993-94, to Zimbabwe and New Zealand 1996-97, to West Indies 1997-98, to South Africa and Zimbabwe 1999-2000, to Kenya (ICC Knockout Trophy) 2000-01, to Pakistan and Sri Lanka 2000-01, to India (one-day series) and New Zealand 2001-02, to Sri Lanka (ICC Champions Trophy) 2002-03, to Australia 2002-03, to Africa (World Cup) 2002-03
Career highlights to date: 'Bowling West Indies out at Lord's [2000] and thus getting my name up on the board'
Cricketers particularly admired: Dennis Lillee, Richard Hadlee, Robin Smith, Jimmy Cook
Other sports followed: 'Mostly all'
Relaxations: Golf
Extras: Rapid Cricketline 2nd XI Championship Player of the Year 1991. Whyte and Mackay Bowler of the Year 1997. Took 105 first-class wickets in 1998 season. Leading wicket-taker in the single-division four-day era of the County Championship with 422 wickets (av. 22.48) 1993-99. Cornhill England Player of the Year 1999-2000. Took
5-16 from 13 overs as West Indies were bowled out for 54 in their second innings in the second Test at Lord's 2000. Took 5-14 in fourth Test v West Indies at Headingley 2000, becoming the fifth England bowler to take four wickets in an over in a Test match. One of *Wisden*'s Five Cricketers of the Year 2001. Took 200th Test wicket (Craig McMillan) in the third Test v New Zealand at Auckland 2001-02. Recorded maiden Test ten-wicket match return (3-121/7-94) in the fifth Test v Australia at Sydney 2002-03, in the process moving above Darren Gough into seventh place in the list of England Test wicket-takers. His international awards include England's Man of the Series v New Zealand 1999 and joint Man of the Match (with Gary Kirsten) in the third Test at Durban 1999-2000, having returned 7-46 in South Africa's first innings. Retired from ODI cricket in March 2003. Took 56 first-class wickets in 2004, including four five-wicket innings returns, after almost a year out with injury. Is a qualified helicopter pilot
Best batting: 92 Somerset v Worcestershire, Worcester 1995
Best bowling: 9-32 Somerset v Lancashire, Taunton 1993

2004 Season

	M	Inns	NO	Runs	HS	Avge	100s	50s	Ct	St	O	M	Runs	Wkts	Avge	Best	5wI	10wM
Test																		
All First	14	14	4	204	54	20.40	-	1	5	-	578.5	110	2026	56	36.17	6-80	4	-
1-day Int																		
C & G	2	1	0	5	5	5.00	-	-	-	-	15	0	100	2	50.00	1-42	-	
totesport	10	4	2	25	21	12.50	-	-	1	-	73	5	364	13	28.00	3-32	-	
Twenty20																		

Career Performances

	M	Inns	NO	Runs	HS	Avge	100s	50s	Ct	St	Balls	Runs	Wkts	Avge	Best	5wI	10wM
Test	62	95	12	861	49 *	10.37	-	-	21	-	13558	6999	234	29.91	7-46	13	1
All First	217	287	55	3360	92	14.48	-	6	75	-	47635	24322	953	25.52	9-32	65	15
1-day Int	54	38	18	249	36	12.45	-	-	9	-	2937	1965	69	28.47	4-19	-	
C & G	30	15	6	34	8	3.77	-	-	5	-	1784	1040	47	22.12	6-30	2	
totesport	106	43	14	317	39	10.93	-	-	15	-	4625	3380	131	25.80	4-18	-	
Twenty20																	

CARBERRY, M. A. — Kent

Name: Michael Alexander Carberry
Role: Left-hand bat, right-arm medium bowler
Born: 29 September 1980, Croydon
Height: 5ft 11in **Weight:** 14st 7lbs
Nickname: Carbs
County debut: 2001 (Surrey), 2003 (Kent)
1st-Class 50s: 11
1st-Class 100s: 4
1st-Class catches: 15
Place in batting averages: 70th av. 42.60 (2003 101st av. 35.82)
Strike rate: 81.00 (career 100.00)
Parents: Maria and Neville
Marital status: Single
Family links with cricket: 'My dad played club cricket'
Education: St John Rigby College
Qualifications: 10 GCSEs
Career outside cricket: DJ
Overseas tours: Surrey U17 to South Africa 1997; England U19 to New Zealand 1998-99, to Malaysia and (U19 World Cup) Sri Lanka 1999-2000

Overseas teams played for: Portland CC, Melbourne; University CC, Perth 2005
Career highlights to date: 'Every day is a highlight'
Cricket moments to forget: 'None'
Cricketers particularly admired: Ricky Ponting, Brian Lara
Relaxations: 'Sleeping'
Extras: Second schoolboy to score a century for Croydon U13 since Ali Brown. Scored century (126*) for ECB U18 v Pakistan U19 at Abergavenny 1998. Represented England U19 at home 1999, 2000. NBC Denis Compton Award for the most promising young Surrey player 1999, 2000. Left Surrey during the 2002-03 off-season and joined Kent for 2003. Scored century (137) on Kent debut v Cambridge UCCE at Fenner's 2003. Scored 112 and shared in a fifth-wicket partnership of 236 with Matthew Walker (151*) as Kent scored a county record fourth-innings 429-5 to beat Worcestershire at Canterbury 2004
Best batting: 153* Surrey v CUCCE, Fenner's 2002
Best bowling: 1-45 Kent v Surrey, The Oval 2003

2004 Season

	M	Inns	NO	Runs	HS	Avge	100s	50s	Ct	St	O	M	Runs	Wkts	Avge	Best	5wI	10wM
Test																		
All First	12	19	4	639	112	42.60	2	4	5	-	27	0	157	2	78.50	1-56	-	-
1-day Int																		
C & G	2	2	0	60	51	30.00	-	1	3	-								
totesport	11	11	0	245	76	22.27	-	2	4	-	3	0	20	0	-	-	-	
Twenty20	5	5	1	15	10 *	3.75	-	-	1	-								

Career Performances

	M	Inns	NO	Runs	HS	Avge	100s	50s	Ct	St	Balls	Runs	Wkts	Avge	Best	5wI	10wM
Test																	
All First	34	57	6	1997	153 *	39.15	4	11	15	-	300	251	3	83.66	1-45	-	-
1-day Int																	
C & G	5	4	0	83	51	20.75	-	1	3	-							
totesport	27	26	1	451	79	18.04	-	3	7	-	42	41	1	41.00	1-21	-	
Twenty20	10	9	2	44	10 *	6.28	-	-	4	-							

CARTER, N. M. Warwickshire

Name: Neil Miller Carter
Role: Left-hand bat, left-arm fast bowler
Born: 29 January 1975, Cape Town, South Africa
Height: 6ft 2in **Weight:** 14st 4lbs
Nickname: Carts
County debut: 2001
1st-Class 50s: 2
1st-Class 100s: 1
1st-Class 5 w. in innings: 4
1st-Class catches: 12
One-Day 5 w. in innings: 1
Place in batting averages: 201st av. 22.27 (2003 238th av. 16.85)
Place in bowling averages: 134th av. 44.77
Strike rate: 81.70 (career 66.08)
Parents: John and Heather
Marital status: Single
Education: Hottentots Holland High School; Cape Technikon
Qualifications: Diploma in Financial Information Systems, Certified Novell Engineer, Level 2 coaching
Career outside cricket: Computers, accounting
Overseas tours: SA Country Schools U15 to England 1992; Warwickshire to Cape Town 2001, 2002
Overseas teams played for: Boland 1998-99 – 2001-02
Cricket moments to forget: 'Any performance under par'
Cricketers particularly admired: Jacques Kallis, Shaun Pollock, Allan Donald
Other sports played: Golf, swimming
Other sports followed: Rugby union (Stormers, Springboks), football (Sheffield Wednesday)
Relaxations: Steam train photography ('gricing')
Extras: Made first-class debut for Boland during the 1999-2000 season. Won Man of the Match award in first one-day match for Warwickshire (4-21 and a 43-ball 40), in C&G Trophy v Essex at Edgbaston 2001. Swept his first ball (the last of the game) for a match-winning four in the B&H semi-final v Lancashire at Old Trafford 2002. Scored maiden first-class century (103) v Sussex at Hove 2002; his 67-ball hundred was the second fastest for Warwickshire since centuries began to be recorded in terms of balls received. Struck an 18-ball 43 v Northamptonshire at Edgbaston in the C&G 2004, including a competition record 28 from one over. Is not considered an overseas player

Best batting: 103 Warwickshire v Sussex, Hove 2002
Best bowling: 6-63 Boland v Griqualand West, Kimberley 2000-01

2004 Season

	M	Inns	NO	Runs	HS	Avge	100s	50s	Ct	St	O	M	Runs	Wkts	Avge	Best	5wI	10wM
Test																		
All First	14	15	4	245	95	22.27	-	1	3	-	367.4	79	1209	27	44.77	4-50	-	-
1-day Int																		
C & G	4	4	0	110	43	27.50	-	-	2	-	35	4	149	2	74.50	1-19	-	
totesport	16	16	1	220	40	14.66	-	-	1	-	103.5	5	494	21	23.52	3-37	-	
Twenty20	6	6	0	86	42	14.33	-	-	1	-	20	0	123	4	30.75	2-25	-	

Career Performances

	M	Inns	NO	Runs	HS	Avge	100s	50s	Ct	St	Balls	Runs	Wkts	Avge	Best	5wI	10wM
Test																	
All First	43	53	12	812	103	19.80	1	2	12	-	6873	4094	104	39.36	6-63	4	-
1-day Int																	
C & G	8	6	0	156	43	26.00	-	-	3	-	411	291	10	29.10	4-21	-	
totesport	45	42	6	547	75	15.19	-	1	4	-	1932	1565	59	26.52	5-31	1	
Twenty20	13	13	0	231	47	17.76	-	-	3	-	258	288	11	26.18	3-19	-	

CAWDRON, M. J. — Northamptonshire

Name: Michael (Mike) John Cawdron
Role: Left-hand bat, right-arm medium-fast bowler
Born: 7 October 1974, Luton
Height: 6ft 3in **Weight:** 13st 7lbs
Nickname: Muscles
County debut: 1995 (one-day, Gloucestershire), 1999 (first-class, Gloucestershire), 2002 (Northamptonshire)
1st-Class 5 w. in innings: 6
1st-Class 10 w. in match: 1
1st-Class catches: 5
Place in batting averages: (2003 272nd av. 10.50)
Place in bowling averages: (2003 30th av. 25.20)
Strike rate: 120.00 (career 51.25)
Parents: William and Mandy
Marital status: Single
Family links with cricket: Father and brother played local village cricket

Education: Cheltenham College
Qualifications: 10 GCSEs, 3 A-levels, NCA coaching award
Overseas tours: West of England U14 to Holland; Cheltenham College to Zimbabwe 1992; Gloucestershire YC to Sri Lanka 1993-94; Gloucestershire Gypsies to Zimbabwe 1994-95, to Cape Town 1997; Christians in Sport to Zimbabwe 1998, to South Africa 2000; Gloucestershire to Kimberley and Cape Town 2001
Career highlights to date: 'Playing in 1999 NatWest final v Somerset'
Cricketers particularly admired: Jack Russell, Jeremy Snape, Kim Barnett ('they are all very tough players who have made the most of their talents')
Other sports followed: Rugby, hockey, rackets, clay-pigeon shooting, golf
Relaxations: Cinema, videos, eating and going out with friends
Extras: Winner of the *Daily Telegraph* Regional Bowling Award 1993. Captain of MCC Schools and ESCA U19 1993. 'Made 50 off 32 balls on Sunday League debut against Essex at my old school' (Cheltenham College). Scored 42 and took 5-35 on first-class debut, v Hampshire at Bristol 1999; went on to take two more five-wicket hauls in his next two Championship games. Released by Gloucestershire at the end of the 2001 season and joined Northamptonshire for 2002; retired at the end of the 2004 season
Best batting: 42 Gloucestershire v Hampshire, Bristol 1999
Best bowling: 6-25 First-Class Counties XI v New Zealand A, Milton Keynes 2000

2004 Season

	M	Inns	NO	Runs	HS	Avge	100s	50s	Ct	St	O	M	Runs	Wkts	Avge	Best	5wI	10wM
Test																		
All First	1	0	0	0	0	-	-	-	1	-	20	7	46	1	46.00	1-46	-	-
1-day Int																		
C & G	1	1	1	2	2*	-	-	-	-	-								
totesport	1	0	0	0	0	-	-	-	-	-	3	0	33	0	-	-	-	
Twenty20																		

Career Performances

	M	Inns	NO	Runs	HS	Avge	100s	50s	Ct	St	Balls	Runs	Wkts	Avge	Best	5wI	10wM
Test																	
All First	25	32	4	396	42	14.14	-	-	5	-	3793	1848	74	24.97	6-25	6	1
1-day Int																	
C & G	11	8	4	36	17	9.00	-	-	1	-	480	333	14	23.78	4-34	-	
totesport	51	30	11	319	50	16.78	-	1	6	-	1994	1649	53	31.11	4-17	-	
Twenty20	5	1	0	1	1	1.00	-	-	1	-	108	157	7	22.42	3-24	-	

CHAMBERS, M. A. — Essex

Name: Maurice Anthony Chambers
Role: Right-hand bat, right-arm fast bowler
Born: 14 September 1987, Portland, Jamaica
Nickname: Moza
County debut: No first-team appearance
Parents: Melinda Fenton
Marital status: Single
Education: Homerton College of Technology; Sir George Monoux College
Career outside cricket: 'Study'
Career highlights to date: 'Winter training with Essex'
Cricket moments to forget: 'There isn't a cricketing moment that I would like to forget because I try my best to learn from my mistakes'
Cricketers particularly admired: Andrew Strauss, Stephen Harmison, Courtney Walsh, Curtly Ambrose
Other sports played: Basketball, badminton
Other sports followed: Football (Manchester United)
Extras: London Schools Cricket Association Best Bowling Award 2003. Played for MCC Young Cricketers 2004

> 16. Which wicket-keeper became only the third person to score a double century on Test debut when he made 201* v New Zealand in the first of only four Test appearances?

CHANDANA, U. D. U. Gloucestershire

Name: Umagiliya Durage Upul Chandana
Role: Right-hand bat, leg-break bowler
Born: 7 May 1972, Galle, Sri Lanka
County debut: No first-team appearance
Test debut: 1998-99
Tests: 14
One-Day Internationals: 128
1st-Class 50s: 28
1st-Class 100s: 8
1st-Class 5 w. in innings: 15
1st-Class 10 w. in match: 1
1st-Class catches: 101
One-Day 5 w. in innings: 1
Strike rate: (career 47.87)
Overseas tours: Sri Lanka to Sharjah (Pepsi Austral-Asia Cup) 1993-94, to South Africa 1997-98, to England 1998, to Malaysia (Commonwealth Games) 1998, to Bangladesh (Wills International Cup) 1998-99, to UK, Ireland and Holland (World Cup) 1999, to Pakistan 1999-2000, to Kenya (ICC Knockout Trophy) 2000-01, to South Africa 2000-01, to England 2002, to Zimbabwe 2004, to Australia 2004, to England (ICC Champions Trophy) 2004, plus other one-day series and tournaments in Sharjah, Singapore, West Indies, Kenya, New Zealand, Pakistan, India, Australia, Zimbabwe, Morocco, South Africa
Overseas teams played for: Tamil Union Cricket and Athletic Club 1991-92 – 2002-03; Nondescripts 2003-04 –
Extras: Represented Sri Lanka Board President's XI and Sri Lanka A against several touring sides and was captain of Sri Lanka A in series v Kenya 2001-02. Represented Sri Lanka in the Asian Test Championship 1998-99 and the ICC Champions Trophy 2002-03. Man of the Match v Bloomfield Cricket and Athletic Club in the final of the Hatna Trophy 1996-97 at Colombo (72). His international awards include Man of the Match in the second ODI v West Indies at Bridgetown 2003 (71-ball 89); in the fourth ODI v Zimbabwe at Harare 2004 (51/2-23); and in the fifth ODI v South Africa at Colombo 2004 (5-61). Has joined Gloucestershire as an overseas player for 2005
Best batting: 194 Sri Lanka A v Kenya, Matara 2001-02
Best bowling: 7-80 Tamil Union v Bloomfield, Colombo 1998-99

2004 Season

	M	Inns	NO	Runs	HS	Avge	100s	50s	Ct	St	O	M	Runs	Wkts	Avge	Best	5wI	10wM
Test																		
All First																		
1-day Int	2	1	1	20	20 *	-	-	-	2	-	18	0	103	2	51.50	2-39	-	
C & G																		
totesport																		
Twenty20																		

Career Performances

	M	Inns	NO	Runs	HS	Avge	100s	50s	Ct	St	Balls	Runs	Wkts	Avge	Best	5wI	10wM
Test	14	21	1	548	92	27.40	-	2	7	-	2277	1303	35	37.22	6-179	3	1
All First	129	174	13	5096	194	31.65	8	28	101	-	16804	8219	351	23.41	7-80	15	1
1-day Int	128	96	12	1440	89	17.14	-	5	70	-	5301	4112	130	31.63	5-61	1	
C & G																	
totesport																	
Twenty20																	

CHAPMAN, J. R. — Derbyshire

Name: James Robert Chapman
Role: Left-hand bat, right-arm medium bowler
Born: 19 May 1986, Nottingham
Height: 6ft 2in **Weight:** 13st
Nickname: Chappy
County debut: 2004
Parents: John and Rosemarie
Marital status: Single
Family links with cricket: 'Dad played local league cricket'
Education: St John Houghton School
Qualifications: 8 GCSEs, Level 1 coaching award
Career highlights to date: 'Making my first-team debut (aged 18) 2004'
Cricket moments to forget: 'Getting a pair against Leicestershire 2nd XI 2004'
Cricket superstitions: 'Left pad on first'
Cricketers particularly admired: Brian Lara
Young players to look out for: Jake Needham, Paul Borrington
Other sports followed: Football (Man Utd), snooker

Favourite band: Eminem
Relaxations: 'Sleeping, listening to music, going out with friends, gym'
Extras: Jack Briggs Award. Played for England U17 and U18. Has played for Derbyshire from U11, including Academy
Opinions on cricket: 'Young players should be given a good chance at playing first-class cricket!'
Best batting: 7 Derbyshire v DUCCE, Derby 2004

2004 Season

	M	Inns	NO	Runs	HS	Avge	100s	50s	Ct	St	O	M	Runs	Wkts	Avge	Best	5wI	10wM
Test																		
All First	1	1	0	7	7	7.00	-	-	-	-								
1-day Int																		
C & G																		
totesport																		
Twenty20																		

Career Performances

	M	Inns	NO	Runs	HS	Avge	100s	50s	Ct	St	Balls	Runs	Wkts	Avge	Best	5wI	10wM
Test																	
All First	1	1	0	7	7	7.00	-	-	-	-							
1-day Int																	
C & G																	
totesport																	
Twenty20																	

CHAPPLE, G. — Lancashire

Name: Glen Chapple
Role: Right-hand bat, right-arm medium-fast bowler
Born: 23 January 1974, Skipton, Yorkshire
Height: 6ft 2in **Weight:** 12st 7lbs
Nickname: Chappy, Boris, Boomor, Cheeky
County debut: 1992
County cap: 1994
Benefit: 2004
50 wickets in a season: 4
1st-Class 50s: 19
1st-Class 100s: 6
1st-Class 5 w. in innings: 21
1st-Class 10 w. in match: 1
1st-Class catches: 57
One-Day 5 w. in innings: 4

Place in batting averages: 115th av. 34.57 (2003 88th av. 37.72)
Place in bowling averages: 113th av. 38.89 (2003 91st av. 35.59)
Strike rate: 77.51 (career 57.13)
Parents: Eileen and Michael
Marital status: Single
Family links with cricket: Father played in Lancashire League for Nelson and was a professional for Darwen and Earby
Education: West Craven High School; Nelson and Colne College
Qualifications: 8 GCSEs, 2 A-levels
Overseas tours: England U18 to Canada (International Youth Tournament) 1991; England YC to New Zealand 1990-91; England U19 to Pakistan 1991-92, to India 1992-93; England A to India 1994-95, to Australia 1996-97; England VI to Hong Kong 2002, 2003, 2004
Cricketers particularly admired: Dennis Lillee, Robin Smith
Other sports followed: Football (Liverpool), golf
Relaxations: 'Watching films, music, socialising'
Extras: Set record for fastest century in first-class cricket (21 minutes; against declaration bowling) v Glamorgan at Old Trafford 1993. Man of the Match in the 1996 NatWest final against Essex at Lord's for his 6-18. Shared in a record eighth-wicket partnership for Lancashire in matches against Northamptonshire (136*) with Warren Hegg at Northampton 2001, scoring 72*; also scored 31 in the first innings and took nine wickets in the match. Scored 155 v Somerset at Old Trafford 2001, equalling Wasim Akram's record, set in 1998 v Nottinghamshire, for the highest score by a Lancashire No. 8. Lancashire Player of the Year 2002. Called up to England squad for the third Test v South Africa at Trent Bridge 2003
Best batting: 155 Lancashire v Somerset, Old Trafford 2001
Best bowling: 6-30 Lancashire v Somerset, Blackpool 2002

2004 Season

	M	Inns	NO	Runs	HS	Avge	100s	50s	Ct	St	O	M	Runs	Wkts	Avge	Best	5wI	10wM
Test																		
All First	14	22	1	726	112	34.57	2	4	3	-	374.4	80	1128	29	38.89	5-136	1	-
1-day Int																		
C & G	2	2	0	19	12	9.50	-	-	-	-	20	5	74	3	24.66	3-44	-	
totesport	13	9	2	136	35	19.42	-	-	11	-	98.5	12	464	16	29.00	3-32	-	
Twenty20	6	3	1	16	11	8.00	-	-	2	-	18	0	145	5	29.00	2-14	-	

Career Performances

	M	Inns	NO	Runs	HS	Avge	100s	50s	Ct	St	Balls	Runs	Wkts	Avge	Best	5wI	10wM
Test																	
All First	176	242	52	4683	155	24.64	6	19	57	-	29480	15191	516	29.43	6-30	21	1
1-day Int																	
C & G	29	19	3	258	81 *	16.12	-	1	6	-	1520	1087	33	32.93	6-18	2	
totesport	147	77	21	942	77 *	16.82	-	4	35	-	5955	4626	167	27.70	6-25	1	
Twenty20	11	8	2	87	55 *	14.50	-	1	3	-	222	246	14	17.57	2-13	-	

CHERRY, D. D. Glamorgan

Name: Daniel David Cherry
Role: Left-hand bat, right-arm off-cutter bowler
Born: 7 February 1980, Newport, Gwent
Height: 5ft 9in **Weight:** 12st 9lbs
Nickname: Rhino, Banners, DC, Kiwi
County debut: 1998
1st-Class catches: 4
Parents: David and Elizabeth
Marital status: Single
Family links with cricket: Father played club cricket for Cresselly CC and now coaches
Education: Tonbridge School, Kent; University of Wales, Swansea
Qualifications: 10 GCSEs, 3 A-levels, BA History, Level 2 coach
Off-season: 'Training hard and coaching'
Overseas tours: Tonbridge School to Australia 1996-97; Glamorgan to Cape Town 2002
Overseas teams played for: Doutta Stars, Melbourne 2002-03
Career highlights to date: 'First-class debut'
Cricket moments to forget: 'Bagging a pair on 2nd XI Championship debut'
Cricket superstitions: 'None'
Cricketers particularly admired: Michael Atherton, Graham Thorpe, Steve James
Other sports played: Rugby, rackets (Public Schools doubles champion)
Other sports followed: Rugby (Neath-Swansea Ospreys), football (Everton)
Injuries: Out for 10 days with split webbing of right hand
Favourite band: Super Furry Animals
Relaxations: Reading true crime books, listening to music; 'socialising with the

high-quality clientele that frequents Pembrokeshire's premier nightspot – "The Sands Discotheque Deluxe"'

Extras: Played for ECB U19 XI v Pakistan U19 1998. Played in Old Tonbridgians *Cricketer* Cup winning side 1998. Awarded Glamorgan 2nd XI cap 2002

Opinions on cricket: 'The gap between 1st and 2nd XI cricket appears to be growing. Second XI cricket needs to be played on 1st XI standard wickets to improve the game. EU players and Kolpaks (*see page 9*) – what are the counties doing?'

Best batting: 47 Glamorgan v Gloucestershire, Cheltenham 2002

2004 Season

	M	Inns	NO	Runs	HS	Avge	100s	50s	Ct	St	O	M	Runs	Wkts	Avge	Best	5wI	10wM
Test																		
All First	3	5	1	107	29	26.75	-	-	-	-								
1-day Int																		
C & G																		
totesport	2	2	0	28	24	14.00	-	-	1	-	1	0	9	0	-	-	-	
Twenty20																		

Career Performances

	M	Inns	NO	Runs	HS	Avge	100s	50s	Ct	St	Balls	Runs	Wkts	Avge	Best	5wI	10wM
Test																	
All First	10	15	1	256	47	18.28	-	-	4	-	18	0	0	-	-	-	-
1-day Int																	
C & G																	
totesport	2	2	0	28	24	14.00	-	-	1	-	6	9	0	-	-	-	
Twenty20	2	2	0	12	11	6.00	-	-	1	-	6	6	2	3.00	2-6	-	

17. Which Bangladesh cricketer won the Man of the Match award in his country's first Test victory, against Zimbabwe?

CHILTON, M. J. Lancashire

Name: Mark James Chilton
Role: Right-hand bat, right-arm medium bowler, county captain
Born: 2 October 1976, Sheffield
Height: 6ft 2in **Weight:** 12st 10lbs
Nickname: Dip, Chill
County debut: 1997
County cap: 2002
1000 runs in a season: 1
1st-Class 50s: 17
1st-Class 100s: 12
1st-Class catches: 80
One-Day 100s: 4
One-Day 5 w. in innings: 1
Place in batting averages: 129th av. 32.36 (2003 29th av. 50.17)
Strike rate: 144.00 (career 163.71)
Parents: Jim and Sue
Marital status: Single
Family links with cricket: Father played local cricket
Education: Manchester Grammar School; Durham University
Qualifications: 10 GCSEs, 3 A-levels, BA (Hons) Business Economics, senior coaching award
Overseas tours: Manchester Grammar School to Barbados 1993-94, to South Africa 1995-96; Durham University to Zimbabwe 1997-98
Overseas teams played for: East Torrens, Adelaide 2000-01; North Sydney CC, Sydney 2002-03
Cricket moments to forget: 'Losing two semi-finals in last over'
Cricket superstitions: 'None'
Cricketers particularly admired: Michael Atherton, David Gower
Young players to look out for: Kyle Hogg, Steven Crook
Other sports played: Football, golf
Other sports followed: 'Interest in most sports', football (Manchester United)
Favourite band: Oasis
Relaxations: 'Music, guitar, relaxing with friends and family'
Extras: Represented England U14, U15, U17. England U15 Batsman of the Year award 1992. Played for North of England v New Zealand U19 in 1996. Played for British Universities in 1997 Benson and Hedges Cup, winning the Gold Award against Sussex (34/5-26). C&G Man of the Match awards for his 76* v Derbyshire at Old Trafford 2002 and for his 62 v Sussex at Hove 2004. Scored century (115) v Surrey at Whitgift School in the totesport League 2004, in the process sharing with Iain Sutcliffe

(102*) in a new Lancashire record opening stand for the one-day league (223). Appointed captain of Lancashire for 2005

Opinions on cricket: 'The increase in overseas and EU players is a worry. The money should be spent on grass-roots cricket and academies. There must be a minimum of six or seven players in each team eligible to play for England. We need to look at restructuring club cricket and creating a pyramid system where the best players are concentrated into one league and play with and against each other every week. This will raise standards and help identify talent.'

Best batting: 125 Lancashire v Middlesex, Old Trafford 2003

Best bowling: 1-1 Lancashire v Sri Lanka A, Old Trafford 1999

2004 Season

	M	Inns	NO	Runs	HS	Avge	100s	50s	Ct	St	O	M	Runs	Wkts	Avge	Best	5wI	10wM
Test																		
All First	16	27	2	809	124 *	32.36	2	2	9	-	24	3	84	1	84.00	1-39	-	-
1-day Int																		
C & G	3	3	0	107	62	35.66	-	1	3	-	5	0	40	2	20.00	2-26	-	
totesport	16	15	3	498	115	41.50	1	4	7	-	23	0	138	7	19.71	3-27	-	
Twenty20	7	5	3	52	23 *	26.00	-	-	2	-								

Career Performances

	M	Inns	NO	Runs	HS	Avge	100s	50s	Ct	St	Balls	Runs	Wkts	Avge	Best	5wI	10wM
Test																	
All First	96	156	10	4688	125	32.10	12	17	80	-	1146	590	7	84.28	1-1	-	-
1-day Int																	
C & G	12	12	1	450	76 *	40.90	-	4	8	-	84	91	4	22.75	2-26	-	
totesport	77	71	8	1748	115	27.74	2	9	18	-	550	522	22	23.72	3-20	-	
Twenty20	8	6	3	75	23 *	25.00	-	-	2	-							

18. Which current cricket coach was Man of the Match when Zimbabwe beat Australia by 13 runs in the 1983 World Cup?

CLARK, S. R. Middlesex

Name: Stuart Rupert Clark
Role: Right-hand bat, right-arm fast-medium bowler
Born: 28 September 1975, Sutherland, Sydney, Australia
Height: 6ft 5½in **Weight:** 15st 9lbs
Nickname: Sarfraz
County debut: 2004
1st-Class 5 w. in innings: 5
1st-Class catches: 11
Place in bowling averages: 6th av. 21.70
Strike rate: 53.40 (career 69.61)
Overseas tours: Australia A to South Africa (one-day series) 2002-03
Overseas teams played for: New South Wales 1997-98 –
Career highlights to date: 'First game for NSW; winning the Pura Cup'
Extras: Opened the bowling for Sutherland club with Glenn McGrath. Has represented Australia A against several touring sides. New South Wales Player of the Year 2001-02 after taking 45 Pura Cup wickets (av. 23.27). Man of the Match in the ING Cup final 2002-03 v Western Australia at Perth (3-34). Was an overseas player with Middlesex August to September 2004, taking over from Glenn McGrath
Best batting: 35 New South Wales v Western Australia, Newcastle 2002-03
Best bowling: 6-84 New South Wales v Tasmania, Hobart 2002-03

2004 Season

	M	Inns	NO	Runs	HS	Avge	100s	50s	Ct	St	O	M	Runs	Wkts	Avge	Best	5wI	10wM
Test																		
All First	3	3	0	69	34	23.00	-	-	-	-	89	23	217	10	21.70	3-28	-	-
1-day Int																		
C & G																		
totesport	1	0	0	0	0	-	-	-	-	-	7.3	1	30	1	30.00	1-30	-	
Twenty20																		

Career Performances

	M	Inns	NO	Runs	HS	Avge	100s	50s	Ct	St	Balls	Runs	Wkts	Avge	Best	5wI	10wM
Test																	
All First	41	59	16	557	35	12.95	-	-	11	-	8911	4286	128	33.48	6-84	5	-
1-day Int																	
C & G																	
totesport	1	0	0	0	0	-	-	-	-	-	45	30	1	30.00	1-30	-	
Twenty20																	

CLARKE, A. J. — Essex

Name: Andrew (Andy) John Clarke
Role: Left-hand bat, right-arm fast-medium bowler
Born: 9 November 1975, Harold Wood, Essex
Height: 6ft 2in **Weight:** 12st 8lbs
Nickname: Vicram, Nobby, Ken
County debut: 2001 (one-day), 2002 (first-class)
1st-Class 5 w. in innings: 1
1st-Class catches: 4
Place in batting averages: 274th av. 8.33
Place in bowling averages: 98th av. 37.00
Strike rate: 65.50 (career 52.26)
Parents: Mary and John (both deceased)
Marital status: Single
Family links with cricket: 'Dad played club cricket'
Education: St Martins School, Hutton; Brentwood College of Higher Education
Qualifications: 7 GCSEs, 1 AS-level, 2 A-levels, Level 2 coaching
Overseas tours: MCC to Amsterdam 1998
Cricketers particularly admired: 'My dad'
Other sports played: Football, squash
Other sports followed: Football (West Ham)
Relaxations: 'Listening to music; time with family and friends'
Extras: MCC Young Cricketers cap and Player of the Year 1998. Recorded maiden first-class five-wicket return on first-class debut v Glamorgan at Swansea 2002; his 5-54 included three wickets in his first six overs
Best batting: 41 Essex v Warwickshire, Chelmsford 2003
Best bowling: 5-54 Essex v Glamorgan, Swansea 2002

2004 Season

	M	Inns	NO	Runs	HS	Avge	100s	50s	Ct	St	O	M	Runs	Wkts	Avge	Best	5wI	10wM
Test																		
All First	5	6	0	50	28	8.33	-	-	2	-	131	25	444	12	37.00	3-32	-	-
1-day Int																		
C & G	1	0	0	0	0	-	-	-	-	-	3	0	20	0	-	-	-	
totesport	5	3	1	30	18	15.00	-	-	1	-	34	2	155	8	19.37	3-40	-	
Twenty20	4	3	2	11	6	11.00	-	-	1	-	12	1	92	2	46.00	1-18	-	

Career Performances

	M	Inns	NO	Runs	HS	Avge	100s	50s	Ct	St	Balls	Runs	Wkts	Avge	Best	5wI	10wM
Test																	
All First	10	14	2	179	41	14.91	-	-	4	-	1359	762	26	29.30	5-54	1	-
1-day Int																	
C & G	6	2	0	9	9	4.50	-	-	2	-	222	175	2	87.50	1-19	-	
totesport	27	14	5	51	18	5.66	-	-	6	-	1076	877	38	23.07	4-28	-	
Twenty20	4	3	2	11	6	11.00	-	-	1	-	72	92	2	46.00	1-18	-	

CLARKE, M. J. — Hampshire

Name: Michael John Clarke
Role: Right-hand bat, slow left-arm bowler
Born: 2 April 1981, Liverpool, New South Wales, Australia
Height: 5ft 10in **Weight:** 11st
Nickname: Pup
County debut: 2004
County cap: 2004
One-Day Internationals: 34
1st-Class 50s: 11
1st-Class 100s: 11
1st-Class catches: 50
One-Day 100s: 1
One-Day 5 w. in innings: 1
Place in batting averages: 106th av. 35.45
Strike rate: 253.00 (career 138.16)
Overseas tours: Australia U19 to England 1999 (vice-captain), to Sri Lanka (U19 World Cup) 1999-2000 (captain); Australia A to South Africa (one-day series) 2002-03; Australia to West Indies 2002-03, to India (TVS Cup) 2003-04, to Sri Lanka 2003-04 (one-day series), to Zimbabwe (one-day series) 2004, to Holland (Videocon Cup) 2004, to England (ICC Champions Trophy) 2004, to India 2004-05, to New Zealand 2004-05

Overseas teams played for: New South Wales 1999-2000 –
Other sports followed: Rugby league
Cricketers admired: Mark Waugh
Favourite band: Bon Jovi
Relaxations: Beach, watching rugby
Extras: Attended Commonwealth Bank [Australian] Cricket Academy 2000. Scored 75* and took three catches in the third ODI v West Indies at Gros Islet 2002-03, winning Man of the Match award. Scored 44* and took 2-36 in the final of the TVS Cup v India at Kolkata (Calcutta) 2003-04, winning Man of the Match award. Recorded maiden ODI five-wicket return (5-35) v Sri Lanka at Dambulla 2003-04. Overseas player with Hampshire 2004. Scored maiden ODI century (105*) in the third ODI v Zimbabwe at Harare 2004. Scored century in each innings (140/103) v Nottinghamshire at Trent Bridge 2004 and another (109) in his next Championship innings v Glamorgan at Cardiff. Awarded Hampshire cap 2004
Best batting: 140 Hampshire v Nottinghamshire, Trent Bridge 2004
Best bowling: 2-25 New South Wales v Tasmania, Hobart 2001-02
Stop press: Scored maiden Test century (151) on debut in the first Test v India at Bangalore 2004-05, winning Man of the Match award. Recorded maiden first-class five-wicket return (6-9 from 6.2 overs) in the fourth Test v India at Mumbai 2004-05. Scored century (141) in the first Test v New Zealand at Brisbane 2004-05, achieving feat of scoring a Test century on home and away debuts and winning Man of the Match award. Man of the Match v Pakistan at Hobart (97) and at Sydney (103*) in the VB Series 2004-05. Winner of the 2005 Allan Border Medal. Man of the Match in the third ODI v New Zealand at Auckland 2004-05 (71*)

2004 Season

	M	Inns	NO	Runs	HS	Avge	100s	50s	Ct	St	O	M	Runs	Wkts	Avge	Best	5wI	10wM
Test																		
All First	12	20	0	709	140	35.45	3	2	20	-	42.1	8	160	1	160.00	1-52	-	-
1-day Int	4	2	0	73	42	36.50	-	-	1	-	2	0	13	0	-	-	-	
C & G	1	1	0	13	13	13.00	-	-	-	-	10	0	30	1	30.00	1-30	-	
totesport	11	10	0	285	68	28.50	-	3	6	-	19	0	99	5	19.80	2-17	-	
Twenty20	6	6	0	151	46	25.16	-	-	4	-	8.3	0	76	1	76.00	1-27	-	

Career Performances

	M	Inns	NO	Runs	HS	Avge	100s	50s	Ct	St	Balls	Runs	Wkts	Avge	Best	5wI	10wM
Test																	
All First	48	86	5	3065	140	37.83	11	11	50	-	829	454	6	75.66	2-25	-	-
1-day Int	34	30	8	900	105 *	40.90	1	4	14	-	593	509	17	29.94	5-35	1	
C & G	1	1	0	13	13	13.00	-	-	-	-	60	30	1	30.00	1-30	-	
totesport	11	10	0	285	68	28.50	-	3	6	-	114	99	5	19.80	2-17	-	
Twenty20	6	6	0	151	46	25.16	-	-	4	-	51	76	1	76.00	1-27	-	

CLARKE, R. Surrey

Name: Rikki Clarke
Role: Right-hand bat, right-arm fast-medium bowler; all-rounder
Born: 29 September 1981, Orsett, Essex
Height: 6ft 4in **Weight:** 14st
Nickname: Clarkey, Crouchy, 50 Pence
County debut: 2001 (one-day), 2002 (first-class)
Test debut: 2003-04
Tests: 2
One-Day Internationals: 17
1st-Class 50s: 10
1st-Class 100s: 5
1st-Class catches: 42
Place in batting averages: 137th av. 31.17 (2003 78th av. 39.35)
Place in bowling averages: (2003 121st av. 41.70)
Strike rate: 73.00 (career 61.34)
Parents: Bob and Janet
Marital status: Single
Family links with cricket: 'Dad plays cricket for Shirenewton in the Welsh League'
Education: Broadwater; Godalming College
Qualifications: 5 GCSEs, GNVQ Leisure and Tourism
Career outside cricket: 'Relaxing'
Off-season: 'England academy'
Overseas tours: Surrey U19 to Barbados; MCC Young Cricketers to Cape Town; England to Sri Lanka (ICC Champions Trophy) 2002-03, to Bangladesh and Sri Lanka 2003-04, to West Indies 2003-04; ECB National Academy to Australia and Sri Lanka 2002-03; England A to Sri Lanka 2004-05
Career highlights to date: 'Making England debut in Test and one-day cricket'
Cricket moments to forget: 'Getting bowled second ball round my legs on one-day England debut'
Cricket superstitions: 'Left pad first'
Cricketers particularly admired: Andrew Flintoff, Adam Hollioake, Darren Gough
Young players to look out for: Alastair Cook, Luke Wright, Kadeer Ali, Tim Murtagh
Other sports played: Golf, snooker, football, 'any really'
Other sports followed: Football ('massive Spurs fan')
Injuries: Out for a month with a pulled hip flexor
Favourite band: Usher, Mario Winans
Relaxations: 'Watching films, playing PlayStation and going to restaurants'

Extras: Named after former Tottenham Hotspur and Argentina footballer Ricky Villa. Represented England U17. Scored maiden first-class century (107*) on first-class debut v Cambridge University CCE at Fenner's 2002. NBC Denis Compton Award for the most promising young Surrey player 2002. Cricket Writers' Club Young Player of the Year 2002. Surrey Supporters' Young Player of the Year 2002. Surrey Sponsors' Young Player of the Year 2002. Made ODI debut v Pakistan at Old Trafford in the NatWest Challenge 2003, taking the wicket of Imran Nazir with his first ball in international cricket. Made Test debut in the first Test v Bangladesh at Dhaka 2003-04. ECB National Academy 2004-05
Opinions on cricket: 'One overseas [player] per county.'
Best batting: 153* Surrey v Somerset, Taunton 2002
Best bowling: 4-21 Surrey v Leicestershire, Leicester 2003

2004 Season

	M	Inns	NO	Runs	HS	Avge	100s	50s	Ct	St	O	M	Runs	Wkts	Avge	Best	5wI	10wM
Test																		
All First	10	17	0	530	112	31.17	1	2	15	-	109.3	16	518	9	57.55	3-47	-	-
1-day Int	1	1	0	11	11	11.00	-	-	-	-	4	0	30	0	-	-	-	
C & G																		
totesport	11	10	0	201	70	20.10	-	1	5	-	37	1	232	7	33.14	4-50	-	
Twenty20	5	5	1	60	20	15.00	-	-	3	-	16	0	122	3	40.66	1-16	-	

Career Performances

	M	Inns	NO	Runs	HS	Avge	100s	50s	Ct	St	Balls	Runs	Wkts	Avge	Best	5wI	10wM
Test	2	3	0	96	55	32.00	-	1	1	-	174	60	4	15.00	2-7	-	-
All First	37	59	5	2059	153 *	38.12	5	10	42	-	2883	2062	47	43.87	4-21	-	-
1-day Int	17	10	0	99	37	9.90	-	-	11	-	404	351	10	35.10	2-28	-	
C & G	8	7	0	122	55	17.42	-	1	1	-	205	231	4	57.75	2-56	-	
totesport	37	36	5	737	98 *	23.77	-	4	15	-	962	934	26	35.92	4-50	-	
Twenty20	7	6	1	75	20	15.00	-	-	4	-	120	142	3	47.33	1-16	-	

19. Who was captain of Sri Lanka's World Cup winning team of 1995-96?

CLEARY, M. F. — Leicestershire

Name: Mark Francis Cleary
Role: Left-hand bat, right-arm fast-medium bowler
Born: 19 July 1980, Moorabbin, Melbourne, Australia
County debut: 2004
County cap: 2004
1st-Class 50s: 1
1st-Class 5 w. in innings: 3
1st-Class catches: 11
Place in batting averages: 146th av. 29.83
Place in bowling averages: 80th av. 35.03
Strike rate: 51.11 (career 49.23)
Overseas teams played for: South Australia 2002-03 –
Extras: Represented Australia A v South Africa A 2002-03 and v Zimbabwe 2003-04. Commonwealth Bank [Australian] Cricket Academy 2003. Man of the Match v New South Wales at Adelaide in the ING Cup 2003-04 (74-ball 70 and 2-43). Joined Leicestershire as an overseas player for 2004, originally as a temporary stand-in for Garnett Kruger; has returned for 2005. Awarded Leicestershire cap 2004
Best batting: 58 South Australia v Tasmania, Hobart 2003-04
Best bowling: 7-80 Leicestershire v Derbyshire, Oakham School 2004

2004 Season

	M	Inns	NO	Runs	HS	Avge	100s	50s	Ct	St	O	M	Runs	Wkts	Avge	Best	5wI	10wM
Test																		
All First	11	14	8	179	38	29.83	-	-	3	-	230	29	946	27	35.03	7-80	2	-
1-day Int																		
C & G																		
totesport	15	8	5	44	20	14.66	-	-	2	-	88	2	456	14	32.57	3-17	-	
Twenty20	7	2	2	27	24 *	-	-	-	3	-	25	0	199	15	13.26	3-11	-	

Career Performances

	M	Inns	NO	Runs	HS	Avge	100s	50s	Ct	St	Balls	Runs	Wkts	Avge	Best	5wI	10wM
Test																	
All First	24	34	8	480	58	18.46	-	1	11	-	3594	2189	73	29.98	7-80	3	-
1-day Int																	
C & G																	
totesport	15	8	5	44	20	14.66	-	-	2	-	528	456	14	32.57	3-17	-	
Twenty20	7	2	2	27	24 *	-	-	-	3	-	150	199	15	13.26	3-11	-	

CLIFFORD, I. J. — Warwickshire

Name: Ian Jeffrey Clifford
Role: Right-hand bat, wicket-keeper
Born: 12 October 1982, Birmingham
Height: 5ft 6in **Weight:** 9st 12lbs
Nickname: Cliffy
County debut: 2002
1st-Class catches: 15
1st-Class stumpings: 1
Parents: Michael and Sheila
Marital status: Single
Education: Park Hall Secondary School
Qualifications: Level 1 coaching
Overseas tours: Warwickshire Development squad to West Indies 1999-2000
Career highlights to date: 'Taking four catches and a stumping as a substitute fielder'
Cricket moments to forget: 'Coming 317th (bottom) in the County Championship batting averages 2002'
Cricket superstitions: 'Always walk on the pitch left foot first'
Cricketers particularly admired: Keith Piper, Jack Russell, Ian Healy
Young players to look out for: Naqaash Tahir, Moeen Munir
Other sports played: Cycling
Other sports followed: Football (Aston Villa)
Extras: Played for Warwickshire Board XI in the C&G 2001 and 2002. Appeared in Championship match v Leicestershire at Edgbaston 2002 as substitute wicket-keeper after Tony Frost suffered a broken finger, later making full debut v Somerset, also at Edgbaston. Released by Warwickshire at the end of the 2004 season
Best batting: 7 Warwickshire v Kent, Edgbaston 2002

2004 Season

	M	Inns	NO	Runs	HS	Avge	100s	50s	Ct	St	O	M	Runs	Wkts	Avge	Best	5wI	10wM
Test																		
All First																		
1-day Int																		
C & G																		
totesport	1	1	0	4	4	4.00	-	-	3	-								
Twenty20																		

Career Performances

	M	Inns	NO	Runs	HS	Avge	100s	50s	Ct	St	Balls	Runs	Wkts	Avge	Best	5wI	10wM
Test																	
All First	4	6	0	20	7	3.33	-	-	15	1							
1-day Int																	
C & G	2	2	1	8	5 *	8.00	-	-	2	1							
totesport	4	2	0	5	4	2.50	-	-	8	-							
Twenty20																	

CLINTON, R. S. Surrey

Name: Richard Selvey Clinton
Role: Left-hand opening bat, right-arm medium bowler
Born: 1 September 1981, Sidcup, Kent
Height: 6ft 3in **Weight:** 15st 9lbs
Nickname: Clint
County debut: 2001 (Essex), 2004 (Surrey)
1st-Class 50s: 4
1st-Class 100s: 1
1st-Class catches: 14
Place in batting averages: 189th av. 24.09
Strike rate: (career 36.00)
Parents: Cathy and Grahame
Marital status: 'Girlfriend (Katie)'
Family links with cricket: 'Father played for Surrey. Uncles, cousin and brother play high standard of club cricket in Kent Premier League'
Education: Colfes School, London; Loughborough University
Qualifications: 9 GCSEs, 3 A-levels
Overseas teams played for: Kensington CC, Adelaide; Valleys CC, Brisbane 2000-02
Career highlights to date: 'Running Christopher Coulsen out against Sussex in '98 season'
Cricket moments to forget: 'Being bowled by Terrance Howes twice in as many games'
Cricket superstitions: 'Just a tried and tested routine'
Cricketers particularly admired: Graham Thorpe, Mark Butcher, Christopher Coulsen, James Watson, Terrance Howes
Young players to look out for: Christopher Coulsen, James Watson, Terrance Howes
Other sports played: Football, squash
Other sports followed: Motor racing (Formula One)

Favourite band: Aqua, The Sometime Maybes
Extras: Scored 36 and 58* on first-class debut v Surrey at Ilford 2001; scored 56 the following day on Norwich Union League debut v Durham at the same ground. Released by Essex at the end of the 2002 season. Played for Loughborough University CCE 2004. Represented British Universities v Sri Lanka A at Grace Road 2004. Joined Surrey during the 2004 season, scoring 73 on Championship debut v Worcestershire at The Oval
Opinions on cricket: 'Too many players and counties are abusing Kolpak ruling (*see page 9*) which is denying the genuine wealth of talent at youth level the chance to progress. This will be to the detriment of the English game in the long term.'
Best batting: 107 Essex v CUCCE, Fenner's 2002
Best bowling: 2-30 Essex v Australians, Chelmsford 2001

2004 Season

	M	Inns	NO	Runs	HS	Avge	100s	50s	Ct	St	O	M	Runs	Wkts	Avge	Best	5wI	10wM
Test																		
All First	7	12	1	265	73	24.09	-	2	10	-	3	0	30	0	-	-	-	-
1-day Int																		
C & G																		
totesport																		
Twenty20																		

Career Performances

	M	Inns	NO	Runs	HS	Avge	100s	50s	Ct	St	Balls	Runs	Wkts	Avge	Best	5wI	10wM
Test																	
All First	20	35	3	790	107	24.68	1	4	14	-	72	60	2	30.00	2-30	-	-
1-day Int																	
C & G	1	1	0	13	13	13.00	-	-	-	-							
totesport	12	9	3	140	56	23.33	-	1	2	-	18	25	0	-	-	-	
Twenty20																	

20. Which all-rounder has scored the most ODI runs for Scotland and has also played Test cricket against South Africa?

CLOUGH, G. D. Nottinghamshire

Name: Gareth David Clough
Role: Right-hand bat, right-arm medium bowler; all-rounder
Born: 23 May 1978, Leeds
Height: 6ft **Weight:** 12st 7lbs
Nickname: Banga, Cloughie
County debut: 1998 (Yorkshire), 2001 (Nottinghamshire)
1st-Class 50s: 1
1st-Class catches: 3
Strike rate: (career 93.33)
Parents: David and Gillian
Wife: Fiona
Education: Pudsey Grangefield
Qualifications: 9 GCSEs, 3 A-levels, Level 1 cricket coach
Overseas tours: Yorkshire to Durban and Cape Town 1999; Nottinghamshire to Johannesburg 2001-03
Overseas teams played for: Somerset West, Cape Town 1996-97; Deepdene Bears, Melbourne 1999-2000, 2001-02
Career highlights to date: 'Making my first-class debut – Yorkshire v Glamorgan 1998, Sophia Gardens'
Cricket moments to forget: 'B&H semi-final v Surrey at The Oval 2001' (*Nottinghamshire conceded 361 runs, more than any other first-class county in B&H history, and were then dismissed for 187*)
Cricket superstitions: 'None'
Cricketers particularly admired: Steve Waugh, Ian Botham
Young players to look out for: Mark Footitt, Andrew Parkin-Coates
Other sports played: Golf, football
Other sports followed: Football (Everton FC), rugby league (Leeds Rhinos)
Favourite band: Little Me
Relaxations: 'Socialising with friends; watching films; eating good food and drinking good wine'
Extras: Formerly with Yorkshire. Played for Nottinghamshire 2nd XI in 2000, topping the bowling averages with 37 wickets at 19.05 and scoring 400 runs
Best batting: 55 Nottinghamshire v India A, Trent Bridge 2003
Best bowling: 3-69 Nottinghamshire v Gloucestershire, Trent Bridge 2001

2004 Season

	M	Inns	NO	Runs	HS	Avge	100s	50s	Ct	St	O	M	Runs	Wkts	Avge	Best	5wI	10wM
Test																		
All First																		
1-day Int																		
C & G	2	1	0	0	0	0.00	-	-	1	-	19	0	93	1	93.00	1-59	-	
totesport	14	9	6	101	40 *	33.66	-	-	3	-	60.5	2	313	9	34.77	2-27	-	
Twenty20	5	5	1	53	28	13.25	-	-	3	-	16	0	118	6	19.66	2-18	-	

Career Performances

	M	Inns	NO	Runs	HS	Avge	100s	50s	Ct	St	Balls	Runs	Wkts	Avge	Best	5wI	10wM
Test																	
All First	9	13	1	133	55	11.08	-	1	3	-	840	544	9	60.44	3-69	-	-
1-day Int																	
C & G	5	3	1	38	27 *	19.00	-	-	2	-	228	206	4	51.50	3-47	-	
totesport	41	27	12	377	42 *	25.13	-	-	12	-	1482	1288	38	33.89	4-32	-	
Twenty20	10	8	1	94	29	13.42	-	-	3	-	204	265	11	24.09	2-18	-	

COETZER, K. J. — Durham

Name: Kyle James Coetzer
Role: Right-hand bat, right-arm medium bowler
Born: 14 April 1984, Aberdeen
Height: 5ft 11in
Nickname: Costa
County debut: 2004
1st-Class 50s: 1
Place in batting averages: 212th av. 21.20
Parents: Peter and Megan
Marital status: Single
Family links with cricket: 'All of my family plays, including two older brothers'
Education: Aberdeen Grammar School
Qualifications: Standard grades, 4 Intermediate 2s
Off-season: 'Cape Town CC until Christmas; in Perth from January to March'
Overseas tours: Scotland U19 to New Zealand (U19 World Cup) 2001-02, to Holland (ECC U19 Championships) 2003 (captain), to Bangladesh (U19 World Cup) 2003-04 (captain), to Ireland, to Denmark; Scotland to UAE (ICC Inter-Continental Cup) 2004-05

Overseas teams played for: Cape Town CC 2002-04; Western Cape Cricket Academy 2002-04
Career highlights to date: '67 against Glamorgan – first-class debut'
Cricket moments to forget: 'Being run out first ball on Scotland debut in NCL'
Cricket superstitions: 'Putting the bat in the crease when "over" is called after each over'
Cricketers particularly admired: Jacques Kallis, Allan Donald, Brian McMillan
Young players to look out for: Moneeb Iqbal, Gordon Muchall
Other sports played: Golf, basketball, football
Other sports followed: Rugby, football (Arsenal, Aberdeen)
Favourite band: Red Hot Chili Peppers
Relaxations: 'Socialising with friends'
Extras: Man of the Match (146*) v Italy in the ECC U19 Championships at Deventer 2003. Played for Scottish Saltires in NCL 2003. Played for Durham Board XI in the C&G 2003 and for Scotland in the first round of the C&G 2004, which was played in August 2003. Scored 67 on first-class debut v Glamorgan at Cardiff 2004. Is a Durham Development Player
Best batting: 67 Durham v Glamorgan, Cardiff 2004
Stop press: Played in Scotland side that won the ICC Inter-Continental Cup in the UAE, November 2004, scoring maiden first-class century (133*) in the semi-final v Kenya in Abu Dhabi

2004 Season

	M	Inns	NO	Runs	HS	Avge	100s	50s	Ct	St	O	M	Runs	Wkts	Avge	Best	5wI	10wM
Test																		
All First	6	10	0	212	67	21.20	-	1	-	-	1	0	2	0	-	-	-	-
1-day Int																		
C & G																		
totesport																		
Twenty20																		

Career Performances

	M	Inns	NO	Runs	HS	Avge	100s	50s	Ct	St	Balls	Runs	Wkts	Avge	Best	5wI	10wM
Test																	
All First	6	10	0	212	67	21.20	-	1	-	-	6	2	0	-	-	-	-
1-day Int																	
C & G	2	2	0	40	30	20.00	-	-	2	-							
totesport	3	3	1	16	16 *	8.00	-	-	1	-							
Twenty20																	

COLLINGWOOD, P. D. Durham

Name: Paul David Collingwood
Role: Right-hand bat, right-arm medium bowler, county vice-captain
Born: 26 May 1976, Shotley Bridge, Tyneside
Height: 5ft 11in **Weight:** 12st
Nickname: Colly
County debut: 1995 (one-day), 1996 (first-class)
County cap: 1998
Test debut: 2003-04
Tests: 2
One-Day Internationals: 59
1000 runs in a season: 1
1st-Class 50s: 31
1st-Class 100s: 8
1st-Class catches: 108
One-Day 100s: 3
Place in batting averages: 151st av. 29.27 (2003 157th av. 28.16)
Place in bowling averages: 107th av. 37.91
Strike rate: 68.50 (career 84.53)
Parents: David and Janet
Marital status: Single
Family links with cricket: Father and brother play in the Tyneside Senior League for Shotley Bridge CC
Education: Blackfyne Comprehensive School; Derwentside College
Qualifications: 9 GCSEs and 2 A-levels
Overseas tours: Durham Cricket Academy to Sri Lanka 1996 (captain); England VI to Hong Kong 2001, 2002; England to Zimbabwe (one-day series) 2001-02, to India and New Zealand 2001-02 (one-day series), to Australia 2002-03, to Africa (World Cup) 2002-03, to Bangladesh and Sri Lanka 2003-04, to West Indies 2003-04, to Zimbabwe (one-day series) 2004-05, to South Africa 2004-05
Overseas teams played for: Bulleen CC, Melbourne 1995-96, 1996-97 ('won flag on both occasions'); Cornwall CC, Auckland 1997-98; Alberton CC, Johannesburg 1998-99; Richmond CC, Melbourne 2000-01
Cricket moments to forget: 'Being Matthew Walker's (Kent) first first-class wicket'
Cricket superstitions: 'Left pad on first, and wearing them on the wrong legs'
Cricketers particularly admired: Steve Waugh, Jacques Kallis, Glenn McGrath, Shane Warne
Young players to look out for: Gordon Muchall
Other sports played: Golf (9 handicap)

Other sports followed: Football ('The Red and Whites' – Sunderland)
Extras: Took wicket (David Capel) with first ball on first-class debut against Northants, then scored 91 in Durham's first innings. Durham Player of the Year 2000. Awarded the Ron Brierley Scholarship 2000 through the ECB in conjunction with the Victorian Cricket Association, Australia; joint winner of the Jack Ryder Medal, awarded by the umpires, for his performances in Victorian Premier Cricket 2000-01. Made Test debut in the first Test v Sri Lanka at Galle 2003-04. Passed 1000 runs in ODIs in the first ODI v West Indies at Georgetown 2003-04. Set record for fastest one-day league century by a Durham batsman with his 72-ball hundred (ended on 102*) v Worcestershire at Worcester in the totesport League 2004. Scored 79* v India at The Oval in the NatWest Challenge 2004, in the process sharing with Andrew Flintoff (99) in a new England record stand for the fifth wicket in ODIs (174). His ODI awards include Man of the Match v India at Cuttack 2001-02 for his all-round performance, including 71*; v Sri Lanka in the VB Series at Perth 2002-03 (100; his maiden ODI century); and v Zimbabwe at Edgbaston in the ICC Champions Trophy 2004 (80*). Appointed vice-captain of Durham for 2005
Best batting: 190 Durham v Sri Lankans, Riverside 2002
Best bowling: 4-31 Durham v Derbyshire, Derby 2002

2004 Season

	M	Inns	NO	Runs	HS	Avge	100s	50s	Ct	St	O	M	Runs	Wkts	Avge	Best	5wI	10wM
Test																		
All First	6	11	0	322	68	29.27	-	3	4	-	137	37	455	12	37.91	3-49	-	-
1-day Int	12	10	3	252	80 *	36.00	-	2	5	-	30.2	0	174	4	43.50	2-22	-	
C & G																		
totesport	7	7	2	257	102 *	51.40	1	1	7	-	47	3	209	7	29.85	2-52	-	
Twenty20																		

Career Performances

	M	Inns	NO	Runs	HS	Avge	100s	50s	Ct	St	Balls	Runs	Wkts	Avge	Best	5wI	10wM
Test	2	4	0	89	36	22.25	-	-	6	-	96	37	0	-	-	-	-
All First	105	182	11	5344	190	31.25	8	31	108	-	6509	3121	77	40.53	4-31	-	-
1-day Int	59	55	16	1346	100	34.51	1	7	27	-	855	856	20	42.80	4-38	-	
C & G	11	10	1	262	60	29.11	-	2	1	-	246	196	4	49.00	2-7	-	
totesport	96	92	9	2553	118 *	30.75	2	16	55	-	2252	1751	57	30.71	3-20	-	
Twenty20																	

COMPTON, N. R. D. Middlesex

Name: Nicholas (Nick) Richard Denis Compton
Role: Right-hand bat, right-arm off-spin bowler; batting all-rounder
Born: 26 June 1983, Durban, South Africa
Height: 6ft 2in **Weight:** 13st 10lbs
Nickname: Compo, Ledge, Cheser
County debut: 2001 (one-day), 2004 (first-class)
1st-Class catches: 3
Parents: Richard and Glynis
Marital status: Single
Family links with cricket: Grandfather Denis Compton played football and cricket for England
Education: Hilton College, South Africa/Harrow School; Durham University
Qualifications: AAC (A-levels), ECB coach Level 1

Overseas tours: England U19 to Australia and (U19 World Cup) New Zealand 2001-02
Overseas teams played for: DHS Old Boys, Durban 1997-98; University of Western Australia, Perth 2001
Career highlights to date: '86 not out for Middlesex XI against Lancashire at Denis Compton Oval, Shenley'
Cricket moments to forget: 'Dropping three catches against Australia 2002'
Sportsmen particularly admired: Jacques Kallis, Rahul Dravid, Muhammad Ali (boxer)
Young players to look out for: Hashim Amla (South African), Shaun Marsh (Australian), Brett Jones (Australian), Bilal Shafayat, Chris Whelan
Other sports played: Golf (6 handicap), represented Natal at junior level at tennis, football and hockey
Other sports followed: Football (Arsenal), golf, rugby union (Natal Sharks)
Relaxations: 'Chilling with a few boys on a beach; music and girls'
Extras: Played for Natal U13 and U15. Natal Academy award 1997. Represented Harrow v Eton in 1999 (match abandoned), 2000, and 2001 (captain). Middlesex U17 Batsman of the Season 1999. Middlesex U19 Player of the Season 2000. NBC Denis Compton Award for the most promising young Middlesex player 2001 and 2002. Represented England U19 v India U19 2002
Opinions on cricket: 'A lack of passion and character in the English game to date.'
Best batting: 40 Middlesex v Worcestershire, Worcester 2004

2004 Season

	M	Inns	NO	Runs	HS	Avge	100s	50s	Ct	St	O	M	Runs	Wkts	Avge	Best	5wI	10wM
Test																		
All First	4	7	2	111	40	22.20	-	-	3	-								
1-day Int																		
C & G																		
totesport	10	8	1	85	33	12.14	-	-	2	-								
Twenty20	4	3	0	5	5	1.66	-	-	2	-								

Career Performances

	M	Inns	NO	Runs	HS	Avge	100s	50s	Ct	St	Balls	Runs	Wkts	Avge	Best	5wI	10wM
Test																	
All First	4	7	2	111	40	22.20	-	-	3	-							
1-day Int																	
C & G																	
totesport	15	13	4	214	86 *	23.77	-	1	2	-	30	20	0	-	-	-	
Twenty20	4	3	0	5	5	1.66	-	-	2	-							

COOK, A. N. — Essex

Name: Alastair (Ali) Nathan Cook
Role: Left-hand opening bat, right-arm off-spin bowler
Born: 25 December 1984, Gloucester
Height: 6ft 2in **Weight:** 12st 10lbs
Nickname: Cooky, Chef
County debut: 2003
1st-Class 50s: 8
1st-Class 100s: 1
1st-Class catches: 24
Place in batting averages: 128th av. 32.63
Parents: Graham and Elizabeth
Marital status: Single
Family links with cricket: 'Dad played for village side; brothers play for Maldon CC'
Education: Bedford School
Qualifications: 9 GCSEs, 3 A-levels
Off-season: 'Part-time [ECB] Academy. Paul Terry Academy, Perth'
Overseas tours: Bedford School to Barbados 2001; England U19 to Bangladesh (U19 World Cup) 2003-04 (captain); England A to Sri Lanka 2004-05
Career highlights to date: 'Maiden first-class 100'

Cricket moments to forget: 'Running myself out first ball in U15 World Cup game against India'
Cricket superstitions: 'A few!'
Cricketers particularly admired: Graham Thorpe, Andy Flower, Graham Gooch
Young players to look out for: Ravi Bopara, James Hildreth, Mark Pettini
Other sports played: Squash, golf
Other sports followed: 'All sports'
Favourite band: Mouldy Lookin' Stain
Relaxations: 'Spending time with friends'
Extras: Played for England U15 in U15 World Cup 2000. Holds Bedford School season record and career record with 19 hundreds. Made debut for Essex 2nd XI aged 15. Scored century in each innings (137/143) for Essex 2nd XI v Surrey 2nd XI at The Oval 2003. Represented England U19 2003 and captained England U19 v Bangladesh U19 2004. Scored 69* on first-class debut v Nottinghamshire at Chelmsford 2003 and a further two half-centuries in his next two Championship matches. Had consecutive scores of 108*, 108* and 87 in the U19 World Cup 2003-04 in Bangladesh. NBC Denis Compton Award for the most promising young Essex player 2003. Scored maiden first-class century (126) v Leicestershire at Chelmsford 2004, in the process sharing with Will Jefferson (128) in Essex's third-highest first-class opening partnership (265). ECB National Academy 2004-05 (part-time)
Opinions on cricket: 'Tea should be longer.'
Best batting: 126 Essex v Leicestershire, Chelmsford 2004
Stop press: Called up to England A tour to Sri Lanka 2004-05 as replacement for Kevin Pietersen

2004 Season

	M	Inns	NO	Runs	HS	Avge	100s	50s	Ct	St	O	M	Runs	Wkts	Avge	Best	5wI	10wM
Test																		
All First	14	24	2	718	126	32.63	1	5	21	-	1	0	12	0	-	-	-	-
1-day Int																		
C & G	2	2	0	16	16	8.00	-	-	2	-								
totesport	5	4	0	29	11	7.25	-	-	1	-								
Twenty20																		

Career Performances

	M	Inns	NO	Runs	HS	Avge	100s	50s	Ct	St	Balls	Runs	Wkts	Avge	Best	5wI	10wM
Test																	
All First	17	30	3	957	126	35.44	1	8	24	-	18	23	0	-	-	-	-
1-day Int																	
C & G	3	3	0	43	27	14.33	-	-	3	-							
totesport	6	5	0	54	25	10.80	-	-	2	-							
Twenty20																	

COOK, J. W. Northamptonshire

Name: Jeffrey William Cook
Role: Left-hand bat, right-arm medium bowler
Born: 2 February 1972, Sydney, Australia
Height: 6ft 4in **Weight:** 14st
Nickname: Cookie
County debut: 2000
1st-Class 50s: 13
1st-Class 100s: 3
1st-Class 5 w. in innings: 1
1st-Class catches: 20
One-Day 100s: 2
Place in batting averages: 181st av. 24.66 (2003 176th av. 25.85)
Place in bowling averages: (2003 31st av. 25.21)
Strike rate: 84.85 (career 73.58)
Parents: Roma and Les
Wife and date of marriage: Fiona, 10 October 1998
Children: Alexander, 21 April 2000
Family links with cricket: Mother represented New South Wales
Education: James Cook High School, Kogarah, NSW
Qualifications: NCA Level 2 coaching award, ACB Level 1 coaching award
Overseas tours: Northamptonshire to Grenada 2000, 2001
Overseas teams played for: St George DCC, Sydney 1987-93; Easts CC, Sydney 1999-2002
Career highlights to date: 'First [first-class] century (137) v Glos in my second game. Winning second division of Championship in 2000 with Northants. Fielding for England v Pakistan at Lord's 2001'
Cricket moments to forget: 'First ever pair – v Yorkshire at Headingley 2001'
Cricketers particularly admired: David Gower, Mark Taylor, Mark Waugh, Steve Waugh
Other sports played: Football, tennis
Other sports followed: Football (Liverpool), rugby league (Parramatta)
Relaxations: 'Time with family'
Extras: Represented NSW at U17, U19 and Colts levels. Represented New South Wales and Australia at indoor cricket. Played for Northants Board XI in 1999 NatWest, scoring 130 v Wiltshire at Northampton and winning the Man of the Match award. Shared in record second-wicket stand for Northants in matches v Surrey (172) with Mike Hussey at Northampton 2001. Left Northamptonshire during the 2004-05 off-season. Is not considered an overseas player, having qualified by residency

Best batting: 137 Northamptonshire v Gloucestershire, Cheltenham 2000
Best bowling: 5-31 Northamptonshire v Durham, Northampton 2003

2004 Season

	M	Inns	NO	Runs	HS	Avge	100s	50s	Ct	St	O	M	Runs	Wkts	Avge	Best	5wI	10wM
Test																		
All First	6	9	0	222	114	24.66	1	1	4	-	99	19	307	7	43.85	3-42	-	-
1-day Int																		
C & G	2	2	0	50	33	25.00	-	-	-	-	5	0	42	0	-	-	-	
totesport	5	5	1	93	38	23.25	-	-	1	-	7	0	49	0	-	-	-	
Twenty20	1	1	0	0	0	0.00	-	-	1	-								

Career Performances

	M	Inns	NO	Runs	HS	Avge	100s	50s	Ct	St	Balls	Runs	Wkts	Avge	Best	5wI	10wM
Test																	
All First	55	88	7	2378	137	29.35	3	13	20	-	2649	1391	36	38.63	5-31	1	-
1-day Int																	
C & G	9	9	0	412	130	45.77	1	2	-	-	168	150	2	75.00	1-5	-	
totesport	58	53	5	954	102	19.87	1	2	17	-	1113	931	40	23.27	4-35	-	
Twenty20	6	6	0	35	18	5.83	-	-	3	-	36	60	1	60.00	1-24	-	

COOK, S. J. Kent

Name: Simon James Cook
Role: Right-hand bat, right-arm medium-fast bowler
Born: 15 January 1977, Oxford
Height: 6ft 4in **Weight:** 13st
Nickname: Donk, Cookie
County debut: 1997 (one-day, Middlesex), 1999 (first-class, Middlesex)
County cap: 2003 (Middlesex)
1st-Class 50s: 3
1st-Class 5 w. in innings: 4
1st-Class catches: 23
One-Day 5 w. in innings: 2
Place in batting averages: 240th av. 16.73 (2003 251st av. 15.07)
Place in bowling averages: 52nd av. 30.62 (2003 109th av. 38.81)
Strike rate: 63.60 (career 60.80)
Parents: Phil and Sue

Marital status: Single
Education: Matthew Arnold School
Qualifications: GCSEs, NVQ Business Administration II, Level 3 ECB coach
Off-season: Coaching
Overseas tours: Middlesex to South Africa 2000
Overseas teams played for: Rockingham, Perth 2000-01
Cricketers particularly admired: Angus Fraser, Mark Waugh, Glenn McGrath
Young players to look out for: Jamie Dalrymple, Ed Joyce, Nick Compton, John Maunders
Other sports followed: Football (Liverpool), 'any other ball sport'
Relaxations: 'Sleeping, playing any sport, watching television and videos'
Extras: Scored career best 93* v Nottinghamshire at Lord's 2001, helping Middlesex to avoid the follow-on, then took a wicket with the first ball of his opening spell. Recorded maiden one-day five-wicket return (6-37) v Leicestershire at Leicester in the totesport League 2004. Equalled Adam Hollioake's record for the most wickets in a one-day league season (39) 2004. Left Middlesex at the end of the 2004 season and has joined Kent for 2005
Best batting: 93* Middlesex v Nottinghamshire, Lord's 2001
Best bowling: 8-63 Middlesex v Northamptonshire, Northampton 2002

2004 Season

	M	Inns	NO	Runs	HS	Avge	100s	50s	Ct	St	O	M	Runs	Wkts	Avge	Best	5wI	10wM
Test																		
All First	12	15	0	251	40	16.73	-	-	6	-	371	82	1072	35	30.62	6-89	2	-
1-day Int																		
C & G	3	2	2	35	32 *	-	-	-	-	-	17	0	84	0	-	-	-	
totesport	18	10	5	62	21 *	12.40	-	-	2	-	133.4	6	599	39	15.35	6-37	2	
Twenty20	4	3	2	13	12 *	13.00	-	-	-	-	14	0	104	7	14.85	3-25	-	

Career Performances

	M	Inns	NO	Runs	HS	Avge	100s	50s	Ct	St	Balls	Runs	Wkts	Avge	Best	5wI	10wM
Test																	
All First	66	87	11	1347	93 *	17.72	-	3	23	-	10215	5410	168	32.20	8-63	4	-
1-day Int																	
C & G	10	9	5	145	39 *	36.25	-	-	1	-	444	337	9	37.44	3-37	-	
totesport	87	59	16	626	67 *	14.55	-	2	12	-	3728	2890	111	26.03	6-37	2	
Twenty20	9	6	3	41	19 *	13.66	-	-	1	-	194	228	16	14.25	3-14	-	

CORK, D. G. Lancashire

Name: Dominic Gerald Cork
Role: Right-hand bat, right-arm fast-medium bowler
Born: 7 August 1971, Newcastle-under-Lyme, Staffordshire
Height: 6ft 2½in **Weight:** 14st
Nickname: Corky
County debut: 1990 (Derbyshire), 2004 (Lancashire)
County cap: 1993 (Derbyshire), 2004 (Lancashire)
Benefit: 2001 (Derbyshire)
Test debut: 1995
Tests: 37
One-Day Internationals: 32
50 wickets in a season: 7
1st-Class 50s: 44
1st-Class 100s: 5
1st-Class 200s: 1
1st-Class 5 w. in innings: 31
1st-Class 10 w. in match: 5
1st-Class catches: 173
One-Day 5 w. in innings: 4
Place in batting averages: 186th av. 24.27 (2003 204th av. 22.80)
Place in bowling averages: 48th av. 30.10 (2003 43rd av. 27.26)
Strike rate: 52.55 (career 53.15)
Parents: Gerald and Mary
Wife and date of marriage: Donna, 28 August 2000
Children: Ashleigh, 28 April 1990; Gregory, 29 September 1994
Family links with cricket: 'Father and two brothers played in the same side at Betley CC in Staffordshire'
Education: St Joseph's College, Trent Vale, Stoke-on-Trent; Newcastle College
Qualifications: 2 O-levels, Level 2 coach
Career outside cricket: 'None at the moment, but once I retire I would like to go into the media side'
Overseas tours: England YC to Australia 1989-90; England A to Bermuda and West Indies 1991-92, to Australia 1992-93, to South Africa 1993-94, to India 1994-95; England to South Africa 1995-96, to India and Pakistan (World Cup) 1995-96, to New Zealand 1996-97, to Australia 1998-99, to Pakistan and Sri Lanka 2000-01, to Sri Lanka (ICC Champions Trophy) 2002-03
Overseas teams played for: East Shirley, Christchurch, New Zealand 1990-91

Career highlights to date: 'Making my debut for England'
Cricket moments to forget: 'Every time the team loses'
Cricket superstitions: 'None'
Cricketers particularly admired: Kim Barnett, Mike Atherton, Ian Botham, Malcolm Marshall
Young players to look out for: Kyle Hogg, Luke Sutton
Other sports played: Golf, football
Other sports followed: Football (Stoke City)
Favourite band: 'Anything R&B'
Relaxations: 'Listening to music'
Extras: Played Minor Counties cricket for Staffordshire 1989 and 1990. In 1990 he took a wicket in his first over in first-class cricket, v New Zealanders at Derby, and scored a century as nightwatchman for England U19 v Pakistan at Taunton. Took 8-53 before lunch on his 20th birthday, v Essex at Derby 1991. Selected for England A in 1991 – his first full season of first-class cricket. PCA Young Player of the Year 1991. Achieved first-class hat-trick against Kent 1994. Took 7-43 on Test debut against West Indies at Lord's 1995, the best innings figures by an England debutant. Took hat-trick against the West Indies at Old Trafford in the fourth Test 1995. PCA Player of the Year 1995. Finished at the top of the Whyte and Mackay ratings for bowling in 1995. Cornhill England Player of the Year 1995-96. One of *Wisden*'s Five Cricketers of the Year 1996. Man of the Match in the second Test v West Indies at Lord's 2000; on his recall to the Test side he recorded match figures of 7-52 followed by a match-winning 33* in England's second innings. Scored maiden first-class 200 (200*, the highest score by a Derbyshire No. 8) v Durham at Derby 2000, sharing in the process in a new record seventh-wicket partnership for Derbyshire (258) with Mathew Dowman. Took 700th first-class wicket (Jon Lewis) v Durham at Derby 2003. Derbyshire captain 1998-2003. Left Derbyshire at the end of the 2003 season and joined Lancashire for 2004; awarded Lancashire cap 2004. Took Twenty20 hat-trick (Pietersen, Ealham, Patel) v Nottinghamshire at Old Trafford 2004
Best batting: 200* Derbyshire v Durham, Derby 2000
Best bowling: 9-43 Derbyshire v Northamptonshire, Derby 1995

2004 Season

	M	Inns	NO	Runs	HS	Avge	100s	50s	Ct	St	O	M	Runs	Wkts	Avge	Best	5wI	10wM
Test																		
All First	14	20	2	437	109	24.27	1	2	17	-	332.5	59	1144	38	30.10	7-120	3	-
1-day Int																		
C & G	2	2	1	66	54 *	66.00	-	1	1	-	13.4	0	75	1	75.00	1-25	-	
totesport	16	11	1	187	57	18.70	-	1	4	-	112	13	494	16	30.87	3-35	-	
Twenty20	7	6	2	61	25	15.25	-	-	1	-	15	0	124	5	24.80	3-9	-	

Career Performances

	M	Inns	NO	Runs	HS	Avge	100s	50s	Ct	St	Balls	Runs	Wkts	Avge	Best	5wI	10wM
Test	37	56	8	864	59	18.00	-	3	18	-	7678	3906	131	29.81	7-43	5	-
All First	236	354	46	7742	200 *	25.13	6	44	173	-	40397	20077	760	26.41	9-43	31	5
1-day Int	32	21	3	180	31 *	10.00	-	-	6	-	1772	1368	41	33.36	3-27	-	
C & G	27	24	5	684	93	36.00	-	8	13	-	1599	1006	49	20.53	5-18	2	
totesport	139	116	13	2046	83 *	19.86	-	8	60	-	6101	4483	166	27.00	6-21	1	
Twenty20	12	11	2	106	25	11.77	-	-	1	-	138	163	6	27.16	3-9	-	

COSKER, D. A. — Glamorgan

Name: Dean Andrew Cosker
Role: Right-hand bat, left-arm spin bowler
Born: 7 January 1978, Weymouth, Dorset
Height: 5ft 11in **Weight:** 12st 7lbs
Nickname: Lurks
County debut: 1996
County cap: 2000
1st-Class 5 w. in innings: 2
1st-Class catches: 78
One-Day 5 w. in innings: 1
Place in batting averages: (2003 265th av. 13.33)
Place in bowling averages: 49th av. 30.17 (2003 120th av. 40.88)
Strike rate: 61.47 (career 78.15)
Parents: Des and Carol
Marital status: Living with partner Katie
Education: Millfield School
Qualifications: 10 GCSEs, 4 A-levels
Overseas tours: West of England U15 to West Indies 1993-94; Millfield School to Sri Lanka 1994-95; England U17 to Holland 1995; England U19 to Pakistan 1996-97; England A to Kenya and Sri Lanka 1997-98, to Zimbabwe and South Africa 1998-99; Glamorgan CCC to Cape Town and Jersey
Overseas teams played for: Gordon CC, Sydney 1996-97; Crusaders, Durban 2001-02
Career highlights to date: 'County cap 2000. My England A tours. Championship with Glamorgan 1997. One-day [league] champs 2002'
Cricket moments to forget: 'Losing Benson and Hedges final 2001. And most Twenty20 games!'
Cricketers particularly admired: 'All the veterans of Glamorgan!'

Young players to look out for: Adam Harrison
Other sports played: Football
Other sports followed: Football (Spurs)
Favourite band: Nickelback
Relaxations: 'Lurking, golf'
Extras: *Daily Telegraph* Regional Bowling Award. England U15, U17 and U19. Played for U19 TCCB Development of Excellence XI v South Africa U19 1995. Leading wicket-taker on England A tour of Zimbabwe and South Africa 1998-99 (22; av. 22.90). Third youngest Glamorgan player to receive county cap. Shared with Robert Croft in a new record tenth-wicket partnership for Glamorgan in matches against Derbyshire (81) at Swansea 2003
Opinions on cricket: 'Enjoy.'
Best batting: 49 Glamorgan v Sussex, Cardiff 1999
Best bowling: 6-140 Glamorgan v Lancashire, Colwyn Bay 1998

2004 Season

	M	Inns	NO	Runs	HS	Avge	100s	50s	Ct	St	O	M	Runs	Wkts	Avge	Best	5wI	10wM
Test																		
All First	7	9	6	68	21 *	22.66	-	-	8	-	174.1	42	513	17	30.17	3-40	-	-
1-day Int																		
C & G																		
totesport	10	4	2	9	4	4.50	-	-	9	-	76	0	354	8	44.25	2-48	-	
Twenty20	6	1	1	1	1 *	-	-	-	5	-	11	0	104	5	20.80	2-30	-	

Career Performances

	M	Inns	NO	Runs	HS	Avge	100s	50s	Ct	St	Balls	Runs	Wkts	Avge	Best	5wI	10wM
Test																	
All First	109	130	41	1015	49	11.40	-	-	78	-	20085	9411	257	36.61	6-140	2	-
1-day Int																	
C & G	10	6	4	18	5	9.00	-	-	1	-	482	365	8	45.62	3-26	-	
totesport	90	41	17	213	27 *	8.87	-	-	35	-	3839	3096	97	31.91	5-54	1	
Twenty20	11	3	3	8	7 *	-	-	-	6	-	168	232	10	23.20	2-24	-	

COTTEY, P. A. — Sussex

Name: Phillip Anthony (Tony) Cottey
Role: Right-hand bat, right-arm off-spin bowler
Born: 2 June 1966, Swansea
Height: 5ft 5in **Weight:** 10st 7lbs
Nickname: Cotts, TC
County debut: 1986 (Glamorgan), 1999 (Sussex)
County cap: 1992 (Glamorgan), 1999 (Sussex)
1000 runs in a season: 8

1st-Class 50s: 73
1st-Class 100s: 30
1st-Class 200s: 1
1st-Class catches: 182
One-Day 5 w. in innings: 1
Place in batting averages: 144th av. 30.00 (2003 43rd av. 45.96)
Strike rate: (career 95.87)
Parents: Bernard John and Ruth
Wife and date of marriage: Gail, 5 October 1992
Children: Lowri Rhiannon, 16 October 1993; Seren Nia, 6 August 1997
Family links with cricket: Father played club cricket for Swansea CC
Education: Bishopston Comprehensive, Swansea; Coleg Sir Gar, Llanelli
Qualifications: 9 O-levels, HND Sports Science, Level 3 cricket coach, Certificate of Professional Competence
Career outside cricket: 'New business, Ysbryd Ltd – Welsh leisurewear'
Overseas tours: Glamorgan to La Manga, Barbados, Trinidad, Zimbabwe and Cape Town 1987-96, to Jersey 1998; Sussex to Grenada 2002
Overseas teams played for: Penrith, Sydney 1986-88; Benoni, Johannesburg 1990-93; Eastern Transvaal 1991-92
Career highlights: 'Winning Championship in 1997 with Glamorgan and in 2003 with Sussex'
Cricket moments to forget: 'Any of the four semi-final losses at Glamorgan and the semi-final loss at Gloucestershire 1999 in Super Cup with Sussex'
Cricketers particularly admired: Ian Botham, Matthew Maynard, Sachin Tendulkar, Mark Robinson
Young players to look out for: Tim Ambrose, Matt Prior
Other sports played: Football ('pro player with Swansea City 1982-85')
Other sports followed: Rugby (Dunvant RFC), football (Swansea City AFC)
Favourite band: Rolling Stones
Relaxations: 'Golf, road running; spending time with family; following all sports'
Extras: Three Welsh Youth caps (one as captain). Glamorgan Player of the Year in 1994. Ran the New York Marathon in 1995 and the Athens Marathon in 1996. Left Glamorgan at the end of the 1998 season and joined Sussex. Sussex Clubman of the Year 1999. Scored 703 runs (three centuries; four fifties) in seven Championship innings June/July 2003. In 2003 joined select band of players who have won the Championship with two counties (Glamorgan 1997; Sussex 2003 – 'the only Welshman to achieve this'). Sussex Team Man of the Year 2003. Recorded maiden one-day five-wicket return (5-49) v Somerset at Taunton in the totesport League 2004. Retired at the end of the 2004 season

Opinions on cricket: 'A bit concerned about the influx of dual-passport-holding cricketers from around the world flooding into the domestic game.'
Best batting: 203 Glamorgan v Leicestershire, Swansea 1996
Best bowling: 4-49 Glamorgan v Leicestershire, Swansea 1996

2004 Season

	M	Inns	NO	Runs	HS	Avge	100s	50s	Ct	St	O	M	Runs	Wkts	Avge	Best	5wI	10wM
Test																		
All First	11	17	0	510	185	30.00	1	-	7	-								
1-day Int																		
C & G																		
totesport	12	9	0	146	50	16.22	-	1	3	-	7	0	49	5	9.80	5-49	1	
Twenty20																		

Career Performances

	M	Inns	NO	Runs	HS	Avge	100s	50s	Ct	St	Balls	Runs	Wkts	Avge	Best	5wI	10wM
Test																	
All First	277	448	51	14567	203	36.69	31	73	182	-	1534	954	16	59.62	4-49	-	-
1-day Int																	
C & G	31	30	7	610	68	26.52	-	4	8	-	186	135	3	45.00	1-9	-	
totesport	194	166	28	3273	92 *	23.71	-	17	64	-	629	635	20	31.75	5-49	1	
Twenty20																	

COVERDALE, P. S. Northamptonshire

Name: Paul Stephen Coverdale
Role: Right-hand bat, right-arm medium bowler
Born: 24 July 1983, Harrogate
Height: 5ft 10in **Weight:** 11st 8lbs
Nickname: Covers, Flaps, Drill Sergeant, Incredible Hulk
County debut: No first-team appearance
Parents: Stephen and Jane
Marital status: Single
Family links with cricket: Father played for Yorkshire CCC and Cambridge University and was Chief Executive of Northamptonshire
Education: Wellingborough School; Loughborough University
Qualifications: 9 GCSEs, 3 A-levels, ECB Level I coaching

Overseas tours: Northamptonshire U19 to South Africa 2000
Overseas teams played for: Swanbourne, Perth 2002
Cricket moments to forget: 'Leaving a straight one first ball in a 2nd XI match and then breaking my hand on the changing room wall in anger. Was too embarrassed to announce it immediately and so attempted to field through it!'
Cricketers particularly admired: Allan Lamb, Steve Waugh, Michael Atherton, David Capel, Mike Hussey
Young players to look out for: Adam Shantry, Monty Panesar, Chris Munns
Other sports played: Rugby, golf
Other sports followed: Rugby (Northampton Saints), football
Favourite band: Dire Straits
Relaxations: 'Socialising and going out with friends; ruining a great classic on the karaoke; watching and playing sports'
Extras: Played county age groups, captaining at U14, U15, U17 and U19. Represented East England Schools U18. Played for Northamptonshire Board XI in the C&G 2001, 2002 and 2003. Joined the Northants Academy in 2000. Joined Loughborough UCCE Academy in 2002. Represented English Universities in the Home Nations Tournament 2003
Opinions on cricket: 'In general it seems that county 2nd XIs are getting younger and there are a lot of young players involved in first-class cricket now. This can only be good for the future of the game, and is a tribute to the investment made by the ECB and the counties in the academy set-ups.'

2004 Season (did not make any first-class or one-day appearances)

Career Performances

	M	Inns	NO	Runs	HS	Avge	100s	50s	Ct	St	Balls	Runs	Wkts	Avge	Best	5wI	10wM
Test																	
All First																	
1-day Int																	
C & G	3	3	0	33	19	11.00	-	-	2	-	96	48	1	48.00	1-21	-	
totesport																	
Twenty20																	

21. Who was the Egyptian-born off-spinner who made his Test debut in 1969-70 for South Africa and returned to Test cricket 22 years later, taking 5-86 against India?

COWAN, A. P. Essex

Name: Ashley Preston Cowan
Role: Right-hand bat, right-arm fast-medium bowler, 'benefit-only wicket-keeper'
Born: 7 May 1975, Hitchin, Hertfordshire
Height: 6ft 5in **Weight:** 15st
Nickname: Dic Dic, Wallace, Vic
County debut: 1995
County cap: 1997
50 wickets in a season: 1
1st-Class 50s: 9
1st-Class 5 w. in innings: 8
1st-Class catches: 51
One-Day 5 w. in innings: 2
Place in bowling averages: 85th av. 35.61
Strike rate: 68.30 (career 60.26)
Parents: Jeff and Pam
Wife and date of marriage: Cath, 14 October 2001
Family links with cricket: 'Father played village cricket. Mother made the teas'
Education: Framlingham College
Qualifications: 8 GCSEs, 3 A-levels
Overseas tours: England to West Indies 1997-98; MCC to Namibia and Uganda 2004-05
Overseas teams played for: Zingari CC, Durban 1995-97
Career highlights to date: 'Getting England blazer. Winning finals at Lord's'
Cricket moments to forget: 'Any time I get smashed around the park. Losing [NatWest] final at Lord's 1996'
Cricketers particularly admired: Ian Botham, Allan Donald, Curtly Ambrose, Glenn McGrath
Young players to look out for: Mark Pettini, Justin Bishop
Other sports played: Rugby, hockey (Chelmsford), golf (single-figure handicap), squash
Other sports followed: Rugby (Saracens), golf, football ('anybody who plays Man U')
Relaxations: Sports, sleeping, reading
Extras: Played rugby and hockey for East of England U18. Was the youngest person to play for Cambridgeshire. Became first Essex player to take a first-class hat-trick at Castle Park, Colchester, v Gloucestershire in 1996. Took three wickets in four balls in the final over of National League match at Southend 2000 to prevent Glamorgan scoring the six runs needed for victory; the over also contained a run-out

Opinions on cricket: 'More day/night cricket.'
Best batting: 94 Essex v Leicestershire, Leicester 1998
Best bowling: 6-47 Essex v Glamorgan, Cardiff 1999

2004 Season

	M	Inns	NO	Runs	HS	Avge	100s	50s	Ct	St	O	M	Runs	Wkts	Avge	Best	5wI	10wM
Test																		
All First	5	7	2	63	25	12.60	-	-	3	-	148	39	463	13	35.61	3-44	-	-
1-day Int																		
C & G	1	0	0	0	0	-	-	-	-	-	8	0	47	3	15.66	3-47	-	
totesport	9	3	1	52	31	26.00	-	-	4	-	41.5	3	236	6	39.33	2-42	-	
Twenty20	3	2	1	21	14 *	21.00	-	-	1	-	12	0	88	3	29.33	2-20	-	

Career Performances

	M	Inns	NO	Runs	HS	Avge	100s	50s	Ct	St	Balls	Runs	Wkts	Avge	Best	5wI	10wM
Test																	
All First	105	156	30	2241	94	17.78	-	9	51	-	17056	9240	283	32.65	6-47	8	-
1-day Int																	
C & G	18	12	4	67	17 *	8.37	-	-	5	-	1031	690	26	26.53	4-27	-	
totesport	99	72	17	704	40 *	12.80	-	-	40	-	4183	3128	120	26.06	5-14	1	
Twenty20	3	2	1	21	14 *	21.00	-	-	1	-	72	88	3	29.33	2-20	-	

COX, J. — Somerset

Name: Jamie Cox
Role: Right-hand bat, off-spin bowler
Born: 15 October 1969, Burnie, Tasmania
Height: 6ft **Weight:** 12st 7lbs
Nickname: Buzz, Skippy
County debut: 1999
County cap: 1999
1000 runs in a season: 4
1st-Class 50s: 78
1st-Class 100s: 47
1st-Class 200s: 4
1st-Class catches: 118
One-Day 100s: 6
Place in batting averages: 29th av. 53.31 (2003 49th av. 45.29)
Strike rate: (career 143.40)
Parents: David and Kaye
Wife: Helen
Children: Lachlan William Joseph, November 2001; Madeleine Grace, January 2003

Family links with cricket: Father played State Colts and is life member of local club
Education: Wynyard High; Deakin University
Qualifications: School Certificate, Diploma of Management, Bachelor of Business degree; currently studying for Diploma of Drafting
Off-season: Playing for Tasmania
Overseas tours: Australia U19 to West Indies 1988; Australia A to Zimbabwe 1989, to Malaysia (Super 8s) 1997; Australia XI to Zimbabwe 1991-92; Tasmania to Zimbabwe 1995-96
Overseas teams played for: Tasmania 1987-88 –
Cricketers particularly admired: Ian Botham, Geoff Marsh, David Boon, Steve Waugh
Other sports played: Golf, soccer ('poorly')
Other sports followed: Australian Rules football (Western Bulldogs)
Relaxations: Music, home design
Extras: First Tasmania player to attend the Australian Cricket Academy, in 1988. Scored 1349 runs in the 1996-97 season, with five 100s, including two in one match v New South Wales. Players' Player of the Year 1996-97. Tasmanian Cricket Player of the Year 1996-97. Scored 115* in the first innings of the 1997-98 Sheffield Shield final v Western Australia, becoming the first player to carry his bat in a Shield final. Became the first Somerset player to score a 200 (216) and a 100 (129*) in a match, v Hampshire at Southampton 1999. Scored 1070 runs (av. 66.88) in the Pura Cup 2000-01, passing during the season David Boon's record of 9096 career first-class runs for Tasmania to become the state's leading run-scorer. *Wisden Australia* Pura Cup Cricketer of the Year 2000-01; also Pura Cup Player of the Year 2000-01 (voted on by the umpires). Captain of Tasmania 1999-2001. Played in his 140th first-class match for Tasmania against Western Australia at Hobart 2001-02, overtaking David Boon's record of 139 matches to become Tasmania's most-capped first-class player. Became the third player to pass 10,000 first-class runs in Australian domestic cricket, v South Australia 2002-03. Scored 50th first-class century of his career (124) v Durham at Taunton 2004. Somerset overseas player 1999-2003 (captain 1999-2002); was an overseas player with Somerset 2004, alternating with Ricky Ponting; left Somerset at the end of the 2004 season
Best batting: 250 Somerset v Nottinghamshire, Trent Bridge 2004
Best bowling: 3-46 Somerset v Middlesex, Taunton 1999

2004 Season

	M	Inns	NO	Runs	HS	Avge	100s	50s	Ct	St	O	M	Runs	Wkts	Avge	Best	5wI	10wM
Test																		
All First	13	20	1	1013	250	53.31	3	4	7	-	1	0	8	0	-	-	-	-
1-day Int																		
C & G	2	2	0	136	131	68.00	1	-	-	-								
totesport	12	12	0	356	71	29.66	-	4	3	-								
Twenty20	3	3	1	11	8 *	5.50	-	-	-	-								

Career Performances

	M	Inns	NO	Runs	HS	Avge	100s	50s	Ct	St	Balls	Runs	Wkts	Avge	Best	5wI	10wM
Test																	
All First	256	451	31	18252	250	43.45	51	78	118	-	717	450	5	90.00	3-46	-	-
1-day Int																	
C & G	19	19	2	756	131	44.47	2	3	6	-	42	33	1	33.00	1-33	-	
totesport	80	78	1	2542	130	33.01	4	16	31	-	96	82	3	27.33	3-28	-	
Twenty20	7	7	1	139	53	23.16	-	1	2	-							

CRAVEN, V. J. Yorkshire

Name: Victor John Craven
Role: Left-hand middle/top-order bat, right-arm medium bowler
Born: 31 July 1980, Harrogate
Height: 6ft **Weight:** 13st 8lbs
Nickname: Cow, Magoo
County debut: 2000
1st-Class 50s: 6
1st-Class catches: 18
Place in batting averages: 154th av. 28.85 (2003 159th av. 28.10)
Strike rate: 51.66 (career 65.06)
Parents: Vic and Sue
Marital status: Single
Family links with cricket: 'Father played local cricket and introduced me to the game'
Education: Harrogate Grammar School
Qualifications: 10 GCSEs, GNVQ (Advanced) Business, Level 2 cricket coaching
Career outside cricket: Gym instructor
Overseas tours: Yorkshire to South Africa
Overseas teams played for: Tatura CC, Victoria 1998-99; Deepdene Bears, Melbourne 2000-01
Career highlights to date: 'Playing against West Indies and scoring 53 [for Yorkshire in 2000]'
Cricket moments to forget: 'All bad drops and misfields'
Cricketers particularly admired: Michael Atherton, Graham Thorpe
Young players to look out for: John Sadler, Michael Lumb
Other sports played: Soccer, golf, snooker
Other sports followed: Football (Leeds United), rugby league (Leeds Rhinos)
Relaxations: 'Cinema, gym, socialising with pals'

Extras: Has Yorkshire 2nd XI cap. Released by Yorkshire at the end of the 2004 season
Best batting: 81* Yorkshire v Derbyshire, Derby 2004
Best bowling: 2-18 Yorkshire v Derbyshire, Derby 2004

2004 Season

	M	Inns	NO	Runs	HS	Avge	100s	50s	Ct	St	O	M	Runs	Wkts	Avge	Best	5wI	10wM
Test																		
All First	6	8	1	202	81 *	28.85	-	1	2	-	51.4	8	191	6	31.83	2-18	-	-
1-day Int																		
C & G	1	0	0	0	0	-	-	-	1	-	6	0	20	2	10.00	2-20	-	
totesport	11	9	2	111	26	15.85	-	-	3	-	16.1	2	106	9	11.77	4-50	-	
Twenty20	4	4	2	59	44 *	29.50	-	-	2	-	6	0	62	0	-	-	-	

Career Performances

	M	Inns	NO	Runs	HS	Avge	100s	50s	Ct	St	Balls	Runs	Wkts	Avge	Best	5wI	10wM
Test																	
All First	33	55	6	1206	81 *	24.61	-	6	18	-	976	584	15	38.93	2-18	-	-
1-day Int																	
C & G	4	3	1	38	26	19.00	-	-	2	-	57	41	2	20.50	2-20	-	
totesport	36	34	4	540	59	18.00	-	2	11	-	326	297	18	16.50	4-22	-	
Twenty20	6	6	4	76	44 *	38.00	-	-	3	-	42	67	0	-	-	-	

CRAWLEY, J. P. — Hampshire

Name: John Paul Crawley
Role: Right-hand bat, occasional wicket-keeper
Born: 21 September 1971, Maldon, Essex
Height: 6ft 2in **Weight:** 13st 7lbs
Nickname: Creepy, Jonty, JC
County debut: 1990 (Lancashire), 2002 (Hampshire)
County cap: 1994 (Lancashire), 2002 (Hampshire)
Test debut: 1994
Tests: 37
One-Day Internationals: 13
1000 runs in a season: 8
1st-Class 50s: 112
1st-Class 100s: 36
1st-Class 200s: 6
1st-Class 300s: 1

1st-Class catches: 185
One-Day 100s: 6
Place in batting averages: 33rd av. 52.11 (2003 110th av. 33.76)
Strike rate: (career 156.00)
Parents: Frank and Jean (deceased)
Marital status: Married
Family links with cricket: Father played in Manchester Association; brother Mark played for Lancashire and Nottinghamshire; brother Peter plays for Warrington CC and has played for Scottish Universities and Cambridge University; uncle was excellent fast bowler; godfather umpires in Manchester Association
Education: Manchester Grammar School; Trinity College, Cambridge; Open University Business School
Qualifications: 10 O-levels, 2 AO-Levels, 3 A-levels, 2 S-levels, BA in History, MA (Cantab), Professional Certificate in Management
Overseas tours: England YC to Australia 1989-90, to New Zealand 1990-91 (captain); England A to South Africa 1993-94, to West Indies 2000-01; England to Australia 1994-95, 1998-99, 2002-03, to South Africa 1995-96, to Zimbabwe and New Zealand 1996-97, to West Indies 1997-98
Overseas teams played for: Midland-Guildford, Perth 1990
Cricketers particularly admired: Michael Atherton, Neil Fairbrother, Graham Gooch, Alec Stewart, David Gower, Allan Donald, Ian Salisbury
Other sports followed: Football (Manchester United), golf
Relaxations: 'Playing or trying to play the guitar'
Extras: Sir John Hobbs Silver Jubilee Memorial Prize 1987. Played for England YC in home series 1989, 1990 and (as captain) 1991; first to score 1000 runs in U19 'Tests'. Scored 281* v Somerest at Southport 1994, becoming the youngest player (22 years 248 days) to score a Championship double century for Lancashire. Lancashire vice-captain 1998. Topped English first-class batting averages for 1998 season (1851 runs; av. 74.04). Lancashire Player of the Year 1998. Lancashire captain 1999-2001. Left Lancashire during the 2001-02 off-season and joined Hampshire for 2002. Scored 272 on debut for Hampshire v Kent at Canterbury 2002, a Hampshire debut record. Recalled to Test side in 2002 for first time since 1998-99 and scored 64 and 100* in second Test after recall, v India at Lord's. Captain of Hampshire 2003. Scored maiden first-class triple century (301*) v Nottinghamshire at Trent Bridge 2004 to record the third-highest individual score by a Hampshire batsman in first-class cricket
Best batting: 301* Hampshire v Nottinghamshire, Trent Bridge 2004
Best bowling: 1-90 Lancashire v Sussex, Hove 1992

2004 Season

	M	Inns	NO	Runs	HS	Avge	100s	50s	Ct	St	O	M	Runs	Wkts	Avge	Best	5wI	10wM
Test																		
All First	13	21	3	938	301 *	52.11	1	5	4	-	4	1	24	0	-	-	-	-
1-day Int																		
C & G	1	1	0	15	15	15.00	-	-	-	-								
totesport	10	9	1	296	70 *	37.00	-	4	3	-								
Twenty20	6	6	0	61	21	10.16	-	-	2	-								

Career Performances

	M	Inns	NO	Runs	HS	Avge	100s	50s	Ct	St	Balls	Runs	Wkts	Avge	Best	5wI	10wM
Test	37	61	9	1800	156 *	34.61	4	9	29	-							
All First	287	471	48	19788	301 *	46.78	43	112	185	-	156	225	1	225.00	1-90	-	-
1-day Int	13	12	1	235	73	21.36	-	2	1	1							
C & G	29	28	4	946	113 *	39.41	2	5	9	-	6	4	0	-	-	-	
totesport	148	144	13	3965	102	30.26	2	29	44	3							
Twenty20	10	10	1	107	23	11.88	-	-	3	-							

CROFT, R. D. B. — Glamorgan

Name: Robert Damien Bale Croft
Role: Right-hand bat, off-spin bowler, county captain
Born: 25 May 1970, Morriston, Swansea
Height: 5ft 11in **Weight:** 13st 7lbs
Nickname: Crofty
County debut: 1989
County cap: 1992
Benefit: 2000
Test debut: 1996
Tests: 21
One-Day Internationals: 50
50 wickets in a season: 7
1st-Class 50s: 42
1st-Class 100s: 6
1st-Class 5 w. in innings: 36
1st-Class 10 w. in match: 6
1st-Class catches: 145
One-Day 100s: 4
One-Day 5 w. in innings: 1
Place in batting averages: 121st av. 33.90 (2003 147th av. 29.56)
Place in bowling averages: 81st av. 35.19 (2003 59th av. 29.66)

Strike rate: 70.94 (career 78.45)
Parents: Malcolm and Susan
Wife: Marie
Children: Callum James Bale Croft
Family links with cricket: Father and grandfather played league cricket
Education: St John Lloyd Catholic School, Llanelli; Neath Tertiary College; West Glamorgan Institute of Higher Education
Qualifications: 6 O-levels, OND Business Studies, HND Business Studies, NCA senior coaching certificate
Overseas tours: England A to Bermuda and West Indies 1991-92, to South Africa 1993-94; England to Zimbabwe and New Zealand 1996-97, to West Indies 1997-98, to Australia 1998-99, to Sharjah (Coca-Cola Cup) 1998-99, to Sri Lanka 2000-01, to Sri Lanka 2003-04; England VI to Hong Kong 2003
Career highlights to date: 'Playing for England and winning the Championship with Glamorgan in 1997'
Cricket moments to forget: 'None. This career is too short to forget any of it'
Cricketers particularly admired: Ian Botham, Viv Richards, Shane Warne
Young players to look out for: 'Everyone at Glamorgan'
Other sports played: 'Give anything a go'
Other sports followed: Football (Liverpool FC), rugby (Llanelli and Wales)
Interests/relaxations: 'Everything'
Extras: Captained England South to victory in International Youth Tournament 1989 and was voted Player of the Tournament. Glamorgan Young Player of the Year 1992. Scored Test best 37* in the third Test at Old Trafford 1998, resisting for 190 minutes to deny South Africa victory. Represented England in the 1999 World Cup. Made his 16th England Test appearance v West Indies at Edgbaston 2000, passing Jeff Jones's total of 15 Tests to become the most capped Welshman. Honorary fellow of West Glamorgan Institute of Higher Education. Scored 69-ball 119 v Surrey at The Oval in the C&G 2002, striking each of Martin Bicknell's first five balls for four as Glamorgan made 429 in reply to Surrey's 438-5. Scored 64 v Essex at Cardiff 2003, sharing with Jimmy Maher (142) in a new record opening partnership for Glamorgan in the one-day league. Glamorgan Player of the Year 2003 (jointly with Michael Kasprowicz), 2004. Glamorgan vice-captain 2002-03; appointed captain of Glamorgan during 2003, taking over from the injured Steve James. Man of the Match in England's victory v Pakistan in the final of the Hong Kong Sixes 2003. Retired from international cricket in January 2004. Took 800th first-class wicket (Ian Blackwell) v Somerset at Swansea 2004 and 200th one-day league wicket (Alex Gidman) v Gloucestershire four days later at the same ground. Scored century (106) v Lancashire at Colwyn Bay as Glamorgan clinched the totesport League division one title 2004. Cricket Society's Wetherell Award 2004 for the leading all-rounder in English first-class cricket
Best batting: 143 Glamorgan v Somerset, Taunton 1995
Best bowling: 8-66 Glamorgan v Warwickshire, Swansea 1992

2004 Season

	M	Inns	NO	Runs	HS	Avge	100s	50s	Ct	St	O	M	Runs	Wkts	Avge	Best	5wI	10wM
Test																		
All First	17	25	4	712	138	33.90	2	1	2	-	674	146	2006	57	35.19	4-52	-	-
1-day Int																		
C & G	2	2	0	144	143	72.00	1	-	-	-	20	0	95	2	47.50	2-40	-	
totesport	16	16	0	490	106	30.62	1	4	4	-	123	1	595	19	31.31	3-30	-	
Twenty20	7	5	1	45	23 *	11.25	-	-	5	-	26	0	176	8	22.00	2-27	-	

Career Performances

	M	Inns	NO	Runs	HS	Avge	100s	50s	Ct	St	Balls	Runs	Wkts	Avge	Best	5wI	10wM
Test	21	34	8	421	37 *	16.19	-	-	10	-	4619	1825	49	37.24	5-95	1	-
All First	300	440	83	9378	143	26.26	6	42	145	-	65746	30037	838	35.84	8-66	36	6
1-day Int	50	36	12	344	32	14.33	-	-	11	-	2466	1743	45	38.73	3-51	-	
C & G	38	32	6	755	143	29.03	2	3	5	-	2260	1460	45	32.44	4-47	-	
totesport	200	173	29	3548	114 *	24.63	2	19	55	-	8454	6314	212	29.78	6-20	1	
Twenty20	12	9	1	150	53	18.75	-	1	7	-	276	356	16	22.25	3-32	-	

CROFT, S. J. — Lancashire

Name: Steven John Croft
Role: Right-hand bat, right-arm medium-fast bowler
Born: 11 October 1984, Blackpool
Height: 5ft 11in **Weight:** 14st 6lbs
Nickname: Crofty, Stifler, Snakebite
County debut: No first-team appearance
Parents: Elizabeth and Lawrence
Marital status: Single
Family links with cricket: 'Dad played for his work side'
Education: Highfield High, Blackpool; Myerscough College
Qualifications: 8 GCSEs, FD Sports Studies, Level 2 cricket coach
Career outside cricket: Cricket coach
Off-season: 'Training hard'
Career highlights to date: 'Signing for Lancashire CCC'
Cricket moments to forget: 'Duck on 2nd XI debut'
Cricket superstitions: 'Left pad on first'
Cricketers particularly admired: Andrew Flintoff, Jacques Kallis, Michael Atherton, Stuart Law

Young players to look out for: Oliver Newby, Steven Crook, Gaz Cross, Tim Rees
Other sports played: Football (county trials)
Other sports followed: Football (Newcastle and Blackpool)
Favourite band: Oasis, Snow Patrol, Scissor Sisters
Relaxations: 'Music, movies, going out with friends and spending time with girlfriend'
Extras: Played for Lancashire Board XI in the C&G 2003
Opinions on cricket: 'Longer time for tea!'

2004 Season (did not make any first-class or one-day appearances)

Career Performances

	M	Inns	NO	Runs	HS	Avge	100s	50s	Ct	St	Balls	Runs	Wkts	Avge	Best	5wI	10wM
Test																	
All First																	
1-day Int																	
C & G	2	2	1	11	7	11.00	-	-	-	-	48	34	1	34.00	1-27	-	
totesport																	
Twenty20																	

CROOK, A. R. — Lancashire

Name: Andrew Richard Crook
Role: Right-hand bat, right-arm off-spin bowler
Born: 14 October 1980, Adelaide, Australia
Height: 6ft 3in
Nickname: Crooky
County debut: 2004
Strike rate: 150.00 (career 190.00)
Parents: Sue (mother) and Doug (stepfather); Martyn (father)
Marital status: Engaged to Michelle ('getting married in December 2005')
Family links with sport: 'Brother Steven Crook – Lancashire all-rounder; Martyn Crook, Dad, played professional football'
Education: Rostrevor College
Career outside cricket: 'Have worked in the finance industry and completed half of a finance degree from University of South Australia'
Overseas teams played for: South Australia 1998-99; Northern Districts, South Australia 2004-05

Career highlights to date: 'Unexpected debut game for Lancashire v Worcestershire 2004, while still on trial'
Cricket moments to forget: 'The entire final Championship game of 2004 season v Gloucestershire at Old Trafford'
Cricket superstitions: 'Left pad on first'
Cricketers particularly admired: Gary Kirsten, Adam Gilchrist, Daniel Vettori
Young players to look for: Steven Croft, Steven Crook, Damian Brandy
Other sports followed: Football (Blackburn Rovers), Australian Rules football (Essendon FC – 'the Bombers')
Favourite band: U2, Counting Crows, Coldplay
Relaxations: 'Golf, relaxing with friends and family'
Extras: Made first-class debut for South Australia v England XI at Adelaide 1998-99. Is not considered an overseas player
Opinions on cricket: 'Twenty20 is a great game and could be the way of the future. Anything that gets the crowds in through the gates like Twenty20 does can only be good for the future of cricket.'
Best batting: 27 Lancashire v Worcestershire, Worcester 2004
Best bowling: 1-8 Lancashire v Worcestershire, Worcester 2004

2004 Season

	M	Inns	NO	Runs	HS	Avge	100s	50s	Ct	St	O	M	Runs	Wkts	Avge	Best	5wI	10wM
Test																		
All First	2	4	0	68	27	17.00	-	-	-	-	50	6	212	2	106.00	1-8	-	-
1-day Int																		
C & G																		
totesport																		
Twenty20																		

Career Performances

	M	Inns	NO	Runs	HS	Avge	100s	50s	Ct	St	Balls	Runs	Wkts	Avge	Best	5wI	10wM
Test																	
All First	3	5	0	69	27	13.80	-	-	-	-	570	377	3	125.66	1-8	-	-
1-day Int																	
C & G																	
totesport																	
Twenty20																	

CROOK, S. P. Lancashire

Name: Steven Paul Crook
Role: Right-hand bat, right-arm medium-fast bowler; all-rounder
Born: 28 May 1983, Adelaide, Australia
Height: 5ft 11in **Weight:** 13st 3lbs
Nickname: Crooky, Crookster
County debut: 2003
1st-Class 50s: 1
1st-Class catches: 2
Strike rate: 68.16 (career 79.00)
Parents: 'Dad – Martyn, mum – Sue and stepfather – Doug'
Marital status: Single
Family links with sport: 'Brother Andrew – Lancs. Dad, Martyn, played pro football'
Education: Rostrevor College
Qualifications: Matriculation
Career outside cricket: 'Business interests – Emerald Street Clothing Company'
Off-season: 'Recovering from knee op'
Overseas tours: Lancashire to Cape Town 2003, 2004
Overseas teams played for: Northern Districts, South Australia 2004
Career highlights to date: 'Playing semi-final of Twenty20 2004'
Cricket moments to forget: 'Getting beaten in semi of Twenty20 2004'
Cricketers particularly admired: Andrew Flintoff, Stuart Law
Young players to look out for: Tom Smith, Steve Croft, Andy Crook
Other sports followed: Football (Tottenham Hotspur FC)
Favourite band: The Doors, The Strokes
Relaxations: 'Hanging out with mates'
Extras: Attended South Australia Cricket Academy. Represented South Australia U13-U19. Selected for Australia U19 preliminary World Cup squad 2001-02. Is not considered an overseas player
Opinions on cricket: 'More Twenty20!!'
Best batting: 68 Lancashire v Kent, Tunbridge Wells 2004
Best bowling: 2-33 Lancashire v Northamptonshire, Liverpool 2004

2004 Season

	M	Inns	NO	Runs	HS	Avge	100s	50s	Ct	St	O	M	Runs	Wkts	Avge	Best	5wI	10wM
Test																		
All First	4	5	0	157	68	31.40	-	1	1	-	68.1	5	309	6	51.50	2-33	-	-
1-day Int																		
C & G																		
totesport	6	5	0	57	21	11.40	-	-	2	-	34	0	225	4	56.25	2-62	-	
Twenty20	6	5	0	73	27	14.60	-	-	-	-	1	0	17	0	-	-	-	

Career Performances

	M	Inns	NO	Runs	HS	Avge	100s	50s	Ct	St	Balls	Runs	Wkts	Avge	Best	5wI	10wM
Test																	
All First	6	6	0	184	68	30.66	-	1	2	-	632	464	8	58.00	2-33	-	-
1-day Int																	
C & G																	
totesport	9	6	0	58	21	9.66	-	-	3	-	270	308	5	61.60	2-62	-	
Twenty20	6	5	0	73	27	14.60	-	-	-	-	6	17	0	-	-	-	

CROSS, G. D. — Lancashire

Name: Gareth David Cross
Role: Right-hand bat, wicket-keeper
Born: 20 June 1984, Bury
Height: 5ft 9in **Weight:** 11st 9lbs
Nickname: Crossy
County debut: No first-team appearance
Parents: Duncan and Margaret
Marital status: Single ('girlfriend Kim')
Family links with cricket: 'Dad played for Prestwich. Brother Matthew plays for Monton and Weaste'
Education: Moorside High School; Eccles College
Qualifications: 9 GCSEs, GNVQ Science
Off-season: 'Training'
Overseas teams played for: St Kilda, Melbourne 2002-04
Career highlights to date: 'Playing for Lancashire 2nd XI'
Cricket moments to forget: 'Tim Rees, who is now my team-mate, top-edging the ball into my head whilst I was keeping for Salford against Bolton'
Cricket superstitions: 'Just putting batting gear on in the same order'

Cricketers particularly admired: Ian Healy, Adam Gilchrist, Graeme Rummans
Young players to look out for: Steven Croft, Steven Crook
Other sports played: Football ('had a trial for Man United when I was 13')
Other sports followed: Football (Man United)
Favourite band: Eminem, Oasis
Relaxations: 'Watching football; five-a-side football'
Extras: Manchester Association Young Player of the Year. Bolton Association Young Player of the Year 2000. ECB Premier League Young Player of the Year. Liverpool Competition Player of the Year 2004. Played for Lancashire Board XI in the C&G 2003
Opinions on cricket: 'Bigger crowds because of Twenty20. More cricket in schools.'

2004 Season (did not make any first-class or one-day appearances)

Career Performances

	M	Inns	NO	Runs	HS	Avge	100s	50s	Ct	St	Balls	Runs	Wkts	Avge	Best	5wI	10wM
Test																	
All First																	
1-day Int																	
C & G	2	2	0	23	21	11.50	-	-	4	1							
totesport																	
Twenty20																	

CUSDEN, S. M. J. — Kent

Name: Simon Mark James Cusden
Role: Right-hand lower-middle-order bat, right-arm fast-medium bowler
Born: 21 February 1985, Margate
Height: 6ft 5in **Weight:** 15st 7lbs
Nickname: Cuzzy, Big Vil, Bungle, Village, Ronnie, Freak
County debut: 2004
1st-Class catches: 2
Place in bowling averages: 54th av. 31.07
Strike rate: 46.38 (career 46.38)
Parents: Mark and Karen
Marital status: 'Girlfriend'
Family links with cricket: 'Dad's a village legend'
Education: Simon Langton GS for Boys
Qualifications: 9 GCSEs, 4 AS-levels, 1 A-level

Off-season: 'Working hard in gym and Ames Levett school'
Overseas tours: Simon Langton GS to Barbados 2001; England U19 to Australia 2002-03; England U18 to Holland 2003
Career highlights to date: 'Wicket with my first ball for Kent'
Cricket moments to forget: 'Not going for the win against Bromley CC last season. Cost us the league. You were right, Ferls'
Cricket superstitions: 'None'
Cricketers particularly admired: Allan Donald, 'Fred' Flintoff, Mark Ealham
Young players to look out for: Paul Dixey, Charlie Hemphrey, Daniel Wenham, Kevin Jones
Other sports followed: Football (Chelsea FC)
Favourite band: Foo Fighters
Relaxations: 'Spending time with mates; gym, guitar'
Extras: Part of St Lawrence and Highland Court's Kent League Premier Division winning side in first season with the club. Represented England U19 v Bangladesh U19 2004. Took wicket (Mal Loye) with his first ball for Kent, v Lancashire at Tunbridge Wells in the totesport League 2004. Kent Academy Scholar of the Year 2004
Opinions on cricket: 'Too many overseas [players]. Television replays for lbw and caught behind.'
Best batting: 12* Kent v Sussex, Canterbury 2004
Best bowling: 4-68 Kent v Northamptonshire, Canterbury 2004

2004 Season

	M	Inns	NO	Runs	HS	Avge	100s	50s	Ct	St	O	M	Runs	Wkts	Avge	Best	5wI	10wM
Test																		
All First	4	6	4	22	12 *	11.00	-	-	2	-	100.3	17	404	13	31.07	4-68	-	-
1-day Int																		
C & G																		
totesport	4	2	0	4	3	2.00	-	-	-	-	21	0	126	2	63.00	1-29	-	
Twenty20																		

Career Performances

	M	Inns	NO	Runs	HS	Avge	100s	50s	Ct	St	Balls	Runs	Wkts	Avge	Best	5wI	10wM
Test																	
All First	4	6	4	22	12 *	11.00	-	-	2	-	603	404	13	31.07	4-68	-	-
1-day Int																	
C & G																	
totesport	4	2	0	4	3	2.00	-	-	-	-	126	126	2	63.00	1-29	-	
Twenty20																	

DAGNALL, C. E. Leicestershire

Name: Charles Edward Dagnall
Role: Right-hand bat, right-arm medium-fast bowler
Born: 10 July 1976, Bury, Lancashire
Height: 6ft 3in **Weight:** '14st on a bowling day; 17st on a batting day'
Nickname: Daggers
County debut: 1999 (Warwickshire), 2002 (Leicestershire)
1st-Class 5 w. in innings: 2
1st-Class catches: 5
Place in batting averages: 280th av. 7.50 (2003 236th av. 17.16)
Place in bowling averages: 61st av. 31.82 (2003 94th av. 35.89)
Strike rate: 53.10 (career 55.72)
Parents: Mike and Jackie
Marital status: Single
Family links with cricket: 'Dad ran town team'
Education: Bridgewater School, Worsley; UMIST
Qualifications: 9 GCSEs, 4 A-levels, BSc (Hons) Chemistry
Career outside cricket: Singer and radio presenter
Overseas tours: Warwickshire to Bloemfontein 2000, to Cape Town 2001
Overseas teams played for: Newtown and Chilwell, Geelong, Australia 1994-95; St Josephs, Geelong 1998-99
Career highlights to date: 'Winning B&H Gold Award v Worcestershire [at Worcester] in 2001'
Cricket moments to forget: 'Alan Richardson getting 91 v Hampshire'
Young players to look out for: Luke Wright
Other sports played: Golf, football, tennis, Scrabble
Other sports followed: Football (Burnley FC, 'still hate Stoke'); NFL (Tampa Bay Buccaneers)
Relaxations: 'Educating the masses about music; meeting new people; talking'
Extras: Played for Cumberland. Man of the Match in the Board XI final 1999 (Warwickshire v Essex). Topped Warwickshire 2nd XI batting averages 1998 and was third in bowling averages. Awarded Warwickshire 2nd XI cap 1999. Took a wicket with his fourth ball in first-class cricket v Oxford University at The Parks 1999. B&H Gold Award for his 21* batting at No. 11 (following 2-18) v Worcestershire at Worcester 2001. Left Warwickshire at the end of the 2001 season and joined Leicestershire for 2002
Best batting: 23* Leicestershire v Surrey, The Oval 2003
Best bowling: 6-50 Warwickshire v Derbyshire, Derby 2001

2004 Season

	M	Inns	NO	Runs	HS	Avge	100s	50s	Ct	St	O	M	Runs	Wkts	Avge	Best	5wI	10wM
Test																		
All First	11	12	2	75	17	7.50	-	-	4	-	256.4	46	923	29	31.82	4-37	-	-
1-day Int																		
C & G																		
totesport	8	4	2	18	7 *	9.00	-	-	1	-	53	9	205	9	22.77	3-21	-	
Twenty20	4	0	0	0	0	-	-	-	1	-	15	0	110	5	22.00	4-22	-	

Career Performances

	M	Inns	NO	Runs	HS	Avge	100s	50s	Ct	St	Balls	Runs	Wkts	Avge	Best	5wI	10wM
Test																	
All First	31	32	10	223	23 *	10.13	-	-	5	-	4848	2746	87	31.56	6-50	2	-
1-day Int																	
C & G	4	4	2	32	24 *	16.00	-	-	-	-	206	128	7	18.28	3-39	-	
totesport	45	20	5	132	28	8.80	-	-	5	-	1918	1360	58	23.44	4-34	-	
Twenty20	6	1	0	2	2	2.00	-	-	1	-	120	161	6	26.83	4-22	-	

DAKIN, J. M. — Leicestershire

Name: Jonathan Michael Dakin
Role: Left-hand bat, right-arm medium-fast bowler
Born: 28 February 1973, Hitchin, Herts
Height: 6ft 6in **Weight:** 16st
Nickname: JD, Babe, Slim
County debut: 1993 (Leicestershire), 2002 (Essex)
County cap: 2000 (Leicestershire), 2003 (Essex)
1st-Class 50s: 14
1st-Class 100s: 5
1st-Class 5 w. in innings: 1
1st-Class catches: 22
One-Day 100s: 2
One-Day 5 w. in innings: 1
Place in batting averages: 110th av. 35.00 (2003 190th av. 24.17)
Place in bowling averages: (2003 46th av. 27.47)
Strike rate: 102.75 (career 65.08)
Parents: Fred and Gloria
Marital status: Engaged

Family links with cricket: 'Brother keeps winning trophies with Ivanhoe'
Education: King Edward VII School, Johannesburg, South Africa
Qualifications: Matriculation
Career outside cricket: 'Tried many; mastered none'
Off-season: North Hobart Demons (Tasmania)
Overseas tours: Rutland Tourists to Jersey 1992; Leicestershire CCC to South Africa 1996, 1997, to Barbados, to Sri Lanka, to Anguilla
Overseas teams played for: Wanderers, South Africa 1986-92; Alberts, South Africa 1993; Kaponga CC, New Zealand 1995-96; North Hobart, Tasmania 2001-05
Career highlights to date: 'Winning two Championships; winning Twenty20 this year [2004]'
Cricket moments to forget: 'Losing three Lord's finals'
Cricket superstitions: 'Some'
Cricketers particularly admired: Brad Hodge, Darren Maddy
Young players to look out for: Tim Mason, Stu Broad
Other sports played: Golf
Other sports followed: Rugby union (Leicester Tigers)
Injuries: Out for two weeks with a hamstring injury
Favourite band: Matchbox Twenty
Relaxations: 'Fishing, going to beach'
Extras: Won three Bain Hogg trophies in four years; scored 193 against Middlesex in the Bain Hogg in 1996. C&G Man of the Match award for his 179 v Wales at Swansea 2001; at the time it was the fourth highest individual score in Gillette/NatWest/C&G history and the highest in the 50-over format of the competition. Left Leicestershire at the end of the 2001 season and joined Essex for 2002. Awarded Essex cap 2003. Left Essex at the end of the 2003 season and rejoined Leicestershire for 2004; released by Leicestershire at the end of the 2004 season
Opinions on cricket: 'Sunday league should be 40 overs.'
Best batting: 190 Leicestershire v Northamptonshire, Northampton 1997
Best bowling: 5-86 Essex v Middlesex, Lord's 2003

2004 Season

	M	Inns	NO	Runs	HS	Avge	100s	50s	Ct	St	O	M	Runs	Wkts	Avge	Best	5wI	10wM
Test																		
All First	5	9	3	210	71 *	35.00	-	1	1	-	137	28	490	8	61.25	2-66	-	-
1-day Int																		
C & G	1	1	0	7	7	7.00	-	-	1	-	8	0	40	3	13.33	3-40	-	
totesport	5	4	0	53	27	13.25	-	-	-	-	13.1	0	80	4	20.00	3-17	-	
Twenty20	6	4	1	22	14	7.33	-	-	1	-	11	1	75	2	37.50	1-11	-	

Career Performances

	M	Inns	NO	Runs	HS	Avge	100s	50s	Ct	St	Balls	Runs	Wkts	Avge	Best	5wI	10wM
Test																	
All First	79	119	14	2937	190	27.97	5	14	22	-	10543	5572	162	34.39	5-86	1	-
1-day Int																	
C & G	16	14	1	314	179	24.15	1	-	2	-	636	451	17	26.52	3-30	-	
totesport	128	111	17	1725	68 *	18.35	-	2	23	-	3562	3015	109	27.66	5-30	1	
Twenty20	11	8	2	45	14	7.50	-	-	3	-	186	235	8	29.37	2-31	-	

DALE, A. — Glamorgan

Name: Adrian Dale
Role: Right-hand bat, right-arm medium bowler
Born: 24 October 1968, Johannesburg, South Africa
Height: 5ft 11in **Weight:** 12st
Nickname: Arthur
County debut: 1989
County cap: 1992
Benefit: 2002 (£110,983)
1000 runs in a season: 4
1st-Class 50s: 58
1st-Class 100s: 21
1st-Class 200s: 2
1st-Class 5 w. in innings: 4
1st-Class catches: 107
One-Day 100s: 2
One-Day 5 w. in innings: 2
Place in batting averages: 187th av. 24.10 (2003 183rd av. 25.26)
Strike rate: (career 71.32)
Parents: John and Maureen
Wife and date of marriage: Ruth, 9 January 1999
Children: Jessica, 12 January 2001; Luke, December 2002
Family links with cricket: Father played occasionally for Glamorgan 2nd XI
Education: Chepstow Comprehensive; Swansea University
Qualifications: 9 O-levels, 3 A-levels, BA (Hons) Economics
Overseas tours: Welsh Schools U16 to Australia 1986-87; Combined Universities to Barbados 1988-89; Glamorgan to Trinidad 1989-90, 1991-92, to Zimbabwe 1990-91, to Cape Town 1992-93, 1999, 2002; England A to South Africa 1993-94
Overseas teams played for: Bionics, Zimbabwe 1990-91; Cornwall, New Zealand 1991-93, 1995-97

Career highlights: '1997 County Championship win'
Cricket moments to forget: 'Losing the 2000 B&H Cup final at Lord's'
Cricket superstitions: 'None'
Cricketers particularly admired: Ian Botham, Michael Holding, Mike Gatting
Young players to look out for: 'There's good young talent at Glamorgan'
Other sports followed: Football (Arsenal), rugby union (Wales)
Relaxations: Travelling, eating out
Extras: Played in successful Combined Universities sides of 1989 and 1990. Only batsman to score two half-centuries against the West Indies tourists in the same match in 1991 (62/51* at Swansea). Took a wicket with his first delivery at Lord's. Recorded Glamorgan's then best one-day bowling figures, 6-22, v Durham at Colwyn Bay in the Sunday League 1993. Scored 214* v Middlesex at Cardiff 1993, in the process sharing with Viv Richards (224*) in Glamorgan's highest ever partnership for any wicket – 425*. Scored two centuries in a match (108/113) v Gloucestershire at Cardiff 1999. Glamorgan CCC Player of the Year 2000, 2001. Vice-captain of Glamorgan in 2001. Glamorgan Supporters' Player of the Year 2001. Retired at the end of the 2004 season
Best batting: 214* Glamorgan v Middlesex, Cardiff 1993
Best bowling: 6-18 Glamorgan v Warwickshire, Cardiff 1993

2004 Season

	M	Inns	NO	Runs	HS	Avge	100s	50s	Ct	St	O	M	Runs	Wkts	Avge	Best	5wI	10wM
Test																		
All First	7	13	3	241	44	24.10	-	-	3	-	13	2	42	0	-	-	-	-
1-day Int																		
C & G	2	2	1	31	30	31.00	-	-	-	-	7	0	45	1	45.00	1-24	-	
totesport	12	6	2	58	26	14.50	-	-	2	-	47.2	1	260	4	65.00	1-19	-	
Twenty20	4	3	2	13	8 *	13.00	-	-	1	-	14	0	109	6	18.16	2-26	-	

Career Performances

	M	Inns	NO	Runs	HS	Avge	100s	50s	Ct	St	Balls	Runs	Wkts	Avge	Best	5wI	10wM
Test																	
All First	251	413	35	12586	214 *	33.29	23	58	107	-	15477	8274	217	38.12	6-18	4	-
1-day Int																	
C & G	40	37	5	950	110	29.68	1	3	7	-	1527	1122	32	35.06	3-15	-	
totesport	220	183	25	4380	82	27.72	-	25	48	-	6672	5669	178	31.84	6-22	1	
Twenty20	9	8	2	42	18	7.00	-	-	2	-	174	248	11	22.54	2-15	-	

DALRYMPLE, J. W. M. Middlesex

Name: James (Jamie) William Murray Dalrymple
Role: Right-hand bat, off-spin bowler
Born: 21 January 1981, Nairobi, Kenya
Height: 6ft **Weight:** 13st 7lbs
Nickname: JD, Pest
County debut: 2000 (one-day), 2001 (first-class)
County cap: 2004
1st-Class 50s: 6
1st-Class 100s: 2
1st-Class 200s: 2
1st-Class 5 w. in innings: 1
1st-Class catches: 25
One-Day 100s: 2
Place in batting averages: 77th av. 40.38 (2003 76th av. 39.66)
Place in bowling averages: 110th av. 38.67 (2003 132nd av. 44.08)
Strike rate: 65.75 (career 86.26)
Parents: Douglas and Patricia
Marital status: Single
Family links with cricket: 'Dad played lots of club cricket.' Brother Simon played for Oxford University in 2002 and 2004
Education: Radley College, Abingdon; St Peter's College, Oxford University
Qualifications: 10 GCSEs, 5 A-levels, degree in History
Overseas tours: Middlesex to South Africa 2000
Cricket moments to forget: 'Middlesex v Warwickshire at Edgbaston 2003 – being part of the loss of eight wickets in a session, and the match'
Cricketers particularly admired: David Gower, Carl Hooper, Ian Botham, Mark Waugh
Young players to look out for: Tom Mees
Other sports played: Rugby (college), hockey (university)
Other sports followed: Rugby (Northampton RUFC)
Favourite band: 'Don't have a favourite'
Relaxations: Reading, golf
Extras: Represented England U19 v Sri Lanka U19 2000. Played for Oxford University CCE 2001 and (as captain) 2002. Represented British Universities 2001 and (as captain) 2002. Oxford Blue 2001, 2002 (captain) and 2003 (captain). Became third ever Oxford University batsman to score a double century in the Varsity Match (236*) at Fenner's 2003, in the process sharing with Neil Millar (108) in a record

third-wicket partnership for the match (263); also took 5-49 in the Cambridge first innings and scored 105* in the 50-over Varsity Match at Lord's. Scored maiden one-day century (104*; second fifty in 14 balls) v Wales Minor Counties at Lamphey in the C&G 2004, winning Man of the Match award; scored another century (107) v Glamorgan at Lord's in the following round, also winning Man of the Match award. Scored maiden Championship double century (244; the highest score by a Middlesex batsman v Surrey) at The Oval 2004, in the process sharing with Ed Joyce (123) in a record fifth-wicket partnership for Middlesex in matches against Surrey (298). Awarded Middlesex cap 2004

Opinions on cricket: 'How about some turning wickets?'

Best batting: 244 Middlesex v Surrey, The Oval 2004

Best bowling: 5-49 Oxford University v Cambridge University, Fenner's 2003

2004 Season

	M	Inns	NO	Runs	HS	Avge	100s	50s	Ct	St	O	M	Runs	Wkts	Avge	Best	5wI	10wM
Test																		
All First	16	25	4	848	244	40.38	1	4	9	-	306.5	47	1083	28	38.67	4-66	-	-
1-day Int																		
C & G	3	3	1	231	107	115.50	2	-	3	-	17	0	65	3	21.66	2-42	-	
totesport	18	13	1	201	58	16.75	-	1	5	-	81	2	385	11	35.00	2-29	-	
Twenty20	4	3	0	48	31	16.00	-	-	2	-	10	0	101	2	50.50	2-38	-	

Career Performances

	M	Inns	NO	Runs	HS	Avge	100s	50s	Ct	St	Balls	Runs	Wkts	Avge	Best	5wI	10wM
Test																	
All First	36	60	8	1943	244	37.36	4	6	25	-	4831	2657	56	47.44	5-49	1	-
1-day Int																	
C & G	3	3	1	231	107	115.50	2	-	3	-	102	65	3	21.66	2-42	-	
totesport	50	42	10	670	58	20.93	-	2	18	-	1503	1224	39	31.38	4-14	-	
Twenty20	4	3	0	48	31	16.00	-	-	2	-	60	101	2	50.50	2-38	-	

22. Who did Sri Lanka beat by 149 runs at Colombo in September 1985 to claim their first Test match victory?

DANISH KANERIA Essex

Name: Danish Prabha Shanker Kaneria
Role: Right-hand bat, right-arm leg-spin and googly bowler
Born: 16 December 1980, Karachi, Pakistan
Height: 6ft 1in
Nickname: Danny Boy, Dani
County debut: 2004
County cap: 2004
Test debut: 2000-01
Tests: 18
One-Day Internationals: 10
50 wickets in a season: 1
1st-Class 5 w. in innings: 24
1st-Class 10 w. in match: 3
1st-Class catches: 22
Place in batting averages: 276th av. 7.83
Place in bowling averages: 21st av. 25.53
Strike rate: 53.61 (career 51.13)
Parents: Prabha Shanker Kaneria and Babita P. Kaneria
Wife and date of marriage: Dharmeta Danish Kaneria, 15 February 2004
Family links with cricket: Cousin, wicket-keeper Anil Dalpat, played nine Tests for Pakistan 1983-84
Education: St Patrick's High School, Karachi
Off-season: Playing cricket
Overseas tours: Pakistan U19 to Sri Lanka (U19 World Cup) 1999-2000; Pakistan A to Kenya 2000, to Sri Lanka 2001; Pakistan to Bangladesh 2001-02, to Sharjah (v West Indies) 2001-02, to Sharjah (v Australia) 2002-03, to England (NatWest Challenge) 2003, to New Zealand 2003-04, to Australia 2004-05, to India 2004-05, plus other one-day tournaments in Sharjah and Sri Lanka
Overseas teams played for: Pakistan National Shipping Corporation 1998-99; Karachi Whites 1998-99, 2000-02; Pakistan Reserves 1999-2000; Habib Bank 1999-2004; Karachi 2003-04; Karachi Blues 2004-05
Career highlights to date: 'Playing for Pakistan. English county cricket'
Cricket moments to forget: 'The first Test match played for Pakistan' (*2-89/0-30 in the drawn second Test at Faisalabad 2000-01*)
Cricket superstitions: 'I kiss the ground when taking the field'
Cricketers particularly admired: Abdul Qadir, Viv Richards, Joel Garner
Other sports played: Football, table tennis
Other sports followed: Football (Brazil)
Favourite band: 'I like Indian music'
Relaxations: 'Listening to music and being with family'

Extras: Represented Pakistan U19 v South Africa U19 1998-99. Only the second Hindu to play in Tests for Pakistan, after his cousin Anil Dalpat. Had match figures of 12-94 (6-42/6-52) v Bangladesh at Multan in the first match of the Asian Test Championship 2001-02. Man of the [Test] Series, Pakistan in Bangladesh 2001-02. Had match figures of 7-111 (2-65/5-46) in the first Test v South Africa at Lahore 2003-04, winning Man of the Match award. Joined Essex as an overseas player for 2004; has returned for 2005. Had match figures of 13-186 (6-121/7-65) v Yorkshire at Chelmsford 2004, the best return for Essex since Mark Ilott's 14-105 v Northamptonshire at Luton 1995. Awarded Essex cap 2004
Best batting: 42 Habib Bank v Allied Bank, Sheikhupura 2001-02
Best bowling: 7-39 Karachi Whites v Gujranwala, Karachi 2000-01
Stop press: Had match figures of 10-190 (3-72/7-118) in the second Test v Sri Lanka at Karachi 2004-05, winning Man of the Match award. Returned first innings figures of 7-188 (from 49.3 overs) in the third Test v Australia at Sydney 2004-05, in the process taking his 100th Test wicket (Shane Warne)

2004 Season

	M	Inns	NO	Runs	HS	Avge	100s	50s	Ct	St	O	M	Runs	Wkts	Avge	Best	5wI	10wM
Test																		
All First	11	13	7	47	13 *	7.83	-	-	7	-	563	123	1609	63	25.53	7-65	4	1
1-day Int																		
C & G	2	1	0	2	2	2.00	-	-	-	-	20	1	62	5	12.40	3-30	-	
totesport	9	4	0	9	7	2.25	-	-	1	-	54.3	2	246	6	41.00	2-17	-	
Twenty20																		

Career Performances

	M	Inns	NO	Runs	HS	Avge	100s	50s	Ct	St	Balls	Runs	Wkts	Avge	Best	5wI	10wM
Test	18	21	10	57	15	5.18	-	-	4	-	4459	2087	72	28.98	7-77	5	1
All First	64	74	37	271	42	7.32	-	-	22	-	16159	7318	316	23.15	7-39	24	3
1-day Int	10	5	4	4	3 *	4.00	-	-	-	-	542	382	9	42.44	3-31	-	
C & G	2	1	0	2	2	2.00	-	-	-	-	120	62	5	12.40	3-30	-	
totesport	9	4	0	9	7	2.25	-	-	1	-	327	246	6	41.00	2-17	-	
Twenty20																	

23. Where is the 2005 ICC Trophy tournament, which determines the final five qualifiers for the 2007 World Cup, scheduled to be played?

DAVIES, A. P. Glamorgan

Name: Andrew Philip Davies
Role: Left-hand bat, right-arm medium-fast bowler
Born: 7 November 1976, Neath
Height: 6ft **Weight:** 12st 3lbs
Nickname: Diver
County debut: 1995
1st-Class 5 w. in innings: 1
1st-Class catches: 4
One-Day 5 w. in innings: 2
Strike rate: 111.33 (career 65.31)
Parents: Anne and Phil
Wife and date of marriage: Nerys, 1 February 2003
Children: 'Twins on the way!'
Family links with cricket: 'Brother plays local league cricket. Dad used to play'
Education: Dwr-y-Felin, Neath; Christ College, Brecon
Qualifications: 7 GCSEs, 1 A-level, Level 2 coach
Career outside cricket: '12-month contracts now'
Off-season: 'Training, cooking and preparing a nursery'
Overseas tours: Wales MC to Barbados; Glamorgan to Pretoria, to Cape Town (twice)
Overseas teams played for: Marist CC, Whangarei, New Zealand 1995-96; Marist Old Boys, Napier, New Zealand
Career highlights to date: '2 x Sunday League champions'
Cricket moments to forget: 'Surrey scoring 400 against us in 50 overs [in the C&G 2002]. We gave them a scare, though!'
Cricket superstitions: 'None'
Cricketers particularly admired: Matt Maynard, Robert Croft, Matthew Elliott
Young players to look out for: 'Some good batters but don't want to let them know'
Other sports played: 'Try to play golf'
Other sports followed: Football
Injuries: Out for six weeks with a torn oblique
Favourite band: Oasis, Stereophonics
Relaxations: 'Reading, crosswords; trying to get a pint off Crofty'
Extras: Wales U19 Player of the Year 1995. Wales Player of the Year 1996. 2nd XI cap 1998. 2nd XI Player of the Year 1998, 1999. 1st XI Player of the Month August-September 1998. Glamorgan's leading wicket-taker (21) in the NUL 2001
Best batting: 40 Glamorgan v Essex, Cardiff 2001
Best bowling: 5-79 Glamorgan v Worcestershire, Cardiff 2002

2004 Season

	M	Inns	NO	Runs	HS	Avge	100s	50s	Ct	St	O	M	Runs	Wkts	Avge	Best	5wI	10wM
Test																		
All First	2	3	0	10	6	3.33	-	-	-	-	55.4	7	203	3	67.66	2-95	-	-
1-day Int																		
C & G	2	1	1	7	7 *	-	-	-	-	-	20	3	96	3	32.00	2-58	-	
totesport	12	5	3	12	8 *	6.00	-	-	-	-	86.1	1	471	23	20.47	4-29	-	
Twenty20	6	1	0	4	4	4.00	-	-	2	-	23.1	1	159	10	15.90	3-17	-	

Career Performances

	M	Inns	NO	Runs	HS	Avge	100s	50s	Ct	St	Balls	Runs	Wkts	Avge	Best	5wI	10wM
Test																	
All First	23	28	4	264	40	11.00	-	-	4	-	2939	1792	45	39.82	5-79	1	-
1-day Int																	
C & G	6	4	3	17	7 *	17.00	-	-	-	-	270	263	9	29.22	5-19	1	
totesport	56	23	13	95	24	9.50	-	-	8	-	2321	1909	91	20.97	5-39	1	
Twenty20	6	1	0	4	4	4.00	-	-	2	-	139	159	10	15.90	3-17	-	

DAVIES, M. A. Durham

Name: Mark Anthony Davies
Role: Right-hand bat, right-arm fast-medium bowler
Born: 4 October 1980, Stockton-on-Tees
Height: 6ft 3in **Weight:** 13st
Nickname: Davo
County debut: 1998 (one-day), 2002 (first-class)
50 wickets in a season: 1
1st-Class 5 w. in innings: 5
1st-Class catches: 5
Place in batting averages: 260th av. 12.22
Place in bowling averages: 3rd av. 18.76 (2003 134th av. 46.27)
Strike rate: 36.52 (career 50.17)
Parents: Howard and Mandy
Marital status: Single
Education: Northfield School, Billingham; Stockton Sixth Form College
Qualifications: 5 GCSEs, NVQ Level 3 Sport and Recreation
Overseas tours: Durham to South Africa 2002
Overseas teams played for: North Kalgoorlie CC, Western Australia

Career highlights to date: 'Gaining promotion in the NUL 2001'
Cricketers particularly admired: Glenn McGrath
Other sports played: Football, golf, boxing
Other sports followed: Football (Middlesbrough)
Injuries: Out from late July 2004 due to a side injury
Relaxations: Socialising, golf
Extras: Represented England U19 v Sri Lanka U19 2000. Played for Durham Board XI in the NatWest 2000 and for Durham Board XI and Durham in the C&G 2001. Attended Durham Academy. Took 50 first-class wickets in a season for the first time and was the first bowler to reach the milestone in 2004
Best batting: 33 Durham v Derbyshire, Darlington 2002
Best bowling: 6-44 Durham v Derbyshire, Riverside 2004

2004 Season

	M	Inns	NO	Runs	HS	Avge	100s	50s	Ct	St	O	M	Runs	Wkts	Avge	Best	5wI	10wM
Test																		
All First	10	17	8	110	29	12.22	-	-	2	-	304.2	75	938	50	18.76	6-44	4	-
1-day Int																		
C & G	1	1	0	3	3	3.00	-	-	-	-	8	1	41	1	41.00	1-41	-	
totesport	12	4	2	12	8 *	6.00	-	-	2	-	67	9	326	9	36.22	3-16	-	
Twenty20	5	3	2	8	6	8.00	-	-	-	-	18	0	97	6	16.16	2-14	-	

Career Performances

	M	Inns	NO	Runs	HS	Avge	100s	50s	Ct	St	Balls	Runs	Wkts	Avge	Best	5wI	10wM
Test																	
All First	29	49	18	358	33	11.54	-	-	5	-	4867	2389	97	24.62	6-44	5	-
1-day Int																	
C & G	9	6	1	11	6	2.20	-	-	-	-	390	261	6	43.50	1-11	-	
totesport	47	24	9	134	31 *	8.93	-	-	9	-	1938	1357	50	27.14	4-13	-	
Twenty20	9	4	3	11	6	11.00	-	-	2	-	204	241	8	30.12	2-14	-	

DAVIES, S. M. — Worcestershire

Name: Steven (Steve) Michael Davies
Role: Left-hand bat, wicket-keeper
Born: 17 June 1986, Bromsgrove
Height: 5ft 11in **Weight:** 11st 6lbs
Nickname: Davo
County debut: No first-team appearance (*see **Extras***)
Parents: Lin and Michael
Marital status: Single
Education: King Charles I School
Qualifications: 9 GCSEs, 1 A-level, 2 AS-levels

Off-season: Part-time student at ECB National Academy
Overseas tours: England U17 to Holland 2003; England U19 to Bangladesh (U19 World Cup) 2003-04, to India 2004-05 (captain)
Career highlights to date: 'Semi-final of U19 World Cup against West Indies. First-team debut for Worcestershire against Sri Lanka A'
Cricketers particularly admired: Matthew Hayden, Ian Healy, Sachin Tendulkar, Brian Lara, Steve Rhodes, Virender Sehwag
Young players to look out for: Adam Harrison, James Hildreth, Luke Wright, Will Gifford
Other sports played: Basketball (trials for England), golf
Other sports followed: Football (Arsenal)
Favourite band: Oasis
Relaxations: 'Listening to music, playing golf'
Extras: Played for Worcestershire Board XI in the C&G 2003. Represented England U19 v Bangladesh U19 2004. Played for Worcestershire v Sri Lanka A in a limited overs fixture at Worcester 2004 but has yet to appear for the county in first-class cricket or domestic competition. ECB National Academy 2004-05 (part-time)
Opinions on cricket: 'More Twenty20 cricket as it brings in the crowds!'

2004 Season (did not make any first-class or one-day appearances)

Career Performances

	M	Inns	NO	Runs	HS	Avge	100s	50s	Ct	St	Balls	Runs	Wkts	Avge	Best	5wI	10wM
Test																	
All First																	
1-day Int																	
C & G	2	1	0	13	13	13.00	-	-	-	-							
totesport																	
Twenty20																	

DAVIS, M. J. G. Sussex

Name: Mark Jeffrey Gronow Davis
Role: Right-hand bat, right-arm off-spin bowler
Born: 10 October 1971, Port Elizabeth, South Africa
Height: 6ft 2in **Weight:** 12st 8lbs
Nickname: Davo, Doxy, Sparky
County debut: 2001
County cap: 2002
1st-Class 50s: 7
1st-Class 100s: 2
1st-Class 5 w. in innings: 5
1st-Class 10 w. in match: 1
1st-Class catches: 67
Place in batting averages: 247th av. 15.54 (2003 175th av. 25.90)
Place in bowling averages: 60th av. 31.52 (2003 144th av. 50.73)
Strike rate: 67.28 (career 78.72)
Parents: Jeremy and Marilyn
Wife and date of marriage: Candice, 8 April 2000
Family links with cricket: 'Father supports Sussex. My brothers, William and Patrick, play league cricket in Sussex'
Education: Grey High School; University of Pretoria
Qualifications: BA Psychology and English
Career outside cricket: Coach of UPE International Cricket Academy in Port Elizabeth
Overseas tours: South Africa U24 to Sri Lanka 1995; Northern Transvaal to Zimbabwe 1992-93, to Kenya 1994-95, 1995-96
Overseas teams played for: Northern Transvaal/Northerns 1991-92 – 2000-01
Career highlights to date: 'Winning the County Championship [2003]. It was second to none, unbelievable! That and my 168 v Middlesex the same season'
Cricket superstitions: 'None'
Cricketers particularly admired: 'All my team-mates', Tim May, Shane Warne
Young players to look out for: Matt Prior, Tim Ambrose
Other sports played: Golf, tennis
Other sports followed: Rugby ('support the Springboks'), football (Middlesbrough)
Favourite band: 'Very eclectic tastes – no real favourite'
Relaxations: 'Golf, music, going out with friends, watching good movies'
Extras: Made first-class debut for Northern Transvaal B 1990-91. Captain of Northern Transvaal/Northerns 1997-2000, during which time the province won the first two

trophies in its history. Represented South Africa A v Zimbabwe 1995. Member of MCC. Scored maiden first-class century (111) v Somerset at Taunton 2002, in the process sharing with Robin Martin-Jenkins (205*) in a record eighth-wicket partnership for Sussex (291); the stand fell one run short of the record eighth-wicket partnership in English first-class cricket, set in 1896. Scored career best 168 v Middlesex at Hove 2003, sharing with Matt Prior (148) in a record seventh-wicket partnership for Sussex in matches against Middlesex (195) and with Billy Taylor (35*) in a record tenth-wicket partnership for Sussex in matches against Middlesex (106). Is not considered an overseas player

Best batting: 168 Sussex v Middlesex, Hove 2003

Best bowling: 8-37 Northerns B v North West, Potchefstroom 1994-95

2004 Season

	M	Inns	NO	Runs	HS	Avge	100s	50s	Ct	St	O	M	Runs	Wkts	Avge	Best	5wI	10wM
Test																		
All First	10	14	3	171	43	15.54	-	-	6	-	235.3	40	662	21	31.52	4-57	-	-
1-day Int																		
C & G	1	1	0	1	1	1.00	-	-	-	-	7	0	29	0	-	-	-	
totesport	15	10	4	98	21	16.33	-	-	3	-	101.4	3	494	15	32.93	4-40	-	
Twenty20	4	3	0	17	12	5.66	-	-	2	-	13	0	94	5	18.80	2-24	-	

Career Performances

	M	Inns	NO	Runs	HS	Avge	100s	50s	Ct	St	Balls	Runs	Wkts	Avge	Best	5wI	10wM
Test																	
All First	121	181	30	2857	168	18.92	2	7	67	-	18029	8191	229	35.76	8-37	5	1
1-day Int																	
C & G	8	6	5	96	32 *	96.00	-	-	-	-	450	296	4	74.00	2-37	-	
totesport	62	41	13	486	37	17.35	-	-	13	-	2676	2061	64	32.20	4-14	-	
Twenty20	9	7	3	52	18 *	13.00	-	-	4	-	192	222	11	20.18	3-13	-	

24. Which former Leicestershire and Lancashire coach was appointed Holland coach in late 2004?

DAWOOD, I. — Yorkshire

Name: Ismail Dawood
Role: Right-hand bat, wicket-keeper
Born: 23 July 1976, Dewsbury
Height: 5ft 8in
County debut: 1994 (Northamptonshire), 1996 (Worcestershire), 1998 (Glamorgan), 2004 (Yorkshire)
1st-Class 50s: 2
1st-Class 100s: 1
1st-Class catches: 60
1st-Class stumpings: 5
Place in batting averages: 118th av. 34.44
Family links with cricket: Grandfather and father played local league cricket
Education: Batley Grammar School
Qualifications: 8 GCSEs, NCA Coaching Award
Overseas tours: Glamorgan to South Africa 1998-99; England U19 to Sri Lanka 1993-94, to West Indies 1994-95
Overseas teams played for: Grafton, Auckland 1992-93
Extras: Represented England U19 v India U19 1994 and v South Africa U19 1995. Left Northamptonshire at the end of the 1995 season and joined Worcestershire in 1996. Joined Glamorgan for the 1998 season. Scored maiden first-class century (102) v Gloucestershire at Cardiff 1999; took five catches at short leg in the same match. Conceded no byes in Lancashire's 556-6 dec. at Blackpool 1999, setting a Glamorgan record for a clean sheet. Left Glamorgan at the end of the 1999 season. Played for Herefordshire in the Minor Counties 2000-03, the NatWest 2000 and the C&G 2001-04. Represented ECB XI in the Triple Crown Tournament 2001. Played for Bradford/Leeds University CCE 2003-04. Represented British Universities v Zimbabweans 2003 and v New Zealanders and Sri Lanka A 2004
Best batting: 102 Glamorgan v Gloucestershire, Cardiff 1999

2004 Season

	M	Inns	NO	Runs	HS	Avge	100s	50s	Ct	St	O	M	Runs	Wkts	Avge	Best	5wI	10wM
Test																		
All First	9	14	5	310	75	34.44	-	1	13	2								
1-day Int																		
C & G	1	1	0	30	30	30.00	-	-	2	-								
totesport	9	6	3	37	20	12.33	-	-	7	3								
Twenty20	3	2	1	5	5 *	5.00	-	-	1	-								

Career Performances

	M	Inns	NO	Runs	HS	Avge	100s	50s	Ct	St	Balls	Runs	Wkts	Avge	Best	5wI	10wM
Test																	
All First	27	44	8	796	102	22.11	1	2	60	5							
1-day Int																	
C & G	12	11	0	330	60	30.00	-	2	13	3							
totesport	23	19	6	179	57	13.76	-	1	20	6							
Twenty20	3	2	1	5	5 *	5.00	-	-	1	-							

DAWSON, R. K. J. — Yorkshire

Name: Richard Kevin James Dawson
Role: Right-hand bat, right-arm off-spin bowler
Born: 4 August 1980, Doncaster
Height: 6ft 4in **Weight:** 11st 4lbs
Nickname: Billy Dog
County debut: 2001
County cap: 2004
Test debut: 2001-02
Tests: 7
1st-Class 50s: 7
1st-Class 5 w. in innings: 5
1st-Class catches: 35
Place in batting averages: 183rd av. 24.52 (2003 152nd av. 29.18)
Place in bowling averages: 79th av. 34.86 (2003 140th av. 49.41)
Strike rate: 63.27 (career 73.91)
Parents: Kevin and Pat
Marital status: Single
Family links with cricket: Brother Gareth plays for Doncaster Town CC
Education: Batley GS; Exeter University
Qualifications: 10 GCSEs, 4 A-levels, degree in Exercise and Sports Science
Overseas tours: England U18 to Bermuda 1997; England U19 to New Zealand 1998-99; England to India and New Zealand 2001-02, to Australia 2002-03; ECB National Academy to Sri Lanka 2002-03; England A to Sri Lanka 2004-05
Cricketers particularly admired: Steve Waugh, Graeme Swann
Other sports played: Football
Other sports followed: Football (Doncaster Rovers FC)
Relaxations: Sleeping, listening to music
Extras: Captained England U15. Sir John Hobbs Silver Jubilee Memorial Prize 1995.

Played for Devon 1999 and 2000. Represented England U19 v Australia U19 in 1999. Captained British Universities 2000. NBC Denis Compton Award for the most promising young Yorkshire player 2001. Made Test debut in first Test v India at Mohali 2001-02, taking 4-134 in India's first innings. Awarded Yorkshire cap 2004
Best batting: 87 Yorkshire v Kent, Canterbury 2002
Best bowling: 6-82 Yorkshire v Glamorgan, Scarborough 2001

2004 Season

	M	Inns	NO	Runs	HS	Avge	100s	50s	Ct	St	O	M	Runs	Wkts	Avge	Best	5wI	10wM
Test																		
All First	15	23	0	564	81	24.52	-	3	11	-	379.4	71	1255	36	34.86	5-40	1	-
1-day Int																		
C & G	4	1	0	4	4	4.00	-	-	1	-	22	3	109	1	109.00	1-36	-	
totesport	17	10	4	34	6 *	5.66	-	-	8	-	100.5	5	436	22	19.81	4-20	-	
Twenty20	5	1	0	0	0	0.00	-	-	-	-	17	0	142	6	23.66	2-23	-	

Career Performances

	M	Inns	NO	Runs	HS	Avge	100s	50s	Ct	St	Balls	Runs	Wkts	Avge	Best	5wI	10wM
Test	7	13	3	114	19 *	11.40	-	-	3	-	1116	677	11	61.54	4-134	-	-
All First	66	101	12	2012	87	22.60	-	7	35	-	10718	5923	145	40.84	6-82	5	-
1-day Int																	
C & G	13	4	0	18	7	4.50	-	-	3	-	567	448	10	44.80	4-34	-	
totesport	47	33	6	188	41	6.96	-	-	17	-	1639	1254	52	24.11	4-20	-	
Twenty20	5	1	0	0	0	0.00	-	-	-	-	102	142	6	23.66	2-23	-	

DEAN, K. J. — Derbyshire

Name: Kevin James Dean
Role: Left-hand bat, left-arm medium bowler
Born: 16 October 1975, Derby
Height: 6ft 5in **Weight:** 14st
Nickname: Deany, Red Face, The Wall, George
County debut: 1996
County cap: 1998
50 wickets in a season: 2
1st-Class 50s: 2
1st-Class 5 w. in innings: 15
1st-Class 10 w. in match: 4
1st-Class catches: 20
One-Day 5 w. in innings: 1
Place in batting averages: 221st av. 19.50 (2003 288th av. 7.04)
Place in bowling averages: 44th av. 29.85 (2003 110th av. 38.85)

Strike rate: 43.20 (career 44.08)
Parents: Ken and Dorothy
Marital status: Single
Education: Leek High School; Leek College of Further Education
Qualifications: 8 GCSEs, 1 AS-level, 3 A-levels, ECB Level 2 coaching
Career outside cricket: Working for Ladbrokes
Off-season: 'Being a member of the ATR and Racing UK crew'
Overseas tours: MCC to Australia 2002-03
Overseas teams played for: Sturt CC, Adelaide 1996-97
Career highlights to date: 'Can't split – 1) Hitting the winning runs against Australia for Derbyshire in 1997; 2) Getting either hat-trick'
Cricket moments to forget: 'Spending time out injured'
Cricket superstitions: 'Last person out of changing room for first session of fielding'
Cricketers particularly admired: Dominic Cork, Wasim Akram, Michael Holding
Young players to look out for: Simon Cusden, Ross Whitely
Other sports played: Football, golf, tennis, snooker
Other sports followed: Football (Derby County), horse racing
Injuries: 'Red face – due to continual running into wind'
Favourite band: Stereophonics, Oasis, Pink, DJ Sammy
Relaxations: 'Going horse racing. Talking with Sutts and trying to keep it vaguely interesting. Fleecing fruit machines with Tetley, but not casinos, yet! Short-term financial investments'
Extras: A member of the Staffordshire U16 Texaco winning team. Achieved first-class hat-trick (E. Smith, Hooper, Llong) against Kent at Derby 1998. Took second first-class hat-trick (Habib, Kumble, Ormond) v Leicestershire at Leicester 2000. Joint leading wicket-taker in English first-class cricket 2002 (with Martin Saggers) with 83 wickets (av. 23.50). Derbyshire Player of the Year 2002 (jointly with Michael DiVenuto)
Opinions on cricket: 'I feel we have everything about right now as regards divisions, amount of cricket, academies. Just give it a chance without wanting to change something almost every season.'
Best batting: 54* Derbyshire v Worcestershire, Derby 2002
Best bowling: 8-52 Derbyshire v Kent, Canterbury 2000

2004 Season

	M	Inns	NO	Runs	HS	Avge	100s	50s	Ct	St	O	M	Runs	Wkts	Avge	Best	5wI	10wM
Test																		
All First	7	10	4	117	35	19.50	-	-	3	-	144	18	597	20	29.85	5-86	1	-
1-day Int																		
C & G																		
totesport	6	5	1	7	6	1.75	-	-	-	-	41.3	5	208	2	104.00	1-42	-	
Twenty20																		

Career Performances

	M	Inns	NO	Runs	HS	Avge	100s	50s	Ct	St	Balls	Runs	Wkts	Avge	Best	5wI	10wM
Test																	
All First	96	130	41	1059	54 *	11.89	-	2	20	-	15518	8866	352	25.18	8-52	15	4
1-day Int																	
C & G	15	5	2	12	8	4.00	-	-	6	-	822	546	28	19.50	3-6	-	
totesport	89	44	23	195	16 *	9.28	-	-	14	-	3863	2988	93	32.12	5-32	1	
Twenty20																	

DE BRUYN, Z. Worcestershire

Name: Zander de Bruyn
Role: Right-hand bat, right-arm fast-medium bowler
Born: 5 July 1975, Johannesburg, South Africa
County debut: No first-team appearance
1st-Class 50s: 17
1st-Class 100s: 4
1st-Class 200s: 1
1st-Class 5 w. in innings: 1
1st-Class catches: 28
One-Day 100s: 1
Strike rate: (career 59.34)
Education: Hoerskool Helpmekaar; Hoerskool Randburg
Overseas tours: South Africa A to Zimbabwe 2004; South Africa to India 2004-05
Overseas teams played for: Transvaal/Gauteng 1995-96 – 2000-01; Easterns 2002-03 – 2003-04; Titans 2004-05 –
Extras: Represented South Africa Schools. Played for MCC v New Zealand A and v Zimbabwe 2000. Played for Surrey Board XI in the NatWest 2000 and C&G 2001,

winning Man of the Match award v Huntingdonshire at Cheam 2001 (113*/2-22). Scored 169 v Western Province in the final of the SuperSport Series 2002-03 at Benoni. Scored 1015 runs (av. 72.50) in the SuperSport Series 2003-04, becoming only the second player (after Barry Richards) to record 1000 runs in a season in the South African domestic first-class competition. Has won numerous domestic awards in South Africa, including Man of the Match v Western Province in the semi-finals of the Standard Bank Cup at Cape Town 2003-04 (5-44/29). Has joined Worcestershire as an overseas player for 2005

Best batting: 266* Easterns v Griqualand West, Kimberley 2003-04

Best bowling: 6-120 Transvaal B v Western Province B, Cape Town 1996-97

Stop press: Made Test debut in the first Test v India at Kanpur 2004-05

2004 Season (did not make any first-class or one-day appearances)

Career Performances

	M	Inns	NO	Runs	HS	Avge	100s	50s	Ct	St	Balls	Runs	Wkts	Avge	Best	5wI	10wM
Test																	
All First	48	87	11	3018	266 *	39.71	5	17	28	-	4095	2229	69	32.30	6-120	1	-
1-day Int																	
C & G	3	3	1	158	113 *	79.00	1	-	-	-	18	22	2	11.00	2-22	-	
totesport																	
Twenty20																	

DEFREITAS, P. A. J. Leicestershire

Name: Phillip Anthony Jason DeFreitas

Role: Right-hand bat, right-arm fast-medium bowler

Born: 18 February 1966, Scotts Head, Dominica

Height: 6ft **Weight:** 13st 7lbs

Nickname: Padge, Daffy, Linchy

County debut: 1985 (Leics), 1989 (Lancs), 1994 (Derbys)

County cap: 1986 (Leics), 1989 (Lancs), 1994 (Derbys)

Benefit: 2004 (Leics)

Test debut: 1986-87

Tests: 44

One-Day Internationals: 103

50 wickets in a season: 14

1st-Class 50s: 54

1st-Class 100s: 10
1st-Class 5 w. in innings: 61
1st-Class 10 w. in match: 6
1st-Class catches: 127
One-Day 5 w. in innings: 7
Place in batting averages: 192nd av. 23.17 (2003 214th av. 21.43)
Place in bowling averages: 74th av. 34.32 (2003 23rd av. 24.05)
Strike rate: 66.51 (career 57.76)
Parents: Sybil and Martin
Marital status: Divorced
Children: Alexandra Elizabeth Jane, 5 August 1991
Family links with cricket: Father played in Windward Islands. All six brothers play
Education: Willesden High School
Qualifications: 2 O-levels
Overseas tours: England YC to West Indies 1984-85; England to Australia 1986-87, to Pakistan, Australia and New Zealand 1987-88, to India (Nehru Cup) and West Indies 1989-90, to Australia 1990-91, to New Zealand 1991-92, to India and Sri Lanka 1992-93, to Australia 1994-95, to South Africa 1995-96, to India and Pakistan (World Cup) 1995-96; England XI to New Zealand (Cricket Max) 1997
Overseas teams played for: Port Adelaide, South Australia 1985; Mosman, Sydney 1988; Boland, South Africa 1993-94, 1995-96
Cricketers particularly admired: Ian Botham, Geoff Boycott, Mike Gatting, Viv Richards, Malcolm Marshall, David Hughes, Neil Fairbrother
Other sports followed: Football (Manchester City)
Extras: Left Leicestershire and joined Lancashire at end of 1988 season. Man of the Match in 1990 NatWest Trophy final at Lord's (5-26). One of *Wisden*'s Five Cricketers of the Year 1992. Man of the Tournament in the Hong Kong Sixes 1993. Left Lancashire at the end of the 1993 season and joined Derbyshire. England Player of the [Test] Series against New Zealand 1994. Captained Derbyshire for part of 1997 season after the departure of Dean Jones. Is the only playing English cricketer to have appeared in two World Cup finals. Took 1000th first-class wicket (Usman Afzaal) v Notts at Trent Bridge 1999. Left Derbyshire at end of 1999 season and rejoined Leicestershire for 2000. Shared in a Leicestershire record eighth-wicket partnership for the one-day league (116) with Neil Burns v Northamptonshire at Leicester in the NUL 2001. Took 6-65 v Glamorgan at Cardiff 2001, in the process achieving the feat of having recorded a five-wicket innings return against all 18 counties. Passed 10,000 runs in first-class cricket v Somerset at Leicester 2002 to achieve the career double of 10,000 runs and 1000 wickets. Scored 103 v Sussex at Leicester 2003, following up with 5-55 in Sussex's first innings. Captain of Leicestershire 2003 until standing down in July 2004
Best batting: 123* Leicestershire v Lancashire, Leicester 2000
Best bowling: 7-21 Lancashire v Middlesex, Lord's 1989

2004 Season

	M	Inns	NO	Runs	HS	Avge	100s	50s	Ct	St	O	M	Runs	Wkts	Avge	Best	5wI	10wM
Test																		
All First	13	20	3	394	78	23.17	-	1	1	-	343.4	81	1064	31	34.32	4-49	-	-
1-day Int																		
C & G	1	1	0	0	0	0.00	-	-	-	-	10	3	16	1	16.00	1-16	-	
totesport	11	6	0	66	26	11.00	-	-	1	-	55.3	5	291	4	72.75	2-17	-	
Twenty20	3	2	1	5	3 *	5.00	-	-	-	-	6	0	56	2	28.00	1-17	-	

Career Performances

	M	Inns	NO	Runs	HS	Avge	100s	50s	Ct	St	Balls	Runs	Wkts	Avge	Best	5wI	10wM
Test	44	68	5	934	88	14.82	-	4	14	-	9838	4700	140	33.57	7-70	4	-
All First	368	526	50	10929	123 *	22.96	10	54	127	-	71397	34403	1236	27.83	7-21	61	6
1-day Int	103	66	23	690	67	16.04	-	1	26	-	5712	3775	115	32.82	4-35	-	
C & G	49	33	4	526	69	18.13	-	1	9	-	2937	1495	63	23.73	5-13	4	
totesport	238	184	29	2969	90	19.15	-	8	44	-	9692	7029	249	28.22	5-26	2	
Twenty20	9	8	1	54	18	7.71	-	-	-	-	138	204	8	25.50	3-39	-	

DENLY, J. L. Kent

Name: Joseph (Joe) Liam Denly
Role: Right-hand opening bat, leg-spin bowler
Born: 16 March 1986, Canterbury
Height: 6ft **Weight:** 11st 9lbs
Nickname: No Pants, Commando, Sweet, Dougie, Denners
County debut: 2004
Parents: Jayne and Nick
Marital status: Single
Family links with cricket: 'Dad and bro are league legends'
Education: Chaucer Technology School
Qualifications: 10 GCSEs, Level 1 coach
Off-season: England U19
Overseas tours: England U18 to Holland 2003; England U19 to India 2004-05
Overseas teams played for: Hammersley Carine, Perth 2003
Career highlights to date: 'Playing on Sky Sports for England U19'
Cricket moments to forget: 'Getting run out without facing a ball for England U19'
Cricket superstitions: 'Left pad on first'

Cricketers particularly admired: Sachin Tendulkar, Steve Waugh
Young players to look out for: Richard Piesley, Charlie Hemphrey
Other sports played: Football (Charlton Athletic U14)
Other sports followed: Football (Arsenal)
Injuries: Out for the first two games of the season with a broken thumb
Favourite band: Westlife
Relaxations: 'Sleeping'
Extras: Has represented England U17 and U18. Represented England U19 v Bangladesh U19 2004

2004 Season

	M	Inns	NO	Runs	HS	Avge	100s	50s	Ct	St	O	M	Runs	Wkts	Avge	Best	5wI	10wM
Test																		
All First	1	1	0	0	0	0.00	-	-	-	-								
1-day Int																		
C & G																		
totesport																		
Twenty20	3	1	0	4	4	4.00	-	-	2	-								

Career Performances

	M	Inns	NO	Runs	HS	Avge	100s	50s	Ct	St	Balls	Runs	Wkts	Avge	Best	5wI	10wM
Test																	
All First	1	1	0	0	0	0.00	-	-	-	-							
1-day Int																	
C & G																	
totesport																	
Twenty20	3	1	0	4	4	4.00	-	-	2	-							

DENNINGTON, M. J. — Kent

Name: Matthew (Matt) John Dennington
Role: Right-hand bat, right-arm medium-fast bowler
Born: 16 October 1982, Durban, South Africa
Height: 6ft 1in **Weight:** 12st 10lbs
Nickname: Denners, Denzel
County debut: 2003 (one-day), 2004 (first-class)
1st-Class 50s: 1
1st-Class catches: 2
Place in batting averages: 248th av. 15.42
Strike rate: 62.00 (career 62.00)
Parents: John and Yvonne
Marital status: Single

Education: Northwood Boys, Durban; Varsity College and University of South Africa (UNISA)
Qualifications: 'Matric; currently studying for degree in marketing'
Career outside cricket: Student
Off-season: 'Training in Australia; studying'
Overseas teams played for: Crusaders CC, Durban 1998-2002; KwaZulu-Natal B 2002-03
Career highlights to date: 'Taking three wickets in a Championship game against Surrey and getting 50* to save the game'
Cricket moments to forget: 'Colliding with team-mate going for a catch on the boundary and breaking my kneecap'
Cricket superstitions: 'Not a superstitious cricketer' 
Cricketers particularly admired: Paddy Clift, Allan Donald
Young players to look out for: James Tredwell, Michael Carberry, Chad Keegan
Other sports played: Golf
Other sports followed: Rugby (Natal Sharks)
Injuries: Out for four to six weeks with a broken hand
Favourite band: Red Hot Chili Peppers
Relaxations: 'Going to gym; surfing and other watersports; playing golf'
Extras: Natal Schools 1999-2000. Natal Academy 2001-02. Natal B 2002
Opinions on cricket: 'The game is quicker in modern times – bowlers are bowling faster, batsmen are hitting the ball further. Twenty20 has exploited this. It has brought crowds in because of its exciting nature.'
Best batting: 50* Kent v Surrey, Canterbury 2004
Best bowling: 3-48 Kent v Sussex, Canterbury 2004

25. Which Sri Lanka batsman has scored six Test match double hundreds, placing him equal with Javed Miandad and behind only Don Bradman, Wally Hammond and Brian Lara on the all-time Test double hundred list?

2004 Season

	M	Inns	NO	Runs	HS	Avge	100s	50s	Ct	St	O	M	Runs	Wkts	Avge	Best	5wI	10wM
Test																		
All First	7	9	2	108	50 *	15.42	-	1	2	-	93	13	368	9	40.88	3-48	-	-
1-day Int																		
C & G	1	1	0	13	13	13.00	-	-	-	-	10	0	47	0	-	-	-	
totesport	8	6	2	39	26 *	9.75	-	-	3	-	42	0	288	5	57.60	3-53	-	
Twenty20	1	1	0	6	6	6.00	-	-	1	-	4	0	44	0	-	-	-	

Career Performances

	M	Inns	NO	Runs	HS	Avge	100s	50s	Ct	St	Balls	Runs	Wkts	Avge	Best	5wI	10wM
Test																	
All First	7	9	2	108	50 *	15.42	-	1	2	-	558	368	9	40.88	3-48	-	-
1-day Int																	
C & G	2	2	0	14	13	7.00	-	-	-	-	108	98	1	98.00	1-51	-	
totesport	10	8	4	67	26 *	16.75	-	-	3	-	300	339	5	67.80	3-53	-	
Twenty20	5	3	0	22	12	7.33	-	-	1	-	114	164	8	20.50	4-28	-	

26. Who top-scored for Kenya in their victory over West Indies in the 1995-96 World Cup and also made 147 in the 1996-97 ICC Trophy final v Bangladesh?

DERNBACH, J. Surrey

Name: Jade Dernbach
Role: Right-hand bat, right-arm fast bowler
Born: 3 March 1986, South Africa
Height: 6ft 2in **Weight:** 13st
County debut: 2003
Strike rate: (career 78.00)
Parents: Carmen and Graeme
Marital status: Single
Education: St John the Baptist
Overseas tours: La Manga tournament, Spain 2003
Career highlights to date: 'Making my first-team debut for Surrey against India A'
Cricket moments to forget: 'Going out first ball in the ECB U17 final in 2003'
Cricketers particularly admired: Jacques Kallis, Jonty Rhodes, James Anderson, Rikki Clarke
Other sports played: Rugby (Surrey U16)
Other sports followed: Football (Arsenal)
Favourite band: Usher
Relaxations: 'Going out with friends; swimming, playing football and rugby; listening to music'
Extras: Sir Jack Hobbs Fair Play Award. Surrey U19 Player of the Year. Made first-class debut v India A at The Oval 2003 aged 17, becoming the youngest player for 30 years to play first-class cricket for Surrey. Surrey Academy 2003, 2004
Best batting: 3 Surrey v India A, The Oval 2003
Best bowling: 1-74 Surrey v India A, The Oval 2003

2004 Season (did not make any first-class or one-day appearances)

Career Performances

	M	Inns	NO	Runs	HS	Avge	100s	50s	Ct	St	Balls	Runs	Wkts	Avge	Best	5wI	10wM
Test																	
All First	1	1	0	3	3	3.00	-	-	-	-	78	74	1	74.00	1-74	-	-
1-day Int																	
C & G																	
totesport																	
Twenty20																	

DIGHTON, M. G. — Hampshire

Name: Michael Gray Dighton
Role: Right-hand bat, leg-break bowler, occasional wicket-keeper
Born: 24 April 1976, Toowoomba, Queensland, Australia
Height: 6ft 4in **Weight:** 14st 1lb
Nickname: Dights
County debut: 2004 (one-day)
1st-Class 50s: 12
1st-Class 100s: 6
1st-Class catches: 32
Overseas teams played for: Western Australia 1997-98 – 1999-2000; Tasmania 2001-02 –
Extras: Captained Western Australia U17 and U19. Australian Cricket Academy 1996. Played for Holland in the NatWest 2000. Has won several domestic match awards. Tasmania's Pura Cup Player of the Year 2003-04. Was an overseas player with Hampshire in May 2004, deputising for Michael Clarke, absent on international duty; struck a 64-ball 74 on debut v Gloucestershire at Bristol in the totesport League
Best batting: 182* Western Australia v Queensland, Perth 1999-2000

2004 Season

	M	Inns	NO	Runs	HS	Avge	100s	50s	Ct	St	O	M	Runs	Wkts	Avge	Best	5wI	10wM
Test																		
All First																		
1-day Int																		
C & G	1	1	0	12	12	12.00	-	-	-	-								
totesport	1	1	0	74	74	74.00	-	1	-	-								
Twenty20																		

Career Performances

	M	Inns	NO	Runs	HS	Avge	100s	50s	Ct	St	Balls	Runs	Wkts	Avge	Best	5wI	10wM
Test																	
All First	41	70	4	2610	182 *	39.54	6	12	32	-	18	31	0	-	-	-	-
1-day Int																	
C & G	2	2	0	23	12	11.50	-	-	-	-							
totesport	1	1	0	74	74	74.00	-	1	-	-							
Twenty20																	

DIVENUTO, M. J. Derbyshire

Name: Michael James DiVenuto
Role: Left-hand bat, right-arm medium/ leg-break bowler, county vice-captain
Born: 12 December 1973, Hobart, Tasmania
Height: 5ft 11in **Weight:** 12st 12lbs
Nickname: Diva
County debut: 1999 (Sussex), 2000 (Derbyshire)
County cap: 1999 (Sussex), 2000 (Derbyshire)
One-Day Internationals: 9
1000 runs in a season: 4
1st-Class 50s: 84
1st-Class 100s: 27
1st-Class 200s: 1
1st-Class catches: 208
One-Day 100s: 5
Place in batting averages: (2003 32nd av. 49.03)
Strike rate: (career 160.20)
Parents: Enrico and Elizabeth
Wife and date of marriage: Renae, 31 December 2003
Family links with cricket: 'Dad and older brother Peter both played grade cricket in Tasmania.' Brother Peter also played for Italy
Education: St Virgil's College, Hobart
Qualifications: HSC (5 x Level III subjects), Level 3 cricket coach
Off-season: Playing for Tasmania
Overseas tours: Australian Cricket Academy to India and Sri Lanka 1993, to South Africa 1996; Australia A to Malaysia (Super 8s) 1997 (captain), to Scotland and Ireland 1998 (captain), to Los Angeles 1999; Australia to South Africa 1996-97 (one-day series), to Hong Kong (Super 6s) 1997, to Malaysia (Super 8s) 1998; Tasmania to Zimbabwe 1995-96
Overseas teams played for: North Hobart CC, Tasmania; Kingborough, Tasmania; Tasmania 1991-92 –
Career highlights to date: 'Playing for Australia. Man of the Match award v South Africa at Johannesburg 1997. Dismissing Jamie Cox at Taunton in 1999, my first wicket in first-class cricket'
Cricket moments to forget: 'Being dismissed by Jamie Cox at Taunton in 1999, *his* first wicket in first-class cricket'
Cricketers particularly admired: David Boon, Dean Jones, Kepler Wessels, Mark and Steve Waugh
Young players to look out for: 'My nephew Jack DiVenuto'

Other sports played: Australian Rules (Tasmanian U15, U16 and Sandy Bay FC)
Other sports followed: Australian Rules football (Geelong Cats)
Injuries: Out for the entire 2004 season after back surgery
Favourite band: U2
Relaxations: Golf, sleeping and eating
Extras: Man of the Match for his 89 in fifth ODI v South Africa at Johannesburg 1997. Scored then career best 189 v Western Australia in 1997-98 Sheffield Shield final. Joined Sussex as overseas player for 1999. Joined Derbyshire as overseas player for 2000. Scored 173* v Derbyshire Board XI at Derby in NatWest 2000, a record for Derbyshire in one-day cricket. Carried his bat for 192* v Middlesex at Lord's 2002; also scored 113 in the second innings. Derbyshire Player of the Year 2002 (jointly with Kevin Dean). First batsman to 1000 Championship runs 2003. Vice-captain of Derbyshire since 2002 (was appointed captain for 2004 but was unable to take up post due to back surgery)
Opinions on cricket: 'The game is in good shape and moving forward as it should be. Twenty20 cricket has been a breath of fresh air. Big crowds, great atmospheres and some brilliant cricket have been a winner with the players and supporters.'
Best batting: 230 Derbyshire v Northamptonshire, Derby 2002
Best bowling: 1-0 Tasmania v Queensland, Brisbane 1999-2000

2004 Season (did not make any first-class or one-day appearances)

Career Performances

	M	Inns	NO	Runs	HS	Avge	100s	50s	Ct	St	Balls	Runs	Wkts	Avge	Best	5wI	10wM
Test																	
All First	189	331	16	13331	230	42.32	28	84	208	-	801	480	5	96.00	1-0	-	-
1-day Int	9	9	0	241	89	26.77	-	2	1	-							
C & G	9	9	1	434	173 *	54.25	1	3	6	-							
totesport	70	69	4	2290	130	35.23	3	14	20	-	30	30	0	-	-	-	
Twenty20	5	5	2	198	67	66.00	-	2	-	-	78	88	5	17.60	3-19	-	

DOSHI, N. D. Surrey

Name: Nayan Dilip Doshi
Role: Right-hand bat, left-arm spin bowler
Born: 6 October 1978, Nottingham
Height: 6ft 4in
Nickname: Dosh, Troll, Turtlehead
County debut: 2004
1st-Class 5 w. in innings: 4
1st-Class 10 w. in match: 2
1st-Class catches: 3
Place in batting averages: 255th av. 13.40

Place in bowling averages: 27th av. 26.51
Strike rate: 48.24 (career 67.44)
Parents: Dilip and Kalindi
Marital status: Engaged
Family links with cricket: Father is former India Test and ODI spin bowler Dilip Doshi, who also played for Nottinghamshire and Warwickshire
Education: King Alfred School, London; 'Life'
Career outside cricket: Family business
Overseas teams played for: Saurashtra, India 2001-02 – 2003-04
Career highlights to date: 'Twenty20 semi-final 2004'
Cricket moments to forget: 'Too many'
Cricketers particularly admired: Viv Richards, Sachin Tendulkar, Garfield Sobers
Favourite band: 'Like lots of them'
Relaxations: Wildlife photography
Extras: Played for Buckinghamshire in the C&G 2001. Made first-class debut for Saurashtra v Baroda at Rajkot 2001-02. Recorded maiden first-class ten-wicket match return (5-125/6-57) v Lancashire at Old Trafford 2004 and another (3-73/7-110) v Sussex at Hove in the following Championship match. Is not considered an overseas player
Best batting: 29* Surrey v Lancashire, Croydon 2004
Best bowling: 7-110 Surrey v Sussex, Hove 2004

2004 Season

	M	Inns	NO	Runs	HS	Avge	100s	50s	Ct	St	O	M	Runs	Wkts	Avge	Best	5wI	10wM
Test																		
All First	9	13	3	134	29 *	13.40	-	-	2	-	265.2	45	875	33	26.51	7-110	3	2
1-day Int																		
C & G																		
totesport	10	4	3	35	18 *	35.00	-	-	2	-	50	0	259	4	64.75	1-28	-	
Twenty20	7	1	0	1	1	1.00	-	-	3	-	26	0	161	8	20.12	3-26	-	

Career Performances

	M	Inns	NO	Runs	HS	Avge	100s	50s	Ct	St	Balls	Runs	Wkts	Avge	Best	5wI	10wM
Test																	
All First	19	29	4	206	29 *	8.24	-	-	3	-	3170	1530	47	32.55	7-110	4	2
1-day Int																	
C & G	1	1	0	0	0	0.00	-	-	-	-	18	12	1	12.00	1-12	-	
totesport	10	4	3	35	18 *	35.00	-	-	2	-	300	259	4	64.75	1-28	-	
Twenty20	7	1	0	1	1	1.00	-	-	3	-	156	161	8	20.12	3-26	-	

DUMELOW, N. R. C. Derbyshire

Name: Nathan Robert Charles Dumelow
Role: Right-hand bat, right-arm off-spin bowler
Born: 30 April 1981, Derby
Height: 5ft 10in **Weight:** 12st 2lbs
Nickname: Pig
County debut: 2001
1st-Class 50s: 6
1st-Class 5 w. in innings: 3
1st-Class 10 w. in match: 1
1st-Class catches: 5
Place in batting averages: 273rd av. 8.33 (2003 186th av. 24.78)
Place in bowling averages: (2003 129th av. 43.11)
Strike rate: 84.00 (career 81.46)
Parents: Kate and Robert
Marital status: Single
Family links with cricket: 'Dad plays for Derbyshire Over 50s'
Education: Denstone College
Qualifications: 7 GCSEs
Career outside cricket: Farmer
Overseas tours: Derbyshire U16 to Barbados; Derbyshire U17 to South Africa
Overseas teams played for: Schoeman Park CC, Bloemfontein 2000-01
Cricket moments to forget: 'Day/night game v Worcestershire' (*Took 2-59 from five overs as Worcs posted 288-6 and beat Derbys by 138 runs at Derby in the NUL 2001*)
Cricketers particularly admired: Viv Richards
Young players to look out for: Chris Bassano, Tom Lungley
Other sports played: Golf, snooker
Other sports followed: Football (Derby County FC)
Relaxations: Fishing, shooting
Extras: Won all Derbyshire age-group awards. Took 4-81 on first-class debut v Pakistanis at Derby 2001, including the wickets of Yousuf Youhana, Inzamam-ul-Haq and Abdul Razzaq. Scored 50* on Championship debut v Hampshire at Derby 2001. Derbyshire's Most Improved Player 2001. Won eight awards while playing club cricket in Tasmania 2001-02, including those for best batting and bowling averages and for fair play. Recorded maiden first-class five-wicket return (5-82) v Northamptonshire at Northampton 2003 and took 5-78 in the second innings for a maiden ten-wicket match. Returned first innings figures of 5-51 v West Indians at Derby 2004. Left Derbyshire during the 2004-05 off-season
Best batting: 75 Derbyshire v Hampshire, West End 2003
Best bowling: 5-51 Derbyshire v West Indians, Derby 2004

2004 Season

	M	Inns	NO	Runs	HS	Avge	100s	50s	Ct	St	O	M	Runs	Wkts	Avge	Best	5wI	10wM
Test																		
All First	4	6	0	50	18	8.33	-	-	-	-	126	20	488	9	54.22	5-51	1	-
1-day Int																		
C & G	1	1	0	5	5	5.00	-	-	-	-	9	0	55	0	-	-	-	
totesport	13	8	1	60	26	8.57	-	-	1	-	74.5	1	459	10	45.90	2-37	-	
Twenty20	1	0	0	0	0	-	-	-	-	-	2	0	17	1	17.00	1-17	-	

Career Performances

	M	Inns	NO	Runs	HS	Avge	100s	50s	Ct	St	Balls	Runs	Wkts	Avge	Best	5wI	10wM
Test																	
All First	25	41	4	781	75	21.10	-	6	5	-	3340	2132	41	52.00	5-51	3	1
1-day Int																	
C & G	6	6	0	86	32	14.33	-	-	-	-	246	192	2	96.00	2-21	-	
totesport	41	33	6	416	52	15.40	-	1	2	-	1583	1419	41	34.60	3-24	-	
Twenty20	6	4	0	17	12	4.25	-	-	-	-	65	86	8	10.75	3-8	-	

DURSTON, W. J. Somerset

Name: Wesley (Wes) John Durston
Role: Right-hand bat, right-arm off-spin bowler; all-rounder
Born: 6 October 1980, Taunton
Height: 5ft 10in **Weight:** 12st
Nickname: Ace, Pringles
County debut: 2002
1st-Class 50s: 1
1st-Class catches: 13
Strike rate: 52.50 (career 66.75)
Parents: Gillian and Steven
Wife and date of marriage: Christina, 4 October 2003
Children: Daisy, 4 July 2004
Family links with cricket: 'Dad and my two brothers, Dan and Greg, all play. On occasions all four played in same local team (Compton Dundon)'
Education: Millfield School; University College, Worcester
Qualifications: 10 GCSEs, 2 A-levels, BSc Sports Studies, ECB Level II cricket coaching
Career outside cricket: Coaching

Overseas tours: West of England to West Indies 1996
Career highlights to date: 'Three centuries (106, 162*, 126) in three days at Tonbridge Festival for Millfield School 1999. First-class debut v West Indies A 2002, scoring 26 and 55, and the match tied chasing 454 to win'
Cricket moments to forget: 'Scoring 0 v Kent, being lbw and breaking left big toe in NUL 2002'
Cricket superstitions: 'Right foot on and off field first. Placing my right inner glove in my pocket while I bat'
Cricketers particularly admired: Brian Lara, Graham Gooch, Muttiah Muralitharan
Young players to look out for: James Hildreth, Richard Timms, Jack Cooper
Other sports played: Hockey (Taunton Vale), football, golf
Other sports followed: Football 'passionately' (Man Utd), 'any sport that's on TV'
Relaxations: 'Spending time with wife and new daughter; all sport (viewing); going to the gym'
Extras: Captained winning Lord's Taverners team v Shrewsbury School at Trent Bridge 1996. Wetherell Schools All-rounder Award 1999; scored 956 runs and took 35 wickets. Has captained Somerset 2nd XI on occasion. Scored 44-ball 55 on first-class debut at Taunton 2002 as Somerset, chasing 454 to win, tied with West Indies A
Best batting: 55 Somerset v West Indies A, Taunton 2002
Best bowling: 3-23 Somerset v Sri Lanka A, Taunton 2004

2004 Season

	M	Inns	NO	Runs	HS	Avge	100s	50s	Ct	St	O	M	Runs	Wkts	Avge	Best	5wI	10wM
Test																		
All First	2	3	0	86	47	28.66	-	-	8	-	35	6	115	4	28.75	3-23	-	-
1-day Int																		
C & G																		
totesport	1	1	0	9	9	9.00	-	-	-	-								
Twenty20																		

Career Performances

	M	Inns	NO	Runs	HS	Avge	100s	50s	Ct	St	Balls	Runs	Wkts	Avge	Best	5wI	10wM
Test																	
All First	5	9	1	215	55	26.87	-	1	13	-	534	305	8	38.12	3-23	-	-
1-day Int																	
C & G	2	2	0	75	50	37.50	-	1	-	-	84	75	2	37.50	1-32	-	
totesport	10	9	2	154	51 *	22.00	-	1	1	-	90	92	0	-	-	-	
Twenty20	5	4	0	85	34	21.25	-	-	1	-	36	65	3	21.66	3-31	-	

DUTCH, K. P. Somerset

Name: Keith Philip Dutch
Role: Right-hand bat, off-spin bowler
Born: 21 March 1973, Harrow, Middlesex
Height: 5ft 9in **Weight:** 11st 4lbs
Nickname: Dutchy, Oik
County debut: 1993 (Middlesex), 2001 (Somerset)
County cap: 2001 (Somerset)
1st-Class 50s: 11
1st-Class 100s: 1
1st-Class 5 w. in innings: 3
1st-Class catches: 72
One-Day 5 w. in innings: 2
Place in batting averages: 107th av. 35.42 (2003 244th av. 16.10)
Place in bowling averages: 13th av. 23.57
Strike rate: 39.15 (career 67.59)
Parents: Alan and Ann
Wife and date of marriage: Emma, 11 November 2000
Children: Lauren Beth Amy, 15 January 1999
Family links with cricket: Father coached
Education: Nower Hill High School, Pinner; Weald College, Harrow
Qualifications: 5 GCSEs, 1 AS-level, staff tutor coach
Overseas tours: MCC to Central and East Africa 1997, to Canada 2000-01
Overseas teams played for: Worcester United, South Africa 1992-93; Geelong City, Australia, 1994; Rygersdal CC, Cape Town 1997-98
Career highlights to date: 'Man of the Match award in C&G semi-final and winning C&G final 2001'
Cricketers particularly admired: Mark Ramprakash, John Emburey
Other sports followed: Football (Arsenal FC)
Relaxations: Music, TV and shopping for clothes
Extras: Middlesex 2nd XI Player of the Year 1995. In 1996 scored over 1000 2nd XI Championship runs and took 63 wickets, setting in the process a record for the highest-ever individual innings (261 v Somerset) and best bowling figures (15 for 157 v Leicestershire) by a Middlesex player in the history of the 2nd XI Championship. 2nd XI Championship Player of the Year in 1993, 1996 and 1999. Scored 91 and took 6-62 (both then career bests) in a single day v Essex at Chelmsford 2000. Released by Middlesex at the end of the 2000 season and joined Somerset for 2001. C&G Man of the Match award for his 54-ball 61 in the semi-final v Warwickshire at Taunton 2001. Left Somerset during the 2004-05 off-season
Best batting: 118 Somerset v Essex, Taunton 2001
Best bowling: 6-62 Middlesex v Essex, Chelmsford 2000

2004 Season

	M	Inns	NO	Runs	HS	Avge	100s	50s	Ct	St	O	M	Runs	Wkts	Avge	Best	5wI	10wM
Test																		
All First	6	8	1	248	72	35.42	-	2	2	-	124	21	448	19	23.57	5-26	2	-
1-day Int																		
C & G	2	2	0	10	9	5.00	-	-	-	-	6	0	42	0	-	-	-	
totesport	15	14	2	260	79 *	21.66	-	1	5	-	92.5	2	461	10	46.10	2-45	-	
Twenty20	5	5	0	158	47	31.60	-	-	2	-	12	0	81	2	40.50	2-25	-	

Career Performances

	M	Inns	NO	Runs	HS	Avge	100s	50s	Ct	St	Balls	Runs	Wkts	Avge	Best	5wI	10wM
Test																	
All First	72	102	10	1868	118	20.30	1	11	72	-	7773	4187	115	36.40	6-62	3	-
1-day Int																	
C & G	23	18	8	292	61 *	29.20	-	1	16	-	852	610	16	38.12	3-26	-	
totesport	125	110	22	1716	79 *	19.50	-	6	45	-	4294	3493	119	29.35	6-40	2	
Twenty20	10	10	1	291	70	32.33	-	1	3	-	132	164	5	32.80	2-14	-	

EALHAM, M. A. — Nottinghamshire

Name: Mark Alan Ealham
Role: Right-hand bat, right-arm medium bowler; all-rounder
Born: 27 August 1969, Ashford, Kent
Height: 5ft 10in **Weight:** 14st
Nickname: Ealy, Border, Skater
County debut: 1989 (Kent), 2004 (Nottinghamshire)
County cap: 1992 (Kent), 2004 (Nottinghamshire)
Benefit: 2003 (Kent)
Test debut: 1996
Tests: 8
One-Day Internationals: 64
1000 runs in a season: 1
1st-Class 50s: 56
1st-Class 100s: 10
1st-Class 5 w. in innings: 19
1st-Class 10 w. in match: 1
1st-Class catches: 109
One-Day 100s: 1
One-Day 5 w. in innings: 4

Place in batting averages: 46th av. 48.38 (2003 98th av. 36.44)
Place in bowling averages: 95th av. 36.61 (2003 40th av. 26.65)
Strike rate: 73.15 (career 60.92)
Parents: Alan and Sue
Wife and date of marriage: Kirsty, 24 February 1996
Children: George, 8 March 2002
Family links with cricket: Father played for Kent
Education: Stour Valley Secondary School
Qualifications: 9 CSEs
Career outside cricket: Plumber
Overseas tours: England A to Australia 1996-97, to Kenya and Sri Lanka 1997-98; England VI to Hong Kong 1997, 2001; England to Sharjah (Champions Trophy) 1997-98, to Bangladesh (Wills International Cup) 1998-99, to Australia 1998-99 (CUB Series), to Sharjah (Coca-Cola Cup) 1998-99, to South Africa and Zimbabwe 1999-2000 (one-day series), to Kenya (ICC Knockout Trophy) 2000-01, to Pakistan and Sri Lanka 2000-01 (one-day series)
Overseas teams played for: South Perth, Australia 1992-93; University, Perth 1993-94
Cricketers particularly admired: Ian Botham, Viv Richards, Robin Smith, Steve Waugh, Paul Blackmore and Albert 'for his F and G'
Other sports followed: Football (Manchester United), 'and most other sports'
Relaxations: Playing golf and snooker, watching films
Extras: Set then record for fastest Sunday League century (44 balls), v Derbyshire at Maidstone 1995. Represented England in the 1999 World Cup. Returned a new England best ODI bowling analysis with his 5-15 v Zimbabwe at Kimberley in January 2000; all five were lbw. Vice-captain of Kent 2001. Left Kent at the end of the 2003 season and joined Nottinghamshire for 2004; awarded Nottinghamshire cap 2004
Best batting: 153* Kent v Northamptonshire, Canterbury 2001
Best bowling: 8-36 Kent v Warwickshire, Edgbaston 1996

2004 Season

	M	Inns	NO	Runs	HS	Avge	100s	50s	Ct	St	O	M	Runs	Wkts	Avge	Best	5wI	10wM
Test																		
All First	16	20	2	871	139	48.38	3	4	13	-	317	90	952	26	36.61	4-43	-	-
1-day Int																		
C & G	1	1	0	8	8	8.00	-	-	-	-	10	0	54	1	54.00	1-54	-	
totesport	15	13	5	269	56	33.62	-	1	8	-	112.5	12	378	22	17.18	3-22	-	
Twenty20	5	5	0	115	91	23.00	-	1	-	-	18	0	113	3	37.66	1-17	-	

Career Performances

	M	Inns	NO	Runs	HS	Avge	100s	50s	Ct	St	Balls	Runs	Wkts	Avge	Best	5wI	10wM
Test	8	13	3	210	53 *	21.00	-	2	4	-	1060	488	17	28.70	4-21	-	-
All First	208	324	49	9012	153 *	32.77	10	56	109	-	27479	13085	451	29.01	8-36	19	1
1-day Int	64	45	4	716	45	17.46	-	-	9	-	3222	2193	67	32.73	5-15	2	
C & G	31	27	7	562	58 *	28.10	-	2	8	-	1661	873	37	23.59	4-10	-	
totesport	195	165	42	3195	112	25.97	1	14	56	-	7940	5728	202	28.35	6-53	2	
Twenty20	10	10	0	184	91	18.40	-	1	-	-	214	229	8	28.62	2-31	-	

EDWARDS, N. J. Somerset

Name: Neil James Edwards
Role: Left-hand bat, occasional right-arm medium bowler
Born: 14 October 1983, Truro, Cornwall
Height: 6ft 3in **Weight:** 14st
Nickname: Toastie, Shanksy
County debut: 2002
1st-Class 50s: 3
1st-Class 100s: 1
1st-Class catches: 13
Place in batting averages: 157th av. 28.26 (2003 75th av. 40.00)
Strike rate: 75.00 (career 131.50)
Parents: Lynn and John
Marital status: Single
Family links with cricket: 'Cousin played first-class cricket for Worcestershire'
Education: Cape Cornwall School; Richard Huish College
Qualifications: 11 GCSEs, 3 A-levels, Level 1 coach
Overseas tours: Cornwall U13 to South Africa 1997; West of England to West Indies 1999; Somerset Academy to Australia 2002; England U19 to Australia 2002-03
Career highlights to date: '160 for Somerset v Hampshire in County Championship 2003'
Cricket moments to forget: 'Duck on debut for Cornwall'
Cricket superstitions: 'Never change batting gloves when batting'
Cricketers particularly admired: Marcus Trescothick, Matthew Hayden
Young players to look out for: Ryan Edwards, Tom Edwards, Kerry Matthew, Nicole Richards
Other sports played: Football
Other sports followed: Football (Stoke City FC)

Favourite band: 'I listen to any music'
Relaxations: 'Spending time at home in Cornwall with girlfriend, family and friends; playing on my Xbox'
Extras: Scored 213 for Cornwall U19 v Dorset U19 at 16 years old. Scored a second innings 97 in England U19's victory over Australia U19 in the first 'Test' at Adelaide 2002-03. Represented England U19 v South Africa U19 2003. Somerset Wyverns Award for Best Performance by an Uncapped Player 2003 (160 v Hampshire)
Opinions on cricket: 'More one-day cricket with the use of floodlights. Twenty20 introduced into 2nd XI cricket, as well as more one-day cricket.'
Best batting: 160 Somerset v Hampshire, Taunton 2003
Best bowling: 1-16 Somerset v Derbyshire, Taunton 2004

2004 Season

	M	Inns	NO	Runs	HS	Avge	100s	50s	Ct	St	O	M	Runs	Wkts	Avge	Best	5wI	10wM
Test																		
All First	10	19	0	537	93	28.26	-	2	11	-	25	1	110	2	55.00	1-16	-	-
1-day Int																		
C & G																		
totesport																		
Twenty20																		

Career Performances

	M	Inns	NO	Runs	HS	Avge	100s	50s	Ct	St	Balls	Runs	Wkts	Avge	Best	5wI	10wM
Test																	
All First	16	30	0	955	160	31.83	1	3	13	-	263	181	2	90.50	1-16	-	-
1-day Int																	
C & G																	
totesport																	
Twenty20	1	1	0	1	1	1.00	-	-	-	-							

27. Who scored 121 against India as captain in Zimbabwe's first Test, coached Worcestershire and also represented his country as a hockey goalkeeper?

ELLIOTT, M. T. G. Glamorgan

Name: Matthew Thomas Gray Elliott
Role: Left-hand bat, left-arm orthodox bowler
Born: 28 September 1971, Chelsea, Victoria, Australia
Height: 6ft 3in **Weight:** 13st 8lbs
Nickname: Hoarse, Herb
County debut: 2000 (Glamorgan), 2002 (Yorkshire)
County cap: 2000 (Glamorgan)
Test debut: 1996-97
Tests: 21
One-Day Internationals: 1
1000 runs in a season: 2
1st-Class 50s: 66
1st-Class 100s: 45
1st-Class 200s: 2
1st-Class catches: 195
One-Day 100s: 6
Place in batting averages: 25th av. 53.84
Strike rate: (career 111.00)
Parents: John and Glenda
Wife and date of marriage: Megan, 11 December 1994
Children: Zachary, 22 November 1997; Samuel, 18 February 2000; William, June 2004
Education: Kyabram Secondary College
Qualifications: VCE
Off-season: 'Playing for Victoria'
Overseas tours: Young Australia (Australia A) to England and Netherlands 1995; Australia to South Africa 1996-97, to England 1997, to West Indies 1998-99; FICA World XI to New Zealand 2004-05
Overseas teams played for: Victoria 1992-93 –
Career highlights to date: 'Taking the 2002 C&G Trophy through Scarborough on an open-top bus with a police escort!'
Cricket moments to forget: 'Being dismissed by Dean Cosker at Sophia Gardens in '97!'
Cricket superstitions: 'Always put left shoe on first'
Cricketers particularly admired: Shane Warne, Allan Border, Steve Waugh
Other sports played: Australian Rules football
Other sports followed: Australian Rules football (Collingwood FC)
Relaxations: 'Fishing; reading biographies; drinking Corona'

Extras: Scored 556 runs (av. 55.60) in the 1997 Ashes series, including 199 in the fourth Test at Headingley. One of *Wisden*'s Five Cricketers of the Year 1998. Sheffield Shield Player of the Year 1995-96 and 1998-99. Was Glamorgan's overseas player in 2000, returning in 2004 and for 2005. Scored century (117) in his first Championship innings for Glamorgan, v Warwickshire at Edgbaston 2000. Scored 177 in helping to set county record first-wicket partnership of 374 with Stephen James v Sussex at Colwyn Bay 2000. Victoria's one-day captain 2001-02, becoming overall skipper for the remainder of the campaign on the retirement of Paul Reiffel during the season. Was Yorkshire's overseas player for the latter part of 2002. C&G Man of the Match award for his 128* in the final v Somerset at Lord's 2002. Pura Cup Player of the Year 2003-04 (a competition record 1381 runs at 81.23 including seven centuries) and Man of the Match in the final v Queensland at Melbourne (155/55*). *Wisden Australia*'s Pura Cup Cricketer of the Year 2003-04. Carried his bat for 77* in the second innings v Hampshire at Cardiff 2004
Best batting: 203 Victoria v Tasmania, Melbourne 1995-96
Best bowling: 1-3 Victoria v Tasmania, Melbourne 1998-99

2004 Season

	M	Inns	NO	Runs	HS	Avge	100s	50s	Ct	St	O	M	Runs	Wkts	Avge	Best	5wI	10wM
Test																		
All First	15	26	1	1346	157	53.84	4	6	15	-	1.3	0	26	0	-	-	-	-
1-day Int																		
C & G	2	2	0	172	87	86.00	-	2	-	-								
totesport	12	12	5	686	112 *	98.00	2	4	6	-	2	0	13	0	-	-	-	
Twenty20	2	2	0	63	48	31.50	-	-	1	-								

Career Performances

	M	Inns	NO	Runs	HS	Avge	100s	50s	Ct	St	Balls	Runs	Wkts	Avge	Best	5wI	10wM
Test	21	36	1	1172	199	33.48	3	4	14	-	12	4	0	-	-	-	-
All First	173	316	26	14810	203	51.06	47	66	195	-	1110	666	10	66.60	1-3	-	-
1-day Int	1	1	0	1	1	1.00	-	-	-	-							
C & G	6	6	1	481	156	96.20	2	2	-	-							
totesport	28	28	9	1381	115 *	72.68	4	8	11	-	30	23	0	-	-	-	
Twenty20	2	2	0	63	48	31.50	-	-	1	-							

28. Who caught both Alec Stewart and Angus Fraser as a substitute fielder in the 1990-91 Brisbane Test and later played for Holland in the 1995-96 World Cup?

ERVINE, S. M. — Hampshire

Name: Sean Michael Ervine
Role: Left-hand bat, right-arm medium-fast bowler
Born: 6 December 1982, Harare, Zimbabwe
Height: 6ft 2in **Weight:** 14st 8lbs
Nickname: Siuc
County debut: No first-team appearance
Test debut: 2003
Tests: 5
One-Day Internationals: 42
1st-Class 50s: 8
1st-Class 100s: 4
1st-Class 5 w. in innings: 2
1st-Class catches: 36
One-Day 100s: 1
Strike rate: (career 62.34)
Family links with cricket: Brother Craig plays for Midlands in Zimbabwe

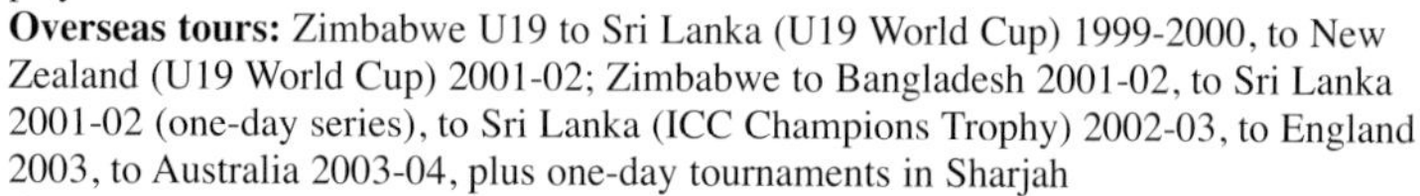

Overseas tours: Zimbabwe U19 to Sri Lanka (U19 World Cup) 1999-2000, to New Zealand (U19 World Cup) 2001-02; Zimbabwe to Bangladesh 2001-02, to Sri Lanka 2001-02 (one-day series), to Sri Lanka (ICC Champions Trophy) 2002-03, to England 2003, to Australia 2003-04, plus one-day tournaments in Sharjah
Overseas teams played for: Midlands, Zimbabwe 2001-02 – 2003-04; Western Australia 2004-05 –
Extras: CFX [Zimbabwean] Academy 2000-01. Represented Zimbabwe in the World Cup 2002-03. Struck 99-ball century (100) at Adelaide in the VB Series 2003-04 as Zimbabwe fell just three runs short of India's 280-7. Man of the Match in the first Test v Bangladesh at Harare 2003-04 (86/74). Has joined Hampshire for 2005; is not considered an overseas player
Best batting: 126 Midlands v Manicaland, Mutare 2002-03
Best bowling: 6-82 Midlands v Mashonaland, Kwekwe 2002-03

2004 Season (did not make any first-class or one-day appearances)

Career Performances

	M	Inns	NO	Runs	HS	Avge	100s	50s	Ct	St	Balls	Runs	Wkts	Avge	Best	5wI	10wM
Test	5	8	0	261	86	32.62	-	3	7	-	570	388	9	43.11	4-146	-	-
All First	30	48	6	1510	126	35.95	4	8	36	-	3429	2183	55	39.69	6-82	2	-
1-day Int	42	34	7	698	100	25.85	1	2	5	-	1649	1561	41	38.07	3-29	-	
C & G																	
totesport																	
Twenty20																	

FERLEY, R. S. Kent

Name: Robert Steven Ferley
Role: Right-hand bat, left-arm spin bowler
Born: 4 February 1982, Norwich
Height: 5ft 8in **Weight:** 12st 4lbs
Nickname: Mr Shaky Shake, Billy Bob, Bob Turkey
County debut: 2003
1st-Class 50s: 2
1st-Class catches: 8
Place in batting averages: (2003 173rd av. 26.20)
Place in bowling averages: (2003 128th av. 43.00)
Strike rate: 62.00 (career 67.86)
Parents: Pam and Tim (divorced)
Marital status: Single
Education: King Edward VII High School; Sutton Valence School (A-levels); Grey College, Durham University
Qualifications: 10 GCSEs, 3 A-levels
Overseas tours: England U19 to India 2000-01; British Universities to South Africa 2002
Career highlights to date: 'Dismissing Charles Clarke for a golden duck. Dismissing Charles Clarke to all parts of the boundary'
Cricketers particularly admired: Steve Waugh, Steve Marsh, Min Patel, Charles Clarke
Young players to look out for: James Tredwell
Other sports played: Rugby, hockey, tennis, football
Other sports followed: Football (Liverpool)
Relaxations: 'Films, interior design, keeping fit'
Extras: Represented England U17 at the ECC Colts Festival in Northern Ireland 1999. Took 4-32 on his 19th birthday v India U19 in the second 'ODI' at Vijayawada 2000-01. Played for Durham University CCE 2001, 2002 and 2003. Represented British Universities 2001, 2002 and 2003. Represented England U19 v West Indies U19 2001. Took 4-76 on Championship debut v Surrey at The Oval 2003. Scored 29 v Surrey at Canterbury 2004, in the process sharing with Ian Butler (68) in a new record ninth-wicket stand for Kent in matches v Surrey (103)
Best batting: 78* DUCCE v Durham, Durham 2003
Best bowling: 4-76 Kent v Surrey, The Oval 2003

2004 Season

	M	Inns	NO	Runs	HS	Avge	100s	50s	Ct	St	O	M	Runs	Wkts	Avge	Best	5wI	10wM
Test																		
All First	4	5	0	34	29	6.80	-	-	1	-	51.4	6	192	5	38.40	3-107	-	-
1-day Int																		
C & G																		
totesport	10	9	3	156	42	26.00	-	-	4	-	78.4	0	338	11	30.72	2-20	-	
Twenty20	1	1	1	16	16 *	-	-	-	-	-	1	0	9	1	9.00	1-9	-	

Career Performances

	M	Inns	NO	Runs	HS	Avge	100s	50s	Ct	St	Balls	Runs	Wkts	Avge	Best	5wI	10wM
Test																	
All First	22	29	7	433	78 *	19.68	-	2	8	-	2986	1864	44	42.36	4-76	-	-
1-day Int																	
C & G	2	1	0	6	6	6.00	-	-	-	-	82	43	3	14.33	2-30	-	
totesport	11	9	3	156	42	26.00	-	-	4	-	526	397	14	28.35	3-59	-	
Twenty20	1	1	1	16	16 *	-	-	-	-	-	6	9	1	9.00	1-9	-	

FERRABY, N. J. — Leicestershire

Name: Nicholas (Nick) John Ferraby
Role: Right-hand bat, right-arm medium bowler
Born: 31 May 1983, Market Harborough, Leicestershire
Height: 6ft **Weight:** 12st
Nickname: Furbs, Ferrers
County debut: No first-team appearance
Parents: Paul and Jill
Marital status: Single
Family links with cricket: 'My grandmother played for Oxfordshire! Both my older brothers, Robin and Alex, played at school but didn't carry it on'
Education: Oakham School; Loughborough University
Qualifications: 9 GCSEs, 2 A-levels, 2.1 in Sport and Leisure Management, Level 1 coaching
Off-season: 'Playing abroad – South Africa this winter'
Overseas tours: Leicestershire U19 to Johannesburg 2000-01; Kibworth CC to Barbados (Fred Rumsey Cricket Festival) 2004
Overseas teams played for: Belville CC, Cape Town 2004-05

Career highlights to date: 'Scoring my first century for Leicestershire 2nd XI'
Cricket moments to forget: 'Any time I get out!'
Cricket superstitions: 'Don't believe in superstition'
Cricketers particularly admired: Ricky Ponting
Young players to look out for: Chris Benham, Chris Liddle
Other sports played: Hockey (England U16, U18 – 'gold medal in European competition' – and U21; Loughborough Students – 'National Prem'); 'like most sports but play just recreationally'
Other sports followed: Rugby (Leicester Tigers), ice hockey (Nottingham Panthers)
Favourite band: Red Hot Chili Peppers, Delirious
Relaxations: 'Working out in the gym; watching films; listening to music (all sorts); and most importantly spending time with friends'
Extras: Leicestershire Young Batsman of the Year 2000. Played for Leicestershire Board XI in the C&G 2003

2004 Season (did not make any first-class or one-day appearances)

Career Performances

	M	Inns	NO	Runs	HS	Avge	100s	50s	Ct	St	Balls	Runs	Wkts	Avge	Best	5wI	10wM
Test																	
All First																	
1-day Int																	
C & G	2	2	0	1	1	0.50	-	-	-	-	42	31	0	-	-	-	
totesport																	
Twenty20																	

29. Muttiah Muralitharan took 9-65 in England's second innings at The Oval in 1998. Who was the batsman not dismissed by him and how was he out?

FISHER, I. D. Gloucestershire

Name: Ian Douglas Fisher
Role: Left-hand bat, left-arm spin bowler
Born: 31 March 1976, Bradford
Height: 5ft 11in **Weight:** 13st 6lbs
Nickname: Fish, Flash, Fishy
County debut: 1995-96 (Yorkshire), 2002 (Gloucestershire)
County cap: 2004
1st-Class 50s: 7
1st-Class 100s: 1
1st-Class 5 w. in innings: 7
1st-Class 10 w. in match: 1
1st-Class catches: 17
Place in batting averages: 225th av. 18.82 (2003 188th av. 24.33)
Place in bowling averages: 140th av. 46.65 (2003 44th av. 27.39)
Strike rate: 83.65 (career 73.95)
Parents: Geoff and Linda
Marital status: Single
Family links with cricket: Father played club cricket
Education: Beckfoot Grammar School
Qualifications: 9 GCSEs, NCA coaching award, sports leader's award, lifesaver (bronze), YMCA gym instructor
Overseas tours: Yorkshire to Zimbabwe 1996, to South Africa 1998, 1999, 2001, to Perth 2000; MCC to Sri Lanka 2001
Overseas teams played for: Somerset West, Cape Town 1994-95; Petone Riverside, Wellington, New Zealand 1997-98
Career highlights to date: 'Winning the Championship with Yorkshire [2001]'
Cricket moments to forget: 'My pair'
Cricketers particularly admired: Darren Lehmann, Shane Warne
Young players to look out for: Tim Bresnan
Other sports played: Football (Westbrook)
Other sports followed: Football (Leeds United)
Relaxations: Music, movies, catching up with friends, shopping, eating out
Extras: Played England U17 and Yorkshire Schools U15, U16 and Yorkshire U19. Yorkshire 2nd XI cap. Bowled the last first-class ball delivered at Northlands Road, Southampton, September 2000. Released by Yorks at the end of the 2001 season and joined Glos for 2002. Scored maiden first-class century (103*) v Essex at Gloucester 2002, sharing with Jack Russell (107) in a record seventh-wicket stand for Glos in matches v Essex (207). Recorded three Championship five-wicket returns in successive innings 2003, including maiden ten-wicket match (5-30/5-93) v Durham at Bristol

Best batting: 103* Gloucestershire v Essex, Gloucester 2002
Best bowling: 5-30 Gloucestershire v Durham, Bristol 2003

2004 Season

	M	Inns	NO	Runs	HS	Avge	100s	50s	Ct	St	O	M	Runs	Wkts	Avge	Best	5wI	10wM
Test																		
All First	11	17	0	320	45	18.82	-	-	4	-	320.4	61	1073	23	46.65	5-114	1	-
1-day Int																		
C & G																		
totesport	8	6	3	27	23	9.00	-	-	5	-	52	3	219	11	19.90	3-18	-	
Twenty20	5	2	1	9	8	9.00	-	-	4	-	8	0	61	6	10.16	4-22	-	

Career Performances

	M	Inns	NO	Runs	HS	Avge	100s	50s	Ct	St	Balls	Runs	Wkts	Avge	Best	5wI	10wM
Test																	
All First	61	87	15	1652	103 *	22.94	1	7	17	-	9318	4949	126	39.27	5-30	7	1
1-day Int																	
C & G	3	1	0	5	5	5.00	-	-	2	-	150	87	3	29.00	1-21	-	
totesport	35	20	7	100	23	7.69	-	-	8	-	1282	925	39	23.71	3-18	-	
Twenty20	5	2	1	9	8	9.00	-	-	4	-	48	61	6	10.16	4-22	-	

FLEMING, S. P. Nottinghamshire

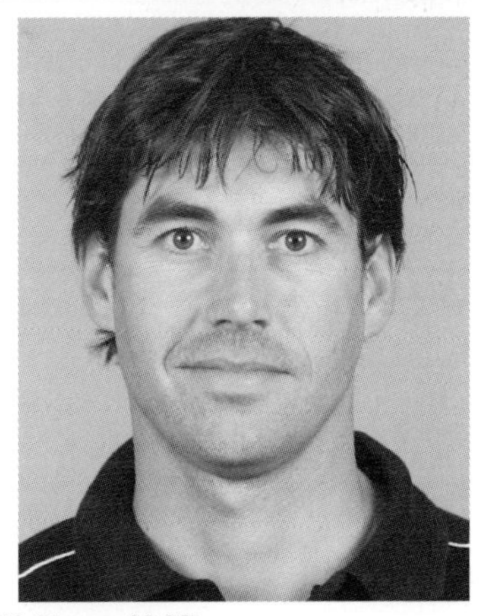

Name: Stephen Paul Fleming
Role: Left-hand bat, occasional right-arm slow-medium bowler, county captain
Born: 1 April 1973, Christchurch, New Zealand
Height: 6ft 3in
County debut: 2001 (Middlesex), 2003 (Yorkshire)
County cap: 2001 (Middlesex)
Test debut: 1993-94
Tests: 85
One-Day Internationals: 226
1000 runs in a season: 1
1st-Class 50s: 67
1st-Class 100s: 21
1st-Class 200s: 1
1st-Class catches: 235
One-Day 100s: 7
Place in batting averages: 26th av. 53.55 (2003 81st av. 39.08)
Education: Cashmere High School; Christchurch College of Education

Overseas tours: New Zealand U19 to India 1991-92; New Zealand to England 1994, to South Africa 1994-95, to India 1995-96, to India and Pakistan (World Cup) 1995-96, to West Indies 1995-96, to Pakistan 1996-97, to Zimbabwe 1997-98 (captain), to Australia 1997-98 (captain), to Sri Lanka 1997-98 (captain), to UK, Ireland and Holland (World Cup) 1999 (captain), to England 1999 (captain), to India 1999-2000 (captain), to Zimbabwe 2000-01 (captain), to Kenya (ICC Knockout Trophy) 2000-01 (captain), to South Africa 2000-01 (captain), to Australia 2001-02 (captain), to Pakistan 2002 (captain), to West Indies 2002 (captain), to Sri Lanka (ICC Champions Trophy) 2002-03 (captain), to Africa (World Cup) 2002-03 (captain), to Sri Lanka 2003 (captain), to India 2003-04 (captain), to England 2004 (captain), to England (ICC Champions Trophy) 2004 (captain), to Bangladesh 2004-05 (captain), to Australia 2004-05 (captain), plus other one-day tournaments
Overseas teams played for: Canterbury 1991-92 – 1999-2000; Wellington 2001-02 –
Extras: Captain of New Zealand since 1996-97. Led his country to series victory in England in 1999, which included New Zealand's first wins at Lord's and The Oval. Led New Zealand to victory in the ICC Knockout Trophy in Kenya 2000-01. Scored 60 v Pakistan at Dunedin 2000-01, in the process sharing with Nathan Astle in a record partnership for any wicket for New Zealand in ODIs (193). Was Middlesex overseas player in 2001. Scored 274* and 69* in the first Test v Sri Lanka at Colombo 2003. His Test awards include Man of the Match in the first Test v West Indies at Bridgetown 2002 (130) and Man of the Match in the first Test v Pakistan at Hamilton 2003-04 (192). Has won numerous ODI awards, including Man of the Match for his 134* v South Africa at Johannesburg in the 2002-03 World Cup and Man of the NatWest Series in England 2004. Was a Yorkshire overseas player in 2003. One of *New Zealand Cricket Almanack*'s two Players of the Year 1998, 2003, 2004. National Bank [New Zealand] Player of the Year 2003-04. Has joined Nottinghamshire as an overseas player and as captain for 2005
Best batting: 274* New Zealand v Sri Lanka, Colombo 2002-03
Stop press: Made 87th Test appearance in the second Test v Bangladesh at Chittagong 2004-05 to become New Zealand's most capped Test player; scored double century (202) in the match to also become New Zealand's highest Test run-scorer, passing Martin Crowe's 5444 runs

2004 Season

	M	Inns	NO	Runs	HS	Avge	100s	50s	Ct	St	O	M	Runs	Wkts	Avge	Best	5wI	10wM
Test	3	6	0	308	117	51.33	1	1	4	-								
All First	5	9	0	482	117	53.55	1	3	6	-								
1-day Int	8	7	0	298	99	42.57	-	2	3	-								
C & G																		
totesport																		
Twenty20																		

Career Performances

	M	Inns	NO	Runs	HS	Avge	100s	50s	Ct	St	Balls	Runs	Wkts	Avge	Best	5wI	10wM
Test	85	148	10	5335	274 *	38.65	7	35	125	-							
All First	179	299	27	11320	274 *	41.61	22	67	235	-	102	129	0	-	-	-	-
1-day Int	226	217	18	6428	134 *	32.30	6	37	107	-	29	28	1	28.00	1-8	-	
C & G																	
totesport	17	16	1	392	139 *	26.13	1	1	5	-							
Twenty20	4	4	0	62	58	15.50	-	1	1	-							

FLINTOFF, A. Lancashire

Name: Andrew Flintoff
Role: Right-hand bat, right-arm fast-medium bowler
Born: 6 December 1977, Preston
Height: 6ft 4in
County debut: 1995
County cap: 1998
Test debut: 1998
Tests: 40
One-Day Internationals: 80
1st-Class 50s: 34
1st-Class 100s: 14
1st-Class 5 w. in innings: 2
1st-Class catches: 138
One-Day 100s: 5
Place in batting averages: 13th av. 60.30 (2003 5th av. 72.46)
Place in bowling averages: 18th av. 24.50 (2003 139th av. 48.46)
Strike rate: 48.33 (career 73.31)
Parents: Colin and Susan
Wife and date of marriage: Rachael, 5 March 2005
Children: Holly, 6 September 2004
Family links with cricket: Brother Chris and father both play local league cricket
Education: Ribbleton Hall High School
Qualifications: 9 GCSEs
Off-season: Touring with England
Overseas tours: England Schools U15 to South Africa 1993; England U19 to West Indies 1994-95, to Zimbabwe 1995-96, to Pakistan 1996-97 (captain); England A to Kenya and Sri Lanka 1997-98, to Zimbabwe and South Africa 1998-99; England to Sharjah (Coca-Cola Cup) 1998-99, to South Africa and Zimbabwe 1999-2000, to

Kenya (ICC Knockout Trophy) 2000-01, to Pakistan and (one-day series) Sri Lanka 2000-01, to Zimbabwe (one-day series) 2001-02, to India and New Zealand 2001-02, to Australia 2002-03, to Africa (World Cup) 2002-03, to Bangladesh and Sri Lanka 2003-04, to West Indies 2003-04, to South Africa 2004-05; ECB National Academy to Australia 2001-02; England VI to Hong Kong 2001
Other sports/games played: Represented Lancashire Schools at chess
Extras: Represented England U14 to U19. Captained England U19 v Zimbabwe U19 1997. Scored 61 off 24 balls in Championship match v Surrey at Old Trafford 1998, including 34 from one over. Became the 50th recipient of the Cricket Writers' Club Young Player of the Year award 1998. PCA Young Player of the Year 1998. Scored 143 off 66 balls, including nine sixes, in National League v Essex at Chelmsford 1999. His 160 v Yorkshire at Old Trafford 1999 included 111 runs before lunch, the first century before lunch by a Lancashire batsman in a Roses match. Won the EDS Walter Lawrence Trophy 1999 (for the fastest first-class century of the season) for his hundred off 61 balls (before lunch) v Gloucestershire at Bristol. Represented England in the 1999 World Cup. Lancashire Player of the Year 2000. Vice-captain of Lancashire 2002. Scored maiden Test century (137) v New Zealand in the first Test at Christchurch 2001-02, in the process sharing with Graham Thorpe in a stand of 281 that set several new records, including that for the highest sixth-wicket partnership for England in Tests. Scored 28-ball 50* (the fastest ODI fifty by an England player) v Sri Lanka at Trent Bridge in the NatWest Series 2002. BBC North West Sports Personality of the Year 2003. Recorded maiden Test five-wicket return (5-58) in the third Test v West Indies at Bridgetown 2003-04. One of *Wisden*'s Five Cricketers of the Year 2004. Vodafone England Cricketer of the Year 2003-04. Scored century (123) v West Indies at Lord's in the NatWest Series 2004, in the process sharing with Andrew Strauss (100) in a new record partnership for England in ODIs (226). His Test awards include England's Man of the Series v South Africa 2003 and v West Indies 2004. His ODI awards include Man of the NatWest Series v Zimbabwe and South Africa 2003 and Man of the Series v Bangladesh 2003-04, during which he passed Ian Botham's England career record of 44 sixes in ODIs. Winner of inaugural ICC One-Day Player of the Year award 2003-04. Book *My Life in Pictures* (with Patrick Murphy) published 2004. PCA Player of the Year award 2004. ECB contract 2004-05
Best batting: 167 England v West Indies, Edgbaston 2004
Best bowling: 5-24 Lancashire v Hampshire, Southampton 1999
Stop press: Took 100th Test wicket (Herschelle Gibbs) in the third Test v South Africa at Cape Town 2004-05, in the process achieving double of 1000 runs and 100 wickets in Tests. Missed ODIs v South Africa 2004-05, returning home after the Test series to undergo ankle surgery

2004 Season

	M	Inns	NO	Runs	HS	Avge	100s	50s	Ct	St	O	M	Runs	Wkts	Avge	Best	5wI	10wM
Test	7	11	1	603	167	60.30	1	6	7	-	193.2	41	588	24	24.50	3-25	-	-
All First	7	11	1	603	167	60.30	1	6	7	-	193.2	41	588	24	24.50	3-25	-	-
1-day Int	9	9	2	512	123	73.14	3	1	1	-	46.3	2	185	11	16.81	3-11	-	
C & G	1	1	0	35	35	35.00	-	-	-	-	10	1	28	2	14.00	2-28	-	
totesport																		
Twenty20	3	3	0	131	85	43.66	-	1	1	-	5.5	0	39	2	19.50	2-15	-	

Career Performances

	M	Inns	NO	Runs	HS	Avge	100s	50s	Ct	St	Balls	Runs	Wkts	Avge	Best	5wI	10wM
Test	40	63	2	2012	167	32.98	4	12	28	-	6699	3254	87	37.40	5-58	1	-
All First	124	191	13	6509	167	36.56	14	34	138	-	12390	5895	169	34.88	5-24	2	-
1-day Int	80	71	11	2111	123	35.18	3	13	28	-	2807	1966	82	23.97	4-14	-	
C & G	24	20	4	706	135 *	44.12	1	3	16	-	774	501	19	26.36	3-54	-	
totesport	59	58	3	1378	143	25.05	1	6	17	-	1391	1043	47	22.19	4-24	-	
Twenty20	3	3	0	131	85	43.66	-	1	1	-	35	39	2	19.50	2-15	-	

FLOWER, A. — Essex

Name: Andrew (Andy) Flower
Role: Left-hand bat, wicket-keeper, occasional right-arm medium/off-spin bowler
Born: 28 April 1968, Cape Town, South Africa
Height: 5ft 10in
Nickname: Petals
County debut: 2002
County cap: 2002
Test debut: 1992-93
Tests: 70
One-Day Internationals: 213
1000 runs in a season: 3
1st-Class 50s: 68
1st-Class 100s: 33
1st-Class 200s: 3
1st-Class catches: 333
1st-Class stumpings: 21
One-Day 100s: 7
Place in batting averages: 67th av. 43.11 (2003 34th av. 47.84)
Strike rate: (career 96.83)
Family links with cricket: Younger brother Grant played for Zimbabwe and also plays for Essex

Education: Vainona High School
Overseas tours: Zimbabwe to Australia and New Zealand (World Cup) 1991-92, to India 1992-93, to Pakistan 1993-94 (captain), to Australia 1994-95 (captain), to New Zealand 1995-96 (captain), to India and Pakistan (World Cup) 1995-96 (captain), to Sri Lanka and Pakistan 1996-97, to Sri Lanka and New Zealand 1997-98, to Bangladesh (Wills International Cup) 1998-99, to Pakistan 1998-99, to UK, Ireland and Holland (World Cup) 1999, to South Africa 1999-2000, to West Indies 1999-2000 (captain), to England 2000 (captain), to Kenya (ICC Knockout Trophy) 2000-01, to India 2000-01, to New Zealand and Australia 2000-01, to Bangladesh, Sri Lanka and India 2001-02, to Sri Lanka (ICC Champions Trophy) 2002-03, plus other one-day tournaments
Overseas teams played for: Mashonaland 1993-94 – 2002-03; South Australia 2003-04
Other sports played: Tennis, squash; rugby, hockey (at school)
Extras: Captained Zimbabwe Schools. Made first-class debut for ZCU President's XI v Young West Indies at Harare 1986. First represented Zimbabwe 1988-89. Scored century (115*) on ODI debut v Sri Lanka at New Plymouth in the 1992 World Cup, batting right through the Zimbabwe innings. Appeared in Zimbabwe's inaugural Test, v India at Harare 1992-93, scoring 59. Scored 156 v Pakistan at Harare 1994-95 in Zimbabwe's first Test win, in the process sharing with Grant Flower (201*) in a fourth-wicket stand of 269, the highest partnership between brothers in Test cricket. Scored 100* v Pakistan at Bulawayo 1997-98, in the process sharing with Murray Goodwin in a new record partnership for Zimbabwe for any wicket in Tests (277*). Man of the Series v India 2000-01, with scores of 232*, 183*, 70 and 55 for a series average of 270.00. Scored 73 v Bangladesh at Bulawayo 2000-01, in the process equalling Everton Weekes's world record, set 1947-49, of seven consecutive Test half-centuries. FICA International Player of the Year 2001. Scored 142 and 199* v South Africa in the first Test at Harare 2001, becoming the first wicket-keeper to score a century in each innings of a Test match; his performance took him to the top of the PricewaterhouseCoopers ratings for Test batsmen, making him the first wicket-keeper/batsman to achieve the feat. Equalled Zimbabwe's then highest individual score in ODIs with his 142* v England at Harare 2001-02, in the process sharing with Heath Streak in a new world record seventh-wicket partnership for ODIs (130). One of *Wisden*'s Five Cricketers of the Year 2002. Joined Essex as overseas player 2002. A former captain of Zimbabwe. Represented Zimbabwe in the 2002-03 World Cup, retiring from international cricket after the competition. Scored 106 v Nottinghamshire at Trent Bridge in the C&G 2004, in the process sharing in an Essex record partnership for one-day cricket (248) with Will Jefferson (126). Is no longer considered an overseas player
Best batting: 232* Zimbabwe v India, Nagpur 2000-01
Best bowling: 1-1 Mashonaland v Mashonaland CD, Harare South 1993-94

2004 Season

	M	Inns	NO	Runs	HS	Avge	100s	50s	Ct	St	O	M	Runs	Wkts	Avge	Best	5wI	10wM
Test																		
All First	17	29	3	1121	172	43.11	2	6	18	-								
1-day Int																		
C & G	3	3	1	186	106	93.00	1	1	-	-								
totesport	16	14	1	394	70	30.30	-	3	6	-								
Twenty20	5	5	0	135	58	27.00	-	1	1	-								

Career Performances

	M	Inns	NO	Runs	HS	Avge	100s	50s	Ct	St	Balls	Runs	Wkts	Avge	Best	5wI	10wM
Test	70	126	19	5136	232 *	48.00	12	29	153	9	3	4	0	-	-	-	-
All First	190	320	57	13495	232 *	51.31	36	68	333	21	581	250	6	41.66	1-1	-	-
1-day Int	213	208	16	6785	145	35.33	4	55	141	32	30	23	0	-	-	-	
C & G	7	6	1	388	106	77.60	1	3	4	-							
totesport	45	43	6	1431	103	38.67	2	11	30	6							
Twenty20	10	10	0	401	83	40.10	-	3	4	-							

FLOWER, G. W. — Essex

Name: Grant William Flower
Role: Right-hand bat, slow left-arm bowler
Born: 20 December 1970, Harare, Zimbabwe
Height: 5ft 10in
County debut: 2002 (Leicestershire)
Test debut: 1992-93
Tests: 67
One-Day Internationals: 219
1st-Class 50s: 51
1st-Class 100s: 16
1st-Class 200s: 3
1st-Class 5 w. in innings: 3
1st-Class catches: 137
One-Day 100s: 6
Strike rate: (career 76.57)
Family links with cricket: Younger brother of Andy Flower (also plays for Essex)
Education: St George's College, Harare
Overseas tours: Zimbabwe to India 1992-93, to Pakistan 1993-94, to Australia (one-day series) 1994-95, to New Zealand 1995-96, to India and Pakistan (World Cup) 1995-96, to Sri Lanka and Pakistan 1996-97, to Sri Lanka and New Zealand 1997-98, to Bangladesh (Wills International Cup) 1998-99, to Pakistan 1998-99, to UK, Ireland

and Holland (World Cup) 1999, to South Africa 1999-2000, to West Indies 1999-2000, to England 2000, to Kenya (ICC Knockout Trophy) 2000-01, to India 2000-01, to New Zealand and Australia 2000-01, to Bangladesh, Sri Lanka and India 2001-02, to Sri Lanka (ICC Champions Trophy) 2002-03, to England 2003, to Australia 2003-04 (VB Series), plus other one-day series and tournaments
Overseas teams played for: Mashonaland 1996-97 – 2003-04
Extras: Made first-class debut for Zimbabwe v England A at Bulawayo 1989-90. Appeared in Zimbabwe's inaugural Test, v India at Harare 1992-93, scoring 82. Scored 201* v Pakistan at Harare 1994-95 in Zimbabwe's first Test win, in the process sharing with Andy Flower (156) in a fourth-wicket stand of 269, the highest partnership between brothers in Test cricket. Became the first player to score a hundred in each innings of a Test for Zimbabwe (104/151) in the first Test v New Zealand at Harare 1997-98. Scored 156* in the first Test v Pakistan at Bulawayo 1997-98, in the process becoming the first Zimbabwe player to score five Test centuries. Was Leicestershire's overseas player during June 2002. Scored century (105*) in the fourth ODI v Pakistan at Harare 2002-03 to help post a total of 210; at one point Zimbabwe had been 41-6. Represented Zimbabwe in the 2002-03 World Cup. His Test awards include Man of the Series v New Zealand 1997-98. His ODI awards include Zimbabwe's Man of the Series v Pakistan 1996-97, as well as Man of the Match v England at Trent Bridge in the NatWest Series 2003 (96*) and v Australia at Adelaide in the VB Series 2003-04 (94). Has joined Essex for 2005; is no longer considered an overseas player
Best batting: 242* Mashonaland v Matabeleland, Harare 1996-97
Best bowling: 7-31 Zimbabweans v Lahore City, Lahore 1998-99

2004 Season (did not make any first-class or one-day appearances)

Career Performances

	M	Inns	NO	Runs	HS	Avge	100s	50s	Ct	St	Balls	Runs	Wkts	Avge	Best	5wI	10wM
Test	67	123	6	3457	201 *	29.54	6	15	42	-	3378	1537	25	61.48	4-41	-	-
All First	149	259	22	9306	242 *	39.26	19	51	137	-	11103	4866	145	33.55	7-31	3	-
1-day Int	219	212	18	6535	142 *	33.68	6	40	85	-	5420	4187	104	40.25	4-32	-	
C & G	2	2	0	11	8	5.50	-	-	1	-	66	33	2	16.50	2-33	-	
totesport	3	2	0	22	19	11.00	-	-	-	-	86	62	1	62.00	1-43	-	
Twenty20																	

30. Which batsman who represented West Indies in the 1983 World Cup later played for USA and then coached them in the 2004 ICC Champions Trophy tournament?

FOSTER, J. S. — Essex

Name: James Savin Foster
Role: Right-hand bat, wicket-keeper
Born: 15 April 1980, Whipps Cross, London
Height: 6ft **Weight:** 12st
Nickname: Fozzy, Chief
County debut: 2000
County cap: 2001
Test debut: 2001-02
Tests: 7
1000 runs in a season: 1
50 dismissals in a season: 2
1st-Class 50s: 11
1st-Class 100s: 4
1st-Class 200s: 1
1st-Class catches: 176
1st-Class stumpings: 19
Place in batting averages: 34th av. 51.85 (2003 168th av. 26.50)
Parents: Martin and Diana
Marital status: Single
Family links with cricket: 'Dad played for Essex Amateurs'
Education: Forest School; Durham University
Qualifications: 10 GCSEs, 3 A-levels, hockey and cricket Level 1 coaching awards
Overseas tours: BUSA to South Africa 1999; Durham University to South Africa 1999, to Vienna (European Indoor Championships) 1999; England A to West Indies 2000-01; England to Zimbabwe (one-day series) 2001-02, to India and New Zealand 2001-02, to Australia 2002-03
Career highlights to date: 'Playing for my country'
Cricket moments to forget: 'None yet'
Cricketers particularly admired: Nasser Hussain, Stuart Law, Robert Rollins, Ian Healy, Jack Russell, Alec Stewart, Adam Gilchrist
Young players to look out for: John Chambers, Adnan Akram, Arfan Akram, Tony Palladino, Ravi Bopara, Michael Brown, Steven Miel
Other sports played: Hockey (Essex U21), tennis (played for GB U14 v Sweden U14; national training squad)
Other sports followed: Football (Wimbledon FC)
Relaxations: Socialising
Extras: Essex U17 Player of the Year 1997. Represented ECB U19 1998 and England U19 1999. Represented BUSA 1999, 2000 and 2001. Scored 52 on Championship debut v Glamorgan at Southend 2000. Voted Essex Cricket Society 2nd XI Player of the Year 2000. Scored 53 on England A debut v Guyana in Grenada 2000-01. Played

for Durham University CCE 2001. NBC Denis Compton Award for the most promising young Essex player 2001. Scored 40 in second Test v India at Ahmedabad 2001-02, in the process sharing with Craig White in a record seventh-wicket partnership for England in Tests in India (105). His 110* for MCC v Sussex on 11 April 2004 is the earliest hundred recorded at Lord's in an English season. Scored maiden first-class double century (212) v Leicestershire at Chelmsford 2004. Scored 1000 first-class runs in a season for the first time and achieved double (1037 runs plus 51 dismissals) 2004
Best batting: 212 Essex v Leicestershire, Chelmsford 2004

2004 Season

	M	Inns	NO	Runs	HS	Avge	100s	50s	Ct	St	O	M	Runs	Wkts	Avge	Best	5wI	10wM
Test																		
All First	17	25	5	1037	212	51.85	4	1	45	6								
1-day Int																		
C & G	3	2	1	26	18 *	26.00	-	-	8	1								
totesport	16	10	2	152	46 *	19.00	-	-	20	2								
Twenty20	5	3	0	25	16	8.33	-	-	2	1								

Career Performances

	M	Inns	NO	Runs	HS	Avge	100s	50s	Ct	St	Balls	Runs	Wkts	Avge	Best	5wI	10wM
Test	7	12	3	226	48	25.11	-	-	17	1							
All First	72	108	13	2995	212	31.52	5	11	176	19	12	6	0	-	-	-	-
1-day Int																	
C & G	6	5	1	91	33	22.75	-	-	13	1							
totesport	48	41	11	606	56 *	20.20	-	1	59	7							
Twenty20	9	6	0	26	16	4.33	-	-	3	1							

FRANCE, B. J. — Derbyshire

Name: Benjaman (Ben) John France
Role: Left-hand bat, right-arm seam bowler
Born: 14 May 1982, Brunei
Height: 5ft 11in **Weight:** 12st 7lbs
Nickname: Benny, Frenchy, Froggy
County debut: 2004
1st-Class 50s: 1
1st-Class catches: 2
Place in batting averages: 231st av. 18.00
Parents: Joseph and Jackie
Marital status: Single
Family links with cricket: Brother played Minor Counties cricket for Oxfordshire and

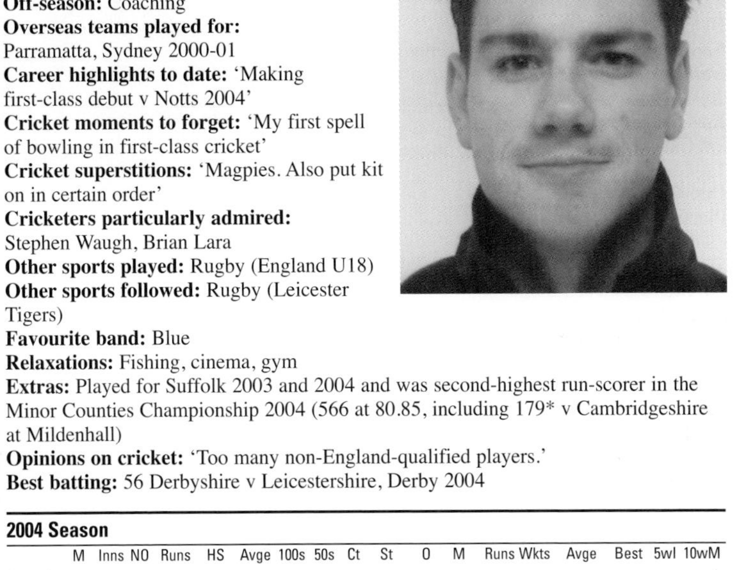

also played for the Combined Services
Education: Bromsgrove School; Oxford College
Qualifications: 9 GCSEs, BTEC National Diploma in Sports Science
Off-season: Coaching
Overseas teams played for: Parramatta, Sydney 2000-01
Career highlights to date: 'Making first-class debut v Notts 2004'
Cricket moments to forget: 'My first spell of bowling in first-class cricket'
Cricket superstitions: 'Magpies. Also put kit on in certain order'
Cricketers particularly admired: Stephen Waugh, Brian Lara
Other sports played: Rugby (England U18)
Other sports followed: Rugby (Leicester Tigers)
Favourite band: Blue
Relaxations: Fishing, cinema, gym
Extras: Played for Suffolk 2003 and 2004 and was second-highest run-scorer in the Minor Counties Championship 2004 (566 at 80.85, including 179* v Cambridgeshire at Mildenhall)
Opinions on cricket: 'Too many non-England-qualified players.'
Best batting: 56 Derbyshire v Leicestershire, Derby 2004

2004 Season

	M	Inns	NO	Runs	HS	Avge	100s	50s	Ct	St	O	M	Runs	Wkts	Avge	Best	5wI	10wM
Test																		
All First	4	7	0	126	56	18.00	-	1	2	-	4	0	20	0	-	-	-	-
1-day Int																		
C & G																		
totesport	1	1	0	13	13	13.00	-	-	-	-								
Twenty20																		

Career Performances

	M	Inns	NO	Runs	HS	Avge	100s	50s	Ct	St	Balls	Runs	Wkts	Avge	Best	5wI	10wM
Test																	
All First	4	7	0	126	56	18.00	-	1	2	-	24	20	0	-	-	-	-
1-day Int																	
C & G	1	1	0	8	8	8.00	-	-	-	-							
totesport	1	1	0	13	13	13.00	-	-	-	-							
Twenty20																	

FRANCIS, J. D. Somerset

Name: John Daniel Francis
Role: Left-hand bat, slow left-arm bowler
Born: 13 November 1980, Bromley, Kent
Height: 5ft 11in **Weight:** 13st
Nickname: Long John, Franky, Junior
County debut: 2001 (Hampshire), 2004 (Somerset)
1st-Class 50s: 9
1st-Class 100s: 2
1st-Class catches: 19
One-Day 100s: 1
Place in batting averages: 90th av. 36.93 (2003 227th av. 19.42)
Strike rate: 109.50 (career 66.75)
Parents: Linda and Daniel
Marital status: Single
Family links with cricket: Brother Simon played for Hampshire 1997-2001; now plays for Somerset. Father played club cricket. Grandfather played in the services
Education: King Edward VI, Southampton; Durham and Loughborough Universities
Qualifications: 10 GCSEs, 3 A-levels, BSc Sports Science, ECB Level 1 coaching award
Off-season: 'Training and working at my game in Taunton before Christmas, then playing in Sydney, Australia, for three months after Christmas'
Overseas tours: Twyford School to Barbados 1993; West of England U15 to West Indies 1995; King Edward VI, Southampton to South Africa 1998; Durham University to South Africa 2000; British Universities to South Africa 2002
Career highlights to date: 'Scoring maiden first-class century for Somerset v Yorkshire at Scarborough 2004, sharing in a partnership of 197 runs with Ricky Ponting'
Cricket moments to forget: 'Getting first ever pair, in a match v Yorkshire'
Cricket superstitions: 'Too many to say'
Cricketers particularly admired: Graham Thorpe, Adam Hollioake, Mike Hussey, Simon Francis
Young players to look out for: James Hildreth, Matt Wood, Ben Riches, Andrew Dunn
Other sports played: Hockey (England U18), golf, squash
Injuries: Out for one and a half weeks with concussion; for four weeks with a broken finger; for one and half weeks with hip bursitis
Favourite band: David Gray
Relaxations: Drawing and painting, socialising

Extras: Hampshire Young Sportsman of the Year 1995. Sir John Hobbs Silver Jubilee Memorial Prize for outstanding U16 player of the year 1996. Leading run-scorer in U15 World Cup 1996. Played for Loughborough University CCE in 2001, 2002 and 2003; scored a century (107) v Leicestershire at Leicester 2001. Scored 189* for British Universities v South Africa Universities in South Africa 2002. NBC Denis Compton Award for the most promising young Hampshire player 2002. Represented British Universities 2002 and 2003. Left Hampshire at the end of the 2003 season and joined Somerset for 2004. Scored maiden first-class century (109) v Yorkshire at Scarborough 2004
Best batting: 110 Somerset v Hampshire, Taunton 2004
Best bowling: 1-1 Hampshire v Leicestershire, Leicester 2002

2004 Season

	M	Inns	NO	Runs	HS	Avge	100s	50s	Ct	St	O	M	Runs	Wkts	Avge	Best	5wI	10wM
Test																		
All First	10	16	1	554	110	36.93	2	3	6	-	36.3	9	120	2	60.00	1-4	-	-
1-day Int																		
C & G	1	1	0	3	3	3.00	-	-	1	-								
totesport	13	12	0	342	79	28.50	-	2	3	-								
Twenty20	5	5	2	116	31	38.66	-	-	-	-								

Career Performances

	M	Inns	NO	Runs	HS	Avge	100s	50s	Ct	St	Balls	Runs	Wkts	Avge	Best	5wI	10wM
Test																	
All First	32	56	3	1445	110	27.26	2	9	19	-	267	155	4	38.75	1-1	-	-
1-day Int																	
C & G	1	1	0	3	3	3.00	-	-	1	-							
totesport	40	39	7	1160	103 *	36.25	1	8	7	-							
Twenty20	5	5	2	116	31	38.66	-	-	-	-							

31. Which Kenyan cricketer scored 15 first-class centuries for Nottinghamshire between 1966 and 1985?

FRANCIS, S. R. G. Somerset

Name: Simon Richard George Francis
Role: Right-hand bat, right-arm medium-fast bowler
Born: 15 August 1978, Bromley, Kent
Height: 6ft 1in **Weight:** 14st
Nickname: Franco, Guru
County debut: 1997 (Hampshire), 2002 (Somerset)
1st-Class 5 w. in innings: 3
1st-Class catches: 11
One-Day 5 w. in innings: 1
Place in batting averages: (2003 267th av. 12.09)
Place in bowling averages: 92nd av. 36.39 (2003 83rd av. 33.68)
Strike rate: 53.78 (career 59.38)
Parents: Daniel and Linda
Marital status: Single
Family links with cricket: Brother John plays at Somerset. Father played club cricket. Grandfather played for the Navy
Education: King Edward VI, Southampton; Durham University
Qualifications: 9 GCSEs, 1 AS-Level, 3 A-levels, BA (Hons) Sport in the Community, Level 1 coaching in hockey, Level III coaching in cricket
Career outside cricket: Cricket and hockey coaching
Overseas tours: England U17 to Holland (International Youth Tournament) 1995; England U19 to Pakistan 1996-97; Durham University to Zimbabwe 1997-98; Hampshire to Boland 2001; England A to Malaysia and India 2003-04
Overseas teams played for: Maties (Stellenbosch University), South Africa 2000; Melville CC, Perth 2001
Cricket moments to forget: 'Whole of the B&H competition 2002'
Cricketers particularly admired: Malcolm Marshall, Richard Hadlee, Allan Donald, Graham Dilley
Young players to look out for: John Francis
Other sports played: Golf, hockey (England U18 1995)
Relaxations: 'Films, sleeping, reading, listening to music'
Extras: *Daily Telegraph* West Region Bowling Award U15. Played in Durham University's BUSA Championship-winning side 1999. Released by Hampshire at the end of the 2001 season and joined Somerset for 2002. Took hat-trick v Loughborough UCCE at Taunton 2003. ECB National Academy 2003-04. His 8-66 v Derbyshire at Derby in the C&G 2004 (his maiden one-day five-wicket return) are the best figures by a Somerset bowler in one-day cricket

Best batting: 44 Somerset v Yorkshire, Taunton 2003
Best bowling: 5-42 Somerset v Glamorgan, Taunton 2004

2004 Season

	M	Inns	NO	Runs	HS	Avge	100s	50s	Ct	St	O	M	Runs	Wkts	Avge	Best	5wI	10wM
Test																		
All First	11	10	6	46	15	11.50	-	-	6	-	295.5	51	1201	33	36.39	5-42	2	-
1-day Int																		
C & G	1	0	0	0	0	-	-	-	-	-	9.5	0	66	8	8.25	8-66	1	
totesport	14	7	3	36	17	9.00	-	-	1	-	100.1	8	536	16	33.50	3-24	-	
Twenty20	5	3	1	11	9 *	5.50	-	-	-	-	15	0	157	1	157.00	1-27	-	

Career Performances

	M	Inns	NO	Runs	HS	Avge	100s	50s	Ct	St	Balls	Runs	Wkts	Avge	Best	5wI	10wM
Test																	
All First	49	63	27	337	44	9.36	-	-	11	-	7483	4764	126	37.80	5-42	3	-
1-day Int																	
C & G	3	0	0	0	0	-	-	-	-	-	155	95	9	10.55	8-66	1	
totesport	43	25	12	176	33 *	13.53	-	-	10	-	1734	1580	44	35.90	4-60	-	
Twenty20	10	7	3	30	9 *	7.50	-	-	3	-	192	303	5	60.60	2-22	-	

FRANKLIN, J. E. C. — Gloucestershire

Name: James Edward Charles Franklin
Role: Left-hand bat, left-arm fast-medium bowler
Born: 7 November 1980, Wellington, New Zealand
County debut: 2004
County cap: 2004
Test debut: 2000-01
Tests: 3
One-Day Internationals: 28
1st-Class 50s: 7
1st-Class 100s: 1
1st-Class 5 w. in innings: 4
1st-Class catches: 14
One-Day 5 w. in innings: 1
Place in bowling averages: 12th av. 23.05
Strike rate: 42.11 (career 48.01)
Overseas tours: New Zealand U19 to South Africa (U19 World Cup) 1997-98, to Sri Lanka (U19 World Cup) 1999-2000; New Zealand A to South Africa 2004-05; New Zealand to Australia 2001-02 (VB Series),

to England 2004, to Bangladesh 2004-05, to Australia 2004-05, plus one-day tournaments in Sharjah
Overseas teams played for: Wellington 1998-99 –
Extras: Represented New Zealand U19 v England U19 1998-99. New Zealand Academy 1999-2000. Called up from club cricket in Lancashire to New Zealand squad in England 2004. Man of the Match v England at Riverside in the NatWest Series 2004 (5-42). Was an overseas player with Gloucestershire July to early August 2004 as a replacement for Shoaib Malik/Shabbir Ahmed. Took 7-60 v Lancashire at Cheltenham 2004, the best figures by a bowler on Championship debut for Gloucestershire since 1900
Best batting: 108* Wellington v Otago, Dunedin 2003-04
Best bowling: 7-60 Gloucestershire v Lancashire, Cheltenham 2004
Stop press: Took 5-28 in Bangladesh's first innings of the first Test at Dhaka 2004-05, becoming in the process the second New Zealand cricketer to take a Test hat-trick (Manjural Islam Rana, Mohammad Rafique, Tapash Baisya)

2004 Season

	M	Inns	NO	Runs	HS	Avge	100s	50s	Ct	St	O	M	Runs	Wkts	Avge	Best	5wI	10wM
Test	1	2	1	21	17	21.00	-	-	1	-	43.1	6	163	6	27.16	4-104	-	-
All First	4	8	3	155	44	31.00	-	-	2	-	126.2	33	415	18	23.05	7-60	1	-
1-day Int	4	0	0	0	0	-	-	-	-	-	29	2	157	6	26.16	5-42	1	
C & G	1	1	0	8	8	8.00	-	-	-	-	10	0	60	1	60.00	1-60	-	
totesport																		
Twenty20	2	2	0	52	36	26.00	-	-	-	-	8	0	48	0	-	-	-	

Career Performances

	M	Inns	NO	Runs	HS	Avge	100s	50s	Ct	St	Balls	Runs	Wkts	Avge	Best	5wI	10wM
Test	3	4	1	21	17	7.00	-	-	2	-	588	313	13	24.07	4-26	-	-
All First	48	72	13	1656	108 *	28.06	1	7	14	-	7538	3731	157	23.76	7-60	4	-
1-day Int	28	16	3	116	25 *	8.92	-	-	7	-	1224	1064	26	40.92	5-42	1	
C & G	1	1	0	8	8	8.00	-	-	-	-	60	60	1	60.00	1-60	-	
totesport																	
Twenty20	2	2	0	52	36	26.00	-	-	-	-	48	48	0	-	-	-	

32. Which Holland player was Hampshire's leading County Championship wicket-taker in 1989?

FRANKS, P. J. Nottinghamshire

Name: Paul John Franks
Role: Left-hand bat, right-arm fast-medium bowler
Born: 3 February 1979, Sutton-in-Ashfield
Height: 6ft 1½in **Weight:** 13st 10lbs
Nickname: Pike, Franno, The General
County debut: 1996
County cap: 1999
One-Day Internationals: 1
50 wickets in a season: 2
1st-Class 50s: 17
1st-Class 100s: 2
1st-Class 5 w. in innings: 11
1st-Class catches: 43
One-Day 5 w. in innings: 2
Place in batting averages: 88th av. 37.29 (2003 71st av. 40.50)
Place in bowling averages: 46th av. 29.93 (2003 122nd av. 42.03)
Strike rate: 49.11 (career 54.44)
Parents: Pat and John
Marital status: Single
Family links with cricket: 'Dad was a local league legend'
Education: Minster School, Southwell; West Notts College
Qualifications: 7 GCSEs, GNVQ (Advanced) Leisure Management, coaching Level 1
Overseas tours: England U19 to Pakistan 1996-97, to South Africa (including U19 World Cup) 1997-98; England A to Zimbabwe and South Africa 1998-99, to Bangladesh and New Zealand 1999-2000, to West Indies 2000-01, to Sri Lanka 2004-05; Notts CCC to South Africa 1998, 1999
Career highlights to date: 'England [one-day] debut v West Indies on home ground in 2000'
Cricket moments to forget: 'Any time I get my poles removed or go the distance'
Cricketers particularly admired: Glenn McGrath, Mike Atherton, Allan Donald, Phil 'bowls like me' DeFreitas
Young players to look out for: Kyle Hogg, Nadeem Malik, Bilal Shafayat, Matt Prior
Other sports played: Golf
Other sports followed: Football (Mansfield Town)
Relaxations: 'Taking it generally steady'
Extras: Became youngest ever Notts player (and third-youngest player ever in English first-class cricket, aged 18 years 163 days) to take a hat-trick, v Warwickshire at Trent Bridge 1997. Won U19 World Cup winner's medal in Johannesburg 1998. NBC Denis

Compton Award 1999. Cricket Writers' Young Player of the Year 2000. Vice-captain of Nottinghamshire 2003-04. ECB National Academy 2004-05
Best batting: 123* Nottinghamshire v Leicestershire, Leicester 2003
Best bowling: 7-56 Nottinghamshire v Middlesex, Lord's 2000

2004 Season

	M	Inns	NO	Runs	HS	Avge	100s	50s	Ct	St	O	M	Runs	Wkts	Avge	Best	5wI	10wM
Test																		
All First	17	22	5	634	57 *	37.29	-	5	2	-	352	68	1287	43	29.93	7-72	2	-
1-day Int																		
C & G	2	1	0	27	27	27.00	-	-	-	-	19	2	86	5	17.20	3-27	-	
totesport	10	9	0	193	64	21.44	-	1	2	-	42.1	2	229	10	22.90	3-37	-	
Twenty20	3	3	0	31	17	10.33	-	-	-	-								

Career Performances

	M	Inns	NO	Runs	HS	Avge	100s	50s	Ct	St	Balls	Runs	Wkts	Avge	Best	5wI	10wM
Test																	
All First	115	169	34	3577	123 *	26.49	2	17	43	-	18292	9832	336	29.26	7-56	11	-
1-day Int	1	1	0	4	4	4.00	-	-	1	-	54	48	0	-	-	-	
C & G	15	10	4	225	84 *	37.50	-	1	4	-	726	560	23	24.34	3-7	-	
totesport	84	69	19	1027	64	20.54	-	3	14	-	3352	2760	104	26.53	6-27	2	
Twenty20	8	7	2	93	29 *	18.60	-	-	3	-	39	51	3	17.00	2-31	-	

FRIEND, T. J. — Derbyshire

Name: Travis John Friend
Role: Right-hand bat, right-arm fast-medium bowler
Born: 7 January 1981, Kwekwe, Zimbabwe
Nickname: Chunks
County debut: No first-team appearance
Test debut: 2001
Tests: 13
One-Day Internationals: 51
1st-Class 50s: 6
1st-Class 100s: 3
1st-Class 5 w. in innings: 2
1st-Class catches: 31
Strike rate: (career 70.98)
Family links with cricket: Father, Ian, played for Rhodesia B; grandfather and great uncles also played
Education: St George's College, Harare

Overseas tours: Zimbabwe U19 to Sri Lanka (U19 World Cup) 1999-2000; Zimbabwe to Sharjah (Coca-Cola Champions Trophy) 2000-01, to India 2000-01, to New Zealand 2000-01, to Australia (CUB Series) 2000-01, to Bangladesh 2001-02, to Sri Lanka 2001-02, to India 2001-02, to England 2003, to Australia 2003-04 (VB Series), plus other one-day tournaments in Sharjah
Overseas teams played for: Midlands 2000-01 – 2003-04
Cricketers particularly admired: Jacques Kallis
Other sports played: Rugby (provincial age-group), golf
Extras: Represented Zimbabwe at U14 (captain), U16 and U19. Attended CFX [Zimbabwe] Academy 2000, making first-class debut v Mashonaland at Harare Country Club. Played for Helmsley, North Yorkshire 2000. Represented Zimbabwe in the World Cup 2002-03. Man of the Match in the first Test v Bangladesh at Dhaka 2001-02 (5-31/81/2-26). Man of the [ODI] Series v Kenya 2002-03. Has joined Derbyshire for 2005; is not considered an overseas player
Best batting: 183 Midlands v Manicaland, Kwekwe 2003-04
Best bowling: 5-16 Midlands v Matabeleland, Kwekwe 2003-04

2004 Season (did not make any first-class or one-day appearances)

Career Performances

	M	Inns	NO	Runs	HS	Avge	100s	50s	Ct	St	Balls	Runs	Wkts	Avge	Best	5wI	10wM
Test	13	19	4	447	81	29.80	-	3	2	-	2000	1090	25	43.60	5-31	1	-
All First	41	60	9	1671	183	32.76	3	6	31	-	5608	3154	79	39.92	5-16	2	-
1-day Int	51	39	5	548	91	16.11	-	3	17	-	1930	1779	37	48.08	4-55	-	
C & G																	
totesport																	
Twenty20																	

33. Which former Leicestershire all-rounder coached Zimbabwe in the 2004 ICC Champions Trophy tournament?

FROST, T. Warwickshire

Name: Tony Frost
Role: Right-hand bat, wicket-keeper
Born: 17 November 1975, Stoke-on-Trent
Height: 5ft 10in **Weight:** 10st 6lbs
County debut: 1997
County cap: 1999
50 dismissals in a season: 1
1st-Class 50s: 10
1st-Class 100s: 3
1st-Class catches: 162
1st-Class stumpings: 15
Place in batting averages: 62nd av. 43.69 (2003 195th av. 23.85)
Parents: Ivan and Christine
Marital status: Single
Family links with cricket: Father played for Staffordshire
Education: James Brinkley High School; Stoke-on-Trent College
Qualifications: 5 GCSEs
Overseas tours: Kidsgrove U18 to Australia 1990-91
Other sports followed: Football, golf
Extras: Represented Staffordshire at all levels from U11 to U19. Won Texaco U16 competition with Staffordshire in 1992. Played for Development of Excellence XI U17 v South Africa and U18 v West Indies and U19 v India. Scored century (135*) v Sussex at Horsham 2004, in the process equalling with Ian Bell (262*) Warwickshire's record partnership for the seventh wicket (289). Made 50 first-class dismissals in a season for the first time 2004
Best batting: 135* Warwickshire v Sussex, Horsham 2004

2004 Season

	M	Inns	NO	Runs	HS	Avge	100s	50s	Ct	St	O	M	Runs	Wkts	Avge	Best	5wI	10wM
Test																		
All First	17	19	6	568	135 *	43.69	1	2	47	6								
1-day Int																		
C & G	4	1	0	4	4	4.00	-	-	3	-								
totesport	10	7	4	69	21	23.00	-	-	11	6								
Twenty20	5	2	1	8	5	8.00	-	-	5	6								

Career Performances

	M	Inns	NO	Runs	HS	Avge	100s	50s	Ct	St	Balls	Runs	Wkts	Avge	Best	5wI	10wM
Test																	
All First	68	96	14	2265	135 *	27.62	3	10	162	15	12	15	0	-	-	-	-
1-day Int																	
C & G	8	5	0	65	47	13.00	-	-	8	1							
totesport	42	22	9	217	22 *	16.69	-	-	34	12							
Twenty20	6	3	1	39	31	19.50	-	-	5	6							

FULTON, D. P. Kent

Name: David (Dave) Paul Fulton
Role: Right-hand top-order bat, left-arm spin bowler, occasional wicket-keeper, county captain
Born: 15 November 1971, Lewisham
Height: 6ft 2in **Weight:** 12st 7lbs
Nickname: Tav, Rave
County debut: 1992
County cap: 1998
1000 runs in a season: 3
1st-Class 50s: 42
1st-Class 100s: 23
1st-Class 200s: 2
1st-Class catches: 243
Place in batting averages: 75th av. 40.96 (2003 91st av. 37.44)
Strike rate: (career 175.00)
Parents: John and Ann
Wife and date of marriage: Claudine Kay Tomlin, 19 December 2003
Children: Freddie Tom, 30 September 2004
Family links with cricket: Father played for village
Education: The Judd School, Tonbridge; University of Kent at Canterbury
Qualifications: 10 GCSEs, 3 A-levels, BA (Hons) Politics and International Relations, advanced cricket coach, rugby coach, gym instructor qualification
Career outside cricket: Journalist
Off-season: 'Perth for six weeks – training'
Overseas tours: Kent SCA U17 to Singapore and New Zealand 1987-88; Kent to France 1998, to Port Elizabeth 2001
Overseas teams played for: Avendale CC, Cape Town 1993-94; Victoria CC, Cape Town 1994-95; University of WA, Perth 1995-96; Petersham-Marrickville CC, Sydney 1998-99, 1999-2000

Career highlights to date: 'Will Kendall caught and bowled Fulton (first and only first-class victim). PCA Player of the Year 2001'
Cricket moments to forget: 'Already forgotten'
Cricketers particularly admired: Gordon Greenidge, Graham Gooch, Courtney Walsh, Steve Waugh
Young players to look out for: Joe Denly
Other sports played: Chess (England junior), table tennis ('top 10 in UK as a junior'; played for South England juniors); rugby, football, tennis, golf, squash
Other sports followed: Football (Nottingham Forest), rugby (Harlequins)
Relaxations: 'Reading, music, fitness; walking Poppy, our dog'
Extras: Was the last person to catch Viv Richards in a first-class match, in 1993. Set record for the longest innings ever played by a Kent batsman in scoring his 207 v Yorkshire at Maidstone 1998. Has best catching strike rate in Kent fielding history. Scored double century (208*) and century (104*) v Somerset at Canterbury 2001, also taking seven catches in the match. Scored 196 v Northamptonshire at Canterbury 2001, in the process equalling Arthur Fagg's 1938 season tally of nine centuries for Kent, one behind Frank Woolley's Kent record of ten. First batsman to 1000 first-class runs in 2001 and the season's leading English batsman in terms of runs scored and average with 1892 runs (av. 75.68). Kent Batsman of the Year (Denness Award) 2001. PCA Player of the Year 2001. Captain of Kent in County Championship 2002; overall captain of Kent since 2003
Best batting: 208* Kent v Somerset, Canterbury 2001
Best bowling: 1-37 Kent v Oxford University, Canterbury 1996

2004 Season

	M	Inns	NO	Runs	HS	Avge	100s	50s	Ct	St	O	M	Runs	Wkts	Avge	Best	5wI	10wM
Test																		
All First	16	28	1	1106	122	40.96	5	3	21	-								
1-day Int																		
C & G	2	1	0	78	78	78.00	-	1	1	-								
totesport	15	13	2	249	48	22.63	-	-	2	-								
Twenty20																		

Career Performances

	M	Inns	NO	Runs	HS	Avge	100s	50s	Ct	St	Balls	Runs	Wkts	Avge	Best	5wI	10wM
Test																	
All First	169	297	18	10323	208 *	37.00	25	42	243	-	175	112	1	112.00	1-37	-	-
1-day Int																	
C & G	18	17	1	429	78	26.81	-	3	10	-	6	9	0	-	-	-	
totesport	67	62	4	1062	82	18.31	-	2	27	-							
Twenty20	5	4	2	40	15	20.00	-	-	1	-							

GAIT, A. I. Derbyshire

Name: Andrew Ian Gait
Role: Right-hand opening bat
Born: 19 December 1978, Bulawayo, Zimbabwe
Height: 6ft 1in **Weight:** 13st 7lbs
Nickname: Bob, Gaitor
County debut: 2002
1st-Class 50s: 19
1st-Class 100s: 4
1st-Class catches: 55
Place in batting averages: 211th av. 21.20 (2003 166th av. 26.56)
Parents: Roger and Hazel
Marital status: Single
Education: Kearsney College, KwaZulu-Natal; 'studying through Open University in the UK'
Qualifications: Level 2 coaching
Overseas tours: South African National Academy to Kenya and Zimbabwe 1998
Overseas teams played for: Free State 1998-2001
Career highlights to date: 'Chasing 400-plus in fourth innings and winning v Natal 1999-2000; scored 101'
Cricketers particularly admired: Allan Donald, Steve Waugh, Jacques Kallis
Other sports played: Running, cycling, keeping fit, surfing
Other sports followed: Rugby (Natal Sharks)
Favourite band: U2, Goo Goo Dolls, Matchbox Twenty
Relaxations: Gym, running; beach, outdoors; music
Extras: Represented South Africa U19 in U19 World Cup 1997-98. Scored 101 in the highest successful fourth-innings run chase by a South African province – 443 by Free State v KwaZulu-Natal at Durban 1999-2000. Set Free State record for highest individual score in one-day cricket (138*) v Griqualand West at Bloemfontein in the Standard Bank Cup 2000-01. Scored 87* v Glamorgan at Cardiff in the C&G 2003, sharing with Chris Bassano (121) in a new competition record third-wicket partnership for Derbyshire (191). Released by Derbyshire at the end of the 2004 season. Holds a British passport and is not considered an overseas player
Opinions on cricket: 'I still believe that the English season is too long and the standard of the pitches needs to improve.'
Best batting: 175 Derbyshire v Northamptonshire, Northampton 2002

2004 Season

	M	Inns	NO	Runs	HS	Avge	100s	50s	Ct	St	O	M	Runs	Wkts	Avge	Best	5wI	10wM
Test																		
All First	14	25	1	509	81	21.20	-	2	12	-								
1-day Int																		
C & G	1	1	0	17	17	17.00	-	-	-	-								
totesport	6	6	1	116	49	23.20	-	-	2	-								
Twenty20																		

Career Performances

	M	Inns	NO	Runs	HS	Avge	100s	50s	Ct	St	Balls	Runs	Wkts	Avge	Best	5wI	10wM
Test																	
All First	63	118	2	3093	175	26.66	4	19	55	-							
1-day Int																	
C & G	5	5	1	113	87 *	28.25	-	1	-	-							
totesport	21	21	2	330	49	17.36	-	-	9	-							
Twenty20	2	1	0	2	2	2.00	-	-	-	-							

GALE, A. W. — Yorkshire

Name: Andrew William Gale
Role: Left-hand bat
Born: 28 November 1983, Dewsbury
Height: 6ft 2in **Weight:** 13st 5lbs
Nickname: Galey
County debut: 2004
1st-Class catches: 2
Place in batting averages: 264th av. 11.14
Parents: Denise and Alan
Marital status: 'Attached'
Family links with cricket: Grandfather keen cricketer
Education: Heckmondwike Grammar
Qualifications: 10 GCSEs, 3 A-levels, Level 2 cricket coaching
Overseas tours: England U17 to Australia 2001; England U19 to Australia 2002-03; Yorkshire to Grenada 2002
Career highlights to date: '164 for Yorkshire 2nd XI v Leicestershire 2nd XI 2002. Being on Yorkshire staff. Captaining England U19'
Cricket superstitions: 'Don't like odd numbers'
Cricketers particularly admired: Marcus Trescothick, Mark Butcher, Graeme Smith

Young players to look out for: Tim Bresnan, Joe Sayers, Chris Taylor, Richard Pyrah
Other sports played: Football, golf
Other sports followed: Football (Huddersfield Town)
Relaxations: 'Golf and listening to music; spending time with girlfriend; playing PlayStation'
Extras: Has played for England since U15 level. Played for Yorkshire Board XI in the C&G 2002 and 2003. Yorkshire League Young Batsman of the Year 2002
Opinions on cricket: 'Should have just one overseas player; if we have two it could take the places of youngsters who may have the potential to be as good as the overseas.'
Best batting: 29 Yorkshire v Derbyshire, Headingley 2004

2004 Season

	M	Inns	NO	Runs	HS	Avge	100s	50s	Ct	St	O	M	Runs	Wkts	Avge	Best	5wI	10wM
Test																		
All First	4	7	0	78	29	11.14	-	-	2	-								
1-day Int																		
C & G	1	1	0	16	16	16.00	-	-	-	-								
totesport	9	9	1	213	70 *	26.62	-	1	5	-								
Twenty20	3	3	0	56	38	18.66	-	-	2	-								

Career Performances

	M	Inns	NO	Runs	HS	Avge	100s	50s	Ct	St	Balls	Runs	Wkts	Avge	Best	5wI	10wM
Test																	
All First	4	7	0	78	29	11.14	-	-	2	-							
1-day Int																	
C & G	4	4	0	51	17	12.75	-	-	1	-							
totesport	9	9	1	213	70 *	26.62	-	1	5	-							
Twenty20	3	3	0	56	38	18.66	-	-	2	-							

34. Which ground became the fifty-fourth Test match venue when Australia met Sri Lanka for the first time in Test cricket?

GALLIAN, J. E. R. Nottinghamshire

Name: Jason Edward Riche Gallian
Role: Right-hand bat, right-arm medium bowler
Born: 25 June 1971, Manly, NSW, Australia
Height: 6ft **Weight:** 14st
Nickname: Gal
County debut: 1990 (Lancashire), 1998 (Nottinghamshire)
County cap: 1994 (Lancashire), 1998 (Nottinghamshire)
Test debut: 1995
Tests: 3
1000 runs in a season: 5
1st-Class 50s: 55
1st-Class 100s: 28
1st-Class 300s: 1
1st-Class 5 w. in innings: 1
1st-Class catches: 160
One-Day 100s: 8
One-Day 5 w. in innings: 1
Place in batting averages: 45th av. 48.73 (2003 37th av. 47.71)
Strike rate: (career 72.61)
Parents: Ray and Marilyn
Wife and date of marriage: Charlotte, 2 October 1999
Children: Tom, 12 April 2001; Harry, 8 September 2003
Family links with cricket: Father played for Stockport
Education: The Pittwater House Schools, Australia; Oxford University
Qualifications: Higher School Certificate, Diploma in Social Studies (Keble College, Oxford)
Career outside cricket: 'Director of a media training company – Red Letter Sports Media'
Off-season: 'Organising my benefit for 2005'
Overseas tours: Australia U20 to West Indies 1989-90; England A to India 1994-95, to Pakistan 1995-96, to Australia 1996-97; England to South Africa 1995-96; Nottinghamshire to Johannesburg 2000, to South Africa 2001; MCC to UAE and Oman 2004
Overseas teams played for: NSW U19 1988-89; NSW Colts and NSW 2nd XI 1990-91; Manly 1993-94
Career highlights to date: 'Playing Test cricket'
Cricket moments to forget: 'Breaking a finger in my first Test match'
Cricket superstitions: 'None'

Cricketers particularly admired: Desmond Haynes, Mike Gatting
Young players to look out for: Samit Patel
Other sports followed: Rugby league and union, football
Favourite band: INXS
Relaxations: Listening to music, playing golf
Extras: Represented Australia YC 1988-90; was captain v England YC 1989-90. Represented Australia U20 and U21 1991-92. Took wicket of D. A. Hagan of Oxford University with his first ball in first-class cricket 1990. Played for Oxford University and Combined Universities 1992; captained Oxford University 1993. Recorded highest individual score in history of Old Trafford with his 312 v Derbyshire in 1996. Left Lancashire during the 1997-98 off-season and joined Nottinghamshire for 1998. Scored 91 v Leicestershire at Trent Bridge in the NUL 2002, in the process sharing with Nicky Boje (86) in a record fourth-wicket partnership for Nottinghamshire in the one-day league (190). Carried his bat for 112* (out of 211) v Surrey at Trent Bridge 2003. Captain of Nottinghamshire from part-way through the 1998 season to 2002 and in 2004; Nottinghamshire club captain and captain in first-class cricket 2003. Granted a benefit for 2005
Best batting: 312 Lancashire v Derbyshire, Old Trafford 1996
Best bowling: 6-115 Lancashire v Surrey, Southport 1996

2004 Season

	M	Inns	NO	Runs	HS	Avge	100s	50s	Ct	St	O	M	Runs	Wkts	Avge	Best	5wI	10wM
Test																		
All First	17	25	2	1121	190	48.73	3	8	16	-								
1-day Int																		
C & G	2	2	0	26	18	13.00	-	-	-	-								
totesport	16	16	0	580	109	36.25	1	5	11	-								
Twenty20	3	3	0	9	8	3.00	-	-	-	-								

Career Performances

	M	Inns	NO	Runs	HS	Avge	100s	50s	Ct	St	Balls	Runs	Wkts	Avge	Best	5wI	10wM
Test	3	6	0	74	28	12.33	-	-	1	-	84	62	0	-	-	-	-
All First	187	323	31	11334	312	38.81	29	55	160	-	6898	3919	95	41.25	6-115	1	-
1-day Int																	
C & G	20	20	1	559	101 *	29.42	1	4	10	-	210	164	2	82.00	1-11	-	
totesport	132	130	11	3910	130	32.85	5	23	47	-	904	888	30	29.60	2-10	-	
Twenty20	8	8	0	152	62	19.00	-	1	1	-							

GAZZARD, C. M. — Somerset

Name: Carl Matthew Gazzard
Role: Right-hand bat, wicket-keeper
Born: 15 April 1982, Penzance
Height: 6ft **Weight:** 13st
Nickname: Gazza, Sling Boy, Coral
County debut: 2002
1st-Class catches: 11
1st-Class stumpings: 1
One-Day 100s: 1
Parents: Paul and Alison
Marital status: Single
Family links with cricket: Father and brother both played for Cornwall Schools; mother's a keen follower
Education: Mounts Bay Comprehensive; Richard Huish College, Taunton
Qualifications: 10 GCSEs, 2 A-levels, Level 1 and 2 coaching
Off-season: 'Training, coaching; Perth in New Year'
Overseas tours: Cornwall Schools U13 to Johannesburg; West of England U15 to West Indies; Somerset Academy to Durban 1999
Overseas teams played for: Subiaco-Floreat, Perth 2000-01; Scarborough, Perth 2002-03
Career highlights to date: '157 v Derby in totesport game [2004]'
Cricket moments to forget: 'Dislocating my shoulder in Perth – kept me out for 2001 season'
Cricket superstitions: 'None'
Cricketers particularly admired: Marcus Trescothick, Graham Rose
Young players to look out for: James Hildreth
Other sports played: Football (played through the age groups for Cornwall)
Other sports followed: Football (West Ham United)
Injuries: Out for six weeks with a broken finger
Favourite band: Red Hot Chili Peppers
Relaxations: 'Walking Stella and Elle. Following the Pilgrims with JP'
Extras: Played for England U13, U14, U15, U19. Won the Graham Kersey Award for Best Wicket-keeper at Bunbury Festival. Played for Cornwall in Minor Counties aged 16 and in the NatWest Trophy 1999. Scored 58 on NCL debut v Nottinghamshire at Taunton 2003. Scored maiden one-day century (157 off 136 balls) v Derbyshire at Derby in the totesport League 2004
Opinions on cricket: 'Great to have England performing well. Twenty20 cricket is great fun; good for everyone.'
Best batting: 44* Somerset v Sri Lanka A, Taunton 2004

2004 Season

	M	Inns	NO	Runs	HS	Avge	100s	50s	Ct	St	O	M	Runs	Wkts	Avge	Best	5wI	10wM
Test																		
All First	2	3	1	97	44 *	48.50	-	-	3	-								
1-day Int																		
C & G	2	2	0	19	10	9.50	-	-	2	-								
totesport	9	9	1	282	157	35.25	1	-	4	-								
Twenty20																		

Career Performances

	M	Inns	NO	Runs	HS	Avge	100s	50s	Ct	St	Balls	Runs	Wkts	Avge	Best	5wI	10wM
Test																	
All First	6	10	2	237	44 *	29.62	-	-	11	1							
1-day Int																	
C & G	3	3	0	35	16	11.66	-	-	4	-							
totesport	23	22	1	640	157	30.47	1	3	20	1							
Twenty20	5	5	0	105	39	21.00	-	-	3	-							

GIBSON, O. D. — Leicestershire

Name: Ottis Delroy Gibson
Role: Right-hand bat, right-arm fast bowler
Born: 16 March 1969, St Peter, Barbados
Height: 6ft 2in
County debut: 1994 (Glamorgan), 2004 (Leicestershire)
County cap: 2004 (Leicestershire)
Test debut: 1995
Tests: 2
One-Day Internationals: 15
50 wickets in a season: 2
1st-Class 50s: 21
1st-Class 100s: 1
1st-Class 5 w. in innings: 22
1st-Class 10 w. in match: 5
1st-Class catches: 55
One-Day 100s: 1
One-Day 5 w. in innings: 2
Place in batting averages: 145th av. 30.00
Place in bowling averages: 14th av. 24.08
Strike rate: 42.48 (career 49.89)
Education: Ellerslie Secondary School, Barbados

Qualifications: Level 4 coach
Overseas tours: West Indies A to Sri Lanka 1996-97, to South Africa 1997-98; West Indies to England 1995, to Australia 1995-96, to India and Pakistan (World Cup) 1995-96, to Malaysia (Commonwealth Games) 1998-99, to South Africa 1998-99, plus one-day tournament in Sharjah
Overseas teams played for: Barbados 1990-91 – 1997-98; Border 1992-93 – 1994-95; Griqualand West 1998-99 – 1999-2000; Gauteng 2000-01
Cricketers particularly admired: Malcolm Marshall, Ian Botham, Viv Richards, Brian Lara
Extras: One of *South African Cricket Annual*'s five Cricketers of the Year 1993. Was Glamorgan overseas player 1994-96. Scored maiden first-class century (101*) from 69 balls, batting at No. 9, for West Indians v Somerset at Taunton 1995. Has won numerous domestic match awards and was also Man of the Match v Australia at Brisbane in B&H World Series Cup 1995-96 (40-ball 52/2-38). Called up from Griqualand West by West Indies for the fourth Test v South Africa at Cape Town 1998-99. Appointed ECB National Coach for Northwest England 2001. Played for Staffordshire in the C&G 2001-02. Joined Leicestershire as player/bowling coach for 2004 having not played a first-class match for three years, taking 60 first-class wickets at 24.08 (including two ten-wicket match returns); awarded Leicestershire cap 2004. Is UK resident and not considered an overseas player
Best batting: 101* West Indians v Somerset, Taunton 1995
Best bowling: 7-55 Border v KwaZulu-Natal, Durban 1994-95

2004 Season

	M	Inns	NO	Runs	HS	Avge	100s	50s	Ct	St	O	M	Runs	Wkts	Avge	Best	5wI	10wM
Test																		
All First	15	19	3	480	60 *	30.00	-	4	5	-	424.5	97	1445	60	24.08	6-43	5	2
1-day Int																		
C & G	1	1	0	20	20	20.00	-	-	1	-	8	3	17	2	8.50	2-17	-	
totesport	16	12	3	152	32	16.88	-	-	4	-	94	12	425	22	19.31	3-36	-	
Twenty20	7	5	1	59	17	14.75	-	-	1	-	21.1	0	163	7	23.28	2-37	-	

Career Performances

	M	Inns	NO	Runs	HS	Avge	100s	50s	Ct	St	Balls	Runs	Wkts	Avge	Best	5wI	10wM
Test	2	4	0	93	37	23.25	-	-	-	-	472	275	3	91.66	2-81	-	-
All First	134	198	26	4051	101 *	23.55	1	21	55	-	24201	13516	485	27.86	7-55	22	5
1-day Int	15	11	1	141	52	14.10	-	1	3	-	739	621	34	18.26	5-40	2	
C & G	7	7	1	231	102 *	38.50	1	-	2	-	360	230	10	23.00	3-34	-	
totesport	45	36	11	514	47 *	20.56	-	-	12	-	1581	1210	44	27.50	3-36	-	
Twenty20	7	5	1	59	17	14.75	-	-	1	-	127	163	7	23.28	2-37	-	

GIDMAN, A. P. R. Gloucestershire

Name: Alexander (Alex) Peter Richard Gidman
Role: Right-hand bat, right-arm medium bowler; batting all-rounder
Born: 22 June 1981, High Wycombe
Height: 6ft 2in **Weight:** 14st
Nickname: G, Giddo
County debut: 2001 (one-day), 2002 (first-class)
County cap: 2004
1st-Class 50s: 15
1st-Class 100s: 1
1st-Class catches: 25
Place in batting averages: 114th av. 34.76 (2003 153rd av. 29.07)
Place in bowling averages: 146th av. 51.68
Strike rate: 78.75 (career 79.93)
Parents: Alistair and Jane
Marital status: Single
Family links with cricket: Brother is an MCC Young Cricketer
Education: Wycliffe College
Qualifications: 6 GCSEs, 1 A-level, GNVQ Level 2 in Leisure and Tourism
Off-season: 'National Academy'
Overseas tours: MCC Young Cricketers to Cape Town 1999; Gloucestershire to South Africa; England A to Malaysia and India 2003-04 (captain), to Sri Lanka 2004-05
Overseas teams played for: Albion CC, New Zealand 2001
Career highlights to date: 'Two C&G Trophy final victories. Academy captain'
Cricket moments to forget: 'C&G quarter-final loss to Kent 2002'
Cricket superstitions: 'None'
Cricketers particularly admired: Steve Waugh
Young players to look out for: Steve Snell
Other sports played: Golf
Other sports followed: Football (Wolves), rugby (Gloucester)
Injuries: 'A nagging finger injury obtained in the Academy 2003'
Favourite band: Matchbox Twenty, Train
Relaxations: 'Just chilling out; movies, golf'
Extras: Scored 67 on first-class debut v Derbyshire at Derby 2002. Gloucestershire Young Player of the Year 2002 and 2003. NBC Denis Compton Award for the most promising young Gloucestershire player 2002, 2003. ECB National Academy 2003-04, 2004-05. Forced to return home early from England A tour to India 2003-04 with a hand injury. Included in preliminary England one-day squad of 30 for ICC Champions

Trophy 2004. 'I hate people that are too involved with stats and figures instead of team's success'

Opinions on cricket: 'County cricket is a great breeding ground for international cricket. However, I don't feel that I have enough time to work on things in the season. You can play with bad habits for long periods of time.'

Best batting: 117 Gloucestershire v Northamptonshire, Bristol 2002

Best bowling: 3-33 Gloucestershire v Middlesex, Cheltenham 2002

2004 Season

	M	Inns	NO	Runs	HS	Avge	100s	50s	Ct	St	O	M	Runs	Wkts	Avge	Best	5wI	10wM
Test																		
All First	17	25	0	869	91	34.76	-	9	13	-	210	39	827	16	51.68	2-12	-	-
1-day Int																		
C & G	4	3	0	17	11	5.66	-	-	3	-	15	1	89	0	-	-	-	
totesport	11	11	2	199	70	22.11	-	1	3	-	29	0	170	1	170.00	1-11	-	
Twenty20																		

Career Performances

	M	Inns	NO	Runs	HS	Avge	100s	50s	Ct	St	Balls	Runs	Wkts	Avge	Best	5wI	10wM
Test																	
All First	35	58	3	1834	117	33.34	1	15	25	-	2478	1710	31	55.16	3-33	-	-
1-day Int																	
C & G	12	11	2	180	41	20.00	-	-	4	-	304	242	5	48.40	2-12	-	
totesport	34	31	5	715	73	27.50	-	3	16	-	474	416	8	52.00	3-26	-	
Twenty20	6	4	1	122	61	40.66	-	1	4	-	12	25	1	25.00	1-25	-	

35. Which Sri Lanka wicket-keeper made his highest Test score, 132*, on debut v Australia in 1992-93?

GIFFORD, W. M. Worcestershire

Name: William (Will) McLean Gifford
Role: Right-hand middle-order bat, right-arm medium bowler
Born: 10 October 1985, Sutton Coldfield
Height: 5ft 11in **Weight:** 12st
Nickname: Giff
County debut: No first-team appearance
Parents: Andy and Kim
Marital status: Single
Family links with cricket: 'Dad played local cricket. Brother plays at school'
Education: Malvern College; Loughborough University
Qualifications: 10 GCSEs, 3 A-levels
Career outside cricket: 'Studying at Loughborough Uni'
Off-season: 'Studying at university/England U19 tour to India'
Overseas tours: Staffordshire U16 to Barbados 2000; Malvern College to South Africa 2001; England U19 to India 2004-05
Career highlights to date: 'Being selected for England U19. Offer of contract from Worcestershire'
Cricket superstitions: 'Left pad on first'
Cricketers particularly admired: Ricky Ponting, Michael Clarke, Vikram Solanki
Young players to look out for: Steve Davies, Moeen Ali, Adam Harrison
Other sports played: Hockey (Midlands U15), football, golf
Other sports followed: Football (West Brom)
Favourite band: Busted
Extras: Made 2nd XI Championship debut for Worcestershire 2003
Opinions on cricket: 'Introduction of Twenty20 has been brilliant for domestic cricket.'

GILES, A. F. — Warwickshire

Name: Ashley Fraser Giles
Role: Right-hand bat, slow left-arm bowler
Born: 19 March 1973, Chertsey, Surrey
Height: 6ft 4in **Weight:** 15st 7lbs
Nickname: Splash, Skinny, Gilo
County debut: 1993
County cap: 1996
Test debut: 1998
Tests: 40
One-Day Internationals: 44
50 wickets in a season: 2
1st-Class 50s: 20
1st-Class 100s: 3
1st-Class 5 w. in innings: 23
1st-Class 10 w. in match: 3
1st-Class catches: 65
One-Day 100s: 1
One-Day 5 w. in innings: 3
Place in batting averages: 99th av. 36.12 (2003 121st av. 32.70)
Place in bowling averages: 31st av. 26.82 (2003 146th av. 52.09)
Strike rate: 62.08 (career 69.23)
Parents: Michael and Paula
Wife and date of marriage: Stine, 9 October 1999
Children: Anders Fraser, 29 May 2000; Matilde, February 2002
Family links with cricket: Father played and brother Andrew a club cricketer at Ripley, Surrey
Education: George Abbott County Secondary, Burpham, Guildford
Qualifications: 9 GCSEs, 2 A-levels, coaching certificate
Off-season: Touring with England
Overseas tours: Surrey U19 to Barbados 1990-91; Warwickshire to Cape Town 1996, 1997, to Bloemfontein 1998; England A to Australia 1996-97, to Kenya and Sri Lanka 1997-98; England to Sharjah (Champions Trophy) 1997-98, to Bangladesh (Wills International Cup) 1998-99, to Australia 1998-99 (CUB Series), to South Africa and Zimbabwe 1999-2000 (one-day series), to Kenya (ICC Knockout Trophy) 2000-01, to Pakistan and Sri Lanka 2000-01, to India and New Zealand 2001-02, to Sri Lanka (ICC Champions Trophy) 2002-03, to Australia 2002-03, to Africa (World Cup) 2002-03, to Bangladesh and Sri Lanka 2003-04, to West Indies 2003-04, to Zimbabwe (one-day series) 2004-05, to South Africa 2004-05
Overseas teams played for: Vredenburg/Saldanha, Cape Town 1992-95; Avendale CC, Cape Town 1995-96
Cricketers particularly admired: Dermot Reeve, Tim Munton, Dougie Brown, Ian Botham

Young players to look out for: Ian Bell
Other sports played: Golf (14 handicap), football
Other sports followed: Football (QPR)
Relaxations: 'Cinema, music, spending lots of time with my family'
Extras: Surrey Young Cricketer of the Year 1991. NBC Denis Compton Award for Warwickshire in 1996. Warwickshire Player of the Year 1996 and 2000. Warwickshire Most Improved Player 1996. Cricket Society's Leading Young All-rounder 1996. Scored hundred (123*) and took five wickets in an innings (5-28) in same match (v Oxford University at The Parks) in 1999, the first time this feat had been performed by a Warwickshire player since 1961. Scored 128*, the best by a Warwickshire No. 8, v Sussex at Hove 2000, in the process sharing with Dougie Brown in a record seventh-wicket partnership for Warwickshire (289; equalled by Ian Bell and Tony Frost 2004). Took 17 Test wickets in series v Pakistan 2000-01, the highest total by an England bowler in a series in Pakistan. Man of the Match in ODI v India at Delhi 2001-02 (5-57). Scored 71* v Essex at Edgbaston in the C&G 2003, sharing with Dougie Brown (108) in a competition record seventh-wicket partnership (170). Man of the Match in the first Test v West Indies at Lord's 2004 for his match return of 9-210 (4-129/5-81); his second innings figures contained his 100th Test wicket (Brian Lara). Had match figures of 9-122 (4-65/5-57) in the second Test v West Indies at Edgbaston 2004 to become the highest ranked England spinner since 1986 in the PricewaterhouseCoopers ratings (tenth) and the first England spinner since Tony Lock in 1958 to take nine or more wickets in successive Tests. ECB contract 2004-05
Best batting: 128* Warwickshire v Sussex, Hove 2000
Best bowling: 8-90 Warwickshire v Northamptonshire, Northampton 2000
Stop press: Passed 1000 Test runs in the third Test v South Africa at Cape Town 2004-05, in the process achieving double of 1000 runs and 100 wickets in Tests

2004 Season

	M	Inns	NO	Runs	HS	Avge	100s	50s	Ct	St	O	M	Runs	Wkts	Avge	Best	5wI	10wM
Test	7	9	2	219	52	31.28	-	1	3	-	300.1	62	811	31	26.16	5-57	2	-
All First	8	10	2	289	70	36.12	-	2	3	-	362.1	79	939	35	26.82	5-57	2	-
1-day Int	9	6	2	93	39	23.25	-	-	5	-	59	3	214	9	23.77	3-26	-	
C & G	3	1	0	10	10	10.00	-	-	1	-	23	0	115	3	38.33	2-32	-	
totesport																		
Twenty20	2	1	1	0	0*	-	-	-	-	-	7	0	34	2	17.00	2-21	-	

Career Performances

	M	Inns	NO	Runs	HS	Avge	100s	50s	Ct	St	Balls	Runs	Wkts	Avge	Best	5wI	10wM
Test	40	55	8	935	52	19.89	-	3	20	-	9439	4270	116	36.81	5-57	5	-
All First	158	213	39	4643	128*	26.68	3	20	65	-	33442	13876	483	28.72	8-90	23	3
1-day Int	44	26	10	252	39	15.75	-	-	16	-	1914	1398	40	34.95	5-57	1	
C & G	26	18	6	506	107	42.16	1	3	4	-	1385	954	39	24.46	5-21	1	
totesport	90	59	14	845	61*	18.77	-	2	29	-	3408	2466	119	20.72	5-36	1	
Twenty20	2	1	1	0	0*	-	-	-	-	-	42	34	2	17.00	2-21	-	

GODDARD, L. J. Derbyshire

Name: Lee James Goddard
Role: Right-hand bat, wicket-keeper
Born: 22 October 1982, Dewsbury
Height: 5ft 10in **Weight:** 11st 3lbs
Nickname: Godders, Goddy
County debut: 2004
1st-Class catches: 9
Parents: Steven and Lynda
Marital status: Single
Education: Batley Grammar School; Huddersfield Technical College; Loughborough University
Qualifications: 10 GCSEs, BTEC National Diploma in Sports Science, Foundation degree in Sports Science, ECB Level 1 coaching, National Pool Lifeguard
Career outside cricket: Student
Off-season: 'Working hard on my fitness and improving my technique at Derbyshire'
Overseas teams played for: Parramatta, Sydney 2001-02
Career highlights to date: 'First-class debut v Somerset. Taking five catches on my County Championship debut for Derbyshire'
Cricket moments to forget: 'None'
Cricket superstitions: 'Always put my left pad on first'
Cricketers particularly admired: Damien Martyn, Adam Gilchrist
Young players to look out for: Mark Loker, Paul Huddlestone
Other sports played: Football (Huddersfield Town 9-15 years), golf (12 handicap), snooker ('handicap – cue')
Other sports followed: Football (Leeds United), rugby league (Leeds Rhinos)
Favourite band: Maroon 5
Relaxations: 'Socialising, spending time with my girlfriend (Kelly), general relaxing; playing golf'
Extras: Played in Yorkshire's U17 County Championship winning side. Played for Yorkshire Board XI in the C&G 2003. Played for Loughborough University CCE in 2003. Was in British Universities squad for match v Zimbabweans 2003. Derbyshire CCC 2nd XI Player of the Year 2004
Opinions on cricket: 'The emergence of the Twenty20 Cup has rejuvenated cricket for the better. Home-grown young players should be given more of an opportunity rather than importing players under the Kolpak ruling (*see page 9*).'
Best batting: 23* LUCCE v Somerset, Taunton 2003

2004 Season

	M	Inns	NO	Runs	HS	Avge	100s	50s	Ct	St	O	M	Runs	Wkts	Avge	Best	5wI	10wM
Test																		
All First	2	1	0	8	8	8.00	-	-	7	-								
1-day Int																		
C & G																		
totesport																		
Twenty20																		

Career Performances

	M	Inns	NO	Runs	HS	Avge	100s	50s	Ct	St	Balls	Runs	Wkts	Avge	Best	5wI	10wM
Test																	
All First	5	6	2	56	23 *	14.00	-	-	9	-							
1-day Int																	
C & G	2	2	1	19	19 *	19.00	-	-	5	-							
totesport																	
Twenty20																	

GODLEMAN, B-A. Middlesex

Name: Billy-Ashley Godleman
Role: Left-hand bat, right-arm leg-spin bowler
Born: 11 February 1989, Islington
Height: 6ft 3in **Weight:** 13st 3lbs
County debut: No first-team appearance
Parents: Ashley Fitzgerald and Johnny Godleman
Marital status: Single
Family links with cricket: 'Father introduced me and showed me exactly how to play in all areas'
Education: Islington Green School
Off-season: 'Middlesex Academy; National Academy; tour of South Africa (England U16)'
Overseas tours: England U16 to South Africa 2004-05
Career highlights to date: 'Getting signed by Middlesex. Representing my nation at age-group level'
Cricket moments to forget: 'Dropping an absolute sitter on square leg boundary for club team Brondesbury v Finchley at Enfield in 2003 Ibex Cup final'
Cricket superstitions: 'Always check my bat alignment before every delivery'

Cricketers particularly admired: Andy Flower, Graeme Smith ('batsmen'); Jason Gillespie ('bowler'); Johnny Godleman ('wicket-keeper')
Young players to look out for: Steven Finn, Johnny Godleman Jnr
Other sports played: Football, rugby union, snooker
Other sports followed: Football ('love Liverpool FC'), rugby union, cricket (Middlesex CCC)
Favourite band: Solos, Nasir Jones (Nas), Tupac Shakur
Relaxations: 'Biggest interest and relaxation is listening to music; also playing football, watching Liverpool; collect Ralph Lauren baseball caps'
Extras: Named best player in country U13, U14 and U15 at regional tournaments; scored 168-ball 143 for South v West at Bunbury U15 Festival at Nottingham 2004. Made 2nd XI Trophy debut for Middlesex 2003
Opinions on cricket: 'You get what you put in.'

GOODE, C. M. Northamptonshire

Name: Christopher (Chris) Martin Goode
Role: Right-hand middle-order bat, right-arm medium-fast bowler
Born: 12 October 1984, Kettering
Height: 6ft 2in **Weight:** 12st 6lbs
Nickname: Goose, Pro, Premiership, Goodey
County debut: 2004
Strike rate: 96.00 (career 96.00)
Parents: Martin and Carla
Marital status: Single
Family links with cricket: 'Old man played club cricket'
Education: Huxlow Comprehensive, Irthlingborough; Tresham College, Kettering
Qualifications: 9 GCSEs, 1 AS-level, 2 A-levels, Level 2 coach
Career outside cricket: Coaching
Off-season: 'Sydney for four to five months'

Overseas tours: Northamptonshire U15 to South Africa 2000; Northamptonshire U19 to South Africa 2002
Overseas teams played for: Randwick-Petersham, Sydney 2004-05
Career highlights to date: 'First-class debut v Worcestershire 2004'
Cricket moments to forget: 'Being hit for six all the way along the ground first ball in first-class cricket – was a no-ball and four'
Cricket superstitions: 'None'
Cricketers particularly admired: Allan Donald, Andy Bichel

Young players to look out for: Craig Jennings, Alex Wakely, Brad Kruger
Other sports played: Football (Rothwell Town FC, semi-pro 2003-04)
Other sports followed: Football (Man Utd)
Favourite band: 'Finedon Saints'
Relaxations: Music, snooker
Extras: Represented England U15 in Costcutter U15 World Challenge 2000, taking 4-22 v India in opening game. Is a Northamptonshire Emerging Player
Opinions on cricket: 'Twenty20 great for the game.'
Best bowling: 1-70 Northamptonshire v Worcestershire, Worcester 2004

2004 Season

	M	Inns	NO	Runs	HS	Avge	100s	50s	Ct	St	O	M	Runs	Wkts	Avge	Best	5wI	10wM
Test																		
All First	1	1	0	0	0	0.00	-	-	-	-	16	3	70	1	70.00	1-70	-	-
1-day Int																		
C & G																		
totesport																		
Twenty20																		

Career Performances

	M	Inns	NO	Runs	HS	Avge	100s	50s	Ct	St	Balls	Runs	Wkts	Avge	Best	5wI	10wM
Test																	
All First	1	1	0	0	0	0.00	-	-	-	-	96	70	1	70.00	1-70	-	-
1-day Int																	
C & G																	
totesport																	
Twenty20																	

36. Which Australia Test off-spinner was Singapore's coach at the 2001 ICC Trophy in Canada?

GOODWIN, M. W. Sussex

Name: Murray William Goodwin
Role: Right-hand bat, right-arm medium/ leg-spin bowler
Born: 11 December 1972, Harare, Zimbabwe
Height: 5ft 9in **Weight:** 11st 2lbs
Nickname: Muzza, Fuzz, Goodie
County debut: 2001
County cap: 2001
Test debut: 1997-98
Tests: 19
One-Day Internationals: 71
1000 runs in a season: 3
1st-Class 50s: 46
1st-Class 100s: 30
1st-Class 200s: 3
1st-Class 300s: 1
1st-Class catches: 97
One-Day 100s: 8

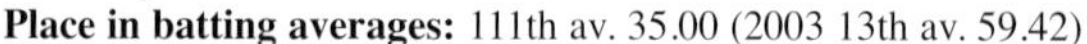

Place in batting averages: 111th av. 35.00 (2003 13th av. 59.42)
Strike rate: (career 98.57)
Parents: Penny and George
Wife and date of marriage: Tarsha, 13 December 1997
Children: Jayden William
Family links with cricket: 'Dad is a coach. Eldest brother played for Zimbabwe'
Education: St John's, Harare, Zimbabwe; Newtonmoore Senior High, Bunbury, Western Australia
Qualifications: Level II coach
Career outside cricket: Coaching, commentating; business
Off-season: Playing for Western Australia
Overseas tours: Australian Cricket Academy to South Africa 1992, to Sri Lanka and India 1993; Zimbabwe to Sri Lanka and New Zealand 1997-98, to Bangladesh (Wills International Cup) 1998-99, to Pakistan 1998-99, to UK, Ireland and Holland (World Cup) 1999, to South Africa 1999-2000, to West Indies 1999-2000, to England 2000
Overseas teams played for: Excelsior, Holland 1997; Mashonaland 1997-98 – 1998-99; Western Australia 1994-95 – 1996-97, 2000-01 –
Career highlights to date: 'Becoming the highest individual scorer in Sussex's history – 335* v Leicestershire, September 2003 at Hove. Broke Duleepsinhji's record of 333 in 1930'
Cricket moments to forget: 'Test against Sri Lanka – we felt the umpiring to be very dubious' (*In the second Test v Zimbabwe 1997-98 at Colombo, chasing 326 to win, Sri Lanka won by five wickets having been 137 for five*)

Cricketers particularly admired: Allan Border, Steve Waugh, Curtly Ambrose, Sachin Tendulkar
Young players to look out for: Shaun Marsh
Other sports played: Hockey (WA Country), golf, tennis
Other sports followed: 'All'
Favourite band: 'No real favourites; I have a very eclectic collection'
Relaxations: 'Socialising with friends'
Extras: Emigrated to Australia aged 13. Attended Australian Cricket Academy. Made first-class debut for Western Australia v England, Perth 1994-95, scoring 91 and 77. Scored century (111) in only his second ODI, v Sri Lanka at Colombo 1997-98, winning Man of the Match award. Scored 166* v Pakistan at Bulawayo 1997-98, in the process sharing with Andy Flower (100*) in the highest partnership for Zimbabwe for any wicket in Tests (277*). His other international awards include Man of the Match in the second Test v England at Trent Bridge 2000 (148*). Retired from international cricket in 2000. Scored 167 for Western Australia v New South Wales at Perth in the Mercantile Mutual Cup 2000-01, a then record for the highest individual score in Australian domestic one-day cricket. Joined Sussex as overseas player for 2001. Scored maiden first-class double century (203*) v Nottinghamshire at Trent Bridge 2001, having already scored a century (115) in the first innings; in the process of scoring his 203* he shared with Richard Montgomerie in a record partnership for any wicket for Sussex in matches against Notts (372*). Joint Sussex Player of the Year (with Richard Montgomerie) 2001. Scored century (118*) v Middlesex at Hove in the NCL 2003, sharing with Chris Adams (115*) in a new record third-wicket partnership for the one-day league and a competition record for any wicket for Sussex (228*). Scored maiden first-class triple century (335*) v Leicestershire at Hove 2003, surpassing K. S. Duleepsinhji's 333 in 1930 to set a new record for the highest individual score for Sussex (and winning the Sussex Outstanding Performance of the Year Award 2003). Scored 1183 Pura Cup runs at 65.72 for Western Australia 2003-04. Is no longer considered an overseas player
Best batting: 335* Sussex v Leicestershire, Hove 2003
Best bowling: 2-23 Zimbabweans v Lahore Division, Lahore 1998-99

2004 Season

	M	Inns	NO	Runs	HS	Avge	100s	50s	Ct	St	O	M	Runs	Wkts	Avge	Best	5wI	10wM
Test																		
All First	17	27	2	875	119	35.00	3	4	9	-								
1-day Int																		
C & G	2	2	0	47	47	23.50	-	-	1	-								
totesport	18	18	1	600	91	35.29	-	5	7	-								
Twenty20	4	3	0	26	17	8.66	-	-	1	-								

Career Performances

	M	Inns	NO	Runs	HS	Avge	100s	50s	Ct	St	Balls	Runs	Wkts	Avge	Best	5wI	10wM
Test	19	37	4	1414	166 *	42.84	3	8	10	-	119	69	0	-	-	-	-
All First	149	261	20	11212	335 *	46.52	34	46	97	-	690	355	7	50.71	2-23	-	-
1-day Int	71	70	3	1818	112 *	27.13	2	8	20	-	248	210	4	52.50	1-12	-	
C & G	10	10	1	367	110 *	40.77	1	1	1	-	42	56	1	56.00	1-28	-	
totesport	67	66	9	2165	129 *	37.98	4	15	22	-							
Twenty20	9	8	0	92	38	11.50	-	-	3	-							

GOUGH, D. Essex

Name: Darren Gough
Role: Right-hand bat, right-arm fast bowler, county vice-captain
Born: 18 September 1970, Barnsley
Height: 5ft 11in **Weight:** 13st 9lbs
Nickname: Rhino, Dazzler
County debut: 1989 (Yorkshire), 2004 (Essex)
County cap: 1993 (Yorkshire), 2004 (Essex)
Benefit: 2001 (Yorkshire)
Test debut: 1994
Tests: 58
One-Day Internationals: 138
50 wickets in a season: 4
1st-Class 50s: 15
1st-Class 100s: 1
1st-Class 5 w. in innings: 28
1st-Class 10 w. in match: 3
1st-Class catches: 44
One-Day 5 w. in innings: 6
Place in batting averages: 243rd av. 16.00 (2003 222nd av. 20.66)
Place in bowling averages: 10th av. 22.40 (2003 130th av. 43.30)
Strike rate: 45.33 (career 50.54)
Parents: Trevor and Christine
Children: Liam James, 24 November 1994; Brennan Kyle, 9 December 1997
Education: Priory Comprehensive; Airedale and Wharfedale College (part-time)
Qualifications: 2 O-levels, 5 CSEs, BTEC Leisure, NCA coaching award
Overseas tours: England YC to Australia 1989-90; Yorkshire to Barbados 1989-90, to South Africa 1991-92, 1992-93; England A to South Africa 1993-94; England to Australia 1994-95, 1998-99, 2002-03, to South Africa 1995-96, 2004-05 (one-day series), to India and Pakistan (World Cup) 1995-96, to Zimbabwe and New Zealand

1996-97, to Sharjah (Coca-Cola Cup) 1998-99, to South Africa and Zimbabwe 1999-2000, to Kenya (ICC Knockout Trophy) 2000-01, to Pakistan and Sri Lanka 2000-01, to India and New Zealand 2001-02 (one-day series), to West Indies 2003-04 (one-day series), to Zimbabwe (one-day series) 2004-05
Overseas teams played for: East Shirley, Christchurch, New Zealand 1991-92
Cricketers particularly admired: Shane Warne, Steve Waugh, Ian Botham, Michael Atherton, Malcolm Marshall
Young players to look out for: Michael Lumb
Other sports played: Golf, football
Other sports followed: Football (Barnsley and Tottenham Hotspur)
Relaxations: Golf, cinema
Extras: Scored 65 in his first Test innings, v New Zealand at Old Trafford 1994, batting at No. 9. Yorkshire Sports Personality of the Year 1994. Cornhill England Player of the Year 1994-95 and 1998-99. Took hat-trick against Kent at Headingley in 1995. Whyte and Mackay Bowler of the Year 1996. Took Test hat-trick (Healy, MacGill, Miller) v Australia at Sydney 1998-99, the first Ashes hat-trick by an England bowler since 1899. *Sheffield Star* Sports Personality of the Year. One of *Wisden*'s Five Cricketers of the Year 1999. Represented England in the 1999 World Cup. Won Freeserve Fast Ball award 2000 (for the fastest recorded ball bowled in a televised match) for a delivery timed at 93.1 mph during the first Test v Zimbabwe at Lord's. Vodafone England Cricketer of the Year 2000-01. *GQ* Sportsman of the Year 2001. Took 200th Test wicket (Rashid Latif) v Pakistan at Lord's 2001 in his 50th Test, in the same match moving above John Snow into seventh place in the list of England Test wicket-takers (*see entry on Andrew Caddick*). Man of the Match in the NatWest Series final v South Africa at Lord's 2003. His other international awards include England Player of the Series in the Texaco one-day rubber v South Africa 1998, England's Man of the [Test] Series v West Indies 2000 and Man of the [Test] Series v Sri Lanka 2000-01. Retired from Test cricket after the second Test v South Africa at Lord's 2003. Left Yorkshire during the 2003-04 off-season and joined Essex for 2004. Granted Freedom of the City of London in March 2004. Took 200th ODI wicket (Harbhajan Singh) v India at Lord's in the NatWest Challenge 2004, becoming the first England bowler to reach the milestone. Awarded Essex cap 2004. Appointed vice-captain of Essex for 2005
Best batting: 121 Yorkshire v Warwickshire, Headingley 1996
Best bowling: 7-28 Yorkshire v Lancashire, Headingley 1995

2004 Season

	M	Inns	NO	Runs	HS	Avge	100s	50s	Ct	St	O	M	Runs	Wkts	Avge	Best	5wI	10wM
Test																		
All First	7	10	1	144	50	16.00	-	1	-	-	226.4	52	672	30	22.40	5-57	1	-
1-day Int	12	4	0	30	13	7.50	-	-	5	-	100.1	13	440	14	31.42	4-50	-	
C & G	2	1	0	11	11	11.00	-	-	-	-	16	0	77	3	25.66	2-49	-	
totesport	11	5	1	24	11	6.00	-	-	-	-	62.3	3	262	12	21.83	3-19	-	
Twenty20	3	3	2	35	17	35.00	-	-	-	-	11	0	67	3	22.33	2-29	-	

Career Performances

	M	Inns	NO	Runs	HS	Avge	100s	50s	Ct	St	Balls	Runs	Wkts	Avge	Best	5wI	10wM
Test	58	86	18	855	65	12.57	-	2	13	-	11821	6503	229	28.39	6-42	9	-
All First	209	283	52	3771	121	16.32	1	15	44	-	38259	20250	757	26.75	7-28	28	3
1-day Int	138	79	33	514	45	11.17	-	-	23	-	7424	5337	206	25.90	5-44	2	
C & G	30	16	1	245	46	16.33	-	-	3	-	1859	1111	61	18.21	7-27	2	
totesport	125	80	22	773	72 *	13.32	-	1	20	-	5317	3788	155	24.43	5-13	2	
Twenty20	3	3	2	35	17	35.00	-	-	-	-	66	67	3	22.33	2-29	-	

GRANT, R. N. Glamorgan

Name: Richard Neil Grant
Role: Right-hand bat, right-arm medium bowler
Born: 5 June 1984, Neath
Height: 5ft 11in **Weight:** 14st
Nickname: Granty, Moth, Big Nose, Shelf
County debut: 2004 (one-day)
Parents: Kevin and Moira
Marital status: Single
Family links with cricket: 'Father played local league cricket and is chairman of Neath Cricket Club. Brother Gareth plays league cricket and was a member of MCC Young Cricketers; also represented Glamorgan 2nd XI. Mum does teas'
Education: Cefn Saeson Comprehensive, Neath; Neath Port Talbot College
Qualifications: 6 GCSEs, NVQ Level II Carpentry, Level II Coaching award
Off-season: Fitness training, coaching
Overseas tours: South Wales Junior League to Australia 1998; Wales U16 to Jersey 2000; Neath Port Talbot College to Goa 2001, to Malta 2002, to South Africa 2003
Overseas teams played for: Havelock North, Napier, New Zealand 2003-04
Career highlights to date: 'totesport League debut 2004'
Cricket moments to forget: 'None, they have all been great'
Cricket superstitions: 'Left pad on first'
Cricketers particularly admired: Simon Jones ('for his courage in returning from serious injury'), Sachin Tendulkar
Young players to look out for: Gareth Rees
Other sports played: Golf, squash, snooker
Other sports followed: Football (Swansea City), rugby (Neath-Swansea Ospreys)

Favourite band: Stereophonics, Queen
Relaxations: PlayStation, cinema
Extras: Neath Port Talbot College Sportsman of the Year 2002; Neath Port Talbot County Borough Council Sportsman of the Year 2002
Opinions on cricket: 'Haven't played long enough at a higher level to form any particular opinion.'

2004 Season

	M	Inns	NO	Runs	HS	Avge	100s	50s	Ct	St	O	M	Runs	Wkts	Avge	Best	5wI	10wM
Test																		
All First																		
1-day Int																		
C & G																		
totesport	2	2	0	26	21	13.00	-	-	-	-	8	0	54	1	54.00	1-26	-	
Twenty20																		

Career Performances

	M	Inns	NO	Runs	HS	Avge	100s	50s	Ct	St	Balls	Runs	Wkts	Avge	Best	5wI	10wM
Test																	
All First																	
1-day Int																	
C & G																	
totesport	2	2	0	26	21	13.00	-	-	-	-	48	54	1	54.00	1-26	-	
Twenty20																	

37. Who was Sri Lanka's first Test captain, later banned by Sri Lanka for joining the 1982-83 Arosa tour to South Africa?

GRAY, A. K. D. — Yorkshire

Name: Andrew (Andy) Kenneth Donovan Gray
Role: Right-hand bat, right-arm off-spin bowler
Born: 19 May 1974, Armadale, Western Australia
Nickname: Graysie
County debut: 2001
1st-Class 50s: 2
1st-Class 100s: 1
1st-Class catches: 16
Place in batting averages: (2003 87th av. 37.72)
Place in bowling averages: (2003 148th av. 53.23)
Strike rate: 93.00 (career 90.66)
Overseas teams played for: Willetton, Western Australia
Extras: Played for Worcestershire 2nd XI v Yorkshire 2nd XI at Scarborough 2001 before joining Yorkshire. Scored maiden first-class century (104) v Somerset at Taunton 2003. Released by Yorkshire at the end of the 2004 season. Is not considered an overseas player
Best batting: 104 Yorkshire v Somerset, Taunton 2003
Best bowling: 4-128 Yorkshire v Surrey, The Oval 2001

2004 Season

	M	Inns	NO	Runs	HS	Avge	100s	50s	Ct	St	O	M	Runs	Wkts	Avge	Best	5wI	10wM
Test																		
All First	2	3	0	37	27	12.33	-	-	2	-	31	3	89	2	44.50	1-20	-	-
1-day Int																		
C & G	1	0	0	0	0	-	-	-	1	-	8	0	78	1	78.00	1-78	-	
totesport	6	1	0	2	2	2.00	-	-	3	-	21	0	101	2	50.50	1-28	-	
Twenty20	3	1	0	0	0	0.00	-	-	1	-	9.1	0	71	5	14.20	3-18	-	

Career Performances

	M	Inns	NO	Runs	HS	Avge	100s	50s	Ct	St	Balls	Runs	Wkts	Avge	Best	5wI	10wM
Test																	
All First	18	26	3	649	104	28.21	1	2	16	-	2720	1359	30	45.30	4-128	-	-
1-day Int																	
C & G	3	1	0	0	0	0.00	-	-	3	-	168	152	5	30.40	3-37	-	
totesport	24	14	6	111	30 *	13.87	-	-	5	-	739	612	17	36.00	4-34	-	
Twenty20	8	3	0	17	13	5.66	-	-	4	-	141	211	9	23.44	3-18	-	

GRAYSON, A. P. Essex

Name: Adrian Paul Grayson
Role: Right-hand opening bat, slow left-arm bowler
Born: 31 March 1971, Ripon
Height: 6ft 1in **Weight:** 12st 7lbs
Nickname: Larry
County debut: 1990 (Yorkshire), 1996 (Essex)
County cap: 1996 (Essex)
One-Day Internationals: 2
1000 runs in a season: 4
1st-Class 50s: 43
1st-Class 100s: 16
1st-Class 5 w. in innings: 1
1st-Class catches: 121
Place in batting averages: 95th av. 36.50 (2003 189th av. 24.25)
Strike rate: (career 93.73)
Parents: Adrian and Carol
Wife and date of marriage: Alison, 30 September 1994
Children: Oliver, 30 January 1997; Beth, 3 February 1999
Family links with cricket: 'Father is a staff coach; brother plays'
Education: Bedale Comprehensive School
Qualifications: 8 CSEs, BTEC in Leisure Studies, Level 2 cricket coach
Overseas tours: England YC to Australia 1989-90; England to Kenya (ICC Knockout Trophy) 2000-01, to Pakistan 2000-01 (one-day series), to Zimbabwe (one-day series) 2001-02; Yorkshire to Barbados 1989-90, to Cape Town 1991, 1992, 1993, to Leeward Islands 1994
Overseas teams played for: Petone, Wellington 1991-92, 1995-96
Career highlights to date: 'Playing for England. All the trophies won with Essex'
Cricket moments to forget: 'Two dropped catches in five minutes v Glamorgan'
Cricket superstitions: 'Have a lucky vest. Left pad on first'
Cricketers particularly admired: Graham Gooch, Martyn Moxon, Darren Gough
Young players to look out for: Ravi Bopara, Oliver Grayson, Tom Westley
Other sports played: Golf (16 handicap), football (Essex CCC charity side; was offered apprentice forms with Middlesbrough FC at 16 but signed for Yorkshire)
Other sports followed: Football (Leeds United)
Favourite band: U2, Coldplay
Relaxations: Golf
Extras: Played for England YC v New Zealand YC 1989 and v Pakistan YC 1990. Yorkshire Player of the Year 1994. Released by Yorkshire at the end of 1995 and

joined Essex for 1996. Essex Player of the Year 1997, 2001. Scored two centuries (173/149) in match v Northamptonshire at Northampton 2001. Vice-captain of Essex 2002-04. Appointed Essex 2nd XI captain for 2005. Granted a benefit for 2005
Best batting: 189 Essex v Glamorgan, Chelmsford 2001
Best bowling: 5-20 Essex v Yorkshire, Scarborough 2001

2004 Season

	M	Inns	NO	Runs	HS	Avge	100s	50s	Ct	St	O	M	Runs	Wkts	Avge	Best	5wI	10wM
Test																		
All First	6	10	0	365	119	36.50	1	2	-	-	40.1	2	167	0	-	-	-	-
1-day Int																		
C & G	1	0	0	0	0	-	-	-	-	-								
totesport	12	10	1	205	58 *	22.77	-	1	3	-	34	0	167	1	167.00	1-29	-	
Twenty20	4	3	0	68	55	22.66	-	1	-	-	3	0	22	0	-	-	-	

Career Performances

	M	Inns	NO	Runs	HS	Avge	100s	50s	Ct	St	Balls	Runs	Wkts	Avge	Best	5wI	10wM
Test																	
All First	181	298	25	8655	189	31.70	16	43	121	-	12748	6038	136	44.39	5-20	1	-
1-day Int	2	2	0	6	6	3.00	-	-	1	-	90	60	3	20.00	3-40	-	
C & G	29	22	3	494	82 *	26.00	-	3	9	-	1151	891	25	35.64	3-24	-	
totesport	169	139	19	2338	69 *	19.48	-	7	47	-	5501	4643	144	32.24	4-25	-	
Twenty20	9	8	3	154	55	30.80	-	1	1	-	126	171	5	34.20	2-36	-	

GREENIDGE, C. G. — Gloucestershire

Name: Carl Gary Greenidge
Role: Right-hand bat, right-arm fast-medium bowler
Born: 20 April 1978, Basingstoke
Height: 5ft 10in **Weight:** 12st 8lbs
Nickname: Carlos, Gs, Jackal
County debut: 1998 (one-day, Surrey), 1999 (first-class, Surrey), 2002 (Northamptonshire)
50 wickets in a season: 1
1st-Class 5 w. in innings: 4
1st-Class catches: 12
Place in bowling averages: 77th av. 34.60 (2003 137th av. 47.22)
Strike rate: 50.00 (career 52.98)
Parents: Gordon and Anita
Marital status: Single
Family links with cricket: Father Gordon played for Hampshire and West Indies, as did cousin (on mother's side) Andy Roberts

Education: St Michael's, Barbados; Heathcote School, Chingford; City of Westminster College
Qualifications: GNVQ Leisure and Tourism, NCA senior coaching award
Cricket moments to forget: 'Yorkshire v Northants, April 2003, first game of the season – easily my worst ever game' (*Northants conceded 673 runs and lost by an innings*)
Cricket superstitions: 'None'
Cricketers particularly admired: Malcolm Marshall, Michael Holding, Viv Richards
Young players to look out for: Scott Newman, Michael Carberry
Other sports played: Football ('PlayStation!')
Other sports followed: Football (Arsenal), basketball (LA Lakers)
Favourite band: Bob Marley and the Wailers
Relaxations: 'PlayStation, movies, reading, music'
Extras: Spent a year on Lord's groundstaff. Took 5-60 (8-124 the match) on Championship debut for Surrey, v Yorkshire at The Oval 1999. Released by Surrey at the end of the 2001 season and joined Northamptonshire for 2002. Released by Northamptonshire at the end of the 2004 season and has joined Gloucestershire for 2005
Opinions on cricket: 'The game is slowly moving forward, what with the introduction and success of the Twenty20 Cup, which can only be good for English cricket. I think that 2nd XI matches should be played in the same conditions as 1st XI – it would go a long way towards creating a more competitive atmosphere. Also, let's have shorter sessions in the Championship; one hour for lunch and half an hour for tea!'
Best batting: 46 Northamptonshire v Derbyshire, Derby 2002
Best bowling: 6-40 Northamptonshire v Durham, Riverside 2002

2004 Season

	M	Inns	NO	Runs	HS	Avge	100s	50s	Ct	St	O	M	Runs	Wkts	Avge	Best	5wI	10wM
Test																		
All First	4	4	1	13	8 *	4.33	-	-	-	-	83.2	14	346	10	34.60	3-71	-	-
1-day Int																		
C & G																		
totesport	6	4	1	18	11	6.00	-	-	1	-	50.5	2	303	8	37.87	2-49	-	
Twenty20	4	1	1	2	2 *	-	-	-	2	-	11	1	106	5	21.20	2-22	-	

Career Performances

	M	Inns	NO	Runs	HS	Avge	100s	50s	Ct	St	Balls	Runs	Wkts	Avge	Best	5wI	10wM
Test																	
All First	32	34	5	234	46	8.06	-	-	12	-	5140	3403	97	35.08	6-40	4	-
1-day Int																	
C & G	3	1	0	12	12	12.00	-	-	1	-	144	160	1	160.00	1-73	-	
totesport	38	16	4	69	20	5.75	-	-	13	-	1600	1476	45	32.80	3-22	-	
Twenty20	4	1	1	2	2 *	-	-	-	2	-	66	106	5	21.20	2-22	-	

GRIFFITHS, D. A. Hampshire

Name: David Andrew Griffiths
Role: Left-hand bat, right-arm medium-fast bowler
Born: 10 September 1985, Newport, Isle of Wight
Height: 6ft **Weight:** 11st 7lbs
Nickname: Griff
County debut: No first-team appearance
Parents: Mrs L. J. Porter ('mum') and Mr D. Porter ('stepdad'); Mr A. Griffiths ('father')
Marital status: Single
Family links with cricket: Father played for Wales/Wales Minor Counties; vice-captain 1995-96. Stepfather captained Isle of Wight for eight years in the 1980s
Education: Sandown High School, Isle of Wight
Qualifications: BTEC Sports Science, Level 1 cricket coaching
Off-season: 'England U19 tour to Malaysia and India Jan/Feb '05'
Overseas tours: West of England U15 to West Indies 2000; England U19 to India 2004-05
Career highlights to date: 'England U19 v Essex 2nd XI – 5-9 in seven overs, including a hat-trick'
Cricket moments to forget: 'India tour with England U19 – four overs for 48 runs in a one-day game'
Cricketers particularly admired: Glenn McGrath, Brian Lara
Young players to look out for: Joe Denly, Kevin Latouf
Other sports played: Football (Isle of Wight Youth team), rugby
Other sports followed: Rugby league (St Helens), football (Man Utd)
Injuries: Out for one week with a groin strain; also suffered a side strain at the end of the season

Favourite band: Lighthouse Family, REM
Relaxations: 'Try to play golf'
Extras: Represented England U19 v Bangladesh U19 2004. Southern League Young Player of the Season 2004. Attended Hampshire Academy
Opinions on cricket: 'High fitness levels. New forms of cricket are bringing lots of new supporters to watch. Very exciting. Cricket is going in the right direction – up.'

GUNTER, N. E. L. — Derbyshire

Name: Neil Edward Lloyd Gunter
Role: Left-hand bat, right-arm medium-fast bowler
Born: 12 May 1981, Basingstoke
Height: 6ft
Nickname: Gunts, Wolfman
County debut: 2002
1st-Class catches: 5
Strike rate: 54.20 (career 49.94)
Parents: Tim and Caroline
Marital status: Single
Family links with cricket: 'Dad played cricket for The Mote, Maidstone'
Education: The Clere School; Newbury College
Qualifications: GCSEs and A-levels
Overseas teams played for: Port Adelaide, South Australia 2002-03
Cricket moments to forget: 'NUL debut' (*Had figures of 0-80 from nine overs and was out first ball v Gloucestershire at Bristol 2002*)
Cricketers particularly admired: Dominic Cork, Michael DiVenuto
Other sports played: Snooker
Other sports followed: 'Passing interest in most sports'
Favourite band: Embrace, The Music, Richard Ashcroft
Relaxations: 'Watching movies; music; sofas'
Extras: Berkshire Young Player of the Year 2000. MCC groundstaff 2001. Took 4-14 from eight overs (plus 2-39 in the first innings) on first-class debut v West Indies A at Derby 2002. Released by Derbyshire at the end of the 2004 season
Best batting: 20* Derbyshire v Hampshire, West End 2003
Best bowling: 4-14 Derbyshire v West Indies A, Derby 2002

2004 Season

	M	Inns	NO	Runs	HS	Avge	100s	50s	Ct	St	O	M	Runs	Wkts	Avge	Best	5wI	10wM
Test																		
All First	2	3	1	27	15 *	13.50	-	-	2	-	45.1	5	215	5	43.00	3-52	-	-
1-day Int																		
C & G																		
totesport	2	1	0	4	4	4.00	-	-	-	-	7	0	57	2	28.50	2-34	-	
Twenty20	1	0	0	0	0	-	-	-	-	-	1	0	14	0	-	-	-	

Career Performances

	M	Inns	NO	Runs	HS	Avge	100s	50s	Ct	St	Balls	Runs	Wkts	Avge	Best	5wI	10wM
Test																	
All First	7	8	3	74	20 *	14.80	-	-	5	-	849	602	17	35.41	4-14	-	-
1-day Int																	
C & G	1	1	0	5	5	5.00	-	-	-	-	24	25	0	-	-	-	
totesport	7	3	0	9	5	3.00	-	-	2	-	186	234	2	117.00	2-34	-	
Twenty20	4	2	2	11	9 *	-	-	-	-	-	78	75	1	75.00	1-12	-	

GUY, S. M. — Yorkshire

Name: Simon Mark Guy
Role: Right-hand bat, wicket-keeper
Born: 17 November 1978, Rotherham
Height: 5ft 7in **Weight:** 10st 7lbs
Nickname: Rat
County debut: 2000
1st-Class catches: 58
1st-Class stumpings: 6
Place in batting averages: 266th av. 10.33 (2003 279th av. 9.12)
Parents: Darrell and Denise
Wife and date of marriage: Suzanne, 13 October 2001
Children: Isaac Simon, 15 January 2004
Family links with cricket: 'Father played for Notts and Worcs 2nd XI and for Rotherham Town CC. Brothers play local cricket for Treeton CC'
Education: Wickersley Comprehensive School
Qualifications: GNVQ in Leisure and Recreation, qualified cricket coach, 'two years at the Yorkshire Cricket School under Ralph Middlebrook'
Overseas tours: Yorkshire to South Africa 1999, 2001, to Grenada 2002
Overseas teams played for: Orange CYMS, NSW 1999-2000

Career highlights to date: 'Playing the last ever County Championship game at Southampton and winning off the last ball with 13 Yorkshire and past Yorkshire men on the pitch at the same time'
Cricket moments to forget: 'On my debut against the Zimbabweans, smashing a door after getting out – but I still say it was an accident'
Cricket superstitions: 'This book is not big enough'
Cricketers particularly admired: Darren Lehmann, Jack Russell
Young players to look out for: Joe Sayers
Other sports played: 'I like to play all sports', rugby (currently Darlington RUFC; also played for South Yorkshire and Yorkshire)
Other sports followed: Rugby (Rotherham RUFC), 'Treeton Welfare CC, where all my family play'
Relaxations: 'Playing all sports, socialising with friends, watching cartoons, and eating a lot'
Extras: Set fifth-wicket partnership record in Yorkshire League (199 unbroken). Topped Yorkshire 2nd XI batting averages 1998 (106.00). Awarded 2nd XI cap 2000. Took five catches in an innings for first time for Yorkshire 1st XI v Surrey at Scarborough 2000
Best batting: 42 Yorkshire v Somerset, Taunton 2000

2004 Season

	M	Inns	NO	Runs	HS	Avge	100s	50s	Ct	St	O	M	Runs	Wkts	Avge	Best	5wI	10wM
Test																		
All First	8	12	0	124	26	10.33	-	-	21	2								
1-day Int																		
C & G	1	0	0	0	0	-	-	-	3	-								
totesport	5	3	0	36	29	12.00	-	-	5	3								
Twenty20																		

Career Performances

	M	Inns	NO	Runs	HS	Avge	100s	50s	Ct	St	Balls	Runs	Wkts	Avge	Best	5wI	10wM
Test																	
All First	21	31	3	345	42	12.32	-	-	58	6	24	8	0	-	-	-	-
1-day Int																	
C & G	1	0	0	0	0	-	-	-	3	-							
totesport	7	4	0	37	29	9.25	-	-	8	3							
Twenty20																	

HABIB, A. Leicestershire

Name: Aftab Habib
Role: Right-hand bat, 'very, very slow bowler'
Born: 7 February 1972, Reading
Height: 5ft 9in **Weight:** 13st
Nickname: Afie, Tabby, Inzy, Habiby
County debut: 1992 (Middlesex), 1995 (Leicestershire), 2002 (Essex)
County cap: 1998 (Leicestershire), 2002 (Essex)
Test debut: 1999
Tests: 2
1000 runs in a season: 2
1st-Class 50s: 43
1st-Class 100s: 19
1st-Class 200s: 1
1st-Class catches: 71
One-Day 100s: 1
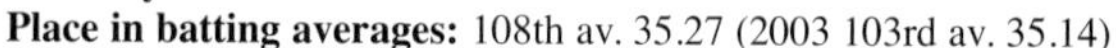
Place in batting averages: 108th av. 35.27 (2003 103rd av. 35.14)
Strike rate: (career 106.00)
Parents: Tahira (deceased) and Hussain
Marital status: Single
Family links with cricket: Cousin of Zahid Sadiq (ex-Surrey and Derbyshire)
Education: Taunton School
Qualifications: 7 GCSEs, Level 2 coaching
Career outside cricket: Property management
Off-season: 'Travelling; relaxing at home'
Overseas tours: Berkshire CCC to South Africa 1996; England YC to Australia 1989-90, to New Zealand 1990-91; England A to Bangladesh and New Zealand 1999-2000, to West Indies 2000-01
Overseas teams played for: Globe Wakatu, Nelson, New Zealand 1992-93, 1996-97; Riccarton CC, Christchurch, New Zealand 1997-98; Kingborough CC, Hobart
Career highlights to date: 'Playing for England in 1999'
Cricket moments to forget: 'Losing three one-day finals and a Test match at Lord's'
Cricketers particularly admired: Sachin Tendulkar, Mark Waugh, Ricky Ponting
Young players to look out for: Ravi Bopara, 'cousin Fuhraz Amjad'
Other sports played: 'Enjoy most sports', football (Reading Schools)
Other sports followed: Football (Reading FC, Liverpool), rugby (Leicester Tigers, New Zealand All Blacks)
Favourite band: Adnan Sami

Relaxations: 'Music, reading, golf, cinema'
Extras: Played for England U15-U19. Middlesex 2nd XI Seaxe Player of the Year 1992. Released by Middlesex at the end of the 1994 season. Leicestershire 2nd XI Player of the Year 1995. Championship medals with Leicestershire in 1996 and 1998. Scored 101* for England A v New Zealand A to help save the first 'Test' at Lincoln 1999-2000. Left Leicestershire during the 2001-02 off-season and joined Essex for 2002; left Essex at the end of the 2004 season and has rejoined Leicestershire for 2005
Opinions on cricket: 'Not happy with the amount of Kolpak players (*see page 9*) now being signed by counties. This is not helping our own young players' development.'
Best batting: 215 Leicestershire v Worcestershire, Leicester 1996
Best bowling: 1-10 Essex v Kent, Chelmsford 2003

2004 Season

	M	Inns	NO	Runs	HS	Avge	100s	50s	Ct	St	O	M	Runs	Wkts	Avge	Best	5wI	10wM
Test																		
All First	14	22	0	776	157	35.27	1	5	3	-	7	1	18	0	-	-	-	-
1-day Int																		
C & G	1	1	1	32	32 *	-	-	-	-	-	6	0	29	0	-	-	-	
totesport	4	3	0	41	21	13.66	-	-	-	-	1	0	4	0	-	-	-	
Twenty20																		

Career Performances

	M	Inns	NO	Runs	HS	Avge	100s	50s	Ct	St	Balls	Runs	Wkts	Avge	Best	5wI	10wM
Test	2	3	0	26	19	8.66	-	-	-	-							
All First	145	219	27	8164	215	42.52	20	43	71	-	106	80	1	80.00	1-10	-	-
1-day Int																	
C & G	19	15	3	358	67	29.83	-	2	6	-	46	40	2	20.00	2-5	-	
totesport	92	81	17	1743	99 *	27.23	-	8	28	-	13	18	0	-	-	-	
Twenty20	2	2	1	26	16 *	26.00	-	-	1	-							

38. Who was 'Chicken George', the first Zimbabwe player to claim an ODI hat-trick – Nick Knight, John Crawley and Nasser Hussain – in 1996-97?

HALL, A. J. Kent

Name: Andrew James Hall
Role: Right-hand bat, right-arm fast-medium bowler; all-rounder
Born: 31 July 1975, Johannesburg, South Africa
County debut: 2003 (Worcestershire)
County colours: 2003 (Worcestershire)
Test debut: 2001-02
Tests: 10
One-Day Internationals: 43
1st-Class 50s: 26
1st-Class 100s: 3
1st-Class 5 w. in innings: 9
1st-Class 10 w. in match: 1
1st-Class catches: 65
Place in batting averages: 127th av. 32.82 (2003 125th av. 31.78)
Place in bowling averages: 102nd av. 37.46 (2003 19th av. 23.51)
Strike rate: 69.40 (career 55.63)
Wife: Leanie
Education: Hoërskool Alberton
Overseas tours: South Africa to Sri Lanka (Singer Triangular Series) 2000, to Australia (Super Challenge) 2000, to Singapore (Godrej Singapore Challenge) 2000-01, to Kenya (ICC Knockout Trophy) 2000-01, to Bangladesh (TVS Cup) 2003, to England 2003, to Pakistan 2003-04, to India 2004-05
Overseas teams played for: Transvaal/Gauteng 1994-95 – 2000-01; Easterns 2001-02 – 2003-04; Lions 2004-05 –
Extras: Played indoor cricket for South Africa. Played for South Africa Academy in series v New Zealand Academy 1997. Was shot in the hand and face by a mugger in Johannesburg in 1999 and was car-jacked in 2002. Man of the Match in tied indoor ODI v Australia at Melbourne 2000. Made Test debut in the second Test v Australia at Cape Town 2001-02, scoring 70 batting at No. 8. One of *South African Cricket Annual*'s five Cricketers of the Year 2002. His domestic awards include Man of the SuperSport Series 2002-03 and Man of the Match in the final (6-77/5-22). Represented South Africa in the 2002-03 World Cup. Joined Worcestershire as an overseas player for 2003. Man of the Match v Lancashire in the C&G semi-final at Worcester 2003 (20-ball 26 and 4-36, including double wicket maiden in final over of game). Became only the fifth player in Test history to run out of partners on 99*, in the fourth Test v England at Headingley 2003. Left Worcestershire at the end of the 2004 season and has joined Kent as an overseas player for 2005

Best batting: 153 Easterns v North West, Benoni 2001-02
Best bowling: 6-77 Easterns v Western Province, Benoni 2002-03
Stop press: Scored maiden Test century (163) in the first Test v India at Kanpur 2004-05, winning Man of the Match award

2004 Season

	M	Inns	NO	Runs	HS	Avge	100s	50s	Ct	St	O	M	Runs	Wkts	Avge	Best	5wI	10wM
Test																		
All First	12	19	2	558	81	32.82	-	5	16	-	347	72	1124	30	37.46	3-10	-	-
1-day Int																		
C & G	4	3	0	41	34	13.66	-	-	-	-	25.4	0	129	4	32.25	3-37	-	
totesport	14	12	4	177	70 *	22.12	-	1	3	-	88	7	376	21	17.90	4-26	-	
Twenty20	6	6	0	54	18	9.00	-	-	-	-	22.5	0	196	8	24.50	2-18	-	

Career Performances

	M	Inns	NO	Runs	HS	Avge	100s	50s	Ct	St	Balls	Runs	Wkts	Avge	Best	5wI	10wM
Test	10	14	3	297	99 *	27.00	-	2	11	-	1447	761	24	31.70	3-1	-	-
All First	81	118	17	3456	153	34.21	3	26	65	-	13742	6345	247	25.68	6-77	9	1
1-day Int	43	32	7	586	81	23.44	-	2	17	-	1218	901	28	32.17	3-32	-	
C & G	12	11	0	262	78	23.81	-	2	4	-	515	378	17	22.23	4-33	-	
totesport	19	17	5	292	70 *	24.33	-	1	3	-	726	536	22	24.36	4-26	-	
Twenty20	8	8	0	102	46	12.75	-	-	-	-	185	230	10	23.00	2-17	-	

HAMBLIN, J. R. C. — Hampshire

Name: James Rupert Christopher Hamblin
Role: Right-hand bat, right-arm fast-medium bowler; all-rounder
Born: 16 August 1978, Pembury, Kent
Height: 6ft **Weight:** 14st
Nickname: Hambo
County debut: 2001
1st-Class 50s: 3
1st-Class 5 w. in innings: 1
1st-Class catches: 5
Place in batting averages: (2003 46th av. 45.50)
Strike rate: (career 71.57)
Parents: Bryan and Amanda
Marital status: Single
Family links with cricket: 'Father (C.B. Hamblin) played for Oxford University 1971-73 and scored a first-class hundred'

Education: Charterhouse School; University of the West of England, Bristol
Qualifications: 9 GCSEs, 2 A-levels, BA (Hons) Social Science
Overseas tours: BUSA to South Africa 2000; Hampshire to Cape Town 2000
Overseas teams played for: Harare Sports Club, Zimbabwe 1996-97; Old Edwardians, Johannesburg 2000-01; Melville, Perth 2001-03
Career highlights: 'First Twenty20 match – Man of the Match. [Also] 6-93 and 96 v Derbyshire 2003'
Cricket superstitions: 'None'
Cricketers particularly admired: James Kirtley
Young players to look out for: James Tomlinson
Other sports played: Rackets, golf, tennis
Other sports followed: 'All sports'
Favourite band: Matchbox Twenty
Relaxations: Playing golf and snooker
Extras: 2nd XI Player of the Month for August/September 1999 and for August/September 2001. Played in Charterhouse Friars' *Cricketer* Cup winning side 2000. Took 3-23 and scored a 42-ball 61 (50 from 28 balls) v Sussex at Hove in the Norwich Union League 2001. Recorded maiden first-class five-wicket return (6-93) v Derbyshire at Derby 2003, following up with a career best 96 in Hampshire's first innings. Retired at the end of the 2004 season
Opinions on cricket: 'I think that we play too much cricket. Twenty20 is a fantastic innovation – need to get people watching more live cricket at county level.'
Best batting: 96 Hampshire v Derbyshire, Derby 2003
Best bowling: 6-93 Hampshire v Derbyshire, Derby 2003

2004 Season

	M	Inns	NO	Runs	HS	Avge	100s	50s	Ct	St	O	M	Runs	Wkts	Avge	Best	5wI	10wM
Test																		
All First																		
1-day Int																		
C & G	2	2	0	23	20	11.50	-	-	-	-	2.1	0	37	0	-	-	-	
totesport	6	5	0	86	42	17.20	-	-	2	-								
Twenty20																		

Career Performances

	M	Inns	NO	Runs	HS	Avge	100s	50s	Ct	St	Balls	Runs	Wkts	Avge	Best	5wI	10wM
Test																	
All First	11	18	2	440	96	27.50	-	3	5	-	1002	723	14	51.64	6-93	1	-
1-day Int																	
C & G	3	3	0	27	20	9.00	-	-	-	-	13	37	0	-	-	-	
totesport	39	32	2	527	61	17.56	-	2	13	-	756	650	25	26.00	4-29	-	
Twenty20	5	5	0	124	38	24.80	-	-	1	-	48	71	7	10.14	3-31	-	

HAMILTON, G. M. Durham

Name: Gavin Mark Hamilton
Role: Left-hand bat, right-arm medium-fast bowler
Born: 16 September 1974, Broxburn
Height: 6ft 3in **Weight:** 13st
Nickname: Hammy, Jock, Dits, 'anything Scottish'
County debut: 1994 (Yorkshire), 2004 (Durham)
County cap: 1998 (Yorkshire)
Test debut: 1999-2000
Tests: 1
One-Day Internationals: 5
50 wickets in a season: 1
1st-Class 50s: 17
1st-Class 100s: 1
1st-Class 5 w. in innings: 9
1st-Class 10 w. in match: 2
1st-Class catches: 31
One-Day 5 w. in innings: 2
Place in batting averages: 196th av. 22.85
Strike rate: 59.25 (career 49.38)
Parents: Gavin and Wendy
Marital status: Single
Family links with cricket: Father 'long-term fast bowler at club level' (Sidcup, Kent; West Lothian, Scotland). Brother opening bat for Sidcup CC and has opened batting for Scotland
Education: Hurstmere School, Sidcup
Qualifications: 10 GCSEs and two coaching awards
Overseas tours: England to South Africa and Zimbabwe 1999-2000; Yorkshire pre-season tours to South Africa, Zimbabwe and West Indies; Scotland to UAE (ICC Six Nations Challenge) 2003-04, to UAE (ICC Inter-Continental Cup) 2004-05
Overseas teams played for: Welling, Municipals, and Stellenbosch University – all South Africa; Spotswood, Melbourne
Cricketers particularly admired: Craig White, Mark Robinson, Chris Adams
Other sports played: Golf ('a lot of it'), football (Arsenal YTS)
Other sports followed: Football (Falkirk FC)
Relaxations: Listening to music and reading the paper
Extras: Took ten wickets (5-69/5-43) and scored 149 runs (79/70) v Glamorgan at Cardiff in 1998, the second best all-round contribution in Yorkshire history. Wetherell Award for the Cricket Society's leading all-rounder in English first-class cricket 1998;

Yorkshire Players' Player of the Year 1998; Yorkshire Supporters' Player of the Year 1998. Scored 76 for Scotland v Pakistan at Chester-le-Street in the 1999 World Cup, the first 50 scored by a Scotland player in World Cup cricket; scored 217 runs (av. 54.25) in the 1999 World Cup, more than any England batsman. Finished in top 15 of first-class batting and bowling averages 1999. Released by Yorkshire at the end of the 2003 season and joined Durham for 2004
Best batting: 125 Yorkshire v Hampshire, Headingley 2000
Best bowling: 7-50 Yorkshire v Surrey, Headingley 1998
Stop press: Played in Scotland side that won the ICC Inter-Continental Cup in the UAE, November 2004, scoring century (115) in the final v Canada in Sharjah

2004 Season

	M	Inns	NO	Runs	HS	Avge	100s	50s	Ct	St	O	M	Runs	Wkts	Avge	Best	5wI	10wM
Test																		
All First	8	15	1	320	58	22.85	-	2	3	-	79	11	288	8	36.00	3-30	-	-
1-day Int																		
C & G																		
totesport	3	3	1	169	76	84.50	-	2	-	-	14.2	1	68	0	-	-	-	
Twenty20																		

Career Performances

	M	Inns	NO	Runs	HS	Avge	100s	50s	Ct	St	Balls	Runs	Wkts	Avge	Best	5wI	10wM
Test	1	2	0	0	0	0.00	-	-	-	-	90	63	0	-	-	-	-
All First	89	123	21	2641	125	25.89	1	17	31	-	12198	6355	247	25.72	7-50	9	2
1-day Int	5	5	1	217	76	54.25	-	2	1	-	214	149	3	49.66	2-36	-	
C & G	11	9	3	148	39	24.66	-	-	3	-	504	340	19	17.89	3-27	-	
totesport	77	55	13	912	76	21.71	-	4	12	-	2521	2101	81	25.93	5-16	2	
Twenty20	3	3	1	41	41 *	20.50	-	-	1	-							

HAMILTON-BROWN, R. J. Surrey

Name: Rory James Hamilton-Brown
Role: Right-hand bat, right-arm off-spin bowler; batting all-rounder
Born: 3 September 1987, London ('overlooking Lord's')
Height: 6ft **Weight:** 13st 6lbs
Nickname: Razza
County debut: No first-team appearance
Parents: Roger and Holly
Marital status: Single
Family links with cricket: 'Father played at Warwickshire. Dennis Amiss is my godfather'
Education: Millfield School

Career outside cricket: 'Still at school until summer 2006'
Overseas tours: England U16 to South Africa
Career highlights to date: 'Scoring 84 as a 16-year-old on 2nd XI Surrey debut against Sussex'
Cricketers particularly admired: Jacques Kallis
Young players to look out for: Tom Maynard, Kieron Powell
Other sports played: Rugby (England U16 – full back)
Favourite band: 'Any R&B'
Relaxations: 'Music, dancing, and my girlfriend when I have time'
Extras: Captained England U15. *Daily Telegraph* Bunbury Scholar (Batsman) 2003. Broke Millfield batting record 2004 at 16. Made 2nd XI Championship debut 2004, scoring 43 and 84 v Sussex 2nd XI at Hove

HANCOCK, N. D. Somerset

Name: Neil David Hancock
Role: Right-hand bat, right-arm medium-fast bowler; all-rounder
Born: 13 April 1976, Casino, New South Wales
Height: 6ft **Weight:** 15st
Nickname: Hanks
County debut: 2004 (one-day)
One-Day 100s: 1
Parents: Terrence and Beatrice
Wife and date of marriage: Claire, 24 April 2000
Education: Casino High School, New South Wales
Qualifications: ACB Level 2 cricket coach
Career outside cricket: Sales representative for Howdens Joinery, selling kitchens
Off-season: 'In the gym'
Overseas tours: Northern NSW Emu Colts to New Zealand 1996

Overseas teams played for: NSW Country 1999-2000; Toombul DCC, Brisbane
Career highlights to date: 'Playing for Somerset against Glamorgan in the Twenty20 competition, which was live on Sky'
Cricket moments to forget: 'Being bowled off the last ball of the game to lose the final of the Australian Indoor Cricket Championships, played in Sydney'
Cricket superstitions: 'None'
Cricketers particularly admired: Steve Waugh
Other sports played: Golf ('handicap of four at the age of 16')
Other sports followed: Football (Manchester United)
Injuries: Hamstring strain; also loss of flexibility after back operation in 2002
Favourite band: Savage Garden
Relaxations: 'Fishing, ferreting, movies'
Extras: Selected for Australia U17 indoor cricket team. Played for Devon in the NatWest 1999 and in the C&G 2001-04. Had first innings figures of 7-80 for Devon v Bedfordshire in the final of the Minor Counties Championship at Exmouth 2004. Played for Somerset in two Twenty20 games and one totesport match during July 2004
Opinions on cricket: 'The Twenty20 competition is a great way to bring the crowds back to the game.'

2004 Season

	M	Inns	NO	Runs	HS	Avge	100s	50s	Ct	St	O	M	Runs	Wkts	Avge	Best	5wI	10wM
Test																		
All First																		
1-day Int																		
C & G	2	2	0	24	23	12.00	-	-	2	-	20	3	97	3	32.33	2-29	-	
totesport	1	1	0	12	12	12.00	-	-	-	-	8	0	48	1	48.00	1-48	-	
Twenty20	2	2	0	9	7	4.50	-	-	-	-	2	0	25	1	25.00	1-9	-	

Career Performances

	M	Inns	NO	Runs	HS	Avge	100s	50s	Ct	St	Balls	Runs	Wkts	Avge	Best	5wI	10wM
Test																	
All First																	
1-day Int																	
C & G	9	9	3	284	113 *	47.33	1	1	5	-	471	351	14	25.07	3-18	-	
totesport	1	1	0	12	12	12.00	-	-	-	-	48	48	1	48.00	1-48	-	
Twenty20	2	2	0	9	7	4.50	-	-	-	-	12	25	1	25.00	1-9	-	

HANCOCK, T. H. C. Gloucestershire

Name: Timothy (Tim) Harold Coulter Hancock
Role: Right-hand bat, right-arm medium bowler
Born: 20 April 1972, Reading
Height: 5ft 11in **Weight:** 12st 7lbs
Nickname: Herbie
County debut: 1991
County cap: 1998
1000 runs in a season: 1
1st-Class 50s: 51
1st-Class 100s: 6
1st-Class 200s: 1
1st-Class catches: 113
One-Day 100s: 2
One-Day 5 w. in innings: 1
Place in batting averages: 79th av. 40.08 (2003 104th av. 34.28)
Strike rate: 111.00 (career 68.02)
Parents: John and Jennifer
Wife and date of marriage: Rachael, 26 September 1998
Children: George, 30 January 2000; Annabel Rachael, 28 August 2001
Family links with cricket: 'Dad and brother very keen players'
Education: St Edward's, Oxford; Henley College
Qualifications: 8 GCSEs, senior coaching award
Overseas tours: Gloucestershire to Kenya 1991, to Sri Lanka 1992-93, to Zimbabwe (two visits)
Overseas teams played for: CBC Old Boys, Bloemfontein 1991-92; Wynnum Manley, Brisbane 1992-93; Harlequins, Durban 1994-95
Career highlights to date: 'Winning at Lord's … and doing the treble in one-day competitions in 2000'
Cricket moments to forget: 'Breaking my hand in fielding practice days before the 2001 B&H final'
Cricketers particularly admired: Viv Richards, Gordon Greenidge, Ian Botham
Other sports played: Hockey, golf
Other sports followed: 'I like to play and watch rugby, but don't do either enough'
Relaxations: 'Family life and a round of golf'
Extras: Played hockey for Oxfordshire U19. Vice-captain of Gloucestershire 2000-02. Scored maiden one-day century (110) to win Man of the Match award in the NatWest quarter-final v Northamptonshire at Bristol 2000. Granted a benefit for 2005
Best batting: 220* Gloucestershire v Nottinghamshire, Trent Bridge 1998
Best bowling: 3-5 Gloucestershire v Essex, Colchester 1998

2004 Season

	M	Inns	NO	Runs	HS	Avge	100s	50s	Ct	St	O	M	Runs	Wkts	Avge	Best	5wI	10wM
Test																		
All First	9	13	1	481	77 *	40.08	-	4	4	-	37	8	105	2	52.50	2-7	-	-
1-day Int																		
C & G	1	0	0	0	0	-	-	-	1	-								
totesport	5	5	2	149	53 *	49.66	-	1	1	-	1	0	5	0	-	-	-	
Twenty20	5	4	0	110	56	27.50	-	1	2	-								

Career Performances

	M	Inns	NO	Runs	HS	Avge	100s	50s	Ct	St	Balls	Runs	Wkts	Avge	Best	5wI	10wM
Test																	
All First	180	313	20	8344	220 *	28.47	7	51	113	-	3129	1785	46	38.80	3-5	-	-
1-day Int																	
C & G	21	19	0	803	135	42.26	2	5	8	-	233	178	13	13.69	6-58	1	
totesport	142	130	4	2428	82	19.26	-	10	50	-	702	659	22	29.95	3-18	-	
Twenty20	5	4	0	110	56	27.50	-	1	2	-							

HARBHAJAN SINGH — Surrey

Name: Harbhajan Singh
Role: Right-hand bat, right-arm off-spin bowler
Born: 3 July 1980, Jalandhar, Punjab
Nickname: Bhajji
County debut: No first-team appearance
Test debut: 1997-98
Tests: 36
One-Day Internationals: 90
1st-Class 50s: 5
1st-Class 5 w. in innings: 21
1st-Class 10 w. in match: 3
1st-Class catches: 39
One-Day 5 w. in innings: 1
Strike rate: (career 56.69)
Overseas tours: India U19 to South Africa (U19 World Cup) 1997-98; India to Sharjah (Coca-Cola Cup) 1997-98, to Malaysia (Commonwealth Games) 1998-99, to Zimbabwe 1998-99, to New Zealand 1998-99, to Sri Lanka (Asian Test Championship) 1998-99, to Australia 1999-2000, to Zimbabwe 2001, to Sri Lanka 2001, to South Africa 2001-02, to West Indies 2001-02, to England 2002, to Sri Lanka (ICC Champions Trophy) 2002-03, to New Zealand

2002-03, to Africa (World Cup) 2002-03, to Australia 2003-04, to England (NatWest Challenge) 2004, to England (ICC Champions Trophy) 2004, to Bangladesh 2004-05, plus one-day tournaments in Sri Lanka, Los Angeles and Bangladesh
Overseas teams played for: Punjab (India) 1997-98 –
Extras: Popularly nicknamed the 'Turbanator'. Represented India U19 v South Africa U19 1995-96. Became the first Indian to take a Test hat-trick (Ponting, Gilchrist, Warne), in the second Test v Australia at Kolkata 2000-01. Took 32 wickets (av. 17.03) in three-Test series v Australia 2000-01, breaking Bishen Bedi's 1977-78 Indian series record v Australia of 31 wickets (in five Tests), and was Man of the Series. His other Test awards include Man of the Match in the second Test v Zimbabwe at Delhi 2001-02 (2-70/6-62) and Man of the Series v West Indies 2002-03 (20 wickets; av. 16.75). One of *Indian Cricket*'s five Cricketers of the Year 2001. His 33-ball fifty (out for 54) in the second Test v England at Trent Bridge 2002 was the second fastest for India in Tests behind Kapil Dev's 30-ball fifty v Pakistan at Karachi 1982-83. Was due to join Lancashire as an overseas player for 2003 but was unable to take up post because of finger injury; has joined Surrey as an overseas player for 2005
Best batting: 84 Punjab v Haryana, Amritsar 2000-01
Best bowling: 8-84 India v Australia, Chennai (Madras) 2000-01
Stop press: Had match figures of 11-224 (5-146/6-78) in the first Test v Australia at Bangalore 2004-05. Man of the Match in the second Test v South Africa at Kolkata 2004-05 (2-54/7-87)

2004 Season

	M	Inns	NO	Runs	HS	Avge	100s	50s	Ct	St	O	M	Runs	Wkts	Avge	Best	5wI	10wM
Test																		
All First																		
1-day Int	4	3	2	44	41 *	44.00	-	-	2	-	40	6	112	8	14.00	3-28	-	
C & G																		
totesport																		
Twenty20																		

Career Performances

	M	Inns	NO	Runs	HS	Avge	100s	50s	Ct	St	Balls	Runs	Wkts	Avge	Best	5wI	10wM
Test	36	51	11	540	66	13.50	-	2	14	-	9647	4299	151	28.47	8-84	11	2
All First	86	113	25	1640	84	18.63	-	5	39	-	20071	9275	354	26.20	8-84	21	3
1-day Int	90	49	13	417	46	11.58	-	-	26	-	4794	3263	116	28.12	5-43	1	
C & G																	
totesport																	
Twenty20																	

HARDINGES, M. A. — Gloucestershire

Name: Mark Andrew Hardinges
Role: Right-hand bat, right-arm medium-fast bowler
Born: 5 February 1978, Gloucester
Height: 6ft 1in **Weight:** 13st 7lbs
Nickname: Dinges
County debut: 1999
County cap: 2004
1st-Class 50s: 1
1st-Class 100s: 1
1st-Class catches: 6
Strike rate: 180.00 (career 94.71)
Parents: David and Jean
Marital status: Single
Family links with cricket: Brother and father played club cricket
Education: Malvern College; Bath University
Qualifications: 10 GCSEs, 3 A-levels, BSc (Hons) Economics and Politics
Overseas tours: Malvern College to South Africa 1996; Gloucestershire to South Africa 1999, 2000
Overseas teams played for: Newtown and Chilwell, Geelong, Australia 1997
Career highlights to date: 'Norwich Union debut v Notts 2001 – scored 65 and set domestic one-day seventh-wicket partnership record (164) with J. Snape. Also Lord's final v Surrey'
Cricket moments to forget: 'Glos v Somerset [Norwich Union 2001] – bowled three overs for 30 and was run out for 0 on Sky TV'
Cricketers particularly admired: Kim Barnett, Steve Waugh, Mark Alleyne
Other sports played: Golf, tennis (Gloucester U14), football (university first team)
Other sports followed: Football (Tottenham)
Relaxations: Golf
Extras: Represented British Universities 2000. Scored 65 v Nottinghamshire at Trent Bridge on NUL debut 2001, in the process sharing in a then record seventh-wicket partnership for domestic one-day competitions (164) with Jeremy Snape. Scored maiden first-class century (172) on his only first-class appearance of 2002, v Oxford University CCE at The Parks. C&G Man of the Match award for his 4-19 v Shropshire at Shrewsbury School 2002. Scored 68* v Warwickshire at Bristol 2004, in the process sharing with Roger Sillence (92) in a new record eighth-wicket stand for Gloucestershire in matches v Warwickshire (154)
Best batting: 172 Gloucestershire v OUCCE, The Parks 2002
Best bowling: 2-16 Gloucestershire v Essex, Bristol 2000

2004 Season

	M	Inns	NO	Runs	HS	Avge	100s	50s	Ct	St	O	M	Runs	Wkts	Avge	Best	5wI	10wM
Test																		
All First	1	1	1	68	68 *	-	-	1	3	-	30	4	120	1	120.00	1-78	-	-
1-day Int																		
C & G																		
totesport																		
Twenty20	4	2	0	6	6	3.00	-	-	1	-	4	0	35	0	-	-	-	

Career Performances

	M	Inns	NO	Runs	HS	Avge	100s	50s	Ct	St	Balls	Runs	Wkts	Avge	Best	5wI	10wM
Test																	
All First	11	12	2	327	172	32.70	1	1	6	-	1326	737	14	52.64	2-16	-	-
1-day Int																	
C & G	5	4	0	14	12	3.50	-	-	2	-	120	73	6	12.16	4-19	-	
totesport	20	18	4	194	65	13.85	-	1	7	-	690	589	14	42.07	3-40	-	
Twenty20	8	5	1	50	24	12.50	-	-	1	-	48	72	3	24.00	3-37	-	

HARMISON, S. J. — Durham

Name: Stephen James Harmison
Role: Right-hand bat, right-arm fast bowler
Born: 23 October 1978, Ashington, Northumberland
Height: 6ft 4in **Weight:** 14st
Nickname: Harmy
County debut: 1996
County cap: 1999
Test debut: 2002
Tests: 23
One-Day Internationals: 23
50 wickets in a season: 2
1st-Class 5 w. in innings: 9
1st-Class catches: 18
Place in batting averages: (2003 281st av. 8.66)
Place in bowling averages: 20th av. 25.42 (2003 42nd av. 27.08)
Strike rate: 47.52 (career 57.00)
Parents: Jimmy and Margaret
Wife and date of marriage: Hayley, 8 October 1999

Children: Emily Alice, 1 June 1999; Abbie
Family links with cricket: Brother James has played for Northumberland; brother Ben has also played for Northumberland and plays for England U19
Education: Ashington High School
Off-season: Touring with England
Overseas tours: England U19 to Pakistan 1996-97; England A to Zimbabwe and South Africa 1998-99; ECB National Academy to Australia 2001-02; England to Australia 2002-03, to Africa (World Cup) 2002-03, to Bangladesh 2003-04, to West Indies 2003-04, to South Africa 2004-05
Cricketers particularly admired: David Boon, Courtney Walsh
Young players to look out for: Gordon Muchall, Kyle Hogg
Other sports played: Football (played for Ashington in Northern League), golf, snooker
Other sports followed: Football (Newcastle United)
Relaxations: Spending time with family
Extras: Represented Northumberland U17. Returned then Test best figures of 4-55 (6-77 in match) in the second Test v Zimbabwe 2003, the inaugural Test at Riverside, his home ground. Had match figures of 9-79 (5-35/4-44) in the first Test v Bangladesh at Dhaka 2003-04, winning Man of the Match award. Man of the [Test] Series v West Indies 2003-04 for his 23 wickets at 14.86 (including ground record Test innings figures of 7-12 at Kingston) and England's Man of the [Test] Series v New Zealand 2004 for his 21 wickets at 22.09. Man of the Match v West Indies at Headingley in the NatWest Series 2004 (3-31). Had match figures of 9-121 (6-46/3-75) in the fourth Test v West Indies at The Oval 2004 to go to the top of the PricewaterhouseCoopers ratings for Test bowlers; his return included his 100th Test wicket (Sylvester Joseph) in his 23rd Test (only Ian Botham among post-war England bowlers has reached the milestone in fewer Tests – 19). Became second England bowler (after James Anderson) to take an ODI hat-trick (Kaif, Balaji, Nehra), v India at Trent Bridge in the NatWest Challenge 2004. ECB contract 2004-05
Best batting: 36* England v West Indies, The Oval 2004
Best bowling: 7-12 England v West Indies, Kingston 2003-04
Stop press: Took an England record 67 Test wickets in the calendar year 2004. Scored 42 in the third Test v South Africa at Cape Town 2004-05 to become the first No. 11 to top-score in an England Test innings

2004 Season

	M	Inns	NO	Runs	HS	Avge	100s	50s	Ct	St	O	M	Runs	Wkts	Avge	Best	5wI	10wM
Test	7	8	4	80	36 *	20.00	-	-	2	-	301	64	966	38	25.42	6-46	1	-
All First	7	8	4	80	36 *	20.00	-	-	2	-	301	64	966	38	25.42	6-46	1	-
1-day Int	12	4	2	21	13 *	10.50	-	-	2	-	108.5	11	438	22	19.90	4-22	-	
C & G																		
totesport	1	1	1	2	2 *	-	-	-	-	-	9	2	22	1	22.00	1-22	-	
Twenty20	1	0	0	0	0	-	-	-	-	-	4	0	19	1	19.00	1-19	-	

Career Performances

	M	Inns	NO	Runs	HS	Avge	100s	50s	Ct	St	Balls	Runs	Wkts	Avge	Best	5wI	10wM
Test	23	30	8	191	36 *	8.68	-	-	3	-	5144	2523	102	24.73	7-12	4	-
All First	99	137	36	861	36 *	8.52	-	-	18	-	19269	9739	338	28.81	7-12	9	-
1-day Int	23	9	6	33	13 *	11.00	-	-	5	-	1161	911	31	29.38	4-22	-	
C & G	5	4	2	4	2 *	2.00	-	-	3	-	252	184	4	46.00	2-37	-	
totesport	32	12	6	29	11 *	4.83	-	-	3	-	1462	1214	39	31.12	4-43	-	
Twenty20	1	0	0	0	0	-	-	-	-	-	24	19	1	19.00	1-19	-	

HARRIS, A. J. — Nottinghamshire

Name: Andrew James Harris
Role: Right-hand bat, right-arm fast-medium bowler
Born: 26 June 1973, Ashton-under-Lyne, Lancashire
Height: 6ft **Weight:** 11st 9lbs
Nickname: AJ, Honest
County debut: 1994 (Derbyshire), 2000 (Nottinghamshire)
County cap: 1996 (Derbyshire), 2000 (Nottinghamshire)
50 wickets in a season: 1
1st-Class 5 w. in innings: 12
1st-Class 10 w. in match: 3
1st-Class catches: 28
One Day 5 w. in innings: 1
Place in batting averages: (2003 296th av. 3.36)
Place in bowling averages: (2003 150th av. 56.66)
Strike rate: 44.66 (career 53.19)
Parents: Norman (deceased) and Joyce
Wife and date of marriage: Kate, 7 October 2000
Children: Jacob Alexander, 28 August 2002
Education: Hadfield Comprehensive School; Glossopdale Community College
Qualifications: 6 GCSEs, 1 A-level
Overseas tours: England A to Australia 1996-97
Overseas teams played for: Ginninderra West Belconnen, Australian Capital Territory 1992-93; Victoria University of Wellington CC, New Zealand 1997-98
Cricket moments to forget: 'Having forgotten my shirt I had to walk out to field in the last Norwich Union game of the 2001 season (which happened to be on TV) wearing the diminutive Guy Welton's shirt'

Cricket superstitions: 'None'
Cricketers particularly admired: Merv Hughes, Allan Donald
Young players to look out for: Bilal Shafayat
Other sports played: Golf, snooker, football
Other sports followed: Football (Man City)
Relaxations: 'Good food, good wine and the odd game of golf'
Extras: Left Derbyshire at end of the 1999 season and joined Nottinghamshire for 2000. Scored 41* v Northamptonshire at Northampton 2002, in the process sharing with Paul McMahon in a record last-wicket stand for Nottinghamshire in matches v Northamptonshire (68). Nottinghamshire Player of the Year 2002. Had the misfortune to be 'timed out' v Durham UCCE at Trent Bridge 2003 (was suffering from groin injury)
Best batting: 41* Nottinghamshire v Northamptonshire, Northampton 2002
Best bowling: 7-54 Nottinghamshire v Northamptonshire, Trent Bridge 2002

2004 Season

	M	Inns	NO	Runs	HS	Avge	100s	50s	Ct	St	O	M	Runs	Wkts	Avge	Best	5wI	10wM
Test																		
All First	2	3	1	24	13	12.00	-	-	-	-	67	15	196	9	21.77	4-22	-	-
1-day Int																		
C & G																		
totesport	5	0	0	0	0	-	-	-	1	-	33	5	133	5	26.60	2-31	-	
Twenty20	5	1	0	0	0	0.00	-	-	1	-	10	0	106	4	26.50	2-30	-	

Career Performances

	M	Inns	NO	Runs	HS	Avge	100s	50s	Ct	St	Balls	Runs	Wkts	Avge	Best	5wI	10wM
Test																	
All First	92	129	33	836	41 *	8.70	-	-	28	-	15958	9511	300	31.70	7-54	12	3
1-day Int																	
C & G	11	5	3	21	11 *	10.50	-	-	1	-	601	402	11	36.54	3-10	-	
totesport	84	28	13	109	16 *	7.26	-	-	21	-	3575	3127	102	30.65	5-35	1	
Twenty20	6	1	0	0	0	0.00	-	-	1	-	84	138	5	27.60	2-30	-	

39. Which team at the 1996-97 ICC Trophy tournament boasted an Adams, a Kallicharran and a Benjamin?

HARRISON, A. J. Glamorgan

Name: Adam James Harrison
Role: Right-hand bat, right-arm medium-fast bowler
Born: 30 October 1985
Height: 6ft **Weight:** 13st
Nickname: Harry, Junior Haz, Junior Roof, Junior Moore, Tasty
County debut: No first-team appearance
Strike rate: 51.33 (career 51.33)
Parents: Stuart and Susan
Marital status: Single
Family links with cricket: 'Father played for Glamorgan in early 1970s. Brother David currently playing for Glamorgan and in ECB National Academy 2004-05'
Education: West Monmouth Comprehensive School; St Albans RC High School
Qualifications: 10 GCSEs, 2 A-levels, Level 1 coaching award
Off-season: 'Training as part-time National Academy student; hopefully touring with England U19; boxing training with Gary Lockett'
Overseas tours: West of England to West Indies 2001; England U18 to Holland 2003; England U19 to Qatar 2003, to Bangladesh (U19 World Cup) 2003-04, to India 2004-05
Career highlights to date: 'Making first-class debut 2004 for MCC against champions Sussex. Playing for England U19 in World Cup, Bangladesh 2004'
Cricket moments to forget: 'Losing semi-final of U19 World Cup 2004 against West Indies'
Cricket superstitions: 'Always put left pad on first'
Cricketers particularly admired: Jacques Kallis, Andrew Flintoff, Steve Watkin, Alex Wharf
Young players to look out for: David Harrison ('big bro'), Steve Davies, Liam Plunkett, Mark Turner, Tom Maynard
Other sports played: Golf, squash (Wales U11-U13), football (goalkeeper; played for Football Association of Wales 2001-02)
Other sports followed: Football (Manchester United)
Injuries: Out for three months with an ankle injury requiring surgery
Relaxations: 'PlayStation 2 (Tiger Woods), Sky Digital'
Extras: BBC *Test Match Special* U15 Cricketer of the Year 2001. Sir John Hobbs Memorial Award 2001. Royal Variety Club Outstanding Newcomer Award 2002. NBC Denis Compton Award for the most promising young Glamorgan player 2003.

Represented England U19 2003 and v Bangladesh U19 2004; scored 33 in the first 'Test' v Bangladesh U19 at Headingley, in the process sharing with Luke Wright (78) in a new England U19 record stand for the eighth wicket (114). Made first-class debut for MCC v Sussex at Lord's 2004. ECB National Academy 2004-05 (part-time)
Opinions on cricket: 'Tea breaks should be longer (30 minutes).'
Best batting: 34* MCC v Sussex, Lord's 2004
Best bowling: 2-65 MCC v Sussex, Lord's 2004

2004 Season (did not make any first-class or one-day appearances for his county)

Career Performances

	M	Inns	NO	Runs	HS	Avge	100s	50s	Ct	St	Balls	Runs	Wkts	Avge	Best	5wI	10wM
Test																	
All First	1	1	1	34	34 *	-	-	-	-	-	154	108	3	36.00	2-65	-	-
1-day Int																	
C & G																	
totesport																	
Twenty20																	

HARRISON, D. S. — Glamorgan

Name: David Stuart Harrison
Role: Right-hand bat, right-arm fast-medium bowler, occasional wicket-keeper; all-rounder
Born: 31 July 1981, Newport
Height: 6ft 4in **Weight:** 15st
Nickname: Harry, Hazza, Roof
County debut: 1999
50 wickets in a season: 1
1st-Class 50s: 2
1st-Class 5 w. in innings: 4
1st-Class catches: 11
One-Day 5 w. in innings: 1
Place in batting averages: 203rd av. 21.94 (2003 263rd av. 13.55)
Place in bowling averages: 35th av. 27.78 (2003 70th av. 32.10)
Strike rate: 50.57 (career 54.50)
Parents: Stuart and Susan
Marital status: Single
Family links with cricket: 'Dad bowled some wily old school seamers for Glamorgan in early 1970s. Brother Adam is on Glamorgan staff and with England Academy for 2004-05'

Education: West Monmouth Comprehensive, Pontypool; Usk College; 'Glamorgan dressing room!'
Qualifications: 8 GCSEs, 2 A-levels, Levels 1 and 2 coaching awards
Career outside cricket: 'Qualified school caretaker; modelling "syrups" (hair)'
Off-season: 'Spending winter with England Academy'
Overseas tours: Gwent U15 to Cape Town 1996; Wales U16 to Jersey 1996, 1997; England U19 to Malaysia and (U19 World Cup) Sri Lanka 1999-2000; Glamorgan to Cape Town 2002; England A to Sri Lanka 2004-05
Overseas teams played for: Claremont, Cape Town 2002 (during Glamorgan tour)
Career highlights to date: 'Making Glamorgan debut; winning NUL at Canterbury 2002; playing at Lord's; being selected for England Academy'
Cricket moments to forget: 'Wouldn't want to forget anything!'
Cricketers particularly admired: Nasser Hussain, Mike Kasprowicz
Young players to look out for: Jimmy Adams
Other sports played: Squash (Welsh Junior Champion U12-U14), rugby (Welsh caps as a junior), 'enjoy a round of golf'
Other sports followed: Rugby (Newport Gwent Dragons), boxing, golf
Favourite band: 'Just a general music fan'
Relaxations: 'Going for a beer with the boys; Sky Digital; walking my dog Jake; spending time with girlfriend Maxine'
Extras: Played for Glamorgan from U12. Represented England at U17, U18 and U19 levels. Recorded maiden one-day five-wicket return (5-26), then struck 37* from 35 balls v Yorkshire at Headingley in the NUL 2002. Recorded maiden first-class five-wicket return (5-80) then scored maiden first-class fifty (66) v Gloucestershire at Cardiff 2003. Glamorgan Young Player of the Year 2003, 2004. Took 50 first-class wickets in a season for the first time 2004. ECB National Academy 2004-05
Opinions on cricket: 'It's a great thing to get paid for something you love doing. Make the most of it because you never know what's around the corner. Too many EU players; too many Kolpaks (*see page 9*) – give the young English players a chance!'
Best batting: 88 Glamorgan v Essex, Chelmsford 2004
Best bowling: 5-48 Glamorgan v Somerset, Swansea 2004

2004 Season

	M	Inns	NO	Runs	HS	Avge	100s	50s	Ct	St	O	M	Runs	Wkts	Avge	Best	5wI	10wM
Test																		
All First	17	22	4	395	88	21.94	-	1	8	-	480.3	123	1584	57	27.78	5-48	3	-
1-day Int																		
C & G	2	1	1	10	10 *	-	-	-	-	-	18	1	78	2	39.00	2-45	-	
totesport	9	3	0	7	3	2.33	-	-	-	-	60	2	301	7	43.00	2-27	-	
Twenty20																		

Career Performances

	M	Inns	NO	Runs	HS	Avge	100s	50s	Ct	St	Balls	Runs	Wkts	Avge	Best	5wI	10wM
Test																	
All First	37	52	9	722	88	16.79	-	2	11	-	5505	3109	101	30.78	5-48	4	-
1-day Int																	
C & G	2	1	1	10	10 *	-	-	-	-	-	108	78	2	39.00	2-45	-	
totesport	26	17	6	145	37 *	13.18	-	-	3	-	1020	873	23	37.95	5-26	1	
Twenty20	2	1	0	4	4	4.00	-	-	-	-	30	61	1	61.00	1-43	-	

HARRITY, M. A. — Worcestershire

Name: Mark Andrew Harrity
Role: Right-hand bat, left-arm fast bowler
Born: 9 March 1974, Adelaide, Australia
Height: 6ft 4in **Weight:** 13st 9lbs
Nickname: Hags
County debut: 2003
County colours: 2003
1st-Class 5 w. in innings: 2
1st-Class catches: 26
Place in bowling averages: (2003 141st av. 49.90)
Strike rate: 70.50 (career 71.37)
Parents: Judith and Stuart
Marital status: Engaged to Laura
Children: Lachlan, 1 August 2000
Education: Taperoo High School
Overseas tours: Young Australia (Australia A) to England and Netherlands 1995
Overseas teams played for: South Australia 1993-94 – 2002-03; West Torrens, South Australia 2001-02 – 2003-04
Career highlights to date: 'Winning the Sheffield Shield with South Australia in 1995-96'
Cricket moments to forget: 'Bringing up Dean Jones's 100 after kicking the ball into the boundary for four runs in 1994'
Cricket superstitions: 'Always wear sweatband'
Cricketers particularly admired: Dean Jones, Jason Gillespie
Young players to look out for: Michael Clarke (NSW), Kadeer Ali
Other sports played: Australian Rules football ('past player')
Other sports followed: Australian Rules football (Port Power, Port Magpies)
Favourite band: Bon Jovi, U2
Relaxations: 'Play guitar, piano'

Extras: Selected for Prime Minister's XI v West Indians at Canberra 1995-96 and for Prime Minister's XI v England tourists at Canberra 1998-99, taking 3-46. Played for Australian XI v West Indians at Brisbane 1995-96. One of South Australia's leading wicket-takers for several seasons (one-day and four-day), topping the state's wicket-taking list in the ING Cup 2001-02 with 17 wickets (av. 19.76). Has name on Adelaide Oval locker for ten years' service (locker was previously that of Sir Donald Bradman and Les Favell). Left Worcestershire at the end of the 2004 season. Is not considered an overseas player

Opinions on cricket: 'Lots of exciting young talent coming through. Twenty20 good concept!'

Best batting: 19 South Australia v Victoria, Melbourne 2001-02

Best bowling: 5-65 South Australia v Tasmania, Hobart 2001-02

2004 Season

	M	Inns	NO	Runs	HS	Avge	100s	50s	Ct	St	O	M	Runs	Wkts	Avge	Best	5wI	10wM
Test																		
All First	4	3	1	3	3 *	1.50	-	-	-	-	94	19	382	8	47.75	3-111	-	-
1-day Int																		
C & G																		
totesport	1	0	0	0	0	-	-	-	-	-	9	0	44	2	22.00	2-44	-	
Twenty20																		

Career Performances

	M	Inns	NO	Runs	HS	Avge	100s	50s	Ct	St	Balls	Runs	Wkts	Avge	Best	5wI	10wM
Test																	
All First	84	103	53	254	19	5.08	-	-	26	-	15418	8491	216	39.31	5-65	2	-
1-day Int																	
C & G	1	0	0	0	0	-	-	-	1	-	47	23	3	7.66	3-23	-	
totesport	8	3	1	17	15	8.50	-	-	1	-	294	304	11	27.63	3-27	-	
Twenty20	5	3	1	0	0 *	0.00	-	-	2	-	106	143	7	20.42	2-20	-	

40. Which Sri Lanka batsman became to first player to record two identical three-figure scores in the same Test match, v India 1982-83?

HARVEY, I. J. Yorkshire

Name: Ian Joseph Harvey
Role: Right-hand bat, right-arm fast-medium bowler
Born: 10 April 1972, Wonthaggi, Victoria, Australia
Height: 5ft 9in **Weight:** 12st 8lbs
Nickname: Freak
County debut: 1999 (Gloucestershire), 2004 (Yorkshire)
County cap: 1999 (Gloucestershire)
One-Day Internationals: 73
1st-Class 50s: 36
1st-Class 100s: 9
1st-Class 5 w. in innings: 14
1st-Class 10 w. in match: 2
1st-Class catches: 94
One-Day 100s: 2
One-Day 5 w. in innings: 8
Place in batting averages: 178th av. 24.81 (2003 52nd av. 44.88)
Place in bowling averages: (2003 15th av. 23.14)
Strike rate: 132.00 (career 56.38)
Family links with cricket: Brothers play club cricket in Australia
Education: Wonthaggi Technical College
Overseas tours: Australian Academy to New Zealand 1994-95; Australia to Sharjah (Coca-Cola Cup) 1997-98, to New Zealand 1999-2000 (one-day series), to Kenya (ICC Knockout Trophy) 2000-01, to India 2000-01 (one-day series), to England 2001 (one-day series), to South Africa 2001-02 (one-day series), to Africa (World Cup) 2002-03, to West Indies 2002-03 (one-day series), to India (TVS Cup) 2003-04, to Sri Lanka 2003-04 (one-day series), to Zimbabwe (one-day series) 2004, to Holland (Videocon Cup) 2004, to England (ICC Champions Trophy) 2004; Australia A to South Africa 2002-03; FICA World XI to New Zealand 2004-05
Overseas teams played for: Victoria 1993-94 –
Extras: The nickname 'Freak' is a reference to his brilliant fielding and was reportedly coined by Shane Warne. Attended Commonwealth Bank [Australian] Cricket Academy 1994. Took a wicket (Jonty Rhodes) with his second ball in ODI cricket v South Africa at Sydney in the CUB Series 1997-98. Joined Gloucestershire in 1999 as overseas player. Man of the Match in the Carlton Series first final v West Indies at Sydney 2000-01 (47* at No. 8/2-5 from six overs). Won the Walter Lawrence Trophy for the season's fastest first-class hundred with his 61-ball century v Derbyshire at Bristol 2001; also took 5-89 in Derbyshire's second innings. Took hat-

trick (Knight, N. Smith, Bell) v Warwickshire at Bristol in the B&H 2002. Has won numerous Australian and English domestic awards, including C&G Man of the Match in the quarter-final v Warwickshire at Edgbaston 2003 (5-23 and a run out) and in the final v Worcestershire at Lord's 2003 (2-37 and a 36-ball 61). Scored the first ever century in the Twenty20 (100* from 50 balls), v Warwickshire at Edgbaston 2003. Left Gloucestershire at the end of the 2003 season and joined Yorkshire as an overseas player for 2004. One of *Wisden*'s Five Cricketers of the Year 2004. Struck his second Twenty20 century (108* from 59 balls) v Lancashire at Headingley 2004
Best batting: 136 Victoria v South Australia, Melbourne 1995-96
Best bowling: 8-101 Australia A v South Africa A, Adelaide 2002-03

2004 Season

	M	Inns	NO	Runs	HS	Avge	100s	50s	Ct	St	O	M	Runs	Wkts	Avge	Best	5wI	10wM
Test																		
All First	7	11	0	273	95	24.81	-	1	4	-	154	41	430	7	61.42	3-38	-	-
1-day Int																		
C & G	1	1	0	20	20	20.00	-	-	-	-	9	0	46	1	46.00	1-46	-	
totesport	11	10	1	209	49	23.22	-	-	3	-	61.3	5	289	16	18.06	3-38	-	
Twenty20	2	2	1	122	108 *	122.00	1	-	1	-	8	0	54	2	27.00	2-30	-	

Career Performances

	M	Inns	NO	Runs	HS	Avge	100s	50s	Ct	St	Balls	Runs	Wkts	Avge	Best	5wI	10wM
Test																	
All First	127	211	18	6222	136	32.23	9	36	94	-	19962	9712	354	27.43	8-101	14	2
1-day Int	73	51	11	715	48 *	17.87	-	-	17	-	3279	2577	85	30.31	4-16	-	
C & G	17	16	0	310	61	19.37	-	1	6	-	894	564	36	15.66	5-23	1	
totesport	65	63	4	1743	96	29.54	-	9	17	-	2848	1996	124	16.09	5-19	4	
Twenty20	8	8	3	370	108 *	74.00	2	1	1	-	191	207	12	17.25	3-28	-	

41. Which current international wicket-keeper is training to be a lawyer in between cricket tours?

HASSAN ADNAN Derbyshire

Name: Mohammad Hassan Adnan Syed
Role: Right-hand bat, right-arm off-spin bowler
Born: 15 May 1975, Lahore, Punjab
Height: 5ft 9in **Weight:** 12st 5lbs
Nickname: Hass
County debut: 2003
County cap: 2004
1000 runs in a season: 1
1st-Class 50s: 36
1st-Class 100s: 7
1st-Class catches: 44
Place in batting averages: 36th av. 51.11
Strike rate: 225.00 (career 243.00)
Parents: Hassan Adnan
Marital status: Single
Education: MAO College, Lahore
Off-season: Playing as overseas player in Lahore
Overseas teams played for: Islamabad 1994-95, 2000-01; Gujranwala 1997-98 – 1998-99; Water and Power Development Authority (WAPDA) 1997-98 –
Career highlights to date: '140 v Notts at Derby. 113* v New Zealand [both 2004]'
Cricketers particularly admired: Steve Waugh
Young players to look out for: 'All players at DCCC!'
Other sports played: Badminton
Other sports followed: Badminton
Favourite music: Rock
Relaxations: Music, watching TV
Extras: Won two Man of the Match awards in the Tissot Cup domestic competition in Pakistan. Scored century (113*) as Derbyshire beat New Zealanders in 50-over match at Derby 2004. Scored 1000 (1247) County Championship runs in his first full season 2004. Derbyshire Supporters' Club Player of the Year 2004. Awarded Derbyshire cap 2004. Is not considered an overseas player
Best batting: 140 Derbyshire v Nottinghamshire, Derby 2004
Best bowling: 1-4 Derbyshire v Yorkshire, Derby 2004

2004 Season

	M	Inns	NO	Runs	HS	Avge	100s	50s	Ct	St	O	M	Runs	Wkts	Avge	Best	5wI	10wM
Test																		
All First	18	31	4	1380	140	51.11	3	8	11	-	37.3	2	154	1	154.00	1-4	-	-
1-day Int																		
C & G	1	1	0	78	78	78.00	-	1	-	-								
totesport	18	17	2	395	57	26.33	-	5	8	-	19.1	0	107	3	35.66	2-13	-	
Twenty20	4	4	0	61	32	15.25	-	-	2	-	4	0	31	1	31.00	1-18	-	

Career Performances

	M	Inns	NO	Runs	HS	Avge	100s	50s	Ct	St	Balls	Runs	Wkts	Avge	Best	5wI	10wM
Test																	
All First	78	125	19	4884	140	46.07	7	36	44	-	243	174	1	174.00	1-4	-	-
1-day Int																	
C & G	1	1	0	78	78	78.00	-	1	-	-							
totesport	19	18	2	424	57	26.50	-	5	10	-	115	107	3	35.66	2-13	-	
Twenty20	4	4	0	61	32	15.25	-	-	2	-	24	31	1	31.00	1-18	-	

HAVELL, P. M. R. Derbyshire

Name: Paul Matthew Roger Havell
Role: Left-hand bat, right-arm fast-medium bowler
Born: 4 July 1980, Melbourne, Australia
Height: 6ft 3in **Weight:** 14st 2lbs
Nickname: Havler, Two Tone Malone, Trigger, William Hill, Ladbrokes, Einstein
County debut: 2001 (Sussex), 2003 (Derbyshire)
1st-Class catches: 4
Place in bowling averages: 111th av. 38.76 (2003 90th av. 35.57)
Strike rate: 50.90 (career 50.02)
Parents: Roger and Caroline
Marital status: Single
Family links with cricket: 'Brother Mark played for Sussex U19 until his back had problems'
Education: Warden Park School
Qualifications: 9 GCSEs, 1 A-level, Level 2 coach, Ambulance Driving Certificate
Off-season: 'Driving ambulances and sleeping'
Overseas tours: Sussex U19 to Barbados 1997-98; Sussex to Grenada 2000-01

Overseas teams played for: East Doncaster CC, Australia 1998-99; Carlton CC, Melbourne 2000-01; Fairfield-Liverpool, Sydney 2002-03
Career highlights to date: 'Going 10 overs without bowling a no-ball'
Cricket moments to forget: 'Bowling no-balls'
Cricket superstitions: 'Don't like being dropped'
Cricketers particularly admired: Viv Richards, David Gower, Ian Botham, David Houghton, Karl Krikken, Mike Hendrick
Young players to look out for: 'Any from DCCC'
Other sports played: 'The roulette wheel'
Other sports followed: 'Anything the "south coast mincers" play'
Injuries: Out for six weeks early in the season with an elbow injury
Favourite band: 'Abba, Bros, Five Star, any 80s retro, classical music'
Relaxations: 'Playing cards; reading Shakespeare, listening to Schubert, and attending the Last Night of the Proms; playing any slot machine'
Extras: Sussex Young Cricketer of the Year 1995. Released by Sussex at the end of the 2002 season; joined Derbyshire during 2003, taking 4-129 on debut v South Africans at Derby
Opinions on cricket: 'Work hard, play hard, Matthew Maynard. Keep cricket simple – it's not rocket surgery.'
Best batting: 13* Derbyshire v Yorkshire, Derby 2004
Best bowling: 4-75 Derbyshire v Durham, Riverside 2004

2004 Season

	M	Inns	NO	Runs	HS	Avge	100s	50s	Ct	St	O	M	Runs	Wkts	Avge	Best	5wI	10wM
Test																		
All First	8	10	6	32	13 *	8.00	-	-	2	-	178.1	20	814	21	38.76	4-75	-	-
1-day Int																		
C & G																		
totesport	3	3	0	8	4	2.66	-	-	-	-	16.5	1	79	3	26.33	3-28	-	
Twenty20	1	0	0	0	0	-	-	-	-	-	4	0	32	2	16.00	2-32	-	

Career Performances

	M	Inns	NO	Runs	HS	Avge	100s	50s	Ct	St	Balls	Runs	Wkts	Avge	Best	5wI	10wM
Test																	
All First	13	16	11	42	13 *	8.40	-	-	4	-	1751	1328	35	37.94	4-75	-	-
1-day Int																	
C & G																	
totesport	5	3	0	8	4	2.66	-	-	-	-	137	116	3	38.66	3-28	-	
Twenty20	1	0	0	0	0	-	-	-	-	-	24	32	2	16.00	2-32	-	

HAYNES, J. J. Lancashire

Name: Jamie Jonathan Haynes
Role: Right-hand bat, wicket-keeper
Born: 5 July 1974, Bristol
Height: 5ft 10½in **Weight:** 13st
Nickname: JJ, Wolf, Monkey
County debut: 1996
1st-Class 50s: 3
1st-Class catches: 47
1st-Class stumpings: 4
Parents: Steve Haynes and Moiya Ford
Wife and date of marriage: Michelle, 20 December 2003
Family links with cricket: 'Dad and uncle played for Gloucestershire. [American] uncle number one cricket authority in New York'
Education: St Edmunds College, Canberra; University of Canberra
Qualifications: Year 12 Certificate, coaching certificate, 'partially complete BA Journalism'
Overseas tours: Lancashire pre-season tours
Overseas teams played for: Weston Creek CC, Canberra; Queanbeyan CC, Canberra; Tuggeranong Valley CC, Canberra 1995-96; South Canberra CC 1996-97
Career highlights to date: 'Winning any trophies'
Cricket moments to forget: 'Losing four front teeth while keeping wicket'
Cricket superstitions: 'Don't cross on stairs unless fingers crossed'
Cricketers particularly admired: Warren Hegg, 'Cool' Carl Hooper, Jack Russell, Carl Butrum
Young players to look out for: Kyle Hogg, Steven Crook
Other sports played: Australian Rules football (Queanbeyan Tigers), golf, rugby
Other sports followed: Football (Manchester United), rugby (Sale Sharks), Australian Rules (Carlton)
Favourite band: Counting Crows, REM
Relaxations: 'Cooking, golf'
Extras: Top scorer with 80 as nightwatchman in Lancashire's first innings v Sri Lanka A at Old Trafford 1999. Released by Lancashire at the end of the 2004 season
Opinions on cricket: 'I think it would be nice if people stopped bagging the system that they made a lot of money out of.'
Best batting: 80 Lancashire v Sri Lanka A, Old Trafford 1999

2004 Season

	M	Inns	NO	Runs	HS	Avge	100s	50s	Ct	St	O	M	Runs	Wkts	Avge	Best	5wI	10wM
Test																		
All First	4	5	0	48	24	9.60	-	-	12	2								
1-day Int																		
C & G																		
totesport	7	4	1	27	13	9.00	-	-	7	4								
Twenty20	2	0	0	0	0	-	-	-	3	2								

Career Performances

	M	Inns	NO	Runs	HS	Avge	100s	50s	Ct	St	Balls	Runs	Wkts	Avge	Best	5wI	10wM
Test																	
All First	20	29	4	491	80	19.64	-	3	47	4							
1-day Int																	
C & G	1	1	1	59	59 *	-	-	1	1	-							
totesport	17	9	2	59	13	8.42	-	-	20	7							
Twenty20	3	1	0	9	9	9.00	-	-	3	2							

HAYWARD, M. — Middlesex

Name: Mornantau (Nantie) Hayward
Role: Right-hand bat, right-arm fast bowler
Born: 6 March 1977, Uitenhage, South Africa
Height: 6ft 1in **Weight:** 13st 7lbs
County debut: 2003 (Worcestershire), 2004 (Middlesex)
County colours: 2003 (Worcestershire)
Test debut: 1999-2000
Tests: 16
One-Day Internationals: 21
50 wickets in a season: 1
1st-Class 50s: 1
1st-Class 5 w. in innings: 9
1st-Class 10 w. in match: 2
1st-Class catches: 30
One-Day 5 w. in innings: 1
Place in batting averages: 285th av. 5.00 (2003 286th av. 7.68)
Place in bowling averages: 42nd av. 29.61 (2003 13th av. 22.88)
Strike rate: 55.93 (career 52.40)
Parents: Maruis and Emmarencia

Wife and date of marriage: Marlize, 6 March 2004
Education: Daniel Pienaar Technical High
Overseas tours: South Africa U19 to India 1995-96; South Africa to England 1998, to India 1999-2000, to Sharjah (Coca-Cola Sharjah Cup) 1999-2000, to Sri Lanka 2000, to Australia (Super Challenge) 2000, to Australia 2001-02, to Sri Lanka 2004
Overseas teams played for: Eastern Province 1995-96 – 2003-04; Warriors 2004-05 –
Cricket moments to forget: 'Tour to Sri Lanka' (*South Africa lost Test series 1-0 and ODI series 5-0 in 2004*)
Cricketers particularly admired: Allan Donald, Lance Klusener
Young players to look out for: Scott Newman
Other sports followed: Rugby (South Africa; 'just nice to beat Australia 2004 in Durban')
Relaxations: Fishing
Extras: Represented South Africa Schools 1995. Represented South Africa Academy 1997. Made Test debut in second Test v England at Port Elizabeth 1999-2000, taking 4-75 in England's first innings. Man of the Match award for his 4-31 in fifth Coca-Cola Cup match v India at Sharjah 1999-2000. One of *South African Cricket Annual*'s five Cricketers of the Year 2000. Joined Worcestershire as an overseas player for 2003, taking 5-70 (9-165 in match) on Championship debut v Hampshire at Worcester. Joined Middlesex as an overseas player for 2004; has returned for 2005
Best batting: 55* Eastern Province v Boland, Port Elizabeth 1997-98
Best bowling: 6-31 Eastern Province v Easterns, Port Elizabeth 1999-2000

2004 Season

	M	Inns	NO	Runs	HS	Avge	100s	50s	Ct	St	O	M	Runs	Wkts	Avge	Best	5wI	10wM
Test																		
All First	11	13	5	40	9	5.00	-	-	4	-	289	54	918	31	29.61	4-41	-	-
1-day Int																		
C & G	3	0	0	0	0	-	-	-	1	-	26	1	113	6	18.83	2-15	-	
totesport	10	1	1	0	0 *	-	-	-	1	-	62.1	3	308	12	25.66	4-21	-	
Twenty20	1	0	0	0	0	-	-	-	-	-	3	0	33	0	-	-	-	

Career Performances

	M	Inns	NO	Runs	HS	Avge	100s	50s	Ct	St	Balls	Runs	Wkts	Avge	Best	5wI	10wM
Test	16	17	7	73	14	7.30	-	-	3	-	2821	1609	54	29.79	5-56	1	-
All First	102	110	38	821	55 *	11.40	-	1	30	-	18551	9999	354	28.24	6-31	9	2
1-day Int	21	5	1	12	4	3.00	-	-	4	-	993	858	21	40.85	4-31	-	
C & G	7	1	0	4	4	4.00	-	-	2	-	330	256	14	18.28	5-49	1	
totesport	18	4	3	14	11	14.00	-	-	1	-	721	597	24	24.87	4-21	-	
Twenty20	3	1	0	2	2	2.00	-	-	-	-	62	86	3	28.66	3-21	-	

HEGG, W. K. Lancashire

Name: Warren Kevin Hegg
Role: Right-hand bat, wicket-keeper
Born: 23 February 1968, Manchester
Height: 5ft 9in **Weight:** 12st 10lbs
Nickname: Chucky
County debut: 1986
County cap: 1989
Benefit: 1999 (£178,000)
Test debut: 1998-99
Tests: 2
50 dismissals in a season: 6
1st-Class 50s: 52
1st-Class 100s: 7
1st-Class catches: 816
1st-Class stumpings: 89
Place in batting averages: 149th av. 29.42 (2003 130th av. 31.07)
Parents: Kevin (deceased) and Glenda
Wife and date of marriage: Joanne, 29 October 1994
Children: Chloe Louise, 13 November 1998
Family links with cricket: Brother Martin local league cricketer
Education: Unsworth High School; Stand College, Whitefield
Qualifications: 5 O-levels, 7 CSEs, qualified coach
Overseas tours: NCA North U19 to Bermuda 1985; England YC to Sri Lanka 1986-87, to Australia (U19 World Cup) 1987-88; England A to Pakistan and Sri Lanka 1990-91, to Australia 1996-97; England to Australia 1998-99, to India and New Zealand 2001-02
Overseas teams played for: Sheffield, Tasmania 1988-90, 1992-93
Cricketers particularly admired: Ian Botham, Alan Knott, Bob Taylor, Gehan Mendis, Ian Healy
Other sports played: Football (Old Standians)
Other sports followed: Rugby league (Salford City Reds), football (Man United)
Relaxations: 'Golf, golf, golf'
Extras: Became youngest player for 30 years to score a century for Lancashire with his 130 v Northamptonshire at Northampton in 1987 aged 19 (in his fourth first-class game). Took 11 catches in match v Derbyshire at Chesterfield 1989, equalling world first-class record. Wombwell Cricket Lovers' Society joint Wicket-keeper of the Year 1993. Vice-captain of Lancashire 1999 and 2001. Lancashire Player of the Year 2001. Lancashire captain 2002-04, the first wicket-keeper to hold the post in an official capacity
Best batting: 134 Lancashire v Leicestershire, Old Trafford 1996

2004 Season

	M	Inns	NO	Runs	HS	Avge	100s	50s	Ct	St	O	M	Runs	Wkts	Avge	Best	5wI	10wM
Test																		
All First	12	17	3	412	54	29.42	-	1	23	5								
1-day Int																		
C & G	3	3	1	8	3 *	4.00	-	-	4	-								
totesport	9	6	1	138	37	27.60	-	-	11	-								
Twenty20	5	4	2	31	20	15.50	-	-	1	5								

Career Performances

	M	Inns	NO	Runs	HS	Avge	100s	50s	Ct	St	Balls	Runs	Wkts	Avge	Best	5wI	10wM
Test	2	4	0	30	15	7.50	-	-	8	-							
All First	333	483	93	10800	134	27.69	7	52	816	89	6	7	0	-	-	-	-
1-day Int																	
C & G	50	28	2	431	60	16.57	-	1	61	7							
totesport	250	154	55	2015	54	20.35	-	2	266	42							
Twenty20	10	8	2	85	45	14.16	-	-	5	7							

HEMP, D. L. — Glamorgan

Name: David Lloyd Hemp
Role: Left-hand bat
Born: 15 November 1970, Hamilton, Bermuda
Height: 6ft 1in **Weight:** 12st 10lbs
Nickname: Hempy, Mad Dog
County debut: 1991 (Glamorgan), 1997 (Warwickshire)
County cap: 1994 (Glamorgan), 1997 (Warwickshire)
1000 runs in a season: 4
1st-Class 50s: 61
1st-Class 100s: 19
1st-Class catches: 133
One-Day 100s: 5
Place in batting averages: 59th av. 44.80 (2003 112th av. 33.72)
Strike rate: (career 60.70)
Parents: Clive and Elisabeth
Wife and date of marriage: Angela, 16 March 1996
Children: Cameron, January 2002
Family links with cricket: Father and brother both played for Swansea CC

Education: Olchfa Comprehensive School; Millfield School; Birmingham University
Qualifications: 5 O-levels, 2 A-levels, MBA, Level III coaching award
Career outside cricket: PR/marketing; coaching
Off-season: Working for PR/marketing company; coaching
Overseas tours: Welsh Cricket Association U18 to Barbados 1986; Welsh Schools U19 to Australia 1987-88; Glamorgan to Trinidad 1990; South Wales Cricket Association to New Zealand and Australia 1991-92; England A to India 1994-95
Overseas teams played for: Crusaders, Durban 1992-98
Career highlights to date: '99* England A v India A, Calcutta "Test" match 1994-95'
Cricket moments to forget: 'None'
Cricket superstitions: 'None'
Cricketers particularly admired: David Gower, Viv Richards
Young players to look out for: Mark Wallace, Jon Hughes, Moeen Ali
Other sports played: Football
Other sports followed: Football (Swansea City, West Ham United)
Favourite band: Nickelback, Manic Street Preachers, Lostprophets
Relaxations: 'Golf, reading'
Extras: In 1989 scored 104* and 101* for Welsh Schools U19 v Scottish Schools U19 and 120 and 102* v Irish Schools U19. Scored 258* for Wales v MCC 1991. Left Glamorgan at the end of the 1996 season and joined Warwickshire. Scored two 100s (138/114*) v Hampshire at Southampton 1997. Vice-captain of Warwickshire 2001. Left Warwickshire in the 2001-02 off-season and rejoined Glamorgan for 2002. Scored 88-ball 102 v Surrey at The Oval in the C&G 2002 as Glamorgan made 429 in reply to Surrey's 438-5. Won Glamorgan's Byron Denning Award 2004
Opinions on cricket: 'Reduce amount of cricket played, which would allow for more quality practice in between games. Bowlers would remain fairly fresh all season. Batters should become more disciplined because of less innings, which would hopefully raise standard and competitiveness of cricket played. Away captain should have choice of whether to bat or bowl. Cricketers are only as good as the surface they play on. Improve the wickets, which will improve the standard of players. Pitch inspectors less tolerant; more points deducted for poor surfaces. Keep two divisions with three up/three down as majority of games will remain competitive up till end of season. Twelve-month contracts for all players – therefore under control of county all year which, if done properly, will/should lead to better/quicker development of players.'
Best batting: 186* Warwickshire v Worcestershire, Edgbaston 2001
Best bowling: 3-23 Glamorgan v South Africa A, Cardiff 1996

2004 Season

	M	Inns	NO	Runs	HS	Avge	100s	50s	Ct	St	O	M	Runs	Wkts	Avge	Best	5wI	10wM
Test																		
All First	17	29	4	1120	102 *	44.80	1	10	15	-								
1-day Int																		
C & G	2	2	1	60	36	60.00	-	-	-	-								
totesport	16	11	3	181	40	22.62	-	-	8	-	2	1	11	3	3.66	3-11	-	
Twenty20	7	7	1	217	74	36.16	-	1	5	-								

Career Performances

	M	Inns	NO	Runs	HS	Avge	100s	50s	Ct	St	Balls	Runs	Wkts	Avge	Best	5wI	10wM
Test																	
All First	202	338	33	10697	186 *	35.07	19	61	133	-	1032	778	17	45.76	3-23	-	-
1-day Int																	
C & G	26	25	3	940	112	42.72	4	3	6	-	48	43	1	43.00	1-40	-	
totesport	151	128	18	2395	83 *	21.77	-	10	64	-	86	97	6	16.16	3-11	-	
Twenty20	12	12	2	292	74	29.20	-	1	7	-							

HENDERSON, C. W. Leicestershire

Name: Claude William Henderson
Role: Right-hand bat, left-arm spin bowler
Born: 14 June 1972, Worcester, South Africa
Height: 6ft 2in **Weight:** 14st
Nickname: Hendo, Hendy
County debut: 2004
County cap: 2004
Test debut: 2001-02
Tests: 7
One-Day Internationals: 4
1st-Class 50s: 5
1st-Class 5 w. in innings: 15
1st-Class catches: 50
One-Day 5 w. in innings: 1
Place in batting averages: 241st av. 16.38
Place in bowling averages: 83rd av. 35.20
Strike rate: 72.15 (career 71.58)
Parents: Henry and Susan
Wife and date of marriage: Nicci, 29 March 2003
Family links with cricket: Brother James an opening batsman for Free State; father played league cricket and for Boland B
Education: Worcester High School
Qualifications: 2 A-levels, Level 2 coaching

Off-season: 'Coaching, South Africa, sightseeing'
Overseas tours: South Africa A to Sri Lanka 1998; South Africa to Zimbabwe 2001-02, to Australia 2001-02
Overseas teams played for: Boland 1990 – 1996-97; Western Province 1997-2004
Career highlights to date: 'Playing for South Africa against Australia at Adelaide (seven wickets in the match)'
Cricket moments to forget: 'Losing to Devon in the C&G Trophy [2004]'
Cricketers particularly admired: Jacques Kallis, Shane Warne
Other sports played: Golf, fishing
Other sports followed: Rugby (South Africa, Western Province, Leicester Tigers)
Favourite band: U2
Relaxations: 'Sightseeing, cinema; spending time with family and friends'
Extras: Has won several match awards in South African domestic cricket. Played for Worcestershire Board XI in the NatWest 2000 and C&G 2001. Scored fifty (63) and recorded five-wicket innings return (5-28) on Championship debut for Leicestershire v Glamorgan at Leicester 2004; recorded a further five-wicket return (5-24) on one-day debut v Yorkshire at Headingley in the totesport League 2004. Awarded Leicestershire cap 2004. Is not considered an overseas player
Best batting: 71 Western Province v KwaZulu-Natal, Cape Town 2003-04
Best bowling: 7-57 Boland v Eastern Province, Paarl 1994-95

2004 Season

	M	Inns	NO	Runs	HS	Avge	100s	50s	Ct	St	O	M	Runs	Wkts	Avge	Best	5wI	10wM
Test																		
All First	16	21	3	295	63	16.38	-	2	6	-	469	132	1373	39	35.20	7-74	2	-
1-day Int																		
C & G	1	1	0	2	2	2.00	-	-	1	-	10	2	27	2	13.50	2-27	-	
totesport	18	10	4	64	27	10.66	-	-	-	-	109.1	8	473	28	16.89	5-24	1	
Twenty20	7	3	1	4	2	2.00	-	-	3	-	20	1	138	9	15.33	3-26	-	

Career Performances

	M	Inns	NO	Runs	HS	Avge	100s	50s	Ct	St	Balls	Runs	Wkts	Avge	Best	5wI	10wM
Test	7	7	0	65	30	9.28	-	-	2	-	1962	929	22	42.22	4-116	-	-
All First	131	175	44	2074	71	15.83	-	5	50	-	33931	14032	474	29.60	7-57	15	-
1-day Int	4	0	0	0	0	-	-	-	-	-	217	132	7	18.85	4-17	-	
C & G	4	2	0	34	32	17.00	-	-	2	-	240	110	7	15.71	2-8	-	
totesport	18	10	4	64	27	10.66	-	-	-	-	655	473	28	16.89	5-24	1	
Twenty20	7	3	1	4	2	2.00	-	-	3	-	120	138	9	15.33	3-26	-	

HEWSON, D. R. — Derbyshire

Name: Dominic (Dom) Robert Hewson
Role: Right-hand bat, right-arm medium bowler
Born: 3 October 1974, Cheltenham
Height: 5ft 9in **Weight:** 13st
Nickname: Chopper
County debut: 1996 (Gloucestershire), 2002 (Derbyshire)
1st-Class 50s: 15
1st-Class 100s: 3
1st-Class catches: 34
Place in batting averages: (2003 259th av. 13.87)
Strike rate: 69.00 (career 90.00)
Parents: Robert and Julie
Wife and date of marriage: Amy, 14 October 2000
Education: Cheltenham College; University of West of England
Qualifications: 10 GCSEs, 3 A-levels, City and Guilds in Tree Surgery
Career outside cricket: Tree surgeon
Overseas teams played for: Constantia, Cape Town 1995-96; Central Hawke's Bay, New Zealand 1998-99
Career highlights to date: 'Playing at Gloucestershire CCC during their successes of 1999 and 2000'
Cricketers particularly admired: Courtney Walsh
Other sports followed: Rugby (Gloucester RFC)
Relaxations: Seeing friends, fishing, and watching sport
Extras: Left Gloucestershire in the 2001-02 off-season and joined Derbyshire for 2002. Scored century (102*) on debut for Derbyshire v Glamorgan at Cardiff 2002
Best batting: 168 Gloucestershire v Derbyshire, Bristol 2001
Best bowling: 3-39 Derbyshire v Somerset, Taunton 2004

2004 Season

	M	Inns	NO	Runs	HS	Avge	100s	50s	Ct	St	O	M	Runs	Wkts	Avge	Best	5wI	10wM
Test																		
All First	2	2	0	9	9	4.50	-	-	-	-	46	18	112	4	28.00	3-39	-	-
1-day Int																		
C & G	1	1	0	7	7	7.00	-	-	-	-	6	0	37	0	-	-	-	
totesport	7	6	2	34	23 *	8.50	-	-	-	-	25.5	1	177	5	35.40	2-33	-	
Twenty20	3	2	0	26	21	13.00	-	-	2	-	3	0	22	1	22.00	1-22	-	

Career Performances

	M	Inns	NO	Runs	HS	Avge	100s	50s	Ct	St	Balls	Runs	Wkts	Avge	Best	5wI	10wM
Test																	
All First	73	132	8	2796	168	22.54	3	15	34	-	450	203	5	40.60	3-39	-	-
1-day Int																	
C & G	11	10	0	351	69	35.10	-	2	4	-	114	87	2	43.50	1-18	-	
totesport	48	41	3	598	52	15.73	-	2	10	-	534	526	20	26.30	4-25	-	
Twenty20	8	5	0	68	36	13.60	-	-	3	-	132	131	11	11.90	4-18	-	

HICK, G. A. Worcestershire

Name: Graeme Ashley Hick
Role: Right-hand bat, off-spin bowler
Born: 23 May 1966, Harare, Zimbabwe
Height: 6ft 3in **Weight:** 14st 4lbs
Nickname: Hicky, Ash
County debut: 1984
County cap: 1986; colours 2002
Benefit: 1999
Test debut: 1991
Tests: 65
One-Day Internationals: 120
1000 runs in a season: 18
1st-Class 50s: 142
1st-Class 100s: 110
1st-Class 200s: 13
1st-Class 300s: 2
1st-Class 400s: 1
1st-Class 5 w. in innings: 5
1st-Class 10 w. in match: 1
1st-Class catches: 597
One-Day 100s: 35
One-Day 5 w. in innings: 1
Place in batting averages: 9th av. 63.56 (2003 114th av. 33.50)
Strike rate: 54.00 (career 90.03)
Parents: John and Eve
Wife and date of marriage: Jackie, 5 October 1991
Children: Lauren Amy, 12 September 1992; Jordan Ashley, 5 September 1995
Family links with cricket: Father has served on Zimbabwe Cricket Union Board of Control and played representative cricket in Zimbabwe
Education: Prince Edward Boys' High School, Zimbabwe
Qualifications: 4 O-levels, NCA coaching award

Overseas tours: Zimbabwe to England (World Cup) 1983, to Sri Lanka 1983-84, to England 1985; England to Australia and New Zealand (World Cup) 1991-92, to India and Sri Lanka 1992-93, to West Indies 1993-94, to Australia 1994-95, to South Africa 1995-96, to India and Pakistan (World Cup) 1995-96, to Sharjah (Akai Singer Champions Trophy) 1997-98, to West Indies 1997-98 (one-day series), to Bangladesh (Wills International Cup) 1998-99, to Australia 1998-99, to Sharjah (Coca-Cola Cup) 1998-99, to South Africa and Zimbabwe 1999-2000 (one-day series), to Kenya (ICC Knockout Trophy) 2000-01, to Pakistan and Sri Lanka 2000-01; FICA World XI to New Zealand 2004-05
Overseas teams played for: Old Hararians, Zimbabwe 1982-90; Northern Districts, New Zealand 1987-89; Queensland 1990-91; Auckland 1997-98
Cricketers particularly admired: Steve Waugh, Glenn McGrath
Other sports played: Golf ('relaxation'), hockey (played for Zimbabwe)
Other sports followed: Football (Liverpool FC), golf, tennis, squash, hockey
Extras: In 1986, at age 20, he became the youngest player to score 2000 runs in an English season. One of *Wisden*'s Five Cricketers of the Year 1987. In 1988 he made 405* v Somerset at Taunton, the highest individual first-class score in England since 1895, and scored 1000 first-class runs by the end of May, hitting a record 410 runs in April. In 1990 became youngest batsman ever to make 50 first-class centuries and the fastest to 10,000 runs in county cricket (179 innings). Qualified to play for England 1991. Finished top of the first-class batting averages 1997. Scored hundredth first-class 100 (132) v Sussex at Worcester 1998; at the age of 32, he became the second youngest player after Wally Hammond to score one hundred 100s. Represented England in the 1999 World Cup. Won ODI Man of the Match awards v Zimbabwe, the country of his birth, for his match-winning 87* at Bulawayo and his 80 and 5-33 at Harare, February 2000; scored 101 in England's only innings in his first Test v Zimbabwe at Lord's 2000. Scored 200* v Durham at Riverside 2001, in the process achieving the feat of having recorded centuries against each of the other 17 counties, both home and away. Scored 315* v Durham at Worcester 2002, the highest individual score by a Worcestershire batsman at the ground. Captain of Worcestershire 2000-02. Scored 262 v Gloucestershire at Worcester 2004, in the process sharing with Ben Smith (187) in the highest first-class partnership ever made at Worcester (417). Set record for the highest individual score in the Twenty20 Cup (116*, equalled only hours later by Ian Thomas) v Northamptonshire at Luton 2004. Scored century (120) v Middlesex at Lord's in the totesport League 2004, in the process moving to the top of the one-day league century-makers' list with 15 career hundreds. Scored 126th career first-class century (178) v Gloucestershire at Cheltenham 2004 to draw level with W.G. Grace in tenth spot on the all-time first-class century-makers' list
Best batting: 405* Worcestershire v Somerset, Taunton 1988
Best bowling: 5-18 Worcestershire v Leicestershire, Worcester 1995

2004 Season

	M	Inns	NO	Runs	HS	Avge	100s	50s	Ct	St	O	M	Runs	Wkts	Avge	Best	5wI	10wM
Test																		
All First	17	29	4	1589	262	63.56	4	6	25	-	9	1	40	1	40.00	1-1	-	-
1-day Int																		
C & G	5	4	0	60	41	15.00	-	-	2	-								
totesport	16	16	1	544	120	36.26	2	3	5	-	2	0	18	0	-	-	-	
Twenty20	6	6	1	199	116 *	39.80	1	1	3	-								

Career Performances

	M	Inns	NO	Runs	HS	Avge	100s	50s	Ct	St	Balls	Runs	Wkts	Avge	Best	5wI	10wM
Test	65	114	6	3383	178	31.32	6	18	90	-	3057	1306	23	56.78	4-126	-	-
All First	470	777	76	37505	405 *	53.50	126	142	597	-	20889	10308	232	44.43	5-18	5	1
1-day Int	120	118	15	3846	126 *	37.33	5	27	64	-	1236	1026	30	34.20	5-33	1	
C & G	55	54	8	2337	172 *	50.80	7	10	27	-	1283	817	24	34.04	4-54	-	
totesport	259	248	38	8964	141 *	42.68	15	63	85	-	2954	2564	88	29.13	4-21	-	
Twenty20	6	6	1	199	116 *	39.80	1	1	3	-							

HILDRETH, J. C. Somerset

Name: James Charles Hildreth
Role: Right-hand bat, right-arm medium bowler; all-rounder
Born: 9 September 1984, Milton Keynes
Height: 5ft 10in **Weight:** 12st
Nickname: Hildy, Hildz
County debut: 2003
1st-Class 50s: 5
1st-Class 100s: 2
1st-Class catches: 12
Place in batting averages: 71st av. 42.22
Strike rate: 51.00 (career 51.00)
Parents: David and Judy
Marital status: Single
Family links with cricket: 'Dad played county league cricket in Kent and Northants'
Education: Millfield School
Qualifications: 10 GCSEs, 3 A-levels, ECB Level 1 coaching
Off-season: 'National Academy'
Overseas tours: 'West' to West Indies 1999, 2000; Millfield to Sri Lanka 2001; England U19 to Bangladesh (U19 World Cup) 2003-04

Career highlights to date: 'Maiden first-class hundred [101] v Durham 2004; 210 for England U19 v Bangladesh U19 2004; first-class hundred [108] v Notts 2004'
Cricket moments to forget: 'Being bowled first ball by Shoaib Akhtar'
Cricket superstitions: 'Left pad before right when getting padded up'
Other sports played: Hockey (West of England), squash (South of England), tennis (South of England), football (England Independent Schools, Luton Town), rugby (Millfield)
Other sports followed: Football (Charlton Athletic)
Favourite band: Jack Johnson
Relaxations: Travelling, snowboarding, music
Extras: Member of Stony Stratford CC and Glastonbury CC. NBC Denis Compton Award for the most promising young Somerset player 2003. Scored maiden first-class century (101) plus 72 in the second innings v Durham at Taunton 2004 in his second Championship match. Represented England U19 v Bangladesh U19 2004, scoring 210 in second 'Test' at Taunton. Nominated for PCA Young Player of the Year award. Cricket Society's Most Promising Young Cricketer of the Year 2004. ECB National Academy 2004-05 (part-time)
Best batting: 108 Somerset v Nottinghamshire, Trent Bridge 2004
Best bowling: 2-39 Somerset v Hampshire, Taunton 2004

2004 Season

	M	Inns	NO	Runs	HS	Avge	100s	50s	Ct	St	O	M	Runs	Wkts	Avge	Best	5wI	10wM
Test																		
All First	13	20	2	760	108	42.22	2	5	12	-	17	1	76	2	38.00	2-39	-	-
1-day Int																		
C & G																		
totesport	14	14	2	384	85	32.00	-	2	6	-	1	0	6	0	-	-	-	
Twenty20	5	5	0	145	66	29.00	-	2	1	-								

Career Performances

	M	Inns	NO	Runs	HS	Avge	100s	50s	Ct	St	Balls	Runs	Wkts	Avge	Best	5wI	10wM
Test																	
All First	14	22	2	769	108	38.45	2	5	12	-	102	76	2	38.00	2-39	-	-
1-day Int																	
C & G	1	1	0	4	4	4.00	-	-	1	-	36	44	1	44.00	1-44	-	
totesport	23	22	2	504	85	25.20	-	2	9	-	6	6	0	-	-	-	
Twenty20	5	5	0	145	66	29.00	-	2	1	-							

HINDLEY, R. J. E. Hampshire

Name: Richard James Edward Hindley
Role: Left-hand bat, right-arm off-spin bowler
Born: 25 April 1975, Portsmouth
Height: 6ft 3in **Weight:** 14st 2lbs
Nickname: Richie
County debut: 2003
1st-Class 50s: 1
Parents: William and Julie
Marital status: Single
Education: Havant College; New College of Southampton
Qualifications: BSc (Hons) Sports Studies, ECB Level III coach
Overseas teams played for: Cardiff Boolaroo DCC, New South Wales 1999-2001, 2002-04
Career highlights to date: 'Hampshire first-team debut v Glamorgan, July 2003'
Cricket moments to forget: 'Any time I get out cheaply, which happens a lot'
Cricket superstitions: 'None'
Cricketers particularly admired: David Gower, Viv Richards, Ian Botham, Shane Warne
Other sports played: Golf, football, tennis – 'not talented enough to have achieved anything'
Other sports followed: Australian rugby league (Newcastle Knights), football (Aston Villa FC)
Relaxations: 'Reading books (autobiographies); playing golf, football, tennis etc; travelling to see friends'
Extras: Has taken hat-trick and four wickets in four balls in club cricket. Played for Hampshire Board XI in the C&G 2001, 2002 and 2003. Scored 70-ball 68* on first-class debut v Glamorgan at West End 2003, after being called up from club cricket to replace the injured Shaun Udal
Best batting: 68* Hampshire v Glamorgan, West End 2003

2004 Season (did not make any first-class or one-day appearances)

Career Performances

	M	Inns	NO	Runs	HS	Avge	100s	50s	Ct	St	Balls	Runs	Wkts	Avge	Best	5wI	10wM
Test																	
All First	1	2	1	76	68 *	76.00	-	1	-	-	54	46	0	-	-	-	-
1-day Int																	
C & G	4	4	2	50	38	25.00	-	-	2	-	124	92	3	30.66	2-27	-	
totesport																	
Twenty20																	

HODD, A. J. — Surrey

Name: Andrew John Hodd
Role: Right-hand bat, wicket-keeper
Born: 12 January 1984, Chichester
Height: 5ft 10in **Weight:** 11st
Nickname: Hoddy, Hodd-dog
County debut: 2003 (Sussex; *see **Extras***)
1st-Class catches: 2
Parents: Karen and Adrian
Marital status: Single
Family links with cricket: 'Long line of club cricketers'
Education: Bexhill High School; Bexhill College 'and a brief stint at Loughborough University'
Qualifications: 9 GCSEs, 4 A-levels, ECB Level 1 coach
Off-season: 'Four months playing club cricket and training in Perth WA; beasting myself in the gym!'
Overseas tours: South of England U14 to West Indies 1998; Sussex Academy to South Africa 1999, to Sri Lanka 2001; England U17 to Australia 2000-01; England U19 to Australia 2002-03
Overseas teams played for: Bayswater-Morley, Perth 2004-05
Career highlights to date: 'Being involved in Twenty20 Surrey v Middlesex at Lord's in front of 26,500'
Cricket moments to forget: 'Too many to remember!'
Cricket superstitions: 'Loads, from order of putting kit on to having even numbers on any digital display'
Cricketers particularly admired: Matt Prior, Tim Ambrose, Adam Hollioake, Nadeem Shahid

Young players to look out for: Luke Wright, Rory Hamilton-Brown, Krishna Singh
Other sports played: Football ('county at Youth level'), golf
Other sports followed: 'All sports'
Injuries: 'Very bruised hands – part of the job!'
Favourite band: 'O-Zone … amazing!'
Relaxations: 'Seeing friends, music, cinema, Buffy the Vampire Slayer!'
Extras: Played for England U14, U15, U17 and U19. Graham Kersey Trophy, Bunbury 1999. Several junior Player of the Year awards at Sussex. Played for Sussex Board XI in the C&G 2003. Sussex County League Young Player of the Year 2002. Attended Sussex Academy. Made first-team debut for Sussex v West Indies A in a limited overs fixture at Hove 2002 but did not appear for the county in first-class cricket or domestic competition until 2003. Sussex 2nd XI Player of the Year 2003. Left Sussex during the 2003-04 off-season and joined Surrey for 2004
Opinions on cricket: 'Too much cricket is played which does not produce an elite standard. Far too many non-English players preventing the development of home-grown talent!'

2004 Season (did not make any first-class or one-day appearances)

Career Performances

	M	Inns	NO	Runs	HS	Avge	100s	50s	Ct	St	Balls	Runs	Wkts	Avge	Best	5wI	10wM
Test																	
All First	1	0	0	0	0	-	-	-	2	-							
1-day Int																	
C & G	1	1	0	1	1	1.00	-	-	1	-							
totesport																	
Twenty20																	

HODGE, B. J. — Lancashire

Name: Bradley (Brad) John Hodge
Role: Right-hand bat, right-arm off-spin bowler
Born: 29 December 1974, Sandringham, Melbourne, Australia
Height: 5ft 7½in **Weight:** 12st 8lbs
Nickname: Bunk
County debut: 2002 (Durham), 2003 (Leicestershire)
County cap: 2003 (Leicestershire)
1000 runs in a season: 2
1st-Class 50s: 40
1st-Class 100s: 27
1st-Class 200s: 5
1st-Class 300s: 1
1st-Class catches: 78

One-Day 100s: 2
Place in batting averages: 10th av. 61.92 (2003 8th av. 62.29)
Place in bowling averages: 93rd av. 36.50
Strike rate: 57.50 (career 72.89)
Parents: John and Val
Wife: Megan
Education: St Bede's College, Mentone; Deakin University
Off-season: Playing for Victoria
Overseas tours: Australia U19 to New Zealand 1992-93; Commonwealth Bank [Australian] Cricket Academy to Zimbabwe 1998-99; Australia A to Los Angeles (Moov America Challenge) 1999; Australia to India 2004-05, to New Zealand 2004-05
Overseas teams played for: Victoria 1993-94 –

Cricketers particularly admired: Allan Border, Dennis Lillee, Dean Jones, Sachin Tendulkar
Other sports played/followed: Australian Rules football (Melbourne), golf, tennis, soccer, skiing
Extras: Attended Commonwealth Bank [Australian] Cricket Academy 1993. Leading run-scorer for Victoria in the Sheffield Shield in his first season (1993-94) with 903 runs (av. 50.16). Has represented Australia A against various touring sides since 1998-99. Victoria's Pura Cup Player of the Year 2000-01 (973 runs; av. 54.06). Victoria's Pura Cup Player of the Year for the second successive season 2001-02 (858 runs; av. 57.20) and winner of the national Pura Cup Player of the Season Award 2001-02 (jointly with Jimmy Maher of Queensland). Was Durham's overseas player 2002 from late July; joined Leicestershire as an overseas player for 2003. Scored 202* v Loughborough UCCE at Leicester 2003, in the process sharing with Darren Maddy (229*) in a record partnership for any wicket for Leicestershire and the second highest partnership for the third wicket in English first-class cricket history (436*). His maiden triple century (302* from 280 balls) v Nottinghamshire 2003 is the highest individual first-class score by a Leicestershire player and the highest individual Championship score recorded at Trent Bridge. ING Cup Player of the Year 2003-04. Became first Leicestershire player since 1965 to score two centuries in a match (105/158), v Glamorgan at Leicester 2004. Scored 122-ball 154* v Sussex at Horsham in the totesport League 2004 to set a new Leicestershire record individual score for the one-day league. Scored 262 v Durham at Leicester 2004 to record the second-highest individual score by a Leicestershire player and the highest by a Leicestershire player at Grace Road. Man of the Match in the Twenty20 Cup final at Edgbaston 2004 for his 53-ball 77*. Appointed vice-captain of Leicestershire for 2004; assumed the captaincy in July on the resignation of Phillip DeFreitas. Left Leicestershire at the end of the 2004 season and has joined Lancashire as an overseas player for 2005

Best batting: 302* Leicestershire v Nottinghamshire, Trent Bridge 2003
Best bowling: 4-17 Australia A v West Indians, Hobart 2000-01

2004 Season

	M	Inns	NO	Runs	HS	Avge	100s	50s	Ct	St	O	M	Runs	Wkts	Avge	Best	5wI	10wM
Test																		
All First	15	25	0	1548	262	61.92	5	4	6	-	95.5	14	365	10	36.50	2-18	-	-
1-day Int																		
C & G	1	1	0	20	20	20.00	-	-	2	-	5	0	22	0	-	-	-	
totesport	17	15	2	454	154 *	34.92	1	-	8	-	38	0	187	5	37.40	2-11	-	
Twenty20	7	7	1	223	78	37.16	-	2	4	-	5	0	39	0	-	-	-	

Career Performances

	M	Inns	NO	Runs	HS	Avge	100s	50s	Ct	St	Balls	Runs	Wkts	Avge	Best	5wI	10wM
Test																	
All First	145	259	23	10977	302 *	46.51	33	40	78	-	4155	2395	57	42.01	4-17	-	-
1-day Int																	
C & G	4	4	0	25	20	6.25	-	-	3	-	30	22	0	-	-	-	
totesport	36	34	3	1124	154 *	36.25	2	4	17	-	558	472	12	39.33	3-34	-	
Twenty20	13	13	1	524	97	43.66	-	5	7	-	108	128	6	21.33	3-6	-	

HOGG, G. B. — Warwickshire

Name: George Bradley (Brad) Hogg
Role: Left-hand bat, left-arm wrist-spin bowler
Born: 6 February 1971, Narrogin, Western Australia
Height: 6ft 1in **Weight:** 12st 9lbs
Nickname: Hoggy
County debut: 2004
Test debut: 1996-97
Tests: 4
One-Day Internationals: 50
1st-Class 50s: 23
1st-Class 100s: 3
1st-Class 5 w. in innings: 4
1st-Class catches: 49
One-Day 5 w. in innings: 2
Place in batting averages: 3rd av. 70.60
Place in bowling averages: 149th av. 53.11
Strike rate: 99.11 (career 81.83)
Overseas tours: Australia to Sri Lanka (Singer World Series) 1996, to India 1996-97,

to Africa (World Cup) 2002-03, to West Indies 2002-03, to India (TVS Cup) 2003-04, to Sri Lanka 2003-04 (one-day series), to Zimbabwe (one-day series) 2004, to Holland (Videocon Cup) 2004, to England (ICC Champions Trophy) 2004, to New Zealand 2004-05 (one-day series); Australia A to South Africa (one-day series) 2002-03
Overseas teams played for: Willetton; Western Australia 1993-94 –
Extras: Played for Australian XI v West Indians 1995-96 and 1996-97. Shared in a Mercantile Cup competition record sixth-wicket partnership of 173* with Mike Hussey v Victoria at Melbourne 1999-2000. Won Man of the Match award for Australia A v South Africa A at Centurion 2002-03 (3-38). Recorded maiden ODI five-wicket return (5-41) in the first ODI v Sri Lanka at Dambulla 2003-04, winning Man of the Match award. Joined Warwickshire as an overseas player for 2004. C&G Man of the Match award for his 61-ball 94* v Northamptonshire at Edgbaston 2004. Left Warwickshire at the end of the 2004 season
Best batting: 158 Warwickshire v Surrey, Edgbaston 2004
Best bowling: 5-53 Western Australia v New South Wales, Sydney 1999-2000
Stop press: Man of the Match in the second ODI v New Zealand at Sydney 2004-05 (41*/3-45). Man of the Match v West Indies at Melbourne in the VB Series 2004-05 (5-32)

2004 Season

	M	Inns	NO	Runs	HS	Avge	100s	50s	Ct	St	O	M	Runs	Wkts	Avge	Best	5wI	10wM
Test																		
All First	12	13	3	706	158	70.60	1	7	6	-	297.2	54	956	18	53.11	4-90	-	-
1-day Int																		
C & G	3	2	1	112	94 *	112.00	-	1	2	-	22.5	1	111	4	27.75	2-14	-	
totesport	15	14	3	355	74	32.27	-	1	4	-	106.2	4	456	19	24.00	5-23	1	
Twenty20	6	6	0	118	54	19.66	-	1	2	-	21.5	0	142	13	10.92	4-9	-	

Career Performances

	M	Inns	NO	Runs	HS	Avge	100s	50s	Ct	St	Balls	Runs	Wkts	Avge	Best	5wI	10wM
Test	4	5	1	38	17 *	9.50	-	-	-	-	774	452	9	50.22	2-40	-	-
All First	85	124	27	3328	158	34.30	3	23	49	-	10557	5804	129	44.99	5-53	4	-
1-day Int	50	31	14	351	71 *	20.64	-	2	13	-	2329	1693	54	31.35	5-41	1	
C & G	3	2	1	112	94 *	112.00	-	1	2	-	137	111	4	27.75	2-14	-	
totesport	15	14	3	355	74	32.27	-	1	4	-	638	456	19	24.00	5-23	1	
Twenty20	6	6	0	118	54	19.66	-	1	2	-	131	142	13	10.92	4-9	-	

HOGG, K. W. — Lancashire

Name: Kyle William Hogg
Role: Left-hand bat, right-arm fast-medium bowler; all-rounder
Born: 2 July 1983, Birmingham
Height: 6ft 4in **Weight:** 13st
Nickname: Boss, Hoggy
County debut: 2001
1st-Class 50s: 3
1st-Class 5 w. in innings: 2
1st-Class catches: 8
Place in batting averages: 267th av. 10.28
Strike rate: 85.20 (career 60.75)
Parents: Sharon and William
Marital status: Single
Family links with cricket: Father played for Lancashire and Warwickshire; grandfather Sonny Ramadhin played for Lancashire and West Indies
Education: Saddleworth High School
Qualifications: GCSEs
Off-season: 'Training (12-month contract)'
Overseas tours: England U19 to India 2000-01, to Australia and (U19 World Cup) New Zealand 2001-02; Lancashire to South Africa, to Grenada; ECB National Academy to Australia and Sri Lanka 2002-03
Career highlights to date: 'Winning second division of one-day league'
Cricket moments to forget: '[B&H 2002] semi-final v Warwickshire'
Cricket superstitions: 'None'
Cricketers particularly admired: Andrew Flintoff, David Byas, Stuart Law, Carl Hooper
Young players to look out for: 'All Lancs 2nd XI'
Other sports played: Football
Other sports followed: Football (Man Utd)
Favourite band: Stone Roses, Red Hot Chili Peppers, Bob Marley
Relaxations: 'Relaxing with friends'
Extras: Represented England U19 v West Indies U19 2001, taking 5-88 in the second 'Test' at Trent Bridge; and v India U19 2002, scoring century (103) in second 'ODI' at Taunton. NBC Denis Compton Award for the most promising young Lancashire player 2001. Recorded maiden first-class five-wicket return (5-48) on Championship debut v Leicestershire at Old Trafford 2002. Included in provisional England squad of 30 for the 2002-03 World Cup
Opinions on cricket: 'Too much cricket. Not enough time to prepare for games, which leads to some games not played at full intensity.'

Best batting: 53 Lancashire v Nottinghamshire, Trent Bridge 2003
Best bowling: 5-48 Lancashire v Leicestershire, Old Trafford 2002

2004 Season

	M	Inns	NO	Runs	HS	Avge	100s	50s	Ct	St	O	M	Runs	Wkts	Avge	Best	5wI	10wM
Test																		
All First	4	7	0	72	23	10.28	-	-	-	-	71	10	259	5	51.80	2-16	-	-
1-day Int																		
C & G	2	2	1	9	8	9.00	-	-	-	-	19	1	90	1	90.00	1-40	-	
totesport	10	5	1	88	37 *	22.00	-	-	2	-	60.2	1	344	7	49.14	2-18	-	
Twenty20																		

Career Performances

	M	Inns	NO	Runs	HS	Avge	100s	50s	Ct	St	Balls	Runs	Wkts	Avge	Best	5wI	10wM
Test																	
All First	20	26	1	434	53	17.36	-	3	8	-	2491	1497	41	36.51	5-48	2	-
1-day Int																	
C & G	5	4	2	9	8	4.50	-	-	-	-	210	168	3	56.00	2-27	-	
totesport	37	19	6	230	37 *	17.69	-	-	7	-	1345	1114	40	27.85	4-20	-	
Twenty20	2	2	0	9	7	4.50	-	-	-	-	25	47	1	47.00	1-16	-	

HOGGARD, M. J. — Yorkshire

Name: Matthew James Hoggard
Role: Right-hand bat, right-arm fast-medium bowler
Born: 31 December 1976, Leeds
Height: 6ft 2in **Weight:** 14st
Nickname: Oggie
County debut: 1996
County cap: 2000
Test debut: 2000
Tests: 33
One-Day Internationals: 20
50 wickets in a season: 1
1st-Class 50s: 1
1st-Class 5 w. in innings: 11
1st-Class catches: 26
One-Day 5 w. in innings: 4
Place in batting averages: 228th av. 18.38
Place in bowling averages: 66th av. 32.38 (2003 55th av. 28.85)
Strike rate: 55.11 (career 53.41)

Parents: Margaret and John
Wife and date of marriage: Sarah, 2 October 2004
Family links with cricket: 'Dad is a cricket badger'
Education: Pudsey Grangefield
Qualifications: GCSEs and A-levels
Off-season: Touring with England
Overseas tours: Yorkshire CCC to South Africa; England U19 to Zimbabwe 1995-96; England to Kenya (ICC Knockout Trophy) 2000-01, to Pakistan and Sri Lanka 2000-01, to Zimbabwe (one-day series) 2001-02, to India and New Zealand 2001-02, to Sri Lanka (ICC Champions Trophy) 2002-03, to Australia 2002-03, to Africa (World Cup) 2002-03, to Bangladesh and Sri Lanka 2003-04, to West Indies 2003-04, to South Africa 2004-05
Overseas teams played for: Pirates, Johannesburg 1995-97; Free State 1998-2000
Career highlights to date: 'Taking my first Test wicket (Younis Khan)'
Cricketers particularly admired: Allan Donald, Courtney Walsh
Young players to look out for: Joe Sayers, Michael Lumb, Tim Bresnan
Other sports played: Rugby
Other sports followed: Rugby league (Leeds Rhinos)
Relaxations: Dog walking
Extras: Was top wicket-taker in the 2000 National League competition with 37 wickets at 12.37, in the process surpassing Howard Cooper's Yorkshire one-day league season record of 29 wickets set in 1975. PCA Young Player of the Year 2000. Took 7-63 v New Zealand in the first Test at Christchurch 2001-02, the best innings return by an England opening bowler in Tests v New Zealand. Took Test hat-trick (Sarwan, Chanderpaul, Ryan Hinds) in the third Test v West Indies at Bridgetown 2003-04. His international awards include Man of the Match in the second ODI v Zimbabwe at Harare 2001-02 (3-37) and in the second Test v Sri Lanka at Edgbaston 2002 (2-55/5-92), as well as Man of the [Test] Series v Bangladesh 2003-04. Took 100th Test wicket (Kyle Mills) in the third Test v New Zealand at Trent Bridge 2004. Scored 265-minute 89* as nightwatchman to help save match v Glamorgan at Headingley 2004. ECB contract 2004-05
Best batting: 89* Yorkshire v Glamorgan, Headingley 2004
Best bowling: 7-49 Yorkshire v Somerset, Headingley 2003
Stop press: Had match figures of 12-205 (5-144/7-61; his maiden first-class ten-wicket match return and the best England bowling figures since Ian Botham's 13-106 v India in 1980) in the fourth Test v South Africa at Johannesburg 2004-05, winning Man of the Match award

42. Which Kent and Nottinghamshire all-rounder was the first Zimbabwe player to score a century and record a five-wicket innings return in the same Test?

2004 Season

	M	Inns	NO	Runs	HS	Avge	100s	50s	Ct	St	O	M	Runs	Wkts	Avge	Best	5wI	10wM
Test	7	8	2	107	38	17.83	-	-	2	-	235	52	877	25	35.08	4-75	-	-
All First	13	18	5	239	89 *	18.38	-	1	4	-	385.5	80	1360	42	32.38	4-32	-	-
1-day Int																		
C & G	3	0	0	0	0	-	-	-	-	-	28	4	107	3	35.66	2-33	-	
totesport	8	2	1	2	2	2.00	-	-	-	-	49.3	3	248	9	27.55	3-35	-	
Twenty20	1	1	1	1	1 *	-	-	-	-	-	4	0	23	3	7.66	3-23	-	

Career Performances

	M	Inns	NO	Runs	HS	Avge	100s	50s	Ct	St	Balls	Runs	Wkts	Avge	Best	5wI	10wM
Test	33	43	18	254	38	10.16	-	-	11	-	6986	3809	117	32.55	7-63	2	-
All First	104	129	47	745	89 *	9.08	-	1	26	-	19389	9726	363	26.79	7-49	11	-
1-day Int	20	5	2	10	5	3.33	-	-	3	-	976	817	27	30.25	5-49	1	
C & G	9	1	1	7	7 *	-	-	-	1	-	425	281	14	20.07	5-65	1	
totesport	46	18	10	18	5 *	2.25	-	-	5	-	2043	1438	75	19.17	5-28	2	
Twenty20	1	1	1	1	1 *	-	-	-	-	-	24	23	3	7.66	3-23	-	

HOLLIOAKE, A. J. Surrey

Name: Adam John Hollioake
Role: Right-hand bat, right-arm medium bowler
Born: 5 September 1971, Melbourne, Australia
Height: 5ft 11in **Weight:** 14st
Nickname: Smokey
County debut: 1992 (one-day), 1993 (first-class)
County cap: 1995
Benefit: 2004
Test debut: 1997
Tests: 4
One-Day Internationals: 35
1000 runs in a season: 2
1st-Class 50s: 55
1st-Class 100s: 17
1st-Class 200s: 1
1st-Class 5 w. in innings: 1
1st-Class catches: 157
One-Day 100s: 2
One-Day 5 w. in innings: 9

Place in batting averages: 195th av. 22.88 (2003 84th av. 38.22)
Strike rate: 67.28 (career 73.45)
Parents: John and Daria
Wife: Sherryn
Children: Bennaya, 25 May 2002
Education: St Joseph's College, Sydney; St Patrick's College, Ballarat (Australia); St George's College, Weybridge; Surrey Tutorial College, Guildford
Qualifications: GCSEs, A-levels
Career outside cricket: Property developer
Overseas tours: School trip to Zimbabwe; Surrey YC to Australia; England YC to New Zealand 1990-91; England A to Australia 1996-97 (captain); England VI to Hong Kong 1997 (captain), 2002; England to Sharjah (Champions Trophy) 1997-98 (captain), to West Indies 1997-98 (captain in one-day series), to Bangladesh (Wills International Cup) 1998-99 (captain), to Australia 1998-99 (CUB Series), to Sharjah (Coca-Cola Cup) 1998-99, to Australia 2002-03 (VB Series)
Overseas teams played for: Fremantle, Western Australia 1990-91; North Shore, Sydney 1992-93; Geelong, Victoria; North Perth, Western Australia 1995-97
Career highlights: 'Getting my first wicket bowling leg spin'
Cricket moments to forget: 'Getting hit on my helmet by Glen Chapple'
Cricket superstitions: 'None'
Cricketers particularly admired: 'Every cricketer who gives their best and takes up the challenge to compete'
Young players to look out for: Rikki Clarke, Tim Murtagh, Scott Newman
Other sports played: Rugby (played for London Counties, Middlesex and South of England; England U18 trialist)
Extras: Scored a century (123) on first-class debut v Derbyshire at Ilkeston 1993. Surrey Young Player of the Year 1993. Scored fastest ever one-day 50 – 15 balls v Yorkshire in the Sunday League at Scarborough 1994. Scored two centuries in match (128/117*) v Somerset at Taunton 1996. His 39 wickets in the Sunday League 1996 is a season record for the domestic one-day league (equalled by Simon Cook 2004). Surrey Supporters' Player of the Year and Surrey Players' Player of the Year 1996. England's Man of the [ODI] Series v Australia 1997. Captained England in the Texaco Trophy one-day series v South Africa 1998. Represented England in the 1999 World Cup. Coached Hong Kong in the Asian Cricket Council Trophy in Sharjah 2000. C&G Man of the Match award for his 59-ball 117* (century from 52 balls) in the quarter-final v Sussex at Hove 2002. Scored a 103-ball 122* (out of 225) as Surrey avoided the follow-on v Kent at Canterbury 2002; the innings contained 98 in boundaries, one six striking an elderly woman spectator, to whom Hollioake later presented the ball, signed. One of *Wisden*'s Five Cricketers of the Year 2003. Captain of Surrey 1997-2003. Completed a 2000-mile walk/cycle/sail from Edinburgh to Tangier during autumn 2003 to raise money for the Ben Hollioake Memorial Fund. Leading wicket-taker in the Twenty20 Cup 2003 (16; av. 12.31) and 2004 (20; av. 10.40). Retired at the end of the 2004 season
Best batting: 208 Surrey v Leicestershire, The Oval 2002
Best bowling: 5-62 Surrey v Glamorgan, Swansea 1998

2004 Season

	M	Inns	NO	Runs	HS	Avge	100s	50s	Ct	St	O	M	Runs	Wkts	Avge	Best	5wI	10wM
Test																		
All First	11	19	1	412	106	22.88	1	2	6	-	78.3	7	290	7	41.42	3-69	-	-
1-day Int																		
C & G	1	1	0	52	52	52.00	-	1	-	-	2	0	18	0	-	-	-	
totesport	14	13	2	312	80 *	28.36	-	2	2	-	50	0	334	9	37.11	3-13	-	
Twenty20	7	7	4	183	65 *	61.00	-	1	2	-	25	0	208	20	10.40	5-34	1	

Career Performances

	M	Inns	NO	Runs	HS	Avge	100s	50s	Ct	St	Balls	Runs	Wkts	Avge	Best	5wI	10wM
Test	4	6	0	65	45	10.83	-	-	4	-	144	67	2	33.50	2-31	-	-
All First	173	263	21	9376	208	38.74	18	55	157	-	8814	4931	120	41.09	5-62	1	-
1-day Int	35	30	6	606	83 *	25.25	-	3	13	-	1208	1019	32	31.84	4-23	-	
C & G	31	25	4	755	117 *	35.95	1	4	11	-	963	866	35	24.74	5-77	1	
totesport	168	154	20	3604	111	26.89	1	16	47	-	5215	4844	232	20.87	6-17	6	
Twenty20	14	13	4	257	65 *	28.55	-	1	2	-	301	405	36	11.25	5-21	2	

HOOPER, C. L. — Lancashire

Name: Carl Llewellyn Hooper
Role: Right-hand bat, off-spin bowler
Born: 15 December 1966, Georgetown, Guyana
Height: 6ft **Weight:** 13st
County debut: 1992 (Kent), 2003 (Lancashire)
County cap: 1992 (Kent), 2003 (Lancashire)
Test debut: 1987-88
Tests: 102
One-Day Internationals: 227
1000 runs in a season: 8
1st-Class 50s: 104
1st-Class 100s: 64
1st-Class 200s: 5
1st-Class 5 w. in innings: 18
1st-Class catches: 375
One-Day 100s: 13
One-Day 5 w. in innings: 1
Place in batting averages: 84th av. 38.50 (2003 7th av. 67.72)
Place in bowling averages: 118th av. 39.66 (2003 62nd av. 30.40)
Strike rate: 93.60 (career 83.87)

Overseas tours: West Indies B to Zimbabwe 1986-87; Young West Indies to Zimbabwe 1989-90; West Indies to New Zealand 1986-87, to India and Pakistan (World Cup) 1987-88, to India 1987-88, to England 1988, to Australia 1988-89, to Pakistan 1990-91, to England 1991, to Australia and New Zealand (World Cup) 1991-92, to Australia 1992-93, to South Africa (Total International Series) 1992-93, to Sri Lanka 1993-94, to India 1994-95, to England 1995, to Australia 1995-96, 1996-97, to Pakistan 1997-98, to Sharjah (Singer-Akai Champions Trophy) 1997-98, to South Africa 1998-99, to Bangladesh (Wills International Cup) 1998-99, to Zimbabwe and Kenya 2001 (captain), to Sri Lanka 2001-02 (captain), to Sharjah (v Pakistan) 2001-02 (captain), to Sri Lanka (ICC Champions Trophy) 2002-03 (captain), to India 2002-03 (captain), to Africa (World Cup) 2002-03 (captain), plus other one-day series and tournaments
Overseas teams played for: Guyana 1984-85 – 2002-03
Extras: Made first-class debut for Demerara v Berbice at Georgetown in the final of the Jones Cup 1983-84. Represented West Indies YC v England YC 1984-85. Made maiden Test century (100*) in his second Test, v India at Calcutta 1987-88. Was Kent's overseas player 1992-94, 1996, 1998. One of *Indian Cricket*'s five Cricketers of the Year 1995. Retired from international cricket in 1999 but returned in 2001 and was captain of West Indies until 2002-03. Scored 149* for Guyana in the final of the Busta International Shield v Jamaica at Kingston 2001-02, winning the Man of the Match award. Has won several Test awards, including Man of the Match for his match-winning 94* v England in the second Test at Port of Spain 1997-98 and for his 233 in the first Test v India at his home ground of Georgetown 2001-02. Has also won numerous ODI awards, including Man of the Series in the Singer-Akai Champions Trophy 1997-98 and Man of the Match for his 112* v Pakistan in Sharjah 2001-02. Joined Lancashire as an overseas player for 2003. Scored 201 v Middlesex at Old Trafford 2003, in the process becoming the second batsman (after Mark Ramprakash) to score a century against all 18 counties. Scored century (177) v Warwickshire at Edgbaston 2003, sharing with Stuart Law (168) in a Lancashire record fifth-wicket partnership of 360 as the county scored 781
Best batting: 236* Kent v Glamorgan, Canterbury 1993
Best bowling: 7-93 Kent v Surrey, The Oval 1998

2004 Season

	M	Inns	NO	Runs	HS	Avge	100s	50s	Ct	St	O	M	Runs	Wkts	Avge	Best	5wI	10wM
Test																		
All First	13	21	3	693	115	38.50	2	4	19	-	234	51	595	15	39.66	4-56	-	-
1-day Int																		
C & G	3	3	1	115	66	57.50	-	1	-	-	19	0	102	1	102.00	1-51	-	
totesport	12	10	3	181	50 *	25.85	-	1	5	-	69	2	311	8	38.87	2-26	-	
Twenty20	5	4	1	106	49 *	35.33	-	-	2	-	16	0	102	3	34.00	1-13	-	

Career Performances

	M	Inns	NO	Runs	HS	Avge	100s	50s	Ct	St	Balls	Runs	Wkts	Avge	Best	5wI	10wM
Test	102	173	15	5762	233	36.46	13	27	115	-	13794	5635	113	49.86	5-26	4	-
All First	339	535	52	23034	236 *	47.68	69	104	375	-	46464	19594	554	35.36	7-93	18	-
1-day Int	227	206	43	5762	113 *	35.34	7	29	120	-	9573	6957	193	36.04	4-34	-	
C & G	19	18	2	649	136 *	40.56	1	3	10	-	1011	656	10	65.60	2-12	-	
totesport	110	100	19	3843	145	47.44	5	31	61	-	4280	3034	90	33.71	5-41	1	
Twenty20	10	9	2	162	49 *	23.14	-	-	6	-	204	197	8	24.62	4-18	-	

HOPKINSON, C. D. Sussex

Name: Carl Daniel Hopkinson
Role: Right-hand bat, right-arm medium-fast bowler; 'batter that bowls'
Born: 14 September 1981, Brighton
Height: 5ft 11in
Nickname: Hoppo
County debut: 2001 (one-day), 2002 (first-class)
1st-Class catches: 2
Strike rate: 60.00 (career 57.00)
Parents: Jane and Jerry
Marital status: Single
Family links with cricket: 'Dad played in the local team, which got me interested, and coached me from a young age'
Education: Chailey; Brighton College
Qualifications: 7 GCSEs, 3 A-levels, Level 1 coaching
Overseas tours: Tours to India 1997-98, to South Africa 1999
Overseas teams played for: Rockingham-Mandurah, Western Australia 2000-01
Career highlights to date: 'Playing in my first day/night game on TV; also my debut'
Cricket moments to forget: 'Playing on my debut and taking guard before the incoming batsman was announced; in other words, they didn't know who I was!'
Cricketers particularly admired: Dennis Lillee, Ian Botham, Viv Richards, Graham Thorpe
Young players to look out for: Krishna Singh
Other sports played: Rugby ('won Rosslyn Park National Sevens'), squash, football
Other sports followed: Football (West Ham)
Favourite band: 50 Cent
Relaxations: 'Going out in Brighton with my mates, cinema etc.'
Extras: South of England and England squads until U17. Sussex Young Player of the

Year 2000. Sussex 2nd XI Fielder of the Year 2001, 2003. Took wicket (John Wood) with his third ball on county debut, in the Norwich Union League v Lancashire at Hove 2001. Took four catches and achieved a run out v Glamorgan at Hove in the Norwich Union League 2001. Took 3-19 and scored a match-winning 67* v Scotland at Edinburgh in the NCL 2003
Best batting: 33 Sussex v Warwickshire, Hove 2002
Best bowling: 1-20 Sussex v LUCCE, Hove 2004

2004 Season

	M	Inns	NO	Runs	HS	Avge	100s	50s	Ct	St	O	M	Runs	Wkts	Avge	Best	5wI	10wM
Test																		
All First	1	2	0	13	13	6.50	-	-	-	-	10	2	34	1	34.00	1-20	-	-
1-day Int																		
C & G																		
totesport	5	4	0	88	41	22.00	-	-	2	-	6.5	0	40	3	13.33	3-40	-	
Twenty20	1	0	0	0	0	-	-	-	-	-								

Career Performances

	M	Inns	NO	Runs	HS	Avge	100s	50s	Ct	St	Balls	Runs	Wkts	Avge	Best	5wI	10wM
Test																	
All First	3	5	1	62	33	15.50	-	-	2	-	114	77	2	38.50	1-20	-	-
1-day Int																	
C & G	2	2	0	58	43	29.00	-	-	1	-	90	88	0	-	-	-	
totesport	22	17	2	264	67 *	17.60	-	1	14	-	323	308	11	28.00	3-19	-	
Twenty20	2	1	0	4	4	4.00	-	-	-	-							

HORTON, P. J. — Lancashire

Name: Paul James Horton
Role: Right-hand bat, right-arm medium/off-spin bowler
Born: 20 September 1982, Sydney, Australia
Height: 5ft 10in **Weight:** 11st 3lbs
Nickname: Horts, Ozzy
County debut: 2003
1st-Class catches: 1
Parents: Donald William and Norma
Marital status: Single
Education: Colo High School, Sydney/Broadgreen Comprehensive, Liverpool; St Margaret's High School
Qualifications: 11 GCSEs, 3 A-levels, Level 2 ECB coach
Overseas tours: Hawkesbury U15 to New Zealand 1997; Lancashire to Cape Town 2002-03, to Grenada 2003

Overseas teams played for: Hawkesbury, Sydney 1992-93 – 1997-98; Penrith, NSW 2002-03
Career highlights to date: 'First-class debut v Durham UCCE 2003'
Cricket moments to forget: 'First 2nd XI game for Lancashire at Old Trafford – out for 0'
Cricket superstitions: 'None'
Cricketers particularly admired: Dean Jones, Sachin Tendulkar, Mark Waugh
Young players to look out for: Steven Crook, Chris Whelan, Kyle Hogg
Other sports played: Football, golf, squash, tennis, badminton
Other sports followed: Football (Liverpool)
Favourite band: Red Hot Chili Peppers
Relaxations: 'Golf, socialising with friends, watching sport'
Extras: Captained Lancashire U17 and U19. Captained Lancashire Board XI in the C&G 2003. Lancashire Young Player of the Year Award 2001, 2002. Played for Lancashire side that won the inaugural ECB 38-County U21 Competition 2003. Leading run-scorer for Lancashire 2nd XI in the 2nd XI Championship 2003 (861 runs; av. 50.65)
Best batting: 22 Lancashire v Warwickshire, Stratford-upon-Avon 2004

2004 Season

	M	Inns	NO	Runs	HS	Avge	100s	50s	Ct	St	O	M	Runs	Wkts	Avge	Best	5wI	10wM
Test																		
All First	1	1	0	22	22	22.00	-	-	-	-								
1-day Int																		
C & G	1	0	0	0	0	-	-	-	-	-								
totesport	3	2	0	46	42	23.00	-	-	-	-								
Twenty20																		

Career Performances

	M	Inns	NO	Runs	HS	Avge	100s	50s	Ct	St	Balls	Runs	Wkts	Avge	Best	5wI	10wM
Test																	
All First	2	2	1	24	22	24.00	-	-	1	-							
1-day Int																	
C & G	3	2	0	49	26	24.50	-	-	-	-							
totesport	3	2	0	46	42	23.00	-	-	-	-							
Twenty20																	

HUGGINS, T. B. Northamptonshire

Name: Thomas (Tom) Benjamin Huggins
Role: Right-hand opening bat, right-arm occasional off-spin bowler
Born: 8 March 1983, Peterborough
Height: 6ft 3in **Weight:** 15st
Nickname: Huggo, Sheep's Head, The Viking
County debut: 2003
1st-Class 50s: 2
1st-Class catches: 3
Place in batting averages: 148th av. 29.58
Parents: John and Elizabeth
Marital status: Single
Family links with cricket: 'Dad's a coach; brother plays'
Education: Kimbolton School; De Montfort University, Bedford
Qualifications: 9 GCSEs, 3 A-levels, Level 3 coach
Off-season: 'Uni; coaching'
Overseas tours: Huntingdon Cricket 2000 to Zimbabwe 1999
Career highlights to date: 'First-class debut; getting a double hundred against Worcestershire 2nd XI 2003; playing at Lord's'
Cricket moments to forget: 'First TV game against Kent at Canterbury – fielding was distinctly average'
Cricket superstitions: 'Quite a few'
Cricketers particularly admired: Usman Afzaal, Mike Hussey
Young players to look out for: Adam Shantry, Tim Roberts
Other sports played: Football, hockey
Favourite band: Oasis, Libertines, Jay-Z
Relaxations: 'Music; playing snooker; going out with friends'
Extras: Huntingdonshire Young Player of the Year 1997, 1998, 2000. Recorded highest individual score in Huntingdonshire Youth cricket (185* v Norfolk U19 2000). Set three records for Kimbolton School 1st XI in 2001. Played for Cambridgeshire in the C&G 2002
Opinions on cricket: 'County sides should contain a minimum number of players who can (and want to) play for England. Standards are improving but would improve further with more practice time.'
Best batting: 82* Northamptonshire v Middlesex, Lord's 2004

2004 Season

	M	Inns	NO	Runs	HS	Avge	100s	50s	Ct	St	O	M	Runs	Wkts	Avge	Best	5wI	10wM
Test																		
All First	9	14	2	355	82 *	29.58	-	2	3	-								
1-day Int																		
C & G																		
totesport	4	4	1	28	16	9.33	-	-	-	-								
Twenty20																		

Career Performances

	M	Inns	NO	Runs	HS	Avge	100s	50s	Ct	St	Balls	Runs	Wkts	Avge	Best	5wI	10wM
Test																	
All First	10	16	2	395	82 *	28.21	-	2	3	-							
1-day Int																	
C & G	1	1	0	2	2	2.00	-	-	-	-							
totesport	4	4	1	28	16	9.33	-	-	-	-							
Twenty20																	

HUGHES, J. — Glamorgan

Name: Jonathan Hughes
Role: Right-hand bat, right-arm medium bowler
Born: 30 June 1981, Pontypridd
Height: 5ft 11in
Nickname: Jonny, Tuck Box, Hughesy
County debut: 2001
1st-Class 50s: 4
1st-Class 100s: 1
1st-Class catches: 17
Place in batting averages: 190th av. 24.06 (2003 212th av. 21.88)
Parents: Steve and Anne
Marital status: Single
Family links with cricket: 'Dad and brothers Matthew and Gareth play for Hopkinstown'
Education: Coed y Lan Comprehensive, Pontypridd
Qualifications: MCC coaching badges
Overseas tours: Hopkinstown to Barbados 1998
Overseas teams played for: Easts-Redlands, Brisbane 2000, 2001
Career highlights to date: 'Debut v Surrey for Glamorgan in County Championship'
Cricketers particularly admired: Matthew Maynard, Ian Botham

Young players to look out for: Mark Wallace
Other sports played: Football (Hopkinstown)
Other sports followed: Rugby (Pontypridd), football (Everton)
Relaxations: Going to the pub
Extras: Captained Welsh Schools. Was on Lord's groundstaff 1998-99. Glamorgan 2nd XI Player of the Year 2001. Glamorgan Young Player of the Year 2001. Scored 74, including 14 fours, v Worcestershire at Worcester 2002 in his second first-class match. NBC Denis Compton Award for the most promising young Glamorgan player 2002. Scored maiden first-class century (110) v Leicestershire at Cardiff 2004
Best batting: 110 Glamorgan v Leicestershire, Cardiff 2004

2004 Season

	M	Inns	NO	Runs	HS	Avge	100s	50s	Ct	St	O	M	Runs	Wkts	Avge	Best	5wI	10wM
Test																		
All First	11	15	0	361	110	24.06	1	1	5	-								
1-day Int																		
C & G																		
totesport																		
Twenty20	2	1	0	7	7	7.00	-	-	-	-								

Career Performances

	M	Inns	NO	Runs	HS	Avge	100s	50s	Ct	St	Balls	Runs	Wkts	Avge	Best	5wI	10wM
Test																	
All First	29	44	1	1045	110	24.30	1	4	17	-							
1-day Int																	
C & G	1	1	0	51	51	51.00	-	1	-	-							
totesport	3	3	0	40	30	13.33	-	-	1	-							
Twenty20	3	2	0	8	7	4.00	-	-	-	-							

HUNT, T. A. — Somerset

Name: Thomas (Thos) Aaron Hunt
Role: Left-hand bat, right-arm medium-fast bowler
Born: 19 January 1982, Melbourne, Australia
Height: 6ft 3in **Weight:** 13st 4lbs
Nickname: Hopalong, Peg-leg
County debut: 2002 (Middlesex; *see **Extras***), 2004 (Somerset)
Strike rate: 84.00 (career 58.44)
Parents: Jennifer Hunt and Tim Woodbridge
Marital status: Single
Education: Acton High; St Clement Danes
Qualifications: 9 GCSEs, 1 A-level, Level 1 coaching award

Cricket moments to forget: '1st XI debut at Lord's [for Middlesex v Australians 2001]'
Cricketers particularly admired: Curtly Ambrose, Waqar Younis
Other sports played: 'Keen skier, also played school and Sunday league football'
Other sports followed: Football (Man Utd)
Relaxations: 'Music; spending time with girlfriend'
Extras: Made 1st XI debut for Middlesex v Australians in a one-day fixture at Lord's 2001 but did not appear for the county in first-class cricket or domestic competition until 2002. Released by Middlesex at the end of the 2003 season and joined Somerset for 2004; released by Somerset at the end of the 2004 season
Best batting: 3 Middlesex v Sri Lankans, Shenley 2002
Best bowling: 3-43 Middlesex v CUCCE, Fenner's 2002

2004 Season

	M	Inns	NO	Runs	HS	Avge	100s	50s	Ct	St	O	M	Runs	Wkts	Avge	Best	5wI	10wM
Test																		
All First	1	1	1	1	1*	-	-	-	-	-	28	4	124	2	62.00	2-85	-	-
1-day Int																		
C & G																		
totesport	1	1	0	0	0	0.00	-	-	-	-	7	0	46	0	-	-	-	
Twenty20	3	2	0	6	4	3.00	-	-	-	-	4	0	45	0	-	-	-	

Career Performances

	M	Inns	NO	Runs	HS	Avge	100s	50s	Ct	St	Balls	Runs	Wkts	Avge	Best	5wI	10wM
Test																	
All First	4	2	1	4	3	4.00	-	-	-	-	526	409	9	45.44	3-43	-	-
1-day Int																	
C & G																	
totesport	4	2	0	0	0	0.00	-	-	1	-	132	126	1	126.00	1-24	-	
Twenty20	3	2	0	6	4	3.00	-	-	-	-	24	45	0	-	-	-	

HUNTER, I. D. — Derbyshire

Name: Ian David Hunter
Role: Right-hand bat, right-arm fast-medium bowler
Born: 11 September 1979, Durham City
Height: 6ft 2in **Weight:** 12st 7lbs
Nickname: Sticks, Hunts
County debut: 1999 (one-day, Durham), 2000 (first-class, Durham), 2004 (Derbyshire)
1st-Class 50s: 2
1st-Class catches: 6
Strike rate: 29.00 (career 65.31)
Parents: Ken and Linda
Marital status: Single
Family links with cricket: Brother local village cricketer
Education: Fyndoune Community College, Sacriston; New College, Durham
Qualifications: 9 GCSEs, 1 A-level (PE), BTEC National Diploma in Sports Science, Level I and II cricket coaching awards
Overseas tours: Durham U21 to Sri Lanka 1996; Durham to Cape Town 2002
Career highlights to date: 'Scoring 63 on first-class debut' (*v Leicestershire at Riverside 2000 as nightwatchman*)
Cricket superstitions: 'Always put my left pad on first'
Cricketers particularly admired: Allan Donald, Steve Waugh
Other sports played: Football, golf
Other sports followed: Football (Durham City AFC)
Relaxations: Socialising with friends; keeping fit, golf, football
Extras: Set a new Durham best analysis for the 2nd XI Championship with his 11-155 v Lancashire 2nd XI 1999. Represented England U19 v Australia U19 1999. Played for Durham Board XI in the C&G 2001, 2002 and 2003. Released by Durham at the end of the 2003 season; joined Derbyshire towards the end of the 2004 season
Best batting: 65 Durham v Northamptonshire, Northampton 2002
Best bowling: 4-55 Durham v Warwickshire, Edgbaston 2001

2004 Season

	M	Inns	NO	Runs	HS	Avge	100s	50s	Ct	St	O	M	Runs	Wkts	Avge	Best	5wI	10wM
Test																		
All First	1	2	0	6	6	3.00	-	-	-	-	14.3	1	52	3	17.33	3-32	-	-
1-day Int																		
C & G																		
totesport																		
Twenty20																		

Career Performances

	M	Inns	NO	Runs	HS	Avge	100s	50s	Ct	St	Balls	Runs	Wkts	Avge	Best	5wI	10wM
Test																	
All First	22	34	4	583	65	19.43	-	2	6	-	3135	1946	48	40.54	4-55	-	-
1-day Int																	
C & G	3	3	0	16	13	5.33	-	-	1	-	138	92	3	30.66	2-45	-	
totesport	36	21	4	131	21	7.70	-	-	8	-	1518	1212	41	29.56	4-29	-	
Twenty20	3	2	1	27	25 *	27.00	-	-	-	-	60	92	2	46.00	1-21	-	

HUSSAIN, N. — Essex

Name: Nasser Hussain
Role: Right-hand bat, leg-break bowler
Born: 28 March 1968, Madras, India
Height: 6ft **Weight:** 12st 7lbs
Nickname: Nashwan
County debut: 1987
County cap: 1989
Benefit: 1999 (£271,500)
Test debut: 1989-90
Tests: 96
One-Day Internationals: 88
1000 runs in a season: 5
1st-Class 50s: 108
1st-Class 100s: 50
1st-Class 200s: 2
1st-Class catches: 349
One-Day 100s: 9
Place in batting averages: (2003 42nd av. 46.05)
Strike rate: (career 156.00)
Parents: Joe and Shireen
Wife and date of marriage: Karen, 24 September 1993
Children: Jacob, 8 June 2001; Joel, 18 November 2002
Family links with cricket: Father played zonal cricket in India. Played for Madras in Ranji Trophy 1966-67. Brother Mel played for Hampshire. Brother Abbas played for Essex 2nd XI
Education: Forest School, Snaresbrook; Durham University
Qualifications: 10 O-levels, 3 A-levels, BSc (Hons) in Natural Sciences, NCA cricket coaching award
Overseas tours: England YC to Sri Lanka 1986-87, to Australia (U19 World Cup) 1987-88; England A to Pakistan and Sri Lanka 1990-91, to Bermuda and West Indies

1991-92, to Pakistan 1995-96 (captain); England to India (Nehru Cup) 1989-90, to West Indies 1989-90, 1993-94, 1997-98, 2003-04, to Zimbabwe and New Zealand 1996-97, to Australia 1998-99, 2002-03 (captain), to South Africa and Zimbabwe 1999-2000 (captain), to Kenya (ICC Knockout Trophy) 2000-01 (captain), to Pakistan and Sri Lanka 2000-01 (captain), to Zimbabwe (one-day series) 2001-02 (captain), to India and New Zealand 2001-02 (captain), to Sri Lanka (ICC Champions Trophy) 2002-03 (captain), to Africa (World Cup) 2002-03 (captain), to Bangladesh and Sri Lanka 2003-04

Overseas teams played for: Madras 1986-87; Adelaide University 1990; Petersham, Sydney 1992-93; Stellenbosch University, South Africa 1994-95; Primrose, Cape Town

Cricketers particularly admired: Mark Waugh, Graham Gooch, Sachin Tendulkar

Other sports played: Golf (10 handicap), football

Other sports followed: Football (Leeds United)

Relaxations: Listening to music; watching television

Extras: Cricket Writers' Club Young Cricketer of the Year 1989. Set records for third (347* v Lancashire at Ilford 1992), fourth (314 v Surrey at The Oval 1991) and fifth (316 v Leicestershire at Leicester 1991) wicket partnerships for Essex (with Mark Waugh, Salim Malik and Mike Garnham respectively). Essex Player of the Year 1993. Finished 2nd in the Whyte and Mackay batting ratings 1995. Appointed Essex vice-captain 1996. Appointed England vice-captain 1996-97. Scored 207 in the first Test v Australia at Edgbaston 1997, in the process sharing with Graham Thorpe (138) in record fourth-wicket partnership for England in Tests v Australia (288) and winning Man of the Match award. Represented England in the 1999 World Cup. Appointed England captain after 1999 World Cup. In 2000 led England to victory in the NatWest triangular one-day series, to a Test series win over Zimbabwe, and to a first Test series win over West Indies for 31 years; followed up with series wins in Pakistan and Sri Lanka in the winter of 2000-01, which made England only the second touring side to win two Test rubbers on the sub-continent in the same season. npower Contribution to Cricket Award 2001. Awarded OBE in New Year honours list 2001-02. Vodafone England Cricketer of the Year 2001-02. One of *Wisden*'s Five Cricketers of the Year 2003. Other Test awards include [England's] Man of the Series v India 1996 and Man of the Match in the first Test v India at Lord's 2002. Resigned as England one-day captain and retired from ODI cricket after the 2002-03 World Cup and stood down as England Test captain after the first Test v South Africa at Edgbaston 2003. Scored his 50th first-class century (116) in the third Test v South Africa 2003. Essex captain 1999; handed over 1st XI captaincy to Ronnie Irani at the start of the 2000 season but remained club captain. Retired from all cricket after the first Test v New Zealand at Lord's 2004, having taken England to victory with a century (103*). Received ECB Special Award at the PCA awards dinner at the Royal Albert Hall 2004. Book *Playing with Fire* (with Paul Newman) published 2004. Has joined Sky Sports as a commentator

Best batting: 207 England v Australia, Edgbaston 1997

Best bowling: 1-38 Essex v Worcestershire, Kidderminster 1992

2004 Season

	M	Inns	NO	Runs	HS	Avge	100s	50s	Ct	St	O	M	Runs	Wkts	Avge	Best	5wI	10wM
Test	1	2	1	137	103 *	137.00	1	-	3	-								
All First	3	5	1	309	103 *	77.25	2	1	5	-								
1-day Int																		
C & G	1	1	0	85	85	85.00	-	1	-	-								
totesport	2	2	1	64	40 *	64.00	-	-	2	-								
Twenty20																		

Career Performances

	M	Inns	NO	Runs	HS	Avge	100s	50s	Ct	St	Balls	Runs	Wkts	Avge	Best	5wI	10wM
Test	96	171	16	5764	207	37.18	14	33	66	-	30	15	0	-	-	-	-
All First	334	545	53	20698	207	42.06	52	108	349	-	312	323	2	161.50	1-38	-	-
1-day Int	88	87	10	2332	115	30.28	1	16	40	-							
C & G	34	32	4	1190	108	42.50	2	7	23	-							
totesport	152	141	21	4187	161 *	34.89	3	26	66	-							
Twenty20																	

HUSSEY, D. J. — Nottinghamshire

Name: David (Dave) John Hussey
Role: Right-hand middle-order bat, right-arm off-spin bowler
Born: 15 July 1977, Perth, Western Australia
Height: 5ft 11in **Weight:** 13st 5lbs
Nickname: Hussa, Husscat, Huss
County debut: 2004
County cap: 2004
1000 runs in a season: 1
1st-Class 50s: 5
1st-Class 100s: 10
1st-Class 200s: 1
1st-Class catches: 36
One-Day 100s: 1
Place in batting averages: 4th av. 69.21
Strike rate: 217.00 (career 147.50)
Parents: Helen and Ted
Marital status: Single
Family links with cricket: Brother Mike plays for Western Australia and Durham and played for Northamptonshire 2001-03 and Gloucestershire 2004
Education: Prendiville Catholic College; Edith Cowan University
Off-season: Playing for Victoria in Australia

Overseas tours: Commonwealth Bank [Australian] Cricket Academy to Sri Lanka 1997-98
Overseas teams played for: Prahran, Victoria 2002 –; Victoria 2002-03 –
Career highlights to date: 'Winning Pura Cup final with Victoria 2003-04'
Cricket moments to forget: 'Debut for Victoria – dropped S. Waugh on four; he went on to make 211'
Cricket superstitions: 'Left shoe on first'
Cricketers particularly admired: Damien Martyn, Mark Waugh, Brendon Julian
Young players to look out for: Aaron Finch, Andrew Hodd, Mark Nash
Other sports played: Australian Rules football, squash
Other sports followed: Football (Brighton & Hove Albion)
Favourite band: Counting Crows
Relaxations: Movies, crime novels, shopping
Extras: Played for Western Australia U19 and 2nd XI. Represented Australia U19 v New Zealand U19 1995-96. Played for Sussex Board XI in the C&G 2001, 2002. Man of the Match v New South Wales at Melbourne in the Pura Cup 2003-04 (120/50). Scored 212* and won Man of the Match award as Victoria scored 455-7 to beat New South Wales at Newcastle in the Pura Cup 2003-04; it was the second highest successful fourth innings run chase in Australian domestic cricket history. Man of the Match v South Australia at Adelaide in the ING Cup 2003-04 (113). Joined Nottinghamshire as an overseas player for 2004, originally as cover for Damien Martyn while on international duty; awarded Nottinghamshire cap 2004; has returned for 2005. Scored third consecutive Championship century (140) v Leicestershire at Trent Bridge 2004, in the process passing 1000 Championship runs in his first season of county cricket
Opinions on cricket: 'Bowlers should be allowed to bowl as many bouncers per over as they like. No-ball/free hit in first-class cricket.'
Best batting: 212* Victoria v New South Wales, Newcastle 2003-04
Best bowling: 1-6 Victoria v Western Australia, Melbourne 2002-03
1-6 Nottinghamshire v OUCCE, The Parks 2004
Stop press: Represented Australia A v West Indians and Pakistanis 2004-05

2004 Season

	M	Inns	NO	Runs	HS	Avge	100s	50s	Ct	St	O	M	Runs	Wkts	Avge	Best	5wI	10wM
Test																		
All First	17	23	4	1315	170	69.21	7	2	24	-	72.2	10	290	2	145.00	1-6	-	-
1-day Int																		
C & G	2	2	0	2	2	1.00	-	-	-	-	3	0	21	0	-	-	-	
totesport	16	16	4	444	87 *	37.00	-	2	2	-	13	0	77	2	38.50	1-5	-	
Twenty20	5	5	0	59	33	11.80	-	-	5	-								

Career Performances

	M	Inns	NO	Runs	HS	Avge	100s	50s	Ct	St	Balls	Runs	Wkts	Avge	Best	5wI	10wM
Test																	
All First	32	44	6	2281	212 *	60.02	11	5	36	-	590	375	4	93.75	1-6	-	-
1-day Int																	
C & G	5	5	1	166	118 *	41.50	1	-	4	-	179	182	6	30.33	3-48	-	
totesport	16	16	4	444	87 *	37.00	-	2	2	-	78	77	2	38.50	1-5	-	
Twenty20	5	5	0	59	33	11.80	-	-	5	-							

HUSSEY, M. E. K. Durham

Name: Michael Edward Killeen Hussey
Role: Left-hand bat, right-arm medium bowler, county captain
Born: 27 May 1975, Perth, Western Australia
Height: 6ft **Weight:** 12st 8lbs
Nickname: Huss
County debut: 2001 (Northamptonshire), 2004 (Gloucestershire)
County cap: 2001 (Northamptonshire), 2004 (Gloucestershire)
One-Day Internationals: 1
1000 runs in a season: 3
1st-Class 50s: 59
1st-Class 100s: 26
1st-Class 200s: 3
1st-Class 300s: 3
1st-Class catches: 164
One-Day 100s: 6
Place in batting averages: 92nd av. 36.83 (2003 2nd av. 89.31)
Strike rate: (career 97.11)
Parents: Helen and Ted
Wife and date of marriage: Amy, 6 April 2002
Children: Jasmin, 9 February 2004
Family links with cricket: Brother plays for Victoria and Nottinghamshire
Education: Prendiville College; Curtin University
Qualifications: Bachelor of Education
Career outside cricket: Teacher
Off-season: Playing cricket in Australia
Overseas tours: Australia U19 to India 1993-94; Australian Cricket Academy to Pakistan 1995; Australia A to Scotland and Ireland 1998, to South Africa (one-day series) 2002-03; Australia to New Zealand (one-day series) 2004-05

Overseas teams played for: Western Australia 1994-95 –
Career highlights to date: 'ODI debut v India, 1 February 2004'
Cricket moments to forget: 'Any loss or duck'
Cricket superstitions: 'None'
Cricketers particularly admired: Sachin Tendulkar, Mark Taylor
Young players to look out for: Beau Casson (Western Australia)
Other sports played: Squash
Other sports followed: Australian Rules (West Coast Eagles), football (Man Utd)
Favourite band: U2
Relaxations: Movies
Extras: Attended Commonwealth Bank [Australian] Cricket Academy 1995 and has represented Australia A against various touring sides. Finished third in the Sheffield Shield Player of the Year award in his first full season 1995-96. Sir Donald Bradman Young Cricketer of the Year 1998. Excalibur Award (Western Australia) 1998-2000. Scored maiden Mercantile Cup century (100*) v Victoria at Melbourne 1999-2000, sharing in a competition record sixth-wicket partnership of 173* with Brad Hogg. Joined Northamptonshire as overseas player for 2001. Scored maiden first-class triple century (329*) v Essex at Northampton 2001, in the process overtaking Mal Loye's record for the highest individual score by a Northants player (322*); was on the field for the entire match. Leading run-scorer in English first-class cricket 2001 with 2055 runs (all in the Championship) at 79.03. Northamptonshire Player of the Year 2001 and 2002, the first player to win the award twice in succession. Was first batsman to reach 1000 first-class runs in the 2002 season. Scored 310* v Gloucestershire at Bristol 2002; was once again on the field for the entire match. Scored third triple century in successive seasons (331*), v Somerset at Taunton 2003, breaking his own record for the highest individual score by a Northamptonshire player. Captain of Northamptonshire 2002-03. Vice-captain of Western Australia since 2003-04. Made ODI debut v India in the VB Series 2003-04 at Perth. Was an overseas player with Gloucestershire July to September 2004 as a replacement for Shoaib Malik/Shabbir Ahmed. Has joined Durham as an overseas player and as captain for 2005
Opinions on cricket: 'I think the game is in good hands. We provide great entertainment to people of all levels from the traditionalists in the four-day game to the youngsters with Twenty20 and one-day cricket. The players are also learning and enhancing new skills with the different forms of the game.'
Best batting: 331* Northamptonshire v Somerset, Taunton 2003
Best bowling: 2-21 Western Australia v Queensland, Perth 1998-99

2004 Season

	M	Inns	NO	Runs	HS	Avge	100s	50s	Ct	St	O	M	Runs	Wkts	Avge	Best	5wI	10wM
Test																		
All First	7	13	1	442	78	36.83	-	2	10	-	8	2	22	0	-	-	-	-
1-day Int																		
C & G	2	2	0	55	35	27.50	-	-	3	-	6	0	38	0	-	-	-	
totesport	7	7	1	357	107 *	59.50	1	2	1	-	9.3	0	55	0	-	-	-	
Twenty20	2	2	0	47	32	23.50	-	-	-	-								

Career Performances

	M	Inns	NO	Runs	HS	Avge	100s	50s	Ct	St	Balls	Runs	Wkts	Avge	Best	5wI	10wM
Test																	
All First	154	276	20	13169	331 *	51.44	32	59	164	-	874	467	9	51.88	2-21	-	-
1-day Int	1	1	1	17	17 *	-	-	-	1	-	18	15	0	-	-	-	
C & G	7	7	0	154	59	22.00	-	1	5	-	66	68	1	68.00	1-20	-	
totesport	50	50	7	2081	123	48.39	5	15	19	-	87	99	1	99.00	1-12	-	
Twenty20	7	7	1	326	88	54.33	-	3	5	-							

HUTCHISON, P. M. Middlesex

Name: Paul Michael Hutchison
Role: Left-hand bat, left-arm seamer
Born: 9 June 1977, Leeds
Height: 6ft 3in **Weight:** 13-14st
Nickname: Hutch, Mantis
County debut: 1995-96 (Yorkshire), 2002 (Sussex), 2004 (Middlesex)
County cap: 1998 (Yorkshire)
50 wickets in a season: 1
1st-Class 5 w. in innings: 7
1st-Class 10 w. in match: 1
1st-Class catches: 12
Place in batting averages: 287th av. 3.57
Place in bowling averages: 154th av. 58.63
Strike rate: 99.63 (career 48.98)
Parents: Rita Laycock (deceased) and David Hutchison
Wife and date of marriage: Emma, 18 October 2003
Family links with cricket: 'Brother Richard has just hung up his boots after 17 years at Pudsey St Lawrence CC'
Education: Pudsey Crawshaw
Qualifications: 8 GCSEs, GNVQ Leisure and Tourism, qualified cricket coach, basic IT ('thanks to PCA')
Career outside cricket: 'Master IT developer'
Off-season: 'Working on my IT course, then heading out to Wellington, NZ, January-March 2005'
Overseas tours: England U19 to Zimbabwe 1995-96; England A to Kenya and Sri Lanka 1997-98, to Zimbabwe and South Africa 1998-99; Yorkshire to Zimbabwe and Botswana 1996, to South Africa 1998, 1999, 2001; Sussex to Grenada 2002; MCC to Namibia and Uganda 2004-05
Overseas teams played for: Upper Valley Bears, Wellington, New Zealand 2003-05

Career highlights to date: 'My Championship debut 7-50. My two England A tours. My two Championship winner's medals'
Cricket moments to forget: 'More and more as the seasons pass by!'
Cricket superstitions: 'Not really'
Cricketers particularly admired: Glenn McGrath
Young players to look out for: Ben Scott, Chris Whelan, Eoin Morgan
Other sports played: Golf, football
Other sports followed: 'Most sports; anything on Sky Sports; any team from my area (Leeds/Bradford)'
Injuries: Out for two months with a stress fracture of the right foot
Favourite band: Drifters
Relaxations: 'Looking to compete in a triathlon with my training partners while in NZ Jan-March '05'
Extras: Represented England at U17, U18 and U19 levels. Played for Pudsey St Lawrence in the Bradford League. Had a place at the Yorkshire Academy. Took 7-38 on first first-class appearance of 1997, against Pakistan A. Took 7-50 against Hampshire at Portsmouth 1997, the best Championship debut figures for Yorkshire since Wilfred Rhodes took 7-24 v Somerset in 1898. Voted Wombwell Cricket Lovers' Young Player of the Year for 1997. Released by Yorkshire at the end of the 2001 season and joined Sussex for 2002. Left Sussex at the end of the 2003 season and joined Middlesex for 2004
Opinions on cricket: 'In the last few years cricket balls were "dulled down" to redress the imbalance between bat and ball due to poor pitches. Now the pitches in general are much better, the balls need to be improved, as the balance has swung back too much to the batters. Just look at the amount of double and triple hundreds scored in the 2004 season compared to previous seasons.'
Best batting: 30 Yorkshire v Essex, Scarborough 1998
Best bowling: 7-31 Yorkshire v Sussex, Hove 1998

2004 Season

	M	Inns	NO	Runs	HS	Avge	100s	50s	Ct	St	O	M	Runs	Wkts	Avge	Best	5wI	10wM
Test																		
All First	8	10	3	25	8	3.57	-	-	3	-	182.4	28	645	11	58.63	3-50	-	-
1-day Int																		
C & G																		
totesport	2	0	0	0	0	-	-	-	1	-	16	1	56	2	28.00	1-23	-	
Twenty20																		

43. Which former England ODI batsman was Scotland's coach during the 1999 World Cup?

Career Performances

	M	Inns	NO	Runs	HS	Avge	100s	50s	Ct	St	Balls	Runs	Wkts	Avge	Best	5wI	10wM
Test																	
All First	60	63	30	277	30	8.39	-	-	12	-	8769	5001	179	27.93	7-31	7	1
1-day Int																	
C & G	3	1	1	4	4 *	-	-	-	-	-	132	62	5	12.40	3-18	-	
totesport	38	17	7	86	20	8.60	-	-	6	-	1622	1200	49	24.48	4-29	-	
Twenty20	3	1	1	0	0 *	-	-	-	1	-	60	72	3	24.00	2-22	-	

HUTTON, B. L. — Middlesex

Name: Benjamin (Ben) Leonard Hutton
Role: Left-hand bat, right-arm medium bowler, county captain
Born: 29 January 1977, Johannesburg, South Africa
Height: 6ft 1½in **Weight:** 12st
Nickname: Gibbo
County debut: 1999
County cap: 2003
1000 runs in a season: 1
1st-Class 50s: 13
1st-Class 100s: 13
1st-Class catches: 93
One-Day 5 w. in innings: 1
Place in batting averages: 78th av. 40.32 (2003 73rd av. 40.04)
Strike rate: 84.75 (career 83.87)
Parents: Charmaine and Richard
Marital status: Single
Family links with cricket: Sir Leonard Hutton (grandfather) Yorkshire and England; Richard Hutton (father) Yorkshire and England; Ben Brocklehurst (grandfather) Somerset; Oliver Hutton (brother) Oxford University
Education: Radley College; Durham University
Qualifications: 10 GCSEs, 3 A-levels, BA (Hons) Social Sciences, NCA coaching award
Career outside cricket: 'Trainee insurance broker'
Off-season: 'Working for RP Hodson Group'
Overseas tours: Durham University to Zimbabwe 1997-98; Middlesex to Portugal 1996, 1997, 1998, to South Africa 1999, to Malta 2001, to Bombay 2003; MCC to Italy
Overseas teams played for: Pirates CC, Johannesburg 1996; Wanderers CC, Johannesburg 1997; Gosnells, Perth 2001-02

Career highlights to date: 'Scoring 73 v Aussies in 2001. Winning second division of totesport League [2004]. Being capped by Middlesex 2003. Captaining Middlesex to two consecutive Championship wins 2004'
Cricket moments to forget: 'Breaking my hand v Gloucestershire 2001. Two Championship pairs'
Cricket superstitions: 'None'
Cricketers particularly admired: Sir Leonard Hutton, Justin Langer, Mark Ramprakash, Andy Flower
Young players to look out for: Nick Compton, Eoin Morgan
Other sports played: Golf (12 handicap)
Other sports followed: 'All sport, except motor racing'
Favourite band: 'Too many to mention'
Relaxations: 'Reading and listening to music'
Extras: Played in Durham University's BUSA Championship winning side 1997, 1998 (shared) and 1999. Opened for Middlesex v Essex at Southend 1999 with Andrew Strauss, his former opening partner at Radley. His maiden first-class century, 133 v Oxford University CCE at The Parks, was the first first-class century of the 2001 season. Scored century in each innings (100/107) v Kent at Southgate 2004. Scored century (100) v Northamptonshire at Northampton 2004, in the process passing 1000 first-class runs in a season for the first time. Appointed captain of Middlesex for 2005
Opinions on cricket: 'We should increase the length of the tea break to half an hour. Twenty20 great success that has really improved the profile of the game. Individuals should stop criticising the game's structure in this country and be more pro-active in trying to ensure that our system produces cricketers who can compete with the best in the world.'
Best batting: 139 Middlesex v Derbyshire, Southgate 2001
Best bowling: 4-37 Middlesex v Sri Lankans, Shenley 2002

2004 Season

	M	Inns	NO	Runs	HS	Avge	100s	50s	Ct	St	O	M	Runs	Wkts	Avge	Best	5wI	10wM
Test																		
All First	16	29	1	1129	126	40.32	5	3	23	-	113	23	353	8	44.12	3-14	-	-
1-day Int																		
C & G	3	3	1	44	17	22.00	-	-	3	-	3	0	16	1	16.00	1-16	-	
totesport	18	17	1	318	70 *	19.87	-	1	7	-	39	0	212	9	23.55	2-10	-	
Twenty20	4	3	0	42	25	14.00	-	-	2	-	7	0	47	3	15.66	2-21	-	

Career Performances

	M	Inns	NO	Runs	HS	Avge	100s	50s	Ct	St	Balls	Runs	Wkts	Avge	Best	5wI	10wM
Test																	
All First	78	131	12	3923	139	32.96	13	13	93	-	2600	1554	31	50.12	4-37	-	-
1-day Int																	
C & G	8	7	1	86	27	14.33	-	-	7	-	96	104	4	26.00	2-42	-	
totesport	68	57	12	985	77	21.88	-	4	26	-	988	894	29	30.82	5-45	1	
Twenty20	9	6	1	57	25	11.40	-	-	4	-	54	72	4	18.00	2-21	-	

INNES, K. J. Sussex

Name: Kevin John Innes
Role: Right-hand bat, right-arm medium bowler; all-rounder
Born: 24 September 1975, Wellingborough
Height: 5ft 10in **Weight:** 11st 5lbs
Nickname: KJ, Squirrel, Ernie
County debut: 1994 (Northamptonshire), 2002 (Sussex)
1st-Class 50s: 3
1st-Class 100s: 1
1st-Class catches: 15
One-Day 5 w. in innings: 1
Place in batting averages: (2003 199th av. 23.50)
Strike rate: 93.00 (career 56.58)
Parents: Peter and Jane
Wife and date of marriage: Caroline, 2001
Education: Weston Favell Upper School, Northampton
Qualifications: 10 GCSEs, Level 3 Staff 1 coach
Career outside cricket: Cricket coaching
Off-season: 'Working at Northamptonshire CCC'
Overseas tours: England U18 to South Africa 1992-93, to Denmark 1993; England U19 to Sri Lanka 1993-94
Overseas teams played for: Karori, New Zealand 1995-97
Career highlights: 'Taking five wickets at Lord's. Scoring my maiden hundred against Nottinghamshire'
Cricket moments to forget: 'A pair on debut'
Cricket superstitions: 'I change them'
Cricketers particularly admired: Mushtaq Ahmed
Other sports played: Golf, snooker, fishing
Favourite band: Crowded House, Coldplay, Travis, Oasis
Relaxations: 'Spending time with my wife; sleeping and eating out; music, reading books/magazines'
Extras: Won the MCC Lord's Taverners Award U13 and U15. Became youngest player to play for Northants 2nd XI, aged 14 years 9 months. Played for England U19 v India U19 1994. 2nd XI Championship Player of the Year 1998. Left Northamptonshire during the 2001-02 off-season and joined Sussex for 2002. Scored maiden first-class century (103*) v Nottinghamshire at Horsham 2003 before being replaced in the Sussex side by James Kirtley (released by England), thus becoming the first 12th man to score a first-class hundred. Retired at the end of the 2004 season

Best batting: 103* Sussex v Nottinghamshire, Horsham 2003
Best bowling: 4-41 Sussex v Surrey, Hove 2002

2004 Season

	M	Inns	NO	Runs	HS	Avge	100s	50s	Ct	St	O	M	Runs	Wkts	Avge	Best	5wI	10wM
Test																		
All First	3	4	0	68	38	17.00	-	-	1	-	46.3	7	156	3	52.00	2-50	-	-
1-day Int																		
C & G	1	1	1	14	14 *	-	-	-	-	-	6	0	43	1	43.00	1-43	-	
totesport	2	1	0	6	6	6.00	-	-	-	-	14	1	68	3	22.66	2-29	-	
Twenty20																		

Career Performances

	M	Inns	NO	Runs	HS	Avge	100s	50s	Ct	St	Balls	Runs	Wkts	Avge	Best	5wI	10wM
Test																	
All First	45	70	17	1256	103*	23.69	1	3	15	-	4470	2461	79	31.15	4-41	-	-
1-day Int																	
C & G	9	6	3	52	25	17.33	-	-	5	-	285	293	6	48.83	3-26	-	
totesport	63	43	14	644	55	22.20	-	2	19	-	2033	1794	65	27.60	5-41	1	
Twenty20	5	5	1	22	10	5.50	-	-	-	-	51	72	1	72.00	1-28	-	

IRANI, R. C. — Essex

Name: Ronald (Ronnie) Charles Irani
Role: Right-hand bat, right-arm medium-fast bowler, county captain
Born: 26 October 1971, Leigh, Lancashire
Height: 6ft 4in **Weight:** 14st 8lbs
Nickname: Reggie
County debut: 1990 (Lancashire), 1994 (Essex)
County cap: 1994 (Essex)
Benefit: 2003 (Essex)
Test debut: 1996
Tests: 3
One-Day Internationals: 31
1000 runs in a season: 5
50 wickets in a season: 1
1st-Class 50s: 56
1st-Class 100s: 21
1st-Class 200s: 1
1st-Class 5 w. in innings: 9
1st-Class catches: 69
One-Day 100s: 5

One-Day 5 w. in innings: 4
Place in batting averages: 18th av. 57.91 (2003 128th av. 31.42)
Strike rate: (career 60.14)
Parents: Jimmy and Anne
Wife: Lorraine
Children: Simone, 25 September 2000; Maria, 6 January 2002
Family links with cricket: 'Father played league cricket for over 30 years. Mum did teas for years as well'
Education: Smithills Comprehensive School
Qualifications: 9 GCSEs
Overseas tours: England YC to Australia 1989-90; England A to Pakistan 1995-96, to Bangladesh and New Zealand 1999-2000; England to Zimbabwe and New Zealand 1996-97, to Sri Lanka (ICC Champions Trophy) 2002-03, to Australia 2002-03 (VB Series), to Africa (World Cup) 2002-03; England VI to Hong Kong 2002
Overseas teams played for: Technicol Natal, Durban 1992-93; Eden-Roskill, Auckland 1993-94
Career highlights to date: 'Playing for England. Winning one-day trophies with Essex'
Cricket moments to forget: 'Admiring lady streaker and getting caught on TV cameras doing it!'
Cricketers particularly admired: Graham Gooch, Javed Miandad, Viv Richards, Wasim Akram
Young players to look out for: Will Jefferson, Justin Bishop
Other sports played: Golf, pool
Other sports followed: Football (Manchester United), Muay Thai boxing
Favourite band: Manic Street Preachers, Travis, Joyce Simms, Alexander O'Neal
Relaxations: Fly fishing
Extras: Bull Man of the Series, England YC v Australia YC 1991. Appointed vice-captain of Essex 1999. Achieved double of 1000 first-class runs and 50 first-class wickets 1999. Took over 1st XI captaincy of Essex at the start of the 2000 season, Nasser Hussain remaining as club captain until his retirement in 2004. Recorded a five-wicket innings return (5-58) and scored a century (119) for Essex v Surrey at Ilford 2001. Took a season record 20 wickets in the 2002 B&H. Man of the Match award v India at The Oval in the NatWest Series 2002 for his 53 (his maiden ODI fifty) and 5-26 (his maiden ODI five-wicket return and the best ODI analysis recorded at The Oval); also named 'Fans' Player of the Series'. Captained England XI v Sir Donald Bradman XI at Bowral 2002-03. Granted Freedom of the City of London in April 2003. Forced by knee injury to give up bowling 2003. Scored century (122*) v Nottinghamshire at Southend 2004, in the process sharing with Scott Brant (19) in the first century partnership for the tenth wicket in first-class cricket at the Southchurch Park ground (105)
Opinions on cricket: 'Three-day cricket to return to allow for a Twenty20 league. "The trend is my friend!"'
Best batting: 207* Essex v Northamptonshire, Ilford 2002
Best bowling: 6-71 Essex v Nottinghamshire, Trent Bridge 2002

2004 Season

	M	Inns	NO	Runs	HS	Avge	100s	50s	Ct	St	O	M	Runs	Wkts	Avge	Best	5wI	10wM
Test																		
All First	10	16	4	695	164	57.91	3	2	1	-								
1-day Int																		
C & G	2	2	0	18	17	9.00	-	-	2	-								
totesport	14	13	3	546	158 *	54.60	2	1	2	-								
Twenty20	5	5	1	124	64 *	31.00	-	1	1	-								

Career Performances

	M	Inns	NO	Runs	HS	Avge	100s	50s	Ct	St	Balls	Runs	Wkts	Avge	Best	5wI	10wM
Test	3	5	0	86	41	17.20	-	-	2	-	192	112	3	37.33	1-22	-	-
All First	196	321	40	10730	207 *	38.18	22	56	69	-	20389	10007	339	29.51	6-71	9	-
1-day Int	31	30	5	360	53	14.40	-	1	6	-	1283	989	24	41.20	5-26	1	
C & G	28	25	3	897	124	40.77	1	7	10	-	1526	1042	37	28.16	4-41	-	
totesport	166	158	25	3901	158 *	29.33	4	20	38	-	5210	3912	165	23.70	5-33	1	
Twenty20	10	10	1	242	64 *	26.88	-	1	2	-							

JAQUES, P. A. — Yorkshire

Name: Philip Anthony Jaques
Role: Left-hand bat, left-arm spin bowler
Born: 3 May 1979, Wollongong, Australia
Height: 6ft 1in
Nickname: Jakesy, Poop
County debut: 2003 (Northamptonshire), 2004 (Yorkshire)
County cap: 2003 (Northamptonshire)
1000 runs in a season: 2
1st-Class 50s: 15
1st-Class 100s: 7
1st-Class 200s: 2
1st-Class catches: 28
One-Day 100s: 3
Place in batting averages: 16th av. 58.84 (2003 16th av. 58.70)
Parents: Mary and Stuart
Marital status: Engaged
Family links with cricket: 'Dad played league cricket in South Lancashire League'
Education: Figtree High School; Australian College of Physical Education (PE degree)
Qualifications: Fitness trainer, Level II coach

Career outside cricket: Coaching
Off-season: New South Wales Blues
Overseas tours: New South Wales to New Zealand 2000-01
Overseas teams played for: Sutherland DCC, Sydney; New South Wales Blues 2000-01 – 2001-02, 2003-04 –
Career highlights to date: '243 v Hampshire [2004] and maiden first-class hundred for NSW'
Cricket moments to forget: 'Any duck really'
Cricketers particularly admired: Steve Waugh
Favourite band: Coldplay
Extras: Attended Australian Cricket Academy 2000. Scored maiden first-class century (149*) v Worcestershire at Worcester 2003 on his 24th birthday and maiden first-class double century (222) in his next Championship innings v Yorkshire at Northampton 2003. Scored 1409 first-class runs in his first season of county cricket, 2003. Holds a British passport and was not considered an overseas player with Northamptonshire in 2003. Was an overseas player with Yorkshire in 2004 (having played for New South Wales 2003-04), deputising for Ian Harvey and Darren Lehmann; has returned for 2005. Scored century (105) on one-day debut for Yorkshire v Sussex at Headingley in the totesport League 2004
Best batting: 243 Yorkshire v Hampshire, West End 2004

2004 Season

	M	Inns	NO	Runs	HS	Avge	100s	50s	Ct	St	O	M	Runs	Wkts	Avge	Best	5wI	10wM
Test																		
All First	11	19	0	1118	243	58.84	3	5	11	-	2	0	18	0	-	-	-	-
1-day Int																		
C & G	2	2	0	60	55	30.00	-	1	-	-								
totesport	9	8	1	366	105	52.28	1	3	5	-								
Twenty20	5	5	1	180	92	45.00	-	1	1	-								

Career Performances

	M	Inns	NO	Runs	HS	Avge	100s	50s	Ct	St	Balls	Runs	Wkts	Avge	Best	5wI	10wM
Test																	
All First	39	68	1	3249	243	48.49	9	15	28	-	66	61	0	-	-	-	-
1-day Int																	
C & G	3	3	0	65	55	21.66	-	1	-	-							
totesport	27	26	2	1169	117	48.70	3	9	9	-							
Twenty20	10	10	1	277	92	30.77	-	1	2	-							

JEFFERSON, W. I. Essex

Name: William (Will) Ingleby Jefferson
Role: Right-hand bat, right-arm medium bowler
Born: 25 October 1979, Derby ('but native of Norfolk')
Height: 6ft 10½in **Weight:** 15st 2lbs
Nickname: Santa, Lemar, Jeffo
County debut: 2000
County cap: 2002
1000 runs in a season: 1
1st-Class 50s: 13
1st-Class 100s: 8
1st-Class 200s: 1
1st-Class catches: 47
One-Day 100s: 4
Place in batting averages: 20th av. 55.53 (2003 108th av. 33.95)
Parents: Richard and Pauline
Marital status: Single
Family links with cricket: Grandfather Jefferson played for the Army and Combined Services in the 1920s. Father, R. I. Jefferson, played for Cambridge University 1961 and Surrey 1961-66
Education: Oundle School, Northants; Durham University
Qualifications: 9 GCSEs, 3 A-levels, BA (Hons) Sport in the Community, Levels 1 and 2 cricket coaching awards
Off-season: 'Four months playing and coaching for Papatoetoe CC, near Auckland NZ'
Overseas tours: Oundle School to South Africa 1995
Overseas teams played for: Young People's Club, Paarl, South Africa 1998-99; South Perth, Western Australia 2002-03
Career highlights to date: 'Being awarded county cap on final day of the 2002 season. Scoring 165* to help beat Notts and secure 2002 second division Championship. 222 v Hampshire at Rose Bowl [2004]'
Cricket moments to forget: 'Any dropped catch; any time bowled playing across the line'
Cricketers particularly admired: Andy Flower, Nasser Hussain
Young players to look out for: Jamie Dalrymple, Justin Ontong
Other sports played: Golf (12 handicap), tennis, swimming
Other sports followed: 'Follow most sports'
Injuries: 'Chronic hamstring injury – played through it'
Favourite band: Coldplay

Relaxations: 'Listening to music; seeing friends outside cricket'
Extras: Aged 15, received a letter handwritten by Sir Colin Cowdrey congratulating him on scoring 83 and 106* in his two games in the Sun Life of Canada U15 Club Championships. Holmwoods School Cricketer of the Year 1998. Represented British Universities 2000, 2001 and 2002. Played for Durham University CCE 2001 and 2002. NBC Denis Compton Award for the most promising young Essex player 2002. Scored century before lunch on the opening day for Essex v Cambridge UCCE at Fenner's 2003. C&G Man of the Match awards for his 97 v Scotland at Edinburgh 2004 and for his 126 v Nottinghamshire at Trent Bridge in the next round; during the latter he shared in an Essex record partnership for one-day cricket (248) with Andy Flower (106). Scored century (128) v Leicestershire at Chelmsford 2004, in the process sharing with Alastair Cook (126) in Essex's third-highest first-class opening partnership (265). Scored maiden first-class double century (222) v Hampshire at West End 2004. Scored century in each innings (167/100*) v Nottinghamshire at Trent Bridge 2004. Scored 1000 first-class runs in a season for the first time 2004 and was fifth highest run-scorer in first-class cricket (1555). Essex Player of the Year 2004. Essex Boundary Club Trophy for scoring most runs for Essex 1st XI 2004
Best batting: 222 Essex v Hampshire, West End 2004

2004 Season

	M	Inns	NO	Runs	HS	Avge	100s	50s	Ct	St	O	M	Runs	Wkts	Avge	Best	5wI	10wM
Test																		
All First	17	29	1	1555	222	55.53	6	5	15	-								
1-day Int																		
C & G	3	3	0	242	126	80.66	1	1	1	-								
totesport	14	13	2	415	97	37.72	-	2	4	-								
Twenty20	4	4	1	27	11 *	9.00	-	-	1	-								

Career Performances

	M	Inns	NO	Runs	HS	Avge	100s	50s	Ct	St	Balls	Runs	Wkts	Avge	Best	5wI	10wM
Test																	
All First	51	93	9	3357	222	39.96	9	13	47	-							
1-day Int																	
C & G	5	5	0	374	132	74.80	2	1	3	-							
totesport	45	44	3	1427	111 *	34.80	2	9	21	-							
Twenty20	7	7	1	59	19	9.83	-	-	1	-							

44. Who was Sanath Jayasuriya's partner in a stand of 576 against India in 1997-98, the highest partnership in Test cricket?

JENNINGS, C. J. R. — Northamptonshire

Name: Craig James Robert Jennings
Role: Right-hand bat, right-arm fast bowler
Born: 13 November 1984, Rugeley
Height: 6ft **Weight:** 12st 10lbs
Nickname: Jenno
County debut: 2004
Strike rate: 84.00 (career 84.00)
Parents: John and Frances
Marital status: Single
Family links with cricket: 'Dad and brother play very high standard of league cricket'
Education: Hageley Park, Staffordshire
Qualifications: 8 GCSEs
Career outside cricket: Taxi driver
Overseas tours: Staffordshire U15 to Barbados; MCC to Papua New Guinea and Fiji 2003
Career highlights to date: 'Playing against New Zealand in June 2004'
Cricket moments to forget: 'My first over on my Championship debut – it went for at least 20'
Cricketers particularly admired: Mike Hussey, Andre Nel, Adam Shantry
Young players to look out for: Adam Shantry, Alex Wakely, Graeme White
Other sports played: Football (county), rugby
Other sports followed: Rugby, football (Birmingham City FC)
Favourite band: Green Day
Relaxations: Playing golf
Extras: Played for Northamptonshire Board XI in the C&G 2002. Left Northamptonshire at the end of the 2004 season
Opinions on cricket: 'There are too many Kolpak players (*see page 9*).'
Best batting: 6 Northamptonshire v Worcestershire, Worcester 2004
Best bowling: 1-64 Northamptonshire v Worcestershire, Worcester 2004

2004 Season

	M	Inns	NO	Runs	HS	Avge	100s	50s	Ct	St	O	M	Runs	Wkts	Avge	Best	5wI	10wM
Test																		
All First	1	1	0	6	6	6.00	-	-	-	-	14	3	64	1	64.00	1-64	-	-
1-day Int																		
C & G																		
totesport	1	1	0	3	3	3.00	-	-	-	-	8	0	36	1	36.00	1-36	-	
Twenty20	1	1	0	2	2	2.00	-	-	-	-	2	0	16	0	-	-	-	

Career Performances

	M	Inns	NO	Runs	HS	Avge	100s	50s	Ct	St	Balls	Runs	Wkts	Avge	Best	5wI	10wM
Test																	
All First	1	1	0	6	6	6.00	-	-	-	-	84	64	1	64.00	1-64	-	-
1-day Int																	
C & G	1	1	1	12	12 *	-	-	-	1	-							
totesport	1	1	0	3	3	3.00	-	-	-	-	48	36	1	36.00	1-36	-	
Twenty20	1	1	0	2	2	2.00	-	-	-	-	12	16	0	-	-	-	

JOHNSON, R. L. Somerset

Name: Richard Leonard Johnson
Role: Right-hand bat, right-arm fast-medium bowler
Born: 29 December 1974, Chertsey, Surrey
Height: 6ft 2in **Weight:** 14st 3lbs
Nickname: Jono, Lenny, The Greek
County debut: 1992 (Middlesex), 2001 (Somerset)
County cap: 1995 (Middlesex), 2001 (Somerset)
Test debut: 2003
Tests: 3
One-Day Internationals: 10
50 wickets in a season: 4
1st-Class 50s: 7
1st-Class 100s: 2
1st-Class 5 w. in innings: 19
1st-Class 10 w. in match: 3
1st-Class catches: 55
One-Day 5 w. in innings: 1
Place in batting averages: 180th av. 24.75 (2003 174th av. 26.16)
Place in bowling averages: 75th av. 34.36 (2003 33rd av. 25.64)
Strike rate: 61.34 (career 50.77)
Parents: Roger and Mary Anne
Wife and date of marriage: Nikki, 4 October 2003
Family links with cricket: Father and grandfather played club cricket
Education: Sunbury Manor School; Spelthorne College
Qualifications: 9 GCSEs, A-level in Physical Education, NCA senior coaching award
Overseas tours: England U18 to South Africa 1992-93; England U19 to Sri Lanka 1993-94; England A to India 1994-95; MCC to Bangladesh 1999-2000, to Canada 2000-01; England to India 2001-02, to Bangladesh and Sri Lanka 2003-04

Career highlights to date: 'Playing in a domestic final for Somerset. Making England debut'
Cricket moments to forget: 'Losing C&G final [2002]'
Cricketers particularly admired: Ian Botham, Richard Hadlee, Angus Fraser
Young players to look out for: James Hildreth
Other sports followed: Football (Tottenham), rugby (London Irish)
Injuries: Out for five weeks with injured ankle ligaments – 'trod on cricket ball; not advisable!'
Relaxations: 'Eating out with wife and friends; having a few beers with Nashy'
Extras: Represented Middlesex at all levels from U11. Took 10 for 45 v Derbyshire at Derby 1994, becoming the first person to take ten wickets in an English first-class innings since 1964. Left Middlesex at the end of the 2000 season and joined Somerset for 2001. Took five wickets in an innings in his first two Championship matches for Somerset – 5-107 v Lancashire and 5-106 v Glamorgan. Took 6-33 on Test debut in the second Test v Zimbabwe at Riverside 2003, including wickets with his third and fourth balls in Test cricket, winning Man of the Match award. Had match figures of 9-93 (5-49/4-44) in the second Test v Bangladesh at Chittagong 2003-04, winning second Man of the Match award in his second Test. Won the Walter Lawrence Trophy (for the season's fastest hundred) in 2004 for his 63-ball century (ending up 101*) v Durham at Riverside
Best batting: 118 Somerset v Gloucestershire, Bristol 2003
Best bowling: 10-45 Middlesex v Derbyshire, Derby 1994

2004 Season

	M	Inns	NO	Runs	HS	Avge	100s	50s	Ct	St	O	M	Runs	Wkts	Avge	Best	5wI	10wM
Test																		
All First	15	14	2	297	101 *	24.75	1	1	3	-	449.5	104	1512	44	34.36	7-69	2	-
1-day Int																		
C & G	1	1	0	3	3	3.00	-	-	-	-	4.3	1	30	0	-	-	-	
totesport	7	5	3	25	17	12.50	-	-	-	-	45	9	204	5	40.80	3-25	-	
Twenty20																		

Career Performances

	M	Inns	NO	Runs	HS	Avge	100s	50s	Ct	St	Balls	Runs	Wkts	Avge	Best	5wI	10wM
Test	3	4	0	59	26	14.75	-	-	-	-	547	275	16	17.18	6-33	2	-
All First	143	196	27	3068	118	18.15	2	7	55	-	24370	12945	480	26.96	10-45	19	3
1-day Int	10	4	1	16	10	5.33	-	-	-	-	402	239	11	21.72	3-22	-	
C & G	27	16	3	184	45 *	14.15	-	-	4	-	1407	1044	38	27.47	5-50	1	
totesport	103	71	20	667	53	13.07	-	1	10	-	4262	3607	109	33.09	4-45	-	
Twenty20																	

JONES, G. O. Kent

Name: Geraint Owen Jones
Role: Right-hand bat, wicket-keeper
Born: 14 July 1976, Kundiawa, Papua New Guinea
Height: 5ft 10in **Weight:** 11st
Nickname: Jonesy
County debut: 2001
County cap: 2003
Test debut: 2003-04
Tests: 8
One-Day Internationals: 12
50 dismissals in a season: 1
1st-Class 50s: 10
1st-Class 100s: 4
1st-Class catches: 102
1st-Class stumpings: 10
Place in batting averages: 101st av. 36.08 (2003 54th av. 44.77)
Parents: Emrys, Carol (deceased), Maureen (stepmother)
Marital status: Single
Family links with cricket: 'Father was star off-spinner in local school side'
Education: Harristown State High School, Toowoomba, Queensland; MacGregor SHS, Brisbane
Qualifications: Level 1 coach
Off-season: Touring with England
Overseas tours: Beenleigh-Logan U19 to New Zealand 1995; Kent to Port Elizabeth 2001-02; England to Bangladesh and Sri Lanka 2003-04, to West Indies 2003-04, to Zimbabwe (one-day series) 2004-05, to South Africa 2004-05
Overseas teams played for: Beenleigh-Logan, Brisbane 1995-98; Valleys, Brisbane 2001-02
Cricket moments to forget: 'Third-ball nought in last innings [of 2003] against Warwickshire'
Cricket superstitions: 'Left pad first'
Cricketers particularly admired: Jack Russell, Alec Stewart
Young players to look out for: James Tredwell, Rob Ferley
Other sports played: Golf
Other sports followed: Rugby (Crickhowell RFC)
Favourite band: Matchbox Twenty
Extras: Scored a 39-ball 39 on Norwich Union League debut v Surrey at The Oval 2001, having arrived at the crease with his side on 59 for 5. Scored maiden first-class 50 (76*) v Sri Lankans at Canterbury 2002 in only his second first-class match. Set

new record for a season's tally of wicket-keeping dismissals in the one-day league (33; 27/6) 2003; also equalled record for number of wicket-keeping catches in one match, six v Leicestershire at Canterbury 2003. Made 59 first-class dismissals plus 985 first-class runs in his first full season of county cricket 2003. Made Test debut in the fourth Test v West Indies in Antigua 2003-04. Man of the Match in the second Test v New Zealand at Headingley 2004, in which he scored his maiden Test century (100). Made ODI debut v West Indies at Trent Bridge in the NatWest Series 2004. Scored 74 in the second Test v West Indies at Edgbaston 2004, in the process sharing with Andrew Flintoff (167) in a new ground record sixth-wicket stand for England v West Indies (170). ECB contract 2004-05

Opinions on cricket: 'Great game; love playing it. Definitely play too much; needs to be looked at and evaluated.'

Best batting: 108* Kent v Essex, Chelmsford 2003

Stop press: Man of the Match in the fourth ODI v Zimbabwe at Bulawayo 2004-05 (80). Stumped Andrew Hall off Kabir Ali off the final ball of the second ODI v South Africa at Bloemfontein 2004-05 to tie the match

2004 Season

	M	Inns	NO	Runs	HS	Avge	100s	50s	Ct	St	O	M	Runs	Wkts	Avge	Best	5wI	10wM
Test	7	9	0	311	100	34.55	1	1	27	2								
All First	11	13	1	433	101	36.08	2	1	34	3								
1-day Int	12	9	3	111	38	18.50	-	-	21	-								
C & G	2	1	0	0	0	0.00	-	-	1	-								
totesport	4	4	0	38	22	9.50	-	-	5	-								
Twenty20	2	2	0	30	22	15.00	-	-	2	-								

Career Performances

	M	Inns	NO	Runs	HS	Avge	100s	50s	Ct	St	Balls	Runs	Wkts	Avge	Best	5wI	10wM
Test	8	11	1	359	100	35.90	1	1	27	2							
All First	37	49	8	1704	108 *	41.56	4	10	102	10	6	4	0	-	-	-	-
1-day Int	12	9	3	111	38	18.50	-	-	21	-							
C & G	5	3	1	64	34	32.00	-	-	3	1							
totesport	31	28	3	493	74 *	19.72	-	2	33	6							
Twenty20	7	6	1	71	22	14.20	-	-	7	-							

45. Who scored 428 for Sind in 1973-74 (the seventh-highest score in first-class history), played two Tests for Pakistan (the first when he was only 16) and coached Nepal in the 2001 ICC Trophy?

JONES, P. S. Northamptonshire

Name: Philip Steffan Jones
Role: Right-hand bat, right-arm fast-medium bowler
Born: 9 February 1974, Llanelli
Height: 6ft 1in **Weight:** 15st
Nickname: Jona
County debut: 1997 (Somerset), 2004 (Northamptonshire)
50 wickets in a season: 1
1st-Class 50s: 3
1st-Class 100s: 1
1st-Class 5 w. in innings: 5
1st-Class 10 w. in match: 1
1st-Class catches: 17
One-Day 5 w. in innings: 2
Place in batting averages: 236th av. 17.37 (2003 161st av. 27.30)
Place in bowling averages: 155th av. 79.20 (2003 124th av. 42.27)
Strike rate: 132.00 (career 65.62)
Parents: Lyndon and Ann
Wife and date of marriage: Alex, 12 October 2002
Family links with cricket: Father played at a high standard and played first-class rugby
Education: Ysgol Gyfun y Strade, Llanelli; Loughborough University; Homerton College, Cambridge University
Qualifications: BSc Sports Science, PGCE in Physical Education
Career outside cricket: Personal fitness trainer
Overseas tours: Wales Minor Counties to Barbados 1996; Somerset CCC to South Africa 1999, 2000
Career highlights to date: 'Winning C&G Trophy with Somerset CCC'
Cricket superstitions: 'Always give 110 per cent effort'
Young players to look out for: Aaron Laraman
Other sports played: Rugby union (Wales Schools, U18, Youth; Swansea, Bristol, Exeter and Moseley)
Other sports followed: Baseball, rugby union, athletics
Favourite band: Will Young
Relaxations: 'Spending time with my wife and close friends; going back to Wales to see my family'
Extras: Represented Wales Minor Counties. Played first-class cricket and first-class rugby for two years. Took nine wickets (6-67/3-81) in the Varsity Match at Lord's

1997. Took 59 first-class wickets in 2001, 'Somerset's most successful season'. Left Somerset at the end of the 2003 season and joined Northamptonshire for 2004. Took one-day career best 6-56 v Ireland at Dublin in the C&G 2004
Best batting: 105 Somerset v New Zealanders, Taunton 1999
Best bowling: 6-67 Cambridge University v Oxford University, Lord's 1997

2004 Season

	M	Inns	NO	Runs	HS	Avge	100s	50s	Ct	St	O	M	Runs	Wkts	Avge	Best	5wI	10wM
Test																		
All First	8	9	1	139	37	17.37	-	-	1	-	220	33	792	10	79.20	3-75	-	-
1-day Int																		
C & G	3	2	1	3	2 *	3.00	-	-	1		25	1	149	6	24.83	6-56	1	
totesport	7	3	1	5	5	2.50	-	-	2	-	54	5	253	7	36.14	2-23	-	
Twenty20																		

Career Performances

	M	Inns	NO	Runs	HS	Avge	100s	50s	Ct	St	Balls	Runs	Wkts	Avge	Best	5wI	10wM
Test																	
All First	77	93	24	1244	105	18.02	1	3	17	-	12993	7705	198	38.91	6-67	5	1
1-day Int																	
C & G	22	7	5	58	26 *	29.00	-	-	3	-	1112	995	31	32.09	6-56	1	
totesport	92	53	27	281	27	10.80	-	-	19	-	4085	3650	137	26.64	5-23	1	
Twenty20	5	4	2	26	24 *	13.00	-	-	-	-	96	159	5	31.80	2-24	-	

JONES, S. P. — Glamorgan

Name: Simon Philip Jones
Role: Left-hand bat, right-arm fast bowler
Born: 25 December 1978, Morriston, Swansea
Height: 6ft 3in **Weight:** 15st
Nickname: Horse
County debut: 1998
County cap: 2002
Test debut: 2002
Tests: 8
1st-Class 5 w. in innings: 9
1st-Class 10 w. in match: 1
1st-Class catches: 13
Place in batting averages: 279th av. 7.50
Place in bowling averages: 72nd av. 33.97
Strike rate: 54.73 (career 53.47)
Parents: Irene and Jeff
Marital status: Single

Family links with cricket: 'Dad played for Glamorgan and England (15 Tests)'
Education: Coedcae Comprehensive School; Millfield School
Qualifications: 12 GCSEs, 1 A-level, basic and senior coaching awards
Career outside cricket: 'Fitness instructor/excavator of Sophia Gardens'
Off-season: England tour of South Africa
Overseas tours: Dyfed Schools to Zimbabwe 1994; Glamorgan to South Africa 1998; ECB National Academy to Australia 2001-02; England to Australia 2002-03, to West Indies 2003-04, to Zimbabwe (one-day series) 2004-05, to South Africa 2004-05; England A to Malaysia and India 2003-04
Career highlights to date: 'Playing on lightning fast tracks at Cardiff'
Cricket moments to forget: 'Injuring my right knee in Australia'
Cricket superstitions: 'Right boot on first'
Cricketers particularly admired: 'Dad', Allan Donald
Young players to look out for: 'ERJ Mustafa'
Other sports played: Football (trials with Leeds United)
Injuries: Stress lesion of left foot
Favourite band: 50 Cent
Relaxations: 'Having a few pots in Cardiff with ERJ Mustafa'
Extras: Struck a 14-ball 46 (including six sixes and two fours) v Yorkshire at Scarborough 2001. NBC Denis Compton Award for the most promising young Glamorgan player 2001. Made Test debut in the first Test v India at Lord's 2002, striking a 43-ball 44 (more runs than his father scored in his Test career); the Joneses are the eleventh father and son to have played in Tests for England. ECB National Academy 2003-04. Recorded maiden first-class ten-wicket match return (5-57/5-31) for England A v Tamil Nadu at Chennai 2003-04. Recorded maiden Test five-wicket return (5-57) in the second Test v West Indies at Port-of-Spain 2003-04; the Joneses thus became the first father and son to have taken five-wicket hauls for England. ECB contract 2004-05
Opinions on cricket: 'Game is progressing. Becoming more professional. Just need more sunshine.'
Best batting: 46 Glamorgan v Yorkshire, Scarborough 2001
Best bowling: 6-45 Glamorgan v Derbyshire, Cardiff 2002
Stop press: Made ODI debut in the third ODI v Zimbabwe at Bulawayo 2004-05. Had second innings figures of 4-39 and took match-turning catch to dismiss Graeme Smith in the first Test v South Africa at Port Elizabeth 2004-05

2004 Season

	M	Inns	NO	Runs	HS	Avge	100s	50s	Ct	St	O	M	Runs	Wkts	Avge	Best	5wI	10wM
Test	2	2	0	8	4	4.00	-	-	-	-	71	19	245	5	49.00	3-82	-	-
All First	11	11	5	45	20	7.50	-	-	2	-	310.1	53	1155	34	33.97	5-77	2	-
1-day Int																		
C & G	1	0	0	0	0	-	-	-	-	-	9.1	0	64	1	64.00	1-64	-	
totesport	1	0	0	0	0	-	-	-	-	-	9	0	34	1	34.00	1-34	-	
Twenty20																		

Career Performances

	M	Inns	NO	Runs	HS	Avge	100s	50s	Ct	St	Balls	Runs	Wkts	Avge	Best	5wI	10wM
Test	8	7	0	75	44	10.71	-	-	2	-	1260	780	21	37.14	5-57	1	-
All First	60	69	19	527	46	10.54	-	-	13	-	8770	5511	164	33.60	6-45	9	1
1-day Int																	
C & G	2	0	0	0	0	-	-	-	-	-	85	94	1	94.00	1-64	-	
totesport	2	1	1	12	12 *	-	-	-	-	-	96	73	2	36.50	1-34	-	
Twenty20																	

JOSEPH, R. H. — Kent

Name: Robert Hartman Joseph Jnr
Role: Right-hand bat, right-arm fast-medium bowler
Born: 20 January 1982, Antigua
Height: 6ft 1in **Weight:** 13st 7lbs
Nickname: RJ, Blueie
County debut: 2004
1st-Class catches: 3
Place in batting averages: 258th av. 12.83
Place in bowling averages: 73rd av. 34.10
Strike rate: 52.21 (career 57.10)
Education: Sutton Valence School; St Mary's University College
Off-season: 'Doing my MSc in Sporting Performance'
Overseas tours: Antigua Young Lions to England 1997; Antigua and Leeward Islands U15 to Trinidad and St Lucia
Career highlights to date: 'Playing for the ECB First-Class XI against New Zealand A'
Cricket moments to forget: 'Losing in a local school final – getting out on 47 needing one to win with four wickets in hand and losing'

Cricketers particularly admired: Sir Vivian Richards, Andy Roberts
Young players to look out for: James Kingstone (Berkshire)
Other sports played: Golf
Other sports followed: Football (Arsenal)
Favourite band: Maroon 5
Relaxations: Listening to music
Extras: Made first-class debut for First-Class Counties XI v New Zealand A at Milton Keynes 2000
Opinions on cricket: 'It's evolving into a faster, more interesting spectator sport, which is in the best interests of the game.'
Best batting: 26 Kent v Middlesex, Canterbury 2004
Best bowling: 3-47 Kent v Middlesex, Canterbury 2004

2004 Season

	M	Inns	NO	Runs	HS	Avge	100s	50s	Ct	St	O	M	Runs	Wkts	Avge	Best	5wI	10wM
Test																		
All First	7	9	3	77	26	12.83	-	-	3	-	165.2	31	648	19	34.10	3-47	-	-
1-day Int																		
C & G																		
totesport	6	3	3	6	3*	-	-	-	-	-	42	2	197	7	28.14	2-30	-	
Twenty20																		

Career Performances

	M	Inns	NO	Runs	HS	Avge	100s	50s	Ct	St	Balls	Runs	Wkts	Avge	Best	5wI	10wM
Test																	
All First	8	10	4	77	26	12.83	-	-	3	-	1142	704	20	35.20	3-47	-	-
1-day Int																	
C & G																	
totesport	6	3	3	6	3*	-	-	-	-	-	252	197	7	28.14	2-30	-	
Twenty20																	

46. Which Gloucestershire and Northamptonshire all-rounder made his ODI debut for Zimbabwe against Australia at Trent Bridge in the 1983 World Cup?

JOYCE, E. C. — Middlesex

Name: Edmund (Ed) Christopher Joyce
Role: Left-hand middle-order bat, occasional right-arm medium bowler
Born: 22 September 1978, Dublin
Height: 5ft 10in **Weight:** 12st 7lbs
Nickname: Joycey, Spud, Piece
County debut: 1999
County cap: 2002
1000 runs in a season: 3
1st-Class 50s: 18
1st-Class 100s: 11
1st-Class catches: 49
One-Day 100s: 1
Place in batting averages: 56th av. 45.86 (2003 79th av. 39.34)
Strike rate: 82.00 (career 134.00)
Parents: Maureen and Jimmy
Marital status: Single
Family links with cricket: 'Two brothers played for Ireland; two sisters currently play for Ireland Ladies'
Education: Presentation College, Bray, County Wicklow; Trinity College, Dublin
Qualifications: Irish Leaving Certificate, BA (Hons) Economics and Geography, Level II coach
Off-season: MCC tour to Namibia and Uganda
Overseas tours: Ireland U19 to Bermuda (International Youth Tournament) 1997, to South Africa (U19 World Cup) 1997-98; Ireland to Zimbabwe (ICC Emerging Nations Tournament) 1999-2000, to Canada (ICC Trophy) 2001; MCC to Namibia and Uganda 2004-05
Overseas teams played for: Coburg CC, Melbourne 1996-97; University CC, Perth 2001-02
Career highlights to date: 'Making hundred at Lord's in 2001'
Cricket moments to forget: 'All the dropped catches at the start of [2003] season'
Cricket superstitions: 'None'
Cricketers particularly admired: Larry Gomes, Brian Lara
Young players to look out for: Eoin Morgan, Nick Compton
Other sports played: Golf, rugby, soccer, snooker
Other sports followed: Rugby (Leinster), football (Manchester United)
Favourite band: The Mars Volta
Relaxations: Cinema, eating out, listening to music
Extras: Leinster U19 to Oxford Festival. Was only player to score a century (105 v Denmark Colts) at the International Youth Tournament, Bermuda 1997. Represented

Ireland senior side 1997-2001. NBC Denis Compton Award for the most promising young Middlesex player 2000. Scored maiden first-class century (104) v Warwickshire at Lord's 2001, becoming the first Irish-born-and-bred player to record a 100 in the County Championship. C&G Man of the Match award for his 72 v Northamptonshire at Northampton 2003. Scored century (123) v Surrey at The Oval 2004, in the process sharing with Jamie Dalrymple (244) in a record fifth-wicket partnership for Middlesex in matches against Surrey (298). Appointed vice-captain of Middlesex in June 2004, captaining the county in the absence of Andrew Strauss on international duty. Is not considered an overseas player

Opinions on cricket: 'Twenty20 cricket is great and will be around for a while. Still too much National League cricket.'

Best batting: 134 Middlesex v CUCCE, Fenner's 2004

Best bowling: 2-34 Middlesex v CUCCE, Fenner's 2004

2004 Season

	M	Inns	NO	Runs	HS	Avge	100s	50s	Ct	St	O	M	Runs	Wkts	Avge	Best	5wI	10wM
Test																		
All First	14	25	2	1055	134	45.86	2	7	12	-	41	3	169	3	56.33	2-34	-	-
1-day Int																		
C & G	3	3	1	181	100 *	90.50	1	1	-	-								
totesport	14	12	3	400	74 *	44.44	-	3	3	-	2	0	17	0	-	-	-	
Twenty20																		

Career Performances

	M	Inns	NO	Runs	HS	Avge	100s	50s	Ct	St	Balls	Runs	Wkts	Avge	Best	5wI	10wM
Test																	
All First	62	101	11	3865	134	42.94	11	18	49	-	804	564	6	94.00	2-34	-	-
1-day Int																	
C & G	12	12	3	471	100 *	52.33	1	3	1	-							
totesport	58	53	9	1378	77	31.31	-	9	22	-	66	79	2	39.50	2-10	-	
Twenty20	4	4	1	53	31	17.66	-	-	1	-	6	12	0	-	-	-	

47. Which current Yorkshire bowler in 1996 became the then youngest player to represent the Scotland national team, aged 17, and was his country's top wicket-taker in the 1999 World Cup?

KASPROWICZ, M. S. — Glamorgan

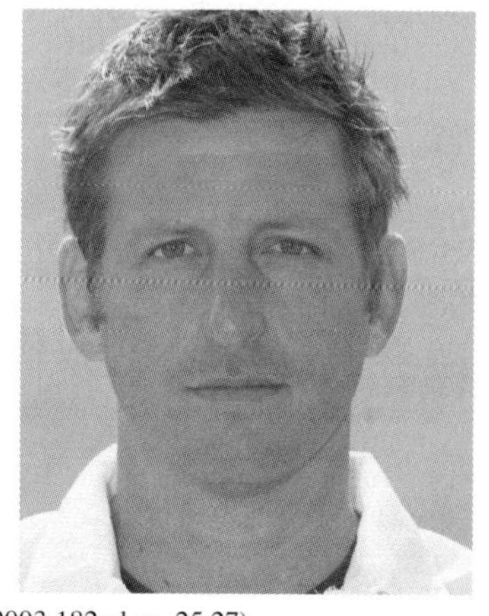

Name: Michael Scott Kasprowicz
Role: Right-hand bat, right-arm fast bowler
Born: 10 February 1972, Brisbane, Australia
Height: 6ft 4in **Weight:** 15st 5lbs
Nickname: Kasper
County debut: 1994 (Essex), 1999 (Leicestershire), 2002 (Glamorgan)
County cap: 1994 (Essex), 1999 (Leicestershire), 2002 (Glamorgan)
Test debut: 1996-97
Tests: 22
One-Day Internationals: 29
50 wickets in a season: 4
1st-Class 50s: 11
1st-Class 5 w. in innings: 47
1st-Class 10 w. in match: 6
1st-Class catches: 84
One-Day 5 w. in innings: 3
Place in batting averages: 252nd av. 14.00 (2003 182nd av. 25.27)
Place in bowling averages: 124th av. 42.52 (2003 6th av. 21.15)
Strike rate: 77.76 (career 51.29)
Parents: Wally and Joan
Wife and date of marriage: Lindsay, 5 December 2002
Family links with cricket/rugby: 'Brother Adam represented Queensland U17 and U19. Brother Simon played for NSW Waratahs in Super 12 rugby competition'
Education: Brisbane State High School
Qualifications: Level 2 cricket coaching
Overseas tours: Australia YC to England 1991; Young Australia (Australia A) to England and Netherlands 1995; Australia to England 1997, to India 1997-98, to Sharjah (Coca-Cola Cup) 1997-98, to Malaysia (Commonwealth Games) 1998-99, to Pakistan 1998-99, to Bangladesh (Wills International Cup) 1998-99, to New Zealand 1999-2000, to India 2000-01, to India (TVS Cup) 2003-04, to Sri Lanka 2003-04, to Zimbabwe (one-day series) 2004, to Holland (Videocon Cup) 2004, to England (ICC Champions Trophy) 2004, to India 2004-05, to New Zealand 2004-05
Overseas teams played for: Queensland 1989-90 –
Career highlights to date: 'Representing Australia and receiving baggy green cap'
Cricketers particularly admired: Dennis Lillee, Steve Waugh
Young players to look out for: Mark Wallace, David Harrison
Other sports played: Rugby (Australian Schoolboys 1989, including tour of New Zealand)
Other sports followed: Rugby league (Brisbane Broncos), Australian Rules football (Brisbane Lions)

Relaxations: 'Fishing, beach, music'

Extras: Played for Queensland U17 and U19 and made his Queensland debut aged 17. Played for Australia U17. Attended Australian Cricket Academy 1991. Was Essex's overseas player 1994. Took 7-36 in the second innings of the sixth Test v England at The Oval 1997. Took 5-28 from 18 overs in the second innings of the third Test v India at Bangalore 1997-98. Was Leicestershire's overseas player 1999. Was leading wicket-taker in the Pura Cup 2001-02 with 49 wickets at 22.08, including match figures of
9-163 in the final v Tasmania at Brisbane. Overseas player at Glamorgan since 2002. Took 9-36 in Durham's second innings at Cardiff 2003; took 9-45 in Durham's second innings in the return match at Riverside 2003. Glamorgan Player of the Year 2003 (jointly with Robert Croft). Cricket Society's Wetherell Award 2003 for the leading all-rounder in English first-class cricket. His international awards include Man of the Match in the fourth ODI v Sri Lanka at Colombo 2003-04 (5-45; his maiden five-wicket return in ODIs). Took 7-39 in Sri Lanka's second innings of the first Test at Darwin 2004. Queensland's leading wicket-taker in Sheffield Shield/Pura Cup (387 to end of 2003-04 season)

Best batting: 92 Australians v India A, Nagpur 2000-01

Best bowling: 9-36 Glamorgan v Durham, Cardiff 2003

2004 Season

	M	Inns	NO	Runs	HS	Avge	100s	50s	Ct	St	O	M	Runs	Wkts	Avge	Best	5wI	10wM
Test																		
All First	7	11	2	126	42	14.00	-	-	2	-	272.1	54	893	21	42.52	5-54	1	-
1-day Int	4	1	1	0	0 *	-	-	-	3	-	36.2	3	145	12	12.08	5-47	1	
C & G	1	0	0	0	0	-	-	-	-	-	7	3	8	0	-	-	-	
totesport	7	1	0	11	11	11.00	-	-	3	-	57.3	5	210	11	19.09	3-27	-	
Twenty20	1	1	0	2	2	2.00	-	-	-	-	3	0	16	1	16.00	1-16	-	

Career Performances

	M	Inns	NO	Runs	HS	Avge	100s	50s	Ct	St	Balls	Runs	Wkts	Avge	Best	5wI	10wM
Test	22	33	8	282	25	11.28	-	-	10	-	4391	2243	67	33.47	7-36	3	-
All First	210	285	61	4024	92	17.96	-	11	84	-	43444	22303	847	26.33	9-36	47	6
1-day Int	29	11	8	62	28 *	20.66	-	-	7	-	1485	1097	49	22.38	5-45	2	
C & G	7	5	0	90	25	18.00	-	-	1	-	407	279	14	19.92	5-60	1	
totesport	62	40	10	409	38	13.63	-	-	13	-	2805	2046	76	26.92	4-28	-	
Twenty20	6	6	1	65	31	13.00	-	-	1	-	126	145	5	29.00	2-25	-	

KATICH, S. M. Hampshire

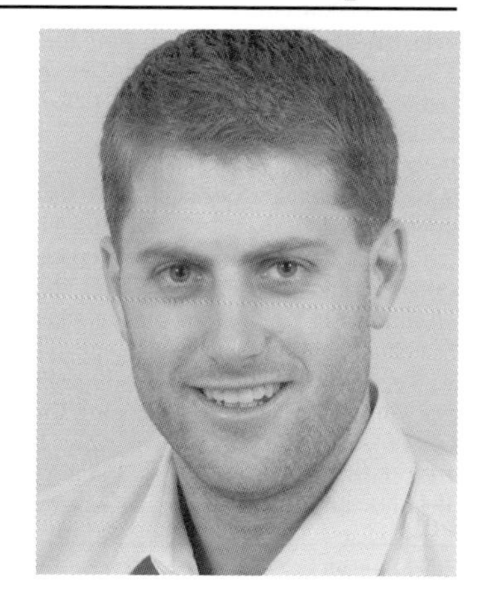

Name: Simon Mathew Katich
Role: Left-hand bat, left-arm wrist-spin bowler
Born: 21 August 1975, Midland, Western Australia
Height: 6ft **Weight:** 12st 8lbs
Nickname: Kat
County debut: 2000 (Durham), 2002 (Yorkshire), 2003 (Hampshire)
County cap: 2000 (Durham), 2003 (Hampshire)
Test debut: 2001
Tests: 9
One-Day Internationals: 6
1000 runs in a season: 2
1st-Class 50s: 46
1st-Class 100s: 25
1st-Class 200s: 1
1st-Class 5 w. in innings: 3
1st-Class catches: 120
One-Day 100s: 2
Place in batting averages: (2003 11th av. 60.15)
Place in bowling averages: (2003 86th av. 34.76)
Strike rate: (career 64.01)
Parents: Vince and Kerry
Marital status: Engaged to Georgie
Education: Trinity College, Perth; University of Western Australia
Qualifications: Bachelor of Commerce degree
Career outside cricket: Entrepreneur
Off-season: Playing in Australia
Overseas tours: Australian Cricket Academy to South Africa 1996; Australia to Sri Lanka and Zimbabwe 1999-2000, to England 2001, to Sri Lanka 2003-04, to India 2004-05, to New Zealand 2004-05; Australia A to South Africa (one-day series) 2002-03 (vice-captain)
Overseas teams played for: Western Australia 1996-97 – 2001-02; New South Wales 2002-03 –; Randwick-Petersham, Sydney
Career highlights to date: 'Making my maiden Test century v India at the SCG'
Cricket moments to forget: 'Any time I drop a catch'
Cricket superstitions: 'Like to wear old gear'
Cricketers particularly admired: Viv Richards
Young players to look out for: Doug Bollinger (NSW), Chris Tremlett

Other sports played: Australian Rules, hockey
Other sports followed: Australian Rules (Richmond), football (Newcastle United)
Favourite band: U2
Relaxations: 'Golf, watching movies and going to the beach in Sydney'
Extras: Attended Commonwealth Bank [Australian] Cricket Academy 1996. Scored 115 in Western Australia's first innings in their 1998-99 Sheffield Shield final victory. *Wisden Australia*'s Sheffield Shield Cricketer of the Year 1998-99. Was Durham's overseas player in 2000. Took over as captain of Western Australia during 2000-01 season after retirement of Tom Moody. Finished the 2000-01 season with a then Western Australian record 1145 Pura Cup runs (av. 71.56), having become the first WA batsman to score a century against each of the other states (including two v Queensland, home and away) in a single season. Was Yorkshire's overseas player during June 2002. Joined New South Wales for 2002-03. Man of the Match in the Pura Cup final v Queensland at Brisbane 2002-03. Joined Hampshire as an overseas player for 2003; returned August to September 2004, deputising for Michael Clarke, absent on international duty; has returned for 2005. Hampshire Cricket Society Player of the Year 2003. Recorded maiden Test five-wicket return (6-65) in the second Test v Zimbabwe at Sydney 2003-04. Scored maiden Test century (125) in the fourth Test v India at Sydney 2003-04, following up with 77* in the second innings. Named State Player of the Year at the 2004 Allan Border Medal awards. Captain of New South Wales since 2004-05
Opinions on cricket: 'The game needs less of the third umpire.'
Best batting: 228* Western Australia v South Australia, Perth 2000-01
Best bowling: 7-130 New South Wales v Victoria, Melbourne 2002-03

2004 Season

	M	Inns	NO	Runs	HS	Avge	100s	50s	Ct	St	O	M	Runs	Wkts	Avge	Best	5wI	10wM
Test																		
All First	4	5	0	183	66	36.60	-	1	3	-	18	1	61	0	-	-	-	-
1-day Int																		
C & G																		
totesport	2	2	0	60	58	30.00	-	1	2	-								
Twenty20																		

Career Performances

	M	Inns	NO	Runs	HS	Avge	100s	50s	Ct	St	Balls	Runs	Wkts	Avge	Best	5wI	10wM
Test	9	15	2	546	125	42.00	1	4	6	-	575	349	11	31.72	6-65	1	-
All First	119	206	30	9030	228 *	51.30	26	46	120	-	4673	2790	73	38.21	7-130	3	-
1-day Int	6	4	2	44	18 *	22.00	-	-	1	-							
C & G	4	4	2	166	82 *	83.00	-	1	2	-							
totesport	38	38	5	1425	106	43.18	2	13	25	-	290	278	8	34.75	2-25	-	
Twenty20	5	5	2	179	59 *	59.66	-	2	1	-							

KEEDY, G. Lancashire

Name: Gary Keedy
Role: Left-hand bat, slow left-arm bowler
Born: 27 November 1974, Wakefield
Height: 5ft 11in **Weight:** 12st 6lbs
Nickname: Keeds
County debut: 1994 (Yorkshire), 1995 (Lancashire)
County cap: 2000 (Lancashire)
50 wickets in a season: 2
1st-Class 50s: 1
1st-Class 5 w. in innings: 18
1st-Class 10 w. in match: 4
1st-Class catches: 36
One-Day 5 w. in innings: 1
Place in batting averages: 278th av. 7.50
Place in bowling averages: 23rd av. 25.68 (2003 38th av. 26.55)
Strike rate: 53.79 (career 70.30)
Parents: Roy and Pat
Wife and date of marriage: Andrea, 12 October 2002
Family links with cricket: Twin brother plays for Castleford in the Yorkshire League
Education: Garforth Comprehensive
Qualifications: 8 GCSEs, Level 2 coaching award
Off-season: 12-month contract
Overseas tours: England U18 to South Africa 1992-93, to Denmark 1993; England U19 to Sri Lanka 1993-94; Lancashire to Portugal 1995, to Jamaica 1996, to South Africa 1997
Overseas teams played for: Frankston, Melbourne 1995-96
Career highlights to date: 'Probably bowling Yorkshire out at Headingley. My involvement with Lancashire in general; receiving my county cap was a proud moment'
Cricketers particularly admired: Shane Warne, Graham Gooch
Young players to look out for: Kyle Hogg
Other sports played: Football, snooker
Other sports followed: Football (Leeds United), rugby league (Leeds Rhinos)
Relaxations: PlayStation
Extras: Player of the Series for England U19 v West Indies U19 1993; also played v India U19 1994. Graduate of the Yorkshire Cricket Academy. His match return of 10-155 v Durham at Old Trafford 2000 included second innings figures of 6-56 from 50 overs. Had match figures of 14-227 (7-95/7-132) v Gloucestershire at Old Trafford 2004, the best return by an English spinner since Martyn Ball's 14-169 in 1993. Leading English wicket-taker (second overall) in the Championship 2004 (72 at 25.68)

Opinions on cricket: 'Too many Italian-looking, Greek-speaking Dutchmen who were educated in South Africa and live in Australia who have played for New Zealand but aren't considered to be overseas players in the English domestic game!'
Best batting: 57 Lancashire v Yorkshire, Headingley 2002
Best bowling: 7-95 Lancashire v Gloucestershire, Old Trafford 2004

2004 Season

	M	Inns	NO	Runs	HS	Avge	100s	50s	Ct	St	O	M	Runs	Wkts	Avge	Best	5wI	10wM
Test																		
All First	16	20	8	90	17	7.50	-	-	7	-	645.3	122	1849	72	25.68	7-95	6	1
1-day Int																		
C & G																		
totesport	5	3	2	6	3 *	6.00	-	-	-	-	39	1	168	6	28.00	2-33	-	
Twenty20	7	1	0	0	0	0.00	-	-	1	-	23	0	138	10	13.80	3-25	-	

Career Performances

	M	Inns	NO	Runs	HS	Avge	100s	50s	Ct	St	Balls	Runs	Wkts	Avge	Best	5wI	10wM
Test																	
All First	123	141	71	769	57	10.98	-	1	36	-	25519	11887	363	32.74	7-95	18	4
1-day Int																	
C & G	1	0	0	0	0	-	-	-	-	-	60	40	1	40.00	1-40	-	
totesport	20	7	4	19	10 *	6.33	-	-	1	-	772	664	21	31.61	5-30	1	
Twenty20	7	1	0	0	0	0.00	-	-	1	-	138	138	10	13.80	3-25	-	

48. Two non-Test-playing teams appeared in the 1975 World Cup. Sri Lanka, at the time, was one of these. Which was the other?

KEEGAN, C. B. Middlesex

Name: Chad Blake Keegan
Role: Right-hand bat, right-arm fast-medium bowler
Born: 30 July 1979, Sandton, Johannesburg, South Africa
Height: 6ft 1in **Weight:** 12st
Nickname: Wick
County debut: 2001
County cap: 2003
50 wickets in a season: 1
1st-Class 5 w. in innings: 5
1st-Class catches: 11
One-Day 5 w. in innings: 2
Place in batting averages: (2003 246th av. 15.88)
Place in bowling averages: 33rd av. 27.50 (2003 63rd av. 30.55)
Strike rate: 48.30 (career 56.42)
Parents: Sharon and Blake
Marital status: Single
Education: Durban High School
Qualifications: YMCA fitness instructor
Overseas tours: MCC to Argentina and Chile 2001
Overseas teams played for: Durban High School Old Boys 1994-97; Crusaders, Durban 1998-99
Career highlights to date: 'Being awarded Player of the Year for Middlesex 2003'
Cricket moments to forget: 'Losing my pants diving for a ball at Lord's'
Cricket superstitions: 'Tapping the bat either side of the crease three times'
Cricketers particularly admired: Malcolm Marshall, Neil Johnson
Other sports played: 'Any extreme sports, golf'
Other sports followed: Football (Liverpool)
Favourite band: Jack Johnson
Relaxations: 'Making and listening to music (guitar); sketching'
Extras: Represented KwaZulu-Natal U13, KwaZulu-Natal Schools, KwaZulu-Natal U19, KwaZulu-Natal Academy. MCC Young Cricketer. Middlesex Player of the Year 2003. Is not considered an overseas player
Best batting: 44 Middlesex v Surrey, The Oval 2004
Best bowling: 6-114 Middlesex v Leicestershire, Southgate 2003

2004 Season

	M	Inns	NO	Runs	HS	Avge	100s	50s	Ct	St	O	M	Runs	Wkts	Avge	Best	5wI	10wM
Test																		
All First	5	4	0	75	44	18.75	-	-	2	-	161	29	550	20	27.50	5-36	2	-
1-day Int																		
C & G	3	2	0	52	26	26.00	-	-	-	-	24	1	122	4	30.50	3-47	-	
totesport	10	6	1	40	11 *	8.00	-	-	6	-	69	5	346	13	26.61	3-28	-	
Twenty20	1	1	0	42	42	42.00	-	-	2	-	4	0	40	0	-	-	-	

Career Performances

	M	Inns	NO	Runs	HS	Avge	100s	50s	Ct	St	Balls	Runs	Wkts	Avge	Best	5wI	10wM
Test																	
All First	38	44	5	448	44	11.48	-	-	11	-	6771	3918	120	32.65	6-114	5	-
1-day Int																	
C & G	6	5	3	97	29 *	48.50	-	-	1	-	322	234	10	23.40	4-35	-	
totesport	52	33	8	357	50	14.28	-	1	13	-	2392	1858	75	24.77	5-17	2	
Twenty20	6	6	1	122	42	24.40	-	-	3	-	138	191	5	38.20	3-34	-	

KENDALL, W. S. Hampshire

Name: William (Will) Salwey Kendall
Role: Right-hand bat, right-arm medium bowler
Born: 18 December 1973, Wimbledon, London
Height: 5ft 10in **Weight:** 12st 7lbs
Nickname: Villy, Wilbur, Baldy, Fish
County debut: 1996
County cap: 1999
1000 runs in a season: 3
1st-Class 50s: 33
1st-Class 100s: 9
1st-Class 200s: 1
1st-Class catches: 118
One-Day 100s: 1
Place in batting averages: 229th av. 18.30 (2003 140th av. 30.07)
Strike rate: 36.00 (career 86.40)
Parents: Tom and Sue
Wife and date of marriage: Emily, 27 September 2002
Children: Lucia Charlotte, 20 May 2004
Family links with cricket: Father played club cricket with East Horsley, Hampshire

Hogs and MCC. Older brother James played for Durham University. Younger brother, Ed, took new ball for Nottingham University
Education: Bradfield College, Berkshire; Keble College, Oxford University
Qualifications: 10 GCSEs, 3 A-levels, 1 AS-level, BA (Hons) Modern History
Career outside cricket: 'Considering a few options'
Off-season: 'Mapping out a new career'
Overseas tours: Bradfield College to Barbados 1991; Troubadours to Argentina 1997; Hampshire CCC to Anguilla 1997, to Cape Town 2001; MCC to Kenya 2001-02, to West Africa 2003
Overseas teams played for: Frankston Peninsula CC, Melbourne 1997-98; Alma Marist CC, Cape Town 2003
Career highlights: 'Being part of the Hampshire side that beat the Aussies in 2001 – an unforgettable three days. Receiving my county cap on the same day I made my career best score v Sussex 1999'
Cricket moments to forget: 'Any very short innings'
Cricket superstitions: 'None'
Cricketers particularly admired: Robin Smith, Graham Thorpe, Mark Ramprakash, Shane Warne, 'and anyone playing over 36'
Young players to look out for: Jimmy Adams, James Tomlinson, Kevin Latouf, Tom Burrows
Other sports played: Hockey (Oxford Blue), football (Independent Schools 1992, Old Bradfieldians, Corinthian Casuals; offered terms by Reading), squash, golf
Other sports followed: 'All sports; an interest in Tottenham Hotspur FC'
Favourite band: Rolling Stones
Relaxations: 'Playing or watching sport; spending time with friends and family; hacking up golf courses; travelling; and quiet days with wife, Emily'
Extras: Surrey Young Cricketer of the Year 1992. Awarded Gray-Nicolls Trophy for Schoolboy Cricketer of the Year in memory of Len Newbery 1992. Made first-class debut for Oxford University in 1994. Hampshire Exiles Player of the Year for 1996. Hampshire Cricket Society Player of the Year 2000. Vice-captain of Hampshire 2001-02. Retired from county cricket at the end of the 2004 season
Opinions on cricket: 'We clearly need to up the standard, but regional cricket is not the answer. Why not restrict full-time county staffs to 17-18, abandon registration and allow all players outside of this core to be free agents? Counties could receive less central funding and be allowed to sink or swim – the cream will soon rise. And bring back an "A" side for summer and winter matches. They should truly be England's 2nd XI. [Also] every county should be compelled to field at least eight current English-qualified players in every team. How they fill the three remaining places is up to them.'
Best batting: 201 Hampshire v Sussex, Southampton 1999
Best bowling: 3-37 Oxford University v Derbyshire, The Parks 1995

2004 Season

	M	Inns	NO	Runs	HS	Avge	100s	50s	Ct	St	O	M	Runs	Wkts	Avge	Best	5wI	10wM
Test																		
All First	8	14	1	238	50	18.30	-	1	7	-	12	2	44	2	22.00	1-12	-	-
1-day Int																		
C & G	2	2	0	55	53	27.50	-	1	-	-	2.5	0	23	1	23.00	1-23	-	
totesport	6	5	1	107	55 *	26.75	-	1	2	-								
Twenty20																		

Career Performances

	M	Inns	NO	Runs	HS	Avge	100s	50s	Ct	St	Balls	Runs	Wkts	Avge	Best	5wI	10wM
Test																	
All First	140	230	25	6822	201	33.27	10	33	118	-	1296	736	15	49.06	3-37	-	-
1-day Int																	
C & G	14	11	2	203	53	22.55	-	1	8	-	59	49	2	24.50	1-8	-	
totesport	93	81	12	1588	110 *	23.01	1	6	45	-	84	98	1	98.00	1-32	-	
Twenty20	4	3	0	13	12	4.33	-	-	1	-							

KENWAY, D. A. — Hampshire

Name: Derek Anthony Kenway
Role: Right-hand bat, right-arm off-spin bowler, part-time wicket-keeper
Born: 12 June 1978, Fareham
Height: 5ft 11in **Weight:** 14st
Nickname: Kenners
County debut: 1997
County cap: 2001
1000 runs in a season: 1
1st-Class 50s: 20
1st-Class 100s: 7
1st-Class catches: 82
1st-Class stumpings: 1
One-Day 100s: 1
Place in batting averages: 177th av. 25.09 (2003 158th av. 28.14)
Strike rate: (career 37.50)
Parents: Keith and Geraldine
Marital status: Single
Family links with cricket: 'Brother Richard plays local cricket and has played some 2nd XI'
Education: St George's, Southampton; Barton Peveril College

Qualifications: 6 GCSEs, Level 2 coaching
Career outside cricket: 'Family own roofing company'
Overseas tours: West of England U15 to West Indies 1993; ECB National Academy to Australia 2001-02
Overseas teams played for: Beaumaris CC, Melbourne 1997-98
Career highlights to date: 'The win against Australia for Hants [2001]'
Cricket moments to forget: 'Leaving a straight one from Welchy on debut'
Cricketers particularly admired: Robin Smith
Young players to look out for: Dave Adams, Jon Doe
Other sports played: Golf, football ('locally')
Other sports followed: Football (Southampton FC)
Favourite band: U2
Relaxations: 'Quiet pint down the local; spending time with my girlfriend'
Extras: *Daily Telegraph* Batting Award (West) 1994. Southern League Young Player of the Year 1996. NBC Denis Compton Award 1999. Hampshire Cricket Society Player of the Year 2001. Scored half-century (60) in ECB National Academy's innings victory over Commonwealth Bank [Australian] Cricket Academy at Adelaide 2001-02
Opinions on cricket: 'Standard has improved with two overseas players. Things should be left alone for a while as too many changes can't be good for the English game.'
Best batting: 166 Hampshire v Nottinghamshire, West End 2001
Best bowling: 1-5 Hampshire v Warwickshire, Southampton 1997

2004 Season

	M	Inns	NO	Runs	HS	Avge	100s	50s	Ct	St	O	M	Runs	Wkts	Avge	Best	5wI	10wM
Test																		
All First	14	23	1	552	101	25.09	1	1	9	-	2	2	0	0	-	-	-	-
1-day Int																		
C & G	2	2	0	18	18	9.00	-	-	2	-	2.5	0	16	1	16.00	1-16	-	
totesport	9	8	0	101	41	12.62	-	-	7	-								
Twenty20																		

Career Performances

	M	Inns	NO	Runs	HS	Avge	100s	50s	Ct	St	Balls	Runs	Wkts	Avge	Best	5wI	10wM
Test																	
All First	92	161	15	4362	166	29.87	7	20	82	1	150	159	4	39.75	1-5	-	-
1-day Int																	
C & G	7	7	0	250	76	35.71	-	2	3	1	17	16	1	16.00	1-16	-	
totesport	79	74	2	1809	115	25.12	1	12	46	5							
Twenty20	5	5	0	115	40	23.00	-	-	2	-							

KEY, R. W. T. Kent

Name: Robert William Trevor Key
Role: Right-hand bat, off-spin bowler
Born: 12 May 1979, Dulwich, London
Height: 6ft 1in **Weight:** 12st 7lbs
Nickname: Keysy
County debut: 1998
County cap: 2001
Test debut: 2002
Tests: 12
One-Day Internationals: 5
1000 runs in a season: 3
1st-Class 50s: 31
1st-Class 100s: 23
1st-Class 200s: 1
1st-Class catches: 84
One-Day 100s: 1
Place in batting averages: 1st av. 79.00 (2003 90th av. 37.70)
Parents: Trevor and Lynn
Marital status: Single
Family links with cricket: Mother played for Kent Ladies. Father played club cricket in Derby. Sister Elizabeth played for her junior school side
Education: Langley Park Boys' School
Qualifications: 10 GCSEs, NCA coaching award, GNVQ Business Studies
Overseas tours: Kent U13 to Holland; England U17 to Bermuda (International Youth Tournament) 1997 (captain); England U19 to South Africa (including U19 World Cup) 1997-98; England A to Zimbabwe and South Africa 1998-99; ECB National Academy to Australia 2001-02, to Sri Lanka 2002-03; England to Australia 2002-03, to South Africa 2004-05
Overseas teams played for: Greenpoint CC, Cape Town 1996-97
Cricket moments to forget: 'Any time I have lost to Min at cards'
Cricketers particularly admired: Min Patel, Neil Taylor, Alan Wells, Mark Ealham 'for his enthusiasm'
Other sports played: Hockey, football, snooker, tennis (played for county)
Other sports followed: Football (Chelsea), basketball (Chicago Bulls)
Extras: Played for England U19 v Zimbabwe U19 1997 and captained England U17 to victory in the International Youth Tournament in Bermuda in July. Played for England U19 World Cup winning side in South Africa 1997-98; England U19 Man of the Series v Pakistan U19 1998 (award shared with Graeme Swann). NBC Denis Compton Award for the most promising young Kent player 2001. Scored 174* for England XI v Australia A at Hobart 2002-03. Scored two centuries in match

(114/117*) v New Zealanders at Canterbury 2004, becoming the third batsman to score twin centuries for Kent against a touring team. Scored 180 (his fifth century in seven first-class innings) v Lancashire at Tunbridge Wells on 2 June 2004, in the process becoming the quickest to 1000 first-class runs in a season since Graeme Hick in 1988. Scored maiden first-class double century (221; his maiden Test century) in the first Test v West Indies at Lord's 2004, in the process sharing with Andrew Strauss (137) in a record second-wicket stand for Test cricket at Lord's (291). Scored 93* to help England to victory in the third Test v West Indies at Old Trafford 2004. Leading run-scorer in English first-class cricket 2004 with 1896 runs at 79.00, including nine centuries

Best batting: 221 England v West Indies, Lord's 2004

Stop press: Scored 83 in the fourth Test v South Africa at Johannesburg 2004-05, in the process sharing with Andrew Strauss (147) in a ground record stand for the second wicket in Tests (182)

2004 Season

	M	Inns	NO	Runs	HS	Avge	100s	50s	Ct	St	O	M	Runs	Wkts	Avge	Best	5wI	10wM
Test	4	7	1	378	221	63.00	1	1	3	-								
All First	16	27	3	1896	221	79.00	9	3	8	-								
1-day Int	3	3	0	43	19	14.33	-	-	-	-								
C & G	2	2	1	106	61 *	106.00	-	1	-	-								
totesport	9	9	0	116	29	12.88	-	-	1	-								
Twenty20	3	3	1	114	66 *	57.00	-	1	-	-								

Career Performances

	M	Inns	NO	Runs	HS	Avge	100s	50s	Ct	St	Balls	Runs	Wkts	Avge	Best	5wI	10wM
Test	12	20	1	622	221	32.73	1	2	9	-							
All First	127	217	11	8061	221	39.13	24	31	84	-	74	44	0	-	-	-	-
1-day Int	5	5	0	54	19	10.80	-	-	-	-							
C & G	15	15	2	611	77	47.00	-	6	2	-							
totesport	72	68	6	1777	114	28.66	1	11	10	-							
Twenty20	3	3	1	114	66 *	57.00	-	1	-	-							

49. Which former Essex opener played for Argentina in the 1979 ICC Trophy?

KHALID, S. A. — Worcestershire

Name: Shaftab Ahmad Khalid
Role: Right-hand bat, right-arm off-spin bowler
Born: 6 October 1982, Pakistan
Height: 5ft 11in **Weight:** 10st 6lbs
Nickname: Shafi
County debut: 2003
County colours: 2003
1st-Class catches: 3
Place in bowling averages: (2003 80th av. 33.40)
Strike rate: 129.75 (career 84.57)
Parents: Dr Khalid Mahmood and Mrs Nuzhat Bano
Marital status: Single
Education: Dormers Wells High School; West Thames College
Qualifications: 11 GCSEs, 3 A-levels, studying for LLB degree
Overseas tours: England A to Malaysia and India 2003-04
Extras: ECB National Academy 2003-04. NBC Denis Compton Award for the most promising young Worcestershire player 2003
Best batting: 15 England A v Tamil Nadu, Chennai 2003-04
Best bowling: 4-131 Worcestershire v Northamptonshire, Northampton 2003

2004 Season

	M	Inns	NO	Runs	HS	Avge	100s	50s	Ct	St	O	M	Runs	Wkts	Avge	Best	5wI	10wM
Test																		
All First	3	3	2	7	6 *	7.00	-	-	1	-	86.3	17	277	4	69.25	2-20	-	-
1-day Int																		
C & G	1	1	1	9	9 *	-	-	-	-	-								
totesport	3	0	0	0	0	-	-	-	1	-	13	2	46	0	-	-	-	
Twenty20																		

Career Performances

	M	Inns	NO	Runs	HS	Avge	100s	50s	Ct	St	Balls	Runs	Wkts	Avge	Best	5wI	10wM
Test																	
All First	9	7	2	44	15	8.80	-	-	3	-	1184	673	14	48.07	4-131	-	-
1-day Int																	
C & G	1	1	1	9	9 *	-	-	-	-	-							
totesport	6	2	2	4	3 *	-	-	-	1	-	174	138	2	69.00	2-40	-	
Twenty20	1	0	0	0	0	-	-	-	-	-	6	13	0	-	-	-	

KHAN, A. Kent

Name: Amjad Khan
Role: Right-hand bat, right-arm fast bowler
Born: 14 October 1980, Copenhagen, Denmark
Height: 6ft **Weight:** 11st 6lbs
Nickname: Ammy
County debut: 2001
50 wickets in a season: 1
1st-Class 50s: 2
1st-Class 5 w. in innings: 4
1st-Class catches: 6
Place in batting averages: 249th av. 15.28 (2003 198th av. 23.60)
Place in bowling averages: 105th av. 37.80 (2003 136th av. 46.88)
Strike rate: 51.15 (career 49.23)
Parents: Aslam and Raisa
Marital status: Single
Education: Skolen på Duevej, Denmark; Falkonĕrgårdens Gymnasium
Off-season: 'Winter training in Perth'
Overseas tours: Denmark U19 to Canada 1996, to Bermuda 1997, to South Africa (U19 World Cup) 1997-98, to Wales 1998, to Ireland 1999; Denmark to Holland 1998, to Zimbabwe (ICC Emerging Nations Tournament) 1999-2000, to Canada (ICC Trophy) 2001
Overseas teams played for: Kjøbenhavns Boldklub, Denmark
Cricket moments to forget: 'I try to forget most of the games where I didn't perform as well as I would like'
Cricketers particularly admired: Wasim Akram, Dennis Lillee
Young players to look out for: Kashif Qureshi
Other sports followed: Football (Denmark)
Favourite band: Marvin Gaye, George Michael, Nerd (Neptunes)
Relaxations: 'Music, sleeping, reading'
Extras: Youngest Danish international ever, at age of 17. Played for Denmark in the NatWest Trophy 1999 and 2000. Recorded maiden first-class five-wicket return (6-52) v Yorkshire at Canterbury 2002 in his third Championship match. Took 6-56 and then scored maiden first-class fifty (58) v Sussex at Hove 2002. Took 50 first-class wickets (63) in his first full season 2002. NBC Denis Compton Award for the most promising young Kent player 2002. Is not considered an overseas player
Best batting: 78 Kent v Middlesex, Lord's 2003
Best bowling: 6-52 Kent v Yorkshire, Canterbury 2002

2004 Season

	M	Inns	NO	Runs	HS	Avge	100s	50s	Ct	St	O	M	Runs	Wkts	Avge	Best	5wI	10wM
Test																		
All First	9	9	2	107	29	15.28	-	-	-	-	170.3	24	756	20	37.80	4-47	-	-
1-day Int																		
C & G	1	0	0	0	0	-	-	-	1	-	9	2	34	2	17.00	2-34	-	
totesport	3	2	1	14	9	14.00	-	-	-	-	14	1	83	2	41.50	2-42	-	
Twenty20	5	3	0	16	15	5.33	-	-	-	-	19	0	160	8	20.00	2-25	-	

Career Performances

	M	Inns	NO	Runs	HS	Avge	100s	50s	Ct	St	Balls	Runs	Wkts	Avge	Best	5wI	10wM
Test																	
All First	34	38	7	556	78	17.93	-	2	6	-	4973	3603	101	35.67	6-52	4	-
1-day Int																	
C & G	6	3	0	15	13	5.00	-	-	3	-	279	232	7	33.14	2-34	-	
totesport	13	10	3	62	21	8.85	-	-	1	-	486	414	15	27.60	4-26	-	
Twenty20	5	3	0	16	15	5.33	-	-	-	-	114	160	8	20.00	2-25	-	

KHAN, R. M. — Derbyshire

Name: Rawait Mahmood Khan
Role: Right-hand bat
Born: 5 March 1982, Birmingham
Height: 5ft 9in **Weight:** 9st 7lbs
Nickname: Ray
County debut: 2001
1st-Class 50s: 3
1st-Class catches: 10
Place in batting averages: (2003 219th av. 21.00)
Parents: Hashim Khan and Barish Begum
Marital status: Single
Family links with cricket: Father played for Warwickshire 2nd XI. Brother Zubair was also with Derbyshire
Education: Moseley School; Solihull College
Cricketers particularly admired: Steve Waugh
Other sports played: Football, badminton
Relaxations: 'Socialising with friends'

Extras: Played for Derbyshire Board XI in the NatWest 2000. Scored 91 v Indians at Derby 2002 in his second first-class match. Released by Derbyshire at the end of the 2004 season

Best batting: 91 Derbyshire v Indians, Derby 2002

2004 Season

	M	Inns	NO	Runs	HS	Avge	100s	50s	Ct	St	O	M	Runs	Wkts	Avge	Best	5wI	10wM
Test																		
All First																		
1-day Int																		
C & G																		
totesport	1	1	0	2	2	2.00	-	-	-	-	2	0	20	0	-	-	-	
Twenty20																		

Career Performances

	M	Inns	NO	Runs	HS	Avge	100s	50s	Ct	St	Balls	Runs	Wkts	Avge	Best	5wI	10wM
Test																	
All First	18	31	1	611	91	20.36	-	3	10	-	36	28	0	-	-	-	-
1-day Int																	
C & G	1	1	0	29	29	29.00	-	-	-	-							
totesport	3	3	0	9	5	3.00	-	-	1	-	12	20	0	-	-	-	
Twenty20																	

KHAN, Z. Surrey

Name: Zaheer Khan

Role: Right-hand bat, left-arm fast-medium bowler

Born: 7 October 1978, Shrirampur, Maharashtra, India

County debut: 2004

Test debut: 2000-01

Tests: 29

One-Day Internationals: 86

1st-Class 5 w. in innings: 13

1st-Class 10 w. in match: 3

1st-Class catches: 21

Strike rate: 160.00 (career 54.06)

Overseas tours: India to Kenya (ICC Knockout Trophy) 2000-01, to Bangladesh 2000-01, to Zimbabwe 2001, to Sri Lanka 2001, to South Africa 2001-02, to West Indies 2001-02, to England 2002, to Sri Lanka (ICC

Champions Trophy) 2002-03, to New Zealand 2002-03, to Africa (World Cup) 2002-03, to Australia 2003-04, to Pakistan 2003-04, to Bangladesh 2004-05, plus other one-day tournaments in Abu Dhabi (India A), Sharjah, Bangladesh and Sri Lanka
Overseas teams played for: Baroda 1999-2000 –
Extras: One of *Indian Cricket*'s five Cricketers of the Year 2002. His match awards include Man of the Match in the Ranji Trophy final 2000-01 v Railways at Vadodara (3-92/5-43) and v New Zealand at Centurion in the World Cup 2002-03 (4-42). Struck a six off each of the final four balls of the Indian innings in the third ODI v Zimbabwe at Jodhpur 2000-01. Played two games for Surrey as an amateur in May 2004 as a replacement for the injured Saqlain Mushtaq, taking a wicket (Will Jefferson) with his first ball for the county v Essex at The Oval in the totesport League
Best batting: 48 Baroda v Maharashtra, Pune 1999-2000
Best bowling: 6-25 Baroda v Punjab, Vadodara 2001-02
Stop press: Scored 75 in the first Test v Bangladesh at Dhaka 2004-05, setting a new record highest score for a No. 11 in Tests

2004 Season

	M	Inns	NO	Runs	HS	Avge	100s	50s	Ct	St	O	M	Runs	Wkts	Avge	Best	5wI	10wM
Test																		
All First	1	1	1	2	2 *	-	-	-	-	-	26.4	2	101	1	101.00	1-48	-	-
1-day Int																		
C & G																		
totesport	1	1	0	0	0	0.00	-	-	1	-	7	0	36	2	18.00	2-36	-	
Twenty20																		

Career Performances

	M	Inns	NO	Runs	HS	Avge	100s	50s	Ct	St	Balls	Runs	Wkts	Avge	Best	5wI	10wM
Test	29	37	7	278	46	9.26	-	-	9	-	5355	2918	83	35.15	5-29	3	-
All First	55	69	12	731	48	12.82	-	-	21	-	10812	5870	200	29.35	6-25	13	3
1-day Int	86	45	18	326	34 *	12.07	-	-	20	-	4236	3439	128	26.86	4-19	-	
C & G																	
totesport	1	1	0	0	0	0.00	-	-	1	-	42	36	2	18.00	2-36	-	
Twenty20																	

50. Which Aberdeen-born batsman scored 133* for Scotland v Kenya in the 2004 ICC Inter-Continental Cup semi-finals and made six first-class appearances for Durham in the same year?

KILLEEN, N. Durham

Name: Neil Killeen
Role: Right-hand bat, right-arm medium-fast bowler
Born: 17 October 1975, Shotley Bridge
Height: 6ft 1in **Weight:** 15st
Nickname: Killer, Bully, Quinny, Squeaky, Bull
County debut: 1995
County cap: 1999
50 wickets in a season: 1
1st-Class 5 w. in innings: 7
1st-Class catches: 20
One-Day 5 w. in innings: 4
Place in batting averages: 246th av. 15.82 (2003 285th av. 7.85)
Place in bowling averages: 153rd av. 55.57 (2003 98th av. 36.38)
Strike rate: 108.52 (career 62.78)
Parents: Glen and Thora
Wife and date of marriage: Clare Louise, 5 February 2000
Children: Jonathan David
Family links with cricket: 'Dad best armchair player in the game'
Education: Greencroft Comprehensive School; Derwentside College, University of Teesside
Qualifications: 8 GCSEs, 2 A-levels, first year Sports Science, Level III coaching award, Level I staff coach
Career outside cricket: Cricket coaching
Overseas tours: Durham CCC to Zimbabwe 1992; England U19 to West Indies 1994-95; MCC to Bangladesh 1999-2000
Career highlights to date: 'My county cap and first-class debut'
Cricket moments to forget: 'Injury causing me to miss most of 2001 season'
Cricketers particularly admired: Ian Botham, Curtly Ambrose, Courtney Walsh, David Boon
Other sports played: Athletics (English Schools javelin)
Sports followed: Football (Sunderland AFC), cricket (Anfield Plain CC)
Relaxations: 'Good food, good wine; golf; spending time with wife and family'
Extras: Was first Durham bowler to take five wickets in a Sunday League game (5-26 v Northamptonshire at Northampton 1995). Scored 35 batting at No. 10 as Durham made 453-9 to beat Somerset at Taunton 2004 in the fourth-highest successful run chase in the history of the County Championship. Had figures of 8.3-7-5-2 v Derbyshire at Riverside in the totesport League 2004

Best batting: 48 Durham v Somerset, Riverside 1995
Best bowling: 7-70 Durham v Hampshire, Riverside 2003

2004 Season

	M	Inns	NO	Runs	HS	Avge	100s	50s	Ct	St	O	M	Runs	Wkts	Avge	Best	5wI	10wM
Test																		
All First	13	22	5	269	35 *	15.82	-	-	1	-	343.4	83	1056	19	55.57	2-39	-	-
1-day Int																		
C & G	1	1	0	29	29	29.00	-	-	-	-	9.4	2	27	1	27.00	1-27	-	
totesport	18	9	5	24	7	6.00	-	-	4	-	128.2	30	458	24	19.08	4-24	-	
Twenty20	5	3	1	20	8	10.00	-	-	-	-	17.1	1	111	9	12.33	4-7	-	

Career Performances

	M	Inns	NO	Runs	HS	Avge	100s	50s	Ct	St	Balls	Runs	Wkts	Avge	Best	5wI	10wM
Test																	
All First	84	126	26	1186	48	11.86	-	-	20	-	13875	7005	221	31.69	7-70	7	-
1-day Int																	
C & G	11	7	1	52	29	8.66	-	-	1	-	586	346	14	24.71	2-15	-	
totesport	120	69	29	408	32	10.20	-	-	21	-	5403	3920	172	22.79	6-31	4	
Twenty20	10	6	3	40	17 *	13.33	-	-	1	-	216	261	18	14.50	4-7	-	

KING, R. D. — Durham

Name: Reon Dane King
Role: Right-hand bat, right-arm fast-medium bowler
Born: 6 October 1975, Good Fortune, West Coast Demerara, Guyana
County debut: 2004
Test debut: 1998-99
Tests: 14
One-Day Internationals: 48
1st-Class 5 w. in innings: 10
1st-Class 10 w. in match: 1
1st-Class catches: 10
Strike rate: 46.60 (career 53.04)
Overseas tours: West Indies U19 to Pakistan 1995-96; West Indies A to South Africa 1997-98, to Bangladesh (one-day series) 1998-99, to India 1998-99, to England 2002; West Indies to Bangladesh (Wills International Cup) 1998-99, to South Africa 1998-99, to UK, Ireland and Holland (World Cup) 1999, to Bangladesh 1999-2000, to New Zealand 1999-2000, to England 2000,

to Zimbabwe and Kenya 2001, to Sri Lanka 2001-02, to Australia 2004-05 (VB Series), plus one-day tournaments in Singapore, Toronto and Sharjah
Overseas teams played for: Northerns, South Africa 2003-04; Guyana 1994-95 –
Extras: Represented West Indies U19 v England U19 1994-95. His match awards include Man of the Match in ODI v Pakistan in Grenada 1999-2000 (3-38). Was an overseas player with Durham at the start of 2004, deputising for Shoaib Akhtar, absent on international duty
Best batting: 30 Guyana v Leeward Islands, Charlestown 1996-97
Best bowling: 7-82 Guyana v Indians, Georgetown 1996-97

2004 Season

	M	Inns	NO	Runs	HS	Avge	100s	50s	Ct	St	O	M	Runs	Wkts	Avge	Best	5wI	10wM
Test																		
All First	2	4	0	4	3	1.00	-	-	1	-	38.5	6	206	5	41.20	3-120	-	-
1-day Int																		
C & G																		
totesport																		
Twenty20																		

Career Performances

	M	Inns	NO	Runs	HS	Avge	100s	50s	Ct	St	Balls	Runs	Wkts	Avge	Best	5wI	10wM
Test	14	19	5	50	12 *	3.57	-	-	2	-	2485	1222	44	27.77	5-51	1	-
All First	76	96	32	391	30	6.10	-	-	10	-	13262	6496	250	25.98	7-82	10	1
1-day Int	48	22	13	62	12 *	6.88	-	-	4	-	2483	1696	73	23.23	4-25	-	
C & G																	
totesport																	
Twenty20																	

KING, R. E. — Northamptonshire

Name: Richard Eric King
Role: Right-hand bat, left-arm medium-fast bowler; all-rounder
Born: 3 January 1984, Hitchin
Height: 6ft **Weight:** 13st
Nickname: Kingy
County debut: No first-team appearance
Strike rate: (career 351.00)
Parents: Roger and Rosemary
Marital status: Single
Education: Bedford Modern School; Loughborough University
Qualifications: 10 GCSEs, 3 A-levels, Level 2 ECB coach
Overseas tours: Bedford Modern to Barbados 1999; Northamptonshire YC to South Africa 2002

Cricket superstitions: 'Right pad on before left'
Cricketers particularly admired: Ian Botham, Shane Warne, Viv Richards, Chris Park
Young players to look out for: Jono Shantry, Matt Hooke, Emily Kortlang
Other sports played: Rugby (East Midlands), golf
Other sports followed: Football (Arsenal)
Favourite band: Lifehouse
Relaxations: 'Listening to music, socialising, extra training'
Extras: MCC Taverners U15 Young Cricketer of the Year. Broke school record with 200* (from 140 balls) in 2001. Played for Northamptonshire Board XI in the C&G 2002 and 2003. Northamptonshire Academy 2002. Captained ECB Schools XI v India U19 at Wellington College 2002. Played for Loughborough University CCE 2003. Is a Northamptonshire Emerging Player

Opinions on cricket: 'Too much cricket played in summer means players often not performing at full capacity. Two overseas players per team is hindering progression of young home-grown cricketers, especially when the ECB are pumping funds into county academies.'
Best batting: 17 LUCCE v Somerset, Taunton 2003
Best bowling: 1-108 LUCCE v Surrey, The Oval 2003

2004 Season (did not make any first-class or one-day appearances)

Career Performances

	M	Inns	NO	Runs	HS	Avge	100s	50s	Ct	St	Balls	Runs	Wkts	Avge	Best	5wI	10wM
Test																	
All First	3	5	0	19	17	3.80	-	-	-	-	351	313	1	313.00	1-108	-	-
1-day Int																	
C & G	2	2	0	2	2	1.00	-	-	1	-	90	66	2	33.00	2-39	-	
totesport																	
Twenty20																	

KIRBY, S. P. — Gloucestershire

Name: Steven Paul Kirby
Role: Right-hand bat, right-arm fast bowler
Born: 4 October 1977, Bury, Lancashire
Height: 6ft 3in **Weight:** 13st 5lbs
Nickname: Tango
County debut: 2001 (Yorkshire)
County cap: 2003 (Yorkshire)
50 wickets in a season: 1
1st-Class 50s: 1
1st-Class 5 w. in innings: 9
1st-Class 10 w. in match: 3
1st-Class catches: 13
Place in batting averages: 288th av. 3.54 (2003 284th av. 8.07)
Place in bowling averages: 94th av. 36.51 (2003 36th av. 26.40)
Strike rate: 63.32 (career 46.72)
Parents: Paul and Alison
Wife and date of marriage: Sasha, 11 October 2003
Education: Elton High School, Walshaw, Bury, Lancs; Bury College
Qualifications: 10 GCSEs, BTEC/GNVQ Advanced Leisure and Tourism
Career outside cricket: 'Coaching, teaching'
Off-season: 'Coaching award Level 3; studying to be a teacher'
Overseas tours: Yorkshire to Grenada 2001; ECB National Academy to Australia 2001-02; England A to India 2003-04
Overseas teams played for: Egmont Plains, New Zealand 1997-98
Career highlights to date: 'Getting Yorkshire county cap; Australia tour with England academy'
Cricket moments to forget: 'Being knocked out by Nixon McLean trying to take a return catch'
Cricketers particularly admired: Steve Waugh, Richard Hadlee, Glenn McGrath, Michael Atherton, Curtly Ambrose, Sachin Tendulkar
Young players to look out for: Tim Bresnan, John Sadler, Joe Sayers, Liam Plunkett
Other sports played: Basketball, table tennis, squash, golf – 'anything sporty and competitive'
Other sports followed: Football (Manchester United), rugby (Leicester Tigers)
Relaxations: 'Walking the dog; shooting; spending time with family; socialising with friends'
Extras: Formerly with Leicestershire but did not appear for first team. Took 14 wickets (41-18-47-14) in one day for Egmont Plains v Hawera in a New Zealand club match 1997-98. Took 7-50 in Kent's second innings at Headingley 2001, the best

bowling figures by a Yorkshire player on first-class debut (Paul Hutchison's similar figures were on his Championship debut only); Kirby had replaced Matthew Hoggard (called up for England) halfway through the match. Took 12-72 against Leicestershire, his former club, at Headingley 2001. Returned first innings figures of 4-100 in ECB National Academy's victory over Commonwealth Bank [Australian] Cricket Academy in Adelaide 2001-02. Took 13-154 (5-74/8-80) v Somerset at Taunton 2003, the best match return by a Yorkshire bowler for 36 years. Left Yorkshire at the end of the 2004 season and has joined Gloucestershire for 2005

Opinions on cricket: '1. We play too much cricket, which reduces a) intensity; b) recovery; c) preparation. 2. Pitches are too inconsistent, which contributes to a) bad techniques; b) lack of hungry, Test-quality bowlers. 3. Too many EU overseas players with no intentions of playing for England. Reduces opportunity for true English players to improve.'

Best batting: 57 Yorkshire v Hampshire, Headingley 2002

Best bowling: 8-80 Yorkshire v Somerset, Taunton 2003

2004 Season

	M	Inns	NO	Runs	HS	Avge	100s	50s	Ct	St	O	M	Runs	Wkts	Avge	Best	5wI	10wM
Test																		
All First	13	16	5	39	14 *	3.54	-	-	2	-	327.1	53	1132	31	36.51	3-64	-	-
1-day Int																		
C & G																		
totesport	8	1	1	3	3 *	-	-	-	2	-	38.4	1	206	5	41.20	2-27	-	
Twenty20	3	0	0	0	0	-	-	-	1	-	12	0	119	4	29.75	2-22	-	

Career Performances

	M	Inns	NO	Runs	HS	Avge	100s	50s	Ct	St	Balls	Runs	Wkts	Avge	Best	5wI	10wM
Test																	
All First	48	63	14	342	57	6.97	-	1	13	-	8597	5231	184	28.42	8-80	9	3
1-day Int																	
C & G	2	1	0	0	0	0.00	-	-	-	-	102	74	2	37.00	1-21	-	
totesport	25	10	3	38	15	5.42	-	-	6	-	986	919	22	41.77	3-27	-	
Twenty20	3	0	0	0	0	-	-	-	1	-	72	119	4	29.75	2-22	-	

51. Which Kent 'keeper won the Man of the Match award in Ireland's six-wicket one-day victory over the West Indians in 2004?

KIRTLEY, R. J. Sussex

Name: Robert James Kirtley
Role: Right-hand bat, right-arm fast-medium bowler, county vice-captain
Born: 10 January 1975, Eastbourne
Height: 6ft **Weight:** 12st
Nickname: Ambi
County debut: 1995
County cap: 1998
Test debut: 2003
Tests: 4
One-Day Internationals: 11
50 wickets in a season: 6
1st-Class 50s: 3
1st-Class 5 w. in innings: 27
1st-Class 10 w. in match: 4
1st-Class catches: 43
One-Day 5 w. in innings: 3
Place in batting averages: 242nd av. 16.30 (2003 208th av. 22.30)
Place in bowling averages: 100th av. 37.32 (2003 41st av. 26.80)
Strike rate: 72.45 (career 49.92)
Parents: Bob and Pip
Wife and date of marriage: Jenny, 26 October 2002
Family links with cricket: Brother plays league cricket
Education: St Andrews School, Eastbourne; Clifton College, Bristol
Qualifications: 9 GCSEs, 2 A-levels, NCA coaching first level
Career outside cricket: 'Teaching?'
Off-season: 'Spending some time at home'
Overseas tours: Sussex YC to Barbados 1993, to Sri Lanka 1995; Sussex to Grenada 2001; England A to Bangladesh and New Zealand 1999-2000; England to Zimbabwe (one-day series) 2001-02, to Sri Lanka (ICC Champions Trophy) 2002-03, to Australia 2002-03 (VB Series), to Bangladesh and Sri Lanka 2003-04, to West Indies 2003-04 (one-day series)
Overseas teams played for: Mashonaland, Zimbabwe 1996-97; Namibian Cricket Board/Wanderers, Windhoek, Namibia 1998-99
Career highlights to date: 'My Test debut at Trent Bridge'
Cricket moments to forget: 'The three times I've bagged a pair'
Cricket superstitions: 'Put my left boot on first!'
Cricketers particularly admired: Curtly Ambrose, Jim Andrew, Darren Gough
Young players to look out for: Tim Ambrose, Matt Prior
Other sports followed: Rugby (England), football (Brighton & Hove Albion)

Relaxations: 'Inviting friends round for a braai (barbeque) and enjoying a cold beer with them'

Extras: Played in the Mashonaland side which defeated England on their 1996-97 tour of Zimbabwe, taking seven wickets in the match. Winner of an NBC Denis Compton Award for promising cricketers 1997. Took hat-trick (A. Morris, Z. Morris, Aymes) in the B&H v Hampshire at West End 2001. Leading wicket-taker in English first-class cricket 2001 with 75 wickets (av. 23.32); took 102 wickets in all county cricket 2001. Sussex Player of the Year 2002. Made Test debut in the third Test v South Africa at Trent Bridge 2003, taking 6-34 in South Africa's second innings and winning Man of the Match award. Took 50 first-class wickets in a season for six consecutive years 1998-2003. Took 500th first-class wicket (Mark Wagh) v Warwickshire at Edgbaston 2004. Vice-captain of Sussex since 2001

Best batting: 59 Sussex v Durham, Eastbourne 1998

Best bowling: 7-21 Sussex v Hampshire, Southampton 1999

2004 Season

	M	Inns	NO	Runs	HS	Avge	100s	50s	Ct	St	O	M	Runs	Wkts	Avge	Best	5wI	10wM
Test																		
All First	13	18	5	212	53 *	16.30	-	1	3	-	446.5	97	1381	37	37.32	4-32	-	-
1-day Int																		
C & G	1	1	1	18	18 *	-	-	-	-	-	10	1	29	1	29.00	1-29	-	
totesport	16	6	3	11	4 *	3.66	-	-	3	-	108.1	7	563	13	43.30	3-11	-	
Twenty20	4	3	0	0	0	0.00	-	-	-	-	16	1	122	6	20.33	2-8	-	

Career Performances

	M	Inns	NO	Runs	HS	Avge	100s	50s	Ct	St	Balls	Runs	Wkts	Avge	Best	5wI	10wM
Test	4	7	1	32	12	5.33	-	-	3	-	1079	561	19	29.52	6-34	1	-
All First	133	185	55	1567	59	12.05	-	3	43	-	25612	13444	513	26.20	7-21	27	4
1-day Int	11	2	0	2	1	1.00	-	-	5	-	549	481	9	53.44	2-33	-	
C & G	13	5	3	61	30 *	30.50	-	-	1	-	745	510	27	18.88	5-39	2	
totesport	108	47	24	234	19 *	10.17	-	-	27	-	4458	3528	142	24.84	4-21	-	
Twenty20	6	3	0	0	0	0.00	-	-	1	-	136	161	8	20.12	2-8	-	

52. Who became the first Sri Lanka batsman to score a century in a home Test, against New Zealand at Colombo in 1983-84?

KLUSENER, L. Middlesex

Name: Lance Klusener
Role: Left-hand bat, right-arm medium-fast bowler
Born: 4 September 1971, Durban, South Africa
Height: 6ft **Weight:** 12st 10lbs
Nickname: Zulu
County debut: 2002 (Nottinghamshire), 2004 (Middlesex)
Test debut: 1996-97
Tests: 49
One-Day Internationals: 171
1st-Class 50s: 27
1st-Class 100s: 6
1st-Class 5 w. in innings: 13
1st-Class 10 w. in match: 4
1st-Class catches: 69
One-Day 100s: 2
One-Day 5 w. in innings: 6
Place in batting averages: 185th av. 24.28
Place in bowling averages: 147th av. 51.76
Strike rate: 78.69 (career 56.60)
Parents: Peter and Dawn
Wife and date of marriage: Isabelle, 13 May 2000
Children: Matthew, 17 February 2002
Education: Durban High School; Durban Technikon
Overseas tours: South Africa U24 to Sri Lanka 1995; South Africa A to England 1996; South Africa to India 1996-97, to Pakistan 1997-98, to Australia 1997-98, to England 1998, to New Zealand 1998-99, to UK, Ireland and Holland (World Cup) 1999, to Kenya (LG Cup) 1999-2000, to Zimbabwe 1999-2000, to India 1999-2000, to Sharjah (Coca-Cola Sharjah Cup) 1999-2000, to Sri Lanka 2000, to Australia (Super Challenge) 2000, to Singapore (Singapore Challenge) 2000, to Kenya (ICC Knockout Trophy) 2000-01, to West Indies 2000-01, to Zimbabwe 2001-02, to Australia 2001-02, to Morocco (Morocco Cup) 2002, to Sri Lanka (ICC Champions Trophy) 2002-03, to New Zealand 2003-04 (one-day series), to Sri Lanka 2004, to England (ICC Champions Trophy) 2004; FICA World XI to New Zealand 2004-05
Overseas teams played for: Natal/KwaZulu-Natal 1993-94 – 2003-04; Dolphins 2004-05 –
Career highlights to date: 'World Cup Man of the Tournament [1999]'
Cricketers particularly admired: Malcolm Marshall
Young players to look out for: Kevin Pietersen, Hashim Amla

Other sports played: Golf
Other sports followed: Rugby (Sharks)
Extras: Returned the best analysis by a South African on Test debut – 8-64 in India's second innings of the second Test at Kolkata 1996-97. Struck his maiden Test century (102*) off an even 100 balls in the second Test v India at Cape Town 1996-97, setting record for the quickest Test hundred by a South African in terms of balls faced. One of *South African Cricket Annual*'s five Cricketers of the Year 1997, 1999. Scored 174 in the second Test v England at Port Elizabeth 1999-2000, winning Man of the Match award. One of *Wisden*'s Five Cricketers of the Year 2000. His other Test awards include Man of the Series v Sri Lanka 2000. Has won numerous ODI awards, including Player of the Tournament in the World Cup 1999 and Man of the Match v Kenya at Potchefstroom in the World Cup 2002-03 (4-16). Was Nottinghamshire's overseas player at the start of the 2002 season. Man of the Match in the SuperSport Series final v Western Province at Cape Town 2003-04 (7-70/5-90). Was a Middlesex overseas player 2004
Best batting: 174 South Africa v England, Port Elizabeth 1999-2000
Best bowling: 8-34 Natal v Western Province, Durban 1995-96

2004 Season

	M	Inns	NO	Runs	HS	Avge	100s	50s	Ct	St	O	M	Runs	Wkts	Avge	Best	5wI	10wM
Test																		
All First	6	8	1	170	68 *	24.28	-	2	2	-	170.3	18	673	13	51.76	4-89	-	-
1-day Int	2	1	1	12	12 *	-	-	-	-	-	13	2	44	0	-	-	-	
C & G	3	2	0	14	11	7.00	-	-	1	-	24	2	88	2	44.00	1-20	-	
totesport	9	4	3	85	56 *	85.00	-	1	2	-	66	0	332	9	36.88	2-31	-	
Twenty20	3	2	1	88	53	88.00	-	1	1	-	11	0	98	4	24.50	2-32	-	

Career Performances

	M	Inns	NO	Runs	HS	Avge	100s	50s	Ct	St	Balls	Runs	Wkts	Avge	Best	5wI	10wM
Test	49	69	11	1906	174	32.86	4	8	34	-	6881	3033	80	37.91	8-64	2	-
All First	125	173	35	4731	174	34.28	6	27	69	-	20548	9874	363	27.20	8-34	13	4
1-day Int	171	137	50	3576	103 *	41.10	2	19	36	-	7334	5750	192	29.94	6-49	6	
C & G	3	2	0	14	11	7.00	-	-	1	-	144	88	2	44.00	1-20	-	
totesport	9	4	3	85	56 *	85.00	-	1	2	-	396	332	9	36.88	2-31	-	
Twenty20	3	2	1	88	53	88.00	-	1	1	-	66	98	4	24.50	2-32	-	

KNAPPETT, J. P. T. — Worcestershire

Name: Joshua (Josh) Philip Thomas Knappett
Role: Right-hand bat, wicket-keeper
Born: 15 April 1985, Westminster
Height: 6ft **Weight:** 11st 9lbs
Nickname: Badger, Knappo, Edwin
County debut: No first-team appearance
1st-Class catches: 2
Parents: Phil and Janie
Marital status: Single
Family links with cricket: Father is Middlesex Cricket Development Officer
Education: East Barnet School; Oxford Brookes University
Qualifications: 9 GCSEs, 3 A-levels, Level 3 cricket coach and staff coach
Career outside cricket: 'Student and cricket coach and coach education'
Off-season: 'University and training'
Career highlights to date: 'Winning *Evening Standard* Cup with club Finchley (Middlesex Premier League). Playing for Oxford UCCE in first-class games. Playing "Twenty20" for OUCCE v Oxfordshire'
Cricket moments to forget: 'Getting hit on the head by James Ormond when playing for OUCCE against Surrey'
Cricketers particularly admired: Jack Russell, Adam Gilchrist
Young players to look out for: Tim Linley, Billy Godleman, Eoin Morgan
Other sports played: Football, golf, skiing
Other sports followed: Football (Tottenham Hotspur)
Favourite band: Gomez, Jack Johnson, Counting Crows
Relaxations: 'Music, films, sleeping, cooking badly'
Extras: Played for Oxford University CCE 2004
Best batting: 45 OUCCE v Surrey, The Parks 2004

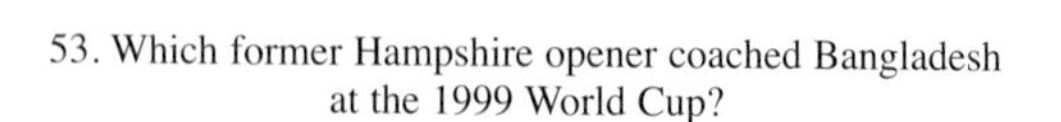
53. Which former Hampshire opener coached Bangladesh at the 1999 World Cup?

2004 Season (did not make any first-class or one-day appearances for his county)

Career Performances

	M	Inns	NO	Runs	HS	Avge	100s	50s	Ct	St	Balls	Runs	Wkts	Avge	Best	5wI	10wM
Test																	
All First	2	2	0	45	45	22.50	-	-	2	-							
1-day Int																	
C & G																	
totesport																	
Twenty20																	

KNIGHT, N. V. — Warwickshire

Name: Nicholas (Nick) Verity Knight
Role: Left-hand bat, right-arm medium-fast bowler, close fielder, county captain
Born: 28 November 1969, Watford
Height: 6ft 1in **Weight:** 13st
Nickname: Stitch, Fungus
County debut: 1991 (Essex), 1995 (Warwickshire)
County cap: 1994 (Essex), 1995 (Warwickshire)
Benefit: 2004 (Warwickshire)
Test debut: 1995
Tests: 17
One-Day Internationals: 100
1000 runs in a season: 5
1st-Class 50s: 66
1st-Class 100s: 30
1st-Class 200s: 3
1st-Class 300s: 1
1st-Class catches: 262
One-Day 100s: 22
Place in batting averages: 22nd av. 55.16 (2003 56th av. 44.00)
Strike rate: (career 195.00)
Parents: John and Rosemary
Wife and date of marriage: Trudie, 3 October 1998
Family links with cricket: Father played for Cambridgeshire. Brother Andy club cricketer in local Cambridge leagues
Education: Felsted School; Loughborough University
Qualifications: 9 O-levels, 3 A-levels, BSc (Hons) Sociology, coaching qualification

Overseas tours: Felsted School to Australia 1986-87; England A to India 1994-95, to Pakistan 1995-96, to Kenya and Sri Lanka 1997-98; England to Zimbabwe and New Zealand 1996-97, to Sharjah (Champions Trophy) 1997-98, to West Indies 1997-98 (one-day series), to Bangladesh (Wills International Cup) 1998-99, to Australia 1998-99 (CUB Series), to Sharjah (Coca-Cola Cup) 1998-99, to South Africa and Zimbabwe 1999-2000 (one-day series), to Sri Lanka 2000-01 (one-day series), to Zimbabwe (one-day series) 2001-02, to India and New Zealand 2001-02 (one-day series), to Sri Lanka (ICC Champions Trophy) 2002-03, to Australia 2002-03 (VB Series), to Africa (World Cup) 2002-03; FICA World XI to New Zealand 2004-05
Overseas teams played for: Northern Districts, Sydney 1991-92; East Torrens, Adelaide 1992-94
Cricketers particularly admired: David Gower, Graham Gooch
Other sports played: Rugby (Eastern Counties), hockey (Essex and Young England)
Relaxations: Eating good food, painting
Extras: Captained English Schools 1987 and 1988, England YC v New Zealand 1989 and Combined Universities 1991. Won *Daily Telegraph* award 1988; voted Gray-Nicolls Cricketer of the Year 1988, Cricket Society Most Promising Young Cricketer of the Year 1989, Essex Young Player of the Year 1991 and Essex U19 Player of the Year. Left Essex at the end of the 1994 season to join Warwickshire. Warwickshire vice-captain 1999. Member of England's 1999 World Cup squad. Scored century (126*) v Somerset at Edgbaston in the B&H 2002, in the process passing Alvin Kallicharran's record of 12 one-day centuries for Warwickshire. Carried his bat for 255* v Hampshire at Edgbaston 2002, in the process sharing with Alan Richardson (91) in a tenth-wicket stand of 214, which was a county best for the last wicket and the fifth highest tenth-wicket partnership in Championship history overall. Leading English player (second overall) in the 2002 first-class batting averages with 1520 runs at 95.00. Warwickshire Batsman of the Year 2002. Leading run-scorer in the VB Series 2002-03 with 461 runs (av. 51.22). His international awards include Man of the Match in the first Test v Zimbabwe at Bulawayo 1996-97, Man of the [ODI] Series v Zimbabwe 2001-02 (302 runs; av. 100.67), and successive ODI Man of the Match awards v West Indies 1997-98. Retired from international cricket in April 2003. Scored maiden first-class triple century (303*; his first hundred at Lord's) v Middlesex 2004. Captain of Warwickshire since 2004
Best batting: 303* Warwickshire v Middlesex, Lord's 2004
Best bowling: 1-61 Essex v Middlesex, Uxbridge 1994

2004 Season

	M	Inns	NO	Runs	HS	Avge	100s	50s	Ct	St	O	M	Runs	Wkts	Avge	Best	5wI	10wM
Test																		
All First	16	30	6	1324	303 *	55.16	2	8	9	-								
1-day Int																		
C & G	4	4	2	180	74 *	90.00	-	1	2	-								
totesport	14	14	2	568	122 *	47.33	2	2	3	-								
Twenty20	3	3	0	86	63	28.66	-	1	1	-								

Career Performances

	M	Inns	NO	Runs	HS	Avge	100s	50s	Ct	St	Balls	Runs	Wkts	Avge	Best	5wI	10wM
Test	17	30	0	719	113	23.96	1	4	26	-							
All First	206	349	39	13880	303 *	44.77	34	66	262	-	195	230	1	230.00	1-61	-	-
1-day Int	100	100	10	3637	125 *	40.41	5	25	44	-							
C & G	34	34	4	1325	151	44.16	4	6	17	-							
totesport	163	151	18	4643	134	34.90	8	22	68	-	84	85	2	42.50	1-14	-	
Twenty20	10	10	1	361	89	40.11	-	4	4	-	5	4	0	-	-	-	

KOENIG, S. G. Middlesex

Name: Sven Gaëtan Koenig
Role: Left-hand bat
Born: 9 December 1973, Durban, South Africa
Height: 5ft 9in **Weight:** 12st 2lbs
Nickname: Blackie, Kuala
County debut: 2002
County cap: 2002
1000 runs in a season: 3
1st-Class 50s: 50
1st-Class 100s: 16
1st-Class catches: 64
One-Day 100s: 1
Place in batting averages: 97th av. 36.29 (2003 38th av. 47.50)
Strike rate: (career 91.00)
Parents: Gaëtan and Barbara
Wife and date of marriage: Catherine, 27 December 2002
Education: Highbury; Hilton College; University of Cape Town
Qualifications: Law degree, Economics degree, Level 2 coach
Career outside cricket: Business
Overseas tours: Western Province to Australia 1995; South Africa A to England 1996; Transvaal to Australia 1997
Overseas teams played for: Western Province 1993-96; Transvaal/Gauteng 1997-2000; Easterns 2003-04
Career highlights to date: 'Playing at Lord's – debut at Lord's v Notts'
Cricket moments to forget: 'First-ball duck – lbw Malcolm Marshall – on Currie Cup debut, Western Province v Natal'
Cricket superstitions: 'None'
Cricketers particularly admired: Desmond Haynes, Steve Waugh, Gary Kirsten

Other sports played: Golf, surfing
Other sports followed: Rugby (Springboks), football (Newcastle United)
Interests/relaxations: Surfing, fishing, business
Extras: South African Young Player of the Year 1994. Leading run-scorer in South African domestic first-class cricket 2000-01 with 789 runs (av. 60.69). Gauteng Player of the Year 2000-01. Scored century (141*) on first-class debut for Middlesex v Cambridge University CCE at Fenner's and another (100) on Championship debut for the county v Durham at Riverside 2002. Scored 1000 (1110) Championship runs in his debut season for Middlesex 2002. Left Middlesex at the end of the 2004 season. Holds an Italian passport and is not considered an overseas player
Opinions on cricket: 'A little less cricket would be good for the game. Twenty20 fantastic. Only need one one-day competition in county cricket.'
Best batting: 171 Middlesex v Lancashire, Old Trafford 2004
Best bowling: 1-0 Gauteng/Northerns v Sri Lanka A, Johannesburg 1999-2000

2004 Season

	M	Inns	NO	Runs	HS	Avge	100s	50s	Ct	St	O	M	Runs	Wkts	Avge	Best	5wI	10wM
Test																		
All First	18	33	2	1125	171	36.29	2	6	6	-	3	1	7	0	-	-	-	-
1-day Int																		
C & G																		
totesport																		
Twenty20																		

Career Performances

	M	Inns	NO	Runs	HS	Avge	100s	50s	Ct	St	Balls	Runs	Wkts	Avge	Best	5wI	10wM
Test																	
All First	135	234	13	8820	171	39.90	16	50	64	-	182	102	2	51.00	1-0	-	-
1-day Int																	
C & G	1	1	0	116	116	116.00	1	-	-	-							
totesport	12	11	1	104	43 *	10.40	-	-	3	-							
Twenty20																	

54. What was the name of the Holland captain who knocked back the off stump of England captain Michael Atherton when the two sides met at Peshawar in the 1995-96 World Cup?

KUMAR, P. — Durham

Name: Pallav Kumar
Role: Right-hand bat, right-arm fast-medium bowler
Born: 13 July 1981, Patna, Bihar, India
Height: 6ft 1in
County debut: 2004
Strike rate: 42.00 (career 42.00)
Parents: Balbir Kumar Singh and Bimla Kumari
Marital status: Single
Education: Central School, Patna; Trinity School, Carlisle; City of Sunderland College
Off-season: Playing in India
Overseas teams played for: Sports Club of India, Delhi
Other sports played: Basketball, badminton
Other sports followed: Football (Newcastle United)
Extras: Plays club cricket for Carlisle and Newcastle City. Played for Cumberland in the first round of the C&G 2004, which was played in August 2003. Released by Durham at the end of the 2004 season
Best batting: 21 Durham v Nottinghamshire, Trent Bridge 2004
Best bowling: 3-78 Durham v Glamorgan, Riverside 2004

2004 Season

	M	Inns	NO	Runs	HS	Avge	100s	50s	Ct	St	O	M	Runs	Wkts	Avge	Best	5wI	10wM
Test																		
All First	2	4	1	36	21	12.00	-	-	-	-	42	5	219	6	36.50	3-78	-	-
1-day Int																		
C & G																		
totesport																		
Twenty20																		

Career Performances

	M	Inns	NO	Runs	HS	Avge	100s	50s	Ct	St	Balls	Runs	Wkts	Avge	Best	5wI	10wM
Test																	
All First	2	4	1	36	21	12.00	-	-	-	-	252	219	6	36.50	3-78	-	-
1-day Int																	
C & G	1	1	0	0	0	0.00	-	-	-	-	60	33	2	16.50	2-33	-	
totesport																	
Twenty20																	

LAMB, G. A. — Hampshire

Name: Gregory (Greg) Arthur Lamb
Role: Right-hand bat, right-arm off-spin or medium bowler; all-rounder
Born: 4 March 1981, Harare, Zimbabwe
Height: 6ft **Weight:** 12st
Nickname: Lamby
County debut: 2004
1st-Class 50s: 3
1st-Class 100s: 1
1st-Class 5 w. in innings: 1
1st-Class catches: 9
Strike rate: (career 39.84)
Parents: Terry and Jackie
Marital status: Single
Children: Isabella Grace Saskia Lamb
Education: Lomagundi College; Guildford College (both Zimbabwe)
Qualifications: School and coaching qualifications
Overseas tours: Zimbabwe U19 to South Africa (U19 World Cup) 1997-98, to Sri Lanka (U19 World Cup) 1999-2000; Zimbabwe A to Sri Lanka 1999-2000
Overseas teams played for: CFX [Zimbabwe] Academy 1999-2000; Mashonaland A 2000-01
Career highlights to date: 'Playing against Australia. Making my first first-class hundred'
Cricket superstitions: 'Every time I hit a four I have to touch the other side of the pitch'
Cricketers particularly admired: Aravinda de Silva
Other sports played: 'All sports'
Favourite band: Matchbox Twenty
Relaxations: 'Fishing, playing sport'
Extras: Played for Zimbabwe U12, U15 and U19. Represented CFX [Zimbabwe] Academy, Zimbabwe Cricket Union President's XI and Zimbabwe A against various touring sides. Played in Hampshire's 2nd XI Trophy winning side 2003. Scored 94 on Championship debut for Hampshire v Derbyshire at Derby 2004
Best batting: 100* CFX Academy v Manicaland, Mutare 1999-2000
Best bowling: 7-73 CFX Academy v Midlands, Kwekwe 1999-2000

2004 Season

	M	Inns	NO	Runs	HS	Avge	100s	50s	Ct	St	O	M	Runs	Wkts	Avge	Best	5wI	10wM
Test																		
All First	1	2	1	101	94	101.00	-	1	-	-	5	2	15	0	-	-	-	-
1-day Int																		
C & G																		
totesport	6	6	0	129	54	21.50	-	1	5	-	2	0	12	0	-	-	-	
Twenty20	6	5	0	38	12	7.60	-	-	1	-								

Career Performances

	M	Inns	NO	Runs	HS	Avge	100s	50s	Ct	St	Balls	Runs	Wkts	Avge	Best	5wI	10wM
Test																	
All First	17	25	4	592	100 *	28.19	1	3	9	-	1036	574	26	22.07	7-73	1	-
1-day Int																	
C & G																	
totesport	6	6	0	129	54	21.50	-	1	5	-	12	12	0	-	-	-	
Twenty20	6	5	0	38	12	7.60	-	-	1	-							

LARAMAN, A. W. — Somerset

Name: Aaron William Laraman
Role: Right-hand bat, right-arm medium-fast bowler
Born: 10 January 1979, London
Height: 6ft 5in **Weight:** 14st 7lbs
Nickname: Az, Lazza, Shanky, Long
County debut: 1998 (Middlesex), 2003 (Somerset)
1st-Class 50s: 5
1st-Class 100s: 1
1st-Class 5 w. in innings: 1
1st-Class catches: 15
One-Day 5 w. in innings: 2
Place in batting averages: 215th av. 20.66 (2003 44th av. 45.92)
Place in bowling averages: 40th av. 29.00 (2003 119th av. 40.79)
Strike rate: 49.22 (career 56.87)
Parents: William and Lynda
Marital status: Single
Education: Enfield Grammar School
Qualifications: 8 GCSEs

Overseas tours: England U17 to Holland 1995; England U19 to South Africa 1997-98
Overseas teams played for: Burnside CC, Christchurch, New Zealand 1999-2000; Willetton CC, Perth 2000-01
Career highlights to date: 'Making my debut at Lord's in 1998'
Cricketers particularly admired: Steve Waugh, Glenn McGrath, Michael Atherton
Other sports followed: Football (Arsenal)
Relaxations: Working out at the gym, football, golf
Extras: Enfield Grammar School cap at the age of 13. Middlesex Colts cap. Seaxe 2nd XI Player of the Year 1997. Took 4-39 on NatWest debut v Nottinghamshire at Lord's 2000. Left Middlesex at the end of the 2002 season and joined Somerset for 2003. Scored maiden first-class century (148*, having arrived at 136 for 5) v Gloucestershire at Taunton 2003. Recorded maiden first-class five-wicket return (5-58) v Derbyshire at Taunton 2004
Best batting: 148* Somerset v Gloucestershire, Taunton 2003
Best bowling: 5-58 Somerset v Derbyshire, Taunton 2004

2004 Season

	M	Inns	NO	Runs	HS	Avge	100s	50s	Ct	St	O	M	Runs	Wkts	Avge	Best	5wI	10wM
Test																		
All First	11	11	2	186	66 *	20.66	-	1	5	-	180.3	43	638	22	29.00	5-58	1	-
1-day Int																		
C & G	1	1	1	50	50 *	-	-	1	1	-	8	0	36	0	-	-	-	
totesport	10	9	2	94	24	13.42	-	-	1	-	59	3	321	10	32.10	2-39	-	
Twenty20	5	3	0	7	5	2.33	-	-	-	-	14.3	0	105	7	15.00	4-15	-	

Career Performances

	M	Inns	NO	Runs	HS	Avge	100s	50s	Ct	St	Balls	Runs	Wkts	Avge	Best	5wI	10wM
Test																	
All First	38	43	10	1142	148 *	34.60	1	5	15	-	4493	2612	79	33.06	5-58	1	-
1-day Int																	
C & G	6	3	2	68	50 *	68.00	-	1	3	-	249	161	9	17.88	4-39	-	
totesport	32	28	7	253	33	12.04	-	-	6	-	1204	1057	35	30.20	6-42	2	
Twenty20	7	5	1	35	28 *	8.75	-	-	-	-	123	151	9	16.77	4-15	-	

55. Kenyan-born, who in 2003 became only the third Oxford batsman to score a double hundred in the Varsity Match and in 2004 cracked a career-best 244 against Surrey for his county side?

LATOUF, K. J. Hampshire

Name: Kevin John Latouf
Role: Right-hand bat, right-arm medium bowler
Born: 7 September 1985, Pretoria, South Africa
Height: 5ft 10in **Weight:** 12st
Nickname: Poindexter, Mushy, Latsy, Kev
County debut: No first-team appearance
Parents: Colin and Josephine
Marital status: Single
Family links with cricket: 'Uncle Brian Venables was a batsman who played in Dublin and now plays cricket in Kent'
Education: Millfield School; Barton Peveril Sixth Form College
Qualifications: 11 GCSEs, 4 AS-Levels
Overseas tours: West of England U15 to West Indies 2000, 2001
Overseas teams played for: Melville CC, Perth ('briefly')
Career highlights to date: '68 v Glamorgan 2nd XI which included Simon Jones. 80* on 2nd XI debut – both 2003'
Cricket moments to forget: 'Golden duck in England U15 trial match'
Cricket superstitions: 'Don't believe in superstition'
Cricketers particularly admired: Ricky Ponting, Jonty Rhodes, Allan Donald
Young players to look out for: Anthony Latouf, James Hildreth, Tom Burrows, Chris Benham, Tom Cledwyn
Other sports played: Tennis (county trials), rugby (Bristol and Somerset trials), golf ('fun'), surfing, snowboarding
Other sports followed: Rugby (Natal Sharks), football (Arsenal), AFL (Collingwood)
Favourite band: Coldplay
Relaxations: 'Prefer listening to R&B and hip hop; going out with mates from cricket, Millfield and BP'
Extras: Played for West of England U13, U14 and U15. Played for ECB U17 and ECB U19 v India U19 2002. Played for ECB U19 v South Africa U19 2003. Played in Hampshire's 2nd XI Trophy winning side 2003
Opinions on cricket: 'People are too opinionated.'

LAW, S. G. Lancashire

Name: Stuart Grant Law
Role: Right-hand bat, right-arm leg-spin bowler, county vice-captain
Born: 18 October 1968, Brisbane, Australia
Height: 6ft 1in **Weight:** 13st
Nickname: Lawry, Judge, LA
County debut: 1996 (Essex), 2002 (Lancashire)
County cap: 1996 (Essex), 2002 (Lancashire)
Test debut: 1995-96
Tests: 1
One-Day Internationals: 54
1000 runs in a season: 8
1st-Class 50s: 107
1st-Class 100s: 63
1st-Class 200s: 5
1st-Class 5 w. in innings: 1
1st-Class catches: 343
One-Day 100s: 13
Place in batting averages: 37th av. 51.00 (2003 1st av. 91.00)
Strike rate: (career 101.67)
Parents: Grant and Pam
Wife and date of marriage: Debbie-Lee, 31 December 1998
Children: Max, 9 January 2002
Family links with cricket: 'Cricket has always been in the family'
Education: Craigslea State High School; Brisbane State High School
Qualifications: Level 2 cricket coach
Overseas tours: Australia B to Zimbabwe 1991-92; Young Australia (Australia A) to England and Netherlands 1995 (captain); Australia to India and Pakistan (World Cup) 1995-96, to Sri Lanka (Singer World Series) 1996, to India (Titan World Series) 1996-97, to South Africa 1996-97 (one-day series), to New Zealand (one-day series) 1997-98
Overseas teams played for: Queensland Bulls 1988-89 – 2003-04
Career highlights to date: 'Playing for Australia. Captaining Queensland to their first Sheffield Shield [title] win [1994-95]'
Cricket superstitions: 'None'
Cricketers particularly admired: Viv Richards, Greg Chappell
Other sports played: Golf, tennis
Other sports followed: Rugby league (Brisbane Broncos)
Relaxations: 'Spending time with family, friends; going to the beach'

Extras: Made his first-class debut for Queensland as a 19-year-old, scoring 179 on only his second appearance, v Tasmania at Brisbane 1988-89. Sheffield Shield Player of the Year 1990-91. Shared with Martin Love in record third-wicket partnership for Queensland (326), v Tasmania at Brisbane 1994-95. Is the most successful captain in Australian domestic cricket history, having captained Queensland to five Sheffield Shield/Pura Cup titles (to equal Richie Benaud's feat of captaining his state to five titles) and to three one-day titles. One of *Wisden*'s Five Cricketers of the Year 1998. Topped the English first-class batting averages for 1999 (1833 runs at 73.32). PCA Player of the Year 1999. Left Essex at the end of the 2001 season and joined Lancashire as overseas player for 2002. Became Queensland's most-capped player in first-class cricket, v Tasmania at Brisbane 2001-02. Stood down as captain of Queensland at the end of the 2001-02 Australian season. Scored century (168) v Warwickshire at Edgbaston 2003, sharing with Carl Hooper (177) in a Lancashire record fifth-wicket partnership of 360 as the county scored 781. Topped the English first-class batting averages for 2003 (1820 runs at 91.00). Lancashire Player of the Year 2003. Scored 69-ball century v Tasmania at Hobart in the ING Cup 2003-04, breaking his own record for the fastest century in Australian domestic one-day cricket. Scored century (146*) v New South Wales at Brisbane 2003-04, in the process becoming Queensland's all-time leading run-scorer in first-class cricket. Retired from Australian cricket at the end of 2003-04, having scored 1053 Pura Cup runs (av. 65.81) and 570 ING Cup runs (av. 57.00) in his final season; has been awarded life membership of Queensland Cricket. Appointed vice-captain of Lancashire for 2005. Is a UK citizen and no longer considered an overseas player
Best batting: 263 Essex v Somerset, Chelmsford 1999
Best bowling: 5-39 Queensland v Tasmania, Brisbane 1995-96

2004 Season

	M	Inns	NO	Runs	HS	Avge	100s	50s	Ct	St	O	M	Runs	Wkts	Avge	Best	5wI	10wM
Test																		
All First	12	18	1	867	171 *	51.00	3	1	17	-	5	1	16	0	-	-	-	-
1-day Int																		
C & G	3	3	0	87	48	29.00	-	-	2	-								
totesport	9	9	0	275	83	30.55	-	3	2	-								
Twenty20	3	3	0	63	31	21.00	-	-	1	-								

Career Performances

	M	Inns	NO	Runs	HS	Avge	100s	50s	Ct	St	Balls	Runs	Wkts	Avge	Best	5wI	10wM
Test	1	1	1	54	54 *	-	-	1	1	-	18	9	0	-	-	-	-
All First	307	507	56	23099	263	51.21	68	107	343	-	8337	4165	82	50.79	5-39	1	-
1-day Int	54	51	5	1237	110	26.89	1	7	12	-	807	635	12	52.91	2-22	-	
C & G	25	22	1	889	107	42.33	3	4	19	-	439	366	8	45.75	2-36	-	
totesport	121	118	7	4093	133	36.87	8	20	42	-	954	832	25	33.28	4-37	-	
Twenty20	8	8	0	122	31	15.25	-	-	2	-	6	10	0	-	-	-	

LAWSON, M. A. K. Yorkshire

Name: Mark Anthony Kenneth Lawson
Role: Right-hand bat, right-arm leg-spin bowler
Born: 24 November 1985, Leeds
Height: 5ft 8in **Weight:** 12st ('approx')
Nickname: Sauce
County debut: 2004
1st-Class 5 w. in innings: 1
1st-Class catches: 1
Strike rate: 50.33 (career 50.33)
Parents: Anthony and Dawn
Marital status: Single
Family links with cricket: 'Father played local league cricket and encouraged me to take up the game'
Education: Castle Hall Language College, Mirfield, West Yorkshire
Qualifications: 11 GCSEs
Overseas tours: England U19 to Australia 2002-03, to Bangladesh (U19 World Cup) 2003-04, to India 2004-05
Cricketers particularly admired: Shane Warne, Gareth Batty
Young players to look out for: Christopher Batchelor, Phillip Holdsworth
Other sports played: Football (school), rugby union (school, Cleckheaton 'in early teens'), rugby league (Dewsbury Moor ARLFC 'in early teens')
Other sports followed: Rugby league (Bradford Bulls)
Relaxations: Music, dining out, cinema
Extras: Played for Yorkshire Schools U11-U16 (captain U13-U15); ESCA North of England U14 and U15; North of England Development of Excellence U17 and U19. Represented England U15, U17 and U19, including v Bangladesh U19 2004. Awarded Brian Johnston Scholarship. Part of Terry Jenner Elite Wrist Spin Program. Voted Yorkshire Supporters' Young Player of the Year 2003. Recorded maiden first-class five-wicket return (5-62) v Durham at Scarborough 2004
Best batting: 14 Yorkshire v Durham, Scarborough 2004
Best bowling: 5-62 Yorkshire v Durham, Scarborough 2004

2004 Season

	M	Inns	NO	Runs	HS	Avge	100s	50s	Ct	St	O	M	Runs	Wkts	Avge	Best	5wI	10wM
Test																		
All First	3	5	1	33	14	8.25	-	-	1	-	75.3	6	308	9	34.22	5-62	1	-
1-day Int																		
C & G																		
totesport																		
Twenty20																		

Career Performances

	M	Inns	NO	Runs	HS	Avge	100s	50s	Ct	St	Balls	Runs	Wkts	Avge	Best	5wI	10wM
Test																	
All First	3	5	1	33	14	8.25	-	-	1	-	453	308	9	34.22	5-62	1	-
1-day Int																	
C & G																	
totesport																	
Twenty20																	

LEATHERDALE, D. A. — Worcestershire

Name: David Anthony Leatherdale
Role: Right-hand bat, right-arm medium bowler, cover fielder
Born: 26 November 1967, Bradford
Height: 5ft 10in **Weight:** 11st
Nickname: Lugsy, Spock
County debut: 1988
County cap: 1994; colours 2002
Benefit: 2003
1000 runs in a season: 1
1st-Class 50s: 54
1st-Class 100s: 14
1st-Class 5 w. in innings: 2
1st-Class catches: 151
One-Day 5 w. in innings: 2
Place in batting averages: (2003 200th av. 23.42)
Strike rate: (career 53.51)
Parents: Paul and Rosalyn
Wife: Vanessa
Children: Callum Edward, 6 July 1990; Christian Ellis, 21 March 1995
Family links with cricket: Father played local cricket; brother-in-law played for England YC in 1979

Education: Pudsey Grangefield Secondary School
Qualifications: 8 O-levels, 3 A-levels, NCA coaching award (stage 1)
Career outside cricket: Commercial director at Worcestershire CCC
Overseas tours: England Indoor to Australia and New Zealand 1994-95
Overseas teams played for: Pretoria Police, South Africa 1987-88
Career highlights to date: '5-10 v Australia 1997' (*In one-day match against the Australian tourists at Worcester*)
Cricketers particularly admired: Mark Scott, George Batty, Peter Kippax
Other sports followed: Football, American football
Relaxations: Golf
Extras: Scored century (120) v Nottinghamshire at Trent Bridge 2002, in the process sharing with Steve Rhodes (124) in a new record seventh-wicket partnership for Worcestershire (256). Recorded career best C&G/NatWest score (80) v Yorkshire at Worcester 2003, winning Man of the Match award. Worcestershire One-Day Player of the Year 2003. Scored 63 v Middlesex at Lord's in the totesport League 2004, in the process sharing with Graeme Hick (120) in a new Worcestershire record fourth-wicket stand for the one-day league (160)
Opinions on cricket: 'Two overseas players will only work and improve county cricket if they are of the highest quality and committed to the county they are playing for!'
Best batting: 157 Worcestershire v Somerset, Worcester 1991
Best bowling: 5-20 Worcestershire v Gloucestershire, Worcester 1998

2004 Season

	M	Inns	NO	Runs	HS	Avge	100s	50s	Ct	St	O	M	Runs	Wkts	Avge	Best	5wI	10wM
Test																		
All First																		
1-day Int																		
C & G	5	4	1	148	66	49.33	-	1	1	-	16.2	1	74	5	14.80	3-9	-	
totesport	16	16	2	279	63	19.92	-	1	4	-	74.3	5	406	13	31.23	3-28	-	
Twenty20	6	6	2	67	52 *	16.75	-	1	4	-	13	0	98	5	19.60	2-15	-	

Career Performances

	M	Inns	NO	Runs	HS	Avge	100s	50s	Ct	St	Balls	Runs	Wkts	Avge	Best	5wI	10wM
Test																	
All First	214	346	41	10003	157	32.79	14	54	151	-	7011	4111	131	31.38	5-20	2	-
1-day Int																	
C & G	40	34	4	776	80	25.86	-	4	18	-	636	530	19	27.89	3-9	-	
totesport	220	187	27	3295	70 *	20.59	-	13	91	-	3251	2679	121	22.14	5-9	2	
Twenty20	11	11	4	123	52 *	17.57	-	1	6	-	150	187	9	20.77	2-14	-	

LEHMANN, D. S. Yorkshire

Name: Darren Scott Lehmann
Role: Left-hand bat, slow left-arm bowler
Born: 5 February 1970, Gawler, South Australia
Nickname: Boof
Height: 5ft 11in **Weight:** 14st 2lbs
County debut: 1997
County cap: 1997
Test debut: 1997-98
Tests: 20
One-Day Internationals: 108
1000 runs in a season: 4
1st-Class 50s: 98
1st-Class 100s: 60
1st-Class 200s: 9
1st-Class catches: 125
One-Day 100s: 11
Place in batting averages: 15th av. 59.20
Place in bowling averages: 1st av. 17.40
Strike rate: 42.26 (career 73.41)
Wife: Andrea
Off-season: Playing for South Australia and Australia
Overseas tours: Australia to Sri Lanka (Singer World Series) 1996-97, to New Zealand (one-day series) 1997-98, to Sharjah (Coca-Cola Cup) 1997-98, to India 1997-98, to Pakistan 1998-99, to Bangladesh (Wills International Cup) 1998-99, to West Indies 1998-99 (one-day series), to UK, Ireland and Holland (World Cup) 1999, to Sri Lanka 1999-2000 (one-day series), to Zimbabwe 1999-2000 (one-day series), to India 2000-01 (one-day series), to South Africa 2001-02, to Sri Lanka (ICC Champions Trophy) 2002-03, to Africa (World Cup) 2002-03, to West Indies 2002-03, to Sri Lanka 2003-04, to Zimbabwe (one-day series) 2004, to Holland (Videocon Cup) 2004, to England (ICC Champions Trophy) 2004, to India 2004-05
Overseas teams played for: Salisbury District CC (now Northern Districts), Adelaide; South Australia 1987-88 – 1989-90; Victoria 1990-91 – 1992-93; South Australia 1993-94 –
Other sports followed: Australian Football League (Adelaide Crows)
Relaxations: Golf, watching sport
Extras: Represented South Australia at all age groups. Scored 1142 runs (av. 57.10) in his first full Australian season 1989-90. Played in Australia's 1999 World Cup winning side, striking the winning runs in the final v Pakistan at Lord's. Pura Milk Cup Player of the Year 1999-2000. Was voted Interstate Cricketer of the Year 1999-2000 at the inaugural Allan Border Medal awards January 2000, also winning the award in 2000-01 and 2001-02. Won the EDS Walter Lawrence Trophy for the fastest first-class

century of the 2000 season – 89 balls for Yorkshire v Kent at Canterbury. Top run-scorer in English first-class cricket 2000 with 1477 runs at 67.13. One of *Wisden*'s Five Cricketers of the Year 2001. Won three B&H Gold Awards in eight days 2001. Yorkshire Player of the Year 2001. Became the highest scoring batsman in Sheffield Shield/Pura Cup history, v Victoria at Melbourne 2001-02. His international awards include Man of the Match in the CUB second final v England at Melbourne 1998-99, in the VB Series v Sri Lanka at Perth 2002-03, and in the third Test v Sri Lanka at Colombo 2003-04 (153 plus match figures of 6-92). Vice-captain of Yorkshire 2001; captain of Yorkshire 2002, the first overseas player to be appointed to the office. Did not play for Yorkshire 2003 but returned for 2004. Captain of South Australia since 1998-99. *Wisden Australia*'s Cricketer of the Year 2003-04. Book *Darren Lehmann: Worth the Wait* published 2004
Best batting: 255 South Australia v Queensland, Adelaide 1996-97
Best bowling: 4-35 Yorkshire v Essex, Chelmsford 2004

2004 Season

	M	Inns	NO	Runs	HS	Avge	100s	50s	Ct	St	O	M	Runs	Wkts	Avge	Best	5wI	10wM
Test																		
All First	7	11	1	592	120	59.20	1	5	2	-	105.4	19	261	15	17.40	4-35	-	-
1-day Int	4	2	0	47	38	23.50	-	-	2	-	16	0	68	1	68.00	1-16	-	
C & G	3	2	1	142	80 *	142.00	-	2	1	-	19.2	0	84	2	42.00	2-14	-	
totesport	8	8	2	194	88 *	32.33	-	2	1	-	45	1	213	10	21.30	3-34	-	
Twenty20																		

Career Performances

	M	Inns	NO	Runs	HS	Avge	100s	50s	Ct	St	Balls	Runs	Wkts	Avge	Best	5wI	10wM
Test	20	32	2	1549	177	51.63	5	8	9	-	740	287	13	22.07	3-42	-	-
All First	239	405	27	21573	255	57.07	69	98	125	-	6901	3214	94	34.19	4-35	-	-
1-day Int	108	93	19	2887	119	39.01	4	15	24	-	1520	1184	45	26.31	4-7	-	
C & G	16	13	3	492	105	49.20	1	4	3	-	416	268	16	16.75	4-26	-	
totesport	73	73	10	2963	191	47.03	3	23	24	-	1537	1143	46	24.84	3-31	-	
Twenty20																	

56. Which former Derbyshire and England bowler coached Ireland from 1995 to 1999?

LEWIS, J. Gloucestershire

Name: Jonathan (Jon) Lewis
Role: Right-hand bat, right-arm fast-medium bowler
Born: 26 August 1975, Aylesbury
Height: 6ft 3in **Weight:** 14st
Nickname: Lewy, JJ, King Black
County debut: 1995
County cap: 1998
50 wickets in a season: 5
1st-Class 50s: 3
1st-Class 5 w. in innings: 24
1st-Class 10 w. in match: 3
1st-Class catches: 29
One-Day 5 w. in innings: 1
Place in batting averages: 235th av. 17.54 (2003 234th av. 17.71)
Place in bowling averages: 19th av. 25.26 (2003 25th av. 24.32)
Strike rate: 49.75 (career 52.67)
Parents: John and Jane
Marital status: Married
Education: Churchfields School, Swindon; Swindon College
Qualifications: 9 GCSEs, BTEC in Leisure and Hospitality, Level III coach
Overseas tours: Bath Schools to New South Wales 1993; England A to West Indies 2000-01, to Sri Lanka 2004-05; England to South Africa 2004-05
Overseas teams played for: Marist, Christchurch, New Zealand 1994-95; Richmond City, Melbourne 1995-96; Wanderers, Johannesburg 1996-98; Techs CC, Cape Town 1998-99; Randwick-Petersham, Sydney 2003-04
Cricket moments to forget: 'Any injury'
Cricket superstitions: 'I always get a haircut if I go for a gallon'
Cricketers particularly admired: Courtney Walsh, Jack Russell, Jonty Rhodes
Young players to look out for: Alex Gidman
Other sports played: Golf (7 handicap), football (Bristol North West FC)
Other sports followed: Football (Swindon Town FC)
Favourite band: Brand New Heavies
Relaxations: Movies
Extras: Was on Northamptonshire staff in 1994 but made no first-team appearance. His 62 v Worcestershire at Cheltenham 1999 is the highest score by a Gloucestershire No. 11. Took Championship hat-trick (Gallian, Afzaal and Morris) v Nottinghamshire at Trent Bridge 2000. Leading first-class wicket-taker among English bowlers in 2000 with 72 wickets (av. 20.91). Gloucestershire Player of the Year 2000. C&G Man of the

Match award for his 4-39 v Hampshire at Bristol 2004. Included in preliminary England one-day squad of 30 for ICC Champions Trophy 2004. ECB National Academy 2004-05; placed on standby for England Test tour of South Africa 2004-05
Opinions on cricket: 'County cricket is hard work – we need a few less games. But most of all we need better practice facilities and playing surfaces. More time to prepare will make English cricketers better players. County cricket is not to blame for poor England performances!'
Best batting: 62 Gloucestershire v Worcestershire, Cheltenham 1999
Best bowling: 8-95 Gloucestershire v Zimbabweans, Gloucester 2000
Stop press: Called up to England Test squad in South Africa 2004-05 as cover in the pace bowling department

2004 Season

	M	Inns	NO	Runs	HS	Avge	100s	50s	Ct	St	O	M	Runs	Wkts	Avge	Best	5wI	10wM
Test																		
All First	16	15	4	193	34 *	17.54	-	-	1	-	472.4	121	1440	57	25.26	7-72	4	-
1-day Int																		
C & G	5	2	1	3	2 *	3.00	-	-	-	-	43	6	173	11	15.72	4-39	-	
totesport	13	6	0	18	6	3.00	-	-	1	-	98.3	7	440	24	18.33	5-23	1	
Twenty20	4	1	1	1	1 *	-	-	-	-	-	13	0	86	8	10.75	3-21	-	

Career Performances

	M	Inns	NO	Runs	HS	Avge	100s	50s	Ct	St	Balls	Runs	Wkts	Avge	Best	5wI	10wM
Test																	
All First	132	185	39	1920	62	13.15	-	3	29	-	24704	12527	469	26.71	8-95	24	3
1-day Int																	
C & G	15	8	5	26	9 *	8.66	-	-	6	-	784	474	22	21.54	4-39	-	
totesport	83	48	16	295	27 *	9.21	-	-	13	-	3541	2835	98	28.92	5-23	1	
Twenty20	8	1	1	1	1 *	-	-	-	-	-	174	212	15	14.13	3-21	-	

LEWIS, J. J. B. — Durham

Name: Jonathan (Jon) James Benjamin Lewis
Role: Right-hand bat
Born: 21 May 1970, Isleworth, Middlesex
Height: 5ft 9in **Weight:** 'slightly heavier than' 12st
Nickname: Judge, JJ, Jonzy
County debut: 1990 (Essex), 1997 (Durham)
County cap: 1994 (Essex), 1998 (Durham)
Benefit: 2004 (Durham)
1000 runs in a season: 4
1st-Class 50s: 61
1st-Class 100s: 15

1st-Class 200s: 1
1st-Class catches: 104
One-Day 100s: 1
Place in batting averages: 175th av. 25.23 (2003 95th av. 37.12)
Strike rate: (career 120.00)
Parents: Ted and Nina
Wife and date of marriage: Fiona, 6 July 1999
Family links with cricket: Father played County Schools. Uncle is a lifelong Somerset supporter. Sister is right-arm medium-fast bowler for Cisco
Education: King Edward VI School, Chelmsford; Roehampton Institute of Higher Education
Qualifications: 5 O-levels, 3 A-levels, BSc (Hons) Sports Science, NCA Senior Coach
Career outside cricket: 'Beginning to look very seriously'
Off-season: 'See above'
Overseas tours: Durham to Cape Town 2002
Overseas teams played for: Old Hararians, Zimbabwe 1991-92; Taita District, New Zealand 1992-93; Eshowe and Zululand, South Africa 1994-95; Richards Bay, South Africa 1996-97; Empangeni, Natal 1997-98; Eshowe 1998-2002
Career highlights to date: 'Captaining Durham CCC'
Cricket moments to forget: 'Even the bad days are worth remembering: you always learn something'
Cricketers particularly admired: John Childs, Greg Matthews, Alan Walker, Shane Warne
Other sports followed: Soccer (West Ham United), rugby (Newcastle Falcons), 'most sports really'
Relaxations: Sleep
Extras: Hit century (116*) on first-class debut in Essex's final Championship match of the 1990 season, v Surrey at The Oval. Joined Durham for the 1997 season. Scored a double century on his debut for Durham (210* v Oxford University at The Parks 1997), placing him in a small club, alongside Peter Bowler and Neil Taylor, of players who have scored centuries on debut for two different counties. Scored 112 v Nottinghamshire at Riverside 2001, in the process sharing in Durham's highest Championship partnership for any wicket (258) with Martin Love. Became Durham's leading first-class run-scorer when he passed John Morris's record of 5670 runs during his 124 v Yorkshire at Headingley 2003. Durham Player of the Year and Batsman of the Year 2003. Carried his bat for 35* out of 91 v Derbyshire at Riverside 2004. Captain of Durham 2000-04
Best batting: 210* Durham v Oxford University, The Parks 1997
Best bowling: 1-73 Durham v Surrey, Riverside 1998

2004 Season

	M	Inns	NO	Runs	HS	Avge	100s	50s	Ct	St	O	M	Runs	Wkts	Avge	Best	5wI	10wM
Test																		
All First	17	31	1	757	127	25.23	1	4	7	-								
1-day Int																		
C & G	1	1	0	10	10	10.00	-	-	-	-								
totesport	17	15	2	327	48	25.15	-	-	2	-								
Twenty20	5	4	2	91	49*	45.50	-	-	1	-								

Career Performances

	M	Inns	NO	Runs	HS	Avge	100s	50s	Ct	St	Balls	Runs	Wkts	Avge	Best	5wI	10wM
Test																	
All First	186	332	25	9971	210*	32.47	16	61	104	-	120	121	1	121.00	1-73	-	-
1-day Int																	
C & G	20	19	4	307	65*	20.46	-	1	1	-							
totesport	163	144	32	3147	102	28.09	1	15	27	-	8	35	0	-		-	-
Twenty20	10	9	4	132	49*	26.40	-	-	6	-							

LEWIS, M. L. — Glamorgan

Name: Michael (Mick) Llewellyn Lewis
Role: Right-hand bat, right-arm fast bowler
Born: 29 June 1974, Greensborough, Victoria, Australia
Height: 6ft **Weight:** 13st 3lbs
Nickname: Brown Snake
County debut: 2004
1st-Class 50s: 1
1st-Class 5 w. in innings: 4
1st-Class catches: 23
Strike rate: 53.16 (career 55.60)
Parents: Melva and Graeme
Marital status: Single
Family links with cricket: 'Older brother played'
Education: Parade College, Victoria
Qualifications: Horticultural Certificate III (Turf Management)
Career outside cricket: Greenkeeper
Off-season: 'No such thing these days'
Overseas teams played for: Northcote CC, Victoria; Victorian Bushrangers 1999-2000 –

Career highlights to date: '2003-04 Pura Cup final (winning)'
Cricket moments to forget: '2000-01 Pura Cup final (losing)'
Cricket superstitions: 'None'
Cricketers particularly admired: Michael Holding, Rodney Hogg
Young players to look out for: Cameron White
Other sports played: Aussie Rules (Greensborough Football Club)
Other sports followed: AFL (Carlton)
Favourite band: Live
Relaxations: Golf, horse racing
Extras: Played for Prime Minister's XI v England at Canberra 2002-03, taking 3-22. Represented Australia A v South Africa A at Perth 2002-03. Victoria's leading wicket-taker in the Pura Cup 2002-03 with 32 wickets (av. 28.53) and 2003-04 with 34 wickets (av. 27.85), including 6-59 in Queensland's second innings in the 2003-04 final at the MCG. Was an overseas player with Glamorgan August to September 2004, deputising for Michael Kasprowicz, absent on international duty
Opinions on cricket: 'We don't need to change the game that much. There is still too much tradition, but some should be kept forever.'
Best batting: 54* Victoria v New South Wales, Sydney 2001-02
Best bowling: 6-59 Victoria v Queensland, Melbourne 2003-04

2004 Season

	M	Inns	NO	Runs	HS	Avge	100s	50s	Ct	St	O	M	Runs	Wkts	Avge	Best	5wI	10wM
Test																		
All First	3	1	0	0	0	0.00	-	-	1	-	53.1	5	253	6	42.16	4-39	-	-
1-day Int																		
C & G																		
totesport	4	1	0	0	0	0.00	-	-	1	-	30	3	157	6	26.16	2-24	-	
Twenty20																		

Career Performances

	M	Inns	NO	Runs	HS	Avge	100s	50s	Ct	St	Balls	Runs	Wkts	Avge	Best	5wI	10wM
Test																	
All First	41	52	15	363	54 *	9.81	-	1	23	-	7229	4057	130	31.20	6-59	4	-
1-day Int																	
C & G																	
totesport	4	1	0	0	0	0.00	-	-	1	-	180	157	6	26.16	2-24	-	
Twenty20																	

LEWRY, J. D. Sussex

Name: Jason David Lewry
Role: Left-hand bat, left-arm fast-medium bowler
Born: 2 April 1971, Worthing
Height: 6ft 3in **Weight:** 14st 7lbs ('depending on time of year!')
Nickname: Lewie, Urco
County debut: 1994
County cap: 1996
Benefit: 2002
50 wickets in a season: 4
1st-Class 50s: 2
1st-Class 5 w. in innings: 25
1st-Class 10 w. in match: 4
1st-Class catches: 28
Place in batting averages: 245th av. 15.90 (2003 232nd av. 17.91)
Place in bowling averages: 58th av. 31.44 (2003 39th av. 26.61)
Strike rate: 57.62 (career 49.67)
Parents: David and Veronica
Wife and date of marriage: Naomi Madeleine, 18 August 1997
Children: William, 14 February 1998; Louis, 20 November 2000
Family links with cricket: Father coaches
Education: Durrington High School, Worthing; Worthing Sixth Form College
Qualifications: 6 O-levels, 3 GCSEs, City and Guilds, NCA Award
Career outside cricket: 'Still looking, but with more urgency with each passing year!'
Off-season: 'Hurt me, "Gunter" (aka Ben Haining)'
Overseas tours: Goring CC to Isle of Wight 1992, 1993; England A to Zimbabwe and South Africa 1998-99
Career highlights to date: 'Winning County Championship 2003 and the month of debauchery that followed'
Cricket moments to forget: 'King pair, Eastbourne 1995'
Cricketers particularly admired: David Gower, Martin Andrews
Other sports played: Golf, squash; darts, pool ('anything you can do in a pub')
Other sports followed: Football (West Ham United)
Injuries: Removal of torn knee cartilage
Favourite band: REM
Relaxations: Golf, pub games, films
Extras: Took seven wickets in 14 balls v Hampshire at Hove 2001, the second most

(most by a seamer) outstanding spell of wicket-taking in first-class cricket (after Pat Pocock's seven in 11 for Surrey v Sussex at Eastbourne in 1972). His 8-106 v Leicestershire at Hove 2003 included a spell of 5-6 in 25 balls
Opinions on cricket: 'A return to "English county cricket" would be good.'
Best batting: 72 Sussex v Surrey, The Oval 2004
Best bowling: 8-106 Sussex v Leicestershire, Hove 2003

2004 Season

	M	Inns	NO	Runs	HS	Avge	100s	50s	Ct	St	O	M	Runs	Wkts	Avge	Best	5wI	10wM
Test																		
All First	11	14	4	159	72	15.90	-	1	2	-	259.2	64	849	27	31.44	5-66	1	-
1-day Int																		
C & G	1	1	0	2	2	2.00	-	-	1	-	8	2	24	1	24.00	1-24	-	
totesport	4	3	1	18	16 *	9.00	-	-	-	-	25.5	4	135	6	22.50	3-26	-	
Twenty20	3	2	1	8	8 *	8.00	-	-	2	-	11	0	62	4	15.50	2-16	-	

Career Performances

	M	Inns	NO	Runs	HS	Avge	100s	50s	Ct	St	Balls	Runs	Wkts	Avge	Best	5wI	10wM
Test																	
All First	124	170	39	1430	72	10.91	-	2	28	-	21458	11683	432	27.04	8-106	25	4
1-day Int																	
C & G	9	6	3	37	16	12.33	-	-	1	-	552	354	16	22.12	4-42	-	
totesport	43	25	8	83	16 *	4.88	-	-	9	-	1799	1455	57	25.52	4-29	-	
Twenty20	8	3	1	9	8 *	4.50	-	-	2	-	167	201	13	15.46	3-34	-	

57. Who made 159 for Barbados v Mike Denness's MCC tourists of 1973-74 and in 1995-96 became the oldest player (aged 47) so far to appear in the World Cup?

LIDDLE, C. J. Leicestershire

Name: Christopher (Chris) John Liddle
Role: Right-hand lower-order bat, left-arm fast bowler
Born: 1 February 1984, Middlesbrough
Height: 6ft 4in **Weight:** 12st 7lbs
Nickname: Lids
County debut: No first-team appearance
Parents: Pat and John
Marital status: 'Girlfriend Joanne'
Family links with cricket: 'Brother plays for Marton CC and Cleveland Schools county team'
Education: Nunthorpe Comprehensive School, Middlesbrough; Teesside Tertiary College; TTE Advanced Modern Apprenticeship
Qualifications: 9 GCSEs, qualified instrument technician, Level 1 coaching

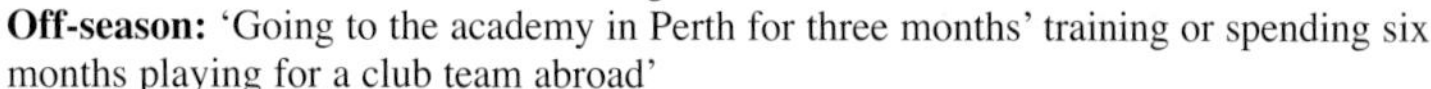

Off-season: 'Going to the academy in Perth for three months' training or spending six months playing for a club team abroad'
Career highlights to date: 'Signing professional for Leicestershire'
Cricket superstitions: 'Right bowling boot on first for bowling; left pad on first for batting'
Cricketers particularly admired: Brett Lee, Brad Hodge
Young players to look out for: John Sadler, Tom New, John Maunders, Liam Plunkett, Andrew Liddle
Other sports played: Football, squash
Other sports followed: Football (Middlesbrough)
Favourite band: 'Have not really got a favourite band – just like lots of different songs, mostly R&B'
Relaxations: 'Going to the gym; playing Championship Manager on the PC or Tiger Woods Golf on the PlayStation'
Extras: Yorkshire area Bowler of the Year 2001-02
Opinions on cricket: 'There should be a limit on Kolpak players (*see page 9*) at each club.'

LOGAN, R. J. Hampshire

Name: Richard James Logan
Role: Right-hand bat, right-arm fast bowler
Born: 28 January 1980, Cannock
Height: 6ft 1in **Weight:** 14st
Nickname: Bungle
County debut: 1999 (Northants), 2001 (Notts)
1st-Class 5 w. in innings: 4
1st-Class catches: 14
One-Day 5 w. in innings: 2
Place in bowling averages: 84th av. 35.30
Strike rate: 45.10 (career 52.87)
Parents: Margaret and Robert
Marital status: Single
Family links with cricket: 'Dad played local cricket for Cannock'
Education: Wolverhampton Grammar School
Qualifications: 11 GCSEs, 1 A-level
Overseas tours: England U17 to Bermuda (International Youth Tournament) 1997; England U19 to South Africa (including U19 World Cup) 1997-98, to New Zealand 1998-99
Overseas teams played for: St George, Sydney 1999-2000; Lancaster Park, New Zealand; Rovers, Durban; Northerns Goodwood, Cape Town
Career highlights to date: 'Winning junior World Cup'
Cricketers particularly admired: Malcolm Marshall, Dennis Lillee
Other sports played: Hockey
Other sports followed: Football (Wolverhampton Wanderers)
Relaxations: 'Spending time with my mates. Training'
Extras: Played for Staffordshire at every level from U11 to U19, and as captain from U13 to U17. Played for Midlands U14 and U15 (both as captain) and HMC Schools U15. 1995 *Daily Telegraph*/Lombard U15 Midlands Bowler and Batsman of the Year. Played for Northamptonshire U17 and U19 national champions 1997. Played for England U15, U17 and U19. Left Northamptonshire in the 2000-01 off-season and joined Nottinghamshire for 2001. C&G Man of the Match award for his 5-24 v Suffolk at Mildenhall 2001; it was his maiden one-day five-wicket return. Released by Nottinghamshire at the end of the 2004 season and has joined Hampshire for 2005
Opinions on cricket: 'I still believe we play too much cricket – therefore recovery is limited and quality suffers. The Twenty20 competition is fantastic. It's great to play in and by the looks of the crowds it's great to watch.'
Best batting: 37* Nottinghamshire v Hampshire, Trent Bridge 2001
Best bowling: 6-93 Nottinghamshire v Derbyshire, Trent Bridge 2001

2004 Season

	M	Inns	NO	Runs	HS	Avge	100s	50s	Ct	St	O	M	Runs	Wkts	Avge	Best	5wI	10wM
Test																		
All First	3	4	2	45	25 *	22.50	-	-	3	-	75.1	9	353	10	35.30	4-34	-	-
1-day Int																		
C & G	1	0	0	0	0	-	-	-	-	-	10	1	25	0	-	-	-	
totesport	6	4	3	27	15 *	27.00	-	-	1	-	41.4	1	239	6	39.83	4-50	-	
Twenty20	5	4	3	30	11 *	30.00	-	-	-	-	8.3	0	89	5	17.80	2-7	-	

Career Performances

	M	Inns	NO	Runs	HS	Avge	100s	50s	Ct	St	Balls	Runs	Wkts	Avge	Best	5wI	10wM
Test																	
All First	37	52	11	425	37 *	10.36	-	-	14	-	5658	3723	107	34.79	6-93	4	-
1-day Int																	
C & G	4	2	0	9	9	4.50	-	-	1	-	240	134	7	19.14	5-24	1	
totesport	41	22	8	161	24	11.50	-	-	13	-	1613	1637	43	38.06	4-32	-	
Twenty20	10	7	4	39	11 *	13.00	-	-	-	-	160	200	12	16.66	5-26	1	

LOUDON, A. G. R. — Warwickshire

Name: Alexander Guy Rushworth Loudon
Role: Right-hand bat, right-arm off-spin bowler
Born: 6 September 1980, London
Height: 6ft 3in **Weight:** 14st 8lbs
Nickname: Noisy, Minor, A-Lo, Minotaur
County debut: 2002 (one-day, Kent), 2003 (first-class, Kent)
1st-Class 50s: 7
1st-Class 100s: 1
1st-Class 5 w. in innings: 2
1st-Class catches: 16
Place in batting averages: 109th av. 35.11 (2003 62nd av. 42.70)
Place in bowling averages: 55th av. 31.09
Strike rate: 54.95 (career 62.53)
Parents: Jane and James
Marital status: Single
Family links with cricket: Brother and father played for Hampshire 2nd XI
Education: Eton College; Durham University
Qualifications: 9 GCSEs, 1 AO-level, 3 A-levels, 2.1 degree, ECB Level 1 coaching
Off-season: 'Working in London; cricket in Perth and Mumbai'

Overseas tours: Kent U12 to Holland 1991; Eton College to South Africa 1995; England U19 to Malaysia and (U19 World Cup) Sri Lanka 1999-2000 (captain); Kent to South Africa 2002
Career highlights to date: '172 v Durham at Racecourse'
Cricket moments to forget: 'Being bowled by Gimli in the nets'
Cricket superstitions: 'Avoiding them'
Cricketers particularly admired: Steve Waugh, Michael Atherton, Michael Bevan, Brian Lara
Young players to look out for: Michael Klingleffer (aka 'The Living')
Other sports played: Golf, squash, rackets, tennis
Other sports followed: Rugby (England), football (Man Utd)
Favourite band: Red Hot Chili Peppers
Relaxations: 'Eating, sleeping, reading, Sky Sports and MTV'
Extras: Captained England U15 in U15 World Cup 1996 and England U19 in U19 World Cup 1999-2000. Len Newbery Award for Best Schools Cricketer 1999. NBC Denis Compton Award for the most promising young Kent player 1999. Silk Trophy batting award 1999. Played for Durham University CCE 2001, 2002 and 2003, and was captain of Durham's BUSA winning side 2003. Played for the Eton Ramblers *Cricketer* Cup winning side 2001, scoring 64 in the final. Represented British Universities 2003. Recorded maiden first-class five-wicket return (5-53) v Middlesex at Southgate 2004. Left Kent at the end of the 2004 season and has joined Warwickshire for 2005
Opinions on cricket: 'Twenty20 has heightened interest in the game. The competition's expansion should be considered, perhaps with more games being played throughout the season. The Kolpak situation (*see page 9*) needs attention.'
Best batting: 172 DUCCE v Durham, Durham 2003
Best bowling: 6-47 Kent v Middlesex, Canterbury 2004

2004 Season

	M	Inns	NO	Runs	HS	Avge	100s	50s	Ct	St	O	M	Runs	Wkts	Avge	Best	5wI	10wM
Test																		
All First	11	17	0	597	92	35.11	-	6	6	-	192.2	32	653	21	31.09	6-47	2	-
1-day Int																		
C & G																		
totesport	12	12	2	234	52	23.40	-	2	5	-	37.3	0	201	9	22.33	4-48	-	
Twenty20	5	5	0	78	25	15.60	-	-	2	-								

Career Performances

	M	Inns	NO	Runs	HS	Avge	100s	50s	Ct	St	Balls	Runs	Wkts	Avge	Best	5wI	10wM
Test																	
All First	22	35	1	1120	172	32.94	1	7	16	-	1876	1205	30	40.16	6-47	2	-
1-day Int																	
C & G	1	1	0	53	53	53.00	-	1	-	-	6	4	0	-	-	-	
totesport	15	15	2	266	52	20.46	-	2	5	-	225	201	9	22.33	4-48	-	
Twenty20	5	5	0	78	25	15.60	-	-	2	-							

LOUW, J. Northamptonshire

Name: Johann Louw
Role: Right-hand bat, right-arm medium-fast bowler
Born: 12 April 1979, Cape Town, South Africa
County debut: 2004
50 wickets in a season: 1
1st-Class 50s: 5
1st-Class 100s: 1
1st-Class 5 w. in innings: 4
1st-Class catches: 21
One-Day 5 w. in innings: 1
Place in batting averages: 232nd av. 18.00
Place in bowling averages: 28th av. 26.51
Strike rate: 46.35 (career 57.18)
Overseas teams played for: Griqualand West 2000-01 – 2002-03; Eastern Province 2003-04; Dolphins 2004-05 –
Extras: Man of the Match for Griqualand West v Northerns at Kimberley in the Standard Bank Cup 2002-03 (4-25). Scored maiden first-class century (124) and had match figures of 5-131 v Boland at Port Elizabeth in the SuperSport Series 2003-04, winning Man of the Match award. Man of the Match v North West at Potchefstroom in the Standard Bank Cup 2003-04. Joined Northamptonshire as an overseas player for 2004, taking 60 first-class wickets at 26.51 and finishing as leading wicket-taker in Division One of the totesport League with 34 wickets at 15.67. Had figures of 2-6, including double wicket maiden, from his four overs v Warwickshire at Edgbaston in the Twenty20 Cup 2004. Is no longer considered an overseas player
Best batting: 124 Eastern Province v Boland, Port Elizabeth, 2003-04
Best bowling: 6-108 Griqualand West v Border, East London 2002-03

2004 Season

	M	Inns	NO	Runs	HS	Avge	100s	50s	Ct	St	O	M	Runs	Wkts	Avge	Best	5wI	10wM
Test																		
All First	16	22	3	342	63	18.00	-	1	8	-	463.3	89	1591	60	26.51	5-44	3	-
1-day Int																		
C & G	3	2	0	30	20	15.00	-	-	2	-	26	2	150	4	37.50	2-83	-	
totesport	16	12	2	144	36	14.40	-	-	3	-	135.2	14	533	34	15.67	5-27	1	
Twenty20	5	4	1	32	17	10.66	-	-	-	-	15.2	1	115	5	23.00	2-6	-	

Career Performances

	M	Inns	NO	Runs	HS	Avge	100s	50s	Ct	St	Balls	Runs	Wkts	Avge	Best	5wI	10wM
Test																	
All First	39	60	8	1151	124	22.13	1	5	21	-	6919	3640	121	30.08	6-108	4	-
1-day Int																	
C & G	3	2	0	30	20	15.00	-	-	2	-	156	150	4	37.50	2-83	-	
totesport	16	12	2	144	36	14.40	-	-	3	-	812	533	34	15.67	5-27	1	
Twenty20	5	4	1	32	17	10.66	-	-	-	-	92	115	5	23.00	2-6	-	

LOVE, M. L. Northamptonshire

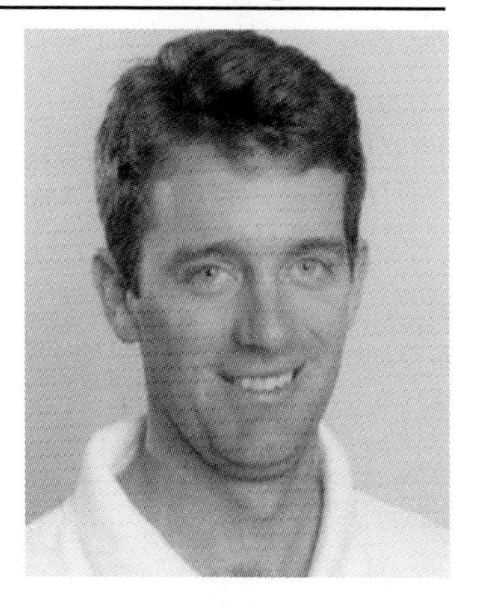

Name: Martin Lloyd Love
Role: Right-hand bat
Born: 30 March 1974, Mundubbera, Queensland, Australia
Height: 6ft **Weight:** 13st
Nickname: Handles
County debut: 2001 (Durham), 2004 (Northamptonshire)
County cap: 2001 (Durham)
Test debut: 2002-03
Tests: 5
1000 runs in a season: 1
1st-Class 50s: 61
1st-Class 100s: 23
1st-Class 200s: 7
1st-Class 300s: 1
1st-Class catches: 190
Place in batting averages: (2003 12th av. 59.84)
Strike rate: (career 30.00)
Parents: Ormond and Evelyn
Wife: Deborah
Education: Toowoomba Grammar School; University of Queensland
Qualifications: Bachelor of Physiotherapy, Level 2 coach
Career outside cricket: Physiotherapist
Off-season: Playing for Queensland Bulls
Overseas tours: Australia U19 to New Zealand 1992-93; Young Australia (Australia A) to England and Netherlands 1995; Australia to West Indies 2002-03
Overseas teams played for: Queensland Bulls 1992-93 –
Career highlights to date: 'Member of Queensland's first ever Sheffield Shield winning team 1994-95'
Cricket moments to forget: 'Any duck'

Cricket superstitions: 'Left pad on first'
Cricketers particularly admired: Allan Border
Young players to look out for: Gordon Muchall
Other sports played: Golf
Other sports followed: AFL (Brisbane Lions), rugby union (Queensland Reds)
Relaxations: 'Home renovation'
Extras: Represented Queensland U17 (1990-91) and U19 (1991-93). Made debut for Queensland in 1992-93 Sheffield Shield final v New South Wales. Shared with Stuart Law in record third-wicket partnership for Queensland (326), v Tasmania at Brisbane 1994-95. Shared with Matthew Hayden in record second-wicket partnership for Queensland (368*), v Tasmania at Hobart 1995-96. Won the Ian Healy Trophy for Queensland Player of the Year 2000-01. Joined Durham as overseas player in 2001. Scored his first century for Durham (149*) v Nottinghamshire at Riverside 2001, in the process sharing in Durham's highest Championship partnership for any wicket (258) with Jon Lewis. Leading run-scorer in the Pura Cup 2001-02 with 1108 (av. 65.18). Scored two double centuries against the England touring side 2002-03 – 250 for Queensland at Brisbane and 201* for Australia A at Hobart. Named State Player of the Year at the 2003 Allan Border Medal awards. Set a new record for the highest individual score made at the Riverside ground (273), v Hampshire 2003, breaking his own record for the highest score made by a Durham batsman. Left Durham at the end of the 2003 season. Scored 300* v Victoria at Melbourne 2003-04, becoming the first player to score a first-class triple century for Queensland. Was an overseas player with Northamptonshire July to August 2004, deputising for Martin van Jaarsveld, absent on international duty; has returned for 2005. Scored undefeated century in each innings (133*/161*) v Worcestershire at Worcester 2004
Best batting: 300* Queensland v Victoria, Melbourne 2003-04
Best bowling: 1-5 Queensland v Western Australia, Brisbane 1997-98

2004 Season

	M	Inns	NO	Runs	HS	Avge	100s	50s	Ct	St	O	M	Runs	Wkts	Avge	Best	5wI	10wM
Test																		
All First	2	4	3	394	161 *	394.00	2	1	3	-								
1-day Int																		
C & G																		
totesport	5	5	0	79	27	15.80	-	-	1	-								
Twenty20																		

Career Performances

	M	Inns	NO	Runs	HS	Avge	100s	50s	Ct	St	Balls	Runs	Wkts	Avge	Best	5wI	10wM
Test	5	8	3	233	100 *	46.60	1	1	7	-							
All First	161	279	29	12980	300 *	51.92	31	61	190	-	30	11	1	11.00	1-5	-	-
1-day Int																	
C & G	5	4	0	132	51	33.00	-	1	1	-							
totesport	31	31	1	848	89	28.26	-	4	13	-	12	7	0	-	-	-	
Twenty20	3	3	0	62	51	20.66	-	1	2	-							

LOWE, J. A. Durham

Name: James Adam Lowe
Role: Right-hand bat, right-arm off-spin bowler
Born: 4 November 1982, Bury St Edmunds
Height: 6ft 2in **Weight:** 14st 10lbs
Nickname: Lowey, J-Lo
County debut: 2003
1st-Class 50s: 1
1st-Class catches: 2
Parents: Jim and Pat
Marital status: Single
Family links with cricket: 'Dad played for Northallerton CC and is a qualified coach'
Education: Northallerton College
Qualifications: Coaching Level 2
Career outside cricket: 'Worked in local leisure centre. Qualified lifeguard'
Overseas tours: Durham to India 2004
Overseas teams played for: Gosnells CC, Perth 2003-04
Career highlights to date: '80 on my first-class debut v Hampshire'
Cricketers particularly admired: Ritchie Storr, Paul Collingwood, Danny Law
Young players to look out for: Liam Plunkett, Graham Onions
Other sports played: Football ('played for school and town as a youngster')
Other sports followed: Football (Middlesbrough)
Favourite band: Stone Roses
Relaxations: Eating out; watching Middlesbrough
Extras: Scored 80 on first-class debut v Hampshire at West End 2003. Is a Durham Development Player
Opinions on cricket: 'Too many EU players.'
Best batting: 80 Durham v Hampshire, West End 2003

2004 Season

	M	Inns	NO	Runs	HS	Avge	100s	50s	Ct	St	O	M	Runs	Wkts	Avge	Best	5wI	10wM
Test																		
All First	2	4	0	91	41	22.75	-	-	2	-								
1-day Int																		
C & G																		
totesport																		
Twenty20																		

Career Performances

	M	Inns	NO	Runs	HS	Avge	100s	50s	Ct	St	Balls	Runs	Wkts	Avge	Best	5wI	10wM
Test																	
All First	3	6	0	171	80	28.50	-	1	2	-							
1-day Int																	
C & G																	
totesport																	
Twenty20																	

LOYE, M. B. Lancashire

Name: Malachy Bernard Loye
Role: Right-hand bat, off-spin bowler, occasional wicket-keeper
Born: 27 September 1972, Northampton
Height: 6ft 3in **Weight:** 14st
Nickname: Mal, Chairman, Jacko, Shermenator
County debut: 1991 (Northamptonshire), 2003 (Lancashire)
County cap: 1994 (Northamptonshire), 2003 (Lancashire)
1000 runs in a season: 3
1st-Class 50s: 43
1st-Class 100s: 26
1st-Class 200s: 1
1st-Class 300s: 1
1st-Class catches: 87
One-Day 100s: 6
Place in batting averages: 43rd av. 49.15 (2003 27th av. 50.57)
Strike rate: (career 55.00)
Parents: Patrick and Anne
Marital status: Single
Family links with cricket: Father and brother played for Cogenhoe CC in Northampton
Education: Moulton Comprehensive School
Qualifications: GCSEs, 'numerous coaching certificates'
Overseas tours: England U18 to Canada (International Youth Tournament) 1991; England U19 to Pakistan 1991-92; England A to South Africa 1993-94, to Zimbabwe and South Africa 1998-99; Northamptonshire to Cape Town 1993, to Zimbabwe 1995, 1998, to Johannesburg 1996, to Grenada 2001, 2002
Overseas teams played for: Riccarton, Christchurch, New Zealand 1992-95; Onslow,

Wellington, New Zealand 1995-96; North Perth, Australia 1997-98; Claremont, Perth 2001
Career highlights to date: 'PCA Player of the Year 1998'
Cricket moments to forget: 'Not being picked for 1995 and 1996 cup finals'
Cricket superstitions: 'None'
Cricketers particularly admired: Wayne Larkins, Gordon Greenidge, Curtly Ambrose, Devon Malcolm, Peter Carlstein, David Capel
Other sports followed: Football (Liverpool, Northampton Town), rugby union (Ireland), boxing
Relaxations: 'Playing the guitar, swimming, singing, reading. Having the odd large night out!'
Extras: Played for England YC and for England U19. PCA Young Player of the Year and Whittingdale Young Player of the Year 1993. Shared in a county then record opening stand of 372 with Richard Montgomerie as Northamptonshire followed on v Yorkshire at Northampton 1996. His 322* v Glamorgan at Northampton 1998 was the then highest individual first-class score for the county; during his innings, Loye put on 401 with David Ripley, setting a new fifth-wicket record for first-class cricket in England. PCA Player of the Year 1998. Left Northamptonshire at the end of the 2002 season and joined Lancashire for 2003. Scored century (126) on Championship debut for Lancashire v Surrey at The Oval 2003 and another (113) in the next match v Nottinghamshire at Old Trafford to become the first batsman to score centuries in his first two matches for the county. C&G Man of the Match award for his 74 v Middlesex in the quarter-final at Old Trafford 2003. Scored century (184) v Warwickshire at Stratford-upon-Avon 2004, in the process passing 10,000 runs in first-class cricket
Best batting: 322* Northamptonshire v Glamorgan, Northampton 1998
Best bowling: 1-8 Lancashire v Kent, Blackpool 2003

2004 Season

	M	Inns	NO	Runs	HS	Avge	100s	50s	Ct	St	O	M	Runs	Wkts	Avge	Best	5wI	10wM
Test																		
All First	14	22	3	934	184	49.15	2	6	8	-	1	0	1	0	-	-	-	-
1-day Int																		
C & G	3	3	0	141	54	47.00	-	2	-	-								
totesport	11	11	0	297	70	27.00	-	2	2	-								
Twenty20	6	6	1	152	64 *	30.40	-	1	2	-								

Career Performances

	M	Inns	NO	Runs	HS	Avge	100s	50s	Ct	St	Balls	Runs	Wkts	Avge	Best	5wI	10wM
Test																	
All First	180	287	27	10345	322 *	39.78	28	43	87	-	55	61	1	61.00	1-8	-	-
1-day Int																	
C & G	28	27	6	865	124 *	41.19	2	4	6	-							
totesport	149	145	14	4295	122	32.78	4	29	37	-							
Twenty20	11	11	1	227	64 *	22.70	-	1	3	-							

LUCAS, D. S. Yorkshire

Name: David Scott Lucas
Role: Right-hand bat, left-arm medium-fast bowler
Born: 19 August 1978, Nottingham
Height: 6ft 3in **Weight:** 13st 3lbs
Nickname: Muke, Lukey
County debut: 1999 (Nottinghamshire)
1st-Class 5 w. in innings: 1
1st-Class catches: 3
Strike rate: (career 60.30)
Parents: Mary and Terry
Marital status: Married
Education: Djanogly City Technology College, Nottingham
Qualifications: 6 GCSEs, pass in Computer-Aided Design
Overseas tours: England (Indoor) to Australia (Indoor Cricket World Cup) 1998
Overseas teams played for: Bankstown-Canterbury Bulldogs, Sydney 1996-97; Wanneroo, Perth 2001-02
Career highlights to date: 'Getting Man of the Match against Derbyshire in a close fixture'
Cricket superstitions: 'Always walk back to the left of my mark when bowling. Always put left pad on first'
Cricketers particularly admired: Wasim Akram, Glenn McGrath, Steve Waugh, Damien Martyn
Young players to look out for: Bilal Shafayat
Other sports played: Indoor cricket, football
Other sports followed: Football (Arsenal FC)
Relaxations: 'Food, cars, PS2, movies'
Extras: Won Yorkshire League with Rotherham in 1996. NBC Denis Compton Award for the most promising young Nottinghamshire player 2000. Released by Nottinghamshire at the end of the 2004 season and has joined Yorkshire for 2005
Best batting: 49 Nottinghamshire v DUCCE, Trent Bridge 2002
Best bowling: 5-104 Nottinghamshire v Essex, Trent Bridge 1999

2004 Season (did not make any first-class or one-day appearances)

Career Performances

	M	Inns	NO	Runs	HS	Avge	100s	50s	Ct	St	Balls	Runs	Wkts	Avge	Best	5wI	10wM
Test																	
All First	22	28	8	436	49	21.80	-	-	3	-	3136	1909	52	36.71	5-104	1	-
1-day Int																	
C & G	1	1	1	14	14 *	-	-	-	-	-	36	40	0	-	-	-	
totesport	26	9	2	52	19 *	7.42	-	-	3	-	1113	1036	39	26.56	4-27	-	
Twenty20																	

LUMB, M. J. — Yorkshire

Name: Michael John Lumb
Role: Left-hand bat, right-arm medium bowler
Born: 12 February 1980, Johannesburg, South Africa
Height: 6ft **Weight:** 13st
Nickname: China, Joe
County debut: 2000
County cap: 2003
1000 runs in a season: 1
1st-Class 50s: 17
1st-Class 100s: 4
1st-Class catches: 28
Place in batting averages: 179th av. 24.81 (2003 69th av. 41.52)
Strike rate: (career 37.50)
Parents: Richard and Sue
Marital status: Single
Family links with cricket: Father played for Yorkshire. Uncle played for Natal
Education: St Stithians College
Qualifications: Matriculation
Overseas tours: Transvaal U19 to Barbados; Yorkshire to Cape Town 2001, to Grenada 2002; England A to Malaysia and India 2003-04
Overseas teams played for: Pirates CC, Johannesburg; Wanderers CC, Johannesburg
Career highlights to date: 'Getting my Yorkshire cap'
Cricket moments to forget: 'Relegation in 2002'
Cricket superstitions: 'None'
Cricketers particularly admired: Graham Thorpe, Darren Lehmann, Craig White, Stephen Fleming

Young players to look out for: Grant Elliott, Matthew Prior
Other sports played: Golf
Other sports followed: Rugby union (Sharks in Super 12, Leeds Tykes)
Favourite band: Oasis
Relaxations: 'Golf, socialising with friends'
Extras: Scored 66* on first-class debut v Zimbabweans at Headingley 2000. Scored maiden first-class century (122) v Leicestershire at Headingley 2001; the Lumbs thus became only the fourth father and son to have scored centuries for Yorkshire. Yorkshire Young Player of the Year 2002, 2003. ECB National Academy 2003-04
Best batting: 124 Yorkshire v Surrey, Guildford 2002
Best bowling: 2-10 Yorkshire v Kent, Canterbury 2001

2004 Season

	M	Inns	NO	Runs	HS	Avge	100s	50s	Ct	St	O	M	Runs	Wkts	Avge	Best	5wI	10wM
Test																		
All First	13	23	1	546	83	24.81	-	4	8	-	1	0	2	0	-	-	-	-
1-day Int																		
C & G	3	3	1	115	77	57.50	-	1	1	-								
totesport	13	12	0	267	71	22.25	-	1	6	-								
Twenty20	5	5	1	17	9 *	4.25	-	-	1	-								

Career Performances

	M	Inns	NO	Runs	HS	Avge	100s	50s	Ct	St	Balls	Runs	Wkts	Avge	Best	5wI	10wM
Test																	
All First	54	91	6	2739	124	32.22	4	17	28	-	150	114	4	28.50	2-10	-	-
1-day Int																	
C & G	9	8	1	261	82	37.28	-	2	3	-							
totesport	46	44	3	1107	92	27.00	-	7	16	-							
Twenty20	10	10	1	164	55	18.22	-	2	1	-	36	65	3	21.66	3-32	-	

LUNGLEY, T. — Derbyshire

Name: Tom Lungley
Role: Left-hand bat, right-arm medium bowler
Born: 25 July 1979, Derby
Height: 6ft 2in **Weight:** 13st
Nickname: Lungfish, Monkfish, Sweaty, Full Moon, Half Moon, Lungo
County debut: 2000
1st-Class catches: 6
Place in batting averages: (2003 268th av. 11.42)
Strike rate: (career 46.14)
Parents: Richard and Christina
Marital status: 'Taken'

Family links with cricket: 'Dad was captain of Derby Road CC. Grandad was bat maker in younger days'
Education: Saint John Houghton School; South East Derbyshire College
Qualifications: 9 GCSEs, Sport and Recreation Levels 1 and 2, pool lifeguard qualification, coaching qualifications in cricket, tennis, basketball, football and volleyball
Career outside cricket: Painter and decorator
Overseas teams played for: Delacombe Park, Melbourne 1999-2000
Cricket moments to forget: 'Unable to speak when interviewed by Sybil Ruscoe on *Channel 4 Cricket Roadshow* (live)'
Cricket superstitions: 'Always eat Jaffa Cake before play'
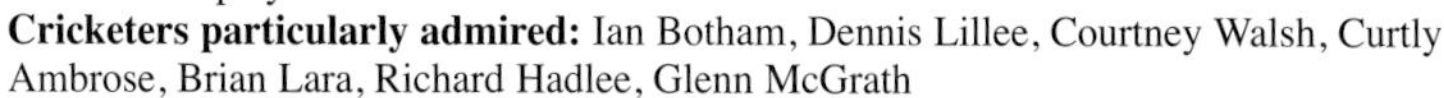
Cricketers particularly admired: Ian Botham, Dennis Lillee, Courtney Walsh, Curtly Ambrose, Brian Lara, Richard Hadlee, Glenn McGrath
Other sports played: 'Enjoy playing most sports, mainly football and basketball'
Other sports followed: Football (Derby County), basketball (Derby Storm)
Extras: First home-grown cricketer to become professional from Ockbrook and Borrowash CC. Scored 109 in Derbyshire Cup final 2000, winning Man of the Match award. Took 4-13 v Nottinghamshire at Derby in the Twenty20 2003. NBC Denis Compton Award for the most promising young Derbyshire player 2003
Best batting: 47 Derbyshire v Warwickshire, Derby 2001
Best bowling: 4-101 Derbyshire v Glamorgan, Swansea 2003

2004 Season (did not make any first-class or one-day appearances)

Career Performances

	M	Inns	NO	Runs	HS	Avge	100s	50s	Ct	St	Balls	Runs	Wkts	Avge	Best	5wI	10wM
Test																	
All First	19	32	5	356	47	13.18	-	-	6	-	1938	1334	42	31.76	4-101	-	-
1-day Int																	
C & G	5	4	1	7	3	2.33	-	-	2	-	179	145	4	36.25	2-18	-	
totesport	25	16	5	198	45	18.00	-	-	4	-	1077	884	37	23.89	4-28	-	
Twenty20	5	3	1	37	18 *	18.50	-	-	1	-	102	126	6	21.00	4-13	-	

MacGILL, S. C. G. Nottinghamshire

Name: Stuart Charles Glyndwr MacGill
Role: Right-hand bat, right-arm leg-spin bowler
Born: 25 February 1971, Perth, Australia
Height: 6ft **Weight:** 14st 2lbs
Nickname: Gorilla
County debut: 1997 (Somerset), 2002 (Nottinghamshire)
County cap: 2002 (Nottinghamshire)
Test debut: 1997-98
Tests: 32
One-Day Internationals: 3
1st-Class 50s: 1
1st-Class 5 w. in innings: 34
1st-Class 10 w. in match: 6
1st-Class catches: 62
Place in batting averages: 259th av. 12.60 (2003 277th av. 9.33)
Place in bowling averages: 82nd av. 35.20 (2003 81st av. 33.52)
Strike rate: 61.50 (career 53.59)
Parents: Terry and Jenny
Wife: Rachel
Children: Alexander
Family links with cricket: Father (T. M. D. MacGill) and grandfather (C. W. T. MacGill) played for Western Australia
Education: Christ Church GS, Perth
Off-season: 'Cricket in Oz'
Overseas tours: Australia to India 1997-98, to Pakistan 1998-99, to West Indies 1998-99, to Sri Lanka and Zimbabwe 1999-2000, to South Africa 2001-02, to West Indies 2002-03, to Sri Lanka 2003-04
Overseas teams played for: Western Australia 1993-94; New South Wales 1996-97 –
Career highlights to date: 'Mick Newell fielding at bat-pad ten years after he retired'
Cricket moments to forget: '2003 for Notts'
Cricket superstitions: 'None'
Cricketers particularly admired: Mick Newell
Young players to look out for: Paul McMahon, Ed Joyce
Other sports followed: Australian Rugby League (Newcastle), football (Newcastle United)
Favourite band: Coldplay
Relaxations: 'Reading, drinking, eating; listening to quality tunes'
Extras: Attended Commonwealth Bank [Australian] Cricket Academy 1991. Played one first-class match for Somerset 1997, v Pakistan A at Taunton. Was leading wicket-

taker in Test series v England 1998-99 with 27 wickets (av. 17.70), including match figures of 12-107 in the fifth Test at Sydney. Took 4-19 on ODI debut v Pakistan at Sydney in the Carlton and United Series 1999-2000, winning Man of the Match award. Was leading wicket-taker in the ING Cup 2001-02 with 21 at 18.14. Was Nottinghamshire's overseas player for two periods during the 2002 season; returned to Nottinghamshire as an overseas player for 2003. Took 5-63 v Worcestershire at Kidderminster 2002, becoming the first bowler since Garfield Sobers in 1968 to record a five-wicket innings return on Championship debut for Nottinghamshire; took 40 wickets (av. 23.25) overall in his six Championship matches for Nottinghamshire 2002. Took 100th Test wicket (Carlton Baugh) in the second Test v West Indies at Port of Spain 2002-03. His other international awards include Man of the Match in the third Test at Bridgetown 2002-03 (4-107/5-75) and Man of the Series v Bangladesh 2003 (17 wickets; av. 12.88). Left Nottinghamshire at the end of the 2004 season
Best batting: 53 New South Wales v South Australia, Sydney 2001-02
Best bowling: 8-111 Nottinghamshire v Middlesex, Trent Bridge 2002
Stop press: Scored 27 v Western Australia in the Pura Cup at Sydney 2004-05, in the process sharing with Dominic Thornely (261*) in a last-wicket stand of 219. Had match figures of 8-170 (5-87/3-83) in the third Test v Pakistan at Sydney 2004-05, winning Man of the Match award

2004 Season

	M	Inns	NO	Runs	HS	Avge	100s	50s	Ct	St	O	M	Runs	Wkts	Avge	Best	5wI	10wM
Test																		
All First	15	12	2	126	28	12.60	-	-	3	-	410	80	1408	40	35.20	7-109	2	1
1-day Int																		
C & G	2	1	1	7	7 *	-	-	-	-	-	9	0	74	0	-	-	-	
totesport	13	1	0	26	26	26.00	-	-	1	-	99.2	7	493	25	19.72	4-18	-	
Twenty20																		

Career Performances

	M	Inns	NO	Runs	HS	Avge	100s	50s	Ct	St	Balls	Runs	Wkts	Avge	Best	5wI	10wM
Test	32	37	6	264	43	8.51	-	-	16	-	8447	4441	152	29.21	7-50	9	2
All First	135	164	41	1183	53	9.61	-	1	62	-	30549	17228	570	30.22	8-111	34	6
1-day Int	3	2	1	1	1	1.00	-	-	2	-	180	105	6	17.50	4-19	-	
C & G	5	4	1	11	7 *	3.66	-	-	1	-	234	171	2	85.50	1-29	-	
totesport	29	8	3	50	26	10.00	-	-	6	-	1275	1037	45	23.04	4-18	-	
Twenty20	5	2	1	13	8 *	13.00	-	-	1	-	104	144	6	24.00	3-42	-	

MADDY, D. L. Leicestershire

Name: Darren Lee Maddy
Role: Right-hand opening bat, right-arm medium bowler, county vice-captain
Born: 23 May 1974, Leicester
Height: 5ft 9in **Weight:** 12st 7lbs
Nickname: Roaster, Dazza, Fire Starter
County debut: 1993 (one-day), 1994 (first-class)
County cap: 1996
Test debut: 1999
Tests: 3
One-Day Internationals: 8
1000 runs in a season: 4
1st-Class 50s: 48
1st-Class 100s: 16
1st-Class 200s: 2
1st-Class 5 w. in innings: 4
1st-Class catches: 195
One-Day 100s: 6
Place in batting averages: 133rd av. 32.14 (2003 63rd av. 42.69)
Place in bowling averages: 137th av. 45.73 (2003 48th av. 27.83)
Strike rate: 67.73 (career 55.83)
Parents: William Arthur and Hilary Jean
Wife and date of marriage: Justine Marie, 7 October 2000
Family links with cricket: Father and younger brother, Greg, play club cricket
Education: Roundhill, Thurmaston; Wreake Valley, Syston
Qualifications: 8 GCSEs, Level 1 coach
Career outside cricket: Fitness advisor
Off-season: 'Travelling and studying'
Overseas tours: Leicestershire to Bloemfontein 1995, to Western Transvaal 1996, to Durban 1997, to Barbados 1998, to Anguilla 2000, to Potchefstroom 2001; England A to Kenya and Sri Lanka 1997-98, to Zimbabwe and South Africa 1998-99; England to South Africa and Zimbabwe 1999-2000; England VI to Hong Kong 2003, 2004
Overseas teams played for: Wanderers, Johannesburg 1992-93; Northern Free State, South Africa 1993-95; Rhodes University, South Africa 1995-97; Sunshine CC, Grenada 2002; Perth CC, 2002-04
Career highlights to date: 'Winning two Championship medals. Playing for England. Winning Twenty20 final [2004]'
Cricket moments to forget: 'Too many to mention. I hate losing a cricket match and I hate getting out – losing two Lord's finals, finishing second in the Norwich Union League, and being relegated [in Championship 2003]'

Cricket superstitions: 'Always put my left pad on first'
Cricketers particularly admired: Graham Gooch, Michael Atherton, Ian Botham, Viv Richards, Richard Hadlee
Young players to look out for: Stuart Broad
Other sports played: Touch rugby, golf, squash, 5-a-side football
Other sports followed: Rugby (Leicester Tigers), football (Leicester City), baseball, golf, boxing – 'most sports really except for horse racing and motor racing'
Injuries: Broken thumb, bad neck, bruised rib – no time off required
Favourite band: 'Too many to mention – Two Tone Deaf, Bon Jovi, Def Leppard, Stereophonics, Aerosmith'
Relaxations: 'Going to the gym, playing sport, spending time with my wife, Justine; listening to music, watching TV, going on holiday, scuba diving, bungee jumping, playing the drums'
Extras: In 1994, set a new 2nd XI Championship run aggregate record (1498) and won the Rapid Cricketline 2nd XI Championship Player of the Year award. Was leading run-scorer on England A's 1997-98 tour with 687 runs at 68.7. In 1998, broke the record for the number of runs scored in the B&H competition in one season (629), also setting a record for the most B&H Gold Awards won in one season (five). Scored 110 for First Class Counties Select XI in one-day match v Sri Lanka A at Riverside 1999. Scored 133 for England XI in one-day match v Combined Border/Eastern Province Invitation XI at Alice 1999-2000. Had first innings figures of 5-104 and then scored 81 and 94 v Surrey at Leicester 2002. Scored 229* v Loughborough UCCE at Leicester 2003, in the process sharing with Brad Hodge (202*) in a record partnership for any wicket for Leicestershire and the second highest partnership for the third wicket in English first-class cricket (436*). Struck 60-ball 111 v Yorkshire at Headingley in the Twenty20 Cup 2004, in the process sharing with Brad Hodge (78) in a competition record partnership for any wicket (167). Struck 40-ball 72 v Glamorgan in Twenty20 Cup semi-final at Edgbaston 2004, in the process becoming the first player to pass 500 runs in the competition. President of the Leicestershire School Sports Federation. Vice-captain of Leicestershire since July 2004
Opinions on cricket: 'If we are trying to improve the standard of English cricket, then why do we have to play the first round of an important competition on club grounds that (although they try their best) are not up to the requirements of first-class cricket and thus bring the standard of cricket down to club/village level? I'm sure these opposing teams would love to have the opportunity to play at a first-class venue. There are too many non-English players playing county cricket. If we don't put some kind of restriction on the influx of such players it will have a detrimental effect on the England team in the very near future! We've already started to see counties releasing home-grown players and substituting them with non-English-qualified players who are not necessarily any better cricketers.'
Best batting: 229* Leicestershire v LUCCE, Leicester 2003
Best bowling: 5-37 Leicestershire v Hampshire, West End 2002

2004 Season

	M	Inns	NO	Runs	HS	Avge	100s	50s	Ct	St	O	M	Runs	Wkts	Avge	Best	5wI	10wM
Test																		
All First	17	30	2	900	145	32.14	1	7	24	-	169.2	24	686	15	45.73	2-41	-	-
1-day Int																		
C & G	1	1	0	3	3	3.00	-	-	-	-	1	0	6	0	-	-	-	
totesport	18	15	0	408	95	27.20	-	3	5	-	57.5	4	293	13	22.53	2-25	-	
Twenty20	7	7	0	356	111	50.85	1	3	1	-	10	0	88	1	88.00	1-22	-	

Career Performances

	M	Inns	NO	Runs	HS	Avge	100s	50s	Ct	St	Balls	Runs	Wkts	Avge	Best	5wI	10wM
Test	3	4	0	46	24	11.50	-	-	4	-	84	40	0	-	-	-	-
All First	188	306	20	9475	229 *	33.12	18	48	195	-	8319	4602	149	30.88	5-37	4	-
1-day Int	8	6	0	113	53	18.83	-	1	1	-							
C & G	24	22	2	455	89	22.75	-	2	10	-	521	425	15	28.33	3-44	-	
totesport	168	152	19	3675	106 *	27.63	1	25	56	-	3169	2815	94	29.94	4-16	-	
Twenty20	13	13	0	532	111	40.92	1	4	2	-	164	212	5	42.40	2-23	-	

MAHMOOD, S. I. — Lancashire

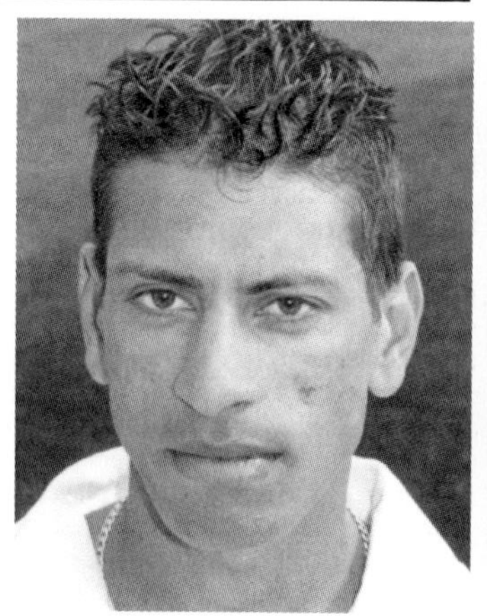

Name: Sajid Iqbal Mahmood
Role: Right-hand bat, right-arm fast-medium bowler
Born: 21 December 1981, Bolton
Height: 6ft 4in **Weight:** 12st 7lbs
Nickname: Saj, King
County debut: 2002
One-Day Internationals: 1
1st-Class 50s: 1
1st-Class 5 w. in innings: 2
1st-Class catches: 3
Place in batting averages: 213th av. 21.18
Place in bowling averages: 131st av. 43.91 (2003 57th av. 29.60)
Strike rate: 60.00 (career 54.04)
Parents: Shahid and Femida
Marital status: Single
Family links with cricket: Father played in Bolton League; younger brother plays in Bolton League
Education: Smithills School; North College, Bolton (sixth form)
Qualifications: 9 GCSEs, 3 A-levels
Off-season: ECB National Academy 2004-05

Overseas tours: Lancashire to South Africa 2003; England A to Malaysia and India 2003-04, to Sri Lanka 2004-05
Overseas teams played for: Napier, New Zealand 2002-03
Career highlights to date: 'Making first-team debut and selection for academy'
Cricket moments to forget: 'None'
Cricket superstitions: 'None'
Cricketers particularly admired: Brett Lee, Shoaib Akhtar
Favourite band: Nelly, Eminem
Relaxations: 'Music and chillin' with mates'
Extras: Scored fastest hundred in Bolton League U15 (42 balls). Took 5-62 for England A v East Zone at Amritsar 2003-04. NBC Denis Compton Award for the most promising young Lancashire player 2003. Struck 66-ball 94 in Championship v Sussex at Old Trafford 2004. Made ODI debut v New Zealand at Bristol in the NatWest Series 2004. ECB National Academy 2003-04, 2004-05. Is cousin of Olympic silver medal winning boxer Amir Khan
Opinions on cricket: 'Too much cricket played.'
Best batting: 94 Lancashire v Sussex, Old Trafford 2004
Best bowling: 5-37 Lancashire v DUCCE, Durham 2003

2004 Season

	M	Inns	NO	Runs	HS	Avge	100s	50s	Ct	St	O	M	Runs	Wkts	Avge	Best	5wI	10wM
Test																		
All First	11	14	3	233	94	21.18	-	1	2	-	230	26	1010	23	43.91	4-59	-	-
1-day Int	1	1	0	1	1	1.00	-	-	-	-	7	0	56	0	-	-	-	
C & G	3	1	0	29	29	29.00	-	-	-	-	25	2	134	6	22.33	3-56	-	
totesport	13	6	4	27	10 *	13.50	-	-	-	-	104.2	12	486	24	20.25	4-39	-	
Twenty20	4	1	0	1	1	1.00	-	-	-	-	13	0	101	1	101.00	1-20	-	

Career Performances

	M	Inns	NO	Runs	HS	Avge	100s	50s	Ct	St	Balls	Runs	Wkts	Avge	Best	5wI	10wM
Test																	
All First	19	24	4	348	94	17.40	-	1	3	-	2486	1685	46	36.63	5-37	2	-
1-day Int	1	1	0	1	1	1.00	-	-	-	-	42	56	0	-	-	-	
C & G	5	3	1	45	29	22.50	-	-	-	-	189	179	8	22.37	3-56	-	
totesport	21	7	4	30	10 *	10.00	-	-	1	-	932	775	33	23.48	4-39	-	
Twenty20	8	4	0	22	21	5.50	-	-	-	-	168	216	3	72.00	1-20	-	

58. Born in Copenhagen, who represented Denmark in the 1999 and 2000 NatWest Trophy competitions and took 63 first-class wickets for Kent in his first full season in 2002?

MALIK, M. N. Worcestershire

Name: Muhammad Nadeem Malik
Role: Right-hand bat, right-arm fast-medium bowler
Born: 6 October 1982, Nottingham
Height: 6ft 5in **Weight:** 14st 7lbs
Nickname: Nad, Busta, Nigel, Gerz
County debut: 2001 (Nottinghamshire), 2004 (Worcestershire)
County colours: 2004 (Worcestershire)
1st-Class 5 w. in innings: 3
1st-Class catches: 3
Place in batting averages: 281st av. 6.85
Place in bowling averages: 67th av. 32.54
Strike rate: 51.00 (career 52.03)
Parents: Abdul and Arshad
Marital status: Single
Family links with cricket: Brother plays club cricket for Carrington
Education: Wilford Meadows Secondary School; Bilborough College
Qualifications: 9 GCSEs
Career outside cricket: Personal trainer
Off-season: Playing club cricket in Perth
Overseas tours: ZRK to Pakistan 2000; Nottinghamshire to South Africa 2001; England U19 to India 2000-01, to Australia and (U19 World Cup) New Zealand 2001-02
Career highlights to date: '5-57 against Derbyshire 2001'
Cricket moments to forget: 'Norwich Union match v Yorkshire at Scarborough 2001 – Lehmann 191'
Cricketers particularly admired: Glenn McGrath, Wasim Akram, Curtly Ambrose
Young players to look out for: Steve Davies, Will Gifford
Other sports played: Football ('beating Usman Afzaal in 5-a-side games')
Other sports followed: Football, boxing
Relaxations: Music, games consoles
Extras: Made Nottinghamshire 2nd XI debut in 1999, aged 16, and took 15 wickets at an average of 19.40 for the 2nd XI 2000. Represented England U19 v West Indies U19 2001 and v India U19 2002. Left Nottinghamshire in the 2003-04 off-season and joined Worcestershire for 2004
Best batting: 39* Worcestershire v New Zealanders, Worcester 2004
Best bowling: 5-57 Nottinghamshire v Derbyshire, Trent Bridge 2001

2004 Season

	M	Inns	NO	Runs	HS	Avge	100s	50s	Ct	St	O	M	Runs	Wkts	Avge	Best	5wI	10wM
Test																		
All First	8	9	2	48	39 *	6.85	-	-	2	-	204	35	781	24	32.54	5-88	1	-
1-day Int																		
C & G	1	0	0	0	0	-	-	-	-	-	7	0	51	0	-	-	-	
totesport	11	5	3	14	6 *	7.00	-	-	1	-	77.5	10	363	18	20.16	4-42	-	
Twenty20	6	2	2	4	3 *	-	-	-	1	-	20	0	156	10	15.60	3-23	-	

Career Performances

	M	Inns	NO	Runs	HS	Avge	100s	50s	Ct	St	Balls	Runs	Wkts	Avge	Best	5wI	10wM
Test																	
All First	22	25	9	148	39 *	9.25	-	-	3	-	3070	1984	59	33.62	5-57	3	-
1-day Int																	
C & G	3	1	1	1	1 *	-	-	-	-	-	90	83	0	-	-	-	
totesport	22	11	7	35	11	8.75	-	-	4	-	929	797	24	33.20	4-42	-	
Twenty20	6	2	2	4	3 *	-	-	-	1	-	120	156	10	15.60	3-23	-	

MARSHALL, S. J. Lancashire

Name: Simon James Marshall
Role: Right-hand bat, right-arm leg-spin bowler; all-rounder
Born: 20 September 1982, Wirral
Height: 6ft 3in **Weight:** 12st 12lbs
Nickname: Marsh
County debut: No first-team appearance
1st-Class 50s: 3
1st-Class 100s: 1
1st-Class 5 w. in innings: 1
1st-Class catches: 3
Place in batting averages: 96th av. 36.33
Strike rate: 96.00 (career 155.76)
Parents: Jim and Dinah
Marital status: Single
Family links with cricket: Father captained Radley School and Liverpool University
Education: Birkenhead School; Cambridge University
Qualifications: 9 GCSEs, 4 A-levels, BA (Cantab) Land Economy
Off-season: 'Adelaide Buffalos CC, South Australia'
Overseas tours: ESCA and ECB age-group tours 1996-2001; British Universities to South Africa 2004

Overseas teams played for: Adelaide Buffalos CC, South Australia 2004-05
Career highlights to date: 'Taking 6-128 and scoring 99 against Essex in my debut first-class season for Cambridge. Maiden first-class century. The 2005 A-Grade one-day final for Adelaide under lights at the Adelaide Oval'
Cricket moments to forget: 'Making a 27-ball duck against Kent 2003, which only included two balls hitting the bat, both of which were dropped at first slip by Greg Blewett'
Cricketers particularly admired: Carl Hooper, Jack Smith, Ben Johnson, Luke Williams
Young players to look out for: Dan Cullen
Other sports played: Hockey (Cambridge Blue)
Other sports followed: Football (Everton FC), hockey (Cambridge University HC)
Favourite band: Dire Straits
Relaxations: 'Spending time with a fantastic group of friends; painting'
Extras: Played for Cheshire in the C&G 2002, 2003. Played for Cambridge University CCE 2002, (as captain) 2003, and 2004; recorded maiden first-class five-wicket return (6-128), then followed up with 99 in CUCCE's second innings v Essex at Fenner's 2002. Cambridge Blue 2002-04, scoring maiden first-class century (126*) in the four-day Varsity Match at Fenner's 2003 and 98 in the corresponding match at The Parks 2004. Represented British Universities v New Zealanders at Fenner's 2004. Cambridge University Sportsman of the Year 2004
Opinions on cricket: 'Having recently experienced a season of Australian grade cricket, it seems that the league set-up in the UK is hugely inadequate for developing cricketers into first-class players. The best players need to be playing against each other week in week out, allowing county selectors to have a realistic chance of selecting proven run-scorers and wicket-takers to take the next step. The grade system also allows young players to see a clear path into the first-class game through consistent performances rather than the talent-spotting of junior representative coaches.'
Best batting: 126* Cambridge University v Oxford University, Fenner's 2003
Best bowling: 6-128 CUCCE v Essex, Fenner's 2002

2004 Season (did not make any first-class or one-day appearances for his county)

Career Performances

	M	Inns	NO	Runs	HS	Avge	100s	50s	Ct	St	Balls	Runs	Wkts	Avge	Best	5wI	10wM
Test																	
All First	12	20	3	629	126 *	37.00	1	3	3	-	2648	1463	17	86.05	6-128	1	-
1-day Int																	
C & G	2	2	0	7	4	3.50	-	-	-	-	96	85	0	-	-	-	
totesport																	
Twenty20																	

MARTIN, P. J. Lancashire

Name: Peter James Martin
Role: Right-hand bat, right-arm fast-medium bowler
Born: 15 November 1968, Accrington
Height: 6ft 5in **Weight:** 16st
Nickname: Digger
County debut: 1989
County cap: 1994
Benefit: 2002
Test debut: 1995
Tests: 8
One-Day Internationals: 20
50 wickets in a season: 3
1st-Class 50s: 7
1st-Class 100s: 2
1st-Class 5 w. in innings: 17
1st-Class 10 w. in match: 1
1st-Class catches: 55
One-Day 5 w. in innings: 6
Place in batting averages: (2003 274th av. 10.00)
Place in bowling averages: 62nd av. 31.90 (2003 68th av. 31.58)
Strike rate: 69.50 (career 60.56)
Parents: Keith and Catherine
Wife and date of marriage: Bethan, 3 October 1998
Children: Oliver Gilbert, 14 August 2001; Louis David, 8 May 2004
Education: Danum School, Doncaster; University of Central Lancashire, Preston
Qualifications: 6 O-levels, 2 A-levels, PGCM (UCLAN), Advanced Certificate (WSET), Levels 1 and 2 coaching certificates
Career outside cricket: Wine trade and painting
Off-season: Wine trade and painting
Overseas tours: England YC to Australia (U19 World Cup) 1987-88, 'and various other tours with English Schools and NAYC'; England to South Africa 1995-96, to India and Pakistan (World Cup) 1995-96, to Sharjah (Champions Trophy) 1997-98, to Bangladesh (Wills International Cup) 1998-99
Overseas teams played for: Southern Districts, Beerwah, Queensland 1988-89; South Launceston, Tasmania 1989-90; South Canberra, ACT 1990-92
Career highlights: 'Playing for this long. Playing for England. Lord's finals. Playing for the most part in a successful Lancs team all my career – not much to complain about!'
Cricket moments to forget: 'Being injured'
Cricket superstitions: 'None'

Cricketers particularly admired: Ian Botham, Allan Border, Clive Lloyd, Viv Richards, Courtney Walsh, Curtly Ambrose, Dennis Lillee, Malcolm Marshall, Andrew Flintoff, Angus Fraser
Young players to look out for: Oliver Newby
Other sports followed: Football (Man Utd), golf
Injuries: 'Right knee strongly objected most of the season'
Favourite band: 'At the moment, Keane – Chilly's mate's brother does the yodelling'
Relaxations: 'Outdoor stuff, being with family, wine, painting, soccer, reading, golf, cooking'
Extras: Played for England A v Sri Lankans 1991. Made ODI debut v West Indies at The Oval 1995, winning Man of the Match award (4-44). His 78* v Durham at Old Trafford 1997 is the equal highest score by a Lancashire No. 11 (although Paul Allott was dismissed v Gloucestershire at Bristol in 1985). Scored 117* v Warwickshire at Old Trafford 2002, setting a new record for the highest score by a Lancashire No. 10. Retired from county cricket at the end of the 2004 season due to a persistent knee injury
Opinions on cricket: 'Non-England-qualified folk must be reduced (other than overseas bods).'
Best batting: 133 Lancashire v Durham, Gateshead Fell 1992
Best bowling: 8-32 Lancashire v Middlesex, Uxbridge 1997

2004 Season

	M	Inns	NO	Runs	HS	Avge	100s	50s	Ct	St	O	M	Runs	Wkts	Avge	Best	5wI	10wM
Test																		
All First	6	7	2	59	33 *	11.80	-	-	1	-	115.5	34	319	10	31.90	4-81	-	-
1-day Int																		
C & G	2	1	1	0	0 *	-	-	-	-	-	16	2	52	3	17.33	2-12	-	
totesport	2	1	1	5	5 *	-	-	-	-	-	18	1	96	3	32.00	2-43	-	
Twenty20																		

Career Performances

	M	Inns	NO	Runs	HS	Avge	100s	50s	Ct	St	Balls	Runs	Wkts	Avge	Best	5wI	10wM
Test	8	13	0	115	29	8.84	-	-	6	-	1452	580	17	34.11	4-60	-	-
All First	212	246	61	3594	133	19.42	2	7	55	-	36700	16677	606	27.51	8-32	17	1
1-day Int	20	13	7	38	6	6.33	-	-	1	-	1048	806	27	29.85	4-44	-	
C & G	35	14	9	107	31 *	21.40	-	-	1	-	1982	1124	67	16.77	5-16	2	
totesport	149	48	26	289	35 *	13.13	-	-	30	-	6115	4273	195	21.91	5-21	4	
Twenty20	4	3	2	18	10 *	18.00	-	-	-	-	90	85	7	12.14	3-20	-	

MARTIN-JENKINS, R. S. C. Sussex

Name: Robin Simon Christopher Martin-Jenkins
Role: Right-hand bat, right-arm fast-medium bowler
Born: 28 October 1975, Guildford
Height: 6ft 5in **Weight:** 14st
Nickname: Tucker
County debut: 1995
County cap: 2000
1000 runs in a season: 1
1st-Class 50s: 22
1st-Class 100s: 2
1st-Class 200s: 1
1st-Class 5 w. in innings: 5
1st-Class catches: 29
Place in batting averages: 223rd av. 19.27 (2003 97th av. 36.86)
Place in bowling averages: 112th av. 38.86 (2003 118th av. 40.58)
Strike rate: 77.73 (career 64.48)
Parents: Christopher and Judy
Wife and date of marriage: Flora, 19 February 2000
Family links with cricket: Father is *The Times* chief cricket correspondent and BBC *TMS* commentator. Brother captains the Radley Rangers
Education: Radley College, Oxon; Durham University
Qualifications: 10 GCSEs, 3 A-levels, 1 AS-level, Grade 3 bassoon (with merit), BA (Hons) Social Sciences, Don Mackenzie School of Professional Photography Certificate, SWPP (Society of Wedding and Portrait Photographers), BPPA (British Professional Photographers Associates)
Career outside cricket: 'Weekly columnist for *Brighton Argus*. Photographer for "Goodnightie Company"'
Overseas tours: Radley College to Barbados 1992; Sussex U19 to Sri Lanka 1995; Durham University to Vienna 1995; MCC to Kenya 1999; Sussex to Grenada 2001, 2002
Overseas teams played for: Lima CC, Peru 1994; Bellville CC, Cape Town 2000-01
Career highlights to date: 'Winning National League Division Two in 1999. Scoring maiden first-class century in same match that Sussex won to take second division Championship 2001. Scoring maiden first-class 200 v Somerset at Taunton 2002. Winning first division Championship 2003'
Cricket superstitions: 'Never bowl first at Colwyn Bay'
Cricketers particularly admired: Angus Fraser, Robin Smith, Umer Rashid, Ben Hollioake, Adam Hollioake

Other sports played: Golf, tennis, Rugby fives
Other sports followed: Rugby, football (Liverpool)
Relaxations: Photography, guitar, reading, TV, films
Extras: Played for ESCA from U15 to U19. *Daily Telegraph* Bowling Award 1994. European Player of the Year, Vienna 1995. Best Performance Award for Sussex 1998. NBC Denis Compton Award for the most promising young Sussex player 1998, 1999, 2000. Scored maiden first-class double century (205*) v Somerset at Taunton 2002, in the process sharing with Mark Davis (111) in a record eighth-wicket partnership for Sussex (291); the stand fell one run short of the record eighth-wicket partnership in English first-class cricket, set by Bobby Peel and Lord Hawke for Yorkshire v Warwickshire at Birmingham in 1896. BBC South Cricketer of the Year 2002
Opinions on cricket: 'Scrap National League and C&G Trophy – they're getting stale, and why are we still the only country that plays 45 overs? In their place have a one-day mini-league in regions, followed by quarters/semis/final knockout. Like old Benson and Hedges except the best Minor Counties and Scotland could be included. Keep Championship as it is with two divisions (but only two up/two down) except everyone to play each other only once and include a regional tournament in early season – best against the best.'
Best batting: 205* Sussex v Somerset, Taunton 2002
Best bowling: 7-51 Sussex v Leicestershire, Horsham 2002

2004 Season

	M	Inns	NO	Runs	HS	Avge	100s	50s	Ct	St	O	M	Runs	Wkts	Avge	Best	5wI	10wM
Test																		
All First	16	23	1	424	64 *	19.27	-	2	6	-	388.4	101	1166	30	38.86	5-96	1	-
1-day Int																		
C & G	2	2	1	65	61 *	65.00	-	1	1	-	17.4	0	74	2	37.00	1-21	-	
totesport	18	13	4	104	22	11.55	-	-	2	-	135.4	20	553	28	19.75	4-39	-	
Twenty20	3	3	0	2	1	0.66	-	-	2	-	9	1	69	2	34.50	1-7	-	

Career Performances

	M	Inns	NO	Runs	HS	Avge	100s	50s	Ct	St	Balls	Runs	Wkts	Avge	Best	5wI	10wM
Test																	
All First	101	160	18	4179	205 *	29.42	3	22	29	-	14768	7731	229	33.75	7-51	5	-
1-day Int																	
C & G	9	8	3	156	61 *	31.20	-	1	3	-	466	285	10	28.50	2-24	-	
totesport	105	76	9	864	68 *	12.89	-	2	26	-	4457	3055	112	27.27	4-39	-	
Twenty20	8	8	2	135	56 *	22.50	-	1	2	-	169	225	10	22.50	4-20	-	

MASCARENHAS, D. A. — Hampshire

Name: Dimitri Adrian Mascarenhas
Role: Right-hand bat, right-arm medium bowler
Born: 30 October 1977, Chiswick, London
Height: 6ft 1in **Weight:** 12st 2lbs
Nickname: Dimi, D-Train
County debut: 1996
County cap: 1998
50 wickets in a season: 1
1st-Class 50s: 15
1st-Class 100s: 4
1st-Class 5 w. in innings: 10
1st-Class catches: 49
One-Day 5 w. in innings: 2
Place in batting averages: 205th av. 21.68 (2003 184th av. 25.00)
Place in bowling averages: 2nd av. 18.67 (2003 72nd av. 32.17)
Strike rate: 43.32 (career 62.54)
Parents: Malik and Pauline
Marital status: Single
Family links with cricket: Uncle played in Sri Lanka and brothers both play for Melville CC in Perth, Western Australia
Education: Trinity College, Perth
Qualifications: Level 2 coaching
Career outside cricket: Personal trainer
Overseas tours: England VI to Hong Kong 2004
Overseas teams played for: Melville CC, Perth 1991 –
Career highlights to date: 'Debut for Hampshire 1996 – 6-88 v Glamorgan'
Cricketers particularly admired: Sir Viv Richards, Malcolm Marshall, Shane Warne
Young players to look out for: Beau Casson (Western Australia)
Other sports followed: Australian Rules (Collingwood)
Favourite band: Red Hot Chili Peppers
Relaxations: Tennis, golf, Australian Rules
Extras: Played for Western Australia at U17 and U19 level as captain. Took 6-88 on first-class debut, for Hampshire v Glamorgan at Southampton 1996, the best analysis by a Hampshire bowler on first-class debut since 1899. Won NatWest Man of the Match awards in semi-final v Lancashire at Southampton 1998 (3-28 and 73) and in quarter-final v Middlesex at Lord's 2000 (4-25). Scorer of the first Championship century recorded at the Rose Bowl (104) v Worcestershire 2001. Took 5-14 v Sussex at

Hove in the Twenty20 Cup 2004, including the competition's first hat-trick (Davis, Mushtaq Ahmed, Lewry). Took 50 first-class wickets (56 at 18.67) in a season for the first time 2004 and finished second in the bowling averages
Opinions on cricket: 'I think that two overseas players is great for the game. It definitely raises the standard, and you also get a chance to play against the best players worldwide.'
Best batting: 104 Hampshire v Worcestershire, West End 2001
104 Hampshire v Durham, Riverside 2004
Best bowling: 6-25 Hampshire v Derbyshire, West End 2004

2004 Season

	M	Inns	NO	Runs	HS	Avge	100s	50s	Ct	St	O	M	Runs	Wkts	Avge	Best	5wI	10wM
Test																		
All First	16	24	2	477	104	21.68	1	-	8	-	404.2	132	1046	56	18.67	6-25	4	-
1-day Int																		
C & G	2	2	0	105	53	52.50	-	2	-	-	12	1	39	1	39.00	1-15	-	
totesport	13	12	3	308	79	34.22	-	2	5	-	90.4	7	349	11	31.72	3-54	-	
Twenty20	6	6	2	152	52	38.00	-	1	3	-	20.5	2	121	12	10.08	5-14	1	

Career Performances

	M	Inns	NO	Runs	HS	Avge	100s	50s	Ct	St	Balls	Runs	Wkts	Avge	Best	5wI	10wM
Test																	
All First	119	178	17	3755	104	23.32	4	15	49	-	17011	7867	272	28.92	6-25	10	-
1-day Int																	
C & G	16	14	4	413	73	41.30	-	4	2	-	786	455	24	18.95	4-25	-	
totesport	113	100	17	1637	79	19.72	-	8	34	-	4714	3341	147	22.72	5-27	1	
Twenty20	11	11	3	214	52	26.75	-	1	6	-	197	252	15	16.80	5-14	1	

MASON, M. S. Worcestershire

Name: Matthew (Matt) Sean Mason
Role: Right-hand bat, right-arm fast-medium bowler
Born: 20 March 1974, Claremont, Perth, Western Australia
Height: 6ft 5in **Weight:** 16st
Nickname: Mase, Moose
County debut: 2002
County colours: 2002
50 wickets in a season: 2
1st-Class 50s: 3
1st-Class 5 w. in innings: 4
1st-Class catches: 9
Place in batting averages: 250th av. 14.64 (2003 247th av. 15.62)
Place in bowling averages: 50th av. 30.42 (2003 7th av. 21.58)

Strike rate: 68.90 (career 61.84)
Parents: Bill and Sue
Marital status: Single
Family links with cricket: Brother Simon plays for Wanneroo District CC
Education: Mazenod College, Perth
Qualifications: Level 1 ACB coach
Career outside cricket: Sales consultant with Nissan Motor Company
Off-season: 'Spending time in Australia with my girlfriend and visiting family'
Overseas teams played for: Western Australia 1996-1998
Career highlights to date: 'Two consecutive C&G Lord's finals in 2003 and 2004'
Cricket moments to forget: 'Losing both finals 2003 and 2004'
Cricket superstitions: 'None'
Cricketers particularly admired: Justin Langer, Graeme Hick, Dennis Lillee
Young players to look out for: Kadeer Ali, Steve Davies
Other sports played: Golf, tennis, Australian Rules football
Other sports followed: Rugby union (Wallabies)
Favourite band: Jack Johnson
Relaxations: 'Listening to live music; long walks; my car'
Extras: Scored maiden first-class fifty (50) from 27 balls v Derbyshire at Worcester 2002. Dick Lygon Award to the [Worcestershire] Clubman of the Year 2003. Holds an Irish passport and is not considered an overseas player
Opinions on cricket: 'The county game is going from strength to strength and the success of the England cricket team is testament to that. Long may it continue.'
Best batting: 63 Worcestershire v Warwickshire, Worcester 2004
Best bowling: 6-68 Worcestershire v Durham, Worcester 2003

2004 Season

	M	Inns	NO	Runs	HS	Avge	100s	50s	Ct	St	O	M	Runs	Wkts	Avge	Best	5wI	10wM
Test																		
All First	17	20	6	205	63	14.64	-	1	5	-	597.1	181	1582	52	30.42	5-62	1	-
1-day Int																		
C & G	5	3	1	2	1 *	1.00	-	-	2	-	45	4	158	6	26.33	2-16	-	
totesport	10	6	2	31	25	7.75	-	-	3	-	76	4	354	11	32.18	3-32	-	
Twenty20																		

Career Performances

	M	Inns	NO	Runs	HS	Avge	100s	50s	Ct	St	Balls	Runs	Wkts	Avge	Best	5wI	10wM
Test																	
All First	42	53	13	572	63	14.30	-	3	9	-	8102	3588	131	27.38	6-68	4	-
1-day Int																	
C & G	12	7	3	7	3 *	1.75	-	-	2	-	633	401	16	25.06	3-28	-	
totesport	35	17	5	120	25	10.00	-	-	7	-	1559	1128	41	27.51	4-34	-	
Twenty20	4	2	0	3	3	1.50	-	-	1	-	91	103	3	34.33	1-22	-	

MASTERS, D. D. Leicestershire

Name: David Daniel Masters
Role: Right-hand bat, right-arm medium-fast bowler
Born: 22 April 1978, Chatham
Height: 6ft 4ins **Weight:** 12st 5lbs
Nickname: Hod, Race Horse, Hoddy
County debut: 2000 (Kent), 2003 (Leicestershire)
1st-Class 50s: 1
1st-Class 100s: 1
1st-Class 5 w. in innings: 4
1st-Class catches: 16
One-Day 5 w. in innings: 1
Place in batting averages: 268th av. 9.25 (2003 264th av. 13.45)
Place in bowling averages: 109th av. 38.07 (2003 126th av. 42.72)
Strike rate: 63.85 (career 62.37)
Parents: Kevin and Tracey
Marital status: Single
Family links with cricket: 'Dad was on staff at Kent 1983-86'
Education: Fort Luton High School; Mid-Kent College
Qualifications: 8 GCSEs, GNVQ in Leisure and Tourism, qualified coach in cricket, football and athletics, bricklayer and plasterer
Career outside cricket: Builder
Overseas teams played for: Double View, Perth 1998-99
Cricketers particularly admired: Ian Botham
Other sports played: Football, boxing 'and most other sports'
Other sports followed: Football (Manchester United)
Relaxations: 'Going out with mates'
Extras: Joint Kent Player of the Year 2000 (with Martin Saggers). NBC Denis

Compton Award for the most promising young Kent player 2000. Left Kent at the end of the 2002 season and joined Leicestershire for 2003
Best batting: 119 Leicestershire v Sussex, Hove 2003
Best bowling: 6-27 Kent v Durham, Tunbridge Wells 2000

2004 Season

	M	Inns	NO	Runs	HS	Avge	100s	50s	Ct	St	O	M	Runs	Wkts	Avge	Best	5wI	10wM
Test																		
All First	6	9	1	74	31	9.25	-	-	3	-	149	29	533	14	38.07	4-74	-	-
1-day Int																		
C & G																		
totesport	2	1	0	5	5	5.00	-	-	-	-	10.3	0	78	1	78.00	1-38	-	
Twenty20																		

Career Performances

	M	Inns	NO	Runs	HS	Avge	100s	50s	Ct	St	Balls	Runs	Wkts	Avge	Best	5wI	10wM
Test																	
All First	51	62	13	539	119	11.00	1	1	16	-	8046	4418	129	34.24	6-27	4	-
1-day Int																	
C & G	4	3	1	25	24 *	12.50	-	-	-	-	185	132	5	26.40	4-15	-	
totesport	37	26	10	154	27	9.62	-	-	3	-	1405	1251	26	48.11	5-20	1	
Twenty20	6	3	1	1	1	0.50	-	-	1	-	108	135	7	19.28	2-19	-	

MAUNDERS, J. K. Leicestershire

Name: John Kenneth Maunders
Role: Left-hand opening bat, right-arm medium bowler
Born: 4 April 1981, Ashford, Middlesex
Height: 5ft 10in **Weight:** 13st
Nickname: Rod, Weaz
County debut: 1999 (Middlesex), 2003 (Leicestershire)
1st-Class 50s: 5
1st-Class 100s: 3
1st-Class catches: 10
Place in batting averages: 214th av. 20.95 (2003 83rd av. 38.85)
Strike rate: 66.00 (career 93.00)
Parents: Lynn and Kenneth
Marital status: Single
Family links with cricket: Grandfather and two uncles club cricketers for Thames Valley Ramblers

Education: Ashford High School; Spelthorne College
Qualifications: 10 GCSEs, coaching certificates
Career outside cricket: Cricket coach
Overseas tours: England U19 to New Zealand 1998-99, to Malaysia and (U19 World Cup) Sri Lanka 1999-2000
Overseas teams played for: University CC, Perth 2001-02
Career highlights to date: 'Scoring maiden first-class hundred v Surrey at Grace Road'
Cricket moments to forget: 'Not any one in particular; getting 0 and dropping catches are not great moments!'
Cricket superstitions: 'Just a few small ones'
Cricketers particularly admired: Brad Hodge, Justin Langer
Other sports played: 'Played football, hockey and squash (consistently wiping the floor with Spencer Collins)'
Other sports followed: Horse racing
Extras: Has been Seaxe Player of Year. Represented England U17 and U19. NBC Denis Compton Award 1999. Released by Middlesex at the end of the 2002 season and joined Leicestershire for 2003
Opinions on cricket: 'Twenty20 cricket has been a great success, and it will continue to be, and can only be positive for cricket in general. The amount of EU players should be assessed, as it seems they take the place of promising young English cricketers, who could possibly do just as good a job. Not against two overseas players, as it does improve standards of our game, which can only be good for English players looking to play at the highest level.'
Best batting: 171 Leicestershire v Surrey, Leicester 2003
Best bowling: 1-11 Leicestershire v Durham, Riverside 2004

2004 Season

	M	Inns	NO	Runs	HS	Avge	100s	50s	Ct	St	O	M	Runs	Wkts	Avge	Best	5wI	10wM
Test																		
All First	11	22	0	461	116	20.95	1	2	6	-	22	6	84	2	42.00	1-11	-	-
1-day Int																		
C & G																		
totesport																		
Twenty20																		

Career Performances

	M	Inns	NO	Runs	HS	Avge	100s	50s	Ct	St	Balls	Runs	Wkts	Avge	Best	5wI	10wM
Test																	
All First	24	46	2	1251	171	28.43	3	5	10	-	186	122	2	61.00	1-11	-	-
1-day Int																	
C & G	3	3	0	36	14	12.00	-	-	-	-	13	18	0	-	-	-	
totesport	7	7	0	84	49	12.00	-	-	1	-							
Twenty20																	

MAYNARD, M. P. Glamorgan

Name: Matthew Peter Maynard
Role: Right-hand middle-order bat, right-arm medium bowler, occasional wicket-keeper
Born: 21 March 1966, Oldham, Lancashire
Height: 5ft 11in **Weight:** 13st
Nickname: Ollie, Wilf
County debut: 1985
County cap: 1987
Benefit: 1996
Test debut: 1988
Tests: 4
One-Day Internationals: 14
1000 runs in a season: 12
1st-Class 50s: 131
1st-Class 100s: 56
1st-Class 200s: 3
1st-Class catches: 371
1st-Class stumpings: 7
One-Day 100s: 15
Place in batting averages: 66th av. 43.14 (2003 41st av. 46.32)
Strike rate: (career 195.16)
Parents: Ken (deceased) and Pat
Wife and date of marriage: Susan, 27 September 1986
Children: Tom, 25 March 1989; Ceri Lloyd, 5 August 1993
Family links with cricket: Father played for many years for Duckinfield. Brother Charles plays for St Fagans. Son Tom plays
Education: Ysgol David Hughes, Menai Bridge, Anglesey
Qualifications: Level 3 coach
Off-season: England VI to Hong Kong; assistant coach to England ODI squad in Zimbabwe and South Africa
Overseas tours: North Wales XI to Barbados 1982; Glamorgan to Barbados 1982, to South Africa 1993; unofficial England XI to South Africa 1989-90; HKCC (Australia) to Bangkok and Hong Kong 1990; England VI to Hong Kong 1992, 1994, 2001 (captain), 2002 (captain), 2003 (captain), 2004 (captain); England to West Indies 1993-94; England XI to New Zealand (Cricket Max) 1997 (captain); England Classics to Grenada (Grenada Classics) 2003-04
Overseas teams played for: St Joseph's, Whakatane, New Zealand 1986-88; Gosnells, Perth, Western Australia 1988-89; Papakura and Northern Districts, New Zealand 1990-91; Morrinsville College and Northern Districts, New Zealand 1991-92; Otago, New Zealand 1996-97
Career highlights to date: 'Leading Glamorgan to the County Championship in 1997. Playing for England'

Cricket moments to forget: 'Losing B&H final in 2000' (*Was neverthelesss Gold Award winner for his 118-ball 104*)
Cricketers particularly admired: Ian Botham, Viv Richards, David Gower
Young players to look out for: Tom Maynard
Other sports played: Golf, football
Other sports followed: Rugby, football
Relaxations: 'Spending time with my wife and family and relaxing'
Extras: Scored century (102) on first-class debut v Yorkshire at Swansea in 1985, reaching his 100 with three successive straight sixes and becoming the youngest centurion for Glamorgan and the first Glamorgan debutant to score a century since F. B. Pinch did so in 1921; scored 1000 first-class runs in his first full season 1986. In 1987 set record for fastest 50 for Glamorgan (14 mins) v Yorkshire at Cardiff, and became youngest player to be awarded Glamorgan cap. Voted Young Cricketer of the Year 1988 by the Cricket Writers' Club. Scored 987 runs in July 1991, including a century in each innings (129/126) v Gloucestershire at Cheltenham. His 243 v Hampshire at Southampton 1991 is the highest score by a Glamorgan No. 4. Captained Glamorgan for most of 1992 in Alan Butcher's absence; Glamorgan captain 1996-2000. Voted Wombwell Cricket Lovers' Society captain of the year for 1997. Was one of *Wisden*'s Five Cricketers of the Year 1998. Appointed honorary fellow of University of Wales, Bangor. Shared in Glamorgan one-day record stand for third wicket (204) with Jacques Kallis in National League match v Surrey at Pontypridd 1999. Published *On the Attack: the Batsman's Story* (with Paul Rees) 2001. Scored a century in each innings (140/118*) v Gloucestershire at Cheltenham 2002 (as he also did in 1991), in the process passing 20,000 runs in first-class cricket for Glamorgan. Glamorgan Player of the Year 2002. Scored his 53rd century (114) for Glamorgan v Leicestershire at Cardiff 2004 to become the county's leading century-maker in first-class cricket (having already become the county's leading scorer and century-maker in one-day cricket). Scored 136 v Essex at Chelmsford 2004, in the process becoming Glamorgan's third highest run-scorer in first-class cricket. Appointed assistant coach to England one-day squad for tours to Zimbabwe and South Africa 2004-05. Granted a testimonial for 2005
Best batting: 243 Glamorgan v Hampshire, Southampton 1991
Best bowling: 3-21 Glamorgan v Oxford University, The Parks 1987

2004 Season

	M	Inns	NO	Runs	HS	Avge	100s	50s	Ct	St	O	M	Runs	Wkts	Avge	Best	5wI	10wM
Test																		
All First	15	24	3	906	163	43.14	3	4	14	-	7	0	27	0	-	-	-	-
1-day Int																		
C & G	2	2	0	61	36	30.50	-	-	-	-								
totesport	15	14	5	612	117	68.00	1	5	6	-								
Twenty20	7	7	0	182	53	26.00	-	1	4	-								

Career Performances

	M	Inns	NO	Runs	HS	Avge	100s	50s	Ct	St	Balls	Runs	Wkts	Avge	Best	5wI	10wM
Test	4	8	0	87	35	10.87	-	-	3	-							
All First	394	641	60	24779	243	42.64	59	131	371	7	1171	895	6	149.16	3-21	-	-
1-day Int	14	12	1	156	41	14.18	-	-	3	-							
C & G	49	47	4	1893	151 *	44.02	3	13	23	1	18	8	0	-	-	-	
totesport	271	260	32	8027	132	35.20	6	53	120	4	64	64	1	64.00	1-13	-	
Twenty20	12	12	0	424	72	35.33	-	4	9	-							

McCOUBREY, A. G. A. M. Essex

Name: Adrian George Agustus Mathew McCoubrey
Role: Right-hand bat, right-arm fast-medium bowler
Born: 3 April 1980, Ballymena, Northern Ireland
Height: 5ft 10in **Weight:** 11st
Nickname: Scoobie, Coubs, Coubsy
County debut: 2003
1st-Class catches: 3
Place in bowling averages: 103rd av. 37.53
Strike rate: 50.66 (career 51.26)
Parents: Ronald and Josephine
Marital status: Single
Family links with cricket: Father played town cricket
Education: Cambridge House Boys' Grammar School; Queen's University of Belfast
Qualifications: 9 GCSEs, 3 A-levels, BEng (Hons) Aeronautical Engineering (2.1)
Career outside cricket: Engineer
Overseas tours: Ireland to Canada (ICC Trophy) 2001
Career highlights to date: 'First Irish senior cap 1999. Playing against Australia at Ormeau, Belfast 2001. Signing professional contract with Essex'
Cricket moments to forget: 'Not qualifying for 2003 World Cup'
Cricket superstitions: 'Will not play any match without wearing the Star of David around my neck'
Cricketers particularly admired: Darren Gough, Glenn McGrath
Other sports played: Football, hockey
Other sports followed: Football (Liverpool FC)
Relaxations: 'Swimming, reading, surfing the Net'

Extras: Has represented Ireland since 1999, including in the C&G 2002 and 2003. Ballymena Adult Sportsperson of the Year 2001. Released by Essex at the end of the 2004 season
Best batting: 2* Essex v Yorkshire, Headingley 2004
Best bowling: 4-16 Essex v CUCCE, Fenner's 2004

2004 Season

	M	Inns	NO	Runs	HS	Avge	100s	50s	Ct	St	O	M	Runs	Wkts	Avge	Best	5wI	10wM
Test																		
All First	6	7	4	4	2*	1.33	-	-	3	-	126.4	22	563	15	37.53	4-16	-	-
1-day Int																		
C & G																		
totesport	1	1	1	4	4*	-	-	-	-	-	9	1	43	1	43.00	1-43	-	
Twenty20																		

Career Performances

	M	Inns	NO	Runs	HS	Avge	100s	50s	Ct	St	Balls	Runs	Wkts	Avge	Best	5wI	10wM
Test																	
All First	10	12	6	6	2*	1.00	-	-	3	-	1179	842	23	36.60	4-16	-	-
1-day Int																	
C & G	4	3	0	13	11	4.33	-	-	-	-	162	85	3	28.33	2-20	-	
totesport	3	1	1	4	4*	-	-	-	-	-	102	84	1	84.00	1-43	-	
Twenty20																	

McGRATH, A. Yorkshire

Name: Anthony McGrath
Role: Right-hand bat, right-arm medium bowler
Born: 6 October 1975, Bradford
Height: 6ft 2in **Weight:** 14st 7lbs
Nickname: Gripper, Mags, Terry
County debut: 1995
County cap: 1999
Test debut: 2003
Tests: 4
One-Day Internationals: 14
1st-Class 50s: 32
1st-Class 100s: 13
1st-Class 5 w. in innings: 1
1st-Class catches: 84
One-Day 100s: 2
Place in batting averages: 57th av. 45.50 (2003 65th av. 42.50)
Place in bowling averages: (2003 21st av. 23.70)

Strike rate: 76.50 (career 59.00)
Parents: Terry and Kath
Marital status: Single
Education: Yorkshire Martyrs Collegiate School
Qualifications: 9 GCSEs, BTEC National Diploma in Leisure Studies, senior coaching award
Overseas tours: England U19 to West Indies 1994-95; England A to Pakistan 1995-96, to Australia 1996-97; MCC to Bangladesh 1999-2000; England to Bangladesh and Sri Lanka 2003-04 (one-day series), to West Indies 2003-04 (one-day series)
Overseas teams played for: Deep Dene, Melbourne 1998-99; Wanneroo, Perth 1999-2001
Cricket moments to forget: 'Losing semi-final to Lancashire 1996. Relegation to Division Two 2002'
Cricketers particularly admired: Darren Lehmann, Robin Smith
Young players to look out for: Michael Lumb, John Sadler
Other sports followed: 'Most sports', football (Manchester United)
Relaxations: 'Music; spending time with friends; eating out'
Extras: Captained Yorkshire Schools U13, U14, U15 and U16; captained English Schools U17. Bradford League Young Cricketer of the Year 1992 and 1993. Played for England U17 and U19. C&G Man of the Match for his 72* in the quarter-final v Essex at Chelmsford 2002. Scored 165 v Lancashire at Headingley 2002, in the process sharing with Darren Lehmann (187) in a record third-wicket partnership for Yorkshire at Headingley (317). Captain of Yorkshire 2003. Made Test debut in the first Test v Zimbabwe at Lord's 2003, scoring 69 in England's only innings and taking 3-16 in Zimbabwe's second innings. Recorded maiden first-class five-wicket return (5-39) v Derbyshire at Derby 2004, scoring career best 174 in the same match
Best batting: 174 Yorkshire v Derbyshire, Derby 2004
Best bowling: 5-39 Yorkshire v Derbyshire, Derby 2004

2004 Season

	M	Inns	NO	Runs	HS	Avge	100s	50s	Ct	St	O	M	Runs	Wkts	Avge	Best	5wI	10wM
Test																		
All First	9	16	0	728	174	45.50	3	1	6	-	102	21	280	8	35.00	5-39	1	-
1-day Int	4	3	0	23	12	7.66	-	-	-	-	12	1	49	2	24.50	1-13	-	
C & G	3	3	1	79	64 *	39.50	-	1	1	-	17.1	1	98	5	19.60	4-56	-	
totesport	12	11	3	327	96 *	40.87	-	2	4	-	51.5	0	298	8	37.25	2-15	-	
Twenty20	4	3	0	47	37	15.66	-	-	1	-	7.5	0	98	1	98.00	1-46	-	

Career Performances

	M	Inns	NO	Runs	HS	Avge	100s	50s	Ct	St	Balls	Runs	Wkts	Avge	Best	5wI	10wM
Test	4	5	0	201	81	40.20	-	2	3	-	102	56	4	14.00	3-16	-	-
All First	139	238	16	7098	174	31.97	13	32	84	-	3599	1762	61	28.88	5-39	1	-
1-day Int	14	12	2	166	52	16.60	-	1	4	-	228	175	4	43.75	1-13	-	
C & G	24	21	4	779	84	45.82	-	8	9	-	271	246	7	35.14	4-56	-	
totesport	114	105	19	2723	102	31.66	1	17	35	-	1214	989	32	30.90	4-41	-	
Twenty20	4	3	0	47	37	15.66	-	-	1	-	47	98	1	98.00	1-46	-	

McGRATH, G. D. — Middlesex

Name: Glenn Donald McGrath
Role: Right-hand bat, right-arm fast bowler
Born: 9 February 1970, Dubbo, New South Wales, Australia
Height: 6ft 6in **Weight:** 14st
Nickname: Pigeon
County debut: 2000 (Worcestershire), 2004 (Middlesex)
County cap: 2000 (Worcestershire)
Test debut: 1993-94
Tests: 97
One-Day Internationals: 193
50 wickets in a season: 1
1st-Class 50s: 1
1st-Class 5 w. in innings: 37
1st-Class 10 w. in match: 7
1st-Class catches: 43
One-Day 5 w. in innings: 6
Strike rate: 67.11 (career 49.83)
Parents: Kevin and Bev
Wife and date of marriage: Jane, 17 July 1999
Children: James, 20 January 2000
Education: Narromine High School
Off-season: Playing cricket for Australia
Overseas tours: Australia to South Africa 1993-94, to Pakistan 1994-95, to West Indies 1994-95, to India, Pakistan and Sri Lanka (World Cup) 1995-96, to India 1996-97, to South Africa 1996-97, to England 1997, to Pakistan 1998-99, to West Indies 1998-99, to UK, Ireland and Holland (World Cup) 1999, to Sri Lanka and Zimbabwe 1999-2000, to New Zealand 1999-2000, to Kenya (ICC Knockout Trophy) 2000-01, to India 2000-01, to England 2001, to South Africa 2001-02, to Sri Lanka (ICC Champions Trophy) 2002-03, to Sri Lanka and Sharjah (v Pakistan) 2002-03, to Africa

(World Cup) 2002-03, to West Indies 2002-03, to Zimbabwe (one-day series) 2004, to Holland (Videocon Cup) 2004, to England (ICC Champions Trophy) 2004, to India 2004-05, to New Zealand 2004-05, plus other one-day tournaments in Sharjah, Sri Lanka, New Zealand, South Africa and Kenya
Overseas teams played for: New South Wales 1992-93 –
Cricketers particularly admired: Dennis Lillee, Rod Marsh
Other sports played: Golf
Other sports followed: Rugby league (Cronulla Sharks)
Relaxations: 'Going to my property in outback NSW'
Extras: Commonwealth Bank [Australian] Cricket Academy 1992-93. One of *Wisden*'s Five Cricketers of the Year 1998. *Wisden Australia*'s Cricketer of the Year 1998-99 and Test Cricketer of the Year 2000-01. Was leading Test wicket-taker of 1999 with 67 (av. 21.27). Winner of the inaugural Allan Border Medal 2000 and was also named Test Player of the Year at the 2000 awards. FICA International Cricketer of the Year 2000. Worcestershire overseas player 2000. Top wicket-taker in English first-class cricket 2000 with 80 wickets at an average of 13.21; also took 30 National League wickets at an average of 8.13 in 2000. Worcestershire Supporters' Club Player of the Year 2000. Named ODI Player of the Year at the 2001 Allan Border Medal awards. Took 300th Test wicket (Brian Lara) in the middle of his maiden first-class hat-trick (Campbell, Lara, Adams) v West Indies in the second Test at Perth 2000-01. Took 400th Test wicket (Waqar Younis) in the third Test v Pakistan at Sharjah 2002-03. Took 7-15 v Namibia at Potchefstroom in the World Cup 2002-03, the best bowling return in World Cups and the second best in ODIs overall. His Test awards include Australia's Man of the Series v England 1997 and 2001 and Man of the Series v West Indies 1996-97 and 2000-01. His ODI awards include Australia's Man of the Series in the CUB Series 1998-99 and Man of the Match v New Zealand at Colombo in the ICC Champions Trophy 2002-03 (5-37). Was an overseas player with Middlesex July to August 2004, deputising for Lance Klusener, absent on international duty
Best batting: 55 Worcestershire v Nottinghamshire, Worcester 2000
Best bowling: 8-38 Australia v England, Lord's 1997
Stop press: Made 100th Test appearance in the third Test v India at Nagpur 2004-05, returning first innings figures of 25-13-27-3. Man of the [Test] Series v New Zealand 2004-05 (in which he scored his maiden Test half-century – 61 – in the first Test at Brisbane). Took 8-24 in the first Test v Pakistan at Perth 2004-05, the second best innings return for Australia in Tests. Took 300th ODI wicket (Mohammad Hafeez) v Pakistan at Melbourne in the VB Series first final 2004-05 (his 200th ODI) and was Man of the Match at Sydney in the second final (5-27). Man of the Match in the first ODI v New Zealand at Wellington 2004-05 (4-16)

2004 Season

	M	Inns	NO	Runs	HS	Avge	100s	50s	Ct	St	O	M	Runs	Wkts	Avge	Best	5wI	10wM
Test																		
All First	2	3	0	28	24	9.33	-	-	-	-	100.4	41	215	9	23.88	4-59	-	-
1-day Int	3	1	1	0	0 *	-	-	-	-	-	24	1	98	3	32.66	3-39	-	
C & G																		
totesport	4	2	1	5	5 *	5.00	-	-	4	-	30.4	1	128	3	42.66	1-10	-	
Twenty20																		

Career Performances

	M	Inns	NO	Runs	HS	Avge	100s	50s	Ct	St	Balls	Runs	Wkts	Avge	Best	5wI	10wM
Test	97	107	38	450	39	6.52	-	-	29	-	22860	9509	440	21.61	8-38	24	3
All First	160	162	54	786	55	7.27	-	1	43	-	35086	14631	704	20.78	8-38	37	7
1-day Int	193	51	28	94	11	4.08	-	-	26	-	10127	6553	289	22.67	7-15	6	
C & G	2	1	1	1	1 *	-	-	-	1	-	120	46	4	11.50	4-23	-	
totesport	18	9	4	6	5 *	1.20	-	-	5	-	860	372	33	11.27	4-9	-	
Twenty20																	

McLEAN, J. J. — Hampshire

Name: Jonathan (Jono) James McLean
Role: Right-hand bat, right-arm seam bowler
Born: 11 July 1980, Johannesburg, South Africa
Height: 6ft 1in **Weight:** 12st 8lbs
County debut: No first-team appearance
Parents: Brian and Rosey
Marital status: Single
Education: St Stithians College, Gauteng
Career outside cricket: 'Studying part-time'
Off-season: 'Playing overseas'
Overseas teams played for: University of Cape Town 2000-04; Western Province 2001-02 – 2003-04
Career highlights to date: 'Making my first-class debut'
Cricketers particularly admired: Sachin Tendulkar, Jacques Kallis
Other sports played: Hockey (Provincial U15), golf (social)
Other sports followed: Rugby
Injuries: Out for four weeks with a broken finger
Relaxations: Golf, listening to music, reading

Extras: Made first-class debut for Western Province v Northerns at Centurion 2001-02. Played for Hampshire 2nd XI 2004
Opinions on cricket: 'The game is getting more exciting and challenging all the time, which means players and teams are having to adjust their tactics quicker to stay ahead of the pack. With Twenty20, specialised skills are being tested to the limit.'

2004 Season (did not make any first-class or one-day appearances)

Career Performances

	M	Inns	NO	Runs	HS	Avge	100s	50s	Ct	St	Balls	Runs	Wkts	Avge	Best	5wI	10wM
Test																	
All First	6	8	0	162	57	20.25	-	1	7	-							
1-day Int																	
C & G																	
totesport																	
Twenty20																	

McLEAN, N. A. M. — Somerset

Name: Nixon Alexei McNamara McLean
Role: Left-hand bat, right-arm fast bowler
Born: 20 July 1973, Stubbs, St Vincent
Height: 6ft 5in
Nickname: Nicko
County debut: 1998 (Hampshire), 2003 (Somerset)
County cap: 1998 (Hampshire), 2003 (Somerset)
Test debut: 1997-98
Tests: 19
One-Day Internationals: 45
50 wickets in a season: 2
1st-Class 50s: 3
1st-Class 5 w. in innings: 19
1st-Class 10 w. in match: 3
1st-Class catches: 41
Place in batting averages: 277th av. 7.62 (2003 239th av. 16.73)
Place in bowling averages: 26th av. 26.20 (2003 54th av. 28.80)
Strike rate: 44.95 (career 51.65)
Marital status: Single
Education: Carapan SS, St Vincent
Overseas tours: West Indies to Australia 1996-97, to Bangladesh (Wills International

Cup) 1998-99, to South Africa 1998-99, to Singapore (Coca-Cola Singapore Challenge) 1999, to Bangladesh (Biman Millennium Cup) 1999-2000, to Sharjah (Coca-Cola Champions Trophy) 1999-2000, to England 2000, to Kenya (ICC Knockout Trophy) 2000-01, to Australia 2000-01, to Africa (World Cup) 2002-03; West Indies A to South Africa 1997-98

Overseas teams played for: Windward Islands 1992-93 – 2000-01; St Vincent and the Grenadines 2002-03; KwaZulu-Natal 2001-02 – 2003-04

Extras: Was Hampshire's overseas player 1998-99, taking 62 first-class wickets (av. 25.40) in 1998. Took 44 wickets (av. 16.27) in KwaZulu-Natal's Supersport Series title win 2001-02, including 6-84 in the Northerns first innings in the final at Durban; also took 15 wickets at 15.33 in KwaZulu-Natal's successful Standard Bank Cup campaign 2001-02. Joined Somerset as an overseas player for 2003, taking 5-87 on debut for the county v Gloucestershire at Bristol. Scored 39 v Derbyshire at Taunton 2003, in the process sharing with Ian Blackwell (247*) in a new record tenth-wicket partnership for Somerset (163)

Best batting: 76 Somerset v Gloucestershire, Taunton 2003

Best bowling: 7-28 West Indians v Free State, Bloemfontein 1998-99

2004 Season

	M	Inns	NO	Runs	HS	Avge	100s	50s	Ct	St	O	M	Runs	Wkts	Avge	Best	5wI	10wM
Test																		
All First	10	11	3	61	22 *	7.62	-	-	1	-	322.1	62	1127	43	26.20	6-79	3	1
1-day Int																		
C & G	2	1	1	0	0 *	-	-	-	1	-	14	1	61	1	61.00	1-23	-	
totesport	10	5	2	17	12	5.66	-	-	2	-	75	5	418	16	26.12	4-35	-	
Twenty20																		

Career Performances

	M	Inns	NO	Runs	HS	Avge	100s	50s	Ct	St	Balls	Runs	Wkts	Avge	Best	5wI	10wM
Test	19	32	2	368	46	12.26	-	-	5	-	3299	1873	44	42.56	3-53	-	-
All First	139	209	31	2399	76	13.47	-	3	41	-	25001	13142	484	27.15	7-28	19	3
1-day Int	45	34	8	314	50 *	12.07	-	1	8	-	2120	1729	46	37.58	3-21	-	
C & G	10	8	4	118	36	29.50	-	-	1	-	511	295	12	24.58	3-27	-	
totesport	53	38	9	430	32	14.82	-	-	7	-	2217	1902	77	24.70	4-35	-	
Twenty20																	

59. Who played for Zimbabwe in their pre-Test days and has a son who became the first Zimbabwe cricketer to take 100 Test wickets?

McMAHON, P. J. Nottinghamshire

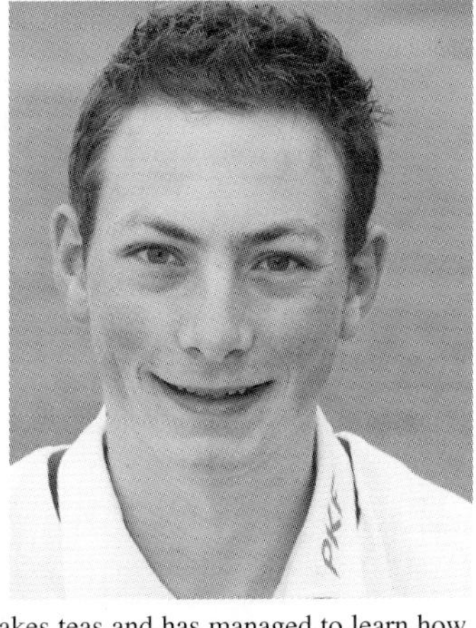

Name: Paul Joseph McMahon
Role: Right-hand bat, off-spin bowler
Born: 12 March 1983, Wigan
Height: 6ft 1in **Weight:** 11st 8lbs
Nickname: Vince, Macca, Boffin
County debut: 2002
1st-Class 50s: 1
1st-Class catches: 6
Place in batting averages: (2003 273rd av. 10.33)
Place in bowling averages: 138th av. 45.91 (2003 75th av. 33.05)
Strike rate: 86.00 (career 74.71)
Parents: Gerry and Teresa
Marital status: Single
Family links with cricket: 'Dad was club professional in Lancashire and Cheshire leagues; now plays for Notts Over 50s and for Wollaton in Notts Premier League. Mum makes teas and has managed to learn how to find scores on Ceefax'

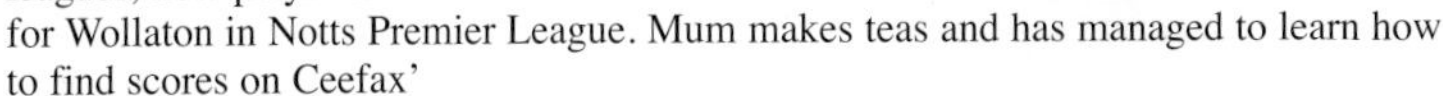

Education: Trinity RC Comprehensive, Nottingham; Wadham College, Oxford University
Qualifications: 11 GCSEs, 4 A-levels
Career outside cricket: Student
Off-season: 'Final year of law degree at Oxford University'
Overseas tours: England U19 to Australia and (U19 World Cup) New Zealand 2001-02; Nottinghamshire to South Africa 2002, 2003; WCA spin bowling camp, Mumbai 2004
Career highlights to date: 'Captaining England U19 against India U19, and taking eight wickets [4-47 and 4-58] in the victory at Northampton in the deciding final "Test"'
Cricketers particularly admired: Mike Atherton, Steve Waugh, Nasser Hussain
Young players to look out for: Michael Munday, Will Smith, Jamie Dalrymple, Joe Sayers
Other sports played: Football (Oxford University AFC), hockey (Wadham College HC), darts (Wadham College 2nd VIII)
Other sports followed: Football (AFC Wimbledon)
Favourite band: Oasis
Relaxations: Music, reading, current affairs, 'doing the Wheelhouse quiz'
Extras: Has played for Notts at every level from U11 to 1st XI. Second graduate of Nottinghamshire CCC Academy. Man of the Match in England's opening game of the 2001-02 U19 World Cup, taking 5-25 against Nepal. Captain of England U19 against

India U19 2002; leading wicket-taker in 'Test' series with ten wickets (av. 22.20). Shared with Andrew Harris (41*) in a record last-wicket stand for Nottinghamshire in matches v Northamptonshire (68), at Northampton 2002. Nottinghamshire Young Player of the Year 2003. NBC Denis Compton Award for the most promising young Nottinghamshire player 2003. Captained Oxford University CCE team which won the UCCE Championship and One-Day Challenge 2004. Oxford University captain 2004 (re-elected for 2005), scoring 99 and returning match figures of 7-140 from 72 overs in the four-day Varsity Match at The Parks. Represented British Universities v New Zealanders at Fenner's 2004. Passed 100 2nd XI Championship wickets in 23 games
Best batting: 99 Oxford University v Cambridge University, The Parks 2004
Best bowling: 4-59 Nottinghamshire v Essex, Chelmsford 2003

2004 Season

	M	Inns	NO	Runs	HS	Avge	100s	50s	Ct	St	O	M	Runs	Wkts	Avge	Best	5wI	10wM
Test																		
All First	6	6	2	153	99	38.25	-	1	3	-	172	36	551	12	45.91	4-68	-	-
1-day Int																		
C & G																		
totesport																		
Twenty20																		

Career Performances

	M	Inns	NO	Runs	HS	Avge	100s	50s	Ct	St	Balls	Runs	Wkts	Avge	Best	5wI	10wM
Test																	
All First	14	18	2	261	99	16.31	-	1	6	-	2391	1249	32	39.03	4-59	-	-
1-day Int																	
C & G																	
totesport	1	1	0	0	0	0.00	-	-	-	-	30	33	0	-	-	-	
Twenty20																	

MEES, T. Warwickshire

Name: Thomas (<u>Tom</u>) Mees
Role: Right-hand bat, right-arm fast-medium bowler
Born: 8 June 1981, Wolverhampton
Height: 6ft 3in **Weight:** 13st
Nickname: Meesy, Meesdog
County debut: No first-team appearance
1st-Class 5 w. in innings: 1
1st-Class catches: 1
Strike rate: (career 71.55)
Parents: Mark and Christina
Marital status: Single

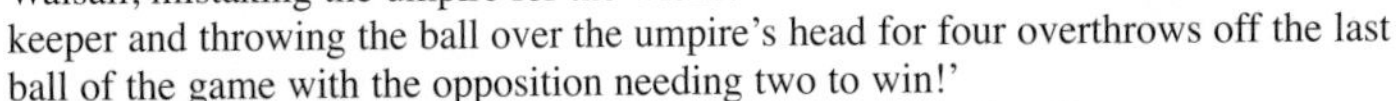

Family links with cricket: 'Cousin Simon played for Worcestershire Youth. Dad played for Cosely and umpires'
Education: Worcester Royal Grammar School; King Edward VI College, Stourbridge; Oxford Brookes University
Qualifications: 9 GCSEs, 3 A-levels, ECB Level 1 coaching award
Overseas tours: British Universities to South Africa 2002
Overseas teams played for: Railways, Albany, Western Australia 1999-2000
Career highlights to date: 'Taking 6-64 v Middlesex on first-class debut for Oxford UCCE 2001'
Cricket moments to forget: 'Playing in a Birmingham League match for Old Hill v Walsall, mistaking the umpire for the wicket-keeper and throwing the ball over the umpire's head for four overthrows off the last ball of the game with the opposition needing two to win!'
Cricketers particularly admired: Ian Botham, Andrew Flintoff
Young players to look out for: Jamie Dalrymple, Matt Stillwell, Patrick Wolff
Other sports played: Golf, football, tennis
Other sports followed: Football (Liverpool FC)
Relaxations: Playing golf, spending time with friends, shopping, going out
Extras: Played for Worcestershire Board XI in the NatWest 1999. Has played for Warwickshire 2nd XI. Played for Oxford University CCE in 2001, 2002 and 2003. Played for Warwickshire Board XI in the C&G 2001 and 2002, taking 3-19 v Cambridgeshire at March in the 2002 competition and winning the Man of the Match award. Recorded maiden first-class five-wicket return (6-64) for OUCCE on first-class debut v Middlesex at The Parks 2001. Represented British Universities 2002 and 2003
Best batting: 36* OUCCE v Hampshire, The Parks 2003
Best bowling: 6-64 OUCCE v Middlesex, The Parks 2001

2004 Season (did not make any first-class or one-day appearances)

Career Performances

	M	Inns	NO	Runs	HS	Avge	100s	50s	Ct	St	Balls	Runs	Wkts	Avge	Best	5wI	10wM
Test																	
All First	8	12	2	110	36 *	11.00	-	-	1	-	1431	917	20	45.85	6-64	1	-
1-day Int																	
C & G	4	2	1	4	4 *	4.00	-	-	-	-	198	144	3	48.00	3-19	-	
totesport																	
Twenty20																	

MIDDLEBROOK, J. D. — Essex

Name: James Daniel Middlebrook
Role: Right-hand bat, off-spin bowler
Born: 13 May 1977, Leeds
Height: 6ft 1in **Weight:** 13st
Nickname: Brooky, Midi, Midders, Midhouse, Dog
County debut: 1998 (Yorkshire), 2002 (Essex)
County cap: 2003 (Essex)
50 wickets in a season: 1
1st-Class 50s: 7
1st-Class 100s: 2
1st-Class 5 w. in innings: 5
1st-Class 10 w. in match: 1
1st-Class catches: 32
Place in batting averages: 126th av. 32.86 (2003 224th av. 20.16)
Place in bowling averages: 126th av. 42.91 (2003 87th av. 35.33)
Strike rate: 69.61 (career 70.17)
Parents: Ralph and Mavis
Marital status: Single
Family links with cricket: 'Dad is a senior staff coach'
Education: Crawshaw, Pudsey ('at this school with Paul Hutchison')
Qualifications: NVQ Level 2 in Coaching Sport and Recreation, ECB senior coach
Overseas tours: Yorkshire CCC to Guernsey
Overseas teams played for: Stokes Valley CC, New Zealand; Gold Coast Dolphins, Brisbane; Surfers Paradise CC, Brisbane
Career highlights to date: 'Beating Yorkshire in the NCL [2003] so we stayed up'
Cricket superstitions: 'Always put my batting gear on the same way'
Cricketers particularly admired: John Emburey, Ian Botham
Young players to look out for: Alastair Cook, Ravinder Bopara
Other sports played: Golf, tennis, squash, badminton
Other sports followed: Football (Leeds United), athletics
Relaxations: 'Any music – MTV – sleeping, socialising, catching up with old friends'
Extras: Played for Pudsey Congs from age of seven. Played for Yorkshire at all age levels U11 to 1st XI. Awarded Yorkshire 2nd XI cap 1998. His maiden first-class five-wicket return (6-82) v Hampshire at Southampton 2000 included a spell of four wickets in five balls. Released by Yorkshire at the end of the 2001 season and joined Essex for 2002. Took Championship hat-trick (Saggers, Muralitharan, Sheriyar) v Kent at Canterbury 2003. Scored maiden first-class century (101*) v Cambridge UCCE at Fenner's 2004 and maiden Championship century (115) v Somerset at Taunton 2004

Best batting: 115 Essex v Somerset, Taunton 2004
Best bowling: 6-82 Yorkshire v Hampshire, Southampton 2000

2004 Season

	M	Inns	NO	Runs	HS	Avge	100s	50s	Ct	St	O	M	Runs	Wkts	Avge	Best	5wI	10wM
Test																		
All First	16	24	2	723	115	32.86	2	3	4	-	394.3	57	1459	34	42.91	5-26	1	-
1-day Int																		
C & G	3	1	0	47	47	47.00	-	-	1	-	21.2	1	83	4	20.75	2-42	-	
totesport	15	10	2	160	40	20.00	-	-	1	-	74	2	321	8	40.12	2-17	-	
Twenty20	5	4	0	40	12	10.00	-	-	2	-	9	0	63	2	31.50	2-17	-	

Career Performances

	M	Inns	NO	Runs	HS	Avge	100s	50s	Ct	St	Balls	Runs	Wkts	Avge	Best	5wI	10wM
Test																	
All First	73	108	10	2109	115	21.52	2	7	32	-	12421	6632	177	37.46	6-82	5	1
1-day Int																	
C & G	7	3	2	59	47	59.00	-	-	4	-	254	194	5	38.80	2-42	-	
totesport	58	39	11	400	46 *	14.28	-	-	13	-	2076	1611	50	32.22	4-33	-	
Twenty20	5	4	0	40	12	10.00	-	-	2	-	54	63	2	31.50	2-17	-	

MILLER, D. J. — Surrey

Name: Daniel James Miller
Role: Left-hand bat, right-arm fast bowler
Born: 12 June 1983, Hammersmith, London
Height: 6ft 4in **Weight:** 14st 4lbs
Nickname: Windy, Funky
County debut: 2002 (one-day)
Parents: Gillian and Keith
Marital status: Single
Family links with cricket: 'My dad's got the name but no ability'
Education: Ewell Castle Senior School; Kingston College
Qualifications: 9 GCSEs, 4 A-levels
Overseas tours: Surrey Cricket Board to Barbados 1999
Career highlights to date: 'Making first-team debut at Surrey in NUL'
Cricket superstitions: 'Copying the preparation of a good day'

Cricketers particularly admired: David Morgan, Ian Botham, Alec Stewart, Graham Thorpe, Glenn McGrath
Young players to look out for: Neil Saker, Chris Murtagh, Simon Day
Other sports played: Football (Kingstonian Youth)
Other sports followed: Football (Tottenham Hotspur), 'all rugby union'
Extras: Attended Surrey Academy

2004 Season (did not make any first-class or one-day appearances)

Career Performances

	M	Inns	NO	Runs	HS	Avge	100s	50s	Ct	St	Balls	Runs	Wkts	Avge	Best	5wI	10wM
Test																	
All First																	
1-day Int																	
C & G																	
totesport	1	1	0	1	1	1.00	-	-	-	-	42	32	0	-	-	-	
Twenty20																	

MITCHELL, D. K. H. — Worcestershire

Name: Daryl Keith Henry Mitchell
Role: Right-hand bat, part-time right-arm medium bowler
Born: 25 November 1983, Evesham
Height: 5ft 10in **Weight:** 11st 4lbs
Nickname: Mitch, Peggy
County debut: No first-team appearance (*see* ***Extras***)
Parents: Keith and Jane
Marital status: Single
Family links with cricket: 'Dad played club cricket and coaches WYC U13'
Education: Prince Henry's, Evesham; University College Worcester
Qualifications: 10 GCSEs, 3 A-levels, 1 AS-level
Career outside cricket: 'Student and barman'

Off-season: University
Career highlights to date: 'Winning 2nd XI Trophy 2004. 142* v Glamorgan 2nd XI'
Cricket moments to forget: '2nd XI Championship v Warwickshire – lbw first ball of game, dropped two catches, bowled two overs 0-22'
Cricket superstitions: 'Put gloves on before helmet'

Cricketers particularly admired: Michael Atherton, Ian Botham, Graeme Hick
Young players to look out for: Steve Davies
Other sports played: Football (Bretforton Sports)
Other sports followed: Football (Aston Villa)
Favourite band: Oasis
Relaxations: 'Watching any sport; playing golf'
Extras: Played for Worcestershire v Cardiff University CCE at Worcester 2004 but has yet to appear for the county in first-class cricket or domestic competition
Opinions on cricket: 'Best game in the world! The more cricket the better!'

MOHAMMAD AKRAM Surrey

Name: Mohammad Akram Awan
Role: Right-hand bat, right-arm fast bowler
Born: 10 September 1974, Islamabad, Pakistan
Height: 6ft 2in **Weight:** 13st 7lbs
Nickname: Haji
County debut: 1997 (Northamptonshire), 2003 (Essex), 2004 (Sussex)
Test debut: 1995-96
Tests: 9
One-Day Internationals: 23
1st-Class 5 w. in innings: 14
1st-Class 10 w. in match: 1
1st-Class catches: 27
Place in batting averages: 220th av. 19.90
Place in bowling averages: 76th av. 34.36 (2003 51st av. 28.00)
Strike rate: 56.36 (career 47.20)
Parents: Mohammad Akbar
Marital status: Married, May 1999
Children: Imaan Akram, 2002
Education: Gordon College, Rawalpindi
Career outside cricket: Business
Overseas tours: Pakistan to Australia 1995-96, to England 1996, to South Africa and Zimbabwe 1997-98, to Australia 1999-2000, to West Indies 1999-2000, to New Zealand 2000-01, plus one-day tournaments in Sharjah, Singapore, Toronto, Bangladesh and Sri Lanka
Overseas teams played for: Rawalpindi Cricket Association 1992-93 – 2002-03; Allied Bank 1996-97 – 2000-01
Cricket superstitions: 'None'
Cricketers particularly admired: Wasim, Waqar

Other sports played: Tennis, swimming
Other sports followed: Football
Relaxations: 'Friends, going to different countries, pool'
Extras: Was Northamptonshire's overseas player in 1997. Recorded maiden Test five-wicket innings return (5-138) in third Test v Australia at Perth 1999-2000. Was an overseas player with Essex for the latter part of the 2003 season. Took 5-98 on Championship debut for Essex v Sussex at Colchester 2003. Took career best 8-49 v Surrey at The Oval 2003, including the first four wickets without conceding a run. Joined Sussex for 2004; was no longer classed as an overseas player, having qualified by residency. Left Sussex at the end of the 2004 season and has joined Surrey for 2005
Best batting: 35* Sussex v Warwickshire, Edgbaston 2004
Best bowling: 8-49 Essex v Surrey, The Oval 2003

2004 Season

	M	Inns	NO	Runs	HS	Avge	100s	50s	Ct	St	O	M	Runs	Wkts	Avge	Best	5wI	10wM
Test																		
All First	14	18	8	199	35 *	19.90	-	-	2	-	432.1	76	1581	46	34.36	4-85	-	-
1-day Int																		
C & G	2	2	0	2	1	1.00	-	-	-	-	20	2	108	6	18.00	4-61	-	
totesport	9	4	0	24	14	6.00	-	-	2	-	69	5	324	10	32.40	2-35	-	
Twenty20	1	1	1	7	7 *	-	-	-	1	-	3	0	35	1	35.00	1-35	-	

Career Performances

	M	Inns	NO	Runs	HS	Avge	100s	50s	Ct	St	Balls	Runs	Wkts	Avge	Best	5wI	10wM
Test	9	15	6	24	10 *	2.66	-	-	4	-	1477	859	17	50.52	5-138	1	-
All First	94	123	34	784	35 *	8.80	-	-	27	-	15341	8891	325	27.35	8-49	14	1
1-day Int	23	9	7	14	7 *	7.00	-	-	8	-	989	790	19	41.57	2-28	-	
C & G	3	3	1	2	1	1.00	-	-	-	-	192	150	7	21.42	4-61	-	
totesport	20	10	5	35	14	7.00	-	-	5	-	876	654	19	34.42	4-19	-	
Twenty20	1	1	1	7	7 *	-	-	-	1	-	18	35	1	35.00	1-35	-	

60. Against which team did Sri Lanka record their highest score in ODI cricket (398-5) in the 1995-96 World Cup?

MOHAMMAD ALI — Derbyshire

Name: Syed Mohammad Ali Bukhari
Role: Right-hand bat, left-arm fast-medium bowler
Born: 8 November 1973, Bahawalpur, Punjab
County debut: 2002
1st-Class 50s: 4
1st-Class 5 w. in innings: 11
1st-Class 10 w. in match: 2
1st-Class catches: 25
Place in batting averages: (2003 287th av. 7.21)
Place in bowling averages: 143rd av. 48.60 (2003 105th av. 37.85)
Strike rate: 70.00 (career 51.84)
Family links with cricket: Uncle Taslim Arif played for Pakistan 1979-80
Overseas teams played for: Numerous, including Bahawalpur, Islamabad Cricket Association, Lahore Cricket Association, Railways and United Bank
Extras: Played for Glamorgan 2nd XI 2000 and 2001. Struck a 38-ball 53 on debut for Derbyshire v Durham at Derby 2002, batting at No. 9. Released by Derbyshire at the end of the 2004 season. Is not considered an overseas player
Best batting: 92 Bahawalpur v Lahore City, Rahimyarkhan 1998-99
Best bowling: 6-37 Railways v National Bank, Faisalabad 1993-94

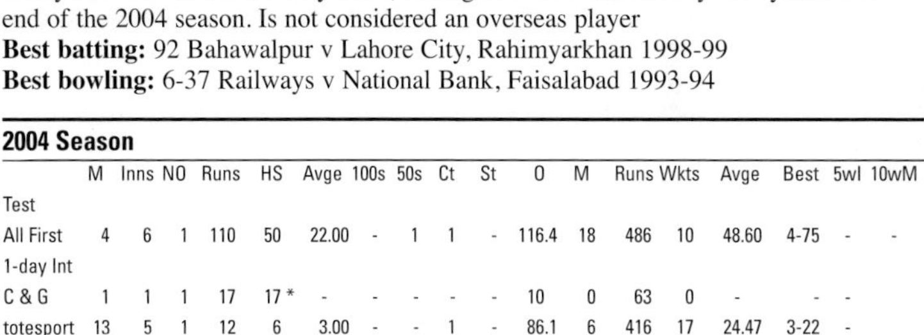

2004 Season

	M	Inns	NO	Runs	HS	Avge	100s	50s	Ct	St	O	M	Runs	Wkts	Avge	Best	5wI	10wM
Test																		
All First	4	6	1	110	50	22.00	-	1	1	-	116.4	18	486	10	48.60	4-75	-	-
1-day Int																		
C & G	1	1	1	17	17 *	-	-	-	-	-	10	0	63	0	-	-	-	
totesport	13	5	1	12	6	3.00	-	-	1	-	86.1	6	416	17	24.47	3-22	-	
Twenty20	4	0	0	0	0	-	-	-	-	-	15	0	95	10	9.50	3-24	-	

Career Performances

	M	Inns	NO	Runs	HS	Avge	100s	50s	Ct	St	Balls	Runs	Wkts	Avge	Best	5wI	10wM
Test																	
All First	84	112	26	1247	92	14.50	-	5	25	-	13688	8607	264	32.60	6-37	11	2
1-day Int																	
C & G	3	2	1	36	19	36.00	-	-	-	-	138	113	1	113.00	1-28	-	
totesport	19	10	5	37	10 *	7.40	-	-	1	-	778	660	25	26.40	3-22	-	
Twenty20	4	0	0	0	0	-	-	-	-	-	90	95	10	9.50	3-24	-	

MOHAMMAD SAMI Kent

Name: Mohammad Sami
Role: Right-hand bat, right-arm fast bowler
Born: 24 February 1981, Karachi, Pakistan
County debut: 2003
Test debut: 2000-01
Tests: 15
One-Day Internationals: 61
1st-Class 5 w. in innings: 10
1st-Class 10 w. in match: 2
1st-Class catches: 13
One-Day 5 w. in innings: 2
Place in batting averages: 271st av. 8.66
Place in bowling averages: 104th av. 37.57
Strike rate: 60.00 (career 53.24)
Overseas tours: Pakistan U19 to Sri Lanka (U19 World Cup) 1999-2000; Pakistan to New Zealand 2000-01, to England 2001, to Bangladesh 2001-02, to Sharjah (v West Indies) 2001-02, to Sri Lanka (ICC Champions Trophy) 2002-03, to Sri Lanka and Sharjah (v Australia) 2002-03, to Zimbabwe 2002-03, to South Africa 2002-03, to Africa (World Cup) 2002-03, to England (NatWest Challenge) 2003, to New Zealand 2003-04, to Holland (Videocon Cup) 2004, to England (ICC Champions Trophy) 2004, to Australia 2004-05, to India 2004-05, plus other one-day tournaments in Sharjah, Australia, Morocco, Kenya and Sri Lanka
Overseas teams played for: Pakistan Customs 1999-2000; Karachi Whites 2000-01; National Bank of Pakistan 2000-01 – 2002-03; Karachi 2003-04; Karachi Blues 2004-05 –
Extras: Had match figures of 8-106 (3-70/5-36) on Test debut in the first Test v New Zealand at Auckland 2000-01, winning Man of the Match award. Took hat-trick (T. C. B. Fernando, Zoysa, Muralitharan) v Sri Lanka in the final of the Asian Test Championship at Lahore 2001-02. Was an overseas player with Kent late June and early July 2003 before injuring an ankle; returned for 2004; left Kent at the end of the 2004 season. Took 15-114 (8-64/7-50) v Nottinghamshire at Maidstone 2003, the best match figures by a Kent bowler since 1939. ODI Man of the Match awards v South Africa at Lahore 2003-04 (3-20) and v New Zealand at Lahore 2003-04 (5-10)
Best batting: 49 Pakistan v India, Rawalpindi 2003-04
Best bowling: 8-64 Kent v Nottinghamshire, Maidstone 2003

2004 Season

	M	Inns	NO	Runs	HS	Avge	100s	50s	Ct	St	O	M	Runs	Wkts	Avge	Best	5wI	10wM
Test																		
All First	5	6	0	52	29	8.66	-	-	1	-	140	32	526	14	37.57	6-99	1	1
1-day Int	4	2	0	10	10	5.00	-	-	-	-	27	4	143	3	47.66	2-56	-	
C & G	1	1	0	5	5	5.00	-	-	-	-	8	0	43	1	43.00	1-43	-	
totesport	3	2	2	20	13 *	-	-	-	1	-	24.5	1	102	7	14.57	6-20	1	
Twenty20																		

Career Performances

	M	Inns	NO	Runs	HS	Avge	100s	50s	Ct	St	Balls	Runs	Wkts	Avge	Best	5wI	10wM
Test	15	22	9	161	49	12.38	-	-	-	-	3282	1831	39	46.94	5-36	2	-
All First	47	63	28	407	49	11.62	-	-	13	-	8785	5071	165	30.73	8-64	10	2
1-day Int	61	32	18	191	23	13.64	-	-	15	-	3009	2431	94	25.86	5-10	1	
C & G	1	1	0	5	5	5.00	-	-	-	-	48	43	1	43.00	1-43	-	
totesport	4	2	2	20	13 *	-	-	-	2	-	203	132	10	13.20	6-20	1	
Twenty20	2	2	1	13	8	13.00	-	-	-	-	47	54	2	27.00	1-23	-	

MONGIA, D. — Leicestershire

Name: Dinesh Mongia
Role: Left-hand bat, slow left-arm bowler
Born: 17 April 1977, Chandigarh, India
County debut: 2004 (Lancashire)
One-Day Internationals: 48
1st-Class 50s: 20
1st-Class 100s: 14
1st-Class 200s: 3
1st-Class 300s: 1
1st-Class catches: 95
One-Day 100s: 2
Place in batting averages: 6th av. 67.14
Strike rate: 60.40 (career 75.57)
Overseas tours: India to Zimbabwe 2001 (Coca-Cola Cup), to Sri Lanka 2001, to West Indies 2001-02, to England 2002, to Sri Lanka (ICC Champions Trophy) 2002-03, to New Zealand 2002-03 (one-day series), to Africa (World Cup) 2002-03, to Bangladesh (TVS Cup) 2003, to Bangladesh 2004-05 (one-day series)

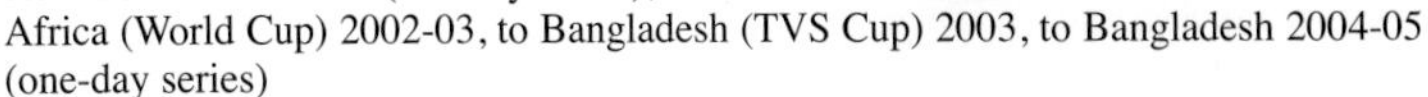

Overseas teams played for: Punjab (India) 1995-96 –
Extras: Represented India U19 v South Africa U19 1995-96. Awards include Man of

the Match in ODI v Zimbabwe at Guwahati 2001-02 (159*; also Man of the Series) and in ODI v West Indies in Barbados 2001-02 (74). Played for Staffordshire in the C&G 2004. Was an overseas player with Lancashire June to August 2004, deputising first for the injured Carl Hooper, then for the injured Stuart Law. Has joined Leicestershire as an overseas player for 2005
Best batting: 308* Punjab v Jammu & Kashmir, Jullundur 2000-01
Best bowling: 4-34 Punjab v Kerala, Palakkad 2003-04

2004 Season

	M	Inns	NO	Runs	HS	Avge	100s	50s	Ct	St	O	M	Runs	Wkts	Avge	Best	5wI	10wM
Test																		
All First	6	9	2	470	111	67.14	2	2	2	-	50.2	9	157	5	31.40	1-1	-	-
1-day Int																		
C & G	1	1	0	31	31	31.00	-	-	3	-	10	0	42	2	21.00	2-42	-	
totesport	8	7	2	241	104 *	48.20	1	1	1	-	39.1	1	200	3	66.66	1-32	-	
Twenty20	4	3	0	112	50	37.33	-	1	2	-	13	0	52	8	6.50	3-19	-	

Career Performances

	M	Inns	NO	Runs	HS	Avge	100s	50s	Ct	St	Balls	Runs	Wkts	Avge	Best	5wI	10wM
Test																	
All First	79	115	12	5493	308 *	53.33	18	20	95	-	1436	659	19	34.68	4-34	-	-
1-day Int	48	42	5	1028	159 *	27.78	1	3	21	-	315	280	8	35.00	3-31	-	
C & G	1	1	0	31	31	31.00	-	-	3	-	60	42	2	21.00	2-42	-	
totesport	8	7	2	241	104 *	48.20	1	1	1	-	235	200	3	66.66	1-32	-	
Twenty20	4	3	0	112	50	37.33	-	1	2	-	78	52	8	6.50	3-19	-	

MONTGOMERIE, R. R. — Sussex

Name: Richard Robert Montgomerie
Role: Right-hand opening bat, occasional right-arm slow bowler
Born: 3 July 1971, Rugby
Height: 5ft 10in **Weight:** 13st
Nickname: Monty
County debut: 1991 (Northamptonshire), 1999 (Sussex)
County cap: 1995 (Northamptonshire), 1999 (Sussex)
1000 runs in a season: 5
1st-Class 50s: 63
1st-Class 100s: 24
1st-Class catches: 189
One-Day 100s: 3
Place in batting averages: 102nd av. 36.07 (2003 113th av. 33.62)
Strike rate: (career 123.00)
Parents: Robert and Gillian

Wife and date of marriage: Frances Elizabeth, 23 October 2004
Family links with cricket: Father captained Oxfordshire
Education: Rugby School; Worcester College, Oxford University
Qualifications: 12 O-levels, 4 A-levels, BA (Hons) Chemistry, Level II coaching
Career outside cricket: 'Sports admin or teaching – still investigating'
Off-season: 'Getting married! Working for Sussex marketing department'
Overseas tours: Oxford University to Namibia 1991; Northamptonshire to Zimbabwe and Johannesburg; Christians in Sport to South Africa 2000; Sussex to Grenada 2001, 2002
Overseas teams played for: Sydney University CC 1995-96
Career highlights to date: 'Winning Championship 2003 crowns it all'
Cricket moments to forget: 'Running [Northants] captain Allan Lamb out on my Championship debut … as his runner'
Other sports followed: Golf, rackets, real tennis 'and many others'
Favourite band: The Police
Relaxations: Any sport, good television, reading and 'occasionally testing my brain'
Extras: Oxford rackets Blue 1990. Scored unbeaten 50 in each innings of 1991 Varsity match. Faced first ball delivered by Durham in first-class cricket, for Oxford University at The Parks 1992. Captained Oxford University and Combined Universities 1994. Released by Northants at the end of the 1998 season and joined Sussex for 1999. Scored his first 100 for Sussex (113*) against his former county at Hove 1999. Scored 160* v Nottinghamshire at Trent Bridge 2001; in the process he shared with Murray Goodwin in a record partnership for any wicket for Sussex in matches against Notts (372*), superseding his own record (292) set with Michael Bevan at Hove in 2000. Scored 108 v Essex at Hove in the Norwich Union League 2001, in the process sharing with Murray Goodwin in a Sussex record opening partnership in the one-day league (176). Man of the Match award for his 157 in the Vodafone Challenge match against the Australians at Hove 2001. Joint Sussex Player of the Year (with Murray Goodwin) 2001. C&G Man of the Match award for his 126* v Leicestershire at Leicester 2002. Sussex 1st XI Fielder of the Year 2003. Carried his bat for 60* in Sussex's first innings v Lancashire at Hove 2004. 'Two first-class wickets!'
Opinions on cricket: 'England are winning – does that mean county cricket is thriving? Four-day, two-division cricket is still improving the standard and Twenty20 has been a great success, hopefully bringing in much-needed gate money. The first county academy players are starting to break into sides. I think this will improve standards further.'

Best batting: 196 Sussex v Hampshire, Hove 2002
Best bowling: 1-0 Sussex v Middlesex, Lord's 2001

2004 Season

	M	Inns	NO	Runs	HS	Avge	100s	50s	Ct	St	O	M	Runs	Wkts	Avge	Best	5wI	10wM
Test																		
All First	18	29	1	1010	85	36.07	-	10	12	-	8	0	26	0	-	-	-	-
1-day Int																		
C & G	1	1	0	0	0	0.00	-	-	-	-								
totesport	2	2	1	30	17 *	30.00	-	-	1	-								
Twenty20																		

Career Performances

	M	Inns	NO	Runs	HS	Avge	100s	50s	Ct	St	Balls	Runs	Wkts	Avge	Best	5wI	10wM
Test																	
All First	199	346	30	11452	196	36.24	24	63	189	-	246	134	2	67.00	1-0	-	-
1-day Int																	
C & G	18	18	4	799	126 *	57.07	2	6	5	-							
totesport	107	105	9	2923	108	30.44	1	21	30	-							
Twenty20																	

MOORE, S. C. — Worcestershire

Name: Stephen Colin Moore
Role: Right-hand opening bat, right-arm medium bowler
Born: 4 November 1980, Johannesburg, South Africa
Height: 6ft **Weight:** 13st
Nickname: Circles, Mandy, Mork
County debut: 2003
County colours: 2003
1000 runs in a season: 1
1st-Class 50s: 4
1st-Class 100s: 3
1st-Class catches: 9
Place in batting averages: 83rd av. 38.61
Strike rate: 54.00 (career 54.00)
Parents: Shane and Carrol
Marital status: Single
Education: Exeter University
Qualifications: MEng (Hons) Electronic Engineering
Overseas teams played for: Midland-Guildford, Perth 2003-04

Career highlights to date: 'Hundred at Lord's in my first innings at the home of cricket. One of the most difficult I've had to play'
Cricket moments to forget: 'Getting a duck in the Lord's final [2004] and losing the match'
Cricketers particularly admired: Steve Waugh ('for ability to score runs when team in trouble'), Daryll Cullinan ('for elegant strokeplay all around the wicket')
Other sports played: Hockey, tennis (both Exeter University 1st team), golf, squash
Other sports followed: Rugby (Springboks)
Favourite band: The Big, On the Case
Relaxations: 'My music (guitar and saxophone); watersports and wildlife'
Extras: Scored maiden first-class century (108*) v Kent at Canterbury 2004 in his third Championship match. Scored 1000 first-class runs in his first full season 2004. Is not considered an overseas player
Best batting: 146 Worcestershire v Surrey, Worcester 2004
Best bowling: 1-13 Worcestershire v Lancashire, Worcester 2004

2004 Season

	M	Inns	NO	Runs	HS	Avge	100s	50s	Ct	St	O	M	Runs	Wkts	Avge	Best	5wI	10wM
Test																		
All First	17	29	3	1004	146	38.61	3	4	7	-	27	3	127	3	42.33	1-13	-	-
1-day Int																		
C & G	4	3	0	104	57	34.66	-	1	-	-								
totesport	13	13	2	367	93 *	33.36	-	3	4	-	1.3	0	10	1	10.00	1-1	-	
Twenty20	6	4	0	15	12	3.75	-	-	4	-								

Career Performances

	M	Inns	NO	Runs	HS	Avge	100s	50s	Ct	St	Balls	Runs	Wkts	Avge	Best	5wI	10wM
Test																	
All First	19	33	4	1101	146	37.96	3	4	9	-	162	127	3	42.33	1-13	-	-
1-day Int																	
C & G	4	3	0	104	57	34.66	-	1	-	-							
totesport	14	14	2	379	93 *	31.58	-	3	4	-	15	20	1	20.00	1-1	-	
Twenty20	11	9	3	131	39 *	21.83	-	-	6	-							

61. Which team made their first World Cup appearance against South Africa in the 1995-96 World Cup and included only one local-born player in their team, captain Sultan Zarawani?

MORGAN, E. J. G. Middlesex

Name: Eoin Joseph Gerard Morgan
Role: Left-hand bat, right-arm medium bowler
Born: 10 September 1986, Dublin
Height: 5ft 10in **Weight:** 11st 11lbs
Nickname: Moggie
County debut: No first-team appearance
Parents: Joseph and Olivia
Marital status: Single
Family links with cricket: 'My father, three brothers, two sisters, grandfather and great-grandfather all played cricket'
Education: CUS, Dublin
Overseas tours: Ireland U15 to Holland (European U15 Championships) 2000, to Denmark (European U15 Championships) 2002; Ireland U17 to Scotland (European U17 Championships) 2002; Ireland U19 to
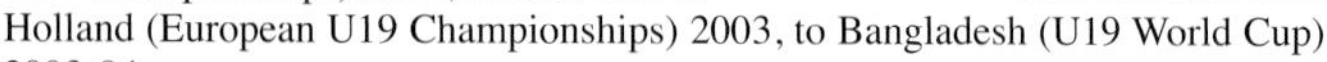
Holland (European U19 Championships) 2003, to Bangladesh (U19 World Cup) 2003-04
Overseas teams played for: St Henry's Marist School U19, Durban 2003
Career highlights to date: 'The contract with Middlesex CCC and playing for the senior Irish cricket team'
Cricket moments to forget: 'None'
Cricket superstitions: 'None'
Cricketers particularly admired: Brian Lara, Ricky Ponting
Young players to look out for: Billy Godleman
Other sports played: Rugby (Schools), Gaelic football (Schools)
Other sports followed: Rugby, football, snooker, darts, golf
Favourite band: Paddy Casey, Eminem, 2Pac, Jay Z, Joe Budden
Relaxations: 'Watching sports on television, listening to music and going out'
Extras: Player of the Tournament in European U15 Championships 2000, 2002 and in European U17 Championships 2002. Became youngest player to represent senior Ireland team 2003. NBC Denis Compton Award for the most promising young Middlesex player 2003. Represented Ireland in the C&G 2004, including the first round, played in August 2003. Made first-class debut for Ireland v Scotland at Dublin in the ICC Inter-Continental Cup 2004
Best batting: 7 Ireland v Scotland, Dublin 2004

2004 Season (did not make any first-class or one-day appearances for his county)

Career Performances

	M	Inns	NO	Runs	HS	Avge	100s	50s	Ct	St	Balls	Runs	Wkts	Avge	Best	5wI	10wM
Test																	
All First	1	2	0	7	7	3.50	-	-	-	-							
1-day Int																	
C & G	3	1	1	13	13 *	-	-	-	2	-	30	44	0	-	-	-	
totesport																	
Twenty20																	

MOSS, J. Derbyshire

Name: Jonathan Moss
Role: Right-hand bat, right-arm medium bowler; all-rounder
Born: 4 May 1975, Manly, Sydney, Australia
Height: 6ft 1in **Weight:** 13st 7lbs
Nickname: Mossy
County debut: 2004
County cap: 2004
1st-Class 50s: 17
1st-Class 100s: 4
1st-Class catches: 17
One-Day 100s: 1
Place in batting averages: 123rd av. 33.77
Place in bowling averages: 139th av. 46.14
Strike rate: 89.07 (career 67.80)
Parents: David and Shirley
Wife and date of marriage: Lori, 16 April 2004
Family links with cricket: 'Father grew up in Manchester and played league cricket with Didsbury; also went to strong cricket school, Manchester Grammar'
Education: Sydney C of E Grammar School (Shore), Sydney; Australian College of Physical Education
Qualifications: Bachelor of Physical Education, Level 2 cricket coach
Career outside cricket: Business development in sport (possible player-manager); public relations in sport
Off-season: Playing for Victoria in Australia
Overseas tours: Antipodeans to UK 1991
Overseas teams played for: Gordon DCC, Sydney 1992-97; Manly-Warringah DCC, Sydney 1998-2000; Prahran CC, Melbourne 2000 –; Victorian Bushrangers 2000-01 –

Career highlights to date: 'Debut for Victorian Bushrangers 2001; winning Pura Cup with Victoria 2003-04; captaining Victoria v Western Australia, December 2003; maiden first-class hundred v NSW at SCG; contributing with 98 and three wickets in Pura Cup final at MCG v Queensland 2003-04'
Cricket moments to forget: 'Without forgetting the man himself, the death of David Hookes – a coach who helped me achieve new and greater heights with my cricket'
Cricket superstitions: 'A couple of pieces of toast with honey morning of game day'
Cricketers particularly admired: Mark Waugh, Shane Warne, Darren Berry
Young players to look out for: David Hussey, Cameron White
Other sports played: Soccer, golf
Other sports followed: Football (Manchester United)
Injuries: Out for three weeks with a displaced disc in the neck
Favourite band: U2, INXS
Relaxations: 'Travelling the world; reading a newspaper sipping on a latte at a nice cafe'
Extras: Played for Berkshire in the C&G Trophy 2001. Awarded inaugural Bill Lawry Medal for Victorian Pura Cup Cricketer of the Year 2002-03. Joined Derbyshire as an overseas player for 2004; awarded Derbyshire cap 2004; has returned for 2005
Opinions on cricket: 'The Twenty20 competition has invigorated the game and has shown what success can be achieved by a progressive and innovative attitude – great concept. I think county cricket is primarily quite strong in terms of talent. However, due to the amount of cricket played, the intensity is poor and the levels of desire to achieve lack. Essentially I think first-class and one-day league games should be modelled on international cricket to fully prepare players for the next level (i.e. 50 overs per side and less than 104 overs per day – compromise in between).'
Best batting: 172* Victoria v Western Australia, Perth 2003-04
Best bowling: 4-50 Victoria v Western Australia, Perth 2002-03

2004 Season

	M	Inns	NO	Runs	HS	Avge	100s	50s	Ct	St	O	M	Runs	Wkts	Avge	Best	5wI	10wM
Test																		
All First	12	20	2	608	147 *	33.77	1	4	5	-	207.5	39	646	14	46.14	3-30	-	-
1-day Int																		
C & G	1	1	0	6	6	6.00	-	-	1	-	10	2	56	0	-	-	-	
totesport	15	14	2	439	104	36.58	1	3	7	-	79.2	5	431	11	39.18	4-45	-	
Twenty20	4	4	0	148	68	37.00	-	1	-	-	11	1	73	2	36.50	1-16	-	

Career Performances

	M	Inns	NO	Runs	HS	Avge	100s	50s	Ct	St	Balls	Runs	Wkts	Avge	Best	5wI	10wM
Test																	
All First	40	64	6	2483	172 *	42.81	4	17	17	-	4068	1912	60	31.86	4-50	-	-
1-day Int																	
C & G	3	3	0	34	28	11.33	-	-	1	-	180	144	5	28.80	3-52	-	
totesport	15	14	2	439	104	36.58	1	3	7	-	476	431	11	39.18	4-45	-	
Twenty20	4	4	0	148	68	37.00	-	1	-	-	66	73	2	36.50	1-16	-	

MUCHALL, G. J. — Durham

Name: Gordon James Muchall
Role: Right-hand bat, right-arm medium-fast bowler
Born: 2 November 1982, Newcastle upon Tyne
Height: 6ft **Weight:** 13st 5lbs
Nickname: Manson, West, Cannon, Melon, Lecter
County debut: 2002
1st-Class 50s: 13
1st-Class 100s: 5
1st-Class catches: 35
Place in batting averages: 124th av. 33.62 (2003 177th av. 25.83)
Strike rate: 43.00 (career 55.33)
Parents: Mary and Arthur
Marital status: Single
Family links with cricket: Grandfather played for Northumberland. Younger brother (Paul) was in England U15 squad
Education: Durham School
Qualifications: 8 GCSEs, 2 A-levels
Overseas tours: England U19 to India 2000-01, to Australia and (U19 World Cup) New Zealand 2001-02; ECB National Academy to Australia and Sri Lanka 2002-03
Overseas teams played for: Fremantle 2001-02
Career highlights to date: '127 at Lord's for Durham. 254 for England U19 v India U19'
Cricket moments to forget: 'With the opposition needing four off the last ball to win, going into the long barrier position and the ball bouncing over my head for four'
Cricketers particularly admired: Jacques Kallis, Ian Botham, Steve Waugh, Darren Gough
Young players to look out for: Paul Muchall, Kyle Hogg, Kadeer Ali, Nadeem Malik
Other sports played: Rugby (at school)
Other sports followed: Football (Newcastle United), rugby (Newcastle Falcons and England)
Relaxations: Listening to music, socialising with friends
Extras: Represented England U19 2001 and v India U19 2002, scoring 254 in the first 'Test' at Cardiff 2002; it was the third highest individual score in the history of U19 international cricket. Cricket Society's Most Promising Young Cricketer of the Year Award 2002. NBC Denis Compton Award for the most promising young Durham player 2002

Best batting: 142* Durham v Yorkshire, Scarborough 2004
Best bowling: 3-26 Durham v Yorkshire, Headingley 2003

2004 Season

	M	Inns	NO	Runs	HS	Avge	100s	50s	Ct	St	O	M	Runs	Wkts	Avge	Best	5wI	10wM
Test																		
All First	16	30	1	975	142 *	33.62	1	5	14	-	43	7	161	6	26.83	1-1	-	-
1-day Int																		
C & G	1	1	0	22	22	22.00	-	-	-	-	5	0	31	0	-	-	-	
totesport	8	5	3	92	28 *	46.00	-	-	2	-	5	0	20	0	-	-	-	
Twenty20	5	4	1	61	45 *	20.33	-	-	4	-								

Career Performances

	M	Inns	NO	Runs	HS	Avge	100s	50s	Ct	St	Balls	Runs	Wkts	Avge	Best	5wI	10wM
Test																	
All First	48	87	2	2573	142 *	30.27	5	13	35	-	830	571	15	38.06	3-26	-	-
1-day Int																	
C & G	5	4	0	48	22	12.00	-	-	2	-	84	76	0	-	-	-	
totesport	29	26	4	703	87	31.95	-	3	9	-	78	61	1	61.00	1-15	-	
Twenty20	8	6	1	88	45 *	17.60	-	-	4	-	12	8	1	8.00	1-8	-	

MULLALLY, A. D. — Hampshire

Name: Alan David Mullally
Role: Right-hand bat, left-arm fast bowler
Born: 12 July 1969, Southend
Height: 6ft 4in **Weight:** 14st
Nickname: Spider
County debut: 1988 (Hampshire), 1990 (Leicestershire)
County cap: 1993 (Leicestershire), 2000 (Hampshire; *see* ***Extras***)
Test debut: 1996
Tests: 19
One-Day Internationals: 50
50 wickets in a season: 5
1st-Class 50s: 2
1st-Class 5 w. in innings: 31
1st-Class 10 w. in match: 4
1st-Class catches: 44
One-Day 5 w. in innings: 2
Place in batting averages: (2003 293rd av. 5.42)
Place in bowling averages: 117th av. 39.50 (2003 112th av. 39.05)

Strike rate: 81.88 (career 61.64)
Parents: Mick and Ann
Wife and date of marriage: Chelsey, 1997
Education: Cannington High School, Perth, Australia; Wembley and Carlisle Technical College
Overseas tours: Western Australia to India 1989-90; Leicestershire to Jamaica 1992-93; England to Zimbabwe and New Zealand 1996-97, to Australia 1998-99, to Sharjah (Coca-Cola Cup) 1998-99, to South Africa and Zimbabwe 1999-2000, to Sri Lanka 2000-01 (one-day series)
Overseas teams played for: Western Australia 1987-90; Victoria 1990-91
Career highlights to date: 'Career best 9-93 v Derbyshire. Man of the Match in World Cup [v Zimbabwe 1999] and CUB Series v Australia [1998-99]'
Cricket moments to forget: 'Sunday League v Middlesex' (*At the Rose Bowl in 2001, Middlesex took 35 runs off the last 13 deliveries of the game to win*)
Cricketers particularly admired: Robin Smith
Other sports followed: Australian Rules football, basketball, most sports
Relaxations: Fishing, music
Extras: Made first-class debut for Western Australia in the 1987-88 Sheffield Shield final v Queensland at Perth. Represented Australia YC v West Indies YC and in the U19 World Cup 1987-88. Played one match for Hampshire in 1988 before joining Leicestershire. Represented England in the 1999 World Cup. Left Leicestershire at end of 1999 season and rejoined Hampshire for 2000. Took 5-18 as Hampshire bowled out the Australians for 97 at West End 2001. Granted a benefit for 2005
Best batting: 75 Leicestershire v Middlesex, Leicester 1996
Best bowling: 9-93 Hampshire v Derbyshire, Derby 2000

2004 Season

	M	Inns	NO	Runs	HS	Avge	100s	50s	Ct	St	O	M	Runs	Wkts	Avge	Best	5wI	10wM
Test																		
All First	10	10	5	67	22 *	13.40	-	-	1	-	245.4	69	711	18	39.50	6-68	1	-
1-day Int																		
C & G	2	1	1	0	0 *	-	-	-	-	-	15	3	48	4	12.00	3-29	-	
totesport	14	7	2	27	10	5.40	-	-	1	-	108.1	16	452	18	25.11	2-18	-	
Twenty20	1	1	0	0	0	0.00	-	-	-	-	2	0	19	0	-	-	-	

Career Performances

	M	Inns	NO	Runs	HS	Avge	100s	50s	Ct	St	Balls	Runs	Wkts	Avge	Best	5wI	10wM
Test	19	27	4	127	24	5.52	-	-	6	-	4525	1812	58	31.24	5-105	1	-
All First	230	258	70	1615	75	8.59	-	2	44	-	43645	19953	708	28.18	9-93	31	4
1-day Int	50	25	10	86	20	5.73	-	-	8	-	2698	1728	63	27.42	4-18	-	
C & G	30	11	6	58	19 *	11.60	-	-	3	-	1806	1027	50	20.54	5-18	1	
totesport	152	68	29	297	38	7.61	-	-	27	-	6845	4753	164	28.98	5-15	1	
Twenty20	6	3	0	0	0	0.00	-	-	1	-	102	123	2	61.50	1-16	-	

MUNDAY, M. K. Somerset

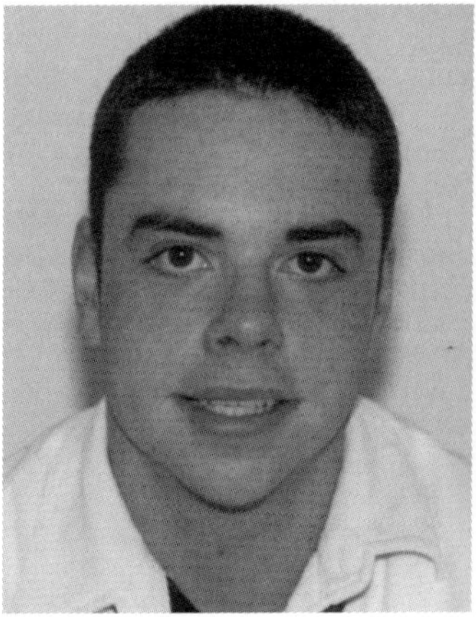

Name: Michael Kenneth Munday
Role: Right-hand bat, leg-spin bowler
Born: 22 October 1984, Nottingham
Height: 5ft 8in **Weight:** 12st
County debut: No first-team appearance
1st-Class 5 w. in innings: 1
1st-Class catches: 2
Place in bowling averages: 24th av. 25.70 (2003 8th av. 21.78)
Strike rate: 36.30 (career 35.12)
Parents: John and Maureen
Marital status: Single
Family links with cricket: 'Dad, brother and sister have played league cricket in Cornwall'
Education: Truro School; Corpus Christi College, Oxford University
Qualifications: 10 GCSEs, 3 A-levels
Career outside cricket: Student
Off-season: Studying chemistry at Oxford University (third year)
Overseas tours: Cornwall Schools U13 to South Africa 1998; ESCA West U15 to West Indies 2000
Career highlights to date: 'Playing in the Oxford University side that beat Cambridge by an innings at Fenner's 2003 and representing England U19 in summer 2004'
Cricket moments to forget: 'Being part of a Cornwall Minor Counties team that dropped 17 catches against Dorset'
Cricket superstitions: 'None'
Cricketers particularly admired: Shane Warne, Graham Gooch
Young players to look out for: Carl Gazzard, Joe Sayers
Other sports played: Chess ('Yes, it is a sport')
Other sports followed: Football (Liverpool)
Favourite band: 'None in particular'
Relaxations: Swimming, reading
Extras: Played for Cornwall in the C&G 2001. Played for Oxford University CCE 2003, 2004. Oxford Blue 2003, 2004, recording maiden first-class five-wicket return (5-83) v Cambridge University in the Varsity Match at Fenner's 2003. Represented England U19 v Bangladesh U19 2004
Opinions on cricket: 'Less cricket during the summer to enable more time for practice.'
Best batting: 14 OUCCE v Surrey, The Parks 2004
Best bowling: 5-83 Oxford University v Cambridge University, Fenner's 2003

2004 Season (did not make any first-class or one-day appearances for his county)

Career Performances

	M	Inns	NO	Runs	HS	Avge	100s	50s	Ct	St	Balls	Runs	Wkts	Avge	Best	5wI	10wM
Test																	
All First	8	6	3	15	14	5.00	-	-	2	-	843	562	24	23.41	5-83	1	-
1-day Int																	
C & G	1	0	0	0	0	-	-	-	-	-	30	39	1	39.00	1-39	-	
totesport																	
Twenty20																	

MURALITHARAN, M. Lancashire

Name: Muttiah Muralitharan
Role: Right-hand bat, off-spin bowler
Born: 17 April 1972, Kandy, Sri Lanka
Height: 5ft 5in
Nickname: Murali
County debut: 1999 (Lancashire), 2003 (Kent)
County cap: 1999 (Lancashire), 2003 (Kent)
Test debut: 1992-93
Tests: 91
One-Day Internationals: 237
50 wickets in a season: 2
1st-Class 50s: 1
1st-Class 5 w. in innings: 87
1st-Class 10 w. in match: 25
1st-Class catches: 97
One-Day 5 w. in innings: 9
Place in batting averages: (2003 289th av. 7.00)
Place in bowling averages: (2003 1st av. 13.54)
Strike rate: (career 49.26)
Marital status: Single
Education: St Anthony's College, Kandy
Overseas tours: Sri Lanka U24 to South Africa 1992-93; FICA World XI to New Zealand 2004-05; Sri Lanka to England 1991, to India 1993-94, to Zimbabwe 1994-95, to South Africa 1994-95, to New Zealand 1994-95, to Pakistan 1995-96, to Australia 1995-96, to India and Pakistan (World Cup) 1995-96, to New Zealand 1996-97, to West Indies 1996-97, to India 1997-98, to South Africa 1997-98, to England 1998, to Bangladesh (Wills International Cup) 1998-99, to UK, Ireland and Holland

(World Cup) 1999, to Zimbabwe 1999-2000, to Pakistan 1999-2000, to Kenya (ICC Knockout Trophy) 2000-01, to South Africa 2000-01, to England 2002, to South Africa 2002-03, to Africa (World Cup) 2002-03, to West Indies 2003, to Zimbabwe 2004, plus numerous other one-day series and tournaments in Sharjah, India, Singapore, West Indies, Kenya, Pakistan, Australia, Bangladesh, New Zealand and Morocco

Overseas teams played for: Tamil Union Cricket and Athletic Club 1991-92 –

Extras: Had match figures of 16-220 (7-155/9-65) from 113.5 overs v England at The Oval 1998. One of *Wisden*'s Five Cricketers of the Year 1999. Was Lancashire's overseas player 1999, taking 66 wickets in the 12 Championship innings in which he bowled. Lancashire Player of the Year 1999. Took 13-171 in the first Test at Galle 2000 in Sri Lanka's first Test win over South Africa. Took 7-30 v India in the Champions Trophy in Sharjah 2000, at the time the best return in ODI history. Highest wicket-taker in Test cricket for the calendar year 2000 with 75 wickets in ten matches. Returned as Lancashire's overseas player for 2001, taking 50 Championship wickets (av. 19.42) in only seven matches. Highest wicket-taker in Test cricket for the calendar year 2001 with 80 wickets in 12 matches. Took 9-51 in Zimbabwe's first innings in the second Test at Kandy 2001-02. Reached 400 Test wickets in a record 72 matches when he dismissed Henry Olonga in the third Test v Zimbabwe at Galle 2001-02. Has won numerous international awards, including Man of the [Test] Series v India 2001 and v England 2003-04. Was an overseas player with Kent July to September 2003, taking 33 wickets at 13.54 in the five Championship matches he played. Took 500th Test wicket (Michael Kasprowicz) in the second Test v Australia on his home ground, Kandy, 2003-04, becoming the third bowler to reach the milestone. Scored 43 in the second Test v Australia at Kandy 2003-04, in the process sharing with Chaminda Vaas (68*) in a record tenth-wicket stand for Sri Lanka in Tests (79). Took 520th Test wicket (Mluleki Nkala) in the first Test v Zimbabwe at Harare 2004, passing Courtney Walsh's 519 to move to the top of the all-time Test wicket-takers' list (*see entry on Shane Warne*). Has rejoined Lancashire as an overseas player for 2005

Best batting: 67 Sri Lanka v India, Kandy 2001-02

Best bowling: 9-51 Sri Lanka v Zimbabwe, Kandy 2001-02

2004 Season (did not make any first-class or one-day appearances)

Career Performances

	M	Inns	NO	Runs	HS	Avge	100s	50s	Ct	St	Balls	Runs	Wkts	Avge	Best	5wI	10wM
Test	91	117	42	942	67	12.56	-	1	50	-	31125	12165	532	22.86	9-51	44	13
All First	175	214	62	1737	67	11.42	-	1	97	-	50006	19388	1015	19.10	9-51	87	25
1-day Int	237	110	45	385	19	5.92	-	-	97	-	12871	8102	366	22.13	7-30	8	
C & G	5	2	0	15	15	7.50	-	-	-	-	288	186	5	37.20	3-21	-	
totesport	20	6	3	40	13 *	13.33	-	-	5	-	986	549	28	19.60	5-34	1	
Twenty20																	

MURTAGH, C. P. — Surrey

Name: Christopher (Chris) Paul Murtagh
Role: Right-hand bat, 'very occasional' leg-spin bowler
Born: 14 October 1984, Lambeth, London
Height: 5ft 11in **Weight:** 11st
Nickname: Murts, Baby, Brow
County debut: No first-team appearance
Parents: Dominic and Elizabeth
Marital status: Single
Family links with cricket: Elder brother Tim plays for Surrey; Uncle Andy (A. J. Murtagh) played for Hampshire
Education: John Fisher, Purley, Surrey; Loughborough University
Qualifications: 10 GCSEs, 2 A-levels
Career outside cricket: Student
Overseas tours: Surrey U19 to Sri Lanka 2002, to Perth 2004
Overseas teams played for: Parramatta, Sydney 2004
Career highlights to date: 'Three 2nd XI hundreds, the first against Northants 2003'
Cricket moments to forget: 'Dislocating finger in first training session in Australia – unable to play for two weeks'
Cricket superstitions: 'Left pad on first'
Cricketers particularly admired: Sachin Tendulkar, Andrew Flintoff, Curtly Ambrose
Young players to look out for: Tim Murtagh, Danny Miller, Neil Saker, Jade Dernbach
Other sports played: Rugby, football, golf
Other sports followed: Football (Liverpool FC)
Relaxations: 'Playing golf; watching sport'
Extras: Played for Surrey age groups and attended Surrey Academy. Made 2nd XI Championship debut 2002
Opinions on cricket: 'Too many EU-type players in county cricket. Twenty20 a good idea.'

MURTAGH, T. J. Surrey

Name: Timothy (Tim) James Murtagh
Role: Left-hand bat, right-arm fast-medium bowler
Born: 2 August 1981, Lambeth, London
Height: 6ft 2in **Weight:** 12st
Nickname: Hairy Faced Dingo
County debut: 2000 (one-day), 2001 (first-class)
1st-Class 50s: 4
1st-Class 5 w. in innings: 3
1st-Class catches: 11
Place in batting averages: 74th av. 41.55 (2003 261st av. 13.57)
Place in bowling averages: 129th av. 43.65 (2003 145th av. 51.25)
Strike rate: 73.05 (career 57.71)
Parents: Dominic and Elizabeth
Marital status: Single
Family links with cricket: Younger brother Chris plays for Surrey; Uncle Andy (A. J. Murtagh) played for Hampshire
Education: John Fisher, Purley, Surrey; St Mary's University, Twickenham
Qualifications: 10 GCSEs, 2 A-levels
Overseas tours: Surrey U17 to South Africa 1997; England U19 to Malaysia and (U19 World Cup) Sri Lanka 1999-2000; British Universities to South Africa 2002
Cricketers particularly admired: Darren Gough, Glenn McGrath
Young players to look out for: Neil Saker, Chris Murtagh, Danny Miller
Other sports played: Rugby (was captain of John Fisher 2nd XV), skiing ('in the past')
Other sports followed: Football (Liverpool FC), rugby
Relaxations: Playing golf, watching sport, films, reading
Extras: Represented British Universities 2000, 2001, 2002 and 2003. Represented England U19 v Sri Lanka U19 2000; named Player of the Series. NBC Denis Compton Award for the most promising young Surrey player 2001
Best batting: 74* Surrey v Middlesex, The Oval 2004
Best bowling: 6-86 British Universities v Pakistanis, Trent Bridge 2001

2004 Season

	M	Inns	NO	Runs	HS	Avge	100s	50s	Ct	St	O	M	Runs	Wkts	Avge	Best	5wI	10wM
Test																		
All First	11	17	8	374	74 *	41.55	-	4	8	-	243.3	50	873	20	43.65	5-74	1	-
1-day Int																		
C & G																		
totesport	8	7	4	115	28	38.33	-	-	1	-	51.3	2	319	5	63.80	2-48	-	
Twenty20	5	3	0	12	4	4.00	-	-	1	-	13	0	125	4	31.25	2-26	-	

Career Performances

	M	Inns	NO	Runs	HS	Avge	100s	50s	Ct	St	Balls	Runs	Wkts	Avge	Best	5wI	10wM
Test																	
All First	26	39	17	555	74 *	25.22	-	4	11	-	3290	2032	57	35.64	6-86	3	-
1-day Int																	
C & G	2	2	0	13	11	6.50	-	-	1	-	108	86	2	43.00	1-40	-	
totesport	30	22	11	167	28	15.18	-	-	5	-	1397	1236	35	35.31	4-31	-	
Twenty20	9	4	0	12	4	3.00	-	-	2	-	174	253	10	25.30	3-37	-	

MUSHTAQ AHMED Sussex

Name: Mushtaq Ahmed
Role: Right-hand bat, leg-spin bowler
Born: 28 June 1970, Sahiwal, Pakistan
Height: 5ft 4in
Nickname: Mushie
County debut: 1993 (Somerset), 2002 (Surrey), 2003 (Sussex)
County cap: 1993 (Somerset), 2003 (Sussex)
Test debut: 1991-92
Tests: 52
One-Day Internationals: 144
50 wickets in a season: 4
100 wickets in a season: 1
1st-Class 50s: 17
1st-Class 5 w. in innings: 76
1st-Class 10 w. in match: 23
1st-Class catches: 105
One-Day 5 w. in innings: 3
Place in batting averages: 199th av. 22.31 (2003 165th av. 26.82)
Place in bowling averages: 34th av. 27.59 (2003 27th av. 24.65)
Strike rate: 56.52 (career 52.76)
Wife and date of marriage: Uzma, 18 December 1994

Children: Bazal, Nawal, Habiba
Overseas tours: Pakistan YC to Australia (U19 World Cup) 1987-88; Pakistan to Sharjah (Sharjah Cup) 1988-89, to Australia 1989-90, 1995-96, 1999-2000, to New Zealand and Australia (World Cup) 1991-92, to England 1992, 1996, 2001, to New Zealand 1992-93, 1993-94, 1995-96, 2000-01, to West Indies 1992-93, 1999-2000, to Sri Lanka 1994-95, 1996-97, 2000, to South Africa 1997-98, to Zimbabwe 1997-98, to India 1998-99, to UK, Ireland and Holland (World Cup) 1999, plus numerous other one-day tournaments in India, Sharjah, Australia, South Africa, Zimbabwe, Singapore, Toronto and Bangladesh
Overseas teams played for: Numerous, including Multan, United Bank, and National Bank 2001-02 –
Career highlights to date: 'Winning the 1992 cricket World Cup final'
Cricket moments to forget: 'Losing the 1996 World Cup quarter-final to India at Bangalore'
Cricket superstitions: 'None'
Cricketers particularly admired: Imran Khan
Young players to look out for: Tim Ambrose, Matt Prior
Other sports followed: Hockey, football (Brazil)
Relaxations: 'Spending time with family, prayer'
Extras: Made first-class debut for Multan v Hyderabad 1986-87. Had first innings figures of 6-81 for Punjab Chief Minister's XI against England tourists at Sahiwal 1987-88. Took 16 wickets in the 1991-92 World Cup, finishing as second highest wicket-taker for Pakistan after Wasim Akram. Somerset's overseas player 1993-95 and 1997-98; Player of the Year 1993. Had match figures of 9-198 and 9-186 in successive Tests v Australia 1995-96, following up with 10-171 (including 7-56) in next Test v New Zealand eight days later. Represented Pakistan in 1995-96 World Cup. His international awards include Man of the [Test] Series v England 1996 and v South Africa 1997-98. One of *Wisden*'s Five Cricketers of the Year 1997. Was Surrey's overseas player during August 2002. Joined Sussex as an overseas player for 2003, taking 103 Championship wickets (av. 24.65). Sussex Player of the Year 2003. PCA Player of the Year 2003. Took 1000th first-class wicket (Martin Bicknell) v Surrey at The Oval 2004. Leading wicket-taker in English first-class cricket for the second season running 2004 with 84 wickets at 27.59, including 13-140 (6-67/7-73) v Worcestershire at Hove
Opinions on cricket: 'Credit should be given for first innings leads in the Championship. Fewer overs in a day's play in the Championship (say 90 not 104).'
Best batting: 90 Somerset v Sussex, Taunton 1993
Best bowling: 9-93 Multan v Peshawar, Sahiwal 1990-91

2004 Season

	M	Inns	NO	Runs	HS	Avge	100s	50s	Ct	St	O	M	Runs	Wkts	Avge	Best	5wI	10wM
Test																		
All First	17	24	5	424	62	22.31	-	2	6	-	791.2	164	2318	84	27.59	7-73	6	2
1-day Int																		
C & G	2	2	0	8	7	4.00	-	-	-	-	20	0	77	3	25.66	2-44	-	
totesport	15	8	5	56	19 *	18.66	-	-	1	-	100	3	492	14	35.14	4-46	-	
Twenty20	4	3	0	11	10	3.66	-	-	-	-	13	0	80	4	20.00	1-3	-	

Career Performances

	M	Inns	NO	Runs	HS	Avge	100s	50s	Ct	St	Balls	Runs	Wkts	Avge	Best	5wI	10wM
Test	52	72	16	656	59	11.71	-	2	23	-	12531	6100	185	32.97	7-56	10	3
All First	248	312	42	4279	90	15.84	-	17	105	-	56991	28231	1080	26.13	9-93	76	23
1-day Int	144	76	34	399	34 *	9.50	-	-	30	-	7543	5361	161	33.29	5-36	1	
C & G	15	10	3	119	35	17.00	-	-	4	-	994	518	26	19.92	5-26	1	
totesport	81	55	17	454	41	11.94	-	-	7	-	3481	2454	77	31.87	4-46	-	
Twenty20	8	5	0	28	16	5.60	-	-	-	-	174	174	9	19.33	2-12	-	

MUSTARD, P. — Durham

Name: Philip Mustard
Role: Left-hand bat, wicket-keeper
Born: 8 October 1982, Sunderland
Nickname: Colonel
County debut: 2002
1st-Class 50s: 3
1st-Class catches: 53
1st-Class stumpings: 3
Place in batting averages: (2003 210th av. 22.09)
Parents: Maureen
Marital status: Single
Education: Usworth Comprehensive
Cricket moments to forget: 'The first game I played I went out to bat and got a first-ball duck, then went out to keep wicket and dropped catches'
Cricketers particularly admired: Mike Atherton ('professionalism')
Young players to look out for: Nicky Peng
Other sports followed: Football (Middlesbrough)
Relaxations: 'Socialising with friends down the pub'

Extras: Scored 77-ball 75 on first-class debut v Sri Lankans at Riverside 2002. Represented England U19 v India U19 2002
Best batting: 75 Durham v Sri Lankans, Riverside 2002

2004 Season

	M	Inns	NO	Runs	HS	Avge	100s	50s	Ct	St	O	M	Runs	Wkts	Avge	Best	5wI	10wM
Test																		
All First	3	5	0	148	60	29.60	-	1	9	-								
1-day Int																		
C & G																		
totesport	3	1	0	1	1	1.00	-	-	1	-								
Twenty20	5	5	0	132	64	26.40	-	1	-	-								

Career Performances

	M	Inns	NO	Runs	HS	Avge	100s	50s	Ct	St	Balls	Runs	Wkts	Avge	Best	5wI	10wM
Test																	
All First	17	29	1	709	75	25.32	-	3	53	3							
1-day Int																	
C & G	7	6	1	47	33	9.40	-	-	9	3							
totesport	16	13	0	166	41	12.76	-	-	15	1							
Twenty20	10	10	0	235	64	23.50	-	2	-	3							

NAMBIAR, A. P. Middlesex

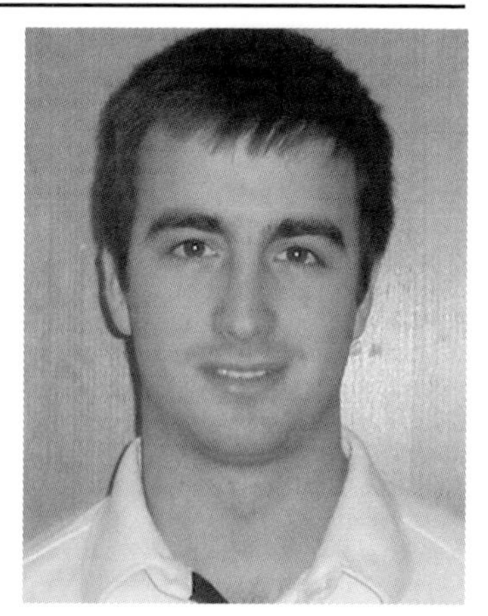

Name: Aneil Padman (<u>Johnny</u>) Nambiar
Role: Right-hand bat, right-arm medium bowler
Born: 2 March 1984, Thiruvananthapuram, Kerala, India
Height: 5ft 11in **Weight:** 11st 11lbs
County debut: No first-team appearance
Parents: Sunny and Anette
Marital status: Single
Education: Mallya Aditi International School, Bangalore, India; University of Surrey
Qualifications: BEng
Off-season: 'In training in India and/or Australia'
Overseas tours: Brijesh Patel Cricket Academy to Singapore 2000-01
Career highlights to date: 'Scoring 151 against Surrey 2nd XI on debut in 2nd XI cricket!' (*At Sutton 2004*)

Cricket moments to forget: 'This one game in Premier League club cricket – I scored four, went for eight runs an over and dropped two catches. I don't think it was my day!'
Cricket superstitions: 'None'
Cricketers particularly admired: Rahul Dravid, Mark Waugh
Young players to look out for: Robin Uthappa, Deepak Chogale (both Indian)
Other sports played: Squash, football, table tennis, badminton
Injuries: Out for eight weeks with a broken thumb
Favourite band: 3 Doors Down
Relaxations: 'Playing the guitar, reading, movies, travelling etc.'
Extras: Represented Karnataka U16. Played for Oxfordshire in the first round of the C&G 2004, which was played in August 2003
Opinions on cricket: 'Fast, with good entertainment value.'

2004 Season (did not make any first-class or one-day appearances)

Career Performances

	M	Inns	NO	Runs	HS	Avge	100s	50s	Ct	St	Balls	Runs	Wkts	Avge	Best	5wI	10wM
Test																	
All First																	
1-day Int																	
C & G	1	1	0	0	0	0.00	-	-	-	-							
totesport																	
Twenty20																	

62. Who is the only Bangladesh player to have scored a century and taken five wickets in an innings in Tests?

NAPIER, G. R. Essex

Name: Graham Richard Napier
Role: Right-hand bat, right-arm medium bowler
Born: 6 January 1980, Colchester
Height: 5ft 10in **Weight:** 12st 7lbs
Nickname: Plank, Napes
County debut: 1997
1st-Class 50s: 12
1st-Class 100s: 2
1st-Class 5 w. in innings: 2
1st-Class catches: 27
One-Day 5 w. in innings: 1
Place in batting averages: 125th av. 33.52 (2003 141st av. 30.00)
Place in bowling averages: 108th av. 37.97 (2003 133rd av. 45.63)
Strike rate: 57.64 (career 59.52)
Parents: Roger and Carol
Marital status: Single
Family links with cricket: Father played for Palmers Boys School 1st XI (1965-68), Essex Police divisional teams, and Harwich Immigration CC
Education: Gilberd School, Colchester
Qualifications: NCA coaching award
Overseas tours: England U17 to Bermuda (International Youth Tournament) 1997; England U19 to South Africa (including U19 World Cup) 1997-98; England A to Malaysia and India 2003-04; England VI to Hong Kong 2004; MCC to Namibia and Uganda 2004-05
Overseas teams played for: Campbelltown CC, Sydney 2000-01; North Perth, Western Australia 2001-02
Career highlights to date: 'Testing myself against the world's best and scoring some runs'
Cricket moments to forget: 'Being 12th man at Lord's and after a drinks break dropping the empties on a tray, towels, jumpers and anything else thrown at me in front of the MCC members'
Young players to look out for: Will Jefferson, Mark Pettini
Other sports followed: Football ('The Tractor Boys' – Ipswich Town FC)
Extras: Represented England U19 v Australia U19 1999. Man of the Match award for Essex Board XI v Lancashire Board XI in the NatWest 2000. Scored 73 (losing three cricket balls in the process) and recorded maiden one-day five-wicket return (6-29) v Worcestershire at Chelmsford in the Norwich Union League 2001. ECB National Academy 2003-04. Included in preliminary England one-day squad of 30 for ICC

Champions Trophy 2004. Scored maiden Championship century (106* from 85 balls) v Nottinghamshire at Trent Bridge 2004
Best batting: 106* Essex v Nottinghamshire, Trent Bridge 2004
Best bowling: 5-56 Essex v Derbyshire, Derby 2004

2004 Season

	M	Inns	NO	Runs	HS	Avge	100s	50s	Ct	St	O	M	Runs	Wkts	Avge	Best	5wI	10wM
Test																		
All First	15	23	4	637	106 *	33.52	1	5	7	-	403.3	65	1595	42	37.97	5-56	1	-
1-day Int																		
C & G	3	2	0	13	13	6.50	-	-	1	-	17	1	89	4	22.25	3-11	-	
totesport	16	11	2	161	32	17.88	-	-	2	-	94.3	6	391	25	15.64	4-23	-	
Twenty20	5	5	0	72	38	14.40	-	-	-	-	18.2	1	125	6	20.83	3-13	-	

Career Performances

	M	Inns	NO	Runs	HS	Avge	100s	50s	Ct	St	Balls	Runs	Wkts	Avge	Best	5wI	10wM
Test																	
All First	57	88	17	2145	106 *	30.21	2	12	27	-	6964	4562	117	38.99	5-56	2	-
1-day Int																	
C & G	10	8	1	141	79	20.14	-	1	2	-	339	295	13	22.69	3-11	-	
totesport	83	66	9	967	78	16.96	-	5	19	-	2159	1710	90	19.00	6-29	1	
Twenty20	10	8	0	105	38	13.12	-	-	1	-	230	280	13	21.53	3-13	-	

NASH, C. D. Sussex

Name: Christopher (Chris) David Nash
Role: Right-hand bat, right-arm off-spin bowler
Born: 19 May 1983, Cuckfield
Height: 5ft 11in **Weight:** 12st 8lbs
Nickname: Nashy, Nashdog, Spidey
County debut: 2002
1st-Class 50s: 4
1st-Class catches: 4
Strike rate: 39.00 (career 112.40)
Parents: Nick and Jane
Marital status: Single
Family links with cricket: Brother played Sussex 2nd XI and Sussex age groups
Education: Collyers Sixth Form College; Loughborough University
Qualifications: 11 GCSEs, 3 A-levels

Overseas tours: Sussex Academy to Cape Town 1999
Career highlights to date: 'First-class debut v Warwickshire at Edgbaston July 2002, taking first wicket in third over'
Cricket moments to forget: 'Getting out first ball on debut (lbw Carter), then having to stand at the non-striker's end for four balls to see if I had to face on a pair in the second innings'
Other sports played: Squash (county level; Loughborough University team), football (Horsham FC)
Other sports followed: Rugby, football (Horsham), cricket (Horsham)
Relaxations: 'Fishing, listening to music, going out with friends, training, squash'
Extras: Represented England U15, U17, U18, U19, captaining at U17 and U18 levels. Sussex League Young Player of the Year 2001. Played for Loughborough University CCE 2002, 2003, 2004, scoring a fifty in each innings (63/54*) v Somerset at Taunton 2004. Represented British Universities v New Zealanders at Fenner's 2004
Best batting: 63 LUCCE v Somerset, Taunton 2004
Best bowling: 1-5 LUCCE v Sussex, Hove 2004

2004 Season (did not make any first-class or one-day appearances for his county)

Career Performances

	M	Inns	NO	Runs	HS	Avge	100s	50s	Ct	St	Balls	Runs	Wkts	Avge	Best	5wI	10wM
Test																	
All First	8	13	2	363	63	33.00	-	4	4	-	562	457	5	91.40	1-5	-	-
1-day Int																	
C & G																	
totesport																	
Twenty20																	

NASH, D. C. — Middlesex

Name: David Charles Nash
Role: Right-hand bat, wicket-keeper
Born: 19 January 1978, Chertsey
Height: 5ft 7in **Weight:** 11st 5lbs
Nickname: Nashy, Knocker
County debut: 1995 (one-day), 1997 (first-class)
County cap: 1999
50 dismissals in a season: 1
1st-Class 50s: 20
1st-Class 100s: 7
1st-Class catches: 239
1st-Class stumpings: 19

Place in batting averages: 76th av. 40.69 (2003 77th av. 39.57)
Strike rate: (career 61.00)
Parents: David and Christine
Marital status: Single
Family links with cricket: 'Father played club cricket; brother plays now and again for Ashford CC; mother is avid watcher and tea lady'
Education: Sunbury Manor; Malvern College
Qualifications: 9 O-levels, 1 A-level, Levels 1 and 2 cricket coaching, qualified football referee
Career outside cricket: Qualified cricket coach
Overseas tours: England U15 to South Africa 1993; British Airways Youth Team to West Indies 1993-94; England U19 to Zimbabwe 1995-96, to Pakistan 1996-97; England A to Kenya and Sri Lanka 1997-98
Overseas teams played for: Fremantle, Perth 2000-01, 2002-03
Career highlights to date: 'Touring with England A and scoring first hundred for Middlesex at Lord's v Somerset'
Cricket moments to forget: 'All golden ducks'
Cricket superstitions: 'Too many to mention'
Cricketers particularly admired: Angus Fraser
Young players to look out for: Ed Joyce
Other sports played: Rugby, football ('played for Millwall U15 and my district side'), 'and most other sports'
Other sports followed: Rugby (London Irish), football (Chelsea)
Relaxations: 'Listening to music, watching sport and socialising with friends'
Extras: Represented Middlesex at all ages. Played for England U14, U15, U17 and U19. Once took six wickets in six balls when aged 11 – 'when I could bowl!' *Daily Telegraph* Southern England Batting Award 1993. Seaxe Young Player of the Year 1993. Scored 67 in the B&H v Sussex at Lord's 2002, in the process sharing with Ashley Noffke (58) in a record eighth-wicket partnership for the competition (112)
Best batting: 114 Middlesex v Somerset, Lord's 1998
Best bowling: 1-8 Middlesex v Essex, Chelmsford 1997

2004 Season

	M	Inns	NO	Runs	HS	Avge	100s	50s	Ct	St	O	M	Runs	Wkts	Avge	Best	5wI	10wM
Test																		
All First	12	17	4	529	113	40.69	1	3	26	2	2	0	8	0	-	-	-	-
1-day Int																		
C & G	1	0	0	0	0	-	-	-	1	-								
totesport	6	5	0	58	35	11.60	-	-	-	-								
Twenty20																		

Career Performances

	M	Inns	NO	Runs	HS	Avge	100s	50s	Ct	St	Balls	Runs	Wkts	Avge	Best	5wI	10wM
Test																	
All First	115	162	33	4283	114	33.20	7	20	239	19	61	52	1	52.00	1-8	-	-
1-day Int																	
C & G	8	5	1	95	58	23.75	-	1	5	-							
totesport	84	64	13	1034	62	20.27	-	3	59	11							
Twenty20																	

NEW, T. J. — Leicestershire

Name: Thomas (Tom) James New
Role: Left-hand bat, wicket-keeper
Born: 18 January 1985, Sutton-in-Ashfield
Height: 5ft 10in **Weight:** 9st 8lbs
Nickname: Newy
County debut: 2004
1st-Class 50s: 1
1st-Class catches: 11
1st-Class stumpings: 1
Parents: Martin and Louise
Marital status: Single
Education: Quarrydale Comprehensive
Qualifications: GCSEs
Overseas tours: England U19 to Bangladesh (U19 World Cup) 2003-04
Overseas teams played for: Geelong Cement, Victoria 2001-02
Career highlights to date: 'Captaining England U15 in Costcutter World Challenge 2000'
Cricket moments to forget: 'Losing semi-final of Costcutter World Challenge 2000 to Pakistan'
Cricket superstitions: 'None'

Cricketers particularly admired: Ian Healy, Jack Russell
Young players to look out for: Luke Wright
Other sports played: Rugby (County U14/U15), football
Other sports followed: Football (Mansfield Town FC)
Relaxations: 'Golf, music'
Extras: Played for Notts U12, U13, U15, U16 and Midlands U13, U14, U15. Captained England U15 in Costcutter World Challenge [U15 World Cup] 2000. Sir John Hobbs Silver Jubilee Memorial Prize 2000. Represented England U19 2003 and v Bangladesh U19 2004. Played for Leicestershire Board XI in the C&G 2001 and 2003. NBC Denis Compton Award for the most promising young Leicestershire player 2003
Best batting: 51* Leicestershire v Durham, Riverside 2004

2004 Season

	M	Inns	NO	Runs	HS	Avge	100s	50s	Ct	St	O	M	Runs	Wkts	Avge	Best	5wI	10wM
Test																		
All First	5	7	3	94	51 *	23.50	-	1	11	1								
1-day Int																		
C & G																		
totesport																		
Twenty20																		

Career Performances

	M	Inns	NO	Runs	HS	Avge	100s	50s	Ct	St	Balls	Runs	Wkts	Avge	Best	5wI	10wM
Test																	
All First	5	7	3	94	51 *	23.50	-	1	11	1							
1-day Int																	
C & G	2	2	0	9	6	4.50	-	-	-	-							
totesport																	
Twenty20																	

63. Which Scottish-born all-rounder, played in nine ODIs for England and coached Namibia at the 2002-03 World Cup?

NEWBY, O. J. — Lancashire

Name: Oliver James Newby
Role: Right-hand bat, right-arm fast-medium bowler
Born: 26 August 1984, Blackburn
Height: 6ft 5in **Weight:** 13st
Nickname: Newbz, Uncle, Flipper
County debut: 2003
Strike rate: 105.00 (career 128.00)
Parents: Frank and Carol
Marital status: Single
Family links with cricket: 'Dad played league cricket for Read CC'
Education: Ribblesdale High School; Myerscough College
Qualifications: 10 GCSEs, ND Sports Science, Level 1 coaching
Career highlights to date: 'First-class debut'
Other sports played: Golf
Favourite band: Eminem, Counting Crows
Relaxations: Music
Extras: Played for Lancashire Board XI in the C&G 2003. Played for Lancashire v India A in a 50-over match at Blackpool 2003, taking a wicket in each of his first two overs
Best bowling: 2-32 Lancashire v Northamptonshire, Liverpool 2004

2004 Season

	M	Inns	NO	Runs	HS	Avge	100s	50s	Ct	St	O	M	Runs	Wkts	Avge	Best	5wI	10wM
Test																		
All First	1	1	1	0	0 *	-	-	-	-	-	35	6	107	2	53.50	2-32	-	-
1-day Int																		
C & G																		
totesport	1	1	1	2	2 *	-	-	-	-	-	4	0	37	2	18.50	2-37	-	
Twenty20	1	0	0	0	0	-	-	-	-	-	3	0	20	1	20.00	1-20	-	

Career Performances

	M	Inns	NO	Runs	HS	Avge	100s	50s	Ct	St	Balls	Runs	Wkts	Avge	Best	5wI	10wM
Test																	
All First	2	1	1	0	0 *	-	-	-	-	-	384	189	3	63.00	2-32	-	-
1-day Int																	
C & G	2	1	1	3	3 *	-	-	-	1	-	110	104	1	104.00	1-45	-	
totesport	1	1	1	2	2 *	-	-	-	-	-	24	37	2	18.50	2-37	-	
Twenty20	2	0	0	0	0	-	-	-	-	-	24	32	1	32.00	1-20	-	

NEWMAN, S. A. Surrey

Name: Scott Alexander Newman
Role: Left-hand bat
Born: 3 November 1979, Epsom
Height: 6ft 1in **Weight:** 13st 7lbs
Nickname: Ronaldo
County debut: 2001 (one-day), 2002 (first-class)
1000 runs in a season: 1
1st-Class 50s: 11
1st-Class 100s: 4
1st-Class catches: 18
One-Day 100s: 1
Place in batting averages: 60th av. 44.03
Parents: Ken and Sandy
Marital status: Married
Children: Lemoy, 1985; Brandon, 8 September 2002
Family links with cricket: 'Dad and brother both played'
Education: Trinity School, Croydon; Brighton University
Qualifications: 10 GCSEs, GNVQ (Advanced) Business Studies
Career outside cricket: 'Father'
Overseas tours: SCB to Barbados; England A to Malaysia and India 2003-04
Overseas teams played for: Mount Lawley CC, Perth
Career highlights to date: 'Partnership of 552 v Derbyshire II with N. Shahid (Shahid 266; Newman 284)'
Cricket moments to forget: 'Any time I fail'
Cricket superstitions: 'None'
Cricketers particularly admired: 'All of Surrey CCC'
Young players to look out for: Alastair Cook, Neil Saker, Brandon Newman, Ben Scott
Other sports played: 'Most sports'
Other sports followed: Football (Man Utd)
Favourite band: Nas
Relaxations: 'Music, relaxing with family'
Extras: Scored 99 on first-class debut v Hampshire at The Oval 2002. Scored maiden first-class century (183) v Leicestershire at The Oval 2002, in the process sharing with Ian Ward (118) in a new record opening partnership for Surrey in matches v Leicestershire (227). Scored 284 v Derbyshire 2nd XI at The Oval 2003, in the process sharing with Nadeem Shahid (266) in an opening partnership of 552, just three runs short of the English all-cricket record first-wicket stand of 555 set by Percy Holmes

and Herbert Sutcliffe for Yorkshire v Essex at Leyton 1932. ECB National Academy 2003-04. Scored 1000 first-class runs in a season for the first time 2004
Opinions on cricket: 'Less EU players.'
Best batting: 183 Surrey v Leicestershire, The Oval 2002

2004 Season

	M	Inns	NO	Runs	HS	Avge	100s	50s	Ct	St	O	M	Runs	Wkts	Avge	Best	5wI	10wM
Test																		
All First	17	30	1	1277	131	44.03	3	9	11	-								
1-day Int																		
C & G																		
totesport	12	11	0	210	106	19.09	1	-	1	-								
Twenty20	6	6	0	96	38	16.00	-	-	2	-								

Career Performances

	M	Inns	NO	Runs	HS	Avge	100s	50s	Ct	St	Balls	Runs	Wkts	Avge	Best	5wI	10wM
Test																	
All First	25	45	2	1759	183	40.90	4	11	18	-	6	5	0	-	-	-	-
1-day Int																	
C & G	3	3	0	100	49	33.33	-	-	1	-							
totesport	20	19	0	324	106	17.05	1	-	2	-							
Twenty20	8	8	0	174	59	21.75	-	1	4	-							

NIXON, P. A. — Leicestershire

Name: Paul Andrew Nixon
Role: Left-hand bat, wicket-keeper
Born: 21 October 1970, Carlisle
Height: 6ft **Weight:** 12st 10lbs
Nickname: Badger, Nico, Nobby
County debut: 1989 (Leicestershire), 2000 (Kent)
County cap: 1994 (Leicestershire), 2000 (Kent)
1000 runs in a season: 1
50 dismissals in a season: 7
1st-Class 50s: 40
1st-Class 100s: 14
1st-Class catches: 703
1st-Class stumpings: 58
Place in batting averages: 217th av. 20.05 (2003 151st av. 29.39)

Parents: Brian and Sylvia
Wife and date of marriage: Jen, 9 October 1999
Family links with cricket: 'Grandad and father played local league cricket. Mum made the teas for Edenhall CC, Penrith'
Education: Ullswater High
Qualifications: 2 O-levels, 6 GCSEs, coaching certificates
Overseas tours: Cumbria Schools U15 to Denmark 1985; Leicestershire to Barbados, to Jamaica, to Holland, to Johannesburg, to Bloemfontein; MCC to Bangladesh 1999-2000; England A to India and Bangladesh 1994-95; England to Pakistan and Sri Lanka 2000-01
Overseas teams played for: Melville, Western Australia; North Fremantle, Western Australia; Mitchells Plain, Cape Town 1993; Primrose CC, Cape Town 1995-96
Career highlights to date: 'Winning the Championship in 1996 with Leicestershire. Receiving phone call from David Graveney advising me of England [tour] selection'
Cricket moments to forget: 'Losing Lord's one-day finals'
Cricketers particularly admired: David Gower, Ian Botham, Ian Healy, Viv Richards
Other sports played: Golf
Other sports followed: Football (Leicester City, Carlisle United, Liverpool), rugby (Leicester Tigers)
Relaxations: Watching England rugby
Extras: County captain of Cumbria at football, cricket and rugby. Youngest person to score a century against Yorkshire (at U15). Played for England U15. Played in Minor Counties Championship for Cumberland at 16. MCC Young Pro in 1988. Took eight catches in debut match v Warwickshire at Hinckley 1989. Played for Carlisle United. Leicestershire Young Player of the Year two years running. In 1994 became only second Leicestershire wicket-keeper to score 1000 runs in a season (1046). Voted Cumbria Sports Personality of the Year 1994-95. Was part of Leicestershire's County Championship winning side in 1996 and 1998. Left Leicestershire at end of 1999 season and joined Kent for 2000. Captained First-Class Counties Select XI v New Zealand A at Milton Keynes 2000. Scored 60 v Worcestershire at Canterbury in the NUL 2002, in the process sharing with Matthew Walker (94) in a record sixth-wicket partnership for Kent in the one-day league (116). Released by Kent at the end of the 2002 season and rejoined Leicestershire for 2003
Opinions on cricket: '1. Too many people running the game with their own personal agendas – the big picture is what matters. 2. No more ideas from me regarding the marketing of English cricket until the ECB pay me a fee for using all my previous ideas!'
Best batting: 134* Kent v Hampshire, Canterbury 2000

2004 Season

	M	Inns	NO	Runs	HS	Avge	100s	50s	Ct	St	O	M	Runs	Wkts	Avge	Best	5wI	10wM
Test																		
All First	12	21	3	361	63 *	20.05	-	1	34	6								
1-day Int																		
C & G	1	1	1	33	33 *	-	-	-	1	-								
totesport	18	14	2	230	37	19.16	-	-	24	7								
Twenty20	7	6	1	52	23	10.40	-	-	3	1								

Career Performances

	M	Inns	NO	Runs	HS	Avge	100s	50s	Ct	St	Balls	Runs	Wkts	Avge	Best	5wI	10wM
Test																	
All First	265	387	84	9519	134 *	31.41	14	40	703	58	33	22	0	-	-	-	-
1-day Int																	
C & G	35	29	11	598	57	33.22	-	2	46	10							
totesport	218	191	33	3439	96 *	21.76	-	14	216	52							
Twenty20	13	12	1	161	43	14.63	-	-	5	4							

NOFFKE, A. A. Durham

Name: Ashley Allan Noffke
Role: Right-hand bat, right-arm fast bowler; all-rounder
Born: 30 April 1977, Sunshine Coast, Queensland, Australia
Height: 6ft 3in **Weight:** 14st
Nickname: Noffers, Wombat
County debut: 2002 (Middlesex)
County cap: 2003 (Middlesex)
1st-Class 50s: 4
1st-Class 100s: 1
1st-Class 5 w. in innings: 9
1st-Class 10 w. in match: 1
1st-Class catches: 19
Place in batting averages: (2003 207th av. 22.33)
Place in bowling averages: (2003 95th av. 35.90)
Strike rate: (career 56.75)
Parents: Rob and Lesley Simpson, and Allan Noffke
Wife and date of marriage: Michelle, 8 April 2000
Family links with cricket: Father played club cricket

Education: Immanuel Lutheran College; Sunshine Coast University
Qualifications: Bachelor of Business, ACB Level 2 coaching certificate
Off-season: Playing cricket for Queensland
Overseas tours: Commonwealth Bank [Australian] Cricket Academy to Zimbabwe 1998-99; Australia to England 2001, to West Indies 2002-03
Overseas teams played for: Queensland 1998 –
Career highlights to date: 'Man of the Match in a winning Pura Cup final for Queensland. Being selected for Australia for 2001 Ashes tour'
Cricket moments to forget: 'Rolling my ankle playing for Australia v Sussex, forcing me home from the Ashes tour'
Cricket superstitions: 'None'
Cricketers particularly admired: Steve Waugh
Young players to look out for: Ed Joyce
Other sports played: Golf
Other sports followed: Rugby league, rugby union, 'enjoy all sports'
Favourite band: Powderfinger
Relaxations: Fishing
Extras: Made first-class debut for Commonwealth Bank [Australian] Cricket Academy v Zimbabwe Cricket Academy XI 1998-99. Queensland Academy of Sport Player of the Year 1998-99. Man of the Match in the Pura Cup final v Victoria 2000-01 for his 7-120 and 43 runs batting as nightwatchman. Awarded an ACB contract 2001-02 after just six first-class matches. Sunshine Coast Sportstar of the Year 2001. Was Middlesex's overseas player for two periods during the 2002 season; returned as an overseas player for 2003. Scored 58 in the B&H v Sussex at Lord's 2002, in the process sharing with David Nash (67) in a record eighth-wicket partnership for the competition (112). Took a career-best 8-24 from 15 overs v Derbyshire at Derby 2002, including a spell of 7-6 from 35 balls. Represented Australia A v England and Sri Lanka tourists 2002-03. Scored maiden first-class century (114*) and had match figures of 6-85 v South Australia at Brisbane in the Pura Cup 2003-04, winning Man of the Match award. Has joined Durham as an overseas player for 2005
Best batting: 114* Queensland v South Australia, Brisbane 2003-04
Best bowling: 8-24 Middlesex v Derbyshire, Derby 2002

2004 Season (did not make any first-class or one-day appearances)

Career Performances

	M	Inns	NO	Runs	HS	Avge	100s	50s	Ct	St	Balls	Runs	Wkts	Avge	Best	5wI	10wM
Test																	
All First	55	63	13	1293	114 *	25.86	1	4	19	-	10841	5770	191	30.20	8-24	9	1
1-day Int																	
C & G	2	1	0	19	19	19.00	-	-	3	-	120	84	1	84.00	1-47	-	
totesport	7	4	2	13	4 *	6.50	-	-	-	-	292	189	6	31.50	2-24	-	
Twenty20	3	1	0	7	7	7.00	-	-	2	-	72	97	8	12.12	3-22	-	

NOON, W. M. — Nottinghamshire

Name: Wayne Michael Noon
Role: Right-hand bat, wicket-keeper
Born: 5 February 1971, Grimsby
Height: 5ft 9in **Weight:** 11st 7lbs
Nickname: Noonie, Spain Boon
County debut: 1988 (one-day, Northants), 1989 (first-class, Northants), 1994 (Notts)
County cap: 1995 (Notts)
Benefit: 2003 (Notts)
1st-Class 50s: 12
1st-Class catches: 195
1st-Class stumpings: 20
Parents: Trafford and Rosemary
Marital status: Married
Education: Caistor Grammar School
Qualifications: 5 O-levels
Overseas tours: Lincolnshire U15 to Pakistan 1984; Rutland tourists to South Africa 1988; England YC to Australia 1989-90 (captain); Northamptonshire to Durban 1992, to Cape Town 1993
Overseas teams played for: Burnside West, Christchurch, New Zealand 1989-90, 1995-96; Rivertonians, Cape Town 1993-94; Canterbury, Christchurch 1994-95
Cricketers particularly admired: Ian Botham
Other sports followed: Football (Lincoln City), horse racing (flat)
Relaxations: 'Having a bet. Eating out and having a pint'
Extras: Played for England YC v New Zealand YC 1989; captain v Pakistan YC 1990. Was the 1000th player to appear in the Sunday League competition. Broke the Northants record for most 2nd XI hundreds in one season in 1993. Took seven catches for Notts in Kent's first innings at Trent Bridge 1999, breaking Bruce French's county record of six. Notts 2nd XI captain since 2003
Best batting: 83 Nottinghamshire v Northamptonshire, Northampton 1997

2004 Season (did not make any first-class or one-day appearances)

Career Performances

	M	Inns	NO	Runs	HS	Avge	100s	50s	Ct	St	Balls	Runs	Wkts	Avge	Best	5wI	10wM
Test																	
All First	92	145	23	2527	83	20.71	-	12	195	20	30	34	0	-	-	-	-
1-day Int																	
C & G	8	5	1	82	34	20.50	-	-	4	2							
totesport	83	53	14	495	38	12.69	-	-	62	16							
Twenty20	4	2	0	13	12	6.50	-	-	-	3							

NORTH, M. J. Durham

Name: Marcus James North
Role: Left-hand bat, right-arm off-spin bowler
Born: 28 July 1979, Pakenham, Melbourne, Australia
Height: 6ft 1in **Weight:** 12st 10lbs
County debut: 2004
1st-Class 50s: 17
1st-Class 100s: 7
1st-Class 200s: 2
1st-Class catches: 39
One-Day 100s: 2
Place in batting averages: 131st av. 32.30
Strike rate: 29.28 (career 74.28)
Wife: Joanne
Overseas tours: Australia U19 to Pakistan 1996-97, to South Africa (U19 World Cup) 1997-98; Commonwealth Bank [Australian] Cricket Academy to Zimbabwe 1998-99
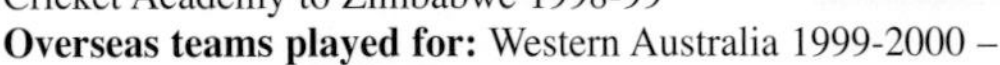
Overseas teams played for: Western Australia 1999-2000 –
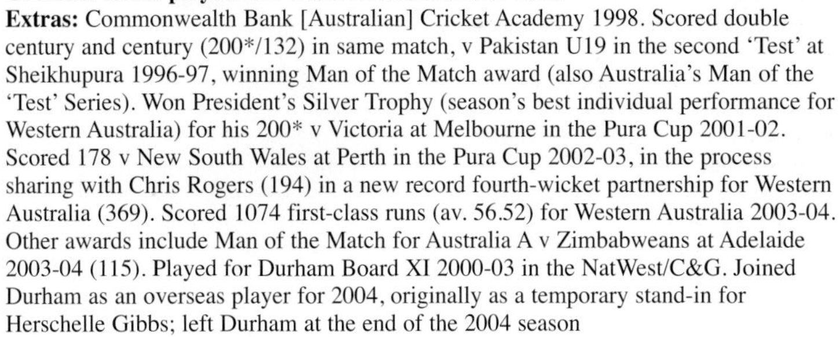
Extras: Commonwealth Bank [Australian] Cricket Academy 1998. Scored double century and century (200*/132) in same match, v Pakistan U19 in the second 'Test' at Sheikhupura 1996-97, winning Man of the Match award (also Australia's Man of the 'Test' Series). Won President's Silver Trophy (season's best individual performance for Western Australia) for his 200* v Victoria at Melbourne in the Pura Cup 2001-02. Scored 178 v New South Wales at Perth in the Pura Cup 2002-03, in the process sharing with Chris Rogers (194) in a new record fourth-wicket partnership for Western Australia (369). Scored 1074 first-class runs (av. 56.52) for Western Australia 2003-04. Other awards include Man of the Match for Australia A v Zimbabweans at Adelaide 2003-04 (115). Played for Durham Board XI 2000-03 in the NatWest/C&G. Joined Durham as an overseas player for 2004, originally as a temporary stand-in for Herschelle Gibbs; left Durham at the end of the 2004 season
Best batting: 219 Durham v Glamorgan, Cardiff 2004
Best bowling: 4-16 Durham v DUCCE, Riverside 2004

2004 Season

	M	Inns	NO	Runs	HS	Avge	100s	50s	Ct	St	O	M	Runs	Wkts	Avge	Best	5wI	10wM
Test																		
All First	17	31	1	969	219	32.30	2	4	8	-	34.1	6	109	7	15.57	4-16	-	-
1-day Int																		
C & G	1	1	0	30	30	30.00	-	-	2	-	9	0	45	2	22.50	2-45	-	
totesport	16	16	1	511	121 *	34.06	2	2	2	-	22	0	118	4	29.50	2-10	-	
Twenty20	2	2	0	25	21	12.50	-	-	1	-	2	0	10	0	-	-	-	

Career Performances

	M	Inns	NO	Runs	HS	Avge	100s	50s	Ct	St	Balls	Runs	Wkts	Avge	Best	5wI	10wM
Test																	
All First	58	101	7	3540	219	37.65	9	17	39	-	2080	1171	28	41.82	4-16	-	-
1-day Int																	
C & G	7	7	1	201	69 *	33.50	-	1	4	-	318	223	7	31.85	4-26	-	
totesport	16	16	1	511	121 *	34.06	2	2	2	-	132	118	4	29.50	2-10	-	
Twenty20	2	2	0	25	21	12.50	-	-	1	-	12	10	0	-	-	-	

O'BRIEN, N. J. — Kent

Name: Niall John O'Brien
Role: Left-hand bat, leg-spin bowler, wicket-keeper
Born: 8 November 1981, Dublin
Height: 5ft 7in **Weight:** 10st 7lbs
Nickname: Nobby, Spud, Paddy, Irish
County debut: 2004
1st-Class 50s: 3
1st-Class catches: 33
1st-Class stumpings: 5
Place in batting averages: 152nd av. 29.26
Parents: Brendan and Camilla
Marital status: Single
Family links with cricket: Father a past captain of Ireland; brother Kevin a current U19 international and an MCC Young Cricketer
Education: Marian College, Ballsbridge, Dublin
Qualifications: Cricket coach
Off-season: 'Training in Ireland and playing hockey'
Overseas tours: Ireland U15 to Holland; Ireland U17 to Holland; Ireland U19 to Sri Lanka (U19 World Cup) 1999-2000, to Holland

Overseas teams played for: Railway Union CC, Dublin; Mosman DCC, Sydney 2000-02; University of Port Elizabeth Academy, South Africa 2002; North Sydney DCC 2003-04
Career highlights to date: 'Gaining first international cap for Ireland; first hundred for Ireland (111 v MCC); making first-class debut for Kent'
Cricket moments to forget: 'Getting a duck on Sky, bowled Warne'
Cricket superstitions: 'None'
Cricketers particularly admired: Steve Waugh, Brett Lee
Young players to look out for: Kevin O'Brien ('brother')
Other sports played: Hockey (Railway Union, Dublin), 'love soccer (especially beating the old guys at warm-ups)'
Other sports followed: Football (Everton), rugby (Ireland)
Favourite band: Oasis
Relaxations: 'Music; walking dog; going to my local in the winter with mates'
Extras: Made Ireland senior debut v Denmark 2002 and played for Ireland in the C&G 2003. Scored 111 for Ireland v MCC at Cork 2002. Ireland Cricketer of the Year 2002. Scored 58* as Ireland defeated West Indians in 50-over game in Belfast 2004, winning Man of the Match award
Best batting: 69 Kent v Warwickshire, Edgbaston 2004

2004 Season

	M	Inns	NO	Runs	HS	Avge	100s	50s	Ct	St	O	M	Runs	Wkts	Avge	Best	5wI	10wM
Test																		
All First	14	19	4	439	69	29.26	-	3	33	5								
1-day Int																		
C & G																		
totesport	12	6	1	56	19	11.20	-	-	9	3								
Twenty20	3	2	0	23	12	11.50	-	-	-	-								

Career Performances

	M	Inns	NO	Runs	HS	Avge	100s	50s	Ct	St	Balls	Runs	Wkts	Avge	Best	5wI	10wM
Test																	
All First	14	19	4	439	69	29.26	-	3	33	5							
1-day Int																	
C & G	1	1	0	13	13	13.00	-	-	-	-							
totesport	12	6	1	56	19	11.20	-	-	9	3							
Twenty20	3	2	0	23	12	11.50	-	-	-	-							

O'SHEA, M. P. — Glamorgan

Name: Michael (Mike) Peter O'Shea
Role: Right-hand bat, right-arm off-spin bowler
Born: 4 October 1987, Cardiff
Height: 5ft 11in **Weight:** 12st 3lbs
Nickname: Rik, O'Sh
County debut: No first-team appearance
Parents: Paul Michael and June Leslie
Marital status: Single
Education: Barry Comprehensive School
Qualifications: 12 GCSEs
Career outside cricket: Student
Overseas tours: England U19 to India 2004-05
Career highlights to date: 'Representing England U19 in India. Being signed by Glamorgan for 2005 season'
Cricket superstitions: 'Put left pad on first'
Cricketers particularly admired: Damien Martyn
Young players to look out for: Greg Wood
Other sports played: Rugby (Millfield 1st XV)
Other sports followed: Rugby (Wales)
Favourite band: Usher
Extras: Has represented England U15, U16, U17, U19. Is on a development contract at Glamorgan
Opinions on cricket: 'Exciting and growing sport. Privilege to play the game at the highest standard possible.'

ONIONS, G. — Durham

Name: Graham Onions
Role: Right-hand bat, right-arm medium bowler
Born: 9 September 1982, Gateshead
Height: 6ft 1in **Weight:** 11st 2lbs
Nickname: Thierry Williamson
County debut: 2004
1st-Class catches: 2
Place in batting averages: 265th av. 10.85
Strike rate: 97.77 (career 97.77)

Parents: Maureen and Richard
Marital status: Single
Family links with cricket: 'My uncle played for local club Gateshead Fell'
Education: St Thomas More RC School, Blaydon
Qualifications: 10 GCSEs, GNVQ Advanced Science (Distinction), Level 2 coach
Career outside cricket: 'Comedian. Clerical work for major building society'
Off-season: 'Working on fitness and strength'
Overseas tours: 'Toured South Africa (Port Elizabeth) 2002, Australia (Perth) 2004'
Overseas teams played for: South Perth CC 2004
Career highlights to date: 'Making first-class debut 2004'
Cricket moments to forget: 'Double stress fracture of my shin – missing end of 2000 season'
Cricket superstitions: 'Licking index finger before bowling – in case the ball slips'
Cricketers particularly admired: Stephen Harmison, Paul Collingwood, Darren Gough
Young players to look out for: Mark Turner, Liam Plunkett
Other sports played: Badminton (England U17, Durham County first team), golf
Other sports followed: Football (Newcastle)
Injuries: Out for five weeks with a torn hamstring
Favourite band: 'No favourite, prefer R&B'
Relaxations: 'Sleep, music'
Extras: 'Voted player of the tour when training in South Africa 2002.' Played for Durham Board XI in the C&G 2003
Opinions on cricket: 'Twenty20 was a massive success. Sessions in Championship games should be two hours only.'
Best batting: 20* Durham v Leicestershire, Riverside 2004
Best bowling: 3-110 Durham v Leicestershire, Leicester 2004

2004 Season

	M	Inns	NO	Runs	HS	Avge	100s	50s	Ct	St	O	M	Runs	Wkts	Avge	Best	5wI	10wM
Test																		
All First	8	12	5	76	20 *	10.85	-	-	2	-	146.4	32	593	9	65.88	3-110	-	-
1-day Int																		
C & G																		
totesport	12	2	2	5	4 *	-	-	-	1	-	64.2	3	300	10	30.00	2-24	-	
Twenty20	4	1	0	0	0	0.00	-	-	1	-	16	0	84	4	21.00	2-25	-	

Career Performances

	M	Inns	NO	Runs	HS	Avge	100s	50s	Ct	St	Balls	Runs	Wkts	Avge	Best	5wI	10wM
Test																	
All First	8	12	5	76	20 *	10.85	-	-	2	-	880	593	9	65.88	3-110	-	-
1-day Int																	
C & G	1	1	0	5	5	5.00	-	-	-	-	60	59	2	29.50	2-59	-	
totesport	12	2	2	5	4 *	-	-	-	1	-	386	300	10	30.00	2-24	-	
Twenty20	4	1	0	0	0	0.00	-	-	1	-	96	84	4	21.00	2-25	-	

ORMOND, J. — Surrey

Name: James Ormond
Role: Right-hand bat, right-arm fast-'ish' bowler, can also bowl off spin
Born: 20 August 1977, Walsgrave, Coventry
Height: 6ft 3in **Weight:** 15st
Nickname: Jimmy, Horse
County debut: 1995 (Leicestershire), 2002 (Surrey)
County cap: 1999 (Leicestershire), 2003 (Surrey)
Test debut: 2001
Tests: 2
50 wickets in a season: 4
1st-Class 50s: 2
1st-Class 5 w. in innings: 19
1st-Class 10 w. in match: 1
1st-Class catches: 24
One-Day 5 w. in innings: 1
Place in batting averages: 237th av. 17.36 (2003 205th av. 22.60)
Place in bowling averages: 96th av. 36.71 (2003 50th av. 28.00)
Strike rate: 70.30 (career 54.03)
Parents: Richard and Margaret
Marital status: Single
Family links with cricket: 'Dad played years of cricket in Warwickshire'
Education: St Thomas More, Nuneaton; North Warwickshire College of Further Education
Qualifications: 6 GCSEs
Overseas tours: England U19 to Zimbabwe 1995-96; England A to Kenya and Sri Lanka 1997-98; England to India and New Zealand 2001-02
Overseas teams played for: Sydney University CC 1996, 1998, 1999
Cricketers particularly admired: Curtly Ambrose, Courtney Walsh, Allan Donald, Sachin Tendulkar, Brian Lara, Steve Griffin

Other sports played: Football, mountain biking, 'anything'
Other sports followed: Football (Coventry City)
Relaxations: Spending time with friends and family
Extras: Played for the Development of Excellence side and England U19. Won Leicestershire's 2nd XI bowling award. NBC Denis Compton Award for the most promising young Leicestershire player 1998, 1999, 2000. Left Leicestershire in the 2001-02 off-season and joined Surrey for 2002. Took 5-26 v Middlesex at The Oval in the Twenty20 2003 and was Man of the Match (4-11) at Trent Bridge in the inaugural final. Took four wickets in an over, including hat-trick (Hutton, Joyce, Weekes), v Middlesex at Guildford 2003
Best batting: 57 Surrey v Gloucestershire, Bristol 2004
Best bowling: 6-33 Leicestershire v Somerset, Leicester 1998

2004 Season

	M	Inns	NO	Runs	HS	Avge	100s	50s	Ct	St	O	M	Runs	Wkts	Avge	Best	5wI	10wM
Test																		
All First	17	24	5	330	57	17.36	-	1	4	-	609.2	143	1909	52	36.71	6-62	1	-
1-day Int																		
C & G	1	1	1	1	1 *	-	-	-	-	-	9	0	48	0	-	-	-	
totesport	9	7	3	20	7 *	5.00	-	-	3	-	60.3	3	319	11	29.00	4-48	-	
Twenty20	4	2	2	5	5 *	-	-	-	1	-	15	1	82	3	27.33	2-14	-	

Career Performances

	M	Inns	NO	Runs	HS	Avge	100s	50s	Ct	St	Balls	Runs	Wkts	Avge	Best	5wI	10wM
Test	2	4	1	38	18	12.66	-	-	-	-	372	185	2	92.50	1-70	-	-
All First	110	133	32	1553	57	15.37	-	2	24	-	20586	11044	381	28.98	6-33	19	1
1-day Int																	
C & G	16	9	5	39	18 *	9.75	-	-	3	-	829	643	15	42.86	3-53	-	
totesport	72	42	22	209	18	10.45	-	-	16	-	3138	2248	92	24.43	4-12	-	
Twenty20	9	3	2	8	5 *	8.00	-	-	2	-	210	193	14	13.78	5-26	1	

64. Who captained Holland in the 2002-03 World Cup and once took 7-15 for Somerset v Devon in the NatWest Trophy?

OSTLER, D. P. Warwickshire

Name: Dominic Piers Ostler
Role: Right-hand bat, right-arm medium bowler
Born: 15 July 1970, Solihull
Height: 6ft 2in **Weight:** 14st
Nickname: Ossie
County debut: 1990
County cap: 1991
Benefit: 2000
1000 runs in a season: 6
1st-Class 50s: 67
1st-Class 100s: 14
1st-Class 200s: 2
1st-Class catches: 259
One-Day 100s: 3
Place in batting averages: (2003 252nd av. 14.87)
Strike rate: (career 251.00)
Parents: Mike and Ann
Wife and date of marriage: Karen, 14 October 2000
Family links with cricket: Brother used to play for Knowle and Dorridge CC
Education: Princethorpe College; Solihull College of Technology
Qualifications: 4 O-levels, A-levels, City and Guilds Recreation Course
Overseas tours: Gladstone Small's Benefit Tour to Barbados 1991; England A to Pakistan 1995-96; England XI to New Zealand (Cricket Max) 1997; Andy Moles' Benefit Tour to Barbados 1997
Overseas teams played for: Avendale CC, Cape Town 1991-92
Career highlights: 'Winning eight trophies'
Cricket moments to forget: 'Dropping a slip catch in final at Lord's'
Cricket superstitions: 'None'
Cricketers particularly admired: Jason Ratcliffe, Simon Millington, Graeme Welch
Young players to look out for: Nick Warren
Other sports played: Golf, snooker
Other sports followed: Football (Birmingham City FC)
Relaxations: 'Spending time with wife, Karen; snooker and golf'
Extras: Was a member of the Warwickshire U19 side that won the Esso U19 County Festivals in 1988 and 1989. Has collected winner's medals for the B&H Cup, County Championship, NatWest Trophy and Sunday League. Scored 134* off 114 balls v Gloucestershire at Edgbaston in the NUL 2001, equalling Nick Knight's Warwickshire record for the highest individual score in the one-day league (although Knight was dismissed). Scored 175 v Somerset at Edgbaston 2002, in the process passing 10,000 runs in first-class cricket. Retired at the end of the 2004 season

PALLADINO, A. P.

Name: Antonio (Tony) Paul Palladino
Role: Right-hand bat, right-arm fast-medium bowler
Born: 29 June 1983, Whitechapel, London
Height: 6ft **Weight:** 11st 6lbs
Nickname: Dino, TP, Italian Stallion
County debut: 2003
1st-Class 5 w. in innings: 1
1st-Class catches: 2
Place in bowling averages: (2003 149th av. 54.00)
Strike rate: 124.00 (career 96.00)
Parents: Antonio and Kathleen
Marital status: 'Officially single but attached (Stephanie)'
Family links with cricket: 'Dad played cricket in the Kent League'
Education: Cardinal Pole Secondary School; Anglia Polytechnic University
Qualifications: 9 GCSEs, Advanced GNVQ Leisure and Tourism
Career outside cricket: Student
Off-season: 'Possible MCC tour and hitting the gym hard'
Career highlights to date: 'Taking 6-41 against Kent in my second Championship match for Essex'
Cricket moments to forget: 'Getting hit for 78 off 10 overs against Durham in AON Trophy semi-final'
Cricket superstitions: 'Paint three dots as my run-up mark'
Cricketers particularly admired: Ian Botham
Young players to look out for: Toby Hembry, 'Ron Weasley', Craig Matey
Other sports played: Football, golf, snooker
Other sports followed: Football (Chelsea), baseball (Boston Red Sox)
Injuries: Out for two months with a torn stomach muscle
Favourite band: 'Various artists'
Relaxations: Playing computer games; watching films
Extras: Hackney Young Sportsman of the Year. London Schools Bowler of the Year five years running. Represented England U17 v Yorkshire Academy. Represented ECB U19 v Sri Lanka U19 2000 and v West Indies U19 2001. Played for Cambridge University CCE 2003, 2004. Recorded maiden first-class five-wicket return (6-41) v Kent at Canterbury 2003 in only his second Championship match
Opinions on cricket: 'Tea should be longer.'
Best batting: 41 Essex v Nottinghamshire, Trent Bridge 2004
Best bowling: 6-41 Essex v Kent, Canterbury 2003

04 Season

	M	Inns	NO	Runs	HS	Avge	100s	50s	Ct	St	O	M	Runs	Wkts	Avge	Best	5wI	10wM
Test																		
All First	3	2	0	41	41	20.50	-	-	-	-	62	7	267	3	89.00	1-28	-	-
1-day Int																		
C & G																		
totesport																		
Twenty20																		

Career Performances

	M	Inns	NO	Runs	HS	Avge	100s	50s	Ct	St	Balls	Runs	Wkts	Avge	Best	5wI	10wM
Test																	
All First	9	7	3	65	41	16.25	-	-	2	-	1344	861	14	61.50	6-41	1	-
1-day Int																	
C & G	2	1	0	16	16	16.00	-	-	1	-	113	90	3	30.00	3-56	-	
totesport	5	2	1	1	1*	1.00	-	-	-	-	205	156	7	22.28	3-32	-	
Twenty20																	

PANESAR, M. S. Northamptonshire

Name: Mudhsuden Singh Panesar
Role: Left-hand bat, slow left-arm bowler
Born: 25 April 1982, Luton
Height: 6ft 1in **Weight:** 12st 7lbs
Nickname: Monty
County debut: 2001
1st-Class 5 w. in innings: 1
1st-Class catches: 8
Place in bowling averages: (2003 127th av. 42.84)
Strike rate: 103.20 (career 67.27)
Parents: Paramjit and Gursharan
Marital status: Single
Family links with cricket: 'Dad played local cricket'
Education: Stopsley High School; Bedford Modern School; Loughborough University
Qualifications: 10 GCSEs, 3 A-levels
Overseas tours: Bedford Modern School to Barbados 1999; England U19 to India 2000-01; Northamptonshire to Grenada 2001-02; British Universities to South Africa 2002; ECB National Academy to Australia and Sri Lanka 2002-03
Cricketers particularly admired: Sachin Tendulkar, Steve Waugh, Matthew Hayden, Rahul Dravid

Other sports played: Badminton, tennis, snooker
Other sports followed: Football (Arsenal)
Relaxations: Music, cars, wildlife
Extras: Represented England U19. Had match figures of 8-131 on first-class debut v Leicestershire at Northampton 2001, including 4-11 in the second innings. NBC Denis Compton Award for the most promising young Northamptonshire player 2001. Played for Loughborough University CCE 2002, 2004. Represented British Universities 2002 and v Sri Lanka A 2004
Best batting: 28 Northamptonshire v CUCCE, Fenner's 2003
Best bowling: 5-77 ECB Academy v Sri Lanka Academy XI, Colombo 2002-03

2004 Season (did not make any first-class or one-day appearances for his county)

Career Performances

	M	Inns	NO	Runs	HS	Avge	100s	50s	Ct	St	Balls	Runs	Wkts	Avge	Best	5wI	10wM
Test																	
All First	20	22	10	81	28	6.75	-	-	8	-	3969	2032	59	34.44	5-77	1	-
1-day Int																	
C & G																	
totesport	2	2	2	22	16 *	-	-	-	-	-	90	62	1	62.00	1-36	-	
Twenty20																	

65. Which South Australia cricketer scored the fastest century in World Cup history for Canada v West Indies at Centurion in 2002-03?

PARSONS, K. A. — Somerset

Name: Keith Alan Parsons
Role: Right-hand bat, right-arm medium bowler
Born: 2 May 1973, Taunton
Height: 6ft 1in **Weight:** 14st 7lbs
Nickname: Pilot, Pars, Orv
County debut: 1992
County cap: 1999
Benefit: 2004
1st-Class 50s: 24
1st-Class 100s: 5
1st-Class 5 w. in innings: 2
1st-Class catches: 101
One-Day 100s: 2
One-Day 5 w. in innings: 1
Strike rate: (career 76.65)
Parents: Alan and Lynne
Wife and date of marriage: Sharon, 12 January 2002
Children: Joseph Luke, 17 October 2002
Family links with cricket: Identical twin brother, Kevin, was on the Somerset staff 1992-94 and then captained the Somerset Board XI. Father played six seasons for Somerset 2nd XI and captained National Civil Service XI
Education: The Castle School, Taunton; Richard Huish Sixth Form College, Taunton
Qualifications: 8 GCSEs, 3 A-levels, NCA senior coach
Overseas tours: Castle School to Barbados 1989; Somerset CCC to Cape Town 1999, 2000, 2001
Overseas teams played for: Kapiti Old Boys, Horowhenua, New Zealand 1992-93; Taita District, Wellington, New Zealand 1993-96; Wembley Downs CC, Perth 1998
Career highlights to date: 'C&G final 2001 v Leicestershire – great to win a trophy, and Man of the Match capped a dream day'
Cricket moments to forget: 'Any bad days at Taunton'
Cricket superstitions: 'None'
Cricketers particularly admired: Andy Caddick, Marcus Trescothick, Glenn McGrath, Saqlain Mushtaq
Other sports followed: Rugby union (Bath RFC), football (Nottingham Forest FC), golf, horse racing
Relaxations: Playing golf, watching movies, listening to music 'and the odd social pint of beer'
Extras: Captained two National Cup winning sides – Taunton St Andrews in National U15 Club Championship and Richard Huish College in National U17 School Championship. Represented English Schools at U15 and U19 level. Somerset Young

Player of the Year 1993. C&G Man of the Match award for his 52-ball 60* (including sixes from the last two balls of the innings) and 2-40 in the final v Leicestershire at Lord's 2001. C&G Man of the Match award for his 100-ball 121 (his maiden one-day century) in the quarter-final v Worcestershire at Taunton 2002 (also took 2-37, two catches and completed a run out). Recorded maiden one-day five-wicket return (5-39) v Derbyshire at Derby in the totesport League 2004

Best batting: 193* Somerset v West Indians, Taunton 2000

Best bowling: 5-13 Somerset v Lancashire, Taunton 2000

2004 Season

	M	Inns	NO	Runs	HS	Avge	100s	50s	Ct	St	O	M	Runs	Wkts	Avge	Best	5wI	10wM
Test																		
All First	3	4	1	114	55	38.00	-	1	2	-	37	7	183	0	-	-	-	-
1-day Int																		
C & G	2	2	0	5	3	2.50	-	-	1	-	6	0	33	1	33.00	1-33	-	
totesport	17	17	2	530	115 *	35.33	1	5	11	-	76.5	2	386	16	24.12	5-39	1	
Twenty20	5	5	2	89	37 *	29.66	-	-	1	-								

Career Performances

	M	Inns	NO	Runs	HS	Avge	100s	50s	Ct	St	Balls	Runs	Wkts	Avge	Best	5wI	10wM
Test																	
All First	112	182	18	4412	193 *	26.90	5	24	101	-	6746	3858	88	43.84	5-13	2	-
1-day Int																	
C & G	31	28	8	818	121	40.90	1	3	9	-	1292	969	37	26.18	4-43	-	
totesport	150	129	18	3107	115 *	27.99	1	18	60	-	3389	2861	79	36.21	5-39	1	
Twenty20	10	10	3	125	37 *	17.85	-	-	3	-	48	83	2	41.50	2-26	-	

66. Who, when they opened the batting for Sri Lanka against New Zealand in 1982-83, became the third set of brothers to open in Tests, after W. G. and E. M. Grace and Hanif and Sadiq Mohammed?

PARSONS, M. Somerset

Name: Michael Parsons
Role: Right-hand bat, right-arm fast-medium bowler
Born: 26 November 1984, Taunton
Height: 6ft **Weight:** 11st 11lbs
Nickname: Pars
County debut: 2002 (one-day)
Parents: Dave and Hilary
Marital status: Single
Education: Ladymead; Richard Huish College
Qualifications: 10 GCSEs, 1 A-level, Level 1 ECB coach
Off-season: 'Training'
Overseas tours: ESCA West Region U15 to West Indies 2000; Somerset Academy U19 to Australia 2002
Career highlights to date: 'Somerset v New Zealand 2004 – 10-1-30-6'
Cricket moments to forget: 'Dropped catch live on Sky TV'
Cricket superstitions: 'None'
Cricketers particularly admired: Allan Donald, Glenn McGrath
Young players to look out for: James Hildreth
Other sports followed: Football (Man United)
Injuries: Out for six weeks with a broken wrist
Relaxations: 'Music, PlayStation'
Extras: England U15 and U17. Bowler of ESCA West Region U15 tour to West Indies 2000. Played for Somerset Board XI in the C&G 2003. Represented England U19 v South Africa U19 2003. Took 6-30 in 10 overs v New Zealanders in 50-over match at Taunton 2004
Opinions on cricket: 'More day/night cricket.'

2004 Season

	M	Inns	NO	Runs	HS	Avge	100s	50s	Ct	St	O	M	Runs	Wkts	Avge	Best	5wI	10wM
Test																		
All First																		
1-day Int																		
C & G																		
totesport	4	2	1	1	1*	1.00	-	-	2	-	29	1	161	4	40.25	2-60	-	
Twenty20																		

Career Performances

	M	Inns	NO	Runs	HS	Avge	100s	50s	Ct	St	Balls	Runs	Wkts	Avge	Best	5wI	10wM
Test																	
All First																	
1-day Int																	
C & G	1	1	0	0	0	0.00	-	-	-	-	60	70	3	23.33	3-70	-	
totesport	7	4	1	1	1 *	0.33	-	-	2	-	285	262	5	52.40	2-60	-	
Twenty20																	

PATEL, M. M. Kent

Name: Minal (Min) Mahesh Patel
Role: Right-hand bat, slow left-arm orthodox bowler
Born: 7 July 1970, Mumbai, India
Height: 5ft 7in **Weight:** 10st
Nickname: Ho Chi, Diamond, Geez
County debut: 1989
County cap: 1994
Benefit: 2004
Test debut: 1996
Tests: 2
50 wickets in a season: 3
1st-Class 50s: 11
1st-Class 5 w. in innings: 25
1st-Class 10 w. in match: 9
1st-Class catches: 89
Place in batting averages: 256th av. 13.22
Place in bowling averages: 39th av. 28.89
Strike rate: 58.16 (career 72.19)
Parents: Mahesh and Aruna
Wife and date of marriage: Karuna, 8 October 1995
Family links with cricket: Father played good club cricket in India, Africa and England
Education: Dartford Grammar School; Manchester Polytechnic
Qualifications: 6 O-levels, 3 A-levels, BA (Hons) Economics
Overseas tours: Dartford GS to Barbados 1988; England A to India and Bangladesh 1994-95; MCC to Malta 1997, 1999, to Fiji, Sydney and Hong Kong 1998, to East and Central Africa 1999, to Bangladesh 1999-2000 (captain), to Argentina and Chile 2001, to Namibia and Uganda 2004-05 (captain); Kent to Port Elizabeth 2001; Club Cricket Conference to Australia 2002
Overseas teams played for: St Augustine's, Cape Town 1993-94; Alberton, Johannesburg 1997-98

Career highlights to date: 'Winning 2001 Norwich Union League at Edgbaston. First Test cap. Any match-winning performance for Kent'
Cricket moments to forget: 'Being left out of the final XI for the Lord's Test v India 1996'
Cricketers particularly admired: Derek Underwood, Aravinda de Silva
Other sports played: Golf, snooker
Other sports followed: Football (Tottenham Hotspur), 'most sports that you can name'
Favourite band: 'A lot of 1970s/80s soul – Phyllis Hyman, Loose Ends, Keni Burke etc.'
Extras: Played for English Schools 1988, 1989 and NCA England South 1989. Was voted Kent League Young Player of the Year 1987 while playing for Blackheath. Whittingdale Young Player of the Year 1994. Took 49 first-class wickets (av. 28.89) 2004 after missing the whole of the 2003 season with a back injury
Best batting: 82 Kent v Leicestershire, Canterbury 2002
Best bowling: 8-96 Kent v Lancashire, Canterbury 1994

2004 Season

	M	Inns	NO	Runs	HS	Avge	100s	50s	Ct	St	O	M	Runs	Wkts	Avge	Best	5wI	10wM
Test																		
All First	13	19	1	238	44	13.22	-	-	1	-	475	91	1416	49	28.89	5-56	2	-
1-day Int																		
C & G																		
totesport	1	1	0	26	26	26.00	-	-	-	-	8	0	52	0	-	-	-	
Twenty20																		

Career Performances

	M	Inns	NO	Runs	HS	Avge	100s	50s	Ct	St	Balls	Runs	Wkts	Avge	Best	5wI	10wM
Test	2	2	0	45	27	22.50	-	-	2	-	276	180	1	180.00	1-101	-	-
All First	173	233	45	3163	82	16.82	-	11	89	-	37471	15900	519	30.63	8-96	25	9
1-day Int																	
C & G	14	5	2	45	27 *	15.00	-	-	5	-	662	399	11	36.27	2-29	-	
totesport	42	25	7	148	26	8.22	-	-	13	-	1762	1335	50	26.70	3-22	-	
Twenty20																	

67. Who scored Holland's first ODI hundred when sharing a second-wicket stand of 228 with Klaas-Jan van Noortwijk (134*) v Namibia in the 2002-03 World Cup?

PATEL, S. R. Nottinghamshire

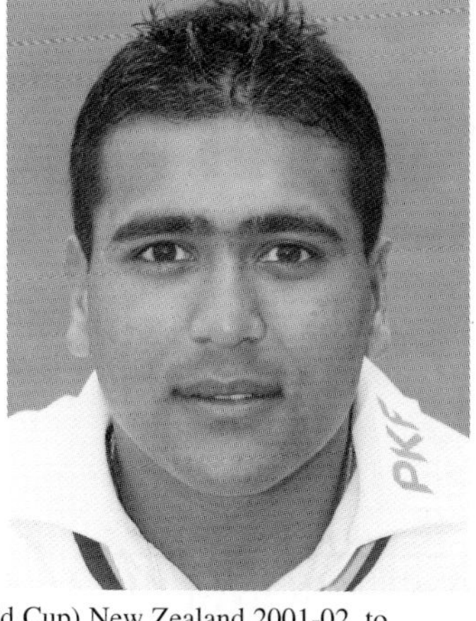

Name: Samit Rohit Patel
Role: Right-hand bat, left-arm orthodox spin bowler; all-rounder
Born: 30 November 1984, Leicester
Height: 5ft 8in **Weight:** 12st
Nickname: Pilchy Patel
County debut: 2002
1st-Class 50s: 1
1st-Class catches: 1
Parents: Rohit and Sejal
Marital status: Single
Family links with cricket: Father local league cricketer and brother has played for Notts U15
Education: Worksop College
Qualifications: 7 GCSEs, 2 A-levels
Career outside cricket: 'Want to be a coach'
Overseas tours: England U17 to Australia 2001; England U19 to Australia and (U19 World Cup) New Zealand 2001-02, to Australia 2002-03, to Bangladesh (U19 World Cup) 2003-04
Career highlights to date: 'Scoring 122 against South Africa U19 at Arundel [2003], because we were 90-6 at the time'
Cricket moments to forget: 'Playing at Headingley in the Twenty20 Cup against Yorkshire, where I got hit for 28 in an over by Michael Lumb'
Cricket superstitions: 'Put my right pad on first'
Cricketers particularly admired: Sachin Tendulkar, Brian Lara
Young players to look out for: Akhil Patel, Bilal Shafayat, Ravinder Bopara
Other sports played: Rugby, hockey (both for Worksop College 1st XI)
Other sports followed: Football (Nottingham Forest)
Favourite band: G-Unit
Relaxations: 'Listening to music; playing snooker; just generally relaxing'
Extras: Made Nottinghamshire 2nd XI debut in 1999, aged 14. Winner of inaugural BBC *Test Match Special* U15 Young Cricketer of the Year Award 2000. Represented England U19 2002, 2003 (captain in one-day series 2003) and v Bangladesh U19 2004. Christopher Martin-Jenkins's promising young cricketer of the year 2003. Scored 102* in England U19 victory over New Zealand U19 at Dhaka in the U19 World Cup 2003-04
Opinions on cricket: 'Lunch and tea should be longer, and batters should get second chances, especially off the first ball.'
Best batting: 55 Nottinghamshire v Lancashire, Trent Bridge 2003

2004 Season

	M	Inns	NO	Runs	HS	Avge	100s	50s	Ct	St	O	M	Runs	Wkts	Avge	Best	5wI	10wM
Test																		
All First																		
1-day Int																		
C & G																		
totesport	4	4	1	26	10	8.66	-	-	-	-	15	0	74	3	24.66	2-28	-	
Twenty20	5	5	2	71	25	23.66	-	-	2	-	7	0	55	2	27.50	1-14	-	

Career Performances

	M	Inns	NO	Runs	HS	Avge	100s	50s	Ct	St	Balls	Runs	Wkts	Avge	Best	5wI	10wM
Test																	
All First	2	3	0	99	55	33.00	-	1	1	-	48	10	0	-	-	-	-
1-day Int																	
C & G																	
totesport	12	9	2	134	44	19.14	-	-	1	-	204	174	7	24.85	2-14	-	
Twenty20	7	7	3	82	25	20.50	-	-	3	-	48	83	2	41.50	1-14	-	

PATTISON, I. — Durham

Name: Ian Pattison
Role: Right-hand bat, right-arm medium bowler
Born: 5 May 1982, Sunderland
Height: 5ft 11in **Weight:** 13st 5lbs ('-ish')
Nickname: Patta, Patto, Mr C
County debut: 2002
1st-Class 50s: 1
1st-Class catches: 5
Strike rate: 117.00 (career 69.14)
Parents: Stewart and Janice
Marital status: Single
Family links with cricket: 'Brother plays in local premier league'
Education: Seaham Comprehensive
Qualifications: 6 GCSEs, Level 1 coaching award
Overseas tours: England U19 to Malaysia and (U19 World Cup) Sri Lanka 1999-2000, to India 2000-01
Overseas teams played for: Bayswater-Morley, Perth 2002-03
Career highlights to date: 'Scoring 50 at Headingley'
Cricket moments to forget: 'Dislocating shoulder day after getting 50, whilst bowling'

Cricketers particularly admired: Darren Gough, Craig White, Damien Martyn, Steve Waugh, Graeme Smith, Jacques Kallis
Young players to look out for: Liam Plunkett, John Sadler
Other sports played: Golf
Other sports followed: Football (Sunderland AFC)
Relaxations: Horse racing
Extras: Played for Durham Board XI in the NatWest 2000 and in the C&G 2002 and 2003; also played for Durham in the C&G 2003. Released by Durham at the end of the 2004 season
Opinions on cricket: 'More day/night cricket.'
Best batting: 62 Durham v Yorkshire, Headingley 2003
Best bowling: 3-41 Durham v Essex, Riverside 2002

2004 Season

	M	Inns	NO	Runs	HS	Avge	100s	50s	Ct	St	O	M	Runs	Wkts	Avge	Best	5wI	10wM
Test																		
All First	3	4	0	92	33	23.00	-	-	3	-	39	7	129	2	64.50	1-30	-	-
1-day Int																		
C & G	1	1	0	8	8	8.00	-	-	-	-	10	1	45	3	15.00	3-45	-	
totesport	7	4	0	19	10	4.75	-	-	4	-	14.4	0	96	2	48.00	1-9	-	
Twenty20	3	2	0	8	7	4.00	-	-	1	-								

Career Performances

	M	Inns	NO	Runs	HS	Avge	100s	50s	Ct	St	Balls	Runs	Wkts	Avge	Best	5wI	10wM
Test																	
All First	7	11	0	215	62	19.54	-	1	5	-	484	303	7	43.28	3-41	-	-
1-day Int																	
C & G	7	7	2	81	48 *	16.20	-	-	3	-	246	213	6	35.50	3-45	-	
totesport	8	5	0	19	10	3.80	-	-	4	-	112	125	2	62.50	1-9	-	
Twenty20	3	2	0	8	7	4.00	-	-	1	-							

68. Which county side did Ireland defeat in the second round of the Cheltenham & Gloucester Trophy in May 2004?

PEARSON, J. A. — Gloucestershire

Name: James Alexander Pearson
Role: Left-hand bat
Born: 11 September 1983, Bristol
Height: 5ft 10in **Weight:** 12st 7lbs
Nickname: JP
County debut: 2002
1st-Class 50s: 1
1st-Class catches: 2
Parents: Milverton and Faith
Marital status: Single
Family links with cricket: 'Dad played club cricket'
Education: Clifton College
Qualifications: 5 GCSEs, 3 A-levels, GNVQ
Overseas tours: England U19 to Australia 2002-03
Career highlights to date: 'Making 51 opening the batting on debut v Northamptonshire'
Cricketers particularly admired: Brian Lara, Courtney Walsh, Ricky Ponting
Young players to look out for: Alex Gidman, Liam Plunkett
Other sports played: 'A bit of footy now and then'
Other sports followed: Football (Arsenal)
Relaxations: 'Listening to music and going clubbing'
Extras: Played for Gloucestershire Board XI in the C&G 2001 and 2002. Scored 51 on debut v Northamptonshire at Bristol 2002. Represented England U19 2002
Best batting: 51 Gloucestershire v Northamptonshire, Bristol 2002

2004 Season (did not make any first-class or one-day appearances)

Career Performances

	M	Inns	NO	Runs	HS	Avge	100s	50s	Ct	St	Balls	Runs	Wkts	Avge	Best	5wI	10wM
Test																	
All First	3	6	1	114	51	22.80	-	1	2	-							
1-day Int																	
C & G	2	2	0	7	7	3.50	-	-	-	-	18	29	1	29.00	1-29	-	
totesport																	
Twenty20																	

PENG, N. — Durham

Name: Nicky Peng
Role: Right-hand bat
Born: 18 September 1982, Newcastle upon Tyne
Height: 6ft 3in **Weight:** 12st
Nickname: Pengy, King
County debut: 2000
County cap: 2001
1st-Class 50s: 11
1st-Class 100s: 4
1st-Class catches: 35
One-Day 100s: 3
Place in batting averages: 193rd av. 23.16 (2003 146th av. 29.72)
Parents: Linda and Wilf
Marital status: Single
Education: Royal Grammar School, Newcastle upon Tyne
Qualifications: 10 GCSEs
Overseas tours: England U19 to India 2000-01, to Australia and (U19 World Cup) New Zealand 2001-02 (captain); ECB National Academy to Australia 2001-02; Durham to South Africa 2002
Cricket moments to forget: 'Every time I get out!'
Cricketers particularly admired: Mike Atherton, Steve Waugh
Young players to look out for: Gordon Muchall, Mark Wallace
Other sports followed: Football, rugby (Newcastle, and especially England)
Relaxations: Socialising with friends; music and films
Extras: Full name Nicky Peng Gillender. Has represented England at U14, U15, U17 and U19 levels. Represented Minor Counties at age 15. Sir John Hobbs Silver Jubilee Memorial Prize 1998. Scored 98 on Championship debut, v Surrey at Riverside 2000. NBC Denis Compton Award for the most promising young Durham player 2000, 2001. C&G Man of the Match award for his 119 v Hampshire at Riverside 2001. Durham CCC Young Player of the Year 2001. PCA Young Player of the Year 2001. Scored century before lunch on the opening day v Durham UCCE at Durham 2003. Scored 99 v Derbyshire at Derby 2003, in the process sharing with Vince Wells (106) in a new record fifth-wicket partnership for Durham (197). Scored 88 as Durham made 453-9 to beat Somerset at Taunton 2004 in the fourth-highest successful run chase in the history of the County Championship
Best batting: 158 Durham v DUCCE, Durham 2003

2004 Season

	M	Inns	NO	Runs	HS	Avge	100s	50s	Ct	St	O	M	Runs	Wkts	Avge	Best	5wI	10wM
Test																		
All First	10	18	0	417	88	23.16	-	3	6	-								
1-day Int																		
C & G	1	1	0	0	0	0.00	-	-	-	-								
totesport	14	14	0	280	65	20.00	-	2	4	-								
Twenty20																		

Career Performances

	M	Inns	NO	Runs	HS	Avge	100s	50s	Ct	St	Balls	Runs	Wkts	Avge	Best	5wI	10wM
Test																	
All First	58	101	2	2450	158	24.74	4	11	35	-	6	2	0	-	-	-	-
1-day Int																	
C & G	8	8	0	243	119	30.37	1	-	1	-							
totesport	60	60	4	1465	121	26.16	2	7	16	-							
Twenty20	5	5	0	110	49	22.00	-	-	6	-							

PENNEY, T. L. Warwickshire

Name: Trevor Lionel Penney
Role: Right-hand bat, leg-break bowler, occasional wicket-keeper
Born: 12 June 1968, Harare, Zimbabwe
Height: 6ft **Weight:** 11st 2lbs
Nickname: TP, Blondie
County debut: 1992
County cap: 1994
Benefit: 2003
1000 runs in a season: 2
1st-Class 50s: 36
1st-Class 100s: 15
1st-Class catches: 94
1st-Class stumpings: 2
Strike rate: (career 43.16)
Parents: George and Bets
Wife and date of marriage: Deborah-Anne, 19 December 1992
Children: Samantha Anne, 20 August 1995; Kevin, 7 June 1998
Family links with cricket: Father played club cricket. Brother Stephen captained Zimbabwe Schools
Education: Prince Edward Boys High School, Zimbabwe

Qualifications: 3 O-levels
Overseas tours: Zimbabwe U24 to England 1984; Zimbabwe to Sri Lanka 1987; ICC Associates to Australia (U19 World Cup) 1987-88 (captain)
Overseas teams played for: Old Hararians, Zimbabwe 1983-89, 1992-98; Scarborough, Perth 1989-90; Avendale, South Africa 1990-91; Boland, South Africa 1991-92; Mashonaland, Zimbabwe 1993-94, 1997-98 – 2000-01
Cricketers particularly admired: Colin Bland, Ian Botham, Allan Donald, Steve Waugh
Other sports played: Hockey (Zimbabwe and Africa), squash, tennis, golf and white water rafting
Other sports followed: Basketball (Chicago Bulls), American football (San Francisco 49ers), Formula One motor racing
Relaxations: 'Spending time with my family'
Extras: Played for Zimbabwe v Sri Lanka 1987. Scored century (102*) on first-class debut for Warwickshire, v Cambridge University at Fenner's 1992. Qualified to play for England in 1992. Captained Old Hararians to victory in three Zimbabwe domestic trophies 1998-99. C&G Man of the Match award for his 58* in the quarter-final v Yorkshire at Headingley 2001. Warwickshire 2nd XI captain in 2002 and 2003; took part in a third-wicket stand of 397 with Jonathan Trott v Somerset 2nd XI at Knowle & Dorridge 2002. Has coached Zimbabwe Board XI and Zimbabwe A
Best batting: 151 Warwickshire v Middlesex, Lord's 1992
Best bowling: 3-18 Mashonaland v Mashonaland U24, Harare 1993-94

2004 Season

	M	Inns	NO	Runs	HS	Avge	100s	50s	Ct	St	O	M	Runs	Wkts	Avge	Best	5wI	10wM
Test																		
All First																		
1-day Int																		
C & G	3	1	0	41	41	41.00	-	-	-	-								
totesport	8	8	2	145	44	24.16	-	-	2	-								
Twenty20	5	4	2	40	32 *	20.00	-	-	2	-								

Career Performances

	M	Inns	NO	Runs	HS	Avge	100s	50s	Ct	St	Balls	Runs	Wkts	Avge	Best	5wI	10wM
Test																	
All First	158	248	45	7975	151	39.28	15	36	94	2	259	184	6	30.66	3-18	-	-
1-day Int																	
C & G	42	37	10	878	90	32.51	-	3	22	-	13	16	1	16.00	1-8	-	
totesport	171	146	49	2885	88 *	29.74	-	12	61	1	6	2	0	-	-	-	
Twenty20	12	11	3	240	52	30.00	-	1	4	-							

PEPLOE, C. T. Middlesex

Name: Christopher (Chris) Thomas Peploe
Role: Left-hand lower-order bat, slow-left arm bowler
Born: 26 April 1981, Hammersmith, London
Height: 6ft 4in **Weight:** 13st 7lbs
Nickname: Peps, Pepsy
County debut: 2003
1st-Class catches: 5
Place in batting averages: 253rd av. 14.00
Place in bowling averages: 130th av. 43.82
Strike rate: 85.52 (career 97.05)
Parents: Trevor and Margaret
Marital status: Single
Education: Twyford C of E High School; University of Surrey, Roehampton
Qualifications: 9 GCSEs, 3 A-levels, Sports Science degree, ECB Level 2 coach, YMCA gym instructor
Career outside cricket: Cricket coach
Off-season: 'Training and working'
Overseas tours: MCC Young Cricketers to South Africa 2002, to Sri Lanka 2003; Middlesex to India 2004
Career highlights to date: 'Making my debut at Lord's for Middlesex. Taking career best figures against Sussex (4-65) at Hove'
Cricket moments to forget: 'Bowling at Nick Knight and Craig Spearman when they both scored 300-plus in '04'
Cricket superstitions: 'None'
Cricketers particularly admired: Daniel Vettori, Andrew Strauss, Phil Tufnell
Young players to look out for: Ed Joyce
Other sports played: Golf
Other sports followed: English rugby
Favourite band: Linkin Park
Relaxations: 'Music, movies, golf'
Extras: MCC Young Cricketer 2002-03; also played for Derbyshire 2nd XI and Surrey 2nd XI
Opinions on cricket: 'Twenty20 great for game.'
Best batting: 28* Middlesex v Gloucestershire, Gloucester 2004
Best bowling: 4-65 Middlesex v Sussex, Hove 2004

2004 Season

	M	Inns	NO	Runs	HS	Avge	100s	50s	Ct	St	O	M	Runs	Wkts	Avge	Best	5wI	10wM
Test																		
All First	8	12	2	140	28 *	14.00	-	-	3	-	242.2	59	745	17	43.82	4-65	-	-
1-day Int																		
C & G																		
totesport	1	0	0	0	0	-	-	-	-	-	3	0	19	0	-	-	-	
Twenty20																		

Career Performances

	M	Inns	NO	Runs	HS	Avge	100s	50s	Ct	St	Balls	Runs	Wkts	Avge	Best	5wI	10wM
Test																	
All First	10	14	3	153	28 *	13.90	-	-	5	-	1844	984	19	51.78	4-65	-	-
1-day Int																	
C & G																	
totesport	1	0	0	0	0	-	-	-	-	-	18	19	0	-	-	-	
Twenty20																	

PETERS, S. D. — Worcestershire

Name: Stephen David Peters
Role: Right-hand bat, leg-break bowler
Born: 10 December 1978, Harold Wood, Essex
Height: 5ft 11in **Weight:** 11st 7lbs
Nickname: Pedro, Geezer
County debut: 1996 (Essex), 2002 (Worcestershire)
County colours: 2002 (Worcestershire)
1000 runs in a season: 1
1st-Class 50s: 25
1st-Class 100s: 9
1st-Class catches: 80
Place in batting averages: 135th av. 31.27 (2003 70th av. 40.58)
Strike rate: (career 35.00)
Parents: Lesley and Brian
Marital status: Single
Family links with cricket: 'All family is linked with Upminster CC'
Education: Coopers Company and Coborn School
Qualifications: 9 GCSEs, Level 2 coaching
Off-season: Coaching, training

Overseas tours: Essex U14 to Barbados; Essex U15 to Hong Kong; England U19 to Pakistan 1996-97, to South Africa (including U19 World Cup) 1997-98
Overseas teams played for: Cornwall CC, Auckland 2001-02; Willetton CC, Perth 2002-03
Career highlights to date: 'Winning B&H Cup in 1998 with Essex'
Cricket moments to forget: 'Running myself out for a pair against Durham in 2003'
Cricket superstitions: 'Binned most in 2002'
Cricketers particularly admired: 'Anyone who has played at the top level'
Young players to look out for: Mark Davis (Worcestershire)
Other sports played: Football, golf
Other sports followed: Football (West Ham United)
Favourite band: Maroon 5, Matchbox Twenty
Relaxations: 'My sofa'
Extras: Sir John Hobbs Silver Jubilee Memorial Prize 1994; a *Daily Telegraph* Regional Batting Award 1994. Represented England at U14, U15, U17 and U19. Scored century (110) on county debut v Cambridge University at Fenner's 1996, in the process becoming (at 17 years 194 days) the youngest player to score a first-class century for Essex. Essex Young Player of the Year 1996. Scored a century (107) and was Man of the Match in the U19 World Cup final in South Africa 1997-98. Left Essex during the 2001-02 off-season and joined Worcestershire for 2002. Scored century in each innings (123/117) v Kent at Worcester 2004
Opinions on cricket: 'Twenty20 great for crowds. EU/Kolpak (*see page 9*) – is it good for the future of English cricket?'
Best batting: 165 Worcestershire v Somerset, Bath 2003
Best bowling: 1-19 Essex v Oxford University, Chelmsford 1999

2004 Season

	M	Inns	NO	Runs	HS	Avge	100s	50s	Ct	St	O	M	Runs	Wkts	Avge	Best	5wI	10wM
Test																		
All First	17	29	0	907	123	31.27	3	3	13	-	2	0	12	0	-	-	-	-
1-day Int																		
C & G	3	3	0	16	7	5.33	-	-	1	-								
totesport	7	7	0	106	27	15.14	-	-	3	-								
Twenty20	1	0	0	0	0	-	-	-	-	-								

Career Performances

	M	Inns	NO	Runs	HS	Avge	100s	50s	Ct	St	Balls	Runs	Wkts	Avge	Best	5wI	10wM
Test																	
All First	107	177	16	4996	165	31.03	9	25	80	-	35	31	1	31.00	1-19	-	-
1-day Int																	
C & G	11	11	0	127	58	11.54	-	1	5	-							
totesport	81	72	3	1285	82	18.62	-	6	20	-							
Twenty20	4	3	0	28	23	9.33	-	-	3	-							

PETTINI, M. L. — Essex

Name: Mark Lewis Pettini
Role: Right-hand bat, occasional wicket-keeper
Born: 7 August 1983, Brighton
Height: 5ft 11in **Weight:** 11st 7lbs
Nickname: Swampy, Michelle
County debut: 2001
1st-Class 50s: 5
1st-Class catches: 7
Parents: Pauline and Max
Marital status: Single
Family links with cricket: 'Brother Tom plays. Mum and Dad watch'
Education: Comberton Village College and Hills Road Sixth Form College, Cambridge; Cardiff University
Qualifications: 10 GCSEs, 3 A-levels, Level 1 cricket coaching award
Overseas tours: England U19 to Australia and (U19 World Cup) New Zealand 2001-02; MCC to Sierra Leone and Nigeria; Essex to Cape Town

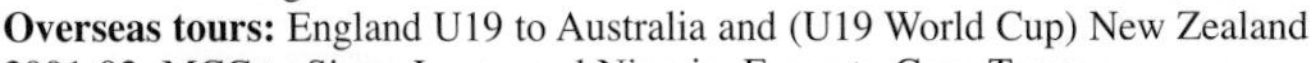

Career highlights to date: 'Any first-team cricket played'
Cricket moments to forget: 'Losing three U19 ODIs to India [2002]'
Cricket superstitions: 'Drive round the car park twice before parking before a game. Never cut toenails during season'
Cricketers particularly admired: 'All the Essex first team', Graham Gooch, Damien West
Young players to look out for: Ryan Bradshaw, Ravi Bopara, Ali Cook, 'brother Tom'
Extras: Captained Cambridgeshire county sides U11-U16. Took hat-trick against Bedfordshire U12. Highest score of 173* v Hampshire U16 1999. Played for Development of Excellence XI (South) v West Indies U19 at Arundel 2001. Represented England U19 v India U19 2002. Essex 2nd XI Player of the Year 2002. Scored an 81-ball 92* v Warwickshire at Edgbaston in the C&G 2003. Represented British Universities 2003 and v Sri Lanka A 2004
Opinions on cricket: 'Tea should be half an hour.'
Best batting: 78 Essex v Warwickshire, Chelmsford 2003

2004 Season

	M	Inns	NO	Runs	HS	Avge	100s	50s	Ct	St	O	M	Runs	Wkts	Avge	Best	5wI	10wM
Test																		
All First	3	5	0	104	67	20.80	-	1	1	-								
1-day Int																		
C & G	1	1	1	18	18 *	-	-	-	-	-								
totesport	4	4	0	65	27	16.25	-	-	-	-								
Twenty20	2	2	2	30	29 *	-	-	-	1	-								

Career Performances

	M	Inns	NO	Runs	HS	Avge	100s	50s	Ct	St	Balls	Runs	Wkts	Avge	Best	5wI	10wM
Test																	
All First	10	18	1	475	78	27.94	-	5	7	-							
1-day Int																	
C & G	3	3	2	113	92 *	113.00	-	1	2	-							
totesport	29	26	1	487	75	19.48	-	3	4	-							
Twenty20	6	6	3	98	32 *	32.66	-	-	4	-							

PHILLIPS, B. J. Northamptonshire

Name: Ben James Phillips
Role: Right-hand bat, right-arm fast-medium bowler
Born: 30 September 1975, Lewisham, London
Height: 6ft 6in **Weight:** 15st
Nickname: Bennyphil, Bus
County debut: 1996 (Kent), 2002 (Northamptonshire)
1st-Class 50s: 5
1st-Class 100s: 1
1st-Class 5 w. in innings: 3
1st-Class catches: 11
Place in batting averages: 230th av. 18.16 (2003 225th av. 19.83)
Place in bowling averages: 106th av. 37.90 (2003 3rd av. 19.04)
Strike rate: 79.06 (career 59.04)
Parents: Glynis and Trevor
Wife and date of marriage: Sarah Jane, 20 January 2003
Family links with cricket: Father and brother both keen club cricketers for Hayes CC (Kent)
Education: Langley Park School for Boys, Beckenham; Langley Park Sixth Form

Qualifications: 9 GCSEs, 3 A-levels
Overseas tours: Northamptonshire to Grenada 2002
Overseas teams played for: University of Queensland, Australia 1993-94; Cape Technikon Greenpoint, Cape Town 1994-95, 1996-98; University of Western Australia, Perth 1998-99; Valley, Brisbane 2001-02
Career highlights to date: '100* v Lancashire, Old Trafford 1997'
Cricket moments to forget: 'Having to leave the field in a televised game against Worcestershire with a shoulder injury that kept me out for most of [2002] season – that would be up there'
Cricket superstitions: 'Arrive at the ground early – hate rushing!'
Cricketers particularly admired: Glenn McGrath, Jason Gillespie
Young players to look out for: Jake Phillips, Monty Panesar
Other sports followed: Football (West Ham United), rugby (Northampton Saints)
Relaxations: 'Enjoy swimming, watching a good movie, and just generally like spending time with family and friends'
Extras: Represented England U19 Schools in 1993-94. Set Langley Park School record for the fastest half-century, off 11 balls. Released by Kent at the end of the 2001 season and joined Northamptonshire for 2002
Best batting: 100* Kent v Lancashire, Old Trafford 1997
Best bowling: 5-47 Kent v Sussex, Horsham 1997

2004 Season

	M	Inns	NO	Runs	HS	Avge	100s	50s	Ct	St	O	M	Runs	Wkts	Avge	Best	5wI	10wM
Test																		
All First	15	21	3	327	90	18.16	-	3	2	-	408.3	107	1175	31	37.90	5-106	1	-
1-day Int																		
C & G	3	2	0	35	33	17.50	-	-	-	-	24	1	126	1	126.00	1-60	-	
totesport	16	11	2	206	44 *	22.88	-	-	5	-	124	12	534	20	26.70	3-21	-	
Twenty20	5	4	2	18	10 *	9.00	-	-	1	-	15	0	108	7	15.42	2-24	-	

Career Performances

	M	Inns	NO	Runs	HS	Avge	100s	50s	Ct	St	Balls	Runs	Wkts	Avge	Best	5wI	10wM
Test																	
All First	50	69	9	1047	100 *	17.45	1	5	11	-	7144	3530	121	29.17	5-47	3	-
1-day Int																	
C & G	6	4	1	63	33	21.00	-	-	2	-	276	231	4	57.75	3-14	-	
totesport	46	27	5	350	44 *	15.90	-	-	14	-	1804	1389	48	28.93	4-25	-	
Twenty20	9	8	4	90	29 *	22.50	-	-	3	-	186	265	8	33.12	2-24	-	

PHILLIPS, T. J. Essex

Name: Timothy (Tim) James Phillips
Role: Left-hand bat, slow left-arm bowler
Born: 13 March 1981, Cambridge
Height: 6ft 1in **Weight:** 13st
Nickname: Pips
County debut: 1999
1st-Class 50s: 1
1st-Class catches: 7
Strike rate: (career 80.59)
Parents: Carolyn and Martin (deceased)
Marital status: Single
Family links with cricket: 'Father played in Lancashire League then village cricket in Essex. Brother Nick plays for local village, Lindsell'
Education: Felsted School; Durham University
Qualifications: 10 GCSEs, 3 A-levels, BA (Hons) Sport in the Community
Off-season: 'Paul Terry Academy, Perth, Oct-Feb; World Cricket Association, Mumbai, Feb'
Overseas tours: Felsted School to Australia 1995-96; England U19 to Malaysia and (U19 World Cup) Sri Lanka 1999-2000
Career highlights to date: '4-42 on first-class debut v Sri Lanka A'
Cricket moments to forget: '2003 season' (*Out for the whole of the season with cartilage and ligament damage to a knee*)
Cricketers particularly admired: Phil Tufnell
Other sports played: Golf, hockey (Essex Schools U14, U15; East of England U21 trials)
Other sports followed: Rugby union
Favourite band: The Libertines, Coldplay, The White Stripes
Relaxations: 'Music, gigs, socialising, fishing'
Extras: Winner of *Daily Telegraph* U14 National Bowling Award 1995. Holmwoods School Cricketer of the Year runner-up 1997 and 1998. Broke Nick Knight's and Elliott Wilson's record for runs in a season for Felsted School, scoring 1213 in 1999. NBC Denis Compton Award 1999. Played for Durham University CCE 2001 and 2002, scoring 75 v Durham at Riverside 2002
Best batting: 75 DUCCE v Durham, Riverside 2002
Best bowling: 4-42 Essex v Sri Lanka A, Chelmsford 1999

2004 Season (did not make any first-class or one-day appearances)

Career Performances

	M	Inns	NO	Runs	HS	Avge	100s	50s	Ct	St	Balls	Runs	Wkts	Avge	Best	5wI	10wM
Test																	
All First	17	25	3	388	75	17.63	-	1	7	-	2579	1704	32	53.25	4-42	-	-
1-day Int																	
C & G	1	1	1	4	4 *	-	-	-	-	-	30	27	0	-	-	-	
totesport	6	6	2	16	6	4.00	-	-	2	-	210	182	6	30.33	2-36	-	
Twenty20																	

PHYTHIAN, M. J. Northamptonshire

Name: Mark John Phythian
Role: Right-hand bat, wicket-keeper
Born: 26 April 1985, Peterborough
Height: 5ft 9in **Weight:** 12st
Nickname: Phythers, Frodo
County debut: No first-team appearance
Parents: John and Julie
Marital status: Single
Family links with cricket: 'Both parents are incredibly keen supporters'
Education: Oundle School; Durham University
Qualifications: 10 GCSEs, 1 AS-level, 3 A-levels, ECB Level 1 coaching award
Career outside cricket: 'Student of Sociology at Durham University'
Off-season: 'Studying at Durham University and training hard with DUCCE'
Overseas tours: Oundle School to Sri Lanka 2003; Northamptonshire U17 to South Africa 2000; Northamptonshire U19 to South Africa 2002; MCC to Namibia and Uganda 2004-05
Overseas teams played for: Young Peoples CC, Paarl, South Africa 2003-04
Career highlights to date: 'Winning the ECB Northamptonshire Premier League with the Northants Academy 2004'
Cricket moments to forget: 'Being run out without facing for Midlands U15 v North U15 at the Bunbury Festival'
Cricket superstitions: 'None'
Cricketers particularly admired: Jack Russell, Mark Boucher, Adam Gilchrist, Andrew Strauss

Young players to look out for: Riki Wessels, Cameron Wake, Alex Wakely
Other sports played: Rugby (school and county), football (school), golf, squash
Other sports followed: Rugby (Leicester Tigers)
Favourite band: Matchbox Twenty, Live, The Killers
Relaxations: 'Spending time with friends away from cricket and enjoying the student life in Durham'
Extras: Made 2nd XI Championship debut 2003. Is a Northamptonshire Emerging Player
Opinions on cricket: 'I feel that it's important for promising young players to be given the opportunities to prove themselves and that when given these opportunities they take them so that counties are not forced to look overseas to bring in established foreign players on EU passports and Kolpak (*see page 9*).'

PIESLEY, R. L. — Kent

Name: Richard Liam Piesley
Role: Right-hand bat, wicket-keeper
Born: 16 June 1986, Chatham
Height: 5ft 10in **Weight:** 10st
Nickname: Pilo
County debut: No first-team appearance (*see* ***Extras***)
Parents: Graham and Arlene
Marital status: Single
Family links with cricket: 'Father played club cricket and two of my younger brothers represent Kent'
Education: Fulston Manor School, Sittingbourne
Qualifications: 10 GCSEs, GNVQ Leisure and Tourism, ECB Level 1 coach
Off-season: 'Playing and training in Queensland, Australia'
Overseas teams played for: Redlands Tigers, Queensland 2004-05
Career highlights to date: 'To have been given a professional contract'
Cricket moments to forget: 'Forgetting my kit for a Kent U16 game'
Cricket superstitions: 'None'
Cricketers particularly admired: Mark Waugh, Steve Marsh, Keith Piper
Young players to look out for: Joe Denly, Simon Cusden, Charlie Hemphrey
Other sports played: Football ('played for local teams')
Other sports followed: Football (Gillingham FC, Sittingbourne FC)
Favourite band: Oasis

Relaxations: 'Socialising with friends; playing snooker'
Extras: Kent Academy Scholar. Selected for England U17. Appeared for Kent as substitute wicket-keeper v Northamptonshire at Canterbury 2004, deputising for the injured Niall O'Brien, but has yet to make full debut

PIETERSEN, C. — Northamptonshire

Name: Charl Pietersen
Role: Left-hand bat, left-arm medium-fast opening bowler
Born: 6 January 1983, Kimberley, South Africa
Height: 6ft **Weight:** 12st 12lbs
County debut: No first-team appearance
1st-Class 5 w. in innings: 1
1st-Class catches: 2
Strike rate: (career 67.97)
Parents: Thinus and Dalena
Marital status: Single
Education: Northern Cape High School, Kimberley
Qualifications: Grade 12 (Matriculation)
Off-season: 'Going back to South Africa and preparing for the next cricket season'
Overseas teams played for: Griqualand West 2001-02 – 2003-04
Career highlights to date: 'SA Schools team 2001. Griqualand West provincial team 2001-04'
Cricket moments to forget: 'When in 2004 there was no longer a place for me in SA cricket'
Cricket superstitions: 'None'
Cricketers particularly admired: Allan Donald, Steve Harmison, Gary Kirsten, Steve Waugh, Shane Warne
Young players to look out for: Kevin Pietersen (no relation), A. B. de Villiers
Other sports played: Indoor cricket (Griqualand West)
Other sports followed: Rugby (Blue Bulls)
Favourite band: Rolling Stones, Blink-182
Relaxations: 'Play a little bit of golf'
Extras: South African indoor cricketer of 1999. Represented South African Schools 2001. Man of the Match v KwaZulu-Natal at Pietermaritzburg in the Standard Bank Cup 2002-03 (4-32). Has joined Northamptonshire for 2005; is not considered an overseas player

Best batting: 45 Griqualand West v North West, Kimberley 2003-04
Best bowling: 6-43 Griqualand West v Boland, Kimberley 2002-03

2004 Season (did not make any first-class or one-day appearances)

Career Performances

	M	Inns	NO	Runs	HS	Avge	100s	50s	Ct	St	Balls	Runs	Wkts	Avge	Best	5wI	10wM
Test																	
All First	14	25	7	326	45	18.11	-	-	2	-	2447	1400	36	38.88	6-43	1	-
1-day Int																	
C & G																	
totesport																	
Twenty20																	

PIETERSEN, K. P. Hampshire

Name: Kevin Peter Pietersen
Role: Right-hand bat, right-arm off-spin bowler
Born: 27 June 1980, Pietermaritzburg, South Africa
Height: 6ft 4in **Weight:** 14st 9lbs
Nickname: KP, Kelv, Kapes
County debut: 2001 (Nottinghamshire)
County cap: 2002 (Nottinghamshire)
1000 runs in a season: 3
1st-Class 50s: 24
1st-Class 100s: 16
1st-Class 200s: 3
1st-Class catches: 76
One-Day 100s: 4
Place in batting averages: 32nd av. 52.20 (2003 25th av. 51.53)
Place in bowling averages: (2003 111th av. 38.90)
Strike rate: 70.14 (career 84.72)
Parents: Jannie and Penny
Marital status: Single
Education: Maritzburg College; University of South Africa
Qualifications: 3 A-levels
Off-season: ECB National Academy and touring with England
Overseas tours: Natal to Zimbabwe 1999-2000, to Australia 2000-01; Nottinghamshire to South Africa 2001, 2002; England A to Malaysia and India 2003-

04; England to Zimbabwe (one-day series) 2004-05, to South Africa 2004-05 (one-day series)
Overseas teams played for: Berea Rovers, Durban 1997 – 2001-02; KwaZulu-Natal 1997-98 – 2000-01; Sydney University 2002-03
Cricket moments to forget: 'Breaking my leg against Glamorgan in August 2002 in an NUL game'
Cricket superstitions: 'Left pad first'
Cricketers particularly admired: Shaun Pollock, Errol Stewart
Young players to look out for: Ed Joyce, Jamie Troughton, Rich Logan
Other sports played: Golf, swimming ('represented my state in 1992-93'), running
Other sports followed: Formula One (Ferrari), rugby (Natal Sharks)
Extras: Played for South African Schools B 1997. Merit award for cricket from Natal 1997. Scored 61* and had figures of 4-141 from 56 overs for KwaZulu-Natal v England on their 1999-2000 tour of South Africa. Youngest Notts player (21 years 33 days) to score a 200 in a first-class match (218* v Derbyshire at Derby 2001). Scored 1275 runs in first season of county cricket 2001. Scored 254* v Middlesex at Trent Bridge 2002, the highest post-war Championship score by a Nottinghamshire batsman, following up with further centuries in each of his next three innings in all cricket. NUL Player of the Month and PCA Player of the Month August 2002. Became first batsman to hit a ball over the pavilion at Riverside, v Durham in the NCL 2003. Scored 131 for England A v India A in second 'ODI' at Bangalore 2003-04. Scored century in each innings (104/115) for England A v South Zone at Gurgaon in the Duleep Trophy 2003-04. ECB National Academy 2003-04, 2004-05. Left Nottinghamshire at the end of the 2004 season and has joined Hampshire for 2005
Best batting: 254* Nottinghamshire v Middlesex, Trent Bridge 2002
Best bowling: 4-31 Nottinghamshire v DUCCE, Trent Bridge 2003
Stop press: Made ODI debut in the first ODI v Zimbabwe at Harare 2004-05. Man of the Match in the second ODI v Zimbabwe at Harare 2004-05 (77*). Added to England ODI squad for tour of South Africa 2004-05 and was Player of the Series (454 runs at 151.33, including the fastest hundred for England in ODIs, from 69 balls). Originally selected for England A tour to Sri Lanka 2004-05 but withdrawn after ODI series in South Africa and replaced by Alastair Cook

2004 Season

	M	Inns	NO	Runs	HS	Avge	100s	50s	Ct	St	O	M	Runs	Wkts	Avge	Best	5wI	10wM
Test																		
All First	16	21	1	1044	167	52.20	4	4	19	-	81.5	7	365	7	52.14	3-72	-	-
1-day Int																		
C & G	2	2	0	8	8	4.00	-	-	1	-	4	0	19	1	19.00	1-19	-	
totesport	16	15	2	531	82 *	40.84	-	4	4	-	30	0	147	6	24.50	3-14	-	
Twenty20	5	5	0	106	67	21.20	-	1	-	-	7	0	56	4	14.00	2-9	-	

Career Performances

	M	Inns	NO	Runs	HS	Avge	100s	50s	Ct	St	Balls	Runs	Wkts	Avge	Best	5wI	10wM
Test																	
All First	72	113	11	5512	254 *	54.03	19	24	76	-	4660	2598	55	47.23	4-31	-	-
1-day Int																	
C & G	7	5	0	52	24	10.40	-	-	4	-	108	81	1	81.00	1-19	-	
totesport	61	59	10	2208	147	45.06	4	13	26	-	1012	953	21	45.38	3-14	-	
Twenty20	10	10	0	256	67	25.60	-	2	-	-	108	136	6	22.66	2-9	-	

PIPE, D. J. — Worcestershire

Name: David James Pipe
Role: Right-hand bat, wicket-keeper
Born: 16 December 1977, Bradford
Height: 5ft 11in **Weight:** 12st
Nickname: Pipey
County debut: 1998
County colours: 2002
1st-Class 50s: 1
1st-Class 100s: 1
1st-Class catches: 38
1st-Class stumpings: 5
Place in batting averages: (2003 136th av. 30.66)
Parents: David and Dorothy
Marital status: 'Girlfriend Emma'
Family links with cricket: 'My dad and uncle played in the local league'
Education: Queensbury Upper School; BICC
Qualifications: 8 GCSEs, BTEC National in Business and Finance, HND Leisure Management, senior coaching award, Diploma in Personal Training, Diploma in Sports Therapy
Overseas teams played for: Leeming Spartans CC/South Metropolitan Cricket Association, Perth 1998-99; Manly CC, Australia 1999-2004
Career highlights to date: 'Getting first hundred'
Cricket moments to forget: 'Any game we lose'
Cricketers particularly admired: Adam Gilchrist, Ian Healy
Other sports followed: Rugby league (Bradford Bulls, Manly Sea Eagles), boxing ('all British fighters'), AFL (West Coast Eagles)
Relaxations: Training
Extras: MCC School of Merit Wilf Slack Memorial Trophy winner 1995. Scored 54 on Championship debut v Warwickshire at Worcester 2000. Took eight catches v

Hertfordshire at Hertford in the C&G 2001 to set a new NatWest/C&G record for most catches in a match by a wicket-keeper. Dick Lygon Award 2002 (Worcestershire Club Man of the Year)
Best batting: 104* Worcestershire v Hampshire, West End 2003

2004 Season

	M	Inns	NO	Runs	HS	Avge	100s	50s	Ct	St	O	M	Runs	Wkts	Avge	Best	5wI	10wM
Test																		
All First	3	3	0	20	12	6.66	-	-	-	-								
1-day Int																		
C & G																		
totesport																		
Twenty20	6	3	1	19	14	9.50	-	-	3	-								

Career Performances

	M	Inns	NO	Runs	HS	Avge	100s	50s	Ct	St	Balls	Runs	Wkts	Avge	Best	5wI	10wM
Test																	
All First	19	28	3	455	104 *	18.20	1	1	38	5							
1-day Int																	
C & G	3	2	0	60	56	30.00	-	1	11	-							
totesport	14	13	3	187	45	18.70	-	-	6	5							
Twenty20	6	3	1	19	14	9.50	-	-	3	-							

PIPER, K. J. — Warwickshire

Name: Keith John Piper
Role: Right-hand bat, wicket-keeper
Born: 18 December 1969, Leicester
Height: 5ft 7in **Weight:** 10st 8lbs
Nickname: Tubbsy, Garden Boy
County debut: 1989
County cap: 1992
Benefit: 2001
50 dismissals in a season: 2
1st-Class 50s: 14
1st-Class 100s: 2
1st-Class catches: 502
1st-Class stumpings: 34
Place in batting averages: (2003 226th av. 19.57)
Strike rate: (career 34.00)
Parents: John and Charlotte

Marital status: Single
Family links with cricket: Father club cricketer in Leicester
Education: Somerset Senior
Qualifications: Senior coaching award, basketball coaching award, volleyball coaching award
Overseas tours: Haringey Cricket College to Barbados 1986, to Trinidad 1987, to Jamaica 1988; Warwickshire to La Manga 1989, to St Lucia 1990; England A to India 1994-95, to Pakistan 1995-96
Overseas teams played for: Desmond Haynes's XI, Barbados v Haringey Cricket College
Cricketers particularly admired: Jack Russell, Alec Stewart, Dermot Reeve, Colin Metson
Other sports followed: Snooker, football, tennis
Relaxations: Music, eating
Extras: London Young Cricketer of the Year 1989 and in the last five 1992. Played for England YC 1989. Was batting partner (116*) to Brian Lara when he reached his 501*, v Durham at Edgbaston 1994. Took six catches v Leicestershire at Edgbaston in the NCL 2003, equalling the record for the one-day league. Took 500th first-class catch during the 2003 season
Best batting: 116* Warwickshire v Durham, Edgbaston 1994
Best bowling: 1-57 Warwickshire v Nottinghamshire, Edgbaston 1992

2004 Season

	M	Inns	NO	Runs	HS	Avge	100s	50s	Ct	St	O	M	Runs	Wkts	Avge	Best	5wI	10wM
Test																		
All First																		
1-day Int																		
C & G																		
totesport	5	0	0	0	0	-	-	-	5	3								
Twenty20	1	0	0	0	0	-	-	-	-	1								

Career Performances

	M	Inns	NO	Runs	HS	Avge	100s	50s	Ct	St	Balls	Runs	Wkts	Avge	Best	5wI	10wM
Test																	
All First	199	275	44	4618	116 *	19.99	2	14	502	34	34	60	1	60.00	1-57	-	-
1-day Int																	
C & G	41	21	10	181	19	16.45	-	-	47	7							
totesport	145	71	35	548	38 *	15.22	-	-	148	38							
Twenty20	6	2	2	1	1 *	-	-	-	3	1							

PLUNKETT, L. E. Durham

Name: Liam Edward Plunkett
Role: Right-hand bat, right-arm fast bowler
Born: 6 April 1985, Middlesbrough
Height: 6ft 3in **Weight:** 13st
Nickname: Pudsey
County debut: 2003
1st-Class 50s: 1
1st-Class 5 w. in innings: 2
1st-Class catches: 4
Place in batting averages: 176th av. 25.16 (2003 201st av. 23.42)
Place in bowling averages: 56th av. 31.09 (2003 88th av. 35.36)
Strike rate: 47.96 (career 49.42)
Parents: Alan and Marie
Marital status: Engaged to Lisa
Education: Nunthorpe Comprehensive; Teesside Tertiary
Qualifications: 9 GCSEs, volleyball coaching badge
Off-season: 'Part-time with ECB Academy; Australia 2005 (maybe)'
Overseas tours: England U19 to Australia 2002-03, to Bangladesh (U19 World Cup) 2003-04
Career highlights to date: 'Taking five wickets on Championship debut against Yorkshire'
Cricket moments to forget: 'Bowling too many wides in first game on TV'
Cricket superstitions: 'None'
Cricketers particularly admired: Glenn McGrath, Stephen Harmison, Allan Donald, Jacques Kallis
Young players to look out for: Ravinder Bopara
Other sports played: Football, swimming
Other sports followed: Football (Arsenal, Middlesbrough)
Injuries: Out for three to four weeks with sore shins; for three weeks with an inflamed disc in back
Favourite band: 'Any R&B'
Relaxations: Swimming, gym, cinema
Extras: Became only the second bowler to record a five-wicket innings return on Championship debut for Durham, 5-53 v Yorkshire at Headingley 2003. Represented England U19 2003. NBC Denis Compton Award for the most promising young Durham player 2003. ECB National Academy 2004-05 (part-time)
Opinions on cricket: 'Twenty20 good game, which brings the crowds in, and is fun to watch.'

Best batting: 54 Durham v Nottinghamshire, Riverside 2004
Best bowling: 6-74 Durham v Hampshire, Riverside 2004

2004 Season

	M	Inns	NO	Runs	HS	Avge	100s	50s	Ct	St	O	M	Runs	Wkts	Avge	Best	5wI	10wM
Test																		
All First	10	16	4	302	54	25.16	-	1	2	-	247.5	37	964	31	31.09	6-74	1	-
1-day Int																		
C & G																		
totesport	8	7	2	88	21	17.60	-	-	2	-	56	3	261	5	52.20	3-35	-	
Twenty20																		

Career Performances

	M	Inns	NO	Runs	HS	Avge	100s	50s	Ct	St	Balls	Runs	Wkts	Avge	Best	5wI	10wM
Test																	
All First	17	28	9	466	54	24.52	-	1	4	-	2471	1636	50	32.72	6-74	2	-
1-day Int																	
C & G	2	1	0	3	3	3.00	-	-	1	-	84	87	4	21.75	3-63	-	
totesport	10	8	3	89	21	17.80	-	-	2	-	444	335	10	33.50	3-35	-	
Twenty20	2	1	0	2	2	2.00	-	-	2	-	48	50	4	12.50	2-18	-	

PONTING, R. T. — Somerset

Name: Ricky Thomas Ponting
Role: Right-hand bat, right-arm medium or off-spin bowler
Born: 19 December 1974, Launceston, Tasmania
Nickname: Punter
County debut: 2004
Test debut: 1995-96
Tests: 79
One-Day Internationals: 207
1st-Class 50s: 55
1st-Class 100s: 47
1st-Class 200s: 5
1st-Class catches: 173
One-Day 100s: 16
Strike rate: (career 102.23)
Parents: Graeme and Lorraine
Wife: Rianna
Family links with cricket: Father played for Mowbray CC in Tasmania; uncle Greg Campbell played for Tasmania and Australia

Education: Brooks Senior HS, Launceston
Overseas tours: Young Australia (Australia A) to England and Netherlands 1995; Tasmania to Zimbabwe 1995-96; Australia to New Zealand (Bank of New Zealand Centenary Series) 1994-95, to West Indies 1994-95, to India and Pakistan (World Cup) 1995-96, to India 1996-97, to England 1997, to India 1997-98, to Malaysia (Commonwealth Games) 1998-99, to Bangladesh (Wills International Cup) 1998-99, to Pakistan 1998-99, to West Indies 1998-99, to UK, Ireland and Holland (World Cup) 1999, to Sri Lanka 1999, to Zimbabwe 1999-2000, to Kenya (ICC Knockout Trophy) 2000-01, to India 2000-01, to England 2001, to South Africa 2001-02, to Sri Lanka (ICC Champions Trophy) 2002-03 (captain), to Sri Lanka and Sharjah (v Pakistan) 2002-03, to Africa (World Cup) 2002-03 (captain), to West Indies 2002-03 (vice-captain), to Sri Lanka 2003-04 (captain), to Zimbabwe (one-day series) 2004 (captain), to Holland (Videocon Cup) 2004 (captain), to England (ICC Champions Trophy) 2004 (captain), to India 2004-05 (captain), to New Zealand 2004-05 (captain), plus other one-day series and tournaments in Sri Lanka, India, New Zealand, Sharjah and Kenya
Overseas teams played for: Tasmania 1992-93 –
Extras: Attended Commonwealth Bank [Australian] Cricket Academy 1992-93. Made first-class debut for Tasmania v South Australia at Adelaide 1992-93 aged 17, scoring 56. Made Test debut in the first Test v Sri Lanka at Perth 1995-96, scoring 96. One of *Indian Cricket*'s five Cricketers of the Year 1998. *Wisden Australia*'s Cricketer of the Year 2002-03. Named One-Day International Player of the Year at the 2002 Allan Border Medal awards and Test Player of the Year at the 2003 awards; winner of the 2004 Allan Border Medal as well as being named Test Player of the Year for the second year running. Has won numerous Test awards, including Man of the Series in Sri Lanka 1999 and in West Indies 2002-03 (523 runs; av. 130.75), and Man of the Match in the third Test v India at Melbourne 2003-04 (257). Has also won numerous ODI awards, including Man of the Series in South Africa 2001-02 (his first as captain), three match awards in the NatWest Series in England 2001, and Man of the Match v Sri Lanka at Centurion in the World Cup 2002-03 (114). Also won Man of the Match award in the final of the World Cup 2002-03, in which he scored 140* and shared with Damien Martyn (88*) in a new Australian record partnership for any wicket in ODIs (234*). Captain of Tasmania since 2001-02. One-day captain of Australia since February 2002; Test captain of Australia (the first from Tasmania) since January 2004. Scored 1503 Test runs (av. 100.20) and 1154 ODI runs (av. 46.16) in 2003. Was named *Wisden*'s inaugural Leading Cricketer in the World 2003. Was an overseas player with Somerset July to August 2004; has not returned for 2005. Scored century (112) on Championship debut for Somerset v Yorkshire at Scarborough 2004 and another (113) on totesport League debut, also v Yorkshire at Scarborough 2004
Best batting: 257 Australia v India, Melbourne 2003-04
Best bowling: 2-10 Australians v Mumbai, Mumbai 2000-01
Stop press: Scored fourth Test double century (207) in the third Test v Pakistan at Sydney 2004-05. Man of the Match in the fifth ODI v New Zealand at Napier 2004-05 (141*)

2004 Season

	M	Inns	NO	Runs	HS	Avge	100s	50s	Ct	St	O	M	Runs	Wkts	Avge	Best	5wI	10wM
Test																		
All First	3	4	1	297	117	99.00	2	1	7	-	5	2	6	0	-	-	-	-
1-day Int	4	4	1	55	29	18.33	-	-	-	-								
C & G																		
totesport	4	4	1	298	113	99.33	1	2	5	-								
Twenty20	1	1	0	20	20	20.00	-	-	-	-								

Career Performances

	M	Inns	NO	Runs	HS	Avge	100s	50s	Ct	St	Balls	Runs	Wkts	Avge	Best	5wI	10wM
Test	79	127	15	6086	257	54.33	20	22	91	-	437	190	4	47.50	1-0	-	-
All First	171	285	39	14219	257	57.80	52	55	173	-	1329	714	13	54.92	2-10	-	-
1-day Int	207	202	26	7360	145	41.81	15	41	82	-	144	104	3	34.66	1-12	-	
C & G																	
totesport	4	4	1	298	113	99.33	1	2	5	-							
Twenty20	1	1	0	20	20	20.00	-	-	-	-							

POTHAS, N. — Hampshire

Name: Nicolas (Nic) Pothas
Role: Right-hand bat, wicket-keeper
Born: 18 November 1973, Johannesburg, South Africa
Height: 6ft 1in **Weight:** 13st 7lbs
Nickname: Skeg
County debut: 2002
County cap: 2003
One-Day Internationals: 3
50 dismissals in a season: 1
1st-Class 50s: 30
1st-Class 100s: 12
1st-Class catches: 351
1st-Class stumpings: 33
Place in batting averages: 81st av. 39.71 (2003 51st av. 44.94)
Parents: Emmanuel and Penelope
Marital status: 'Very single'
Family links with cricket: 'Greek by nationality, therefore clearly none'
Education: King Edward VII High School; Rand Afrikaans University
Career outside cricket: 'Own two clothing businesses – 1) sport and corporate clothing; 2) fashion clothing. Own fabricare business in UK with my brother'

Overseas tours: South Africa A to England 1996, to Sri Lanka 1998-99, to West Indies 2000-01; Gauteng to Australia 1997; South Africa to Singapore (Singapore Challenge) 2000-01
Overseas teams played for: Transvaal/Gauteng 1993-94 – 2001-02
Career highlights to date: 'First tour for South Africa A. Playing for South Africa'
Cricket superstitions: 'Too many to mention'
Cricketers particularly admired: Ray Jennings, Jimmy Cook, Robin Smith
Young players to look out for: John Francis, Chris Tremlett
Other sports played: Hockey (South Africa U21, Transvaal)
Other sports followed: Football (Manchester United)
Favourite band: Counting Crows, Gin Blossoms, Just Jinger
Relaxations: 'Shopping; designing clothes; sleeping; gym'
Extras: Scored maiden first-class century (147) for South African Students v England tourists at Pietermaritzburg 1995-96. Benson and Hedges Young Player of the Year 1996. Transvaal Player of the Year 1996, 1998. Was stand-by wicket-keeper for South Africa's tour to West Indies 2000-01. Made 50 first-class dismissals in a season for the first time 2004, also scoring 834 first-class runs. Holds a Greek passport and is not considered an overseas player
Best batting: 165 Gauteng v KwaZulu-Natal, Johannesburg 1998-99

2004 Season

	M	Inns	NO	Runs	HS	Avge	100s	50s	Ct	St	O	M	Runs	Wkts	Avge	Best	5wI	10wM
Test																		
All First	16	24	3	834	131 *	39.71	3	4	45	5								
1-day Int																		
C & G	2	2	0	41	25	20.50	-	-	3	-								
totesport	13	13	4	395	83 *	43.88	-	3	11	6								
Twenty20	6	5	3	49	16 *	24.50	-	-	8	1								

Career Performances

	M	Inns	NO	Runs	HS	Avge	100s	50s	Ct	St	Balls	Runs	Wkts	Avge	Best	5wI	10wM
Test																	
All First	131	203	31	6130	165	35.63	12	30	351	33	6	5	0	-	-	-	-
1-day Int	3	1	0	24	24	24.00	-	-	4	1							
C & G	5	4	1	91	40	30.33	-	-	6	-							
totesport	37	33	15	959	83 *	53.27	-	7	40	9							
Twenty20	11	8	4	81	22 *	20.25	-	-	8	1							

POWELL, D. B. Derbyshire

Name: Daren Brentlyle Powell
Role: Right-hand bat, right-arm fast-medium bowler
Born: 15 April 1978, Malvern, St Elizabeth, Jamaica
County debut: 2004
Test debut: 2002
Tests: 4
One-Day Internationals: 2
1st-Class 5 w. in innings: 5
1st-Class catches: 13
Strike rate: 42.30 (career 51.83)
Overseas tours: West Indies A to England 2002; West Indies to India 2002-03, to Bangladesh 2002-03
Overseas teams played for: Gauteng 2003-04; Jamaica 2000-01 –
Extras: Man of the Match v Bangladesh A in the Busta Cup 2001-02 in Jamaica (3-39/5-37) and v West Indies B in the Carib Beer Cup 2002-03 also in Jamaica (5-34/2-36). Called up from local league cricket (Belper Meadows CC) as an overseas player for Derbyshire late May to June 2004, deputising for the injured Jonathan Moss and Chris Rogers
Best batting: 38 Jamaica v Bangladesh A, Spanish Town 2001-02
Best bowling: 6-49 Derbyshire v DUCCE, Derby 2004

2004 Season

	M	Inns	NO	Runs	HS	Avge	100s	50s	Ct	St	O	M	Runs	Wkts	Avge	Best	5wI	10wM
Test																		
All First	2	3	0	33	17	11.00	-	-	1	-	70.3	14	253	10	25.30	6-49	1	-
1-day Int																		
C & G																		
totesport	1	1	1	18	18 *	-	-	-	-	-	4	0	24	1	24.00	1-24	-	
Twenty20																		

Career Performances

	M	Inns	NO	Runs	HS	Avge	100s	50s	Ct	St	Balls	Runs	Wkts	Avge	Best	5wI	10wM
Test	4	5	0	19	16	3.80	-	-	1	-	770	354	12	29.50	3-36	-	-
All First	36	44	7	392	38	10.59	-	-	13	-	5495	2941	106	27.74	6-49	5	-
1-day Int	2	0	0	0	0	-	-	-	-	-	114	71	1	71.00	1-34	-	
C & G																	
totesport	1	1	1	18	18 *	-	-	-	-	-	24	24	1	24.00	1-24	-	
Twenty20																	

POWELL, M. J. Northamptonshire

Name: Mark John Powell
Role: Right-hand bat, right-arm medium bowler
Born: 4 November 1980, Northampton
Height: 5ft 11in **Weight:** 11st
Nickname: Piggy, Perfect, Powelly
County debut: 2000
1st-Class 50s: 4
1st-Class 100s: 2
1st-Class catches: 40
Place in batting averages: 219th av. 19.91 (2003 213th av. 21.47)
Parents: David and Philippa
Marital status: 'Girlfriend'
Education: Campion School, Bugbrooke, Northants; Loughborough University
Qualifications: 10 GCSEs, 3 A-levels, BSc (Hons) Information Management and Business Studies, Level 1 coach
Career outside cricket: Training to be a chartered accountant
Off-season: Working in London
Overseas tours: Northamptonshire U19 to South Africa 2000
Overseas teams played for: Rockingham-Mandurah, Western Australia 2002-03; Sutherland, Sydney 2003-04
Career highlights to date: 'Scoring maiden first-class hundred against Gloucestershire and breaking Northants opening partnership record at the same time. Captaining Loughborough to the "clean sweep" of university trophies for the second year running [2002]'
Cricket moments to forget: 'Bagging a pair on 2nd XI debut when 16'
Cricket superstitions: 'Always put right pad on first'
Cricketers particularly admired: Mike Hussey, Michael Vaughan, Rahul Dravid
Young players to look out for: Alex Wakely
Other sports played: Golf
Other sports followed: Football (Tottenham Hotspur), rugby union (Northampton Saints)
Injuries: Out for four weeks with a fractured knuckle
Favourite band: Matchbox Twenty
Relaxations: 'Cinema, watching sport'
Extras: Played for England U15 in inaugural U15 World Cup 1996. Played for Midlands U19 v Australia U19 1999. 2nd XI Player of the Month August/September 2000. Scored 50 in Loughborough University's BUSA Championship final win at

Fenner's 2000; captained Loughborough University to BUSA Championship and UCCE titles in 2001 and 2002. Scored century (124*) for Loughborough UCCE v Hampshire at West End 2002. Scored maiden first-class century (107) v Gloucestershire at Northampton 2002 in his third Championship match, in the process sharing with Rob White (277; also a maiden first-class century) in a new record opening partnership for Northamptonshire (375); followed up with a second century (108*) in next Championship match v Glamorgan at Cardiff. NBC Denis Compton Award for the most promising young Northamptonshire player 2003. Released by Northamptonshire at the end of the 2004 season

Opinions on cricket: 'Something has to be done about the number of foreigners in county cricket. If people are here to play for England then fine; if not, then why are we developing overseas players or lining the pockets of Kolpak players (*see page 9*) that are no better than the next guy?'

Best batting: 108* Northamptonshire v Glamorgan, Cardiff 2002

2004 Season

	M	Inns	NO	Runs	HS	Avge	100s	50s	Ct	St	O	M	Runs	Wkts	Avge	Best	5wI	10wM
Test																		
All First	7	12	0	239	49	19.91	-	-	2	-								
1-day Int																		
C & G																		
totesport	1	1	0	13	13	13.00	-	-	-	-								
Twenty20																		

Career Performances

	M	Inns	NO	Runs	HS	Avge	100s	50s	Ct	St	Balls	Runs	Wkts	Avge	Best	5wI	10wM
Test																	
All First	27	44	3	1024	108 *	24.97	2	4	40	-	12	12	0	-	-	-	-
1-day Int																	
C & G																	
totesport	13	12	1	241	70	21.90	-	2	3	-							
Twenty20																	

POWELL, M. J. — Warwickshire

Name: Michael James Powell
Role: Right-hand opening/middle-order bat, right-arm medium bowler
Born: 5 April 1975, Bolton
Height: 5ft 10in **Weight:** 12st 2lbs
Nickname: Arthur, Powelly
County debut: 1996
County cap: 1999
1000 runs in a season: 1

1st-Class 50s: 33
1st-Class 100s: 10
1st-Class 200s: 1
1st-Class catches: 81
One-Day 100s: 1
One-Day 5 w. in innings: 1
Place in batting averages: 61st av. 43.80 (2003 105th av. 34.27)
Strike rate: (career 112.80)
Parents: Terry and Pat
Marital status: Single
Family links with cricket: 'Father loves the game. Brother John played for Warwickshire youth teams'
Education: Lawrence Sheriff Grammar School, Rugby
Qualifications: 6 GCSEs, 2 A-levels, Levels I-III ECB coaching awards
Career outside cricket: 'Coaching – any other ideas would be welcome'
Off-season: 'South Africa'
Overseas tours: England U18 to South Africa 1992-93 (captain), to Denmark 1993 (captain); England U19 to Sri Lanka 1993-94; England A to West Indies 2000-01
Overseas teams played for: Avendale CC, Cape Town 1994-95, 1996-97, 2000-01; Griqualand West, South Africa 2001-02
Career highlights to date: 'B&H Cup winners 2002. Frizzell County Champions 2004'
Cricket moments to forget: 'My first pair against my old friend Gary Keedy v Lancs 2004'
Cricket superstitions: 'None'
Cricketers particularly admired: Dermot Reeve, Shaun Pollock, Allan Donald
Young players to look out for: Moeen Ali
Other sports played: Golf, rugby (Warwickshire U16-U18)
Other sports followed: Football
Favourite band: 'No band, just Robbie!! (Williams, that is)'
Relaxations: 'Enjoying just one glass of wine with my girlfriend Michelle'
Extras: Captained Warwickshire U14-U19. Captained England U17 and U18. Became first uncapped Warwickshire player for 49 years to carry his bat, for 70* out of 130 v Nottinghamshire at Edgbaston 1998. Scored 96 v Barbados at Bridgetown 2000-01, in the process sharing with Ian Ward (135) in a record opening stand for England A (224). Scored century (110) v Surrey at Guildford 2004, in the process equalling with Ian Bell (155) the ground record stand for any wicket against Surrey (214). Captain of Warwickshire 2001-03
Opinions on cricket: 'The England set-up is superb. If this is to be maintained, then two quality overseas players is a must, with nine English-born players learning from

them. "Kolpak" (*see page 9*) will do to English cricket what "quota system" is doing to South African first-class and Zimbabwean cricket.'
Best batting: 236 Warwickshire v OUCCE, The Parks 2001
Best bowling: 2-16 Warwickshire v Oxford University, The Parks 1998

2004 Season

	M	Inns	NO	Runs	HS	Avge	100s	50s	Ct	St	O	M	Runs	Wkts	Avge	Best	5wI	10wM
Test																		
All First	10	17	2	657	134	43.80	2	2	5	-	8	0	51	0	-	-	-	-
1-day Int																		
C & G																		
totesport	1	1	1	10	10 *	-	-	-	-	-								
Twenty20																		

Career Performances

	M	Inns	NO	Runs	HS	Avge	100s	50s	Ct	St	Balls	Runs	Wkts	Avge	Best	5wI	10wM
Test																	
All First	112	186	7	5903	236	32.97	11	33	81	-	1128	627	10	62.70	2-16	-	-
1-day Int																	
C & G	11	11	1	171	39	17.10	-	-	8	-	42	40	5	8.00	5-40	1	
totesport	59	47	7	987	78	24.67	-	2	25	-	467	415	14	29.64	3-44	-	
Twenty20																	

POWELL, M. J. Glamorgan

Name: Michael John Powell
Role: Right-hand bat
Born: 3 February 1977, Abergavenny
Height: 6ft 1in **Weight:** 14st 8lbs
Nickname: Powelly
County debut: 1997
County cap: 2000
1000 runs in a season: 3
1st-Class 50s: 35
1st-Class 100s: 15
1st-Class 200s: 1
1st-Class catches: 74
Place in batting averages: 103rd av. 36.00 (2003 64th av. 42.55)
Strike rate: (career 82.00)
Parents: Linda and John
Marital status: Single

Family links with cricket: 'Dad John and Uncle Mike both played for Abergavenny'
Education: Crickhowell Secondary School; Pontypool College
Qualifications: 5 GCSEs, BTEC National Diploma in Sports Science, Level 1 coaching award
Overseas tours: Glamorgan to Cape Town 1999, 2002; England A to Sri Lanka 2004-05
Overseas teams played for: Wests, Brisbane 1996-97; Cornwall CC, Auckland 1998-99, 2000-01
Cricket moments to forget: 'You wouldn't want to forget any of it'
Cricket superstitions: 'None'
Cricketers particularly admired: Adam Hollioake
Other sports played: Rugby (Crickhowell RFC)
Other sports followed: Rugby (Cardiff)
Relaxations: Eating and sleeping
Extras: Scored 200* on first-class debut v Oxford University at The Parks 1997, becoming the youngest player (20 years 122 days) to score a first-class double century for Glamorgan. Scored 1210 runs at 75.63 in the 1997 2nd XI Championship and was 2nd XI Championship Player of the Year. NBC Denis Compton Award for the most promising young Glamorgan player 2000. Acted as 12th man in the third Test v Sri Lanka at Old Trafford 2002, taking the catch that ended Sri Lanka's second innings and left England with a victory target of 50 runs in six overs. Scored century in each innings (125/142) v Worcestershire at Cardiff 2003. Included in England one-day squad for NatWest Series 2004 and in preliminary England one-day squad of 30 for ICC Champions Trophy 2004. ECB National Academy 2004-05
Best batting: 200* Glamorgan v Oxford University, The Parks 1997
Best bowling: 2-39 Glamorgan v Oxford University, The Parks 1999

2004 Season

	M	Inns	NO	Runs	HS	Avge	100s	50s	Ct	St	O	M	Runs	Wkts	Avge	Best	5wI	10wM
Test																		
All First	16	27	2	900	124	36.00	1	7	14	-								
1-day Int																		
C & G	2	2	0	19	17	9.50	-	-	1	-	4	0	26	1	26.00	1-26	-	
totesport	16	16	1	411	73	27.40	-	3	4	-								
Twenty20	6	6	0	53	19	8.83	-	-	3	-								

Career Performances

	M	Inns	NO	Runs	HS	Avge	100s	50s	Ct	St	Balls	Runs	Wkts	Avge	Best	5wI	10wM
Test																	
All First	119	197	18	6996	200 *	39.08	16	35	74	-	164	132	2	66.00	2-39	-	-
1-day Int																	
C & G	13	13	2	167	52	15.18	-	1	5	-	24	26	1	26.00	1-26	-	
totesport	110	103	15	2603	91 *	29.57	-	12	35	-							
Twenty20	10	10	1	149	66 *	16.55	-	1	5	-							

PRATT, A. Durham

Name: Andrew Pratt
Role: Left-hand bat, wicket-keeper
Born: 4 March 1975, Bishop Auckland
Height: 5ft 11in **Weight:** 12st
Nickname: The Claw
County debut: 1997
County cap: 2001
50 dismissals in a season: 1
1st-Class 50s: 10
1st-Class catches: 150
1st-Class stumpings: 12
Place in batting averages: 158th av. 28.09 (2003 248th av. 15.50)
Parents: Gordon and Brenda
Wife: Laura
Family links with cricket: One brother was with MCC Young Cricketers for four years. Younger brother Gary also plays for Durham. Father played for many years in Durham
Education: Willington Parkside Comprehensive School; Durham New College

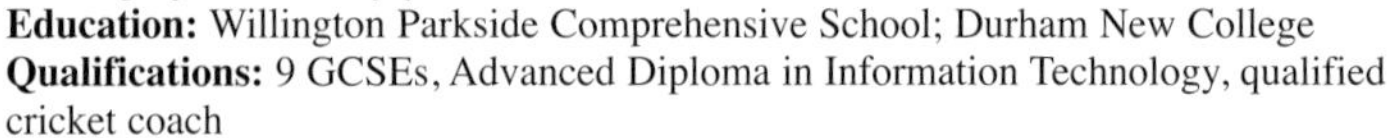

Qualifications: 9 GCSEs, Advanced Diploma in Information Technology, qualified cricket coach
Overseas tours: Durham Academy to Sri Lanka
Overseas teams played for: Hallam, Melbourne 1997-98
Career highlights to date: 'Making debut for Durham'
Cricketers particularly admired: Alan Knott, Jack Russell
Other sports followed: Football (Middlesbrough FC)
Relaxations: 'Music, drinking'
Extras: Played for Durham County Schools at all levels and for the North of England U15. Played for MCC Young Cricketers for three years. He and brother Gary became the first brothers to play in a Championship match for Durham, against Lancashire at Old Trafford 2000. Durham Player of the Year 2001
Best batting: 93 Durham v Gloucestershire, Riverside 2002

2004 Season

	M	Inns	NO	Runs	HS	Avge	100s	50s	Ct	St	O	M	Runs	Wkts	Avge	Best	5wI	10wM
Test																		
All First	14	25	3	618	68	28.09	-	4	33	2								
1-day Int																		
C & G	1	1	0	44	44	44.00	-	-	3	1								
totesport	18	12	1	196	53	17.81	-	1	18	2								
Twenty20	5	5	0	74	35	14.80	-	-	2	2								

Career Performances

	M	Inns	NO	Runs	HS	Avge	100s	50s	Ct	St	Balls	Runs	Wkts	Avge	Best	5wI	10wM
Test																	
All First	62	105	14	1974	93	21.69	-	10	150	12							
1-day Int																	
C & G	7	5	1	96	44	24.00	-	-	13	2							
totesport	63	49	10	769	86	19.71	-	4	67	18							
Twenty20	5	5	0	74	35	14.80	-	-	2	2							

PRATT, G. J. Durham

Name: Gary Joseph Pratt
Role: Left-hand bat, right-arm spin bowler, wicket-keeper ('if I need to')
Born: 22 December 1981, Bishop Auckland
Height: 5ft 10in **Weight:** 10st 7lbs
Nickname: Gonzo, Gazza, Gates
County debut: 2000
1000 runs in a season: 1
1st-Class 50s: 14
1st-Class 100s: 1
1st-Class catches: 32
One-Day 100s: 1
Place in batting averages: 224th av. 19.05 (2003 119th av. 32.96)
Parents: Gordon and Brenda
Marital status: Single
Family links with cricket: Father played for many years in Durham and one brother was on Lord's groundstaff (MCC Young Cricketers). Brother Andrew also plays for Durham
Education: Parkside Comprehensive
Qualifications: 9 GCSEs
Overseas tours: England U19 to Malaysia and (U19 World Cup) Sri Lanka 1999-2000, to India 2000-01
Overseas teams played for: Melville, Perth 2001-02
Career highlights to date: 'Scoring first first-class 150 v Northants 2003 at Riverside'
Cricket moments to forget: 'Getting my first pair in my cricket career v Gloucestershire'
Cricket superstitions: 'Right pad first'
Cricketers particularly admired: Steve Waugh, Graham Thorpe, David Gower

Young players to look out for: Liam Plunkett, Mark Turner
Other sports played: Golf (14 handicap)
Other sports followed: Football ('all northern teams')
Favourite band: Stereophonics
Relaxations: 'Golf, TV, singing, socialising'
Extras: Represented England U17 and U19. NBC Denis Compton Award 1999. On his first-class debut, against Lancashire at Old Trafford 2000, he and brother Andrew became the first brothers to play in a Championship match for Durham. Durham Player of the Year 2002. Durham Fielder of the Year 2002, 2003. Scored 79-ball hundred (101*; his maiden county century) v Somerset at Taunton 2003 to equal then record for the fastest one-day league century by a Durham player. Durham Young Player of the Year 2003
Opinions on cricket: 'Too many games; not enough prep. Two-hour sessions would be good, after all it's quality not quantity.'
Best batting: 150 Durham v Northamptonshire, Riverside 2003

2004 Season

	M	Inns	NO	Runs	HS	Avge	100s	50s	Ct	St	O	M	Runs	Wkts	Avge	Best	5wI	10wM
Test																		
All First	9	17	0	324	71	19.05	-	2	7	-	2	0	2	0	-	-	-	-
1-day Int																		
C & G	1	1	0	10	10	10.00	-	-	-	-								
totesport	18	15	4	396	67 *	36.00	-	4	10	-								
Twenty20	5	5	1	83	36	20.75	-	-	2	-								

Career Performances

	M	Inns	NO	Runs	HS	Avge	100s	50s	Ct	St	Balls	Runs	Wkts	Avge	Best	5wI	10wM
Test																	
All First	47	84	1	2217	150	26.71	1	14	32	-	33	19	0	-	-	-	-
1-day Int																	
C & G	6	6	1	154	89	30.80	-	1	-	-							
totesport	51	47	12	1212	101 *	34.62	1	9	27	-							
Twenty20	10	10	2	179	62 *	22.37	-	1	3	-							

69. Which Kenya player picked up 13 wickets at 28.76, including 5-24 v Sri Lanka at Nairobi, in the 2002-03 World Cup, a performance that led to a one-year contract with Warwickshire?

PRETORIUS, D. Warwickshire

Name: Dewald Pretorius
Role: Right-hand bat, right-arm fast bowler
Born: 6 December 1977, Pretoria, South Africa
County debut: 2003 (Durham), 2004 (Warwickshire)
Test debut: 2001-02
Tests: 4
1st-Class 5 w. in innings: 7
1st-Class catches: 13
Place in batting averages: (2003 290th av. 7.00)
Place in bowling averages: 115th av. 39.00 (2003 77th av. 33.19)
Strike rate: 61.25 (career 48.64)
Overseas tours: South African Academy to Ireland and Scotland 1999; South Africa A to Australia 2002-03; South Africa to England 2003
Overseas teams played for: Free State 1998-99 – 2003-04

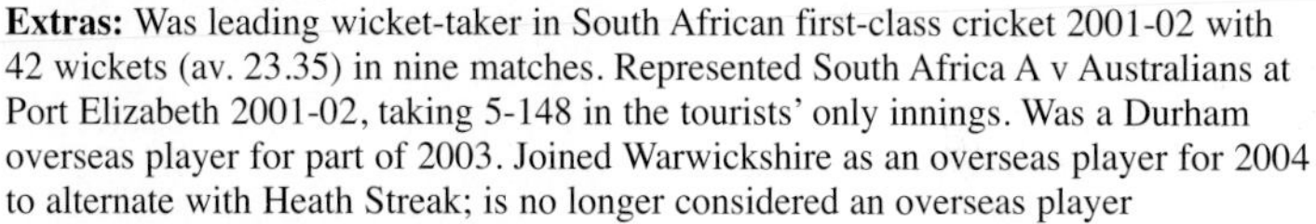

Extras: Was leading wicket-taker in South African first-class cricket 2001-02 with 42 wickets (av. 23.35) in nine matches. Represented South Africa A v Australians at Port Elizabeth 2001-02, taking 5-148 in the tourists' only innings. Was a Durham overseas player for part of 2003. Joined Warwickshire as an overseas player for 2004 to alternate with Heath Streak; is no longer considered an overseas player
Best batting: 43 Free State v Western Province, Bloemfontein 1998-99
Best bowling: 6-49 South Africa A v India A, Bloemfontein 2001-02

2004 Season

	M	Inns	NO	Runs	HS	Avge	100s	50s	Ct	St	O	M	Runs	Wkts	Avge	Best	5wI	10wM
Test																		
All First	9	6	3	31	14	10.33	-	-	1	-	245	43	936	24	39.00	4-119	-	-
1-day Int																		
C & G	2	0	0	0	0	-	-	-	1	-	20	3	71	5	14.20	3-43	-	
totesport	7	5	0	2	2	0.40	-	-	3	-	48	5	249	11	22.63	4-36	-	
Twenty20	2	0	0	0	0	-	-	-	1	-	5	0	40	2	20.00	2-27	-	

Career Performances

	M	Inns	NO	Runs	HS	Avge	100s	50s	Ct	St	Balls	Runs	Wkts	Avge	Best	5wI	10wM
Test	4	4	1	22	9	7.33	-	-	-	-	570	430	6	71.66	4-115	-	-
All First	61	65	17	452	43	9.41	-	-	13	-	10654	5866	219	26.78	6-49	7	-
1-day Int																	
C & G	3	1	0	2	2	2.00	-	-	1	-	180	103	8	12.87	3-32	-	
totesport	10	6	1	9	7 *	1.80	-	-	4	-	416	314	19	16.52	4-31	-	
Twenty20	2	0	0	0	0	-	-	-	1	-	30	40	2	20.00	2-27	-	

PRICE, R. W. Worcestershire

Name: Raymond (Ray) William Price
Role: Right-hand bat, slow left-arm spin bowler
Born: 12 June 1976, Harare, Zimbabwe
Height: 6ft 1in **Weight:** 13st
Nickname: Razor, Razorback
County debut: 2004
County colours: 2004
Test debut: 1999-2000
Tests: 18
One-Day Internationals: 26
1st-Class 50s: 6
1st-Class 100s: 1
1st-Class 5 w. in innings: 15
1st-Class 10 w. in match: 3
1st-Class catches: 18
Place in bowling averages: 121st av. 42.00
Strike rate: 101.50 (career 69.44)
Parents: Tim and Pam
Wife and date of marriage: Julie, 13 July 2003
Family links with cricket: Father captained Zimbabwe Schools XI
Education: Watershed College, Zimbabwe
Qualifications: 7 GCEs, 2 A-levels, refrigeration and air conditioning mechanic
Career outside cricket: 'Fishing'
Off-season: 'Fishing'
Overseas tours: Zimbabwe A to Sri Lanka 1999-2000, to Kenya 2001-02; Zimbabwe to India 2001-02, to Sri Lanka (ICC Champions Trophy) 2002-03, to Sharjah (Cherry Blossom Sharjah Cup) 2002-03, to England 2003, to Australia 2003-04
Overseas teams played for: Midlands, Zimbabwe 1996-2003; Old Hararians 1994-2005
Career highlights to date: 'Six wickets v Australia at Sydney 2003-04. Tendulkar twice in same Test' (*In the second Test v India at Delhi 2001-02*)

Cricket moments to forget: 'Missed stumping off first ball in Test cricket'
Cricket superstitions: 'None'
Cricketers particularly admired: Steve Waugh, Heath Streak, Andy Flower, Sachin Tendulkar, Shane Warne
Young players to look out for: Brendan Taylor (Zimbabwe)
Other sports played: Tennis, squash, golf
Other sports followed: BASS League USA (Jerry Joost)
Favourite band: Dire Straits
Relaxations: Fishing, walking
Extras: Took 33 wickets in six Tests 2003-04, including 6-121 in Australia's first innings of the second Test at Sydney and 19 wickets (av. 20.84) in two-Test home series v West Indies. Zimbabwe Cricketer of the Year. Is nephew of golfer Nick Price. Is not considered an overseas player
Opinions on cricket: 'Twenty20 should be played at schools to get more young people interested.'
Best batting: 117* Midlands v Manicaland, Mutare 2003-04
Best bowling: 8-35 Midlands v CFX Academy, Kwekwe 2001-02

2004 Season

	M	Inns	NO	Runs	HS	Avge	100s	50s	Ct	St	O	M	Runs	Wkts	Avge	Best	5wI	10wM
Test																		
All First	3	5	2	146	76 *	48.66	-	1	1	-	169.1	50	420	10	42.00	4-83	-	-
1-day Int																		
C & G	1	1	1	2	2 *	-	-	-	-	-	9	0	51	1	51.00	1-51	-	
totesport	3	0	0	0	0	-	-	-	-	-	11	1	64	2	32.00	2-48	-	
Twenty20																		

Career Performances

	M	Inns	NO	Runs	HS	Avge	100s	50s	Ct	St	Balls	Runs	Wkts	Avge	Best	5wI	10wM
Test	18	30	7	224	36	9.73	-	-	3	-	5135	2475	69	35.86	6-73	5	1
All First	61	101	19	1401	117 *	17.08	1	6	18	-	15626	7206	225	32.02	8-35	15	3
1-day Int	26	12	5	90	20 *	12.85	-	-	1	-	1322	917	15	61.13	2-16	-	
C & G	1	1	1	2	2 *	-	-	-	-	-	54	51	1	51.00	1-51	-	
totesport	3	0	0	0	0	-	-	-	-	-	66	64	2	32.00	2-48	-	
Twenty20																	

70. Who was Scotland's captain (and the Man of the Match) when they gained their first victory in the B&H Cup, by three runs over Lancashire at Perth in 1986?

PRIOR, M. J. Sussex

Name: Matthew (Matt) James Prior
Role: Right-hand bat, wicket-keeper
Born: 26 February 1982, Johannesburg, South Africa
Height: 5ft 11in **Weight:** 13st
Nickname: MP, Cheese
County debut: 2001
County cap: 2003
1000 runs in a season: 2
1st-Class 50s: 18
1st-Class 100s: 7
1st-Class 200s: 1
1st-Class catches: 135
1st-Class stumpings: 6
One-Day 100s: 1
Place in batting averages: 52nd av. 46.32 (2003 33rd av. 47.90)
Parents: Michael and Teresa
Marital status: Single
Education: Brighton College, East Sussex
Qualifications: 9 GCSEs, 3 A-levels, Level 1 coaching certificate
Off-season: ECB National Academy
Overseas tours: Brighton College to India 1997-98; Sussex Academy to Cape Town 1999; Sussex to Grenada 2001, 2002; England A to Malaysia and India 2003-04, to Sri Lanka 2004-05; England to Zimbabwe (one-day series) 2004-05
Cricket moments to forget: 'Falling on to stumps at the Rose Bowl on Sky TV!'
Cricket superstitions: 'Too many to name all of them'
Cricketers particularly admired: Steve Waugh, Alec Stewart, Mushtaq Ahmed, Murray Goodwin
Young players to look out for: Bilal Shafayat, Michael Lumb
Other sports played: Golf
Other sports followed: Football (Arsenal), golf, rugby
Favourite band: Red Hot Chili Peppers
Relaxations: 'Gym, listening to music'
Extras: Has played for Sussex since U12. Represented England U14-U19, captaining England U17. Attended Sussex Academy. NBC Denis Compton Award for the most promising young Sussex player 2001, 2002, 2003. Umer Rashid Award for Most Improved [Sussex] Player 2003. Scored maiden first-class double century (201*) v Loughborough University CCE at Hove 2004. ECB National Academy 2003-04, 2004-05
Opinions on cricket: 'The game is moving forward at a rapid rate – e.g. training techniques, work ethics etc. – and until everyone grasps hold of this idea then the

game will stand still. There is so much scope for one and two per cent improvements in all areas, which makes it a very exciting game to be associated with.'
Best batting: 201* Sussex v LUCCE, Hove 2004
Stop press: Made ODI debut in the fourth ODI v Zimbabwe at Bulawayo 2004-05

2004 Season

	M	Inns	NO	Runs	HS	Avge	100s	50s	Ct	St	O	M	Runs	Wkts	Avge	Best	5wI	10wM
Test																		
All First	18	26	1	1158	201 *	46.32	3	6	25	2								
1-day Int																		
C & G	2	2	0	28	20	14.00	-	-	4	-								
totesport	18	18	2	641	119	40.06	1	4	12	2								
Twenty20	4	4	1	117	68 *	39.00	-	1	1	1								

Career Performances

	M	Inns	NO	Runs	HS	Avge	100s	50s	Ct	St	Balls	Runs	Wkts	Avge	Best	5wI	10wM
Test																	
All First	69	107	10	3648	201 *	37.60	8	18	135	6							
1-day Int																	
C & G	9	8	0	88	34	11.00	-	-	12	-							
totesport	55	47	5	1000	119	23.80	1	6	28	5							
Twenty20	9	9	1	204	68 *	25.50	-	1	6	1							

PRITTIPAUL, L. R. — Hampshire

Name: Lawrence Roland Prittipaul
Role: Right-hand bat, right-arm medium-fast bowler; all-rounder
Born: 19 October 1979, Portsmouth
Height: 6ft **Weight:** 12st 7lbs
Nickname: Lozza, Lawrie, Throat
County debut: 1999 (one-day), 2000 (first-class)
1st-Class 50s: 4
1st-Class 100s: 1
1st-Class catches: 17
Place in batting averages: 172nd av. 25.66
Strike rate: 126.00 (career 84.33)
Parents: Roland and Christine
Marital status: Single
Family links with cricket: Cousin Shivnarine Chanderpaul plays for West Indies
Education: St John's College, Southsea

Qualifications: GCSEs, GNVQ, Level 2 coaching, first aid
Career outside cricket: 'Working for Fleet UK car sales/Exbury Developments'
Off-season: 'Going to Melbourne'
Overseas tours: Hampshire to Cape Town 2001; MCC to Sierra Leone and Nigeria 2003
Overseas teams played for: Milnerton, Cape Town 2000-02; Old Edwardian (Old Eds), Johannesburg 2003; Rockingham, Perth 2003-04
Career highlights to date: '152 v Derbyshire on home debut'
Cricketers particularly admired: Carl Hooper, Shane Warne
Young players to look out for: David Griffiths, Archie Ayling, Deano Wilson
Other sports played: Football
Other sports followed: Football ('Pompey!!')
Favourite band: Counting Crows
Relaxations: 'Films, spending time with friends, holidays'
Extras: Played for Hants Colts from age 11 to 18. Represented England U17. Won Player of the Year award in Southern League 1998. Scored over 1000 runs for Hants 2nd XI in 1999. Scored 152 on home debut, v Derbyshire at Southampton 2000, breaking Dennis Baldry's Hampshire home Championship debut record of 151 set in 1959. Hampshire Young Player of the Year 2000
Opinions on cricket: 'More games need to end in results – need to play to win more.'
Best batting: 152 Hampshire v Derbyshire, Southampton 2000
Best bowling: 3-17 Hampshire v Worcestershire, West End 2003

2004 Season

	M	Inns	NO	Runs	HS	Avge	100s	50s	Ct	St	O	M	Runs	Wkts	Avge	Best	5wI	10wM
Test																		
All First	5	9	0	231	49	25.66	-	-	3	-	21	4	71	1	71.00	1-14	-	-
1-day Int																		
C & G	1	1	0	1	1	1.00	-	-	1	-	4	0	11	3	3.66	3-11	-	
totesport	8	7	0	87	26	12.42	-	-	-	-	5	0	38	1	38.00	1-23	-	
Twenty20	3	2	0	13	11	6.50	-	-	-	-								

Career Performances

	M	Inns	NO	Runs	HS	Avge	100s	50s	Ct	St	Balls	Runs	Wkts	Avge	Best	5wI	10wM
Test																	
All First	23	36	2	975	152	28.67	1	4	17	-	759	443	9	49.22	3-17	-	-
1-day Int																	
C & G	5	5	0	76	30	15.20	-	-	4	-	180	136	7	19.42	3-11	-	
totesport	52	40	5	462	61	13.20	-	1	13	-	748	697	15	46.46	3-33	-	
Twenty20	6	4	0	30	15	7.50	-	-	2	-	59	67	2	33.50	2-17	-	

PYRAH, R. M. Yorkshire

Name: Richard (Rich) Michael Pyrah
Role: Right-hand bat, right-arm medium bowler
Born: 1 November 1982, Dewsbury
Height: 6ft **Weight:** 12st
Nickname: RP, Pyro
County debut: 2004
One-Day 5 w. in innings: 1
Place in batting averages: 168th av. 26.33
Parents: Mick and Lesley
Marital status: Single
Family links with cricket: 'Dad and Grandad both played for Ossett CC'
Education: Ossett High School; Wakefield College
Qualifications: 10 GCSEs, Level 1 coaching
Off-season: 'Decorating new apartment'
Overseas teams played for: Kaponga, New Zealand 2000-2002; Taranaki, New Zealand 2003-04
Career highlights to date: 'Making my debut for Yorkshire on Sky. Man of the Match in my second NCL game at Scarborough'
Cricket moments to forget: 'First ever pair!'
Cricket superstitions: 'Left pad on first. Bat in some whites'
Cricketers particularly admired: Michael Vaughan, Matthew Wood
Young players to look out for: Mark Lawson, John Sadler
Other sports played: Golf
Other sports followed: Football (Leeds United)
Injuries: Out for two weeks pre-season with a calf strain
Favourite band: Oasis, Evanescence
Relaxations: Xbox
Extras: Played for Yorkshire Board XI in the C&G 2001, 2002 and 2003, winning Man of the Match award for his 5-50 (plus 26 runs) v Somerset at Scarborough in the third round 2002
Opinions on cricket: 'Second XI cricket should be played on better playing surfaces. No EU players allowed as it prevents young players coming through.'
Best batting: 39 Yorkshire v Somerset, Taunton 2004

2004 Season

	M	Inns	NO	Runs	HS	Avge	100s	50s	Ct	St	O	M	Runs	Wkts	Avge	Best	5wI	10wM
Test																		
All First	4	7	1	158	39	26.33	-	-	-	-	6	4	2	0	-	-	-	-
1-day Int																		
C & G																		
totesport	2	2	0	44	42	22.00	-	-	-	-	5	0	17	2	8.50	2-17	-	
Twenty20																		

Career Performances

	M	Inns	NO	Runs	HS	Avge	100s	50s	Ct	St	Balls	Runs	Wkts	Avge	Best	5wI	10wM
Test																	
All First	4	7	1	158	39	26.33	-	-	-	-	36	2	0	-	-	-	-
1-day Int																	
C & G	4	4	0	106	27	26.50	-	-	2	-	102	98	7	14.00	5-50	1	
totesport	2	2	0	44	42	22.00	-	-	-	-	30	17	2	8.50	2-17	-	
Twenty20																	

RAMPRAKASH, M. R. — Surrey

Name: Mark Ravindra Ramprakash
Role: Right-hand bat, right arm off-spin bowler, county vice-captain
Born: 5 September 1969, Bushey, Herts
Height: 5ft 10in **Weight:** 12st 4lbs
Nickname: Ramps, Bloodaxe
County debut: 1987 (Middlesex), 2001 (Surrey)
County cap: 1990 (Middlesex), 2002 (Surrey)
Benefit: 2000 (Middlesex)
Test debut: 1991
Tests: 52
One-Day Internationals: 18
1000 runs in a season: 14
1st-Class 50s: 116
1st-Class 100s: 64
1st-Class 200s: 9
1st-Class catches: 201
One-Day 100s: 11
One-Day 5 w. in innings: 1
Place in batting averages: 7th av. 65.16 (2003 4th av. 76.00)

Strike rate: 72.00 (career 122.14)
Parents: Deonarine and Jennifer
Date of marriage: 24 September 1993
Children: Two
Family links with cricket: Father played club cricket in Guyana
Education: Gayton High School; Harrow Weald Sixth Form College
Qualifications: 6 O-levels, 2 A-levels, Level 3 cricket coach, Level 2 FA football coach, 'in first year of Level 4 cricket coaching course'
Off-season: 'Time with family; training; Level 4 course; coach at Surrey Academy'
Overseas tours: England YC to Sri Lanka 1986-87, to Australia (U19 World Cup) 1987-88; England A to Pakistan 1990-91, to West Indies 1991-92, to India 1994-95 (vice-captain); Lion Cubs to Barbados 1993; England to New Zealand 1991-92, to West Indies 1993-94, to Australia 1994-95, to South Africa 1995-96, to West Indies 1997-98, to Australia 1998-99, to South Africa 1999-2000, to Zimbabwe (one-day series) 2001-02, to India and New Zealand 2001-02
Overseas teams played for: Nairobi Jafferys, Kenya 1988; North Melbourne 1989; University of Perth 1996-97; Clico-Preysal, Trinidad 2004
Career highlights to date: 'My two Test hundreds, v West Indies and Australia'
Cricket moments to forget: 'There are so many bad days!'
Cricket superstitions: 'Same piece of chewing gum in innings'
Cricketers particularly admired: 'All the great all-rounders'; Alec Stewart
Young players to look out for: Arun Harinath
Other sports played: Football (Corinthian Casuals FC, Arsenal Pro-Celeb XI)
Other sports followed: Football (Arsenal FC)
Favourite band: 'Have lost touch!'
Relaxations: 'Taking up golf; my two children'
Extras: Played for Middlesex 2nd XI aged 16 and made first-team debut for Middlesex aged 17. Voted Best U15 Schoolboy of 1985 by Cricket Society (Sir John Hobbs Silver Jubilee Memorial Prize), Best Young Cricketer of 1986 and Cricket Society's Most Promising Young Cricketer of the Year in 1988. Man of the Match for his 56 in Middlesex's NatWest Trophy final win in 1988, on his debut in the competition. Represented England YC. Scored century in each innings (100*/125) v Kent at Canterbury 1990, becoming (at 20 years 325 days) the youngest batsman to score twin centuries in the Championship. Won Cricket Writers' Young Cricketer of the Year award 1991. Finished top of the Whyte and Mackay batting ratings 1995 and 1997. Middlesex captain May 1997 to the end of the 1999 season. Scored maiden Test century (154) v West Indies at Bridgetown 1997-98, sharing in a record sixth-wicket partnership for England in Tests v West Indies (205) with Graham Thorpe and winning Man of the Match award. Leading run-scorer in the single-division four-day era of the County Championship with 8392 runs (av. 56.32) 1993-99. Scored two centuries (110*/112) in match v Sussex at Southgate 2000 to become the first Middlesex player to record 100s in each innings of a game on four occasions. Left Middlesex in the 2000-01 off-season and joined Surrey for 2001; his career average with Middlesex was 50.49, second only to that of Mike Gatting. Scored century (146) on Championship debut for Surrey v Kent at The Oval 2001. Became first player to score a

Championship century against all 18 first-class counties with his 110 v Middlesex at Lord's 2003. Scored century in each innings of a Championship match (130/100*) for the fifth time, v Worcestershire at The Oval 2004. Surrey Players' Player of the Year 2003, 2004; Surrey Supporters' Player of the Year 2003, 2004. Vice-captain of Surrey since 2004
Opinions on cricket: 'Now that England are playing well, why are so many demanding a radical overhaul of the county system? I enjoy the current status quo, with the positives far outweighing the negatives.'
Best batting: 279* Surrey v Nottinghamshire, Croydon 2003
Best bowling: 3-32 Middlesex v Glamorgan, Lord's 1998

2004 Season

	M	Inns	NO	Runs	HS	Avge	100s	50s	Ct	St	O	M	Runs	Wkts	Avge	Best	5wI	10wM
Test																		
All First	17	29	5	1564	161	65.16	7	6	7	-	24	4	68	2	34.00	2-35	-	-
1-day Int																		
C & G	1	1	0	34	34	34.00	-	-	-	-								
totesport	13	13	0	285	73	21.92	-	2	2	-								
Twenty20	7	7	2	216	76 *	43.20	-	1	4	-								

Career Performances

	M	Inns	NO	Runs	HS	Avge	100s	50s	Ct	St	Balls	Runs	Wkts	Avge	Best	5wI	10wM
Test	52	92	6	2350	154	27.32	2	12	39	-	895	477	4	119.25	1-2	-	-
All First	357	589	75	24787	279 *	48.22	73	116	201	-	4153	2172	34	63.88	3-32	-	-
1-day Int	18	18	4	376	51	26.85	-	1	8	-	132	108	4	27.00	3-28	-	
C & G	40	39	3	1315	107 *	36.52	3	5	20	-	396	255	10	25.50	2-15	-	
totesport	208	199	34	6842	147 *	41.46	6	51	62	-	558	503	17	29.58	5-38	1	
Twenty20	14	14	4	321	76 *	32.10	-	2	7	-							

71. Who is the only Kenya player to have scored 1000 runs and taken 50 wickets in ODIs?

RANKIN, W. B. — Middlesex

Name: William Boyd Rankin
Role: Left-hand bat, right-arm medium-fast bowler
Born: 5 July 1984, Londonderry
Height: 6ft 8in **Weight:** 17st 4lbs
County debut: No first-team appearance
Parents: Robert and Dawn
Marital status: Single
Family links with cricket: 'Both brothers – Robert and David – play for Ireland under-age teams'
Education: Strabane Grammar School; Harper Adams University College
Qualifications: Level 1 cricket coach
Career outside cricket: Farmer/student
Off-season: University
Overseas tours: Ireland U19 to Bangladesh (U19 World Cup) 2003-04
Career highlights to date: 'Playing for Middlesex; U19 World Cup; and senior debut for Ireland'
Cricket superstitions: 'None'
Cricketers particularly admired: Glenn McGrath, Curtly Ambrose
Young players to look out for: Eoin Morgan
Other sports played: 'Did play rugby; not any more'
Other sports followed: Football (Liverpool FC)
Favourite band: Coldplay
Interests/relaxations: 'Sport in general'
Extras: Attended European Cricket Academy in Spain

72. Which former male model took 5-73 on his Test debut for Zimbabwe and had a brief spell with Durham?

READ, C. M. W. Nottinghamshire

Name: Christopher (Chris) Mark Wells Read
Role: Right-hand bat, wicket-keeper
Born: 10 August 1978, Paignton
Height: 5ft 8in **Weight:** 11st
Nickname: Readie, Reados
County debut: 1997 (one-day, Glos), 1998 (Notts)
County cap: 1999 (Notts)
Test debut: 1999
Tests: 11
One-Day Internationals: 28
50 dismissals in a season: 2
1st-Class 50s: 26
1st-Class 100s: 4
1st-Class catches: 378
1st-Class stumpings: 20
One-Day 100s: 1
Place in batting averages: 38th av. 50.43 (2003 132nd av. 30.95)
Parents: Geoffrey and Carolyn
Wife and date of marriage: Louise, 2 October 2004
Family links with cricket: 'Dad is now "chairman of selectors" at Paignton CC!'
Education: Torquay Boys' Grammar School; University of Bath; Loughborough University
Qualifications: 9 GCSEs, 4 A-levels, senior coaching award
Off-season: 'Touring with England'
Overseas tours: West of England U13 to Holland 1991; West of England U15 to West Indies 1992-93; England U17 to Holland (International Youth Tournament) 1995; England U19 to Pakistan 1996-97; England A to Kenya and Sri Lanka 1997-98, to Zimbabwe and South Africa 1998-99, to West Indies 2000-01; England to South Africa and Zimbabwe 1999-2000, to Australia 2002-03 (VB Series), to Bangladesh and Sri Lanka 2003-04, to West Indies 2003-04, to South Africa 2004-05; British Universities to South Africa 2002; ECB National Academy to Australia and Sri Lanka 2002-03
Career highlights to date: 'Winning Test series v West Indies 2004'
Cricket moments to forget: 'Ducking a slower ball from Chris Cairns in second Test v New Zealand at Lord's 1999'
Cricketers particularly admired: Adam Gilchrist, Bruce French, Alan Knott, Bob Taylor, Jack Russell, Ian Healy
Young players to look out for: James Hildreth
Other sports played: Hockey (Devon U18, U21; West of England U17; South Nottingham)

Other sports followed: Football (Torquay United)
Favourite band: Stereophonics
Relaxations: 'Reading, listening to music, keeping fit and going out with friends'
Extras: Played for Devon 1995-97. Represented England U18 1996 and England U19 1997. Was selected for the England A tour to Kenya and Sri Lanka 1997-98 aged 18 and without having played a first-class game. Joined Nottinghamshire for 1998 season. Recorded eight dismissals on Test debut in the first Test v New Zealand at Edgbaston 1999. Leading wicket-keeper in English first-class cricket 2002 with 68 dismissals (also scored 797 runs at 34.65). Scored 79* v Sussex at Trent Bridge in the NCL 2003, sharing with Chris Cairns (91*) in a new record sixth-wicket partnership for the one-day league (167*). Man of the Match in the first ODI v West Indies at Georgetown 2003-04 after striking a match-winning 15-ball 27 including three sixes and a four
Opinions on cricket: 'Can't understand why we still have a red ball one-day competition. Temporary floodlights at domestic day/night games (totesport League) often inadequate. Too many non-English-qualified players!'
Best batting: 160 Nottinghamshire v Warwickshire, Trent Bridge 1999

2004 Season

	M	Inns	NO	Runs	HS	Avge	100s	50s	Ct	St	O	M	Runs	Wkts	Avge	Best	5wI	10wM
Test																		
All First	13	18	2	807	130	50.43	2	6	35	3								
1-day Int																		
C & G	2	2	1	123	77 *	123.00	-	1	1	1								
totesport	14	11	2	210	45	23.33	-	-	10	8								
Twenty20	5	5	1	104	34 *	26.00	-	-	5	1								

Career Performances

	M	Inns	NO	Runs	HS	Avge	100s	50s	Ct	St	Balls	Runs	Wkts	Avge	Best	5wI	10wM
Test	11	16	3	199	38 *	15.30	-	-	31	4							
All First	139	212	32	5082	160	28.23	4	26	378	20	18	25	0	-	-	-	-
1-day Int	28	17	6	239	30 *	21.72	-	-	36	2							
C & G	16	13	4	318	77 *	35.33	-	2	14	7							
totesport	100	84	19	1703	119 *	26.20	1	3	107	26							
Twenty20	5	5	1	104	34 *	26.00	-	-	5	1							

73. Which former Leicestershire, Hampshire and Ireland all-rounder won three Man of the Match awards at the 1999 World Cup?

REES, G. P. — Glamorgan

Name: Gareth Peter Rees
Role: Left-hand bat, right-arm medium bowler
Born: 8 April 1985, Swansea
Height: 6ft 1in **Weight:** 14st 10lbs
County debut: No first-team appearance
Parents: Peter and Diane
Marital status: Single
Education: Coedcae Comprehensive, Llanelli; Bath University
Qualifications: 10 GCSEs, 3 A-levels
Career outside cricket: Student
Off-season: 'Uni'
Career highlights to date: 'Getting first hundred for 2nd team'
Cricket moments to forget: 'Getting out first ball next game'
Cricketers particularly admired: Brian Lara
Other sports played: Rugby (Wales U17)
Other sports followed: Rugby (Llanelli Scarlets)
Favourite band: Oasis
Extras: Made 2nd XI Championship debut 2003. Played for Wales Minor Counties in the C&G 2004. Is on a development contract at Glamorgan

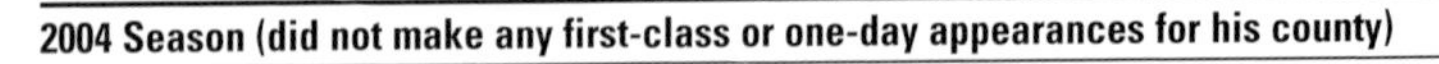

2004 Season (did not make any first-class or one-day appearances for his county)

Career Performances

	M	Inns	NO	Runs	HS	Avge	100s	50s	Ct	St	Balls	Runs	Wkts	Avge	Best	5wI	10wM
Test																	
All First																	
1-day Int																	
C & G	2	2	0	27	15	13.50	-	-	-	-							
totesport																	
Twenty20																	

REES, T. M. Lancashire

Name: Timothy (Tim) Martyn Rees
Role: Right-hand bat, right-arm off-spin bowler
Born: 4 September 1984, Loughborough
Height: 6ft 1in **Weight:** 12st 2lbs
Nickname: Reescy, 50, Tommy
County debut: 2002
1st-Class catches: 1
Parents: Simon and Rosey
Marital status: Single
Family links with cricket: 'Father umpire in Bolton League; used to play in Leicestershire League. Both brothers play in local league, and both have played for Lancashire Schoolboys at various levels'
Education: Canon Slade School, Bolton
Qualifications: 9 GCSEs, 3 A-levels
Off-season: 'Holiday; seeing friends; keeping fit'
Overseas tours: England U17 to Australia 2000-01
Career highlights to date: 'First-team/first-class debut'
Cricket moments to forget: 'My 19th birthday when my girlfriend and friends came to watch me get a third-ball duck, and they still clapped me off!!'
Cricket superstitions: 'Too many'
Cricketers particularly admired: Michael Atherton, Michael Vaughan, Freddie Flintoff
Other sports played: Football, basketball
Other sports followed: Football (Bolton Wanderers FC)
Favourite band: Oasis, Stereophonics
Relaxations: 'PlayStation; watching films and DVDs; spending time with friends'
Extras: Won the A.A. Thomson Fielding Prize 2000 (for the best schoolboy fieldsman) while playing for England U15 in the U15 World Cup
Opinions on cricket: 'Too many matches during the season; too many EU/passport players coming over and taking chances away from younger lads.'
Best batting: 16 Lancashire v Somerset, Taunton 2002

2004 Season (did not make any first-class or one-day appearances)

Career Performances

	M	Inns	NO	Runs	HS	Avge	100s	50s	Ct	St	Balls	Runs	Wkts	Avge	Best	5wI	10wM
Test																	
All First	1	1	0	16	16	16.00	-	-	1	-							
1-day Int																	
C & G																	
totesport	1	1	1	7	7 *	-	-	-	1	-							
Twenty20																	

RHODES, S. J. — Worcestershire

Name: Steven (Steve) John Rhodes
Role: Right-hand bat, wicket-keeper
Born: 17 June 1964, Bradford
Height: 5ft 8in **Weight:** 12st 8lbs
Nickname: Bumpy
County debut: 1981 (Yorkshire), 1985 (Worcestershire)
County cap: 1986 (Worcestershire; colours, 2002)
Benefit: 1996
Test debut: 1994
Tests: 11
One-Day Internationals: 9
1000 runs in a season: 2
50 dismissals in a season: 13
1st-Class 50s: 72
1st-Class 100s: 12
1st-Class catches: 1138
1st-Class stumpings: 124
Place in batting averages: 100th av. 36.08 (2003 179th av. 25.75)
Parents: William Ernest and Norma Kathleen
Wife and date of marriage: Judy Ann, 6 March 1993
Children: Holly Jade, 20 August 1985; George Harry, 26 October 1993; Lily Amber, 3 March 1995
Family links with cricket: Father played for Nottinghamshire 1959-64
Education: Carlton-Bolling Comprehensive, Bradford
Qualifications: 4 O-levels, Level III coach, 'attended Bradford Management Centre for ECB – Coaching and Management Skills course'
Career outside cricket: 'Joining Worcestershire coaching staff as assistant coach'

Overseas tours: England A to Sri Lanka 1986, to Zimbabwe and Kenya 1989-90, to Pakistan 1990-91, to West Indies 1991-92, to South Africa 1993-94; England to Australia 1994-95; MCC to Kenya 1999
Overseas teams played for: Past Bros, Bundaberg, Queensland; Avis Vogeltown, New Plymouth, New Zealand; Melville, Perth, Australia
Cricketers particularly admired: Richard Hadlee, Ian Healy, Glenn McGrath
Young players to look out for: Steve Davies
Other sports followed: Rugby league (Bradford Bulls), horse racing
Favourite band: Robbie Williams
Relaxations: Horse racing
Extras: Played for England YC v Australia YC in 1983 and set record for most victims in an innings for England YC. Youngest wicket-keeper to play for Yorkshire. Released by Yorkshire to join Worcestershire at end of 1984 season. Set one-day record of four stumpings in an innings v Warwickshire in Sunday League at Edgbaston 1986. One of *Wisden*'s Five Cricketers of the Year 1995. Overtook David Bairstow (257) as the wicket-keeper with the most dismissals in the Sunday League, v Essex 1997. Made 1000th first-class dismissal of his career when he caught Graeme Swann off Alamgir Sheriyar v Northants at Northampton 1999. Equalled his own Worcestershire record for the most catches in a match with nine v Gloucestershire at Worcester 2000. Took 1000th first-class catch during the 2001 season. Coach of Zimbabwe U19 squad to U19 World Cup in New Zealand 2001-02. Scored 124 v Nottinghamshire at Trent Bridge 2002, in the process sharing with David Leatherdale (120) in a new record seventh-wicket partnership for Worcestershire (256); also shares in Worcestershire record partnerships for the sixth wicket (265 with Graeme Hick) and the eighth wicket (184 with Stuart Lampitt). Made 400th one-day league dismissal (Jamie Cox) v Somerset at Worcester in the totesport League 2004. Vice-captain of Worcestershire from 2001, taking over as captain from August 2004 after the resignation of Ben Smith. Retired from county cricket at the end of the 2004 season in eighth place in the all-time list of wicket-keepers with 1263 (1139/124) first-class dismissals. Received 'In Safe Hands' award (shared with Jack Russell) at the PCA awards dinner at the Royal Albert Hall 2004
Best batting: 124 Worcestershire v Nottinghamshire, Trent Bridge 2002

2004 Season

	M	Inns	NO	Runs	HS	Avge	100s	50s	Ct	St	O	M	Runs	Wkts	Avge	Best	5wI	10wM
Test																		
All First	17	21	9	433	59 *	36.08	-	2	44	4								
1-day Int																		
C & G	5	3	2	26	15	26.00	-	-	7	-								
totesport	16	10	6	169	71 *	42.25	-	1	16	4								
Twenty20																		

Career Performances

	M	Inns	NO	Runs	HS	Avge	100s	50s	Ct	St	Balls	Runs	Wkts	Avge	Best	5wI	10wM
Test	11	17	5	294	65 *	24.50	-	1	46	3							
All First	440	618	166	14839	124	32.82	12	72	1138	124	6	30	0	-	-	-	-
1-day Int	9	8	2	107	56	17.83	-	1	9	2							
C & G	59	44	17	624	61	23.11	-	3	71	10	6	1	0	-	-	-	
totesport	300	190	65	2587	71 *	20.69	-	1	318	96							
Twenty20	3	2	0	12	9	6.00	-	-	-	5							

RICHARDSON, A. — Middlesex

Name: Alan Richardson
Role: Right-hand bat, right-arm medium bowler
Born: 6 May 1975, Newcastle-under-Lyme, Staffs
Height: 6ft 2in **Weight:** 13st
Nickname: Richo
County debut: 1995 (Derbyshire), 1999 (Warwickshire)
County cap: 2002 (Warwickshire)
1st-Class 50s: 1
1st-Class 5 w. in innings: 4
1st-Class 10 w. in match: 1
1st-Class catches: 18
One-Day 5 w. in innings: 1
Place in batting averages: (2003 269th av. 11.28)
Place in bowling averages: (2003 115th av. 39.81)
Strike rate: 144.00 (career 67.62)
Parents: Roy and Sandra
Marital status: Single
Family links with cricket: 'Dad captained Little Stoke 3rd XI and now patrols the boundary with pint in hand at the Sid Jenkins Cricket Ground'
Education: Alleyne's High School, Stone; Stafford College of Further Education
Qualifications: 8 GCSEs, 2 A-levels, 2 AS-levels, Level 2 cricket coach
Career outside cricket: Landscape gardener
Off-season: 'Following Stoke around the country – getting depressed'
Overseas tours: Derbyshire to Malaga 1995; Warwickshire to Bloemfontein 2000, to Cape Town 2001, 2002, to Portugal 2003
Overseas teams played for: Northern Natal, South Africa 1994-96; Hawkesbury CC,

Sydney 1997-99; Northern Districts, Sydney 1999-2000, 2001-03; Avendale, Cape Town 2000-01; Kyriang Mountains, Australia 2003-04
Career highlights to date: 'Taking 8-51 on home debut for Warwickshire, and any attempted catch by Charlie Dagnall'
Cricket moments to forget: 'Most of last season, either being constantly moved in the field or carrying drinks'
Cricket superstitions: 'None'
Cricketers particularly admired: Angus Fraser, Neil Smith, Ian Carr
Players to look out for: Moeen Ali, Will Speer, Ryan Nelson
Other sports played: 'Play clumsily for Warwickshire football team'
Other sports followed: Football (Stoke City – 'bordering on fanatical')
Injuries: 'Pourer's elbow. It's a repetitive strain injury – started in May; cleared up in September'
Favourite band: The Zutons, Kasabian
Relaxations: 'Socialising down the Station'
Extras: *Cricket World* award for best bowling performance in Oxford U19 Festival (8-60 v Devon). Topped Minor Counties bowling averages with Staffordshire 1998 and won Minor Counties bowling award. Most Improved 2nd XI Player 1999. Outstanding Performance of the Year 1999 for his 8-51 v Gloucestershire on home debut; besides being the season's best analysis, it was the best return by a Warwickshire player on debut at Edgbaston. Scored 91 v Hampshire at Edgbaston 2002; it was the highest score by a Warwickshire No. 11 and in scoring it he shared with Nick Knight (255*) in a tenth-wicket stand of 214, which was a county best for the last wicket and the fifth highest tenth-wicket partnership in Championship history overall. Recorded maiden one-day five-wicket return (5-35) v Staffordshire (his native county) at Stone in the C&G 2002. His 8-46 in the second innings v Sussex at Edgbaston 2002 was the best return by a Warwickshire bowler since 1977. Left Warwickshire at the end of the 2004 season and has joined Middlesex for 2005
Opinions on cricket: 'Longer teas. Less bouncers at tail-enders!'
Best batting: 91 Warwickshire v Hampshire, Edgbaston 2002
Best bowling: 8-46 Warwickshire v Sussex, Edgbaston 2002

2004 Season

	M	Inns	NO	Runs	HS	Avge	100s	50s	Ct	St	O	M	Runs	Wkts	Avge	Best	5wI	10wM
Test																		
All First	7	4	2	26	17	13.00	-	-	2	-	144	28	532	6	88.66	2-62	-	-
1-day Int																		
C & G	2	1	1	0	0 *	-	-	-	1	-	13	2	79	1	79.00	1-46	-	
totesport	8	3	3	3	1 *	-	-	-	1	-	51	3	265	5	53.00	1-20	-	
Twenty20	3	1	1	6	6 *	-	-	-	1	-	9	1	52	3	17.33	3-13	-	

Career Performances

	M	Inns	NO	Runs	HS	Avge	100s	50s	Ct	St	Balls	Runs	Wkts	Avge	Best	5wI	10wM
Test																	
All First	64	62	25	392	91	10.59	-	1	18	-	11226	5419	166	32.64	8-46	4	1
1-day Int																	
C & G	6	5	2	4	3	1.33	-	-	2	-	306	230	7	32.85	5-35	1	
totesport	29	12	8	54	18	13.50	-	-	6	-	1189	968	28	34.57	3-17	-	
Twenty20	3	1	1	6	6 *	-	-	-	1	-	54	52	3	17.33	3-13	-	

ROBERTS, T. W. Northamptonshire

Name: Timothy (Tim) William Roberts
Role: Right-hand bat, right-arm off-spin bowler
Born: 4 March 1978, Kettering
Height: 5ft 8in **Weight:** 11st
Nickname: Robbo
County debut: 2001 (Lancashire), 2003 (Northamptonshire)
1st-Class 50s: 8
1st-Class catches: 21
One-Day 100s: 2
Place in batting averages: 162nd av. 27.70 (2003 172nd av. 26.30)
Strike rate: 78.00 (career 114.00)
Parents: Dave and Shirley
Marital status: Single
Family links with cricket: 'Brother Andy was a leg-spinner at Northants; Dad had trials for Northants'
Education: Bishop Stopford School, Kettering; Durham University
Qualifications: 2.1 degree in Geology, Level 3 cricket coach
Career outside cricket: Teaching/coaching
Overseas tours: England U17 to Holland (International Youth Tournament) 1995; Lancashire to South Africa 2000, 2001
Overseas teams played for: Eastern Suburbs, Wellington, New Zealand 1999-2000
Career highlights to date: 'Getting signed by Northants after having a good year in the league'
Cricketers particularly admired: Andy Roberts, Mike Hussey
Other sports played: Golf, football, squash, badminton
Other sports followed: Football (Rushden & Diamonds FC)
Favourite band: Oasis

Relaxations: 'Having a few Coronas with the lads at Finedon Dolben CC'
Extras: Represented British Universities 1999. Scored a 41-ball 50 (ending up with 55) in his second Norwich Union League match, v Derbyshire at Derby 2001. Released by Lancashire at the end of the 2002 season and joined Northamptonshire from club cricket during 2003. Scored 83 on Championship debut v Somerset at Northampton 2003, his first two scoring strokes being a four and a six
Best batting: 89 Northamptonshire v Lancashire, Northampton 2004
Best bowling: 1-10 Northamptonshire v DUCCE, Northampton 2004

2004 Season

	M	Inns	NO	Runs	HS	Avge	100s	50s	Ct	St	O	M	Runs	Wkts	Avge	Best	5wI	10wM
Test																		
All First	17	29	2	748	89	27.70	-	6	12	-	13	7	10	1	10.00	1-10	-	-
1-day Int																		
C & G	3	3	0	54	39	18.00	-	-	1	-								
totesport	16	16	0	431	112	26.93	1	2	4	-								
Twenty20	5	4	1	90	39	30.00	-	-	1	-								

Career Performances

	M	Inns	NO	Runs	HS	Avge	100s	50s	Ct	St	Balls	Runs	Wkts	Avge	Best	5wI	10wM
Test																	
All First	29	46	2	1121	89	25.47	-	8	21	-	114	20	1	20.00	1-10	-	-
1-day Int																	
C & G	4	4	0	102	48	25.50	-	-	1	-							
totesport	30	30	0	804	131	26.80	2	4	7	-	36	35	0	-	-	-	
Twenty20	5	4	1	90	39	30.00	-	-	1	-							

74. Which former county cricketer once played for South Australia against the 1990-91 England tourists and is now captain of Italy?

ROBINSON, D. D. J. Leicestershire

Name: Darren David John Robinson
Role: Right-hand bat, leg-spin bowler
Born: 2 March 1973, Braintree, Essex
Height: 5ft 11in **Weight:** 14st
Nickname: Pies, Pie Shop, Robbo
County debut: 1993 (Essex), 2004 (Leicestershire)
County cap: 1997 (Essex)
1000 runs in a season: 2
1st-Class 50s: 42
1st-Class 100s: 15
1st-Class 200s: 1
1st-Class catches: 129
One-Day 100s: 4
Place in batting averages: 82nd av. 38.82 (2003 120th av. 32.88)
Strike rate: (career 260.00)
Parents: Dorothy (deceased) and David
Wife and date of marriage: Alyssa, 2 December 2001
Children: Kalli, 20 July 1998; Cameron, 20 May 2000; Evie, 30 October 2002
Family links with cricket: Father club cricketer for Halstead
Education: Tabor High School, Braintree; Chelmsford College of Further Education
Qualifications: 5 GCSEs, BTEC National Diploma in Building and Construction
Career outside cricket: Site investigation and surveying
Overseas tours: England U18 to Canada (International Youth Tournament) 1991; England U19 to Pakistan 1991-92
Overseas teams played for: Waverley, Sydney 1992-94; Eden Roskill CC, Auckland 1995-96
Career highlights to date: 'Every trophy won'
Cricket moments to forget: 'Being bowled out for 57 against Lancashire in the NatWest final [1996]'
Cricket superstitions: 'None'
Cricketers particularly admired: Steve Hale, David Denny
Young players to look out for: Alastair Cook, Ravinder Bopara
Other sports played: Football, golf, squash
Other sports followed: Golf, football, rugby, swimming
Relaxations: Reading, music
Extras: *Daily Telegraph* Batting Award 1988. International Youth Tournament in Canada batting award 1991. Scored two centuries (102/118*) in match v Leicestershire at Chelmsford 2001. Scored Championship career-best 175 v Gloucestershire at Gloucester 2002 while captaining Essex in the absence of Ronnie Irani on international

duty. Essex Player of the Year 2002. Left Essex at the end of the 2003 season and joined Leicestershire for 2004, scoring 1000 first-class runs in his first season
Opinions on cricket: 'Two overseas players [are] too many, especially with so many EU players raping our game. Should be back to one overseas and send the rest back to Greece or Italy where they supposedly come from!'
Best batting: 200 Essex v New Zealanders, Chelmsford 1999
Best bowling: 1-7 Essex v Middlesex, Chelmsford 2003

2004 Season

	M	Inns	NO	Runs	HS	Avge	100s	50s	Ct	St	O	M	Runs	Wkts	Avge	Best	5wI	10wM
Test																		
All First	16	28	0	1087	154	38.82	1	9	18	-	7	0	64	0	-	-	-	-
1-day Int																		
C & G	1	1	0	0	0	0.00	-	-	-	-								
totesport	13	11	2	246	109 *	27.33	1	-	2	-								
Twenty20																		

Career Performances

	M	Inns	NO	Runs	HS	Avge	100s	50s	Ct	St	Balls	Runs	Wkts	Avge	Best	5wI	10wM
Test																	
All First	152	268	13	8236	200	32.29	16	42	129	-	260	279	1	279.00	1-7	-	-
1-day Int																	
C & G	21	19	1	475	70	26.38	-	5	6	-							
totesport	122	117	10	2777	129 *	25.95	2	13	35	-	17	26	1	26.00	1-7	-	
Twenty20	2	2	0	12	7	6.00	-	-	1	-							

75. Which ground hosted the 1982 ICC Trophy final, in which Zimbabwe beat Bermuda by five wickets?

ROBINSON, M. A. Sussex

Name: Mark Andrew Robinson
Role: Right-hand bat, right-arm fast-medium bowler; club coach
Born: 23 November 1966, Hull
Height: 6ft 3in **Weight:** 13st
Nickname: Coddy, Smokie, Tiger, Storm, Rodney
County debut: 1987 (Northamptonshire), 1991 (Yorkshire), 1996 (Sussex)
County cap: 1990 (Northamptonshire), 1992 (Yorkshire), 1997 (Sussex)
50 wickets in a season: 1
1st-Class 5 w. in innings: 13
1st-Class 10 w. in match: 2
1st-Class catches: 41
Strike rate: (career 64.53)
Parents: Malcolm and Joan
Wife and date of marriage: Julia, 8 October 1994
Children: Samuel Lewis, 11 January 1996; Eleanor Grace, 20 July 2000
Family links with cricket: Grandfather a prominent local cricketer and 'father was hostile bowler in the back garden'
Education: Hull Grammar School
Qualifications: 6 O-levels, 2 A-levels, advanced cricket coach ('currently doing Level 4 ECB'), badminton coach, rugby union coach
Off-season: Employed full-time by Sussex CCC
Overseas tours: England U19 North to Bermuda; Yorkshire to Cape Town 1991-92, 1992-93, to West Indies 1993-94; Sussex to Grenada 2001
Overseas teams played for: East Shirley, Canterbury, New Zealand 1987-89; Canterbury, New Zealand 1989-98
Career highlights to date: 'Sussex winning County Championship'
Cricket moments to forget: 'Don't want to forget any moment of what is a privileged existence'
Cricket superstitions: 'Never let Mike Yardy drive'
Cricketers particularly admired: Peter Moores, Keith Greenfield, Tony Cottey 'and any other player who lives for the game'
Young players to look out for: 'Tony Cottey'
Other sports played: Football
Other sports followed: Football (Hull City), 'all sports'
Favourite band: U2
Extras: Took hat-trick with first three balls of innings in Yorkshire League playing for Hull v Doncaster. First player to win Yorkshire U19 Bowler of the Season in two

successive years, 1984 and 1985. Northamptonshire Uncapped Player of the Year in 1989. Endured a world record 12 innings without scoring a run in 1990. Sussex Clubman of the Year 1997 and 1998. Scored 500th first-class run on the same day as he took 500th first-class wicket v Surrey at Hove 1999. Was not out in ten successive innings during 1999-2000, equalling the record for county cricket. His 5-59 v Durham at Hove 2001 included his 200th wicket for Sussex. Sussex club coach since 2003 but is still registered. Granted a testimonial for 2005

Opinions on cricket: 'More support needed for the county game from England's finest.'

Best batting: 27 Sussex v Lancashire, Old Trafford 1997

Best bowling: 9-37 Yorkshire v Northamptonshire, Harrogate 1993

2004 Season (did not make any first-class or one-day appearances)

Career Performances

	M	Inns	NO	Runs	HS	Avge	100s	50s	Ct	St	Balls	Runs	Wkts	Avge	Best	5wI	10wM
Test																	
All First	229	259	112	590	27	4.01	-	-	41	-	37689	17807	584	30.49	9-37	13	2
1-day Int																	
C & G	29	11	7	19	8 *	4.75	-	-	3	-	1908	1042	38	27.42	4-32	-	
totesport	176	69	31	127	15 *	3.34	-	-	16	-	7780	5488	171	32.09	4-23	-	
Twenty20																	

76. Known as the 'Bangla Bradman', who had scored over 2000 runs in 34 Tests to the end of February 2005, including three centuries?

ROFE, P. C. Northamptonshire

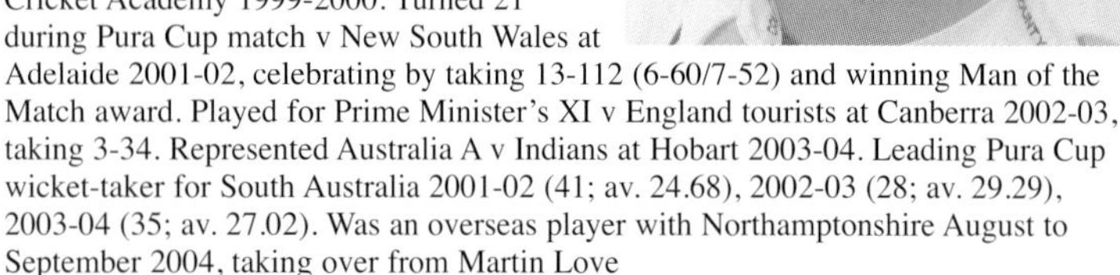

Name: Paul Cameron Rofe
Role: Right-hand bat, right-arm fast-medium bowler
Born: 16 January 1981, Adelaide, Australia
County debut: 2004
1st-Class 5 w. in innings: 6
1st-Class 10 w. in match: 1
1st-Class catches: 10
Place in bowling averages: 122nd av. 42.08
Strike rate: 83.91 (career 67.25)
Overseas tours: Australia U19 to England 1999, to Sri Lanka (U19 World Cup) 1999-2000
Overseas teams played for: South Australia 2000-01 –
Extras: Commonwealth Bank [Australian] Cricket Academy 1999-2000. Turned 21 during Pura Cup match v New South Wales at Adelaide 2001-02, celebrating by taking 13-112 (6-60/7-52) and winning Man of the Match award. Played for Prime Minister's XI v England tourists at Canberra 2002-03, taking 3-34. Represented Australia A v Indians at Hobart 2003-04. Leading Pura Cup wicket-taker for South Australia 2001-02 (41; av. 24.68), 2002-03 (28; av. 29.29), 2003-04 (35; av. 27.02). Was an overseas player with Northamptonshire August to September 2004, taking over from Martin Love
Best batting: 18 South Australia v Queensland, Adelaide 2000-01
Best bowling: 7-52 South Australia v New South Wales, Adelaide 2001-02

2004 Season

	M	Inns	NO	Runs	HS	Avge	100s	50s	Ct	St	O	M	Runs	Wkts	Avge	Best	5wI	10wM
Test																		
All First	5	6	4	20	15 *	10.00	-	-	1	-	167.5	42	505	12	42.08	4-109	-	-
1-day Int																		
C & G																		
totesport	3	1	0	5	5	5.00	-	-	1	-	23	2	114	7	16.28	3-23	-	
Twenty20																		

Career Performances

	M	Inns	NO	Runs	HS	Avge	100s	50s	Ct	St	Balls	Runs	Wkts	Avge	Best	5wI	10wM
Test																	
All First	38	56	20	225	18	6.25	-	-	10	-	8071	3635	120	30.29	7-52	6	1
1-day Int																	
C & G																	
totesport	3	1	0	5	5	5.00	-	-	1	-	138	114	7	16.28	3-23	-	
Twenty20																	

ROGERS, C. J. L. Derbyshire

Name: Christopher (Chris) John Llewellyn Rogers
Role: Left-hand bat, leg-spin/right-arm medium bowler
Born: 31 August 1977, Sydney, Australia
Height: 5ft 11in **Weight:** 12st 8lbs
County debut: 2004
1st-Class 50s: 14
1st-Class 100s: 9
1st-Class catches: 36
Place in batting averages: 21st av. 55.33
Family links with cricket: Father played for New South Wales and became cricket administrator
Overseas teams played for: Western Australia 1998-99 –
Extras: Represented Australia U19 v New Zealand U19 1995-96. Represented Australia A v South Africa A and Indians. Scored two centuries (101*/102*) in Pura Cup match v South Australia at Perth 2001-02, winning Man of the Match award. Scored 194 v New South Wales at Perth in the Pura Cup 2002-03, in the process sharing with Marcus North (178) in a new record fourth-wicket partnership for Western Australia (369). Won three Western Australia awards 2002-03 – Lawrie Sawle Medal (leading first-class and one-day player), President's Silver Trophy (season's best individual performance – for his 194 v NSW *see above*), and Excalibur Award (spirit of WA cricket). Played for Shropshire in round one of the C&G 2004 (contested August 2003). Joined Derbyshire as an overseas player for 2004 but was forced to return home early because of a shoulder injury
Best batting: 194 Western Australia v New South Wales, Perth 2002-03

2004 Season

	M	Inns	NO	Runs	HS	Avge	100s	50s	Ct	St	O	M	Runs	Wkts	Avge	Best	5wI	10wM
Test																		
All First	6	11	2	498	156	55.33	1	3	6	-								
1-day Int																		
C & G	1	1	0	93	93	93.00	-	1	-	-								
totesport	3	3	0	41	27	13.66	-	-	2	-								
Twenty20																		

Career Performances

	M	Inns	NO	Runs	HS	Avge	100s	50s	Ct	St	Balls	Runs	Wkts	Avge	Best	5wI	10wM
Test																	
All First	40	72	6	2908	194	44.06	9	14	36	-	18	12	0	-	-	-	-
1-day Int																	
C & G	2	2	0	142	93	71.00	-	1	-	-							
totesport	3	3	0	41	27	13.66	-	-	2	-							
Twenty20																	

RUSHWORTH, C. Durham

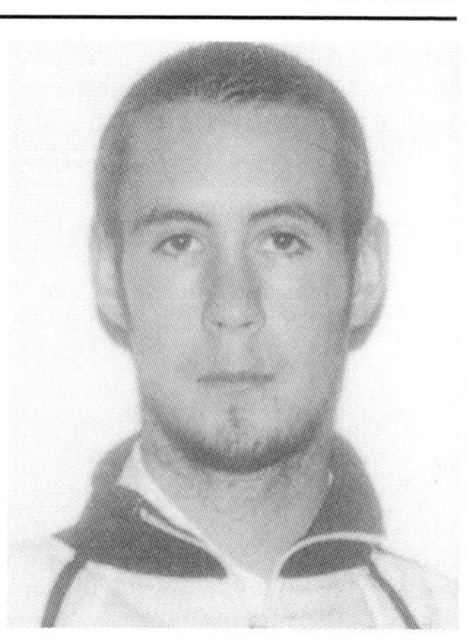

Name: Christopher (Chris) Rushworth
Role: Right-hand bat, right-arm fast bowler
Born: 11 July 1986, Sunderland
Height: 6ft 1in **Weight:** 11st 6lbs
County debut: No first-team appearance (*see* ***Extras***)
Parents: Joseph and Aileen
Marital status: Single
Education: Castle View, Sunderland
Qualifications: Level 2 coach
Off-season: 'Playing in Australia'
Overseas teams played for: Doveton CC, Melbourne 2004-05
Career highlights to date: 'Playing against Sri Lanka A in 2004 season'
Cricket moments to forget: 'Being hit for six first ball in above game'
Cricket superstitions: 'None'
Cricketers particularly admired: Angus Fraser
Young players to look out for: 'Myself'
Other sports played: 'Park football', snooker
Other sports followed: Football (Sunderland AFC)

Favourite band: Travis, Abba
Extras: Is a Durham Academy player. Made 1st XI debut for Durham v Sri Lanka A in a one-day fixture at Riverside 2004 but has yet to appear for the county in first-class cricket or domestic competition
Opinions on cricket: 'Faster and more technical than ever before.'

RUSSELL, R. C. — Gloucestershire

Name: Robert Charles (Jack) Russell
Role: Left-hand bat, wicket-keeper
Born: 15 August 1963, Stroud
Height: 5ft 8¼in **Weight:** 9st 9lbs
County debut: 1981
County cap: 1985
Benefit: 1994; testimonial 2004
Test debut: 1988
Tests: 54
One-Day Internationals: 40
1000 runs in a season: 1
50 dismissals in a season: 15
1st-Class 50s: 89
1st-Class 100s: 11
1st-Class catches: 1193
1st-Class stumpings: 127
One-Day 100s: 2
Place in batting averages: (2003 99th av. 36.33)
Strike rate: (career 56.00)
Parents: John (deceased) and Jennifer
Wife and date of marriage: Aileen Ann, 6 March 1985
Children: Stepson, Marcus Anthony, 1980; Elizabeth Ann, March 1988; Victoria, 1989; Charles David, 1991; Katherine Jane, 1996
Family links with cricket: 'Late father and late brother played club cricket (plus other sports)'
Education: Archway Comprehensive School; Bristol Polytechnic
Qualifications: 7 O-levels, 2 A-levels
Career outside cricket: Professional artist
Off-season: 'Painting'
Overseas tours: England A to Australia 1992-93 (vice-captain); England to Pakistan 1987-88, to India and West Indies 1989-90, to Australia 1990-91, to New Zealand 1991-92, to West Indies 1993-94, to Australia 1994-95, to South Africa 1995-96, to Pakistan and India (World Cup) 1995-96, to Zimbabwe and New Zealand 1996-97, to West Indies 1997-98, to Bangladesh (Wills International Cup) 1998-99

Career highlights: 'Running down the steps and on to the ground at Lord's to make Test debut'
Cricket moments to forget: 'All ducks and missed chances!'
Cricket superstitions: 'None (if you believe that, you'll believe anything!). Too many to mention'
Cricketers particularly admired: Alan Knott, Bob Taylor, Ian Botham, Sir Don Bradman, Rodney Marsh, 'and other greats'
Others sports played: None – 'no time! Too busy painting'
Other sports followed: Football, rugby, snooker, 'anything competitive'
Relaxations: Playing cricket and painting pictures
Extras: Became youngest Gloucestershire wicket-keeper (17 years 307 days) and set record for most dismissals in a match on first-class debut: eight (seven caught, one stumped) for Gloucestershire v Sri Lankans at Bristol 1981. Hat-trick of catches v Surrey at The Oval 1986. Made Test debut v Sri Lanka at Lord's 1988, scoring 94 as nightwatchman in England's first innings. England's Man of the Test Series v Australia 1989, which included his maiden first-class century (128*) in the fourth Test at Old Trafford. One of *Wisden*'s Five Cricketers of the Year 1990. Captain of Gloucestershire and Player of the Year 1995. Whyte and Mackay wicket-keeper/batsman of the year 1995, 1996, 1997. Broke Bob Taylor's long-standing world record for the number of dismissals in a Test match with 11 (all caught) in the second Test v South Africa at Johannesburg 1995-96 (his 27 Test dismissals in the series is a record for England); also partnered Michael Atherton (185*) for 277 minutes in England's second innings to save the match, making 29*. Awarded MBE in 1996 for services to cricket. Set a new NatWest dismissals record by claiming his 67th victim (Adrian Rollins) v Derbyshire at Bristol 1999. Man of the Match in Gloucestershire's NatWest final victory over Somerset 1999. Conceded no byes in Northamptonshire's 746 v Gloucestershire at Bristol 2002, setting a new world record for a clean sheet in first-class cricket. During 2002 season passed Gloucestershire record for most first-class runs by a wicket-keeper and equalled club record for most first-class dismissals (1016 by Jack Board). Winner of Cricket Writers' Club Peter Smith Award (for presentation of cricket to the public) 2002. Opened Jack Russell Gallery (www.jackrussell.co.uk) in Chipping Sodbury, Gloucestershire, 1995; painting commissions include 'The Cenotaph' for Royal British Legion; 'Field Marshals of the British Army' for Army Benevolent Fund (hanging National Army Museum, London); Duke of Edinburgh; Duke of Kent. *Jack Russell – Unleashed*, an autobiography, made the top ten bestsellers in 1997. Retired from county cricket during the 2004 season (due to a persistent back injury) in fifth place in the all-time list of wicket-keepers with 1320 (1193/127) first-class dismissals. Received 'In Safe Hands' award (shared with Steve Rhodes) at the PCA awards dinner at the Royal Albert Hall 2004
Best batting: 129* England XI v Boland, Paarl 1995-96
Best bowling: 1-4 Gloucestershire v West Indians, Bristol 1991

2004 Season

	M	Inns	NO	Runs	HS	Avge	100s	50s	Ct	St	O	M	Runs	Wkts	Avge	Best	5wI	10wM
Test																		
All First	2	2	1	30	28 *	30.00	-	-	1	-								
1-day Int																		
C & G																		
totesport	1	1	0	6	6	6.00	-	-	-	-								
Twenty20																		

Career Performances

	M	Inns	NO	Runs	HS	Avge	100s	50s	Ct	St	Balls	Runs	Wkts	Avge	Best	5wI	10wM
Test	54	86	16	1897	128 *	27.10	2	6	153	12							
All First	465	690	145	16861	129 *	30.93	11	89	1193	127	56	68	1	68.00	1-4	-	-
1-day Int	40	31	7	423	50	17.62	-	1	41	6							
C & G	61	46	12	950	84	27.94	-	4	88	17							
totesport	279	217	47	3843	108	22.60	1	15	233	59							
Twenty20	2	1	1	11	11 *	-	-	-	1	1							

SADLER, J. L. — Leicestershire

Name: John Leonard Sadler
Role: Left-hand top-order bat, leg-spin bowler
Born: 19 November 1981, Dewsbury
Height: 5ft 11in **Weight:** 12st 7lbs
Nickname: Sads
County debut: 2003
1st-Class 50s: 4
1st-Class 100s: 2
1st-Class catches: 12
Place in batting averages: 182nd av. 24.60 (2003 58th av. 43.40)
Strike rate: 40.00 (career 87.00)
Parents: Michael and Sue
Marital status: Single
Family links with cricket: Father played for 25 years and now coaches. Brothers Dave and Jamie play local league cricket; both played for Yorkshire youth teams
Education: St Thomas à Becket RC School, Wakefield
Qualifications: 9 GCSEs, Levels I and II coaching awards
Off-season: 'Batting course in India'

Overseas tours: England U19 to Malaysia and (U19 World Cup) Sri Lanka 1999-2000, to India 2000-01; Yorkshire to Grenada 2002
Overseas teams played for: Tuart Hill, Perth 2001-04
Career highlights to date: 'First first-class 50 v Warwickshire; first first-class century v Surrey; winning Twenty20 competition'
Cricket moments to forget: 'Injury to knee in Sri Lanka January 2000, leading to early return to England from U19 World Cup squad'
Cricket superstitions: 'None'
Cricketers particularly admired: Robin Smith, Sachin Tendulkar, Graham Thorpe, Darren Lehmann, Brian Lara
Young players to look out for: Stuart Broad, Tom New, Richard Pyrah
Other sports played: 'Five-a-side football, squash and occasional golf'
Other sports followed: Football (Leeds United), rugby league (Leeds Rhinos)
Favourite band: Oasis
Relaxations: 'Music, relaxing, socialising with friends, keeping fit, PlayStation 2'
Extras: Played for Yorkshire Schools at all levels and joined Yorkshire Academy 1998. Yorkshire Supporters' Club Young Player of the Year 1998. Represented England at U14, U15, U17, U18 and U19 levels. Awarded Yorkshire 2nd XI cap 2002. Released by Yorkshire at the end of the 2002 season and joined Leicestershire for 2003
Opinions on cricket: 'The best game and the hardest at times.'
Best batting: 145 Leicestershire v Surrey, Leicester 2003
145 Leicestershire v Sussex, Hove 2003
Best bowling: 1-22 Leicestershire v New Zealanders, Leicester 2004

2004 Season

	M	Inns	NO	Runs	HS	Avge	100s	50s	Ct	St	O	M	Runs	Wkts	Avge	Best	5wI	10wM
Test																		
All First	14	25	2	566	95	24.60	-	3	7	-	6.4	0	58	1	58.00	1-22	-	-
1-day Int																		
C & G	1	1	0	10	10	10.00	-	-	-	-								
totesport	17	14	1	287	88	22.07	-	1	2	-								
Twenty20	7	7	2	47	22	9.40	-	-	5	-								

Career Performances

	M	Inns	NO	Runs	HS	Avge	100s	50s	Ct	St	Balls	Runs	Wkts	Avge	Best	5wI	10wM
Test																	
All First	21	36	3	1000	145	30.30	2	4	12	-	87	98	1	98.00	1-22	-	-
1-day Int																	
C & G	3	3	0	27	10	9.00	-	-	-	-							
totesport	27	23	1	405	88	18.40	-	1	4	-							
Twenty20	12	11	4	54	22	7.71	-	-	7	-							

SAGGERS, M. J. — Kent

Name: Martin John Saggers
Role: Right-hand bat, right-arm fast-medium bowler
Born: 23 May 1972, King's Lynn
Height: 6ft 2in **Weight:** 14st 2lbs
Nickname: Saggs, Saggy Bits, Bits of Aloo, Jurgen Burgen
County debut: 1996 (Durham), 1999 (Kent)
County cap: 2001 (Kent)
Test debut: 2003-04
Tests: 3
50 wickets in a season: 4
1st-Class 50s: 2
1st-Class 5 w. in innings: 15
1st-Class catches: 21
One-Day 5 w. in innings: 1
Place in batting averages: 275th av. 8.22 (2003 245th av. 16.00)
Place in bowling averages: 57th av. 31.17 (2003 28th av. 24.84)
Strike rate: 67.78 (career 46.25)
Parents: Brian and Edna
Wife and date of marriage: Samantha, 27 February 2004
Family links with cricket: Grandfather played in the Essex League
Education: Springwood High School; University of Huddersfield
Qualifications: BA (Hons) Architectural Studies International
Career outside cricket: 'Setting up a website for South African wildlife photography'
Off-season: Training in South Africa
Overseas tours: Kent to South Africa 2001; England VI to Hong Kong 2002; England to Bangladesh 2003-04
Overseas teams played for: Randburg CC, Johannesburg 1996-98, 2000-04; Southern Suburbs CC, Johannesburg 1998-99
Career highlights to date: 'Winning the Norwich Union League 2001. Making my Test debut in Bangladesh. Taking a wicket with my first delivery in Test cricket on English soil'
Cricket moments to forget: 'Any form of injury'
Cricket superstitions: 'Getting a corner spot in the changing room'
Cricketers particularly admired: Neil Foster, Graham Dilley, Allan Donald, Richard Ellison
Young players to look out for: Billy Hockley
Other sports played: Golf (10 handicap), 'base jumping, snail racing'
Other sports followed: Football (Spurs), 'any form of motor sport'
Injuries: Out for 10 weeks with patellar tendonitis

Favourite band: Metallica
Relaxations: 'Going on safari in the Kruger National Park in South Africa. Wildlife photography'
Extras: Released by Durham at end of the 1998 season and joined Kent. Took career best 7-79 against his old county, Durham, at Riverside 2000. Won Most Promising Uncapped Player Award 2000. Joint Kent Player of the Year 2000 (with David Masters). Took two hat-tricks in two weeks for Randburg CC, Johannesburg 2000-01, including one spell of five wickets in six balls. Underwood Award (Kent leading wicket-taker) 2001, 2002, 2003. *Kent Messenger* Group Readers Player of the Season 2002. Shepherd Neame Award for Best Bowler 2002. Cowdrey Award (Kent Player of the Year) 2002. Joint leading wicket-taker in English first-class cricket 2002 (with Kevin Dean) with 83 wickets (av. 21.51). Called up to the England Test tour of Bangladesh 2003-04 as replacement for the injured Andrew Flintoff, making Test debut in the second Test at Chittagong. Took wicket (Philip Weston) with his first Championship delivery of the 2004 season v Gloucestershire at Bristol. Scored career best 64 as nightwatchman as Kent scored a county record fourth-innings 429-5 to beat Worcestershire at Canterbury 2004. Took wicket (Mark Richardson) with his first delivery in Test cricket on English soil, in the second Test v New Zealand at Headingley 2004
Opinions on cricket: 'Too many non-English-qualified players playing. Two division system definitely works. However, there should only be two teams promoted and relegated.'
Best batting: 64 Kent v Worcestershire, Canterbury 2004
Best bowling: 7-79 Kent v Durham, Riverside 2000

2004 Season

	M	Inns	NO	Runs	HS	Avge	100s	50s	Ct	St	O	M	Runs	Wkts	Avge	Best	5wI	10wM
Test	2	2	0	0	0	0.00	-	-	-	-	63	16	185	4	46.25	2-80	-	-
All First	9	9	0	74	64	8.22	-	1	4	-	259.5	72	717	23	31.17	4-43	-	-
1-day Int																		
C & G	2	1	0	4	4	4.00	-	-	-	-	13.4	5	40	4	10.00	4-6	-	
totesport	8	5	1	28	16	7.00	-	-	1	-	45	5	201	9	22.33	3-30	-	
Twenty20	2	1	0	5	5	5.00	-	-	1	-	7	0	45	2	22.50	2-14	-	

Career Performances

	M	Inns	NO	Runs	HS	Avge	100s	50s	Ct	St	Balls	Runs	Wkts	Avge	Best	5wI	10wM
Test	3	3	0	1	1	0.33	-	-	1	-	493	247	7	35.28	2-29	-	-
All First	84	104	26	792	64	10.15	-	2	21	-	15126	7666	327	23.44	7-79	15	-
1-day Int																	
C & G	13	6	3	7	4	2.33	-	-	1	-	696	479	19	25.21	4-6	-	
totesport	66	34	16	152	21 *	8.44	-	-	14	-	2841	2117	96	22.05	5-22	1	
Twenty20	2	1	0	5	5	5.00	-	-	1	-	42	45	2	22.50	2-14	-	

SAKER, N. C. — Surrey

Name: Neil Clifford Saker
Role: Right-hand bat, right-arm fast bowler
Born: 20 September 1984, Tooting, London
Height: 6ft 4in **Weight:** 12st
Nickname: Sakes, For Goodness, Bulbus
County debut: 2003
Strike rate: (career 211.00)
Parents: Pauline and Steve
Marital status: Single
Family links with cricket: 'Dad plays for Guildford CC'
Education: Raynes Park High; Nescot College
Qualifications: 2 GCSEs, City & Guilds Carpentry and Joinery
Off-season: 'Staying home working on my fitness'
Overseas tours: Guildford CC to Trinidad and Tobago 2001; Surrey U19 to Sri Lanka 2002
Overseas teams played for: Randwick-Petersham, Sydney 2003-04
Career highlights to date: 'Championship debut v Essex at The Oval 2003'
Cricket moments to forget: 'Once bowled a 13-ball over in a club game'
Cricket superstitions: 'Bowling marker has to be lying on surface, not pushed into ground!'
Cricketers particularly admired: Ian Botham, Brett Lee, Allan Donald
Young players to look out for: Jade Dernbach, Chris Murtagh, Danny Miller
Other sports played: Snooker, 'occasionally like to hack my way around a golf course'
Other sports followed: Football (Tottenham)
Injuries: Out for six weeks with separated joint and torn ligaments in the right shoulder
Favourite band: Powderfinger
Relaxations: 'Spending time with family and friends; also spending time with girlfriend'
Extras: Attended University of Port Elizabeth International Cricket Academy 2002-03
Opinions on cricket: 'Would like to see one overseas [player] as opposed to two – would give youngsters more opportunities to fill their spot in the team.'
Best batting: 5 Surrey v India A, The Oval 2003
Best bowling: 1-71 Surrey v Essex, The Oval 2003

2004 Season (did not make any first-class or one-day appearances)

Career Performances

	M	Inns	NO	Runs	HS	Avge	100s	50s	Ct	St	Balls	Runs	Wkts	Avge	Best	5wI	10wM
Test																	
All First	2	3	0	6	5	2.00	-	-	-	-	211	179	1	179.00	1-71	-	-
1-day Int																	
C & G																	
totesport																	
Twenty20																	

SALES, D. J. G. Northamptonshire

Name: David John Grimwood Sales
Role: Right-hand bat, right-arm medium bowler, county captain
Born: 3 December 1977, Carshalton, Surrey
Height: 6ft **Weight:** 14st 7lbs
Nickname: Jumble
County debut: 1994 (one-day), 1996 (first-class)
County cap: 1999
1000 runs in a season: 2
1st-Class 50s: 35
1st-Class 100s: 7
1st-Class 200s: 4
1st-Class 300s: 1
1st-Class catches: 97
One-Day 100s: 1
Place in batting averages: 12th av. 61.50 (2003 53rd av. 44.85)
Strike rate: (career 35.66)
Parents: Daphne and John
Wife and date of marriage: Abigail, 22 September 2001
Children: James, 11 February 2003
Family links with cricket: 'Father played club cricket, and father-in-law bowls a mean ball in the back garden'
Education: Caterham Boys' School
Qualifications: 7 GCSEs, cricket coach
Career outside cricket: 'Playing golf and working for "Friar Tuck"'
Off-season: Coaching
Overseas tours: England U15 to South Africa 1993; England U19 to West Indies

1994-95, to Zimbabwe 1995-96, to Pakistan 1996-97; England A to Kenya and Sri Lanka 1997-98, to Bangladesh and New Zealand 1999-2000, to West Indies 2000-01; Northants to Grenada 2000
Overseas teams played for: Wellington Firebirds, New Zealand 2001-02
Career highlights to date: '303 not out v Essex; 104 v Pakistan 2003'
Cricket moments to forget: 'Watching White and Powell for five hours, then getting 0' (*Rob White and Mark Powell shared in a new record Northamptonshire opening partnership of 375 v Gloucestershire at Northampton 2002*)
Cricket superstitions: 'None'
Cricketers particularly admired: Graham Gooch, Steve Waugh
Players to look out for: Jason Brown
Other sports followed: Rugby (Northampton Saints), football (Crystal Palace), golf
Favourite band: Coldplay
Relaxations: Fishing and golf
Extras: Sir John Hobbs Silver Jubilee Memorial Prize 1993. In 1994, became youngest batsman (16 years 289 days) to score a 50 in the Sunday League with his 56-ball 70* v Essex at Chelmsford. Scored 210* v Worcs at Kidderminster 1996 to become first player to score a double century on his Championship debut and the youngest ever (18 years 237 days) to score a Championship double century. Became the youngest Englishman to score a first-class 300 (303*) v Essex at Northampton 1999 aged 21 years 240 days (and became the first Englishman to 1000 runs for 1999 in the process). PCA/CGU Young Player of the Year 1999. Scored 62 for Wellington v Canterbury in the final of New Zealand's State Shield at Wellington 2001-02, winning the Man of the Match award. Captain of Northamptonshire since 2004
Best batting: 303* Northamptonshire v Essex, Northampton 1999
Best bowling: 4-25 Northamptonshire v Sri Lanka A, Northampton 1999

2004 Season

	M	Inns	NO	Runs	HS	Avge	100s	50s	Ct	St	O	M	Runs	Wkts	Avge	Best	5wI	10wM
Test																		
All First	16	25	5	1230	171	61.50	1	12	18	-	2	1	2	0	-	-	-	-
1-day Int																		
C & G	3	3	0	168	67	56.00	-	2	3	-								
totesport	16	15	2	321	63	24.69	-	3	12	-								
Twenty20	5	5	1	110	60 *	27.50	-	1	1	-								

Career Performances

	M	Inns	NO	Runs	HS	Avge	100s	50s	Ct	St	Balls	Runs	Wkts	Avge	Best	5wI	10wM
Test																	
All First	122	189	17	6546	303 *	38.05	12	35	97	-	321	169	9	18.77	4-25	-	-
1-day Int																	
C & G	15	15	1	513	67	36.64	-	5	8	-	12	13	0	-	-	-	
totesport	115	108	16	2820	133 *	30.65	1	19	46	-	24	17	0	-	-	-	
Twenty20	10	10	1	157	60 *	17.44	-	1	3	-							

SALISBURY, I. D. K. Surrey

Name: Ian David Kenneth Salisbury
Role: Right-hand bat, leg-break bowler
Born: 21 January 1970, Moulton, Northampton
Height: 5ft 11in **Weight:** 12st 7lbs
Nickname: Solly, Dingle, Sals
County debut: 1989 (Sussex), 1997 (Surrey)
County cap: 1991 (Sussex), 1998 (Surrey)
Test debut: 1992
Tests: 15
One-Day Internationals: 4
50 wickets in a season: 6
1st-Class 50s: 20
1st-Class 100s: 2
1st-Class 5 w. in innings: 34
1st-Class 10 w. in match: 6
1st-Class catches: 180
One-Day 5 w. in innings: 1
Place in batting averages: 191st av. 23.75 (2003 122nd av. 32.50)
Place in bowling averages: 144th av. 50.76 (2003 101st av. 37.09)
Strike rate: 102.53 (career 64.21)
Parents: Dave and Margaret
Wife and date of marriage: Emma Louise, 25 September 1993
Children: Anya-Rose, 10 August 2002
Family links with cricket: 'Dad is vice-president of my first club, Brixworth. He also re-lays cricket squares (e.g. Lord's, Northampton, Leicester)'
Education: Moulton Comprehensive, Northampton
Qualifications: 7 O-levels, NCA coaching certificate
Overseas tours: England A to Pakistan 1990-91, to Bermuda and West Indies 1991-92, to India 1994-95, to Pakistan 1995-96; England to India and Sri Lanka 1992-93, to West Indies 1993-94, to Pakistan 2000-01; World Masters XI v Indian Masters XI November 1996 ('Masters aged 26?')
Overseas teams played for: University of New South Wales, Sydney 1997-2000
Cricketers particularly admired: 'Any that keep performing day in, day out, for both country and county'
Young players to look out for: Jim Troughton, Kyle Hogg, Scott Newman, Rikki Clarke
Other sports played: 'Most sports'
Other sports followed: Football (Southampton FC, Northampton Town FC), rugby union (Northampton Saints), 'any England team'
Relaxations: 'Spending time with wife, Emma; meeting friends and relaxing with them and eating out with good wine'

Extras: In 1992 was named Young Player of the Year by both the Wombwell Cricket Lovers and the Cricket Writers. One of *Wisden*'s Five Cricketers of the Year 1993. Left Sussex during the 1996-97 off-season to join Surrey. Won Bill O'Reilly Medal for Sydney first-grade player of the year 1999-2000
Best batting: 101* Surrey v Leicestershire, The Oval 2003
Best bowling: 8-60 Surrey v Somerset, The Oval 2000

2004 Season

	M	Inns	NO	Runs	HS	Avge	100s	50s	Ct	St	O	M	Runs	Wkts	Avge	Best	5wI	10wM
Test																		
All First	9	13	1	285	77	23.75	-	1	3	-	222.1	39	660	13	50.76	3-30	-	-
1-day Int																		
C & G	1	1	0	4	4	4.00	-	-	-	-	8	0	44	1	44.00	1-44	-	
totesport	3	3	1	79	59 *	39.50	-	1	1	-	9	0	42	1	42.00	1-42	-	
Twenty20																		

Career Performances

	M	Inns	NO	Runs	HS	Avge	100s	50s	Ct	St	Balls	Runs	Wkts	Avge	Best	5wI	10wM
Test	15	25	3	368	50	16.72	-	1	5	-	2492	1539	20	76.95	4-163	-	-
All First	284	367	73	5941	101 *	20.20	2	20	180	-	49639	25160	773	32.54	8-60	34	6
1-day Int	4	2	1	7	5	7.00	-	-	1	-	186	177	5	35.40	3-41	-	
C & G	30	18	5	168	34 *	12.92	-	-	5	-	1745	1024	34	30.11	3-28	-	
totesport	150	101	25	1026	59 *	13.50	-	1	55	-	5485	4533	131	34.60	5-30	1	
Twenty20	5	4	1	20	12 *	6.66	-	-	2	-	84	93	3	31.00	2-20	-	

77. Which former international fast bowler is also an accomplished opera singer?

SAMPSON, P. J. Surrey

Name: Philip James Sampson
Role: Right-hand bat, right-arm fast-medium bowler
Born: 6 September 1980, Manchester
Height: 6ft 1in **Weight:** 14st 7lbs
Nickname: Sammo, Rhino
County debut: 2000 (one-day), 2002 (first-class)
1st-Class 5 w. in innings: 1
Strike rate: 34.50 (career 34.70)
Parents: Les and Kay
Marital status: Girlfriend Sally
Family links with cricket: Father played league cricket and was chairman of the Harlequins club in Pretoria. Brother was captain of Northern Transvaal (Northerns) at Youth level
Education: Pretoria Boys High School
Qualifications: Matriculation (A-level equivalent)
Career outside cricket: 'Golfer'
Off-season: 'Training in South Africa'
Overseas teams played for: Harlequins CC, Pretoria 1990-98, 2002
Career highlights to date: 'Playing in front of 26,000 at Lord's in Twenty20 v Middlesex'
Cricket moments to forget: 'Not getting a hand on a catch in Twenty20 semi-final v Lancs'
Cricket superstitions: 'Tying my left shoelace first'
Cricketers particularly admired: Allan Donald, Adam Hollioake
Young players to look out for: Jade Dernbach, Neil Saker
Other sports played: Football, golf
Other sports followed: Football (Manchester United), 'all sports'
Injuries: Out for two weeks in April with back spasms; for one week in May with a broken finger
Favourite band: Counting Crows, Powderfinger
Relaxations: 'Spending time with my girlfriend, socialising with friends, watching sport'
Extras: Trophy for best all-round cricketer at school. Represented Northerns at U15, U18, U19. Played for Buckinghamshire in the Minor Counties 1999. Recorded maiden first-class five-wicket return (5-121) v Warwickshire at Guildford 2004. Is not considered an overseas player
Opinions on cricket: 'Reduce the number of National League games and increase Twenty20 games.'

Best batting: 42 Surrey v CUCCE, Fenner's 2002
Best bowling: 5-121 Surrey v Warwickshire, Guildford 2004

2004 Season

	M	Inns	NO	Runs	HS	Avge	100s	50s	Ct	St	O	M	Runs	Wkts	Avge	Best	5wI	10wM
Test																		
All First	2	4	2	13	11 *	6.50	-	-	-	-	34.3	4	154	6	25.66	5-121	1	-
1-day Int																		
C & G																		
totesport	9	3	1	2	1 *	1.00	-	-	1	-	57	2	317	9	35.22	3-48	-	
Twenty20	7	1	0	0	0	0.00	-	-	3	-	23	0	164	9	18.22	2-26	-	

Career Performances

	M	Inns	NO	Runs	HS	Avge	100s	50s	Ct	St	Balls	Runs	Wkts	Avge	Best	5wI	10wM
Test																	
All First	5	9	4	91	42	18.20	-	-	-	-	590	415	17	24.41	5-121	1	-
1-day Int																	
C & G	2	2	2	9	5 *	-	-	-	2	-	96	59	0	-	-	-	
totesport	17	7	1	23	16	3.83	-	-	2	-	660	607	17	35.70	3-48	-	
Twenty20	11	3	2	7	4 *	7.00	-	-	5	-	228	287	13	22.07	2-26	-	

SAQLAIN MUSHTAQ — Surrey

Name: Saqlain Mushtaq
Role: Right-hand bat, off-spin bowler
Born: 29 December 1976, Lahore, Pakistan
Height: 5ft 9in **Weight:** 11st 4lbs
Nickname: Saqi, Baba
County debut: 1997
County cap: 1998
Test debut: 1995-96
Tests: 49
One-Day Internationals: 169
50 wickets in a season: 5
1st-Class 50s: 12
1st-Class 100s: 1
1st-Class 5 w. in innings: 56
1st-Class 10 w. in match: 15
1st-Class catches: 60
One-Day 5 w. in innings: 6
Place in batting averages: (2003 123rd av. 32.38)
Place in bowling averages: (2003 78th av. 33.26)

Strike rate: 43.33 (career 53.23)
Parents: Nasim Akhtar and Mushtaq Ahmed
Wife and date of marriage: Sana ('Sunny') Saqlain, 11 April 2000
Education: Lahore MAO College
Overseas tours: Pakistan U19 to New Zealand 1994-95; Pakistan to Australia 1995-96, 1996-97, 1999-2000, to England 1996, 2001, to Sri Lanka 1996-97, 1997-98, to India 1996-97, 1998-99, to South Africa 1997-98, 2002-03, to Zimbabwe 1997-98, 2002-03, to Bangladesh (Wills International Cup) 1998-99, to UK, Ireland and Holland (World Cup) 1999, to West Indies 1999-2000, to Kenya (ICC Knockout Trophy) 2000-01, to New Zealand 2000-01, to Bangladesh 2001-02, to Sharjah (v West Indies) 2001-02, to Morocco (Morocco Cup) 2002, to Sri Lanka and Sharjah (v Australia) 2002-03, to Africa (World Cup) 2002-03, plus other one-day tournaments in Toronto, Sharjah, Kenya, Bangladesh and Singapore
Overseas teams played for: PIA 1994-95 – ; Islamabad 1994-95, 1998
Cricketers particularly admired: Imran Khan, Wasim Akram, Waqar Younis
Other sports played: Squash
Other sports followed: Hockey (Pakistan), football (Manchester United and Arsenal)
Injuries: Out for most of the 2004 season with a knee injury
Relaxations: 'I like listening to music when free or travelling'
Extras: Scored 79 v Zimbabwe in the first Test at Sheikhupura 1996-97, in the process sharing with Wasim Akram (257*) in a world record eighth-wicket partnership in Tests (313). Joined Surrey as overseas player in 1997. Took only the second hat-trick in World Cup cricket (Olonga, Huckle and Mbangwa), v Zimbabwe at The Oval 1999; it was his second hat-trick in ODIs v Zimbabwe. Topped the English first-class bowling averages in 1999, taking 58 wickets at 11.37 in the seven games he played for Surrey. One of *Wisden*'s Five Cricketers of the Year 2000. Took 7-11 from 9.3 overs v Derbyshire at The Oval 2000. His international awards include Man of the [Test] Series v India 1998-99 and v Zimbabwe 2002-03, and Man of the Match in the first Test v England at Lahore 2000-01 (first innings figures of 8-164) and in the third ODI v England at Rawalpindi 2000-01 (5-20). Took 700th first-class wicket (Michael Carberry) v Kent at The Oval 2003, aged 26. Holds record for taking fewest matches to reach 100 (53 matches), 150 (78), 200 (104) and 250 (138) ODI wickets; also holds record for the most ODI wickets in a calendar year (69 in 1997). Left Surrey at the end of the 2004 season
Best batting: 101* Pakistan v New Zealand, Christchurch 2000-01
Best bowling: 8-65 Surrey v Derbyshire, The Oval 1998

2004 Season

	M	Inns	NO	Runs	HS	Avge	100s	50s	Ct	St	O	M	Runs	Wkts	Avge	Best	5wI	10wM
Test																		
All First	3	4	0	17	14	4.25	-	-	1	-	86.4	9	304	12	25.33	4-107	-	-
1-day Int																		
C & G	1	1	0	1	1	1.00	-	-	-	-	10	0	34	1	34.00	1-34	-	
totesport	2	2	0	41	26	20.50	-	-	1	-	9	0	35	2	17.50	2-35	-	
Twenty20																		

Career Performances

	M	Inns	NO	Runs	HS	Avge	100s	50s	Ct	St	Balls	Runs	Wkts	Avge	Best	5wI	10wM
Test	49	78	14	927	101 *	14.48	1	2	14	-	14070	6206	208	29.83	8-164	13	3
All First	171	237	53	3056	101 *	16.60	1	12	60	-	40405	17433	759	22.96	8-65	56	15
1-day Int	169	98	39	709	37 *	12.01	-	-	40	-	8770	6276	288	21.79	5-20	6	
C & G	21	8	2	52	24	8.66	-	-	1	-	1141	764	32	23.87	4-17	-	
totesport	58	36	12	308	38 *	12.83	-	-	13	-	2542	1810	63	28.73	3-12	-	
Twenty20	3	2	0	5	5	2.50	-	-	1	-	66	87	4	21.75	2-35	-	

SAYERS, J. J. — Yorkshire

Name: Joseph (Joe) John Sayers
Role: Left-hand bat, right-arm off-spin bowler
Born: 5 November 1983, Leeds
Height: 6ft **Weight:** 13st
Nickname: Leo, JJ, Ralph
County debut: 2003 (one-day), 2004 (first-class)
1st-Class 50s: 6
1st-Class 100s: 2
1st-Class catches: 3
Place in batting averages: 80th av. 39.84
Parents: Geraldine and Roger
Marital status: Single
Family links with cricket: 'Father played at school, but otherwise none'
Education: St Mary's RC Comprehensive School, Menston; Worcester College, Oxford University
Qualifications: 12 GCSEs, 4 A-levels, BA Physics (Oxon)
Off-season: 'Playing for Manly-Warringah in Sydney'
Overseas tours: Leeds Schools to South Africa 1998; Yorkshire U17 to South Africa 2001; England U17 to Australia 2001
Overseas teams played for: Manly-Warringah, Sydney 2004-05
Career highlights to date: 'Making my Championship debut for Yorkshire. Scoring 147* at Lord's in 2004 Varsity Match victory for Oxford. Maiden first-class century v Hampshire 2003'
Cricketers particularly admired: Rahul Dravid, Andrew Strauss, Michael Vaughan
Young players to look out for: Tim Bresnan
Other sports played: Football ('played as goalkeeper for Bradford City AFC for three years'), rowing (Worcester College)

Favourite band: Coldplay
Relaxations: 'Playing guitar; drawing/painting; reading autobiographies; listening to music'
Extras: Captained England U17 against Australia U17 in Adelaide 2001. Played for Oxford University CCE 2002, 2003 (captain 2003), 2004. Oxford Blue 2002, 2003, 2004, scoring century (144*) in the 50-over Varsity Match at Lord's and century (147) in the four-day Varsity Match at The Parks, both 2004. Represented England U19 v India U19 2002 and v South Africa U19 2003 (captain in the third 'Test'). Scored 62 v Gloucestershire at Headingley on one-day debut in the NCL 2003
Opinions on cricket: 'The presence of two overseas players per county team has led to an improved standard of first-class cricket and has fuelled the development of many emerging young players. However, the introduction and employment of players who are not qualified to play for England must not be allowed to further hinder the progress of future prospects.'
Best batting: 147 Oxford University v Cambridge University, The Parks 2004

2004 Season

	M	Inns	NO	Runs	HS	Avge	100s	50s	Ct	St	O	M	Runs	Wkts	Avge	Best	5wI	10wM
Test																		
All First	8	13	0	518	147	39.84	1	4	1	-								
1-day Int																		
C & G																		
totesport	1	1	0	7	7	7.00	-	-	-	-								
Twenty20																		

Career Performances

	M	Inns	NO	Runs	HS	Avge	100s	50s	Ct	St	Balls	Runs	Wkts	Avge	Best	5wI	10wM
Test																	
All First	16	27	1	913	147	35.11	2	6	3	-	18	12	0	-	-	-	-
1-day Int																	
C & G																	
totesport	2	2	0	69	62	34.50	-	1	-	-							
Twenty20																	

78. Who in 2001-02 became the youngest cricketer to make a Test century, breaking a long-standing record set some 40 years previously by Mushtaq Mohammed?

SCHOFIELD, C. P. Lancashire

Name: Christopher (Chris) Paul Schofield
Role: Left-hand bat, leg-break bowler
Born: 6 October 1978, Rochdale
Height: 6ft 1in **Weight:** 11st 5lbs
Nickname: Scoey, Junior, Scoffer
County debut: 1998
County cap: 2002
Test debut: 2000
Tests: 2
1st-Class 50s: 20
1st-Class 5 w. in innings: 4
1st-Class catches: 40
One-Day 5 w. in innings: 1
Place in batting averages: 51st av. 46.50 (2003 131st av. 31.00)
Place in bowling averages: (2003 125th av. 42.40)
Strike rate: 159.00 (career 62.08)
Parents: David and Judith
Marital status: Single
Family links with cricket: Father played with local club team Whittles and brother plays with local team Littleborough
Education: Wardle High School
Qualifications: 4 GCSEs, NVQ Levels 2 and 3 in Information Technology
Overseas tours: England U17 to Bermuda 1997; England U19 to South Africa (including U19 World Cup) 1997-98; England A to Bangladesh and New Zealand 1999-2000, to West Indies 2000-01; ECB National Academy to Australia 2001-02
Cricketers particularly admired: Shane Warne, Stuart Law
Other sports played: Football (Littleborough FC, Whittles FC), snooker (Wardle Con Club – handicap of four)
Other sports followed: Football ('like watching Liverpool FC')
Relaxations: Listening to music, playing snooker, socialising
Extras: Was part of England U19 World Cup winning squad 1997-98. Won double twice in two years with Littleborough CC (Wood Cup and Lancashire Cup 1997; League and Wood Cup 1998). Won Sir Ron Brierley/Crusaders Scholarship 1998. NBC Denis Compton Award for the most promising young Lancashire player 1998, 1999, 2000. Was the only uncapped player to be contracted to England in 2000. Leading first-class wicket-taker on England A tour to West Indies 2000-01 (22 wickets; av. 26.27). Released by Lancashire at the end of the 2004 season
Best batting: 99 Lancashire v Warwickshire, Old Trafford 2004
Best bowling: 6-120 England A v Bangladesh, Chittagong 1999-2000

2004 Season

	M	Inns	NO	Runs	HS	Avge	100s	50s	Ct	St	O	M	Runs	Wkts	Avge	Best	5wI	10wM
Test																		
All First	3	6	0	279	99	46.50	-	3	-	-	26.3	3	85	1	85.00	1-13	-	-
1-day Int																		
C & G																		
totesport	10	7	1	197	69 *	32.83	-	1	2	-	6	0	63	0	-	-	-	
Twenty20	7	5	1	24	8	6.00	-	-	1	-	5	0	25	4	6.25	2-9	-	

Career Performances

	M	Inns	NO	Runs	HS	Avge	100s	50s	Ct	St	Balls	Runs	Wkts	Avge	Best	5wI	10wM
Test	2	3	0	67	57	22.33	-	1	-	-	108	73	0	-	-	-	-
All First	68	95	14	2423	99	29.91	-	20	40	-	10616	5347	171	31.26	6-120	4	-
1-day Int																	
C & G	11	4	0	88	42	22.00	-	-	6	-	401	317	16	19.81	4-34	-	
totesport	62	47	11	779	69 *	21.63	-	2	13	-	1611	1431	47	30.44	5-31	1	
Twenty20	11	9	2	84	27	12.00	-	-	2	-	54	49	4	12.25	2-9	-	

SCOTT, B. J. M. — Middlesex

Name: Benjamin (Ben) James Matthew Scott
Role: Right-hand bat, wicket-keeper, leg-spin bowler
Born: 4 August 1981, Isleworth
Height: 'Small' (5ft 9in) **Weight:** 11st 7lbs
Nickname: Scotty
County debut: 2002 (one-day, Surrey), 2003 (first-class, Surrey), 2004 (Middlesex)
1st-Class 50s: 1
1st-Class 100s: 1
1st-Class catches: 14
1st-Class stumpings: 3
Place in batting averages: 169th av. 26.22
Parents: Terry and Edna
Marital status: Single
Family links with cricket: Father played for the Primitives; brother played local cricket
Education: Whitton School, Richmond; Richmond College
Qualifications: 9 GCSEs, 3 A-levels studied, ECB Level 1 coach, YMCA Fitness Instructor's Award
Off-season: 'Fixing my nose'

Overseas tours: MCC YC to Cape Town 1999-2000; Mumbai, India 2005
Overseas teams played for: Portland CC, Victoria 1999-2000; Mt Gambia, South Australia 2001-02
Career highlights to date: 'Scoring 101* at Lord's v Northants; just getting there with Nantie Hayward down the other end'
Cricket moments to forget: 'Getting a first-baller against Alex Loudon's "other one" at Kent'
Cricket superstitions: 'None'
Cricketers particularly admired: Alec Stewart, Jack Russell, Nad Shahid
Young players to look out for: 'Brandon Newman', Eoin Morgan
Other sports played: Golf
Favourite band: Michael Jackson, The Jacksons, Usher
Relaxations: Music, golf, TV
Extras: Middlesex YC cap. Represented ESCA U14 and U15. Played for Development of Excellence XI v Australia U19 1999. Finchley CC Player of the Season 2000. Left Surrey at the end of the 2003 season and joined Middlesex for 2004. Scored maiden first-class century (101*) v Northamptonshire at Lord's 2004
Opinions on cricket: 'One-day and Twenty20 cricket has dramatically enhanced the profile of cricket in England. England winning Test matches now is awesome.'
Best batting: 101* Middlesex v Northamptonshire, Lord's 2004

2004 Season

	M	Inns	NO	Runs	HS	Avge	100s	50s	Ct	St	O	M	Runs	Wkts	Avge	Best	5wI	10wM
Test																		
All First	7	13	4	236	101 *	26.22	1	-	8	3								
1-day Int																		
C & G	2	1	1	8	8 *	-	-	-	-	1								
totesport	18	7	1	70	42	11.66	-	-	24	8								
Twenty20	4	3	2	1	1 *	1.00	-	-	1	-								

Career Performances

	M	Inns	NO	Runs	HS	Avge	100s	50s	Ct	St	Balls	Runs	Wkts	Avge	Best	5wI	10wM
Test																	
All First	9	16	5	315	101 *	28.63	1	1	14	3							
1-day Int																	
C & G	3	2	1	19	11	19.00	-	-	-	1							
totesport	19	8	1	74	42	10.57	-	-	24	8							
Twenty20	4	3	2	1	1 *	1.00	-	-	1	-							

SCOTT, G. M. Durham

Name: Gary Michael Scott
Role: Right-hand bat, right-arm off-spin bowler
Born: 21 July 1984, Sunderland
Height: 6ft **Weight:** 13st
Nickname: Scotty, Dirk
County debut: 2001
1st-Class catches: 1
One-Day 100s: 1
Parents: Mary and Michael
Marital status: Single
Family links with cricket: 'Dad and uncle played but only at school; brother (Martin) played club cricket with me (Hetton Lyons CC)'
Education: Hetton Comprehensive
Qualifications: 8 GCSEs
Overseas tours: England U17 to Australia 2000-01
Overseas teams played for: Northern Districts, Adelaide 2002-03
Career highlights to date: 'First-class debut against Derby. Scoring 100 off 64 balls against Herefordshire at Darlington for Durham Board XI'
Cricket moments to forget: 'Getting my first pair against Warwickshire in the same day for the 2nd XI'
Cricket superstitions: 'Not really'
Cricketers particularly admired: Steve Waugh, Jacques Kallis, Paul Collingwood
Young players to look out for: Liam Plunkett, Bilal Shafayat
Other sports played: Football (represented Sunderland Schoolboys), golf
Other sports followed: Football (Newcastle Utd)
Favourite band: U2
Relaxations: 'Golf, pool, eating out and watching TV'
Extras: Sir John Hobbs Silver Jubilee Memorial Prize 1999. Played for Durham Board XI in the C&G 2001, 2002 and 2003, scoring maiden one-day century (100) v Herefordshire at Darlington in the 2003 competition and winning Man of the Match award. Became youngest to play first-class cricket for Durham when he made his debut v Derbyshire at Riverside 2001 aged 17 years and 19 days. Attended Durham Academy; is a Durham Development Player
Opinions on cricket: 'Too much cricket; not enough practice and rest time.'
Best batting: 25 Durham v Derbyshire, Riverside 2001

2004 Season (did not make any first-class or one-day appearances)

Career Performances

	M	Inns	NO	Runs	HS	Avge	100s	50s	Ct	St	Balls	Runs	Wkts	Avge	Best	5wI	10wM
Test																	
All First	1	2	0	33	25	16.50	-	-	1	-	18	11	0	-	-	-	-
1-day Int																	
C & G	3	3	0	130	100	43.33	1	-	2	-	174	107	4	26.75	2-32	-	
totesport																	
Twenty20																	

SELWOOD, S. A. — Derbyshire

Name: Steven (Steve) Andrew Selwood
Role: Left-hand bat, left-arm spin bowler
Born: 24 November 1979, Barnet, London
Height: 5ft 11in **Weight:** 12st
Nickname: Sellers, Hollywood
County debut: 2001
1st-Class 50s: 4
1st-Class catches: 6
Place in batting averages: 272nd av. 8.50 (2003 221st av. 20.81)
Strike rate: (career 60.00)
Parents: Tim and Sarah
Marital status: 'Taken'
Family links with cricket: Father played for Middlesex 1969-74 and Central Districts 1972-73
Education: Mill Hill School; Loughborough University
Qualifications: 9 GCSEs, 2 A-levels, BA (Hons) Politics, Level 1 coaching
Overseas tours: Middlesex Prep Schools to Australia 1990-91; British Universities to South Africa 2002
Overseas teams played for: Manly-Warringah, Sydney 1996-97; Claremont-Nedlands, Perth 1998-99
Career highlights to date: 'Every time we win'
Cricket moments to forget: 'Any time we lose and every time I fail'
Cricket superstitions: 'None'
Cricketers particularly admired: Darren Lehmann, Ian Botham
Other sports played: Football, rugby
Other sports followed: Football (Tottenham Hotspur)

Relaxations: 'Spending time with my girlfriend; travel; going out with friends'
Extras: Represented England U14. Played for Finchley v Uxbridge in the *Evening Standard* final 2000, winning Man of the Match award. Played for Loughborough University CCE 2001 and 2002. Scored 93 v Gloucestershire at Bristol in the NUL 2002, in the process sharing with Mathew Dowman (45) in a new record sixth-wicket partnership for Derbyshire in the one-day league (123). Released by Derbyshire at the end of the 2004 season
Best batting: 99 Derbyshire v Worcestershire, Derby 2002
Best bowling: 1-8 Derbyshire v Essex, Derby 2002

2004 Season

	M	Inns	NO	Runs	HS	Avge	100s	50s	Ct	St	O	M	Runs	Wkts	Avge	Best	5wI	10wM
Test																		
All First	4	8	0	68	38	8.50	-	-	1	-								
1-day Int																		
C & G																		
totesport	5	4	0	108	55	27.00	-	1	1	-								
Twenty20																		

Career Performances

	M	Inns	NO	Runs	HS	Avge	100s	50s	Ct	St	Balls	Runs	Wkts	Avge	Best	5wI	10wM
Test																	
All First	25	48	1	901	99	19.17	-	4	6	-	120	95	2	47.50	1-8	-	-
1-day Int																	
C & G	4	4	1	31	19	10.33	-	-	-	-	12	7	1	7.00	1-7	-	
totesport	33	29	3	849	93	32.65	-	7	8	-	2	8	0	-	-	-	
Twenty20	5	3	0	17	12	5.66	-	-	-	-							

SHABBIR AHMED — Gloucestershire

Name: Shabbir Ahmed Khan
Role: Right-hand bat, right-arm fast-medium bowler
Born: 21 April 1976, Khanewal, Pakistan
Height: 6ft 5in
County debut: 2004
County cap: 2004
Test debut: 2003
Tests: 7
One-Day Internationals: 29
1st-Class 50s: 1
1st-Class 5 w. in innings: 15
1st-Class catches: 15
Place in bowling averages: 69th av. 33.61

Strike rate: 56.33 (career 47.16)
Overseas tours: Pakistan A to Sri Lanka 2001; Pakistan to West Indies 1999-2000, to England (NatWest Challenge) 2003, to New Zealand 2003-04, plus one-day tournaments in Toronto, Sharjah, Bangladesh, Sri Lanka and Holland
Overseas teams played for: Multan 1997-98; WAPDA 1997-98 – 1999-2000; Bahawalpur 1998-99; Pakistan Reserves 1999-2000; REDCO Pakistan 1999-2000; National Bank of Pakistan 2000-01 – 2002-03; Rest of Punjab 2001-02
Extras: Won three match awards in 10 days in the National Bank of Pakistan Cup 1999-2000. Had match figures of 8-109 (3-61/5-48) on Test debut in the first Test v Bangladesh at Karachi 2003-04. Joined Gloucestershire as an overseas player for 2004; left Gloucestershire at the end of the 2004 season
Best batting: 50 National Bank of Pakistan v Allied Bank, Sheikhupura 2000-01
Best bowling: 7-70 National Bank of Pakistan v Lahore Blues, Okara 2002-03

2004 Season

	M	Inns	NO	Runs	HS	Avge	100s	50s	Ct	St	O	M	Runs	Wkts	Avge	Best	5wI	10wM
Test																		
All First	6	6	4	51	34 *	25.50	-	-	1	-	169	38	605	18	33.61	4-96	-	-
1-day Int																		
C & G	2	1	1	10	10 *	-	-	-	-	-	17	4	48	2	24.00	1-23	-	
totesport	3	2	1	62	42	62.00	-	-	-	-	26.2	0	138	0	-	-	-	
Twenty20																		

Career Performances

	M	Inns	NO	Runs	HS	Avge	100s	50s	Ct	St	Balls	Runs	Wkts	Avge	Best	5wI	10wM
Test	7	9	4	82	24 *	16.40	-	-	3	-	1907	841	33	25.48	5-48	2	-
All First	66	89	22	778	50	11.61	-	1	15	-	13158	6587	279	23.60	7-70	15	-
1-day Int	29	10	5	9	2	1.80	-	-	8	-	1484	1071	29	36.93	3-32	-	
C & G	2	1	1	10	10 *	-	-	-	-	-	102	48	2	24.00	1-23	-	
totesport	3	2	1	62	42	62.00	-	-	-	-	158	138	0	-	-	-	
Twenty20																	

SHAFAYAT, B. M. — Northamptonshire

Name: Bilal Mustafa Shafayat
Role: Right-hand bat, right-arm medium-fast bowler, occasional wicket-keeper
Born: 10 July 1984, Nottingham
Height: 5ft 7in **Weight:** 10st 7lbs
Nickname: Billy, Muzzy, Our Kid
County debut: 2001 (Nottinghamshire)
1st-Class 50s: 7
1st-Class 100s: 2
1st-Class catches: 10
1st-Class stumpings: 1
Place in batting averages: (2003 203rd av. 23.17)
Strike rate: (career 242.00)
Parents: Mohammad Shafayat and Mahfooza Begum
Marital status: Single
Family links with cricket: 'Brother Rashid

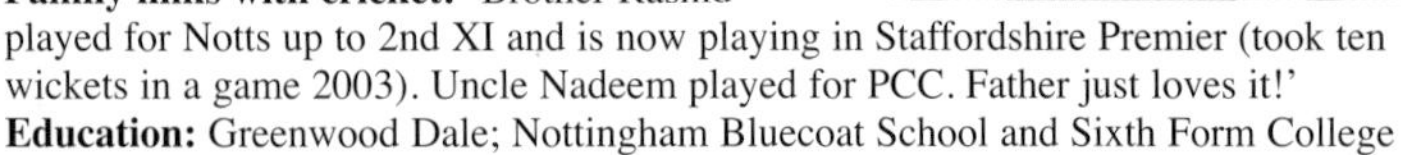

played for Notts up to 2nd XI and is now playing in Staffordshire Premier (took ten wickets in a game 2003). Uncle Nadeem played for PCC. Father just loves it!'
Education: Greenwood Dale; Nottingham Bluecoat School and Sixth Form College
Qualifications: 9 GCSEs, 2 A-levels, Level 1 coaching
Overseas tours: ZRK to Pakistan 2000; Sparkhill ('Kadeer Ali's dad's academy') to Pakistan; England U17 to Australia 2000-01; England U19 to Australia and (U19 World Cup) New Zealand 2001-02, to Australia 2002-03 (captain); Nottinghamshire to South Africa 2002, 2003; England A to Malaysia and India 2003-04
Career highlights to date: 'Making my first-class debut for Notts v Middlesex (scoring 72). Scoring a hundred and double hundred v India in final U19 "Test" 2002. Scoring crucial hundred v Worcestershire for promotion in Championship. Beating Australia U19 in first "Test" 2002-03, scoring 66, 108 and taking six wickets'
Cricket moments to forget: 'Losing U19 "Test" series to Australia'
Cricketers particularly admired: Sachin Tendulkar, Carl Hooper, Andrew Jackman
Young players to look out for: Ravinder Bopara, Samit Patel, Liam Plunkett, Moeen and Kadeer Ali, Nadeem Malik, Aaqib Afzaal, Kamani, Sajid and Rakib Mahmood, Shaftab Khalid
Other sports played: Football, badminton, squash, pool
Other sports followed: Football (Liverpool), boxing (Prince Naseem Hamed), snooker (Ronnie O'Sullivan)
Favourite band: Sean Paul, 50 Cent, Tupac, Nusrat Fateh Ali Khan
Relaxations: 'Praying Namaz; chilling with loved ones'
Extras: Scored 72 on Championship debut v Middlesex at Trent Bridge 2001; aged 16 years 360 days, he became the youngest player to represent Nottinghamshire in the

competition. NBC Denis Compton Award for the most promising young Nottinghamshire player 2001, 2002. Scored maiden first-class century (104) v Worcestershire at Trent Bridge 2002, becoming the youngest Nottinghamshire centurion. Scored record-equalling four 'Test' centuries for England U19, including two (118/201*) in the third 'Test' v India U19 at Northampton 2002 and 108 (along with second innings figures of 6-54) in the first 'Test' v Australia U19 at Adelaide 2002-03. BBC East Midlands Junior Sportsman of the Year 2003. ECB National Academy 2003-04. Left Nottinghamshire at the end of the 2004 season and has joined Northamptonshire for 2005

Opinions on cricket: 'Best [game] in the world.'

Best batting: 105 Nottinghamshire v DUCCE, Trent Bridge 2003

Best bowling: 1-22 Nottinghamshire v DUCCE, Trent Bridge 2003

2004 Season

	M	Inns	NO	Runs	HS	Avge	100s	50s	Ct	St	O	M	Runs	Wkts	Avge	Best	5wI	10wM
Test																		
All First	1	2	0	16	13	8.00	-	-	-	-	2	0	16	0	-	-	-	-
1-day Int																		
C & G																		
totesport	6	4	0	74	27	18.50	-	-	6	1								
Twenty20	2	2	0	13	13	6.50	-	-	-	-	3	0	17	0	-	-	-	

Career Performances

	M	Inns	NO	Runs	HS	Avge	100s	50s	Ct	St	Balls	Runs	Wkts	Avge	Best	5wI	10wM
Test																	
All First	26	48	1	1332	105	28.34	2	7	10	1	242	192	1	192.00	1-22	-	-
1-day Int																	
C & G	6	6	1	76	36	15.20	-	-	-	-	12	21	0	-	-	-	
totesport	31	29	0	535	66	18.44	-	1	15	1	292	261	9	29.00	4-35	-	
Twenty20	7	7	1	78	28	13.00	-	-	2	1	36	54	0	-	-	-	

79. Which Sri Lankan-born batsman played for Sussex and Lancashire between 1973 and 1993 and scored 41 first-class centuries?

SHAH, O. A. — Middlesex

Name: Owais Alam Shah
Role: Right-hand bat, off-spin bowler
Born: 22 October 1978, Karachi, Pakistan
Height: 6ft 1in **Weight:** 13st 7lbs
Nickname: Ace, The Mauler
County debut: 1995 (one-day), 1996 (first-class)
County cap: 1999
One-Day Internationals: 15
1000 runs in a season: 4
1st-Class 50s: 39
1st-Class 100s: 18
1st-Class 200s: 1
1st-Class catches: 91
One-Day 100s: 7
Place in batting averages: 27th av. 53.44 (2003 59th av. 43.07)
Strike rate: 132.00 (career 66.33)
Parents: Jamshed and Mehjabeen
Wife and date of marriage: Gemma, 25 September 2004
Family links with cricket: Father played for his college side
Education: Isleworth and Syon School; Lampton School; Westminster University, Harrow
Qualifications: 7 GCSEs, 2 A-levels
Off-season: 'ECB Academy and then touring'
Overseas tours: England U19 to Zimbabwe 1995-96, to South Africa (including U19 World Cup) 1997-98 (captain); England A to Australia 1996-97, to Kenya and Sri Lanka 1997-98, to Sri Lanka 2004-05; ECB National Academy to Australia 2001-02; England to Zimbabwe (one-day series) 2001-02, to India and New Zealand 2001-02 (one-day series), to Sri Lanka (ICC Champions Trophy) 2002-03, to Australia 2002-03 (VB Series)
Overseas teams played for: University of Western Australia, Perth
Career highlights to date: 'England debut v Australia [2001]. Fifty [62] against Pakistan at Lord's [2001]'
Cricket moments to forget: 'Getting a pair in first-class cricket'
Cricketers particularly admired: Viv Richards, Sachin Tendulkar, Mark Waugh
Young players to look out for: Ben Scott, Chris Whelan
Other sports played: Snooker
Other sports followed: Football ('like to watch Man Utd play')
Favourite band: 'Too many to mention'
Relaxations: 'Movies, eating out'

Extras: Scored record 232 for England U15 against England U16. Man of the Series in U17 'Test' series against India 1994. Captained the England U19 side to success in the 1997-98 U19 World Cup in South Africa, scoring 54* in the final. Captain of England U19 v Pakistan U19 1998. Scored 62 v Pakistan at Lord's in the NatWest Series 2001, in the process sharing in a then record fourth-wicket partnership for England in ODIs (170) with Marcus Trescothick. Cricket Writers' Young Player of the Year 2001. Middlesex Player of the Year 2002. *Evening Standard* Player of the Month August 2004. Vice-captain of Middlesex 2002 to June 2004. ECB National Academy 2004-05
Opinions on cricket: 'Too much cricket played in this country. Need to cut down the amount of four-day cricket.'
Best batting: 203 Middlesex v Derbyshire, Southgate 2001
Best bowling: 3-33 Middlesex v Gloucestershire, Bristol 1999

2004 Season

	M	Inns	NO	Runs	HS	Avge	100s	50s	Ct	St	O	M	Runs	Wkts	Avge	Best	5wI	10wM
Test																		
All First	17	30	5	1336	140 *	53.44	4	9	19	-	22	5	67	1	67.00	1-9	-	-
1-day Int																		
C & G	3	3	0	26	24	8.66	-	-	-	-								
totesport	18	16	3	561	125 *	43.15	2	3	6	-								
Twenty20	4	4	1	85	48 *	28.33	-	-	2	-	0.1	0	1	0	-	-	-	

Career Performances

	M	Inns	NO	Runs	HS	Avge	100s	50s	Ct	St	Balls	Runs	Wkts	Avge	Best	5wI	10wM
Test																	
All First	130	216	18	7617	203	38.46	19	39	91	-	1194	749	18	41.61	3-33	-	-
1-day Int	15	15	2	283	62	21.76	-	2	6	-							
C & G	17	17	1	311	49	19.43	-	-	4	-	30	36	1	36.00	1-36	-	
totesport	122	114	14	3314	134	33.14	6	17	42	-	151	176	3	58.66	1-4	-	
Twenty20	9	9	3	156	48 *	26.00	-	-	5	-	1	1	0	-	-	-	

80. Which slow left-armer was Man of the Match v Australia at Durban in the 2002-03 World Cup and also played Davis Cup tennis for his country?

SHAHID AFRIDI Kent

Name: Sahibzaha Mohammad Shahid Khan Afridi
Role: Right-hand bat, leg-break bowler
Born: 1 March 1980, Kohat, Pakistan
County debut: 2001 (Leicestershire), 2003 (Derbyshire), 2004 (one-day, Kent)
Test debut: 1998-99
Tests: 14
One-Day Internationals: 185
1st-Class 50s: 18
1st-Class 100s: 8
1st-Class 5 w. in innings: 6
1st-Class catches: 53
One-Day 100s: 3
One-Day 5 w. in innings: 2
Place in batting averages: (2003 249th av. 15.33)
Strike rate: (career 55.48)
Family links with cricket: Brother Tariq Afridi played first-class cricket in Pakistan
Overseas tours: Pakistan U19 to West Indies 1996-97; Pakistan to Kenya (one-day series) 1996-97, to Australia (one-day series) 1996-97, to India (one-day series) 1996-97, to Zimbabwe and South Africa 1997-98 (one-day series), to Bangladesh (Wills International Cup) 1998-99, to India 1998-99, to UK, Ireland and Holland (World Cup) 1999, to Australia 1999-2000 (one-day series), to West Indies 1999-2000 (one-day series), to New Zealand 2000-01 (one-day series), to England 2001 (one-day series), to Sharjah (v West Indies) 2001-02, to Australia (Super Challenge II) 2002, to Morocco (Morocco Cup) 2002, to Kenya (Nairobi Triangular) 2002, to Sri Lanka (ICC Champions Trophy) 2002-03, to Zimbabwe 2002-03, to South Africa 2002-03 (one-day series), to Africa (World Cup) 2002-03, to England (ICC Champions Trophy) 2004, to Australia 2004-05, to India 2004-05, plus other one-day tournaments in Toronto, Sharjah, India and Holland
Overseas teams played for: Karachi Whites 1995-96 – 2001-02; Habib Bank 1997-98 – 2002-03; Karachi Blues 1996-97; Karachi 2003-04; Griqualand West 2003-04
Extras: Set record for fastest ODI century – 37 balls (out for 102) v Sri Lanka in Kenya 1996-97 in his first ODI innings, aged 16 years 217 days; innings included a record-equalling 11 sixes. Recorded his maiden Test five-wicket innings return (5-52) on debut v Australia at Karachi 1998-99, going on to score his maiden Test century (141) v India at Chennai (Madras) in his second match. Overseas player with Leicestershire for part of the 2001 season. C&G Man of the Match awards for his 44-ball 67 in the quarter-final v Worcestershire at Worcester and for his 58-ball 95 in the semi-final v Lancashire at Leicester 2001. Has won numerous ODI awards, among

them Man of the Finals in the CUB Series in Australia 1996-97 and Man of the Match v England at Lahore 2000-01 (5-40/61) and v Kenya at Edgbaston in the ICC Champions Trophy 2004 (5-11). Struck 18-ball 55* v Holland at Colombo in the ICC Champions Trophy 2002-03, equalling his own record for the second-fastest fifty in ODIs. His quicker ball was once timed at 86mph. Was an overseas player with Derbyshire April to May 2003. Was an overseas player with Kent in July 2004, pending the arrival of Ian Butler, absent on international duty
Best batting: 164 Leicestershire v Northamptonshire, Northampton 2001
Best bowling: 6-101 Habib Bank v KRL, Rawalpindi 1997-98

2004 Season

	M	Inns	NO	Runs	HS	Avge	100s	50s	Ct	St	O	M	Runs	Wkts	Avge	Best	5wI	10wM
Test																		
All First																		
1-day Int	4	4	0	45	25	11.25	-	-	2	-	17	1	74	6	12.33	5-11	1	
C & G																		
totesport	1	0	0	0	0	-	-	-	-	-								
Twenty20	3	3	0	39	25	13.00	-	-	-	-	10.3	0	66	1	66.00	1-23	-	

Career Performances

	M	Inns	NO	Runs	HS	Avge	100s	50s	Ct	St	Balls	Runs	Wkts	Avge	Best	5wI	10wM
Test	14	25	1	780	141	32.50	2	4	8	-	1331	661	21	31.47	5-52	1	-
All First	75	128	4	3722	164	30.01	8	18	53	-	8766	4479	158	28.34	6-101	6	-
1-day Int	185	180	7	4040	109	23.35	3	23	68	-	6965	5355	143	37.44	5-11	2	
C & G	5	5	0	228	95	45.60	-	2	1	-	276	203	9	22.55	3-47	-	
totesport	13	12	1	317	70	28.81	-	3	1	-	468	369	13	28.38	3-45	-	
Twenty20	3	3	0	39	25	13.00	-	-	-	-	63	66	1	66.00	1-23	-	

81. Which former Essex, Worcestershire and Durham bowler represented Scotland in the 1999 World Cup?

SHAHID, N. Surrey

Name: Nadeem Shahid
Role: Right-hand bat, leg-spin bowler
Born: 23 April 1969, Karachi, Pakistan
Height: 6ft **Weight:** 12st
Nickname: Nad, Gonad, 'too many to mention'
County debut: 1989 (Essex), 1995 (Surrey)
County cap: 1998 (Surrey)
1000 runs in a season: 1
1st-Class 50s: 35
1st-Class 100s: 9
1st-Class catches: 153
One-Day 100s: 2
Place in batting averages: (2003 266th av. 12.66)
Strike rate: (career 72.75)
Parents: Ahmed and Salma
Marital status: Single
Family links with cricket: Brother league cricketer in Suffolk
Education: Ipswich School; Plymouth Polytechnic
Qualifications: 6 O-levels, 1 A-level, coaching certificate
Overseas tours: Ipswich School to Barbados (Sir Garfield Sobers Trophy) 1987; England (South) to Northern Ireland (Youth World Tournament) 1988
Overseas teams played for: Gosnells, Perth, Western Australia 1989-91; Fairfield, Sydney 1992-93
Cricket moments to forget: 'Cannot remember … maybe a dropped catch against Gloucestershire that cost us the game some years back'
Cricket superstitions: 'Not eating duck the night before I'm due to bat'
Cricketers particularly admired: 'All players at Surrey plus Ed Giddins and Gavin Hamilton'
Young players to look out for: Rikki Clarke, Tim Murtagh
Other sports played: 'Golf, tennis, golf, football (centre forward), golf, snooker, golf … most sports'
Other sports followed: Football (Ipswich Town), 'follow most sports'
Relaxations: 'Playing as much golf as possible; eating out; watching movies'
Extras: Youngest Suffolk player, aged 17. Played for HMC, MCC Schools, ESCA U19, NCA Young Cricketers, England U25 and at every level for Suffolk. TSB Young Player of the Year 1987, *Daily Telegraph* Bowling Award 1987 and 1988 and Cricket Society's Leading All-rounder in English Schools Cricket 1988. Laidlaw Young Player of the Year for Essex and Essex Society Player of the Year 1993. Released by Essex at end of 1994 season and signed for Surrey. Member of the Surrey Sunday League

winning side of 1996. Member of Surrey County Championship winning squad of 1999, 2000 and 2002. Surrey Team Man of the Year and Fielder of the Year 2002. Scored 266 v Derbyshire 2nd XI at The Oval 2003, sharing with Scott Newman (284) in an opening partnership of 552, just three runs short of the English all-cricket record first-wicket stand of 555 set by Percy Holmes and Herbert Sutcliffe for Yorkshire v Essex at Leyton 1932; scored 272 v Sussex 2nd XI at Hove in next match. Retired at the end of the 2004 season
Best batting: 150 Surrey v Sussex, The Oval 2002
Best bowling: 3-91 Essex v Surrey, The Oval 1990

2004 Season

	M	Inns	NO	Runs	HS	Avge	100s	50s	Ct	St	O	M	Runs	Wkts	Avge	Best	5wI	10wM
Test																		
All First	3	6	1	109	53	21.80	-	1	2	-	3	3	0	0	-	-	-	-
1-day Int																		
C & G	1	1	0	27	27	27.00	-	-	-	-								
totesport	1	1	1	61	61 *	-	-	1	-	-								
Twenty20	1	1	0	1	1	1.00	-	-	-	-								

Career Performances

	M	Inns	NO	Runs	HS	Avge	100s	50s	Ct	St	Balls	Runs	Wkts	Avge	Best	5wI	10wM
Test																	
All First	148	235	27	6453	150	31.02	9	35	153	-	3274	2146	45	47.68	3-91	-	-
1-day Int																	
C & G	13	10	2	276	85 *	34.50	-	2	6	-	72	30	4	7.50	3-30	-	
totesport	128	114	19	2312	109 *	24.33	2	8	40	-	78	85	0	-	-	-	
Twenty20	1	1	0	1	1	1.00	-	-	-	-							

82. Which West Indies cricketer scored a fifty in each innings of his Test debut v Australia in 1977-78 and later captained USA in the 1986 and 1990 ICC Trophy tournaments?

SHAHZAD, A. Yorkshire

Name: Ajmal Shahzad
Role: Right-hand bat, right-arm fast bowler
Born: 27 July 1985, Huddersfield
Height: 6ft **Weight:** 12st
Nickname: Ajy
County debut: 2004 (one-day)
Parents: Parveen and Mohammed
Marital status: Single
Family links with cricket: 'Dad played some Bradford League cricket'
Education: Woodhouse Grove School; Bradford University
Qualifications: GCSEs and A-levels
Career outside cricket: Studying pharmacology at Bradford University
Off-season: 'Recovering from injury'
Overseas tours: England U18 to Holland 2003; Woodhouse Grove to Grenada 2004

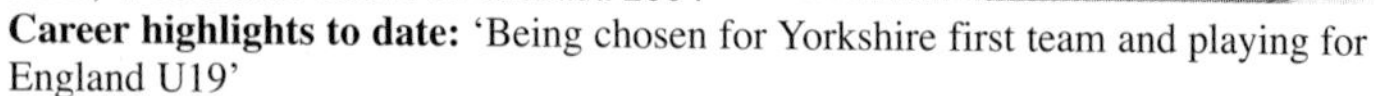

Career highlights to date: 'Being chosen for Yorkshire first team and playing for England U19'
Cricket moments to forget: 'England U19 v Ireland'
Cricketers particularly admired: Wasim Akram
Young players to look out for: Tim Bresnan
Other sports played: Badminton (Yorkshire U15)
Injuries: Suffered stress fracture of lower back in mid-season
Favourite band: Niche
Relaxations: 'Gym, clubbing'
Extras: First British-born Asian to play for Yorkshire first team

2004 Season

	M	Inns	NO	Runs	HS	Avge	100s	50s	Ct	St	O	M	Runs	Wkts	Avge	Best	5wI	10wM
Test																		
All First																		
1-day Int																		
C & G																		
totesport	1	1	0	5	5	5.00	-	-	-	-	6	0	35	0	-		-	-
Twenty20																		

Career Performances

	M	Inns	NO	Runs	HS	Avge	100s	50s	Ct	St	Balls	Runs	Wkts	Avge	Best	5wI	10wM
Test																	
All First																	
1-day Int																	
C & G																	
totesport	1	1	0	5	5	5.00	-	-	-	-	36	35	0	-	-	-	
Twenty20																	

SHANTRY, A. J. Warwickshire

Name: Adam John Shantry
Role: Left-hand bat, left-arm fast-medium bowler; all-rounder
Born: 13 November 1982, Bristol
Height: 6ft 3in **Weight:** 14st 6lbs
Nickname: Shants
County debut: 2003 (Northamptonshire)
1st-Class catches: 2
Strike rate: 70.00 (career 49.00)
Parents: Brian and Josephine
Marital status: Single
Family links with cricket: Father played for Gloucestershire; younger brother plays for Shropshire U17
Education: The Priory School, Shrewsbury; Shrewsbury Sixth Form College
Qualifications: 11 GCSEs, 4 A-levels, Level 2 coaching
Off-season: 'Ten weeks in Perth after Christmas'
Overseas teams played for: Balwyn, Melbourne 2001-02
Career highlights to date: '5-37 v New Zealand 2004; 3-8 on Championship debut v Somerset 2003; four wickets in four balls v Warwickshire 2nd XI 2004'
Cricket moments to forget: 'Any time Chris Park hits me off the square'
Cricket superstitions: 'None'
Cricketers particularly admired: Brian Shantry, Andre Nel
Young players to look out for: Jack Shantry, Chris Park, Craig Jennings ('if he stays calm')
Other sports played: Football (Shrewsbury Area)
Other sports followed: Football (Bristol City – 'only team in Bristol')
Injuries: Side strain
Favourite band: Feeder

Relaxations: 'Listening to proper music – My Chemical Romance, Lostprophets, Bloc Party, Funeral for a Friend'
Extras: England U17 squad. Represented ESCA U18 v West Indies U19 2001. Radio Shropshire Young Player of the Year 2001. Leading wicket-taker for Northamptonshire Colts 2002; took 7-18 v Warwickshire U19 2002. Took 3-8 (including spell of three wickets in five balls before conceding a run) on Championship debut v Somerset at Northampton 2003. Took 5-37 v New Zealanders in 50-over match at Northampton 2004, winning Carlsberg Man of the Match award. His 5-15 v Warwickshire 2nd XI at Kenilworth 2004 included four wickets in four balls (bowled, bowled, lbw, bowled). Left Northamptonshire at the end of the 2004 season and has joined Warwickshire for 2005
Opinions on cricket: 'More cricket on TV and other exposure in the media can only be good for the game.'
Best batting: 38* Northamptonshire v Somerset, Northampton 2003
Best bowling: 3-8 Northamptonshire v Somerset, Northampton 2003

2004 Season

	M	Inns	NO	Runs	HS	Avge	100s	50s	Ct	St	O	M	Runs	Wkts	Avge	Best	5wI	10wM
Test																		
All First	2	3	2	7	5	7.00	-	-	1	-	35	10	110	3	36.66	2-67	-	-
1-day Int																		
C & G																		
totesport																		
Twenty20	1	0	0	0	0	-	-	-	-	-	2	0	31	0	-		-	-

Career Performances

	M	Inns	NO	Runs	HS	Avge	100s	50s	Ct	St	Balls	Runs	Wkts	Avge	Best	5wI	10wM
Test																	
All First	5	6	4	62	38 *	31.00	-	-	2	-	490	263	10	26.30	3-8	-	-
1-day Int																	
C & G	1	1	0	15	15	15.00	-	-	-	-	42	21	2	10.50	2-21	-	
totesport	1	1	0	4	4	4.00	-	-	1	-	12	17	0	-		-	-
Twenty20	1	0	0	0	0	-	-	-	-	-	12	31	0	-		-	-

83. Which former Sussex and Warwickshire batsman scored 172 on his ICC Trophy debut for Hong Kong v Gibraltar in 1986?

SHAW, A. D. Glamorgan

Name: Adrian David Shaw
Role: Right-hand bat, wicket-keeper; 2nd XI captain/coach
Born: 17 February 1972, Neath
Height: 6ft **Weight:** 13st
Nickname: Shawsy ('I'm sure the 2nd XI boys have a few, though!')
County debut: 1992 (one-day), 1994 (first-class)
County cap: 1999
50 dismissals in a season: 1
1st-Class 50s: 9
1st-Class 100s: 1
1st-Class catches: 180
1st-Class stumpings: 14
Parents: David Colin and Christina
Wife and date of marriage: Wendy, December 2002
Children: Seren Georgia, 8 January 2002
Education: Llangatwg Comprehensive; Neath Tertiary College
Qualifications: 9 O-levels, 3 A-levels, 'currently doing Level IV [coaching]; starting rugby awards'
Off-season: 'Coaching our younger players'
Overseas tours: Welsh Schools U17 to Barbados 1987; England YC to New Zealand 1990-91; Glamorgan pre-season tours, including to Cape Town 1999
Overseas teams played for: Welkom Police, Free State 1995-96
Career highlights to date: 'Every time I get offered a new contract!'
Cricket moments to forget: 'Any of the days my team-mates were released'
Cricket superstitions: 'Never whistle with a mouth full of custard'
Cricketers particularly admired: 'Anyone who stays modest with success'
Young players to look out for: 'Doesn't seem to be apparent at a lot of counties any more – they buy 'em in first-class'
Other sports played: Rugby (formerly centre with Neath RFC – Back of the Year 1993-94; Welsh U19 and U21 squad member)
Other sports followed: Rugby (Neath)
Favourite band: Massive Attack
Extras: One of youngest players (18 years 7 days) to play first-class rugby for Neath. Voted Glamorgan 2nd XI Player of the Year and Glamorgan Young Player of the Year 1995. 2nd XI Player of the Month, June 1996. Claimed eight catches in the second innings and 12 for the match v Gloucestershire 2nd XI at Usk 1998, setting two records for the 2nd XI Championship. Awarded county Young Player of the Month for

August 1999 'at the geriatric age of 27'. Scored eleventh century for Glamorgan 2nd XI (103) v Somerset 2nd XI at Cardiff 2003, surpassing Tony Cottey's record of ten centuries in 2nd XI cricket for Glamorgan. Glamorgan 2nd XI player/coach since 2002
Opinions on cricket: 'Young cricketers, don't get disheartened by many counties' attitudes toward you. It's not your fault they can't see past the next six games and really care about what's best for English cricket. And it could all be resolved with a little bit of honesty between counties. Where would we be without the Test team? Stacking shelves? Surely every county should bear this in mind. Our duty is to produce English players.'
Best batting: 140 Glamorgan v Oxford University, The Parks 1999

2004 Season (did not make any first-class or one-day appearances)

Career Performances

	M	Inns	NO	Runs	HS	Avge	100s	50s	Ct	St	Balls	Runs	Wkts	Avge	Best	5wI	10wM
Test																	
All First	77	103	16	1906	140	21.90	1	9	180	14	6	7	0	-	-	-	-
1-day Int																	
C & G	9	8	2	151	47	25.16	-	-	13	-							
totesport	56	38	9	436	48	15.03	-	-	29	10							
Twenty20																	

SHEIKH, M. A. — Derbyshire

Name: Mohammed Avez Sheikh
Role: Left-hand bat, right-arm medium bowler
Born: 2 July 1973, Birmingham
Height: 6ft
Nickname: Sheikhy
County debut: 1997 (Warwickshire), 2004 (Derbyshire)
1st-Class 50s: 2
1st-Class catches: 4
Place in batting averages: 207th av. 21.58
Place in bowling averages: 91st av. 36.34 (2003 100th av. 36.86)
Strike rate: 68.88 (career 76.91)
Education: Broadway School
Overseas teams played for: Western Province CC 1997-98
Extras: Played for Warwickshire U19 and played for both Worcestershire and Essex 2nd XIs in 1995. Played for the

Warwickshire Board side that won the last ECB 38-County competition 2002, taking 4-37 in the final. Released by Warwickshire at the end of the 2003 season and joined Derbyshire for 2004. Returned first innings figures of 11-7-9-4 v Durham at Riverside 2004

Best batting: 58* Warwickshire v Northamptonshire, Northampton 2000

Best bowling: 4-9 Derbyshire v Durham, Riverside 2004

2004 Season

	M	Inns	NO	Runs	HS	Avge	100s	50s	Ct	St	O	M	Runs	Wkts	Avge	Best	5wI	10wM
Test																		
All First	13	18	6	259	42	21.58	-	-	1	-	298.3	69	945	26	36.34	4-9	-	-
1-day Int																		
C & G																		
totesport	14	10	5	112	50 *	22.40	-	1	-	-	72	4	372	12	31.00	3-25	-	
Twenty20	4	1	1	0	0 *	-	-	-	2	-	10.1	0	52	3	17.33	2-20	-	

Career Performances

	M	Inns	NO	Runs	HS	Avge	100s	50s	Ct	St	Balls	Runs	Wkts	Avge	Best	5wI	10wM
Test																	
All First	33	45	13	831	58 *	25.96	-	2	4	-	4769	2336	62	37.67	4-9	-	-
1-day Int																	
C & G	11	7	3	50	14	12.50	-	-	2	-	606	420	10	42.00	2-18	-	
totesport	66	37	15	288	50 *	13.09	-	1	9	-	2745	1965	68	28.89	4-17	-	
Twenty20	4	1	1	0	0 *	-	-	-	2	-	61	52	3	17.33	2-20	-	

84. Which bowler played for Lancashire in the mid-1980s and also represented Denmark in four ICC Trophy tournaments?

SHERIYAR, A. Kent

Name: Alamgir Sheriyar
Role: Right-hand bat, left-arm fast bowler
Born: 15 November 1973, Birmingham
Height: 6ft 1in **Weight:** 13st
Nickname: Sheri
County debut: 1993 (one-day, Leics), 1994 (first-class, Leics), 1996 (Worcs), 2003 (Kent)
County cap: 1997 (Worcs; colours, 2002)
50 wickets in a season: 4
1st-Class 5 w. in innings: 23
1st-Class 10 w. in match: 3
1st-Class catches: 22
Place in batting averages: (2003 280th av. 8.81)
Place in bowling averages: 125th av. 42.88 (2003 76th av. 33.07)
Strike rate: 66.50 (career 51.27)
Parents: Mohammed Zaman (deceased) and Safia Sultana
Marital status: Single
Family links with cricket: Brothers play a bit
Education: George Dixon Secondary School, Birmingham; Joseph Chamberlain Sixth Form College, Birmingham; Oxford Brookes University
Qualifications: 6 O-levels
Overseas tours: Leicestershire to South Africa 1995; Worcestershire to Barbados 1996; England A to Bangladesh and New Zealand 1999-2000
Cricketers particularly admired: Wasim Akram
Other sports followed: Football, basketball
Relaxations: Time at home, music
Extras: Played for English Schools U17 and has also played in the Indoor National League. Became only the second player to take a hat-trick on his Championship debut, for Leicestershire v Durham at Durham University 1994. Asked to be released by Leicestershire at the end of the 1995 season and joined Worcestershire for 1996. First bowler to reach 50 first-class wickets in 1999 and ended season as leading wicket-taker with 92 wickets (av. 24.70). Took second first-class hat-trick of his career v Kent at Worcester 1999. Left Worcestershire at the end of the 2002 season and joined Kent for 2003
Best batting: 21 Worcestershire v Nottinghamshire, Trent Bridge 1997
21 Worcestershire v Pakistan A, Worcester 1997
Best bowling: 7-130 Worcestershire v Hampshire, Southampton 1999

2004 Season

	M	Inns	NO	Runs	HS	Avge	100s	50s	Ct	St	O	M	Runs	Wkts	Avge	Best	5wI	10wM
Test																		
All First	8	8	5	36	12	12.00	-	-	-	-	199.3	33	772	18	42.88	5-94	1	-
1-day Int																		
C & G	2	1	1	2	2 *	-	-	-	-	-	13.1	2	72	1	72.00	1-21	-	
totesport	2	2	1	19	14	19.00	-	-	-	-	13	0	60	0	-	-	-	
Twenty20																		

Career Performances

	M	Inns	NO	Runs	HS	Avge	100s	50s	Ct	St	Balls	Runs	Wkts	Avge	Best	5wI	10wM
Test																	
All First	150	162	64	816	21	8.32	-	-	22	-	25535	14904	498	29.92	7-130	23	3
1-day Int																	
C & G	11	5	2	16	10	5.33	-	-	1	-	468	371	10	37.10	2-47	-	
totesport	80	24	13	88	19	8.00	-	-	5	-	2818	2427	88	27.57	4-18	-	
Twenty20	3	2	2	13	9 *	-	-	-	-	-	60	64	2	32.00	1-18	-	

SHIRAZI, D. C. Hampshire

Name: Damian Cyrus Shirazi
Role: Left-hand bat, right-arm medium bowler
Born: 23 March 1983, Neath
Height: 5ft 11in **Weight:** 13st
Nickname: Shizz, Razu, Virus, Cabernet Blanc
County debut: No first-team appearance
One-Day 100s: 1
Parents: Syed and Elaine
Marital status: 'Very single'
Family links with cricket: 'Dad is a qualified and active cricket coach; Mum was our scorer; and brothers Sam and Dan played up to district level'
Education: Applemore College; Totton Sixth Form College; Southampton Institute
Qualifications: 10 GCSEs, 3 A-levels, 'in final year of BA (Hons) Business and Sport', Level 2 cricket coach, Level 2 volleyball certificate
Career outside cricket: Student ('once sold Slush Puppies on Bondi Beach'), cricket coaching

Off-season: 'Finishing off my degree; getting fit for season'
Overseas tours: West of England U15 to West Indies 1999; MCC YC to La Santa 2003, to Sri Lanka 2004; British Universities to South Africa 2004
Overseas teams played for: University of New South Wales 2001-02
Career highlights to date: 'Breaking MCC YC all-time run record in 2003. Any time I've batted for the whole day!'
Cricket moments to forget: 'Joining the primary club first ball of the season in 2002 after losing my off stump!'
Cricket superstitions: 'Too many to mention'
Cricketers particularly admired: Allan Border, Graham Thorpe, Justin Langer
Young players to look out for: Mark 'Swampy' Pettini, Justin 'Bish' Bishop, Will 'Smudger' Smith
Other sports played: 'Played county football and athletics as a junior'
Other sports followed: Football (Manchester United 'and any English team in Europe except Arsenal!')
Injuries: Out for three weeks with a torn wrist ligament
Favourite band: Snow Patrol
Relaxations: 'Occasional bet on the horses; eating out; listening to talkSPORT radio'
Extras: Captained England at U14, U15 and U17. Southern Premier League Young Player of the Year 2002. Played for Hampshire Board XI in the NatWest 2000 and C&G 2001 and 2003, winning Man of the Match award for his century (101) v Wiltshire at Winchester in the 2003 competition. Scored 1326 runs for MCC Young Cricketers in 2003, breaking the all-time season record for MCC YC and winning Player of the Year award. Scored only century on British Universities tour of South Africa 2004 (100* v Stellenbosch University). Represented British Universities v New Zealanders at Fenner's 2004
Opinions on cricket: 'Cricket in the UK is really on a high at the moment and the introduction of Twenty20 cricket has really raised its profile. Even so, the increased insurgence of Kolpak-qualified overseas players (*see page 9*) plying their trade in the county game may have a detrimental effect on the long-term development of young English players and therefore the chances they receive.'

2004 Season (did not make any first-class or one-day appearances for his county)

Career Performances

	M	Inns	NO	Runs	HS	Avge	100s	50s	Ct	St	Balls	Runs	Wkts	Avge	Best	5wI	10wM
Test																	
All First	1	0	0	0	0	-	-	-	-	-							
1-day Int																	
C & G	4	3	0	117	101	39.00	1	-	-	-							
totesport																	
Twenty20																	

SHOAIB AKHTAR — Worcestershire

Name: Shoaib Akhtar
Role: Right-hand bat, right-arm fast bowler
Born: 13 August 1975, Rawalpindi, Pakistan
Height: 6ft
County debut: 2003 (Durham; *see* ***Extras***)
Test debut: 1997-98
Tests: 32
One-Day Internationals: 113
1st-Class 50s: 1
1st-Class 5 w. in innings: 22
1st-Class 10 w. in match: 2
1st-Class catches: 32
One-Day 5 w. in innings: 4
Place in batting averages: (2003 242nd av. 16.41)
Place in bowling averages: (2003 2nd av. 17.05)
Strike rate: 43.00 (career 43.65)
Education: Elliott High School, Rawalpindi; Asghar Mal Government College, Rawalpindi

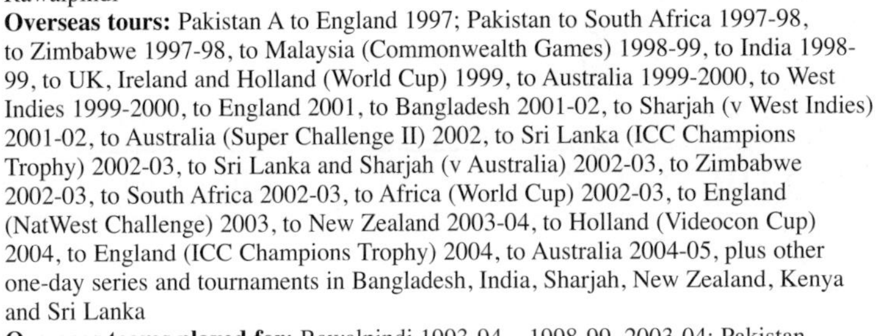

Overseas tours: Pakistan A to England 1997; Pakistan to South Africa 1997-98, to Zimbabwe 1997-98, to Malaysia (Commonwealth Games) 1998-99, to India 1998-99, to UK, Ireland and Holland (World Cup) 1999, to Australia 1999-2000, to West Indies 1999-2000, to England 2001, to Bangladesh 2001-02, to Sharjah (v West Indies) 2001-02, to Australia (Super Challenge II) 2002, to Sri Lanka (ICC Champions Trophy) 2002-03, to Sri Lanka and Sharjah (v Australia) 2002-03, to Zimbabwe 2002-03, to South Africa 2002-03, to Africa (World Cup) 2002-03, to England (NatWest Challenge) 2003, to New Zealand 2003-04, to Holland (Videocon Cup) 2004, to England (ICC Champions Trophy) 2004, to Australia 2004-05, plus other one-day series and tournaments in Bangladesh, India, Sharjah, New Zealand, Kenya and Sri Lanka
Overseas teams played for: Rawalpindi 1993-94 – 1998-99, 2003-04; Pakistan International Airlines 1994-95 – 1995-96; Agriculture Development Bank of Pakistan 1996-97 – 1997-98; Khan Research Labs 2001-02 – 2002-03
Extras: Nicknamed the Rawalpindi Express. Represented Pakistan U19. Played one first-class match for Somerset 2001, v Australians at Taunton. Took 6-11 from 8.2 overs as New Zealand were bowled out for 73 in their first innings of the first Test at Lahore 2001-02. Bowled the first official 100mph delivery (timed at 100.23mph) to Nick Knight v England at Cape Town in the World Cup 2002-03. Was an overseas player with Durham June to September 2003; returned for 2004. Durham Bowler of the Year 2003. Man of the Match in the first Test v West Indies in Sharjah 2001-02

(5-24); in the second Test v Bangladesh at Peshawar 2003-04 (6-50/4-30); and in the second Test v New Zealand at Wellington 2003-04 (5-48/6-30). His ODI awards include Man of the Series in the Coca-Cola Sharjah Cup 1998-99 and in the Super Challenge II v Australia 2002, in which he took 5-25 at Brisbane; also Man of the Match v New Zealand at Old Trafford in the semi-finals of the World Cup 1999. Has joined Worcestershire as an overseas player for 2005
Best batting: 59* KRL v PIA, Lahore 2001-02
Best bowling: 6-11 Pakistan v New Zealand, Lahore 2001-02

2004 Season

	M	Inns	NO	Runs	HS	Avge	100s	50s	Ct	St	O	M	Runs	Wkts	Avge	Best	5wI	10wM
Test																		
All First	2	4	1	94	46	31.33	-	-	2	-	57.2	12	218	8	27.25	4-64	-	-
1-day Int	4	2	2	2	2 *	-	-	-	1	-	29.5	4	134	7	19.14	4-36	-	
C & G																		
totesport	6	5	0	93	32	18.60	-	-	-	-	47.3	8	215	13	16.53	4-15	-	
Twenty20																		

Career Performances

	M	Inns	NO	Runs	HS	Avge	100s	50s	Ct	St	Balls	Runs	Wkts	Avge	Best	5wI	10wM
Test	32	46	10	297	37	8.25	-	-	7	-	5657	3059	125	24.47	6-11	8	2
All First	105	143	44	1170	59 *	11.81	-	1	32	-	16241	9667	372	25.98	6-11	22	2
1-day Int	113	56	29	296	43	10.96	-	-	15	-	5339	4040	183	22.07	6-16	3	
C & G																	
totesport	13	11	0	162	32	14.72	-	-	1	-	621	439	30	14.63	5-35	1	
Twenty20	1	1	0	0	0	0.00	-	-	-	-	24	31	1	31.00	1-31	-	

SHOAIB MALIK — Gloucestershire

Name: Shoaib Malik
Role: Right-hand bat, right-arm off-spin bowler
Born: 1 February 1982, Sialkot, Punjab
County debut: 2003
County cap: 2004
Test debut: 2001-02
Tests: 5
One-Day Internationals: 79
1st-Class 50s: 6
1st-Class 100s: 4
1st-Class 5 w. in innings: 5
1st-Class 10 w. in match: 1
1st-Class catches: 25
One-Day 100s: 4

Place in batting averages: 239th av. 16.75
Place in bowling averages: 148th av. 53.00
Strike rate: 105.60 (career 55.75)
Overseas tours: Pakistan U19 to South Africa 1996-97, to Australia 1997-98, to South Africa (U19 World Cup) 1997-98, to England 1998; Pakistan A to England 1997; Pakistan to Sharjah (Coca-Cola Champions Trophy) 1999-2000, to Australia 1999-2000 (CUB Series), to West Indies 1999-2000 (one-day series), to England 2001 (NatWest Series), to Sharjah (v West Indies) 2001-02 (one-day series), to Australia (Super Challenge II) 2002, to Sri Lanka (ICC Champions Trophy) 2002-03, to Sri Lanka (Bank Alfalah Cup) 2003, to England (NatWest Challenge) 2003, to New Zealand 2003-04, to Holland (Videocon Cup) 2004, to England (ICC Champions Trophy) 2004, to Australia 2004-05, to India 2004-05, plus other one-day series and tournaments in Sharjah, Bangladesh, Sri Lanka, Morocco, Kenya and India
Overseas teams played for: Gujranwala 1997-98 – 1998-99; Pakistan International Airlines 1998-99 – ; Pakistan Reserves (in domestic competition) 1999-2000; Sialkot 2001-02 –
Extras: Represented Pakistan U19. Has won several domestic awards, including Man of the Match for Pakistan International Airlines v Water and Power Development Authority at Faisalabad 2000-01 (83/130* and 7-81/2-56). His ODI awards include Man of the Series in the Bank Alfalah Cup in Sri Lanka 2003 and in the Paktel Cup in Pakistan 2004, as well as Man of the Match v New Zealand at Lahore 2002 (115/3-37), Man of the Match v South Africa at Lahore 2003-04 (82*) and three match awards in the Asia Cup 2004. Was an overseas player with Gloucestershire in late July and early August 2003; returned for 2004; left Gloucestershire at the end of the 2004 season. C&G Man of the Match award v Derbyshire in the semi-final at Bristol 2003 (1-46/74)
Best batting: 130* PIA v WAPDA, Faisalabad 2000-01
Best bowling: 7-81 PIA v WAPDA, Faisalabad 2000-01

2004 Season

	M	Inns	NO	Runs	HS	Avge	100s	50s	Ct	St	O	M	Runs	Wkts	Avge	Best	5wI	10wM
Test																		
All First	6	9	1	134	63	16.75	-	1	2	-	176	30	530	10	53.00	3-109	-	-
1-day Int	4	4	0	24	17	6.00	-	-	4	-	31	1	95	5	19.00	3-15	-	
C & G	2	2	1	75	43	75.00	-	-	-	-	15	0	69	0	-	-	-	
totesport	5	5	1	136	52	34.00	-	2	-	-	44	0	193	8	24.12	3-28	-	
Twenty20																		

Career Performances

	M	Inns	NO	Runs	HS	Avge	100s	50s	Ct	St	Balls	Runs	Wkts	Avge	Best	5wI	10wM
Test	5	7	2	121	47	24.20	-	-	1	-	565	291	7	41.57	4-42	-	-
All First	53	76	10	1544	130 *	23.39	4	6	25	-	8587	4157	154	26.99	7-81	5	1
1-day Int	79	66	8	1708	143	29.44	4	5	29	-	3476	2471	73	33.84	4-19	-	
C & G	3	3	1	149	74	74.50	-	1	-	-	144	115	1	115.00	1-46	-	
totesport	8	7	2	160	52	32.00	-	2	-	-	414	323	9	35.88	3-28	-	
Twenty20																	

SHRECK, C. E. — Nottinghamshire

Name: Charles (Charlie) Edward Shreck
Role: Right-hand bat, right-arm fast-medium bowler
Born: 6 January 1978, Truro
Height: 6ft 7in **Weight:** 15st 7lbs
Nickname: Shrecker, Ogre, Stoat, Chough
County debut: 2002 (one-day), 2003 (first-class)
1st-Class 5 w. in innings: 3
1st-Class catches: 3
One-Day 5 w. in innings: 2
Place in batting averages: (2003 292nd av. 5.66)
Place in bowling averages: 29th av. 26.54 (2003 107th av. 38.17)
Strike rate: 45.48 (career 51.35)
Parents: Peter and Sheila
Marital status: Single
Family links with cricket: 'Grandfather watched Southampton'
Education: Truro School
Qualifications: Level 1 coaching
Career outside cricket: 'Sleeping'
Overseas tours: Cornwall U17 to South Africa 1997
Overseas teams played for: Merewether District CC, NSW 1997-98; Hutt District CC, New Zealand 2000-03
Cricket moments to forget: 'Being run out off the last ball of the game against Shropshire, walking off – we lost!'
Cricket superstitions: 'None'
Cricketers particularly admired: Viv Richards, Michael Holding, Ian Botham
Young players to look out for: Michael Munday, Carl Gazzard
Relaxations: 'Swimming, music'

Extras: Played for Cornwall in the NatWest 2000 and in the C&G 2001, 2002 and 2003, winning Man of the Match award for his 5-19 (his maiden one-day five-wicket return) v Worcestershire at Truro 2002. Took wicket (Vikram Solanki) with his third ball in county cricket v Worcestershire at Trent Bridge in the NUL 2002, going on to record maiden one-day league five-wicket return (5-35)
Best batting: 19 Nottinghamshire v Essex, Chelmsford 2003
Best bowling: 6-46 Nottinghamshire v Durham, Riverside 2004

2004 Season

	M	Inns	NO	Runs	HS	Avge	100s	50s	Ct	St	O	M	Runs	Wkts	Avge	Best	5wI	10wM
Test																		
All First	8	6	4	16	13 *	8.00	-	-	2	-	235	51	823	31	26.54	6-46	2	-
1-day Int																		
C & G																		
totesport																		
Twenty20																		

Career Performances

	M	Inns	NO	Runs	HS	Avge	100s	50s	Ct	St	Balls	Runs	Wkts	Avge	Best	5wI	10wM
Test																	
All First	19	21	10	67	19	6.09	-	-	3	-	2773	1701	54	31.50	6-46	3	-
1-day Int																	
C & G	7	3	1	11	9	5.50	-	-	2	-	360	298	12	24.83	5-19	1	
totesport	2	2	2	3	2 *	-	-	-	1	-	96	97	6	16.16	5-35	1	
Twenty20	1	1	1	1	1 *	-	-	-	-	-	24	25	1	25.00	1-25	-	

85. Who made his Test debut at the age of 40, was South Africa's chairman of selectors prior to England's 2004-05 tour, and featured in Scotland's historic first B&H Cup win over Lancashire in 1986, taking 2-19 in 11 overs?

SIDEBOTTOM, R. J. Nottinghamshire

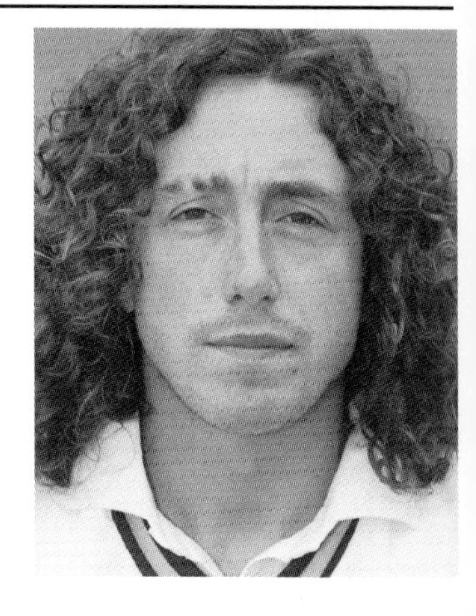

Name: Ryan Jay Sidebottom
Role: Left-hand bat, left-arm fast bowler
Born: 15 January 1978, Huddersfield
Height: 6ft 4in **Weight:** 14st 7lbs
Nickname: Siddy, Sexual, Jazz
County debut: 1997 (Yorkshire), 2004 (Nottinghamshire)
County cap: 2000 (Yorkshire), 2004 (Nottinghamshire)
Test debut: 2001
Tests: 1
One-Day Internationals: 2
1st-Class 50s: 1
1st-Class 5 w. in innings: 9
1st-Class 10 w. in match: 1
1st-Class catches: 26
One-Day 5 w. in innings: 2
Place in batting averages: 283rd av. 6.12 (2003 262nd av. 13.55)
Place in bowling averages: 37th av. 28.63 (2003 4th av. 20.28)
Strike rate: 51.60 (career 51.52)
Parents: Arnie and Gillian
Marital status: Single
Family links with cricket: Father played cricket for Yorkshire and England and football for Manchester United and Huddersfield Town
Education: King James Grammar School, Almondbury
Qualifications: 5 GCSEs
Overseas tours: England U17 to Holland 1995; MCC to Bangladesh 1999-2000; England A to West Indies 2000-01; England to Zimbabwe (one-day series) 2001-02; ECB National Academy to Australia 2001-02
Overseas teams played for: Ringwood, Melbourne 1998
Cricketers particularly admired: Darren Gough, Chris Silverwood, Glenn McGrath
Young players to look out for: Joe Sayers
Other sports played: Football (once with Sheffield United), 'all sports'
Other sports followed: 'Love rugby league (any team)', football (Man Utd)
Relaxations: 'Music (R&B), films, clubbing, going out with my team-mates'
Extras: NBC Denis Compton Award for the most promising young Yorkshire player 1999, 2000. Recorded maiden first-class five-wicket return (5-27) v Kent at Headingley 2000, following up with 6-16 in second innings for maiden ten-wicket match. Top English bowler in first-class averages 2000 (second overall) with 24 wickets at 12.50. Took 5-31 (8-65 in match) in the Busta Cup for England A v Jamaica at Kingston 2000-01, winning the Man of the Match award; topped tour first-class

bowling averages (16 wickets; av. 16.81). Made Test debut in the first Test v Pakistan at Lord's 2001 (England's 100th Test at the ground), becoming the tenth player to follow his father into the England Test team. Left Yorkshire at the end of the 2003 season and joined Nottinghamshire for 2004; awarded Nottinghamshire cap 2004
Best batting: 54 Yorkshire v Glamorgan, Cardiff 1998
Best bowling: 7-97 Yorkshire v Derbyshire, Headingley 2003

2004 Season

	M	Inns	NO	Runs	HS	Avge	100s	50s	Ct	St	O	M	Runs	Wkts	Avge	Best	5wI	10wM
Test																		
All First	10	10	2	49	15 *	6.12	-	-	3	-	258	59	859	30	28.63	5-86	1	-
1-day Int																		
C & G	1	1	0	9	9	9.00	-	-	-	-	8	1	34	0	-	-	-	
totesport	10	0	0	0	0	-	-	-	2	-	66	2	349	5	69.80	2-39	-	
Twenty20	5	2	2	1	1 *	-	-	-	1	-	17	0	134	5	26.80	2-47	-	

Career Performances

	M	Inns	NO	Runs	HS	Avge	100s	50s	Ct	St	Balls	Runs	Wkts	Avge	Best	5wI	10wM
Test	1	1	0	4	4	4.00	-	-	-	-	120	64	0	-	-	-	-
All First	70	89	26	673	54	10.68	-	1	26	-	10769	5288	209	25.30	7-97	9	1
1-day Int	2	1	1	2	2 *	-	-	-	-	-	84	84	2	42.00	1-42	-	
C & G	15	3	1	22	9	11.00	-	-	4	-	702	466	20	23.30	4-39	-	
totesport	76	35	18	218	30 *	12.82	-	-	11	-	3125	2365	77	30.71	6-40	2	
Twenty20	10	3	2	11	10	11.00	-	-	3	-	205	270	12	22.50	3-20	-	

86. Who was the youngest squad member in the 1983 World Cup?

SILLENCE, R. J. Gloucestershire

Name: Roger John Sillence
Role: Right-hand bat, right-arm fast-medium bowler
Born: 29 June 1977, Salisbury, Wiltshire
Height: 6ft 3in **Weight:** 12st 10lbs
Nickname: Silly, Sillo
County debut: 2001
County cap: 2004
1st-Class 50s: 1
1st-Class 100s: 1
1st-Class 5 w. in innings: 2
1st-Class catches: 3
Strike rate: 62.40 (career 53.00)
Parents: Angela
Marital status: Single
Family links with cricket: 'Dad played local cricket'
Education: Highbury, Salisbury; Salisbury Art College
Qualifications: 7 GCSEs, ND and HND Graphic Design, ECB Level II coach
Career outside cricket: Graphic design
Overseas teams played for: Napier Old Boys, New Zealand 1997-98; St Augustine's, Cape Town 1998-99; East Keilor, Melbourne 2000-01; Hamersley Carine, Perth 2001-02; South Melbourne 2002-03
Career highlights to date: 'First 100 v Derby on home debut'
Cricket moments to forget: 'Whenever I drop a catch'
Cricket superstitions: 'Always bowl in a short-sleeved shirt'
Cricketers particularly admired: Mike Smith ('good advice'), Jonty Rhodes
Other sports played: Football ('social')
Other sports followed: Football
Relaxations: 'Design, music, eating out, coffee'
Extras: Wiltshire Player of the Year 2000. Recorded maiden first-class five-wicket return (5-97) on debut v Sussex at Hove 2001. Took 4-35 v West Indies A in a 50-over match at Cheltenham 2002. Scored maiden first-class century (101) v Derbyshire at Bristol 2002 on home debut, batting at No. 9. Scored 92 v Warwickshire at Bristol 2004, in the process sharing with Mark Hardinges (68*) in a new record eighth-wicket stand for Gloucestershire in matches v Warwickshire (154)
Best batting: 101 Gloucestershire v Derbyshire, Bristol 2002
Best bowling: 5-63 Gloucestershire v Durham, Bristol 2002

2004 Season

	M	Inns	NO	Runs	HS	Avge	100s	50s	Ct	St	O	M	Runs	Wkts	Avge	Best	5wI	10wM
Test																		
All First	2	2	0	96	92	48.00	-	1	-	-	52	19	135	5	27.00	2-50	-	-
1-day Int																		
C & G																		
totesport																		
Twenty20																		

Career Performances

	M	Inns	NO	Runs	HS	Avge	100s	50s	Ct	St	Balls	Runs	Wkts	Avge	Best	5wI	10wM
Test																	
All First	12	16	0	367	101	22.93	1	1	3	-	1696	1092	32	34.12	5-63	2	-
1-day Int																	
C & G	4	3	0	89	82	29.66	-	1	-	-	96	75	4	18.75	3-47	-	
totesport	1	1	0	11	11	11.00	-	-	-	-							
Twenty20																	

SILVERWOOD, C. E. W. — Yorkshire

Name: Christopher (Chris) Eric Wilfred Silverwood
Role: Right-hand bat, right-arm fast bowler
Born: 5 March 1975, Pontefract
Height: 6ft 1in **Weight:** 12st 9lbs
Nickname: Spoons, Silvers, Chubby
County debut: 1993
County cap: 1996
Benefit: 2004
Test debut: 1996-97
Tests: 6
One-Day Internationals: 7
50 wickets in a season: 1
1st-Class 50s: 6
1st-Class 5 w. in innings: 20
1st-Class 10 w. in match: 1
1st-Class catches: 34
One-Day 5 w. in innings: 1
Place in batting averages: 226th av. 18.75 (2003 271st av. 10.85)
Place in bowling averages: 25th av. 25.90 (2003 26th av. 24.52)
Strike rate: 47.59 (career 50.48)

Parents: Brenda
Marital status: Single
Family links with cricket: 'Dad played a bit'
Education: Garforth Comprehensive
Qualifications: 8 GCSEs, City and Guilds in Leisure and Recreation
Overseas tours: England A to Kenya and Sri Lanka 1997-98, to Bangladesh and New Zealand 1999-2000, to West Indies 2000-01; England to Zimbabwe and New Zealand 1996-97, to West Indies 1997-98, to Bangladesh (Wills International Cup) 1998-99, to South Africa 1999-2000, to Zimbabwe (one-day series) 2001-02, to Australia 2002-03; England VI to Hong Kong 2002, 2003
Overseas teams played for: Wellington, Cape Town 1993-94, 1995-96
Career highlights to date: 'Making Test debut. Winning the Championship [2001]'
Cricketers particularly admired: Ian Botham, Allan Donald
Other sports played: Karate (black belt), rugby league (Kippax Welfare), athletics (represented Yorkshire)
Other sports followed: Rugby league (Castleford)
Relaxations: 'Listening to music, watching videos, riding my motorbike'
Extras: Attended Yorkshire Academy. Represented England U19. C&G Man of the Match awards for his 61 and 2-35 v Northamptonshire at Northampton 2002 and for his 4-18 v Dorset at Dean Park 2004
Best batting: 70 Yorkshire v Essex, Chelmsford 2001
Best bowling: 7-93 Yorkshire v Kent, Headingley 1997

2004 Season

	M	Inns	NO	Runs	HS	Avge	100s	50s	Ct	St	O	M	Runs	Wkts	Avge	Best	5wI	10wM
Test																		
All First	7	10	2	150	37	18.75	-	-	3	-	174.3	33	570	22	25.90	3-18	-	-
1-day Int																		
C & G	3	1	0	2	2	2.00	-	-	-	-	22	2	99	6	16.50	4-18	-	
totesport	7	4	1	28	10	9.33	-	-	1	-	43.3	4	219	10	21.90	2-14	-	
Twenty20	4	3	1	16	12	8.00	-	-	1	-	15	0	127	3	42.33	2-30	-	

Career Performances

	M	Inns	NO	Runs	HS	Avge	100s	50s	Ct	St	Balls	Runs	Wkts	Avge	Best	5wI	10wM
Test	6	7	3	29	10	7.25	-	-	5	-	828	444	11	40.36	5-91	1	-
All First	142	190	38	2325	70	15.29	-	6	34	-	23275	12269	461	26.61	7-93	20	1
1-day Int	7	4	0	17	12	4.25	-	-	-	-	306	244	6	40.66	3-43	-	
C & G	26	12	3	161	61	17.88	-	1	7	-	1325	841	27	31.14	4-18	-	
totesport	106	64	27	555	58	15.00	-	2	11	-	4420	3168	146	21.69	4-11	-	
Twenty20	9	5	2	32	13 *	10.66	-	-	4	-	204	264	7	37.71	2-22	-	

SINGH, A. Nottinghamshire

Name: Anurag Singh
Role: Right-hand bat, right-arm 'all sorts'
Born: 9 September 1975, Kanpur, India
Height: 5ft 11½in **Weight:** 11st
Nickname: Ragi
County debut: 1995 (Warwickshire), 2001 (Worcestershire), 2004 (Nottinghamshire)
County colours: 2002 (Worcestershire)
1000 runs in a season: 2
1st-Class 50s: 23
1st-Class 100s: 10
1st-Class catches: 40
One-Day 100s: 1
Place in batting averages: 48th av. 47.42 (2003 156th av. 29.00)
Parents: Vijay and Rajul
Marital status: Single
Family links with cricket: 'Brother (Rudi) has played first-class cricket for Cambridge Uni and has a Cambridge Blue'
Education: King Edward's School, Birmingham; Gonville and Caius College, Cambridge; College of Law, London
Qualifications: 12 GCSEs, 1 AO-level, 4 A-levels, passed Law School exams
Career outside cricket: Solicitor
Off-season: 'Working for Wragge & Co Solicitors in Birmingham'
Overseas tours: England U19 to West Indies 1994-95; Warwickshire U21 to South Africa; Warwickshire CCC to South Africa; Quidnuncs to South Africa 2002; Worcestershire to South Africa 2003
Overseas teams played for: Gordon CC, Sydney; Avendale CC, Cape Town
Career highlights to date: 'Scoring 62 v McGrath, Warne & Co at New Road 2001. Reaching the 2000 NatWest final. Scoring 187 v Gloucestershire [2002]. Winning the 2003 C&G semi-final against Lancashire and getting to the final'
Cricket moments to forget: 'Losing two cup finals to Gloucestershire'
Cricket superstitions: 'None'
Cricketers particularly admired: Steve Waugh, Sachin Tendulkar, Michael Atherton, Brian Lara
Young players to look out for: Samit Patel ('if he loses weight'), Mark Footitt ('if he puts some on')
Other sports played: Hockey ('college and school'), football ('college and firm')
Other sports followed: Football (Aston Villa FC)
Injuries: Out for six weeks with a torn hamstring; played the last month of the season with a broken foot

Favourite band: 'Too many to mention'
Relaxations: Reading, socialising with friends
Extras: Cambridge Blue 1996-98; captain of Cambridge University 1997-98. Scored 85 in NatWest semi-final v Hampshire at Edgbaston 2000, in the process sharing with Nick Knight (100) in a Warwickshire record first-wicket stand (185) for one-day cricket. Left Warwickshire at the end of the 2000 season and joined Worcestershire for 2001. Scored 1000 first-class runs in each of his first two full seasons of county cricket (2001 and 2002). Carried his bat for 83* v Gloucestershire at Worcester 2003. C&G Man of the Match award for his 74 v Leicestershire in the quarter-final at Leicester 2003. Left Worcestershire at the end of the 2003 season and joined Nottinghamshire for 2004
Opinions on cricket: 'The effect of Kolpak (*see page 9*), EU and overseas players needs to be carefully regulated, otherwise the game in this country will suffer greatly. I think the number of EU and Kolpak players on a county's staff should affect the number of overseas players they can register – e.g. if you have two Kolpak/EU players, then you can only have one overseas; if you have three or more, then no overseas; if none or one, then two overseas players.'
Best batting: 187 Worcestershire v Gloucestershire, Bristol 2002

2004 Season

	M	Inns	NO	Runs	HS	Avge	100s	50s	Ct	St	O	M	Runs	Wkts	Avge	Best	5wI	10wM
Test																		
All First	5	8	1	332	112 *	47.42	1	2	3	-								
1-day Int																		
C & G	1	1	0	24	24	24.00	-	-	-	-								
totesport	6	6	1	237	67	47.40	-	1	1	-								
Twenty20																		

Career Performances

	M	Inns	NO	Runs	HS	Avge	100s	50s	Ct	St	Balls	Runs	Wkts	Avge	Best	5wI	10wM
Test																	
All First	100	165	7	5136	187	32.50	10	23	40	-	95	111	0	-	-	-	-
1-day Int																	
C & G	13	13	0	471	85	36.23	-	4	3	-							
totesport	67	66	3	1699	97	26.96	-	11	16	-							
Twenty20																	

SMITH, A. M. Gloucestershire

Name: Andrew Michael Smith
Role: Right-hand bat ('put bat to ball!'), left-arm swing bowler
Born: 1 October 1967, Dewsbury
Height: 5ft 9in **Weight:** 12st 3lbs
Nickname: Smudge, Cyril
County debut: 1991
County cap: 1995
Benefit: 2001
Test debut: 1997
Tests: 1
50 wickets in a season: 5
1st-Class 50s: 4
1st-Class 5 w. in innings: 22
1st-Class 10 w. in match: 5
1st-Class catches: 31
One-Day 5 w. in innings: 2
Place in batting averages: (2003 283rd av. 8.28)
Place in bowling averages: (2003 20th av. 23.63)
Strike rate: 40.87 (career 49.66)
Parents: Hugh and Margaret
Wife and date of marriage: Sarah, 2 October 1993
Children: William James, 9 October 1994; Amelia Lucy, 14 June 1997
Family links with cricket: Father (Birstall club) and brother (East Ardsley club) local league cricketers in Yorkshire
Education: Queen Elizabeth Grammar School, Wakefield; Exeter University; University of the West of England, Bristol
Qualifications: 9 O-levels, 4 A-levels, BA (Hons) French and German, PGDip Law
Career outside cricket: Works for law firm Osborne Clarke
Overseas tours: Queen Elizabeth Grammar School to Holland 1985; Bradford Junior Cricket League to Barbados 1986; Exeter University to Barbados 1987; Gloucestershire to Kenya 1990, to Sri Lanka 1992-93, to Zimbabwe 1996, to Cape Town 2000, to South Africa 2001; England A to Pakistan 1995-96; MCC to New Zealand 1999
Overseas teams played for: Waimea, New Zealand 1990; WTTU, New Zealand 1991
Career highlights: 'My one Test match and the 1999 NatWest final v Somerset'
Cricket moments to forget: 'My batting in my one Test match'
Cricket superstitions: 'I try not to rely on superstitions to bring me good luck'
Cricketers particularly admired: Wasim Akram, Malcolm Marshall, Richard Hadlee, Darren Gough, Jacques Kallis, Adam Gilchrist

Young players to look out for: Alex Gidman
Other sports played: Football, golf
Other sports followed: Football (Leeds United), horse racing
Relaxations: Looking after the kids ('hardly relaxing!'), crosswords, computers
Extras: Played for Yorkshire age groups. Played for English Schools U19, NAYC and represented Combined Universities in the B&H Cup in 1988 and 1990. Finished the 1997 English season as leading first-class wicket-taker with 83 wickets (av. 17.63). Gloucestershire Player of the Year 1997. Took 500th first-class wicket when Jack Russell caught David Hemp v Glamorgan at Cardiff 2003. Retired at the end of the 2004 season
Best batting: 61 Gloucestershire v Yorkshire, Gloucester 1998
Best bowling: 8-73 Gloucestershire v Middlesex, Lord's 1996

2004 Season

	M	Inns	NO	Runs	HS	Avge	100s	50s	Ct	St	O	M	Runs	Wkts	Avge	Best	5wI	10wM
Test																		
All First	3	2	1	12	9	12.00	-	-	1	-	54.3	22	127	8	15.87	3-34	-	-
1-day Int																		
C & G	4	0	0	0	0	-	-	-	1	-	39	8	120	6	20.00	2-25	-	
totesport	10	5	3	10	5	5.00	-	-	-	-	79	7	378	10	37.80	2-42	-	
Twenty20	4	0	0	0	0	-	-	-	2	-	11.1	0	85	3	28.33	2-21	-	

Career Performances

	M	Inns	NO	Runs	HS	Avge	100s	50s	Ct	St	Balls	Runs	Wkts	Avge	Best	5wI	10wM
Test	1	2	1	4	4 *	4.00	-	-	-	-	138	89	0	-	-	-	-
All First	157	206	62	1756	61	12.19	-	4	31	-	26470	13158	533	24.68	8-73	22	5
1-day Int																	
C & G	37	11	7	53	13	13.25	-	-	9	-	2083	1110	55	20.18	4-35	-	
totesport	173	86	52	364	26 *	10.70	-	-	27	-	7349	5125	192	26.69	5-30	1	
Twenty20	10	0	0	0	0	-	-	-	2	-	211	182	8	22.75	2-14	-	

SMITH, B. F. Worcestershire

Name: Benjamin (Ben) Francis Smith
Role: Right-hand bat, right-arm medium bowler
Born: 3 April 1972, Corby
Height: 5ft 9in **Weight:** 11st
Nickname: Turnip, Sven
County debut: 1990 (Leicestershire), 2002 (Worcestershire)
County cap: 1995 (Leicestershire), 2002 (Worcestershire colours)
1000 runs in a season: 6
1st-Class 50s: 69
1st-Class 100s: 30

1st-Class 200s: 2
1st-Class catches: 130
One-Day 100s: 1
Place in batting averages: 49th av. 47.09 (2003 36th av. 47.74)
Strike rate: (career 179.66)
Parents: Keith and Janet
Wife and date of marriage: Lisa, 10 October 1998
Family links with cricket: Father, grandfather and uncles all played club and representative cricket
Education: Kibworth High School; Robert Smyth, Market Harborough
Qualifications: 5 O-levels, 8 GCSEs, NCA coaching certificate
Overseas tours: England YC to New Zealand 1990-91; MCC to Bangladesh 1999-2000; 'numerous pre-season tours to South Africa, Caribbean and Sri Lanka'

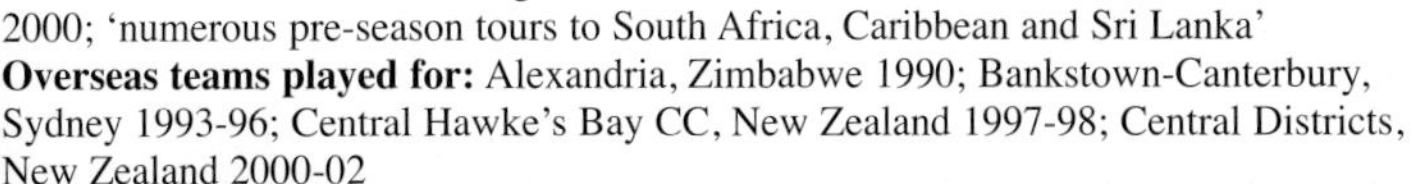

Overseas teams played for: Alexandria, Zimbabwe 1990; Bankstown-Canterbury, Sydney 1993-96; Central Hawke's Bay CC, New Zealand 1997-98; Central Districts, New Zealand 2000-02
Career highlights to date: 'Winning 1996 County Championship'
Cricket moments to forget: 'Lord's finals'
Cricketers particularly admired: Viv Richards, David Gower, Steve Waugh
Other sports played: Tennis (Leicestershire aged 12), golf, touch rugby
Other sports followed: Rugby union (Leicester Tigers)
Favourite band: Coldplay
Relaxations: 'Music, DIY, good wine'
Extras: Cricket Society Young Player of the Year 1991. Took part in Leicestershire record fifth-wicket partnership (322) with Phil Simmons v Notts at Worksop 1998. 'Two Championship medals so far!' Played in the Central Districts Shell Cup winning side in New Zealand 2000-01. Vice-captain of Leicestershire 2001. Left Leicestershire at the end of the 2001 season and joined Worcestershire for 2002. Scored century (137) on first-class debut for Worcestershire v Oxford University CCE at The Parks and another (129) on Championship debut for the county v Gloucestershire at Worcester 2002 to become the first player to achieve this 'double' for Worcestershire. Scored 2024 runs for Worcestershire in all cricket 2002. Worcestershire Supporters' Player of the Year 2002. Worcestershire Player of the Year 2003. Scored 187 v Gloucestershire at Worcester 2004, in the process sharing with Graeme Hick (262) in the highest first-class partnership ever made at New Road (417). Captain of Worcestershire 2003 until standing down in August 2004
Opinions on cricket: 'Twenty20 a huge success for spectators and also in helping develop other aspects of one-day cricket.'

Best batting: 204 Leicestershire v Surrey, The Oval 1998
Best bowling: 1-5 Leicestershire v Essex, Ilford 1991

2004 Season

	M	Inns	NO	Runs	HS	Avge	100s	50s	Ct	St	O	M	Runs	Wkts	Avge	Best	5wI	10wM
Test																		
All First	16	25	3	1036	187	47.09	2	7	17	-								
1-day Int																		
C & G	5	4	0	169	91	42.25	-	2	1	-								
totesport	15	15	2	320	77	24.61	-	3	4	-								
Twenty20	5	5	0	49	34	9.80	-	-	2	-								

Career Performances

	M	Inns	NO	Runs	HS	Avge	100s	50s	Ct	St	Balls	Runs	Wkts	Avge	Best	5wI	10wM
Test																	
All First	248	384	45	13773	204	40.62	32	69	130	-	539	350	3	116.66	1-5	-	-
1-day Int																	
C & G	35	33	5	870	91	31.07	-	6	16	-	24	17	1	17.00	1-2	-	
totesport	203	198	30	5308	115	31.59	1	33	55	-	31	36	0	-	-	-	
Twenty20	10	10	1	103	40 *	11.44	-	-	6	-							

SMITH, B. M. — Essex

Name: Brendan Mitchell Smith
Role: Left-hand bat, left-arm fast bowler
Born: 24 September 1985, Basildon
Height: 5ft 11in **Weight:** 10st 11lbs
Nickname: Brend, Bren, Brenny, Smudger
County debut: No first-team appearance
Parents: Kay and David
Marital status: Single
Education: Woodlands School, Basildon; Palmers College, Grays; Anglia Polytechnic University, Cambridge
Qualifications: BTEC National Diploma for Sport and Exercise Sciences ('triple distinction'), ECB Level 1 coaching certificate
Off-season: 'Studying for my BSc (Hons) Sports Science degree'
Career highlights to date: 'Representing ECB in fixtures against Bangladesh and South Africa U19'

Cricket moments to forget: 'Essex 2nd XI v Suffolk CCC – running in to bowl my first ball and tripping up at the delivery crease'
Cricket superstitions: 'Always pad up in the same order'
Cricketers particularly admired: Glenn McGrath, Courtney Walsh
Other sports followed: Football (Tottenham Hotspur FC)
Favourite band: Razorlight
Relaxations: 'Cinema, music, DVDs'
Extras: Made 2nd XI Championship debut 2004
Opinions on cricket: 'Think that the current England side have made the game appealing to a wider audience. Can further enhance this with a successful Ashes campaign in 2005.'

SMITH, E. T. — Middlesex

Name: Edward (Ed) Thomas Smith
Role: Right-hand bat, right-arm medium bowler
Born: 19 July 1977, Pembury, Kent
Height: 6ft 2in **Weight:** 13st
Nickname: Smudge
County debut: 1996 (Kent)
County cap: 2001 (Kent)
Test debut: 2003
Tests: 3
1000 runs in a season: 5
1st-Class 50s: 37
1st-Class 100s: 20
1st-Class 200s: 2
1st-Class catches: 49
One-Day 100s: 2
Place in batting averages: 44th av. 49.11 (2003 21st av. 52.89)
Parents: Jonathan and Gillie
Marital status: Single
Family links with cricket: 'Dad wrote *Good Enough?* with Chris Cowdrey'
Education: Tonbridge School; Peterhouse, Cambridge University
Qualifications: 11 GCSEs, 3 A-levels, degree in History
Career outside cricket: Journalism; broadcasting
Off-season: 'Cricket in Perth and Bombay'
Overseas tours: England A to Malaysia and India 2003-04
Overseas teams played for: University CC, Perth, Western Australia
Career highlights to date: 'My Test debut'

Cricket moments to forget: 'Getting a pair at Chelmsford 2003'
Cricket superstitions: 'Left pad on first'
Cricketers particularly admired: Steve Waugh, Rahul Dravid
Young players to look out for: Simon Cusden
Other sports played: Squash, golf
Other sports followed: Football (Arsenal FC), baseball (New York Mets)
Favourite band: Bob Dylan
Relaxations: 'Listening to music, reading, going to concerts'
Extras: Scored century (101) on first-class debut v Glamorgan 1996, becoming the youngest player to score a century on debut for Cambridge University; was also the first person to score 50 or more in each of his first six first-class games. Cambridge Blue 1996. Represented England U19. Scored century in each innings (149/113) v Nottinghamshire at Maidstone 2003. Scored maiden double century (203) v Lancashire at Blackpool 2003, in the process becoming the first batsman to pass 1000 first-class runs for the season. Scored 108 v Essex at Canterbury 2003, equalling Kent record of four consecutive first-class centuries. Made Test debut in the third Test v South Africa at Trent Bridge 2003, scoring 64. *Kent Messenger* Readers Player of the Year 2003. Denness Award (Kent leading run-scorer) 2003. Cowdrey Award (Kent Player of the Season) 2003. Slazenger 'Sheer Instinct' award for 2003. Left Kent at the end of the 2004 season and has joined Middlesex for 2005. Books *Playing Hard Ball* (about baseball) published 2001 and *On and Off the Field* published 2004
Opinions on cricket: 'We need good wickets, good practice facilities and enough time between games to prepare properly.'
Best batting: 213 Kent v Warwickshire, Canterbury 2003

2004 Season

	M	Inns	NO	Runs	HS	Avge	100s	50s	Ct	St	O	M	Runs	Wkts	Avge	Best	5wI	10wM
Test																		
All First	18	30	4	1277	189	49.11	4	5	6	-								
1-day Int																		
C & G	2	2	1	38	23 *	38.00	-	-	-	-								
totesport	14	14	1	618	106	47.53	1	5	3	-								
Twenty20																		

Career Performances

	M	Inns	NO	Runs	HS	Avge	100s	50s	Ct	St	Balls	Runs	Wkts	Avge	Best	5wI	10wM
Test	3	5	0	87	64	17.40	-	1	5	-							
All First	134	227	14	8690	213	40.79	22	37	49	-	72	59	0	-	-	-	-
1-day Int																	
C & G	7	7	1	110	25	18.33	-	-	-	-							
totesport	55	52	3	1545	122	31.53	2	11	7	-							
Twenty20	2	2	0	65	56	32.50	-	1	1	-							

SMITH, G. C. Somerset

Name: Graeme Craig Smith
Role: Left-hand bat, right-arm off-spin bowler, county captain
Born: 1 February 1981, Johannesburg, South Africa
County debut: No first-team appearance
Test debut: 2001-02
Tests: 26
One-Day Internationals: 56
1st-Class 50s: 14
1st-Class 100s: 10
1st-Class 200s: 3
1st-Class catches: 68
Strike rate: (career 125.75)
Overseas tours: South Africa U19 to Pakistan 1998-99, to Sri Lanka (U19 World Cup) 1999-2000; South Africa A to West Indies 2000, to Zimbabwe (one-day series) 2002-03; South Africa to Morocco (Morocco Cup) 2002, to Sri Lanka (ICC Champions Trophy) 2002-03, to Bangladesh 2002-03 (captain), to England 2003 (captain), to Pakistan 2003-04 (captain), to New Zealand 2003-04 (captain), to Sri Lanka 2004 (captain), to England (ICC Champions Trophy) 2004 (captain), to India 2004-05 (captain)
Overseas teams played for: Gauteng 1999-2000; Western Province 2000-01 – 2003-04; Western Province Boland 2004-05 –
Extras: Made first-class debut for UCBSA Invitation XI v Griqualand West at Kimberley 1999-2000, scoring 187 in first innings. Played for Hampshire Board XI in the NatWest 2000. Made Test debut in the second Test v Australia at Cape Town 2001-02, scoring 68 in the second innings. One of *South African Cricket Annual*'s Five Cricketers of the Year 2002, 2003. Scored 151 in the second Test v Pakistan at Cape Town 2002-03, sharing with Herschelle Gibbs (228) in a South African record opening partnership for Test cricket (368). Represented South Africa in the 2002-03 World Cup. His 277 in the first Test v England at Edgbaston 2003 is the highest individual score for South Africa in Tests. One of *Wisden*'s Five Cricketers of the Year 2004. Has won numerous domestic awards, including Man of the Match in the SuperSport Series final v Border at Cape Town 2000-01 (183) and Man of the Series in the Standard Bank Cup 2001-02. His international awards include South Africa's Man of the [Test] Series v England 2003 (714 runs at 79.33, including two double centuries; *see above*) and Man of the Match in the third Test v New Zealand at Wellington 2003-04 (47/125*). Captain of South Africa (youngest ever) since March 2003. Has joined Somerset as an overseas player and as captain for 2005

Best batting: 277 South Africa v England, Edgbaston 2003
Best bowling: 1-9 South Africa v Bangladesh, Chittagong 2002-03
Stop press: Scored maiden ODI century (105; the first by a South Africa captain) in the third ODI v England at Port Elizabeth 2004-05, winning Man of the Match award

2004 Season

	M	Inns	NO	Runs	HS	Avge	100s	50s	Ct	St	O	M	Runs	Wkts	Avge	Best	5wI	10wM
Test																		
All First																		
1-day Int	2	2	1	87	45	87.00	-	-	1	-								
C & G																		
totesport																		
Twenty20																		

Career Performances

	M	Inns	NO	Runs	HS	Avge	100s	50s	Ct	St	Balls	Runs	Wkts	Avge	Best	5wI	10wM
Test	26	44	3	2350	277	57.31	7	7	26	-	365	200	3	66.66	1-9	-	-
All First	53	89	6	4369	277	52.63	13	14	68	-	503	295	4	73.75	1-9	-	-
1-day Int	56	55	2	1995	99	37.64	-	15	21	-	224	244	4	61.00	1-24	-	
C & G	1	1	0	4	4	4.00	-	-	-	-							
totesport																	
Twenty20																	

SMITH, G. J. Nottinghamshire

Name: Gregory (Greg) James Smith
Role: Right-hand bat, left-arm fast bowler
Born: 30 October 1971, Pretoria, South Africa
Height: 6ft 4in **Weight:** 15st
Nickname: Claw, Smudge, G
County debut: 2001
County cap: 2001
50 wickets in a season: 2
1st-Class 50s: 2
1st-Class 5 w. in innings: 16
1st-Class 10 w. in match: 2
1st-Class catches: 25
One-Day 5 w. in innings: 1
Place in batting averages: 198th av. 22.33 (2003 275th av. 9.55)
Place in bowling averages: 43rd av. 29.76 (2003 24th av. 24.05)

Strike rate: 51.71 (career 54.73)
Parents: Fred and Nellie
Wife and date of marriage: Thea, 5 September 1999
Children: Rob, 1989; Keeghan, 1999
Education: Pretoria BHS
Overseas tours: South Africa A to England 1996
Overseas teams played for: Northern Transvaal/Northerns Titans 1993-94 – 2001-02
Career highlights to date: 'Playing for South Africa A. Being capped by Notts'
Cricket moments to forget: 'Losing to Surrey in semi-final of B&H Cup [2001]. Losing to Natal in final of Standard Bank Cup [2000-01]'
Cricketers particularly admired: Wasim Akram, Fanie de Villiers, Kepler Wessels
Young players to look out for: Bilal Shafayat, Krier van Wyk
Other sports played: Golf
Other sports followed: Football (Arsenal), South African rugby
Relaxations: 'Spending time with my family and friends'
Extras: Attended National Academy in South Africa. Made first-class debut for Northern Transvaal B v Transvaal B at Johannesburg 1993-94. Took hat-trick (Mitchell, Drakes, Henderson) v Border at East London in semi-final (second leg) of Standard Bank Cup 2000-01; took 3-15 in deciding leg at East London, winning Man of the Match award. Nottinghamshire Player of the Year 2001. Holds a British passport and is not considered an overseas player
Best batting: 68 Northerns v Western Province, Centurion 1995-96
Best bowling: 8-53 Nottinghamshire v Essex, Trent Bridge 2002

2004 Season

	M	Inns	NO	Runs	HS	Avge	100s	50s	Ct	St	O	M	Runs	Wkts	Avge	Best	5wI	10wM
Test																		
All First	13	12	3	201	35	22.33	-	-	2	-	336.1	69	1161	39	29.76	5-35	3	-
1-day Int																		
C & G	2	1	0	0	0	0.00	-	-	1	-	18	2	66	2	33.00	2-28	-	
totesport	13	5	5	28	17 *	-	-	-	5	-	79.1	6	317	19	16.68	4-28	-	
Twenty20																		

Career Performances

	M	Inns	NO	Runs	HS	Avge	100s	50s	Ct	St	Balls	Runs	Wkts	Avge	Best	5wI	10wM
Test																	
All First	125	157	53	1460	68	14.03	-	2	25	-	21567	10919	394	27.71	8-53	16	2
1-day Int																	
C & G	8	3	1	5	4 *	2.50	-	-	1	-	444	293	15	19.53	4-25	-	
totesport	47	20	8	89	17 *	7.41	-	-	7	-	2081	1516	64	23.68	4-28	-	
Twenty20	2	1	0	2	2	2.00	-	-	-	-	42	43	1	43.00	1-18	-	

SMITH, W. R. Nottinghamshire

Name: William (Will) Rew Smith
Role: Right-hand bat, occasional right-arm off-spin bowler, occasional wicket-keeper
Born: 28 September 1982, Luton
Height: 5ft 10in **Weight:** 12st 2lbs
Nickname: Jiggy, Jigs, Posh Kid, Smudger, Swill
County debut: 2002
1st-Class catches: 6
Place in batting averages: (2003 255th av. 14.50)
Strike rate: 105.00 (career 105.00)
Parents: Jim and Barbara
Marital status: Single ('long-term girlfriend Lucy')
Family links with cricket: 'Brother played a lot of club cricket; Dad is an enthusiastic follower'
Education: Bedford School; Durham University
Qualifications: 11 GCSEs, 3 A-levels
Career outside cricket: Student
Off-season: 'Klute'
Overseas tours: Bedford School to Barbados (Sir Garfield Sobers International Tournament) 1998; British Universities to South Africa 2004
Overseas teams played for: Gordon CC, Sydney 2001-02
Career highlights to date: 'Winning a grade final for Gordon CC, scoring 120'
Cricket moments to forget: 'Batting with Ali Maiden!'
Cricket superstitions: 'None'
Cricketers particularly admired: Nick Phillips ('brother of Tim')
Young players to look out for: 'Rick (Phil) Phillips'
Other sports played: Rugby (East Midlands age group), hockey (Eastern Counties age group), five-a-side football
Other sports followed: Football (Rushden & Diamonds, Nottingham Forest)
Injuries: Anterior laxity of shoulder ('ongoing')
Favourite band: Keane
Relaxations: 'Klute; following Phil Phillips and his blossoming cricket career'
Extras: Captained Harrold CC U13 to Ken Barrington Trophy (national club championship). England U16-U18. Played for Durham University CCE 2003, 2004 (captain 2004; reappointed for 2005). Represented British Universities v New Zealanders and v Sri Lanka A 2004
Opinions on cricket: 'I think the two divisional system has had a great effect on competition and aspiration of counties.'

Best batting: 48 DUCCE v Durham, Riverside 2004
Best bowling: 2-83 DUCCE v Derbyshire, Derby 2004

2004 Season

	M	Inns	NO	Runs	HS	Avge	100s	50s	Ct	St	O	M	Runs	Wkts	Avge	Best	5wI	10wM
Test																		
All First	4	6	1	91	48	18.20	-	-	4	-	35	4	127	2	63.50	2-83	-	-
1-day Int																		
C & G																		
totesport																		
Twenty20	1	0	0	0	0	-	-	-	-	-								

Career Performances

	M	Inns	NO	Runs	HS	Avge	100s	50s	Ct	St	Balls	Runs	Wkts	Avge	Best	5wI	10wM
Test																	
All First	8	13	2	216	48	19.63	-	-	6	-	210	127	2	63.50	2-83	-	-
1-day Int																	
C & G																	
totesport	6	5	0	41	16	8.20	-	-	1	-							
Twenty20	2	1	0	1	1	1.00	-	-	1	-							

SNAPE, J. N. — Leicestershire

Name: Jeremy Nicholas Snape
Role: Right-hand bat, off-spin bowler; all-rounder
Born: 27 April 1973, Stoke-on-Trent
Height: 5ft 8in **Weight:** 12st
Nickname: Snapey, Coot, Jez, Snapper
County debut: 1992 (Northamptonshire), 1999 (Gloucestershire), 2003 (Leicestershire)
County cap: 1999 (Gloucestershire)
One-Day Internationals: 10
1st-Class 50s: 22
1st-Class 100s: 3
1st-Class 5 w. in innings: 1
1st-Class catches: 71
One-Day 100s: 1
One-Day 5 w. in innings: 1
Place in batting averages: 218th av. 20.00 (2003 154th av. 29.05)
Place in bowling averages: (2003 151st av. 60.81)
Strike rate: 218.00 (career 94.88)

Parents: Keith and Barbara
Wife and date of marriage: Joanne, 4 October 2003
Family links with cricket: 'Brother Jonathan plays league cricket for Rode Park CC in Cheshire. Dad loves cricket now, and Mum hates the sweep shot!'
Education: Denstone College, Staffordshire; Durham University
Qualifications: 8 GCSEs, 3 A-levels, BSc Natural Science
Career outside cricket: Director of Capetours – tailor-made holidays to Southern Africa (www.capetours.co.uk)
Overseas tours: England U18 to Canada (International Youth Tournament) 1991 (captain); England U19 to Pakistan 1991-92; Durham University to South Africa 1993, to Vienna (European Indoor Championships) 1994; Northamptonshire to Cape Town 1993; Christians in Sport to Zimbabwe 1994-95; Troubadours to South Africa 1997; Gloucestershire to Kimberley, South Africa 1999; England to Zimbabwe (one-day series) 2001-02, to India and New Zealand 2001-02 (one-day series), to Sri Lanka (ICC Champions Trophy) 2002-03, to Australia 2002-03 (VB Series)
Overseas teams played for: Petone, Wellington, New Zealand 1994-95; Wainuiamata, Wellington, New Zealand 1995-96; Techs CC, Cape Town 1996-99
Career highlights to date: 'Playing for England'
Cricket moments to forget: 'Breaking my thumb in Australia 2003 and being ruled out of World Cup'
Cricketers particularly admired: Allan Lamb, Jack Russell
Relaxations: Travelling, music, cooking, good food and wine
Extras: Sir John Hobbs Silver Jubilee Memorial Prize 1988. B&H Gold Award for his 3-34 for Combined Universities v Worcestershire at The Parks 1992. Player of the Tournament at European Indoor 6-a-side Championships in 1994. Left Northants at end of 1998 season and joined Gloucestershire for 1999. Scored maiden one-day century (104*) in the Norwich Union League v Nottinghamshire at Trent Bridge 2001, in the process sharing with Mark Hardinges (65) in a then record seventh-wicket partnership for domestic one-day competitions (164). Made ODI debut in first ODI v Zimbabwe at Harare 2001-02, winning Man of the Match award for his 2-39 and brilliant catch. BBC West Country Sports Cricketer of the Year for 2001. Left Gloucestershire at the end of the 2002 season and joined Leicestershire for 2003. Struck 16-ball 34*, including winning runs, in the Twenty20 Cup final at Edgbaston 2004
Best batting: 131 Gloucestershire v Sussex, Cheltenham 2001
Best bowling: 5-65 Northamptonshire v Durham, Northampton 1995

2004 Season

	M	Inns	NO	Runs	HS	Avge	100s	50s	Ct	St	O	M	Runs	Wkts	Avge	Best	5wI	10wM
Test																		
All First	5	8	1	140	66	20.00	-	1	1	-	36.2	5	133	1	133.00	1-78	-	-
1-day Int																		
C & G	1	1	0	28	28	28.00	-	-	-	-	8	1	18	0	-	-	-	
totesport	18	14	4	391	69	39.10	-	3	7	-	86	2	453	13	34.84	3-42	-	
Twenty20	7	6	3	97	34 *	32.33	-	-	3	-	24	0	161	2	80.50	2-13	-	

Career Performances

	M	Inns	NO	Runs	HS	Avge	100s	50s	Ct	St	Balls	Runs	Wkts	Avge	Best	5wI	10wM
Test																	
All First	111	165	30	3874	131	28.69	3	22	71	-	10343	5361	109	49.18	5-65	1	-
1-day Int	10	7	3	118	38	29.50	-	-	5	-	529	403	13	31.00	3-43	-	
C & G	25	21	4	343	54	20.17	-	1	12	-	625	438	10	43.80	2-19	-	
totesport	141	114	31	2018	104 *	24.31	1	6	43	-	4022	3136	118	26.57	4-27	-	
Twenty20	13	12	7	151	34 *	30.20	-	-	7	-	252	290	7	41.42	3-14	-	

SOLANKI, V. S. Worcestershire

Name: Vikram Singh Solanki
Role: Right-hand bat, right-arm off-spin bowler, county captain
Born: 1 April 1976, Udaipur, India
Height: 6ft **Weight:** 12st
Nickname: Vik
County debut: 1993 (one-day), 1995 (first-class)
County cap: 1998; colours, 2002
One-Day Internationals: 28
1000 runs in a season: 2
1st-Class 50s: 52
1st-Class 100s: 15
1st-Class 5 w. in innings: 4
1st-Class 10 w. in match: 1
1st-Class catches: 209
One-Day 100s: 9
Place in batting averages: 73rd av. 42.05 (2003 167th av. 26.54)
Strike rate: 74.50 (career 77.97)
Parents: Mr Vijay Singh and Mrs Florabel Solanki
Marital status: Single
Family links with cricket: 'Father played in India. Brother Vishal is a keen cricketer'
Education: Regis School, Wolverhampton; Open University
Qualifications: 9 GCSEs, 3 A-levels
Overseas tours: England U18 to South Africa 1992-93, to Denmark (ICC Youth Tournament) 1994; England U19 to West Indies 1994-95; Worcestershire CCC to Barbados 1996, to Zimbabwe 1997; England A to Zimbabwe and South Africa 1998-99, to Bangladesh and New Zealand 1999-2000, to West Indies 2000-01, to Sri Lanka 2004-05; England to South Africa and Zimbabwe 1999-2000 (one-day series),

to Kenya (ICC Knockout Trophy) 2000-01, to Pakistan 2000-01 (one-day series), to Bangladesh and Sri Lanka 2003-04 (one-day series), to Zimbabwe (one-day series) 2004-05, to South Africa 2004-05 (one-day series)
Overseas teams played for: Midland-Guildford, Perth, Western Australia
Career highlights to date: 'Playing for England'
Cricket moments to forget: 'Losing to Scotland (NatWest 1998)'
Cricketers particularly admired: Sachin Tendulkar, Graeme Hick
Other sports played: 'Enjoy most sports'
Relaxations: 'Reading; spending time with family and friends'
Extras: Scored more first-class runs (1339) in 1999 season than any other English player. Topped batting averages with 597 first-class runs (av. 59.70) on England A tour of Bangladesh and New Zealand 1999-2000. C&G Man of the Match award for his 108 v Nottinghamshire at Trent Bridge 2002. Scored maiden ODI century (106) v South Africa at The Oval in the NatWest Series 2003, winning the Man of the Match award and sharing with Marcus Trescothick (114*) in a record England opening partnership in ODIs (200). C&G Man of the Match awards for his 127 (plus three catches and a run-out) in the semi-final v Warwickshire at Edgbaston 2004 and for his 115 in the final v Gloucestershire at Lord's 2004. Appointed captain of Worcestershire for 2005
Best batting: 185 England A v Bangladesh, Chittagong 1999-2000
Best bowling: 5-40 Worcestershire v Middlesex, Lord's 2004
Stop press: Man of the Match in the third ODI v Zimbabwe at Bulawayo 2004-05 (100*)

2004 Season

	M	Inns	NO	Runs	HS	Avge	100s	50s	Ct	St	O	M	Runs	Wkts	Avge	Best	5wI	10wM
Test																		
All First	13	18	0	757	107	42.05	1	6	10	-	74.3	7	240	6	40.00	5-40	1	-
1-day Int	7	7	0	200	62	28.57	-	2	1	-								
C & G	4	4	0	289	126	72.25	2	-	5	-								
totesport	14	14	0	653	122	46.64	2	4	8	-	2	0	5	2	2.50	2-5	-	
Twenty20	6	6	0	138	50	23.00	-	1	4	-								

Career Performances

	M	Inns	NO	Runs	HS	Avge	100s	50s	Ct	St	Balls	Runs	Wkts	Avge	Best	5wI	10wM
Test																	
All First	170	276	19	9167	185	35.66	15	52	209	-	6082	3549	78	45.50	5-40	4	1
1-day Int	28	27	2	573	106	22.92	1	3	7	-							
C & G	24	23	1	923	164 *	41.95	4	3	10	-	225	174	3	58.00	1-25	-	
totesport	144	127	13	3429	122	30.07	4	20	52	-	246	252	7	36.00	2-5	-	
Twenty20	6	6	0	138	50	23.00	-	1	4	-							

SPEARMAN, C. M. Gloucestershire

Name: Craig Murray Spearman
Role: Right-hand opening bat
Born: 4 July 1972, Auckland, New Zealand
Height: 6ft **Weight:** 13st 7lbs
Nickname: Spears
County debut: 2002
County cap: 2002
Test debut: 1995-96
Tests: 19
One-Day Internationals: 51
1000 runs in a season: 2
1st-Class 50s: 46
1st-Class 100s: 19
1st-Class 200s: 1
1st-Class 300s: 1
1st-Class catches: 140
One-Day 100s: 5
Place in batting averages: 19th av. 56.23 (2003 116th av. 33.44)
Strike rate: (career 78.00)
Parents: Murray and Sandra
Wife and date of marriage: Maree, 4 March 2004
Education: Kelston Boys High School, Auckland; Massey University, Palmerston North, New Zealand
Qualifications: Bachelor of Business Studies (BBS; Finance major)
Off-season: 'Going to New Zealand for two months'
Overseas tours: New Zealand to India and Pakistan (World Cup) 1995-96, to West Indies 1995-96, to Sharjah (Singer Champions Trophy) 1996-97, to Pakistan 1996-97, to Zimbabwe 1997-98, to Australia 1997-98 (CUB Series), to Sri Lanka 1998, to India 1999-2000, to Zimbabwe 2000-01, to Kenya (ICC Knockout Trophy) 2000-01, to South Africa 2000-01
Overseas teams played for: Auckland 1993-96; Central Districts 1997-2000-01, 2002-03 –
Career highlights to date: 'Playing international cricket; Test century; winning ICC Knockout Trophy [2000-01] with New Zealand; winning two C&G finals with Gloucestershire; scoring 341 for Gloucestershire v Middlesex (highest score for Gloucestershire)'
Cricket moments to forget: 'Misfielding on the boundary at the SCG in the fifth over and hearing about it for the next 45 overs'
Cricket superstitions: 'None'
Cricketers particularly admired: Gordon Greenidge

Other sports played: Golf, tennis
Other sports followed: Rugby, golf, football
Favourite band: U2
Relaxations: 'Sleeping'
Extras: Scored maiden Test century (112) at Auckland 1995-96, in the process sharing with Roger Twose in a record first-wicket partnership for New Zealand in Tests against Zimbabwe (214). Scored century (111) on Championship debut for Gloucestershire v Worcestershire at Worcester 2002. C&G Man of the Match award for his 77-ball 104* (his maiden one-day century for Gloucestershire) v Durham at Bristol 2002. Gloucestershire Players' Player of the Year 2002. Scored 123-ball 153 v Warwickshire at Gloucester in the NCL 2003 to set a new individual record score for Gloucestershire in the one-day league. Vice-captain of Gloucestershire 2003. Scored a 48-ball 85 for Central Districts v Canterbury in the final of the State Shield 2003-04 at Christchurch. Scored maiden first-class triple century (341; the highest individual score for Gloucestershire in first-class cricket) v Middlesex at Gloucester 2004. C&G Man of the Match award for his 122-ball 143* in the semi-final v Yorkshire at Bristol 2004. His 237 v Warwickshire at Bristol 2004 was the first double century by a Gloucestershire player at the ground since 1946. 'Qualify to play for Gloucestershire because of my mother's Welsh background'
Best batting: 341 Gloucestershire v Middlesex, Gloucester 2004
Best bowling: 1-37 Central Districts v Wellington, New Plymouth 1999-2000
Stop press: Played for FICA World XI v New Zealand at Christchurch 2004-05

2004 Season

	M	Inns	NO	Runs	HS	Avge	100s	50s	Ct	St	O	M	Runs	Wkts	Avge	Best	5wI	10wM
Test																		
All First	17	28	2	1462	341	56.23	4	4	15	-								
1-day Int																		
C & G	5	5	1	364	143 *	91.00	1	3	4	-								
totesport	16	16	0	518	89	32.37	-	3	8	-								
Twenty20	5	4	1	11	8	3.66	-	-	1	-								

Career Performances

	M	Inns	NO	Runs	HS	Avge	100s	50s	Ct	St	Balls	Runs	Wkts	Avge	Best	5wI	10wM
Test	19	36	2	920	112	27.05	1	3	21	-							
All First	149	266	16	9633	341	38.53	21	46	140	-	78	55	1	55.00	1-37	-	-
1-day Int	51	50	0	936	86	18.72	-	5	15	-	3	6	0	-	-	-	
C & G	13	13	2	667	143 *	60.63	2	5	4	-							
totesport	46	45	1	1777	153	40.38	3	10	16	-							
Twenty20	11	10	2	191	88	23.87	-	1	2	-							

SPENDLOVE, B. L. Derbyshire

Name: Benjamin (Ben) Lee Spendlove
Role: Right-hand bat, right-arm off-spin bowler
Born: 4 November 1978, Derby
Height: 6ft 2in **Weight:** 13st
Nickname: Silky
County debut: 1997
1st-Class 50s: 2
1st-Class catches: 10
Parents: Lee and Christine
Marital status: Single
Children: Zack, 8 September 1999
Family links with cricket: Father played local leagues
Education: Trent College, Long Eaton
Qualifications: 9 GCSEs, ECB Level 1 coaching
Overseas tours: England U17 to Holland (International Youth Tournament) 1995
Overseas teams played for: Gold Coast Dolphins, Queensland 1996-97
Career highlights to date: 'Taking two catches as 12th man for England against South Africa at Edgbaston [1998]'
Cricket moments to forget: 'Scoring no runs and ending up on the losing side in the NatWest final [1998]'
Cricketers particularly admired: Robin Smith, Allan Lamb, Alec Stewart
Other sports played: Hockey (Derbyshire U15), rugby (Midlands U16)
Other sports followed: Football (Arsenal, Chesterfield)
Favourite band: Keane, Snow Patrol
Relaxations: 'Eating out with my girlfriend; cinema; shopping (clothes)'
Extras: Represented England U15, U17 and U19. Fielded as 12th man for England in the first Test v South Africa at Edgbaston 1998, taking two catches. Played for Derbyshire 1997-2000; rejoined the county 2004
Opinions on cricket: 'Enjoying seeing the national side playing positive and aggressive Test cricket. Also good to see players I grew up playing with doing really well at the top level.'
Best batting: 63 Derbyshire v Warwickshire, Edgbaston 1999

2004 Season

	M	Inns	NO	Runs	HS	Avge	100s	50s	Ct	St	O	M	Runs	Wkts	Avge	Best	5wI	10wM
Test																		
All First																		
1-day Int																		
C & G																		
totesport	4	4	0	19	13	4.75	-	-	1	-								
Twenty20																		

Career Performances

	M	Inns	NO	Runs	HS	Avge	100s	50s	Ct	St	Balls	Runs	Wkts	Avge	Best	5wI	10wM
Test																	
All First	20	36	2	656	63	19.29	-	2	10	-							
1-day Int																	
C & G	8	7	0	211	58	30.14	-	2	2	-							
totesport	17	16	0	151	26	9.43	-	-	4	-							
Twenty20																	

STEPHENSON, J. P. — Essex

Name: John Patrick Stephenson
Role: Right-hand bat, right-arm medium bowler
Born: 14 March 1965, Stebbing, Essex
Height: 6ft 1in **Weight:** 12st 7lbs
Nickname: Stan
County debut: 1985 (Essex), 1995 (Hants)
County cap: 1989 (Essex), 1995 (Hants)
Benefit: 2001 (Hants; £192,092)
Test debut: 1989
Tests: 1
1000 runs in a season: 5
1st-Class 50s: 78
1st-Class 100s: 24
1st-Class 200s: 1
1st-Class 5 w. in innings: 11
1st-Class 10 w. in match: 1
1st-Class catches: 182
One-Day 100s: 7
One-Day 5 w. in innings: 3
Strike rate: 49.33 (career 58.34)
Parents: Pat and Eve

Wife and date of marriage: Fiona Maria, 24 September 1994
Children: Emma-Lydia, 19 May 1997; Camilla, 30 April 2000
Family links with cricket: 'Father was member of Rugby Meteors *Cricketer* Cup winning side in 1973. Three brothers played in Felsted 1st XI; Guy played for Essex 2nd XI and now plays for Teddington'
Education: Felsted School; Durham University
Qualifications: 7 O-levels, 3 A-levels, BA General Arts, Level 3 coaching award, SFA registered representative
Overseas tours: English Schools U19 to Zimbabwe 1982-83; England A to Kenya and Zimbabwe 1989-90, to Bermuda and West Indies 1991-92; MCC to Kenya 1999
Overseas teams played for: Fitzroy, Melbourne 1982-83, 1987-88; Boland, South Africa 1988-89; Gold Coast Dolphins and Bond University, Australia 1990-91; St George's, Argentina 1994-95; Belgrano, Argentina 1994-95; Victoria CC, South Africa 1995-96
Career highlights to date: 'Playing for England. Winning Championship in 1992 with Essex. Captaining Hampshire. Rejoining Essex and winning second division Championship. B&H final'
Cricketers particularly admired: Brian Hardie
Young players to look out for: Alastair Cook
Favourite band: The Smiths
Relaxations: 'Watching cricket, reading (*Sunday Telegraph*, *Wisden*), alternative music'
Extras: Essex Young Player of the Year 1985. Captained Durham University to victory in UAU Championship 1986 and was captain of Combined Universities team 1987 in the first year that it was drawn from all universities. Was leading wicket-taker on England A tour to Bermuda and West Indies 1991-92. Carried bat in first innings for 113* and scored 159* in the second v Somerset at Taunton in 1992 and was on the field for the whole game (the first Essex player to achieve this). First Essex player to achieve 500 runs and 20 wickets in a Sunday League season 1993. Joined Hampshire for 1995. Scored 107 v Norfolk in the NatWest at Southampton 1996, in the process sharing with Jason Laney (153) in a then competition record stand for the first wicket (269). Took over the captaincy of Hampshire in 1996, but relinquished it at the end of the 1997 season. Founded the One Test Wonder Club in 1996. Scored 83* v Durham 2000, becoming the first opening batsman to carry his bat five times in the Sunday/National League. Released by Hampshire at the end of the 2001 season; rejoined Essex for 2002 as 2nd XI captain/coach and ended up as the county's leading wicket-taker in the Championship with 48 wickets (av. 22.54) as well as scoring 562 runs (av. 35.12). Retired from county cricket in May 2004, becoming Head of Cricket at MCC
Opinions on cricket: 'Young players are given too much support and information. They will learn the game by standing on their own two feet.'
Best batting: 202* Essex v Somerset, Bath 1990
Best bowling: 7-44 Essex v Worcestershire, Worcester 2002

2004 Season

	M	Inns	NO	Runs	HS	Avge	100s	50s	Ct	St	O	M	Runs	Wkts	Avge	Best	5wI	10wM
Test																		
All First	5	7	2	226	71 *	45.20	-	2	1	-	74	11	285	9	31.66	3-28	-	-
1-day Int																		
C & G																		
totesport																		
Twenty20																		

Career Performances

	M	Inns	NO	Runs	HS	Avge	100s	50s	Ct	St	Balls	Runs	Wkts	Avge	Best	5wI	10wM
Test	1	2	0	36	25	18.00	-	-	-	-							
All First	302	510	56	14772	202 *	32.53	25	78	182	-	22871	12782	392	32.60	7-44	11	1
1-day Int																	
C & G	36	31	1	930	107	31.00	1	7	16	-	1225	965	29	33.27	5-34	1	
totesport	202	180	26	4339	110 *	28.17	4	19	85	-	5815	4605	180	25.58	6-33	2	
Twenty20																	

STEVENS, D. I. Kent

Name: Darren Ian Stevens
Role: Right-hand bat, right-arm medium bowler
Born: 30 April 1976, Leicester
Height: 5ft 11in **Weight:** 12st
Nickname: Stevo
County debut: 1997 (Leicestershire)
County cap: 2002 (Leicestershire)
1st-Class 50s: 23
1st-Class 100s: 5
1st-Class catches: 66
One-Day 100s: 2
Place in batting averages: 98th av. 36.26 (2003 124th av. 32.36)
Strike rate: 34.66 (career 111.50)
Parents: Maddy and Bob
Marital status: Engaged to Sue
Family links with cricket: Father and grandfather played league cricket in Leicestershire
Education: Mount Grace High School; John Cleveland College, Hinckley; Hinckley Tech; Charles Klein College
Qualifications: 5 GCSEs, BTEC National in Sports Studies

Overseas tours: Leicestershire U19 to South Africa 1994-95; Leicestershire to Barbados 1998, to Sri Lanka 1999, to Potchefstroom 2001; ECB National Academy to Australia and Sri Lanka 2002-03
Overseas teams played for: Wanderers CC, Johannesburg, South Africa 1996-97; Rhodes University, Grahamstown, South Africa 1997-98; Fairfield CC, Sydney 1998-99; Hawthorn-Waverley, Melbourne 1999-2000; Taita CC, Wellington, New Zealand 2000-01; Ringwood CC, Melbourne 2001-02
Career highlights to date: 'The build-up to my first final at Lord's'
Cricket moments to forget: 'Losing in my first final in the C&G against Somerset 2001'
Cricketers particularly admired: Steve Waugh, Viv Richards, Ian Botham
Young players to look out for: John Maunders, John Sadler, Matt Prior
Other sports played: Golf, squash
Other sports followed: Football (Leicester City), rugby union (Leicester Tigers)
Favourite band: U2
Relaxations: 'Music, spending time with Sue and close friends'
Extras: Received painting from Sir Colin Cowdrey on day of maiden first-class 100 (130 in fourth Championship match), v Sussex at Arundel 1999. Won Sir Ron Brierley/Crusaders Scholarship 1999. Scored a 114-ball 125 v Durham at Riverside in the NUL 2002; it was his maiden one-day league century and the equal highest individual one-day score recorded at Riverside. Included in provisional England squad of 30 for the 2002-03 World Cup. Released by Leicestershire at the end of the 2004 season and has joined Kent for 2005
Best batting: 149 Leicestershire v Essex, Southend 2003
Best bowling: 2-50 Leicestershire v Somerset, Leicester 2004

2004 Season

	M	Inns	NO	Runs	HS	Avge	100s	50s	Ct	St	O	M	Runs	Wkts	Avge	Best	5wI	10wM
Test																		
All First	13	22	3	689	105	36.26	1	5	13	-	17.2	1	80	3	26.66	2-50	-	-
1-day Int																		
C & G	1	1	0	14	14	14.00	-	-	-	-								
totesport	18	16	0	271	83	16.93	-	1	11	-	2	0	14	0	-	-	-	
Twenty20	7	7	1	161	39	26.83	-	-	1	-								

Career Performances

	M	Inns	NO	Runs	HS	Avge	100s	50s	Ct	St	Balls	Runs	Wkts	Avge	Best	5wI	10wM
Test																	
All First	81	135	8	3651	149	28.74	5	23	66	-	669	413	6	68.83	2-50	-	-
1-day Int																	
C & G	14	13	0	438	133	33.69	1	2	5	-	84	82	2	41.00	2-26	-	
totesport	88	82	6	1965	125	25.85	1	13	40	-	201	157	4	39.25	2-28	-	
Twenty20	13	13	1	244	39	20.33	-	-	6	-	12	16	1	16.00	1-16	-	

STIFF, D. A. Kent

Name: David Alexander Stiff
Role: Right-hand bat, right-arm fast bowler
Born: 20 October 1984, Dewsbury
Height: 6ft 6in **Weight:** 15st
Nickname: Stiffy, Stiffler
County debut: 2004
1st-Class catches: 1
Strike rate: 75.42 (career 75.42)
Parents: Christine and Ian
Marital status: Single
Family links with cricket: 'Eldest brother, Peter, played club cricket in Yorkshire and is now trying to increase the profile of the game in Germany, where he now lives.' Youngest brother, William, has played for Yorkshire Schools and North of England Schools age group teams
Education: Batley Grammar School
Qualifications: 6 GCSEs
Overseas tours: England U17 to Australia 2001; Yorkshire to Grenada 2002; England U19 to Australia 2002-03, to Bangladesh (U19 World Cup) 2003-04
Career highlights to date: 'Taking five wickets in the first innings of the third U19 "Test" match v Australia at Bankstown, Sydney [2002-03]'
Cricket moments to forget: 'Losing that same match [*see above*] and the series by 14 runs. My last two years at Yorkshire (2002-03)'
Cricketers particularly admired: Allan Donald, Brett Lee, Jason Gillespie, Courtney Walsh
Young players to look out for: Mark Lawson, Trent Kelly (Australian)
Favourite band: Radiohead
Relaxations: Music
Extras: Yorkshire Cricket Academy 1999-2003. Played for Yorkshire Board XI in the C&G 2002. Took 5-35 for England U19 in the third 'Test' v Australia U19 at Bankstown Oval, Sydney 2002-03. Represented England U19 v Bangladesh U19 2004. ECB National Academy 2004-05 (part-time)
Opinions on cricket: 'Less games, more competitive games. Less players who are happy just to play county cricket and not push themselves to play for England. More time to train during the season.'
Best batting: 18 Kent v Lancashire, Tunbridge Wells 2004
Best bowling: 3-88 Kent v New Zealanders, Canterbury 2004

2004 Season

	M	Inns	NO	Runs	HS	Avge	100s	50s	Ct	St	O	M	Runs	Wkts	Avge	Best	5wI	10wM
Test																		
All First	6	4	1	30	18	10.00	-	-	1	-	88	13	419	7	59.85	3-88	-	-
1-day Int																		
C & G																		
totesport																		
Twenty20																		

Career Performances

	M	Inns	NO	Runs	HS	Avge	100s	50s	Ct	St	Balls	Runs	Wkts	Avge	Best	5wI	10wM
Test																	
All First	6	4	1	30	18	10.00	-	-	1	-	528	419	7	59.85	3-88	-	-
1-day Int																	
C & G	1	0	0	0	0	-	-	-	-	-	30	27	1	27.00	1-27	-	
totesport																	
Twenty20																	

STRAUSS, A. J. — Middlesex

Name: Andrew John Strauss
Role: Left-hand bat, left-arm medium bowler
Born: 2 March 1977, Johannesburg, South Africa
Height: 5ft 11in **Weight:** 13st
Nickname: Straussy, Johann, Levi, Mareman, Muppet, Lord Brocket
County debut: 1997 (one-day), 1998 (first-class)
County cap: 2001
Test debut: 2004
Tests: 7
One-Day Internationals: 18
1000 runs in a season: 3
1st-Class 50s: 31
1st-Class 100s: 13
1st-Class catches: 52
One-Day 100s: 3
Place in batting averages: 41st av. 50.28 (2003 26th av. 50.96)
Strike rate: (career 48.00)
Parents: David and Dawn
Wife and date of marriage: Ruth, 18 October 2003

Education: Radley College; Durham University
Qualifications: 4 A-levels, BA (Hons) Economics
Off-season: England tour to South Africa
Overseas tours: Durham University to Zimbabwe 1997-98; Middlesex to South Africa 2000; ECB National Academy to Australia 2001-02; England to Bangladesh and Sri Lanka 2003-04 (one-day series), to West Indies 2003-04, to Zimbabwe (one-day series) 2004-05, to South Africa 2004-05
Overseas teams played for: Sydney University 1998-99; Mosman, Sydney 1999-2001
Career highlights to date: 'Scoring century on Test debut. Beating the Aussies in semi-final of ICC Champions Trophy'
Cricket moments to forget: 'Getting out second ball of the season 2001'
Cricket superstitions: 'Never borrow David Nash's box'
Cricketers particularly admired: Allan Donald, Brian Lara, Saqlain Mushtaq
Other sports played: Golf (Durham University 1998), rugby (Durham University 1996-97)
Other sports followed: 'Anything with a ball'
Extras: Middlesex Player of the Year 2001. Made ODI debut v Sri Lanka at Dambulla 2003-04. Originally selected for England one-day squad to West Indies 2003-04, then called up to Test squad as cover for Mark Butcher and Graham Thorpe. Man of the Match in the first Test v New Zealand 2004 after becoming only the second England player, after John Hampshire in 1969, to score a century (112) on Test debut at Lord's (his home ground); also scored 83 in the second innings. Scored maiden ODI century (100) v West Indies, also at Lord's, in the NatWest Series 2004, in the process sharing with Andrew Flintoff (123) in a new record partnership for England in ODIs (226). Scored century (137) in the first Test v West Indies, once again at Lord's, 2004, in the process sharing with Robert Key (221) in a ground record second-wicket stand for Test cricket (291). Wombwell Cricket Lovers' Society George Spofforth Cricketer of the Year 2004. Captain of Middlesex 2002-04. ECB contract 2004-05
Opinions on cricket: 'The performance of the England team this summer [2004] shows what can be done with the right training and preparation. Surely the county game must follow suit at some stage and reduce the amount we play.'
Best batting: 176 Middlesex v Durham, Lord's 2001
Best bowling: 1-27 Middlesex v Nottinghamshire, Lord's 2003
Stop press: Scored 126 in the first Test v South Africa at Port Elizabeth 2004-05, achieving feat of scoring a Test century on home and away debuts and becoming first player to score a Test century in his first innings against each of first three opponents; also scored 94* in second innings. Scored 136 in the second Test v South Africa at Durban 2004-05, in the process sharing with Marcus Trescothick (132) in the highest opening partnership for England in Tests since 1960 (273). Scored century (147) in the fourth Test v South Africa at Johannesburg (his birthplace), in the process sharing with Robert Key (83) in a ground record stand for the second wicket in Tests (182). Man of the [Test] Series v South Africa 2004-05 (656 runs at 72.88)

2004 Season

	M	Inns	NO	Runs	HS	Avge	100s	50s	Ct	St	O	M	Runs	Wkts	Avge	Best	5wI	10wM
Test	7	14	1	590	137	45.38	2	3	11	-								
All First	8	16	2	704	137	50.28	2	4	11	-								
1-day Int	12	12	3	403	100	44.77	1	2	2	-								
C & G	2	2	0	31	19	15.50	-	-	-	-								
totesport	4	4	2	234	107 *	117.00	1	2	-	-								
Twenty20	2	2	0	21	11	10.50	-	-	-	-								

Career Performances

	M	Inns	NO	Runs	HS	Avge	100s	50s	Ct	St	Balls	Runs	Wkts	Avge	Best	5wI	10wM
Test	7	14	1	590	137	45.38	2	3	11	-							
All First	89	155	11	6141	176	42.64	13	31	52	-	48	58	1	58.00	1-27	-	-
1-day Int	18	17	3	578	100	41.28	1	4	3	-							
C & G	10	10	0	315	75	31.50	-	3	-	-							
totesport	70	67	4	1806	127	28.66	2	13	10	-							
Twenty20	7	7	0	194	60	27.71	-	2	4	-							

STREAK, H. H. — Warwickshire

Name: Heath Hilton Streak
Role: Right-hand bat, right-arm fast bowler
Born: 16 March 1974, Bulawayo, Zimbabwe
Height: 6ft 1in **Weight:** 15st
Nickname: Streaky, Stack
County debut: 1995 (Hampshire), 2004 (Warwickshire)
Test debut: 1993-94
Tests: 59
One-Day Internationals: 183
50 wickets in a season: 1
1st-Class 50s: 21
1st-Class 100s: 6
1st-Class 5 w. in innings: 12
1st-Class 10 w. in match: 2
1st-Class catches: 46
One-Day 5 w. in innings: 1
Place in batting averages: 171st av. 25.71
Place in bowling averages: 7th av. 21.75
Strike rate: 39.75 (career 60.62)
Parents: Denis and Sheona
Wife and date of marriage: Nadine, 18 August 2000

Children: Holly, 23 December 1992; Charlotte, 14 August 2002
Family links with cricket: 'Denis, my father, played for Rhodesia and Zimbabwe'
Education: Falcon College, Zimbabwe
Qualifications: Pro safari guide
Career outside cricket: Farming/safari guide
Off-season: 'Playing cricket/working family ranch'
Overseas tours: Zimbabwe to England 1993, to India (Hero Cup) 1993-94, to Pakistan 1993-94, to New Zealand 1995-96, to India and Pakistan (World Cup) 1995-96, to Sri Lanka 1996, 1997-98, to New Zealand 1997-98, to Malaysia (Commonwealth Games) 1998-99, to Bangladesh (Wills International Cup) 1998-99, to Pakistan 1998-99, to UK, Ireland and Holland (World Cup) 1999, to West Indies 1999-2000, to England 2000, to Kenya (ICC Knockout Trophy) 2000-01 (captain), to India 2000-01 (captain), to New Zealand 2000-01 (captain), to Bangladesh 2001-02, to Sri Lanka 2001-02, to India 2001-02, to Sri Lanka (ICC Champions Trophy) 2002-03 (captain), to England 2003 (captain), to Australia 2003-04 (captain), to South Africa 2004-05, plus other one-day tournaments in Australia, South Africa, Sharjah, India and Bangladesh; FICA World XI to New Zealand 2004-05
Overseas teams played for: Matabeleland 1993-94 – 2003-04
Career highlights to date: 'Inaugural Test win, v Pakistan [1994-95]'
Cricket moments to forget: 'None – some are embarrassing but funny on reflection!'
Cricket superstitions: 'Nelson!'
Cricketers particularly admired: Dennis Lillee, Ian Botham
Young players to look out for: Ian Bell
Other sports played: Rugby (Zimbabwe U19), fishing
Other sports followed: Football (Liverpool)
Favourite band: U2
Relaxations: 'Time with family and watersports'
Extras: First Zimbabwe player to 100 and 200 wickets in both Tests and ODIs. Has won several ODI awards, including Man of the Match v West Indies at Sydney in the CUB Series 2000-01 (45/4-8) and Man of the Series v Bangladesh 2003-04. His Test awards include Zimbabwe's Man of the Series v England in 2000 and 2003. Scored maiden Test century (127*) in the first Test v West Indies at Harare 2003-04, winning Man of the Match award; it was the highest score by a Zimbabwe number eight and set a new world record of Tests/Test innings from debut to maiden hundred (56/91). Has a share in the record Test partnerships for Zimbabwe for the seventh and eighth wickets (154 and 168 respectively, both with Andy Blignaut). Captain of Zimbabwe 2000-01 and 2002-04, including the 2002-03 World Cup. Was Hampshire's overseas player in 1995. Joined Warwickshire as an overseas player for 2004, sharing post with Dewald Pretorius; has returned for 2005. Had match figures of 13-158 (7-80/6-78), the best return by a debutant in Championship history, in his first game for Warwickshire, v Northamptonshire at Edgbaston 2004; also scored 61 in Warwickshire's first innings
Opinions on cricket: 'Introduction of Twenty20 great for the game. It will generate well needed support for the game and draw youngsters to watch.'
Best batting: 131 Matabeleland v Midlands, Bulawayo 2003-04
Best bowling: 7-55 Matabeleland v Mashonaland, Bulawayo 2003-04

2004 Season

	M	Inns	NO	Runs	HS	Avge	100s	50s	Ct	St	O	M	Runs	Wkts	Avge	Best	5wI	10wM
Test																		
All First	6	9	2	180	61	25.71	-	1	-	-	159	29	522	24	21.75	7-80	2	1
1-day Int																		
C & G																		
totesport	5	2	1	17	9 *	17.00	-	-	1	-	36.1	4	160	7	22.85	3-7	-	
Twenty20	1	1	0	18	18	18.00	-	-	1	-	3	0	32	0	-	-	-	

Career Performances

	M	Inns	NO	Runs	HS	Avge	100s	50s	Ct	St	Balls	Runs	Wkts	Avge	Best	5wI	10wM
Test	59	95	18	1814	127 *	23.55	1	10	17	-	12733	5572	202	27.58	6-87	6	-
All First	134	202	37	4523	131	27.41	6	21	46	-	24553	10974	405	27.09	7-55	12	2
1-day Int	183	153	54	2752	79 *	27.79	-	12	43	-	9192	6894	234	29.46	5-32	1	
C & G																	
totesport	20	13	6	171	32 *	24.42	-	-	2	-	889	816	29	28.13	4-56	-	
Twenty20	1	1	0	18	18	18.00	-	-	1	-	18	32	0	-	-	-	

STUBBINGS, S. D. — Derbyshire

Name: Stephen David Stubbings
Role: Left-hand bat, occasional right-arm medium/spin bowler, 'very occasional wicket-keeper'
Born: 31 March 1978, Huddersfield
Height: 6ft 3in **Weight:** 15st
Nickname: Stubbo
County debut: 1997
County cap: 2001
1000 runs in a season: 2
1st-Class 50s: 19
1st-Class 100s: 6
1st-Class catches: 27
Place in batting averages: 163rd av. 27.51 (2003 30th av. 50.00)
Parents: Marie and David
Marital status: Single
Family links with cricket: 'My father used to play in Cambridge, while my brother Jonathan (20) plays his cricket at my old club Delacombe Park in Melbourne, Australia'
Education: Frankston High School; Swinburne University – both Melbourne, Australia

Qualifications: Victorian Certificate of Education (VCE), ACB Level 1 coaching
Overseas tours: Derbyshire to Portugal 2000
Overseas teams played for: Delacombe Park CC, Melbourne 1990-94; Frankston Peninsula CC, Victoria 1994-2000, 2002-03; Kingborough CC, Tasmania 2000-02
Career highlights to date: 'Being presented with my Derbyshire county cap at the end of the 2001 season and receiving Player of the Year award'
Cricket moments to forget: 'Making a pair of noughts against Glamorgan at Derby during the 2002 season'
Cricket superstitions: 'No sex during a cricket season!'
Cricketers particularly admired: Mark Taylor, Michael Atherton, Steve Waugh, Ricky Ponting 'and a couple of Derbyshire players who shall remain anonymous!'
Young players to look out for: Sam Patel
Other sports followed: Australian Rules football (Essendon Bombers)
Relaxations: 'Chris Bassano fishing adventures; eating, drinking, sleeping'
Extras: Represented Victoria at all junior levels. Spent two years on the cricket programme at the Victorian Institute of Sport. Scored maiden first-class century (135*) v Kent at Canterbury 2000, taking part in an unbroken opening partnership of 293 with Steve Titchard (141*); it was the first occasion on which Derbyshire had batted all day without losing a wicket. Derbyshire Player of the Year 2001
Best batting: 135* Derbyshire v Kent, Canterbury 2000

2004 Season

	M	Inns	NO	Runs	HS	Avge	100s	50s	Ct	St	O	M	Runs	Wkts	Avge	Best	5wI	10wM
Test																		
All First	16	28	1	743	96	27.51	-	6	8	-								
1-day Int																		
C & G																		
totesport	3	3	0	35	23	11.66	-	-	1	-								
Twenty20																		

Career Performances

	M	Inns	NO	Runs	HS	Avge	100s	50s	Ct	St	Balls	Runs	Wkts	Avge	Best	5wI	10wM
Test																	
All First	72	130	6	3697	135 *	29.81	6	19	27	-	54	77	0	-	-	-	-
1-day Int																	
C & G	3	2	0	63	47	31.50	-	-	-	-							
totesport	53	51	3	1034	98 *	21.54	-	4	7	-							
Twenty20																	

STYRIS, S. B. — Middlesex

Name: Scott Bernard Styris
Role: Right-hand bat, right-arm medium-fast bowler
Born: 10 July 1975, Brisbane, Australia
County debut: No first-team appearance
Test debut: 2002
Tests: 15
One-Day Internationals: 89
1st-Class 50s: 15
1st-Class 100s: 5
1st-Class 200s: 1
1st-Class 5 w. in innings: 6
1st-Class catches: 48
One-Day 100s: 2
One-Day 5 w. in innings: 1
Place in batting averages: 155th av. 28.58
Strike rate: 82.71 (career 61.39)

Overseas tours: New Zealand A to England 2002; New Zealand to India 1999-2000 (one-day series), to Zimbabwe and South Africa 2000-01, to Kenya (ICC Knockout Trophy) 2000-01, to Australia 2001-02 (VB Series), to Pakistan 2002, to West Indies 2002, to Sri Lanka (ICC Champions Trophy) 2002-03, to Africa (World Cup) 2002-03, to Sri Lanka 2003, to India 2003-04, to England 2004, to England (ICC Champions Trophy) 2004, to Bangladesh 2004-05, to Australia 2004-05, plus one-day tournaments in Singapore and Sharjah
Overseas teams played for: Northern Districts 1994-95 –
Extras: Represented New Zealand A against various touring teams. Made Test debut in the second Test v West Indies in Grenada 2002, scoring 107 and 69*. Winner of Redpath Cup (New Zealand annual batting award) 2003-04. Scored century (108) in the third Test v England at Trent Bridge 2004, in the process passing 1000 runs in Test cricket. His ODI awards include Man of the Match in the fourth ODI v West Indies at Port of Spain 2002 (63*/6-25) and in the first ODI v Pakistan at Auckland 2003-04 (3-34/101*). Has joined Middlesex as an overseas player for 2005
Best batting: 212* Northern Districts v Otago, Hamilton 2001-02
Best bowling: 6-32 Northern Districts v Otago, Gisborne 1999-2000
Stop press: Man of [ODI] Series v Bangladesh 2004-05

2004 Season

	M	Inns	NO	Runs	HS	Avge	100s	50s	Ct	St	O	M	Runs	Wkts	Avge	Best	5wI	10wM
Test	3	6	0	191	108	31.83	1	-	3	-	69.3	12	224	6	37.33	3-88	-	-
All First	7	13	1	343	108	28.58	1	-	5	-	96.3	18	325	7	46.42	3-88	-	-
1-day Int	8	7	2	129	75	25.80	-	1	4	-	26	1	106	5	21.20	2-12	-	
C & G																		
totesport																		
Twenty20																		

Career Performances

	M	Inns	NO	Runs	HS	Avge	100s	50s	Ct	St	Balls	Runs	Wkts	Avge	Best	5wI	10wM
Test	15	27	2	1072	170	42.88	4	4	10	-	1527	804	16	50.25	3-28	-	-
All First	72	120	15	3398	212 *	32.36	6	15	48	-	8718	4208	142	29.63	6-32	6	-
1-day Int	89	75	12	1758	141	27.90	2	9	35	-	3251	2629	84	31.29	6-25	1	
C & G																	
totesport																	
Twenty20																	

SUPPIAH, A. V. — Somerset

Name: Arul Vivasvan Suppiah
Role: Right-hand bat, left-arm orthodox spin bowler
Born: 30 August 1983, Kuala Lumpur, Malaysia
Height: 6ft **Weight:** 12st 7lbs
Nickname: Ruley, Ja Rule
County debut: 2002
1st-Class catches: 2
Strike rate: 37.50 (career 38.25)
Parents: Suppiah and Baanumathi
Marital status: Single
Family links with cricket: 'Brother Rohan Vishnu plays cricket for Malaysia. Dad plays club cricket in Malaysia. Mum scores for Malaysia'
Education: Millfield School; Exeter University
Qualifications: 9 GCSEs, 4 A-levels, BA in Accounting and Finance, Level 1 coaching qualification
Off-season: 'Looking for a job for the winter'
Overseas tours: Millfield School to South Africa 1997, to Sri Lanka 1999; West of

England U15 to West Indies 1998; Malaysia to Sharjah (Asian Cricket Council Trophy) 2000-01
Career highlights to date: 'Making my first-class debut v West Indies A for Somerset 2002; making my debut in the NUL for Somerset v Durham 2002; being the youngest ever cricketer to play for Malaysia; playing for England through the age groups'
Cricket moments to forget: 'Being bowled out for a golden duck off the seventh ball of the over'
Cricket superstitions: 'Right pad first'
Cricketers particularly admired: Sachin Tendulkar, Wasim Akram, Marcus Trescothick
Young players to look out for: Richard Timms, Bilal Shafayat, Kadeer Ali, Matthew Wood
Other sports played: Hockey (Somerset U16), badminton (Millfield School 1st team)
Other sports followed: Football (Manchester United)
Favourite band: Red Hot Chili Peppers
Relaxations: 'Web surfing, listening to music'
Extras: Youngest ever cricketer to play for Malaysia (aged 15 years). Has represented England at U14, U15, U17 and U18 levels. Somerset U15 Player of the Year 1998. West of England U15 Player of the Year 1998. Most Promising Sportsman for Malaysia 2000. NBC Denis Compton Award for the most promising young Somerset player 2002. Played for Somerset Board XI and Devon in the C&G 2003. Scored 97 for Devon v Bedfordshire in the final of the Minor Counties Championship at Exmouth 2004
Opinions on cricket: 'Fast-moving game. There is always action. The game is moving forward.'
Best batting: 33 Somerset v Sri Lanka A, Taunton 2004
Best bowling: 3-46 Somerset v West Indies A, Taunton 2002

2004 Season

	M	Inns	NO	Runs	HS	Avge	100s	50s	Ct	St	O	M	Runs	Wkts	Avge	Best	5wI	10wM
Test																		
All First	2	3	0	44	33	14.66	-	-	1	-	25	1	105	4	26.25	2-36	-	-
1-day Int																		
C & G	2	2	0	54	36	27.00	-	-	-	-	4	0	42	1	42.00	1-42	-	
totesport	2	2	0	36	30	18.00	-	-	-	-	5	0	29	1	29.00	1-29	-	
Twenty20																		

Career Performances

	M	Inns	NO	Runs	HS	Avge	100s	50s	Ct	St	Balls	Runs	Wkts	Avge	Best	5wI	10wM
Test																	
All First	5	8	0	87	33	10.87	-	-	2	-	306	204	8	25.50	3-46	-	-
1-day Int																	
C & G	4	4	0	134	70	33.50	-	1	2	-	126	102	2	51.00	1-24	-	
totesport	6	6	0	81	30	13.50	-	-	1	-	96	91	3	30.33	2-36	-	
Twenty20																	

SUTCLIFFE, I. J. Lancashire

Name: Iain John Sutcliffe
Role: Left-hand bat, leg-spin bowler
Born: 20 December 1974, Leeds
Height: 6ft 2in **Weight:** 13st
Nickname: Sutty
County debut: 1995 (Leicestershire), 2003 (Lancashire)
County cap: 1997 (Leicestershire), 2003 (Lancashire)
1000 runs in a season: 2
1st-Class 50s: 39
1st-Class 100s: 10
1st-Class 200s: 1
1st-Class catches: 76
One-Day 100s: 4
Place in batting averages: 119th av. 34.26 (2003 48th av. 45.40)
Strike rate: (career 49.00)
Parents: John and Valerie
Marital status: Single
Education: Leeds Grammar School; Oxford University
Qualifications: 10 GCSEs, 4 A-levels, 2.1 PPE degree
Overseas tours: Leeds GS to Kenya; Leicestershire to South Africa, to West Indies, to Sri Lanka
Career highlights to date: 'Championship winner's medal 1998'
Cricketers particularly admired: Brian Lara, David Gower
Other sports played: Boxing (Oxford Blue 1994, 1995; British Universities Light-middleweight Champion 1993)
Other sports followed: Football (Liverpool)
Relaxations: Socialising, cinema
Extras: Played NCA England U14 and NCA Development Team U18/U19. Scored maiden first-class century (163*) v Hampshire at The Parks 1995, in the process sharing with C. Gupte (119) in a record partnership for Oxford University against the county (283). Scored 55 out of Leicestershire's first innings total of 96 v Pakistanis at Leicester 2001. Leicestershire vice-captain 2002. Leicestershire Player of the Year 2002. Left Leicestershire at the end of the 2002 season and joined Lancashire for 2003. Scored century (102*) v Surrey at Whitgift School in the totesport League 2004, in the process sharing with Mark Chilton (115) in a new Lancashire record opening stand for the one-day league (223)
Best batting: 203 Leicestershire v Glamorgan, Cardiff 2001
Best bowling: 2-21 Oxford University v Cambridge University, Lord's 1996

2004 Season

	M	Inns	NO	Runs	HS	Avge	100s	50s	Ct	St	O	M	Runs	Wkts	Avge	Best	5wI	10wM
Test																		
All First	14	24	1	788	104	34.26	1	6	5	-								
1-day Int																		
C & G	2	2	0	57	41	28.50	-	-	4	-								
totesport	14	13	1	380	102 *	31.66	1	1	2	-								
Twenty20																		

Career Performances

	M	Inns	NO	Runs	HS	Avge	100s	50s	Ct	St	Balls	Runs	Wkts	Avge	Best	5wI	10wM
Test																	
All First	147	233	19	7204	203	33.66	11	39	76	-	441	329	9	36.55	2-21	-	-
1-day Int																	
C & G	14	14	3	579	103 *	52.63	1	3	6	-							
totesport	68	66	6	1691	104 *	28.18	2	9	16	-							
Twenty20	4	3	0	4	4	1.33	-	-	-	-							

SUTTON, L. D. — Derbyshire

Name: Luke David Sutton
Role: Right-hand bat, wicket-keeper, 'right-arm rubbish', county captain
Born: 4 October 1976, Keynsham
Height: 5ft 11in **Weight:** 12st 7lbs
Nickname: Sutts
County debut: 1997 (Somerset), 2000 (Derbyshire)
County cap: 2002 (Derbyshire)
1st-Class 50s: 10
1st-Class 100s: 5
1st-Class catches: 129
1st-Class stumpings: 7
Place in batting averages: 138th av. 31.12 (2003 80th av. 39.28)
Parents: David and Molly
Marital status: Single
Education: Millfield School, Street, Somerset; Durham University
Qualifications: 9 GCSEs, 4 A-levels, 2.1 degree in Economics, CeMAP 1, 2 and 3
Career outside cricket: 'Setting up sports camps with Activate Sport; Independent Financial Advisor; raising money for charity with my brother'

Off-season: 'Relaxing, training, coaching; some financial advising; climbing Ben Nevis with my brother for charity called CAH Support Group'
Overseas tours: Various Somerset Schools tours to Holland; West of England U15 to West Indies 1991; Millfield School to Zimbabwe 1993, to Sri Lanka 1994; Durham University to Zimbabwe 1997
Overseas teams played for: UNSW, Sydney 1998-99; Northville, Port Elizabeth, South Africa 1999-2000; Subiaco Marist, Perth 2000-01
Career highlights to date: 'Scoring my maiden first-class 100 v Warwickshire in 2001. Carrying my bat v Sussex in 2001, scoring 140 not out. Captaining Derbyshire in final two games of 2002 season. Being appointed vice-captain of Derbyshire for 2004 season; captaining Derbyshire in 2004 and now into 2005' (*see **Extras***)
Cricket moments to forget: 'Scoring 0 on my Championship debut for Somerset v Leicestershire in 1997. Losing C&G semi in 2003 by one wicket'
Cricket superstitions: 'Plenty, but it's a superstition to keep them a secret'
Cricketers particularly admired: Ian Healy, Jack Russell, Alec Stewart, Steve Waugh
Young players to look out for: 'All the crop of young Derbyshire players'
Other sports followed: Football (Newcastle United), rugby (Bath)
Injuries: Out for one day of cricket with bulging disc in back
Relaxations: 'Quality time with family and friends'
Extras: Captained England U15 and also represented England U18 and U19. Won Sir John Hobbs Silver Jubilee Memorial Prize for the U16 Cricketer of the Year in 1992 and the Gray-Nicolls Award for the English Schools Cricketer of the Year in 1995. Left Somerset at the end of the 1999 season and joined Derbyshire for 2000. Voted Derbyshire 2nd XI Player of the Year 2000. NBC Denis Compton Award for the most promising young Derbyshire player 2000, 2001, 2002. Captain of Derbyshire since 2004 (was originally appointed vice-captain 2004 but assumed the captaincy when back surgery prevented Michael DiVenuto from taking up the post)
Opinions on cricket: 'The fixture list does seem to get more and more packed, but I love the game and it's a great way to live.'
Best batting: 140* Derbyshire v Sussex, Derby 2001

2004 Season

	M	Inns	NO	Runs	HS	Avge	100s	50s	Ct	St	O	M	Runs	Wkts	Avge	Best	5wI	10wM
Test																		
All First	16	27	3	747	131	31.12	1	2	34	3								
1-day Int																		
C & G	1	1	0	0	0	0.00	-	-	1	-								
totesport	17	15	3	231	58 *	19.25	-	1	19	1								
Twenty20	4	4	1	53	19 *	17.66	-	-	4	2								

Career Performances

	M	Inns	NO	Runs	HS	Avge	100s	50s	Ct	St	Balls	Runs	Wkts	Avge	Best	5wI	10wM
Test																	
All First	70	125	16	3265	140 *	29.95	5	10	129	7							
1-day Int																	
C & G	9	7	1	96	45	16.00	-	-	11	-							
totesport	67	58	13	811	83	18.02	-	3	70	7							
Twenty20	8	7	2	95	22 *	19.00	-	-	6	4							

SWANN, A. J. Lancashire

Name: Alec James Swann
Role: Right-hand opening bat, occasional off-spin bowler
Born: 26 October 1976, Northampton
Height: 6ft 2in **Weight:** 13st
Nickname: Ron, Swanny
County debut: 1996 (Northamptonshire), 2002 (Lancashire)
County cap: 2002 (Lancashire)
1000 runs in a season: 1
1st-Class 50s: 14
1st-Class 100s: 8
1st-Class catches: 56
Place in batting averages: 244th av. 16.00 (2003 197th av. 23.66)
Strike rate: 36.00 (career 94.50)
Parents: Ray and Mavis
Marital status: Engaged to Sally
Family links with cricket: Father played for Northumberland, Bedfordshire, Northants 2nd XI and England Amateurs. Brother Graeme plays for Nottinghamshire
Education: Sponne School, Towcester
Qualifications: 9 GCSEs, 4 A-levels, coaching badge
Career outside cricket: 'Hopefully journalism; otherwise golf course abuse'
Overseas tours: Northants to Zimbabwe 1998, to Grenada 1999, 2000; Lancashire to Cape Town 2002, 2003, 2004
Overseas teams played for: Wallsend, NSW 1995-96, 1997-98, 2003-04; Montrose CC, Cape Town 1998-99, 2002-03
Career highlights to date: 'Maiden first-class 100 and first Lancs 100 at Headingley'
Cricket moments to forget: 'My two pairs, the 2000 season, and getting out to my brother'
Cricket superstitions: 'Bar towel in my front pad'

Cricketers particularly admired: Steve and Mark Waugh, Peter Martin
Young players to look out for: Steven Croft, Mark Turner, Joe Sayers
Other sports played: Golf, snooker, 'might play football this winter'
Other sports followed: Football (Newcastle United), rugby league (Warrington)
Injuries: Out for two weeks with an inflamed heel
Favourite band: 'This year The Charlatans'
Relaxations: 'Reading, gambling, arguing and sofa testing'
Extras: Played for England Schools U15 and U19. Opened batting for Bedfordshire with father in Minor Counties game. *Daily Telegraph* U15 Young Cricketer of the Year 1992. Midlands Club Cricket Conference Young Cricketer of the Year 1992. Played for England U19 1996. Released by Northamptonshire at the end of the 2001 season and joined Lancashire for 2002. Scored 112 v Yorkshire at Old Trafford 2002 to become the first Lancashire batsman to score a century in each of his first two Roses matches, having scored 128 at Headingley earlier in the season. Left Lancashire at the end of the 2004 season
Opinions on cricket: 'Let's introduce pairs cricket. It seems the naturally progressive thing to do.'
Best batting: 154 Northamptonshire v Nottinghamshire, Northampton 1999
Best bowling: 2-30 Northamptonshire v Gloucestershire, Northampton 2000

2004 Season

	M	Inns	NO	Runs	HS	Avge	100s	50s	Ct	St	O	M	Runs	Wkts	Avge	Best	5wI	10wM
Test																		
All First	5	7	0	112	34	16.00	-	-	2	-	6	2	18	1	18.00	1-14	-	-
1-day Int																		
C & G	1	1	0	38	38	38.00	-	-	-	-								
totesport	4	3	0	23	22	7.66	-	-	3	-								
Twenty20																		

Career Performances

	M	Inns	NO	Runs	HS	Avge	100s	50s	Ct	St	Balls	Runs	Wkts	Avge	Best	5wI	10wM
Test																	
All First	77	123	4	3305	154	27.77	8	14	56	-	567	326	6	54.33	2-30	-	-
1-day Int																	
C & G	8	6	0	211	74	35.16	-	1	1	-	18	16	0	-		-	-
totesport	40	37	6	708	73 *	22.83	-	4	10	-	18	32	0	-		-	-
Twenty20	4	3	1	86	56	43.00	-	1	1	-							

SWANN, G. P. — Nottinghamshire

Name: Graeme Peter Swann
Role: Right-hand bat, right-arm off-spin bowler, 'benefit wicket-keeper'
Born: 24 March 1979, Northampton
Height: 6ft **Weight:** 13st
Nickname: Swanny, G-spot, Chin
County debut: 1997 (one-day, Northamptonshire), 1998 (first-class, Northamptonshire)
County cap: 1999 (Northamptonshire)
One-Day Internationals: 1
50 wickets in a season: 1
1st-Class 50s: 17
1st-Class 100s: 4
1st-Class 5 w. in innings: 12
1st-Class 10 w. in match: 2
1st-Class catches: 75
One-Day 5 w. in innings: 1
Place in batting averages: 202nd av. 22.04 (2003 216th av. 21.33)
Place in bowling averages: 114th av. 38.93 (2003 14th av. 23.00)
Strike rate: 80.66 (career 62.56)
Parents: Ray and Mavis
Marital status: Single
Family links with cricket: Dad has played Minor Counties cricket for Bedfordshire and Northumberland and also for England Amateurs. Brother was contracted to Northants and Lancs. 'Cat is named after Gus Logie'
Education: Sponne School, Towcester
Qualifications: 10 GCSEs, 4 A-levels, Levels 1 and 2 coaching awards
Career outside cricket: Journalism
Off-season: National Academy
Overseas tours: England U19 to South Africa (including U19 World Cup) 1997-98; England A to Zimbabwe and South Africa 1998-99, to West Indies 2000-01, to Sri Lanka 2004-05; England to South Africa 1999-2000; ECB National Academy to Australia 2001-02
Overseas teams played for: Old Colts, Christchurch 2002-03
Career highlights to date: 'Dismissing my brother in a totesport pyjama game'
Cricket moments to forget: 'Being hit for an enormous six by Peter Such'
Cricketers particularly admired: Neil Foster, Devon Malcolm
Young players to look out for: Cameron Wake, Steve Swann
Other sports played: Golf, rugby (Northants U14, U15, U16), football (Old Northamptonians Chenecks FC – 'dynamic left back')

Other sports followed: Football (Newcastle United)
Injuries: 'Dazed and confused throughout Twenty20'
Favourite band: Oasis, The Libertines, Charlatans, Stone Roses
Relaxations: 'Playing guitar and golf'
Extras: Played for England U14, U15, U17 and U19. *Daily Telegraph* Regional Bowling Award 1994. Gray-Nicolls Len Newbery Schools Cricketer of the Year 1996. Took 8-118 for England U19 in second 'Test' v Pakistan U19 1998, the best ever figures in an U19 'Test'. Completed Championship double of 500 runs and 50 wickets 1999. Had match figures of 9-62 and scored 49 runs for England A v Windward Islands in St Lucia in the Busta Cup 2000-01, winning the Man of the Match award. Scored 183 v Gloucestershire at Bristol 2002, in the process sharing with Mike Hussey (310*) in a stand of 318. Left Northamptonshire at the end of the 2004 season and has joined Nottinghamshire for 2005. ECB National Academy 2004-05
Opinions on cricket: 'Still the greatest game in the world, apart from football and golf.'
Best batting: 183 Northamptonshire v Gloucestershire, Bristol 2002
Best bowling: 7-33 Northamptonshire v Derbyshire, Northampton 2003

2004 Season

	M	Inns	NO	Runs	HS	Avge	100s	50s	Ct	St	O	M	Runs	Wkts	Avge	Best	5wI	10wM
Test																		
All First	14	22	0	485	54	22.04	-	2	13	-	403.2	71	1168	30	38.93	4-94	-	-
1-day Int																		
C & G	3	3	1	106	50	53.00	-	1	2	-	27	2	119	0	-	-	-	
totesport	16	15	2	384	78	29.53	-	3	4	-	136.4	7	516	23	22.43	4-21	-	
Twenty20	5	5	1	71	35 *	17.75	-	-	1	-	17	0	148	1	148.00	1-28	-	

Career Performances

	M	Inns	NO	Runs	HS	Avge	100s	50s	Ct	St	Balls	Runs	Wkts	Avge	Best	5wI	10wM
Test																	
All First	108	161	8	3979	183	26.00	4	17	75	-	17768	8959	284	31.54	7-33	12	2
1-day Int	1	0	0	0	0	-	-	-	-	-	30	24	0	-	-	-	
C & G	13	11	1	285	50	28.50	-	1	8	-	628	483	12	40.25	4-40	-	
totesport	87	71	6	1377	83	21.18	-	9	22	-	3037	2315	92	25.16	5-35	1	
Twenty20	10	9	3	121	42 *	20.16	-	-	2	-	204	240	6	40.00	2-17	-	

87. Who played for Holland in the 1986 ICC Trophy, for Hong Kong in the 1993-94 tournament and was in the Durham team that beat Yorkshire in the 1973 Gillette Cup?

SYMONDS, A. Kent

Name: Andrew Symonds
Role: Right-hand bat, right-arm medium or off-spin bowler
Born: 9 June 1975, Birmingham, England
Height: 6ft 1in **Weight:** 13st 5lbs
Nickname: Roy
County debut: 1995 (Gloucestershire), 1999 (Kent)
County cap: 1999 (Kent)
Test debut: 2003-04
Tests: 2
One-Day Internationals: 102
1000 runs in a season: 2
1st-Class 50s: 45
1st-Class 100s: 32
1st-Class 200s: 1
1st-Class 5 w. in innings: 2
1st-Class catches: 121
One-Day 100s: 4
One-Day 5 w. in innings: 2
Place in batting averages: 2nd av. 72.28 (2003 39th av. 47.07)
Place in bowling averages: 45th av. 29.92 (2003 73rd av. 32.31)
Strike rate: 59.78 (career 72.28)
Parents: Ken and Barbara
Wife and date of marriage: Brooke, April 2004
Family links with cricket: Father played Minor Counties cricket
Education: All Saints Anglican School, Gold Coast, Australia; Ballarat and Clarendon College, Australia
Qualifications: Level 2 coaching, professional fisherman
Off-season: Playing cricket for Queensland and Australia
Overseas tours: Australia U19 to India 1993-94; Australia A to Los Angeles (Moov America Challenge) 1999, to South Africa (one-day series) 2002-03; Australia to Pakistan 1998-99 (one-day series), to Sri Lanka and Zimbabwe 1999-2000 (one-day series), to New Zealand 1999-2000 (one-day series), to India 2000-01 (one-day series), to England 2001 (one-day series), to Kenya (Nairobi Triangular) 2002, to Africa (World Cup) 2002-03, to West Indies 2002-03 (one-day series), to India (TVS Cup) 2003-04, to Sri Lanka 2003-04, to Zimbabwe (one-day series) 2004, to Holland (Videocon Cup) 2004, to England (ICC Champions Trophy) 2004, to New Zealand 2004-05 (one-day series)
Overseas teams played for: Queensland Academy of Sport 1992-93 – 1997-98; Queensland 1994-95 –
Cricketers particularly admired: Viv Richards, Shane Warne, Michael Holding

Other sports followed: Hockey, rugby, football
Relaxations: Fishing, camping and hunting
Extras: Nickname 'Roy' reportedly coined by his father after comic-book character 'Roy of the Rovers'. Attended the Commonwealth Bank [Australian] Cricket Academy 1994. In his first season of first-class cricket he scored a century (108*) for Queensland against England on their 1994-95 tour of Australia. Hit a world record number of sixes in a first-class innings (16) during his 254* for Gloucestershire v Glamorgan at Abergavenny 1995; struck four more sixes in the second innings to set a new world record for a first-class match. PCA Young Player of the Year 1995. Cricket Writers' Club Young Cricketer of the Year 1995. Turned down the invitation to tour with England A in 1995 so that he could remain eligible to play for Australia, for whom he made ODI debut v Pakistan at Lahore 1998. His ODI awards include Man of the Series v Sri Lanka 2003-04 and Man of the Match v Pakistan at Johannesburg in the World Cup 2002-03 (143*; the highest World Cup score for Australia) and v Pakistan at Lord's in one-off NatWest ODI 2004 (104). Overseas player with Kent 1999, 2001-04. C&G Man of the Match award for his 5-21 and 40-ball 39* v Northamptonshire at Canterbury 2001. Man of the Match in the Pura Cup final 2001-02 for his first innings 91 and match figures of 6-65 v Tasmania at Brisbane. Made Test debut in the first Test v Sri Lanka at Galle 2003-04. Scored 110-ball 146 v Lancashire at Tunbridge Wells in the totesport League 2004, setting a new Kent record individual score for the one-day league. Struck 43-ball 112 v Middlesex at Maidstone in the Twenty20 Cup 2004
Best batting: 254* Gloucestershire v Glamorgan, Abergavenny 1995
Best bowling: 6-105 Kent v Sussex, Tunbridge Wells 2002
Stop press: Named One-Day International Player of the Year at the 2005 Allan Border Medal awards. Man of the Match v Pakistan at Melbourne in the VB Series first final 2004-05 (91)

2004 Season

	M	Inns	NO	Runs	HS	Avge	100s	50s	Ct	St	O	M	Runs	Wkts	Avge	Best	5wI	10wM
Test																		
All First	5	8	1	506	156 *	72.28	3	1	6	-	139.3	39	419	14	29.92	5-140	1	-
1-day Int	4	3	2	175	104 *	175.00	1	1	-	-	21	3	94	2	47.00	1-31	-	
C & G	1	0	0	0	0	-	-	-	-	-	10	2	24	3	8.00	3-24	-	
totesport	7	7	1	225	146	37.50	1	-	3	-	45	2	181	11	16.45	3-28	-	
Twenty20	5	5	0	152	112	30.40	1	-	4	-	16	0	103	4	25.75	1-11	-	

Career Performances

	M	Inns	NO	Runs	HS	Avge	100s	50s	Ct	St	Balls	Runs	Wkts	Avge	Best	5wI	10wM
Test	2	4	0	53	24	13.25	-	-	4	-	144	85	1	85.00	1-68	-	-
All First	173	290	28	11130	254 *	42.48	33	45	121	-	12288	6278	170	36.92	6-105	2	-
1-day Int	102	77	17	2287	143 *	38.11	2	11	42	-	3325	2710	76	35.65	4-11	-	
C & G	16	14	1	486	87	37.38	-	3	4	-	497	332	19	17.47	5-21	1	
totesport	74	73	5	2020	146	29.70	1	10	36	-	1707	1272	54	23.55	5-18	1	
Twenty20	10	10	1	322	112	35.77	1	1	7	-	194	233	7	33.28	2-35	-	

TAHIR MUGHAL

Durham

Name: Tahir Mahmood Mughal
Role: Right-hand bat, right-arm fast-medium bowler
Born: 25 April 1977, Daska, Pakistan
County debut: 2004
1st-Class 50s: 6
1st-Class 5 w. in innings: 23
1st-Class 10 w. in match: 5
1st-Class catches: 29
Strike rate: 57.00 (career 39.31)
Overseas teams played for: Gujranwala 1997-98 – 1998-99; Agriculture Development Bank of Pakistan 1997-98 – 2001-02; Sialkot 2001-02 – ; Allied Bank 2003-04
Extras: Had match figures of 15-74 (8-32/ 7-42) for Saga Sports v Pakistan Army at Sialkot in the Kardar Trophy (non-first-class) 2002-03. Man of the Match v National Bank of Pakistan at Sialkot in Patron's Cup 50-over competition 2002-03, taking 2-58 and scoring 118* from 87 balls, as Sialkot successfully chased 343 to win. Played one game for Durham Academy 2003. Called up from Silverdale CC (North Staffs and District League) as a temporary overseas player with Durham at the start of the 2004 season, deputising for Shoaib Akhtar
Best batting: 68* Sialkot v Lahore Blues, Lahore 2001-02
Best bowling: 7-63 Sialkot v Rest of NWFP, Sialkot 2001-02

2004 Season

	M	Inns	NO	Runs	HS	Avge	100s	50s	Ct	St	O	M	Runs	Wkts	Avge	Best	5wI	10wM
Test																		
All First	1	2	1	17	17 *	17.00	-	-	-	-	19	4	54	2	27.00	2-54	-	-
1-day Int																		
C & G																		
totesport																		
Twenty20																		

Career Performances

	M	Inns	NO	Runs	HS	Avge	100s	50s	Ct	St	Balls	Runs	Wkts	Avge	Best	5wI	10wM
Test																	
All First	58	90	11	1524	68 *	19.29	-	6	29	-	10929	5923	278	21.30	7-63	23	5
1-day Int																	
C & G																	
totesport																	
Twenty20																	

TAHIR, N. — Warwickshire

Name: Naqaash Tahir
Role: Right-hand bat, right-arm fast bowler
Born: 14 November 1983, Birmingham
Height: 5ft 10in **Weight:** 11st
Nickname: Naq, Naqy
County debut: 2004
1st-Class catches: 1
Place in batting averages: 209th av. 21.42
Place in bowling averages: 36th av. 28.25
Strike rate: 44.50 (career 44.50)
Parents: Mohammed Amin and Ishrat Nasreen
Marital status: Single
Family links with cricket: 'Dad played club cricket and brother played for Worcestershire and Warwickshire'
Education: Moseley School; Spring Hill College
Qualifications: 3 GCSEs, Level 1 coaching
Overseas tours: Warwickshire U15 to South Africa 1999
Overseas teams played for: Mirpur, Pakistan; Subiaco-Floreat, Perth
Cricket superstitions: 'Putting my pads on in a certain way'
Cricketers particularly admired: Waqar Younis, Wasim Akram, Darren Gough, Brett Lee
Young players to look out for: Moeen Ali
Other sports played: Football
Other sports followed: Football (Man Utd)
Relaxations: 'Watching TV; PlayStation 2'
Extras: Scored 103 in a 20-over match, setting a record for Moseley Ashfield U15. Has been Moseley Ashfield U15 Player of the Year, Warwickshire U15 Youth Player of the Year and top wicket-taker for Warwickshire U16. Warwickshire U19 Players'

Player of the Year. Warwickshire U19 Player of the Year (Coney Edmonds Trophy). Had match figures of 8-90 (4-47/4-43) on Championship debut v Worcestershire at Edgbaston 2004
Opinions on cricket: 'The game is more competitive now.'
Best batting: 49 Warwickshire v Worcestershire, Worcester 2004
Best bowling: 4-43 Warwickshire v Worcestershire, Edgbaston 2004

2004 Season

	M	Inns	NO	Runs	HS	Avge	100s	50s	Ct	St	O	M	Runs	Wkts	Avge	Best	5wI	10wM
Test																		
All First	12	12	5	150	49	21.42	-	-	1	-	207.4	33	791	28	28.25	4-43	-	-
1-day Int																		
C & G																		
totesport																		
Twenty20																		

Career Performances

	M	Inns	NO	Runs	HS	Avge	100s	50s	Ct	St	Balls	Runs	Wkts	Avge	Best	5wI	10wM
Test																	
All First	12	12	5	150	49	21.42	-	-	1	-	1246	791	28	28.25	4-43	-	-
1-day Int																	
C & G																	
totesport																	
Twenty20																	

88. A member of Sri Lanka's 1975 and 1979 World Cup squads, who was chief executive of the Sri Lankan cricket board from 2000 to 2003?

TAIT, S. W. Durham

Name: Shaun William Tait
Role: Right-hand bat, right-arm fast bowler
Born: 22 February 1983, Adelaide, Australia
County debut: 2004
1st-Class 5 w. in innings: 2
1st-Class catches: 3
Strike rate: (career 45.16)
Overseas tours: Australia to Sri Lanka 2003-04
Overseas teams played for: South Australia 2002-03 –
Extras: Commonwealth Bank [Australian] Cricket Academy 2003. Represented Australia A v Indians and Zimbabweans 2003-04. Took 8-43 v Tasmania at Adelaide in the ING Cup 2003-04, becoming the first bowler to return eight wickets in a match in the Australian domestic one-day competition. ING Cup Best New Talent award 2003-04. Named Bradman Young Cricketer of the Year at the 2004 Allan Border Medal awards. Called up for Australia tour to Sri Lanka 2003-04 as a replacement for the injured Brett Lee. Was an overseas player with Durham August 2004 as a replacement for Shoaib Akhtar
Best batting: 12 South Australia v Queensland, Brisbane 2002-03
Best bowling: 5-68 South Australia v Tasmania, Adelaide 2002-03

2004 Season

	M	Inns	NO	Runs	HS	Avge	100s	50s	Ct	St	O	M	Runs	Wkts	Avge	Best	5wI	10wM
Test																		
All First	2	2	0	4	4	2.00	-	-	-	-	18	0	176	0	-	-	-	-
1-day Int																		
C & G																		
totesport																		
Twenty20																		

Career Performances

	M	Inns	NO	Runs	HS	Avge	100s	50s	Ct	St	Balls	Runs	Wkts	Avge	Best	5wI	10wM
Test																	
All First	16	23	10	62	12	4.76	-	-	3	-	2394	1584	53	29.88	5-68	2	-
1-day Int																	
C & G																	
totesport																	
Twenty20																	

TAYLOR, B. V. Hampshire

Name: Billy Victor Taylor
Role: Left-hand bat, right-arm medium-fast bowler
Born: 11 January 1977, Southampton
Height: 6ft 3in **Weight:** 14st
Nickname: Tav
County debut: 1999 (Sussex), 2004 (Hampshire)
1st-Class 5 w. in innings: 2
1st-Class catches: 5
One-Day 5 w. in innings: 1
Place in batting averages: 233rd av. 17.70
Place in bowling averages: 59th av. 31.48 (2003 58th av. 29.60)
Strike rate: 54.21 (career 62.12)
Parents: Jackie and Victor
Marital status: Single
Family links with cricket: 'Learnt from and played cricket with both my brothers, Martin and James'
Education: Bitterne Park; Southampton Tech College; Sparsholt Agricultural College, Hampshire
Qualifications: 5 GCSEs, NVQ Level 2 Carpentry and Joinery, NTPC Tree Surgery, Level 2 coaching
Career outside cricket: 'Tree surgery'
Off-season: 'Getting fitter for next season'
Overseas tours: Sussex/Hampshire to Cyprus 1999; Sussex to Grenada 2002
Overseas teams played for: Central Hawke's Bay, New Zealand 1996-97; Manawatu Foxton CC and Horowhenua rep team, New Zealand 1998-99, 2000-01; Te Puke 2002
Career highlights to date: 'Winning the County Championship in 2003 [with Sussex]. Playing for Hampshire'
Cricket moments to forget: 'Don't want to forget any moments as it's such a great career and too short a one'
Cricket superstitions: 'Have a towel hanging out of back of trousers'
Cricketers particularly admired: Malcolm Marshall, Robin Smith, Mushtaq Ahmed
Young players to look out for: Chris Tremlett
Other sports played: Golf
Other sports followed: Football (Havant & Waterlooville)
Favourite band: Dido, Black Eyed Peas
Relaxations: 'Spending time with girlfriend, going to gym and having a glass of wine and something to eat in Greens Wine Bar, Winchester'
Extras: Took 98 wickets in New Zealand club cricket in 1998-99. Sussex 2nd XI

Player of the Year 1999, 2000. Took hat-trick (Ormond, Sampson, Giddins) v Surrey at Hove in the B&H and another (G. Flower, Maddy, Malcolm) v Leicestershire at Leicester in the C&G, both in 2002. Scored career best 35* v Middlesex at Hove 2003, sharing with Mark Davis (168) in a record tenth-wicket partnership for Sussex in matches against Middlesex (106). Left Sussex at the end of the 2003 season and joined Hampshire for 2004
Opinions on cricket: 'We should play exactly the same format as international cricket, as that should be the aim – to play for England and improve English cricket at international level.'
Best batting: 40 Hampshire v Essex, West End 2004
Best bowling: 5-73 Hampshire v Essex, Chelmsford 2004

2004 Season

	M	Inns	NO	Runs	HS	Avge	100s	50s	Ct	St	O	M	Runs	Wkts	Avge	Best	5wI	10wM
Test																		
All First	11	16	6	177	40	17.70	-	-	3	-	298.1	59	1039	33	31.48	5-73	1	-
1-day Int																		
C & G																		
totesport	12	7	4	24	10 *	8.00	-	-	4	-	80.5	11	348	14	24.85	3-51	-	
Twenty20	6	3	3	15	12 *	-	-	-	2	-	21	0	143	4	35.75	1-14	-	

Career Performances

	M	Inns	NO	Runs	HS	Avge	100s	50s	Ct	St	Balls	Runs	Wkts	Avge	Best	5wI	10wM
Test																	
All First	39	48	17	360	40	11.61	-	-	5	-	6461	3532	104	33.96	5-73	2	-
1-day Int																	
C & G	9	1	0	1	1	1.00	-	-	1	-	498	344	17	20.23	4-26	-	
totesport	72	38	17	144	21 *	6.85	-	-	15	-	3038	2276	91	25.01	4-22	-	
Twenty20	6	3	3	15	12 *	-	-	-	2	-	126	143	4	35.75	1-14	-	

TAYLOR, C. G. — Gloucestershire

Name: Christopher (Chris) Glyn Taylor
Role: Right-hand bat, right-arm off-spin bowler, county four-day captain
Born: 27 September 1976, Bristol
Height: 5ft 8in **Weight:** 10st
Nickname: Tales, Tootsie
County debut: 2000
County cap: 2001
1000 runs in a season: 1
1st-Class 50s: 10
1st-Class 100s: 9
1st-Class catches: 38

Place in batting averages: 58th av. 44.87 (2003 215th av. 21.37)
Strike rate: (career 99.00)
Parents: Chris and Maggie
Wife and date of marriage: Sarah, 8 December 2001
Family links with cricket: Father and grandfather both played local club cricket
Education: Colston's Collegiate School
Qualifications: GCSEs and A-levels
Overseas teams played for: Harbord CC, Manly, Australia 2000
Cricket moments to forget: 'B&H loss to Surrey at Lord's [2001]'
Cricketers particularly admired: Jonty Rhodes, Mark Waugh
Other sports played: Rugby, hockey (both county level); squash, tennis
Other sports followed: Rugby
Relaxations: Fishing
Extras: Represented England Schools U18. In 1995 won the Cricket Society's A. A. Thomson Fielding Prize and Wetherell Award for Leading All-rounder in English Schools Cricket. Set school record of 278* v Hutton Grammar School. Made his highest score of 300* for Gloucestershire 2nd XI v Somerset 2nd XI at Taunton 1999. Scored maiden first-class century (104) v Middlesex 2000, becoming the first player to score a century at Lord's on Championship debut; also the first player to score a century for Gloucestershire in match that was both first-class and Championship debut. NBC Denis Compton Award for the most promising young Gloucestershire player 2000. Four-day captain of Gloucestershire since 2004. Scored 1000 first-class runs in a season for the first time 2004
Best batting: 196 Gloucestershire v Nottinghamshire, Trent Bridge 2001
Best bowling: 3-126 Gloucestershire v Northamptonshire, Cheltenham 2000

2004 Season

	M	Inns	NO	Runs	HS	Avge	100s	50s	Ct	St	O	M	Runs	Wkts	Avge	Best	5wI	10wM
Test																		
All First	16	25	1	1077	177	44.87	4	4	6	-	1	0	2	0	-	-	-	-
1-day Int																		
C & G	5	5	1	52	22 *	13.00	-	-	3	-								
totesport	16	16	2	392	60	28.00	-	2	6	-	9	0	29	3	9.66	2-5	-	
Twenty20	5	4	1	74	36	24.66	-	-	1	-								

Career Performances

	M	Inns	NO	Runs	HS	Avge	100s	50s	Ct	St	Balls	Runs	Wkts	Avge	Best	5wI	10wM
Test																	
All First	59	104	6	3334	196	34.02	9	10	38	-	297	222	3	74.00	3-126	-	-
1-day Int																	
C & G	16	15	4	206	41	18.72	-	-	10	-							
totesport	52	45	6	742	63 *	19.02	-	3	14	1	54	29	3	9.66	2-5	-	
Twenty20	10	8	2	148	36	24.66	-	-	3	-	6	11	0	-	-	-	

TAYLOR, C. R. Yorkshire

Name: Christopher (Chris) Robert Taylor
Role: Right-hand opening bat, right-arm fast-medium bowler
Born: 21 February 1981, Leeds
Height: 6ft 4in **Weight:** 14st 6lbs
Nickname: CT
County debut: 2001
1st-Class 50s: 2
1st-Class catches: 7
Parents: Phil and Elaine
Marital status: Single
Family links with cricket: 'Brother Matthew plays in Bradford League, Dad slogged a few in Dales Council League and Mum gives good throw-downs'
Education: Benton Park High School, Leeds
Qualifications: 9 GCSEs, 4 A-levels
Off-season: Playing for Fairfield-Liverpool Lions in Sydney
Overseas tours: Yorkshire to Grenada 2002
Overseas teams played for: Western Suburbs Magpies, Sydney 1999-2003; Fairfield-Liverpool Lions, Sydney 2003-05
Career highlights to date: 'To have played in County Championship winning team 2001. On a personal note, my maiden first-class half-century v Surrey at Headingley, April 2002' (*A 3¼-hour rearguard action of 52**)
Cricket moments to forget: 'To have bagged 'em in my first Roses match v Lancashire, which also just happened to be my first game live on Sky TV (I turned my phone off for a week after it!)'
Cricket superstitions: 'Keeping them to myself!'
Cricketers particularly admired: Geoffrey Boycott, Michael Vaughan, John Wilkinson ('aka "Mad John"')

Young players to look out for: Mark Lawson
Other sports played: Rugby, football, tennis, basketball (all for Benton Park HS first teams)
Other sports followed: Football (Everton – 'since I was four years old'), 'enjoy watching all sports'
Injuries: Out for two months with a damaged disc in back
Favourite band: Matchbox Twenty
Relaxations: 'Beaches of Sydney; training; nightspots of Leeds; birds!'
Extras: Represented Yorkshire U10-U17. Represented North of England at Bunbury Festival 1996 and was awarded Neil Lloyd Trophy for top run-scorer in festival. Selected for England U15 team for Lombard World Cup 1996. Has also represented England U17 and U19. Yorkshire CCC Supporters' Club Young Player of the Year 1999. Awarded Yorkshire 2nd XI cap 2001
Opinions on cricket: 'I suggest English players should go and qualify as the equivalent of EU/Kolpak players (*see page 9*) for Australian first-class cricket. Just one problem, though – the ACB wouldn't allow it! And who is the best nation in the world?!'
Best batting: 52* Yorkshire v Surrey, Headingley 2002

2004 Season

	M	Inns	NO	Runs	HS	Avge	100s	50s	Ct	St	O	M	Runs	Wkts	Avge	Best	5wI	10wM
Test																		
All First	4	5	1	105	43 *	26.25	-	-	1	-								
1-day Int																		
C & G	1	0	0	0	0	-	-	-	-	-								
totesport	2	2	0	29	27	14.50	-	-	-	-								
Twenty20																		

Career Performances

	M	Inns	NO	Runs	HS	Avge	100s	50s	Ct	St	Balls	Runs	Wkts	Avge	Best	5wI	10wM
Test																	
All First	15	25	2	402	52 *	17.47	-	2	7	-							
1-day Int																	
C & G	1	0	0	0	0	-	-	-	-	-							
totesport	3	3	0	57	28	19.00	-	-	-	-							
Twenty20																	

TAYLOR, D. K. — Derbyshire

Name: David Kenneth Taylor
Role: Left-hand opening bat, right-arm medium bowler
Born: 17 December 1974, Oxford
Height: 6ft 1in **Weight:** 16st
Nickname: The DT
County debut: 2003 (one-day, Worcestershire), 2004 (one-day, Derbyshire)
One-Day 100s: 1
Parents: Mike and Pat
Marital status: Engaged
Children: Josh, 5 October 1991; Lochie, 2 November 1999
Education: Kent St High School, Perth, Western Australia (cricket scholarship)
Career outside cricket: Contracts manager for building company
Career highlights to date: 'Playing my debut [match] for Worcester and getting man of the match'
Cricket moments to forget: 'Being run out while using a runner and going out to bat without my thigh pad in a 2nd XI game against Warwickshire 2nd XI'
Cricket superstitions: 'None'
Cricketers particularly admired: Viv Richards, Ian Botham
Other sports followed: Aussie Rules football (West Coast Eagles)
Favourite band: Bon Jovi
Extras: Played for Oxfordshire in the C&G 2001; for Buckinghamshire in the C&G 2003 (Man of the Match award for his 140 v Suffolk at Dinton in the first round); for Berkshire in the C&G 2004. Joined Worcestershire on short-term contract in 2003. Scored 20-ball 46 on county debut v Northamptonshire at Worcester in the Twenty20 2003, winning Man of the Match award. Broke batting record in Home Counties Premier League 2003. Released by Worcestershire at the end of the 2003 season and joined Derbyshire for 2004; released by Derbyshire at the end of the 2004 season

2004 Season

	M	Inns	NO	Runs	HS	Avge	100s	50s	Ct	St	O	M	Runs	Wkts	Avge	Best	5wI	10wM
Test																		
All First																		
1-day Int																		
C & G	1	1	0	2	2	2.00	-	-	-	-	2	0	15	0	-	-	-	
totesport	3	2	0	38	29	19.00	-	-	2	-								
Twenty20	3	3	0	29	15	9.66	-	-	1	-								

Career Performances

	M	Inns	NO	Runs	HS	Avge	100s	50s	Ct	St	Balls	Runs	Wkts	Avge	Best	5wI	10wM
Test																	
All First																	
1-day Int																	
C & G	3	3	0	156	140	52.00	1	-	1	-	12	15	0	-	-	-	
totesport	4	3	0	45	29	15.00	-	-	2	-							
Twenty20	7	7	0	82	46	11.71	-	-	3	-							

TEN DOESCHATE, R. N. Essex

Name: Ryan Neil ten Doeschate
Role: Right-hand bat, right-arm medium-fast bowler
Born: 30 June 1980, Port Elizabeth, South Africa
Height: 5ft 11in **Weight:** 12st 8lbs
Nickname: Tendo
County debut: 2003
1st-Class catches: 2
Strike rate: 31.57 (career 52.14)
Parents: Boudewyn and Ingrid
Marital status: Single
Education: Fairbairn College; University of Cape Town
Qualifications: Business science degree
Overseas teams played for: Western Province; Western Province B; Bloemendaal, Holland 2002-03
Cricket moments to forget: 'My county debut at Chelmsford'
Cricketers particularly admired: Jacques Kallis, Kepler Wessels
Young players to look out for: Jono McLean
Other sports played: Rugby
Other sports followed: Football (Arsenal), rugby (Stormers)
Favourite band: Phil Collins
Relaxations: Golf, tennis, reading
Extras: Is not considered an overseas player
Best batting: 31 Essex v Sussex, Arundel 2003
Best bowling: 3-29 Essex v CUCCE, Fenner's 2004

2004 Season

	M	Inns	NO	Runs	HS	Avge	100s	50s	Ct	St	O	M	Runs	Wkts	Avge	Best	5wI	10wM
Test																		
All First	2	1	0	7	7	7.00	-	-	1	-	36.5	7	117	7	16.71	3-29	-	-
1-day Int																		
C & G																		
totesport																		
Twenty20																		

Career Performances

	M	Inns	NO	Runs	HS	Avge	100s	50s	Ct	St	Balls	Runs	Wkts	Avge	Best	5wI	10wM
Test																	
All First	4	5	0	55	31	11.00	-	-	2	-	365	239	7	34.14	3-29	-	-
1-day Int																	
C & G																	
totesport	1	0	0	0	0	-	-	-	-	-	48	39	1	39.00	1-39	-	
Twenty20	5	2	0	9	6	4.50	-	-	1	-	109	147	5	29.40	2-27	-	

THOMAS, I. J. Glamorgan

Name: Ian James Thomas
Role: Left-hand bat, right-arm off-spin bowler, wicket-keeper 'when needed'
Born: 9 May 1979, Newport, Gwent
Height: 6ft **Weight:** 14st 7lbs
Nickname: Bolts
County debut: 1998
1st-Class 50s: 6
1st-Class catches: 19
One-Day 100s: 1
Place in batting averages: (2003 241st av. 16.54)
Strike rate: (career 61.00)
Parents: Amanda and Alun
Marital status: Single
Family links with cricket: 'Brother Rhys is captain of local village team, Machen CC; father still slogging for them. Mother brings up the whites lovely'
Education: Bedwas and Bassaleg Comprehensive Schools; University of Wales Institute Cardiff (UWIC)
Qualifications: 9 GCSEs, 2 A-levels, BSc (Hons) Sports Development

Career outside cricket: 'Sports development, marketing, management; possibly police force; or start a DIY business with Mike Powell'
Off-season: 'Working closely with coaching staff at GCCC'
Overseas tours: Wales U16 to Jersey and Isle of Wight; British Universities to Port Elizabeth 1999; Glamorgan to Cape Town 2002; Forest Nomads CC to Trinidad and Tobago 2003
Overseas teams played for: Mt Lawley Hawks, Perth 2001-02; Subiaco Marist CC, Perth 2003-04
Career highlights to date: 'Winning two National League titles 2002, 2004; playing for Glamorgan; holding the joint record (116*) with Graeme Hick in the Twenty20 Cup'
Cricket moments to forget: 'First-class pair, v Derbys 2002'
Cricket superstitions: 'Too many to mention'
Cricketers particularly admired: Matthew Maynard, Brian Lara
Young players to look out for: Michael O'Shea, James Hildreth
Other sports played: Golf (Peterstone Lakes GC), rugby (Machen RFC)
Other sports followed: Rugby (Newport-Gwent Dragons), golf (European Tour)
Favourite band: 'A big fan of Phil Collins'
Relaxations: 'Fishing, golf, swimming'
Extras: Captained Welsh Schools at all age groups. Glamorgan Young Player of the Month June, July, August and September 2000. Scored 82 on Championship debut v Essex at Southend 2000. Equalled record for the highest individual score in the Twenty20 Cup (116*, set only hours earlier by Graeme Hick) v Somerset at Taunton 2004. Underwent major back surgery in 1997
Opinions on cricket: 'I am extremely proud and lucky to play cricket for a living and be part of Glamorgan CCC. If only other counties would not be so narrow-minded in producing first-class cricketers, taking short-term stop-gaps with Kolpak (*see page 9*) and EU-qualified players. When will the ECB control this situation? Two overseas players – do we really need this many?'
Best batting: 82 Glamorgan v Essex, Southend 2000
Best bowling: 1-26 Glamorgan v Nottinghamshire, Colwyn Bay 2002

2004 Season

	M	Inns	NO	Runs	HS	Avge	100s	50s	Ct	St	O	M	Runs	Wkts	Avge	Best	5wI	10wM
Test																		
All First	2	3	0	106	68	35.33	-	1	2	-	1	0	6	0	-	-	-	-
1-day Int																		
C & G																		
totesport	6	6	2	86	38 *	21.50	-	-	-	-	11	0	60	1	60.00	1-27	-	
Twenty20	7	7	1	179	116 *	29.83	1	-	4	-	6	0	58	1	58.00	1-25	-	

Career Performances

	M	Inns	NO	Runs	HS	Avge	100s	50s	Ct	St	Balls	Runs	Wkts	Avge	Best	5wI	10wM
Test																	
All First	28	46	4	941	82	22.40	-	6	19	-	61	38	1	38.00	1-26	-	-
1-day Int																	
C & G	4	4	0	161	93	40.25	-	1	2	-							
totesport	35	34	4	796	72	26.53	-	5	10	-	66	60	1	60.00	1-27	-	
Twenty20	10	10	1	197	116 *	21.88	1	-	4	-	42	63	2	31.50	1-5	-	

THOMAS, S. D. Glamorgan

Name: Stuart Darren Thomas
Role: Left-hand bat, right-arm fast-medium bowler; all-rounder
Born: 25 January 1975, Morriston, Swansea
Height: 6ft **Weight:** 13st
Nickname: Ted, Stu
County debut: 1992
County cap: 1997
50 wickets in a season: 5
1st-Class 50s: 17
1st-Class 100s: 2
1st-Class 5 w. in innings: 18
1st-Class 10 w. in match: 1
1st-Class catches: 56
One-Day 5 w. in innings: 3
Place in batting averages: 104th av. 35.64 (2003 191st av. 24.16)
Place in bowling averages: 97th av. 36.82 (2003 11th av. 22.53)
Strike rate: 56.55 (career 52.08)
Parents: Stu and Ann
Wife and date of marriage: Claire, 30 September 2000
Children: Ellie Sofia, 20 August 2002
Family links with cricket: 'Father was a good striker of the ball for Llanelli CC'
Education: Graig Comprehensive, Llanelli; Neath Tertiary College
Qualifications: 5 GCSEs, BTEC National Diploma in Sports Studies, Level 2 coaching award, 'and all the DIY knowledge in the world'
Career outside cricket: Sales rep
Off-season: 'Going on holiday with family and also starting our new 12-month contracts with Glamorgan'
Overseas tours: Glamorgan to Cape Town 1993, 1999, 2002, to Zimbabwe 1994, to Pretoria 1995, to Portugal 1996, to Jersey 1998; England U18 to South Africa

1992-93; England U19 to Sri Lanka 1993-94; England A to Zimbabwe and South Africa 1998-99, to Bangladesh and New Zealand 1999-2000
Overseas teams played for: Rovers CC, Welkom, Free State 1994; Burnside West University CC, Christchurch, New Zealand 2003
Career highlights to date: 'Winning County Championship 1997 by far, followed by my two England A tours'
Cricket moments to forget: 'There are too many to mention'
Cricket superstitions: 'None'
Cricketers particularly admired: Allan Donald, Malcolm Marshall, Ian Botham, 'and now Freddie'
Young players to look out for: Gareth Rees, Alastair Cook
Other sports followed: 'All kinds on Sky Sports'
Injuries: Out for 'odd games here and there' with a hernia
Favourite band: 'Don't have band but Robbie Williams is quality'
Relaxations: 'Spending time with family; training; enjoy seeing the globe; eating out'
Extras: Became youngest player (17 years 217 days) to take five wickets (5-80) on debut, v Derbyshire 1992, and finished eighth in national bowling averages. BBC Welsh Young Sports Personality 1992. Represented England U19. Returned Glamorgan best B&H bowling figures (6-20) on his competition debut v Combined Universities at Cardiff 1995. Took 7-16 v Surrey at Swansea in the Sunday League 1998, a competition best analysis by a Glamorgan bowler. Glamorgan Player of the Year 1998. Took 8-50 for England A v Zimbabwe A at Harare on 1998-99 tour – the first eight-wicket haul by an England A tourist. Scored maiden first-class century v Essex at Chelmsford 2001, his 138 being a record Championship score by a Glamorgan No. 8. Scored a 41-ball 71* v Surrey at The Oval in the C&G 2002 as Glamorgan made 429 in reply to Surrey's 438-5. Had first innings figures of 4-103, then scored 105* to become the second 12th man (after Kevin Innes) to score a century in a first-class match, before being replaced by Simon Jones v Hampshire at West End 2004
Opinions on cricket: 'The EU and Kolpak system (*see page 9*) is a disgrace. The younger players will suffer by the introduction of these players, and you even might find overseas [players] being barred in the future, which is sad. We have to do something about it!!'
Best batting: 138 Glamorgan v Essex, Chelmsford 2001
Best bowling: 8-50 England A v Zimbabwe A, Harare 1998-99

2004 Season

	M	Inns	NO	Runs	HS	Avge	100s	50s	Ct	St	O	M	Runs	Wkts	Avge	Best	5wI	10wM
Test																		
All First	14	19	5	499	105 *	35.64	1	3	8	-	320.3	32	1252	34	36.82	4-47	-	-
1-day Int																		
C & G																		
totesport	5	3	1	30	22 *	15.00	-	-	2	-	21	0	117	4	29.25	2-36	-	
Twenty20	7	6	3	106	43 *	35.33	-	-	-	-	24	0	209	9	23.22	3-32	-	

Career Performances

	M	Inns	NO	Runs	HS	Avge	100s	50s	Ct	St	Balls	Runs	Wkts	Avge	Best	5wI	10wM
Test																	
All First	162	220	43	3702	138	20.91	2	17	56	-	25783	15412	495	31.13	8-50	18	1
1-day Int																	
C & G	16	13	3	238	71 *	23.80	-	1	3	-	909	770	29	26.55	5-74	1	
totesport	89	67	14	738	38 *	13.92	-	-	15	-	3132	2662	105	25.35	7-16	1	
Twenty20	10	9	3	151	43 *	25.16	-	-	1	-	174	275	10	27.50	3-32	-	

THORNICROFT, N. D. — Yorkshire

Name: Nicholas (Nick) David Thornicroft
Role: Left-hand bat, right-arm fast bowler
Born: 23 January 1985, York
Height: 5ft 11in **Weight:** 12st 8lbs
Nickname: Thorny, Mad Dog, Harry Potter
County debut: 2002
1st-Class catches: 1
One-Day 5 w. in innings: 1
Strike rate: 44.33 (career 71.70)
Parents: Lyn and David
Marital status: Single
Education: Easingwold
Qualifications: 'Common sense'
Overseas tours: Yorkshire U16 to Cape Town, to Jersey; England U19 to Australia 2002-03
Career highlights to date: 'Getting Neil Fairbrother as my first first-class wicket'
Cricket moments to forget: 'Haven't got one yet'
Cricketers particularly admired: Darren Gough, Brett Lee, Ian Botham, Craig White, Andrew Flintoff
Young players to look out for: Charlie Thornicroft, Haroon Rashid, Andrew Gale, Liam Plunkett
Other sports played: Athletics, football, basketball
Other sports followed: Football (York City FC), horse racing
Relaxations: 'Spending time with family; music; shooting'
Extras: Played for Yorkshire Board XI in the C&G 2002. Became youngest ever Roses match debutant, v Lancashire at Old Trafford 2002, aged 17. Represented England U19 2002 and 2003, striking an 11-ball 42* in the second 'Test' v South Africa U19 at Worcester 2003
Best batting: 30 Yorkshire v Nottinghamshire, Headingley 2004
Best bowling: 2-27 Yorkshire v Durham, Riverside 2004

2004 Season

	M	Inns	NO	Runs	HS	Avge	100s	50s	Ct	St	O	M	Runs	Wkts	Avge	Best	5wI	10wM
Test																		
All First	2	3	0	40	30	13.33	-	-	1	-	44.2	10	168	6	28.00	2-27	-	-
1-day Int																		
C & G																		
totesport	3	2	2	8	8 *	-	-	-	-	-	19	2	121	3	40.33	2-57	-	
Twenty20																		

Career Performances

	M	Inns	NO	Runs	HS	Avge	100s	50s	Ct	St	Balls	Runs	Wkts	Avge	Best	5wI	10wM
Test																	
All First	6	10	4	50	30	8.33	-	-	1	-	717	473	10	47.30	2-27	-	-
1-day Int																	
C & G	1	0	0	0	0	-	-	-	-	-	30	19	0	-	-	-	
totesport	7	3	3	8	8 *	-	-	-	1	-	258	252	11	22.90	5-42	1	
Twenty20																	

THORP, C. D. — Durham

Name: Callum David Thorp
Role: Right-hand bat, right-arm medium bowler
Born: 11 February 1975, Mount Lawley, Western Australia
County debut: No first-team appearance
1st-Class catches: 2
Strike rate: (career 93.60)
Overseas teams played for: Western Australia 2002-03 – 2003-04
Extras: Took 4-58 for Western Australia v England XI in two-day match at Perth 2002-03. Attended Commonwealth Bank [Australian] Cricket Academy 2003. Has British parents and is not considered an overseas player
Best batting: 26 Western Australia v New South Wales, Newcastle 2002-03
Best bowling: 3-59 Western Australia v Tasmania, Perth 2003-04

2004 Season (did not make any first-class or one-day appearances)

Career Performances

	M	Inns	NO	Runs	HS	Avge	100s	50s	Ct	St	Balls	Runs	Wkts	Avge	Best	5wI	10wM
Test																	
All First	6	8	0	66	26	8.25	-	-	2	-	936	531	10	53.10	3-59	-	-
1-day Int																	
C & G																	
totesport																	
Twenty20																	

THORPE, G. P. — Surrey

Name: Graham Paul Thorpe
Role: Left-hand bat, occasional right-arm medium bowler
Born: 1 August 1969, Farnham
Height: 5ft 10in **Weight:** 12st 9lbs
Nickname: Chalky
County debut: 1988
County cap: 1991
Benefit: 2000
Test debut: 1993
Tests: 93
One-Day Internationals: 82
1000 runs in a season: 9
1st-Class 50s: 117
1st-Class 100s: 44
1st-Class 200s: 4
1st-Class catches: 277
One-Day 100s: 9
Place in batting averages: 24th av. 55.00 (2003 19th av. 56.61)
Strike rate: (career 91.80)
Parents: 'Mr and Mrs Thorpe'
Children: Henry and Amelia
Education: Weydon Comprehensive; Farnham College
Qualifications: 7 O-levels, PE Diploma
Overseas tours: England A to Zimbabwe and Kenya 1989-90, to Pakistan 1990-91, to Bermuda and West Indies 1991-92, to Australia 1992-93; England to West Indies 1993-94, to Australia 1994-95, to South Africa 1995-96, to India and Pakistan (World Cup) 1995-96, to Zimbabwe and New Zealand 1996-97, to Sharjah (Champions Trophy) 1997-98, to West Indies 1997-98, to Australia 1998-99,

to Sharjah (Coca-Cola Cup) 1998-99, to Kenya (ICC Knockout Trophy) 2000-01, to Pakistan and Sri Lanka 2000-01, to India and New Zealand 2001-02, to Bangladesh and Sri Lanka 2003-04, to West Indies 2003-04, to South Africa 2004-05
Cricketers particularly admired: Grahame Clinton, Waqar Younis, Ian Botham, Viv Richards
Other sports followed: Football (Chelsea FC), golf
Relaxations: Sleeping
Extras: Played for English Schools cricket U15 and U19 and England Schools football U18. Scored a century (114*) v Australia on his Test debut at Trent Bridge 1993. Cornhill England Player of the Year 1997-98. One of *Wisden*'s Five Cricketers of the Year 1998. Represented England in the 1999 World Cup. His century in the first Test v Pakistan at Lahore 2000-01 was the first in Test history to contain only one boundary (he added a second four before being out for 118). Captained England in one-day series v Sri Lanka 2000-01. Scored maiden Test double century (200*) v New Zealand in the first Test at Christchurch 2001-02, sharing with Andrew Flintoff in a stand of 281 that set several new records, including that for the highest sixth-wicket partnership for England in Tests. Has featured in several other record stands in international cricket, including a record fourth-wicket partnership for England in Tests v Australia (288) with Nasser Hussain at Edgbaston 1997. Retired from ODI cricket after the NatWest Series 2002. Recalled to the England Test side for the fifth Test v South Africa 2003 at his home ground of The Oval, scoring century (124) and sharing with Marcus Trescothick (219) in a ground record partnership for the third wicket in Tests (268). His international awards include England's Player of the Series in the 1997 Ashes campaign; Man of the Match in the third Test v Sri Lanka at Colombo 2000-01 (113*/32*); in the third Test v West Indies at Bridgetown 2003-04 (119*); in the third Test v New Zealand at Trent Bridge 2004 (45/104*), during which he became the tenth England batsman to pass 6000 Test runs; and in the third Test v West Indies at Old Trafford 2004 (114). ECB contract 2004-05
Best batting: 223* England XI v South Australia, Adelaide 1998-99
Best bowling: 4-40 Surrey v Australians, The Oval 1993

2004 Season

	M	Inns	NO	Runs	HS	Avge	100s	50s	Ct	St	O	M	Runs	Wkts	Avge	Best	5wI	10wM
Test	6	10	2	523	114	65.37	2	3	6	-								
All First	10	17	3	770	114	55.00	2	4	7	-								
1-day Int																		
C & G																		
totesport	2	2	0	39	39	19.50	-	-	3	-								
Twenty20																		

Career Performances

	M	Inns	NO	Runs	HS	Avge	100s	50s	Ct	St	Balls	Runs	Wkts	Avge	Best	5wI	10wM
Test	93	167	24	6349	200 *	44.39	15	37	97	-	138	37	0	-	-	-	-
All First	325	541	75	21185	223 *	45.46	48	117	277	-	2387	1378	26	53.00	4-40	-	-
1-day Int	82	77	13	2380	89	37.18	-	21	43	-	120	97	2	48.50	2-15	-	
C & G	33	32	9	1303	145 *	56.65	2	9	19	-	13	12	0	-	-	-	
totesport	145	134	21	4362	126 *	38.60	6	29	62	-	318	307	8	38.37	3-21	-	
Twenty20	5	4	0	95	50	23.75	-	1	1	-							

TOMLINSON, J. A. — Hampshire

Name: James Andrew Tomlinson
Role: Left-hand lower-order bat, left-arm fast-medium bowler
Born: 12 June 1982, Appleshaw, Hants
Height: 6ft 1½in **Weight:** 12st 7lbs
Nickname: Tommo, Mr T, T-Mobile, Dangerous Dave, T
County debut: 2002
1st-Class 5 w. in innings: 1
1st-Class catches: 5
Place in batting averages: (2003 295th av. 3.37)
Place in bowling averages: (2003 135th av. 46.70)
Strike rate: 120.00 (career 72.06)
Parents: Ian and Janet
Marital status: Single
Family links with cricket: 'Grandfathers played in the Yorkshire leagues. Brother Ralph captain of Dulwich 3rds. Brother Hugh making comeback from knee injury for South Wilts'
Education: Harrow Way Community School, Andover; Cricklade College, Andover; Cardiff University
Qualifications: 9 GCSEs, 3 A-levels, 2.1 degree in Education and Psychology
Off-season: 'Travelling round Europe with girlfriend, then off to Perth in January to Paul Terry Academy'
Career highlights to date: 'Any Hampshire win'
Cricket moments to forget: 'Southern League debut v Andover for South Wilts – seven overs for 59'
Cricket superstitions: 'None'
Cricketers particularly admired: Dimi Mascarenhas, Shane Warne, Nic Pothas, Shaun Udal

Young players to look out for: David Griffiths, Kevin Latouf, Chris Benham
Other sports played: Darts, golf
Other sports followed: Football (West Ham)
Injuries: Out for two weeks with an ankle ligament injury
Favourite band: Duran Duran, Aha, Spandau Ballet
Relaxations: 'Wildlife (ornithology)'
Extras: Played for Development of Excellence XI (South) v West Indies U19 2001. Part of Hampshire's 2nd XI Championship winning side 2001. Played for Cardiff University CCE 2002 and 2003, taking 5-104 (7-134 the match) v Somerset at Millfield School 2002. Represented British Universities 2002 and 2003. NBC Denis Compton Award for the most promising young Hampshire player 2003. Won Southern Premier League with South Wilts 2004
Opinions on cricket: 'There were too many overseas ("stop-gap" in particular) players used in 2004. County XIs should be limited to only three overseas, Kolpak (*see page 9*), EU or "Lurpak" players. The rest of the team should be made up of English (UK) qualified players.'
Best batting: 23 Hampshire v Indians, West End 2002
Best bowling: 6-63 Hampshire v Derbyshire, Derby 2003

2004 Season

	M	Inns	NO	Runs	HS	Avge	100s	50s	Ct	St	O	M	Runs	Wkts	Avge	Best	5wI	10wM
Test																		
All First	1	1	1	12	12 *	-	-	-	1	-	20	7	43	1	43.00	1-9	-	-
1-day Int																		
C & G																		
totesport	1	0	0	0	0	-	-	-	-	-	9	0	45	0	-	-	-	
Twenty20																		

Career Performances

	M	Inns	NO	Runs	HS	Avge	100s	50s	Ct	St	Balls	Runs	Wkts	Avge	Best	5wI	10wM
Test																	
All First	15	24	11	73	23	5.61	-	-	5	-	2162	1585	30	52.83	6-63	1	-
1-day Int																	
C & G	2	2	0	4	4	2.00	-	-	-	-	102	46	1	46.00	1-29	-	
totesport	12	6	3	10	6	3.33	-	-	1	-	500	413	11	37.54	2-15	-	
Twenty20																	

TREDWELL, J. C. Kent

Name: James Cullum Tredwell
Role: Left-hand bat, right-arm off-spin bowler
Born: 27 February 1982, Ashford, Kent
Height: 5ft 11in **Weight:** 14st 2lbs
Nickname: Tredders, Pingu, Chad
County debut: 2001
1st-Class 50s: 3
1st-Class 5 w. in innings: 1
1st-Class catches: 33
Place in batting averages: 122nd av. 33.85 (2003 240th av. 16.68)
Place in bowling averages: (2003 117th av. 40.17)
Strike rate: 130.42 (career 73.85)
Parents: John and Rosemary
Marital status: Single
Family links with cricket: 'Father played for Ashford and Folkestone in Kent League'
Education: Southlands Community Comprehensive
Qualifications: 10 GCSEs, 2 A-levels, ECB Level 1 coach
Overseas tours: Kent U17 to Sri Lanka 1998-99; Kent to Port Elizabeth 2002; England A to Malaysia and India 2003-04
Overseas teams played for: Redlands Tigers, Brisbane 2000-02
Cricket moments to forget: 'Being hit for six in a crucial B&H Cup match v Essex, which probably cost Kent's qualification to next stage'
Cricketers particularly admired: 'All the great spinners'
Young players to look out for: Rob Ferley, Joe Denly
Extras: Represented England U19 v West Indies U19 2001 (captain in second 'Test'). Captained Kent to victory in the 2nd XI Trophy final at West End 2002, scoring 111. Kent Most Improved Player Award 2003. ECB National Academy 2003-04. Took over captaincy of England A in India after Alex Gidman was forced to return home with a hand injury. Had match figures of 9-231 (5-101/4-130) for England A v East Zone at Amritsar in the Duleep Trophy 2003-04. NBC Denis Compton Award for the most promising young Kent player 2003
Best batting: 61 Kent v Yorkshire, Headingley 2002
Best bowling: 5-101 England A v East Zone, Amritsar 2003-04

2004 Season

	M	Inns	NO	Runs	HS	Avge	100s	50s	Ct	St	O	M	Runs	Wkts	Avge	Best	5wI	10wM
Test																		
All First	8	8	1	237	51 *	33.85	-	1	7	-	152.1	21	583	7	83.28	3-20	-	-
1-day Int																		
C & G	2	1	0	13	13	13.00	-	-	1	-	16	0	60	0	-	-	-	
totesport	14	12	2	156	30 *	15.60	-	-	9	-	92.1	4	389	11	35.36	3-35	-	
Twenty20	5	4	0	40	19	10.00	-	-	-	-	8	0	71	2	35.50	2-23	-	

Career Performances

	M	Inns	NO	Runs	HS	Avge	100s	50s	Ct	St	Balls	Runs	Wkts	Avge	Best	5wI	10wM
Test																	
All First	29	40	6	772	61	22.70	-	3	33	-	4579	2679	62	43.20	5-101	1	-
1-day Int																	
C & G	13	9	1	203	71	25.37	-	2	5	-	540	333	8	41.62	3-7	-	
totesport	40	32	9	287	30 *	12.47	-	-	17	-	1418	1060	36	29.44	3-28	-	
Twenty20	10	9	0	130	34	14.44	-	-	2	-	132	200	5	40.00	2-23	-	

TREMLETT, C. T. — Hampshire

Name: Christopher Timothy Tremlett
Role: Right-hand bat, right-arm fast-medium bowler
Born: 2 September 1981, Southampton
Height: 6ft 7in **Weight:** 16st 1lb
Nickname: Twiggy, Goober
County debut: 2000
County cap: 2004
1st-Class 50s: 1
1st-Class 5 w. in innings: 3
1st-Class catches: 13
Place in batting averages: 222nd av. 19.36 (2003 231st av. 18.09)
Place in bowling averages: 8th av. 22.23 (2003 84th av. 34.40)
Strike rate: 41.28 (career 48.04)
Parents: Timothy and Carolyn
Marital status: Single
Family links with cricket: Grandfather [Maurice] played for Somerset and in three Tests for England. Father played for Hampshire and is now director of cricket at the county
Education: Thornden School, Chandlers Ford; Taunton's College, Southampton

Qualifications: 5 GCSEs, BTEC National Diploma in Sports Science, Level 2 coach
Overseas tours: West of England U15 to West Indies 1997; Hampshire U16 to Jersey; England U17 to Northern Ireland (ECC Colts Festival) 1999; England U19 to India 2000-01; ECB National Academy to Australia 2001-02, to Australia and Sri Lanka 2002-03; England VI to Hong Kong 2004
Career highlights to date: 'Taking first five-wicket haul against Lancashire at the Rose Bowl'
Cricket moments to forget: 'Getting injured against Essex in an NUL game and being put out for the rest of the 2002 season'
Cricketers particularly admired: Glenn McGrath, Mark Waugh, Shane Warne
Young players to look out for: John Francis
Other sports played: Basketball, volleyball
Other sports followed: Football (Arsenal)
Relaxations: 'Socialising with friends; cinema'
Extras: Took wicket (Mark Richardson) with first ball in first-class cricket v New Zealand A at Portsmouth 2000; finished with debut match figures of 6-91. Represented England U19. NBC Denis Compton Award for the most promising young Hampshire player 2000, 2001. Hampshire Young Player of the Year 2001. Included in preliminary England one-day squad of 30 for ICC Champions Trophy 2004. Awarded Hampshire cap 2004
Best batting: 57 Hampshire v Somerset, West End 2004
Best bowling: 6-51 Hampshire v Glamorgan, West End 2003

2004 Season

	M	Inns	NO	Runs	HS	Avge	100s	50s	Ct	St	O	M	Runs	Wkts	Avge	Best	5wI	10wM
Test																		
All First	10	15	4	213	57	19.36	-	1	2	-	268.2	56	867	39	22.23	4-29	-	-
1-day Int																		
C & G	2	2	1	62	38 *	62.00	-	-	-	-	13	3	40	1	40.00	1-10	-	
totesport	8	5	2	35	11 *	11.66	-	-	1	-	56	3	270	14	19.28	4-37	-	
Twenty20	5	3	1	31	13	15.50	-	-	3	-	17	1	110	8	13.75	3-20	-	

Career Performances

	M	Inns	NO	Runs	HS	Avge	100s	50s	Ct	St	Balls	Runs	Wkts	Avge	Best	5wI	10wM
Test																	
All First	42	58	17	723	57	17.63	-	1	13	-	6630	3589	138	26.00	6-51	3	-
1-day Int																	
C & G	7	3	1	72	38 *	36.00	-	-	-	-	320	229	7	32.71	3-20	-	
totesport	45	27	9	179	30 *	9.94	-	-	10	-	2002	1401	70	20.01	4-25	-	
Twenty20	5	3	1	31	13	15.50	-	-	3	-	102	110	8	13.75	3-20	-	

TRESCOTHICK, M. E. Somerset

Name: Marcus Edward Trescothick
Role: Left-hand bat, right-arm swing bowler, reserve wicket-keeper
Born: 25 December 1975, Keynsham, Bristol
Height: 6ft 3in **Weight:** 14st 7lbs
Nickname: Banger, Tres
County debut: 1993
County cap: 1999
Test debut: 2000
Tests: 54
One-Day Internationals: 92
1st-Class 50s: 58
1st-Class 100s: 16
1st-Class 200s: 1
1st-Class catches: 190
One-Day 100s: 16
Place in batting averages: 28th av. 53.41 (2003 24th av. 51.62)
Strike rate: (career 73.44)
Parents: Martyn and Lin
Wife and date of marriage: Hayley, 24 January 2004
Family links with cricket: Father played for Somerset 2nd XI; uncle played club cricket
Education: Sir Bernard Lovell School
Qualifications: 7 GCSEs
Off-season: Touring with England
Overseas tours: England U18 to South Africa 1992-93; England U19 to Sri Lanka 1993-94, to West Indies 1994-95 (captain); England A to Bangladesh and New Zealand 1999-2000; England to Kenya (ICC Knockout Trophy) 2000-01, to Pakistan and Sri Lanka 2000-01, to Zimbabwe (one-day series) 2001-02, to India and New Zealand 2001-02, to Sri Lanka (ICC Champions Trophy) 2002-03, to Australia 2002-03, to Africa (World Cup) 2002-03, to Bangladesh and Sri Lanka 2003-04, to West Indies 2003-04, to South Africa 2004-05
Overseas teams played for: Melville CC, Perth 1997-99
Career highlights to date: 'Scoring my first Test hundred in Galle, Sri Lanka [2001]'
Cricketers particularly admired: Adam Gilchrist, Andy Caddick
Other sports followed: Golf, football (Bristol City FC)
Relaxations: 'Spending time at home (it's such a rare thing), playing golf'
Extras: Scored more than 1000 runs for England U19. Took hat-trick for Somerset v Young Australia at Taunton 1995. Scored 322 v Warwickshire 2nd XI 1997, being the last man out with the score on 605 as Somerset 2nd XI chased 612. Made ODI debut

v Zimbabwe at The Oval in the NatWest Series 2000, scoring 79. Made Test debut in the third Test v West Indies 2000, scoring 66. PCA Player of the Year 2000. Scored three B&H centuries in eight days 2001, winning three Gold Awards. Sports.com Cricketer of the Year 2001. BBC West Country Sports Sportsman of the Year 2001. Scored 109-ball 121 v India at Kolkata (Calcutta) 2001-02, including the then fastest century for England in ODIs (80 balls). Took part in first-wicket stand of 50 in five overs with Michael Vaughan to bring England victory with an over to spare in the third Test v Sri Lanka at Old Trafford 2002. Scored 114* v South Africa at The Oval in the NatWest Series 2003, sharing with Vikram Solanki (106) in a record England opening partnership in ODIs (200). Has featured in several other record stands in international cricket, including a record third-wicket partnership for Tests at The Oval (268) with Graham Thorpe v South Africa 2003. His international awards include Man of the NatWest Series v Sri Lanka and India 2002, Man of the Series in the NatWest Challenge v Pakistan 2003, Man of the [ODI] Series v West Indies 2003-04, and Man of the Match in the fifth Test v South Africa at The Oval 2003 (219/69*). Scored century in each innings (105/107) in the second Test v West Indies at Edgbaston 2004. ECB contract 2004-05
Best batting: 219 England v South Africa, The Oval 2003
Best bowling: 4-36 Somerset v Young Australia, Taunton 1995
Stop press: Scored 132 in the second Test v South Africa at Durban 2004-05, in the process sharing with Andrew Strauss (136) in the highest opening partnership for England in Tests since 1960 (273)

2004 Season

	M	Inns	NO	Runs	HS	Avge	100s	50s	Ct	St	O	M	Runs	Wkts	Avge	Best	5wI	10wM
Test	7	14	2	641	132	53.41	3	2	6	-	4	0	10	0	-	-	-	-
All First	7	14	2	641	132	53.41	3	2	6	-	4	0	10	0	-	-	-	-
1-day Int	12	12	0	403	104	33.58	1	3	9	-	7	0	45	2	22.50	1-17	-	
C & G	1	1	0	24	24	24.00	-	-	1	-								
totesport	1	1	0	36	36	36.00	-	-	-	-								
Twenty20	1	1	0	56	56	56.00	-	1	-	-								

Career Performances

	M	Inns	NO	Runs	HS	Avge	100s	50s	Ct	St	Balls	Runs	Wkts	Avge	Best	5wI	10wM
Test	54	103	10	3982	219	42.81	8	24	58	-	270	144	1	144.00	1-34	-	-
All First	175	302	18	10033	219	35.32	17	58	190	-	2644	1530	36	42.50	4-36	-	-
1-day Int	92	91	3	3370	137	38.29	8	19	38	-	124	117	4	29.25	2-7	-	
C & G	21	19	1	859	133	47.72	4	1	6	-	174	141	4	35.25	2-23	-	
totesport	89	80	11	2011	110	29.14	1	11	30	-	978	823	31	26.54	4-50	-	
Twenty20	1	1	0	56	56	56.00	-	1	-	-							

TROTT, B. J. Kent

Name: Benjamin (Ben) James Trott
Role: Right-hand bat, right-arm fast-medium bowler
Born: 14 March 1975, Wellington, Somerset
Height: 6ft 5in **Weight:** 14st
Nickname: Tony Rott, Trotsky, Trotty
County debut: 1997 (Somerset), 2000 (Kent)
1st-Class 5 w. in innings: 4
1st-Class 10 w. in match: 1
1st-Class catches: 8
One-Day 5 w. in innings: 1
Place in batting averages: 286th av. 4.66 (2003 291st av. 6.16)
Place in bowling averages: 150th av. 53.80 (2003 142nd av. 49.92)
Strike rate: 91.80 (career 55.93)
Parents: Alan Robert and Jane Elizabeth
Marital status: Single
Family links with cricket: Younger brother Thom and father both play
Education: Court Fields Community School, Taunton; Richard Huish College, Taunton; College of St Mark and St John, Plymouth
Qualifications: 8 GCSEs, 3 A-levels, BEd (Hons) Physical Education and Information Technology; sports coaching – cricket, rugby, football, hockey
Career outside cricket: Study support centre manager at Canterbury
Overseas teams played for: Claremont-Nedlands, Perth 1998-99
Career highlights to date: 'Winning the Norwich Union League 2001 with the last game of the season'
Cricketers particularly admired: Glenn McGrath, Darren Gough, Andrew Caddick
Young players to look out for: Alex Loudon, James Tredwell, Robert Ferley
Other sports played: Golf, football
Other sports followed: Football (Manchester United)
Extras: Wellington Young Player of the Year 1993. Wellington Players' Player of the Year 1996. Played for Somerset 1997-99; has also played for Devon. Joined Kent in 2000. Recorded maiden first-class five-wicket return (5-65) v Essex at Tunbridge Wells 2001, going on to take 6-13 in the second innings for a maiden first-class ten-wicket match. Also recorded maiden one-day five-wicket return in 2001, 5-18 v Cumberland at Barrow on C&G debut, winning Man of the Match award. Released by Kent at the end of the 2004 season
Best batting: 26 Kent v Sussex, Tunbridge Wells 2002
Best bowling: 6-13 Kent v Essex, Tunbridge Wells 2001

2004 Season

	M	Inns	NO	Runs	HS	Avge	100s	50s	Ct	St	O	M	Runs	Wkts	Avge	Best	5wI	10wM
Test																		
All First	5	7	1	28	12	4.66	-	-	1	-	153	23	538	10	53.80	4-109	-	-
1-day Int																		
C & G																		
totesport	6	1	0	0	0	0.00	-	-	1	-	33	4	174	6	29.00	2-19	-	
Twenty20	5	3	3	10	5 *	-	-	-	2	-	20	0	171	4	42.75	2-27	-	

Career Performances

	M	Inns	NO	Runs	HS	Avge	100s	50s	Ct	St	Balls	Runs	Wkts	Avge	Best	5wI	10wM
Test																	
All First	34	37	11	150	26	5.76	-	-	8	-	4922	2999	88	34.07	6-13	4	1
1-day Int																	
C & G	5	2	0	3	3	1.50	-	-	1	-	295	168	12	14.00	5-18	1	
totesport	33	15	9	9	2 *	1.50	-	-	6	-	1430	1171	38	30.81	3-19	-	
Twenty20	7	3	3	10	5 *	-	-	-	2	-	162	220	6	36.66	2-17	-	

TROTT, I. J. L. — Warwickshire

Name: Ian Jonathan Leonard Trott
Role: Right-hand bat, right-arm medium bowler; all-rounder
Born: 22 April 1981, Cape Town, South Africa
Height: 6ft **Weight:** 13st 5lbs
Nickname: Booger
County debut: 2003
1000 runs in a season: 1
1st-Class 50s: 22
1st-Class 100s: 3
1st-Class 5 w. in innings: 1
1st-Class catches: 29
Place in batting averages: 30th av. 53.18 (2003 66th av. 42.38)
Strike rate: 62.00 (career 58.42)
Parents: Ian and Donna
Marital status: Single
Family links with cricket: Father a professional cricket coach. Brother (Kenny Jackson) played for Western Province and Boland. Is related to the late-19th-century Test cricketers Albert (Australia and England) and Harry Trott (Australia)
Education: Rondebosch Boys' High School; Stellenbosch University

Qualifications: Level 2 coaching
Overseas tours: South Africa U15 to England (U15 World Cup) 1996; South Africa U19 to Pakistan 1998-99, to Sri Lanka (U19 World Cup) 1999-2000
Overseas teams played for: Boland 1999-2000 – 2000-01; Western Province 2001-02
Cricket moments to forget: 'Losing in the final of the Standard Bank Cup 2002'
Cricket superstitions: 'Personal'
Cricketers particularly admired: Sachin Tendulkar, Adam Hollioake, Steve Waugh
Other sports played: Hockey (Western Province U16, U18, U21), golf
Other sports followed: Football (Tottenham Hotspur)
Favourite band: Roxette, Robbie Williams
Relaxations: 'Music, watching sport'
Extras: Represented South Africa A. Struck a record debut score of 245 for Warwickshire 2nd XI v Somerset 2nd XI at Knowle & Dorridge 2002, sharing in a third-wicket stand of 397 with Trevor Penney. Scored 248 v Worcestershire 2nd XI at Barnt Green 2003, in the process sharing with Ian Westwood (250*) in a record opening partnership for Warwickshire 2nd XI (429). Scored century (134) on Championship debut for Warwickshire v Sussex at Edgbaston 2003. Became the first player to bat for the full 20 overs in the Twenty20, for a 54-ball 65* v Gloucestershire at Edgbaston 2003. Scored 1000 first-class runs in a season for the first time 2004. Is a British passport holder and is not considered an overseas player
Opinions on cricket: 'Should be less cricket, which would make the cricket we play more competitive.'
Best batting: 134 Warwickshire v Sussex, Edgbaston 2003
Best bowling: 7-39 Warwickshire v Kent, Canterbury 2003

2004 Season

	M	Inns	NO	Runs	HS	Avge	100s	50s	Ct	St	O	M	Runs	Wkts	Avge	Best	5wI	10wM
Test																		
All First	17	28	6	1170	115	53.18	1	10	12	-	31	10	96	3	32.00	1-1	-	-
1-day Int																		
C & G	4	2	1	65	65 *	65.00	-	1	-	-	3	0	16	0	-	-	-	
totesport	16	16	3	398	70	30.61	-	1	7	-								
Twenty20	5	5	3	93	39	46.50	-	-	1	-	2	0	20	2	10.00	2-20	-	

Career Performances

	M	Inns	NO	Runs	HS	Avge	100s	50s	Ct	St	Balls	Runs	Wkts	Avge	Best	5wI	10wM
Test																	
All First	44	78	9	2733	134	39.60	3	22	29	-	818	531	14	37.92	7-39	1	-
1-day Int																	
C & G	4	2	1	65	65 *	65.00	-	1	-	-	18	16	0	-	-	-	
totesport	24	24	5	682	70	35.89	-	5	11	-	18	19	0	-	-	-	
Twenty20	10	9	4	179	65 *	35.80	-	1	1	-	18	30	2	15.00	2-20	-	

TROUGHTON, J. O. Warwickshire

Name: Jamie (Jim) Oliver Troughton
Role: Left-hand bat, slow left-arm bowler
Born: 2 March 1979, London
Height: 5ft 11in **Weight:** 12st 12lbs
Nickname: Troughts
County debut: 2001
County cap: 2002
One-Day Internationals: 6
1000 runs in a season: 1
1st-Class 50s: 13
1st-Class 100s: 8
1st-Class catches: 21
One-Day 100s: 1
Place in batting averages: 117th av. 34.52 (2003 68th av. 41.55)
Strike rate: 125.33 (career 160.33)
Parents: Ali and David
Wife and date of marriage: Naomi, 28 September 2002

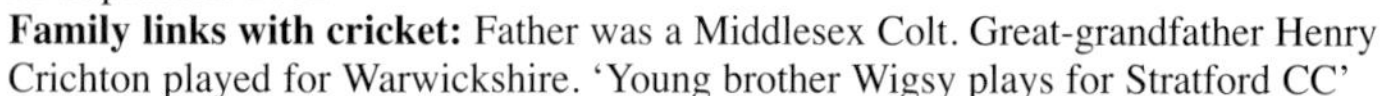

Family links with cricket: Father was a Middlesex Colt. Great-grandfather Henry Crichton played for Warwickshire. 'Young brother Wigsy plays for Stratford CC'
Education: Trinity School, Leamington Spa; Birmingham University
Qualifications: 8 GCSEs, 3 A-levels, BSc Sport & Exercise Psychology
Career outside cricket: Coaching/acting
Off-season: 'Perth for six months, playing for Claremont-Nedlands CC'
Overseas tours: Warwickshire Development of Excellence squad to Cape Town 1998; MCC to Australia and Singapore 2001; ECB National Academy to Australia and Sri Lanka 2002-03
Overseas teams played for: Harvinia CC, Free State, South Africa 2000; Avendale CC, Cape Town 2001-02; Belville CC, Cape Town 2003-04; Claremont-Nedlands CC, Perth 2004-05
Career highlights to date: 'Winning the Championship 2004'
Cricket moments to forget: 'Being relegated in one-day league [2004]'
Cricket superstitions: 'None'
Cricketers particularly admired: Graham Thorpe, Steve Waugh, Allan Donald, Ashley Giles
Young players to look out for: Jonathan Trott, Ian Westwood, Naqaash Tahir, Moeen Ali
Other sports played: Football (Stoke City youth player; 'I enjoy skinning Alan Richardson for a pastime')
Other sports followed: 'Hooked on Manchester United since going to their soccer school aged five'

Injuries: Out for one week with a groin strain
Favourite band: Red Hot Chili Peppers, Coldplay, Stone Roses
Relaxations: 'Music, films, playing my guitar, spending time with Naomi, going abroad'
Extras: Is grandson of *Dr Who* actor Patrick Troughton; father also an actor. County colours U12-U19. Has represented England U15, U16 and U17. Represented ECB Midlands U19 v Pakistan U19 1998. Has won the Alec Hastilow Trophy and the Coney Edmonds Trophy (Warwickshire awards). Warwickshire 2nd XI Player of the Year 2001. Scored 1067 first-class runs in his first full season 2002. NBC Denis Compton Award for the most promising young Warwickshire player 2002. Warwickshire Young Player and Most Improved Player of the Year 2002. Nominated for PCA Young Player of the Year award 2002
Opinions on cricket: 'How does this Kolpak bloke (*see page 9*) sleep at night? There has got to be a gentleman's agreement by all county chairmen not to sign them. With two overseas [players], EU players and Kolpaks we will stifle the English youth and prevent the "cream" rising to the top. We have just turned the corner in terms of catching up the Aussies, but there is a big road block ahead with Kolpak written all over it in bold letters.'
Best batting: 131* Warwickshire v Hampshire, West End 2002
Best bowling: 3-1 Warwickshire v CUCCE, Fenner's 2004

2004 Season

	M	Inns	NO	Runs	HS	Avge	100s	50s	Ct	St	O	M	Runs	Wkts	Avge	Best	5wI	10wM
Test																		
All First	14	18	1	587	120	34.52	1	5	4	-	125.2	28	345	6	57.50	3-1	-	-
1-day Int																		
C & G	1	0	0	0	0	-	-	-	-	-								
totesport	11	8	1	104	36	14.85	-	-	4	-	33	1	164	6	27.33	2-36	-	
Twenty20	4	3	0	39	32	13.00	-	-	2	-	4	0	25	2	12.50	2-10	-	

Career Performances

	M	Inns	NO	Runs	HS	Avge	100s	50s	Ct	St	Balls	Runs	Wkts	Avge	Best	5wI	10wM
Test																	
All First	44	70	7	2640	131 *	41.90	8	13	21	-	962	544	6	90.66	3-1	-	-
1-day Int	6	5	1	36	20	9.00	-	-	1	-							
C & G	9	8	1	361	115 *	51.57	1	2	3	-	130	83	7	11.85	4-23	-	
totesport	33	28	4	528	77	22.00	-	3	9	-	234	196	7	28.00	2-36	-	
Twenty20	6	5	1	73	33 *	18.25	-	-	2	-	24	25	2	12.50	2-10	-	

TUDOR, A. J. Essex

Name: Alexander (Alex) Jeremy Tudor
Role: Right-hand bat, right-arm fast bowler
Born: 23 October 1977, West Brompton, London
Height: 6ft 4in **Weight:** 13st 7lbs
Nickname: Big Al, Bambi, Tudes
County debut: 1995 (Surrey)
County cap: 1999 (Surrey)
Test debut: 1998-99
Tests: 10
One-Day Internationals: 3
1st-Class 50s: 6
1st-Class 100s: 1
1st-Class 5 w. in innings: 13
1st-Class catches: 27
Place in batting averages: (2003 150th av. 29.50)
Place in bowling averages: (2003 147th av. 53.20)
Strike rate: 33.00 (career 47.28)
Parents: Daryll and Jennifer
Marital status: Single
Family links with cricket: Brother was on the staff at The Oval
Education: St Mark's C of E, Fulham; City of Westminster College
Overseas tours: England U15 to South Africa 1992-93; England U19 to Zimbabwe 1995-96, to Pakistan 1996-97; England to Australia 1998-99, to South Africa 1999-2000, to Pakistan 2000-01, to Australia 2002-03; England A to West Indies 2000-01; ECB National Academy to Australia 2001-02, 2002-03
Cricketers particularly admired: Curtly Ambrose, Brian Lara
Other sports followed: Basketball, football (QPR)
Relaxations: Listening to music
Extras: Played for London Schools at all ages from U8. Represented England U17. MCC Young Cricketer. Took 4-89 in Australia's first innings on Test debut at Perth 1998-99; his victims included both Waugh twins. Scored 99* in second innings of the first Test v New Zealand at Edgbaston 1999, bettering the highest score by a nightwatchman for England (Harold Larwood's 98 v Australia at Sydney 1932-33) and winning Man of the Match award; in total he scored 131 unbeaten runs in the match. Cricket Writers' Club Young Cricketer of the Year 1999. Recorded match figures of 7-109 in the third Test v Sri Lanka at Old Trafford 2002, winning Man of the Match award. Released by Surrey at the end of the 2004 season and has joined Essex for 2005

Best batting: 116 Surrey v Essex, The Oval 2001
Best bowling: 7-48 Surrey v Lancashire, The Oval 2000

2004 Season

	M	Inns	NO	Runs	HS	Avge	100s	50s	Ct	St	O	M	Runs	Wkts	Avge	Best	5wI	10wM
Test																		
All First	2	2	1	18	18 *	18.00	-	-	3	-	33	7	157	6	26.16	4-61	-	-
1-day Int																		
C & G																		
totesport	4	4	2	74	56	37.00	-	1	3	-	19.3	1	90	5	18.00	3-31	-	
Twenty20																		

Career Performances

	M	Inns	NO	Runs	HS	Avge	100s	50s	Ct	St	Balls	Runs	Wkts	Avge	Best	5wI	10wM
Test	10	16	4	229	99 *	19.08	-	1	3	-	1512	963	28	34.39	5-44	1	-
All First	92	120	27	2041	116	21.94	1	6	27	-	13241	7908	280	28.24	7-48	13	-
1-day Int	3	2	1	9	6	9.00	-	-	1	-	127	136	4	34.00	2-30	-	
C & G	7	3	2	28	17 *	28.00	-	-	2	-	399	269	10	26.90	4-39	-	
totesport	39	29	9	260	56	13.00	-	1	11	-	1505	1209	52	23.25	4-26	-	
Twenty20																	

TURK, N. R. K. — Sussex

Name: Neil Richard Keith Turk
Role: Left-hand bat, right-arm medium bowler
Born: 28 April 1983, Cuckfield
Height: 6ft **Weight:** 11st 8lbs
Nickname: Turkish, Neilo
County debut: 2002 (one-day)
Parents: Keith and Lorraine
Marital status: Single
Family links with cricket: 'Father PE teacher and grade coach. Brother county junior. Mother junior cricket coach/manager'
Education: Sackville Community College, East Grinstead; Exeter University (Sports Science degree)
Qualifications: 9 GCSEs, 1 AS-level, 3 A-levels, FIFA-approved referee
Career highlights to date: 'County debut 2002 v Essex Eagles. Maiden 2nd XI Championship century (123) v Hampshire'
Cricket moments to forget: 'Being dismissed by Hampshire's wicket-keeper in a

match for Sussex 2nd XI, having scored a century in the first innings; his only wicket to date'
Cricket superstitions: 'I don't believe you need superstitions to help you'
Cricketers particularly admired: Brian Lara, Jacques Kallis
Young players to look out for: Arul Suppiah
Other sports played: Hockey (West of England U21, Exeter University, ISCA HC), golf, football
Other sports followed: Football (Liverpool FC), rugby league (Wigan Warriors), hockey (East Grinstead HC)
Favourite band: Usher
Relaxations: 'I enjoy most sports; I also like to spend time on the golf course when I'm not playing cricket'
Extras: Youngest player ever to score a Sussex League century. Sussex U17 Player of the Year. Played for Sussex Board XI in the C&G 2003. Attended Sussex Academy

2004 Season (did not make any first-class or one-day appearances)

Career Performances

	M	Inns	NO	Runs	HS	Avge	100s	50s	Ct	St	Balls	Runs	Wkts	Avge	Best	5wI	10wM
Test																	
All First																	
1-day Int																	
C & G	1	1	0	20	20	20.00	-	-	-	-	12	21	0	-		-	-
totesport	2	2	0	44	36	22.00	-	-	-	-							
Twenty20																	

TURNER, M. L. — Durham

Name: Mark Leif Turner
Role: Right-hand bat, right-arm medium-fast bowler; lower-order all-rounder
Born: 23 October 1984, Sunderland
Height: 5ft 11in **Weight:** 12st 2lbs
Nickname: Tina, Stella
County debut: No first-team appearance
Parents: Kenneth and Eileen
Marital status: Single
Family links with cricket: 'Brother Ian played for county at schoolboy and junior levels'
Education: Thornhill Comprehensive School
Qualifications: 7 GCSEs, Level 2 coaching
Career outside cricket: 'Winter job at Northern Rock call centre'
Off-season: 'Working and touring'

Overseas tours: England U19 to Bangladesh (U19 World Cup) 2003-04; Durham to India 2004

Career highlights to date: 'Taking five wickets for England U19 in "Test" match'
Cricket moments to forget: 'Dropping a catch on Sky for England U19 (easy chance)'
Cricketers particularly admired: Allan Donald, Alec Stewart, Glenn McGrath
Young players to look out for: Liam Plunkett, Graham Onions, Luke Anderson
Other sports played: 'Played junior football for Manchester Utd and Sunderland boys'
Other sports followed: Football (Sunderland AFC)
Injuries: Out for two to three months after an ankle operation
Favourite band: Keith Sweat, Maxwell
Relaxations: 'Listening to music, socialising, fishing'
Extras: Represented England U19 2003 and v Bangladesh U19 2004, returning match figures of 9-104 (5-57/4-47) in the second 'Test' at Taunton 2004. Is a Durham Development Player
Opinions on cricket: 'More day/night matches. County sides to keep on giving young English players a chance.'

89. Which Oxford-born umpire made his international debut standing in Zimbabwe's inaugural Test against India at Harare in 1992-93 and went on to stand in 28 Tests and 90 ODIs?

TURNER, R. J. Somerset

Name: Robert (Rob) Julian Turner
Role: Right-hand middle-order bat, wicket-keeper
Born: 25 November 1967, Malvern
Height: 6ft 2in **Weight:** 14st
Nickname: Noddy, Turns
County debut: 1991
County cap: 1994
Benefit: 2002
1000 runs in a season: 2
50 dismissals in a season: 9
1st-Class 50s: 45
1st-Class 100s: 10
1st-Class catches: 681
1st-Class stumpings: 49
Place in batting averages: 194th av. 23.06 (2003 89th av. 37.70)
Parents: Derek and Doris
Wife and date of marriage: Lucy, 25 September 1999
Children: Jamie Jonathan Paul, 4 April 2001
Family links with cricket: 'Father and both brothers (Richard and Simon) are closely associated with Weston-super-Mare CC. Simon played for Somerset in 1984, also as a wicket-keeper. My wife, Lucy, plays for MCC Ladies and Somerset Ladies (also as a wicket-keeper!)'
Education: Broadoak Comprehensive, Weston-super-Mare; Millfield School, Street; Magdalene College, Cambridge University
Qualifications: BA (Hons) Engineering, Diploma in Computer Science, NCA coaching award, approved person under the Financial Services Authority
Career outside cricket: Rowan Dartington stockbrokers
Off-season: 'Working at the Taunton branch office of stockbrokers Rowan Dartington'
Overseas tours: Millfield School to Barbados 1985; Combined Universities to Barbados 1989; Qantas Airlines Tournament, Kuala Lumpur, Malaysia 1992-93; English Lions to New Zealand (Cricket Max) 1997; MCC to New Zealand 1999, to Canada 2000, to Italy 2004; England A to Bangladesh and New Zealand 1999-2000 (vice-captain)
Overseas teams played for: Claremont-Nedlands, Perth, Western Australia 1991-93
Career highlights to date: 'Winning the C&G Trophy 2001 at Lord's – especially catching a skyer to remove Afridi'
Cricket moments to forget: 'Any dropped catch!'
Cricket superstitions: 'Being last out on to the pitch (but that is just an excuse for being late, really!)'

Cricketers particularly admired: Jack Russell, Ricky Ponting
Young players to look out for: Lachlan Cox, Adam Burns, Jamie Turner, Robert and Matthew Bowler, Fraser Caddick, Felix Rose, Jack and Thomas Shine, Thomas Dutch, Joseph Parsons
Other sports played: Golf ('badly, but holed in one at the par three fourth at Oake Manor GC!')
Other sports followed: Football ('The Villa'), hockey (Taunton Vale Ladies)
Favourite band: 'Theraband'
Relaxations: 'Being entertained by my son; curry club on away trips'
Extras: Captain of Cambridge University (Blue 1988-91) and Combined Universities 1991. Wombwell Cricket Lovers' Society Wicket-keeper of the Year 1999. Highest-placed Englishman in the 1999 batting averages (6th with 1217 runs at 52.91). Sheffield Cricket Lovers' Society Allrounder of the Year 1999. Was on stand-by for England tours of West Indies 1997-98 and South Africa and Zimbabwe 1999-2000. Made nine dismissals (all caught) in the match v Surrey at Taunton 2001, breaking his own (shared) Somerset record. Took seven catches in an innings v Northamptonshire at Taunton 2001, breaking his own (shared) Somerset record. Wombwell Cricket Lovers' Society Highlight of the Year 2001 (for catching Shahid Afridi in the C&G final)
Opinions on cricket: 'Twenty20 proved to be a great success once more. It shows that the public enjoy this format of the game and I'm sure we'll see more of it in years to come.'
Best batting: 144 Somerset v Kent, Taunton 1997

2004 Season

	M	Inns	NO	Runs	HS	Avge	100s	50s	Ct	St	O	M	Runs	Wkts	Avge	Best	5wI	10wM
Test																		
All First	16	18	3	346	46	23.06	-	-	61	4								
1-day Int																		
C & G	2	2	1	7	5	7.00	-	-	3	-								
totesport	6	5	4	68	24 *	68.00	-	-	9	1								
Twenty20																		

Career Performances

	M	Inns	NO	Runs	HS	Avge	100s	50s	Ct	St	Balls	Runs	Wkts	Avge	Best	5wI	10wM
Test																	
All First	241	367	67	9242	144	30.80	10	45	681	49	79	58	0	-	-	-	-
1-day Int																	
C & G	31	25	10	511	52	34.06	-	2	46	3							
totesport	150	130	43	2086	67	23.97	-	6	141	27							
Twenty20	5	4	0	24	11	6.00	-	-	3	-							

UDAL, S. D. Hampshire

Name: Shaun David Udal
Role: Right-hand bat, off-spin bowler
Born: 18 March 1969, Farnborough, Hants
Height: 6ft 3in **Weight:** 14st
Nickname: Shaggy
County debut: 1989
County cap: 1992
Benefit: 2002
One-Day Internationals: 10
50 wickets in a season: 7
1st-Class 50s: 28
1st-Class 100s: 1
1st-Class 5 w. in innings: 30
1st-Class 10 w. in match: 4
1st-Class catches: 105
One-Day 5 w. in innings: 1
Place in batting averages: 113th av. 34.85 (2003 162nd av. 27.11)
Place in bowling averages: 9th av. 22.28 (2003 71st av. 32.14)
Strike rate: 38.10 (career 67.39)
Parents: Robin and Mary
Wife and date of marriage: Emma Jane, 5 October 1991
Children: Katherine Mary, 26 August 1992; Rebecca Jane, 17 November 1995
Family links with cricket: Grandfather (G. F. Udal) played for Leicestershire and Middlesex. Father played for Camberley CC for over 40 years and also for Surrey Colts; brother Gary plays for Camberley 1st XI
Education: Cove Comprehensive
Qualifications: 8 CSEs, print finisher, company director
Overseas tours: England to Australia 1994-95; England A to Pakistan 1995-96; England XI to New Zealand (Cricket Max) 1997; Hampshire to Anguilla 1998, to Cape Town 2001
Overseas teams played for: Hamilton Wickham, Newcastle, NSW 1989-90
Career highlights to date: 'Winning B&H, NatWest and promotion with Hants. Playing for England'
Cricket moments to forget: 'Getting out twice as nightwatchman hooking'
Cricket superstitions: 'Left side on first'
Cricketers particularly admired: Ian Botham, Shane Warne, Robin Smith
Young players to look out for: Chris Tremlett
Other sports played: Football, golf (12 handicap)
Other sports followed: Football (West Ham Utd, Aldershot Town)
Favourite band: Blue

Relaxations: 'Going out for a beer and meal; living life to the full; my children'
Extras: Has taken two hat-tricks in club cricket. Has scored a double hundred (202) in a 40-over club game. Man of the Match on NatWest debut against Berkshire 1991. Named Hampshire Cricket Association Player of the Year 1993. Vice-captain of Hampshire 1998-2000. Hampshire Players' Player of the Year 2001, 2002. Recorded Hampshire record benefit 2002. Took 600th first-class wicket for Hampshire (Chris Rogers) v Derbyshire at West End 2004
Opinions on cricket: 'Finger spin is slowly dying as batters see it as their chance for quick runs and try to smash you! Keep supporting county cricket – it is where we all started, even the England contracted players!'
Best batting: 117* Hampshire v Warwickshire, Southampton 1997
Best bowling: 8-50 Hampshire v Sussex, Southampton 1992

2004 Season

	M	Inns	NO	Runs	HS	Avge	100s	50s	Ct	St	O	M	Runs	Wkts	Avge	Best	5wI	10wM
Test																		
All First	13	17	3	488	74	34.85	-	3	8	-	247.4	40	869	39	22.28	6-79	1	-
1-day Int																		
C & G	2	2	1	30	17 *	30.00	-	-	-	-	8	0	40	0	-	-	-	
totesport	13	10	3	74	30 *	10.57	-	-	4	-	95	2	429	14	30.64	4-46	-	
Twenty20	6	6	0	81	37	13.50	-	-	1	-	18	0	120	7	17.14	2-22	-	

Career Performances

	M	Inns	NO	Runs	HS	Avge	100s	50s	Ct	St	Balls	Runs	Wkts	Avge	Best	5wI	10wM
Test																	
All First	229	327	61	6269	117 *	23.56	1	28	105	-	43338	21324	643	33.16	8-50	30	4
1-day Int	10	6	4	35	11 *	17.50	-	-	1	-	570	371	8	46.37	2-37	-	
C & G	33	15	7	169	39 *	21.12	-	-	12	-	1803	1077	40	26.92	4-20	-	
totesport	219	148	43	1563	78	14.88	-	8	75	-	9354	7356	246	29.90	5-43	1	
Twenty20	10	9	2	93	37	13.28	-	-	2	-	180	226	10	22.60	2-22	-	

90. Which Sri Lanka seamer took 17 wickets in the 1983 World Cup, finishing one behind Roger Binny of India?

VAAS, W. P. U. J. C. Worcestershire

Name: Warnakulasuriya Patabendige Ushantha Joseph Chaminda Vaas
Role: Left-hand bat, left-arm fast-medium bowler
Born: 27 January 1974, Mattumagala, Sri Lanka
County debut: 2003 (Hampshire)
Test debut: 1994-95
Tests: 80
One-Day Internationals: 244
1st-Class 50s: 13
1st-Class 100s: 1
1st-Class 5 w. in innings: 20
1st-Class 10 w. in match: 2
1st-Class catches: 40
One-Day 5 w. in innings: 3
Strike rate: (career 54.81)
Overseas tours: Sri Lanka U19 to England 1992; Sri Lanka to India 1993-94, to Zimbabwe 1994-95, to South Africa 1994-95, to New Zealand 1994-95, to Pakistan 1995-96, to Australia 1995-96, to India and Pakistan (World Cup) 1995-96, to New Zealand 1996-97, to India 1997-98, to South Africa 1997-98, to Bangladesh (Wills International Cup) 1998-99, to UK, Ireland and Holland (World Cup) 1999, to Zimbabwe 1999-2000, to Pakistan 1999-2000, to Kenya (ICC Knockout Trophy) 2000-01, to South Africa 2000-01, to England 2002, to South Africa 2002-03, to Africa (World Cup) 2002-03, to West Indies 2003, to Zimbabwe 2004, to Australia 2004, to England (ICC Champions Trophy) 2004, to Pakistan 2004-05, to New Zealand 2004-05, plus numerous other one-day series and tournaments in Sharjah, Singapore, West Indies, Kenya, India, Pakistan, Australia, Bangladesh, New Zealand and Morocco; FICA World XI to New Zealand 2004-05
Overseas teams played for: Colts CC, Sri Lanka 1990-91 –
Extras: Had match figures of 14-191 (7-120/7-71) in the third Test v West Indies at Colombo 2001-02, becoming only the second pace bowler (after Imran Khan) to take 14 wickets in a Test on the subcontinent. Five days later took 8-19 v Zimbabwe in the LG Abans Triangular Series at Colombo 2001-02, a new world's best analysis for ODIs; his figures included a hat-trick (Carlisle, Wishart, Taibu) as Zimbabwe were bowled out for 38. Took a hat-trick (Hannan Sarkar, Mohammad Ashraful, Ehsanul Haque) with the first three balls of the match v Bangladesh at Pietermaritzburg in the World Cup 2002-03; took a further wicket in the same over and finished with 6-25. Took 300th ODI wicket (Alester Maregwede) in the third ODI v Zimbabwe at Harare 2004. His Test awards include Man of the Series v South Africa 2004 and Man of the Match in the first Test v New Zealand at Napier 1994-95 (5-47/5-43) and in the following Test at Dunedin. His ODI awards include Man of the Match in the first ODI

v England at Dambulla 2003-04 (3-15) and in the first ODI v South Africa at Colombo 2004 (4-33). Was an overseas player with Hampshire in the latter part of the 2003 season. Has joined Worcestershire as an overseas player for the early part of the 2005 season

Best batting: 104 Uva Province v North Central Province, Dambulla 2003-04
Best bowling: 7-71 Sri Lanka v West Indies, Colombo 2001-02

2004 Season

	M	Inns	NO	Runs	HS	Avge	100s	50s	Ct	St	O	M	Runs	Wkts	Avge	Best	5wI	10wM
Test																		
All First																		
1-day Int	2	0	0	0	0	-	-	-	-	-	20	1	93	3	31.00	2-51	-	
C & G																		
totesport																		
Twenty20																		

Career Performances

	M	Inns	NO	Runs	HS	Avge	100s	50s	Ct	St	Balls	Runs	Wkts	Avge	Best	5wI	10wM
Test	80	114	21	1963	74 *	21.10	-	8	23	-	17598	7778	262	29.68	7-71	9	2
All First	134	174	37	2884	104	21.05	1	13	40	-	26255	11878	479	24.79	7-71	20	2
1-day Int	244	165	54	1557	50 *	14.02	-	1	48	-	11962	8230	315	26.12	8-19	3	
C & G																	
totesport	8	4	2	35	28 *	17.50	-	-	2	-	399	284	9	31.55	2-24	-	
Twenty20																	

91. Which bowler appeared for Derbyshire between 1983 and 1994 and represented Denmark in four ICC Trophy tournaments?

VAN BUNGE, D. L. S. — Middlesex

Name: Daan Lodewijk Samuel van Bunge
Role: Right-hand top-order bat, leg-spin bowler
Born: 19 October 1982, Leidschendam, Holland
Height: 6ft 4in **Weight:** 15st 10lbs
Nickname: Bungey, VB
County debut: 2004 (one-day)
One-Day Internationals: 8
1st-Class catches: 2
Parents: Alfred and Ludy
Marital status: Single
Family links with cricket: 'Brother Job represented Holland senior side and brother Coen played for almost all the junior Holland teams'
Qualifications: 'Finished high school in Holland; have done many courses as part of the MCC Young Cricketers scheme'
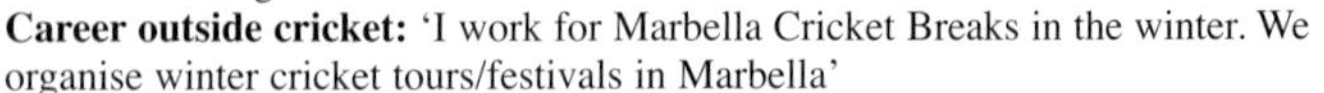
Career outside cricket: 'I work for Marbella Cricket Breaks in the winter. We organise winter cricket tours/festivals in Marbella'
Off-season: 'Going to Dhaka in February 2005'
Overseas tours: Holland U15 to England (U15 World Cup) 1996; Holland U19 to Sri Lanka (U19 World Cup) 1999-2000; Holland to Northern Ireland (European Championships) 2002, to Sri Lanka (ICC Champions Trophy) 2002-03, to Africa (World Cup) 2002-03, to UAE (ICC Six Nations Challenge) 2003-04
Overseas teams played for: Voorburg CC, Holland; Claremont, Cape Town 2000; Northerns-Goodwood, Cape Town 2001-02; Colombo CC, Sri Lanka 2003
Career highlights to date: 'Scoring 62 v India in our opening match at the 2002-03 World Cup and taking 3-16 v England (Vaughan, Flintoff and Knight). Sharing winning partnership with Bas Zuiderent v USA in Dubai in the ICC Champions Trophy qualification tournament. Scoring the fastest 100 in the history of MCC Young Cricketers (*38 balls v Surrey U19 at Weybridge 2004; ended up with 121*)'
Cricket moments to forget: 'Breaking my jaw against an English touring side in 1998. Holland were playing against South Korea in the football World Cup and as a youngster I was sent in to open the batting as everyone else was watching the footie. Quite upset that I had to open and not fully focused, I had my jaw broken by the first ball that was bowled at me. Holland won 5-0, I think; that was the only bright thing that day'
Cricket superstitions: 'While batting, if I see an insect I never kill it. I always brush it gently away'

Cricketers particularly admired: Richie Richardson, Shane Warne, Andy Flower, Tim de Leede
Young players to look out for: Damian Shirazi, Frederik Klokker; Alexei Kervesee, Floris Kingma ('in my eyes the two biggest talents in Holland')
Other sports played: Hockey (scored four goals in final of national U15 club championship in Holland), tennis, golf, squash
Other sports followed: Football ('Premiership and the Dutch League, in particular Ajax FC'), tennis ('all the grand slams'), Olympic Games, 'all the big events, really'
Injuries: Out for three weeks with an injury to the lower back
Favourite band: Bryan Adams
Relaxations: 'Other sports – watching and playing; music, movies, PlayStation'
Extras: Kept wicket for Holland U15 at the U15 World Cup 1996. Attended Dutch Cricket Academy, Cape Town 2000-03. Represented Holland in the C&G 2004, including the first round, which was played in August 2003. Represented Holland in the 2004 European Championships. Made first-class debut for Holland v Scotland at Aberdeen in the ICC Inter-Continental Cup 2004. MCC Young Cricketer 2003-04. Left Middlesex at the end of the 2004 season
Opinions on cricket: 'I think that B-playing cricket nations do not play enough cricket at the highest level. It's really strange that a country like Holland can only compete on the international stage every four years. It's like going from nothing to playing in the biggest scene there is – the World Cup. It takes a lot of time to get to a certain level of cricket and it's obvious that you have to play a lot on that level if you want to close the gap with the likes of the top international teams.'
Best batting: 19 Holland v Scotland, Aberdeen 2004

2004 Season

	M	Inns	NO	Runs	HS	Avge	100s	50s	Ct	St	O	M	Runs	Wkts	Avge	Best	5wI	10wM
Test																		
All First	1	2	0	19	19	9.50	-	-	2	-	5	0	26	0	-	-	-	-
1-day Int																		
C & G	1	1	0	14	14	14.00	-	-	-	-								
totesport	3	2	0	11	11	5.50	-	-	-	-								
Twenty20	3	2	0	8	7	4.00	-	-	-	-								

Career Performances

	M	Inns	NO	Runs	HS	Avge	100s	50s	Ct	St	Balls	Runs	Wkts	Avge	Best	5wI	10wM
Test																	
All First	1	2	0	19	19	9.50	-	-	2	-	30	26	0	-	-	-	-
1-day Int	8	7	0	139	62	19.85	-	1	2	-	72	85	5	17.00	3-16	-	
C & G	2	2	0	50	36	25.00	-	-	-	-							
totesport	3	2	0	11	11	5.50	-	-	-	-							
Twenty20	3	2	0	8	7	4.00	-	-	-	-							

VAN JAARSVELD, M. Kent

Name: Martin van Jaarsveld
Role: Right-hand top-order bat
Born: 18 June 1974, Klerksdorp, South Africa
Height: 6ft 2in **Weight:** 12st 12lbs
Nickname: Jarre
County debut: 2004 (Northamptonshire)
Test debut: 2002-03
Tests: 7
One-Day Internationals: 11
1st-Class 50s: 29
1st-Class 100s: 18
1st-Class 200s: 1
1st-Class catches: 114
Place in batting averages: 89th av. 37.23
Strike rate: (career 112.16)
Parents: Leon and Isobel
Marital status: Single
Education: Warmbads High School; University of Pretoria
Qualifications: BComm (Financial Management)
Overseas tours: South Africa A to Sri Lanka 1998, to Zimbabwe (one-day series) 2002-03, to Australia 2002-03; South African Academy to Zimbabwe 1998-99; South Africa to England 2003, to New Zealand 2003-04, to Sri Lanka 2004, to England (ICC Champions Trophy) 2004, to India 2004-05
Overseas teams played for: Northern Transvaal/Northerns Titans 1994-95 – 2003-04; Titans 2004-05 –
Career highlights to date: 'Playing for South Africa. Being chosen as one of the five Cricketers of the Year in South Africa 2002'
Cricket moments to forget: 'Losing the NatWest Series final at Lord's, July 2003'
Cricket superstitions: 'Left pad first when padding up'
Cricketers particularly admired: Michael Atherton, Kepler Wessels
Other sports played: Golf, tennis
Other sports followed: Rugby, 'and most other sports'
Favourite band: Live
Relaxations: 'Having throw-downs; going to the cinema'
Extras: Made first-class debut for Northern Transvaal B v Natal B at Durban 1994-95. Player of the SuperSport Series 2001-02 for his 934 runs at 84.90; also topped South African first-class averages for the season with 1268 runs at 74.58. Scored 182* and 158* v Griqualand West at Centurion 2001-02, becoming only the second batsman to record two 150s in the same match in South Africa and setting a new record individual aggregate score for South African first-class cricket (340). One of *South African*

Cricket Annual's five Cricketers of the Year 2002. Played for Suffolk in the first round of the C&G 2004, which was played in August 2003. Was an overseas player with Northamptonshire 2004. C&G Man of the Match award for his 93* v Ireland at Dublin 2004. Has joined Kent for 2005; is no longer considered an overseas player
Best batting: 238* Northerns v Griqualand West, Kimberley 1999-2000
Best bowling: 1-1 Northerns v Boland, Centurion 1998-99
Stop press: Man of the Match v Western Province Boland at Benoni in the SuperSport Series 2004-05 (236*). Retired from international cricket in February 2005

2004 Season

	M	Inns	NO	Runs	HS	Avge	100s	50s	Ct	St	O	M	Runs	Wkts	Avge	Best	5wI	10wM
Test																		
All First	7	13	0	484	114	37.23	1	1	7	-	4	2	8	0	-	-	-	-
1-day Int	2	1	0	0	0	0.00	-	-	1	-								
C & G	3	3	1	206	93 *	103.00	-	2	-	-	0.1	0	1	1	1.00	1-1	-	
totesport	7	7	2	246	96 *	49.20	-	2	4	-	3	1	18	1	18.00	1-18	-	
Twenty20	5	5	1	174	61 *	43.50	-	2	3	-	2	0	15	1	15.00	1-15	-	

Career Performances

	M	Inns	NO	Runs	HS	Avge	100s	50s	Ct	St	Balls	Runs	Wkts	Avge	Best	5wI	10wM
Test	7	11	2	332	73	36.88	-	3	9	-	42	28	0	-	-	-	-
All First	98	165	15	6677	238 *	44.51	19	29	114	-	673	374	6	62.33	1-1	-	-
1-day Int	11	7	1	124	45	20.66	-	-	4	-	31	18	2	9.00	1-0	-	
C & G	4	4	1	227	93 *	75.66	-	2	3	-	61	51	1	51.00	1-1	-	
totesport	7	7	2	246	96 *	49.20	-	2	4	-	18	18	1	18.00	1-18	-	
Twenty20	5	5	1	174	61 *	43.50	-	2	3	-	12	15	1	15.00	1-15	-	

92. Which India Test player once hit Bob Willis for 24
in an over at Old Trafford and later coached Kenya to a World Cup
semi-final in 2002-03?

VAUGHAN, M. P. — Yorkshire

Name: Michael Paul Vaughan
Role: Right-hand bat, off-spin bowler
Born: 29 October 1974, Eccles, Manchester
Height: 6ft 2in **Weight:** 11st 7lbs
Nickname: Frankie, Virgil
County debut: 1993
County cap: 1995
Test debut: 1999-2000
Tests: 50
One-Day Internationals: 56
1000 runs in a season: 4
1st-Class 50s: 54
1st-Class 100s: 36
1st-Class catches: 101
One-Day 100s: 2
Place in batting averages: 54th av. 46.00 (2003 86th av. 38.06)
Strike rate: (career 80.65)
Parents: Graham John and Dee
Wife and date of marriage: Nichola, September 2003
Children: Tallulah Grace, 4 June 2004
Family links with cricket: Father played league cricket for Worsley CC. Brother plays for Sheffield Collegiate. Mother is related to the famous Tyldesley family (Lancashire and England)
Education: Silverdale Comprehensive, Sheffield
Qualifications: 7 GCSEs
Off-season: Touring with England
Overseas tours: Yorkshire to West Indies 1994, to South Africa 1995, to Zimbabwe 1996; England U19 to India 1992-93, to Sri Lanka 1993-94 (captain); England A to India 1994-95, to Australia 1996-97, to Zimbabwe and South Africa 1998-99 (captain); England to South Africa 1999-2000, to Pakistan and Sri Lanka 2000-01, to India and New Zealand 2001-02, to Australia 2002-03, to Africa (World Cup) 2002-03, to Bangladesh and Sri Lanka 2003-04 (captain), to West Indies 2003-04 (captain), to Zimbabwe (one-day series) 2004-05 (captain), to South Africa 2004-05 (captain)
Cricketers particularly admired: Darren Lehmann, 'all the Yorkshire and England squads'
Other sports played: Football (Baslow FC), golf (10 handicap)
Other sports followed: Football (Sheffield Wednesday), all golf
Relaxations: Most sports. 'Enjoy a good meal with friends'
Extras: *Daily Telegraph* U15 Batsman of the Year 1990; Maurice Leyland Batting Award 1990; Cricket Society's Most Promising Young Cricketer 1993; A. A. Thompson Memorial Trophy – The Roses Cricketer of the Year 1993. Scored 1066

runs in first full season of first-class cricket 1994. Captained England U19. Scored maiden Test century (120) at Old Trafford 2001, in the process sharing with Graham Thorpe (138) in a record partnership for any wicket for England in Tests v Pakistan (267). Took part in first-wicket stand of 50 in five overs with Marcus Trescothick to bring England victory with an over to spare in the third Test v Sri Lanka at Old Trafford 2002. Scored 195 in the fourth Test v India at The Oval 2002, in the process becoming only the sixth batsman to score four Test centuries in an English summer. PCA Player of the Year 2002. Highest-scoring batsman in Test cricket for the calendar year 2002 with 1481 runs. One of *Wisden*'s Five Cricketers of the Year 2003. Topped PricewaterhouseCoopers rankings for Test batsmen in early summer 2003. Vodafone Cricketer of the Year 2002-03. His international awards include England's Man of the [Test] Series v India 2002 (615 runs at 102.50, including three centuries) and Man of the [Test] Series v Australia 2002-03 (633 runs at 63.30, including three centuries), as well as Man of the Match in the fourth Test v West Indies at his home ground of Headingley 2000, in the second Test v Sri Lanka at Kandy 2003-04 (52/105), and v Australia at Edgbaston in the ICC Champions Trophy 2004 (86/2-42 plus run-out). England one-day captain since May 2003 and England Test captain since July 2003. Book *A Year in the Sun* published 2003. C&G Man of the Match award for his 116* v Lancashire at Old Trafford 2004. Scored century in each innings (103/101*) in the first Test v West Indies 2004, becoming only the third player to score twin Test hundreds at Lord's. Granted a benefit for 2005. ECB contract 2004-05
Best batting: 197 England v India, Trent Bridge 2002
Best bowling: 4-39 Yorkshire v Oxford University, The Parks 1994
Stop press: Passed 4000 runs in Test cricket during his second innings in the fifth Test v South Africa at Centurion 2004-05

2004 Season

	M	Inns	NO	Runs	HS	Avge	100s	50s	Ct	St	O	M	Runs	Wkts	Avge	Best	5wI	10wM
Test	6	10	1	414	103	46.00	2	2	7	-	7	0	25	0	-	-	-	-
All First	6	10	1	414	103	46.00	2	2	7	-	7	0	25	0	-	-	-	-
1-day Int	12	12	0	240	86	20.00	-	2	7	-	26	0	136	2	68.00	2-42	-	
C & G	2	2	1	146	116 *	146.00	1	-	-	-								
totesport	2	2	0	89	57	44.50	-	1	2	-	8	0	46	0	-	-	-	
Twenty20																		

Career Performances

	M	Inns	NO	Runs	HS	Avge	100s	50s	Ct	St	Balls	Runs	Wkts	Avge	Best	5wI	10wM
Test	50	89	6	3777	197	45.50	13	10	32	-	840	487	5	97.40	2-71	-	-
All First	209	368	22	13336	197	38.54	36	54	101	-	9114	5092	113	45.06	4-39	-	-
1-day Int	56	54	4	1228	86	24.56	-	9	17	-	490	414	10	41.40	4-22	-	
C & G	27	26	3	822	116 *	35.73	1	5	7	-	342	217	6	36.16	1-4	-	
totesport	97	95	6	2092	90	23.50	-	10	31	-	1076	891	31	28.74	4-27	-	
Twenty20																	

VOROS, J. A. Sussex

Name: Jason Alexander Voros
Role: Left-hand lower-middle-order bat, left-arm fast-medium bowler
Born: 31 December 1976, Canberra, Australia
Height: 6ft 2in **Weight:** 14st 6lbs
Nickname: JV, Oz
County debut: 2004
Strike rate: 25.00 (career 25.00)
Parents: Peter and Debbie
Marital status: Single
Family links with cricket: 'Dad coached me for five years'
Education: Daramalan College, Canberra
Qualifications: Year 10 and Year 12, Levels 1 and 2 cricket coaching
Career outside cricket: Coaching
Overseas teams played for: Western District CC, ACT 1993-99; Canberra Comets 1998-2000; Sunshine Coast, Queensland 1999-2001; Australian Capital Territory 1998-99
Career highlights to date: 'Man of the Match v Tasmania – took 3-28 and a classic catch in a televised match' (*ACT v Tasmania at Canberra in the Mercantile Mutual Cup 1998-99*)
Cricket moments to forget: 'Going for 85 runs off nine overs at the hands of Adam Gilchrist and Damien Martyn'
Cricket superstitions: 'None'
Cricketers particularly admired: Dennis Lillee, Merv Hughes, Wasim Akram
Young players to look out for: Sam Latus, Jack Latus, Tim Appleyard, Chris Gray
Other sports played: Golf, tennis, rugby union (Australian Schoolboys 1996)
Other sports followed: Football (Arsenal)
Favourite band: Hunters and Collectors, Crowded House
Extras: 'Life-saving back in Oz.' Played for Commonwealth Bank [Australian] Cricket Academy 1999-2001. Was in Queensland Bulls training squad 2000-01. Played for Sussex 2nd XI 2003. Took 4-40 on Sussex debut v Loughborough University CCE at Hove 2004
Opinions on cricket: 'I think there should be more focus on bringing our juniors through. There is not enough four-day and five-day cricket played for younger cricketers.'
Best batting: 3* Sussex v LUCCE, Hove 2004
Best bowling: 4-40 Sussex v LUCCE, Hove 2004

2004 Season

	M	Inns	NO	Runs	HS	Avge	100s	50s	Ct	St	O	M	Runs	Wkts	Avge	Best	5wI	10wM
Test																		
All First	1	1	1	3	3 *	-	-	-	-	-	20.5	6	62	5	12.40	4-40	-	-
1-day Int																		
C & G																		
totesport																		
Twenty20																		

Career Performances

	M	Inns	NO	Runs	HS	Avge	100s	50s	Ct	St	Balls	Runs	Wkts	Avge	Best	5wI	10wM
Test																	
All First	1	1	1	3	3 *	-	-	-	-	-	125	62	5	12.40	4-40	-	-
1-day Int																	
C & G																	
totesport																	
Twenty20																	

WAGG, G. G. — Warwickshire

Name: Graham Grant Wagg
Role: Right-hand bat, left-arm fast-medium bowler
Born: 28 April 1983, Rugby
Height: 6ft **Weight:** 12st 10lbs
Nickname: Stiggy, Waggy, Captain Caveman, Wild Card, Ug
County debut: 2002
1st-Class 50s: 2
1st-Class catches: 2
Strike rate: 27.00 (career 45.60)
Parents: John and Dawn
Marital status: Single
Family links with cricket: Father is qualified coach
Education: Ashlawn School, Rugby
Qualifications: Level 1 cricket coach
Overseas tours: Warwickshire Development tour to South Africa 1998, to West Indies 2000; England A to Malaysia and India 2003-04
Overseas teams played for: Hams Tech, East London, South Africa 1999
Career highlights to date: 'Four wickets and 50 on first-class debut'

Cricketers particularly admired: Stuart MacGill, John Wagg
Other sports played: Golf, carp fishing
Other sports followed: Football (Man United), cricket (Leamington CC)
Relaxations: 'Fishing, music, clubbing'
Extras: Represented England U16, U17, U18 and U19. Member of Warwickshire's ECB U19 County Championship winning squad 2001. Took 5-57 and scored 40* for Development of Excellence (Midlands) XI v West Indies U19 at Oakham School 2001. Scored 42* from 50 balls, 51 from 57 balls and took 4-43 on first-class debut v Somerset at Edgbaston 2002. Took 4-50 on NUL debut v Kent at Edgbaston 2002. Struck 52-ball 74 (including 14 balls to get off the mark) v India A at Edgbaston 2003. ECB National Academy 2003-04. NBC Denis Compton Award for the most promising young Warwickshire player 2003. Suspended from cricket until January 2006 by an ECB disciplinary panel after he failed a drugs test in September 2004 and admitted having taken cocaine; released by Warwickshire
Best batting: 74 Warwickshire v India A, Edgbaston 2003
Best bowling: 4-43 Warwickshire v Somerset, Edgbaston 2002

2004 Season

	M	Inns	NO	Runs	HS	Avge	100s	50s	Ct	St	O	M	Runs	Wkts	Avge	Best	5wI	10wM
Test																		
All First	1	0	0	0	0	-	-	-	-	-	18	7	33	4	8.25	3-21	-	-
1-day Int																		
C & G	1	0	0	0	0	-	-	-	-	-	4	1	17	1	17.00	1-17	-	
totesport	11	8	0	124	35	15.50	-	-	1	-	19	0	111	2	55.50	1-38	-	
Twenty20	4	3	1	59	25	29.50	-	-	1	-								

Career Performances

	M	Inns	NO	Runs	HS	Avge	100s	50s	Ct	St	Balls	Runs	Wkts	Avge	Best	5wI	10wM
Test																	
All First	10	15	2	284	74	21.84	-	2	2	-	1049	726	23	31.56	4-43	-	-
1-day Int																	
C & G	5	4	0	41	21	10.25	-	-	1	-	168	128	4	32.00	3-35	-	
totesport	18	12	1	200	35	18.18	-	-	6	-	402	387	13	29.76	4-50	-	
Twenty20	11	9	1	111	25	13.87	-	-	2	-	102	134	8	16.75	3-33	-	

93. Where did Sri Lanka and Canada contest the final of the first ICC Trophy tournament?

WAGH, M. A. — Warwickshire

Name: Mark Anant Wagh
Role: Right-hand bat, off-spin bowler
Born: 20 October 1976, Birmingham
Height: 6ft 2in **Weight:** 13st
Nickname: Waggy
County debut: 1997
County cap: 2000
1000 runs in a season: 3
1st-Class 50s: 32
1st-Class 100s: 16
1st-Class 200s: 1
1st-Class 300s: 1
1st-Class 5 w. in innings: 2
1st-Class catches: 69
One-Day 100s: 1
Place in batting averages: 91st av. 36.89 (2003 47th av. 45.48)
Place in bowling averages: 145th av. 51.00 (2003 99th av. 36.50)
Strike rate: 91.90 (career 87.27)
Parents: Mohan and Rita
Marital status: Single
Education: King Edward's School, Birmingham; Keble College, Oxford
Qualifications: BA degree, Level 2 coaching award
Overseas tours: Warwickshire U19 to South Africa 1992; ECB National Academy to Australia 2001-02
Career highlights to date: '315 at Lord's 2001'
Cricket moments to forget: 'Too many to mention'
Cricketers particularly admired: Andy Flower
Young players to look out for: Moeen Ali
Favourite band: Dido
Extras: Oxford Blue 1996-98; Oxford University captain 1997. Scored maiden first-class century (116) v Glamorgan at The Parks 1997, following up with another 100 (101) in the second innings to become the first batsman since 1974 to score a century in each innings of a match for Oxford University. Attended Zimbabwe Cricket Academy 1999. His 315 v Middlesex at Lord's 2001 is the second highest score by a batsman for Warwickshire (behind Brian Lara's 501* in 1994) and the equal second highest individual Championship score made at Lord's (behind Jack Hobbs's 316 in 1926). C&G Man of the Match award for his 102* (his maiden one-day century) v Kent at Edgbaston 2004. Included in preliminary England one-day squad of 30 for ICC Champions Trophy 2004

Best batting: 315 Warwickshire v Middlesex, Lord's 2001
Best bowling: 7-222 Warwickshire v Lancashire, Edgbaston 2003

2004 Season

	M	Inns	NO	Runs	HS	Avge	100s	50s	Ct	St	O	M	Runs	Wkts	Avge	Best	5wI	10wM
Test																		
All First	17	30	2	1033	167	36.89	2	5	16	-	306.2	56	1020	20	51.00	3-85	-	-
1-day Int																		
C & G	4	4	1	165	102 *	55.00	1	-	-	-	9	0	61	3	20.33	2-31	-	
totesport	15	13	1	349	83	29.08	-	3	6	-	58.4	0	252	12	21.00	4-35	-	
Twenty20	6	6	0	74	28	12.33	-	-	2	-	12.3	0	106	5	21.20	2-16	-	

Career Performances

	M	Inns	NO	Runs	HS	Avge	100s	50s	Ct	St	Balls	Runs	Wkts	Avge	Best	5wI	10wM
Test																	
All First	125	208	18	7335	315	38.60	18	32	69	-	8553	4553	98	46.45	7-222	2	-
1-day Int																	
C & G	10	10	1	256	102 *	28.44	1	-	1	-	168	142	6	23.66	3-35	-	
totesport	48	44	3	1031	84	25.14	-	8	11	-	754	601	16	37.56	4-35	-	
Twenty20	7	6	0	74	28	12.33	-	-	2	-	75	106	5	21.20	2-16	-	

WAINWRIGHT, D. J. — Yorkshire

Name: David John Wainwright
Role: Left-hand bat, left-arm orthodox spin bowler
Born: 21 March 1985, Pontefract
Height: 5ft 9in **Weight:** 9st 3lbs
Nickname: Wainers
County debut: 2004
Parents: Paul and Debbie
Marital status: Single
Family links with cricket: 'Grandfather (Harry Heritage) represented Yorkshire Schoolboys 1950-51'
Education: Hemsworth High School; Hemsworth Arts and Community College; Loughborough University
Qualifications: 10 GCSEs, 3 A-levels, Level 1 coaching
Off-season: 'Studying Physics and Sports Science at Loughborough University'
Overseas tours: Yorkshire U15 to South Africa 2000

Career highlights to date: 'Making Yorkshire 1st XI debut in 2004 v Somerset'
Cricketers particularly admired: Brian Lara, Daniel Vettori
Young players to look out for: Tim Bresnan, Joe Sayers
Other sports played: Football, golf
Other sports followed: Football (Liverpool FC)
Favourite band: Jackson Five
Relaxations: Listening to music
Extras: Best bowling award at Bunbury Festival for North of England U15. Is a junior professional at Yorkshire
Opinions on cricket: 'I feel that the game is moving forward, with the introduction of Twenty20 helping to widen the fan-base. England's success is also helping to promote the game at grass-roots level.'
Best batting: 5 Yorkshire v Somerset, Taunton 2004

2004 Season

	M	Inns	NO	Runs	HS	Avge	100s	50s	Ct	St	O	M	Runs	Wkts	Avge	Best	5wI	10wM
Test																		
All First	1	1	0	5	5	5.00	-	-	-	-	3	1	5	0	-	-	-	-
1-day Int																		
C & G																		
totesport																		
Twenty20																		

Career Performances

	M	Inns	NO	Runs	HS	Avge	100s	50s	Ct	St	Balls	Runs	Wkts	Avge	Best	5wI	10wM
Test																	
All First	1	1	0	5	5	5.00	-	-	-	-	18	5	0	-	-	-	-
1-day Int																	
C & G																	
totesport																	
Twenty20																	

94. Which former Barbados and Warwickshire bowler took 4-33 for East Africa against Bangladesh at Swindon in the 1982 ICC Trophy competition?

WAKE, C. J. Northamptonshire

Name: Cameron John Wake
Role: Right-hand bat, right-arm outswing bowler; all-rounder
Born: 28 June 1985, Kettering
Height: 5ft 11in **Weight:** 12st
Nickname: Wakey
County debut: No first-team appearance
Parents: John and Susan
Marital status: Single
Family links with cricket: Father, John Wake, former captain of Bedfordshire CCC, ECB staff coach, master i/c cricket Oundle School, ESCA chairman 2005
Education: Oundle School, Northamptonshire; Durham University (October 2005)
Qualifications: 9 GCSEs, 3 A-levels, ECB Level II coach
Career outside cricket: Undergraduate BSc Earth Sciences
Off-season: 'Playing cricket and coaching in Paarl, South Africa'
Overseas tours: Northamptonshire U17 to South Africa 2000; Northamptonshire U19 to South Africa 2002; Oundle School 1st XI to Sri Lanka 2003
Overseas teams played for: Wellington CC, Boland, South Africa 2004-05
Career highlights to date: 'Captaining ECB Schools in 2003 and 2004. Contract with Northamptonshire CCC'
Cricket moments to forget: 'My first pair for Northants 2nd XI v Durham 2nd XI'
Cricketers particularly admired: Steve Waugh ('captain'), Jonty Rhodes ('fielder'), Andrew Strauss ('batsman'), John Wake ('bowler!')
Young players to look out for: Patrick Foster, Greg Smith (Oundle School), Dawid Mallan (Paarl Boys HS, South Africa), Chris Goode, Mark Phythian (Northants CCC)
Other sports played: Football and hockey (Northants), rugby
Other sports followed: Football (Newcastle United – 'Toon Army!')
Injuries: 'RTA in South Africa November 2004 – broken ribs and clavicle, collapsed lung; lost half a season in South Africa'
Favourite band: Coldplay
Relaxations: 'Singing and other extra-mural activities with the Barmy Army on tour!'
Extras: Captained England Schools 2003-04, Oundle School and Northamptonshire U19. Is a Northamptonshire Emerging Player
Opinions on cricket: 'Excessive amount of Kolpak players (*see page 9*) coming into the county game. How are young English players going to be given the opportunity to develop their game?'

WALKER, A. Durham

Name: Alan Walker
Role: Left-hand bat, right-arm medium-fast bowler
Born: 7 July 1962, Emley, near Huddersfield
Height: 5ft 11in **Weight:** 13st 7lbs
Nickname: Wacky, Walks
County debut: 1983 (Northants), 1994 (Durham)
County cap: 1987 (Northants)
1st-Class 5 w. in innings: 6
1st-Class 10 w. in match: 1
1st-Class catches: 43
Strike rate: (career 62.52)
Family links with cricket: Grandfather played in local league
Education: Shelley High School
Qualifications: 2 O-levels, 4 CSEs, qualified coal-face worker
Career outside cricket: On Durham CCC coaching staff
Overseas tours: NCA North U19 to Denmark; Northamptonshire to Durban
Overseas teams played for: Uitenhage, South Africa 1984-85, 1987-88; Sunshine, Melbourne 1994-95
Cricketers particularly admired: Dennis Lillee, Richard Hadlee
Other sports followed: Football (Huddersfield Town and Emley), rugby league (Wakefield Trinity)
Extras: Returned best innings and match figures by a Durham bowler in 1995 (8-118 and 14-177) v Essex at Chelmsford. Retired at the end of the 1998 season and joined Durham coaching staff; recalled to the Durham side v Sussex at Riverside in the C&G 2004 due to injuries in the seam bowling department
Best batting: 41* Northamptonshire v Warwickshire, Edgbaston 1987
Best bowling: 8-118 Durham v Essex, Chelmsford 1995

2004 Season

	M	Inns	NO	Runs	HS	Avge	100s	50s	Ct	St	O	M	Runs	Wkts	Avge	Best	5wI	10wM
Test																		
All First																		
1-day Int																		
C & G	1	1	1	23	23 *	-	-	-	-	-								
totesport																		
Twenty20																		

Career Performances

	M	Inns	NO	Runs	HS	Avge	100s	50s	Ct	St	Balls	Runs	Wkts	Avge	Best	5wI	10wM
Test																	
All First	128	142	63	922	41 *	11.67	-	-	43	-	18694	9667	299	32.33	8-118	6	1
1-day Int																	
C & G	25	10	2	102	23 *	12.75	-	-	5	-	1407	825	24	34.37	4-7	-	
totesport	151	44	19	278	30	11.12	-	-	36	-	6156	4908	168	29.21	4-18	-	
Twenty20																	

WALKER, M. J. — Kent

Name: Matthew (Matt) Jonathan Walker
Role: Left-hand bat, right-arm medium bowler, county vice-captain
Born: 2 January 1974, Gravesend
Height: 5ft 6in **Weight:** 13st
Nickname: Walks, Pumba
County debut: 1992-93
County cap: 2000
1000 runs in a season: 2
1st-Class 50s: 26
1st-Class 100s: 13
1st-Class 200s: 1
1st-Class catches: 98
One-Day 100s: 3
Place in batting averages: 23rd av. 55.04 (2003 57th av. 43.79)
Strike rate: 66.00 (career 93.46)
Parents: Richard and June
Wife and date of marriage: Claudia, 25 September 1999
Children: Charlie Jack, 20 November 2002
Family links with cricket: Grandfather Jack played one game for Kent as a wicket-keeper. Father played for Kent and Middlesex 2nd XIs and was on Lord's groundstaff. Mother coached ex-England Ladies captain Megan Lear
Education: King's School, Rochester
Qualifications: 9 GCSEs, 2 A-levels, advanced coaching award
Career outside cricket: 'Property developer'
Off-season: 'A couple of holidays and teaching at St Edmund's School'
Overseas tours: Kent U17 to New Zealand 1990-91; England U19 to Pakistan 1991-92, to India 1992-93 (captain); Kent to Zimbabwe 1992-93, to Port Elizabeth 2001
Career highlights to date: 'Captaining England U19. Winning Norwich Union League 2001'

Cricket moments to forget: 'Losing Lord's [B&H] final against Surrey 1997'
Cricket superstitions: 'None'
Cricketers particularly admired: Sachin Tendulkar, Darren Lehmann, Damien Martyn
Young players to look out for: Charlie Hemphrey, Richard Piesley
Other sports played: Hockey (England U14-U21 [captain U15-U17], Kent U14-U21, South East U16-U18), rugby (Kent U18), football (trials for Chelsea and Gillingham), athletics (Kent U15 javelin champion)
Other sports followed: Football (Charlton Athletic), hockey (Gore Court HC), rugby union (Wasps)
Favourite band: Ryan Adams, Counting Crows, Gavin DeGraw, Keane
Relaxations: Music and films ('avid collector of both')
Extras: Captained England U16 cricket team and England U16 hockey team in same year. Sir John Hobbs Silver Jubilee Memorial Prize for outstanding U16 cricketer 1989; *Daily Telegraph* U15 batting award 1989. Captained England U19 v West Indies U19 1993. Woolwich Kent League's Young Cricketer of the Year 1994. Scored 275* against Somerset in 1996 – the highest ever individual score by a Kent batsman at Canterbury – and was on the pitch for the whole game. Scored 151* and shared in a fifth-wicket partnership of 236 with Michael Carberry (112) as Kent scored a county record fourth-innings 429-5 to beat Worcestershire at Canterbury 2004. Scored century in each innings (157/100*) for the first time, v Sussex at Canterbury 2004. Ealham Award for Fielding Excellence 2003, 2004. Cowdrey Award for Kent Player of the Year 2004. Appointed vice-captain of Kent for 2005. Became an Eminent Roffensian in 1995
Opinions on cricket: 'Should be two up/two down; only one overseas player. Apart from that it's a great game and the sport is in better shape than the press always make it out to be.'
Best batting: 275* Kent v Somerset, Canterbury 1996
Best bowling: 2-21 Kent v Middlesex, Canterbury 2004

2004 Season

	M	Inns	NO	Runs	HS	Avge	100s	50s	Ct	St	O	M	Runs	Wkts	Avge	Best	5wI	10wM
Test																		
All First	17	27	4	1266	157	55.04	4	8	17	-	66	10	228	6	38.00	2-21	-	-
1-day Int																		
C & G	2	1	0	10	10	10.00	-	-	2	-	7	0	31	0	-	-	-	
totesport	16	13	1	271	61	22.58	-	2	7	-	21.2	0	147	5	29.40	3-28	-	
Twenty20	5	5	2	136	48 *	45.33	-	-	-	-								

Career Performances

	M	Inns	NO	Runs	HS	Avge	100s	50s	Ct	St	Balls	Runs	Wkts	Avge	Best	5wI	10wM
Test																	
All First	133	219	25	6529	275 *	33.65	14	26	98	-	1402	791	15	52.73	2-21	-	-
1-day Int																	
C & G	18	16	4	368	73	30.66	-	2	7	-	174	123	2	61.50	1-33	-	
totesport	144	134	16	2914	101	24.69	1	15	34	-	491	442	20	22.10	4-24	-	
Twenty20	10	10	2	220	48 *	27.50	-	-	1	-							

WALKER, N. G. E. Derbyshire

Name: Nicholas Guy Eades Walker
Role: Right-hand bat, right-arm fast-medium bowler; all-rounder
Born: 7 August 1984, Enfield
Height: 6ft 2in **Weight:** 13st 6lbs
Nickname: Walks
County debut: 2004
1st-Class 50s: 2
1st-Class 5 w. in innings: 1
1st-Class catches: 3
Place in batting averages: 93rd av. 36.83
Place in bowling averages: 99th av. 37.05
Strike rate: 50.44 (career 50.44)
Parents: Amanda and Martin
Marital status: 'Taken'
Family links with cricket: 'Brother Duncan plays village cricket on Sundays; brother Robbie captained Oxford Uni college'
Education: Haileybury Imperial Service College; 'two terms at Durham Uni'
Qualifications: Level 1 coach
Career outside cricket: 'Internet sales'
Overseas tours: Haileybury School to South Africa 2000
Overseas teams played for: South Perth, Western Australia 2001-02
Career highlights to date: 'Five-for against Somerset; 80 against Somerset, breaking Derbyshire record for highest score by number 11'
Cricket moments to forget: 'Missing run-out against Yorkshire to bring in number 11 with two overs to go'
Cricket superstitions: 'Too many'
Cricketers particularly admired: Ian Botham, Kevin Dean, Graeme Welch
Young players to look out for: James Chapman, James Hildreth, Paul Havell
Other sports played: Badminton (county), rackets, real tennis, golf

Other sports followed: Rugby (Wasps)
Injuries: Out for two weeks with a pre-stress fracture of the back
Favourite band: Tracy Chapman
Extras: Played for Hertfordshire in the C&G 2002 and in the first round of the C&G 2004, which was played in August 2003. Struck 57-ball 80 (highest first-class score by a Derbyshire No. 11) in his third Championship innings, then recorded maiden first-class five-wicket return (5-68), both v Somerset at Derby 2004. Struck 24-ball fifty (ending with 63*), batting at No. 11 v Leicestershire at Oakham School 2004
Opinions on cricket: 'Very good game – long days when fielding! A lot of EU players now coming into the game; not sure if good or bad.'
Best batting: 80 Derbyshire v Somerset, Derby 2004
Best bowling: 5-68 Derbyshire v Somerset, Derby 2004

2004 Season

	M	Inns	NO	Runs	HS	Avge	100s	50s	Ct	St	O	M	Runs	Wkts	Avge	Best	5wI	10wM
Test																		
All First	8	9	3	221	80	36.83	-	2	3	-	151.2	17	667	18	37.05	5-68	1	-
1-day Int																		
C & G																		
totesport	6	4	0	73	43	18.25	-	-	1	-	6	0	30	1	30.00	1-19	-	
Twenty20																		

Career Performances

	M	Inns	NO	Runs	HS	Avge	100s	50s	Ct	St	Balls	Runs	Wkts	Avge	Best	5wI	10wM
Test																	
All First	8	9	3	221	80	36.83	-	2	3	-	908	667	18	37.05	5-68	1	-
1-day Int																	
C & G	2	2	0	13	12	6.50	-	-	2	-	104	114	4	28.50	3-49	-	
totesport	6	4	0	73	43	18.25	-	-	1	-	36	30	1	30.00	1-19	-	
Twenty20																	

95. Who was banned by Sri Lanka for taking part in the 1982-83 Arosa tour to South Africa, then played for Holland in the 1995-96 World Cup, taking Gary Kirsten's wicket in his last ODI?

WALLACE, M. A. Glamorgan

Name: Mark Alexander Wallace
Role: Left-hand bat, wicket-keeper
Born: 19 November 1981, Abergavenny
Height: 5ft 9in **Weight:** 12st
Nickname: Wally, Grommit, Wash
County debut: 1999
County cap: 2003
50 dismissals in a season: 2
1st-Class 50s: 12
1st-Class 100s: 4
1st-Class catches: 202
1st-Class stumpings: 9
Place in batting averages: 161st av. 27.71 (2003 149th av. 29.51)
Parents: Ryland and Alvine
Marital status: Single
Family links with cricket: 'Father plays for Abergavenny and Wales Over 50s'
Education: Crickhowell High School
Qualifications: 10 GCSEs, 2 A-levels, Levels 1 and 2 coaching
Off-season: Playing grade cricket in Brisbane
Overseas tours: Gwent U15 to South Africa 1996; Wales U16 to Jersey 1996, 1997; England U19 to New Zealand 1998-99, to Malaysia and (U19 World Cup) Sri Lanka 1999-2000, to India 2000-01; ECB National Academy to Australia 2001-02, to Australia and Sri Lanka 2002-03
Overseas teams played for: Port Adelaide Magpies, South Australia 2002-03
Career highlights to date: 'NCL titles 2002 and 2004. National Academy selections; captaining National Academy. David Harrison's success in 2004; Mike Powell's England call-up'
Cricket moments to forget: 'With 10 to win off two balls v Kent 2004, getting nutmegged for four byes and seeing Adrian Dale's final ball in county cricket go into the car park for six'
Cricket superstitions: 'More and more every year'
Cricketers particularly admired: Ian Healy, Steve Rhodes, Keith Piper, Warren Hegg, Chris Read, Adam Gilchrist, Alec Stewart, Mike Kasprowicz, Darren Berry
Young players to look out for: David Harrison, Jamie Pipe, Johnny Hughes
Other sports played: 'Plenty of golf, football, boxing'
Other sports followed: Football (Merthyr FC), rugby (Cardiff Blues), golf
Favourite band: Bon Jovi, Eminem
Extras: Represented England U17. Represented England U19 v Pakistan U19 1998, Australia U19 1999 and Sri Lanka U19 2000 (captain for second 'Test'). Made first-

class debut v Somerset at Taunton 1999 aged 17 years 287 days – youngest ever Glamorgan wicket-keeper. NBC Denis Compton Award 1999. Took eight catches in match v Kent at Maidstone 2001, one short of Colin Metson's Glamorgan record. Captained ECB National Academy to innings victory over Commonwealth Bank [Australian] Cricket Academy at Adelaide 2001-02. Made 51 first-class dismissals and scored 856 first-class runs 2003. Byron Denning Glamorgan Clubman of the Year Award 2003
Opinions on cricket: 'Pitch inspectors need to start deducting points from sides who are doctoring pitches. EU/Kolpak player situation (*see page 9*) is worrying and is only being fuelled by the increase of foreign coaches. Should get choice of getting extra delivery after a no-ball/wide.'
Best batting: 121 Glamorgan v Durham, Riverside 2003

2004 Season

	M	Inns	NO	Runs	HS	Avge	100s	50s	Ct	St	O	M	Runs	Wkts	Avge	Best	5wI	10wM
Test																		
All First	17	28	0	776	105	27.71	1	3	40	3								
1-day Int																		
C & G	2	1	0	21	21	21.00	-	-	2	-								
totesport	16	8	1	58	23	8.28	-	-	16	3								
Twenty20	7	6	2	103	32 *	25.75	-	-	3	1								

Career Performances

	M	Inns	NO	Runs	HS	Avge	100s	50s	Ct	St	Balls	Runs	Wkts	Avge	Best	5wI	10wM
Test																	
All First	70	113	10	2821	121	27.38	4	12	202	9							
1-day Int																	
C & G	6	4	0	41	21	10.25	-	-	6	-							
totesport	54	37	7	344	37 *	11.46	-	-	61	15							
Twenty20	12	10	4	148	32 *	24.66	-	-	4	2							

96. Which former international cricketer scored a club-record 335* against Leicestershire to seal Sussex's first Championship title in 2003?

WARD, I. J. — Sussex

Name: Ian James Ward
Role: Left-hand bat
Born: 30 September 1973, Plymouth
Height: 5ft 9in **Weight:** 13st
Nickname: Wardy, Cocker, Son of Baboon, Dwarf, Stumpy, Pig in a Passage
County debut: 1992 (Surrey), 2004 (Sussex)
County cap: 2000 (Surrey), 2004 (Sussex)
Test debut: 2001
Tests: 5
1000 runs in a season: 3
1st-Class 50s: 41
1st-Class 100s: 21
1st-Class catches: 68
One-Day 100s: 2
Place in batting averages: 68th av. 43.00 (2003 93rd av. 37.21)
Strike rate: (career 104.33)
Parents: Tony and Mary
Wife and date of marriage: Joanne, 15 February 1998
Children: Robert, 21 September; Lennox, 10 April
Family links with cricket: Grandfather and father played for Devon
Education: Millfield School
Qualifications: 8 GCSEs, 3 A-levels, NCA coaching award
Career outside cricket: 'Sky television/media'
Off-season: 'Working for Sky Sports'
Overseas tours: Surrey U19 to Barbados 1990; Millfield to Jamaica 1991, to Australia; Malden Wanderers to Jersey 1994; England A to Bangladesh and New Zealand 1999-2000, to West Indies 2000-01
Overseas teams played for: North Perth CC, Western Australia 1996-97; Perth CC, Western Australia; Marist Newman Old Boys CC, Perth
Career highlights to date: 'Test debut'
Cricket superstitions: 'None'
Cricketers particularly admired: Alec Stewart, Saqlain Mushtaq, Graham Thorpe
Young players to look out for: Rory Hamilton-Brown, Matt Prior, 'Mark Robinson'
Other sports played: Golf, football, skiing
Other sports followed: Football (Liverpool), Formula One, skiing
Injuries: Out for two weeks with a broken hand
Favourite band: 'The Mark Butcher Band!'
Relaxations: Running, walking dog
Extras: Released by Surrey at 18 and missed four years of cricket, returning to the

county in 1996. Scored centuries in three successive Busta Cup matches for England A in West Indies 2000-01 and was leading first-class run-scorer on tour (769 av. 64.08); during his 135 v Barbados at Bridgetown, he shared in record opening stand for England A (224) with Michael Powell. Made Test debut v Pakistan at Lord's 2001 in England's 100th Test at the ground. Scored 95-ball 97 v Glamorgan at The Oval in the C&G 2002 as Surrey posted 438-5 from 50 overs. Scored four centuries in consecutive Championship innings 2002 – including two centuries in match (112/156) v Hampshire at West End – to equal a Surrey record last achieved by Jack Hobbs in 1925. Leading run-scorer in English first-class cricket 2002 with 1759 runs (av. 62.82). Surrey Player of the Year 2002. Left Surrey at the end of the 2003 season and joined Sussex for 2004; awarded Sussex cap 2004
Opinions on cricket: 'Leave Twenty20 as it's working. Bring back Benson and Hedges-type one-day competition instead of C&G and totesport but play at right time of year. Practice facilities are not good enough in general in this country. More money to Duncan Fletcher for ECB contracts. It's working.'
Best batting: 168* Surrey v Kent, Canterbury 2002
Best bowling: 1-1 Surrey v Hampshire, West End 2002

2004 Season

	M	Inns	NO	Runs	HS	Avge	100s	50s	Ct	St	O	M	Runs	Wkts	Avge	Best	5wI	10wM
Test																		
All First	16	25	1	1032	160	43.00	4	3	5	-								
1-day Int																		
C & G	2	2	0	56	54	28.00	-	1	1	-								
totesport	15	15	1	538	136	38.42	1	3	3	-								
Twenty20	4	4	0	67	27	16.75	-	-	-	-								

Career Performances

	M	Inns	NO	Runs	HS	Avge	100s	50s	Ct	St	Balls	Runs	Wkts	Avge	Best	5wI	10wM
Test	5	9	1	129	39	16.12	-	-	1	-							
All First	128	214	17	7955	168 *	40.38	21	41	68	-	313	197	3	65.66	1-1	-	-
1-day Int																	
C & G	21	19	2	667	108	39.23	1	5	2	-	60	49	0	-		-	-
totesport	104	101	10	2478	136	27.23	1	14	20	-	59	92	0	-		-	-
Twenty20	10	10	0	253	50	25.30	-	1	3	-							

97. Who scored an unbeaten double hundred in Zimbabwe's first ever Test win and has been contracted to two English counties?

WARNE, S. K. — Hampshire

Name: Shane Keith Warne
Role: Right-hand bat, leg-spin bowler, county captain
Born: 13 September 1969, Upper Ferntree Gully, Victoria, Australia
Height: 6ft
Nickname: Warney, Hollywood
County debut: 2000
County cap: 2000
Test debut: 1991-92
Tests: 112
One-Day Internationals: 193
50 wickets in a season: 2
1st-Class 50s: 16
1st-Class 5 w. in innings: 47
1st-Class 10 w. in match: 8
1st-Class catches: 174
One-Day 5 w. in innings: 1
Place in batting averages: 164th av. 27.21
Place in bowling averages: 15th av. 24.13
Strike rate: 48.45 (career 58.03)
Parents: Keith and Brigitte
Wife and date of marriage: Simone, 1 September 1995
Children: Brooke, Jackson and Summer
Education: Mentone Grammar School
Overseas tours: Australia YC to West Indies 1990; Australia B to Zimbabwe 1991-92; Australia to Sri Lanka 1992, to New Zealand 1992-93, to England 1993, to South Africa 1993-94, to Pakistan 1994-95, to West Indies 1994-95, to India, Pakistan and Sri Lanka (World Cup) 1995-96, to South Africa 1996-97, to England 1997, to India 1997-98, to West Indies 1998-99, to UK, Ireland and Holland (World Cup) 1999, to Sri Lanka 1999, to Zimbabwe 1999-2000, to New Zealand 1999-2000, to India 2000-01, to England 2001, to South Africa 2001-02, to Sri Lanka (ICC Champions Trophy) 2002-03, to Sri Lanka and Sharjah (v Pakistan) 2002-03, to Sri Lanka 2003-04, to India 2004-05, to New Zealand 2004-05, plus other one-day series and tournaments in Sharjah, Sri Lanka, Pakistan, New Zealand, India, South Africa and Kenya; FICA World XI to New Zealand 2004-05
Overseas teams played for: St Kilda, Victoria; Victoria 1990-91 –
Cricketers particularly admired: Ian Chappell, Allan Border, Peter Hartley
Other sports played: Golf (14 handicap)
Other sports followed: Football (Chelsea), Australian Rules (St Kilda)
Extras: Attended Australian Cricket Academy 1990. One of *Wisden*'s Five Cricketers

of the Year 1994, one of *South African Cricket Annual*'s five Cricketers of the Year 1994, and one of *Indian Cricket*'s five Cricketers of the Year 1996. Took hat-trick (DeFreitas, Gough, Malcolm) in the second Test v England at Melbourne 1994-95. Was leading wicket-taker in world Test cricket in the 1990s with 351 wickets (av. 25.67). Voted one of *Wisden*'s Five Cricketers of the Century 2000. Voted One-Day International Player of the Year at the inaugural Allan Border Medal awards January 2000. Featured on a limited-edition Australian stamp issued in 2000. Took 400th Test wicket (Alec Stewart) in the fifth Test v England at The Oval 2001. Man of the Match in his 100th Test, v South Africa at Cape Town 2001-02 (2-70/6-161), in which he also became the fourth cricketer to pass 2000 runs and 400 wickets in Tests. Has won numerous other Test awards, among them Man of the Series in the 1993 Ashes (34 wickets; av. 25.79) and v Sri Lanka 2003-04 (26; 20.03); also Man of the Series v Pakistan in Colombo and Sharjah 2002-03 for his 27 wickets (av. 12.66), an Australian three-match-series record. Has also won numerous ODI awards, including Man of the Match in the 1999 World Cup semi-final v South Africa at Edgbaston (4-29) and final v Pakistan at Lord's (4-33). Has captained Australia in ODIs; has now retired from ODI cricket. Was Hampshire's overseas player in 2000; rejoined Hampshire as an overseas player and as captain in 2004. Tops the list of Australian Test wicket-takers; became second bowler to reach 500 Test wickets when he dismissed Hashan Tillakaratne in the second innings of the first Test v Sri Lanka at Galle 2003-04. Took 900th first-class wicket (Greg Smith) v Nottinghamshire at West End 2004

Opinions on cricket: 'Play to win. Never give up!'
Best batting: 99 Australia v New Zealand, Perth 2001-02
Best bowling: 8-71 Australia v England, Brisbane 1994-95
Stop press: Took 533rd Test wicket (Irfan Pathan) in the second Test v India at Chennai 2004-05 to move to the top of the all-time Test wicket-takers' list

2004 Season

	M	Inns	NO	Runs	HS	Avge	100s	50s	Ct	St	O	M	Runs	Wkts	Avge	Best	5wI	10wM
Test																		
All First	12	16	2	381	57	27.21	-	1	9	-	411.5	88	1231	51	24.13	6-65	3	-
1-day Int																		
C & G	2	2	0	1	1	0.50	-	-	-	-	15.5	1	47	4	11.75	4-23	-	
totesport	12	10	0	116	48	11.60	-	-	4	-	103	6	450	18	25.00	4-27	-	
Twenty20	1	1	0	0	0	0.00	-	-	-	-	4	0	22	0	-	-	-	

Career Performances

	M	Inns	NO	Runs	HS	Avge	100s	50s	Ct	St	Balls	Runs	Wkts	Avge	Best	5wI	10wM
Test	112	156	13	2326	99	16.26	-	8	93	-	31489	13425	527	25.47	8-71	27	8
All First	219	296	36	4629	99	17.80	-	16	174	-	54903	24452	946	25.84	8-71	47	8
1-day Int	193	106	28	1016	55	13.02	-	1	79	-	10600	7513	291	25.81	5-33	1	
C & G	5	4	1	21	20	7.00	-	-	-	-	257	131	12	10.91	4-23	-	
totesport	25	23	1	267	48	12.13	-	-	9	-	1296	888	43	20.65	4-23	-	
Twenty20	1	1	0	0	0	0.00	-	-	-	-	24	22	0	-	-	-	

WARREN, N. A. — Warwickshire

Name: Nick Alexander Warren
Role: Right-hand bat, right-arm medium-fast bowler
Born: 26 June 1982, Moseley
Height: 5ft 11in **Weight:** 12st 7lbs
Nickname: Wazza
County debut: 2002
Strike rate: 34.00 (career 44.40)
Parents: Lesley
Marital status: Single
Education: Wheelers Lane Boys School; Solihull Sixth Form College
Qualifications: 9 GCSEs, BTEC Sports Science
Overseas tours: Warwickshire U19 to Cape Town 1998-99; England U17 to Ireland 1999; England U19 to Malaysia and (U19 World Cup) Sri Lanka 1999-2000

Cricketers particularly admired: Allan Donald, Graeme Welch
Other sports played: Football
Other sports followed: Football (Birmingham City)
Relaxations: Watching films; planes, music
Extras: Played for Warwickshire Board XI in the C&G 2002. Played for the Warwickshire Board XI side that won the final ECB 38-County competition 2002
Best batting: 11 Warwickshire v West Indies A, Edgbaston 2002
Best bowling: 3-60 Warwickshire v Northamptonshire, Northampton 2004

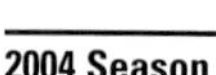
2004 Season

	M	Inns	NO	Runs	HS	Avge	100s	50s	Ct	St	O	M	Runs	Wkts	Avge	Best	5wI	10wM
Test																		
All First	1	1	0	0	0	0.00	-	-	-	-	17	3	60	3	20.00	3-60	-	-
1-day Int																		
C & G																		
totesport																		
Twenty20																		

Career Performances

	M	Inns	NO	Runs	HS	Avge	100s	50s	Ct	St	Balls	Runs	Wkts	Avge	Best	5wI	10wM
Test																	
All First	2	3	1	13	11	6.50	-	-	-	-	222	150	5	30.00	3-60	-	-
1-day Int																	
C & G	1	1	0	0	0	0.00	-	-	2	-	36	29	0	-	-	-	
totesport	2	2	1	2	2	2.00	-	-	-	-	66	76	3	25.33	3-34	-	
Twenty20																	

WARREN, R. J. — Nottinghamshire

Name: Russell John Warren
Role: Right-hand bat, wicket-keeper
Born: 10 September 1971, Northampton
Height: 6ft 2in **Weight:** 13st 4lbs
Nickname: Rab C, Rabbit
County debut: 1992 (Northamptonshire), 2003 (Nottinghamshire)
County cap: 1995 (Northamptonshire), 2004 (Nottinghamshire)
1000 runs in a season: 1
1st-Class 50s: 37
1st-Class 100s: 14
1st-Class 200s: 1
1st-Class catches: 119
1st-Class stumpings: 5
One-Day 100s: 1
Place in batting averages: 53rd av. 46.11 (2003 45th av. 45.87)
Parents: John and Sally
Wife and date of marriage: Kate, November 2004
Education: Kingsthorpe Middle and Upper Schools
Qualifications: 8 O-levels, 2 A-levels
Overseas tours: England YC to New Zealand 1990-91; Northamptonshire to Cape Town 1993, to Zimbabwe 1995, to Johannesburg 1996, to Grenada 2000; Nottinghamshire to Pretoria 2003
Overseas teams played for: Lancaster Park, Christchurch, and Canterbury B, New Zealand 1991-93; Riverside CC, Lower Hutt, New Zealand 1994-95; Petone CC, Wellington, New Zealand 1995-96; Alma Marist CC, Cape Town, South Africa 1997-98
Career highlights to date: '1995 NatWest final'
Cricketers particularly admired: Allan Lamb, Wayne Larkins

Young players to look out for: Samit Patel
Other sports played: Golf, snooker
Other sports followed: Football (Manchester United, Northampton Town, Nottingham Forest), rugby (Northampton Saints), golf, snooker and horse racing
Injuries: Out for the last month of the season with a torn calf muscle
Favourite band: The Thrills
Relaxations: 'Music, watching golf'
Extras: Scored 175 v Glamorgan at Northampton 2001, in the process sharing with Tony Penberthy (132*) in a record sixth-wicket partnership for Northants in matches against Glamorgan (250). Scored 144 v Somerset at Taunton 2001, in the process sharing with Mike Hussey (208) in a record third-wicket partnership for Northants in matches against Somerset (287). Released by Northamptonshire at the end of the 2002 season and joined Nottinghamshire for 2003. Scored century in each innings (123/113*) v Middlesex at Lord's 2003. Awarded Nottinghamshire cap 2004
Best batting: 201* Northamptonshire v Glamorgan, Northampton 1996

2004 Season

	M	Inns	NO	Runs	HS	Avge	100s	50s	Ct	St	O	M	Runs	Wkts	Avge	Best	5wI	10wM
Test																		
All First	13	19	2	784	134	46.11	2	4	4	-								
1-day Int																		
C & G	2	2	1	47	45 *	47.00	-	-	1	-								
totesport	11	11	0	398	81	36.18	-	2	4	-								
Twenty20	1	1	0	26	26	26.00	-	-	-	-								

Career Performances

	M	Inns	NO	Runs	HS	Avge	100s	50s	Ct	St	Balls	Runs	Wkts	Avge	Best	5wI	10wM
Test																	
All First	132	216	24	7285	201 *	37.94	15	37	119	5	6	0	0	-	-	-	-
1-day Int																	
C & G	23	21	4	506	100 *	29.76	1	2	22	1							
totesport	117	106	14	2355	93	25.59	-	11	86	10							
Twenty20	1	1	0	26	26	26.00	-	-	-	-							

98. Which left-arm seamer took 6-81 on Test debut for Bangladesh against Zimbabwe at Bulawayo in April 2001?

WATKINS, R. E. Glamorgan

Name: Ryan Edward Watkins
Role: Left-hand bat, right-arm medium bowler
Born: 9 June 1983, Abergavenny, Monmouthshire
Height: 6ft **Weight:** 13st 7lbs
Nickname: Tetanus
County debut: 2003 (one-day)
Parents: Huw and Gaynor
Marital status: Single
Family links with cricket: 'Father and brother keen club cricketers'
Education: Pontllanfraith CS; Cross Keys College
Qualifications: Level 2 coach
Career outside cricket: Motor trade
Overseas teams played for: North Balwyn CC, Victoria, Australia 2003
Career highlights to date: 'First-team debut in Twenty20 Cup'
Cricket superstitions: 'Always put right pad on before the left'
Cricketers particularly admired: 'Too many to single one out'
Young players to look out for: Adam Harrison, Mike O'Shea
Other sports played: Football (Ynysddu Crusaders)
Other sports followed: Football (Tottenham Hotspur)
Favourite band: 'No one favourite'
Relaxations: Golf, pool
Extras: Made 2nd XI Championship debut 2001

2004 Season

	M	Inns	NO	Runs	HS	Avge	100s	50s	Ct	St	O	M	Runs	Wkts	Avge	Best	5wI	10wM
Test																		
All First																		
1-day Int																		
C & G																		
totesport	1	1	0	0	0	0.00	-	-	-	-	5	0	47	0	-		-	-
Twenty20	1	0	0	0	0	-	-	-	-	-	1	0	11	0	-		-	-

Career Performances

	M	Inns	NO	Runs	HS	Avge	100s	50s	Ct	St	Balls	Runs	Wkts	Avge	Best	5wI	10wM
Test																	
All First																	
1-day Int																	
C & G																	
totesport	1	1	0	0	0	0.00	-	-	-	-	30	47	0	-	-	-	
Twenty20	3	1	1	6	6 *	-	-	-	2	-	30	49	2	24.50	2-8	-	

WATKINSON, M. — Lancashire

Name: Michael Watkinson
Role: Right-hand bat, right-arm medium or off-spin bowler
Born: 1 August 1961, Westhoughton, Greater Manchester
Height: 6ft 1½in **Weight:** 13st
Nickname: Winker
County debut: 1982
County cap: 1987
Benefit: 1996 (£209,000)
Test debut: 1995
Tests: 4
One-Day Internationals: 1
1000 runs in a season: 1
50 wickets in a season: 7
1st-Class 50s: 50
1st-Class 100s: 11
1st-Class 5 w. in innings: 27
1st-Class 10 w. in match: 3
1st-Class catches: 156
One-Day 100s: 2
One-Day 5 w. in innings: 3
Strike rate: (career 64.69)
Parents: Albert and Marian
Wife and date of marriage: Susan, 12 April 1986
Children: Charlotte, 24 February 1989; Liam, 27 July 1991
Education: Rivington and Blackrod High School, Horwich
Qualifications: 8 O-levels, HTC Civil Engineering
Career outside cricket: Draughtsman
Overseas tours: England to South Africa 1995-96
Cricketers particularly admired: Clive Lloyd, Imran Khan

Other sports followed: Football
Relaxations: Watching Bolton Wanderers
Extras: Played for Cheshire in Minor Counties Championship and in NatWest Trophy (v Middlesex) 1982. Man of the Match in the first Refuge Assurance Cup final 1988 and for his 50 plus 2-37 in B&H Cup final 1990. Lancashire captain 1994-97, leading the county to one NatWest and two B&H titles. Lancashire Player of the Year 1995. 2nd XI captain and coach 2000-01. Cricket manager since 2002; retired but registration retained. Assistant England coach for latter part of Test tour to South Africa 2004-05
Best batting: 161 Lancashire v Essex, Old Trafford 1995
Best bowling: 8-30 Lancashire v Hampshire, Old Trafford 1994

2004 Season (did not make any first-class or one-day appearances)

Career Performances

	M	Inns	NO	Runs	HS	Avge	100s	50s	Ct	St	Balls	Runs	Wkts	Avge	Best	5wI	10wM
Test	4	6	1	167	82 *	33.40	-	1	1	-	672	348	10	34.80	3-64	-	-
All First	308	459	49	10939	161	26.68	11	50	156	-	47806	24960	739	33.77	8-30	27	3
1-day Int	1	0	0	0	0	-	-	-	-	-	54	43	0	-	-	-	
C & G	46	40	7	1064	130	32.24	1	7	12	-	2681	1751	46	38.06	3-14	-	
totesport	236	189	38	3262	121	21.60	1	9	59	-	8730	7113	225	31.61	5-46	1	
Twenty20																	

WATSON, S. R. — Hampshire

Name: Shane Robert Watson
Role: Right-hand bat, right-arm fast-medium bowler
Born: 17 June 1981, Ipswich, Queensland, Australia
County debut: 2004
One-Day Internationals: 26
1st-Class 50s: 10
1st-Class 100s: 7
1st-Class 5 w. in innings: 2
1st-Class 10 w. in match: 1
1st-Class catches: 13
Strike rate: (career 46.00)
Overseas tours: Australia U19 to Sri Lanka (U19 World Cup) 1999-2000; Australia to South Africa 2001-02, to Kenya (PSO Tri-Nation Tournament) 2002, to Sri Lanka (ICC Champions Trophy) 2002-03, to Zimbabwe

(one-day series) 2004, to Holland (Videocon Cup) 2004, to England (ICC Champions Trophy) 2004, to India 2004-05
Overseas teams played for: Tasmania 2000-01 – 2003-04; Queensland 2004-05 –
Extras: Played for Queensland U17 aged 15. Commonwealth Bank [Australian] Cricket Academy 2000, 2003. Scored 300* then followed up with 7-29 for Lindisfarne v North Hobart in Tasmanian grade match at Hobart 2003-04. Tasmania's Player of the Year 2003-04. His match awards include Man of the Match v Queensland at Hobart in the Pura Cup 2001-02 (6-32/5-46) and v Victoria at Melbourne in the ING Cup 2003-04 (2-15/63). Joined Hampshire 2004 as an overseas player as cover for Shane Warne and Michael Clarke while on international duty; left Hampshire at the end of the 2004 season. Scored century (112*) on first-class debut for Hampshire v Somerset at West End 2004
Best batting: 157 Tasmania v New South Wales, Sydney 2003-04
Best bowling: 6-32 Tasmania v Queensland, Hobart 2001-02
Stop press: Made Test debut in the third Test v Pakistan at Sydney 2004-05

2004 Season

	M	Inns	NO	Runs	HS	Avge	100s	50s	Ct	St	O	M	Runs	Wkts	Avge	Best	5wI	10wM
Test																		
All First	1	2	1	136	112 *	136.00	1	-	-	-	8.4	2	28	0	-	-	-	-
1-day Int	2	1	1	7	7 *	-	-	-	2	-	15	0	79	0	-	-	-	
C & G																		
totesport	2	2	1	77	54 *	77.00	-	1	1	-	9	0	39	0	-	-	-	
Twenty20	5	5	1	122	97 *	30.50	-	1	3	-								

Career Performances

	M	Inns	NO	Runs	HS	Avge	100s	50s	Ct	St	Balls	Runs	Wkts	Avge	Best	5wI	10wM
Test																	
All First	28	49	6	2038	157	47.39	7	10	13	-	2438	1487	53	28.05	6-32	2	1
1-day Int	26	17	9	313	77 *	39.12	-	1	9	-	959	749	18	41.61	3-27	-	
C & G																	
totesport	2	2	1	77	54 *	77.00	-	1	1	-	54	39	0	-	-	-	
Twenty20	5	5	1	122	97 *	30.50	-	1	3	-							

99. Which Scottish international goalkeeper also played first-class and one-day cricket for Scotland from 1989 to 1991?

WEEKES, P. N. Middlesex

Name: Paul Nicholas Weekes
Role: Left-hand bat, right-arm off-spin bowler; all-rounder
Born: 8 July 1969, Hackney, London
Height: 5ft 10½in **Weight:** 12st 2lbs
Nickname: Twidds, Weekesy
County debut: 1990
County cap: 1993
Benefit: 2002
1000 runs in a season: 2
1st-Class 50s: 50
1st-Class 100s: 18
1st-Class 5 w. in innings: 5
1st-Class catches: 203
One-Day 100s: 5
Place in batting averages: 63rd av. 43.52 (2003 127th av. 31.66)
Place in bowling averages: 135th av. 44.84 (2003 108th av. 38.71)
Strike rate: 75.11 (career 83.62)
Parents: Robert
Marital status: Single
Children: Cherie, 4 September 1993; Shyann, 3 May 1998
Family links with cricket: Father played club cricket
Education: Homerton House, Hackney; Hackney College
Qualifications: Level 2 coaching award
Career outside cricket: Cricket coach – Middlesex Youth squads and Hackney Cricket Academy
Overseas tours: England A to India and Bangladesh 1994-95; Middlesex to Johannesburg; three tours with BWIA to the West Indies
Overseas teams played for: Newcastle University, NSW 1988-89; Sunrise CC, Harare 1990-91
Career highlights to date: 'Scoring 171* and 160 in the same match, v Somerset at Uxbridge 1996'
Cricket moments to forget: 'Getting a pair against Essex'
Cricketers particularly admired: Viv Richards, Courtney Walsh, Brian Lara
Favourite band: Burning Flames, Jay-Z
Relaxations: DIY
Extras: Scored 50 in debut innings for both 2nd and 1st teams. Took two catches whilst appearing as 12th man for England in the second Test against West Indies at Lord's in 1995. Middlesex Player of the Year 1999, 2004. First Englishman to score more than

150 in both innings of a first-class game. Has won six one-day Man of the Match awards (two NatWest; four B&H). Captained Middlesex to their one-day victory over the Australians at Lord's 2001. Passed 50 (including two centuries) in nine out of ten innings in all cricket from 31 May to 27 June 2004, scoring 680 runs. Leading run-scorer in the totesport League 2004 with 807 runs at an average of 57.64
Opinions on cricket: '[Would] still like to see more coverage on TV as youngsters prefer to do what they see or visualise top players doing.'
Best batting: 171* Middlesex v Somerset, Uxbridge 1996
Best bowling: 8-39 Middlesex v Glamorgan, Lord's 1996

2004 Season

	M	Inns	NO	Runs	HS	Avge	100s	50s	Ct	St	O	M	Runs	Wkts	Avge	Best	5wI	10wM
Test																		
All First	16	26	3	1001	118	43.52	2	9	14	-	325.3	34	1166	26	44.84	5-76	1	-
1-day Int																		
C & G	3	3	0	76	66	25.33	-	1	1	-	23.1	5	74	4	18.50	2-8	-	
totesport	18	18	4	807	119 *	57.64	1	7	12	-	90.4	2	469	12	39.08	2-3	-	
Twenty20	4	4	1	150	55 *	50.00	-	1	1	-	9	0	57	2	28.50	2-20	-	

Career Performances

	M	Inns	NO	Runs	HS	Avge	100s	50s	Ct	St	Balls	Runs	Wkts	Avge	Best	5wI	10wM
Test																	
All First	212	331	44	9870	171 *	34.39	18	50	203	-	23833	11656	285	40.89	8-39	5	-
1-day Int																	
C & G	27	27	5	763	143 *	34.68	2	5	7	-	1342	963	27	35.66	3-35	-	
totesport	216	189	26	4691	119 *	28.77	3	27	100	-	7531	6361	222	28.65	4-26	-	
Twenty20	9	9	1	313	56	39.12	-	2	2	-	162	180	4	45.00	2-20	-	

WELCH, G. — Derbyshire

Name: Graeme Welch
Role: Right-hand bat, right-arm medium-fast bowler
Born: 21 March 1972, Durham
Height: 6ft **Weight:** 13st
Nickname: Pop
County debut: 1992 (one-day, Warwickshire), 1994 (first-class, Warwickshire), 2001 (Derbyshire)
County cap: 1997 (Warwickshire), 2001 (Derbyshire)
50 wickets in a season: 3
1st-Class 50s: 15
1st-Class 100s: 1
1st-Class 5 w. in innings: 14
1st-Class 10 w. in match: 1

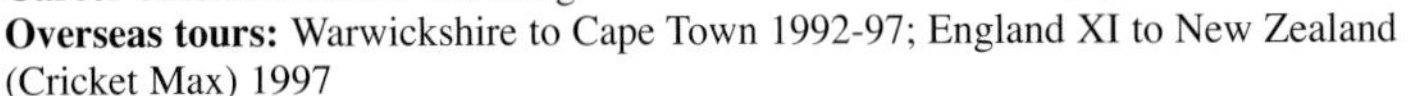

1st-Class catches: 56
One-Day 5 w. in innings: 3
Place in batting averages: 153rd av. 29.00 (2003 223rd av. 20.42)
Place in bowling averages: 70th av. 33.88 (2003 49th av. 27.84)
Strike rate: 62.91 (career 59.85)
Parents: Jean and Robert
Wife and date of marriage: Emma, 4 October 1997
Children: Ethan, 4 April 2000
Family links with cricket: Brother and father club cricketers in Leeds and Durham respectively
Education: Hetton Comprehensive
Qualifications: 9 GCSEs, City and Guilds in Sports and Leisure, senior coaching award
Career outside cricket: Coaching
Overseas tours: Warwickshire to Cape Town 1992-97; England XI to New Zealand (Cricket Max) 1997
Overseas teams played for: Avendale, Cape Town 1992-94; Wellington Collegians and Wellington 1996
Career highlights to date: 'Winning the treble with Warwickshire in 1994'
Cricket moments to forget: 'Benson and Hedges game against Lancashire in 1995' (*Became first bowler to concede 100 runs in B&H match*)
Cricketers particularly admired: Brian Lara, Allan Donald, Sachin Tendulkar
Other sports played: Football
Other sports followed: Football (Newcastle United)
Relaxations: 'A beer at The Brook; spending time with Emma and Ethan'
Extras: Represented England YC. Took two hat-tricks in the 2nd XI, against Durham in 1992 and against Worcestershire. Warwickshire's Most Improved Player 1994. Won seven trophies with Warwickshire 1994-97. Left Warwickshire at the end of the 2000 season and joined Derbyshire for 2001. Scored maiden first-class century (115*) v Leicestershire at Oakham School 2004
Best batting: 115* Derbyshire v Leicestershire, Oakham School 2004
Best bowling: 6-30 Derbyshire v Durham, Riverside 2001

2004 Season

	M	Inns	NO	Runs	HS	Avge	100s	50s	Ct	St	O	M	Runs	Wkts	Avge	Best	5wI	10wM
Test																		
All First	16	25	4	609	115 *	29.00	1	1	12	-	471.5	103	1525	45	33.88	5-57	3	-
1-day Int																		
C & G	1	1	0	22	22	22.00	-	-	-	-	10	1	38	3	12.66	3-38	-	
totesport	18	14	1	276	82	21.23	-	1	4	-	142	18	562	18	31.22	4-26	-	
Twenty20	3	3	2	31	15 *	31.00	-	-	-	-	11	0	71	2	35.50	1-23	-	

Career Performances

	M	Inns	NO	Runs	HS	Avge	100s	50s	Ct	St	Balls	Runs	Wkts	Avge	Best	5wI	10wM
Test																	
All First	139	213	35	3904	115 *	21.93	1	15	56	-	22804	12277	381	32.22	6-30	14	1
1-day Int																	
C & G	23	17	5	248	41	20.66	-	-	1	-	1192	781	21	37.19	4-26	-	
totesport	135	108	27	1473	82	18.18	-	4	23	-	5649	4159	128	32.49	6-31	3	
Twenty20	8	6	2	60	15 *	15.00	-	-	2	-	180	248	4	62.00	1-15	-	

WESSELS, M. H. Northamptonshire

Name: Mattheus Hendrik (Riki) Wessels
Role: Right-hand bat, wicket-keeper
Born: 12 November 1985, Nambour, Australia
Height: 5ft 11in **Weight:** 10st 10lbs
Nickname: Blood, Moose
County debut: No first-team appearance
1st-Class catches: 4
1st-Class stumpings: 1
Parents: Kepler and Sally
Marital status: 'Attached'
Family links with cricket: 'My dad played a little bit'
Education: Woodridge College, Port Elizabeth; University College of Northampton
Qualifications: Coach
Off-season: 'Studying'
Career highlights to date: 'Winning the national cricket week in South Africa'
Cricket moments to forget: 'Losing in the 2nd XI [Trophy] semi-final by nine wickets [2004]'
Cricket superstitions: 'Lucky shirt'
Cricketers particularly admired: 'My dad and Justin Langer'
Young players to look out for: Alex Wakely
Other sports played: Hockey
Other sports followed: Rugby (Queensland Reds)
Favourite band: Linkin Park
Relaxations: 'Reading autobiographies'
Extras: Northamptonshire Academy Players' Player of the Year 2004. Northamptonshire Young Player of the Year (Frank Rudd Trophy) 2004. Highest score for Northamptonshire Academy. Made first-class debut for MCC v West Indians at Arundel 2004. Is a Northamptonshire Emerging Player

Opinions on cricket: 'Always growing and changing to better the game.'
Best batting: 34 MCC v West Indians, Arundel 2004

2004 Season (did not make any first-class or one-day appearances for his county)

Career Performances

	M	Inns	NO	Runs	HS	Avge	100s	50s	Ct	St	Balls	Runs	Wkts	Avge	Best	5wI	10wM
Test																	
All First	1	2	0	35	34	17.50	-	-	4	1							
1-day Int																	
C & G																	
totesport																	
Twenty20																	

WESTFIELD, M. S. — Essex

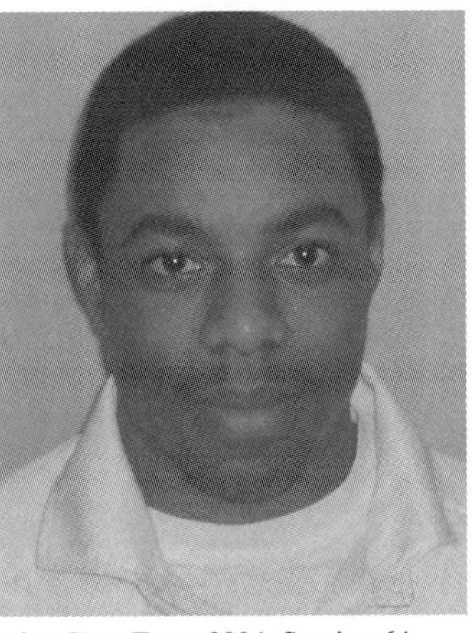

Name: Mervyn Simon Westfield
Role: Right-hand bat, right-arm fast bowler; all-rounder
Born: 5 May 1988, Romford
Height: 6ft **Weight:** 12st 2lbs
Nickname: Swerve
County debut: No first-team appearance
Parents: Pam and Mervyn
Marital status: Single
Family links with cricket: 'Began playing cricket at the age of seven and have been coached, influenced and guided by my father'
Education: The Chafford; Barking College
Qualifications: 8 GCSEs, Level 1 coaching
Career outside cricket: 'Full-time student'
Off-season: 'Training (indoors)'
Overseas tours: ECB U16 to Cape Town 2004
Career highlights to date: 'Playing for ECB U16 at Cape Town 2004. Scoring 64 runs for Wanstead U16 v Ilford U16 at Chelmsford (County Ground) 2002'
Cricket moments to forget: 'None'
Cricket superstitions: 'None'
Cricketers particularly admired: Courtney Walsh, Viv Richards
Young players to look out for: Maurice Chambers, Tom Westley (Essex), Michael O'Shea (Glamorgan)
Other sports followed: Football (Manchester United)
Injuries: Played but did not bowl for six weeks with a shoulder injury

Favourite band: G-Unit
Relaxations: 'Socialising with friends, listening to music'
Extras: Wanstead U11 Young Player of the Year 1997. Wanstead U11 All-Rounder of 1998. Havering District U13 Best Innings 2000. MCC Cricketer of the Year 2003, 2004. *Daily Telegraph* Bunbury Scholar (Best Fast Bowler) 2003
Opinions on cricket: 'Too much sledging is spoiling the spirit of the game. The introduction of Twenty20 cricket has added a fast, furious and fun element to the game. Australia appear to have the correct formula in order to reach success.'

WESTON, W. P. C. — Gloucestershire

Name: William Philip Christopher Weston
Role: Left-hand bat, left-arm medium bowler
Born: 16 June 1973, Durham City
Height: 6ft 4in **Weight:** 14st
Nickname: Tickle, Weso
County debut: 1991 (Worcestershire), 2003 (Gloucestershire)
County cap: 1995; colours, 2002 (both Worcestershire), 2004 (Gloucestershire)
1000 runs in a season: 4
1st-Class 50s: 53
1st-Class 100s: 20
1st-Class 200s: 1
1st-Class catches: 118
One-Day 100s: 4
Place in batting averages: 105th av. 35.59 (2003 111th av. 33.73)
Strike rate: 24.00 (career 200.20)
Parents: Michael and Kate (deceased)
Wife and date of marriage: Sarah, 30 September 2000
Family links with cricket: Brother Robin played for Durham, Derbyshire and Middlesex. Father played Minor Counties cricket for Durham (and rugby union for England)
Education: Durham School
Qualifications: 9 GCSEs, 4 A-levels, Diploma in Business and Management
Career outside cricket: 'Hoping to pursue a career in property'
Off-season: 'Studying for a degree in estate management'
Overseas tours: England U18 to Canada (International Youth Tournament) 1991 (vice-captain); England YC to New Zealand 1990-91; England U19 to Pakistan 1991-92 (captain); Worcestershire to Zimbabwe 1996

Overseas teams played for: Melville, Perth 1992-94, 1996-97; Swanbourne, Perth 1995-96
Career highlights to date: '2004 C&G final'
Cricket moments to forget: 'The 2002 season and the way my career at Worcester ended'
Cricket superstitions: 'Not really'
Cricketers particularly admired: Ian Botham
Young players to look out for: Ian Bell
Other sports played: 'Have a go at most sports'
Other sports followed: Rugby union, football (Sunderland AFC)
Favourite band: U2
Relaxations: 'Spending time with my lovely wife; travelling, films, hanging out with friends'
Extras: Scored century (146) for England YC v Australia YC 1991. Scored century (107) for England U19 v Sri Lanka U19 1992 and was Man of the Series. Cricket Society's Most Promising Young Cricketer 1992. Worcestershire Uncapped Player of the Year 1992. Member of Whittingdale Fringe Squad 1993. Left Worcestershire by mutual agreement before the beginning of the 2003 season with a year left on contract and joined Gloucestershire. C&G Man of the Match award for his 106 v Holland at Amstelveen 2004. Scored century (110*) in the C&G final v Worcestershire at Lord's 2004
Opinions on cricket: 'Pitches and practice facilities remain an ongoing issue at county level. Registration and qualification needs to be sorted to avoid certain teams becoming too cosmopolitan in their composition. Pleased to see the England team doing well.'
Best batting: 205 Worcestershire v Northamptonshire, Northampton 1997
Best bowling: 2-39 Worcestershire v Pakistanis, Worcester 1992

2004 Season

	M	Inns	NO	Runs	HS	Avge	100s	50s	Ct	St	O	M	Runs	Wkts	Avge	Best	5wI	10wM
Test																		
All First	17	28	1	961	135	35.59	2	4	18	-	4	2	8	1	8.00	1-8	-	-
1-day Int																		
C & G	5	5	1	315	110 *	78.75	2	1	1	-								
totesport	16	16	0	444	75	27.75	-	3	2	-								
Twenty20																		

Career Performances

	M	Inns	NO	Runs	HS	Avge	100s	50s	Ct	St	Balls	Runs	Wkts	Avge	Best	5wI	10wM
Test																	
All First	202	354	33	10970	205	34.17	21	53	118	-	1001	658	5	131.60	2-39	-	-
1-day Int																	
C & G	21	21	2	645	110 *	33.94	2	2	4	-							
totesport	120	106	8	2494	134	25.44	2	11	24	-	6	2	1	2.00	1-2	-	
Twenty20																	

WESTWOOD, I. J. Warwickshire

Name: Ian James Westwood
Role: Left-hand opening bat, right-arm off-spinner
Born: 13 July 1982, Birmingham
Height: 5ft 7½in **Weight:** 11st
Nickname: Westy, Tomato Head, Wezzo, Sammy Lee, Tot
County debut: 2003
Parents: Ann and David
Marital status: Single
Family links with cricket: 'Brother represented Warwickshire Schools from 11 to 16'
Education: Wheelers Lane; Solihull Sixth Form College
Qualifications: 8 GCSEs, BTEC Sports Science
Overseas tours: Warwickshire Development squad to Cape Town 1998
Overseas teams played for: Hawkesbury CC, Sydney 2001-02; Subiaco Marist CC, Perth 2002-03
Career highlights to date: 'Took 6-104 and scored 250* in the same game v Worcestershire 2nd XI [2003]'
Cricket moments to forget: 'Being relegated from the Birmingham Premier League after losing the last game of season, for Moseley CC'
Cricket superstitions: 'Put right pad on first'
Cricketers particularly admired: Brian Lara, Nick Knight
Young players to look out for: Nick Chase, Vanraj Padhaal
Other sports played: Football (Coleshill Town FC 2001; Moseley Mariners FC)
Other sports followed: Football (Birmingham City)
Favourite band: Fleetwood Mac
Relaxations: 'Music, films, fruit machines, socialising'
Extras: Played for Warwickshire Board XI in the C&G 2001, 2002 and 2003. Scored 250* v Worcestershire 2nd XI at Barnt Green 2003, sharing with Jonathan Trott (248) in a record opening partnership for Warwickshire 2nd XI (429); also took 6-104 in Worcestershire 2nd XI's only innings
Opinions on cricket: 'Play on too many poor pitches in England, resulting in bowlers not needing to be as good as Australian, South African etc. We don't know how to bowl on flat pitches against quality opposition.'
Best batting: 38 Warwickshire v Northamptonshire, Northampton 2004

2004 Season

	M	Inns	NO	Runs	HS	Avge	100s	50s	Ct	St	O	M	Runs	Wkts	Avge	Best	5wI	10wM
Test																		
All First	1	2	0	41	38	20.50	-	-	-	-								
1-day Int																		
C & G																		
totesport																		
Twenty20																		

Career Performances

	M	Inns	NO	Runs	HS	Avge	100s	50s	Ct	St	Balls	Runs	Wkts	Avge	Best	5wI	10wM
Test																	
All First	2	3	0	60	38	20.00	-	-	-	-	48	57	0	-	-	-	-
1-day Int																	
C & G	4	4	0	78	55	19.50	-	1	1	-	180	139	2	69.50	1-28	-	
totesport																	
Twenty20																	

WHARF, A. G. B. — Glamorgan

Name: Alexander (Alex) George Busfield Wharf
Role: Right-hand bat, right-arm fast-medium bowler; all-rounder
Born: 4 June 1975, Bradford
Height: 6ft 4in **Weight:** 15st
Nickname: Gangster
County debut: 1994 (Yorks), 1998 (Notts), 2000 (Glamorgan)
County cap: 2000 (Glamorgan)
One-Day Internationals: 7
50 wickets in a season: 1
1st-Class 50s: 8
1st-Class 100s: 2
1st-Class 5 w. in innings: 3
1st-Class catches: 33
One-Day 5 w. in innings: 1
Place in batting averages: 204th av. 21.92 (2003 170th av. 26.38)
Place in bowling averages: 101st av. 37.44 (2003 79th av. 33.34)
Strike rate: 55.51 (career 54.15)
Parents: Jane and Derek

Wife and date of marriage: Shelley Jane, 1 December 2001
Children: Tristan Jack Busfield Wharf, 15 November 1997; Alf Alexander Busfield Wharf, 30 June 2001
Family links with cricket: Father played local cricket and brother Simon plays local cricket
Education: Buttershaw Upper School; Thomas Danby College
Qualifications: 6 GCSEs, City and Guilds in Sports Management, NCA coaching award, junior football coaching award
Overseas tours: England to Zimbabwe (one-day series) 2004-05, to South Africa 2004-05 (one-day series); various pre-season tours with Yorks, Notts and Glamorgan
Overseas teams played for: Somerset West, Cape Town 1993-95; Johnsonville CC, Wellington, New Zealand 1996-97; Universities, Wellington 1998-99
Cricket moments to forget: 'Too many to mention'
Cricket superstitions: 'None'
Cricketers particularly admired: Ian Botham
Other sports played: Football
Other sports followed: 'Follow most sports but my passion is Manchester United; also very proud of Bradford City'
Relaxations: 'Spending time with family and friends, movies, PlayStation 2, eating (too much), TV, gym, football'
Extras: Scored 78 v Glamorgan at Colwyn Bay 1999, having arrived at the wicket with Nottinghamshire on 9 for 6. Left Nottinghamshire at end of the 1999 season and joined Glamorgan for 2000. Took hat-trick (Wagg, Knight, Pretorius) v Warwickshire at Edgbaston in the totesport League 2004. Had figures of 6-5 (his maiden one-day five-wicket return) v Kent at Cardiff in the totesport League 2004 (match reduced to 25 overs a side). Made ODI debut v India at Trent Bridge in the NatWest Challenge 2004, taking a wicket in each of his first three overs, finishing with 3-30 and winning Man of the Match award
Best batting: 101* Glamorgan v Northamptonshire, Northampton 2000
Best bowling: 5-63 Glamorgan v Yorkshire, Swansea 2001

2004 Season

	M	Inns	NO	Runs	HS	Avge	100s	50s	Ct	St	O	M	Runs	Wkts	Avge	Best	5wI	10wM
Test																		
All First	10	15	1	307	78	21.92	-	3	4	-	249.5	38	1011	27	37.44	5-93	1	-
1-day Int	7	4	2	16	9	8.00	-	-	1	-	48.2	1	223	6	37.16	3-30	-	
C & G	2	1	0	13	13	13.00	-	-	-	-	11	0	60	0	-	-	-	
totesport	14	12	1	244	72	22.18	-	1	8	-	104.5	9	462	26	17.76	6-5	1	
Twenty20	7	4	1	36	16	12.00	-	-	1	-	25.1	0	202	11	18.36	3-23	-	

Career Performances

	M	Inns	NO	Runs	HS	Avge	100s	50s	Ct	St	Balls	Runs	Wkts	Avge	Best	5wI	10wM
Test																	
All First	72	104	18	1696	101 *	19.72	2	8	33	-	10181	6402	188	34.05	5-63	3	-
1-day Int	7	4	2	16	9	8.00	-	-	1	-	290	223	6	37.16	3-30	-	
C & G	10	7	1	74	24 *	12.33	-	-	-	-	502	309	9	34.33	3-18	-	
totesport	67	44	12	530	72	16.56	-	1	21	-	2666	2217	79	28.06	6-5	1	
Twenty20	7	4	1	36	16	12.00	-	-	1	-	151	202	11	18.36	3-23	-	

WHELAN, C. D. Middlesex

Name: Christopher David Whelan
Role: Right-hand bat, right-arm medium-fast opening bowler
Born: 8 May 1986, Liverpool
Height: 6ft 2in **Weight:** 12st
Nickname: Scouse, Wheelo, Wheels
County debut: 2004 (one-day)
Parents: Sue and Dave
Marital status: Single
Family links with cricket: 'Father played high level of club cricket – Liverpool CC'
Education: St Margaret's High School
Qualifications: 11 GCSEs, 3 A-levels
Career outside cricket: 'Trying for a role in sports psychology'
Off-season: 'Training hard for new season'
Overseas tours: Mumbai 2005
Cricket moments to forget: 'Bowling awfully in front of coaches at trial game! Getting a contract after 0-100!'
Cricketers particularly admired: Jason Gillespie
Young players to look out for: Paul Horton, Billy Godleman, S. Wade
Other sports played: Football (Quarry Bank), golf
Other sports followed: Football (Everton)
Favourite band: Counting Crows, Matchbox Twenty, Keane
Relaxations: 'Playing golf; watching DVDs'
Extras: Spotted by a Middlesex overseas professional while playing at Sefton Park CC
Opinions on cricket: 'Not enough attention paid to young players who may or may not fit into county preferences who are good enough players, and they then slip through the net.'

2004 Season

	M	Inns	NO	Runs	HS	Avge	100s	50s	Ct	St	O	M	Runs	Wkts	Avge	Best	5wI	10wM
Test																		
All First																		
1-day Int																		
C & G																		
totesport	1	1	0	6	6	6.00	-	-	-	-	7	0	40	0	-		-	-
Twenty20																		

Career Performances

	M	Inns	NO	Runs	HS	Avge	100s	50s	Ct	St	Balls	Runs	Wkts	Avge	Best	5wI	10wM
Test																	
All First																	
1-day Int																	
C & G																	
totesport	1	1	0	6	6	6.00	-	-	-	-	42	40	0	-		-	-
Twenty20																	

WHITE, A. R. — Northamptonshire

Name: Andrew Rowland White
Role: Right-hand bat, right-arm off-spin bowler; all-rounder
Born: 3 July 1980, Newtownards, County Down
Height: 6ft **Weight:** 12st 2lbs
Nickname: Whitey
County debut: 2004
1st-Class 50s: 1
1st-Class 100s: 1
1st-Class catches: 1
Strike rate: 81.00 (career 81.00)
Parents: Rowland and Elizabeth
Marital status: Single
Family links with cricket: 'Brother Richard and cousins play league cricket in Northern Ireland'
Education: Regent House Grammar School; University of Ulster
Qualifications: 9 GCSEs, 2 A-levels, honours degree in Sport, Exercise and Leisure, ECB level 2 coach
Career outside cricket: Student – PGCE in Physical Education

Off-season: 'Studying at university'
Overseas tours: Ireland U19 to Sri Lanka (U19 World Cup) 1999-2000; Ireland to South Africa 2001, to Toronto (ICC Trophy) 2001
Overseas teams played for: UPE International Cricket Academy, South Africa 2002
Career highlights to date: 'Scoring the winning runs in Ireland's historic victory over the West Indies in Belfast, June 2004'
Cricket moments to forget: 'Failure to qualify for the 2003 World Cup via the ICC Trophy in Canada in 2001'
Cricket superstitions: 'None'
Cricketers particularly admired: Jonty Rhodes, Steve Waugh
Young players to look out for: Greg Thompson, Eoin Morgan
Other sports played: Football, golf
Other sports followed: Football (Northern Ireland – 'Our Wee Country'), rugby (Ulster)
Favourite band: U2
Relaxations: 'Snooker; eating out'
Extras: Represented Ireland in the C&G 2002, 2003, 2004; Man of the Match v Surrey at Clontarf in the C&G 2004. Made first-class debut for Ireland v Holland at Deventer in the ICC Inter-Continental Cup 2004, scoring maiden first-class century (152*). Youngest player to pass 1000 runs in history of Irish cricket
Opinions on cricket: 'Great initiative by the ECB to expand the C&G Trophy in 2006 and to involve Ireland and Scotland. This is important for the development of cricket in the two countries – both have shown they are well capable of competing at this level.'
Best batting: 152* Ireland v Holland, Deventer 2004
Best bowling: 2-19 Northamptonshire v Warwickshire, Northampton 2004

2004 Season

	M	Inns	NO	Runs	HS	Avge	100s	50s	Ct	St	O	M	Runs	Wkts	Avge	Best	5wI	10wM
Test																		
All First	4	5	1	252	152 *	63.00	1	1	1	-	54	12	159	4	39.75	2-19	-	-
1-day Int																		
C & G	2	2	1	64	44	64.00	-	-	1	-	17	0	85	3	28.33	3-43	-	
totesport																		
Twenty20																		

Career Performances

	M	Inns	NO	Runs	HS	Avge	100s	50s	Ct	St	Balls	Runs	Wkts	Avge	Best	5wI	10wM
Test																	
All First	4	5	1	252	152 *	63.00	1	1	1	-	324	159	4	39.75	2-19	-	-
1-day Int																	
C & G	5	4	1	69	44	23.00	-	-	1	-	180	137	3	45.66	3-43	-	
totesport																	
Twenty20																	

WHITE, C. Yorkshire

Name: Craig White
Role: Right-hand bat, right-arm fast-medium bowler, county captain
Born: 16 December 1969, Morley, Yorkshire
Height: 6ft 1in **Weight:** 11st 11lbs
Nickname: Chalky, Bassey
County debut: 1990
County cap: 1993
Benefit: 2002
Test debut: 1994
Tests: 30
One-Day Internationals: 51
1st-Class 50s: 53
1st-Class 100s: 17
1st-Class 5 w. in innings: 11
1st-Class catches: 148
One-Day 100s: 3
One-Day 5 w. in innings: 3
Place in batting averages: 188th av. 24.09 (2003 31st av. 49.53)
Place in bowling averages: 22nd av. 25.63
Strike rate: 48.18 (career 53.72)
Parents: Fred Emsley and Cynthia Anne
Wife and date of marriage: Elizabeth Anne, 19 September 1992
Family links with cricket: Father played for Pudsey St Lawrence
Education: Flora Hill High School; Bendigo Senior High School (both Victoria, Australia)
Overseas tours: Australia YC to West Indies 1989-90; England A to Pakistan 1995-96, to Australia 1996-97; England to Australia 1994-95, to India and Pakistan (World Cup) 1995-96, to Zimbabwe and New Zealand 1996-97, to South Africa and Zimbabwe 1999-2000 (one-day series), to Kenya (ICC Knockout Trophy) 2000-01, to Pakistan and Sri Lanka 2000-01, to India and New Zealand 2001-02, to Australia 2002-03, to Africa (World Cup) 2002-03
Overseas teams played for: Victoria, Australia 1990-91; Central Districts, New Zealand 1999-2000
Cricketers particularly admired: Graeme Hick, Mark Waugh, Brian Lara
Other sports followed: Leeds RFC, motocross, golf, tennis
Relaxations: Playing guitar, reading, gardening and socialising
Extras: Man of the Match in the second ODI v Zimbabwe at Bulawayo 1999-2000 (5-21/26). Took National League hat-trick (Fleming, Patel, Masters) v Kent at Headingley 2000. Recorded maiden Test five-wicket return (5-57) in the fourth Test v West Indies on his home ground of Headingley 2000. Scored 93 in the first Test at

Lahore 2000-01, in the process sharing with Graham Thorpe (118) in a new record sixth-wicket partnership for England in Tests v Pakistan (166). Scored maiden Test century (121) in the second Test v India at Ahmedabad 2001-02, winning Man of the Match award. C&G Man of the Match award for his 4-35 and 78-ball 100* in the semi-final v Surrey at Headingley 2002. Scored 60 v Essex at Headingley 2004, in the process passing 10,000 first-class career runs. Captain of Yorkshire since 2004
Best batting: 186 Yorkshire v Lancashire, Old Trafford 2001
Best bowling: 8-55 Yorkshire v Gloucestershire, Gloucester 1998

2004 Season

	M	Inns	NO	Runs	HS	Avge	100s	50s	Ct	St	O	M	Runs	Wkts	Avge	Best	5wI	10wM
Test																		
All First	7	12	1	265	60	24.09	-	1	4	-	88.2	18	282	11	25.63	3-50	-	-
1-day Int																		
C & G	3	3	0	71	43	23.66	-	-	1	-	14	1	87	1	87.00	1-42	-	
totesport	9	9	1	278	59	34.75	-	1	2	-	21	0	88	3	29.33	2-15	-	
Twenty20	1	0	0	0	0	-	-	-	-	-								

Career Performances

	M	Inns	NO	Runs	HS	Avge	100s	50s	Ct	St	Balls	Runs	Wkts	Avge	Best	5wI	10wM
Test	30	50	7	1052	121	24.46	2	9	14	-	3959	2220	59	37.62	5-32	3	-
All First	234	371	48	10217	186	31.63	17	53	148	-	20954	11103	390	28.46	8-55	11	-
1-day Int	51	41	5	568	57 *	15.77	-	1	12	-	2364	1727	65	26.56	5-21	1	
C & G	34	31	7	1114	113	46.41	2	7	12	-	1452	967	33	29.30	4-35	-	
totesport	161	145	16	3224	148	24.99	1	10	47	-	4628	3339	146	22.86	5-19	1	
Twenty20	6	5	0	67	24	13.40	-	-	-	-							

100. Who scored 600 runs at 66.66, including three centuries, as an overseas player for the Scottish Saltires in the one-day league 2003?

WHITE, R. A. Northamptonshire

Name: Robert (Rob) Allan White
Role: Right-hand bat, leg-spin bowler
Born: 15 October 1979, Chelmsford, Essex
Height: 5ft 11in **Weight:** 11st 7lbs
Nickname: Chalky, Toff, Zorro, Whitey, Lamb
County debut: 2000
1st-Class 50s: 6
1st-Class 200s: 1
1st-Class catches: 10
One-Day 100s: 1
Place in batting averages: 234th av. 17.55 (2003 229th av. 18.64)
Strike rate: 64.00 (career 53.11)
Parents: Dennis and Ann
Marital status: Single
Family links with cricket: 'Grandfather on Essex committee for many years. Dad flailed the willow and brother travels the local leagues high and low'
Education: Stowe School; St John's College, Durham University; Loughborough University
Qualifications: 9 GCSEs, 3 A-levels
Cricket moments to forget: 'Franklyn Rose telling me my mates had bet £10 that he couldn't injure me, as I walked out to play Lashings'
Cricketers particularly admired: Ian Botham, Viv Richards, Steve Waugh
Young players to look out for: Monty Panesar
Other sports played: Badminton, squash, golf, kabaddi
Other sports followed: Football (West Ham), rugby (Northampton Saints)
Extras: Northamptonshire League Young Player of the Year and Youth Cricketer of the Year 1999. Scored the first ever double century (206) in the history of the *Cricketer* Cup, for Stowe Templars v Old Whitgiftians at Stowe 2001. Northamptonshire Young Player of the Year (Frank Rudd Trophy) 2001. Played for Loughborough University CCE 2001, 2002 and 2003 and was Man of the Match in the first One-Day UCCE Challenge Match at Lord's 2001. Recorded the highest maiden century in the history of English first-class cricket (277, including a hundred before lunch on the first day), v Gloucestershire at Northampton 2002 in his fifth first-class match; in the process he shared with Mark Powell (107) in a new record opening partnership for Northamptonshire (375). NBC Denis Compton Award for the most promising young Northamptonshire player 2002. Represented British Universities 2003
Best batting: 277 Northamptonshire v Gloucestershire, Northampton 2002
Best bowling: 2-30 Northamptonshire v Gloucestershire, Northampton 2002

2004 Season

	M	Inns	NO	Runs	HS	Avge	100s	50s	Ct	St	O	M	Runs	Wkts	Avge	Best	5wI	10wM
Test																		
All First	5	9	0	158	52	17.55	-	1	3	-	32	6	98	3	32.66	2-46	-	-
1-day Int																		
C & G																		
totesport	6	6	0	146	101	24.33	1	-	2	-	2	0	9	0	-	-	-	
Twenty20	2	2	0	1	1	0.50	-	-	1	-								

Career Performances

	M	Inns	NO	Runs	HS	Avge	100s	50s	Ct	St	Balls	Runs	Wkts	Avge	Best	5wI	10wM
Test																	
All First	18	34	1	1012	277	30.66	1	6	10	-	478	319	9	35.44	2-30	-	-
1-day Int																	
C & G																	
totesport	16	16	0	262	101	16.37	1	-	4	-	48	46	2	23.00	2-18	-	
Twenty20	7	7	0	81	28	11.57	-	-	2	-							

WIGLEY, D. H. — Worcestershire

Name: David Harry Wigley
Role: Right-hand bat, right-arm fast-medium bowler
Born: 26 October 1981, Bradford, Yorkshire
Height: 6ft 4in **Weight:** 13st 6lbs
Nickname: Wiggers, Wigsy
County debut: 2002 (Yorkshire), 2003 (Worcestershire)
County colours: 2003 (Worcestershire)
1st-Class catches: 2
Strike rate: 55.80 (career 69.93)
Parents: Max and Judith
Marital status: Girlfriend Sarah
Family links with cricket: 'Dad played league cricket in Liverpool Competition, Bradford League and Durham Senior League'
Education: St Mary's Roman Catholic Comprehensive, Menston; Loughborough University
Qualifications: 9 GCSEs, 3 A-levels, honours degree in sports science, ECB Level I coaching
Off-season: 'Playing and training in Perth, Western Australia'

Overseas tours: British Universities to Cape Town 2004
Overseas teams played for: Gormandale CC, Victoria 2001; Mount Lawley CC, Perth 2004-05
Career highlights to date: 'Taking "five-for" at Lord's in University final 2002. Taking 4-37 in totesport League v Leicestershire 2004. Winning 2nd XI Trophy 2004'
Cricket moments to forget: 'Losing University final at Lord's to Oxford 2004'
Cricket superstitions: 'Prefer to receive ball from right and must turn left to run in when bowling'
Cricketers particularly admired: Darren Gough, Allan Donald, Jason Gillespie, Graeme Hick
Young players to look out for: Joe Sayers, James Pipe, Chris Benham
Other sports played: Rugby union ('played until 17 for district; had county trials')
Other sports followed: Football (Leeds United), rugby (Wales)
Favourite band: Maroon 5
Relaxations: 'Watching films; listening to music'
Extras: Played for ECB Schools v Sri Lanka U19 2000. Yorkshire U19 Bowling Award 2000. Played for Loughborough University CCE 2002 and 2003, taking 5-71 v Hampshire at West End 2002 and 5-52 v Oxford in the UCCE One-Day Challenge at Lord's 2002; captained LUCCE 2004. Left Yorkshire at the end of the 2002 season and joined Worcestershire for 2003. Represented British Universities 2003; captained British Universities v New Zealanders and Sri Lanka A 2004
Opinions on cricket: 'A lot of cricket – less time for preparation. Three up/three down probably one too many. Two overseas one too many.'
Best batting: 23* LUCCE v Somerset, Taunton 2004
Best bowling: 4-133 LUCCE v Somerset, Taunton 2004

2004 Season

	M	Inns	NO	Runs	HS	Avge	100s	50s	Ct	St	O	M	Runs	Wkts	Avge	Best	5wI	10wM
Test																		
All First	4	3	1	34	23 *	17.00	-	-	2	-	93	16	350	10	35.00	4-133	-	-
1-day Int																		
C & G																		
totesport	2	1	0	2	2	2.00	-	-	-	-	15	3	59	6	9.83	4-37	-	
Twenty20	2	1	0	1	1	1.00	-	-	-	-	5	0	33	1	33.00	1-8	-	

Career Performances

	M	Inns	NO	Runs	HS	Avge	100s	50s	Ct	St	Balls	Runs	Wkts	Avge	Best	5wI	10wM
Test																	
All First	7	9	2	91	23 *	13.00	-	-	2	-	1049	746	15	49.73	4-133	-	-
1-day Int																	
C & G																	
totesport	4	2	0	3	2	1.50	-	-	-	-	198	158	7	22.57	4-37	-	
Twenty20	2	1	0	1	1	1.00	-	-	-	-	30	33	1	33.00	1-8	-	

WINDOWS, M. G. N. Gloucestershire

Name: Matthew Guy Newman Windows
Role: Right-hand bat, left-arm medium bowler
Born: 5 April 1973, Bristol
Height: 5ft 7in **Weight:** 11st 7lbs
Nickname: Steamy, Bedos, Boat
County debut: 1992
County cap: 1998
1000 runs in a season: 3
1st-Class 50s: 45
1st-Class 100s: 16
1st-Class catches: 88
One-Day 100s: 3
Place in batting averages: 197th av. 22.63 (2003 134th av. 30.68)
Strike rate: (career 68.50)
Parents: Tony and Carolyn
Wife and date of marriage: Emma, 12 October 2002
Family links with cricket: 'Father (A.R.) played for Gloucestershire (1960-69) and was Cambridge cricket Blue'
Education: Clifton College; Durham University
Qualifications: 9 GCSEs, 3 A-levels, BA (Hons) Sociology (Dunelm), SFA securities representative of the London Stock Exchange
Career outside cricket: Working with Rowan Dartington stockbrokers
Overseas tours: Clifton College to Barbados 1991; England U19 to Pakistan 1991-92; Durham University to South Africa 1992-93; England A to Zimbabwe and South Africa 1998-99; Gloucestershire's annual pre-season tour to South Africa
Overseas teams played for: Gold Coast Dolphins, Queensland 1996-97
Career highlights to date: 'Winning all the Lord's finals, but [especially] being not out against Glamorgan in the 2000 [B&H] final'
Cricketers particularly admired: David Boon, Courtney Walsh
Young players to look out for: Monty Panesar, Alex Gidman
Other sports played: Rackets (British Open runner-up 1997)
Relaxations: 'Travelling and understanding financial jargon'
Extras: Represented England U19. Scored 71 on county debut v Essex at Bristol 1992. Gloucestershire Young Player of the Year 1994. Set record for highest individual score for Durham University (218*), v Hull University in the BUSA Championships 1995. Gloucestershire Player of the Year 1998. Scored three consecutive one-day centuries against Northants 2001-02 – 108* in the B&H 2001, his maiden one-day hundred and for which he won the Gold Award; 117 off 94 balls in the NUL at

Cheltenham 2001, his maiden one-day league century; 112* in the NUL 2002, in which innings he equalled the most sixes (seven) hit in an innings at Bristol
Best batting: 184 Gloucestershire v Warwickshire, Cheltenham 1996
Best bowling: 1-6 Combined Universities v West Indians, The Parks 1995

2004 Season

	M	Inns	NO	Runs	HS	Avge	100s	50s	Ct	St	O	M	Runs	Wkts	Avge	Best	5wI	10wM
Test																		
All First	9	13	2	249	58	22.63	-	1	4	-								
1-day Int																		
C & G	3	3	0	87	62	29.00	-	1	-	-								
totesport	13	13	0	434	79	33.38	-	3	2	-								
Twenty20																		

Career Performances

	M	Inns	NO	Runs	HS	Avge	100s	50s	Ct	St	Balls	Runs	Wkts	Avge	Best	5wI	10wM
Test																	
All First	154	271	19	8497	184	33.71	16	45	88	-	137	131	2	65.50	1-6	-	-
1-day Int																	
C & G	27	24	4	533	82	26.65	-	3	11	-							
totesport	136	129	14	3050	117	26.52	2	15	43	-	48	49	0	-	-	-	
Twenty20	5	3	0	36	27	12.00	-	-	3	-							

WOOD, J. Lancashire

Name: John Wood
Role: Right-hand bat, right-arm fast-medium bowler
Born: 22 July 1970, Crofton, Wakefield
Height: 6ft 3in **Weight:** 16st 7lbs
Nickname: Woody
County debut: 1992 (Durham), 2001 (Lancashire)
County cap: 1998 (Durham), 2003 (Lancashire)
50 wickets in a season: 1
1st-Class 50s: 3
1st-Class 5 w. in innings: 11
1st-Class catches: 28
One-Day 5 w. in innings: 1
Place in batting averages: (2003 270th av. 11.16)

Place in bowling averages: (2003 69th av. 31.62)
Strike rate: 76.50 (career 54.86)
Parents: Brian and Anne
Wife and date of marriage: Emma Louise, 30 October 1994
Children: Alexandra Mae, 7 April 1996; Joseph Samuel, 3 July 1998; Kate Amelia, 22 January 2004
Family links with cricket: Brother Ian plays for Cleckheaton; father played local league cricket for Crofton
Education: Crofton High School; Wakefield District College; Leeds Polytechnic
Qualifications: 6 O-levels, BTEC Diploma Electronic Engineering, HND Electrical and Electronic Engineering, Level III cricket coach
Overseas tours: Durham CCC to South Africa 1994-95
Overseas teams played for: Griqualand West Cricket Union, South Africa 1990-91; TAWA, Wellington and Wellington B, New Zealand 1993-95
Career highlights to date: 'Reaching C&G semi-final'
Cricket moments to forget: 'C&G semi-final' (*Lancashire lost to Leicestershire as Shahid Afridi struck a 58-ball 95*)
Cricketers particularly admired: Wasim Akram, David Boon, Wayne Larkins
Other sports played: Golf
Other sports followed: Football (Leeds United), rugby (England)
Relaxations: 'Spending time with my family; playing golf'
Extras: Played in the Bradford League. Made his debut for Durham (Minor Counties) in 1991. Durham Players' Player of the Year 1998. Left Durham at the end of the 2000 season and joined Lancs for 2001. Released by Lancs at the end of the 2004 season
Opinions on cricket: 'Time to get rid of EU players and give English youth a chance.'
Best batting: 64 Lancashire v Yorkshire, Headingley 2002
Best bowling: 7-58 Durham v Yorkshire, Headingley 1999

2004 Season

	M	Inns	NO	Runs	HS	Avge	100s	50s	Ct	St	O	M	Runs	Wkts	Avge	Best	5wI	10wM
Test																		
All First	2	2	1	48	35	48.00	-	-	1	-	51	5	243	4	60.75	2-70	-	-
1-day Int																		
C & G																		
totesport	2	2	0	4	4	2.00	-	-	1	-	9	0	78	0	-	-	-	
Twenty20	1	0	0	0	0	-	-	-	-	-	2	0	19	0	-	-	-	

Career Performances

	M	Inns	NO	Runs	HS	Avge	100s	50s	Ct	St	Balls	Runs	Wkts	Avge	Best	5wI	10wM
Test																	
All First	115	163	24	1762	64	12.67	-	3	28	-	17446	10787	318	33.92	7-58	11	-
1-day Int																	
C & G	16	8	2	50	25	8.33	-	-	-	-	691	483	16	30.18	4-33	-	
totesport	112	67	24	428	28 *	9.95	-	-	21	-	4820	3852	112	34.39	5-49	1	
Twenty20	5	2	1	15	15 *	15.00	-	-	1	-	95	100	3	33.33	1-15	-	

WOOD, M. J. Somerset

Name: Matthew James Wood
Role: Right-hand bat, occasional right-arm off-spin bowler
Born: 30 September 1980, Exeter
Height: 5ft 11in **Weight:** 11st 12lbs
Nickname: Woody, Grandma
County debut: 2001
1st-Class 50s: 15
1st-Class 100s: 7
1st-Class catches: 13
Place in batting averages: 40th av. 50.33 (2003 187th av. 24.36)
Parents: Jim and Trina
Marital status: Single
Family links with cricket: Father is chairman of Devon Cricket Board
Education: Exmouth Community College; Exeter University
Qualifications: 8 GCSEs, 2 A-levels, ECB Level 3 coach
Off-season: 'Coaching, training'
Overseas tours: West of England U15 to West Indies 1995
Overseas teams played for: Doubleview CC, Perth
Career highlights to date: 'Debut v Yorkshire at Bath 2001. Two hundreds in the match v Surrey 2002'
Cricketers particularly admired: Marcus Trescothick
Young players to look out for: James Hildreth, Arul Suppiah
Other sports followed: Football (Liverpool FC)
Relaxations: 'Music, cinema, spending time with friends'
Extras: Scored 71 on debut v Yorkshire at Bath 2001. NBC Denis Compton Award for the most promising young Somerset player 2001. Scored century in each innings (106/131) v Surrey at Taunton 2002, becoming (at 21 years 279 days) the fourth youngest batsman to score twin centuries in the Championship. Somerset Player of the Year 2002. Has played for Devon
Opinions on cricket: 'There should be a minimum number of English-qualified players per county.'
Best batting: 196 Somerset v Kent, Taunton 2002

2004 Season

	M	Inns	NO	Runs	HS	Avge	100s	50s	Ct	St	O	M	Runs	Wkts	Avge	Best	5wI	10wM
Test																		
All First	11	16	4	604	128 *	50.33	2	3	5	-	2	0	6	0	-	-	-	-
1-day Int																		
C & G																		
totesport	10	10	2	213	56	26.62	-	1	1	-								
Twenty20	2	2	0	65	50	32.50	-	1	-	-								

Career Performances

	M	Inns	NO	Runs	HS	Avge	100s	50s	Ct	St	Balls	Runs	Wkts	Avge	Best	5wI	10wM
Test																	
All First	45	79	5	2640	196	35.67	7	15	13	-	85	68	0	-	-	-	-
1-day Int																	
C & G	4	3	0	38	19	12.66	-	-	1	-							
totesport	31	29	3	695	88 *	26.73	-	5	6	-							
Twenty20	2	2	0	65	50	32.50	-	1	-	-							

WOOD, M. J. — Yorkshire

Name: Matthew James Wood
Role: Right-hand opening bat, off-spin bowler
Born: 6 April 1977, Huddersfield
Height: 5ft 9in **Weight:** 12st
Nickname: Ronnie, Chuddy
County debut: 1997
County cap: 2001
1000 runs in a season: 3
1st-Class 50s: 23
1st-Class 100s: 13
1st-Class 200s: 2
1st-Class catches: 86
One-Day 100s: 4
Place in batting averages: 85th av. 38.20 (2003 20th av. 53.03)
Strike rate: (career 36.00)
Parents: Roger and Kathryn
Marital status: Single
Family links with cricket: 'Father played for local team Emley. Mum made the teas and sister Caroline scored'
Education: Shelley High School and Sixth Form Centre

Qualifications: 9 GCSEs, 2 A-levels, NCA coaching award
Off-season: 'Mosman CC, Sydney'
Overseas tours: England U19 to Zimbabwe 1995-96; Yorkshire CCC to West Indies 1996-97, to Cape Town 1997, 1998; MCC to Kenya 1999, to Bangladesh 1999-2000; ECB National Academy to Australia 2001-02
Overseas teams played for: Somerset West CC, Cape Town 1994-95; Upper Hutt United CC, New Zealand 1997-98; Mosman Park, Western Australia 2000-01; Mosman CC, Sydney 2004-05
Career highlights to date: 'Being on the pitch as fielding 12th man for England series win v South Africa at Headingley [1998]. Winning the Championship in 2001 and winning the C&G 2002 at Lord's'
Cricket moments to forget: 'Most of the 2002 season'
Cricket superstitions: 'Not any more'
Cricketers particularly admired: Darren Lehmann, Matthew Maynard, Stephen Fleming, Michael Vaughan
Young players to look out for: Ben Heritage
Other sports played: Football (Kirkburton FC)
Other sports followed: Football (Liverpool FC)
Favourite band: Atomic Kitten
Relaxations: 'Socialising, eating out, golf, DIY'
Extras: Represented England U17. Attended Yorkshire Academy. Scored 81 on first-class debut v Lancashire at Headingley 1997. Scored 1000 first-class runs in first full season 1998. Yorkshire Coach's Player of the Year, Yorkshire Club Player of the Year and Yorkshire Players' Player of the Year 2003. Set a new Yorkshire record individual score in the NatWest/C&G (160 from 124 balls) v Devon at Exmouth in the C&G 2004, winning Man of the Match award. Carried his bat for 66* (the first Yorkshire batsman to do so since 1985) v Somerset at Scarborough 2004. Vice-captain of Yorkshire 2003-04
Opinions on cricket: 'Away team captains should have choice to bat/bowl. This would eradicate pitch doctoring. Twenty20 is very good. Should be played on Friday nights, home and away; teams would develop their own support following like Superleague/soccer.'
Best batting: 207 Yorkshire v Somerset, Taunton 2003
Best bowling: 1-4 Yorkshire v Somerset, Headingley 2003

2004 Season

	M	Inns	NO	Runs	HS	Avge	100s	50s	Ct	St	O	M	Runs	Wkts	Avge	Best	5wI	10wM
Test																		
All First	16	27	2	955	123	38.20	1	7	24	-	1	0	1	0	-	-	-	-
1-day Int																		
C & G	4	4	1	278	160	92.66	1	1	3	-								
totesport	18	18	3	386	56	25.73	-	2	2	-	3	0	16	0	-	-	-	
Twenty20	5	5	1	139	96 *	34.75	-	1	3	-								

Career Performances

	M	Inns	NO	Runs	HS	Avge	100s	50s	Ct	St	Balls	Runs	Wkts	Avge	Best	5wI	10wM
Test																	
All First	105	183	18	5615	207	34.03	15	23	86	-	72	39	2	19.50	1-4	-	-
1-day Int																	
C & G	16	16	4	730	160	60.83	2	3	7	-	36	45	3	15.00	3-45	-	
totesport	84	75	6	1597	105 *	23.14	1	8	29	-	18	16	0	-	-	-	
Twenty20	9	9	2	253	96 *	36.14	-	2	7	-							

WRIGHT, B. J. Glamorgan

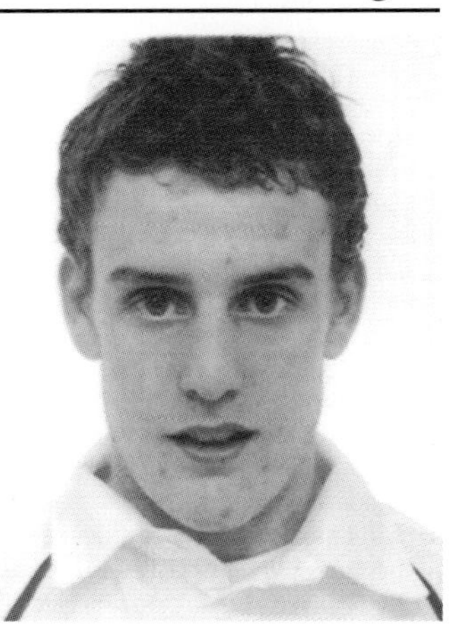

Name: Ben James Wright
Role: Right-hand middle-order bat, right-arm medium bowler
Born: 5 December 1987, Fulwood, Preston
Height: 5ft 9in **Weight:** 11st 9lbs
Nickname: Bej
County debut: No first-team appearance
Parents: Julia and Peter
Marital status: Single
Education: Cowbridge Comprehensive
Off-season: 'Nets at Sophia Gardens'
Overseas tours: West of England U15 to West Indies 2003; England U16 to South Africa 2004
Career highlights to date: 'Playing at Newlands, Western Province, for England U16'
Cricket moments to forget: 'Batting with my father'
Cricket superstitions: 'Always put my right pad on before my left'
Cricketers particularly admired: Andrew Flintoff, Chris Gayle
Young players to look out for: Daniel Roberts
Other sports played: Rugby (Wales U16 A)
Other sports followed: Rugby (Leicester Tigers), football (Man Utd)
Favourite band: Houston
Extras: Sir John Hobbs Memorial Prize 2003. A.A. Thomson Fielding Prize 2003. Young Cricketer of the Year award 2003. Is on a development contract at Glamorgan
Opinions on cricket: 'Enjoy watching, playing. Getting quicker and further by the season.'

WRIGHT, C. J. C. — Middlesex

Name: Christopher (Chris) Julian Clement Wright
Role: Right-hand bat, right-arm medium-fast bowler
Born: 14 July 1985, Chipping Norton, Oxfordshire
Height: 6ft 3in **Weight:** 11st 7lbs
Nickname: Wrighty
County debut: 2004
1st-Class 50s: 1
1st-Class catches: 3
Strike rate: 103.00 (career 103.00)
Parents: Alan and Nikki
Marital status: Single
Family links with cricket: 'Dad plays for Hampshire Seniors'
Education: Eggars School, Alton; Alton College; Anglia Polytechnic University
Qualifications: 11 GCSEs, 3 A-levels
Career outside cricket: Student
Off-season: 'Studying, in gym, playing CM 04-05'
Overseas tours: Cambridge UCCE to Grenada 2004
Career highlights to date: 'Middlesex debut at Headingley v Yorkshire'
Cricket moments to forget: 'Two-ball duck (Kabir Ali slower ball got me out) on live TV under lights with mates watching!'
Cricket superstitions: 'Got rid of them all!'
Cricketers particularly admired: Jason Gillespie, Glenn McGrath
Young players to look out for: Phil Edwards ('Swingers'), Nick Lee, Billy Godleman
Other sports played: Basketball (college)
Other sports followed: Football (Arsenal), basketball (Sacramento Kings)
Favourite band: Rage Against The Machine, Guns N' Roses, Metallica
Relaxations: 'Rock music, table football, movies, Championship Manager, bantering with mates and sleep'
Extras: Played for Cambridge University CCE 2004
Opinions on cricket: 'Players under 20 and batting below eight can't be out in their first six balls! Too many teams have similar kits; perhaps home and away kits should be introduced.'
Best batting: 57 CUCCE v Essex, Fenner's 2004
Best bowling: 2-70 CUCCE v Middlesex, Fenner's 2004

2004 Season

	M	Inns	NO	Runs	HS	Avge	100s	50s	Ct	St	O	M	Runs	Wkts	Avge	Best	5wI	10wM
Test																		
All First	4	5	0	96	57	19.20	-	1	3	-	103	19	379	6	63.16	2-70	-	-
1-day Int																		
C & G																		
totesport	3	1	0	0	0	0.00	-	-	-	-	18	0	104	1	104.00	1-34	-	
Twenty20	1	0	0	0	0	-	-	-	-	-	2	0	15	0	-	-	-	

Career Performances

	M	Inns	NO	Runs	HS	Avge	100s	50s	Ct	St	Balls	Runs	Wkts	Avge	Best	5wI	10wM
Test																	
All First	4	5	0	96	57	19.20	-	1	3	-	618	379	6	63.16	2-70	-	-
1-day Int																	
C & G																	
totesport	3	1	0	0	0	0.00	-	-	-	-	108	104	1	104.00	1-34	-	
Twenty20	1	0	0	0	0	-	-	-	-	-	12	15	0	-	-	-	

WRIGHT, D. G. — Northamptonshire

Name: Damien Geoffrey Wright
Role: Right-hand bat, right-arm fast-medium bowler, gully fielder
Born: 25 July 1975, Casino, NSW, Australia
County debut: 2003
1st-Class 50s: 6
1st-Class 5 w. in innings: 2
1st-Class catches: 24
Strike rate: (career 68.97)
Overseas tours: Australia A to South Africa (one-day series) 2002-03
Overseas teams played for: Tasmania 1997-98 –
Extras: Played for Scotland in the C&G 2002, winning two Man of the Match awards. Has also won several domestic awards in Australia, including Man of the Match v Victoria in the ING Cup at Melbourne 2001-02 (4-23/40). Has represented Australia A against various touring sides. Tasmania's leading wicket-taker in the Pura Cup 2002-03 (31 wickets; av. 27.25) and 2003-04 (37; 26.49). Tasmanian Player of the Year 2002-03. Named in Australia's initial squad of 30 for the 2002-03 World Cup. Was an overseas player with Northamptonshire in June

and July 2003; has returned for 2005. Was due to join Derbyshire as an overseas player for 2004 but was forced to withdraw with a knee injury
Best batting: 65 Tasmania v Western Australia, Perth 2003-04
Best bowling: 6-39 Tasmania v New South Wales, Hobart 2002-03

2004 Season (did not make any first-class or one-day appearances)

Career Performances

	M	Inns	NO	Runs	HS	Avge	100s	50s	Ct	St	Balls	Runs	Wkts	Avge	Best	5wI	10wM
Test																	
All First	52	75	15	1272	65	21.20	-	6	24	-	10622	5051	154	32.79	6-39	2	-
1-day Int																	
C & G	2	2	1	108	55	108.00	-	2	2	-	102	51	3	17.00	2-37	-	
totesport	2	2	0	15	9	7.50	-	-	1	-	93	85	1	85.00	1-52	-	
Twenty20																	

WRIGHT, L. J. Sussex

Name: Luke James Wright
Role: Right-hand bat, right-arm medium-fast bowler; all-rounder
Born: 7 March 1985, Grantham
Height: 5ft 11in **Weight:** 12st 3lbs
Nickname: Wrighty
County debut: 2003 (Leicestershire), 2004 (Sussex)
1st-Class 100s: 1
1st-Class catches: 1
Strike rate: 203.00 (career 317.00)
Parents: Keith and Anna
Marital status: Single
Family links with cricket: 'Father very keen cricketer (Level 2 coach).' Brother Ashley played for Leicestershire
Education: Belvoir High School, Bottesford; Ratcliffe College; Loughborough University
Qualifications: 8 GCSEs, National Diploma in Sports Science and Sports Massage, ECB Level 1 coaching
Overseas tours: Leicestershire U13 to South Africa; Leicestershire U15 to South Africa; England U19 to Australia 2002-03, to Bangladesh (U19 World Cup) 2003-04
Cricket superstitions: 'Too many to name'
Cricketers particularly admired: Andrew Flintoff, Jacques Kallis

Young players to look out for: Ashley Wright, Richard Robinson, Andrew Hodd, Tom New
Other sports played: Football, hockey, squash, tennis
Other sports followed: Football (Newcastle United)
Relaxations: Music, cinema, going out
Extras: Set record for best debut for Ratcliffe College with 130. Scored 86 v MCC, the highest score by a Ratcliffe player against the club. NBC Denis Compton Award for the most promising young Leicestershire player 2002. Took the first ever hat-trick for England U19 in one-day cricket, v South Africa U19 at Hove 2003, finishing with 5-46. Left Leicestershire in the 2003-04 off-season and joined Sussex for 2004. Scored maiden first-class century (100) on Sussex debut v Loughborough University CCE at Hove 2004. Represented England U19 v Bangladesh U19 2004; scored 78 in the first 'Test' at Headingley, sharing with Adam Harrison (33) in a new England U19 record stand for the eighth wicket (114). ECB National Academy 2004-05 (part-time)
Opinions on cricket: 'Too many EU players coming into the game, which is stopping English cricket developing.'
Best batting: 100 Sussex v LUCCE, Hove 2004
Best bowling: 1-74 Sussex v Kent, Canterbury 2004

2004 Season

	M	Inns	NO	Runs	HS	Avge	100s	50s	Ct	St	O	M	Runs	Wkts	Avge	Best	5wI	10wM
Test																		
All First	2	3	0	118	100	39.33	1	-	1	-	33.5	4	104	1	104.00	1-74	-	-
1-day Int																		
C & G	1	1	0	21	21	21.00	-	-	1	-	8	0	43	0	-	-	-	
totesport	14	12	3	134	25 *	14.88	-	-	1	-	85.4	8	418	12	34.83	4-12	-	
Twenty20	4	3	0	19	18	6.33	-	-	1	-	14	0	111	6	18.50	3-39	-	

Career Performances

	M	Inns	NO	Runs	HS	Avge	100s	50s	Ct	St	Balls	Runs	Wkts	Avge	Best	5wI	10wM
Test																	
All First	3	5	1	129	100	32.25	1	-	1	-	317	199	1	199.00	1-74	-	-
1-day Int																	
C & G	2	2	0	37	21	18.50	-	-	1	-	48	43	0	-	-	-	
totesport	16	13	3	141	25 *	14.10	-	-	1	-	520	426	12	35.50	4-12	-	
Twenty20	4	3	0	19	18	6.33	-	-	1	-	84	111	6	18.50	3-39	-	

YARDY, M. H. — Sussex

Name: Michael (Mike) Howard Yardy
Role: Left-hand bat, left-arm medium-fast bowler
Born: 27 November 1980, Pembury, Kent
Height: 6ft **Weight:** 14st 2lbs
Nickname: Yards, Paolo
County debut: 1999 (one-day), 2000 (first-class)
1st-Class 50s: 8
1st-Class 100s: 1
1st-Class catches: 27
Place in batting averages: 120th av. 34.14
Strike rate: 198.00 (career 262.50)
Parents: Beverly and Howard
Marital status: Engaged to Karin Mason
Family links with cricket: 'Brother plays for local team'
Education: William Parker School, Hastings
Qualifications: 5 GCSEs, 2 A-levels, ECB Level 1 coach, Sports Psychology diploma
Overseas tours: Sussex Academy to Barbados 1997; Sussex to Grenada 2001, 2002
Overseas teams played for: Cape Town CC 1999
Career highlights to date: 'Winning County Championship'
Cricket superstitions: 'Loads – all secret'
Cricketers particularly admired: 'All those who have reached the pinnacle of their careers'
Young players to look out for: Greg Hobbs, Russ Jones, Fraser Key, Martin Smith, Jon McSweeney, Richard Chynoweth
Other sports followed: Football (West Ham)
Favourite band: Bluetones
Relaxations: 'Watching West Ham; relaxing with my girlfriend'
Extras: Played in the Sussex U15 side that won the U15 County Championship 1996, the U16 side that won the U16 County Championship 1997 and the U19 side that were runners-up in the NAYC Two-Day Cup 1997. Represented England U17. Attended Sussex Academy. Sussex Most Improved Player 2001. Scored maiden first-class century (115) v Surrey at Hove 2004
Best batting: 115 Sussex v Surrey, Hove 2004
Best bowling: 1-13 Sussex v Derbyshire, Arundel 2001

2004 Season

	M	Inns	NO	Runs	HS	Avge	100s	50s	Ct	St	O	M	Runs	Wkts	Avge	Best	5wI	10wM
Test																		
All First	4	8	1	239	115	34.14	1	-	3	-	33	4	135	1	135.00	1-18	-	-
1-day Int																		
C & G	1	1	0	27	27	27.00	-	-	-	-	2	0	15	0	-	-	-	
totesport	12	12	2	361	88 *	36.10	-	2	8	-	21.4	0	116	1	116.00	1-45	-	
Twenty20	4	3	0	32	17	10.66	-	-	4	-								

Career Performances

	M	Inns	NO	Runs	HS	Avge	100s	50s	Ct	St	Balls	Runs	Wkts	Avge	Best	5wI	10wM
Test																	
All First	38	66	8	1725	115	29.74	1	8	27	-	1050	610	4	152.50	1-13	-	-
1-day Int																	
C & G	10	9	0	129	52	14.33	-	1	4	-	278	266	6	44.33	3-39	-	
totesport	34	31	4	607	88 *	22.48	-	2	13	-	464	416	8	52.00	3-36	-	
Twenty20	4	3	0	32	17	10.66	-	-	4	-							

YATES, G. — Lancashire

Name: Gary Yates
Role: Right-hand bat, right-arm off-spin bowler; 2nd XI captain/coach
Born: 20 September 1967, Ashton-under-Lyne
Height: 6ft 1in **Weight:** 13st 1lb
Nickname: Sweaty, Yugo, Pearly, Backyard, Zippy
County debut: 1990
County cap: 1994
1st-Class 50s: 5
1st-Class 100s: 3
1st-Class 5 w. in innings: 5
1st-Class catches: 38
Strike rate: (career 74.73)
Parents: Alan and Patricia
Wife and date of marriage: Christine, 20 February 2004
Children: Francis Leonard George, 1 May 1999
Family links with cricket: 'Father played for Denton St Lawrence and other teams in the Lancashire League'
Education: Manchester Grammar School

Qualifications: 6 O-levels, ECB Level III coach ('halfway through ECB Level IV coaching course'), Australian Cricket Coaching Council coach
Career outside cricket: 'Sales rep with family business (Digical Ltd), selling diaries, calendars and business gifts'
Off-season: 'Preparing for benefit'
Overseas tours: Lancashire to Tasmania and Western Australia 1990, to Western Australia 1991, to Johannesburg 1992, to Barbados and St Lucia 1992, to Calcutta 1997, to Cape Town 1997-98, to Grenada 2003; MCC to Bangladesh 1999-2000
Overseas teams played for: South Barwon, Geelong, Australia 1987-88; Johnsonville, Wellington, New Zealand 1989-90; Western Suburbs, Brisbane 1991-92; Old Selbornian, East London, South Africa 1992-93; Hermanus CC, South Africa 1995-96
Career highlights to date: 'All trophies won while playing with Lancashire'
Cricket moments to forget: 'Not being selected for a 2nd XI Bain Hogg final after playing all ten round matches and semi-final'
Cricket superstitions: 'They vary'
Cricketers particularly admired: Michael Atherton, Ian Botham, John Emburey
Other sports played: Golf ('represented Lancashire CCC at National *Times* Corporate Golf Challenge, La Manga, Spain, December 2001')
Other sports followed: 'All sports, especially football (Manchester City season-ticket holder), golf, motor rallying'
Relaxations: 'Playing golf, watching football and good films, eating; spending time with my son'
Extras: Scored century (106) on Championship debut v Nottinghamshire at Trent Bridge 1990. Rapid Cricketline Player of the Month April/May 1992. Won the double with Bowdon CC (Cheshire County League) 2002 and 2003; took 77 wickets and scored 930 runs (av. 103.00) in league 2003. Leading wicket-taker for Lancashire 2nd XI. Lancashire 2nd XI captain/coach since 2002. Granted a benefit for 2005
Opinions on cricket: 'Still adamant that relegation and promotion should be two teams only.'
Best batting: 134* Lancashire v Northamptonshire, Old Trafford 1993
Best bowling: 6-64 Lancashire v Kent, Old Trafford 1999

2004 Season (did not make any first-class or one-day appearances)

Career Performances

	M	Inns	NO	Runs	HS	Avge	100s	50s	Ct	St	Balls	Runs	Wkts	Avge	Best	5wI	10wM
Test																	
All First	82	107	36	1789	134 *	25.19	3	5	38	-	13751	7025	184	38.17	6-64	5	-
1-day Int																	
C & G	22	10	5	91	34 *	18.20	-	-	5	-	1266	712	19	37.47	2-15	-	
totesport	115	53	25	435	38	15.53	-	-	28	-	4122	3309	105	31.51	4-34	-	
Twenty20																	

STOP PRESS

BORRINGTON, P. M. Derbyshire

Name: Paul Michael Borrington
Role: Right-hand bat, off-spin bowler
Born: 24 May 1988
Extras: Father, A. J. Borrington, played for Derbyshire 1970-81. Made 2nd XI Championship debut 2004. Is a Derbyshire Academy player

BROWNING, R. Derbyshire

Name: Richard Browning
Role: Right-hand bat, right-arm medium-fast bowler
Born: 9 October 1987
Extras: Is a Derbyshire Academy player

HUGHES, L. Derbyshire

Name: Liam Hughes
Role: Right-hand bat, right-arm medium-fast bowler
Born: 21 March 1988
Extras: Is a Derbyshire Academy player

JAYASURIYA, S. T. Somerset

Name: Sanath Teran Jayasuriya
Role: Left-hand bat, slow left-arm bowler
Born: 30 June 1969, Matara, Sri Lanka
Extras: Has played 92 Tests and 328 ODIs for Sri Lanka; captain 1999-2003. Has joined Somerset as an overseas player for the early part of 2005

KRUIS, G. J. Yorkshire

Name: Gideon (Deon) Jacobus Kruis
Role: Right-hand bat, right-arm fast-medium bowler
Born: 9 May 1974, Pretoria, South Africa
Extras: Has played for Northern Transvaal, Griqualand West and Eagles in South Africa. Has joined Yorkshire for 2005; is not considered an overseas player

NEEDHAM, J. Derbyshire

Name: Jake Needham
Role: Right-hand bat, right-arm off-spin bowler
Born: 30 September 1986, Portsmouth, Hampshire
Extras: Made 2nd XI Championship debut 2004. Is a Derbyshire Academy player

RUDGE, W. D. Gloucestershire

Name: William Douglas Rudge
Role: Right-hand bat, right-arm medium bowler
Born: 15 July 1983, Bristol
Extras: Played for Gloucestershire Board XI in the C&G 2002 and 2003

SNELL, S. D. Gloucestershire

Name: Stephen David Snell
Role: Right-hand bat, wicket-keeper
Born: 27 February 1983, Winchester, Hampshire
Extras: Played for Hampshire Board XI in the C&G 2002

SCOTTISH SALTIRES 2005

WRIGHT, C. M.

Name: Craig McIntyre Wright
Role: Right-hand bat, right-arm medium-fast bowler, captain
Born: 28 April 1974, Paisley
Extras: Scotland debut 1997. International tournaments include Commonwealth Games 1998-99, ICC Trophy 2001, ICC Inter-Continental Cup 2004. First Scotland bowler to record a one-day league five-wicket return (5-44), v Somerset 2004

ASIM BUTT

Name: Asim Butt
Role: Right-hand bat, left-arm medium-fast bowler
Born: 24 October 1967, Lahore, Pakistan
Extras: Scotland debut 1998. Played first-class cricket in Pakistan. Represented Scotland in World Cup 1999, ICC Trophy 2001 and ICC Inter-Continental Cup 2004

BRINKLEY, J. E.

Name: James Edward Brinkley
Role: Right-hand bat, right-arm fast-medium bowler
Born: 13 March 1974, Helensburgh
Extras: Scotland debut 1998. Played for Worcestershire (6-98 on Championship debut 1994), Essex and Durham. International tournaments include Commonwealth Games 1998-99, World Cup 1999, ICC Trophy 2001 and ICC Six Nations Challenge 2003-04

COETZER, S. C.

Name: Stuart Charles Coetzer
Role: Right-hand bat, wicket-keeper
Born: 30 January 1982, Grahamstown, South Africa
Extras: Scotland debut 2004. Represented Scotland in U19 World Cup in New Zealand 2001-02. Represented Scotland against the Bangladeshis 2004

ENGLISH, C. V.

Name: Cedric Vaughan English
Role: Right-hand bat, right-arm fast-medium bowler
Born: 13 September 1973, Kimberley, South Africa
Extras: Scotland debut 2002. Played first-class cricket in South Africa. Qualifies for Scotland by residence; represented Scotland in ICC Inter-Continental Cup 2004

GOUDIE, G.

Name: Gordon Goudie
Role: Right-hand bat, right-arm fast-medium bowler
Born: 12 August 1987, Aberdeen
Extras: Scotland debut 2004. Youngest player ever capped by Scotland (aged 16). Represented Scotland in U19 World Cup in Bangladesh 2003-04

HAQ, R. M.

Name: Rana Majid Haq Khan
Role: Left-hand bat, right-arm off-spin bowler
Born: 11 February 1983, Paisley
Extras: Scotland debut 2002. Took 4-36 v Durham at Riverside in Scotland's debut NCL match 2003. Represented Scotland in ICC Six Nations Challenge 2003-04 and ICC Inter-Continental Cup 2004

HOFFMANN, P. J. C.

Name: Paul Jacob Christopher Hoffmann
Role: Right-hand bat, right-arm fast-medium bowler
Born: 14 January 1970, Rockhampton, Queensland, Australia
Extras: Scotland debut 2001. Leading wicket-taker in Scottish National Cricket League history. Qualifies for Scotland by residence; represented Scotland in ICC Six Nations Challenge 2003-04 and ICC Inter-Continental Cup 2004

KNOX, S. T.

Name: Steven Thomas Knox
Role: Right-hand bat, right-arm medium bowler
Born: 16 February 1974, Barrow-in-Furness, Lancashire
Extras: Scotland debut 2003. Played for Cumberland in Minor Counties (scoring 101*/125* v Bedfordshire at Kendal 2002) and in NatWest and C&G. Represented Scotland in ICC Inter-Continental Cup 2004

LOCKHART, D. R.

Name: Douglas Ross Lockhart
Role: Right-hand bat, wicket-keeper
Born: 19 January 1976, Glasgow
Extras: Scotland debut 1995. Player of the Tournament at International Youth Tournament, Holland 1995. Oxford Blue 1998. International tournaments include ICC Trophy 1996-97 and 2001, Commonwealth Games 1998-99, ICC Six Nations Challenge 2003-04 and ICC Inter-Continental Cup 2004

MAIDEN, G. I.

Name: Gregor Ian Maiden
Role: Right-hand bat, right-arm off-spin bowler
Born: 22 July 1979, Glasgow
Extras: Scotland debut 1998. Represented Scotland in U19 World Cup in South Africa 1997-98. International tournaments include ICC Trophy 2001, ICC Six Nations Challenge 2003-04 and ICC Inter-Continental Cup 2004. Also played one-day cricket for Lancashire 2003

NEL, J. D.

Name: Johann Dewald Nel
Role: Right-hand bat, right-arm fast-medium bowler
Born: 6 June 1980, Klerksdorp, South Africa
Extras: Scotland debut 2004. Represented Scotland U23; represented Scotland in ICC Inter-Continental Cup 2004

SMITH, C. J. O.

Name: Colin John Ogilvie Smith
Role: Right-hand bat, wicket-keeper
Born: 27 September 1972, Aberdeen
Extras: Scotland debut 1999. Represented Scotland age groups and Scotland A. Represented Scotland in ICC Emerging Nations Tournament 1999-2000, ICC Trophy 2001 and ICC Inter-Continental Cup 2004. Top-scored with 79* v Durham at Edinburgh in the totesport League 2004, in the process sharing with Cedric English (53*) in a record fifth-wicket partnership for Scotland in one-day cricket (146*)

SMITH, S. J. S.

Name: Simon James Stevenson Smith
Role: Right-hand bat, wicket-keeper
Born: 8 December 1979, Ashington, Northumberland
Extras: Scotland debut 2004. Represented Scotland U16, U19 and U23; represented Scotland in ICC Inter-Continental Cup 2004

STANGER, I. M.

Name: Ian Michael Stanger
Role: Right-hand bat, right-arm medium-fast bowler
Born: 5 October 1971, Glasgow
Extras: Scotland debut 1992. Scotland Young Cricketer of the Year 1992, 1993. Played for Leicestershire 1994. Represented Scotland in Commonwealth Games 1998-99, World Cup 1999, ICC Six Nations Challenge 2003-04 and ICC Inter-Continental Cup 2004

WATSON, R. R.

Name: Ryan Robert Watson
Role: Right-hand bat, right-arm medium/off-spin bowler, vice-captain
Born: 12 November 1976, Harare, Zimbabwe
Extras: Scotland debut 2002. Represented South Africa Schools B 1995 and captained Transvaal U24 1996. Struck 43-ball century (103*) v Somerset at Edinburgh in the NCL 2003. Qualifies for Scotland by residence; represented Scotland in ICC Six Nations Challenge 2003-04 and ICC Inter-Continental Cup 2004

WATTS, D. F.

Name: David Fraser Watts
Role: Right-hand bat, right-arm medium bowler
Born: 5 June 1979, King's Lynn, Norfolk
Extras: Scotland debut 1998. Represented Scotland in U19 World Cup in South Africa 1997-98. Represented Scotland in ICC Trophy 2001, ICC Six Nations Challenge 2003-04, and ICC Inter-Continental Cup 2004, scoring centuries (118* and 146) against Ireland and Kenya respectively

WILLIAMSON, J. G.

Name: John Greig Williamson
Role: Right-hand bat, right-arm fast-medium bowler
Born: 28 December 1968, Glasgow
Extras: Scotland debut 1989. Represented Scotland in ICC Trophy 1996-97 and 2001, Commonwealth Games 1998-99, World Cup 1999, ICC Emerging Nations Tournament 1999-2000, ICC Six Nations Challenge 2003-04 and ICC Inter-Continental Cup 2004. Became fourth player to win 100 Scotland caps 2001

YASIR ARAFAT

Name: Yasir Arafat Satti
Role: Right-hand bat, right-arm fast-medium bowler
Born: 12 March 1982, Rawalpindi, Pakistan
Extras: Scotland debut 2004. Represented Pakistan U19; represented Pakistan in two ODIs. Is club professional at Clydesdale; joined Scotland as an overseas player for 2004 and has returned for 2005

THE UMPIRES

BENSON, M. R.

Name: Mark Richard Benson
Born: 6 July 1958, Shoreham, Sussex
Height: 5ft 10in
Nickname: Benny
Wife and date of marriage: Sarah Patricia, 20 September 1986
Children: Laurence, 16 October 1987; Edward, 23 June 1990
Education: Sutton Valence School
Off-season: 'Improving my golf and bridge'
Other sports played: Bridge, golf, swimming, cycling
Relaxations: Bridge, golf
Appointed to 1st-Class list: 2000
International panel: 2004 –
Tests umpired: 3 (plus 4 as TV umpire)
One-Day Internationals umpired: 10 (plus 5 as TV umpire)
Other umpiring honours: Stood in the C&G Trophy final 2003
County as player: Kent
Role: Left-hand bat
County debut: 1980
County cap: 1981
Benefit: 1991 (£174,619)
Test debut: 1986
Tests: 1
One-Day Internationals: 1
1000 runs in a season: 11
1st-Class 50s: 99
1st-Class 100s: 47
1st-Class 200s: 1
1st-Class catches: 140
One-Day 100s: 5
Overseas tours: None
Highlights of playing career: '257 v Hampshire. Winning Sunday League as captain of Kent. Two 90s to win a game against Hampshire with Malcolm Marshall bowling.

One of only four cricketers in the history of Kent to have scored more than 10,000 runs and have an average in excess of 40'
Extras: Scored 1000 runs in first full season. Kent captain 1991-95
Opinions on cricket: 'Teams should be permitted a certain number of appeals against poor decisions. As an umpire I would be quite happy for a decision to be overturned if a mistake has been made. If the umpire has been proved to be correct, the team that has appealed loses one of their appeals. This occurs in American football and works very well. Surely the object must be to achieve 100 per cent correct decision-making.'
Best batting: 257 Kent v Hampshire, Southampton 1991
Best bowling: 2-55 Kent v Surrey, Dartford 1986

First-Class Career Performances

	M	Inns	NO	Runs	HS	Avge	100s	Ct	St	Runs	Wkts	Avge	Best	5wI	10wM
Test	1	2	0	51	30	25.50	-	-	-						
All First	292	491	34	18387	257	40.23	48	140	-	493	5	98.60	2-55	-	-

BURGESS, G. I.

Name: Graham Iefvion Burgess
Born: 5 May 1943, Glastonbury, Somerset
Education: Millfield School
Appointed to 1st-Class list: 1991
One-Day Internationals umpired: 2 as TV umpire
County as player: Somerset
Role: Right-hand bat, right-arm medium bowler
County debut: 1966
County cap: 1968
Testimonial: 1977
1st-Class 100s: 2
1st-Class 5 w. in innings: 18
1st-Class 10 w. in match: 2
1st-Class catches: 120
One-Day 5 w. in innings: 2
Extras: Played Minor Counties cricket for Wiltshire 1981-82 and for Cambridgeshire 1983-84
Best batting: 129 Somerset v Gloucestershire, Taunton 1973
Best bowling: 7-43 Somerset v Oxford University, The Parks 1975

First-Class Career Performances

	M	Inns	NO	Runs	HS	Avge	100s	Ct	St	Runs	Wkts	Avge	Best	5wI	10wM
Test															
All First	252	414	37	7129	129	18.90	2	120	-	13543	474	28.57	7-43	18	2

CONSTANT, D. J.

Name: David John Constant
Born: 9 November 1941, Bradford-on-Avon, Wiltshire
Height: 5ft 7in
Nickname: Connie
Wife's name: Rosalyn
Children: Lisa, 6 July 1966; Julie, 21 February 1969
Family links with cricket: Father-in-law, G.E.E. Lambert, played for Gloucestershire
Education: Grove Park Secondary Modern
Off-season: Bowls
Other sports followed: Football (Millwall)
Interests/relaxations: 'Six grandchildren and bowls'
Appointed to 1st-Class list: 1969
First appointed to Test panel: 1971
Tests umpired: 36 (plus 5 as TV umpire)
One-Day Internationals umpired: 33 (plus 5 as TV umpire)
Other umpiring honours: Stood in 1975, 1979 and 1983 World Cups
Counties as player: Kent, Leicestershire
Role: Left-hand bat, slow left-arm bowler
County debut: 1961 (Kent), 1965 (Leicestershire)
1st-Class 50s: 6
1st-Class catches: 33
Extras: County bowls player for Gloucestershire 1984-86 (outdoor). Also represented Somerset at indoor version of the game in the Liberty Trophy
Best batting: 80 Leicestershire v Gloucestershire, Bristol 1966
Best bowling: 1-28 Leicestershire v Surrey, The Oval 1968

First-Class Career Performances

	M	Inns	NO	Runs	HS	Avge	100s	Ct	St	Runs	Wkts	Avge	Best	5wI	10wM
Test															
All First	61	93	14	1517	80	19.20	-	33	-	36	1	36.00	1-28	-	-

COWLEY, N. G.

Name: Nigel Geoffrey Cowley
Born: 1 March 1953, Shaftesbury, Dorset
Height: 5ft 6½in
Marital status: Divorced
Children: Mark Antony, 14 June 1973; Darren James, 30 October 1976
Family links with cricket: Darren played Hampshire Schools U11, U12, U13; Natal Schools 1993, 1994, 1995; and toured India with South Africa U19 1996
Education: Duchy Manor, Mere, Wiltshire
Other sports played: Golf (8 handicap)
Other sports followed: Football (Liverpool FC)
Appointed to 1st-Class list: 2000
Counties as player: Hampshire, Glamorgan
Role: Right-hand bat, off-spin bowler
County debut: 1974 (Hampshire), 1990 (Glamorgan)
County cap: 1978 (Hampshire)
Benefit: 1988 (Hampshire; £88,274)
1000 runs in a season: 1
50 wickets in a season: 2
1st-Class 50s: 36
1st-Class 100s: 2
1st-Class 5 w. in innings: 5
1st-Class catches: 105
One-Day 5 w. in innings: 1
Overseas tours: Hampshire to Barbados 1985, 1986, 1987, to Dubai 1989
Overseas teams played for: Paarl CC, 1982-83; Amanzimtoti, 1984-96 (both South Africa)
Extras: Played for Dorset 1972. NatWest Man of the Match award
Best batting: 109* Hampshire v Somerset, Taunton 1977
Best bowling: 6-48 Hampshire v Leicestershire, Southampton 1982

First-Class Career Performances

	M	Inns	NO	Runs	HS	Avge	100s	Ct	St	Runs	Wkts	Avge	Best	5wI	10wM
Test															
All First	271	375	62	7309	109*	23.35	2	105	-	14879	437	34.04	6-48	5	-

DUDLESTON, B.

Name: Barry Dudleston
Born: 16 July 1945, Bebington, Cheshire
Height: 5ft 9in
Nickname: Danny
Wife and date of marriage: Louise Wendy, 19 October 1994
Children: Sharon Louise, 29 October 1968; Matthew Barry, 12 September 1988; Jack Nicholas, 29 April 1998
Family links with cricket: 'Dad was a league cricketer'
Education: Stockport School
Career outside cricket: Managing director of Sunsport Tours & Travel
Other sports played: Golf
Other sports followed: All sports
Relaxations: Bridge, red wine
Appointed to 1st-Class list: 1984
First appointed to Test panel: 1991
Tests umpired: 2 (plus 14 as TV umpire)
One-Day Internationals umpired: 4 (plus 10 as TV umpire)
Other umpiring honours: Stood in C&G final 2001 and B&H final 2002; also officiated at the inaugural Twenty20 finals day at Trent Bridge 2003, including standing in the final
Players to watch for the future: Ian Bell
Counties as player: Leicestershire, Gloucestershire
Role: Right-hand opening bat, slow left-arm bowler, occasional wicket-keeper
County debut: 1966 (Leicestershire), 1981 (Gloucestershire)
County cap: 1969 (Leicestershire)
Benefit: 1980 (Leicestershire; £25,000)
1000 runs in a season: 8
1st-Class 50s: 64
1st-Class 100s: 31
1st-Class 200s: 1
1st-Class catches: 234
One-Day 100s: 4
Overseas tours: Kent (as guest player) to West Indies 1972; D.H. Robins' XI to West Indies 1973; Wisden XI to West Indies 1984; MCC to Kenya 1993
Overseas teams played for: Rhodesia 1976-80
Highlights of playing career: 'Winning County Championship [with Leicestershire]'

Extras: Played for England U25. Holder with John Steele of the highest first-wicket partnership for Leics, 390 v Derbys at Leicester in 1979. Fastest player in Rhodesian cricket history to 1000 first-class runs in Currie Cup; second fastest ever in Currie Cup
Opinions on cricket: 'My team-mate Duncan Fletcher is doing a great job.'
Best batting: 202 Leicestershire v Derbyshire, Leicester 1979
Best bowling: 4-6 Leicestershire v Surrey, Leicester 1972

First-Class Career Performances

	M	Inns	NO	Runs	HS	Avge	100s	Ct	St	Runs	Wkts	Avge	Best	5wI	10wM
Test															
All First	295	501	47	14747	202	32.48	32	234	7	1365	47	29.04	4-6	-	-

EVANS, J. H.

Name: Jeffrey (Jeff) Howard Evans
Born: 7 August 1954, Llanelli
Height: 5ft 8in
Education: Llanelli Boys Grammar School; Dudley College of Education
Career outside cricket: Supply teacher
Off-season: Teaching; coaching
Other sports followed: 'Most sports, rugby in particular'
Relaxations: Keeping fit, walking, cycling, skiing
Appointed to 1st-Class list: 2001
Other umpiring honours: Toured Namibia and Uganda 2004-05 with MCC (as umpire)
Highlights of umpiring career: 'First Championship match – Yorkshire v Somerset at Headingley 2001'
Cricket moments to forget: 'Any error of judgement!'
County as player: Did not play first-class cricket. Played league cricket in South Wales as a right-hand bat
Extras: Coach to Welsh Schools Cricket Association team on tour to Australia 1993. Taught in the Gwendraeth Grammar School – 'the old "outside-half factory"'
Opinions on cricket: 'Would like to see more honesty throughout the game!'

Did not play first-class cricket

GOULD, I. J.

Name: Ian James Gould
Born: 19 August 1957, Taplow, Bucks
Height: 5ft 7in
Nickname: Gunner
Wife and date of marriage: Joanne, 27 September 1986
Children: Gemma; Michael; George
Education: Westgate Secondary Modern, Slough
Career outside cricket: 'Learning to be a groundsman'
Other sports played: Golf
Other sports followed: Football (Arsenal), racing
Relaxations: 'Spending many hours listening to Richard Edmondson (Racing Correspondent of *The Independent*) telling me what might win tomorrow'
Appointed to 1st-Class list: 2002
Other umpiring honours: Officiated at the Twenty20 finals day at Edgbaston 2004, including standing in the final
Players to watch for the future: John Maunders
Counties as player: Middlesex, Sussex
Role: Left-hand bat, wicket-keeper
County debut: 1975 (Middlesex), 1981 (Sussex)
County cap: 1977 (Middlesex), 1981 (Sussex)
Benefit: 1990 (Sussex; £87,097)
One-Day Internationals: 18
1st-Class 50s: 47
1st-Class 100s: 4
1st-Class catches: 536
1st-Class stumpings: 67
Overseas tours: England YC to West Indies 1976; D.H. Robins' XI to Canada 1978-79; International XI to Pakistan 1980-81; England to Australia and New Zealand 1982-83; MCC to Namibia
Overseas teams played for: Auckland 1979-80
Highlights of playing career: 'Playing in the World Cup'
Extras: Represented England in the 1983 World Cup. Retired from county cricket in 1991
Opinions on cricket: 'Cricket seems to be going the right way. People seem more positive about the game and I feel that they are enjoying playing.'

Best batting: 128 Middlesex v Worcestershire, Worcester 1978
Best bowling: 3-10 Sussex v Surrey, The Oval 1989

First-Class Career Performances

	M	Inns	NO	Runs	HS	Avge	100s	Ct	St	Runs	Wkts	Avge	Best	5wI	10wM
Test															
All First	297	399	63	8756	128	26.06	4	536	67	365	7	52.14	3-10	-	-

HAMPSHIRE, J. H.

Name: John Harry Hampshire
Born: 10 February 1941, Thurnscoe, Yorks
Height: 6ft
Nickname: Hamps
Marital status: Married
Wife and date of marriage: Judith Ann, 5 September 1964 (deceased 20 April 2002); Alison Mary, 11 December 2004
Children: Ian Christopher, 6 January 1969; Paul Wesley, 12 February 1972
Family links with cricket: Father (J.) and brother (A.W.) both played for Yorkshire
Education: Oakwood Technical High School, Rotherham; Sheffield College of Art
Other sports followed: Most sports
Relaxations: Golf, gardening, cooking
Appointed to 1st-Class list: 1985
First appointed to Test panel: 1989
International panel: 1999-2002
Tests umpired: 21 (plus 4 as TV umpire)
One-Day Internationals umpired: 20 (plus 8 as TV umpire)
Other umpiring honours: Umpired four Tests in Pakistan 1989-90. Toured Bangladesh 1999-2000 with MCC (as umpire). Stood in Coca-Cola Cup, Sharjah 2000. Umpired NatWest final 2000, B&H final 2001, 2002, and C&G final 2003. Officiated at the Twenty20 finals day at Edgbaston 2004
Counties as player: Yorkshire, Derbyshire
Role: Right-hand bat, leg-spin bowler
County debut: 1961 (Yorkshire), 1982 (Derbyshire)
County cap: 1963 (Yorkshire), 1982 (Derbyshire)
Benefit: 1976 (Yorkshire)
Test debut: 1969
Tests: 8
One-Day Internationals: 3

1000 runs in a season: 15
1st-Class 50s: 142
1st-Class 100s: 43
1st-Class 5 w. in innings: 2
1st-Class catches: 445
One-Day 100s: 7
Overseas tours: MCC (England) to Australia and New Zealand 1970-71
Overseas teams played for: Tasmania 1966-69, 1977-79
Extras: Captained Yorkshire 1979-80. Scored a century (107) at Lord's on Test debut (v West Indies 1969); the first England player to do so. Retired from county cricket in 1984. Manager/coach of the Zimbabwe squad for their first Test matches against India and New Zealand 1992-93
Best batting: 183* Yorkshire v Surrey, Hove 1971
Best bowling: 7-52 Yorkshire v Glamorgan, Cardiff 1963

First-Class Career Performances

	M	Inns	NO	Runs	HS	Avge	100s	Ct	St	Runs	Wkts	Avge	Best	5wI	10wM
Test	8	16	1	405	107	26.86	1	9	-						
All First	577	924	112	28059	183*	34.55	43	445	-	1637	30	54.56	7-52	2	-

HARRIS, M. J.

Name: Michael John Harris
Born: 25 May 1944, St Just-in-Roseland, Cornwall
Height: 6ft 1in
Nickname: Pasty
Wife and date of marriage: Danielle Ruth, 10 September 1969
Children: Jodie; Richard
Education: Gerrans Comprehensive
Career outside cricket: Sports teacher
Other sports followed: Squash, golf
Appointed to 1st-Class list: 1998
Counties as player: Middlesex, Nottinghamshire
Role: Right-hand bat, leg-break bowler, wicket-keeper
County debut: 1964 (Middlesex), 1969 (Nottinghamshire)
County cap: 1967 (Middlesex), 1970 (Nottinghamshire)
1000 runs in a season: 11
1st-Class 50s: 98

1st-Class 100s: 40
1st-Class 200s: 1
1st-Class catches: 288
1st-Class stumpings: 14
One-Day 100s: 3
Overseas teams played for: Eastern Province 1971-72; Wellington 1975-76
Extras: Shared Middlesex then record first-wicket partnership of 312 with Eric Russell v Pakistanis at Lord's 1967. Scored nine centuries in 1971 to equal Nottinghamshire county record for a season, scoring two centuries in a match twice and totalling 2238 runs at an average of 50.86
Best batting: 201* Nottinghamshire v Glamorgan, Trent Bridge 1973
Best bowling: 4-16 Nottinghamshire v Warwickshire, Trent Bridge 1969

First-Class Career Performances

	M	Inns	NO	Runs	HS	Avge	100s	Ct	St	Runs	Wkts	Avge	Best	5wI	10wM
Test															
All First	344	581	58	19196	201*	36.70	41	288	14	3459	79	43.78	4-16	-	-

HARTLEY, P. J.

Name: Peter John Hartley
Born: 18 April 1960, Keighley, Yorkshire
Height: 6ft
Nickname: Jack
Wife and date of marriage: Sharon, 12 March 1988
Children: Megan, 25 April 1992; Courtney, 25 July 1995
Family links with cricket: Father played local league cricket
Education: Greenhead Grammar School, Keighley; Bradford College
Career outside cricket: Sports footwear agent
Off-season: Development and sales of footwear within cricket
Other sports played: Golf
Other sports followed: Football (Chelsea)
Relaxations: 'Gardening, walking the hound'
Appointed to 1st-Class list: 2003
Counties as player: Warwickshire, Yorkshire, Hampshire
Role: Right-hand bat, right-arm fast-medium bowler
County debut: 1982 (Warwickshire), 1985 (Yorkshire), 1998 (Hampshire)

County cap: 1987 (Yorkshire), 1998 (Hampshire)
Benefit: 1996 (Yorkshire)
50 wickets in a season: 7
1st-Class 50s: 14
1st-Class 100s: 2
1st-Class 5 w. in innings: 23
1st-Class 10 w. in match: 3
1st-Class catches: 68
One-Day 5 w. in innings: 5
Overseas tours: Yorkshire pre-season tours to Barbados 1986-87, to South Africa 1991-92, 1992-93, to Zimbabwe
Overseas teams played for: Melville, New Zealand 1983-84; Adelaide, Australia 1985-86; Harmony and Orange Free State, South Africa 1988-89
Extras: Returned 8-65, his best figures for Hampshire, against Yorkshire, his former county, at Basingstoke 1999. Recorded his highest B&H score (32*) and best one-day analysis (5-20) v Sussex at Hove 2000. Retired at the end of the 2000 season
Best batting: 127* Yorkshire v Lancashire, Old Trafford 1988
Best bowling: 9-41 Yorkshire v Derbyshire, Chesterfield 1995

First-Class Career Performances

	M	Inns	NO	Runs	HS	Avge	100s	Ct	St	Runs	Wkts	Avge	Best	5wI	10wM
Test															
All First	232	283	66	4321	127*	19.91	2	68	-	20635	683	30.21	9-41	23	3

HOLDER, J. W.

Name: John Wakefield Holder
Born: 19 March 1945, Barbados
Height: 5ft 11in
Nickname: Benson
Wife's name: Glenda
Children: Christopher, 1968; Nigel, 1970
Education: Combermere High School, Barbados; Rochdale College
Off-season: 'Relaxing initially, then working part-time for the European Cricket Council; keeping fit'
Other sports followed: Football (Manchester United)
Relaxations: 'Regular visits to the gym trying to keep fit. Love watching wildlife programmes on TV and travel'
Appointed to 1st-Class list: 1983
First appointed to Test panel: 1988
Tests umpired: 11 (plus 5 as TV umpire)
One-Day Internationals umpired: 19 (plus 3 as TV umpire)
Other umpiring honours: Umpired in Nehru Cup in India and in Pakistan v India Test series 1989-90. Umpired in Pepsi Champions Trophy, Sharjah 1993-94 and Masters Cup, Sharjah 1995-96. MCC tours to Kenya 1999, 2002 and to Greece 2003 (as umpire). Has stood in Refuge Assurance Cup, B&H Cup and NatWest Trophy finals and in C&G Trophy final 2002. Officiated at the inaugural Twenty20 finals day at Trent Bridge 2003, including standing in the final
Highlights of umpiring career: 'Umpiring Lord's Ashes Test in 2001, when I met the Queen'
County as player: Hampshire
Role: Right-hand bat, right-arm fast bowler
County debut: 1968
50 wickets in a season: 1
1st-Class 5 w. in innings: 5
1st-Class 10 w. in match: 1
1st-Class catches: 12
Highlights of playing career: 'Taking 6-7 against International Cavaliers in 1968'
Extras: Championship hat-trick v Kent at Southampton 1972. Retired from county cricket in 1972
Opinions on cricket: 'A few years ago at Headingley, about two hours before the start of a National League game, the entire Yorkshire playing staff sat at a row of tables signing autographs for fans. This is an excellent idea which I believe every county

should copy for two matches every year. This would help foster better relations between players and the public.'
Best batting: 33 Hampshire v Sussex, Hove 1971
Best bowling: 7-79 Hampshire v Gloucestershire, Gloucester 1972

First-Class Career Performances

	M	Inns	NO	Runs	HS	Avge	100s	Ct	St	Runs	Wkts	Avge	Best	5wI	10wM
Test															
All First	47	49	14	374	33	10.68	-	12	-	3415	139	24.56	7-79	5	1

HOLDER, V. A.

Name: Vanburn Alonza Holder
Born: 8 October 1945, St Michael, Barbados
Height: 6ft 3in
Nickname: Van
Wife's name: Christine
Children: James Vanburn, 2 September 1981
Education: St Leonard's Secondary Modern; Community High
Other sports followed: Football (Liverpool)
Relaxations: Music, doing crosswords
Appointed to 1st-Class list: 1992
One-Day Internationals umpired: 2 as TV umpire
County as player: Worcestershire
Role: Right-hand bat, right-arm fast-medium bowler
County debut: 1968
County cap: 1970
Benefit: 1979
Test debut: 1969
Tests: 40
One-Day Internationals: 12
1st-Class 50s: 4
1st-Class 100s: 1
1st-Class 5 w. in innings: 38
1st-Class 10 w. in match: 3
1st-Class catches: 98
One-Day 5 w. in innings: 3
Overseas tours: West Indies to England 1969, 1973, 1975 (World Cup), 1976, to India, Sri Lanka and Pakistan 1974-75, to Australia 1975-76, to India and Sri Lanka 1978-79 (vice-captain); Rest of the World to Pakistan 1973-74

Overseas teams played for: Barbados 1966-78
Extras: Made his debut for Barbados in the Shell Shield competition in 1966-67. Won John Player League 1973 and County Championship 1974 with Worcestershire. Played in West Indies 1975 World Cup winning side
Best batting: 122 Barbados v Trinidad, Bridgetown 1973-74
Best bowling: 7-40 Worcestershire v Glamorgan, Cardiff 1974

First-Class Career Performances

	M	Inns	NO	Runs	HS	Avge	100s	Ct	St	Runs	Wkts	Avge	Best	5wI	10wM
Test	40	59	11	682	42	14.20	-	16	-	3627	109	33.27	6-28	3	-
All First	311	354	81	3559	122	13.03	1	98	-	23183	948	24.45	7-40	38	3

JESTY, T. E.

Name: Trevor Edward Jesty
Born: 2 June 1948, Gosport, Hampshire
Height: 5ft 9in
Nickname: Jets
Wife and date of marriage: Jacqueline, 12 September 1970
Children: Graeme Barry, 27 September 1972; Lorna Samantha, 7 November 1976
Family links with cricket: Daughter played for England XI 2000
Education: Privett County Secondary Modern, Gosport
Off-season: Cricket coaching
Other sports followed: Football (Arsenal)
Relaxations: Gardening, reading
Appointed to 1st-Class list: 1994
One-Day Internationals umpired: 3 as TV umpire
Counties as player: Hampshire, Surrey, Lancashire
Role: Right-hand bat, right-arm medium bowler
County debut: 1966 (Hampshire), 1985 (Surrey), 1988 (Lancashire)
County cap: 1971 (Hampshire), 1985 (Surrey), 1990 (Lancashire)
Benefit: 1982 (Hampshire)
One-Day Internationals: 10
1000 runs in a season: 10
50 wickets in a season: 2
1st-Class 50s: 110
1st-Class 100s: 33
1st-Class 200s: 2

1st-Class 5 w. in innings: 19
1st-Class catches: 265
1st-Class stumpings: 1
One-Day 100s: 7
Overseas tours: International XI to West Indies 1982; joined England tour to Australia 1982-83; Lancashire to Zimbabwe 1989
Overseas teams played for: Border, South Africa 1973-74; Griqualand West 1974-76, 1980-81; Canterbury, New Zealand 1979-80
Highlights of playing career: 'Winning Championship with Hampshire in 1973. Playing against Australia for England in one-day match on 1982-83 tour'
Extras: One of *Wisden*'s Five Cricketers of the Year 1983
Best batting: 248 Hampshire v Cambridge University, Fenner's 1984
Best bowling: 7-75 Hampshire v Worcestershire, Southampton 1976

First-Class Career Performances

	M	Inns	NO	Runs	HS	Avge	100s	Ct	St	Runs	Wkts	Avge	Best	5wI	10wM
Test															
All First	490	777	107	21916	248	32.71	35	265	1	16075	585	27.47	7-75	19	-

JONES, A. A.

Name: Allan Arthur Jones
Born: 9 December 1947, Horley, Surrey
Height: 6ft 4in
Nickname: Jonah
Wife and date of marriage: Stephanie, 11 December 2004
Education: St John's College, Horsham
Career outside cricket: Sports tours
Off-season: 'Enjoying life'
Other sports played: Golf
Other sports followed: Football (Arsenal)
Relaxations: English history, reading, cooking
Appointed to 1st-Class list: 1985
First appointed to Test panel: 1996
Tests umpired: 3 as TV umpire
One-Day Internationals umpired: 1 (plus 4 as TV umpire)
Other umpiring honours: Has umpired at Hong Kong Sixes. Chairman of the First-Class Umpires' Association
Players to watch for the future: Ed Joyce
Counties as player: Sussex, Somerset, Middlesex, Glamorgan

Role: Right-hand bat, right-arm fast bowler
County debut: 1964 (Sussex), 1970 (Somerset), 1976 (Middlesex), 1980 (Glamorgan)
County cap: 1972 (Somerset), 1976 (Middlesex)
50 wickets in a season: 4
1st-Class 5 w. in innings: 23
1st-Class 10 w. in match: 3
1st-Class catches: 50
One-Day 5 w. in innings: 5
Overseas teams played for: Northern Transvaal 1971-72; Orange Free State 1976-77; Auckland (Birkenhead)
Highlights of playing career: '9-51 v Sussex 1972'
Extras: Won two Championship medals with Middlesex (1976 and 1977). Was on stand-by for England tour of India 1976-77. Represented MCC v Australians 1977. Was the first person to play for four counties
Best batting: 33 Middlesex v Kent, Canterbury 1978
Best bowling: 9-51 Somerset v Sussex, Hove 1972

First-Class Career Performances

	M	Inns	NO	Runs	HS	Avge	100s	Ct	St	Runs	Wkts	Avge	Best	5wI	10wM
Test															
All First	214	216	68	799	33	5-39	-	50	-	15414	549	28.07	9-51	23	3

KITCHEN, M. J.

Name: Mervyn (Merv) John Kitchen
Born: 1 August 1940, Nailsea, Somerset
Height: 5ft 11in
Nickname: MJ
Wife and date of marriage: Anne, March 1972
Children: Faye, 30 September 1975; Jody, 5 March 1977
Family links with cricket: Father played local cricket for the village of Nailsea
Education: Backwell Secondary Modern, Backwell
Career outside cricket: 'Many varied winter jobs – driver, labourer, decorator, printing; worked on the racetracks, horses and greyhounds, for a bookmaker for ten years'
Other sports played: Golf, bowls, skittles
Other sports followed: 'Love TV football now the coverage is so good; no allegiance to any teams'

Relaxations: 'Like crosswords but very rarely complete one; DIY'
Appointed to 1st-Class list: 1982
First appointed to Test panel: 1990
International panel: 1995-99
Tests umpired: 20 (plus 3 as TV umpire)
One-Day Internationals umpired: 28 (plus 8 as TV umpire)
Other umpiring honours: Stood in 1983 World Cup. Has umpired finals of the domestic one-day competitions. Umpired in a one-day series in Kenya between the hosts, Bangladesh and Zimbabwe, including the final, 1997-98
Highlights of umpiring career: 'My first Test match, England v New Zealand at Lord's with D. Shepherd'
Players to watch for the future: James Troughton
County as player: Somerset
Role: Left-hand bat, occasional right-arm medium bowler
County debut: 1960
County cap: 1966
Testimonial: 1973
1000 runs in a season: 7
1st-Class 50s: 68
1st-Class 100s: 17
1st-Class catches: 157
One-Day 100s: 1
Overseas tours: Whitbread Wanderers to Rhodesia
Highlights of playing career: 'Many happy memories but perhaps playing with such talent as Viv Richards, Ian Botham and Joel Garner all in the same side ranks [at] the top of my list'
Cricket moments to forget: 'I once scored three ducks in three days – one on Saturday in the Championship, one on the Sunday in the John Player League and another, second, Championship innings on the Monday'
Extras: Won two Gillette Cup Man of the Match awards and two B&H Gold Awards. Retired in September 1979 and played local cricket for Mendip Acorns
Opinions on cricket: 'Microscopic examination of umpires and players by TV replays. Tremendous coverage of cricket all over the world by TV, which I think has increased the knowledge of the armchair watcher.'
Best batting: 189 Somerset v Pakistanis, Taunton 1967
Best bowling: 1-4 Somerset v Sussex, Taunton 1969

First-Class Career Performances

	M	Inns	NO	Runs	HS	Avge	100s	Ct	St	Runs	Wkts	Avge	Best	5wI	10wM
Test															
All First	354	612	32	15230	189	26.25	17	157	-	109	2	54.50	1-4	-	-

LEADBEATER, B.

Name: Barrie Leadbeater
Born: 14 August 1943, Leeds
Height: 6ft
Nickname: Leady
Marital status: Widowed
Wife and date of marriage: Jacqueline, 18 September 1971 (deceased 1997)
Children: Richard Barrie, 23 November 1972; Michael Spencer, 21 March 1976; Daniel Mark Ronnie, 19 June 1981
Education: Harehills County Secondary, Leeds
Career outside cricket: LGV Class 1 driver
Other sports played: Golf, snooker, table tennis
Other sports followed: All sport – football (Leeds United), rugby league (Leeds Rhinos)
Relaxations: 'Reading, going to the pub, running'
Appointed to 1st-Class list: 1981
Tests umpired: 2 as TV umpire
One-Day Internationals umpired: 5 (plus 2 as TV umpire)
Other umpiring honours: Stood in 1983 World Cup. MCC tours to New Zealand 1999 and to Argentina and Chile 2001. Former chairman of the First-Class Umpires' Association
County as player: Yorkshire
Role: Right-hand opening bat, right-arm medium bowler, slip fielder
County debut: 1966
County cap: 1969
Benefit: 1980 (joint benefit with G.A. Cope)
1st-Class 50s: 27
1st-Class 100s: 1
1st-Class catches: 82
Overseas tours: Duke of Norfolk's XI to West Indies 1970
Overseas teams played for: Johannesburg Municipals 1978-79
Highlights of playing career: 'Man of the Match in Gillette Cup final 1969'
Cricket moments to forget: 'I've forgotten'
Extras: Took part in London Marathon 1997, 1998, 2000. Retired from county cricket in 1979 and played social cricket
Best batting: 140* Yorkshire v Hampshire, Portsmouth 1976
Best bowling: 1-1 Yorkshire v Middlesex, Headingley 1971

First-Class Career Performances

	M	Inns	NO	Runs	HS	Avge	100s	Ct	St	Runs	Wkts	Avge	Best	5wI	10wM
Test															
All First	147	241	29	5373	140*	25.34	1	82	-	5	1	5.00	1-1	-	-

LLONG, N. J.

Name: Nigel James Llong
Born: 11 February 1969, Ashford, Kent
Height: 6ft
Nickname: Nidge
Wife and date of marriage: Melissa, 20 February 1999
Children: Andrew Stuart, 30 August 2002; Matthew James, 14 December 2004
Family links with cricket: Father and brother played local club cricket
Education: North School for Boys, Ashford
Off-season: Coaching – Kent Cricket Board; Duke of York School, Dover
Other sports followed: Football (Arsenal), 'generally most sports'
Relaxations: Fishing, clay-pigeon shooting
Appointed to 1st-Class list: 2002
International panel: 2004 – (as TV umpire)
Tests umpired: 2 as TV umpire
One-Day Internationals umpired: 5 as TV umpire
Other umpiring honours: Officiated at the Twenty20 finals day at Edgbaston 2004, including standing in the final
County as player: Kent
Role: Left-hand bat, right-arm off-spin bowler
County debut: 1991
County cap: 1993
1st-Class 50s: 16
1st-Class 100s: 6
1st-Class 5 w. in innings: 2
1st-Class catches: 59
One-Day 100s: 2
Overseas tours: Kent to Zimbabwe 1993
Overseas teams played for: Ashburton, Melbourne 1988-90, 1996-97; Greenpoint, Cape Town 1990-95
Highlights of playing career: 'B&H final 1997. Sunday League winners 1995. First Championship hundred, Lord's 1993'

Cricket moments to forget: 'Sunday League [1993], last match against Glamorgan at Canterbury – lost the match and were runners-up. Plus not making the most of my ability'
Extras: Kent Young Player of the Year 1992. Man of the Match in 2nd XI Trophy semi-final and final 1999. Retired from county cricket in September 1999 and played for Norfolk in 2000
Opinions on cricket: 'Good pitches produce good players. With central contracts, we now need two overseas players per club (especially bowlers).'
Best batting: 130 Kent v Hampshire, Canterbury 1996
Best bowling: 5-21 Kent v Middlesex, Canterbury 1996

First-Class Career Performances

	M	Inns	NO	Runs	HS	Avge	100s	Ct	St	Runs	Wkts	Avge	Best	5wI	10wM
Test															
All First	68	108	11	3024	130	31.17	6	59	-	1259	35	35.97	5-21	2	-

LLOYDS, J. W.

Name: Jeremy William Lloyds
Born: 17 November 1954, Penang, Malaya
Height: 5ft 11in
Nickname: Jerry
Wife and date of marriage: Janine, 16 September 1997
Children: Kaeli, 16 November 1991
Family links with cricket: Father played cricket in Malaya. Brother Chris played for Somerset 2nd XI
Education: Blundell's School, Tiverton
Career outside cricket: Coaching and setting up Western Province Youth Programme 1992-95 in South Africa. Works for National Car Rental
Other sports played: Golf (6 handicap)
Other sports followed: Golf, football (Tottenham Hotspur), American football (San Francisco 49ers), Formula One and saloon car racing, rugby (Gloucester)
Relaxations: 'Reading, music and spending time at home with my family'
Appointed to 1st-Class list: 1998
International panel: 2002-2004 as TV umpire; 2004 –
Tests umpired: 4 (plus 7 as TV umpire)
One-Day Internationals umpired: 10 (plus 18 as TV umpire)
Counties as player: Somerset, Gloucestershire

Role: Left-hand bat, off-spin bowler
County debut: 1979 (Somerset), 1985 (Gloucestershire)
County cap: 1982 (Somerset), 1985 (Gloucestershire)
1000 runs in a season: 3
1st-Class 50s: 62
1st-Class 100s: 10
1st-Class 5 w. in innings: 13
1st-Class 10 w. in match: 1
1st-Class catches: 229
Overseas tours: Somerset to Antigua 1982; Gloucestershire to Barbados 1985, to Sri Lanka 1987
Overseas teams played for: St Stithian's Old Boys, Johannesburg 1978-79; Toombull DCC, Brisbane 1980-82; North Sydney District 1982-83; Alberton, Johannesburg 1984; Preston CC, Melbourne 1986; Orange Free State 1987; Fish Hoek CC, Cape Town 1988-92
Highlights of playing career: 'Winning 1983 NatWest final'
Extras: Highest score in Brisbane Premier League 1980-81 (165). Britannic Player of the Month July 1987. Gloucestershire Player of the Year 1987. Leading run-scorer in Western Province Cricket League 1988, 1989
Opinions on cricket: 'Too much overseas influence on how to play the game in England. We have more variations in wickets and weather conditions than in most other countries. Yes, take the best of what they have and work it into our game. Also, too much emphasis on all the various levels of coaching certificates. We have been dragged too far away from the *basics* – batting, bowling and fielding. The game hasn't really changed – people's perception of it has! We show people how to play but not the thinking side of it. At times, some players are too robotic. Whatever happened to natural flair?'
Best batting: 132* Somerset v Northamptonshire, Northampton 1982
Best bowling: 7-88 Somerset v Essex, Chelmsford 1982

First-Class Career Performances

	M	Inns	NO	Runs	HS	Avge	100s	Ct	St	Runs	Wkts	Avge	Best	5wI	10wM
Test															
All First	267	408	64	10679	132*	31.04	10	229	-	12943	333	38.86	7-88	13	1

MALLENDER, N. A.

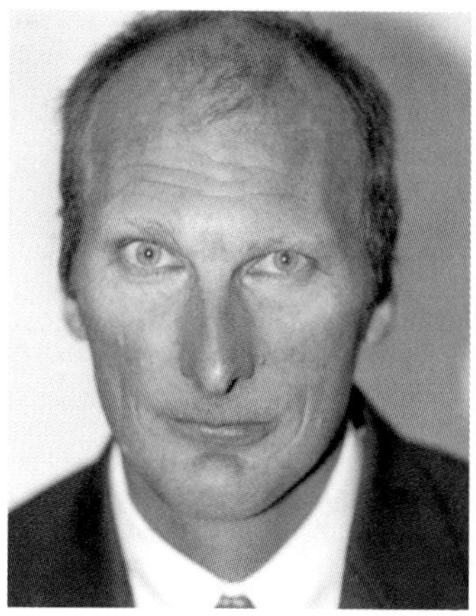

Name: Neil Alan Mallender
Born: 13 August 1961, Kirk Sandall, Doncaster
Height: 6ft
Nickname: Ghostie
Marital status: Divorced
Children: Kirstie, 16; Dominic, 13; Jacob, 8
Education: Beverley Grammar School
Other sports played: Golf (2 handicap)
Other sports followed: 'Most sports'
Relaxations: 'Most sports; music'
Appointed to 1st-Class list: 1999
International panel: 2002-2004
Tests umpired: 3 (plus 5 as TV umpire)
One-Day Internationals umpired: 22 (plus 9 as TV umpire)
Other umpiring honours: Went with MCC to umpire in Namibia March/April 2001. PCA Umpire of the Year 2001, 2002, 2003, 2004. Stood in the 2002-03 World Cup. Umpired the 2004 C&G Trophy final
Highlights of umpiring career: 'First ODI at Lord's, England v Pakistan – and game went to the last ball'
Players to watch for the future: James Hildreth, Liam Plunkett
Counties as player: Northamptonshire, Somerset
Role: Right-hand bat, right-arm fast-medium bowler
County debut: 1980 (Northamptonshire), 1987 (Somerset)
County cap: 1984 (Northamptonshire), 1987 (Somerset)
Benefit: 1994 (Somerset)
Test debut: 1992
Tests: 2
50 wickets in a season: 6
1st-Class 50s: 10
1st-Class 100s: 1
1st-Class 5 w. in innings: 36
1st-Class 10 w. in match: 5
1st-Class catches: 111
One-Day 5 w. in innings: 3
Overseas tours: England YC to West Indies 1979-80
Overseas teams played for: Kaikorai, Dunedin, New Zealand; University, Wellington, New Zealand; Otago, New Zealand 1983-84 – 1992-93
Highlights of playing career: 'Test debut at Headingley'

Extras: Represented England YC 1980-81. Took 5-50 on Test debut v Pakistan at Headingley in 1992. Retired from county cricket in 1996
Opinions on cricket: 'People should be more supportive of the county system. There are some good players and standards in county cricket which will continue to produce good Test players. Too many people seem to criticise it for the sake of it. How much county cricket do these people actually watch?!'
Best batting: 100* Otago v Central Districts, Palmerston North 1991-92
Best bowling: 7-27 Otago v Auckland, Auckland 1984-85

First-Class Career Performances

	M	Inns	NO	Runs	HS	Avge	100s	Ct	St	Runs	Wkts	Avge	Best	5wI	10wM
Test	2	3	0	8	4	2.66	-	-	-	215	10	21.50	5-50	1	-
All First	345	396	122	4709	100*	17.18	1	111	-	24654	937	26.31	7-27	36	5

PALMER, R.

Name: Roy Palmer
Born: 12 July 1942, Hampshire
Height: 6ft 3in
Nickname: Arp
Wife and date of marriage: Alyne, 5 November 1983
Children: Nick, 7 October 1968
Family links with cricket: Brother of Ken Palmer, former Test umpire and Somerset player; nephew Gary also played for Somerset
Education: Southbroom Secondary Modern, Devizes
Off-season: Golf, DIY
Relaxations: Golf
Appointed to 1st-Class list: 1980
First appointed to Test panel: 1992
Tests umpired: 2 (plus 1 as TV umpire)
One-Day Internationals umpired: 8 (plus 2 as TV umpire)
Other umpiring honours: Stood in 1983 World Cup
Players to watch for the future: Ian Bell
County as player: Somerset
Role: Right-hand bat, right-arm fast-medium bowler
County debut: 1965
50 wickets in a season: 1
1st-Class 50s: 1
1st-Class 5 w. in innings: 4

1st-Class catches: 25
One-Day 5 w. in innings: 1
Extras: Won two Man of the Match Awards in the Gillette Cup
Best batting: 84 Somerset v Leicestershire, Taunton 1967
Best bowling: 6-45 Somerset v Middlesex, Lord's 1967

First-Class Career Performances

	M	Inns	NO	Runs	HS	Avge	100s	Ct	St	Runs	Wkts	Avge	Best	5wI	10wM
Test															
All First	74	110	32	1037	84	13.29	-	25	-	5439	172	31.62	6-45	4	-

SHARP, G.

Name: George Sharp
Born: 12 March 1950, West Hartlepool, County Durham
Height: 5ft 11in
Nickname: Sharpy, Blunt, Razor, Toffee
Wife and date of marriage: Audrey, 14 September 1974
Children: Gareth James, 27 June 1984
Education: Elwick Road Secondary Modern, Hartlepool
Career outside cricket: Watching all sports
Off-season: Working as joint director of GSB Loams Ltd for soils and top dressing
Other sports played: Golf (8 handicap)
Other sports followed: Football (Newcastle Utd and Middlesbrough), rugby (Northampton Saints)
Relaxations: Golf; 'spend a lot of time in the gym during the off-season'
Appointed to 1st-Class list: 1992
International panel: 1996-2002
Tests umpired: 15 (plus 1 as TV umpire)
One-Day Internationals umpired: 31 (plus 13 as TV umpire)
Other umpiring honours: Has umpired three B&H finals and one NatWest final and stood in the inaugural C&G final 2001 and the 2002 final; also officiated at the inaugural Twenty20 finals day at Trent Bridge 2003. Has stood in four overseas tournaments, including the Singer Cup (India, Sri Lanka, Pakistan) in Singapore 1995-96 and the Singer Champions Trophy (Pakistan, Sri Lanka, New Zealand) in Sharjah 1996-97
County as player: Northamptonshire

Role: Right-hand bat, wicket-keeper
County debut: 1967
County cap: 1973
Benefit: 1982
1st-Class 50s: 21
1st-Class catches: 565
1st-Class stumpings: 90
Overseas tours: England Counties XI to Barbados and Trinidad 1975
Best batting: 98 Northamptonshire v Yorkshire, Northampton 1983
Best bowling: 1-47 Northamptonshire v Yorkshire, Northampton 1980

First-Class Career Performances

	M	Inns	NO	Runs	HS	Avge	100s	Ct	St	Runs	Wkts	Avge	Best	5wI	10wM
Test															
All First	306	396	81	6254	98	19.85	-	565	90	70	1	70.00	1-47	-	-

SHEPHERD, D. R.

Name: David Robert Shepherd
Born: 27 December 1940, Bideford, Devon
Height: 5ft 10in
Nickname: Shep
Marital status: Single
Family links with cricket: Father: club cricketer and local umpire. Brother Bill: MCC Young Professional, Devon CCC and North Devon CC; local umpire
Education: Barnstaple Grammar School; St Luke's College, Exeter
Career outside cricket: Schoolteacher
Off-season: 'With international umpiring now, there is no close season'
Other sports played: 'Used to play rugby (school, Devon Public & Grammar Schools XV, South Molton RFC)'
Other sports followed: 'All sports'
Relaxations: Stamp collecting
Appointed to 1st-Class list: 1981
First appointed to Test panel: 1985
International panel: 1994-2002
Elite panel: 2002 –
Tests umpired: 86
One-Day Internationals umpired: 164 (plus 16 as TV umpire)

Other umpiring honours: Has stood in each World Cup since 1983, including the 1995-96 final at Lahore, the 1999 final at Lord's and the 2002-03 final between Australia and India at Johannesburg. Umpired the MCC Bicentenary Test, England v Rest of the World, at Lord's in 1987. Has umpired numerous domestic finals. Received National Grid/ICC 'bronze award' in March 1998 for long service as a Test umpire. Umpired 50th Test, India v South Africa, Mumbai (Bombay) February 2000, receiving ICC 'silver award' to acknowledge this achievement. Received inaugural ICC Bronze Bails award in 2004 (along with Rudi Koertzen) in recognition of having umpired 100 ODIs. Known for his superstition regarding 'Nelson' score 111, and multiples – 222, 333 etc.
Highlights of umpiring career: 'Standing in first Test match. Three World Cup finals.'
County as player: Gloucestershire
Role: Right-hand bat, right-arm ('occasional!') medium bowler
County debut: 1965
County cap: 1969
Benefit: 1978 (joint benefit with J. Davey)
1000 runs in a season: 2
1st-Class 50s: 55
1st-Class 100s: 12
1st-Class catches: 95
One-Day 100s: 2
Highlights of playing career: 'Winning two domestic finals with Gloucestershire at Lord's – the Gillette Cup in 1973 and the B&H Cup in 1977'
Extras: Played Minor Counties cricket for Devon 1959-64. First player to score a century for Gloucestershire on his first-class debut, v Oxford University 1965. Retired from county cricket in 1979 and played a little cricket for his original club, North Devon CC. Was awarded the MBE in 1997 for services to cricket. Wrote autobiography (*Shep*) 2001
Opinions on cricket: 'Players at the highest level must realise that they have a tremendous responsibility to the game as a whole. Their behaviour on the field is of the utmost importance, as they set an example to the rest of the sport. We must get some trust back in the game between players and officials and administrators, as well as between players themselves. How I hate the cheats!! Any batsman who stands at the crease knowing he is out is in my book a cheat! Any player who appeals knowing the batsman is not out is also a cheat!'
Best batting: 153 Gloucestershire v Middlesex, Bristol 1968
Best bowling: 1-1 Gloucestershire v Northamptonshire, Gloucester 1968

First-Class Career Performances

	M	Inns	NO	Runs	HS	Avge	100s	Ct	St	Runs	Wkts	Avge	Best	5wI	10wM
Test															
All First	282	476	40	10672	153	24.47	12	95	-	106	2	53.00	1-1	-	-

STEELE, J. F.

Name: John Frederick Steele
Born: 23 July 1946, Stafford
Height: 5ft 10in
Nickname: Steely
Wife and date of marriage: Susan, 17 April 1977
Children: Sarah Jane, 2 April 1982; Robert Alfred, 10 April 1985
Family links with cricket: Uncle Stan played for Staffordshire. Brother David played for Northamptonshire, Derbyshire and England. Cousin Brian Crump played for Northamptonshire and Staffordshire
Education: Endon School, Stoke-on-Trent; Stafford College
Other sports followed: Soccer (Stoke City, Port Vale), golf
Relaxations: Music and walking
Appointed to 1st-Class list: 1997
Counties as player: Leicestershire, Glamorgan
Role: Right-hand bat, slow left-arm bowler
County debut: 1970 (Leicestershire), 1984 (Glamorgan)
County cap: 1971 (Leicestershire), 1984 (Glamorgan)
Benefit: 1983 (Leicestershire)
1000 runs in a season: 6
1st-Class 50s: 69
1st-Class 100s: 21
1st-Class 5 w. in innings: 16
1st-Class catches: 414
One-Day 100s: 1
One-Day 5 w. in innings: 4
Overseas teams played for: Springs HSOB, Northern Transvaal 1971-73; Pine Town CC, Natal 1973-74, 1982-83; Natal 1975-76, 1978-79
Extras: Played for England U25. Was voted Natal's Best Bowler in 1975-76. First-wicket record partnership for Leicestershire of 390 with Barry Dudleston v Derbyshire at Leicester 1979. Won two Man of the Match Awards in the Gillette Cup and four in the Benson and Hedges Cup. Won the award for the most catches in a season in 1984
Best batting: 195 Leicestershire v Derbyshire, Leicester 1971
Best bowling: 7-29 Natal B v Griqualand West, Umzinto 1973-74
7-29 Leicestershire v Gloucestershire, Leicester 1980

First-class career performances

	M	Inns	NO	Runs	HS	Avge	100s	Ct	St	Runs	Wkts	Avge	Best	5wI	10wM
Test															
All First	379	605	85	15053	195	28.94	21	414	-	15793	584	27.04	7-29	16	-

WHITEHEAD, A. G. T.

Name: Alan Geoffrey Thomas Whitehead
Born: 28 October 1940, Butleigh, Somerset
Appointed to 1st-Class list: 1970
First appointed to Test panel: 1982
Tests umpired: 5 (plus 5 as TV umpire)
One-Day Internationals umpired: 14 (plus 2 as TV umpire)
Other umpiring honours: Stood in the 1979 and 1983 World Cups
County as player: Somerset
Role: Left-hand bat, slow left-arm bowler
County debut: 1957
1st-Class 5 w. in innings: 3
1st-Class catches: 20
Best batting: 15 Somerset v Hampshire, Southampton 1959
Best bowling: 6-74 Somerset v Sussex, Eastbourne 1959

First-Class Career Performances

	M	Inns	NO	Runs	HS	Avge	100s	Ct	St	Runs	Wkts	Avge	Best	5wI	10wM
Test															
All First	38	49	25	137	15	5.70	-	20	-	2306	67	34.41	6-74	3	

WILLEY, P.

Name: Peter Willey
Born: 6 December 1949, Sedgefield, County Durham
Height: 6ft 1in
Nickname: Will, 'many unprintable'
Wife and date of marriage: Charmaine, 23 September 1971
Children: Heather Jane, 11 September 1985; David, 28 February 1990
Family links with cricket: Father played local club cricket in County Durham
Education: Seaham Secondary School, County Durham
Other sports followed: All sports
Relaxations: 'Dog-walking, keeping fit (??), fishing'
Appointed to 1st-Class list: 1993
International panel: 1996-2003
Tests umpired: 25 (plus 7 as TV umpire)
One-Day Internationals umpired: 34 (plus 16 as TV umpire)
Other umpiring honours: Stood in the 1999 and 2002-03 World Cups, in the 1999 Benson and Hedges Super Cup final and in the 2004 C&G Trophy final
Counties as player: Northamptonshire, Leicestershire
Role: Right-hand bat, off-break bowler
County debut: 1966 (Northamptonshire), 1984 (Leicestershire)
County cap: 1971 (Northamptonshire), 1984 (Leicestershire)
Benefit: 1981 (Northamptonshire; £31,400)
Test debut: 1976
Tests: 26
One-Day Internationals: 26
1000 runs in a season: 10
50 wickets in a season: 2
1st-Class 50s: 101
1st-Class 100s: 43
1st-Class 200s: 1
1st-Class 5 w. in innings: 26
1st-Class 10 w. in match: 3
1st-Class catches: 235
One-Day 100s: 9
Overseas tours: England to Australia and India 1979-80, to West Indies 1980-81, 1985-86; unofficial England XI to South Africa 1981-82

Overseas teams played for: Eastern Province, South Africa 1982-85
Extras: Became youngest player ever to play for Northamptonshire, at 16 years 180 days, v Cambridge University in 1966. Leicestershire captain 1987. Played for Northumberland in 1992. Offered membership of the ICC Elite Panel of umpires in 2002 but declined because of the amount of time the appointment would require away from his family
Opinions on cricket: 'Game is being made too complicated from U9 to first-class at county level. Kids can't enjoy the game. They have too many different coaches giving different opinions so they get confused. Some of the coaches may have passed all the exams, but they frighten me to death with the things they come out with. Keep it simple. Concentrate more on cricket and less on fitness. [Have] no technique and it doesn't matter how fit you are.'
Best batting: 227 Northamptonshire v Somerset, Northampton 1976
Best bowling: 7-37 Northamptonshire v Oxford University, The Parks 1975

First-Class Career Performances

	M	Inns	NO	Runs	HS	Avge	100s	Ct	St	Runs	Wkts	Avge	Best	5wI	10wM
Test	26	50	6	1184	102*	26.90	2	3	-	456	7	65.14	2-73	-	-
All First	559	918	121	24361	227	30.56	44	235	-	23400	756	30.95	7-37	26	3

THE PRIMARY CLUB

PO Box 12121,Saffron Walden
Essex CB10 2ZF
Telephone: 01799 586507
e-mail: secretary@primaryclub.org
website: www.primaryclub.org

)erek Underwood, the patron of the Primary Club, qualified for nembership in some style in 1965. Playing for Kent against the outh Africans he was out first ball twice in the same match.

However, members do not have to be playing Test or county ricket when the ultimate disaster strikes in order to qualify for he club. As long as you are out first ball at ANY level of cricket ou are eligible to join The Primary Club.

Why join? The Primary Club is a charity (Registered Charity lo. 285285) and all profits from subscriptions, donations and the ange of items for sale (ties, sweaters, shirts, mugs, umbrellas, tc.) go to pay for sporting and recreational facilities for the lind and partially sighted. All the club's workers are olunteers.

For many of us sport is an important part of our every day ves; for the blind and partially sighted, sport can mean so nuch more. The confidence and sense of achievement they get om mastering a physical skill helps them a great deal in ackling the problems of their lives.

MEMBERSHIP APPLICATION

ame

ddress

oining subscription:

To include City tie – £20	
To include Club tie – £20	
To include City & Club tie – £30	
To include 100% silk tie (City) – £30	
To include 100% silk tie (Country) – £30	
To include Bow tie – £20	
Lady, to include brooch – £15	
ONATION	
EMITTANCE TO 'THE PRIMARY CLUB' £	

egistered Charity No. 285285

The value of your remittance to The Primary Club can be increased by 28p for every £1 you give under Gift Aid tax reclaim arrangements, *at no extra cost to you.* To enable the Club to benefit from this scheme, please sign and date the declaration below, provided that you pay income tax, or capital gains tax, of an amount equal to the tax to be reclaimed.

I wish The Primary Club to reclaim tax on all donations I make on or after the date of this declaration.

Signed **Date**

It would be of great benefit to the Club if you pay future donations by banker's standing order. Please tick the box and a form will be sent to you. ☐

ROLL OF HONOUR 2004

FRIZZELL COUNTY CHAMPIONSHIP

Division One

		P	W	L	D	T	Bt	Bl	Pts
1	Warwickshire (I/5)	16	5	0	11	0	65	43	222
2	Kent (I/4)	16	7	3	6	0	43	41	206
3	Surrey (I/3)	16	5	5	6	0	60	42	195.50
4	Middlesex (I/6)	16	4	4	8	0	48	43	179
5	Sussex (I/1)	16	4	5	7	0	46	42	172
6	Gloucestershire (II/3)	16	3	3	10	0	49	41	172
7	Worcestershire (II/1)	16	3	6	7	0	51	40	161
8	Lancashire (I/2)	16	2	4	10	0	44	44	154
9	Northamptonshire (II/2)	16	1	4	11	0	35	41	134

The bottom three counties were relegated to Division Two for the 2005 season

Division Two

		P	W	L	D	T	Bt	Bl	Pts
1	Nottinghamshire (I/8)	16	9	2	5	0	66	40	252
2	Hampshire (II/8)	16	9	2	5	0	42	40	228
3	Glamorgan (II/5)	16	5	2	9	0	48	44	196.50
4	Somerset (II/7)	16	4	5	7	0	47	44	175
5	Essex (I/7)	16	3	6	7	0	50	45	165
6	Leicestershire (I/9)	16	4	5	7	0	39	42	163.50
7	Yorkshire (II/4)	16	3	4	9	0	44	40	162
8	Derbyshire (II/9)	16	1	6	9	0	36	40	126
9	Durham (II/6)	16	2	8	6	0	28	41	118.50

The top three counties were promoted to Division One for the 2005 season

Teams are docked 0.50 points for each over they fail to bowl of the target figure of 16 per hour. The following sides incurred deductions in 2004: Surrey 0.5 points, Lancashire 2, Glamorgan 1.5, Leicestershire 1.5, Durham 2.5.

TOTESPORT LEAGUE

Division One

		P	W	L	T	NR	Pts
1	Glamorgan (I/5)	16	11	5	0	0	44
2	Lancashire (II/1)	16	9	6	0	1	38
3	Hampshire (II/3)	16	7	6	0	3	34
4	Northamptonshire (II/2)	16	8	8	0	0	32
5	Gloucestershire (I/2)	16	7	7	1	1	32
6	Essex (I/3)	16	6	6	1	3	32
7	Warwickshire (I/4)	16	7	8	0	1	30
8	Kent (I/6)	16	5	9	0	2	24
9	Surrey (I/1)	16	4	9	0	3	22

The bottom three counties were relegated to Division Two for the 2005 season

Division Two

		P	W	L	T	NR	Pts
1	Middlesex (II/4)	18	12	6	0	0	48
2	Worcestershire (I/9)	18	11	5	0	2	48
3	Nottinghamshire (II/5)	18	9	4	1	4	46
4	Yorkshire (I/8)	18	10	6	0	2	44
5	Sussex (II/8)	18	9	7	1	1	40
6	Durham (II/7)	18	9	7	0	2	40
7	Leicestershire (I/7)	18	7	8	0	3	34
8	Somerset (II/9)	18	6	11	0	1	26
9	Derbyshire (II/6)	18	5	12	0	1	22
10	Scotland (II/10)	18	2	14	0	2	12

The top three counties were promoted to Division One for the 2005 season

CHELTENHAM & GLOUCESTER TROPHY

Winners: Gloucestershire **Runners-up:** Worcestershire

TWENTY20 CUP

Winners: Leicestershire

Runners-up: Surrey **Semi-finalists:** Lancashire, Glamorgan

2004 AVERAGES (all first-class matches)

BATTING AVERAGES – including fielding
Qualifying requirements: 6 completed innings and an average of over 26.00

Name	*Matches*	*Inns*	*NO*	*Runs*	*HS*	*Avge*	*100s*	*50s*	*Ct*	*St*
R W T Key	16	27	3	1896	221	79.00	9	3	8	-
A Symonds	5	8	1	506	156*	72.28	3	1	6	-
G B Hogg	12	13	3	706	158	70.60	1	7	6	-
D J Hussey	17	23	4	1315	170	69.21	7	2	24	-
I R Bell	18	29	4	1714	262*	68.56	6	7	12	-
D Mongia	6	9	2	470	111	67.14	2	2	2	-
M R Ramprakash	17	29	5	1564	161	65.16	7	6	7	-
S Chanderpaul	6	12	3	583	128*	64.77	2	2	4	-
G A Hick	17	29	4	1589	262	63.56	4	6	25	-
B J Hodge	15	25	0	1548	262	61.92	5	4	6	-
I D Blackwell	11	16	2	864	131	61.71	2	6	5	-
D J G Sales	16	25	5	1230	171	61.50	1	12	18	-
A Flintoff	7	11	1	603	167	60.30	1	6	7	-
U Afzaal	16	28	5	1365	167*	59.34	4	7	9	-
D S Lehmann	7	11	1	592	120	59.20	1	5	2	-
P A Jaques	11	19	0	1118	243	58.84	3	5	11	-
M H Richardson	6	11	1	583	101	58.30	1	3	4	-
R C Irani	10	16	4	695	164	57.91	3	2	1	-
C M Spearman	17	28	2	1462	341	56.23	4	4	15	-
W I Jefferson	17	29	1	1555	222	55.53	6	5	15	-
C J L Rogers	6	11	2	498	156	55.33	1	3	6	-
N V Knight	16	30	6	1324	303*	55.16	2	8	9	-
M J Walker	17	27	4	1266	157	55.04	4	8	17	-
G P Thorpe	10	17	3	770	114	55.00	2	4	7	-
M T G Elliott	15	26	1	1346	157	53.84	4	6	15	-
S P Fleming	5	9	0	482	117	53.55	1	3	6	-
O A Shah	17	30	5	1336	140*	53.44	4	9	19	-
M E Trescothick	7	14	2	641	132	53.41	3	2	6	-
J Cox	13	20	1	1013	250	53.31	3	4	7	-
I J L Trott	17	28	6	1170	115	53.18	1	10	12	-
A D Brown	15	24	2	1155	170	52.50	4	6	15	-
K P Pietersen	16	21	1	1044	167	52.20	4	4	19	-
J P Crawley	13	21	3	938	301*	52.11	1	5	4	-
J S Foster	17	25	5	1037	212	51.85	4	1	45	6
C H Gayle	6	11	0	569	105	51.72	1	4	3	-
Hassan Adnan	18	31	4	1380	140	51.11	3	8	11	-
S G Law	12	18	1	867	171*	51.00	3	1	17	-

Name	*Matches*	*Inns*	*NO*	*Runs*	*HS*	*Avge*	*100s*	*50s*	*Ct*	*St*
C M W Read	13	18	2	807	130	50.43	2	6	35	3
D R Brown	17	22	3	957	162	50.36	3	2	7	-
M J Wood (So)	11	16	4	604	128*	50.33	2	3	5	-
A J Strauss	8	16	2	704	137	50.28	2	4	11	-
P D Bowler	16	27	6	1034	187*	49.23	3	3	11	-
M B Loye	14	22	3	934	184	49.15	2	6	8	-
E T Smith	18	30	4	1277	189	49.11	4	5	6	-
J E R Gallian	17	25	2	1121	190	48.73	3	8	16	-
M A Ealham	16	20	2	871	139	48.38	3	4	13	-
C J Adams	16	25	4	1003	200	47.76	4	2	14	-
A Singh	5	8	1	332	112*	47.42	1	2	3	-
B F Smith	16	25	3	1036	187	47.09	2	7	17	-
B C Lara	5	10	1	420	113*	46.66	1	2	10	-
C P Schofield	3	6	0	279	99	46.50	-	3	-	-
M J Prior	18	26	1	1158	201*	46.32	3	6	25	2
R J Warren	13	19	2	784	134	46.11	2	4	4	-
M P Vaughan	6	10	1	414	103	46.00	2	2	7	-
S C Joseph	4	8	0	367	114	45.87	1	2	2	-
E C Joyce	14	25	2	1055	134	45.86	2	7	12	-
A McGrath	9	16	0	728	174	45.50	3	1	6	-
C G Taylor	16	25	1	1077	177	44.87	4	4	6	-
D L Hemp	17	29	4	1120	102*	44.80	1	10	15	-
S A Newman	17	30	1	1277	131	44.03	3	9	11	-
M J Powell (Wa)	10	17	2	657	134	43.80	2	2	5	-
T Frost	17	19	6	568	135*	43.69	1	2	47	6
P N Weekes	16	26	3	1001	118	43.52	2	9	14	-
C S Baugh	4	8	1	304	150*	43.42	1	1	10	2
D J Bicknell	17	26	1	1080	175	43.20	5	1	4	-
M P Maynard	15	24	3	906	163	43.14	3	4	14	-
A Flower	17	29	3	1121	172	43.11	2	6	18	-
I J Ward	16	25	1	1032	160	43.00	4	3	5	-
C W G Bassano	14	22	3	814	123*	42.84	2	6	4	-
M A Carberry	12	19	4	639	112	42.60	2	4	5	-
J C Hildreth	13	20	2	760	108	42.22	2	5	12	-
A J Bichel	14	18	1	717	142	42.17	3	2	3	-
V S Solanki	13	18	0	757	107	42.05	1	6	10	-
T J Murtagh	11	17	8	374	74*	41.55	-	4	8	-
D P Fulton	16	28	1	1106	122	40.96	5	3	21	-
D C Nash	12	17	4	529	113	40.69	1	3	26	2
J W M Dalrymple	16	25	4	848	244	40.38	1	4	9	-
B L Hutton	16	29	1	1129	126	40.32	5	3	23	-
T H C Hancock	9	13	1	481	77*	40.08	-	4	4	-
J J Sayers	8	13	0	518	147	39.84	1	4	1	-
N Pothas	16	24	3	834	131*	39.71	3	4	45	5

Name	*Matches*	*Inns*	*NO*	*Runs*	*HS*	*Avge*	*100s*	*50s*	*Ct*	*St*
D D J Robinson	16	28	0	1087	154	38.82	1	9	18	-
S C Moore	17	29	3	1004	146	38.61	3	4	7	-
C L Hooper	13	21	3	693	115	38.50	2	4	19	-
M J Wood (Y)	16	27	2	955	123	38.20	1	7	24	-
N J Astle	6	10	1	343	93	38.11	-	3	1	-
S J Adshead	15	23	7	609	61	38.06	-	4	39	2
P J Franks	17	22	5	634	57*	37.29	-	5	2	-
M van Jaarsveld	7	13	0	484	114	37.23	1	1	7	-
J D Francis	10	16	1	554	110	36.93	2	3	6	-
M A Wagh	17	30	2	1033	167	36.89	2	5	16	-
M E K Hussey	7	13	1	442	78	36.83	-	2	10	-
N G E Walker	8	9	3	221	80	36.83	-	2	3	-
M Burns	16	22	2	733	124*	36.65	1	4	17	-
A P Grayson	6	10	0	365	119	36.50	1	2	-	-
S J Marshall	4	6	0	218	98	36.33	-	1	-	-
S G Koenig	18	33	2	1125	171	36.29	2	6	6	-
D I Stevens	13	22	3	689	105	36.26	1	5	13	-
A F Giles	8	10	2	289	70	36.12	-	2	3	-
S J Rhodes	17	21	9	433	59*	36.08	-	2	44	4
G O Jones	11	13	1	433	101	36.08	2	1	34	3
R R Montgomerie	18	29	1	1010	85	36.07	-	10	12	-
M J Powell (Glm)	16	27	2	900	124	36.00	1	7	14	-
S D Thomas	14	19	5	499	105*	35.64	1	3	8	-
W P C Weston	17	28	1	961	135	35.59	2	4	18	-
M J Clarke	12	20	0	709	140	35.45	3	2	20	-
K P Dutch	6	8	1	248	72	35.42	-	2	2	-
A Habib	14	22	0	776	157	35.27	1	5	3	-
A G R Loudon	11	17	0	597	92	35.11	-	6	6	-
J M Dakin	5	9	3	210	71*	35.00	-	1	1	-
M W Goodwin	17	27	2	875	119	35.00	3	4	9	-
C L Cairns	6	10	0	349	82	34.90	-	4	-	-
S D Udal	13	17	3	488	74	34.85	-	3	8	-
A P R Gidman	17	25	0	869	91	34.76	-	9	13	-
G Chapple	14	22	1	726	112	34.57	2	4	3	-
J N Batty	17	29	2	933	145	34.55	3	3	50	6
J O Troughton	14	18	1	587	120	34.52	1	5	4	-
I Dawood	9	14	5	310	75	34.44	-	1	13	2
I J Sutcliffe	14	24	1	788	104	34.26	1	6	5	-
M H Yardy	4	8	1	239	115	34.14	1	-	3	-
R D B Croft	17	25	4	712	138	33.90	2	1	2	-
J C Tredwell	8	8	1	237	51*	33.85	-	1	7	-
J Moss	12	20	2	608	147*	33.77	1	4	5	-
G J Muchall	16	30	1	975	142*	33.62	1	5	14	-
G R Napier	15	23	4	637	106*	33.52	1	5	7	-

Name	*Matches*	*Inns*	*NO*	*Runs*	*HS*	*Avge*	*100s*	*50s*	*Ct*	*St*
J D Middlebrook	16	24	2	723	115	32.86	2	3	4	-
A J Hall	12	19	2	558	81	32.82	-	5	16	-
A N Cook	14	24	2	718	126	32.63	1	5	21	-
M J Chilton	16	27	2	809	124*	32.36	2	2	9	-
G L Brophy	16	25	2	744	181	32.34	1	4	27	2
M J North	17	31	1	969	219	32.30	2	4	8	-
M J Brown	16	28	2	838	109*	32.23	2	6	12	-
D L Maddy	17	30	2	900	145	32.14	1	7	24	-
G J Batty	12	18	3	470	133	31.33	1	2	7	-
S D Peters	17	29	0	907	123	31.27	3	3	13	-
D L Vettori	6	8	0	250	77	31.25	-	2	1	-
R Clarke	10	17	0	530	112	31.17	1	2	15	-
L D Sutton	16	27	3	747	131	31.12	1	2	34	3
M A Butcher	7	14	1	403	184	31.00	1	1	3	-
I G Butler	5	8	2	185	68	30.83	-	1	2	-
C D McMillan	6	9	1	245	86	30.62	-	2	-	-
Azhar Mahmood	12	20	1	577	84	30.36	-	4	8	-
J H K Adams	12	20	3	511	75	30.05	-	2	2	-
P A Cottey	11	17	0	510	185	30.00	1	-	7	-
O D Gibson	15	19	3	480	60*	30.00	-	4	5	-
M F Cleary	11	14	8	179	38	29.83	-	-	3	-
B B McCullum	7	10	0	298	96	29.80	-	3	13	3
T B Huggins	9	14	2	355	82*	29.58	-	2	3	-
W K Hegg	12	17	3	412	54	29.42	-	1	23	5
D S Smith	5	10	0	294	142	29.40	1	-	6	-
P D Collingwood	6	11	0	322	68	29.27	-	3	4	-
N J O'Brien	14	19	4	439	69	29.26	-	3	33	5
G Welch	16	25	4	609	115*	29.00	1	1	12	-
V J Craven	6	8	1	202	81*	28.85	-	1	2	-
S B Styris	7	13	1	343	108	28.58	1	-	5	-
G R Breese	14	25	1	685	165*	28.54	1	3	12	-
N J Edwards	10	19	0	537	93	28.26	-	2	11	-
A Pratt	14	25	3	618	68	28.09	-	4	33	2
O A C Banks	5	10	2	224	90	28.00	-	1	1	-
M P Bicknell	13	19	3	447	47*	27.93	-	-	4	-
M A Wallace	17	28	0	776	105	27.71	1	3	40	3
T W Roberts	17	29	2	748	89	27.70	-	6	12	-
S D Stubbings	16	28	1	743	96	27.51	-	6	8	-
S K Warne	12	16	2	381	57	27.21	-	1	9	-
M H W Papps	5	9	0	241	126	26.77	1	1	4	-
R R Sarwan	6	12	0	319	139	26.58	1	1	7	-
J G E Benning	6	11	1	265	128	26.50	1	-	3	-
R M Pyrah	4	7	1	158	39	26.33	-	-	-	-
B J M Scott	7	13	4	236	101*	26.22	1	-	8	3

BOWLING AVERAGES
Qualifying requirements: 10 wickets taken, having bowled in a minimum of 6 innings and an average of less than 50.00

Name	*Overs*	*Mdns*	*Runs*	*Wkts*	*Avge*	*Best*	*5wI*	*10wM*
D S Lehmann	105.4	19	261	15	17.40	4-35	-	-
D A Mascarenhas	404.2	132	1046	56	18.67	6-25	4	-
M A Davies	304.2	75	938	50	18.76	6-44	4	-
C H Gayle	66.1	13	189	10	18.90	5-34	1	-
M W Alleyne	66.3	19	227	11	20.63	5-71	1	-
S R Clark	89	23	217	10	21.70	3-28	-	-
H H Streak	159	29	522	24	21.75	7-80	2	1
C T Tremlett	268.2	56	867	39	22.23	4-29	-	-
S D Udal	247.4	40	869	39	22.28	6-79	1	-
D Gough	226.4	52	672	30	22.40	5-57	1	-
J M Anderson	181.1	35	593	26	22.80	6-49	1	1
J E C Franklin	126.2	33	415	18	23.05	7-60	1	-
K P Dutch	124	21	448	19	23.57	5-26	2	-
O D Gibson	424.5	97	1445	60	24.08	6-43	5	2
S K Warne	411.5	88	1231	51	24.13	6-65	3	-
D J J Bravo	146.4	29	486	20	24.30	6-55	1	-
A R Adams	157.4	23	561	23	24.39	5-93	1	-
A Flintoff	193.2	41	588	24	24.50	3-25	-	-
J Lewis	472.4	121	1440	57	25.26	7-72	4	-
S J Harmison	301	64	966	38	25.42	6-46	1	-
Danish Kaneria	563	123	1609	63	25.53	7-65	4	1
C White	88.2	18	282	11	25.63	3-50	-	-
G Keedy	645.3	122	1849	72	25.68	7-95	6	1
M K Munday	60.3	13	257	10	25.70	4-36	-	-
C E W Silverwood	174.3	33	570	22	25.90	3-18	-	-
N A M McLean	322.1	62	1127	43	26.20	6-79	3	1
N D Doshi	265.2	45	875	33	26.51	7-110	3	2
J Louw	463.3	89	1591	60	26.51	5-44	3	-
C E Shreck	235	51	823	31	26.54	6-46	2	-
J A R Blain	188	26	804	30	26.80	4-38	-	-
A F Giles	362.1	79	939	35	26.82	5-57	2	-
I R Bell	149.4	34	438	16	27.37	4-4	-	-
C B Keegan	161	29	550	20	27.50	5-36	2	-
Mushtaq Ahmed	791.2	164	2318	84	27.59	7-73	6	2
D S Harrison	480.3	123	1584	57	27.78	5-48	3	-
N Tahir	207.4	33	791	28	28.25	4-43	-	-
R J Sidebottom	258	59	859	30	28.63	5-86	1	-
C L Cairns	143.1	24	516	18	28.66	5-79	1	-
M M Patel	475	91	1416	49	28.89	5-56	2	-
A W Laraman	180.3	43	638	22	29.00	5-58	1	-
M P Bicknell	387	95	1266	43	29.44	5-128	1	-
M Hayward	289	54	918	31	29.61	4-41	-	-
G J Smith	336.1	69	1161	39	29.76	5-35	3	-
K J Dean	144	18	597	20	29.85	5-86	1	-
A Symonds	139.3	39	419	14	29.92	5-140	1	-

Name	*Overs*	*Mdns*	*Runs*	*Wkts*	*Avge*	*Best*	*5wI*	*10wM*
P J Franks	352	68	1287	43	29.93	7-72	2	-
Azhar Mahmood	336.3	77	1138	38	29.94	5-54	1	-
D G Cork	332.5	59	1144	38	30.10	7-120	3	-
D A Cosker	174.1	42	513	17	30.17	3-40	-	-
M S Mason	597.1	181	1582	52	30.42	5-62	1	-
D L Vettori	173.1	22	612	20	30.60	5-92	1	-
S J Cook	371	82	1072	35	30.62	6-89	2	-
G J Batty	492.1	129	1381	45	30.68	7-52	2	1
S M J Cusden	100.3	17	404	13	31.07	4-68	-	-
A G R Loudon	192.2	32	653	21	31.09	6-47	2	-
L E Plunkett	247.5	37	964	31	31.09	6-74	1	-
M J Saggers	259.5	72	717	23	31.17	4-43	-	-
J D Lewry	259.2	64	849	27	31.44	5-66	1	-
B V Taylor	298.1	59	1039	33	31.48	5-73	1	-
M J G Davis	235.3	40	662	21	31.52	4-57	-	-
C E Dagnall	256.4	46	923	29	31.82	4-37	-	-
P J Martin	115.5	34	319	10	31.90	4-81	-	-
Kabir Ali	248	45	899	28	32.10	5-60	1	-
A B Agarkar	93.3	20	323	10	32.30	5-81	1	-
D R Brown	425.4	97	1293	40	32.32	5-53	2	-
M J Hoggard	385.5	80	1360	42	32.38	4-32	-	-
M N Malik	204	35	781	24	32.54	5-88	1	-
T T Bresnan	160.3	31	557	17	32.76	3-32	-	-
Shabbir Ahmed	169	38	605	18	33.61	4-96	-	-
G Welch	471.5	103	1525	45	33.88	5-57	3	-
K M D N Kulasekara	102.1	15	407	12	33.91	6-109	1	-
S P Jones	310.1	53	1155	34	33.97	5-77	2	-
R H Joseph	165.2	31	648	19	34.10	3-47	-	-
P A J DeFreitas	343.4	81	1064	31	34.32	4-49	-	-
R L Johnson	449.5	104	1512	44	34.36	7-69	2	-
Mohammad Akram	432.1	76	1581	46	34.36	4-85	-	-
C G Greenidge	83.2	14	346	10	34.60	3-71	-	-
P T Collins	109	9	453	13	34.84	4-113	-	-
R K J Dawson	379.4	71	1255	36	34.86	5-40	1	-
M F Cleary	230	29	946	27	35.03	7-80	2	-
R D B Croft	674	146	2006	57	35.19	4-52	-	-
S C G MacGill	410	80	1408	40	35.20	7-109	2	1
C W Henderson	469	132	1373	39	35.20	7-74	2	-
R J Logan	75.1	9	353	10	35.30	4-34	-	-
A P Cowan	148	39	463	13	35.61	3-44	-	-
G D Bridge	235	60	680	19	35.78	4-64	-	-
I D Blackwell	345.1	85	972	27	36.00	7-90	2	-
A G Botha	291	62	938	26	36.07	5-55	1	-
A R Caddick	578.5	110	2026	56	36.17	6-80	4	-
J J C Lawson	105.3	13	471	13	36.23	4-94	-	-
M A Sheikh	298.3	69	945	26	36.34	4-9	-	-
S R G Francis	295.5	51	1201	33	36.39	5-42	2	-
B J Hodge	95.5	14	365	10	36.50	2-18	-	-
S P Kirby	327.1	53	1132	31	36.51	3-64	-	-

Name	Overs	Mdns	Runs	Wkts	Avge	Best	5wI	10wM
M A Ealham	317	90	952	26	36.61	4-43	-	-
J Ormond	609.2	143	1909	52	36.71	6-62	1	-
S D Thomas	320.3	32	1252	34	36.82	4-47	-	-
A J Clarke	131	25	444	12	37.00	3-32	-	-
N G E Walker	151.2	17	667	18	37.05	5-68	1	-
R J Kirtley	446.5	97	1381	37	37.32	4-32	-	-
A G Wharf	249.5	38	1011	27	37.44	5-93	1	-
A J Hall	347	72	1124	30	37.46	3-10	-	-
A G A M McCoubrey	126.4	22	563	15	37.53	4-16	-	-
Mohammad Sami	140	32	526	14	37.57	6-99	1	1
A Khan	170.3	24	756	20	37.80	4-47	-	-
B J Phillips	408.3	107	1175	31	37.90	5-106	1	-
P D Collingwood	137	37	455	12	37.91	3-49	-	-
G R Napier	403.3	65	1595	42	37.97	5-56	1	-
D D Masters	149	29	533	14	38.07	4-74	-	-
J W M Dalrymple	306.5	47	1083	28	38.67	4-66	-	-
P M R Havell	178.1	20	814	21	38.76	4-75	-	-
R S C Martin-Jenkins	388.4	101	1166	30	38.86	5-96	1	-
G Chapple	374.4	80	1128	29	38.89	5-136	1	-
G P Swann	403.2	71	1168	30	38.93	4-94	-	-
D Pretorius	245	43	936	24	39.00	4-119	-	-
J M M Averis	285.2	51	1099	28	39.25	6-32	2	-
A D Mullally	245.4	69	711	18	39.50	6-68	1	-
C L Hooper	234	51	595	15	39.66	4-56	-	-
I G Butler	101.3	11	446	11	40.54	4-114	-	-
G R Breese	307.4	44	1163	28	41.53	5-41	2	1
R W Price	169.1	50	420	10	42.00	4-83	-	-
P C Rofe	167.5	42	505	12	42.08	4-109	-	-
J F Brown	584.3	133	1523	36	42.30	5-113	1	-
M S Kasprowicz	272.1	54	893	21	42.52	5-54	1	-
A Sheriyar	199.3	33	772	18	42.88	5-94	1	-
J D Middlebrook	394.3	57	1459	34	42.91	5-26	1	-
T E Savill	96	10	435	10	43.50	3-93	-	-
F H Edwards	139.2	14	610	14	43.57	5-22	2	1
T J Murtagh	243.3	50	873	20	43.65	5-74	1	-
C T Peploe	242.2	59	745	17	43.82	4-65	-	-
S I Mahmood	230	26	1010	23	43.91	4-59	-	-
M M Betts	147.4	30	577	13	44.38	5-89	1	-
C S Martin	161.5	34	624	14	44.57	4-92	-	-
N M Carter	367.4	79	1209	27	44.77	4-50	-	-
P N Weekes	325.3	34	1166	26	44.84	5-76	1	-
M M M Suraj	134.4	21	498	11	45.27	5-40	1	-
D L Maddy	169.2	24	686	15	45.73	2-41	-	-
P J McMahon	172	36	551	12	45.91	4-68	-	-
J Moss	207.5	39	646	14	46.14	3-30	-	-
I D Fisher	320.4	61	1073	23	46.65	5-114	1	-
A J Bichel	398.5	75	1549	33	46.93	5-87	2	-
O A C Banks	131	19	527	11	47.90	3-50	-	-
Mohammad Ali	116.4	18	486	10	48.60	4-75	-	-

INDEX OF PLAYERS BY COUNTY

*denotes not registered for the 2005 season. Where a player is known to have moved in the off-season he is listed under his new county.

DERBYSHIRE

BASSANO, C.W.G.
BORRINGTON, P.M.
BOTHA, A.G.
BROWNING, R.
BRYANT, J.D.C.
CHAPMAN, J.R.
DEAN, K.J.
DIVENUTO, M.J.
DUMELOW, N.R.C.*
FRANCE, B.J.
FRIEND, T.J.
GAIT, A.I.*
GODDARD, L.J.
GUNTER, N.E.L.*
HASSAN ADNAN
HAVELL, P.M.R.
HEWSON, D.R.
HUGHES, L.
HUNTER, I.D.
KHAN, R.M.*
LUNGLEY, T.
MOHAMMAD ALI*
MOSS, J.
NEEDHAM, J.
PAGET, C.D.
POWELL, D.B.*
ROGERS, C.J.L.*
SELWOOD, S.A.*
SHEIKH, M.A.
SPENDLOVE, B.L.
STUBBINGS, S.D.
SUTTON, L.D.
TAYLOR, D.K.*
WALKER, N.G.E.
WELCH, G.

DURHAM

BARRICK, D.J.
BENKENSTEIN, D.M.
BLIGNAUT, A.M.*
BREESE, G.R.
BRIDGE, G.D.
COETZER, K.J.
COLLINGWOOD, P.D.
DAVIES, M.A.
HAMILTON, G.M.
HARMISON, S.J.
HUSSEY, M.E.K.
KILLEEN, N.
KING, R.D.*
KUMAR, P.*
LEWIS, J.J.B.
LOWE, J.A.
MUCHALL, G.J.
MUSTARD, P.
NOFFKE, A.A.
NORTH, M.J.*
ONIONS, G.
PATTISON, I.*
PENG, N.
PLUNKETT, L.E.
PRATT, A.
PRATT, G.J.
RUSHWORTH, C.
SCOTT, G.M.
TAHIR MUGHAL*
TAIT, S.W.*
THORP, C.D.
TURNER, M.L.
WALKER, A.*

ESSEX

ADAMS, A.R.
BISHOP, J.E.
BOPARA, R.S.
BRANT, S.A.*
CHAMBERS, M.A.
CLARKE, A.J.
COOK, A.N.
COWAN, A.P.
DANISH KANERIA
FLOWER, A.
FLOWER, G.W.
FOSTER, J.S.
GOUGH, D.
GRAYSON, A.P.
HUSSAIN, N.*
IRANI, R.C.
JEFFERSON, W.I.
MCCOUBREY, A.G.A.M.*
MIDDLEBROOK, J.D.
NAPIER, G.R.
PALLADINO, A.P.
PETTINI, M.L.
PHILLIPS, T.J.
SMITH, B.M.
STEPHENSON, J.P.*
TEN DOESCHATE, R.N.
TUDOR, A.J.
WESTFIELD, M.S.

GLAMORGAN

CHERRY, D.D.
COSKER, D.A.
CROFT, R.D.B.
DALE, A.*

INDEX OF PLAYERS BY COUNTY

DAVIES, A.P.
ELLIOTT, M.T.G.
GRANT, R.N.
HARRISON, A.J.
HARRISON, D.S.
HEMP, D.L.
HUGHES, J.
JONES, S.P.
KASPROWICZ, M.S.
LEWIS, M.L.*
MAYNARD, M.P.
O'SHEA, M.P.
POWELL, M.J.
REES, G.P.
SHAW, A.D.
THOMAS, I.J.
THOMAS, S.D.
WALLACE, M.A.
WATKINS, R.E.
WHARF, A.G.B.
WRIGHT, B.J.

GLOUCESTERSHIRE

ADSHEAD, S.J.
ALI, KADEER
ALLEYNE, M.W.
AVERIS, J.M.M.
BALL, M.C.J.
BRACKEN, N.W.*
BRESSINGTON, A.N.*
CHANDANA, U.D.U.
FISHER, I.D.
FRANKLIN, J.E.C.*
GIDMAN, A.P.R.
GREENIDGE, C.G.
HANCOCK, T.H.C.
HARDINGES, M.A.
KIRBY, S.P.
LEWIS, J.
PEARSON, J.A.
RUDGE, W.D.
RUSSELL, R.C.*
SHABBIR AHMED*
SHOAIB MALIK*
SILLENCE, R.J.
SMITH, A.M.*
SNELL, S.D.
SPEARMAN, C.M.
TAYLOR, C.G.
WESTON, W.P.C.
WINDOWS, M.G.N.

HAMPSHIRE

ADAMS, J.H.K.
BENHAM, C.C.
BROWN, M.J.
BRUCE, J.T.A.
BURROWS, T.G.
CLARKE, M.J.*
CRAWLEY, J.P.
DIGHTON, M.G.*
ERVINE, S.M.
GRIFFITHS, D.A.
HAMBLIN, J.R.C.*
HINDLEY, R.J.E.
KATICH, S.M.
KENDALL, W.S.*
KENWAY, D.A.
LAMB, G.A.
LATOUF, K.J.
LOGAN, R.J.
MASCARENHAS, D.A.
MCLEAN, J.J.
MULLALLY, A.D.
PIETERSEN, K.P.
POTHAS, N.
PRITTIPAUL, L.R.
SHIRAZI, D.C.
TAYLOR, B.V.
TOMLINSON, J.A.
TREMLETT, C.T.
UDAL, S.D.
WARNE, S.K.
WATSON, S.R.*

KENT

BEVAN, M.G.*
BUTLER, I.G.*
CARBERRY, M.A.
COOK, S.J.
CUSDEN, S.M.J.
DENLY, J.L.
DENNINGTON, M.J.
FERLEY, R.S.
FULTON, D.P.
HALL, A.J.
JONES, G.O.
JOSEPH, R.H.
KEY, R.W.T.
KHAN, A.
MOHAMMAD SAMI*
O'BRIEN, N.J.
PATEL, M.M.
PIESLEY, R.L.
SAGGERS, M.J.
SHAHID AFRIDI*
SHERIYAR, A.
STEVENS, D.I.
STIFF, D.A.
SYMONDS, A.*
TREDWELL, J.C.
TROTT, B.J.*
VAN JAARSVELD, M.
WALKER, M.J.

INDEX OF PLAYERS BY COUNTY

LANCASHIRE

ANDERSON, J.M.
CHAPPLE, G.
CHILTON, M.J.
CORK, D.G.
CROFT, S.J.
CROOK, A.R.
CROOK, S.P.
CROSS, G.D.
FLINTOFF, A.
HAYNES, J.J.*
HEGG, W.K.
HODGE, B.J.
HOGG, K.W.
HOOPER, C.L.
HORTON, P.J.
KEEDY, G.
LAW, S.G.
LOYE, M.B.
MAHMOOD, S.I.
MARSHALL, S.J.
MARTIN, P.J.*
MURALITHARAN, M.
NEWBY, O.J.
REES, T.M.
SCHOFIELD, C.P.*
SUTCLIFFE, I.J.
SWANN, A.J.*
WATKINSON, M.
WOOD, J.*
YATES, G.

LEICESTERSHIRE

ACKERMAN, H.D.
BOYCE, M.A.G.
BRANDY, D.G.*
BRIGNULL, D.S.
BROAD, S.
CLEARY, M.F.
DAGNALL, C.E.
DAKIN, J.M.*
DEFREITAS, P.A.J.
FERRABY, N.J.
GIBSON, O.D.
HABIB, A.
HENDERSON, C.W.
LIDDLE, C.J.
MADDY, D.L.
MASTERS, D.D.
MAUNDERS, J.
MONGIA, D.
NEW, T.J.
NIXON, P.A.
ROBINSON, D.D.J.
SADLER, J.L.
SNAPE, J.N.

MIDDLESEX

AGARKAR, A.B.*
BETTS, M.M.
BLOOMFIELD, T.F.*
CLARK, S.R.*
COMPTON, N.R.D.
DALRYMPLE, J.W.M.
GODLEMAN, B-A.
HAYWARD, M.
HUTCHISON, P.M.
HUTTON, B.L.
JOYCE, E.C.
KEEGAN, C.B.
KLUSENER, L.*
KOENIG, S.G.*
MCGRATH, G.D.*
MORGAN, E.J.G.
NAMBIAR, A.P.
NASH, D.C.
PEPLOE, C.T.
RANKIN, W.B.
RICHARDSON, A.
SCOTT, B.J.M.
SHAH, O.A.
SMITH, E.T.
STRAUSS, A.J.
STYRIS, S.B.
VAN BUNGE, D.L.S.*
WEEKES, P.N.
WHELAN, C.D.
WRIGHT, C.J.C.

NORTHAMPTONSHIRE

AFZAAL, U.
ANDERSON, R.S.G.*
BAILEY, T.M.B.*
BROPHY, G.L.
BROWN, J.F.
CAWDRON, M.J.*
COOK, J.W.*
COVERDALE, P.S.
GOODE, C.M.
HUGGINS, T.B.
JENNINGS, C.J.R.*
JONES, P.S.
KING, R.E.
LOUW, J.
LOVE, M.L.
PANESAR, M.S.
PHILLIPS, B.J.
PHYTHIAN, M.J.
PIETERSEN, C.
POWELL, M.J.*
ROBERTS, T.W.

INDEX OF PLAYERS BY COUNTY

ROFE, P.C.*
SALES, D.J.G.
SHAFAYAT, B.M.
WAKE, C.J.
WESSELS, M.H.
WHITE, A.R.
WHITE, R.A.
WRIGHT, D.G.

NOTTINGHAMSHIRE

ALLEYNE, D.
BICKNELL, D.J.
CLOUGH, G.D.
EALHAM, M.A.
FLEMING, S.P.
FRANKS, P.J.
GALLIAN, J.E.R.
HARRIS, A.J.
HUSSEY, D.J.
MACGILL, S.C.G.*
MCMAHON, P.J.
NOON, W.M.
PATEL, S.R.
READ, C.M.W.
SHRECK, C.E.
SIDEBOTTOM, R.J.
SINGH, A.
SMITH, G.J.
SMITH, W.R.
SWANN, G.P.
WARREN, R.J.

SOMERSET

ANDREW, G.M.
BLACKWELL, I.D.
BOWLER, P.D.*
BURNS, M.
CADDICK, A.R.
COX, J.*
DURSTON, W.J.
DUTCH, K.P.*
EDWARDS, N.J.
FRANCIS, J.D.
FRANCIS, S.R.G.
GAZZARD, C.M.
HANCOCK, N.D.*
HILDRETH, J.C.
HUNT, T.A.*
JAYASURIYA, S.T.
JOHNSON, R.L.
LARAMAN, A.W.
MCLEAN, N.A.M.
MUNDAY, M.K.
PARSONS, K.A.
PARSONS, M.
PONTING, R.T.*
SMITH, G.C.
SUPPIAH, A.V.
TRESCOTHICK, M.E.
TURNER, R.J.
WOOD, M.J.

SURREY

AZHAR MAHMOOD
BATTY, J.N.
BENNING, J.G.E.
BICKNELL, M.P.
BLEWETT, G.S.*
BROWN, A.D.
BUTCHER, M.A.
CLARKE, R.
CLINTON, R.S.
DERNBACH, J.
DOSHI, N.D.
HAMILTON-BROWN, R.J.
HARBHAJAN SINGH
HODD, A.J.
HOLLIOAKE, A.J.*
KHAN, Z.*
MILLER, D.J.
MOHAMMAD AKRAM
MURTAGH, C.P.
MURTAGH, T.J.
NEWMAN, S.A.
ORMOND, J.
RAMPRAKASH, M.R.
SAKER, N.C.
SALISBURY, I.D.K.
SAMPSON, P.J.
SAQLAIN MUSHTAQ*
SHAHID, N.*
THORPE, G.P.

SUSSEX

ADAMS, C.J.
AMBROSE, T.R.
COTTEY, P.A.*
DAVIS, M.J.G.
GOODWIN, M.W.
HOPKINSON, C.D.
INNES, K.J.*
KIRTLEY, R.J.
LEWRY, J.D.
MARTIN-JENKINS, R.S.C.
MONTGOMERIE, R.R.

INDEX OF PLAYERS BY COUNTY

MUSHTAQ AHMED
NASH, C.D.
PRIOR, M.J.
ROBINSON, M.A.
TURK, N.R.K.
VOROS, J.A.
WARD, I.J.
WRIGHT, L.J.
YARDY, M.H.

WARWICKSHIRE

ALI, M.M.
ANYON, J.E.
BELL, I.R.
BROWN, D.R.
CARTER, N.M.
CLIFFORD, I.J.*
FROST, T.
GILES, A.F.
HOGG, G.B.*
KNIGHT, N.V.
LOUDON, A.G.R.
MEES, T.
OSTLER, D.P.*
PENNEY, T.L.
PIPER, K.J.
POWELL, M.J.
PRETORIUS, D.
SHANTRY, A.J.
STREAK, H.H.
TAHIR, N.
TROTT, I.J.L.
TROUGHTON, J.O.
WAGG, G.G.*
WAGH, M.A.
WARREN, N.A.
WESTWOOD, I.J.

WORCESTERSHIRE

ALI, KABIR
BATTY, G.J.
BICHEL, A.J.*
DAVIES, S.M.
DE BRUYN, Z.
GIFFORD, W.M.
HARRITY, M.A.*
HICK, G.A.
KHALID, S.A.
KNAPPETT, J.P.T.
LEATHERDALE, D.A.
MALIK, M.N.
MASON, M.S.
MITCHELL, D.K.H.
MOORE, S.C.
PETERS, S.D.
PIPE, D.J.
PRICE, R.W.
RHODES, S.J.*
SHOAIB AKHTAR
SMITH, B.F.
SOLANKI, V.S.
VAAS, W.P.U.J.C.
WIGLEY, D.H.

YORKSHIRE

BLAIN, J.A.R.
BLAKEY, R.J.
BRESNAN, T.T.
CRAVEN, V.J.*
DAWOOD, I.
DAWSON, R.K.J.
GALE, A.W.
GRAY, A.D.K.*
GUY, S.M.
HARVEY, I.J.
HOGGARD, M.J.
JAQUES, P.A.
KRUIS, G.J.
LAWSON, M.A.K.
LEHMANN, D.S.
LUCAS, D.S.
LUMB, M.J.
MCGRATH, A.
PYRAH, R.M.
SAYERS, J.J.
SHAHZAD, A.
SILVERWOOD, C.E.W.
TAYLOR, C.R.
THORNICROFT, N.D.
VAUGHAN, M.P.
WAINWRIGHT, D.J.
WHITE, C.
WOOD, M.J.

QUIZ ANSWERS

1. The Wills International Cup
2. Don Topley
3. The Grange, Edinburgh
4. Clayton Lambert
5. Dav Whatmore
6. Bas Zuiderent (Sachin Tendulkar was the youngest)
7. Ed Joyce
8. Chaminda Vaas
9. Andy Moles
10. Nairobi (in 2000-01)
11. 25 (Goodwin 5-6, O'Riordan 4-18)
12. John Dyson
13. Mike Denness (Ian 'Mighty Mouse' McLauchlan was the prop)
14. Aravinda de Silva (107*/3-42)
15. Ray Price
16. Brendan Kuruppu (Sri Lanka)
17. Enamul Haque Jnr
18. Duncan Fletcher (69*/4-42)
19. Arjuna Ranatunga
20. Gavin Hamilton
21. John Traicos (his 5-86 was for Zimbabwe)
22. India
23. Ireland
24. Bobby Simpson
25. Marvan Atapattu
26. Steve Tikolo (29 v West Indies)
27. Dave Houghton
28. Peter Cantrell
29. Alec Stewart – run out (Chandana) 32
30. Faoud Bacchus
31. Basharat Hassan
32. Paul-Jan Bakker
33. Phil Simmons
34. Kandy
35. Romesh Kaluwitharana
36. Bruce Yardley
37. Bandula Warnapura
38. Eddo Brandes
39. USA – Compton Adams, Derek Kallicharran (brother of Alvin) and Reginald Benjamin
40. Duleep Mendis (105/105)
41. Kumar Sangakkara
42. Paul Strang (106*/5-212 v Pakistan 1996-97)
43. Jim Love (Yorkshire)
44. Roshan Mahanama
45. Aftab Baloch
46. Kevin Curran
47. John Blain
48. East Africa
49. Brian Ward
50. Kyle Coetzer
51. Niall O'Brien
52. Roy Dias (108)
53. Gordon Greenidge
54. Steven Lubbers
55. Jamie Dalrymple (Middlesex)
56. Mike Hendrick
57. Nolan Clarke (represented Holland in the 1995-96 World Cup)
58. Amjad Khan
59. Denis Streak (father of Heath)
60. Kenya
61. United Arab Emirates
62. Mohammad Rafique
63. Dougie Brown
64. Roland Lefebvre
65. John Davison (67 balls; ended up with 111)
66. S. and M. de S. Wettimuny
67. Feiko Kloppenburg (121)
68. Surrey
69. Collins Obuya
70. Richard Swan
71. Thomas Odoyo
72. Andy Blignaut
73. Neil Johnson (Zimbabwe)
74. Joe Scuderi (Lancashire)
75. Grace Road, Leicester
76. Habibul Bashar
77. Henry Olonga (Zimbabwe)
78. Mohammad Ashraful (114 for Bangladesh v Sri Lanka at Colombo)
79. Gehan Mendis
80. Aasif Karim (Kenya)
81. James Brinkley
82. Sewdatt Shivnarine
83. Simon Myles
84. Soren Henriksen
85. Omar Henry
86. Graeme Hick (Zimbabwe)
87. Steve Atkinson
88. Anura Tennekoon
89. Ian Robinson (Zimbabwe)
90. Ashantha de Mel
91. Ole Mortensen
92. Sandeep Patil
93. Worcester, June 1979
94. Bill Bourne
95. Flavian Aponso
96. Murray Goodwin (Zimbabwe)
97. Grant Flower (Leicestershire and Essex)
98. Manjural Islam
99. Andy Goram
100. Rahul Dravid